Poetry Criticism

Guide to Gale Literary Criticism Series

For criticism on	Consult these Gale series
Authors now living or who died after December 31, 1999	*CONTEMPORARY LITERARY CRITICISM (CLC)*
Authors who died between 1900 and 1999	*TWENTIETH-CENTURY LITERARY CRITICISM (TCLC)*
Authors who died between 1800 and 1899	*NINETEENTH-CENTURY LITERATURE CRITICISM (NCLC)*
Authors who died between 1400 and 1799	*LITERATURE CRITICISM FROM 1400 TO 1800 (LC)* *SHAKESPEAREAN CRITICISM (SC)*
Authors who died before 1400	*CLASSICAL AND MEDIEVAL LITERATURE CRITICISM (CMLC)*
Authors of books for children and young adults	*CHILDREN'S LITERATURE REVIEW (CLR)*
Dramatists	*DRAMA CRITICISM (DC)*
Poets	*POETRY CRITICISM (PC)*
Short story writers	*SHORT STORY CRITICISM (SSC)*
Black writers of the past two hundred years	*BLACK LITERATURE CRITICISM (BLC)* *BLACK LITERATURE CRITICISM SUPPLEMENT (BLCS)*
Hispanic writers of the late nineteenth and twentieth centuries	*HISPANIC LITERATURE CRITICISM (HLC)* *HISPANIC LITERATURE CRITICISM SUPPLEMENT (HLCS)*
Native North American writers and orators of the eighteenth, nineteenth, and twentieth centuries	*NATIVE NORTH AMERICAN LITERATURE (NNAL)*
Major authors from the Renaissance to the present	*WORLD LITERATURE CRITICISM, 1500 TO THE PRESENT (WLC)* *WORLD LITERATURE CRITICISM SUPPLEMENT (WLCS)*

ISSN 1052-4851

Poetry Criticism

*Excerpts from Criticism of the Works
of the Most Significant and Widely
Studied Poets of World Literature*

Volume 40

David Galens
Project Editor

GALE®

THOMSON
™
GALE

Detroit • New York • San Diego • San Francisco • Cleveland • New Haven, Conn. • Waterville, Maine • London • Munich

THOMSON
GALE

Poetry Criticism, Vol. 40

Project Editor
David Galens

Editorial
Jenny Cromie, Kathy D. Darrow, Lisa Gellert, Madeline S. Harris, Allison Marion, Ellen McGeagh, Ron Morelli

Permissions
Debra Freitas, Margaret Chamberlain

Imaging and Multimedia
Kelly A. Quin, Lezlie Light, Dan Newell

Product Design
Michael Logusz

Composition and Electronic Capture
Gary Leach

Manufacturing
Stacy L. Melson

LIBRARY OF CONGRESS CATALOG CARD NUMBER 76-46132

ISBN 0-7876-5966-5
ISSN 0091-3421

Printed in the United States of America
10 9 8 7 6 5 4 3 2 1

Contents

Preface vii

Acknowledgments ix

Literary Criticism Series Advisory Board xi

Preface

Poetry Criticism (PC) presents significant criticism of the world's greatest poets and provides supplementary biographical and bibliographical material to guide the interested reader to a greater understanding of the genre and its creators. Although major poets and literary movements are covered in such Gale Literary Criticism series as *Contemporary Literary Criticism* (CLC), *Twentieth-Century Literary Criticism* (TCLC), *Nineteenth-Century Literature Criticism* (NCLC), *Literature Criticism from 1400 to 1800* (LC), and *Classical and Medieval Literature Criticism* (CMLC), PC offers more focused attention on poetry than is possible in the broader, survey-oriented entries on writers in these Gale series. Students, teachers, librarians, and researchers will find that the generous excerpts and supplementary material provided by PC supply them with the vital information needed to write a term paper on poetic technique, to examine a poet's most prominent themes, or to lead a poetry discussion group.

Scope of the Series

PC is designed to serve as an introduction to major poets of all eras and nationalities. Since these authors have inspired a great deal of relevant critical material, PC is necessarily selective, and the editors have chosen the most important published criticism to aid readers and students in their research. Each author entry presents a historical survey of the critical response to that author's work. The length of an entry is intended to reflect the amount of critical attention the author has received from critics writing in English and from foreign critics in translation. Every attempt has been made to identify and include the most significant essays on each author's work. In order to provide these important critical pieces, the editors sometimes reprint essays that have appeared elsewhere in Gale's Literary Criticism Series. Such duplication, however, never exceeds twenty percent of a PC volume.

Organization of the Book

Each PC entry consists of the following elements:

- The **Author Heading** cites the name under which the author most commonly wrote, followed by birth and death dates. Also located here are any name variations under which an author wrote, including transliterated forms for authors whose native languages use nonroman alphabets. If the author wrote consistently under a pseudonym, the pseudonym will be listed in the author heading and the author's actual name given in parenthesis on the first line of the biographical and critical introduction. Uncertain birth or death dates are indicated by question marks. Single-work entries are preceded by the title of the work and its date of publication.

- The **Introduction** contains background information that introduces the reader to the author and the critical debates surrounding his or her work.

- A **Portrait of the Author** is included when available.

- The list of **Principal Works** is ordered chronologically by date of first publication and lists the most important works by the author. The first section comprises poetry collections and book-length poems. The second section gives information on other major works by the author. For foreign authors, the editors have provided original foreign-language publication information and have selected what are considered the best and most complete English-language editions of their works.

- Reprinted **Criticism** is arranged chronologically in each entry to provide a useful perspective on changes in critical evaluation over time. All individual titles of poems and poetry collections by the author featured in the entry are printed in boldface type. The critic's name and the date of composition or publication of the critical work are given at the beginning of each piece of criticism. Unsigned criticism is preceded by the title of the source in which it appeared. Footnotes are reprinted at the end of each essay or excerpt. In the case of excerpted criticism, only those footnotes that pertain to the excerpted texts are included.

- Critical essays are prefaced by brief **Annotations** explicating each piece.

- A complete **Bibliographical Citation** of the original essay or book precedes each piece of criticism.

- An annotated bibliography of **Further Reading** appears at the end of each entry and suggests resources for additional study. In some cases, significant essays for which the editors could not obtain reprint rights are included here. Boxed material following the further reading list provides references to other biographical and critical sources on the author in series published by Gale.

Cumulative Indexes

A **Cumulative Author Index** lists all of the authors that appear in a wide variety of reference sources published by the Gale Group, including *PC*. A complete list of these sources is found facing the first page of the Author Index. The index also includes birth and death dates and cross references between pseudonyms and actual names.

A **Cumulative Nationality Index** lists all authors featured in *PC* by nationality, followed by the number of the *PC* volume in which their entry appears.

A **Cumulative Title Index** lists in alphabetical order all individual poems, book-length poems, and collection titles contained in the *PC* series. Titles of poetry collections and separately published poems are printed in italics, while titles of individual poems are printed in roman type with quotation marks. Each title is followed by the author's last name and corresponding volume and page numbers where commentary on the work is located. English-language translations of original foreign-language titles are cross-referenced to the foreign titles so that all references to discussion of a work are combined in one listing.

Citing *Poetry Criticism*

When writing papers, students who quote directly from any volume in the Literary Criticism Series may use the following general format to footnote reprinted criticism. The first example pertains to material drawn from periodicals, the second to material reprinted from books.

Sylvia Kasey Marks, "A Brief Glance at George Eliot's *The Spanish Gypsy*," *Victorian Poetry* 20, no. 2 (Summer 1983), 184-90; reprinted in *Poetry Criticism*, vol. 20, ed. Ellen McGeagh (Detroit: The Gale Group), 128-31.

Linden Peach, "Man, Nature and Wordsworth: American Versions," *British Influence on the Birth of American Literature*, (Macmillan Press Ltd., 1982), 29-57; reprinted in *Poetry Criticism*, vol. 20, ed. Ellen McGeagh (Detroit: The Gale Group), 37-40.

Suggestions are Welcome

Readers who wish to suggest new features, topics, or authors to appear in future volumes, or who have other suggestions or comments are cordially invited to call, write, or fax the Managing Editor:

Project Editor, Literary Criticism Series
The Gale Group
27500 Drake Road
Farmington Hills, MI 48331-3535
1-800-347-4253 (GALE)
Fax: 248-699-8054

Acknowledgments

The editors wish to thank the copyright holders of the excerpted criticism included in this volume and the permissions managers of many book and magazine publishing companies for assisting us in securing reproduction rights. We are also grateful to the staffs of the Detroit Public Library, the Library of Congress, the University of Detroit Mercy Library, Wayne State University Purdy/Kresge Library Complex, and the University of Michigan Libraries for making their resources available to us. Following is a list of the copyright holders who have granted us permission to reproduce material in this volume of *PC*. Every effort has been made to trace copyright, but if omissions have been made, please let us know.

COPYRIGHTED EXCERPTS IN *PC*, VOLUME 40, WERE REPRODUCED FROM THE FOLLOWING PERIODICALS:

Concerning Poetry, v. 11, Spring, 1978. Copyright © 1978, Western Washington University. Reproduced by permission.—*Contemporary Literature,* v. 36, Spring, 1995. Copyright © 1995 The Board of Regents of the University of Wisconsin System. All rights reserved. Reproduced by permission.—*Durham University Journal,* July, 1991. Reproduced by permission.—*Eighteenth-Century Life,* v. 13, November, 1989. Copyright © The Johns Hopkins University Press. Reproduced by permission.—*ELH,* v. 57, Winter, 1990. Copyright © The Johns Hopkins University Press. Reproduced by permission.—*Explicator,* v. 54, Winter, 1996. Copyright © 1996 Helen Dwight Reid Educational Foundation. Reproduced with permission of the Helen Dwight Reid Educational Foundation, published by Heldref Publications, 1319 18th Street, NW, Washington, DC 20036-1802.—*Hitting Critical Mass,* v. 6, Spring, 2000. Reproduced by permission.—*Hudson Review,* v. 52, Summer, 1999. Copyright © 1999 by The Hudson Review, Inc. Reproduced by permission.—*James Dickey Newsletter,* v. 6, Fall, 1989. Copyright © 1989 James Dickey Newsletter/James Dickey Society. Reproduced by permission.—*Library Journal,* v. 119, 15 February, 1994 for review of "The Phoenix Gone, The Terrace Empty," by Doris Lynch. Copyright © 1994 by Reed Elsevier, USA. Reproduced by permission of the publisher and the author.—*LIT: Literature Interpretation Theory,* v. 12, April, 2001, for "Mocking My Own Ripeness: Authenticity, Heritage, and Self-Erasure in the Poetry of Marilyn Chin," by John Grey. Copyright © 2001 by OPA (Amsterdam) B.V. All rights reserved. Reproduced by permission of the publisher and the author.—*MELUS,* v. 25, Fall-Winter, 2000. Copyright ©, MELUS: The Society for the Study of Multi-Ethnic Literature of the United States, 2000. Reproduced by permission.—*Modern Poetry Studies,* v. 2, 1972; v. 5, 1974. Copyright © 1972, 1974, by Media Study, Inc. Reproduced by permission.—*The New Republic,* v. 204, 6 May, 1991. Reproduced by permission.— *New Statesman & Society,* v. 4, 15 March, 1991. Copyright © 1991 Statesman & Nation Publishing Company Limited. Reproduced by permission.—*New York Review of Books,* v. 46, 18 November, 1999. Copyright © 1999 Nyrev, Inc. Reproduced with permission from *The New York Review of Books.*—*Parnassus,* v. 13, Spring-Summer, 1986, for "Toward the Abyss: James Dickey at Middle Age," by Paul Christensen. Copyright © 1986 Poetry in Review Foundation, NY. Reproduced by permission of the publisher and the author.—*Prairie Schooner,* v. 52, Spring, 1978. Copyright © 1978 by University of Nebraska Press. Reproduced from *Prairie Schooner* by permission of the University of Nebraska Press.—*The Progressive,* v. 58, May, 1994. Copyright © 1994 by The Progressive, Inc. Reproduced by permission of *The Progressive,* 409 East Main Street, Madison, WI 53703.— *Publishers Weekly,* v. 241, 28 February, 1994; v. 248, 22 October, 2001. Copyright © 1994, 2001 by Reed Publishing USA. Reproduced from *Publishers Weekly,* published by the Bowker Magazine Group of Cahners Publishing Co., a division of Reed Publishing USA., by permission.—*Sewanee Review,* v. 71, Winter, 1963. Copyright © 1963, 1991 by The University of the South. Reproduced by permission of the editor.—*Signs: Journal of Women in Culture and Society,* v. 15, Autumn, 1989 for "The Sapphic-Platonics of Katherine Philips, 1632-1664," by Harrietre Andreadis. Reproduced by permission of the publisher and the author.—*South Carolina Review,* v. 26, Spring, 1994. Copyright © 1994 by Clemson University. Reproduced by permission.—*Southern Review,* v. 21, Winter, 1985, for "James Dickey: From 'The Other' through The Early Motion," by Harold Bloom. / v. 21, Winter, 1985, for "Reflections on 'Puella'" by James Applewhite. / v. 28, Autumn, 1992, for "The Whole Motion," by Richard Tillinghast. Copyright © 1992, by the author. / v. 34, Winter, 1998, for "James Dickey's Dear God of the Wilderness of Poetry," by Russell Fraser. Reproduced by permission of the respective authors.—*Studies in Eighteenth-Century Culture,* v. 7, 1978. Copyright © The Johns Hopkins University Press. Reproduced by permission.—*Studies in English Literature 1500-1900,* v. 27, Summer, 1987; v. 34, Summer, 1994; v. 35, Summer, 1995. Copyright © The Johns Hopkins University Press. Reproduced by permission.—*TriQuarterly,* Winter, 1968 for a review of "Poems 1957-1967 " by Ralph J. Mills, Jr. Copyright © 1968 by TriQuarterly, Northwestern University. Reproduced by permission of the author.—*World Literature Today,* v. 66, Winter, 1992. Reproduced by permission.—*The Yearbook of English Studies,* v. 19, 1989. Copyright © Modern Humanities Research Association 1989. Reproduced by permission of the publisher.

Literary Criticism Series Advisory Board

The members of the Gale Group Literary Criticism Series Advisory Board—reference librarians and subject specialists from public, academic, and school library systems—represent a cross-section of our customer base and offer a variety of informed perspectives on both the presentation and content of our literature criticism products. Advisory board members assess and define such quality issues as the relevance, currency, and usefulness of the author coverage, critical content, and literary topics included in our series; evaluate the layout, presentation, and general quality of our printed volumes; provide feedback on the criteria used for selecting authors and topics covered in our series; provide suggestions for potential enhancements to our series; identify any gaps in our coverage of authors or literary topics, recommending authors or topics for inclusion; analyze the appropriateness of our content and presentation for various user audiences, such as high school students, undergraduates, graduate students, librarians, and educators; and offer feedback on any proposed changes/ enhancements to our series. We wish to thank the following advisors for their advice throughout the year.

Marilyn Chin
1955-

(Full name Marilyn Mei Ling Chin) Chinese-born American poet.

INTRODUCTION

Chin is known for producing spare, often confrontational, poetry that explores her experience as a first-generation Chinese-American and a woman of color in the United States, as well as social and political injustices in her native China.

BIOGRAPHICAL INFORMATION

Chin was born in Hong Kong in 1955 to George and Rose Chin, who emigrated to the American Northwest shortly after her birth. In a well-known poem, "How I Got That Name: An Essay on Assimilation," Chin meditated on the fact that her father, a restaurant proprietor in Oregon, incongruously named her after the American film and cultural icon Marilyn Monroe—an occurrence that helped form Chin's thoughts on the experience of assimilation in America. Chin received her B.A. at the University of Massachusetts at Amherst in 1977 and her M.F.A. at the University of Iowa in 1981. She worked as a translator and editor in the International Writing Program at the University of Iowa from 1978 to 1982. In 1988 Chin took a position as an assistant professor of creative writing at San Diego State University, becoming a full professor of English and Asian-American studies in 1996. Chin has won numerous fellowships and awards for her writing, including a National Endowment for the Arts grant in 1984-1985 and 1991; the Josephine Miles Award from PEN in 1994; and the Pushcart Prize in 1994, 1995, and 1997.

MAJOR WORKS

Chin's first collection of verse, *Dwarf Bamboo* (1987), which she dedicated to the Communist poet and revolutionary Ai Qing, contains many poems that focus on the immigrant experience in the United States. Chin continued this theme in her second collection, *The Phoenix Gone, The Terrace Empty* (1994). In this volume Chin began to more deeply explore the damaging effects of Western standards on women of color, notably in the autobiographical poem "How I Got That Name: An Essay on Assimilation," in which Chin bluntly describes her father's naming

her after "some tragic white woman / swollen with gin and Nembutal." *The Phoenix Gone* also contains a section entitled "Beijing Spring," a group of poems dealing with the 1989 student uprising in China's Tiananmen Square. *Rhapsody in Plain Yellow* (2001), Chin's third volume of poetry, again examines the struggle between heritage and the new world, mostly in poems exploring her relationship with her parents and grandparents. In this collection Chin drew inspiration for the forms and rhythms of her poems from Chinese music as well as Persian ghazals and American blues music.

CRITICAL RECEPTION

Critics have praised Chin's poetry for its unflinching examination of the contradictory feelings brought on by immigration in general and for Asian Americans specifically. Chin's openness about female sexuality and the social roles of women of color—in particular the image of

Asian women as exotic and doll-like—and her frequent references to the revolutionary movement in China have earned her a reputation as an important political feminist poet.

PRINCIPAL WORKS

Poetry

Dwarf Bamboo 1987
The Phoenix Gone, The Terrace Empty 1994
Rhapsody in Plain Yellow 2001

CRITICISM

George Uba (essay date 1992)

SOURCE: Uba, George. "Versions of Identity in Post-Activist Asian American Poetry." In *Reading the Literatures of Asian America,* edited by Shirley Geok-lin Lim and Amy Ling, pp. 33-48. Philadelphia: Temple University Press, 1992.

[*In the following essay, Uba includes Chin in a discussion of Asian-American poets writing after the 1960s and 1970s, noting that Chin, in her poetry, is skeptical of the very source of personal and ethnic identity to which she is drawn.*]

The raw energy of Asian-Pacific American "activist" poets of the late 1960s and early 1970s gave impetus to a literature in the process of self-discovery. By refereeing unexplored spaces of Asian American existence, these poets helped preside over an emerging ethnic consciousness and helped plot the sociopolitical vectors of the age. Seeking to "unmask" poetry by removing it from the elitist academy (which had sealed meanings in the esoteric and the arcane, renounced plainness of speech, and conferred shamanistic status on university professors), the activist writers sought to deliver poetry to the People, who, apprehending its "essentials," would renew it in the spirit of emerging political freedom. The activist spirit survives in the bristling warning contained in Janice Mirikitani's "We, the Dangerous":[1]

> We, the dangerous,
> Dwelling in the ocean.
> Akin to the jungle.
> Close to the earth.

> Hiroshima
> Vietnam
> Tule Lake
> And yet we were not devoured.
> And yet we were not humbled.
> And yet we are not broken.

> *(Ayumi,* 211)

Not uncommonly, activist poems resorted to linguistic shock tactics as well, as in these lines from Merle Woo's "Yellow Woman Speaks":

> Yellow woman, a revolutionary speaks:

> "They have mutilated our genitals, but I will
>   restore them

>   . . . . .

>   I will create armies of . . . descendants.

> And I will expose the lies and ridicule
> the impotence of those who have called us
>   chink
>   yellow-livered
>   slanted cunts
>   exotic
> in order to abuse and exploit us.
>   And I will destroy them."

> *(Bruchac,* 286)

Woo's poem eschews the conventional finesse of Euro-American poetry in an effort to confront directly the oppressors who have developed and perpetuated racist stereotypes. The revolutionary's vow is to multiply and to "destroy." Less confrontational, Mirikitani's approach is to assert the vitalizing power to endure. Nevertheless, she too warns that "we" are "dangerous." The impetus behind these poems is not only politics in the conventional sense but also the politics of poetry. Both poems align themselves self-consciously with an oral tradition. Woo's poem demands that it be spoken aloud ("a revolutionary speaks"); in the process it also contests standard Euro-American definitions of poetry by embracing polemic. Mirikitani's poem violates the contemporary "rules" of poetry by relying heavily on political slogans and the rhetoric of abstraction. Her poem aligns itself not with a theory of poetry as written inscription but with an oral tradition that blurs the distinction between poem and chant, and privileges performance over inscription. Moreover, the poem's paratactical linking of "Hiroshima / Vietnam / Tule Lake" reflects Russell Leong's notion of a "tribal" impulse common to poets of the late 1960s and early 1970s, an impulse that highlighted the "shared experience[s] of subjugation" among people of color and that actively sought to "unlock the . . . keys to memory and to provide a base for unity" (166).

This tribalism was a common way of negotiating identity, especially valuable as an ethnographic signifier of resistance to an oppressive, well-armed, and thoroughly entrenched dominant culture. It was a means of resisting the assimilationist ethic for so long spreading insidiously across the American ethnic landscape by focusing on and celebrating differences between whites and people of color, while acknowledging both similarities and differences among the latter as well.[2] To some degree, much of contemporary Asian American poetry presupposes this activist base.

The situation has altered, however, in the sense that many of today's poets express at once an affinity for and a sense of distance from the activist tradition. In the wake of the profound demographic changes affecting Asian America, changes which have resulted in a diversity unimaginable twenty years ago, the reification of the "tribal" has become increasingly problematic.[3] The dimensions of the effort to achieve a communal or "tribalistic" connection have multiplied, even as the results of such effort have grown less certain. Keenly aware of heterogeneity, as well as the absence of geographical centers, today's poets may yearn for a connection they can only ratify in a compromised form. They have been thrust back upon their sense of an individual self, an alteration implying the forfeiture of oral traditions. Joined with a loss of faith in the efficacy of language as an agent of social reform and as a reliable tool of representation, this individualizing tendency has redirected poets toward Euro-American poetics.

But with a difference. Today's poets tend to appropriate such poetics for their own ethnographic purposes. If, in acknowledging the provisional conduct of poetry, post-activist poets hold that identity, whether tribal or otherwise, is always in doubt, it is not that the issue of identity has ceased to demand their attention. Indeed, the post-activist poem tends to recognize problematics of language and event both as a way of approaching identity and of renouncing its stability. Although these recognitions extend to an increasing number of poets, recent works by Marilyn Chin and David Mura and the special case of John Yau reveal some of the distinct contours that Asian American poetry currently describes. For Chin and Mura—although in different ways—conceiving identity is only possible by foregrounding its partialities, while for Yau every version of identity is radically contestable because of the unstable nature of the tools used to conceptualize it.

. . . . .

In dedicating her book *Dwarf Bamboo* to the Communist poet and revolutionary Ai Qing, Marilyn Chin reveals an affinity with the collectivist politics of the activist poets. However, her skepticism toward unificatory gestures and her intense recognition of identity as process rather than as cultural preserve lead her to question the very impulses toward which she is otherwise drawn. The poem **"Segments of a Bamboo Screen,"** for example, conjoins the centrifugal tendencies of world politics with the inability to negotiate pictorial unity out of the "segments" of the bamboo screen. The speaker questions the bamboo screen artist's ability to "sit there on top of the world" and gain a perspective "that I cannot"(18)—a centrist position around which all others supposedly revolve. For this speaker, the partial replaces the whole: "The moon is gibbous. Just say / She shall no longer pay you her full attention" (17).

Chin is also acutely aware of how historical contingencies intrude upon every version of identity. Rather than stabilizing a connection to her "Parent Node," Chin's frequent use of historicized personae reveals the provisional nature of all identity. The poems **"The Landlord's Wife"** and **"Untrimmed Mourning"** offer contrasting portraits of the widows of two Chinese men, one a wealthy landlord slain in the course of political ferment in 1919 and the other a poor man who had "only small pink babies / and one good hog" (14). Years later in post-revolutionary China, the landlord's wife, who still regrets her loss of status as "the wealthiest woman in Guang Dung," nevertheless repudiates her husband's memory and proclaims her allegiance to Chairman Mao. "'I never loved him, never. / The only man I love now, the only man I believe—/ The man from above, from Yenan'" (12). For the impoverished widow remaining in prerevolutionary China, however, who for ten years has "gulped down / this loneliness," the continuing pressures of survival have forced her to drag the hog to market where she will proclaim in broken dialect, "'Rich man, have you no / dollars to taste?'" (14). The "Chinese" identity of these two survivors is self-consciously multiple, deriving from no acknowledged center but negotiated among historical contingencies. In severing her allegiance to her landlord husband's estate, the rich widow responds to a far-reaching alteration in political circumstances, while the poor widow responds to an immediate change in her personal environment. At the same time, it is evident that each woman's sense of identity is subject to further internal shift, depending on forces beyond her control.

As history destabilizes identity, so can ideology. The poem **"After My Last Paycheck from the Factory . . ."** takes as its epigraph, "For the Chinese Cultural Revolution and all that was wrong with my life" (21)—a satirical thrust at the notion that Mao's Cultural Revolution conferred a stable identity upon everyone of Chinese descent. And, indeed, in the poem a youthful Chinese American expatriate working in a Communist factory experiences a profound revulsion when she invites an elderly Chinese man for an afternoon meal. The sight of old Liu eating dog and smacking "his greasy lips" is enough to make the woman yearn for "home" and her "lover's gentle kisses" (21). Although the sight of two girls wearing uniforms, bandanas, and armbands and "shouting slogans and Mao-ish songs" momentarily reminds her of why she has come to China in the first place, "the realist Liu" disrupts this "mirage" by revealing that the raw conditions of life have not changed for him, for as he declares, "'It's the dog I ordered and am eating still!'" (21). The dog has spots, "rampant colonies of scabies and fleas," and a forehead that "bled with worms" (21-22). The woman says, "I rubbed my eyes, readjusted the world" (22). But through Chin's lenses, the world must be read justed yet again. For a neighboring patron, a "stout provincial governor" who dines for free on fine "Chinese pug, twenty-five yuan a leg" and who afterwards flaunts his wealth, is destined, according to Liu, to pay a drastic penalty for his reactionary ways: "'and he as dead as the four-legged he ate / two short kilometers before home'" (22).

By setting itself skeptically on the shifting borders of ideological rectitude, the poem complicates the leftist political identification that constitutes the radical base of an "authentic" Asian American identity. Obviously, though, it also prohibits the retreat into bourgeois complacency. At the end of the poem, the woman is given no firm ideological hold on her own identity. Whatever she thought it was is now called into question; whatever it may become remains in a state of flux.

If history and ideology move toward the destabilization of identity, their "absence" exacts a similar price. Originally from Hong Kong, Chin has spent most of her life in America. In the poem **"Repulse Bay,"** the "dead and swimming creatures of the sea" are images of the speaker herself, struggling to remain culturally afloat in a defamiliarized locale, a part of "the country I have lost" (64). In the poem **"A Chinaman's Chance,"** Chin acknowledges the special difficulties faced by the American-born Chinese attempting to recover the Chinese American past when only its fragments remain. The inability to pattern oneself after Chinese ancestors in America is stated succinctly in the lines "The railroad killed your great-grandfather / His arms here, his legs there. . . . / *How can we remake ourselves in his image?*" (29). That is, how can a connection be forged with an image that has been rent, scattered, and left unpreserved? With an ancestor who can only be recalled—both physically and otherwise—in pieces? Such a dilemma can be exacerbated by alienation from traditional systems of belief, an alienation manifested in the sardonic question posed at the poem's start:

> If you were a Chinese born in America, who would
>   you believe
> Plato who said what Socrates said
> Or Confucius in his bawdy way:
>   "So a male child is born to you
>   I am happy, very very happy."
>
>   (29)

The repudiation of traditional beliefs further problematizes the effort to recover a "lost" identity.

Yet, despite their instabilities, it is wrong to assume that Chin's views of identity inevitably testify to loss. In the poem **"I confess . . ."** the speaker expresses a dialogic relationship between cultures by reading alternately Bachelard's "The Poetics of Space" and chapters from "The Compassionate Buddha." She pens ironic "letters of progress":

> one day I am filial
> monkey, practicing reading
> and writing. Next day
> I wear ink
> eyeliner, open up
> Mandarin frock for the boys.
>
>   (53-54)

The speaker's mischievous "confession" regarding her obsessive movement between cultures is partly an acknowledgment of the intellectual tradition of the West, which she willingly inherits. But more to the point, it is simultaneously a defense of an identity kept vital by its own instability. For Chin, the question of identity is engaging precisely because it is never still. The alternative—to snatch "a quick decision—/ to marry Chinese, / to succeed in business, / to buy that slow boat" (54)—is to avoid the vexations and rewards of self-examination by impulsive marriage to convention. Attending only to "business" means boarding a "slow boat" bound for a cultural nowhere.

Like Marilyn Chin, David Mura, author of the book *After We Lost Our Way,* acknowledges how activist poets serve as his literary ancestors, even as he insists upon his necessary differences from them. As a third-generation Japanese American, Mura feels a particular connection with the activists of twenty years ago of whom so many were also at least third-generation Asian Americans. The anger, outrage, and alienation they shared are especially manifest in Mura's poems dealing with racism, internment camps, and assimilation. Like Chin, Mura operates from outside the earlier oral tradition, even though he remains attracted to the aural (as is evidenced by several poems bearing the words "suite," "song," and "argument" in their titles). But whereas Chin remains skeptical of the communalistic impulse as a basis for identity, even as she yearns for its retrieval, Mura campaigns at once to recover and expand the impulse by embracing other marginalized lives—the oppressed, wretched, and suffering in all stations and cultures, including (in a singularly bold stroke) the homosexual Italian film director and writer Pasolini. By embracing even a white male European, Mura testifies to the impossibility of containing identity along purely racial and ethnic lines. Identity may also be conceived in the presence of lives outwardly removed from one's own.

Pasolini, as Mura explains in a series of eleven poems strategically placed at the center of his book, frequented the brutal Italian demimonde of "punks, pickpockets, whores," even as he directed brilliant, controversial films—nearly all of them censored, denounced, or involved in lawsuits—that assure his place in film history. From the peasant son of a father devoted to Mussolini to the adult "crazy about Marx and *terza rima*" (25) and from his compassion for slum dwellers to his autocratic desire "to subjugate, to block / his [lover's] ego's light with the shadow of mine" (30), Pasolini was a figure steeped in contradictions. Refusing to abjure "the ambiguous life" (25), Pasolini was persecuted in the popular press and prosecuted in a series of demeaning public trials.

In the majority of these poems Mura assumes a mask, usually that of Pasolini himself—Pasolini describing his seduction at the hands of his young lover Ninetto, Pasolini describing his ambivalence toward Roland Barthes or writing a letter from Nepal to Alberto Moravia, Pasolini transcribing a stunning apologia for his promiscuous, risk-filled life—while interspersing these subjective accounts with neutral ones of his brutal murder by a teenager, a "two-bit thief" (44). Although Pasolini seems as remote from conventional Japanese American experience as humanly imaginable, Mura identifies him as a sort of presiding spirit, joined to the author by his powerful sense of alienation from bourgeois culture, by his artistry, and by his human frailty. Despite the apparent modesty of the title, the centrally placed poem "Intermission: Postcard from Rome" elucidates the nature and depth of the connection between the two artists. In a cemetery in Casarsa the American wife, a descendant of the Mayflower Pilgrims, discovers Pasolini's simple stone marker. It lies "next to the stone of Susanna," his mother; coincidentally, the American wife's name is "Susie" (37). Here, at the grave, the Japanese American poet stares at the stone of the Italian filmmaker and begins to weep, apologizing once because "it seems so predictable." Later, the speaker acknowledges that "in my country, // it's customary to ask why, why Pasolini?" (38). That is, why should a Japanese American poet be drawn so powerfully to Pasolini? The speaker answers, "We are young. We believe in the unconscious, an emotional life" (38). A stream of connection, unconscious and emotional, underlies and proceeds from the two lives despite surface discontinuities. The speaker affirms, "It's no good to say my genes are Japanese" (38), as though that simple biological accident somehow accounts for an entire identity. The speaker acknowledges, "We will never be intimate. Will always be the same" (38). They will always be the same in their lack of intimacy; their distance will never be completely bridged. Their identities are acknowledged as conjunctural, not identical. But at the same time the speaker reaffirms at the end the initiating connection: "Dear ghost, do not go to another house" (38). Only in this one poem is the issue of the speaker's Japanese American identity directly raised. But the affirmation of the connection to Pasolini suggests the plural possibilities of identity within the framework of opposition, rage, and outrage.

Elsewhere, Mura offers a gallery of portraits of the infirm and dying, the lost and the as-good-as lost. The range itself is remarkable—an architect's five-year old son dying, a Cambodian refugee bound for France, a Viet Cong recalling the men he has slain, a man in a pornographic bookstore, another turned informer in South Africa, a brutally beaten woman lying in a hospital emergency room. The nearly unbearable cry of pain, so heterogeneous in its sources yet so alarmingly unified in its despair, contributes to Mura's idea of identity expanded beyond its customary limits.

Ostensibly, then, Mura merely expands what the activist tradition had all along pointed in the direction of—a synthetical identity of the oppressed that resolves all the competing elements of experience. But the difference between him and the activist writers is pronounced, starting with the fact that he acknowledges linguistic limitations, admitting that language can result in "dangling rantings" (71) and averring that even at its best, its value in a world marked by profound suffering remains problematic. Like Marilyn Chin, Mura also acknowledges that all ideas about identity are in some way inadequate, partial, and

contradictory, even as he asserts that it is these very properties that help us to install identity at any moment in history. So imperfect, partial, and inherently contradictory is any expressed notion of identity that it cannot be known through any concrete instance; yet these same partialities and contradictions necessarily point in the direction of identity. As Fredric Jameson so succinctly puts it in describing Adorno's *Negative Dialektik* (Adorno is one of Mura's intellectual affiliations), "a negative dialectic has no choice but to affirm the notion and value of an ultimate synthesis, while negating its possibility and reality in every concrete case that comes before it" (56).

It is in this light that Mura's continual yearning for reconciliation, wholeness, and the unification of identity must be understood. The opening lines of his book's first poem, "Grandfather and Grandmother in Love," elucidate the poet's charge: "Now I will ask for one true word beyond / betrayal" (3). This word should be as true, as authentic, as the speaker takes the sex act between his grandparents in love to have been. Taking this "one true word," the speaker will "crack it, like a seed / between the teeth, spit it out in the world" (3), where, it is hoped, it may take root. The effort seemingly reflects what Adorno describes as "neo-romantic" poetry's endeavor "to recover some of the substantiality of language" (*Aesthetic Theory,* 23). For Mura, to substantialize language would be to re-substantialize his grandparents' pasts, to negotiate identity with an instrument made reliable and whole once again.

But Mura's poetry does not actually suggest either that language can be resubstantialized or identity stabilized in this way. In investigating identities within a given group, Mura repeatedly uncovers contradictions. In "A *Nisei* Picnic: From an Album" he describes an uncle, a veteran of the war, who eventually "ballooned like Buddha, / over three hundred pounds"; an aunt who tried vainly to raise minks instead of children; and the speaker's father who "worked . . . hard to be white" (14). The use of the family photograph to inscribe these disparate selves in a version of unity serves as reminder of how such family presentations constitute a lie collectively assented to, functioning to conceal rather than reveal differences. The speaker, still a young boy in the old photo, sees through the imposture in a burst of helpless sympathy: "Who are these grown-ups? / Why are they laughing? How can I tear / the bewilderment from their eyes?" (14).

Such self-awareness joins with vituperation in "Song for Uncle Tom, Tonto, and Mr. Moto," where Mura savages the unitary mask that racial stereotyping assumes by proclaiming a declaration of war to be waged by the obsequious yes-men of popular culture. These oppressed— African American, American Indian, Hispanic, Asian American—who have been forced to "live in the monstrous sarcophagi" of a "white cultivated heart" (15), have forged an alliance of the oppressed out of their hurt and rage. Here Mura self-consciously aligns himself with the tribal impulse and comes closest to connecting with an oral tradition of song. The creature orchestrating this rage is "Kitsune, the fox," a trickster figure with a "sneaky inscrutable body" (15) who reveals not only the inadequacy of racial stereotypes but also the yearning for an authentic identity. But himself a polymorphous figure, Kitsune cannot help but represent the uncertain nature of the identity aspired to. Linked by a shared outrage over oppression, the identities behind the mask of Kitsune nevertheless are never wholly revealed. By use of Kitsune, the poem necessarily acknowledges its own partialness.

Mura offers no enduring consolation in the form of language or event, no "true word beyond / betrayal" (the poem "The One Who Tells, The One Who Burns" describes a black South African watching the brutal murder of the black man he has informed on). Indeed, the poem "Hope Without Hope" contests the value of writing at all: "Words on the page, prayers, even shouts of rage, / What do they count against tanks, missiles, guns?" (61). Alternating lines of the poem rhyme, often conventionally ("rage"/ "wage"; "guns"/"one"), as if to point up the futility of poetry against the unrhymed brutalities of existence. One's "poems are like roses," we are told, "Washed in the gutter by a dozen hoses" (61). Throughout there persists the feeling that language, no matter how powerfully expressed, changes nothing. And even though the despair is sometimes countered by "moments of release" (76) and affirmation, it is always with the sense of the temporal, with the acute knowledge that every brief burst of "clarity" contains as well the threat of its own extinction.

Only in the poem "The Natives" is an image of perfect unification offered. It is here where "time disappeared" (22), here where soldiers are absorbed into a mysterious, pacifistic "native" culture and gradually transformed into peaceful beings, "like soft-eyed virgins" (22). Gradually, the speaker of the poem says, "our names / fell from our mouths, never heard again" (21). But this note of reconciliation and transcendence recognizes at the same time its own unreality. Indeed, the markedly "unreal" conditions are what allow such a note to sound at all. Thus, the unificatory identity is negated as an actuality even as it is affirmed as an ideal.

Unlike both Chin and Mura, John Yau poses the special instance of the writer who not only eschews communalistic connections and oral traditions of poetry but affiliates with decidedly Western traditions of modern art (he doubles as an art critic). Author of *Corpse and Mirror,* along with at least six other volumes of poetry, Yau utilizes many of the elements associated with experimental writing, including discontinuous narrative, suspended logic, blurred distinctions between animate and inanimate objects, and a network of private symbols. His effort primarily is to disconnect rather than connect, to project a world cut off from certitude—a world in which human beings exist in perpetual exile, their lives an amalgam of absurdity, banality, and insufficiency, and in which politics are the ephemerae of a provisional reality. By contesting myths and other structuring devices as coherent stewards of meaning, as well as language as a reliable epistemologi-

cal tool, Yau posits a world of disorder in which the unstable traces of identity threaten to dissolve as quickly as they appear.

Evidence of such instability can be found in the prose poem "Two Kinds of Story-Telling," which describes an immigrant woman for whom the China of her childhood is recalled as a fairy tale, "a kind of Eden she could never return to" (72). Yet in the second telling of her story, she focuses on "how the present is better, and how the future will be better still." Behind this second version, the narrator asserts, lies the indigenous narrative of "the passage of the *Mayflower* to the New World," even though the names *Mayflower, Pilgrim,* and *Plymouth Rock* are associated in the woman's mind only with a moving van and insurance ads (72). The point is that the woman's sensibility has been incidentally conditioned by things she has come into contact with in America, and in the process she has become more thoroughly imbued with an American myth than even she is aware. The line of demarcation between the exile longing for her Chinese home and the immigrant at home in America becomes hopelessly blurred by such subconscious activity, as does the identity such demarcations are intended to reveal.

Behind the problematics of identity lies Yau's skepticism regarding the organizing properties of myth and other forms of narrative. Consistently foregrounding how writer and readers together create meaning, his poems acknowledge "the human urge to make order while pointing out that the orders we create are just that: human constructs, not natural or given entities" (Hutcheon 41-42). "Missing Pages," which describes an unidentified resort island whose featured attraction is a pair of "jeweled towers" rising out of a bay—"symbols of the miraculous"—parodies one type of mythmaking (33). The creation legend surrounding these towers begins "in daylight and desire" (33), which means that "anyone can add whatever they like to the story, or take some chunk of it away" (34). The precise details are later settled upon by vote of the city council at the beginning of the tourist season, and the story is passed on to the inhabitants' children as the "basis for the entire [school] curriculum" (34).

Yau also challenges language as a reliable epistemological tool. The poem "Persons in the Presence of a Metamorphosis," whose title pays homage to Miró, demonstrates his method. It begins thus:

> The porcelain bayonet of noon scrapes the face
> of a man who has forgotten why he started
> to spit. A uniformed girl,
>
> tiny and tireless, memorizes words
> she believes make accurate mirrors.
> A nun felt damp and gray. . . .
>
> (19)

Just as Miró attempts simultaneously to quicken and release a flux of energies through his biomorphs, Yau disturbs and liberates the individual word from its "inert" positioning within syntax. Words mysteriously appear and reappear, behaving like linguistic particles capable of leaving and reentering this created universe at random points. The "porcelain" reappears as a "porcelain glaze of noon," which then reappears as "porcelain rooms" (19). Likewise, the "bayonet" reappears, as do the man and the girl and the mirrors. And so on. Despite the girl's belief that words "make accurate mirrors," the evidence of the poem is otherwise. In vain the poem, like the plumber, "looks for a word / with none of its pages missing" (19). If the words cannot be trusted as representations of reality, neither can their meanings be managed. So a young Catholic girl in her uniform who earnestly memorizes words (perhaps her catechism) suddenly may "spit" out a different kind of word or be transformed into a different type of person—a woman warrior polishing bayonets (19). Identity, then, is immediately contested by the very means used to construct it. Because these basic units of syntax are subject to almost instantaneous change (metamorphosis), this poem and others like it defy adequate summarizing. Their meanings change in the process of decoding.

"Shanghai Shenanigans" is a poem whose title seems to promise a negotiation between a recognizably Chinese setting and a recognizably non-Chinese set of behaviors. Instead, it is a poem whose lines depend on conjunctures as accidental as the alliterative "sh" sounds that apparently determined the poem's title. Here is how the poem begins:

> The moon emptied its cigarette over a row of clouds
> whose windowsills tremble in the breeze
>
> The breeze pushed my boat through a series
> of telephone conversations started by perfume
>
> Perfume splashed over the words of a nomad
> who believed it was better to starve than to laugh
>
>   (57)

The concluding word of each stanza instigates each succeeding stanza. The connections between stanzas are purely linguistic, however, not logical. Clearly the poem could proceed indefinitely. Closure is possible, but the illusion of inevitability is forfeited. Under such conditions, the geographical bearings implied in the word "Shanghai" fail to assist in the formulation of meaning. Since the poem suggests that language is in some sense always a series of linguistic accidents, then the adequacy of language in formulating identity must always remain problematic. Yau writes at the farthest possible remove from the assumptions of the activist poets.

Nevertheless, in maintaining that identity as a construction of language and myth is always insecure, Yau does not dismiss such constructing activities as useless; on the contrary he serves as an example of the directions these activities may take. His identity formation involves the dissolving of the more apparent evidences of the "ethnic" but not a denial that such evidences, on some level, persist. The poem "Two Kinds of Language" recalls the exclusion that a Chinese American boy felt whenever his immigrant parents spoke Chinese in his presence. As an adult traveling along "the back roads through North Carolina," his radio tuned to, presumably, country music, the Chinese American senses how "all the songs seemed to tell a similar story, and yet the words and music never quite seemed to fit together" (82). In other words, for the Asian American there must always be a recognition of difference, no matter how deeply he or she penetrates into the heart of America. At the same time, what was forfeited by virtue of becoming American may be recovered on some unannounced level. Although the boy did not understand the words of his parents, he realized that "if he listened hard enough, what he thought he understood was the intonation and the voice" (82). Below the level of the conscious and beyond our ability to report, these vestiges persist.

Occasionally, Yau even acknowledges the ability to construct moments of alignment among disparate selves. In his poem "Parallel Lives," he arrives at an astonishing connection between Alexander Pope and a mythological Aztec, a figure who arrives "In the guise of a postcard / Depicting a grim-faced Aztec deity." This god is "bent beneath / A disc meant to represent the sun" (3). Yau recollects that Pope was ravaged by polio in his youth, "And the memory of it grew out of his back / Until he resembled a squat reptile" (4). By the end of the poem, Yau affirms the unexpected "parallel" between the poet and the Aztec god as messengers: "Joined together in their deformity / And the need to deliver something / To its correct destination" (4). To be sure, the parallel is presented provisionally, depending on a momentary agreement to suspend all the disqualifying factors which another moment may restore, but the impetus behind it would be easily recognizable to David Mura and ultimately to the activist poets.

. . . . .

Together, the writings of Marilyn Chin, David Mura, and John Yau reveal some of the depth, range, and sophistication of Asian American poetry today. From the social ferment of the 1960s arose an intense concern over the nature of Asian American identity and the instruments of a new socioeconomic policy. Such concern manifested itself valuably in challenging racial stereotypes and literary conventions alike. Attuned to the increasingly heterogeneous nature of Asian America as well as to the problematics of language, today's poets acknowledge the conditionalities that shape identity without stabilizing it and the provisionality of poetry itself. At the same time, their writings recognize a tradition to which, even in departure, they ultimately refer back.

Notes

1. Janice Mirikitani is probably the best-known of the Asian American activist poets. For additional background, see, for example, her editing of *Time to Greez!* See also Bruce Iwasaki's introductions to the sections on literature in the anthologies Tachiki, ed., *Roots* and Gee, ed., *Counterpoint.*

2. As a corollary to the attack on the assimilationist ethic, Frank Chin, though not an activist writer per

se, has long served as the most outspoken opponent of the concept of the "dual identity," i.e., "half" (white) American, "half" Asian. See, for example, *Aiiieeeee!*, p. viii and passim.

3. A fairly typical anthology of the period, Hsu's 1972 *Asian-American Authors* limited itself to Chinese American, Japanese American, and Filipino American authors. Wand's 1974 *Asian-American Heritage* added Korean Americans and an indigenous Polynesian oral poetry in translation.

Works Cited

Adorno, T. W. *Aesthetic Theory.* Trans. C. Lenhardt. Ed. Gretel Adorno and Rolf Tiedemann. London: Routledge, 1984.

———. *Negative Dialektik.* Frankfurt: Suhrkamp Verlag, 1966.

Bruchac, Joseph, ed. *Breaking Silence: An Anthology of Contemporary Asian American Poets.* Greenfield Center, N.Y.: Greenfield Review Press, 1983.

Chin, Frank, et al., eds. *Aiiieeeee! An Anthology of Asian-American Writers.* Washington, D.C.: Howard University Press, 1975.

Chin, Marilyn. *Dwarf Bamboo.* Greenfield Center, N.Y.: Greenfield Review Press, 1987.

Gee, Emma, ed. *Counterpoint: Perspectives on Asian America.* Los Angeles: Asian American Studies Center, University of California, 1976.

Hsu, Kai-yu, and Helen Palubinskas, eds. *Asian-American Authors.* Boston: Houghton Mifflin, 1972.

Hutcheon, Linda. *A Poetics of Postmodernism.* New York: Routledge, 1988.

Jameson, Fredric. *Marxism and Form: Twentieth-Century Dialectical Theories of Literature.* Princeton, N.J.: Princeton University Press, 1971.

Leong, Russell. "Poetry within Earshot." *Amerasia Journal* 15.1 (1989): 165-193.

Mirikitani, Janice, ed. *Time to Greez!: Incantations from the Third World.* San Francisco: Glide Publications, 1975.

———, ed. *Ayumi.* San Francisco: The Japanese American Anthology Committee, 1980.

Mura, David. *After We Lost Our Way.* New York: Dutton, 1989.

Tachiki, Amy, et al. *Roots: An Asian American Reader.* Los Angeles: Continental Graphics, 1971.

Wand, David Hsin-Fu, ed. *Asian-American Heritage: An Anthology of Prose and Poetry.* New York: Washington Square Press, 1974.

Yau, John. *Corpse and Mirror.* New York: Holt, Rinehart and Winston, 1983.

Doris Lynch (review date 1994)

SOURCE: Lynch, Doris. Review of *The Phoenix Gone, The Terrace Empty,* by Marilyn Chin. *Library Journal* 119, no. 3 (15 February 1994): 164.

[*In the following review, Lynch offers high praise for most of the poems in* The Phoenix Gone, The Terrace Empty.]

The strongest poems in Chin's second collection [*The Phoenix Gone, the Terrace Empty.*] (after *Dwarf Bamboo*, Greenfield, 1987) present an immigrant's view, combining old stories and sensibilities with an American idiom. In **"How I Got That Name,"** the author reveals how she received her name from two cultures. In adopting a new land and renouncing the old, she writes, "My loss is your loss, a dialect here, a memory there." Her verse is full of mysterious images, gifts from another culture, details that enlarge our world: "her lotus feet," "almond grass-jelly and guava," "my umbilical cord wrapped in rice-paper." As in every collection, there are weaker entries, especially those set at Crestwood Psychiatric Hospital. Of particular interest is the section entitled "Beijing Spring," in which Chin writes about Tiananmen Square and the Chinese Democratic Movement from a Chinese American perspective. We take away from these poems "the song within the song, the weeping within the willow."

Publishers Weekly (review date 1994)

SOURCE: Review of *The Phoenix Gone, The Terrace Empty,* by Marilyn Chin. *Publishers Weekly* 241, no. 9 (28 February 1994): 79.

[*In the following review, the critic praises Chin's simplicity of imagery and language in* The Phoenix Gone, The Terrace Empty.]

[In *The Phoenix Gone, The Terrace Empty*] Chin (*Dwarf Bamboo*) writes with a toughened lyricism that persuades us of the poet's firm life knowledge: she never imputes to experience (or poetry) a false or wishful glamour. Yet Chin refuses to sacrifice her sensibility to cynicism, either, though at times she is willing to acknowledge bitterness, contempt or disappointment as her lot. Instead, she seems to strike a balance between ideal and tatty, pure and spoiled, a balance that is literary and also cultural, considering her own position as one whose father, "a petty thug, / who bought a chain of chopsuey joints / in Piss River, Oregon," named his Asian American daughter after Marilyn Monroe: "And there I was, a wayward pink baby, / named after some tragic white woman / swollen with gin and Nembutal." Chin's habit of stalwart declaration gives the poetry a grounded force, line to line; and her imagery, simple and spare, lifts up those same lines. Directness and indirection can be tools of equal use, she shows, and though not all the poetry calls fully on them both, the work that does is unsentimentally courageous.

Matthew Rothschild (review date 1994)

SOURCE: Rothschild, Matthew. "A Feast of Poetry." *Progressive* 58 (May 1994): 48-50.

[*In the following excerpt, Rothschild praises Chin's intensely personal depiction of cultural assimilation.*]

Marilyn Chin has a voice all her own—witty, epigraphic, idiomatic, elegiac, earthy. In *The Phoenix Gone, The Terrace Empty,* she covers the canvas of cultural assimilation with an intensely personal brush. Born in Hong Kong and raised in Oregon, she pours herself into her poetry.

"How I Got That Name: An Essay on Assimilation" begins with the declaration, "I am Marilyn Mei Ling Chin," and recounts how her father "obsessed with a bombshell blonde / transliterated 'Mei Ling' to 'Marilyn,'" honoring her with the name of "some tragic white woman / swollen with gin and Nembutal." She goes on to warn that the stereotypes of Asian Americans are wrong: "We've managed to fool the experts," she writes, ". . . they can use us. / But the 'Model Minority' is a tease."

Worse than that, it can be fatal. Her **"Elegy for Chloe Nguyen"** tells of her precocious childhood friend, "Bipedal in five months, trilingual in a year; / at eleven she had her first lover." At thirty-three, she was dead. The last line reads: "Chloe, we are finally Americans now. Chloe, we are here!".

Similarly affecting are the ten little poems that make up **"Homage to Diana Toy,"** a patient Chin tutored in a psychiatric hospital. When Toy, denied citizenship in the United States and sexually taken advantage of by an administrator, commits suicide, Chin blames herself, an "unworthy tutor," who "failed to tell her about the fifty paltry stars."

Chin concerns herself not only with the United States, but also, poignantly, with China. She dedicates a section of her book to the Chinese Democratic Movement. In **"Beijing Spring,"** she embraces the protesters. "Lover, on Tienanmen Square, near the Avenue of Eternal Peace / believe in the passions of youth, / I believe in eternal spring." She offers to "breathe life into your life" so rebellion can "begin again."

The immense charm that Chin brings to this book comes out in some of her "Love Poesies," as in, **"Where Is the Moralizer, Your Mother?".**

Here and in other poems, Chin parks the reader at the busy intersection of love, sex, family, and politics. This convergence makes for an astonishing conclusion in **"A Portrait of the Nation, 1990-1991."** This six-page poem includes sexual puns, remembrances of past lovers, praise for masturbation, remarks the judge made to her when she became a naturalized citizen, reminders of those denied citizenship, plus reflections on being in bed with a lover when the Persian Gulf war began: "Last night, in our large, rotund bed, / we witnessed the fall. Ours / was an 'aerial war.' Bombs / glittering in the twilight sky / against the Star Spangled Banner."

I've read this book three times now, and each time I go through it, I find it more compelling. For me, the most moving poem is **"Tienanmen, the Aftermath,"** where Chin again juxtaposes being in bed while atrocities are committed: "There was blood and guts all over the road, / I said I'm sorry, darling, and rolled over." The poem closes with this haunting admonition: "leave the innocent ones alone, / those alive, yet stillborn, undead, yet waiting / in a fitful sleep undeserved of an awakening."

Mary Slowik (essay date 2000)

SOURCE: Slowik, Mary. "Beyond Lot's Wife: The Immigration Poems of Marilyn Chin, Garrett Hongo, Li-Young Lee, and David Mura." *MELUS* 25, nos. 3-4 (fall-winter 2000): 221-42.

[*In the following essay, Slowik examines the ways in which Chin and other Asian-American poets address their need to examine their cultural roots while continuing to assimilate into their new culture.*]

When God tells Lot to flee Soddam and Gomorrah, he cautions him not to look back. Lot's wife cannot resist the temptation and, as they rush from the great fire storm erupting behind them, she does look back and is immediately turned into a pillar of salt. The fear of looking back and yet the compulsion to look back at the country that one has left behind infuses much cross-cultural writing in the United States today. The experience of immigration is a central fact in the lives of Asian, Hispanic, Mid-Eastern, Slavic, Irish, and Italian families in America. Even when the immigration is several generations removed, cross-cultural writers searching for their roots must in one way or another grapple with the event itself.

For many families, immigration is a traumatic experience. Expelled out of their homelands, immigrants must suffer the treacherous journey to America and then survive in a different and frequently hostile host culture. Families do not easily talk about these experiences. Migrations are frequently shrouded in silence and an unspoken prohibition not to look back. For Asian immigrants in America, the subject of this paper, silence about origins in Japan or China has been a necessary course as they have attempted to assimilate into a dangerous, frequently racist environment. During the era of the Exclusion Acts and the internment camps of World War II, having Asian origins and cultural identity incurred enormous penalties: job and home loss, deportation, even imprisonment and death.

The writers whom I am discussing in this paper, however, suggest that there are even more painful and damaging silences than those required by survival in a hostile environment. There are the silences families demand of their own members, both out of cultural tradition and also out of profound and unexamined ambivalence about cultural identity. Such silence passed on from one generation to the next robs sons and daughters of a knowledge of their own history and origins. It also places families in a void between cultures, where they can feel paralyzed by an inexplicable shame and guilt. It is the failure to look back, these sons and daughters claim, that turns one into a deathly statue. Lot and their own families may have the curse wrong. One has to look back in order to look forward. It is only by looking back that one escapes death.

Garrett Hongo, Marilyn Chin, David Mura, and Li-Young Lee came of age in the 1960s and 70s and gained literary recognition in the 1980s. One of their central projects, both as poets and as Asian American children of immigrants, is to confront the silence of their families head-on. In doing so, they write an intense and innovative lyric poetry that in complex ways broadens and complicates the first person, meditative poetry of self-examination that dominates American writing today.

Life, these writers insist, does not begin when an immigrant steps on the shore of America. Life does not start with the first sighting of the Statue of Liberty or the Golden Gate Bridge. Rather, immigrants take the history and culture of their country of origin with them and, whether they intend to or not, pass it on to their children who then live in a fragmentary world which speaks always of some other place, some other culture no longer fully realized or acknowledged. "The migrant voice tells us what it is like to feel a stranger and yet at home, to live simultaneously inside and outside one's immediate situation" (King xv).

The dislocation that the children of immigration suffer is not rooted solely in the break-up of personality, examined so fully by American first-person poetry. It also resides in the break-up of history and geography occasioned by abrupt cross-cultural flight. The landscape of immigrant families is strewn not only with personal symbols that are difficult to decipher but also with public symbols wrested out of a larger cultural context that would give them meaning.

The poetry of immigration also pushes beyond the time-span of a single existence. Immigrants see their lives as chapters in a larger family narrative that precedes and follows their own. The task of emigration and assimilation is frequently not completed in one generation: parents and grandparents pass the torch to succeeding generations. Garrett Hongo, Marilyn Chin, David Mura, and Li-Young Lee have taken up the torch, even if ultimately they will douse its flames. Thus, the meaning of their individual lives does not reside in the single span of their own lifetimes as is the case with most confessional poets. Meaning also resides within the earlier generations of their families and in the generations to follow. The poets of immigration are entangled in the obligation of familial respect and in the obligation to interpret and pass on family his-

tory and family story. As part of a larger history of emigration and assimilation, they acknowledge their responsibility to complete an immigration narrative that their parents and grandparents have started, not in an isolated voice but a family's voice discovering its own expression.

The silences these poets face are complex. There is no established tradition of Asian American poetry of immigration to draw on. Immigration itself is surrounded by a disturbing literary silence. There is very little formal writing by actual immigrants about their experience. Many immigrants came out of an oral tradition which expressed itself in stories and songs which were not recorded, and the stress of migration and the demands of mere survival precluded extensive written first-hand history (See Lim). There are efforts to recover Asian American folk and oral traditions by Marlon K. Hom, Robert Lee, and in the collection of Angel Island poems in Island, but, as Sau-Ling Cynthia Wong admits in An Interethnic Companion to Asian American Literature, "the oral tradition among Chinese Americans is, by and large, under-researched and ill-understood" (42-43).

For the poets I am concerned with here, the more troubling silence originates in the fear and cultural shame of their own families. The sense of displacement is particularly exacerbated by the "cultural amnesia" fostered by their parents. King-Kok Cheung, in "Reviewing Asian American Literary Studies," uses the narrator of Maxine Hong King's China Men to pose the central question these poets ask their families: "Do you mean to give us a chance at being real Americans by forgetting the Chinese past?" (6).

For the Japanese-Americans, whose first migration experiences were repeated during the forced removal to internment camps during World War II, the silence crosses several generations: "Although most sansei third-generation Japanese-Americans were not yet born at the time of internment," Stan Yogi writes, "the event has marked the third generation psychically, mainly through the silence issei first-generation and nisei second-generation maintained about the complexities and traumas of the war years" (126). As opposed to the insistence of more recent Asian American writers on diaspora, that is, the scattering of people away from a homeland to which they never quite lose allegiance, or on the cultivation of a state of permanent exile (See preface in King) or on the scenario of immigration and return-to-homeland envisioned by many nineteenth and early twentieth century immigrants (See Kelen and Stone), the poets of my paper are caught within a family culture that takes the American mainstream at its most prosperous as its point of reference. It is the country of destination not the country of origin,—America, not Asia,—that is the family's main concern. For Garrett Hongo, Marilyn Chin, David Mura, and Li-Young Lee, however, American culture does not hold the promise it is supposed to have or, if it does, its promise exacts a terrible price from immigrant families. Their poetry puts an ironic twist on their families' immigrant dreams.

My study does not intend to be exhaustive either concerning the poetry of immigration or of Asian American writing. The experience of immigration is complex, and the writing that comes out of this experience has not yet been systematically studied. Also, the flowering of Asian American writing in the last twenty years has been so rich and diverse and relatively new that I do not claim that the small handful of poems I discuss in this paper represent the entire movement. Furthermore, the poets I have chosen are not meant to represent the entire Asian American community, which is not homogeneous but is composed of many different ethnic groups and is criss-crossed with class and generational divides representing profoundly different attitudes toward America and Asia. I do think, however, that the issues of immigration history and poetic form that these poems address must be faced in one way or another by all Asian American writers who take up the immigration experience of their families.

The four poets I examine have written extensively about migration. David Mura is a third-generation Japanese-American. Garrett Hongo is a fourth-generation Japanese-American born in Hawaii. Both write about the internment of the Japanese during World War II in their poetry but have also written longer prose works inspired by reverse migration, that is, their temporary return to their families' homelands, Mura in *Turning Japanese,* Hongo in *Volcano.* Li-Young Lee's central concern in almost all of his early poetry is his relationship to his father, an eminent Chinese intellectual who fled China with his family and came to America in the 1950s by way of Indonesia. Marilyn Chin is also a first-generation Chinese-American born in Hong Kong and raised in Portland, Oregon. She dedicates the book from which I draw the poems for this paper, *The Phoenix Gone, The Terrace Empty,* to her mother, who was born in China of "strong Southern Cantonese peasant stock," the family that constitutes the subject of many of the book's poems.

Chin, Lee, Hongo, and Mura write a carefully honed and focused poetry that has won them recognition in the American mainstream. Although less experimental and overtly political than some of their contemporaries, the four poets more insistently than others address their own family's silences and their own obligations of familial respect. It is the complex inter-family relations in the face of migration and its effect on poetic form that is the subject of this paper.

A boldness, even a brashness, characterizes the immigration poems of Hongo, Chin, Mura, and Lee. They announce in their poetry that no matter what gaps there are in their histories, no matter what silences suffered, the poets will talk anyway. Theirs is a poetry of assertive statement and declarative force. With Maxine Hong Kingston, they challenge their elders: "I'll tell you what I suppose from your silences and few words, and you can tell me that I'm mistaken. You'll just have to speak up with the real stories if I've got you wrong" (10).

With a declarative force, Garrett Hongo makes a call to witness, a call to public attention and testimony. He commands in "Stepchild": "Is it the Sacramento? / It doesn't

matter / Go out there anyway. / The noises you hear / are the footsteps / of a thousand families / raining on the planks / of the bridge" (51, this and all subsequent Hongo quotes are from *Yellow Light,* 1982, unless otherwise noted). As stubbornly, as intractably, David Mura recounts family history over family objection. Mura's family, however, protests more vocally than Hongo's. Notice, again, the declarative and documentary force of Mura's language:

> *There Rose's Chop Suey and Pino Suke's grocery,*
> *the temple where incense havered and inspired*
> *dense evening chants (prayers for Buddha's mercy*
> *colorless and deep), that day he was fired . . .*

> No, no, no, she tells me. Why bring it back?
> The camps are over. (Also overly dramatic)
> Forget *shoyu*-stained *furoshiki, mochi* on a stick:
> You're like a terrier, David, gnawing a bone,
> an old, old trick. . . .

> (*After We Lost* 10, italics are Mura's).

Marilyn Chin's language is tense, accusatory, bristling with irony. When she is reconstructing the family experience preceding the flight from China, she is assertive, probing, tending toward the imperative: "Do you remember / the shantytowns," she asks and demands of her grandfather in **"The Phoenix Gone, The Terrace Empty."** "Do you remember / mother's first lover . . . Do you know the stare / of a dead man?" she asks her relatives. "Open the gate," she commands them, "Open / the gilded facade / of restaurant 'Double Happiness'. / The man crouched / on the dirty linoleum / fingering dice / is my father" (48-49, this and all subsequent Chin quotes are from **The Phoenix Gone, The Terrace Empty,** unless otherwise noted).

Her commands, however, are countered by the determination of a family to survive and move inexorably forward in time and history: "Upon entering the world—/ there would be no return. / Upon treading the path—/ there would be no detours. / When one plum ripens—/ the others will follow" (72), she writes of the family philosophy in **"Ode to Prized Koi and Baby Finches."** But against this march of fate which forbids looking backward, Chin does just that, boldly naming everything she has lost: "Please forgive my arrogance," she writes to the koi and finches, "but to be human means to never look back. / The lost country of my birth, / the forbidden lovers in the moon, / the broken promises in my heart / give me a sadness that you would never know / being merely, happily, fish and fowl" (73).

Li-Young Lee is more reverent towards his parents, but not any less persistent, even brash, in evoking his father's life as a way of understanding his own. His writing is insistently in the present tense, where past experience and future promise are fused in the confusion of the present moment, intensely and immediately experienced. Note again the terseness, the declarative and documentary force of Lee's voice. Like David Mura, Lee meets a wall of silence when he asks one of his relatives questions. "Which house did we flee by night? Which house did we flee by day?" he probes in "Interrogation" (*City* 33). "Don't ask me," she replies. He persists: "We stood and watched one burn; from one we ran way." She answers: "I'm neatly folding / the nights and days, notes / to be forgotten" (33). By the end of the poem, she is chanting, "I'm through with memory. . . . I'm through with memory," though the last line suggests that the event will not be evaded: "Can't you still smell," she says, "the smoke on my body?" (34).

Yet, in the face of such family resistance, the poems of Hongo, Chin, Mura, and Lee reconstruct the migration experience with an intense omniscience. The speakers in the poems are hyper-observant, pointing out seemingly trivial physical details which attain an eerie significance against the stark background of people fleeing their own countries. Hongo and Chin in their migration poems position themselves high above the scene. Hongo does a wide-angle take of the bridge across which the Japanese-Americans flee in "Stepchild" (*Yellow Light* 51). Chin's narrator hides in the moon that shines over the fields at the moment the Chinese woman decides to leave her home and begin her journey in **"Exile's Letter: After the Failed Revolution"** (*Phoenix Gone* 15). Mura in the voice of an epic documentary evokes heaven and earth: "In 1918, as the sea sparkled like the last tear God / shed before giving up on the world, women / . . . lined the ship's rail like / the horizon of a planet with dozens of moons" (11). While Lee places himself within the scene, a baby held in his fleeing father's arms, the child's innocent point of view and intense sensory awareness give such poems as "Furious Versions," "The Interrogation," "This House and What Is Dead," "Arise, Go Down," and "For a New Citizen of the United States," the same kind of almost preternatural perception of the other migration poems: "We were diminished," he declares in "The Interrogation" (*City* 33). "We were not spared. There was no pity. . . . There were fires in the streets. We stood among men, at the level / of their hands, all those wrists, dead or soon to die."

What the poets notice are the mundane details of ordinary life suddenly and haphazardly wrenched from the ordinary and gaining a terrible significance as people decide which few things they can take with them as they plunge out of one life and into another, the decisions made in haste. The result is a fractured sense of culture, a being on the outside among fragments of an unknown whole. Thus, Mura notices temple incense and Buddhist chants and shoyu-stained furoshiki, mochi on a stick, and tins of utske-mono and eel hidden beneath the bed when he recalls his family's flight from their home in California to an intern-ment camp in Jerome, Arkansas. Hongo notes the heavy clothes, the bundles of kitchenware, a jewel box, "maybe some blankets / wrapped in huge purple / and scarlet pil-lowcases" (*Phoenix Gone* 51) or "furoshiki," as he refers to them later. And then, in order to call attention to the haste of the departure and the respectability of the people who have been turned out of their homes, he points to the mother dressed in evening clothes, a long black gown, the flat-topped round hat, "the white fin of a baggage tag /

pinwheeling like a kite on her breast" (*Phoenix Gone* 52). Chin's exile in **"Exile's Letter: After the Failed Revolution,"** departs a more exotic world, of threshed wheat and silk forced from mulberries (15). She dreams of gazebos and vistas, as abruptly renounced as noticed in the poem when she recognizes they are "not hers, as she walks into exile vowing no return." Li-Young Lee notes clothes hast-ily patched, the question a guard asks, "politely deferring to class," before pistol whipping his father: "What color suit, Professor, would you like to be buried in? Brown or blue?" (*City* 18).

"Migrant literature reflects but also may exaggerate or even invert the social experience that drives it. We may be surprised, and hence illuminated, by the migrant's feel for the quotidian and commonplace, and by migrant percep-tions of the odd and the exotic" (King xv). The sense of the quotidian and the odd in the poets we are examining, however, does not in the end surprise or illuminate. The effect of the omniscient point of view firmly placed on the outside of the experience underscores how fractured the experience is, how, as Chin so frequently images it, culture for the immigrant's children is a kind of empty casing of patched-together fragments with a whole that can only be guessed at, but no longer fully lived, an empty turtle shell, she calls it in **"Turtle Soup,"** "bearing humanity's strange inscriptions" (*Phoenix Gone* 24).

The poets seem to be ethnographers, slightly out of joint. Like ethnographers, they deal with single, sometimes seemingly disconnected artifacts pulled out of a cultural group's everyday life. They invest these artifacts with cultural significance, but then their power falls short. Ethnographers attempt to uncover the fabric of the culture taken as some kind of whole. Not so, with the poetry we have been discussing. The ethnographer's sensibility may be present in the attention given to the details of everyday life, but ultimately significance is no longer clearly present even though the artifacts retain their cultural force. Thus, the poets we are discussing continuously bring a symbolic reading to the worlds their elders have given them. Things brought from the old country have a peculiar though unexplained force on life. The old world and the new world exist side by side without clear bridges between them. Neither culture is secure in the moorings of a larger, fully realized society or history.

In Marilyn Chin's **"Altar,"** a neglected statue of a household god also represents a long silent and neglected grandmother:

> I tell her she has outlived her usefulness.
> I point to the corner where dust gathers,
> where light has never touched. But there she sits,
> a thousand years, hands folded, in a tattered armchair,
> with yesterday's news, "the Golden Mountain Edi-
> tion."
>
> (*Phoenix Gone* 29).

The speaker is situated at the other end of a religious, historical, and family dream gone wrong. The altar con-flates a grandmother who can no longer pass on a living or a vibrant tradition, a religious icon gathering dust for lack of use, an historical figure still holding the local Chinese language newspaper named for the old immigrant dream of America: the gold mountain, the land of promise and plenty. Not only is the meaning sustained by religious or cultural observance dead, but the hope itself is doomed. Above the altar a dead moth hangs in a spider web:

> She, who was attracted to that bare bulb,
> who danced around that immigrant dream,
> will find her end here, this corner,
> this solemn altar.
>
> (***Phoenix Gone*** 29).

For Chin, the fragments of Chinese culture become persistent omens of doom infiltrating her American experience. **"Altar"** emphasizes not only their uselessness, but in the presence of immigrant hope, their power to attract and then kill all who take refuge in them.

In **"The Phoenix Gone, the Terrace Empty"** (46-51), Chin gives the cultural fragments even broader powers. The American speaker, while visiting a Chinese garden, seems to be inhabited by the spirit of an ancestor, "who in the netherworld" the ancestor asks, "walks on my soles as I walk?" (46). In the presence of this unnamed spirit, the poem becomes a dialogue with several spirits, the speaker's father, grandfather, grandmother, and Aunt, who together recall their suffering and ruin in China at the hands of the Japanese, the Nationalists, and the Communists. Their voices overwhelm the speaker with despair: "When you pray to your ancestor," they counsel her, "You are praying / to his her father's hollowness" (50). At the end of the poem, they accompany her to an American garden where she is secretly meeting her boyfriend. They are quick to point out all the bad omens in the garden. The moon looks like a severed car or a snake biting her tail, "eating herself into extinction" (51). The poem ends like a confused fairy tale; the voice of the speaker is crying out like a doomed princess, "Oh dead prince, oh hateful love / shall we meet again / on the bridge of the magpies" (51).

In **"The Phoenix Gone, The Terrace Empty,"** the poet herself takes on the double vision of a second-generation American and a native Chinese woman, where physical reality, even the mundane details of an American courtship, are filled with omens foretelling doom. The poem resonates not only with personal foreboding but also with the weight of a violent history and with the threat of the continued violence visited on women. The place of tender kissing "where the arch meets toe meets ankle" is also "where dried blood warbles" (51).

David Mura's Japanese-American grandparents in *After We Lost Our Way* also live in two worlds, understanding the details of their harsh life in the internment camps against the narrative of their old life in Asia. The symbols of security and prosperity from their old life, the "ancient shrines" (12) and "emperor's food" (6), are ironically turned into the deadly icons of the American internment camps: "And then its Pearl, Heart mountain, mornings / when rifle towers, like ancient shrines / obscure the horizon (12) . . . the putrid gray beans . . . put my stomach / in a permanent revolt shouting no emperor / would ever feed his people so harshly" (6). Most eerie and disturbing is Mura's great-aunt's premonition of the bombing of Japan: "her dream came across seas / and the mountains. / it smelled of ash, a gasless flame" (7). The premonition, however, is spliced into the mundane events of the day: "bending to / the tomatoes, in line to mess / trudging through the desert dust . . . I heard them again. The cries" (8). The intensity of this symbolic perception leads to the poem's final confusion: "please / tell me what country I'm in" (9).

In many of his poems, Mura takes on the double vision of his grandparents. The bi-lingualisms, "teriyaki," "sake," "otoo-san," "okaa-san," suggest that the most intimate worlds of food and affection are not shared with an English-speaking world (3). In "A Nisei Picnic: From an Album" (14), Mura images his family in both traditional Asian and contemporary American ways: an uncle with a rice ball in his mouth eventually "ballooning like a Buddha." There is a wordly aunt who took Mura to "the zoo, movies," gave him "candy," and his father who "worked too hard to be white." The poem ends with the same confusion expressed by the grandparents. He notes "the bewilderment of their eyes." In later poems he expresses the same perplexity: "my grandchildren won't know how bewildered I was / how alone. They'll think I felt American. I was always at home" (20). For Mura, the confusion in identity is realized in intense self-loating which is reversed only when he examines the dual history he outlines in these early poems. Eventually, he learns, particularly through undergoing and writing about a "reverse migration" back to Japan in *Turning Japanese*, which parts of both traditions he can reject, which he can claim for his own.

Garrett Hongo, also Japanese-American, subscribes to a double vision very early in his poetry. After a visit to Japan, he writes in "Roots" (48-51), "I learned there was a signature to all things / the same as my own, and that my own sight / sanctified streetlights and stalled cars / the same as ceremonies in solitude" (48). The poem is about the practice of a religious discipline to strengthen and clarify this ability to read the surroundings symbolically. There is the tutelage of a dream mentor, an old man who ultimately in a mystical moment of ritual and song passes to Hongo an Asian cultural and religious inheritance where "heritage will be an ancient flute / throbbing from its place in my heart / where his heart has found its roots" (50).

In America, however, the heritage is fragmented, broken, silenced. The pieces are too disjointed to easily "sing" into some kind of whole, and the history too silenced for a Japanese-American son to claim for his own. Against the myth of assimilation where Nisei (second-generation Japanese-Americans) supposedly emerge "full grown Americans at birth," Hongo wants to place the as-yet-untold bitter half of the story, the tales of flight and survival and, with them, the larger narratives that give significance. "Where are the histories / our tragedies, our books / of fact and fiction?" he asks at the end of "Stepchild." "Where are the legends . . . where are the myths, the tales?" (58-59).

If Hongo wants to reroot Asian culture in America, he first must discover the missing American story. His growing awareness of the suppressed American history leads him to an angry outburst against both his Japanese family and the Anglo culture that has so injured them: "The Dragon wants me to scream," he writes towards the end of "Stepchild," "to swear at my father / for burying anger / in the red dirt. . . . The Shark wants me to kill / to tear at the throats / of white children" (*After We Lost* 61). If he is under the influence of Japanese gods in his anger, ironically Hongo is also controlled by the equally powerful influence of the pacifist actions of his American wife "who nursed the sick / at Manzanar, / who comforted the crying / at Gila River" (61). The poem ends with the speaker gripped in an impasse, alert to his American surroundings but unable to act within them: "I think about nothing / for a change. . . . And the sun blonds nothing / but the sands outside my window / and melons ripening on the sill, / the yellow ones we call bitter" (63).

For Li-Young Lee, a first-generation Chinese immigrant, it is the subjective presence, the "I" of the poem that slips elusively across the competing cultural fragments of history. In *The City in Which I Love You*, the speaking self can assume any version of the past. It can become the "I" that "will rise and go / out into an American city" (13), or the one that "might run with wife and children to the docks / to bribe an officer . . . for perilous passage" (13), or the self that will go to his father's "snowbound church to dust the pews" (13). But beneath such free choice of histories is a self profoundly threatened by oblivion. "Furious Versions" (13-29) is an act of recovery of this slippery self that requires holding firmly to the horrific physical details of the flight from Indonesia: the pistol blow to the father's head, the drifting boat and bodies in the harbor, the "flesh-laced, mid-century fire / teeth and hair infested / napalm-dressed and skull-hung fire" (18). Lee melds these memories to the immediate perception of an American world, in this case, the presence of three flowers that the poet notices in the dark and the flowers' suggestion of the symbolic possibilities of the Paul's Scarlet rose his father nurtured at their house in Pennsylvania.

The poem seems a strange reversal of the problem of partial meaning that we have been discussing. For Lee, there are continuities in the physical world that the self, so aware of its own dissolution, cannot grasp. The problem is not with the discontinuities imposed by immigration, but with the fragmentation of the self caused by the brutality and horrors of the flight itself. In fact, the American landscape occasionally yields surprising revelations of continuity. Once when Lee and his father are out walking in America, a blind man on the street recognizes his

father's voice. Years ago, in Asia, the father helped the man bury his wife "ten thousand miles away / in an abandoned house in Nan Jing." "Here was a man," Lee claims, "who remembered / the sound of another's footfalls / so well as to call to him / after 20 years / on a sidewalk in America" (23). Lee also comes across Li Bai and Du Fu "on the corner of Argyle and Broadway . . . sending folded paper boats down the gutter: Gold-toothed, cigarettes rolled in their sleeves / they noted my dumb surprise: / *What did you expect? Where else should we be?*" (23-24, italics are Lee's).

Yet Lee makes no easy act of faith in the surprising continuity immigrants sometimes discover on this shore. "All of my visions and interpretation," Lee writes, "depend on what I see and between my eyes is always the rain, the migrant rain" (Rose 68-69). He insists on the immanence of his vision: history is not a narrative sequence moving from past-present-to future, nor is it a sequence of cause-and-effect events, but rather history is an insistent present which keeps revising our most immediate perception of where and who we are. Always spliced into Lee's immediate experiences are the relived experience of the terrifying flight from Asia: "How, then, may I / speak of flowers, here," he asks in "Furious Version" as he meditates on the flowers in his garden and the remembered flower in his father's garden: "where / a world of forms convulses, / here / amidst / drafts—yet / these are not drafts / toward a future form, but / furious versions / of the here and now" (*City* 18-19).

If immigration is seen as a three-part sequence—the expulsion from home, the journey where one's identity is on hold, and the survival in the host country—then the poems we have been discussing suggest that no matter how distant the first immigration from Asia to America, the poets still feel themselves "in the "middle," not having fully left Asia, not having fully embraced America. In part, their displacement is reinforced by the fact that immigration is not a one-time event in their family histories. Asians have repeatedly been uprooted from their homes in America. The Exclusion Laws, enacted immediately after the transcontinental railroad was built and renewed through the late nineteenth and early twentieth centuries, refused citizenship to Asians, particularly the Chinese, who were hounded out of American communities and sent on many cross-country migrations. During World War II, Japanese-Americans were forcefully uprooted from their homes, their property and assets impounded and frequently lost, and the people placed in internment camps.

Thus, while the "original" immigration to the United States from Asia may have taken place several generations before the generation of the writers we are discussing here, the terrible disruption of migration has re-occurred for their parents and grandparents. There is a sense in their poetry that each migration repeats the drama of the first immigration, intensifying the experience and making it accessible across time to the present generation. Garrett Hongo, for instance, does not feel he has to discriminate between bridges in the opening of "Stepchild": "Go out to the bridge over the river / Is it the Sacramento? / It doesn't matter. / Go out there anyway. / The noises you hear / are the footsteps / of a thousand families / raining on the planks / of the bridge" (51). The bridge could be any number of bridges in the United States or Asia.

Marilyn Chin embraces the "Road of Regret" with her ancestor in China. The ancestor addresses her directly and includes her on the journey of exile. Whatever distinction is made between them at the beginning of **"Exile's Letter: After the Failed Revolution"** disappears at the end. "Dear Cousin," the ancestor addresses her directly, "do not mourn me or this empty sky, / for the sky is limitless. Ah yet, there is a limit / to even 'sky.' Like you we are fallow deer, / on Regret Road we must not tarry" (15). Much of Chin's poetry is written from the Road of Regret, out of a sense of loss, displacement, and grief.

There are four migrations in David Mura's "Suite for Grandfather and Grandmother Uyemura: Relocation" (*After We Lost* 11-13): the arrival of the arranged brides from Japan in 1918, the flight to the relocation camps during World War II, the exile to Chicago after internment where the grandmother dies, and the grandfather's return to Japan to remarry. The poem ends in painful and sardonic understatement. The grandfather writes about his life: "*bonsai tree like me you are useless and a little sad*" (*After We Lost* 13, italics are Mura's).

We have already seen how immediate a memory immigration is for Li-Young Lee. Images slide one beneath the other so that the "napalm-dressed and skull hung fire" intrudes on the peace of a later night, but also cuts into the act of writing itself, the pun on the word "draft" intended: "here, where / a world of forms convulses, / here, amidst / drafts—yet / these are not drafts / toward a future form, but / furious versions / of the here and now" (*City* 18-19).

Past immigrations slide over each other and intensify the sense of cultural dislocation. Sons and daughters re-suffer the immigration with their parents and grandparents. Li-Young Lee and Marilyn Chin vividly recall and interpret the immigration made while they were young children, a traumatic event that continues to haunt their own lives. David Mura and Garrett Hongo place the fragments of family stories into the contexts of the repeated immigrations suffered in America. All four poets articulate their own cultural dislocation in terms of the ongoing alienation of families uprooted from whatever real or metaphoric place they call home.

As a repeated event, immigration is vivid in family memory and, while the poets of my study are more insistent about revealing family history than other family members, by virtue of their reimagining immigration in their own poems, they share a common suffering with earlier generations. Ultimately, their poems win from their families an authorization to speak, to break the silence. But it is not simply that the repetitions make immigration

an experience available to the poets. More importantly it is the dialogic form they develop within their poetry that makes room for the voices of those earlier generations expressed without antagonism.

While framing their poems in an intimate first-person lyric voice, Hongo, Chin, Mura, and Lee also write out of an oral tradition which is essentially dialogic in nature. Thus their poems are not dramatic monologues or first-person confessions. Nor are they documentaries or exposés. Rather, their poetry is based on the give-and-take of conversation. They embody intimate revelations made between family members through letter and prayer, through a family's story-telling and religious ritual. The poems revere these connections and are not intended to destroy them. The poems are acts of love and family obligation, which ultimately carry the authority of the older generation but also allow the younger generation to develop family voices freed from shame. In the process, the poets develop a complex dialogic poetic form where the voice in the poem is not wholly the poet's own but shifts between family members and moves across time.

The speaker/writer of David Mura's "Letters from Poston Relocation Camp" (*After We Lost* 6-9), for instance, is a Japanese man in a World War II American internment camp sending letters to his wife outside the camp. In the letters, he juxtaposes the starkness of the camp with his perceptions of beauty in those around him: "our beauty," he calls it, "the way we carry the land / and the life of plants inside us" (6). At the center of the poem, there is the terrible premonition of the bombing of Japan, felt by the letter-writer with the same sensuous intensity that he feels the desert dust and the tomato plants in the prison garden. He ends the letter with an apology for the premonition: "Forgive me. Blessed / with a chance to talk to my wife, . . . all I can do is moan" (8-9). In the final words, however, he justifies writing about his moaning, and in doing so establishes a complicated bond, not only with his wife, but with all who are reading his words later: "And yet, if I didn't tell you, / I would be angry at you for not listening, / blaming you for what I haven't spoken" (9). By breaking silence, the letter-writer creates an audience defined by a relationship of listening and response rather than anger and strangely misplaced responsibility. The poem ends with a definition of this listening audience: "When you write back, please / tell me what country I'm in. / I feel so poor now. / These words are all I own" (9). The poem Mura writes a generation later answers the request. Mura himself owns the words, and in making them known, is both writing back to the letter-writer, his grand-uncle, and also revealing the contours of the country they both inhabit.

Marilyn Chin is also receiving a letter from an ancestor in **"Exile's Letter: After the Failed Revolution"** (15), but, as so frequently happens in Chin's poetry, the give-and-take of conversation suggests the give-and-take of prayer to an ancestral spirit. In **"Exile's Letter,"** Chin seems to be a god or a spirit present in the moon protecting the peasant farmer who is leaving the fields for the last time: "she the exile looks up, finds my face in the moon." What follows is a prayer made to the face in the moon, but the identification of Chin with the farmer becomes so complete that the letter quoted at the end could well originate with either of them, praying one to the other: "Dear Cousin, do not mourn me . . . Like you we are fallow deer; / on Regret Road we must not tarry" (15).

Sometimes, Chin herself is the supplicant looking for the ancestor she might pray to. Her investigation, however, always involves a dialogue with her family or with us, the readers: "Do you know the stare / of a dead man?" she asks in **"The Phoenix Gone, the Terrace Empty"** (49). "My father the ox / without his yoke / sitting on a ridge / of the quay," she answers herself. "Auntie Jade / remembers:" she continues, "Hunger / had spooned / the flesh / from his cheek. . . ." Auntie Jade also warns her, "when you pray / to your ancestors / you are praying / to his hollowness."

In **"Turtle Soup"** (24), Chin recounts a conversation about a turtle cooked by her mother into soup. Almost from the beginning of the poem, Chin's voice becomes dialogic, poised between various speakers and listeners. She uses the second person which in an unsettling way implicates the reader: "You go home one evening tired from work, and your mother boils you turtle soup, . . . You say, 'Ma, you've poached the symbol of long life.'" The mother responds to the daughter coming home from work, Chin, the poet, and us, the reader: "All our ancestors have been fools. / Remember Uncle Wu who rode ten thousand miles / to kill a famous Manchu and ended up / with his head on a pole? . . . Sometimes you're the life, sometimes the sacrifice." Chin then directly enters into the conversation as an outside voice addressing the person coming home from work: "Baby, some high priestess has got it wrong." She then turns to us, the readers, and addresses us with a rhetorical question which also suggests a lament: "Is there nothing left but the shell / and humanity's strange inscriptions, / the songs, the rites, the oracles?" It is apparent that Chin longs to be that priestess who could "get it right."

Less skeptical than Chin, Garrett Hongo also aspires to be a priest for his generation and for those before him, a task which complicates and historicizes the voice in his poems. In "Stepchild" (51-63), he oversees a dialogue that crosses generations. While in part, the poem documents briefly the events about which second-generation Japanese-Americans have kept silent, it also opens up an accusatory dialogue between the generations: "Why," the first-generation Issei ask of the second-generation Nissei: "do you ignore us? / We give you songs of grief / and you run to the liars. . . . Our history is bitter" (54). "This is not beautiful, you the Nissei and third-generation, Sansei say / This is not what we came for. / But who knows this better / than your grandfather / who spent the years / of his internment / sealed in the adobes / at Leuppe in Arizona" (55). Hongo, like Chin, directly enters into the argument in the middle of the poem by bringing the argument into the poem's

own present tense, no matter how far in time from World War II that present may be: "Why do you give me fairy tales?" Hongo asks in the first person. "I am your stepchild. / Tell me, / your one bastard / tell me the truth" (56).

While "Stepchild" is a call to investigate and make known Japanese-American history and to discover and make the myths, stories, and poems that realize the meaning of this history, two other poems, "Roots" and "Something Whispered in the Shakunachi," suggest that myth-making involves a different kind of conversation with the ancestors themselves. Here Hongo's role is priestly, rather accusatory. "Heritage," you will recall him saying in "Roots," will be an "ancient flute / throbbing from its place in my heart / where his ancestor's heart has found its roots" (50). The ancestor is described in "Something Whispered" as a farmer who made flutes out of bamboo and lost his farm during the internment, but managed to raise bamboo again. The "full-throated songs" that memory creates for the farmer come "out of wind, out of bamboo / out of a voice / that only whispers" (78). The image of a voiced wind recalls the powerful story of Chinaman's Hat in Maxine Hong Kingston's *China Men,* where the grasses hold the voices of those who lived among them. In many poems Hongo aspires to be the receptive conduit for this historical and mythic voice although such a role requires him to enter into a complex dialogue with the earlier generations themselves.

In "A Final Thing" (*City* 72-74), Li-Young Lee works out more fully the relation between speaker and listener in a poem based on dialogue. The poet in "A Final Thing" awakens one morning to overhear his wife telling their son a story. Although he cannot hear the words, the poet is especially sensitive to the nuances of his wife's voice and its responsiveness to the listening son:

> she is telling a story,
>
> using a voice which speaks to another,
> weighted with that other's attention,
> and avowing it
> by deepening in intention.
>
> Rich with the fullness of what's declared,
> this voice points
> away from itself
> to some place
> in the hearer,
> sends the hearer back
> to himself
> to find what he knows.
>
> A saying full of hearing,
> a murmuring full of telling
> and compassion for the listener
> and for what's told.
>
> (72-73).

The language that requires a listener and includes in its own words the act of hearing could well describe the letter and prayer forms of Chin and Mura and the inchoate mythic flute songs of Hongo.

But Li-Young Lee goes a step further and frames the conversation between his wife and son with his own unseen presence as he overhears them in a far bedroom:

> My son, my first-born, and his mother
> are involved in a story no longer only theirs
> for I am implicated,
> all three of us now
> clinging to expectancy, riding sound and air . . .
>
> I hear it through the bedroom wall;
> something, someday, I'll close my eyes to recall.
>
> (73-74).

You will recall that Lee is plagued by his own subjectivity: his ability to make up multiple and contradictory versions of the past and his vulnerability in the present where immediate perception is always fragmented, transient, and interrupted by terrifying physical memories. Yet by witnessing the intimate exchange between his wife and child and being implicated in that exchange, Lee transcends his own subjectivity partly because the dialogue does not originate with himself and partly because the dialogue introduces him to a history beyond his own invention. He will later recall words his wife, not he, invented and which his son received. Such words suggest an oral poetry that precedes his own tragic history. Faith in the transcendence of such dialogic language that somehow can sustain itself across time and place ultimately saves Lee from the fragmentation and transience expressed in "Furious Versions."

In "Furious Versions," Lee asks the question: "How, then, may I / speak of flowers / here, where / a world of forms convulses / here, amidst / drafts" (*City* 18-19). Lee writes in a later stanza: "behind the sound / of trees is another / sound. . . . it / ties our human telling / to its course / by momentum, and ours / is merely part / of its unbroken / stream, the human / and otherwise simultaneously / told. The past / doesn't fall away, the past / joins the greater / telling and is" (*City* 26). In "A Final Thing" (*City* 72-74), Lee identifies the origins of the "greater telling" in an oral and dialogic language in which he participates.

Li-Young Lee's poetry, together with the poetry of David Mura, Marilyn Chin, and Garrett Hongo, attests to a faith in the continuity of language, particularly as it enacts a dialogue across generations. To look back at a "homeland" is ultimately not to look back at a burning city and freeze in a deathly paralysis, but rather to overhear in the fire the conversation of ancestors. The task of poetry is to declare the conversation loudly and assertively in a fractured world and then to turn it into a dialogue across and through the fissures of geography and time and grief. This is the challenge and the accomplishment of the poetry of Li-Young Lee, David Mura, Marilyn Chin, and Garrett Hongo.

Works Cited

Brinker-Gabler, Gisela, and Sidonie Smith eds. *Writing New Identities.* Minneapolis: U of Minnesota P, 1997.

Cheung, King-Kok. "Reviewing Asian American Literary Studies." *An Interethnic Companion to Asian American Literature.* Ed. Cheung. Cambridge: Cambridge UP, 1997. 1-37.

Chin, Marilyn. *The Phoenix Gone, The Terrace Empty.* Minneapolis: Milkweed, 1994.

Fuchs, Lawrence. *The American Kaleidoscope.* Hanover NH: Wesleyan UP, 1990.

Hom, Marilyn K., trans. *Songs of Gold Mountain: Cantonese Rhymes from San Francisco Chinatown.* Berkeley and Los Angeles: U of California P, 1987.

Hongo, Garrett Kaoru. *Yellow Light.* Hanover, NH: Wesleyan UP, 1982.

———. *Volcano: A Memoir of Hawaii.* New York: Knopf, 1995.

Kelen, Leslie and Eileen Stone. "Introduction." *An Oral History of Ethnic and Minority Groups in Utah.* Eds. Kelen and Stone. Salt Lake City: U of Utah P, 1996. 4-15.

King, Russell, John Connell, and Paul White, eds. *Writing Across Worlds.* New York: Routledge, 1995.

Kingston, Maxine Hong. *China Men.* New York: Ballantine, 1980.

Lai, Him Mark, Genny Lim, and Judy Yung. *Island: Poetry and History of Chinese Immigrants on Angel Island 1910-1940.* San Francisco: *Hoc Doi* Project, 1980.

Lee, Li-Young. *The City in Which I Love You.* Brockport, NY: BOA Editions, 1990.

———. *Rose.* New York: BOA Editions, 1986.

Lee, Robert. *Singing to Remember.* Prod. and dir. Tony Heriza. New York: Asian American Arts Centre, 1992.

Lim, Shirley Geok-lin. "Immigration and Diaspora." *An Interethnic Companion to Asian American Literature.* Ed. King-Kok Cheung. Cambridge: Cambridge UP, 1997. 289-311.

Mura, David. *After We Lost Our Way.* New York: Dutton, 1989.

———. *Turning Japanese.* New York: Atlantic Monthly, 1991.

Stone, Elizabeth. *Black Sheep and Kissing Cousins.* New York: Penguin, 1989.

Uba, George. "Versions of Identity in Post-Activist Asian American Poetry." *Reading the Literature of Asian America.* Ed. Shirley Geok-lin Lim and Amy Ling. Philadelphia: Temple UP, 1992. 33-48.

Wong, Sau-ling Cynthia. "Chinese American Literature." *An Interethnic Companion to Asian American Literature.* Ed. King-Kok Cheung. Cambridge: Cambridge UP, 1997. 39-61.

Yogi, Stan. "Japanese American Literature." *An Interethnic Companion to Asian American Literature.* Ed. King-Kok Cheung. Cambridge: Cambridge UP, 1997. 125-55.

Adrienne McCormick (essay date 2000)

SOURCE: McCormick, Adrienne. "'Being Without': Marilyn Chin's Poems as Feminist Acts of Theorizing." *Hitting Critical Mass* 6, no. 2 (spring 2000): 1-16.

[*In the following essay, McCormick places Chin's poems that examine the poet's identity in the company of feminist theory that seeks to claim both a history and a language for women of color.*]

Marilyn Chin's "I" poems do not merely reflect the rich and varied modes of Asian American feminist literary theory which predate her work, but are themselves acts of theorizing. By referring to Chin's poems as such, I intentionally riff on the work of Barbara Christian, Katie King, and Lisa Lowe. In the influential article "The Race for Theory," Christian claims that "people of color have always theorized, but in forms quite different from the Western form of abstract knowledge" (336). This statement is quoted in numerous texts, testifying to the importance of Christian's claim to the various practices called theorizing by writers of color. In the book *Theory in Its Feminist Travels: Conversations in U.S. Women's Movements* (1994), Katie King also explores at length the question of "what counts as theory," and voices her "investment in the object 'theory' as those mutually constituting, mutually embedded 'actions': theory building, alliance shifting, and political identity production" (29). As Christian does, King emphasizes the multiple acts that count as theorizing (as process) for different communities of writers. Building upon the work of feminists such as Christian and King in situating Chin's poems as acts of theorizing allows me to approach her work in a manner that challenges traditional relations of power within literary and theoretical communities. One way to avoid the continued marginalization of non-abstract modes of theorizing, Donald Goellnicht argues, "is to read Asian American texts as theoretically informed and informing rather than as transparently referential human documents over which we place a grid of sophisticated Euro-American theory in order to extract meaning" (340).

In keeping with Goellnicht's observation, I situate Chin as firmly rooted within a cohort of contemporary feminist women of color, and Asian American feminists in particular, who situate theorizing within diverse forms of creative and critical writing. By referring to Chin's poems as "feminist acts of theorizing," I particularly play upon Lisa Lowe's language in *Immigrant Acts* (1996). Lowe argues that the phrase "immigrant acts" works in two ways: first, it names the history of racialized oppression and exclusion of Asians within/from the "universality of the political body of the [U.S.] nation," and second, it marks immigrants' acts as a "generative site for the critique of that universality" (8-9). I play on Lowe's use of the word "acts" in particular in order to illustrate how the phrase "acts of theorizing" also serves a dual purpose in approaching Chin's poetry.

First, situating Chin's poems as acts of theorizing claims for the poet the history of Asian American feminist literary

theorizing and the manner in which that history bridges the creative and critical, as do the theorizing practices of many women of color. *The Forbidden Stitch: An Asian American Women's Anthology* (1989), *Making Waves: An Anthology of Writing By and About Asian American Women* (1989), and *Making More Waves: New Writing By Asian American Women* (1997) provide three excellent examples of how Asian American feminist theorizing has bridged creative and critical theoretical practices by bringing together poetry, fiction, memoir, essays, and works of visual art in texts that broaden what we mean when we refer to theoretical practice.[1] Just as these anthologies destabilize the distinction between what counts as a creative and what as a critical work (or theoretical—as Christian does), so too do Chin's poems destabilize the distinction between the poem and the act of theorizing. Her poems critique stereotypes of racialized and gendered identities, revealing the complex intersections between the two. By extending these critiques to questions of national identification, colonization, and sexual exploitation, Chin builds upon the intersectionality that has characterized feminist theorizing by contemporary Asian American feminists such as Trinh T. Minh-ha and Lowe, to name only two, as well as by African American and Latina feminists such as Christian, Audre Lorde, and Chéla Sandoval. Furthermore, Chin's poems as acts of theorizing produce knowledge about new modes of identification and more complex understandings of identity in order to provide alternatives to the limitations—physical, mental, theoretical—embodied in the stereotypes and the status quo she critiques.

Second, situating Chin's poems as "acts of theorizing" marks the manner in which contemporary theory has excluded such poetry from the realm of cultural critique. The "critical marginalization" of Asian American poetry, as Juliana Chang refers to it (84), has a complex history. After the confessional poets and the development of feminist theories of the poetic speaker, the poetic "I" as a transparent referent for the self of the poet has been positioned as either politically liberatory or aesthetically simplistic, depending upon the politics of the particular reader.[2] Traditionally, any speaking voice in a poem can be referred to as the poem's persona, regardless of whether that voice uses an "I" or not. Many scholars would, for instance, refer to the speaking voice in Chin's poems as a "persona," rather than as Chin, regardless of the fact that she uses her own name and clearly refers to herself in several instances. In the introduction to *Stealing the Language: The Emergence of Women's Poetry in America* (1986), Alicia Ostriker warns her readers that this approach to the poetic persona does not apply to women's poetry:

> academic distinctions between the self and what we in the classroom call the 'persona' move to vanishing point [sic], When a woman poet today says 'I,' she is likely to mean herself . . . It is the fact that the ques-

tion of identity is a real one, for which the thinking woman may have no satisfactory answer, that turns her resolutely inward.

(12)

Chin's poetic "I" resembles Ostriker's; she does mean herself, but in a very irresolute manner. However, many contemporary theorists see such self-referential uses of the poetic "I" as outdated and suspect. These contradictory approaches to the poetic "I" contribute to the schism between poetry and contemporary critical theorists who "regard as naive the notion of a unified speaking subject" in any capacity (Keller and Miller 3). The critical neglect of contemporary poetry by many poststructuralist and anti-essentialist theorists—which Lynn Keller and Cristanne Miller describe—suggests that such theorists view poetry as uninteresting, an outdated genre that lags behind the advances of contemporary critical theory.[3] But as several Asian American poets have observed, such arguments result in the silencing of ethnically marked poets in particular.[4] For contemporary multi-ethnic American poets, questions of identity and the construction of self are particulariy complex and central to their work. This is not to say that they produce outdated, simplistic, or nostalgic poetic "I's" or totalized versions of identity; on the contrary, contemporary multi-ethnic American poets produce a range of complex poetic "I's" that critique simplistic notions of ethnic, racial, gender, sexual, and national identities.[5] Marilyn Chin—as a Chinese American poet whose work theorizes feminist responses to racialized and gendered narratives of the Asian woman immigrant—provides some of the best examples of dynamic poetic "I's" that explore the production of specifically racialized, gendered, and national identities.

Chin uses the "I" persona to illustrate the extent to which, for her, neither gender, ethnic, racial nor national identity is a fixed quantity. Chin's work counters the prevailing tendency in many U.S. cultural and socio-political relations and institutions to mark the intersections between gendered, ethnic, and racial identities in overly simplistic terms. Disagreements continue to arise within different ethnic groups over who counts as an authentic or inauthentic member; discussions such as these position ethnic and racial identities as easily knowable and definable.[6] As acts of theorizing that critique such limiting approaches to authenticity and the damaging racist stereotypes which they sustain, Chin's "I" poems function as op/positional tools.[7] She challenges the notion that the genre of poetry still clings to a sense of coherent poetic identity and the presence of an authentic (gendered, ethnic, racial, or national) "I." This challenge extends to notions of the Asian woman as delicate, submissive, and exotic, and by extension, to characterizations of Asia as feminized and submissive to the West. In her foreword to *Making More Waves*, Jessica Hagedorn describes Chin's poem **"A Portrait of the Self as Nation, 1990-1991"** as "an ironic manifesto" for the anthology as a whole, due to the manner in which the poem portrays the self "as battleground and as defiant nation, the self as illuminating poem and

story, the self as dark song of memory and resistance" (x). In situating the self/"I" so complexly, Chin theorizes an "I" that is not in the least bit naive, but which rather makes crucial waves in the already irresolute waters of contemporary cultural and critical theories pertaining to gender, ethnic, racial, and national identities.

READING CHIN'S "I" POEMS

Chin writes poems in which the "I" is un/equivocally linked to Chin as poet. She addresses the contradictions involved in processes of self-identification and in the assigning of ethnic, racial, sexual, and national identities in the United States. Her treatment of Asian American identity in particular addresses national identification and the contradictions involved in being asked, on the one hand, to assimilate to mainstream American culture, while on the other, being made to feel irrevocably foreign. Thus, Chin theorizes identify as something that is constantly being re/produced; it shifts upon entry into "the new country" as much as it shifts with the dying and birthing of old and new customs. Identity, for Chin, is something to kill and regenerate. It is part little bird, part rising phoenix; part lotus, part yellow crowfoot; part confining stereotype, part open space of possibility. These various parts are explored in depth in Chin's **"How I Got That Name," "The Phoenix Gone, The Terrace Empty,"** and **"A Portrait of the Self as Nation, 1990-1991."**[8]

The subtitle of **"How I Got That Name"** is "an essay on assimilation." The subtitle marks the manner in which the poem functions as an act of theorizing. Calling it an "essay" aligns the poem with a "legitimate" critical genre, thus bridging the creative writing of the poem with the critical writing of the essay/theory. The content, of course, also reveals Chin's theorizing. The first line of the poem establishes that the name being referred to is in fact the poet's: "I am Marilyn Mei Ling Chin" (16). The following lines expand upon the sense of "ir/resoluteness" in this statement:

> Oh, how I love the resoluteness
> of that first person singular
> followed by that stalwart indicative
> of "be," without the uncertain i-n-g
> of "becoming."

(16)

The speaker loves the resoluteness because it is something she lacks. She, herself, is constantly in the process of "becoming." The subtitle shows that the resoluteness of the "I am" which begins the poem stands in opposition to the unresolved nature of the speaker's "becoming American" through the process of assimilation. To become a citizen, Chin must assimilate, or in a word, change. The poem embodies this requisite transformation in the lines which address how her name "had been changed / somewhere between Angel Island and the sea" where her father "transliterated 'Mei Ling' to 'Marilyn'" after "some tragic white woman / swollen with gin and Nembutal" (16). This "transliteration" marks the impossibility of identity for Chin. She can state "I am Marilyn Mei Ling Chin," but in doing so, she cannot avoid marking how she is not "Marilyn Monroe," the epitome of blonde American beauty. Chin's "I," therefore, is always multiple and irresolute, even when she states her love for "the resoluteness of that first person singular" (16). Chin theorizes her own Chinese American identities and the poetic "I" attached to them as anything but resolute.

Chin's father dubs her "Marilyn" in a move fraught with the specific binds that women immigrants face after entering the United States. Not only must their names and customs change to match that which is dubbed most "American," but they also enter into the beauty game by which all American women are measured against an archetype of beauty, the "blonde bombshell" (16). Thus, Chin critiques not only the processes of identification by which names and customs are altered to more smoothly assimilate into the new culture, but also marks the specific discontinuities that surface for Asian women immigrants in particular in the process of assimilation. For women immigrants, their appearance becomes something that should also "fit" into a stereotypically American mold but that inevitably cannot. For Chin, this particular contradiction arises from traditions which do not question male decision-making: "nobody dared question / his initial impulse—for we all know / lust drove men to greatness, / not goodness, not decency" (16).

Chin also portrays her mother's response to her renaming:

> And there I was, a wayward pink baby,
> named after some tragic white woman
> swollen with gin and Nembutal.
> My mother couldn't pronounce the "r."
> She dubbed me: "Numba one female offshoot"
> for brevity.
>
> (16)

The story of immigration is a common narrative, as is the taking on of an American name; Chin particularizes her representation of that experience with her wit. She exposes the contradictory positions of the ideal American woman (Marilyn Monroe) and the Asian immigrant woman, illustrated symbolically through the equally awkward names "Marilyn" (which cannot be pronounced correctly) and "Numba one female offshoot" (which is not brief). The tongue-in-cheek tone thus questions the male authority of the father in naming his immigrant daughter after Marilyn Monroe; it exposes the gendered double standards associated with the effects of lust (it drives men to greatness and women to shame); and it destabilizes the resolute "I" of ethnic, national, and gendered identities. Hence, the statement "I am Marilyn Mei Ling Chin" does not enforce a coherent sense of identity at all, but rather theorizes how identities and the names that are so inextricably intertwined with them are produced through complex processes which involve assimilation, cultural contradiction, and, for Chin, struggles with patriarchal power systems.

In the second section, the poem continues to indict what passes for mainstream American culture and how that culture fixes identities and categorizes people by group stereotypes. In order to extend her critique of putatively fixed I-dentities from the individual to the group, Chin chooses to speak as a "we" in this section rather than as an "I." This enables her to expand from her particular experiences as a Chinese American female meeting the myth of beauty in the U.S., and to explore group identities and stereotypes imposed upon Asian Americans. She examines two in particular, the myth of the Model Minority and the racist stereotype of duplicitous Asians:

> How we've managed to fool the experts
> in education, statistics, and demography—
> We're not very creative but not adverse to rote-
> learning.
> Indeed they can use us.
>
> (17)

Chin refers to the demographers and politicians who "use" Asian "successes" as proof that the U.S. is the "land of opportunity," thus erasing inequalities within the Asian American community and redirecting the fault for poverty in other immigrant, ethnic, and racial groups away from the nationally sanctioned dynamics of exclusion, racism, and oppression and onto those groups themselves. Thus, it is not the American democratic, capitalist system that has faults but minority groups who do not work hard enough to achieve the American dream. Chin exposes the Model Minority myth as false by portraying it as something that Asian immigrants connived to trick and tease those in power: "But the 'Model Minority' is a tease. / We know you are watching now, / so we refuse to give you any!" (17). The model minority and those who have constructed them as such are portrayed as engaged in sexual relations—a premonition of the gendering of Asia as feminine and the West/U.S. as masculine that we see in more depth in **"Portrait of the Self as Nation, 1990-1991."** But the refusal of the feminine-gendered Asian Model Minority to "give any" to the masculine-gendered U.S. experts gives the model minority a false sense of power. The power is false since it too derives from a stereotype—the duplicitous Asian.

Chin turns every contradictory stereotype of Asian identity—as model, smart, tricky, lethargic, industrious—on its head. Shifting back from the communal to the single "I," Chin portrays herself as lethargic and as a failed descendent—failed because she is female but also because she is perceived as "ugly"—of the "Great Patriarch Chin": "too listless to fight for my people's destiny . . . I wait for imminent death. / The fact that this death is also metaphorical / is testament to my lethargy" (18). In a characteristic inversion, death in Chin is not seen as a negative, or endpoint, but rather provides an opportunity for the rebirth and reconstruction of a different understanding of identity. Death signs the differences within the "I" that undermine, or make impossible, coherent versions of identity. Trinh T. Minh-ha writes, "If identity refers to the whole pattern of sameness within a human life, the style of a continuing me that permeates all the changes undergone, then difference remains within the boundary of that which distinguishes one identity from another" (95). What Trinh argues for in her writing, and Chin also theorizes in her poetry, is a more complex understanding of difference not only between different I-dentities, but within them as well:

> The differences made between entities comprehended as absolute presences—hence the notions of pure origin and true self—are an outgrowth of a dualistic system of thought peculiar to the Occident (the "ontotheology" which characterizes Western metaphysics). They should be distinguished from the differences grasped both between and within entities, each of these being understood as multiple presence. Not One, not two either. "I" is, therefore, not a unified subject, a fixed identity, or that solid mass covered with layers of superficialities one has gradually to peel off before one can see its true face. "I" is, itself, infinite layers.
>
> (90, 94)

Such an approach to difference, Trinh argues, "undermines the very idea of identity, deferring to infinity the layers whose totality forms 'I'" (96).

In the final section of **"How I Got That Name,"** Chin shifts again from the "I" to the third person "she," thus incorporating layers of identity—as Trinh calls them—into the poem through shifting speaking voices. Chin kills herself metaphorically—"So, here lies Marilyn Mei Ling Chin"—in order to enable revisionings of the poetic "I" and of ethnic, racial, gender, and national identity that are subject neither to stereotype nor fixity, absolute presence nor dualistic systems of thought:

> She was neither black nor white,
> neither cherished nor vanquished,
> just another squatter in her own bamboo grove
> minding her poetry—
>
> (18)

The poem embodies a series of contradictions which Chin positions herself in the middle of in order to disrupt them. She is "neither black nor white," "cherished nor vanquished"; she is also neither "Model" nor "lethargic." She is a (singular) not the (prescriptive) model of an Asian American woman artist, which perhaps has no small amount to do with her disruption of so many binaries. As poet, she teases the language in order to develop a dynamism that stands in opposition to the "mesmerized squatter" she portrays herself as in the poem. She shunts dynamically between these poles of identity that are imposed upon her in order to show that the complex "I" she envisions is "Not One, not two either," but is more associated with ambivalent spaces of possibility, as seen in the chasm referred to below:

> one day heaven was unmerciful,
> and a chasm opened where she stood.
> Like the jowls of a mighty white whale,
> or the jaws of a metaphysical Godzilla,
> it swallowed her whole.
>
> (18)

The chasm is an unmarked space that exists between cultures, at the point of learning a new and unlearning a previous culture. These are symbolized by the white whale and Godzilla: the white whale is Melville's supremely patriarchal and phallic Moby Dick, symbolizing mainstream American male literary culture, and Godzilla is the Japanese movie icon symbolizing all that is Asian, "non-American," and threatening. The subject of the poem, who no longer speaks in the first person, has been split into the "squatter swallowed whole" and Chin/the poet who remains to describe what happens to her after she has been metaphorically killed by the process of assimilation:

> She did not flinch nor writhe,
> nor fret about the afterlife,
> but stayed! Solid as wood, happily
> a little gnawed, tattered, mesmerized
> by all that had been lavished upon her
> and all that was taken away!
>
> (18)

The afterlife is Chin's life after entering the United States. Rather than become split and fractured, she stays "solid" though "gnawed" and "tattered." These gnaws and tatters are evident in the multiple voices of the poem, the "she," "we," and "I" which, though they construct a whole, do not comprise a fixed or necessarily coherent identity. The "she" of the poem remains "mesmerized / by all that had been lavished upon her" in her new life in the United States as well as in her past history, as well as by "all that was taken away" (18). The latter also applies both to the past—she was literally taken away from China—and to the present—the processes of assimilation continue to take things away.

The title poem of the collection—**"The Phoenix Gone, the Terrace Empty"**—likewise addresses the death and regeneration of I-dentity. Chin is again referred to in the first person in the poem; as her father plays dice, he begs her "Mei Ling, child, / Mei Ling, don't cry, / I can change our lives / with one strike" (49). But where the previous poem explores a multiple I-dentity in reaction to processes of immigration, assimilation, and racialization, **"The Phoenix Gone, The Terrace Empty"** is less linear and reactive and reverses the two worlds/lives as seen in **"How I Got That Name."** The afterlife does not refer to life in the U.S., but to China, which is referred to as the "netherworld" (47). In a rhyming, song-like stanza, Chin imagines a double of her Asian American self:

> "Who in the netherworld
> walks on my soles
> as I walk?
> And opens her black mouth
> when I cry?
> Whose lutestrings
> play my sorrow?
> Whose silence
> undulates
> a millenium
> of bells,
> in which

all of history
shall wallow?"

(47)

The use of quotation marks signals that the stanza is a lament or song that Chin quotes from elsewhere and uses to
voice her own concerns with her Other, Chinese self. The
series of questions transmit yearning for knowledge
combined with sorrow, and a plaintive contrast between
Chin's ability to voice these questions in a poem and the
double's resounding silence. This double is not the
"disowned" racial shadow of Asian American literature,
but is perhaps an outgrowth of it.[9] Sau-ling Wong's
analysis of the racial shadow explores texts in which
second generation Asian Americans project their own fears
and insecurities onto less assimilated, recently arrived
Asian immigrant doubles (77-115). These projections
invariably explore what Wong refers to as "the impossibility of the agenda set for Asian Americans: that they are
expected at once to lose their offensive 'Asianness' and to
remain permanently foreign" (91). In **"Phoenix,"** Chin
does not project this Other in order to know herself as less
foreign, nor to produce a more coherent "I," or whole self;
rather, Chin complicates how she knows the Other that is
herself. She does not fear, but seeks, knowledge of that
Other.

The entire poem tells the story of Chin walking down a
staircase, out a door, into a "new world," and then returning with a "strange" boyfriend, whose name a family
member cannot pronounce and who is probably white.
Thus, the motif for the poem is identity as a circle with
constant shifts, deaths, and regenerations: "Shall I walk /
into the new world / in last year's pinafore?" (50). Echoes
of *Prufrock* give further depth to the presence of Chin as
poet, an echo that can be heard in many of her poems.[10]
That she uses the snake to further develop her vision of
identity as a circle also links to subversive symbols of the
powerful woman, from Medusa's snaky locks to Coatli-
cue's serpent skirt:

> The snake bites her own tail,
> meaning harmony at the year's end.
> Or does it mean
> she is eating herself
> into extinction?

(51)

Chin's snake woman both consumes and regenerates
herself. There is no answer to the paradox of the snake
biting her own tail, only an insistent awareness of identity
as again "Not One, not two either," but a constantly
consumed and reproduced circle. I began this paragraph
by stating a surface reading of the poem ("The entire poem
tells the story of . . ."), but I will end by complicating
that reading, for the poem is not simply a story of Chin
leaving and returning to a childhood space of Chineseness.
The poem is also a complex chronicle of how Chin must
wrestle with the "stock signifiers" of what being Chinese
means to her family (47), as well as with how her multiple

identities do and do not satisfy the demands that her family and ethnic history place upon her. The voice of her
Auntie Jade laments, "Ten thousand years of history and
you have come to this. / Four thousand years of tutelage
and you have come to this!" (50). Certainly Chin's use of
powerful female images such as the snake, and her rejection of passive female images such as the lotus, have
something to do with this family member's expression of
dismay.

Yet it is these very images of power and regeneration that
are central to Chin's theorizing of the poetic/ethnic "I."
The final two stanzas of the poem include several
contradictory images which reinforce the dual possibilities
of interpretation embodied in the snake woman as
regenerating and/or self-consuming circle. These are not
Chin's words, but are again spoken to her. They seem to
be spoken to a child by the same voice that is quoted
above, perhaps the Aunt again or some other family
member, so the poem itself is a circle and returns to the
moment of escape:

> Little bird, little bird
> something escaping,
> something escaping . . .
>
> The phoenix gone, the terrace empty.
> Look, Mei Ling,
> yellow crowfoot in the pond
> not lotus, not lily.

(51)

Mei Ling is first associated with the "little bird" trying to
escape, a diminutive image that resonates closely to
stereotypes of Asian women as delicate, passive lotus (or
lily) flowers. But the concluding stanza begins with a
sentence that contradicts the tentativeness of the repetition
in the preceding stanza. The phoenix is defined as a
fabulous, powerful bird who lives for centuries before
burning itself and then rising anew from the ashes; it does
not connote a "little bird." Another connotation for phoenix
is "a person or thing that has been restored after suffering
calamity or apparent annihilation" (*Webster's* 1015). Thus,
Mei Ling is not only the "little bird" produced by the
adult's voice in the poem, but is also associated with the
phoenix, a powerful bird who rises from her own ashes,
who kills herself in order to make herself anew. She is
also one who has suffered the calamity of assimilation and
the "apparent annihilation" of her identity. Being unfixed,
changing, and embodied in a circle, the "I" and identity in
these terms is something that defies annihilation; identity
is not totalized or impermeable, but unfixed and regenerative.

The "yellow crowfoot" is another example of a symbol
used to counter the stereotype of the passive Asian female
identity. Yellow crowfoot is a plant with "divided leaves
suggestive of a bird's foot" (*Webster's* 326). The yellow
crowfoot in the pond is a theorized alternative to the
complex intersections of racist and sexist ideologies which
produce Asian and Asian American women's identities as

passive, exoticized lotus, or lily, blossoms. Chin does not ignore those misrepresentations, but juxtaposes them with other possibilities, with the powerful embodiment of the phoenix and the terrace as yet another unmarked, empty space signifying possibility. Thus, by the end of the poem, Chin's voice has become the silent voice, evoking the racial shadow from the beginning of the poem; Chin structures the poem to end with the voice of her Aunt or some other relative introducing her to the multiple possibilities for self-identification found in the lines quoted above, possibilities which extend to both the Chinese American and the Chinese woman through Chin's theorizing of the multiple poetic "I."

"A Portrait of the Self as Nation, 1990-1991" likewise theorizes a portrait of identity that builds upon the contradictions found in both of the poems by Chin already mentioned. But the contradictions here relate to the self as both person and nation, sadist and masochist, the site of possibility and the internalized enemy. The poem is an extended treatment of the self standing before an inquisitor, in this case the judge granting American citizenship to the Chinese applicant, Marilyn Mei Ling Chin.[11] Chin/China plays the role of the passive, Eastern, masochistic female slave to the judge/U.S. as active, Western, sadistic male Master. The poem begins with two epigraphs which establish these themes. The first is a Latin proverb: "In mastery there is bondage / In bondage there is mastery," another example of the op/positions Chin frequently works into her poems (92). Bondage and mastery circle into one another just as the snake woman did in **"The Phoenix Gone, The Terrace Empty."** The second epigraph is a quote by the poet George Seferis: "The stranger and the enemy / We have seen him in the mirror" (92), which again speaks to the contradictions found within the individual and the manner in which they complicate processes of identity formation and identification.

The poem begins with the female China addressing the male U.S. judge: "Forgive me, Head Master, / but you see I have forgotten / to put on my black lace underwear" (92). The "I" here and throughout the poem is never straightforward, but rather should be read as ironic and thus critical of the power relations that it presents. The reader only learns what questions the judge asks through Chin/China's replies, thus hers is the voice the poem centers: "When was the last time I made love? / The last century?" (92). Speaking as a centuries-old China, she recounts past lovers and remembers that it was the West, represented by the United States, with whom she last "slept":

> You were a conquering barbarian,
> helmeted, halberded,
> beneath the gauntleted moon,
> whispering Hunnish or English—
> so-long Oolong went the racist song
> bye-bye little chinky butterfly.
>
> (94)

Thus, the poem details in sadomasochistic terms the internalization of racism into "self-hate" and the internal-

ization of Asian exoticism into "self-love, both self-erotic notions" (93). The self wishes to challenge how she has become her own enemy, and she attempts to do so by exposing what the other/U.S. finds attractive about her:

> This is the way you want me—
> asleep quiescent, almost dead
> sedated by lush immigrant dreams
> of global bliss, connubial harmony.
>
> (95)

The bliss and harmony are in fact dreams, and the speaker realizes that she is no match for the sexual energies and histories which have determined the systems of inclusion and exclusion that decide what is and is not a valid American identity. Though she gets her citizenship, she must forget who does not in order to celebrate:

> "Congratulations,
> On this day, fifteen of November, 1967,
> Marilyn Mei Ling Chin,
> application # z-z-z-z-z
> you are an American citizen
> naturalized in the name of God
> the father, God the son and the Holy Ghost."
> Time assuages, and even
> the Yellow River becomes clean . . .
>
> (96)

To assuage the pain of not belonging, not being "clean" or "naturally American enough" comes at the cost of forgetting those who are denied citizenship: "Meanwhile we forget / the power of exclusion / what you are walling in or walling out—" (96). These lines refer directly to the Chinese Exclusion Act of 1882, as well as to China's attempts to police its own borders by building the Great Wall.[12] The language of bondage and sexual colonization gives way to the lingo of nationalism and racist, ethnocentric exclusion. Chin's "I" surrounds the voice of the judge, isolating his power over her ability to identity as American or not. Whether she remains in bondage to the feminized, colonized stereotype of the Asian female, or in bondage to an idea of patriotism and national identification through the erasure of her Chineseness, she is still in bondage to a mastery of one form or another. But it is important to remember the epigraph also, that "In mastery there is bondage / In bondage there is mastery." While Chin/China remains in bondage, she also masters the Master. The opening lines say "Forgive me," but the reference to her absent "black lace underwear" is followed by an act of exposure in which Chin takes the power of looking/seeing her body into her own hands: "I have hiked my slip up, up to my waist / so that I can enjoy the breeze. / It feels good to be without" (92). Chin/China here gives herself pleasure, marking her power over her own body in defying the master as much as she marks her bondage to and mastery over the Master/U.S.

Another avenue that Chin goes down in exploring the multiple "I" is its relationship to history and memory. The version of identity Chin constructs in **"A Portrait"** results from amnesia and apathy, a set of characteristics that other feminist theorists and poets have identified as particularly American. In *The Sacred Hoop* (1986), Paula Gunn Allen argues that "Indians think it is important to remember, while Americans believe it is important to forget" (210). This is, of course, a generalization, but one that speaks to the necessity of "forgetting" rich pasts and cultures, as well as agonizing processes of assimilation and deculturation, common experiences for immigrant groups and colonized cultures in the United States. In Chin's poems, and in Allen's assertion, identity is closely intertwined with history. Allen asserts that "the root of oppression is loss of memory," and Chin's poems insist on how cultural memories and histories impact the process of assimilation and identity formation that immigrants undergo (213). For the newly assimilated American Chin whose voice closes the poem **"A Portrait,"** there is little regret over loss and a haunting disregard for political accountability and the progress or regress of history:

> Sir, Master, Dominatrix,
> Fall was a glorious season for the hegemonists,
> We took long melancholy strolls on the beach,
> digressed on art and politics
> in a quaint warfside café in La Jolla,
> The storm grazed our bare arms gently . . .
> History never failed us.

(96-97)

"Art and politics" become digressions on a beach, and "history has never failed us" because "we" control what is remembered and how, and because internalized racism and sadistic international shows of force rule the day. This "we" resembles the one seen in **"How I Got That Name"**; while the ends of each are quite different—the former subsumes Chin into an amorphous American communal voice of arrogance and disregard for cultural difference while the latter positions Chin amongst a community of Asian Americans out to trick the U.S. cultural mainstream—both uses of the communal "we" are ironic, deftly manipulated by Chin as poet to critique the particular values communicated by each. In **"A Portrait,"** the self asserts that the "storm" of war (Desert Storm) does nothing but "graze our arms gently" (97). The internalized racism positions Chin as an unapologetic ally of the western Master of hegemony, who endures in power because he controls the terms of American identity and the historical record and determines when to fight and what to fight for. Other countries only matter when they have something that the United States finds valuable or needs in order to preserve the dominance of its own cultural centers:

> Why save Babylonia or Cathay,
> when we can always have Paris?
> Darling, if we are to remember at all,
> Let us remember it well—
> We were fierce, yet tender,
> fierce and tender.

(97)

Babylonia refers to Iraq, and Cathay to China, both disposable when "we" have Paris, a reference not only to

European cultural origins but to the dominance of U.S. industries, such as the film industry, signified by the iconic stature of films such as *Casablanca* and figures such as Bogart and Bergman.

The question of remembering is, in fact, a question: "If we are to remember" is not a rhetorical structure suggesting that they (Chin/China and Master/U.S.), of course, will. The relationship between the question of cultural remembering and (the question of) membership in the U.S. polity is one that Lowe articulates in Immigrant Acts. Lowe writes:

> Citizens inhabit the political space of the nation, a space that is, at once, juridically legislated, territorially situated, and culturally embodied. Although the law is perhaps the discourse that most literally governs citizenship, U.S. national culture—the collectively forged images, histories, and narratives that place, displace, and replace individuals in relation to the national polity—powerfully shapes who the citizenry is, where they dwell, what they remember, and what they forget.

(2)

For Chin/China to become assimilated into the U.S. and to please her Master, she must be careful about what she remembers and what she forgets. The "I" in this poem will not remember the history she leaves behind in China, nor will she remember any alternative histories to the one the Master/U.S. portrays; she has chosen to "forget / the power of exclusion" in order to continue her "love" affair with her Master. However, the forgotten returns in the contradictoriness of the "love" story she tells. If she and her lover choose to remember their alliance, they must remember its contradictoriness—they were "fierce, yet tender / fierce and tender," both fierce warriors and tender lovers. Thus, the entire poem mocks the posturing involved in U.S. foreign relations, and reduces American concerns with the well-being of other nations, and immigrants from other nations, to a sexual game of role-playing and voluntary bondage. The representation of Chin/China as an amnesiac embodies what Lowe refers to as "critical acts that negate those universals" associated with U.S. citizenship (i.e., this is not a love story, but a story of bondage) (8). Lowe writes that "the cultural productions emerging out of the contradictions of immigrant marginality displace the fiction of reconciliation. [and] disrupt the myth of national identity by revealing its gaps and fissures" (8). Chin's "I" as both Chin/China reproduces the gap between her position as the assimilated American and the unassimilable Asian. But it is a contradictory gap; the bold voice of Chin/China belies a passive, masochistic Asian assimilating to the U.S. Master. Thus, Chin's poem exemplifies the functioning of Asian American cultural productions as "alternative site[s] where the palimpsest of lost memories is reinvented, histories are fractured and retraced, and the unlike varieties of silence emerge into articulacy" (Lowe 6). For while the story that Chin/China tells is one of submission and bondage to the U.S./Master, the story of exclusion and forgetting that she seeks to fracture, retrace, and voice is encoded in the lines of the poem as well, and nothing, in effect, is forgotten.

In summary, Chin theorizes ethnic and racial identities as constructed around national concerns and narratives as much as they are constructed in response to group and individual interactions. She portrays the extent to which becoming an American involves contradictions and shifts in identity and identification, shifts that are affected by national narratives which assign gendered and sexualized characteristics to immigrants seeking citizenship, as much as they assign ethnic and racialized characteristics. Thus, Chin's "I" is hardly simplistic or nostalgic; it theorizes self, nation, gender, race, multiple myths of national and individual identity.

Finally, and perhaps most importantly for the study of contemporary American poetry concerned with differences and identities, Chin situates these acts of theorizing within poems. In **"Moon and Oatgrass,"** Chin envisions poetry as a kind of landscape, perhaps another space of possibility. References to the moon and oatgrass evoke stock images of the poet/self communing with nature, but the poem is not devoid of the concern with identities and differences seen in Chin's other work. On the contrary, **"Moon and Oatgrass"** explicitly draws the reader into Chin's vision of poetry as landscape, a space that she controls—"Only I know where / terrace ends and house begins"—and through which the reader wanders:

> The moon is not over the water,
> as you would have it,
> but one with it, and the house
> is on the precipice
> overlooking a green meadow.
> And you—an eye and not an I—
> are walking through it.
>
> (54)

The reader's "eye" walks through the pages of the poem. By linking the "you" to the reader, Chin expands her critique of identity outward from the pages of her book to the "eye" / "not I" of the reader as well, whose identity can be no more fixed nor coherent than the identities explored throughout her poetry. Thus, Chin's poems emphasize the degree to which all identities are re/ produced and mediated through representation; poems mediate the identities she explores, as much as a camera mediates the image the eye records.

Chin closes the poem by asking, "what is this landscape?" (54). Her answer is simple:

> The moon in oatgrass,
> the oatgrass moon.
> A woman pacing
> the linoleum floor,
> contemplating a poem.
>
> (54-55)

This act of contemplation is also an act of power and an act of theorizing. "A woman" is contemplating a poem, providing a surrogate for the reader, whose contemplation

of Chin's poems is likewise empowering. I end on this note in order to emphasize that approaching the poetic "I" as multiple and asserting the differences found within identities as unfixed and constantly consumed and re/ produced does not reduce the possibilities for political alliance building or action. In a reading of Maxine Hong Kingston's *The Woman Warrior* (1976), Wong writes that "talking means having the power to define oneself, to resist the definition of others" (89). By inserting her critique of identity into the poems she writes, writing poems—for Chin—means having the power to resist the definitions of others. Writing poems which theorize also means having the power to leave herself open to definition, to dwell in the undefined space of the empty terrace, to enjoy being—however momentarily—without.

Notes

1. These anthologies belong to a larger group of anthologies produced by multiple communities of women of color, all of which situate creative and critical works as modes of theorizing. Cherrie Moraga and Gloria Anzaldua's *This Bridge Called My Back: Writings By Radical Women of Color* (1981), and Anzaldua's later *Making Face, Making Soul / Haciendo Caras: Creative and Critical Perspectives by Feminists of Color* (1990) are but two examples of multi-genre anthologies. See Cynthia Franklin for a book length discussion of the politics of such anthologies.

2. See Alicia Ostriker for a discussion of the self-referential "I" as politically liberatory for feminist poets exploring women's subjectivity; see Bob Perelman and Marjorie Perloff for discussions of the self-referential "I" as theoretically unsophisticated.

3. The most obvious exception to this is language poetry, which refuses the referentiality of language in general as well as the concept of a self-referential poetry. See Perelman, Perloff, and Koethe.

4. See John Yau and David Mura.

5. I am currently working on a book project titled *Practicing Poetry, Producing Theory* that explores contemporary multi-ethnic American poets—including Marilyn Chin—whose persona poems theorize new understandings of identity and difference.

6. The most obvious example of this dynamic is Frank Chin's introduction to *The Big Aiiieeeee!*, "Come All Ye Asian American Writers of the Real and the Fake." According to Chin, the fakes are those who write from assimilated, Christian, inauthentic positions (such as Maxine Hong Kingston and Amy Tan), and the real are those who write authentically of their Asian histories and non-Christian cultural heritages (1-35).

7. The book project this essay is taken from examines op/positional poetic practices in contemporary multi-ethnic American poetry. Op/positional poetries: 1)

emphasize the interconnectedness of politics and aesthetics; 2) portray the poetic "I" as dynamic, unfixed, and capable of multiple forms of agency; 3) examine the intersectionality of identities; 4) revise familial, social, and mythic histories; and 5) situate poetry as an important sight for theorizing. In this essay, I analyze how op/positional poets utilize a multiple poetic "I" (number 2 above). The term "op/positional" highlights the importance of oppositional politics (opposing the oversimplification of group traits common to identity politics, and opposing racism, sexism, heterosexism) as well as the importance of the politics of position (learning to hear the specificities of each poet's use of language, as well as the particular intersections of the multiple axes which construct and produce each poet's identities).

8. All poems and quotations are from Chin's second collection of poetry, *The Phoenix Gone, The Terrace Empty* (1994).

9. Sau-ling Cynthia Wong explores several different aspects of the racial shadow in Asian American literature. I differentiate Chin's specifically from Wong's exploration of the "disowned" racial shadow, not from the racial shadow in general. Wong ends her chapter on the racial shadow by postulating some possibilities for future research, one of which includes the possibility for "doubling by multiplication," whereby "differing versions of a basic figure are offered to the protagonist faced with a race- and ethnicity- linked identity crisis" (117). The differing versions that Chin explores in this poem are not, however, of a basic figure but include versions of herself and also imagined others. See the first poem of *The Phoenix Gone, The Terrace Empty*—"Exile's Letter: After the Failed Revolution"—for another image of the racial shadow.

10. "How I Got That Name" has an intertextual reference to William Carlos Williams in the following lines:

> History has turned its stomach
> on a black polluted beach—
> where life doesn't hinge
> on that red, red wheelbarrow,
> but whether or not our new lover
> in the final episode of "Santa Barbara"
> will lean over a scented candle
> and call us a "bitch."

(17)

11. Two important intertexts for reading "A Portrait of the Self as Nation, 1990-1991" are Theresa Hak Kyung Cha's Dictee and the visual art of Yong Soon Min, both of whom situate the body of the woman as a synecdoche for the body of the nation (Korea). Yong Soon Min's work can be found in *Writing Self, Writing Nation* (1994), a collection of essays on Dictee edited by Norma Alarcon and Elaine Kim. Thanks to Helena Grice and to Heike Berner for stimulating my thinking on these connections at the Asian America session of the conference on "Reconfiguring Ethnic America," University of Wales, Aberystwyth. Berner's paper on "Identity and the Self in Contemporary Korean American Art: Yong Soon Min, Young Chung, and Jean Shin" was particularly helpful in thinking about the connections between Chin's theorizing and work being done by Asian American visual artists.

12. Another intertextual echo here is Robert Frost's "Mending Wall."

Works Cited

Allen, Paula Gunn. *The Sacred Hoop: Recovering the Feminine In American Indian Traditions.* Boston: Beacon Press, 1986.

Anzaldua, Gloria. *Making Face, Making Soul / Haciendo Caras: Creative and Critical Perspectives by Feminists of Color.* San Francisco: Aunt Lute, 1990.

Cha, Theresa Hak Kyung. *Dictee.* Berkeley: Third Woman Press, 1995. (Originally published Tanam Press, 1982.)

Chang, Juliana. "Reading Asian American Poetry." *MELUS* 21.1 (1996): 81-98.

Chin, Frank. "Come All Ye Asian American Writers of the Real and the Fake." *The Big AIIIEEEEE! An Anthology of Chinese American and Japanese American Literature.* New York: Meridian Books, 1991. 1-35.

Chin, Marilyn. *The Phoenix Gone, the Terrace Empty.* Minneapolis: Milkweed, 1994.

Christian, Barbara. "The Race for Theory." *Making Face, Making Soul / Haciendo Caras: Creative and Critical Perspectives by Feminists of Color.* San Francisco: Aunt Lute, 1990. 335-345. (Originally published in *Cultural Critique* 6 [1989]).

The Forbidden Stitch: An Asian American Women's Anthology. Ed. Shirley Geok-lin Lim, Mayurni Tsutakawa, and Margarita Donnelly. Corvallis: Calyx Books, 1989.

Franklin, Cynthia G. *Writing Women's Communities: The Politics and Poetics of Contemporary Multi-Genre Anthologies.* Madison: University of Wisconsin Press, 1997.

Goellnicht, Donald C. "Blurring Boundaries: Asian American Literature as Theory." *An Interethnic Companion to Asian American Literature.* Ed. King-Kok Cheung. Cambridge: Cambridge UP, 1997. 338-365.

Hagedorn, Jessica. "There Once Was a Woman . . ." Foreword. *Making More Waves: New Writing by Asian American Women.* Ed. Elaine H. Kim, Lilia V. Villanueva, and Asian Women United of California. Boston: Beacon, 1997.

Keller, Lynn and Cristanne Miller. *Feminist Measures: Soundings in Poetry and Theory.* Ann Arbor: University of Michigan Press, 1994.

Kim, Elaine H., and Norma Alarcon, eds. *Writing Self, Writing Nation.* Berkeley: Third Woman Press, 1994.

King, Katie. *Theory in Its Feminist Travels: Conversations in U.S. Women's Movements.* Bloomington: Indiana UP, 1994.

Koethe, John. "Contrary Impulses: The Tension Between Poetry and Theory." *Critical Inquiry* 18 (1991): 64- 75.

Lowe, Lisa. *Immigrant Acts: On Asian American Cultural Politics.* Durham: Duke UP, 1996.

Making More Waves: New Writing by Asian American Women. Ed. Elaine H. Kim, Lilia V. Villanueva, and Asian Women United of California. Boston: Beacon, 1997.

Making Waves: An Anthology of Writings By and About Asian American Women. Ed. Asian Women United of California. Boston: Beacon, 1989.

Moraga, Cherrie, and Gloria Anzaldua. *This Bridge Called My Back: Writings By Radical Women of Color.* Watertown: Persephone Press, 1981.

Mura, David. "The Margins at the Center, the Center at the Margins." *ReViewing Asian America: Locating Diversity.* Ed. Wendy L. Ng, Soo-Young Chin, James S. Moy, and Gary Y. Okihiro. Pullman: Washington State UP, 1995.171- 183.

Ostriker, Alicia. *Stealing the Language: The Emergence of Women's Poetry in America.* Boston: Beacon, 1986.

Perelman, Bob. *The Marginalization of Poetry: Language Writing and Literary History.* Princeton: Princeton UP, 1996.

Perloff, Marjorie. *Poetic License: Essays on Modernist and Postmodernist Lyric.* Evanston: Northwestern UP, 1990.

Trinh, T. Minh-ha. *Woman, Native, Other: Writing Postcoloniality and Feminism.* Indiana: Bloomington UP, 1989.

Webster's College Dictionary. New York: Random House, 1991.

Wong, Sau-ling Cynthia. *Reading Asian American Literature: From Necessity to Extravagance.* Princeton: Princeton UP, 1993.

Yau, John. "Between the Forest and Its Trees." *Amerasia Journal* 20.3 (1994): 37-43.

John Gery (essay date 2001)

SOURCE: Gery, John. "Mocking My Own Ripeness: Authenticity, Heritage, and Self-Erasure in the Poetry of Marilyn Chin." *LIT: Literature Interpretation Theory* 12, no. 1 (April 2001): 25-45.

[*In the following essay, Gery maintains that Chin finds her own voice, and transcends the constraints confronted by women writers of color, through "articulate emptinesses" and "imaginative reconstruction of the diverse resources she inherits."*]

Although ensnared in a complex nexus of gender, race, ancient traditions, and literary conventions, Marilyn Chin's poetry at its most resilient invites all these cultural and literary forces into it, whether explicitly as subject matter or obliquely in form and language. As Sau-ling Cynthia Wong notes about Chin's first collection, *Dwarf Bamboo* (1987), Chin is "Chinese-literate but open to a host of poetic influences," and because of her "passionate sense of craft" ("Chinese American" 53), what has emerged, even in her poems of cynicism or despair, is a finely honed voice struggling toward self-definition, rather than one resigned to be seen *only* as other, or as others define it. To oppose being labeled as "other" in this way, rather than to draw on it or even assert it as her identity, tends to align Chin with those Asian American writers whom critics such as Wong approach from what Wong calls "a 'minority discourse' framework" (*Reading* 4)—that is, to be read not just in terms of how her work differs from that of the dominant culture surrounding her, but of how it expresses "shared historical experiences of oppression" among different minorities that "cannot be adequately addressed by a model centered on a hegemonic culture" (*Reading* 4).

Adopting a similar perspective to discuss Chin's second collection of poems, *The Phoenix Gone, The Terrace Empty* (1994), Srimati Mukherjee has described her work as a "poetics of depletion," characterized by a "drive for a loss that is irreplaceable" (Mukherjee). As a poet shaping her particular Asian American identity—that is, her own "walk / into the new world" of the West (Chin 50) from her Chinese heritage—Chin, according to Mukherjee, defines her existence less by presences than by absences: Her existence is, as Chin portrays that of the "little bird" in the book's title poem, one of "*something escaping, something escaping*" (Chin 51).[1] Nevertheless, the power of Chin's verse derives not only from its many articulate emptinesses but from its fullnesses, too—that is, from her imaginative reconfiguration of the diverse resources she inherits, even as those same resources persistently threaten to erase her identity. So even as one poem may close, almost bitterly, "Is there nothing left but the shell / and humanity's strange inscriptions, / the songs, the rites, the oracles?" (**"Turtle Soup"** 24), in other poems Chin, if not exactly consoled, grimly affirms her imagination's ability to re-cast what she has inherited—as in "the black ink dried in the receptacle" (**"The Tao and the Art of Leave-taking"** 31), for instance, or "the red eye of morning" that closes **"Moon and Oatgrass"** (55). In **"The Disorder,"** she concludes, almost whimsically: "As you attempt to fill an emptiness / not filled by the sun, as you wait / for your inevitable fall / a small child / within you remembers: *so, these, these / were the* "'*golden mountains!*'" (60).

In order to appreciate the intricate reconstruction of gender, race, and poetic tradition which Chin's best poems perform, it is important first, I think, to situate her in the threefold framework within which she writes: namely, her social, theoretical, and literary context. To begin with the social context, Chin (who was born in 1955 in Hong Kong) may be too young a poet to be directly associated with the wave of Asian American women writers (most notably, Maxine Hong Kingston) who emerged into prominence among the growing community of feminist writers in the U.S. in the 1960s and 1970s. Nonetheless, their accounts of their own racial and gender consciousness help to clarify the social milieu of Chin's later writing. For instance, the Japanese-born American writer Mitsuye Yamada, herself confined to an internment camp in Idaho during the Second World War (Yamada 147), has described poignantly the sense of socio-political exclusion Asian American women felt during feminist gatherings on the West Coast as recently as the 1980s. While these Asian American women fully allied themselves with other American feminists "to know what it means to be a woman in our society, to know the historical and psychological forces that have shaped and are shaping our thoughts which in turn determine the direction of our lives" (148), observes Yamada, they also could not help but notice that too often middle-class women's groups seemed "no different from other organizations that imposed opinions and goals on their members rather than having them shaped by the needs of the members" themselves (148). Consequently, among Asian Pacific American women in particular, at the time, there developed "a pervasive feeling of mistrust toward the women in the movement." "A movement that fights sexism in the social structure must deal with racism," argues Yamada, "and we had hoped the leaders in the women's movement would be able to see the parallels in the lives of the women of color and themselves, and would 'join' us in our struggle and give us 'input.'" The result of their "feeling of disappointment" in the feminist political agenda, Yamada believes, was that activist Asian American women in general have tended to devote themselves to "groups promoting ethnic identity, most notably ethnic studies in universities, ethnic theater groups or ethnic community agencies" (149), rather than to women's organizations per se.

While Yamada maintains, as others have, that ethnic and women's groups are not, nor need be, "at war with one another," she makes it clear how "women of color are often made to feel that we must make a choice" between these two types of social activism (149). Yet the dilemma of having to decide necessarily involves dividing oneself at the center—thereby creating conflict not only in terms of one's social commitment but also, more subtly, in one's very identity. This internal tension in fact is what Chin, an Asian-born female living in the U.S., has inherited and constantly speaks from in her work, as she tries to develop an "authentic" voice as a poet. As George Uba points out about the poems in Dwarf Bamboo, despite Chin's leftist political affinities, her "skepticism toward unificatory gestures and her intense recognition of identity as process rather than as cultural preserve lead her to question the very impulses toward which she is otherwise drawn" (36), creating a kind of "post-activist" poetry that questions the language and action of identity and renounces its stability (35). "For Chin," concludes Uba, "the question of identity is engaging precisely because it is never still" (39).

It is this destabilizing of social identity, as shaped by the ideological context of any "Third World" woman writer searching for "authenticity," that lies at the heart of Trinh T. Minh-ha's deconstructive meditation Woman, Native, Other: Writing Postcoloniality and Feminism (1989). Trinh's book furnishes a second, more theoretical perspective on The Phoenix Gone, the Terrace Empty. Echoing Yamada, Trinh describes what she calls the "triple bind" constraining an Asian American woman writer in a state in which she finds herself "driven into situations where she is made to feel she must choose from among three conflicting identities. Writer of color? Woman writer? Or woman of color? Which comes first? Where does she place her loyalties?" (6). Confronted with these divisive, categorical questions, she is liable to find herself "at odds with language, which partakes in the white-male-is-norm ideology and is used predominantly as a vehicle to circulate established power relations" (6). Yet inevitably, in attempting to establish her own identity, she must locate herself not only according to social norms but to high cultural and literary standards as well.

For instance, Trinh recalls Margaret Atwood's critique of what she calls "The Quiller-Couch Syndrome," referring to the critic Arthur Quiller-Couch's distinction between masculine and feminine writing, with the former "type" (not surprisingly, for the era) characterized as "objective" and "universal" and the latter as "subjective," "confessional," "personal," even "narcissistic" and "neurotic" (27). "She who writes well," goes the line of reasoning which Trinh reiterates, "'writes like a man' and 'thinks like a man' [so that] what is implied here is her capability to write and think differently from other women [. . .]" (27-8). Similarly, in regard to race, adds Trinh, conventional thinking has dictated that

> the white man knows through *reason* and logic—the intelligible. The black man understands through *intuition* and sympathy—the sensible. Old stereotypes deriving from well-defined differences (the apartheid type of difference) govern our thought. Our province, we hear, is the *heart*, not the *mind*, which many of us have come to loathe and despise, for we believe it has a sex, a male one however, for reasons of (in)security. (We are told and we tell ourselves that we need to assert our identities.) But to write well, we must either espouse his cause or transcend our borderlines. *We must forget ourselves* [emphasis added]. We are therefore triply jeopardized: as a writer, as a woman, and as a woman of color.
>
> (28)

In short, this tri-lateral condition Trinh ascribes to the Asian American woman writer—ultimately requiring that she must *forget* herself in order to speak in any semblance of an "authentic" voice—is chiefly what lies behind the proliferation of absences to be found in such a writer's method as well as in her subject matter. As an "author" conscious of playing the role of a creator or "God" over language, yet "eager to create a meaningful world and/or to unveil her ignored/censored deeper self," the Asian

American woman writer, argues Trinh, "adopts a series of strategies liable to ensure a transparency of form through which content, intelligibly constructed, can travel unhindered. Or she plays a hide-and-seek game with her readers, thus preserving the image of the misunderstood genius and leaving the task of guessing-rediscovering-clarifying to the critic" (30). Such a writer's technique, she adds, is concerned "not with inserting a 'me' into language, but with creating an opening where the 'me' disappears while 'I' endlessly come and go, as the nature of language requires" (35). Whereas the "traditional" writer (namely, in this society, one who is male and white in method, at least, if not in fact) may struggle to assert a unique or individual identity, even if in an attempt to "transcend" it, for Trinh the paradoxical position of the "Third World" woman writer is that of a self *hiding behind* or even *disappearing into* the text she creates.

The posture of Marilyn Chin's work epitomizes Trinh's concept, even dangerously so. For example, in a 1998 interview in *The Writer's Chronicle,* Chin consistently dodges Calvin Bedient's questions about the ambiguity of the speaker's identity in several poems in **The Phoenix Gone, The Terrace Empty.** Each time Bedient asks her to identify the source of the speaking voice in a particular poem—whether autobiographical or fictional—Chin stubbornly equivocates, replying, for example, that though the woman in **"The Floral Apron"** may be fashioned after her grandmother, "I tried to universalize her by not naming her" (8). Then she responds to Bedient's query whether the speaker in **"Against War, Against Watchtower"** is a human being or a symbol for China with "I think both" (9). Later, when asked about the use of "I" in her poems, Chin clearly echoes Trinh's ethic of self-erasure as method, expressed as a principle of expressing "multiple identities":

> The "I" in my poems has multiple layers; the "I" always represents something greater than the self. That the "I" has more than one identity, shifting within the poem, is a direct rebellion against what I learned in the workshop days, when the professor would say "you," the addressee, must be a specific person; and "I," the speaker, must be clear.
>
> (10)

Turning Chin's poetics here inside out, Bedient then tries to undermine the insinuated grandiosity of her explanation, by asking, "The first 'I,' then, is just an empty pronoun?" to which Chin replies, as Trinh might, "I think Chinese Americans sometimes feel like empty pronouns. I feel this burden of history, and although I've arrived on the shores of safety, the burden of history is so compelling that the 'I' in the lyric poem seems empty. The 'I' can't stand by itself; it has to have archetypal significance." Later, she adds, "That's what I yearn for: the collective pronoun" (10).

Of course, we might argue that most poets, at least Western poets, "yearn" for "the collective pronoun," too. That is, they, too, want their poems to speak for a larger community. But that Chin, like Trinh, locates her voice in the "displacement" of the collective she hopes to represent draws attention to the "emptiness" or indiscernibility of her "multiple layers." As Trinh defines it,

> "I" is, therefore, not a unified subject, a fixed identity, or that solid mass covered with layers of superficialities one has gradually to peel off before one can see its true face. "I" is, itself, *infinite layers.* Its complexity can hardly be conveyed through such typographic conventions as I, i, or I/i. Thus, I/i am compelled by the will to say/unsay, to resort to the entire gamut of personal pronouns to stay near this fleeing *and* static essence of Not-I.
>
> (94)

Given such a protean sense of self as this, Chin's own ambivalence in response to Bedient's questions about her poems' voices seems not finally an evasive tactic but a "necessary" one (Trinh 94). On the other hand, for Trinh, *"authenticity,"* which she defines "as a need to rely on an 'undisputed origin,'" is also "prey to an obsessive *fear,* that of *losing a connection*" (94). In other words, in reading the work of an Asian American woman poet, our usual critical standards may well be themselves turned inside out, considering that hers is an art in which self-erasure becomes self-assertion, ambivalence signifies identity, and the only authentic voice seems to be one neither confident nor fearless. In her interview with Bedient, Chin echoes this paradoxical condition when describing herself: "In America, I'm always reminded of my difference. The loss of China, the loss of being part of that world, makes me lonely. My poetry is about the fear of assimilation, of being incorporated by the Western world. But I know that that's inevitable" (12).

Before considering the third aspect of Chin's context—namely, the Chinese literary heritage out of which her poems are constructed—one further qualification concerning Trinh T. Minh-ha's account of "authenticity" bears mentioning. While Trinh demonstrates how the Asian American (or "Third World") woman writer's situation deconstructs "authenticity" itself as her working principle—that is, how the concepts of a "true inner self" and authentic self-expression become suspect because of implicit assumptions about "origins" and "my so-called roots" (89)—she is also careful to clarify earlier that by "authenticity" she does *not* mean, simply, one's ethnic or racial "specialness" (88). For an ambitious Third World woman writer, Trinh admits, "Specialness as a soporific soothes, anaesthetizes my sense of justice" in a social environment in which "i am not only given the permission to open up and talk, i am also encouraged to express my difference. My audience expects and demands it; otherwise people would feel as if they had been cheated: We did not come to hear a Third World member speak about the First (?) World, We came to listen to that voice of difference likely to bring us *what we can't have* and to divert us from the monotony of sameness" (88). For a "Third World representative" or writer to yield to such a tempting social identity as the "other," however, therein remaining "more preoccupied with her/his image of the *real* native—the *truly different*—than with the issues of hegemony, racism, feminism, and social change," is, for Trinh, to contort authenticity into "a product that one can buy, arrange to one's liking, and/or preserve" (88).[2] In other words, for the "minority" writer, there is no more solace to be found in embracing one's apparent socio-historical difference than in rejecting it. Again, self-erasure, ambivalence and the "triple jeopardy" of contending among conflicting identities constitute the Third World woman writer's primary legacy in the U.S.

However, for Marilyn Chin, a well-trained Chinese scholar and poet,[3] a third context for, or dimension of, her identity presents itself: While Trinh discusses at length how storytelling (including narrative poetry) has long been a conduit of women's power (120-28)—a tradition which Chin also affirms (Interview 11)—Chin further acknowledges, and her poetry clearly reveals, the impact of her education, not only on her use of diction, idiom, rhythms, imagery, and point of view, all arguably influenced by her training at the University of Iowa Creative Writing Workshop, but more significantly, on her immersion in ancient Chinese (male) poetry. Labeling herself for a national television audience in Bill Moyers' *The Language of Life* (though undoubtedly aware of the contradictions therein) as "a radical, feminist, West Coast, Pacific Rim, Marxist-socialist, neoclassical, Iowa-educated, Asian-American poet" (Interview 6), Chin nonetheless remains consistent about what she calls her "neoclassicism" when she asserts, "I want my feet to be grounded in traditions" so that "to experiment doesn't mean that we have to work against tradition. Sometimes the shift can be very gentle and still make a difference. I think that those of us from the margins must add to the tradition" (Interview 13-14). While she has spoken out against the inherited social inequities of Chinese culture, she expresses an unambiguously high regard for the Chinese literary past.[4]

In particular, Chin has inherited from ancient Chinese poetry, in my observation, three of its most important characteristics—namely, its evocative but heavily symbolic imagery (Liu 101), its decorous style, and, most importantly, its use of indirection as a method of dismantling "authority"—or as one of Maxine Hong Kingston's characters puts it, "That's what Chinese say. We like to say the opposite" (237). My primary source here for characterizing classical Chinese poetry in these ways is James J. Y. Liu's important 1962 work *The Art of Chinese Poetry,* where, in opposition to Ernest Fenollosa's famous essay, *The Chinese Written Character as a Medium for Poetry,* not only does Liu establish an intricate link between the auditory and visual aspects of the Chinese language used in poetry (8-19), but also he demonstrates the central role both language and imagery, whether conventional or idiosyncratic, play in traditional verse. For example, in discussing the interrelationship of imagery and symbolism, Liu argues (as Chin herself has suggested) that the strong associations or allusions attached to traditional images need not be a deterrent to a poet's

particular sensual imagination; such associations may, in fact, provide surprisingly opportune moments for individuality (because of how they function as visual allusions as well as signifiers, to use Derridean terms): "In the case of conventional symbols," writes Liu, "we should consider how the poet has reaffirmed, developed, modified, or changed their significance. Just as poets can use conventional imagery without piling up *cliches,* so can they use conventional symbols with varying implications and associations so as to avoid stereotyped repetition" (128).

Liu discusses the image of the chrysanthemum in particular to illustrate the symbolic variations he has in mind (128-30). But because of their coincidental intersections, we might note instead how Liu interprets the symbolism of a short poem by the poet Li Shang-yin (812?-858), of the Late T'ang Dynasty (618-907), in order to reveal the suggestively different use Marilyn Chin makes of a similar set of images, more than eleven hundred years later, in her poem **"And All I Have Is Tu Fu."** Here is A. C. Graham's 1965 translation of this untitled poem in *Poems of the Late T'ang*:

> Phoenix tail on scented silk, flimsy layer on layer:
> Blue patterns on a round canopy, stitched deep into the night.
> The fan's sliced moon could not hide her shame,
> His coach drove out with the sound of thunder, no time to exchange a word.
> In the silent room the gold of the wick turned dark:
> No message since has ever come, though the pomegranate is red.
> The dappled horse stands tethered only on the bank of drooping willows,
> Where shall she wait for a kind wind to blow from the South West?

> (149)

As Liu explains (139-41), the opening two lines of this poem depict the speaker's employment of sewing the canopy, woven with "Phoenix tail" silk on top, "deep into the night" before her own wedding. But the image of the fan compared to the moon in line three, for a knowledgeable Chinese reader, alludes to several imperial poems where a fan compared to the moon suggests abandonment—especially that of the Lady Pan, a court lady of the Han Dynasty, who compares her circular fan to the moon and notes being put aside when she is no longer needed (i.e. deserted), like a fan in autumn. In addition to revealing the quick departure of the man who has fled, the sound of thunder in line four of Li's poem also alludes to the thunder in two lines in Ssu-ma Hsiang-ju's *Song of the Long Gate,* lines composed for the Empress Ch'en of Palace of Long Gate after she fell out of favor with Emperor Wu. But because in her case she was later restored to her place, the allusion here introduces a similar hope for the return of this speaker's lover. The "gold of the wick" in line five refers to a candle that has burned out after a long time, a symbol of despair familiar to all of us. The pomegranate refers to the red pomegranate wine drunk specifically at weddings. Line seven is equally informative (if equally oblique), in that the "dappled" or "pied" horse alludes to a famous Chinese song of a young man on a "piebald horse" who roams indefinitely, never to return home, so that we know the speaker will remain alone. Yet its standing "tethered only on the bank of drooping willows" tells us its rider has stopped temporarily for "plucking the willow at Chang Terrace," a familiar Chinese euphemism for visiting a courtesan; furthermore, Liu adds, a willow twig is often given to a departing friend (thus, easily passed on to another). Finally, the poem closes with the speaker echoing two lines by the poet Ts'ao Chih (192-232) in which a deserted wife sighs, "I wish to become the south-west wind / To fly far away, into your arms."

Layered though it may be, once we begin to follow the symbolic, imagistic pattern of Li Shang-yin's poem, the individual "subjectivity" of its speaker begins to emerge, even in this English rendering. As Liu points out, in the poem "the allusions are the main means to bring out the underlying meaning, yet because they are combined with imagery [and are not literary for literariness' sake alone], they do not appear pedantic and prosaic" but are in fact "highly sensuous" (140).

Now look how Chin, in a poem also inspired by feelings of abandonment but composed in contemporary American English, can be as allusive as Li Shang-yin, although to different effect:

"And All I Have Is Tu Fu"

Pied horse, pied horse, I am having a dream.
Twenty-five Mongolians on horseback, twenty-five;
their hooves gouging deep trenches into the loess.
Now they enter a hole in the Wall, now they retreat.
Freud snickers; Jung shakes his head.

Then, a soldier comes forward who calls himself Tu
    Fu.
He opens his mouth and issues a cartouche:
all black-bearded, knitted browed,
each meaning "what your viscera look like
after having been disemboweled!"

Pray, promise me, this is not what the dream por-
    tends—
my roommate's in the bathroom fucking my boyfriend,
and all I have is Tu Fu.

                                                                  (79)

In addition to the intricate series of allusions here (most of which I do not pretend to understand, since no gloss yet exists on this poem, as Liu has provided for Li Shang-yin's poem), Chin adds a new dimension—namely, a tone of self-derision, in the references to Freud and Jung in line five, for instance, as well as in her imagining her roommate in the bathroom, a comically internal reference to Tu Fu's proclamation of the speaker's being "disemboweled" that is almost like something out of an *Animal House* movie. The pied horse to whom the poem is addressed, as in Li Shang-yin's poem, suggests the irony of the speaker addressing one who is roaming, never to return, an empty

gesture that anticipates her fear of betrayal in the last strophe. Yet for all the poem's humor and sophistication—with its juxtaposition of the ancient and the modern, war and love, the visual and the literary, the rarified and the vulgar—it is no less poignant in mood: virtually all that is missing is an image of a fan laid aside. As is often true in Chin's poetry, the poem registers the speaker's fear of erasure, expressing that same "drive for a loss that is irreplaceable" that Mukherjee finds elsewhere in her work. That its language is a mixture of the formal ("hooves gouging deep trenches into the loess," "who calls himself Tu Fu," "issues a cartouche," "Pray") and the vernacular ("snickers," "shakes his head," "roommate," "fucking my boyfriend") neither deflates the ancient heritage nor elevates the idiomatic, exactly, but reconfigures both to become part of the poet's own language. In other words, while the poem's tone may mock Chin's Chinese heritage as much as her American lifestyle, it is no less "authentic" in its voice and sensuous in its imagery than Li Shang-yin's poem, once we adjust to the multivocal, ambivalent, self-deprecating style that distinguishes her style—not as an "Asian American" poet per se but as a poet seeking her identity in that cultural and literary context.

Although **"And All I Have Is Tu Fu"** may deliberately draw attention to Chin's self-consciousness of the Eastern and Western patriarchal webs from which she hopes to extricate herself, her best poems, such as **"How I Got That Name," "The Phoenix Gone, the Terrace Empty,"** and **"Moon and Oatgrass,"** even better illustrate how she sometimes ruptures her identity as "woman, native, other" through an ironic, even parodic "dis-play" of self-consciousness capable of linking her internal divisions, as well as connecting her past to her present. While these three poems are all longer (three, six, and two pages, respectively) than **"And All I Have Is Tu Fu,"** they tend to employ shorter lines, especially **"The Phoenix Gone,"** which when considered with their discursive, even conversational diction clearly associate them with it. Furthermore, while self-erasure figures prominently in all three poems (if erasure can *be* "prominent"), all three can also be said to exploit the poet's thinking about identity, ultimately finding their resolution in the emergence of the "authenticity" of her voice, despite each poem's sense of defeat. Or to put it in Trinh's terms, in these poems Chin can be said to adopt "a series of strategies liable to ensure a transparency of form through which content [. . .] can travel unhindered" (30), so that she might create "an opening where the 'me' disappears while 'I' endlessly come and go" (35).

"How I Got That Name," a poem divided into four discrete parts, carries the subtitle, "an essay on assimilation," as though either to deflate or defer the poetics of its author. **"I am Marilyn Mei Ling Chin"** (16) announces the first line, in an apparently proud echo of Whitman, adding with equal vigor, "Oh, how I love the resoluteness / of that first person singular." Initially, the poet seems at least as delighted, in fact, in using the pronoun "I" and the verb "am" ("without the uncertain i-n-g") as she is in stating her own name. Yet the qualifier "Of course" in line seven quickly reveals why and sends the speaker into a downward spiral; she acknowledges that, in fact, not only was her name changed "somewhere between Angel Island and the sea" on her voyage to the U.S., but the new name "Marilyn" was given her by her father because of his infatuation with that "tragic white woman / swollen with gin and Nembutal," Marilyn Monroe. In other words, within the first twenty-five lines, not only does Chin mock the grotesque inappropriateness of her own name (so proudly declaimed at first), but she attributes it to the patriarchy of one whose impulses "nobody dared question" and further discloses, in humiliating detail, how her own mother could not pronounce it and so "dubbed me 'Numba one female off-shoot' / for brevity." By the end of this first section, the speaker descends even deeper into self-mockery and satire, as she describes her father's emigre activities and the sheeplike manners of "his nice, devout daughters / and his bright, industrious sons / as if filial piety were the standard / by which all earthly men were measured" (16-17).

Part two of the poem (its most overt section) mixes Chinese symbols ("Oh, bamboo shoots, bamboo shoots!") with highly allusive American phrasing (invoking not only William Carlos Williams's "red wheelbarrow" and John Berryman's "inner resources" but the television soap opera *Santa Barbara*) in a bitterly satiric depiction of Chinese American stereotypes. Then the third section remarks on the (now dead) "Great Patriarch Chin" peering down at his children "from his kiosk in heaven" and realizing they are "ugly." Chin's self-portrait here traces the same pattern of multiplicity, self-erasure, and ambivalence we have seen elsewhere, as she calls herself "his least favorite—/ 'not quite boiled, not quite cooked,' / a plump pomfret simmering in my juices—/ too listless to fight for my people's destiny" (17-18). Indeed, the section closes with the poet awaiting her "imminent death," one that arrives not with a bang, not even a whimper, but virtually unnoticed, and having almost entirely lost a sense of her self, her identity, she closes this passage sardonically:

> The fact that this death is also metaphorical
> is testament to my lethargy.

(18)

The fourth and final section of the poem then appropriately presents, but doesn't really even "express" (since, after all, the self in this poem is meant to be entirely obliterated), the poet's own epitaph: After a denigrating litany of her ancestors in a mock-Chinese manner, she describes herself in an American context as "neither black nor white / neither cherished nor vanquished / just another squatter in her own bamboo groove / minding her poetry." And the poem closes, ironically, both by iterating the absence of a self in a contemporary American cultural context that ranges from *Moby-Dick* to the movies *and*, surprisingly enough, by celebrating, Whitman-like, her own kind of survival,

> when one day heaven was unmerciful,
> and a chasm opened where she stood.
> Like the jowls of a mighty white whale,
> or the jaws of a metaphysical Godzilla,
> it swallowed her whole.
> She did not flinch nor writhe,
> nor fret about the afterlife,
> but stayed! Solid as wood, happily
> a little gnawed, tattered, mesmerized
> by all that was lavished upon her
> and all that was taken away!

(18)

The end of **"How I Got That Name"** balances precariously between the assimilation into American culture that Chin sees as inevitable, an assimilation that will ultimately eradicate her distinctly Asian heritage, and (by virtue of her own name now having been said in the poem) the "solid," unfettered being who remains, despite "all that was taken away." Its dark humor, irony and contradictions make it cohere. Whether it is finally considered an "essay" or a poem, its having effectively represented how the speaker *isn't* reveals, by its finish, how she *is*.

As the longest poem of the collection, **"The Phoenix Gone, the Terrace Empty"** vacillates between imagining the past and imagining the present. Even more than in **"How I Got That Name,"** its narrow, cryptic lines insinuate a poem almost barely coming into being on the page, as though it were sustained by only the flimsiest of syntactic or cognitive connections. Not so neatly divided into parts as **"How I Got That Name,"** the poem stretches across six pages and eleven strophes ranging from three to fifty-six lines in length. The links between strophes often appear tenuous at best. Yet what binds the poem, in the poet's search to come to terms with the loss of her father (or, more broadly, her patriarchal heritage), is the same mix of allusion and confession, symbolic and sensual imagery, that Liu identifies in ancient Chinese poetry. After an epigraph citing a Chinese verse in Chinese characters together with its English translation, "The river flows without ceasing," the first strophe opens with a direct address to a "shallow river," with the speaker echoing a Chinese poet. Gathering "the hem / of my terry-cloth robe" in order to climb the "steep" stairs into the river, she expresses her longing: "Quietly, / gingerly, / if an inch could sing / I would sing / for miles," she sighs, beyond the rock garden she finds herself in, with its courtyard, mulberries, Bodhi tree "fragrant with jossticks," Buddha ("whose laugh is unmerciful"), nasturtium, and irises (46). Her song, indeed the narrow lines of the poem itself, she addresses directly as "my pink horses, / my tiny soldiers" who will carry her away from where she stands, where "the flagstones / caress my feet," as she commands that they be kissed "tenderly." The second strophe shifts to a quoted (probably translated) passage of a solo voice wondering about the significance of its own being: "'Who in the netherworld walks on my sole / as I walk? / And opens her black mouth / when I cry? / Whose lutestrings / play my sorrow?'" (46-47). Finding comfort in the words of another who also felt isolated from his or her community, Chin establishes an elaborate historical and literary context here for expressing her own displacement, first wishing to efface herself, then ironically finding herself through that effacement by quoting another who has clearly felt the same way.

The poem's third strophe, however, figuratively relocates the poet back in the present:

> This banister
> painted with red lacquer
> where
> my grip turns white.
> These plum blossoms,
> stock signifiers,
> mocking my own ripeness
> I cannot taste.
> Flesh remembers
> what the mind resists.
>
> (47)

Concentrating on the "shallow river" she stands beside, she examines her hands and then the plum blossoms, which she self-consciously dismisses as "stock signifiers" that, despite their beauty in the garden (or on the "terrace"), "mock" the poet's "ripeness" which she "cannot taste." Having been so often used symbolically in Chinese poetry for spring and sexuality, Chin implies here not only that she cannot see the plum blossoms for themselves alone, but that as conventional "signifiers" they in fact *suppress* what they signify, namely, "[her] own ripeness." Despite their richly suggestive nature (and despite the music of the verse itself, with the alliteration on "s" and the *stock/mocking* rhyme), seeing the plum blossoms simultaneously distracts the poet from herself and, paradoxically, draws her more deeply into her own erasure. After all, despite her mind's resistance to what surrounds her, her "flesh remembers," as the rest of the strophe recalls her family heritage: "the warm blur" of her mother, which she associates with love, and "the hard shape" of her father, which she obversely associates with "hate." She imagines her parents as "mugworts, / no, water bison," discussing her future "in a fulcrum / of angry gestures." Then she pictures her grandmother singing a lullaby, her grandfather as an "itinerant tinker" working his bellows at a forge, "the shanty towns / on the hills of Wanchai" with their "tin roofs / crying into the sun" (48), and even "the charred sweetness" in the "raven hair" of her mother's first lover. In other words, while her cultural inheritance may oppress her individual ability to experience the world firsthand, her "flesh remembers" even that which her psyche has been denied.

The following two strophes shift again from an imagined, distant heritage to nearer memories of the poet's father: First, she recalls his words to her as a child, as he "crouched / on the dirty linoleum" of a Chinese restaurant in America in a dice game; "'Mei Ling, don't cry,'" he assures her, "'I can change our lives / with one strike'" (48-49). The next, longer strophe cites the poet's Auntie Jade characterizing the poet's father as "the ox, / without his yoke, / sitting on a ridge / of the quay." The man Auntie

Jade describes is a defeated victim of social forces beyond himself whose "dreams / were robbed / by the Japanese, / his fortune / [. . .] plundered / by the Nationalists" and his home "seared" by the Communists. "When you pray / to your ancestors," Auntie Jade informs the daughter, "you are praying / to his hollowness" (50). Not only is the poet displaced, but what she has been displaced from is a father who himself epitomes emptiness itself.

The last six strophes of **"The Phoenix Gone, the Terrace Empty"** are shorter and even more fragmented than the first five, as the poet tries to gather what she might say without intending to find any resolution. The sixth strophe brings us back to the present and the poet's climbing the terrace steps again, as she asks, "shall I walk / into the new world / in last year's pinafore?" Mocking both her Western context and herself—in the same duplicitous manner in which Ezra Pound in the Pisan Cantos, for instance, cites the Parisian dress designer Paquin in the often quoted passage, "Pull down thy vanity," in Canto LXXXI (541-42)—Chin also alludes to the fashion world: "Chanel says: / black, black / is our century's color," which she then aligns both with what is "proper and elegant" and with her "deep, deep regret." Even the *absence* of color is not without ambiguity for this poet. Abruptly, the following strophe turns to another quoted passage, like that in the second strophe, yet the source here seems to be Auntie Jade again, this time commenting on the poet's bringing her "new boyfriend" Ezekiel home to meet her mother. Not only is he dismissed because her mother can't pronounce his name, but he is belittled for his "demeanor," for being "too thin, too sallow," for not eating beef "in a country / where beef is possible," and for not playing the violin "in a country / where rapture is possible" (50-51). As with the image of her boyfriend in the bathroom at the end of **"And All I Have Is Tu Fu,"** the contrast here to the formal lament quoted earlier is comic, yet not entirely deflated, since whoever Chin is quoting closes by remarking on the image of the "'Moon / which accompanied his arrival'" as "'shaped naughtily / like a woman's severed ear'" (51). This fragmented moon, with its haunting insinuation of the silencing not only of women's speech but of their hearing, again seems to derive from the disrupted, fragmented setting of **"The Phoenix Gone, the Terrace Empty,"** though incidentally it stands in sharp contrast to the moon as it appears in **"Moon and Oatgrass."**

However, perhaps the poem's most telling "symbol" (if we can call it that) appears directly after this "severed ear," in the image of the snake biting her own tail, about which the poet wonders whether it signifies "harmony at year's end," a more or less traditional interpretation, or that "she is eating herself / into extinction." Nowhere else in **"The Phoenix Gone, the Terrace Empty"** do its conflicting forces seem so explicit, as Chin devolves into an ambiguous emptiness resulting from her being severed from her past, her father, her mother, her heritage, her surroundings, and herself. "Oh dead prince, Oh hateful love," she cries in the next strophe, referring to her dead father in the same unsettling manner that has pervaded the whole poem, "shall we meet again / on the bridge of magpies?" She then invokes the "shallow river" of the opening strophe one more time, as she asks the dead prince to "kiss me tenderly / where arch meets toe meets ankle, / where dried blood warbles."

The last seven lines of the poem, all italicized, essentially erase the voice of the poet altogether, as though it were another voice replying, the dead prince's ghost, maybe, or the river, in yet another displacement or erasure. Despite the disappearance of the speaking voice, though, these lines are surprisingly lyrical, in my view, not so hollow as we might expect, given the emptiness they suggest. What we hear here is not the voice of T. S. Eliot or Samuel Beckett:

> *Little bird, little bird.*
> *something escaping*
> *something escaping . . .*
>
> *The phoenix gone, the terrace empty.*
> *Look, Mei Ling.*
> *yellow crowfoot in the pond,*
> *not lotus, not lily.*

(51)

Are these the words that "would sing / for miles / past the courtyard" (46) at the poem's start? Although the bird or phoenix eludes us as *something escaping,* not ascertainable, not a source, finally, of meaning for this poet, is it not still powerfully *present* in the poet's imagination as a thing identified, if not named, as something of "archetypal significance," even as a kind of "collective pronoun" (Interview 10) for the emptiness experienced by the Third World Woman writer? While the poem ends with this disembodied voice telling us what is *not* in the "pond" (or "shallow river")—neither the lotus signifying paradise nor the lily signifying death—the yellow crowfoot *is* there, an image strangely authentic to itself, regardless of any association with emptiness we might bring to it. While lacking the humor of the end of **"And All I Have Is Tu Fu"** and the "solid as wood" (18) sense of survival at the end of **"How I Got That Name,"** the voice of **"The Phoenix Gone, the Terrace Empty"** also coheres, and its disparate parts do express an identity—surely, not an identity easily or "soporifically" recognizable as that of "a radical, feminist, West Coast, Pacific Rim, Marxist-socialist, neo-classical, Iowa-educated, Asian-American poet" (Interview 6), but a self-shaping voice that manifests itself through "mocking my own ripeness / I cannot taste" while at the same time acknowledging what the "Flesh remembers" (47) or what the eye sees in the pond.

Finally, perhaps no poem in ***The Phoenix Gone, the Terrace Empty*** better embodies Trinh's concept of the Asian American woman writer's adaptive strategies than **"Moon and Oatgrass,"** a kind of *ars poetica* for Chin. Not only does this poem's straightforward yet imaginative depiction of a landscape concern self-erasure (both socially and psychically), but it counters that erasure through art; it is in this poem that the speaker celebrates her own power to create as, without fanfare, she exerts that power. The poem opens with the poet seeming to contradict the one whom she addresses. At first it may even seem, in fact, as though she is addressing herself, but in the second and later strophes it becomes clear that the "you" is someone else, presumably the man she is watching from a distance: as he is "walking through" oatgrass by a body of water and under the moon, the speaker observes him from a house "on a precipice / overlooking a green meadow" (54). While he "would have it" that the moon is over the water, she disagrees, since from her perspective the moon is "one with it."

But the crux of the poem lies in its crafty combination of self-erasure and assertion; that is, while in line six Chin characterizes "you" (whether man or woman) as "an *eye* and not an *I*," so that the "you" walking or the "you" watching becomes more aware of the landscape than of the self, nevertheless, she goes on to insist on her own power as the poet to determine reality:

> And whether you live here
> or are visiting
> in your long pilgrimage—
> is my prerogative.
> Whether she is your acolyte,
> the Pearl Concubine,
> or a mere beggarwoman—
> is also my invention.
>
> Only I know where
> terrace ends and house begins,
> whether the country is lost,
> whether rivers and mountains
> will continue.

(54)

While the tone here may seem at first almost antagonistic toward "you," in fact its insistence has more to do with the poet's "prerogative" as artist to create her own world, at least to gauge her own understanding of it for herself, such that she can anticipate that, "after the inkstone is dry, / we shall be together / high in a corner bedroom / with a pale view of hills." Yet she is quick to qualify this eventuality as one to be understood "without pleasure or transcendence." Neither fantasizing nor romanticizing the couple's union, rather she acknowledges the degree of power she does have to see them together as they "penetrate this landscape" (54).

And "what *is* this landscape?" she asks in the penultimate strophe. As the juxtaposition of short lines and fragmented phrases that close the poem graphically convey, it is a landscape of parts, not of a whole, as the two figures and the setting remain distinct, even as the poet links them:

> The moon in oatgrass,
> the oatgrass moon.
> A woman pacing
> the linoleum floor,
> contemplating a poem.

A man dissolving
into the dailiness of rain

and the red eye of morning.

(54-55)

Paradoxically (despite its utter simplicity) this poem reasserts the separateness, the isolation, of the two figures as well as their individual perspectives, even while joining them. But the balance is maintained only momentarily, until both the image of the man and the poem itself dissolve in the presence of the rain and the sun, the latter characterized as yet *another* eye, one that ironically erases what the poet has just seen. Although, as Trinh might describe it, the "I" in **"Moon and Oatgrass"** is "not a unified subject, a fixed identity [. . .] covered with layers of superficialities one has gradually to peel off before one can see its true face" (94), Chin has still discovered an "authentic" means with which to voice her experience—not as "other," not as transcendent or assimilated self, but as "[her] prerogative," "[her] invention."

Ironically, for Marilyn Chin, it is *through* the erasure of the multiple voices that are layered in **"The Phoenix Gone, the Terrace Empty"** and throughout her poetry that she is able to clear the linguistic and imaginary space she needs to contend with the "triple jeopardy" of gender, race and literary heritage that Trinh defines as the inheritance of the Asian American woman artist. While in poem after poem, she discovers a way to undermine, bracket, discount, defray, or mock her own observations, the "poetics of depletion" Mukherjee has discovered in her work strike me as as much a part of her method of creation as of her expression of loss. By evading easy social definitions of the self as "other," by engaging the internal incredulities and insecurities that accompany one who attempts "to fill an emptiness / not filled by the sun, as [she waits] / for [her] inevitable fall" (60), by acknowledging the patriarchal heritage she has been removed from even as she has been enmeshed in another one, yet without being cowed by its intricate language and symbols—in effect, by "mocking her own ripeness" even while allowing it to unfold—Chin's poetry breaks a silence without compromise and speaks in an "authentic" voice, insisting, as she does in the book's "Prelude," dedicated to her mother, that "although the country is lost / rivers and mountains remain. / And we shall always live / in this poetry that you love" (5).

Notes

1. All textual citations of Marilyn Chin's poetry refer to *The Phoenix Gone, the Terrace Empty,* unless specifically noted otherwise.

2. "Today," Trinh points out later, in a veiled comment on "political correctness," I think, "planned authenticity is rife; as a product of hegemony and a remarkable counterpart of universal standardization, it constitutes an efficacious means of silencing the cry of racial oppression. We no longer wish to erase your difference, We demand, on the contrary, that you remember and assert it. At least, to a certain extent. Every path I/i take is edged with thorns" (89).

3. Chin majored in ancient Chinese Literature as an undergraduate at the University of Massachusetts at Amherst (receiving her B.A. in 1977), after which she worked as a translator and editor in the International Writing Program at the University of Iowa, where she earned her M.F.A. in Creative Writing in 1981. She has translated or co-translated two books of Chinese literature, most notably, Eugene Eoyang, Ed., *Selected Poems of Ai Qing,* and continues to work on translations of contemporary Chinese poets ("Chin," *Contemporary Authors* 82).

4. Even when she interviewed Maxine Hong Kingston in 1989, Chin found an opportunity to express her respect for the Chinese literary tradition. At one point in the interview, Kingston remarks with obvious delight that Chinese critics have situated her work within the canon of ancient Chinese literature, and Chin replies (and does not edit from the published text), "that's important, to think that there is continuity. I always think back to the T'ang Dynasty when I write poetry. I feel I am very much a part of that Chinese tradition. I don't want to be cut off from it. That's why I studied classical Chinese. I feel it's very, very important" ("Writing the Other" 94).

Works Cited

Ai, Ch'ing. *Selected Poems of Ai Qing.* Bloomington, IN: Indiana UP, 1982.

Chin, Marilyn. Interview with Calvin Bedient. *The Writer's Chronicle* 31.3 (December 1998): 5-15.

———. *Dwarf Bamboo.* Greenfield Center, NY: Greenfield Review, 1987.

———. *The Phoenix Gone, the Terrace Empty.* Minneapolis: Milkweed, 1994.

"Chin, Marilyn (Mei Ling) 1955-." *Contemporary Authors.* Vol. 129. 82.

Fenollosa, Ernest. *The Chinese Written Character as a Medium for Poetry.* San Francisco: City Lights, 1963.

Graham, A. C., trans. *Poems of the Late T'ang.* Baltimore: Penguin, 1965.

Kingston, Maxine Hong. *The Woman Warrior: Memoirs of a Girlhood Among Ghosts.* New York: Random House, 1976.

———. Interview with Marilyn Chin. "Writing the Other: A Conversation with Maxine Hong Kingston." *Conversations with Maxine Hong Kingston.* Ed. Paul Skenazy and Tera Maltin. Jackson: UP of Mississippi, 1998.

Liu, James J. Y. *The Art of Chinese Poetry.* Chicago: U of Chicago P, 1962.

Mukherjee, Srimati. "Two Asian American Women Writers." Lecture. University of New Orleans. 20 March 1997.

Pound, Ezra. *The Cantos of Ezra Pound.* New York: New Directions, 1993.

Trinh, T. Minh-ha. *Woman, Native, Other: Writing Postco-loniality and Feminism.* Bloomington: Indiana UP, 1989.

Uba, George. "Versions of Identity in Post-Activist Asian American Poetry." *Reading the Literatures of Asian America.* Ed. Shirley Geok-lin Lim and Amy Ling. Philadelphia: Temple UP, 1992. 33-48.

Wong, Sau-ling Cynthia. "Chinese American Literature." *An Interethnic Companion to Asian American Literature.* Ed. King-Kok Cheung. Cambridge: Cambridge UP, 1997. 39-61.

————. *Reading Asian American Literature: From Necessity to Extravagance.* Princeton: Princeton UP, 1993.

Yamada, Mitsuye. "Asian Pacific American Women and Feminism." *Modern Feminisms: Political, Literary, Cultural.* Ed. Maggie Humm. New York: Columbia UP, 1992.

Publishers Weekly (review date 2001)

SOURCE: Review of *Rhapsody in Plain Yellow,* by Marilyn Chin. *Publishers Weekly* 248, no. 43 (22 October 2001): 71.

[*In the following review, the critic offers overall praise for* Rhapsody in Plain Yellow.]

Chin's concerns for heritage and descent, matched with confrontational rhetoric, seem to make her an old-school poet of Asian-American identity, while a liberal use of autobiographical material (her grandmother, her parents, her neighborhood, her lovers, her English department) positions her speaker as a representative witness to modern, multicultural, middle-class California. This third collection's [*Rhapsody in Plain Yellow*] jagged rhythms and fragmented forms, some based on Chinese poetry and music, others derived from blues and Persian ghazals, thus seem a small-scale syncretism of the personal and political. Chin can tear at familial wounds even while expressing dismay at the limits of tradition: "I, my mother's aging girl / Myopic, goat-footed // Got snagged on an unmarked trail / The road diverged; I took / The one less traveled / Blah, blah // I sit at her grave for hours. . . ." In other

elegies for her mother, and in the at times erotic title poem, Chin approaches the sinewy strength of Adrienne Rich. "Poetry is a vast orphanage in which you and I are stars," **"Broken Chord Sequence"** says; "One robe, one bowl, silent pilgrimage, the river filled with martyrs." One poem proclaims "The Colonial Language is English"; others promise musical idyll (**"Summer Sonatina"**) or allegory (**"The True Story of Mortar and Pestle"**). Chin's ambitions can outrun her technique: some poems, especially those in short lines, lack aural or emotional power. Overall, though, this collection's speaker has a strong sense of herself and of her times—a sense to which readers of many concerns could respond.

FURTHER READING

Criticism

Dove, Rita. "Poet's Choice." *Washington Post* (6 February 2000): X12.
  Brief admiration of Chin's poetry by a former U.S. Poet Laureate.

Scott, Whitney. Review of *The Phoenix Gone, The Terrace Empty,* by Marilyn Chin. *Booklist* 90, no. 14 (15 March 1994): 1322.
  Offers a positive assessment of *The Phoenix Gone, The Terrace Empty.*

Seaman, Donna. Review of *Rhapsody in Plain Yellow,* by Marilyn Chin. *Booklist,* (1 January 2002): 796.
  Offers a positive assessment of *Rhapsody in Plain Yellow.*

Zheng, Da. Review of *Dwarf Bamboo,* by Marilyn Chin. *Amerasia Journal* 21, nos. 1–2 (winter-spring 1995): 173–75.
  Offers a mixed assessment of *Dwarf Bamboo.*

————. Review of *The Phoenix Gone, The Terrace Empty,* by Marilyn Chin. *Amerasia Journal* 24, no. 2 (summer 1998): 186–90.
  Offers a positive assessment of *The Phoenix Gone, The Terrace Empty.*

Additional coverage of Chin's life and career is contained in the following sources published by the Gale Group: *Contemporary Authors,* Vol. 129; *Contemporary Authors New Revision Series,* Vol. 70; *Contemporary Women Poets;* **and** *Literature Resource Center.*

William Cowper
1731-1800

English poet, hymn writer, satirist, letter writer, essayist, and translator.

INTRODUCTION

Considered a transitional figure in English poetry whose works embody both eighteenth- and nineteenth-century styles and concerns, Cowper was a forerunner of Romanticism in England and one of the most popular poets of his age. Known for his early comic ballad, "The Journey of John Gilpin," which established his literary reputation, the *Olney Hymns* (1779), now a part of Evangelical liturgy, and his mock-heroic verse satires, Cowper is principally remembered for his discursive and conversational blank-verse masterpiece, *The Task* (1785). A poem composed in response to Lady Austen's flippant remark that he write on the subject of her sofa, the six highly descriptive books of *The Task* demonstrate Cowper's contention that repose in the country lends itself to the cultivation of "piety and virtue," while life in the city degrades humankind by its corruptive influence. The work is viewed as Cowper's lasting poetic expression on nature, society, God, and man, as it regards subjects ranging from the topical and trivial to the national and spiritual. Additionally, Cowper continues to be regarded for the spontaneity and simplicity of his nature lyrics, the earnest, personal tone of his religious poetry, and the wit embodied in his satires and correspondence.

BIOGRAPHICAL INFORMATION

Cowper was born in Great Berkhamsted, Hertfordshire, England, into a distinguished aristocratic family. The death of his mother, a descendant of the seventeenth-century English poet John Donne, in childbirth in 1737 remained one of the poet's most traumatic experiences and many biographers attribute Cowper's mental instability and habitual melancholy to his early loss. In 1738, Cowper entered Dr. Pitman's school at Markyate. There, he was mercilessly bullied by older boys, an ordeal that appeared to haunt Cowper throughout his life. He attended the Westminster school from 1741 to 1748, and then lived in London's Middle Temple, a law court, until 1763, first as a law student and later as Commissioner of Bankrupts. While at the Middle Temple, Cowper befriended other young intellectuals, experimented with writing, and avidly studied classical literature. In 1756, Cowper fell deeply in love with his cousin Theodora, but the romance ended when their parents refused to permit them to marry. This experience contributed to the onset of Cowper's emotional decline. Having transferred to the Inner Temple in 1757, Cowper suffered a nervous breakdown six years later, shortly before he was to sit for a formal examination to become clerk of journals at the House of Lords. His failed suicide attempt led to hospitalization at St. Albans for the next two years. Cowper's recuperation was thought to stem partly from his conversion to Evangelicalism: when he left the hospital, he lived in Huntington with the Unwins, an Evangelical minister and his family. After the death of the Reverend Unwin in 1767, Cowper and the rest of the household moved to Olney, where Cowper pursued a literary career. Here he completed his best work and enjoyed a period of unprecedented happiness. However, in 1773 he suffered a new bout of mental illness, likely derived from anxiety over his announced engagement to Mary Unwin, the widow of the Evangelical minister, and from the religious gloom brought on by his association with the pastor, John Newton. Cowper and Mrs. Unwin never married, but moved together to Weston where the poet experienced two more breakdowns in 1786 and 1794. In 1795, he witnessed the long illness and death of his devoted companion. Despite such personal difficulties, Cowper enjoyed a reputation as one of his generation's greatest poets. Shortly before his death at East Dereham in 1800, he was rewarded with the tribute of a royal pension arranged by his friend, the noted author William Hayley.

MAJOR WORKS

The *Olney Hymns,* Cowper's first major publication, was a collaborative effort with his spiritual mentor, John Newton, who contributed the greatest number of pieces. Among the most popular of Cowper's hymns in the collection, "There is a Fountain Filled with Blood," "God Moves in a Mysterious Way," and "Oh for a Closer Walk with God" have since passed into Evangelical tradition. Highly personal in tone and displaying vivid Biblical imagery, the *Olney Hymns* treat the recurrent theme of humanity's need for salvation. The volume *Poems by William Cowper, of the Inner Temple, Esq.* first appeared in 1782, and includes the long poem "Table Talk," four satires on philosophical subjects, reflective verses on issues of moral and theological import, such as "The Progress of Error" and "Truth," as well as the shorter lyrics "Boadicea" and "Verses Supposed to be Written by Alexander Selkirk." Characterized by Cowper's spontaneous, natural diction and emotional response to nature, many of these poems also demonstrate a didactic tendency as the poet repeatedly explores the proper moral relationship of human beings with nature, society, and God. A discursive poem in six books of blank verse, *The Task* presents a number of Cowper's usual themes, but in a witty and satirical manner that generally departs from the meditative and didactic tone of his earlier poetry. Distinguished by its abundant descriptive detail and conversational mode, *The Task* is credited with introducing new motifs into English poetry, including such subjects as the love of animals and domestic life. Cowper included "The Journey of John Gilpin" in the same volume, which is a ballad ostensibly about the adventures of a tailor, but in reality a raucous parody of poetic conventions. A departure from his otherwise well-received original poetry, Cowper's blank verse translation of *Homer's Iliad and Odyssey* (1791) was generally considered inferior to that of his contemporary Alexander Pope, a work he had hoped it would supersede. A subsequent collection of *Poems* appeared in 1798, containing "On the Receipt of My Mother's Picture," "Yardley Oak," a sonnet "To Mrs Unwin," and the mock-elegy "On the Death of Mrs Throckmorton's Bulfinch"—a number of Cowper's most enduring poems. Among these are found brilliant satirical verses, alongside his most elegiac and ecstatic poems, as well as his darkest and most grief-stricken. The collection was subsequently expanded to include works Cowper composed in his final years, notably "The Castaway," written in 1799, which eloquently documents his anguished feelings of despair and spiritual torment. The poet's *Memoir of the Early Life of William Cowper, Esq.,* published posthumously in 1816, recounts his first attack of mental illness, his subsequent treatment, and his religious rebirth with both candor and an almost analytical detachment. Cowper's letters, first published in *The Life and Works of William Cowper* (1835-37), are unanimously admired for their humor, precise observation, and capacity to express mundane subjects in a lively and engaging manner as they depict Cowper's love of nature and genuine humanitarianism.

CRITICAL RECEPTION

Cowper's historical position as a transitional figure between the Neoclassical and Romantic periods in English literature has inspired a combined critical interest in his life and works. Many critics contend that Cowper's use of blank verse, his interest in nature, his focus on everyday life, and his emotional response to the world around him link him to Romantic poets like George Crabbe, Robert Burns, and William Wordsworth. Nevertheless, early reviewers considered his verse unpoetical; among them the renowned nineteenth-century critic William Hazlitt decried Cowper's weakness in depicting nature. Yet others have praised his shrewd social commentary and self-analysis, and they find that Cowper's poetry, like his life, encompasses both the emotionalism of the Romantic era and elements of Neoclassical order and rationalism. Additionally, many critics contend that Cowper's later *Poems,* especially "Yardley Oak," clearly foreshadow the descriptive and meditative poetic style of high Romanticism. Overall, *The Task* has inspired the most critical commentary among Cowper's poetic works. While early critics tended to disparage the apparent lack of unity and plan in *The Task,* more contemporary scholars have disputed this charge. Citing Cowper's interweaving of themes and counter-themes in the poem, Morris Golden described *The Task* as "a unified recording and communication of an intense emotional perception of reality." At the close of the twentieth century, several critics were attracted to Cowper's status as a public poet, discussing his verse commentary on contemporary English society and British imperialism, as well as his importance as a deeply religious writer concerned with Evangelicalism and Christian Providentialism.

PRINCIPAL WORKS

Poetry

Olney Hymns [with John Newton] (songs) 1779
Anti-Thelyphthora: A Tale, in Verse 1781
Poems by William Cowper, of the Inner Temple, Esq. 1782
The Task 1785
Poems 1798

Other Major Works

Homer's Iliad and Odyssey [translator] 1791

Adelphi: A Sketch of the Character, and an Account of the Last Illness, of the Late Rev. John Cowper (memoirs and biography) 1814

Memoir of the Early Life of William Cowper, Esq. (memoir) 1816

The Life and Works of William Cowper 15 vols. (letters, poetry, songs, and essays) 1835-37

The Correspondence of William Cowper 4 vols. (letters) 1904

CRITICISM

William Hazlitt (essay date 1841)

SOURCE: Hazlitt, William. "On Thomson and Cowper." In *Lectures on the English Poets,* pp. 164-200. 1841. Reprint, New York: Russell & Russell, 1968.

[*In the following excerpt, originally published in 1841, Hazlitt disparages the excessive effeminacy and polish of Cowper's poetry, while praising the merits of elegance, satire, and pathos in his verse.*]

Cowper . . . lived at a considerable distance of time after [James] Thomson; and had some advantages over him, particularly in simplicity of style, in a certain precision and minuteness of graphical description, and in a more careful and leisurely choice of such topics only as his genius and peculiar habits of mind prompted him to treat of. *The Task* has fewer blemishes than the *Seasons*; but it has not the same capital excellence, the "unbought grace" of poetry, the power of moving and infusing the warmth of the author's mind into that of the reader. If Cowper had a more polished taste, Thomson had, beyond comparison, a more fertile genius, more impulsive force, a more entire forgetfulness of himself in his subject. If in Thomson you are sometimes offended with the slovenliness of the author by profession, determined to get through his task at all events; in Cowper you are no less dissatisfied with the finicalness of the private gentleman, who does not care whether he completes his work or not; and, in whatever he does, is evidently more solicitous to please himself than the public. There is an effeminacy about him, which shrinks from and repels common and hearty sympathy. With all his boasted simplicity and love of the country, he seldom launches out into general descriptions of nature: he looks at her over his clipped hedges, and from his well-swept garden-walks; or if he makes a bolder experiment now and then, it is with an air of precaution, as if he were afraid of being caught in a shower of rain, or of not being able, in case of any untoward accident, to make good his retreat home. He shakes hands with nature with a pair of

fashionable gloves on, and leads "his Vashti" forth to public view with a look of consciousness and attention to etiquette, as a fine gentleman hands a lady out to dance a minuet. He is delicate to fastidiousness, and glad to get back, after a romantic adventure with crazy Kate, a party of gypsies or a little child on a common, to the drawing-room and the ladies again, to the sofa and the tea-kettle—No, I beg his pardon, not to the singing, well-scoured tea-kettle, but to the polished and loud-hissing urn. His walks and arbours are kept clear of worms and snails, with as much an appearance of *petit-maitreship* as of humanity. He has some of the sickly sensibility and pampered refinements of Pope; but then Pope prided himself in them: whereas, Cowper affects to be all simplicity and plainness. He had neither Thomson's love of the unadorned beauties of nature, nor Pope's exquisite sense of the elegances of art. He was, in fact, a nervous man, afraid of trusting himself to the seductions of the one, and ashamed of putting forward his pretensions to an intimacy with the other: but to be a coward is not the way to succeed either in poetry, in war, or in love! Still he is a genuine poet, and deserves all his reputation. His worst vices are amiable weaknesses, elegant trifling. Though there is a frequent dryness, timidity, and jejuneness in his manner, he has left a number of pictures of domestic comfort and social refinement, as well as of natural imagery and feeling, which can hardly be forgotten but with the language itself. Such, among others, are his memorable description of the post coming in, that of the preparations for tea in a winter's evening in the country, of the unexpected fall of snow, of the frosty morning (with the fine satirical transition to the Empress of Russia's palace of ice), and, most of all, the winter's walk at noon. Every one of these may be considered as distinct studies, or highly-finished cabinet-pieces arranged without order or coherence. I shall be excused for giving the last of them, as what has always appeared to me one of the most feeling, elegant, and perfect specimens of this writer's manner.

> The night was winter in his roughest mood;
> The morning sharp and clear. But now at noon
> Upon the southern side of the slant hills,
> And where the woods fence off the northern blast,
> The season smiles, resigning all its rage,
> And has the warmth of May. The vault is blue,
> Without a cloud, and white without a speck
> The dazzling splendour of the scene below.
> Again the harmony comes o'er the vale;
> And through the trees I view th' embattled tow'r,
> Whence all the music. I again perceive
> The soothing influence of the wafted strains,
> And settle in soft musings as I tread
> The walk, still verdant, under oaks and elms,
> Whose outspread branches overarch the glade.
> The roof, though moveable through all its length,
> As the wind sways it, has yet well suffic'd,
> And, intercepting in their silent fall
> The frequent flakes, has kept a path for me.
> No noise is here, or none that hinders thought.
> The redbreast warbles still, but is content
> With slender notes, and more than half suppress'd.
> Pleas'd with his solitude, and flitting light

From spray to spray, where'er he rests he shakes
From many a twig the pendent drops of ice
That tinkle in the wither'd leaves below.
Stillness, accompanied with sounds so soft,
Charms more than silence. Meditation here
May think down hours to moments. Here the heart
May give a useful lesson to the head,
And Learning wiser grow without his books.
Knowledge and Wisdom, far from being one,
Have oft-times no connection. Knowledge dwells
In heads replete with thoughts of other men;
Wisdom in minds attentive to their own.
Books are not seldom talismans and spells,
By which the magic art of shrewder wits
Holds an unthinking multitude enthrall'd.
Some to the fascination of a name
Surrender judgment hood-wink'd. Some the style
Infatuates, and through labyrinths and wilds
Of error leads them, by a tune entranc'd.
While sloth seduces more, too weak to bear
The insupportable fatigue of thought,
And swallowing therefore, without pause or choice,
The total grist unsifted, husks and all.
But trees, and rivulets whose rapid course
Defies the check of winter, haunts of deer,
And sheep-walks populous with bleating lambs,
And lanes, in which the primrose ere her time
Peeps through the moss that clothes the hawthorn root,
Deceive no student. Wisdom there, and truth,
Not shy, as in the world, and to be won
By slow solicitation, seize at once
The roving thought, and fix it on themselves.

His satire is also excellent. It is pointed and forcible, with the polished manners of the gentleman, and the honest indignation of the virtuous man. His religious poetry, except where it takes a tincture of controversial heat, wants elevation and fire. His Muse had not a seraph's wing. I might refer, in illustration of this opinion, to the laboured anticipation of the Millennium at the end of the sixth book. He could describe a piece of shell-work as well as any modern poet: but he could not describe the New Jerusalem so well as John Bunyan;—nor are his verses on Alexander Selkirk so good as *Robinson Crusoe*. The one is not so much like a vision, nor is the other so much like the reality.

The first volume of Cowper's poems has, however, been less read than it deserved. The comparison in these poems of the proud and humble believer to the peacock and the pheasant, and the parallel between Voltaire and the poor cottager, are exquisite pieces of eloquence and poetry, particularly the last:

Yon cottager, who weaves at her own door,
Pillow and bobbins all her little store;
Content though mean, and cheerful if not gay,
Shuffling her threads about the live-long day,
Just earns a scanty pittance, and at night,
Lies down secure, her heart and pocket light;
She, for her humble sphere by nature fit,
Has little understanding, and no wit,
Receives no praise; but, though her lot be such,
(Toilsome and indigent) she renders much;

Just knows, and knows no more, her Bible true—
A truth the brilliant Frenchman never knew;
And in that charter reads with sparkling eyes
Her title to a treasure in the skies.
    O happy peasant! Oh unhappy bard!
His the mere tinsel, hers the rich reward;
He prais'd, perhaps, for ages yet to come,
She never heard of half a mile from home:
He lost in errors his vain heart prefers,
She safe in the simplicity of hers.

His character of Whitfield, in the poem on Hope, is one of the most spirited and striking things. It is written *con amore.*

But if, unblameable in word and thought,
A man arise, a man whom God has taught,
With all Elijah's dignity of tone,
And all the love of the beloved John,
To storm the citadels they build in air,
To smite the untemper'd wall ('tis death to spare),
To sweep away all refuges of lies,
And place, instead of quirks themselves devise,
Lama Sabachthani before their eyes;
To show that without Christ all gain is loss,
All hope despair that stands not on his cross;
Except a few his God may have impress'd,
A tenfold phrensy seizes all the rest.

These lines were quoted, soon after their appearance, by the Monthly Reviewers, to show that Cowper was no poet, though they afterwards took credit to themselves for having been the first to introduce his verses to the notice of the public. It is not a little remarkable that these same critics regularly damned, at its first coming out, every work which has since acquired a standard reputation with the public. Cowper's verses on his mother's picture, and his lines to Mary, are some of the most pathetic that ever were written. His stanzas on the loss of the Royal George have a masculine strength and feeling beyond what was usual with him. The story of John Gilpin has perhaps given as much pleasure to as many people as any thing of the same length that ever was written.

His life was an unhappy one. It was embittered by a morbid affection, and by his religious sentiments. Nor are we to wonder at this, or bring it as a charge against religion; for it is the nature of the poetical temperament to carry every thing to excess, whether it be love, religion, pleasure, or pain, as we may see in the case of Cowper and of Burns, and to find torment or rapture in that in which others merely find a resource from *ennui,* or a relaxation from common occupation.

Kenneth MacLean (essay date 1949)

SOURCE: MacLean, Kenneth. "William Cowper." In *The Age of Johnson: Essays Presented to Chauncey Brewster Tinker,* edited by Wilmarth S. Lewis, pp. 257-67. New Haven: Yale University Press, 1949.

[In the following essay, MacLean presents an overview of Cowper's life and writings, suggesting that "neurotic terror" principally informs his poetry and other works.]

Everyone knows Cowper's poems and letters, but how many have seen that small volume, the *Memoir of the Early Life of William Cowper, Esq. Written by Himself?* Beginning ominously, this little piece of psychic Hogarth achieves the ultimate in terror. We see a young man, thirty-two years old, unnerved by the prospect of a public examination for a parliamentary clerkship, for which he had been studying a half year without any perception. He takes a vacation at Margate, but returns little improved for the final push. The day preceding the public examination was one of confused suicidal purposes. No one intent on destroying himself ever turned so quickly from poison to pond to knife to halter. That wayward mind, so evident in Cowper's writings where it assumes runaway symbols, was never more shifting than on this semifatal day. The morning of the examinations found Cowper in a swoon on his chamber floor, the much too elegant garter with which he had attempted to hang himself having broken. Now follow days of paralyzing religious thoughts. The sinner eats alone in the dark. Dreams terrify him at night.

> Satan plied me closely with horrible visions, and more horrible voices. My ears rang with the sound of torments, that seemed to await me. Then did the pains of hell get hold of me, and, before daybreak, the very sorrows of death encompassed me. A numbness seized upon the extremities of my body, and life seemed to retreat before it; my hands and feet became cold and stiff; a cold sweat stood upon my forehead; my heart seemed at every pulse to beat its last, and my soul to cling to my lips, as if on the very brink of departure.

At this moment of final terror madness came upon Cowper with a darkness. He was taken to Dr. Cotton's College for the Insane at St. Albans. Here we will not so much say that his mind was restored as that his sins were forgiven under the care of the pious little physician. He left St. Albans in a state of religious euphoria. Nothing is more terrible than neurotic ecstasy. At Huntingdon, where his brother had found him rooms, we see him praying deliriously in the fields and weeping in church for the love he felt for the faces there. On November 11, 1765, a rather manic Cowper sank down into the comfort of the home of Mrs. Unwin whom hereafter we shall come to associate with mother and chickens, but who will remain for us very much of a quiet mystery.

Cowper's *Memoir* is a document in neurotic terror, and the terror it directly describes is, we feel, central to all his writings. True, he expresses many feelings that seem conventionally and pleasantly romantic—a love of the country, a liking for simplicity, a sentimental taste for tear-stained faces. But such sentiments cannot be understood in reference to a romantic movement: they can be seen properly only in reference to the Cowper whose nerves needed the isolation of Olney, whose neurotic rigor asked for a severe puritan plainness in speech, whose instability

expected tears. Neurosis and not the romantic movement was responsible for everything that he was as a writer—the very need itself to write and enshrine the dying life, the tone of sincerity which cannot still tell quite all the truth, the limited symbolism from the garden of Orchardside. Needless to say, Cowper interests our times greatly, hardly less than Byron whom he so much resembles in their common sense of injury and damnation.

> The world and I fortuitously met;
> I ow'd a trifle, and have paid the debt;
> She did me wrong, I recompens'd the deed . . .

We wonder particularly about his devastating modern nihilism which allowed for daily walks and daily letters and a daily number of verses but left the whole great course of things to a ruining providence.

His early poetry, much of it, was a kind of shiny pastoral addressed to a dazzling Delia, a star seen through that remarkable instrument, "passion's optic." Daydreams, parting, absence, curl-saving—and then this course of true love was suddenly interrupted by illness, and the poetry to Delia becomes something else. Now in a poem Cowper records a dream in which the beloved appears as he is trying to drink from a stream that at once flies and thickens into mud. She gives him water in a goblet, and then takes him strangely into a flight from which he falls with dreamlike gravity. The poem ends with the waking hope that the real Delia will come to him when health, in the unreasonable way of Cowper's causeless world, will suddenly return. This poem of terror is followed by related poems in the next few years, in some of them those painful images of shipwreck which Cowper's imperial English imagination fully explored. Then in his own "storm of '63" which took him to Dr. Cotton's, we come to a poem which, for language and image, could hardly be surpassed in the presentation of terror.

> Man disavows, and Deity disowns me:
> Hell might afford my miseries a shelter;
> Therefore hell keeps her ever hungry mouths all
>   Bolted against me.
>
> Hard lot! encompass'd with a thousand dangers;
> Weary, faint, trembling with a thousand terrors;
> I'm called, if vanquish'd, to receive a sentence
>   Worse than Abiram's.
>
> *Him* the vindictive rod of angry justice
> Sent quick and howling to the centre headlong;
> *I,* fed with judgment, in a fleshly tomb, am
>   Buried above ground.

This has the accent of Hopkins, of the last "terrible sonnets." We suspect that Hopkins knew Cowper, who like himself felt at times that rather sadistic bursting of colored beauty on the senses which excites to divine love. Such affinities might give hints to Cowper's biographers, who as yet have said nothing about the psychology of this poet who has left such a complete account of himself.

Cowper, as we have seen, interpreted his emotional variations in the language of the rising evangelicalism of his day. Elation was a sign of grace and faith, depression of guilt and rejection. It was in a state of elation that he had left Dr. Cotton's to enter the pious Unwin home, and grace still continued with him when, after Mr. Unwin's death, he and Mary left the blue willows of Huntingdon for Olney, a center of experiential religion with the presence of John Newton. He lived closely in the first years in Olney: the ego was hardly ever exposed. He did however attend Newton's prayer meetings, begun in 1769, where with some embarrassment he told the story of his own religious experience, a story that attains the status of a fixed idea in his writings. When after the first years in Olney faith began to give way to depression, Newton urged Cowper to interest himself in the composition of hymns for their prayer meetings. Thus his hymns were composed for the little saints of Olney, who, we trust, were not among those who gossiped to Newton when in later years the poet was seen entering a lady's carriage to visit a charming Catholic family, the Throckmortons, often called in the letters "the Throcks"! The basic imagery of the *Olney Hymns* is, I believe, the country village. We hear indeed as so frequently in Protestant religious writings the language of landholding and property. To speak of the religious experience in the language of the village was to speak closely to the parishes of England, and of New England as well, where the spirit of Cowper, its healthier part so largely exploited by Emerson, has been particularly at home. In these country hymns we feel little of that sense of innocence which Blake is shortly to associate with the village symbol. The *Olney Hymns* are poems in religious, in primitive fear, and emotions of fear, let us remember, were little considered by poets in Cowper's time. Part of the fear stems from a feeling of hatred for God, imaged in materials we think of especially as Emily Dickinson's, steel and stone. The art of these hymns in all ways suggests this New England poet, who perhaps did not overlook one title, **"The Narrow Way."** Cowper has her same restricting wit which will call the Lord's Supper a "treat." He has too some of her expanding imaginative phrasing. And in both poets agony is lyrical. These careful hymns are reassuring to anyone anxious about Cowper's art. He was not above allowing his publisher to emend his poems. Nonetheless, he knew the business of poet.

The writing of the *Olney Hymns* preceded another period of insanity, in 1773 and 1774, accompanied by the "fatal dream" which left with Cowper the lasting impression that he was damned. Hereafter he was never without depression. All religious exercises ended, even grace and private prayer. The withdrawal from church developed into a distaste for the cloth, whom he was known to avoid in his walks. Alone now with Mrs. Unwin at Orchardside, he sought distraction in simple human activities: in gardening, in keeping his pet hares—Tiney, Puss, and Bess—in making furniture for the house. But carpentry was hard on the eyes, and so was sketching, he discovered. The search for proper distraction led Cowper again to poetry, and the greenhouse in the narrow walled garden at Olney, lined with mats and fragrant with flowers, became a poet's room. Poetry was not only easy on the eyes. It becomes clear as

one examines Cowper's life that terror took a vocal form for him. He heard voices, as in that "fatal dream" when he heard the word of despair. From his account of his early troubles in the *Memoir* it is evident that he tried to drive out such voices by quoting reassuring Bible sentences to himself. Hereabouts lies the reason for his life-long battle with the Deists who would destroy the essential, truly saving word of God. In time Cowper discovered that the poetic creation of language was very helpful in drowning out inner voices of despair.

> There is a pleasure in poetic pains
> Which only poets know.

And as he wrote to save his own soul, he developed with his longer poems an aesthetic which had something to do with the saving of the soul of poetry in his day. Before Wordsworth he was spokesman for a prose-like speech in poetry, and though there is much of the homely elegance of a Hitchcock chair in his verse, he sometimes achieved Wordsworthian naturalness, in the blank verse of *The Task* most frequently. He also practiced and preached in his longer poems that free-running, digressive manner which Wordsworth, Keats, and Byron were to exploit in a poetry of association. The winged fancy, the runaway horse, the grasshopper—these varied symbols preside over Cowper's new achievement in free form.

In a period of eleven excited months he wrote the eight long poems comprising the volume of 1782, which we may especially admire for its splendid picture of the England of that day. It is an England that has in a way ceased to be England. The international flavor is everywhere, in tea, in silks, in Negro servants, in Chinese fans and Indian cane. Emporium of this England is London, its wharves fragrant with the spices of ships harbored from India. Here are the merchants investing in foreign trade, and their lawyers. Some merchants are bankrupt and in prison, and their attorney now is the poet Cowper, himself always hard up and ready to plead that "insolvent innocence go free." Behind this London lies the sea, and Cowper who devoured all the voyage literature he could borrow is not deficient in giving us a sense of the sea—its flags and guns and canvas and wind. These poems exhibit that power prized by the modern poet of seeing a society standing on its economic foundations. Cowper could see England as "commercial England." He can give us that whole blue period, of blue sea and blue naval uniforms and Lowestoft china and blue pipe smoke. He pictures commercial England, and then proceeds to draw up a moral balance sheet for a commercial society where luxury has brought weakness. Men are collecting antiques, listening to music, honoring Handel on Sunday, and dancing on softest nights to sweetest music. "Hark! how it floats upon the dewy air!" Cowper's social poems bespeak a horror of effeminacy, a horror felt by his age but felt particularly strongly by this poet who deeply sensed his own personal weakness. Out of this weakness came the strength, comparable to Wordsworth's, with which he spoke for a more masculine England, a more English England, the England of the oak.

The poems of 1782 set some of the themes for *The Task,* an important national poem. But *The Task* is more than just a social poem. Its chief theme is surely nature and the soul. Of all things in nature, air and wind seemed to have interested Cowper most. He was allergic to the bad air of London. The air at Olney he found healthful in summer but in the winter damp and aguish, especially at Orchardside where the rooms were filled with melancholy vapors rising from a water-filled cellar. This circumstance, in part, prompted Cowper and Mrs. Unwin to move from Olney to Weston-Underwood, leaving a home of twenty years, the house associated with nearly all the poetry. Empty, this old home looked like a little House of Usher—"no inapt resemblance of a soul that God has forsaken." Cowper's attention to air is reflected in his interest in flowers and flowering shrubbery. He loved the air of flowers—in the garden, carnation, mignonette, canary lavender—by the summerhouse, pinks and roses—in the Wilderness, honeysuckle and lilac. No one was more sensitive than this poet to the fragrance of England's disappearing commons. It was perhaps Cowper's interest in air which drew him to the Throckmortons' lawn many a time to see a balloon go up in the year after Montgolfier's experiment. Cowper the correspondent always assured his confiding friends that he was "hermetically sealed." But it was the wind moving through the air that the poet was most conscious of, the wind that in the first splendid descriptions in *The Task* sweeps the skirts of the woods, making the sound of waves on a shore. It was Cowper's Leibnizian notion that nature, the dancing girl, is never at rest; and he supposed that the wind was the primary element at the center of this motion. These thoughts are expressed in a passage in the excellent first book of *The Task,* beginning "By ceaseless action all that is subsists." But there is no Leibnizian harmony for Cowper, for like Hopkins he felt God beating in the wind, the God of his own damnation—"He who has commanded me to wither,"—He by whose will "the flow'rs of Eden felt the blast,"—He by whose pleasure still the fiend of famine "blows mildew from between his shrivel'd lips." This presence makes the final experience of nature a fearful one. And so, while there are many rhythmical moments in *The Task,* its essential mood is fear. Aren't we always retreating from the fresh open scene where Wordsworth keeps us into weatherhouses, greenhouses, alcoves, colonnades? Aren't we clinging beside garden walls? Isn't the huge Russian ice palace pictured in the opening of the fifth book simply the greatest and biggest shelter of all? Aren't we shutting shutters on winter evenings, giving ourselves occupational therapy with our books, our weaving of nets for fruit, our twining of silken threads on ivory reels? Peeping at the world through the "loop-holes of retreat"—the newspapers! The stricken deer is hiding in the shade.

But comedy always stands closely beside fear in Cowper's pages. Shy in any company, Cowper found relief for his embarrassment in watching people's motions and gestures. Sterne would call this "translating." Imprisoned in his Olney house, he was devoted to the street window. Obviously a peace treaty had been signed: "Every man's posture bespoke a pacific turn of mind." He saw the surface of human life, and this surface is essentially comic. His delightful poem, **"Conversation,"** is full of the comedy lying before an eye which would see a person conversing with his face too close to the other person's. In his very first poem we are amused simply in watching the walk of a peasant who is missing one heel. *The Task* is rich in comic observation. Indeed, it begins with all the comedy that can slide, twitch, sprawl, or doze on the seat of a chair. Cowper especially loved the comedy that lies in shadows.

With the writing of *The Task* much of his creative work as poet was done. "The mind of man is not a fountain, but a cistern." Poetry had something of a period in his life, but not the letter which he always wrote. He was an authority on the letter, who knew among other things that the "epistolary race" is "always won by him that comes in last." His letters have often been called the finest in English. One claim surely might well be made for them— that they contain as much of the myth of England as any piece of English literature. Here is the English character fully represented in the writings of one whom we should think incapacitated to the point of being unable to represent anything. This may be a commentary at once upon psychological disturbance and upon the suitability of English culture to a human soul. The Cowper of the letters is the complete Englishman—liking a well-cocked hat— taking his exercise—medicating shamelessly—very timid about bathing machines—feminine in his humor—liking privacy—defending the home against polygamous relations—relishing "fine" food, even as much as Hazlitt— like Lamb, deaf to music—gentlemanly but not lordly— charitable—patriotic—independent—bold enough to be ready to thresh Dr. Johnson's old jacket till the pension jingled in his pocket! These letters are an intimate picture of an Englishman. And since they are letters they particularly exhibit an English trait without which there would be no letters—a deep sense of friendship, not unlike a Prospero's.

So much health combined with such weakness, the very health growing out of the disease—this essential but much forgotten irony lies in Cowper's letters. While his despondency, he thought, would not be suspected by a visitor, it is apparent enough in his letters where we hear a good deal, but not too much, about this illness which crippled him in his morning writing hours, allowing him a certain alertness only toward the later afternoon when, as we remember, the pet hares too were more lively. The neurotic death-sense moves all through these letters, growing more intense rather than less with age. Against the stream of time (and Cowper remembered Shakespeare's thought that no man bathes twice in the same stream) we see him and Mary Unwin, who surely shared his terrors, setting up a kind of still life for themselves which a vivacious Lady Austen was not allowed to disrupt. We sense terror as well as melancholy in these letters when Cowper takes us inside his mind where thoughts stand in sober livery, the tallest and loudest among them calling, "It is all over with thee; thou hast perished." We partly see the dreams of this mind, and we hear Cowper express his disturbing and very modern opinion that dreams are true.

The tone of despondency and terror is just as it should be in the letters. Cowper has subdued the direct statement into quiet phrases and sentences. Some of these we shall never forget: "On this very day twenty-two years ago left I London." "Yesterday was one of my terrible seasons . . ." "Nature revives again; but a soul once slain lives no more." "There is a mystery in my destruction . . ." One sentence we shall remember because it puzzles: "Mine is merely a case of relaxation." The sense of terror is restrained in the letters. It is also, we note, most skillfully transferred into the symbols of those excellent poems frequently enclosed in a letter. In some of these Cowper has drawn upon his beloved sea imagery as in **"The Castaway,"** his last poem and an ultimate image in lonely terror. One sea poem in the letters is the splendid Horatian piece on the halibut which survived as an egg in the great immensity of the ocean, only to be devoured by the poet. To swim the wide dangerous seas

> Where flat Batavia just emerging peeps
> Above the brine,

only to lie dead on a poet's plate—this thing was always happening in this Humian world of no proper cause and effect. Out of his deep conviction about such matters Cowper wrote for enclosure in another letter the verses, **"On the Loss of the Royal George."** Eight hundred men on a stout oaken ship safely in harbor, and then a little land breeze shook the shrouds, and not a life was saved! No world is more terrible than one where this kind of thing can happen. And Cowper saw this happening every day. Most of these poems, which are surely Cowper's greatest achievement, draw their imagery from the garden at Orchardside and near by. And this is what we see about this garden. We see the head of a rose snapped off as one is shaking raindrops from it. We see kittens hypnotized by a snake's forked tongue, and we see a large man killing the small snake. We see a pet rabbit going to his last long home. Tiney had been safe in the garden walls from the pursuit of greyhounds. He had known the security of russet apple peels and Turkey carpets. But the protected life had no security from death. We see birds about this garden. There are two goldfinches in separate cages: one works his way out of his cage, but unable perhaps because of his own deep experience of terror to seek his own freedom, he clings to the cage of the other bird. Mirror everywhere for Cowper and Mary Unwin. We see in one of the best of these poems a raven nesting in a neighbor's elm. Ravens may have the gift of prophecy, but this bird has no idea what is going to happen to her, nor does she know the map of danger. Cowper observed her anxiety during an April storm lest the bough break and her eggs be lost. The eggs went not to the storm but to Hodge who climbed the tree to get them as a present for his pregnant wife. Hardy must have loved Cowper.

> An earthquake may be bid to spare
> The man that's strangled by a hair.

> Fate steals along with silent tread,
> Found oft'nest in what least we dread,
> Frowns in the storm with angry brow,
> But in the sunshine strikes the blow.

Cowper's poems and letters are a record of a terror which must interest the modern reader. What is particularly remarkable about this record is its mark, often painful, of sincerity and simple truth. Nothing has been faked. This is human terror. This is terror in a garden.

Morris Golden (essay date 1960)

SOURCE: Golden, Morris. "Solitude and Society." In *In Search of Stability: The Poetry of William Cowper,* pp. 28-54. New York: Bookman Associates, 1960.

[*In the following essay, Golden surveys the myriad ways in which Cowper's mental attitudes and instabilities—including feelings of isolation, delusion, victimization, abandonment, despair, and divine rapture—are reflected in his poetry.*]

Cowper has been pictured variously as a friendly little man eager to proclaim his brotherhood with men, beasts, and insects; as a morose recluse, hating men and the world; as a psychotic hovering on the edge of terror at all times; as a frigidly aloof specimen of the breed that produced Chesterfield and Horace Walpole, the eighteenth-century gentleman. He is in part all of these, and I should like to examine his attitude toward himself in relation to the rest of the world in an attempt to discover whether any one category encloses him most, whether he is a shaky synthesis of all, or whether he is something else completely. Besides his comments on his own situation, it is worth looking at the images and structures of his poems, for these may give unconscious expression of certain basic attitudes that he does not wish to make overt.

The general tone of his letters, the eagerness with which he accepted new correspondents if he was assured of their good will, his 31-year attachment to the unexceptionable Mrs. Unwin, his delight in discovering as close friends first William Unwin, then Lady Austen, then the Throckmortons, then his cousin Lady Hesketh, then Hayley and John Johnson, as well as a number of clergymen in and around Olney and Weston, are all substantiated by his poem **"Friendship,"** by a few minor poems, and by a great many references to his need of friends. In one of his earliest extant letters (1762), he wrote to his old schoolfellow Clotworthy Rowley, "Upon the whole, my dear Rowley, there is a degree of poverty that has no disgrace belonging to it; that degree of it, I mean, in which a man enjoys clean linen and good company; and if I never sink below this degree of it, I care not if I never rise above it" (*Correspondence,* I, 19). His fondness for society, limited to a few similarly disposed people, is further evidenced in a revealing passage in **"Retirement"**:

. . . solitude, however some may rave,
Seeming a sanctuary, proves a grave,
A sepulchre in which the living lie. . . .

(735-7)

The "stricken deer" retreats from the world, as Mr. Gilbert Thomas reminds us,[1] not alone but "with few associates" (**"Garden,"** 117). In Cowper's greenhouse, flowers from many lands "form one social shade" (**"Garden,"** 586); developing an associative connection later in *The Task,* Cowper says that

Man in society is like a flow'r
Blown in its native bed: 'tis there alone
His faculties, expanded in full bloom,
Shine out. . . .

(**"Winter Evening,"** 659-62)

Sympathy among men causes all man's delights, for "'Tis woven in the world's great plan," and those who do not sympathize with others are "sullen elves" (**"To Miss Macartney"**). Friendship, he advises in his poem of that name, must involve decent and polite manners as well as such more elevated requisites as honesty, sincerity, compatibility, and so on. A lonely cottage, described in the **"Sofa,"** is a fine place to visit, but Cowper would not want to live there—it lacks civilized conveniences and is too far from the society of other humans.

In **"The Garden,"** he deals generally with the problem of self and society, and among other things points out that he is a brother of all men and therefore is disturbed by man's folly. One of the reasons that he was drawn to young Unwin, he wrote in 1765, was that Unwin, "having nothing in his heart that makes it necessary for him to keep it barred and bolted, opens it to the perusal even of a stranger" (*Correspondence,* I, 45). More than other people, Cowper wrote in 1766, he himself needed the sympathetic concern of others: "My circumstances are rather particular, such as call upon my friends, those, I mean, who are truly such, to take some little notice of me, and will naturally make those who are not such in sincerity rather shy of doing it. To this, I impute the silence of many with regard to me, who, before the affliction that befel me, were ready enough to converse with me" (*Correspondence,* I, 60). Very soon after this letter, a correspondent asked whether there was any social intercourse in heaven, and Cowper answered that "reason seems to require it so peremptorily, that a society without social intercourse seems to be a solecism and a contradiction in terms. . . ." (*Correspondence,* I, 73). Society, the society of sober friends, he sees pre-eminently as a civilizing influence: in the country,

Such friends prevent what else would soon succeed,
A temper rustic as the life we lead,
And keep the polish of the manners clean,
As their's who bustle in the busiest scene. . . .

(**"Retirement,"** 731-4)

It becomes apparent, I think, that to Cowper heaven was the essence of civilization; the fervors and ecstasies of his faith, though he shared them for a short space after his conversion in 1764, seem essentially alien to his temperament, as many critics and biographers have pointed out. In a fairly late echo of the requirements of breeding in friendship, he wrote in 1788 of a new Vicar of Olney: "He is a man with whom, when I can converse at all, I can converse on terms perfectly agreeable to myself; who does not distress me with forms, nor yet disgust me by the neglect of them; whose manners are easy and natural, and his observations always sensible" (*Correspondence,* III, 275-6). Addison himself could not have put it less evangelically.

Here, then, are the members of Cowper's ideal society: a chosen few friends, with similar interests (as he developed, this included primarily evangelicalism or at least a serious concern with religion), sympathizing warmly with each other's sorrows and joys, and contriving to pour out their hearts to each other and at the same time to maintain the reserves of good breeding and avoid causing embarrassment. There is a touch of aloofness still about this ideal, though the warmheartedness predominates; and in his retreat from anything approaching undue familiarity or lack of proper cultivation in his poem **"Conversation,"** we can see that this state requires a very delicate sense of balance. Furthermore, Cowper sees the ideal of friendship as subsumed under the greater ideal of a cultivated religion—a subtle, though important, step from the Augustans, whose larger goal was a cultivated morality.

Since he so evidently needed proper company and properly solicitous friends, his mental illness exaggerated to him the solitude in which everyone inevitably finds himself. For him more than for most people, the mind and soul were a battlefield, and he alternately bemoaned the impossibility of help from others and its lack. He was alone with God (or was it the Devil? he could never resolve the question), whom he feared far too much for equanimity and whom, after a few years of the ecstatic joy of the convert, he suspected of trickery. It was a solitude made more fearful by his steady brooding over God's huge power, manifest most conspicuously in the excesses of nature (storms, wildernesses, tidal waves) that form so substantial a part of his imagery from the beginning of his writing to its culmination in **"The Castaway."** These internal dangers, the dangers of the battle-field, he twice develops: of nervous fevers like his own, he wrote in 1776, "Other distempers only batter the walls; but *they* creep silently into the citadel, and put the garrison to the sword" (*Correspondence,* I, 139); "Interior mischiefs must be grappled with. There is no flight from them" (*Correspondence,* II, 257). In an early verse letter to his friend Robert Lloyd he had described the fierce banditti that attacked his brain insidiously and kept him confused. And later in his solitude, particularly at night in his sleeping and sleepless moments, in critical times of major decisions, divine or infernal voices threatened him with horrible punishments.

An evil effect of this conviction of being singled out was Cowper's corollary conviction of being isolated from society. Several times, he writes that he is not an inhabitant of this world, and he sometimes adds that he consequently has no interest in it. In the **"Winter Morning Walk"** he beholds the stars

> As one who long detain'd on foreign shores
> Pants to return. . . .

(832-3)

That this is a fairly conventional idea for a religious person is not to the point; many other religious people do not have it, and some that do are not so constantly aware of it. In Huntingdon, though he in time made friends, particularly of the Unwins, he was conscious of being suspected, ever so subtly, even by them. He had arranged for William Unwin to visit his cousin Maria Cowper, he wrote, partly because

> You know I am a Stranger here; all such are suspected characters, unless they bring their Credentials with them. To this moment I believe it is a matter of Speculation in the Place, whence I came, and to whom I belong. My story is of such a Nature that I cannot satisfy this Curiosity by relating it, and to be close and reserved as I am obliged to be, is in a manner to plead guilty to any Charge their Jealousy may bring against me.[2]

He is a poor horseman, he writes: "What nature expressly designed me for I have never been able to conjecture; I seem to myself so universally disqualified for the common and customary occupations and amusements of mankind" (*Correspondence,* I, 314). More specifically, he writes in 1782 on his strangeness: "Reminded as I am continually, and always knowing it to be true, that I am a foreigner to the system I inhabit, I cannot, if I would, deceive myself into an opinion that I have any real interest in anything here" (*Correspondence,* I, 451). This image reveals an attitude essentially the same as that in a letter of two years later: "Had I dropped from the moon into this system eleven years ago, the concerns of a world to which I did not naturally belong would not have engaged me much; and just as little engaged I feel myself under a persuasion which nothing has yet shaken, that I am an extra-mundane character with reference to this globe of yours; and that, though not a native of the moon, I was not, however, made of the dust of this planet" (*Correspondence,* II, 172-3). Similarly, though with a significant variation, he writes in 1786: "It has pleased God that I should, like Joseph, be put into a well; and because there are no Midianites in the way to deliver me, therefore my friends are coming down into the well to see me" (*Correspondence,* III, 3). One of his last letters, of 1795, complains that "I have been tossed like a ball into a far country, from which there is no rebound for me" (*Correspondence,* IV, 494-5). His isolation is, in some moods completely and in others at least partly, that of a being unlike any others in this world (consequently, of one whose relations to its inhabitants cannot be as warm as his social ideal demands). A famous short poem, **"Lines Written During a Period of Insanity"** (1763), much quoted by commentators on Cowper, most terribly conveys this feeling:

> Man disavows, and Deity disowns me:
> Hell might afford my miseries a shelter;
> Therefore hell keeps her ever hungry mouths all
>   Bolted against me.
>   . . . . .
>
> *Him* [Abiram] the vindictive rod of angry justice
> Sent quick and howling to the centre headlong;
> *I,* fed with judgment, in a fleshly tomb, am
>   Buried above ground.

In one of Cowper's visions of his fate during his final illness, this theme became agonizingly specific; according to Mr. Quinlan, John Johnson's letters show that Cowper's "most constant dream was that a group of bailiffs or soldiers were about to seize him and lead him off to a public execution."[3]

Elsewhere, Cowper sees himself as more normally isolated. In an early poem **"On the Death of Sir W. Russell"** (1757), before Cowper's second and permanently affecting attack of melancholy, he wrote:

> See me—ere yet my destin'd course half done,
> Cast forth a wand'rer on a wild unknown!
> See me neglected on the world's rude coast,
> Each dear companion of my voyage lost!

"The Valediction" (1783), on his abandonment by his now-important old friends Thurlow and Colman, complains that though friendship may be professed,

> The heart of man . . .
> . . . summon'd to partake a fellow's woe,
> Starts from its office like a broken bow.

(67-70)

Most to the point here is, of course, **"The Castaway."** In it, what Mr. Fausset has perceptively seen as Cowper's terrible "detached self-possession."[4] his ability to watch reasonably and realistically the irrational nature of his own preoccupations, intensifies the horror of Cowper's position. The friends on the ship do their best—subject, of course, to the limitation that they cannot endanger themselves. The poem strikes deep, it seems to me, because it affirms, with chilling politeness, the awful truth that every man is for himself, and that no man can help himself.

As a foreigner and as one abandoned, Cowper has no interest in politics: "It is truly a matter in which I am so little interested, that were it not that it sometimes serves me for a theme, when I can find no other, I should never mention it" (*Correspondence,* II, 224). Longevity, similarly and necessarily, forces the thought of isolation on Cowper: "We must all leave, or be left; and it is the circumstance of all others that makes long life the least desirable, that others go while we stay,—till at last we find ourselves alone, like a tree on a hill-top" (*Correspondence,* III, 395). This passage, like the next, is important in an understanding of Cowper's conception of his relation to the world, suggesting (as almost always, unhappily) an identification of himself with something above the ordinary course of existence. In one of his last letters, he wrote to Lady Hesketh: "At two miles distance on the coast is a solitary pillar of rock, that the crumbling cliff has left at the high water-mark. I have visited it twice, and have found it an emblem of myself. Torn from my natural connections, I stand alone and expect the storm that shall displace me" (*Correspondence,* IV, 490).

Inevitably, one who considers himself singled out from mankind, whether for good or ill, must necessarily see himself symbolically in a position above it, or at least distinct from it. Goldsmith in *The Traveller,* for example, places himself on a mountain top, where he suffers the disadvantage of loneliness and enjoys the advantage of superiority to mankind; Churchill, Cowper's old schoolfellow, steadily and smugly projects himself above his fellow man in his poems, delighting in the superiority and the dangers of the eminence. But while Cowper, when appraising his position consciously, speaks with humility and denigrates himself, he very often portrays figures reaching above the crowd, and usually their position is unhappy.

Comparing himself to great poets, he writes that they are like nightingales, and

> The nightingale may claim the topmost bough,
> While the poor grasshopper must chirp below:
> Like him, unnotic'd, I, and such as I,
> Spread little wings, and rather skip than fly;
> Perch'd on the meagre produce of the land,
> An ell or two of prospect we command;
> But never peep beyond the thorny bound,
> Or oaken fence, that hems the paddoc round.
>
> **("Table Talk,"** 576-83)

Writing in 1765, after setting up his home in Huntingdon, his first great move from London, he says: "For my own part, who am but as a Thames wherry, in a world full of tempest and commotion, I know . . . well the value of the creek I have put into. . . ." (*Correspondence,* I, 48).

Possessing greatness, being in some way above the crowd, suggests to Cowper danger and the great likelihood of being misunderstood—his horror of conspicuousness, it will be recalled, precipitated his first severe attack of madness. Similarly, he reacted to the possibility of taking orders, in 1766, with

> I have had many anxious thoughts about taking orders, and I believe every new convert is apt to think himself called upon for that purpose; but it has pleased God, by means which there is no need to particularise, to give me full satisfaction as to the propriety of declining it; indeed, they who have the least idea of what I have suffered from the dread of public exhibitions, will readily excuse my never attempting them hereafter
>
> (*Correspondence,* I, 81).

A less exacting, and therefore more revealing, demand on his inconspicuousness nearly caused another breakdown. After the move to Olney, in a new house, Cowper was called on to lead family prayers:

I trembled at the Apprehension of it, and was so dreadfully harrass'd in the Conflict I sustain upon this Occasion in the first Week, that my health was not a little affected by it. But there was no Remedy, and I hope the Lord brought me to that point, to chuse Death rather than a Retreat from Duty. In my first Attempt he was sensibly present with me, and has since favour'd me with every possible Assistance. My Fears begin to wear off, I get rather more Liberty of Speech at least, if not of Spirit, and have some Hope that having open'd my Mouth he will never suffer it closed again, but rather give Increase of Utterance and Zeal to serve him. How much of that Monster Self has he taken Occasion to shew me by this Incident. Pride Ostentation, and Vain glory have always been my Hindrance in these Attempts. These be at the Root of that Evil Tree which the world good natur'dly calls Bashfullness.[5]

Even this objectively trivial prominence Cowper was able to dramatize into a life-and-death battle, in which his antagonist, however kindly, was no less than God. On greater occasions, at more dismal stages in Cowper's life, God does not treat his conspicuousness so gently.

Most images of conspicuousness, as I have said, are for good reason fearful, or at least uneasy; one, however, is quite admiring: the great poet, in a passage which includes Cowper's disclaimer of the title, needs

> . . . as the sun in rising beauty dress'd
> Looks to the westward from the dappled east,
> And marks, whatever clouds may interpose,
> Ere yet his race begins, its glorious close;
> An eye like his to catch the distant goal,
> Or ere the wheels of verse begin to roll;
> Like his to shed illuminating rays
> On ev'ry scene and subject it surveys. . . .
>
> **("Table Talk,"** 706-13)

Cowper's whole attitude toward the fancy (imagination), whose range he considers an index to the poet's greatness, is, as is usual with him, complex and ambivalent; he mistrusts it elsewhere and, though yearning for its consequence, poetic stature, everywhere complains that even greatness as a poet is vanity. The very poem in which this passage appears ends with a firm preference for piety in verse over talent, even if that means supporting Sternhold and Hopkins at the expense of such as Pope. In **"Truth"** Cowper points out that few great or conspicuous people "win one inch of heav'nly ground" (338). A great man (Whitefield)

> Stood pilloried on infamy's high stage . . .
> The very butt of slander, and the blot
> For ev'ry dart that malice ever shot.
>
> **("Hope,"** 556, 558-9)

But a great preacher will "storm the citadels they [wastrels] build in air" (**"Hope,"** 626). Here, applied to conspicuousness, are a pair of pervasive symbols in Cowper that involve himself and the world at large—the target and the attacker. In response to a friend's poem on indifference, Cowper argued that he did not at all want to be indifferent: only

Some Alpine mountain, wrapt in snow,
    Thus braves the whirling blast,
Eternal winter doom'd to know,
    No genial spring to taste.

("To Miss Macartney," 33-36)

The structure of Cowper's most famous jeu d'esprit, **"John Gilpin,"** is pre-eminently a reflection of this same preoccupation: the poem is concerned with a man who, in the course of an ordinary event, becomes ludicrously and disagreeably prominent. In another poem, the first in Cowper's first book (**"Table Talk"**), kings, the chief subjects at the beginning, are, because of their eminent positions, suspected, misunderstood, thwarted, gossiped about by all sorts—the main speaker in the dialogue says that he would not be such a king for anything. In **"The Winter Evening"** Cowper sees himself as temporarily on a more than mortal height, as he surveys the world's doings from his Olney home—but note the emphasis that he has placed on his safety (presumably from darts and other missiles) behind the "loop-holes of retreat" (l. 88). With the lone tree on the hilltop representing those who live while others die and with the imminently endangered pillar in the sea already referred to, it becomes clear that to Cowper any picture of something above the crowd suggests insecurity, danger, warfare. Both consciously and unconsciously, Cowper uses such objects to reflect his own sense of danger.

But this sort of attitude cannot be limited for a man with Cowper's mental fixations; and the image or symbolic structure involving the sympathetic character at bay, even when he is not in any way distinguished above the world, is among the most frequent in his writings. He suffers either the attacks of a deluded world or, in the storm and other natural images which have been so often commented on, he is battered by an arbitrary God (in a letter of 1781, Cowper wrote that one striking aspect of the sea that had always affected his imagination was that it was the most immediate agent of God).[6] We can further extend our understanding of Cowper's themes if we note that objects—England, the quiet countryside, the converted sinner—similarly pictured are, for a short while, being identified with Cowper's own mental states.

In **"Table Talk"** this complex of attitudes affects, among other things, Cowper's homeland:

Poor England! thou art a devoted deer,
Beset with ev'ry ill but that of fear.
The nations hunt; all mark thee for a prey;
They swarm around thee, and thou stand'st at bay.
Undaunted still, though wearied and perplex'd,
Once Chatham sav'd thee; but who saves thee next?

(362-7)

Cowper's self-identification with that which is hunted, evident here, most conspicuous in the famous stricken deer passage in **"The Garden,"** and continuing to the end of his life, helps to explain his humanitarian kindness to animals and his conception of himself as harried by both man and God.

Adherence to the world's requirements makes a man foolish and perhaps even conspicuous; if now truth must be

. . . cut short to make a period round,
I judg'd a man of sense could scarce do worse
Than caper in the morris-dance of verse.

("Table Talk," 517-9)

The world forces us out of our proper human mold. In conversation, fashion makes us talk like apes: though a nightingale will never give up his own song for "the twitt'ring of a meaner bird,"

Yet fashion, leader of a chatt'ring train,
Whom man for his own hurt permits to reign,
Who shifts and changes all things but his shape,
And would degrade her vot'ry to an ape,
The fruitful parent of abuse and wrong,
Holds an usurp'd dominion of his tongue. . . .

("Conversation," 457-62)

The world, grown old,

Claps spectacles on her sagacious nose,
Peruses closely the true Christian's face,
And finds it a mere mask of sly grimace. . . .

("Conversation," 742-4)

Man plunders and enslaves his different-colored brother, "Dooms and devotes him as his lawful prey" (**"Time-Piece,"** 15). Note here the hunting image, again contributing to illuminate the motives for one of those benevolent attitudes for which Cowper is so properly admired. In **"The Garden"** comes the most famous of these hunting images:

I was a stricken deer, that left the herd
Long since; with many an arrow deep infixt
My panting side was charg'd, when I withdrew
To seek a tranquil death in distant shades.
There was I found by one who had himself
Been hurt by th'archers. In his side he bore,
And in his hands and feet, the cruel scars.

(108-14)

The identification with Christ is important in this picture, emphasizing as it does the frequent undercurrent of self-justification in Cowper. He could never convince himself, as his very late **"Spiritual Diary"** shows most painfully,[7] that he had been fairly chosen for such punishment, being well aware that by most standards he was a good man. At the time of his conversion and on through the 1760's he seems to have accepted the obvious theological argument that man, since the fall, was intolerably sinful, and that consequently he himself deserved his punishment; but he cited without comment Lady Hesketh's reaction to his *Memoir*, that he did not seem to have deserved his tortures;[8] and in the *Memoir* itself he suggested that his overpowering sense of guilt during his madness might well have been the work of the devil. The stricken deer passage is, moreover, biographically curious, since it implies that

Cowper had been stricken by the same hunters as Christ, i.e., sinful men. However, this deer has left the herd, and not it him—and of what could the herd be composed but these same sinful, malicious men? In point of fact, Cowper's madness had not been the fault of men but of his own mental constitution—except for the parliamentary group interested in challenging Ashley Cowper's patronage power, Cowper's associates in London seem to have been singularly kindly to him. The inference is, I believe, that Cowper had been stricken by God, in the same way that, in one of his mortality poems for the clerk of Norwich, numbers of crowded forest trees are yearly singled out for death.

His ambivalence is reflected in his attitude toward one aspect of society, the state. When it is a beleaguered, oppressed figure of stability at bay, he sees

> . . . the old castle of the state,
> That promis'd once more firmness, so assail'd
> That all its tempest-beaten turrets shake,
> Stand motionless expectants of its fall.

("The Winter Morning Walk," 525-8)

But when it represents collective society in its oppressive relation to the individual, he fears it and attempts to placate it. If the good man is not violently attacked, he is at least scorned: by kindness within his sphere, the contemplative man

> . . . recompenses well
> The state, beneath the shadow of whose vine
> He sits secure, and in the scale of life
> Holds no ignoble, though a slighted, place.

("The Winter Walk at Noon," 968-71)

But at times the man is in much greater danger from smaller and more intense groups: in an occasional piece thanking Mrs. King for a quilt to which many women had contributed, he is grateful that they are not coming to reclaim their own:

> Thanks then to ev'ry gentle fair
> Who will not come to peck me bare
> As bird of borrow'd feather. . . .

("To Mrs. King")

"Table Talk," significant for its discussion of the discomfort of kings as elevated targets for the crowd, is perhaps even more significant for its general tenor. Placed first in the poems of 1782, it serves as a prologue to the rest, justifying the kind of poetry that Cowper writes and the subjects that he chooses. Its ending is a thorough defense against and disclaimer of anticipated criticism from the world: poor religious poems, he argues, are better than good nonreligious ones. One of the central points of **"Charity,"** in which Cowper refers to himself as "disgrac'd and slighted," is that a man with vision in the land of the blind is derided—note again the faint urgency toward self-justification in the steady battle between himself and society. In **"Retirement,"** one of the character types going

to nature is the melancholy man (Cowper saw his own illness as an aggravation of melancholy), who is laughed at by blockheads without nerves. It is pertinent that the melancholy man is one of those who seek nature for the wrong reasons—the right one is to observe God's appearance in it—and that though Cowper frequently justifies himself against man's misunderstanding on the ground that he sees the truth that the crowd misses, when he addresses God he is more likely to plead for kindness than for justice. After all, the hare is no more "right" than the hunter. Its position is pathetic, and hunting it is an arbitrary exercise of brute power, but its vision of the world is not necessarily a true one.[9]

In his strife with society and its fashions, Cowper argues, in a long passage in **"The Time-Piece,"** that there is a pleasure in overcoming difficulties in the poetic craft, but that readers cannot understand or appreciate the subtlety of technique (lines 285-310). In **"The Garden"** there is, to balance the stricken deer passage, one attacking hunters, who misuse the country (and hunters, in the allegory of Cowper's own soul, often suggest God). Cowper here says that it is good to retreat from the world, since thus one avoids passion, which is caused by the world's temptations aimed at one's senses. **"The Winter Evening"** is a long poetic essay symbolically on the theme of attack on the innocent—the city's staining of the country. In the beginning, the sallies are minor and are easily repulsed: the noisy posthorn announces the arrival of news of the world's doings, but Cowper can overcome it and them from his fortified position of retreat. Later attacks, however, are successful and cause permanent effects—the generic country girl has been corrupted by fashions in dress, the country "clown" has been ruined by his service in the army, the lazy peasant, sick with the drinking contagion derived from sources outside the country, has become a drunken thief. The lesser poems, as well, exhibit these preoccupations: banditti attack Cowper's brain; a sensitive minister (William Unwin) is hurt by coarse farmers' dislike of paying tithes; Gilpin's motives and actions are misconstrued by the world; a rat murders a favorite bullfinch.

In a letter soon after the one complaining that his friends should take more notice of him, he implied (so much was his isolation on his mind during a period supposed to have been happy with rebirth, 1766) that they had deliberately abandoned him: "My friends must excuse me, if I write to none but those who lay it fairly in my way to do so. The inference I am apt to draw from their silence is, that they wish me to be silent too; and my circumstances are such as not only justify that apprehension in point of prudence, but even make it natural" (*Correspondence*, I, 62). He is steadily "Conscious that my religious principles are generally excepted against, and that the conduct they produce, wherever they are heartily maintained, is still more the object of disapprobation than those principles themselves. . . ." (*Correspondence*, I, 7). This sensitivity to the world's opinion, as the last passage shows, and as his reactions to Huntingdon gossip about him and Mrs. Unwin show even more, is overtly connected with the justified group sensitivity of the Evangelicals; but Cowper's reasons for feeling a conspicuous butt of man's and God's derision, as the mass of his work makes clear, are private and inevitable. It seems to me quite likely that his need to feel persecuted (combined with other needs, such as that for certainty) caused him to join so unpopular a movement. Of its unpopularity he was consciously aware, if not before his conversion then very soon after it; in August, 1767, he wrote to Mrs. Madan that "Our Friends here define a Methodist to be—One who committs every Sin he can think of and invents New Ones every Day,—that he may be saved by Faith."[10] I cannot see that the continuing argument, beginning very soon after Cowper's death in 1800 and affecting such comparatively recent work as the studies by Gilbert Thomas, Hugh l'Anson Fausset, and David Cecil, over the issue of whether Evangelicalism contributed to Cowper's madness, has any point except the airing of prejudices. A neurotic of Cowper's cast inevitably seeks some assurance of his unique inadequacy, and if he does not find it in severe Calvinism he will impose rigid moral qualifications on lotus eating.

In the battle between the self and the world, Cowper's imagery and structures show a variety of reactions: defensiveness, coupled with the assertion of his own importance; fearful retreat (which Kenneth MacLean has so brilliantly discussed);[11] superiority toward the world, assertion of its triviality, and downright attacks upon it. Everywhere in his poetry and letters are evidences of the importance of defensiveness in his mental constitution. Poetry, at the end of **"Table Talk,"** is defined as a "gift, whose office is the Giver's praise" (750); it should not be used

> To purchase, at the fool-frequented fair
> Of vanity, a wreath for self to wear
>
> (756-7)

but should be an instrument (as in Cowper it professedly is) to direct men to God's path. Of his writing of satire, he says,

> An individual is a sacred mark,
> Not to be pierc'd in play, or in the dark;
> But public censure speaks a public foe,
> Unless a zeal for virtue guide the blow.
>
> **("Expostulation,"** 434-7)

Here the fear of being misunderstood is immediately answered by an assertion of public-spiritedness. Of his digression and playfulness in **"Charity,"** he writes:

> Thus have I sought to grace a serious lay
> With many a wild, indeed, but flow'ry spray,
> In hopes to gain, what else I must have lost,
> Th'attention pleasure has so much engross'd.
>
> **("Charity,"** 628-31)

Again, defense is mixed with reproof—he blames the world for forcing him out of his proper path to please it. A similar apology for digression appears in **"Conversation"**:

> Digression is so much in modern use,
> Thought is so rare, and fancy so profuse,
> Some never seem so wide of their intent,
> As when returning to the theme they meant;
> As mendicants, whose business is to roam,
> Make ev'ry parish, but their own, their home.
> Though such continual zigzags in a book,
> Such drunken reelings, have an awkward look,
> And I had rather creep to what is true,
> Than rove and stagger with no mark in view;
>
> . . . . .
>
> [but he does not want to] give good company a face severe,
> As if they met around a father's bier. . . .
>
> (855-74)

The contemplative man at the end of *The Task* "recompenses well" the state by his example of kindness. As **"Table Talk"** defends Cowper's techniques and subjects, so **"Truth"** defends the current enthusiasts: the poem begins with the ways to heaven that the world believes to be true, shows that they are false, and goes on to point out that faith (like that of Cowper and his friends) wins heaven while pride goes to hell. In **"Charity,"** besides the essentially defensive description of the contempt in which the man with vision is held by the blind, Cowper again defends his satire—satire that is not virtuously motivated is destructive of man's proper tie to man, but there is no question about the motivation of Cowper's. And the **"Winter Walk at Noon"** ends with the assurance that the man who has a foretaste of Judgment Day is happy though the world neglects him and scorns his pleasures; it is possible, says Cowper, that the world owes its successes to his prayers.

In the retreat from the world that is a favorite way of dealing with its propensity to hurt Cowper, the stricken deer's is again the most conspicuous passage. But note that in it the deer and his associates have found a path that is not merely different from, but also better than, the herd's. They ruminate over the ways of the world and conclude that

> . . . all are wand'rers, gone astray
> Each in his own delusions. . . .
>
> **("The Garden,"** 124-5)

The religious man, in another image combining the two attitudes of retreat and superiority,

> . . . cannot skim the ground like summer birds
> Pursuing gilded flies; and such he deems
> Her [the world's] honours, her emoluments, her joys.
>
> **("Winter Walk at Noon,"** 921-3)

Again, in the **"Winter Walk at Noon"** the fortunate man who sees that God animates every detail of nature is contemptuous of fashionable pleasures. The "Thames wherry" image is primarily of retreat, though in his reference to "a world full of tempest and commotion" there is a suggestion that the world is not worth being in. At the same time, Cowper was occasionally aware that his retreat was also one of the mind, and that it distorted his vision: ". . . when we circumscribe our estimate of all that is clever within the limits of our own acquaintance (which I, at least, have been always apt to do), we are guilty of a very uncharitable censure upon the rest of the world, and of a narrowness of thinking disgraceful to ourselves" (*Correspondence*, I, 54). He could, furthermore, in accordance with his horror of solitude and of oblivion, pity his own retreat: of Olney, he wrote, "It is no attachment to the place that binds me here, but an unfitness for every other. I lived in it once, but now I am buried in it, and have no business with the world on the outside of my sepulchre; my appearance would startle them, and theirs would be shocking to me" (*Correspondence*, I, 175). His letter of 1784 in which he praises the virtue that flies temptation has already been alluded to. In 1785 comes yet another example of the combination of retreat with superiority: walking home with Mrs. Unwin he wrote to her son, "a glimpse of something white, contained in a little hole in the gate-post, caught my eye. I looked again and discovered a bird's nest with two tiny eggs in it. By and by they will be fledged, and tailed, and get wing-feathers, and fly. My case is somewhat similar to that of the parent bird. My nest is in a little nook. Here I brood and hatch, and in due time my progeny takes wing and whistles" (*Correspondence*, II, 318-9). Some years later refusing an invitation to visit a friend some distance away, he wrote, "My fate and fortune have combined with my natural disposition to draw a circle round me which I cannot pass; nor have I been more than thirteen miles from home these twenty years, and so far very seldom" (*Correspondence*, IV, 37).

The assertions of the world's triviality relate, quite obviously, to the superiority just suggested. People unconcerned with religion, he wrote in **"Truth,"**

> Sport for a day, and perish in a night;
> The foam upon the waters not so light.
>
> (42-3)

Those who attack the true religion resemble in their noise

> . . . the clamour of rooks, daws, and kites,
> Th'explosion of the levell'd tube excites,
> Where mould'ring abbey walls o'erhang the glade,
> And oaks coeval spread a mournful shade.
>
> (**"Hope,"** 349-52)

The stricken deer discovers that

> . . . The million flit as gay
> As if created only like the fly,
> That spreads his motley wings in th'eye of noon.
>
> (**"Garden,"** 133-6)

Notice that the image of light and useless matters—ephemeral insects, foam, summer birds pursuing gilded flies—pervades these descriptions of mankind at large.

A most important category of images and structures expanding Cowper's view of himself to all mankind in its stay on earth deals with the confusion of man's lot, the impossibility of man's finding his way in a world arbitrarily uncertain. Though it was Cowper's conscious intention to show that conversion, the acquisition of grace, would clearly guide man's steps, one notices in this steady development of man's inability to see the right way through dangers an undercurrent of Cowper's resentment, or at least suspicion, of God's purposes with respect to him. In the **"Progress of Error"** he gives this view its most direct, and acceptable, theological form: man is "Plac'd for his trail on this bustling stage" (23). In **"Truth,"** which is designed to show the enlightening effect of grace, he writes that

> Man, on the dubious waves of error toss'd,
> His ship half founder'd and his compass lost,
> Sees, far as human optics may command,
> A sleeping fog, and fancies it dry land:
> Spreads all his canvass, ev'ry sinew plies;
> Pants for't, aims at it, enters it, and dies!
>
> (1-6)

The world is a prison house, he says in the **"Time-Piece"**; and a man who has been restored through hope of salvation is like a felon pardoned at the last moment (**"Hope,"** 712-31). It is, note again, the arbitrariness of his Calvinism that he stresses here, as he does also in his **"Spiritual Diary"** and in a letter to Newton. . . . Similarly, **"The Sofa"** contains a long passage on the joy of the long-time prisoner who has been released to savor nature (436-44).

The theme of delusion, as well as its culmination in disaster, is a repeated one: in **"The Sofa,"** among the examples of those who have true love for nature is a sailor who so longs for his native countryside that he mistakes the ocean for it, jumps overboard, and drowns. In another place (**"Hope,"** 674-741) we are given a description of two sinners hoping for grace and of their reactions when one is granted it and the other is not. Similarly, in two parables in **"The Winter Walk at Noon"** the same theme is developed in the same way. Cowper is concerned with the treatment accorded horses by heedless and vicious riders (and the image clusters suggest that in such a situation Cowper identifies himself with the despoiled, the prey, and is likely to identify an arbitrary God with the hunter or exploiter). In one case,

> With unsuspecting readiness he takes
> His murd'rer on his back, and, push'd all day,
> With bleeding sides and flanks that heave for life,
> To the far-distant goal, arrives and dies.
>
> (427-30)

For the expected contrast, there is a moral tale some 100 lines later (possibly the silliest that Cowper ever wrote) of a headstrong youth who twice safely spurred his horse to the edge of a precipice to tempt fate but was finally hurled into the gulf when the horse, on his own initiative, rushed to the edge and stopped short:

So God wrought double justice; made the fool
The victim of his own tremendous choice,
And taught a brute the way to safe revenge.

(557-9)

As has been suggested, Cowper often saw man's lot symbolically as his own; but he also tended to project on general human existence his own special problems. The city, for example, became for him the epitome of the confusion of existence. When he reads the news of the active world in the paper, he is happy in his retirement

To hear the roar she sends through all her gates
At a safe distance, where the dying sound
Falls a soft murmur on th'uninjur'd ear.

(**"The Winter Evening,"** 91-93)

All of fashionable life is the type and symbol of confusion, of wandering from the true path, and is so described again and again. Cowper's aim is to direct it right. His satire, in general, is not of the kind of Juvenal or, in his own period, of Churchill, a kind that often cries, "You are evil. Disappear!" It is, rather, the call, "You are wrong. Change your ways!"

Cowper sees his relation to God and to man in a complex way. From one point of view, in one mood, he can speak as a man who has grace and loves society, and is therefore on a good footing with both. But more frequently the conviction at the root of his melancholy that he was the one sinner of the universe, cast out by both God and society, dominates him; it, and its subtle ramifications, really determine his picture of himself. Overtly, he loves God with ecstasy, as he had loved Him when he was reborn from his violent attack of madness in 1764; but basically, as I shall try to show more fully below, he hates and fears Him. Paradoxically, this fear of God's arbitrariness, hatred because Cowper felt himself the chief sufferer from it, helps much to explain the humanitarianism that Mr. Lodwick Hartley's recent study has so well dealt with.[12] Seeing himself often as a hunted animal—a deer, a hare—and sympathizing with the fears of the animal, he eloquently protested against man's arbitrary commission of acts proper only to God (it is possible that this explanation could be true of the general evangelical objection to blood sports). God has placed man on earth to be judged, without providing at least one man, Cowper, with adequate faculties for choosing, and has arbitrarily decided without concern for human conceptions of justice. Cowper wanted "a closer walk with God," but always in the front of his mind was a great fear of God's might, which is expressed typically in storms, mountains, tidal waves, earthquakes, all the terrors of the natural world.

Not surprising in a man who had good cause to fear solitude, the state that left his mind free to ponder arbitrary damnation, Cowper needed and wanted friends. He felt himself tied to humanity (and indeed to all creation) in a bond of brotherhood. But that brotherhood was primarily one of sinfulness under God's rule. His first step out of

despondence after the overwhelming experience of being nominated for the clerkship occurred when Martin Madan told him that not only he but all men were steeped in sin. Here Cowper felt some glimmering of hope; but its perverseness is borne out by the event, which was that his full attack of madness came *afterwards*. Furthermore, his reminders of man's brotherhood usually come in contexts where he is assailing mankind for forgetting the bond, or where he bids men to unite in the face of an angry God, or both. This is so in **"The Time-Piece,"** in **"The Garden,"** and in **"Expostulation."**

Just as he wants a relationship with God which will be close but not close enough to expose him to destruction, so he seeks a similar relationship with man. Again his attitude is paradoxical. Convinced of his uniqueness, of his foreignness within mankind, he yet needs to stretch out to man for corroboration of his own significance. Repelled by the confusion of man in the mass, a confusion which aggravates his certainty of his own difference and inadequacy to deal with life, he yet needs some contact with man's activities to draw him from the contemplation of his own fearful fate. The consequence is a voluntary retirement from the world combined with a great effort to find a few friends close by with whom he could maintain a precarious balance of openness and restraint, and with a further effort to expand his influence beyond into the world without running the dangers of its forcing itself upon him. He withdraws from human activities, but takes great care, possibly because of his awareness of the danger of complete apathy (to which he succumbed for most of his last five years), to know what these activities are, providing he is safe from them. A powerful strain of self-justification, connected with if not deriving from his need to argue his case before authority (before an angry God), supports him in his relations with the world. Its activities, a huge projection of his own sense of uncertainty and terror, are the consequences of folly, delusion, and triviality; in his own retreat from the world's temptations, he achieves a certain triumph over it, a triumph which, if it were not for the horrors of solitude, would be complete.

The only victory can be in a kind of obscurity (the hare is only safe if the dogs or hunters cannot detect it), for prominence only invites assault. The towering person, like the high hill or promontory, is subjected to God's storms and man's viciousness. Greatness involves just this towering; but greatness is the most dangerous human condition, and while Cowper admires the soaring poet or the passionate statesman or preacher, he is well aware that poetic greatness involves the self-deceiving and self-defeating fancy, that Whitefield has been wrongly aspersed, and that Chatham and Wolfe are dead. Better far to be the brood bird hidden away that sends its fledglings to remind the world of its existence.

Notes

1. Gilbert Thomas, *William Cowper and the Eighteenth Century* (London: Allen & Unwin, 1948), 2d ed., pp. 261-3.

2. Printed in Charles Ryskamp, *William Cowper of the Inner Temple, Esq.* (Cambridge: Cambridge University Press, 1959), p. 223.

3. Maurice J. Quinlan, *William Cowper: A Critical Life* (Minneapolis: University of Minnesota Press, 1953), p. 183.

4. Hugh l'Anson Fausset, *William Cowper* (London: Jonathan Cape, 1928), p. 61.

5. William Cowper, *Unpublished and Uncollected Letters,* ed. Thomas Wright (London: C. J. Farncombe & Sons, 1925), pp. 21-2.

6. "I think with you, that the most magnificent object under heaven is the great deep; and cannot but feel an unpolite species of astonishment, when I consider the multitudes that view it without emotion, and even without reflection. In all its various forms, it is an object of all others the most suited to affect us with lasting impressions of the awful Power that created and controls it . . . at a time of life when I gave as little attention to religious subjects as almost any man, I yet remember that the waves would preach to me, and that in the midst of dissipation I had an ear to hear them" (*Correspondence*, I, 358).

7. Kenneth Povey, ed., "Cowper's Spiritual Diary," *London Mercury*, XV (1927), 493-6.

8. *Unpublished and Uncollected Letters*, p. 27.

9. In his most interesting Harvard dissertation, "The Prisoner and His Crimes: A Psychological Approach to William Cowper's Life and Writings" (1951), Mr. Hoosag K. Gregory discusses Cowper's identification with hunted animals from a Freudian viewpoint (his Chapter 9). Similarly, my study necessarily touches on a number of issues (Cowper and the authority figure, Cowper's obsession with death, Gilpin's ride in relation to Cowper's mind, etc.) which Mr. Gregory also treats. Mr. Gregory uses Cowper's preoccupations and symbols as tools in his psychoanalysis of Cowper, while I am concerned primarily with dissecting the preoccupations and showing their relevance to Cowper's poetry, particularly to *The Task*. See also Hoosag K. Gregory, "The Prisoner and His Crimes: Summary Comments on a Longer Study of the Mind of William Cowper," *Literature and Psychology*, VI (1956), 53-9.

10. *Unpublished and Uncollected Letters*, p. 13.

11. Kenneth MacLean, "William Cowper," in *The Age of Johnson: Essays Presented to Chauncey Brewster Tinker* (New Haven: Yale University Press, 1949), 257-67.

12. Lodwick C. Hartley, *William Cowper, Humanitarian* (Chapel Hill: University of North Carolina Press, 1938).

Patricia Meyer Spacks (essay date 1967)

SOURCE: Spacks, Patricia Meyer. "William Cowper: The Heightened Perception." In *The Poetry of Vision: Five Eighteenth-Century Poets,* pp. 165-206. Cambridge: Harvard University Press, 1967.

[*In the following excerpt, Spacks assesses Cowper as a writer of hymns, considers his poetic technique, and offers a stylistic and thematic survey of* The Task.]

As a writer of hymns, William Cowper is more renowned than [Christopher] Smart; his contributions to the ***Olney Hymns*** have been admired and sung for almost two centuries. If Smart's hymns gain much of their power from a vision turned freshly outward, Cowper's (to which Smart was a subscriber) depend as heavily on the quality of perception directed within. Several commentators have observed that a personal record of psychological distress and recovery is perceptible in his sequence of hymns. The hymns, says Lodwick Hartley, "represent various stages and aspects of the poet's struggle for faith: an ebb and a flow, but withal a progression, in this one respect not unlike the struggle for faith found in a more elaborate but not more poignant manner in *In Memoriam*."[1] Kenneth MacLean suggests that the unique quality of Cowper's hymns depends on the fact that they "are poems in religious, in primitive fear," an emotion "little considered by poets of Cowper's time."[2] And Maurice Quinlan observes that, in Cowper's poetic production as a whole, "even a brief consideration of [his] imagery reveals that he was one of the most subjective of English poets."[3]

What is particularly striking about Cowper's hymns as compared with his other work is their essentially slight dependence on imagery: their strength derives almost entirely from the quality of their psychological insight, and their attempts to translate that insight into images are rarely and incompletely successful. Key images identified by critics[4] include the worm, the thorn, the tempest, the fig tree, and fetters. To this we may add imagery of light, of battle, and of streams or fountains. All are commonplaces of Evangelical discourse; most are common to religious language in general. And, upon examination, few seem truly essential to Cowper's record of religious agony occasionally modified by the faint hope of salvation.

One of the most moving of the ***Olney Hymns*** is **number IX, "The Contrite Heart."**

> The Lord will happiness divine
>   On contrite hearts bestow:
> Then tell me, gracious God, is mine
>   A contrite heart, or no?
>
> I hear, but seem to hear in vain,
>   Insensible as steel;
> If ought is felt, 'tis only pain,
>   To find I cannot feel.
>
> I sometimes think myself inclin'd
>   To love thee, if I could;
> But often feel another mind,
>   Averse to all that's good.

My best desires are faint and few,
 I fain would strive for more;
But when I cry, "My strength renew,"
 Seem weaker than before.

Thy saints are comforted I know,
 And love thy house of pray'r;
I therefore go where others go,
 But find no comfort there.

Oh make this heart rejoice, or ache;
 Decide this doubt for me;
And if it be not broken, break,
 And heal it, if it be.

This is almost bare of figurative language; the only clear metaphor is "Insensible as steel"—the broken heart of the final stanza seems not metaphorical but literal. The hymn's power derives largely from its very bareness, and from the conviction with which the poet describes and analyzes his own emotional tension. Conflict is the essence of the poem. Initially, there seems to be a clash between the conventional—the automatic, easy assurance of the first two lines—and the personal: the bewilderment expressed in the succeeding two lines, underlined by the fact that they address a conventionally "gracious" God. Then Cowper redefines the opposition between conventional and personal as one between the expected (the speaker should "hear" the word of God) and the actual (he hears in vain). He is literally "of two minds": one weakly "inclin'd" toward God; the other, more forceful, "Averse to all that's good." Willing to go through the prescribed motions, the sufferer is constantly brought up short by awareness of his own feelings: he *thinks* himself inclined to love God, but *feels* averse to good; he cries, conventionally, "My strength renew," only to *feel* his own weakness; he *knows* that "saints" love church, does what they do, but *feels* the lack of resultant comfort.

The Donnean appeal of the final stanza is fully justified by the exposition that precedes it. It is an appeal that emotion resolve conflict—not knowledge or even faith: God can "decide" the speaker's doubt only by making him *feel* intensely and unambiguously. The extreme economy of the final two lines helps to make them climactically moving. The poet's heart is unavoidably passive: it either is or is not broken; the stress on passive verb forms (increased by the use of *be* as the final rhyme word) emphasizes the human helplessness which is so often Cowper's theme. In contrast, only God is capable of meaningful action: He can "break" (the strong physical connotations of the word increase its power, suggesting the possibility that the will of God could shatter the whole personality) or "heal" all breaks, all human maladies; and breaking as well as healing may be a mode of salvation—through the restoration of feeling.

This evocation of God as all-powerful, but apparently strangely unwilling to use His power, and of man as forced by his own divided state into a condition of helpless passivity, is central to Cowper's thought. The same ideas

emerge frequently in his other hymns, but rarely with as much energy and conviction as in **"The Contrite Heart."** Here is another presentation of the same problem:

My God, how perfect are thy ways!
 But mine polluted are;
Sin twines itself about my praise,
 And slides into my pray'r.

When I would speak what thou hast done
 To save me from my sin,
I cannot make thy mercies known
 But self-applause creeps in.

Divine desire, that holy flame
 Thy grace creates in me;
Alas! impatience is its name,
 When it returns to thee.

This heart, a fountain of vile thoughts,
 How does it overflow?
While self upon the surface floats
 Still bubbling from below.

Let others in the gaudy dress
 Of fancied merit shine;
The Lord shall be my righteousness;
 The Lord for ever mine.

   (No. XI, "Jehovah Our Righteousness")

Once more, the hymn's theme is the nature and destructiveness of the divided human spirit. This time Cowper concentrates on how good impulses can turn into their opposites: prayer into sin, praise into "self-applause," "Divine desire" into impatience; the heart, traditionally the repository of gentle feelings, is actually "a fountain of vile thoughts." Yet the final stanza somewhat smugly asserts the poet's superiority to others because he recognizes his own inability to achieve virtue and therefore relies solely on the goodness of God.

This conclusion is logical enough: the rational content of the poem consists of an elaboration of the opening two lines, and the concluding stanza defines an attitude toward the facts the poem has described. But that attitude, although logically plausible, contradicts the emotional emphasis of the stanzas that precede its statement. One may object to the imagery of serpent and fountain, but its emotional purport is clear: it insists upon self-disgust as the necessary consequence of man's awareness of his sinful nature. To deny that self-disgust in the conclusion exemplifies the very weakness pointed to in the second stanza: "I cannot make thy mercies known / But self-applause creeps in." Although self-awareness is the subject of the hymn, there is none in the resolution. The disdain for less knowledgeable "others" implied by *gaudy,* the easy assurance of the pronouncement, "The Lord for ever mine"—these are far from the sense of doubt and questioning earlier conveyed.

The most moving stanzas are the second and third, most specifically concerned with the nature of inward contradiction, most direct in their statement of the problem. Their paucity of imagery also distinguishes them: "that holy flame" is the only clear metaphor. ("Creeps in," in the preceding stanza, has undeveloped metaphoric implications.) This rather commonplace image exists in dramatic conjunction with expression of a very different sort: the holy flame of divine desire reveals itself to be simply impatience, and one perceives the relative pretentiousness of the metaphor when the quality it refers to receives a different "name." The problem of using language properly is implicit in all but the final stanzas of this hymn: the sinner's self-examination is largely examination of the difficulty of expressing in words any inner integrity he may have. Sin contaminates the words of prayer; the effort to "speak" God's praises turns to self-applause; the name of divine desire becomes the name *impatience*.

Partly because the poem's concerns are mental (or spiritual) and verbal problems, the concreteness of sin conceived as serpent is disturbing: twining and sliding are motions too physical for the context. On the other hand, when Cowper treats sin simply as spiritual fact, in the second stanza, its force is considerably greater. The heart as "fountain of vile thoughts" is momentarily impressive, but as the image is elaborated its details become so concrete and specific as to remove stress from the main point. We may even find ourselves lost in contemplation of how and why the "self" manages to float on the surface of its own heart. The image is vivid, but its meaning becomes shadowy; the relation between the self and the heart is both obscure and grotesque.

The danger of grotesquerie is often imminent for Cowper because of his singular lack of tact in converting his ideas to images. Norman Nicholson may argue that **"Praise for the Fountain Opened"** ("There is a fountain fill'd with blood") makes us "aware of rituals even older than the Old Testament: of the dying god of the fertility cults and of primitive symbols that probe deeply into the subconscious mind,"[5] but the argument seems singularly irrelevant to the immediate effect of the hymn, which, on non-evangelical readers, is likely to be shocking but not illuminating.

> There is a fountain fill'd with blood
>   Drawn from Emmanuel's veins;
> And sinners, plung'd beneath that flood,
>   Lose all their guilty stains. . . .
>
> E'er since, by faith, I saw the stream
>   Thy flowing wounds supply;
> Redeeming love has been my theme,
>   And shall be till I die.

The effort at fruitful paradox is unsuccessful because the sheer physical specificity of the image, with its insistence on the source of the blood in *veins* (and later *wounds*) is so intense as to overpower its meaning in Christian tradition. Cowper's frequent references to the blood of Christ make it clear that he conceives it not as an image but as a symbol: what it stands for is of course immeasurably more

important than what it *is*. Yet since the poet insists on reminding us in some detail of what precisely it *is*, readers less tradition-steeped than he are likely to have difficulty making the transition from image to meaning. "Comfortable thoughts arise / From the bleeding sacrifice," observes another hymn (**number VIII, "O Lord, I Will Praise Thee"**); it is difficult to imagine anyone but Cowper composing such a couplet. The adjective *bleeding* presumably reminds him of the symbolic import of Christ's sacrifice; for the reader, it turns a relatively abstract noun into a sharp and perhaps unpleasant image. The attempt to evoke a Christian paradox by speaking of *comfortable* thoughts fails; the paradox is too easy to be convincing.

The most vivid single example of Cowper's lack of control of his images is the final hymn of his Olney series, which systematically turns the natural world into a series of emblems for Christ. This can hardly be what Hugh Fausset meant when he maintained that "of all the hymns which Cowper wrote, . . . those come nearest to pure poetry in which God is invoked through Nature."[6] The final stanzas are typical:

> What! has autumn left to say
> Nothing of a Saviour's grace?
> Yes, the beams of milder day
> Tell me of his smiling face.
>
> Light appears with early dawn,
> While the sun makes haste to rise,
> See his bleeding beauties, drawn
> On the blushes of the skies.
>
> Ev'ning, with a silent pace,
> Slowly moving in the west,
> Show an emblem of his grace,
> Points to an eternal rest.

(no. LXVII, "I Will Praise the Lord at All Times")

The grotesque conjunction of "the blushes of the skies" and "his bleeding beauties" is the most startling element in these stanzas, but the flatness of the first one quoted, the padding of its opening lines, the anticlimax of its conclusion, are also characteristic of Cowper the hymn-writer at his worst. Although the implied personification of this stanza is thematically appropriate, in the second stanza the personification emphasizes the awkwardness of the emblematic treatment, and in the final stanza it is simply irrelevant: how does evening conceived as a person "point to an eternal rest" in any way importantly different from that of evening as a physical phenomenon? This is poetry *voulue* with a vengeance, justifiable only by reference to its purpose, not to its effects. One recalls Dr. Johnson's strictures on metaphysical imagery: "the force of metaphors is lost when the mind by the mention of particulars is turned more upon the original than the secondary sense, more upon that from which the illustration is drawn than that to which it is applied."[7] Cowper's images, in his hymns, frequently seem to have a sort of fatality, to call one's attention inexorably to the "original" rather than the "secondary sense." And his imagery is often "metaphysical" in two ways: its references, although they may purport to deal with the realm of concrete actuality, really concern only the realm beyond the physical; and the images often embody "the most heterogeneous ideas . . . yoked by violence together."[8] Unfortunately Cowper at his most "metaphysical" resembles John Cleveland ("my pen's the spout / Where the rain-water of mine eyes runs out") more than John Donne; his extravagances, traditional though they often are, are imperfectly controlled, and likely to alienate rather than to attract the reader.

Yet the imagery of these hymns, when it is less extreme, is strangely revealing. Most deeply-felt of Cowper's images of the sinner's state seem to be those of storm and of battle. God may be a pilot in the storm (**Hymn XXXVIII**), or He may actually calm the storm (**Hymn XLI**); He may control the course of battle and supply the weapons (**IV, V**), or guard the city against besiegers (**XIV**), or brighten the Christian's armor in answer to prayer (**XXIX**); when the satanic "foe" takes the guise of bird of prey, God becomes a sheltering bird, protecting His children beneath His wings (**XXIV**). Only in the last of these functions, though, does God seem vividly present to the poet's imagination. Cowper's reiterated imagery of light (his favorite emblem of God) and of streams and fountains is more convincing. His most typical positive adjectives and nouns (*calm, pleasant, cheerful, peace, comfort*) suggest the state of restored innocence for which he, as a Christian, yearns, a state emblemized by the calm cheer of light, the steady flow of the fountain.

The conjunction of these facts is suggestive; two stanzas from **Hymn LVIII, "The New Convert,"** hint their significance:

> No fears he feels, he sees no foes,
> No conflict yet his faith employs,
> Nor has he learnt to whom he owes
> The strength and peace his soul enjoys.
>
> But sin soon darts its cruel sting,
> And, comforts sinking day by day,
> What seem'd his own, a self-fed spring,
> Proves but a brook that glides away.

The polarities of Cowper's universe are here suggested and partly described. On the one side is the realm of "conflict." The new convert may postpone awareness of it, but he cannot avoid its actuality; he will ultimately be forced to "see" the foes which have existed all along; his comforts will "sink" as inevitably as the brook glides away. Conflict implies depletion of human resources; it involves a falling away from the state of "strength and peace," of enjoyment, calm, cheer, which is Cowper's most potent vision. He dreams, too, of a never-exhausted fountain of grace, as he dreams of, and believes in, a divine source of spiritual light. But faith and perception seem, in this hymn at least, fundamentally opposed: faith temporarily protects a man from "seeing" what is to be seen; as the power of sin counteracts that of faith, he comes to realize that the inexhaustible spring is only a transient brook. In some of the most convincing hymns Cowper's perceptions of nature support him in his non-rational conviction of the essential hostility of the universe he inhabits. Yet his fundamental effort in all his poetry was to justify, and thus to retain, his dream of idyllic peace, in which he might return to the child-like state of the new convert.

In the hymns, by their very nature, Cowper's religious conviction dominates his poetic gifts. It is not necessary to agree with Hugh Fausset that the poet's life and work demonstrate the unalterable and fundamental opposition between his poetic impulses and his religious bias ("Throughout his life Cowper's allegiance was disastrously divided between poetry and religion."[9]); one may still see that the hymn form emphasizes a dichotomy which may elsewhere disappear. In his most successful poetry, Cowper's concern with art and his preoccupation with morality unite—despite the fact that his own utterances on his poetry occasionally suggest a drastic separation between them, insisting even that all artistic devices must be a means for moral instruction. "My principal purpose," he wrote to the Rev. John Newton, of *The Task*, "is to allure the reader, by character, by scenery, by imagery, and such poetical embellishments, to the reading of what may profit him."[10] Newton was far more interested in Cowper's spiritual development than in his artistic achievement; the poet's statement of his intent may have been colored by his sense of what his mentor expected of him. But his sense of a responsibility to make his poetry "useful" emerges elsewhere as well. "I can write nothing without aiming at least at usefulness," he explained to the Reverend William Unwin: "it were beneath my years to do it, and still more dishonourable to my religion."[11]

One reason for Cowper's insistence on the didactic function of poetry seems to have been his conviction that his contemporaries subordinated matter to manner. An important subject of **"Table Talk"** is the deterioration of value implicit in the fact that modern standards of poetic excellence stress technique rather than content: "Manner is all in all, whate'er is writ, / The substitute for genius, sense, and wit" (ll. 542-543). Cowper insists that poets must be judged by their subject matter:

> To dally much with subjects mean and low
> Proves that the mind is weak, or makes it so. . . .
> The man that means success should soar above
> A soldier's feather, or a lady's glove;
> Else, summoning the muse to such a theme,
> The fruit of all her labour is whipt-cream.
>
> (ll. 544-545, 548-551)

Yet Cowper's notion of the poet's proper subject matter was by no means limited to the promulgation of religious doctrine; he had also an idea of imaginative truth. His scorn for "mere matters of fact" is worthy of a nineteenth-century "Romantic": "I do not know," he writes to Newton, "that a poet is obliged to write with a philosopher at his elbow, prepared always to bind down his imagination to mere matters of fact."[12] And his concern for the substance of poetry did not prevent him from being deeply aware of the demands and resources of technique, considered in isolation from content. The struggle for technical dexterity offered a sort of salvation for him. In a touching letter to Newton, Cowper dilates upon his religious despair, describing himself as engaged in "continual listening to the language of a heart hopeless and deserted" and therefore as unfit for conversation about theological matters. He admits, however, that he is able to write verse about subjects he cannot discuss in talk or in written prose. The reason is that "The search after poetical expression, the rhyme, and the numbers, are all affairs of some difficulty; they amuse, indeed, but are not to be attained without study, and engross, perhaps, a larger share of the attention than the subject itself. Persons fond of music will sometimes find pleasure in the tune, when the words afford them none."[13] Cowper was much concerned with the "tune" of his poetry in its very specific aspects. "To make verse speak the language of prose, without being prosaic—to marshal the words of it in such an order as they might naturally take in falling from the lips of an exemplary speaker, yet without meanness, harmoniously, elegantly, and without seeming to displace a syllable for the sake of rhyme, is one of the most arduous tasks a poet can undertake."[14] This is, at least in its opening phrases, such an ideal as Wordsworth was to enunciate, and Cowper appears to have pursued it assiduously.

Yet Donald Davie is surely right in maintaining that Cowper's "work is far more the consummation of one tradition than the prelude to another."[15] Mr. Davie points out that the Augustans in general, like Wordsworth, insisted "that the poet had a duty to the spoken language. . . . But for them this requirement, this duty laid upon the poet, was one among many, others being the observance of decorum, the need for compactness, and metrical felicity" (p. 188). Cowper's adverbs in the passage quoted above (*harmoniously, elegantly*) indicate his concern with decorum and "felicity." The extent to which his poetic principles corresponded to those of his contemporaries and predecessors emerges even more vividly in his ideal of "perspicuity." "Blank verse, by the unusual arrangement of the words, and by the frequent infusion of one line into another, not less than by the style, which requires a kind of tragical magnificence, cannot be chargeable with much obscurity,— must rather be singularly perspicuous,—to be so easily comprehended. It is my labour, and my principal one, to be as clear as possible."[16] Again, six years later: "Only remember, that in writing, perspicuity is always more than half the battle: the want of it is the ruin of more than half the poetry that is published. A meaning that does not stare you in the face is as bad as no meaning, because nobody will take the pains to poke for it."[17] Years before, Fénelon had written, "We shou'd use a simple, exact, easy Stile, that lays every thing open to the Reader, and even prevents his Attention. When an Author writes for the Publick, he shou'd take all the Pains imaginable to prevent his Reader's having any."[18] The goal, and the sense of audience which determines it, remain precisely the same at the century's end as at its beginning. The most authoritative

critics of Cowper's own time were unwavering in their advocacy of perspicuity as a prime—perhaps *the* prime— poetic virtue. Lord Kames exposes the logic of their view: "communication of thought being the chief end of language, it is a rule, That perspicuity ought not to be sacrificed to any other beauty whatever."[19] Blair echoes him with greater elaboration and even more emphasis: "Perspicuity, it will be readily admitted, is the fundamental quality of Style; a quality so essential in every kind of writing, that, for the want of it, nothing can atone. . . . This, therefore, must be our first object, to make our meaning clearly and fully understood, and understood without the least difficulty."[20]

For twentieth-century readers, trained to value complexity as an index to poetic merit, such an ideal may seem to promise a dull and obvious sort of poetry. These adjectives, however, do not describe Cowper's best poetic achievement (any more than they describe much of the other poetry written in the service of the same ideal). One may theorize that Cowper was wiser as a poet than as a commentator on poetry, that he did not actually attempt to achieve the goals to which he pays lip service. But the goal of perspicuity itself implies a more complicated critical perception than one may at first realize, for perspicuity can only be achieved through simultaneous awareness of the demands of form and of content: indeed, it specifically implies a union of these concerns. Style, Hugh Blair pointed out, "is a picture of the ideas which rise in [an author's] mind, and of the manner in which they rise there; and, hence, when we are examining an author's composition, it is, in many cases, extremely difficult to separate the Style from the sentiment. . . . Style is nothing else, than that sort of expression which our thoughts most readily assume."[21]

The style most readily assumed by Cowper's thoughts, in *The Task* for example, is fluent and deceptively simple. "I always write as smoothly as I can," he explained to Joseph Johnson; "but . . . I never did, never will, sacrifice the spirit or sense of a passage to the sound of it."[22] On the other hand, he scorned a poet "Too proud for art, and trusting in mere force" (**"Table Talk,"** l. 683) and articulated a poetic ideal involving both form and content:

> Fervency, freedom, fluency of thought,
> Harmony, strength, words exquisitely sought;
> Fancy, that from the bow that spans the sky
> Brings colours, dipt in heav'n, that never die;
> A soul exalted above earth, a mind
> Skill'd in the characters that form mankind . . .
>
> (**"Table Talk,"** ll. 700-705)

This passage on the poetic character develops an elaborate simile of the poet as resembling the sun:

> Like his to shed illuminating rays
> On ev'ry scene and subject it surveys.
>
> (ll. 712-713)

It was not a new comparison: Daniel Webb, for example, had pointed out that "poetry is to the soul, what the sun is to nature; it calls forth, it cherishes, it adorns her beauties."[23] Yet as an instance of Cowper's poetic technique and as a statement of conviction, this description of the poet's gifts is important. Its insistence on metaphors from nature (the rainbow, the sun) is more than accidental: the best examples of Cowper's successful and quite individual fusion of the claims of form and content characteristically develop from his concern with natural imagery. The intellectual progressions recorded in *The Task* depend heavily on the implications of images often presented quite unemphatically.

Cowper's letters sometimes expressed his worry that *The Task* might not immediately reveal its coherence. In a letter to Unwin he supplied his most detailed account of what he considers himself to have achieved in the poem. His defense of his own achievement rests on his expressed belief that his work demonstrates independence of spirit (in its use of his own experience as the sole basis for descriptions both of human and terrestrial nature, and in its "numbers"), authenticity of feeling and, he strongly implies, a rather more "regular" plan than may be immediately apparent. The explanation is worth quoting in full:

> My descriptions are all from nature: not one of them second-handed. My delineations of the heart are from my own experience: not one of them borrowed from books, or in the least degree conjectural. In my numbers, which I have varied as much as I could (for blank verse without variety of numbers is no better than bladder and string), I have imitated nobody, though sometimes perhaps there may be an apparent resemblance; because at the same time that I would not imitate, I have not affectedly differed.
>
> If the work cannot boast a regular plan (in which respect however I do not think it altogether indefensible), it may yet boast, that the reflections are naturally suggested always by the preceding passage, and that except the fifth book, which is rather of a political aspect, the whole has one tendency: to discountenance the modern enthusiasm after a London life, and to recommend rural ease and leisure, as friendly to the cause of piety and virtue.[24]

Cowper here suggests that the unity of *The Task* derives from its consistent recommendation of country over city life, its insistence that "God made the country, and man made the town" ; but he explicitly excepts the "political" fifth book from the general unity of the whole. Yet the fifth book, too, fits into a more subtly articulated pattern of unity than Cowper ever explicitly claimed, a unity derived largely from the reiteration and elaboration of certain sorts of imagery and reference. Examination of the first book—which contains Cowper's announcement of his intentions in the poem along with certain well-known passages of natural description—and the fifth—largely concerned with political and theological issues—may suggest the nature of that unity.

Book I, entitled **"The Sofa,"** begins with a mock-heroic account of the evolution of the sofa. With a rather heavy-handed piece of levity Cowper announces that, having previously sung "Truth, Hope, and Charity," he now proposes to "seek repose upon an humbler theme" (l. 5). The justification for such a concern is merely that "the Fair commands the song" (l. 7); in an accompanying note the author explains the origin of the poem in the arbitrary and fanciful suggestion of Lady Austen. In the succeeding history of the sofa's development, occasional references suggest the possibility of some allegorical connection between the creation of sofas and the creation of poems. Both may be "employed t'accommodate the fair" (l. 73); both may be based on plans simple or elaborate; both may use shepherds or flowers as decoration (see ll. 35-38). And both attain excellence only as a result of slow, hard labor (ll. 83-85). Such connections are merely hinted; their significance emerges gradually.

The transition from consideration of the sofa to presentation of the poet's experience of the natural world involves a rejection of the indoor life associated with diseases resulting from "libertine excess" (l. 106). The speaker, who prefers the outdoors, recounts his memories of the sights and sounds of the country (ll. 109-364); these lead him to reflections on their significance which occupy most of the rest of the first book. The visual perceptions he offers are organized in "scenes."[25] The value of these, the real point of their inclusion, seems to be their effect on the observer rather than any inherent meaning.

> scenes that sooth'd
> Or charm'd me young, no longer young, I find
> Still soothing, and of pow'r to charm me still.
>
> (ll. 141-143)

> Scenes must be beautiful, which, daily view'd,
> Please daily.
>
> (ll. 177-178)

> Now roves the eye;
> And, posted on this speculative height,
> Exults in its command.
>
> (ll. 288-290)

The observer is more important than the phenomena he perceives. In a revealing sequence, Cowper discusses a small cottage which he has named "the peasant's nest" and romantically yearned to inhabit. Considering the possibilities more carefully, he realizes that life in such rural isolation would offer far too many hardships, and concludes

> thou seeming sweet,
> Be still a pleasing object in my view;
> My visit still, but never mine abode.
>
> (ll. 249-251)

To make external reality into a series of pleasing objects in his view seems to be part of Cowper's goal; a partial justification for this procedure is that it does no harm: "the guiltless eye / Commits no wrong, nor wastes what it enjoys" (ll. 333-334).

The reduction of nature to an object of aesthetic perception implies the possibility of a close relation between nature and art; this relation is a significant part of Cowper's subject, although his concern with it sometimes emerges only through his choice of metaphors. His description of rural scenes frequently insists, explicitly or implicitly, on the fact that nature provides "works of art" for contemplation. Like many eighteenth-century poets, Cowper often perceives landscapes as spatially organized like paintings, but he seems more aware than most of what he is doing. A typical passage is full of indications of spatial relationships: *there, here, there, far beyond.* But it also expresses the perceiver's conscious—or almost conscious—pleasure in having discovered a point of view from which nature and people in the natural world can be considered as purely aesthetic phenomena.

> Thence with what pleasure have we just discern'd
> The distant plough slow moving, and beside
> His lab'ring team, that swerv'd not from the track,
> The sturdy swain diminish'd to a boy!
> Here Ouse, slow-winding through a level plain
> Of spacious meads with cattle sprinkled o'er
> Conducts the eye along its sinuous course
> Delighted. There, fast rooted in their bank,
> Stand, never overlook'd, our fav'rite elms,
> That screen the herdsman's solitary hut;
> While far beyond, and overthwart the stream
> That, as with molten glass, inlays the vale,
> The sloping land recedes into the clouds.

>   (ll. 158-171)

The sturdy swain, visually diminished to a boy, therefore need not be considered as a suffering, striving human being. The pleasures of perspective make it unnecessary to contemplate hard realities. (Cowper elsewhere in *The Task* demonstrates some capacity to participate imaginatively in the difficulties of peasant life. He does so clearly from a sense of duty; the pleasure of contemplating peasants depends on thinking of them as children, or as figures in a landscape). Similarly, the cattle, "sprinkled o'er" the spacious meads, are elements of composition, not real animals; even the "lab'ring team" is described with primary emphasis on its participation in a visual pattern ("swerved not from the track"). The Ouse is significant because, like a river in a painting, it can conduct the eye along its sinuous course and thereby "delight" the perceiver. The final metaphor of the stream "inlaying" the vale "as with molten glass" sums up many implications of the passage. The visual joys of nature are thoroughly analogous to those of art; to see the river as resembling a stream of molten glass is to assert its place in an ordered aesthetic whole. This is nature tamed and methodized in a particularly significant way, nature made comprehensible through analogy, subordinated to the aesthetic needs of the observer.

The scenes Cowper describes frequently have this sort of neatness, orderliness—frequently, but by no means always. The first book, however, describes the natural universe almost entirely from the point of view of the connoisseur of art, whose eye orders even the relative confusion of the forest.

> Nor less attractive is the woodland scene,
> Diversified with trees of ev'ry growth,
> Alike, yet various. Here the gray smooth trunks
> Of ash, or lime, or beech, distinctly shine,
> Within the twilight of their distant shades;
> There, lost behind a rising ground . . .

>   (ll. 300-305)

Once more we have the *here-there* organization; Cowper asserts confidently, "No tree in all the grove but has its charms" (l. 307), and then specifies with sharp visual detail the individual attractions of each, providing a brilliant objectification of that Augustan ideal of "order in variety" hinted by the opening lines of the passage. He can perceive the panorama of hill and valley between wood and water as "a spacious map" (l. 321) with no implied deprecation of its beauty: the fact that it is describable in terms of human achievement suggests its praiseworthy orderliness. The effect of this reference to nature as a map is at the opposite pole from that of Smart's "All scenes of painting crowd the map / Of nature," which dramatizes the poet's impression of an overflowingly rich universe, in which the distinction between the works of God and those of man becomes finally irrelevant. Cowper's metaphor describes a world in which the human need for perceptual order is dominant.

"The love of Nature, and the scene she draws, / Is Nature's dictate," Cowper observes (ll. 412-413) in one of his most explicit uses of the analogy between nature and art. The purpose of the analogy is to insist on the superiority of nature to art:

> Strange! there should be found, . . .
> Who, satisfied with only pencil'd scenes,
> Prefer to the performance of a God
> Th' inferior wonders of an artist's hand!
> Lovely indeed the mimic works of art;
> But Nature's works far lovelier.

>   (ll. 413-421)

Cowper offers a standard argument for the greater loveliness of nature: painting pleases only the eye, "sweet Nature ev'ry sense" (l. 427). But this is only a superficial justification for a preference which is in fact the key to the structure and meaning of the first book and in a sense of the poem as a whole.

The more profound significance of the poet's belief in the aesthetic superiority of nature to art emerges only gradually, although it is implicit even in the early natural descriptions. Immediately after his direct statement that nature's works are lovelier than man's—in the same verse paragraph—Cowper begins exploring the aesthetic principle of contrast which had interested Thomson and Akenside. The prisoner, the invalid, the sailor deprived of sight of land: these appreciate the "feast" spread by nature (l. 433) more than can men to whom that feast is constantly available. (In the case of the sailor, longing for the beauty of nature brings about his destruction: looking into the ocean he sees "visions prompted by intense desire" [l. 451], visions of the fields he has left behind; seeking those fields, he plunges to his death. The destructive agent is not nature but his own imagination. The dangers of fancy are an important subordinate theme of ***The Task***.) Earlier, Cowper had pointed out the principle of contrast operating in other areas: nature herself subsists by constant change (ll. 367-384); man gains the greatest goods through alternation of activity and rest. "Measure life / By its true worth, the comforts it affords," the poet commands (ll. 396-397); then one perceives that only through contrast can genuine pleasure be achieved.

The greatest pleasure for Cowper is unquestionably aesthetic contemplation, contemplation as an observer. Actual participation in life is dangerous and debilitating; life can become "A peddler's pack, that bows the bearer down" (l. 465); men cling to it although it is essentially meaningless, long for society through mere dread of solitude. Cowper's images of all but peasant life are characteristically images of deprivation and desperation. To the horrors of the urban life which, through its very gaiety, "fills the bones with pain, / The mouth with blasphemy, the heart with woe" (ll. 504-505), the poet opposes, once more, his vision of nature as essentially designed for human contemplation:

> The earth was made so various, that the mind
> Of desultory man, studious of change,
> And pleas'd with novelty, might be indulg'd.
>
> (ll. 506-508)

The principle of change and contrast in nature seems now to exist to fulfill man's aesthetic needs: man may become bored with individual "prospects," but other prospects always exist; he may contemplate landscapes interrupted by hedges which provide visual variety; the shapeless gorse offers "ornaments of gold" (l. 529) made more pleasing because opposed to the "deform'd" (l. 527) bush itself.

In the last third of the first book, nature as aesthetic object is not so important. The organization of episodes now begins to seem relatively random; yet subterraneously the same theme remains dominant: the theme of nature's importance as an object of contemplation and a source of the comforts life affords, its superiority in these respects to human art and artifice. We learn about crazy Kate, whose insanity results from an over-active fancy (ll. 534-556); then about the gypsies, lazy and immoral, who none the less enjoy "health and gaiety of heart" (l. 587), direct results of their contact with nature. Then comes, rather surprisingly, an extended passage of praise for civilization (ll. 592-677), in the course of which Cowper considers the limitations of the "noble savage." Finally the book moves into its lengthy denunciation of cities (a denunciation which, however, painstakingly accords credit to urban achievement) and its ultimate praise of the superiority of country life (ll. 678-774).

The need to record the glories of civilization seems to come, in the context, from recognition of the fact that man is, after all, by necessity, a being who must act as well as contemplate. In the first two-thirds of this book, Cowper has insisted upon the value of nature to man, who is the passive recipient of what it has to offer. Partly through reiterated analogies between nature and art, he has stressed the inferiority of art to nature as an object of contemplation, the aesthetic value of nature, the moral innocence of "nature appreciation," the importance of the physical and mental health which nature offers man as recipient. As long as man *sees* rather than *does,* he is secure; he may even be happy, gaining the "comforts" by which the value of life is to be judged. On the other hand, there have also been hints of darker possibility. The sailor is killed, Kate crazed as a result of the operations of fancy. The gypsies steal; as *doers* they are unattractive, though blessed as recipients of nature's power. And we have had a somber sketch of those who give their lives to the pursuit of pleasure in a social environment: a pursuit which makes life empty, valueless. On the other hand, Cowper has asserted the value of "strenuous toil"—but only because it provides, by contrast, "sweetest ease" (l. 388).

In the context of the values implied, Cowper faces a dilemma when he begins to consider the possibility of man's acting positively rather than negatively. In what context can man act properly; and what, precisely, is the relation between action and contemplation? Does action necessarily result in that "sinking" of comfort which the poet so deeply dreads? Only civilization, Cowper concludes, makes possible true and consistent virtue in action. "Here virtue thrives as in her proper soil" (l. 600): repeated uses of natural analogy insist that the patterns of nature are the models to man. Thus civilized virtue is "By culture tam'd, by liberty refresh'd / And all her fruits by radiant truth matur'd" (ll. 606-607). It tends to exist only in temperate climates; the inhabitant of the frozen north feels "severe constraint" (l. 612), and—more interestingly—residents of tropic isles

> Can boast but little virtue; and inert
> Through plenty, lose in morals what they gain
> In manners—victims of luxurious ease.
> These therefore I can pity, plac'd remote
> From all that science traces, art invents,
> Or inspiration teaches.
>
> (ll. 623-628)

The distaste for the inertness of ease and of over-constraint, the admiration for the accomplishments of science and art—these are standard eighteenth-century attitudes, associated with belief in the doctrine of progress. They are not, however, really compatible with Cowper's more fundamental convictions, and his uneasiness with them soon emerges through his expressed consciousness of the gap between the ideal of progress and the actuality. Ideally, civilized virtue is "gentle, kind" (l. 605). Actually, it is Omai, the South Sea Islander, who is gentle—and he is a "gentle savage" (l. 633). The real result of civilization is

> With what superior skill we can abuse
> The gifts of Providence, and squander life.
>
> (ll. 637-638)

"Doing good, / Disinterested good, is not our trade," Cowper explains (ll. 673-674); the conflict between commercial and moral values is fundamental and unalterable. Lacking such conflicts, the South Sea Islander, despite his lack also of civilized graces, seems in all his passivity the moral superior of the energetic Englishman. Like Wordsworth, who advocated a "wise passiveness" toward nature, unlike Thomson, who felt obliged to condemn such passivity as "indolence," Cowper seems to feel the passive relation to nature as an ideal state of being. Indeed, in one of his letters he suggests that man can achieve even active virtue only in a state of nature. "I accede most readily to the justice of your remark on the subject of the truly Roman heroism of the Sandwich islanders," he wrote John Newton. "Proofs of such prowess, I believe, are seldom exhibited by a people who have attained to a high degree of civilization. Refinement and profligacy of principle are too nearly allied, to admit of any thing so noble."[26]

Cowper insists on a distinction between the "civilization" of cities—characterized by "refinement"—and that of the country. Virtue thrives "in the mild / And genial soil of cultivated life" (ll. 678-679)—"Yet not in cities oft" (l. 681), to which flow, as to a sewer, "The dregs and feculence of ev'ry land" (l. 683). In one respect alone are cities truly praiseworthy: they are "nurs'ries of the arts" (l. 693). The poet praises Joshua Reynolds—who can turn "a dull blank" into "A lucid mirror, in which Nature sees / All her reflected features" (ll. 700-702)—the sculptor John Bacon, and the powers of sculpture in general. He also appears to admire the achievements of "philosophy" and of commerce—although his comparison of London as the thriving mart of commerce with ancient Babylon, the city of captivity, qualifies the positive implications of his presentation. His damnation of London is far more emphatic than his praise; it centers on the evils of urban activity, the injustice and hypocrisies of a life where "civilized" forms have quite replaced moral content.

The argument of the first book is now complete: Cowper has both asserted and demonstrated the value of aesthetic contemplation of the natural world; he has opposed to his insistence on nature's aesthetic value an equally clear awareness of the dangers of participation in worldly activity. He has suggested repeatedly that art is necessarily inferior to nature, although art provides useful analogies for the understanding of nature—and nature for the proper appreciation of art. And he has hinted that commitment to the life of imagination may be dangerous: the perception through which man sees, the memory with which he recalls satisfying sights, the judgment with which he guards against moral danger—all these human faculties are more unambiguously valuable than the fancy. The final lines of the book, beginning, "God made the country, and man made the town," sum up these implications.

> What wonder then that health and virtue, gifts
> That can alone make sweet the bitter draught
> That life holds out to all, should most abound
> And least be threaten'd in the fields and groves?
>
> (ll. 750-753)

Nature's lack of threat to passive man is as significant a value as her more positive virtues. But the ultimate value is once more aesthetic. Cowper abandons city-dwellers to their own element: they "taste no scenes / But such as art contrives" (ll. 756-757). Then he returns to the "scenes" which interest him more, the groves and birds and moonlight of the country, whose aesthetic appeal is now systematically contrasted with that achieved by human art and artifice. The conclusion strikes a strong moral note:

> Folly such as your's,
> Grac'd with a sword, and worthier of a fan,
> Has made, what enemies could ne'er have done,
> Our arch of empire, stedfast but for you,
> A multilated structure, soon to fall.
>
> (ll. 770-774)

This final condemnation of those who live in cities is justified by reference to no sin more serious than their preference of opera singers to birds, lamplight to moonlight. In Cowper's ethical system, however, such lapses of judgment, such willing acceptance of inferior sorts of perception, amount to genuine moral failing. He has not yet fully revealed the basis for his consistent association of strong perceptual response to nature with moral uprightness; it emerges completely in the fifth book, paradoxically one of the sections of the poem least obviously concerned with nature.

Book V, despite its title (**"The Winter Morning Walk"**), is a record primarily of man reflecting rather than man perceiving. It begins with a hundred and seventy-five lines of description and meditation on nature and man in nature, but the succeeding seven hundred and thirty lines virtually abandon nature as subject. Yet the problem of perception is once more central to the argument of the book, although liberty and permanence are the subjects which most clearly unify the poet's concerns.

The opening lines present a direct record of perception, visual awareness modulating imperceptibly into moral. The sun, at first an image of great power, loses force as it rises. First "with ruddy orb / Ascending, [it] fires th'horizon" (ll. 1-2); the regal associations of *orb* support the sense of potency in the image of the sun "firing" the whole horizon. By line 4, the sun is no longer an orb, but merely a disk. Two lines later, "his slanting ray / Slides ineffectual down the snowy vale" (ll. 6-7); with an increasing sense of the sun's ineffectuality we learn that now its power consists merely in "tinging all with his own rosy hue" (l. 8)—a considerable falling-off, both visually and conceptually, from the energy which fired the horizon. Finally, the sun creates shadows; the observer in the scene is thus united with "ev'ry herb and ev'ry spiry blade" (l. 9), which, like him, cast their shadows. When the human participant in the natural scene reflects on the import of his shadow he announces, with surprising levity, one of the major themes of this book. The relative impermanence of man and his achievements will come to seem more and more important as the book proceeds; here, on the other hand, the poet's verbal attempt to assert his own transience is immediately counteracted by the enduring reality of nature, which seems infinitely more significant. The transience of man is almost a joke; recognition of it coincides with awareness of the visual grotesqueness of the shadow's transformation of well-proportioned limb to lean shank.

> Mine, spindling into longitude immense,
> In spite of gravity, and sage remark
> That I myself am but a fleeting shade,
> Provokes me to a smile. With eye askance
> I view the muscular proportion'd limb
> Transform'd to a lean shank.

(ll. 11-16)

The observer, perceiving the natural world sharply, feels himself essentially a part of that world; his abstract awareness that he is "but a fleeting shade" is far less compelling than the comic visual reality of distorting shadow, and the pleasure derived from perception of that reality.

The revelatory power of nature is important throughout this description.

> the bents,
> And coarser grass, upspearing o'er the rest,
> Of late unsightly and unseen, now shine
> Conspicuous, and, in bright apparel clad
> And fledg'd with icy feathers, nod superb.

(ll. 22-26)

Frost makes the unseen seeable, the unsightly beautiful. This natural power is meaningful not, as in Thomson, primarily for the kind of energy it manifests, but for the transformed world it displays. The display implies the great kinships of nature—weeds metaphorically unite with men by being "clad" in "apparel," with birds by being "fledged with . . . feathers"—but its chief impact is visual. Similarly, as the vignette continues, it directs our attention chiefly to the visual effect of mourning cattle, working man, scampering dog, and only secondarily to the implications of order and permanence in the description of the haystack, for example, or even of the woodman moving "right toward the mark" (l. 53).

Reflection about what happens to various kinds of animals and insects in winter leads Cowper to the two central images of Book V: the frozen surroundings of the waterfall and the ice palace of Empress Anna of Russia. The waterfall itself is too forceful to be "bound" by frost, but the mist it throws off freezes into fantastic and compelling forms. "See," the poet commands, with Thomsonian emphasis,

> where it [the frost] has hung th' embroider'd banks
> With forms so various, that no pow'rs of art,
> The pencil or the pen, may trace the same!

(ll. 107-109)

Once more the specific "scene" raises the issue of nature's relation to art; once more Cowper insists that neither the painter nor the poet can capture the beauty of natural real-

ity. Art is clearly inadequate as the "mirror" of nature; if it aspires to mirror, it must fail. (Elsewhere in the poem, Cowper explains that the mind of the artist is a mirror, and that the responsibility of the poet is

> T'arrest the fleeting images that fill
> The mirror of the mind, and hold them fast,
> And force them sit till he has pencil'd off
> A faithful likeness of the forms he views.

[II, 290-293]

Art—specifically poetry—may provide a mirror for nature, but in a moral, not an aesthetic sense; Cowper describes his "stream" of poetry as "reflecting clear, / If not the virtues, yet the worth, of brutes" [VI, 723-724].) Continuing to describe the wonders of the frozen landscape, Cowper concentrates on suggestion more than precise visual detail: "Here grotto within grotto safe defies / The sunbeam" (ll. 117-118). The reader is invited to consider the significance, the mystery of the frost's achievement as well as to "see" its manifestations. And the poet concludes his treatment of this magical creation with yet another extended and emphatic statement of nature's superiority to art:

> Thus nature works as if to mock at art,
> And in defiance of her rival pow'rs;
> By these fortuitous and random strokes
> Performing such inimitable feats
> As she with all her rules can never reach.

(ll. 122-126)

Gone is Pope's sense of the essential, inevitable harmony between art and nature; now the two are "rival powers," with nature clearly the victor. Nature's aesthetic superiority to art is clearly explained:

> The growing wonder takes a thousand shapes
> Capricious, in which fancy seeks in vain
> The likeness of some object seen before.

(ll. 119-121)

The fancy, the human creative power which produces art, is limited, Locke had explained, to forming new combinations or interpretations of objects (or parts of objects) previously perceived. It cannot create anything entirely new, completely unrelated to earlier perception. Nature as artist, on the other hand, suffers from no such limitation: its creations bear no likeness to any object seen before. Only nature can provide new material for fancy to work upon. The perceptual grounds for its aesthetic superiority to art are perfectly apparent.

The man-made ice palace contrasted with the nature-created grottoes also offers aesthetic appeals—despite the fact that it is "less worthy of applause, though more admir'd" (l. 126). Its attractiveness, however, derives largely from the illusion it creates of permanence and accordingly of man's dominance over nature.

> though smooth
> And slipp'ry the materials, yet frost-bound

Firm as a rock. Nor wanted aught within,
That royal residence might well befit,
For grandeur or for use.

(ll. 154-158)

But it is, after all, a "brittle prodigy" (l. 154); the moral satisfaction of considering its "evanescent glory, once a stream, / And soon to slide into a stream again" (ll. 167-168) counteracts the aesthetic satisfaction of contemplating its apparent permanence and order. "In such a palace Poetry might place / The armory of Winter" (ll. 138-139), Cowper observes; this idea causes him to consider the power of winter, which produces "snow, that often blinds the trav'ler's course, And wraps him in an unexpected tomb" (ll. 142-143). No human structure adequately contains the menace of winter; if the lamps within the palace seem "Another moon new risen, or meteor fall'n / From heav'n to earth, of lambent flame serene" (ll. 152-153), it is only by an illusion of human perception. The apparently successful manipulation of nature by man is temporary, soon to vanish, offering but the pretence of permanence.

The complex combination of immediately perceived solidity with intellectually recognized evanescence makes the ice palace the type of all human achievement; for this reason it provides an underlying metaphor throughout the rest of Book V. Its metaphoric value is underlined at the end of the description:

Alas; 'twas but a mortifying stroke
Of undesign'd serenity, that glanc'd
(Made by a monarch) on her own estate,
On human grandeur and the courts of kings.
'Twas transient in its nature, as in show
'Twas durable.

(ll. 169-174)

The "mortifying stroke" is the palace's sliding back into a stream. The palace is the emblem of princely endeavor, which may struggle for dominance "by pyramids and mausolean pomp" (l. 182), by building; or by destroying, provoking wars in which kings make "the sorrows of mankind their sport" (l. 186). The desire of kings to assert their power in tangible form causes war, but war originated, Cowper explains, in man's attempt to extend his dominance over nature, when he "had begun to call / These meadows and that range of hills his own" (ll. 222-223). Continuing his discussion of warfare and of the presumption of kings, the poet defines the king's pride: it consists in thinking "the world was made in vain, if not for him" (l. 271). Man persists in believing that he is in some real sense master of the natural world; it is an odd corollary that he should believe that some are fit to be masters of others, even though a king is a man

Compounded and made up like other men
Of elements tumultuous, in whom lust
And folly in as ample measure meet
As in the bosoms of the slaves he rules.

(ll. 307-310)

So it is that man loses his freedom in his political institutions: through a misinterpretation of his own humble position in the universe which remotely parallels the misinterpretation involved in believing an ice palace to be permanent or its lights to be equivalent to the moon.

We are not directly reminded of the ice palace, however, until the very end of the discussion of political liberty, when Cowper returns to the metaphor of building:

We turn to dust, and all our mightiest works
Die too: . . .
We build with what we deem eternal rock:
A distant age asks where the fabric stood.

(ll. 531-532, 534-535)

The state itself can be described as an "old castle" (l. 525); the entire issue of political liberty is evanescent as the ice palace in comparison with the far more fundamental problem of spiritual liberty which Cowper next considers.

The essence of spiritual liberty is its permanence, in comparison with which nature itself seems transient. In His visible works, God,

finding an interminable space
Unoccupied, has fill'd the void so well,
And made so sparkling what was dark before.
But these are not his glory.

(ll. 556-559)

On aesthetic grounds, man supposes that "so fair a scene" (l. 560) must be eternal—as he supposes the permanence of the ice palace on the basis of visual evidence (the adjective *sparkling,* like *glitter* in the lines quoted below, may remind one of the connection between the two phenomena). Yet nature, considered in terms of the divine plan, is merely another sort of artifice, the product of an "artificer divine" (l. 561) who has Himself "pronounc'd it transient, glorious as it is" (l. 563) because He values spiritual, not physical, permanence. Cowper's values are similar; he elaborates for almost two hundred lines on the value, the essentiality, of spiritual liberty. Yet the resolution of the discussion of spiritual freedom accepts once more the profound aesthetic value of nature, and makes the ability to perceive this value a touchstone of one's spiritual state.

He is the freeman whom the truth makes free,
And all are slaves beside. . . .
He looks abroad into the varied field
Of nature, and, though poor perhaps compar'd
With those whose mansions glitter in his sight,
Calls the delightful scen'ry all his own. . . .
Are they not his by a peculiar right,
And by an emphasis of int'rest his,
Whose eye they fill with tears of holy joy,
Whose heart with praise, and whose exalted mind
With worthy thoughts of that unwearied love
That plann'd, and built, and still upholds, a world
So cloth'd with beauty for rebellious man?

(ll. 733-734, 738-741, 748-754)

The beauty of the world is God's special gift to man; visual "possession" of "delightful scenery" is more valuable than wealth. Moreover, true aesthetic response to nature depends on a proper relation with God:

> Acquaint thyself with God, if thou would'st taste
> His works. Admitted once to his embrace,
> Thou shalt perceive that thou wast blind before:
> Thine eye shall be instructed; and thine heart,
> Made pure, shall relish, with divine delight
> Till then unfelt, what hands divine have wrought.
>
> (ll. 779-784)

Understanding of God's dominance over nature (in contrast to the false belief in man's control of nature) produces the perception which distinguishes men from brutes (see ll. 785-790), gives the soul "new faculties" (l. 806) which enable it to discern "in all things, what, with stupid gaze / Of ignorance, till then she overlook'd" (ll. 808-809). When man holds converse with the stars, the special significance of the "shining hosts" (l. 822) is that they "view / Distinctly scenes invisible to man" (ll. 825-826); heightened perception is a metaphysical goal. The "lamp of truth" enables man to "read" nature (l. 845); and liberty itself "like day, / Breaks on the soul, and by a flash from heav'n / Fires all the faculties with glorious joy" (ll. 883-885).

> In that blest moment Nature, throwing wide
> Her veil opaque, discloses with a smile
> The author of her beauties, who, retir'd
> Behind his own creation, works unseen
> By the impure.
>
> (ll. 891-895)

If God is the source of proper perception, He is also the *end* of perception: this is the final word of Book V. The fired faculties which liberty creates lead man ultimately to God, healing the potential and sometimes actual split felt between God and nature as objects of contemplation. The poignant story which Cowper tells in his *Memoir* is well-known: how, exalted and soothed by contemplation of a marine sunset, he was subsequently overwhelmed with guilt at the realization that he had sinfully attributed to the power of nature the psychological healing that could only be due to the power of God. In the logic of Book V of *The Task* such distinctions virtually disappear—not because nature and God are identical ("Nature is but a name for an effect, Whose cause is God" [VI, 223-224]), but because the ability to perceive nature is the result of a proper relation with God, and the heightening of faculties which makes possible an enlightened aesthetic response to nature also produces an awareness of how God expresses Himself through nature. The ability to appreciate the "scenes" which nature provides becomes thus virtually a test of one's spiritual condition; the belief in the aesthetic superiority of nature to art is not a matter merely of personal response, but a product of the realization that nature has intrinsic significance which no work of art can achieve. Elsewhere in *The Task,* some of the most compelling passages of natural description attempt to define and

delineate this significance. The substructure which justifies such attempts is probably most apparent in Book V, itself comparatively bare of description.

For Cowper, then, the act of visual perception, which had provided subject matter and metaphors for poets throughout the eighteenth-century development of the poetry of image rather than action, finally takes on metaphysical importance. Thomson had attempted to "see" significance as well as appearance, Collins had "seen" into a realm of fantasy as well as of reality, Gray had used contrasting "visions" to create a poetry of tension, Smart had seen the natural world and then gone beyond his own seeing to establish connections with a realm of transcendental truth. For Cowper the seeing itself implied the transcendental truth; the physical power of vision became a spiritual reality.

Donald Davie has remarked of Cowper that he is, "after Ben Jonson, . . . the most neglected of our poets."[27] The neglect is of analysis rather than simply of attention: Cowper has been written about voluminously—as a psychological case, as a representative of piety, as a phenomenon of his century. Few critics, however, have made any serious attempt to examine the source or nature of his poetic effects; those who have tried to describe his poetry often take so large a view that all possibility of accuracy vanishes. Thus we are told, for example, that *The Task* resembles the conversation of one dowered with no special gifts of intellect; of an interesting quiet man, of humour and austerity with an intensely human hand-grip.[28] Alternately, its form, "remarquable par sa simplicité audacieuse," is that of fragments of a journal.[29] "To Cowper," another critic observes, "nature is simply a background, . . . essentially a *locus in quo*—a space in which the work and mirth of life pass and are performed."[30] Or we are informed that "his intuition was comparatively superficial, if disinterested, because he never strove to discipline ideas to facts or to interpret facts ideally, but only to invest them with sentiment or reflect upon them."[31] All such statements seem plausible when one considers *The Task* casually as a whole; all lose their plausibility if closely examined in relation to specific passages, which reveal at least a potential unity far more rigorous than that of a conversation or a journal, demonstrate the fundamental importance of nature not as a *locus in quo* but as an object of contemplation, and suggest that Cowper at his best characteristically "interpret[s] facts ideally." It is extremely difficult to generalize accurately about *The Task* because although, as I have attempted to show, an underlying structure of ideas does in fact unify many of its apparently disparate concerns, it remains a poem of details, details which depend upon varied techniques and apparent preoccupations. The poem's variety is particularly confusing with regard to its language. The diction of *The Task* ranges from "poetic" to colloquial, from abstract to concrete, apparently depending on many different principles of control. The magnitude of the poet's concerns emerges vividly through examination of his language.

The prevailing critical attitude toward the diction of *The Task* has been that it is remarkable for its "plainness." In Cowper's own time plainness was thought to be one of his chief poetic merits; thus a reviewer of his first volume observes: "Anxious only to give each image its due prominence and relief, he has wasted no unnecessary attention on grace and embellishment; his language, therefore, though neither strikingly harmonious nor elegant, is plain, forcible, and expressive."[32] Specifically with regard to *The Task,* another of Cowper's contemporaries, remarking "the familiarity of the diction,"[34] observes, "The language may sometimes appear below the poetical standard; but he was such a foe to affectation in any shape, that he seems to have avoided nothing so much as the stiff pomposity so common to blank verse writers."[33] More modern critics have echoed this view: "the language is of the purest and finest, but it is not strikingly ornamented. It is without anything unusual in poetic diction."[34] And Thomas Quayle singles out "the moral and didactic portions" as characterized by language "as a rule, uniformly simple and direct."[35]

Yet these judgments, too, seem perplexing when one examines specific passages of *The Task* to find Cowper writing, "The verdure of the plain lies buried deep / Beneath the dazzling deluge" (V, 21-22), or—for a more extended example—

> Now from the roost, or from the neighb'ring pale,
> Where, diligent to catch the first faint gleam
> Of smiling day, they gossip'd side by side,
> Come trooping at the housewife's well-known call
> The feather'd tribes domestic. Half on wing,
> And half on foot, they brush the fleecy flood,
> Conscious, and fearful of too deep a plunge.
> The sparrows peep, and quit the shelt'ring eaves
> To seize the fair occasion. Well they eye
> The scatter'd grain; and, thievishly resolv'd
> T'escape the' impending famine, often scar'd,
> As oft return—a pert voracious kind.
>
> (V, 58-69)

This is part of the opening description of man, animals and vegetation in a winter landscape. It is not, in its diction, fully characteristic of Cowper's technique, but it demonstrates the dexterity with which the poet turns varied conventions to personal use.

In language and in sentence structure, these lines seem to come from the mid, not the late, eighteenth century. The pseudo-Miltonic inversions, such Thomsonian formulations as "the feather'd tribes domestic," the unrealized personification of "smiling day," the automatic phrase, "the fair occasion," the periphrases of "fleecy flood," "feather'd tribes," "pert voracious kind": all these belong to well-established poetic patterns—patterns which we might expect Cowper to avoid. They seem to be used for familiar reasons: to establish metaphoric links between man and lower forms of nature which will reinforce the reader's sense of some vast natural harmony. One may note Cowper's accuracy of perception in such phrases as

"half on wing / And half on foot," or the vividness of "brush" (in "they brush the fleecy flood"), the figurative appropriateness of "gossip'd"; still, the impression remains that the passage as a whole is almost pure convention, in language and in concept.

To understand its function in *The Task* one must turn to its context, which significantly modifies the effect of the lines considered in isolation. A few lines taken from either side of the description of the birds may suggest the nature of that context. The first of these passages focuses on an individual animal, sharply perceived in his separateness; the second, although it too is rich in specific detail, is more general. The first makes emphatic use of inversion, and offers the Thomsonian "wide-scamp'ring"; the second has no striking structural peculiarities and its diction provides no special associations. Yet these two descriptions resemble one another far more than they resemble the description of domestic fowl. The voice that speaks in them, although it is not emphatically distinctive, is none the less individual in comparison to that which speaks of a "fleecy flood." One sees here the effect of an eye trained steadfastly upon the object, a mind concerned to discriminate and to define not on the basis of relationships or of categories ("kinds") but in terms of specific individual perceptions.

> Shaggy, and lean, and shrewd, with pointed ears
> And tail cropp'd short, half lurcher and half cur—
> His dog attends him. Close behind his heel
> Now creeps he slow; and now, with many a frisk
> Wide-scamp'ring, snatches up the drifted snow
> With iv'ry teeth, or ploughs it with his snout;
> Then shakes his powder'd coat, and barks for joy.
>
> (V, 45-51)
>
> The very rooks and daws forsake the fields,
> Where neither grub, nor root, nor earth-nut, now
> Repays their labour more; and, perch'd aloft
> By the wayside, or stalking in the path,
> Lean pensioners upon the trav'ler's track,
> Pick up their nauseous dole, though sweet to them,
> Of voided pulse or half-digested grain.
> The streams are lost amid the splendid blank,
> O'erwhelming all distinction.
>
> (V, 89-97)

The lines beginning with allusion to the rooks and daws deal with transformations effected by winter, and with the resulting paradoxes: birds forsake their "natural" habitat for traveled roads; the "nauseous dole" voided by the travelers is "sweet to them"; winter creates a "splendid blank, / O'erwhelming all distinction," while the poet insists precisely on the distinctions of the chill landscape. The passage on the dog, with its emphasis on energetic verbs (*snatches, ploughs, shakes, barks*; the noun *frisk* and the participle *wide-scamp'ring* also suggest the energy of action), dramatizes the way in which the power of winter may inform the animal kingdom: if it immobilizes water, it intensely animates dogs.

Each of the three passages, then, represents a different way, almost a different principle, of "seeing." The eye focuses on an individual phenomenon in the lines about the dog, discriminates the details of the animal's appearance ("Shaggy, and lean, and shrewd, with pointed ears / And tail cropp'd short"), then moves on to contemplate the exact nature of his activity. The language of the description is "plain," generally direct, heavily Anglo-Saxon. Interpretation is kept to a minimum, suggested only by the adjective *shrewd* and the phrase "barks for joy"; the scene is self- sufficient, containing its meaning in its details. One sentence is simple, one compound; the coordinate conjunction *and,* occurring six times in the seven lines, is vital in establishing relationships.

In the passage about rooks and daws, a single, elaborate complex sentence occupies seven of the nine lines; the increased complexity of structure is paralleled by heightened dignity of tone. Although direct, simple description remains important, with the plain diction appropriate to it, Latinate words now assume a more significant rôle. They convey the interpretive judgment of the author in such key terms as *labour, pensioners, nauseous, splendid, distinction.* Meaning as well as appearance is important here; this fact accounts for the heightened dignity of language and structure. The central paradox that privation and beauty are by winter mysteriously connected, a paradox embodied in the phrase "splendid blank," is elaborated both through the specificity with which Cowper details the nature of privation and its compensations and through the generality of his final descriptive allusion to the snow which covers everything.

The heavy stress on established poetic diction in the section on domestic fowl does not obscure the clarity of the poet's observation any more than does the complexity of structure or the relative elevation of language in the lines on rooks and daws. Here, though, the principle of "seeing" is to place observed details in the context a tradition, to remind the reader of eternal rather than immediate patterns, to insist on the fundamental kinships of the universe. The descriptive emphasis is on characterization, the special personality of these birds. But unlike the dog's "personality," which is conceived as his specifically animal nature, the character of the birds is at least analogically human: they "gossip," "troop," compose "domestic" tribes, are "conscious, and fearful," sensitive to the "fair occasion," capable of being "thievish." Winter, which increases the dependency of the animal kingdom on man, increases as a consequence human awareness of the links that bind all creation, so that analogies between the look of sheep and of snow, the nature of chickens and of the housewife who feeds them, or between sparrows and children (this barely suggested: but children too might under some circumstances be defined as a "pert voracious kind," although this was not the typical eighteenth-century view of them), take on true significance.

These three modes of "seeing" the panoramas which winter presents, with the dictions appropriate to each mode, suggest how functional Cowper's varieties of perspective and technique can prove. In the early descriptive section of Book V, the poet demonstrates the nature of that true perception which by the end of the book he will assert to be a product of man's right relationship with God. True perception does not depend on anything so simple as constant assertion of the connections between God and His creation, but it does involve completeness, wholeness of vision. Such wholeness is the sum of many parts, many incomplete visions; in this long descriptive portion of his poem, Cowper isolates and emphasizes various ways of seeing in a fashion that may prepare us to believe in the significance of their combination. His variations of technique reflect quite precisely the shifts in emphasis of his subject matter.

One cannot always believe that Cowper's diction conforms exactly to the meanings it is intended to convey. His verse seems dependably good when its content is descriptive, its subject that perception which Cowper found both emotionally and philosophically so important. Large portions of **The Task,** however, are moralistic rather than descriptive; nor does the moralizing always resolve itself, as in Book V, in terms of the poet's commitment to the value of perception. Book II, **"The Time-Piece,"** for example, contains no extended treatment of the external world; it is entirely reflective. Although it includes sections of great vigor and poetic skill, it also displays Cowper at his worst—and his "worst" is characteristically his most rhetorical.

Considering two particularly weak passages, we may find it hard to understand why either of them should be poetry rather than prose. By Coleridge's well-known standard ("whatever lines can be translated into other words of the same language, without diminution of their significance, either in sense, or association, or in any worthy feeling, are so far vicious in their diction"),[36] most of these lines are excellent examples of "vicious diction," in spite of the fact that, with some exceptions, the diction does not call special attention to itself. In the first passage, Cowper considers the institution of preaching; the second deals with an individual exemplar of the institution. Both treatments may be the product of deep conviction, but it is not embodied in any way likely to move a reader. "Men love to be moved, much better than to be instructed," Joseph Warton pointed out;[37] Cowper's calculated rhetoric is only "instructive." Here are the passages:

> The pulpit, therefore (and I name it fill'd
> With solemn awe, that bids me well beware
> With what intent I touch that holy thing)
> The pulpit (when the sat'rist has at last,
> Strutting and vap'ring in an empty school,
> Spent all his force and made no proselyte)
> I say the pulpit (in the sober use
> Of its legitimate, peculiar pow'rs)
> Must stand acknowledged, while the world
> shall stand,
> The most important and effectual guard,
> Support, and ornament, of virtue's cause.

> (II. 326-336)

The second selection describes the bad pastor,

Perverting often, by the stress of lewd
And loose example, whom he should instruct;
[he] Exposes, and holds up to broad disgrace
The noblest function, and discredits much
The brightest truths that man has ever seen.
For ghostly counsel; if it either fall
Below the exigence, or be not back'd
With show of love, at least with hopeful proof
Of some sincerity on th' giver's part;
Or be dishonour'd, in th'exterior form
And mode of its conveyance, by such tricks
As move derision, or by foppish airs
And histrionic mumm'ry, that let down
The pulpit to the level of the stage;
Drops from the lips a disregarded thing.

(II. 551-565)

The repeated, self-conscious parentheses of the first passage, the artifice of the reiterated phrase "the pulpit," which
produces an inadvertent comic effect, the factitious-
seeming indignation in the denunciation of the satirist, the
padding in such phrases as "solemn awe" and "well
beware," even the relatively skillful play on *stand*—all
these contribute to one's sense that the poet as contriver
has here superseded the poet as expresser of felt, perceived
or imagined reality. The passage has almost the effect of
parody. One believes in the existence of the felt reality,
but not that Cowper is committed to it; his obvious concern
with the proper mode of expression seems strangely
isolated from what he has to say, seems not a concern for
the best way to convey emotion or meaning so much as
for the moral posture appropriate to a man of his convictions. In the second passage, the moral posture itself seems
suspect: is "*show* of love," with its conceivable implication of hypocrisy, really adequate for the "good" pastor?
Or is merely "hopeful proof / Of some sincerity"? The
poet concerns himself almost entirely with appearances,
with what he himself calls "th' exterior form / And mode
of . . . . conveyance" of divine truths; yet he appears to
make a distinction between exterior forms and what he
evidently considers inner reality—reality demonstrated by
"show of love" of "proof / Of some sincerity." In the actual
concerns of the passage, then, form and content blur, and
exterior forms assume disproportionate importance—just
such importance as they seem to assume in the poetic
rendering of the ideas, which itself has some aspect of
"histrionic mumm'ry." The language of the passage, with
the possible exception of the word *exigence,* is quite
ordinary and straightforward; its structure, with its deliberate slowness and suspension, moving with measured pace
toward the calculated anticlimax of "disregarded thing,"
seems anything but straight forward, and its contrived
complexity reflects no corresponding complexity of
thought.

One striking fact about the relatively weak moralistic sections of *The Task* is that they are so radically different in
technique from the worst of Cowper's hymns. If the special
talent manifested in the hymns is the ability to turn the
perceptive faculty inward, to define and render directly
certain sorts of psychic activity and psychic stasis without

significant recourse to visual metaphor, the talent which
created *The Task* seems adept at rending inner states by
suggestion, through reference to and reliance on imagery
of the external world. Conversely, the hymns at their worst
depend most heavily on metaphor; *The Task,* whose central
subject is concrete reality in its spiritual context, is at its
worst often almost bare of imagery, lapsing into concern
only with abstractions. There is a kind of metaphor
(although a weak and sketchy one) in "ghostly counsel"
dropping, a "disregarded thing" ; aside from that, and the
vague metaphoric possibilities of *touch* in line 328, *empty
school* in line 330, the only metaphor in the two passages
is "The brightest truth that man has ever seen," a reference
characteristic of Cowper's conventional interest in light as
an emblem of spiritual reality, but hardly more than a
reference

But if these passages manifest little distinct visual awareness, they also demonstrate little psychic awareness. What
"perception" they display seems theoretical ("philosophical," Cowper might say) rather than direct, the product of
what the poet has been told, not what he has himself
"seen." Cut off from his deepest sources of feeling, he
produces impoverished language; the more barren sections
of *The Task,* which by implication deny the validity of
that very perception that the poem at its best strongly affirms, are boring. "Where the Idea is accurate, the terms
will be so too; and wherever you find the words hobble,
you may conclude the notion was lame; otherwise they
wou'd both have had an equal and graceful pace." So
wrote John Constable,[38] and his terms suggest an appropriate vocabulary to indict Cowper at his worst.

But Cowper also had at his disposal strikingly individual
language. Trying to describe the writer characterized by
"simplicity" (a term which in his usage as in Collins's has
rather complex implications), Hugh Blair observes, "There
are no marks of art in his expression; it seems the very
language of nature; you see in the Style, not the writer and
his labour, but the man, in his own natural character."[39]
The distinction he makes is difficult to enforce, but it
seems appropriate to one of Cowper's characteristic modes,
a mode which defines his most personal ways of perceiving. "All we behold is miracle," Cowper points out, "but,
seen / So duly, all is miracle in vain" (VI, 132-133). The
statement might serve as text for *The Task,* which at its
best uncovers the miracle of the commonplace, sometimes
employing a distinctive rhetoric to emphasize its revelations. Divine power operates "all in sight of inattentive
man" (VI, 120); the poet's responsibility is to make man
more attentive, so that his "sight" will be more significant.
Man sees the dearth of winter; he should be conscious
simultaneously of the richness it foretells.

But let the months go by, a few short months,
And all shall be restor'd. These naked shoots,
Barren as lances, among which the wind
Makes wintry music, sighing as it goes,
Shall put their graceful foliage on again,

And, more aspiring, and with ampler spread,
Shall boast new charms, and more than they have lost.

(VI, 140-146)

Both the lines about miracle and the first line of this description employ rhetorical repetition. Unlike the reiteration of "the pulpit" in the moralizing passage, this duplication is a device of progression rather than of suspension. It intensifies an atmosphere of calm assurance (defined particularly by the grand inclusiveness of "all shall be restor'd") instead of creating, like the other repetitive pattern, merely a sense of dogged determination. Now Cowper relies heavily on metaphoric suggestion, both the conventional associations of *aspiring* and *boast,* and a more complex and personal effect in the description of "naked shoots, / Barren as lances." The defencelessness implied by *naked* is immediately denied when the nakedness becomes that of an aggressive weapon. But the implications of *lances* are in turn opposed by the further transformation of lances into musical instruments; and the fact that the music derives from the "sighing" of the wind adds a final degree of perceptual and emotional complexity. The beauty of winter is as real as that of spring, although it is beauty of an entirely different order. Nature embodies the Christian sequence of death and resurrection. The poem directs one's attention to the beauties of winter as well as those of spring, to the beauty of apparent death and that of rebirth, reinforcing the aesthetic contrast by the opposition between the conventional language of personalization applied to spring and the more direct, personal language through which winter is evoked.

This passage continues with one of the catalogues so characteristic of Cowper, introduced by a generalization couched entirely in "poetic diction," in a form which reminds one of the associations of that diction with the language of science.

Then, each in its peculiar honours clad,
Shall publish, even to the distant eye,
Its family and tribe. Laburnum, rich In streaming gold;
   syringa, iv'ry pure;
The scentless and the scented rose; this red
And of an humbler growth, the other tall,
And throwing up into the darkest gloom
Of neighb'ring cypress, or more sable yew,
Her silver globes, light as the foamy surf
That the wind severs from the broken wave;
The lilac, various in array, now white,
Now sanguine, and her beauteous head now set
With purple spikes pyramidal, as if,
Studious of ornament, yet unresolv'd
Which hue she most approv'd, she chose
   them all . . .

(VI,147-161)

This is slightly less than half the full catalogue, but it suggests the technique and quality of the whole. The imagined conjunction of flowers is complexly perceived, with reference to form (*streaming, globes, pyramidal*), color, balance and contrast ("The scentless and the scented rose,"

tall and short, dark and light, white and purple), and metaphor, Metaphors of richness (*gold, iv'ry, silver, ornament*) dominate the scene, and two key images insist on relationships among the parts of the created universe: the emphatic association of the "silver globes" of the rose with the bits of surf "severed" from the wave, and the description of the lilac as a human belle.

The powerful effect of this catalogue depends heavily on the relationship between the directness of the diction (only *sable, sanguine,* possibly *beauteous* and *gloom,* have predominantly poetic associations; the adjectives and nouns which carry the weight of the description are on the whole precise and limited in their individual meanings) and the elaboration of the picture and meaning created by the simple language. As Cowper saw in the naked branches of winter a rapidly shifting range of meanings, he perceives in a static panorama of spring and summer flowers so many sorts of meaning and relationship—visual and "philosophic"—that his presentation of the scene pulses with energy. The source of that energy, and its significance, become explicit at the end:

From dearth to plenty, and from death to life,
Is Nature's progress when she lectures man
In heav'nly truth; evincing, as she makes
The grand transition, that there lives and works
A soul in all things, and that soul is God.
The beauties of the wilderness are his,
That makes so gay the solitary place
Where no eye sees them.

(VI,181-188)

The "lecture" nature offers is the revelation that there is no separation, finally, between the visual glory (or, for that matter, the visual barrenness) of the natural world and its theological meaning. The vibrant "soul in all things" need only be recognized; perception of its energy is part of Cowper's direct relation-seeking poetic perception of the imagined scene itself. The force of that perception, expressed through unpretentious but intricately organized language, leads the poet finally to the realization that meaning and beauty are inherent in the natural world independently of the perceiver—"Where no eye sees them." The perceiver, even at the beginning of this passage, is only a "distant eye" ; the splendor of the scene does not depend on human perception. In this pageant of inanimate nature, the vegetative world finally embodies full richness, dignity, even hints of eroticism ("her beauteous head"). God's plenty is here; religious, aesthetic, emotional meaning fuse. The greatest achievement of *The Task* (not only here; in other "passages as well) is this fusion. In the hymns, Cowper conveyed his fear that man must move inevitably from an infantile state of pure dependence and complete comfort to an anguished awareness of conflict and the loss of peace, comfort. Elsewhere in *The Task* he reminds us that the eye is" guiltless": no blame can attach to aesthetic contemplation; passivity is associated with lack of vice. In the flower passage, contemplation is not merely guiltless; it becomes essentially an act of worship, of such total worship that it involves the poet's entire sensibility—his desire for peace, for beauty, for piety; his emotional and religious yearnings, his intellectual convictions. The act of visual perception has finally become fully inclusive as it leads Cowper back to his ideal state of faith and ease.

Notes

1. Lodwick Hartley, "The Worm and the Thorn: A Study of Cowper's *Olney Hymns,*" *The Journal of Religion,* *XXIX* (1949), 224.

2. Kenneth MacLean, "William Cowper," *The Age of Johnson: Essays Presented to Chauncey Brewster Tinker* (New Haven: Yale University Press, 1949) p. 260.

3. Maurice Quinlan, "Cowper's Imagery," *JEGP,* XLVII (1948), 285.

4. See Quinlan, "Cowper's Imagery," pp. 276-285; Hartley, "The Worm and the Thorn," pp. 220-229.

5. Norman Nicholson, *William Cowper,* Writers and their Work No. 121 (London: Longmans, Green, 1960), p. 16.

6. Hugh Fausset, *William Cowper* (London: Jonathan Cape, 1928), p. 79.

7. Johnson, *Lives of the English Poets,* ed. George Birkbeck Hill, 3 vols. (Oxford: Oxford University Press, 1905), I, 45.

8. Ibid., I, 20.

9. Fausset, *William Cowper,* p. 35.

10. 27 November 1784; *The Correspondence of William Cowper,* ed. Thomas Wright, 4 vols. (London: Hodder and Stoughton, 1904), II, 272.

11. 10 October 1784; *Correspondence,* II, 251.

12. 17 December 1781; *Correspondence,* I, 411.

13. 19 March 1784; *Correspondence,* II, 176-177.

14. To the Rev. William Unwin, 17 January 1782; *Correspondence,* I, 430.

15. Donald Davie, "The Critical Principles of William Cowper," *The Cambridge Journal,* VII (1953), 182.

16. To the Rev. William Unwin, 20 October 1784; *Correspondence,* II 257.

17. To John Johnson, 28 February 1790; *Correspondence,* III, 439.

18. François de Salignac de la Mothe Fénelon, *Dialogues Concerning Eloquence,* tr. William Stevenson (London, 1722), p. 252.

19. Henry Home, Lord Kames, *Elements of Criticism,* 6th ed., 2 vols. (Edinburgh, 1785), II, 19.

20. Hugh Blair, *Lectures on Rhetoric and Belles Lettres,* 2 vols. (London, 1783), I, 185.

21. Ibid., I, 217-218.

22. No date [1784]; *Correspondence,* II, 287.

23. Daniel Webb, *Remarks on the Beauties of Poetry* (London, 1762), p. 56.

24. 10 October 1784; *Correspondence,* II, 252-253.

25. *Scene* is one of the nouns Josephine Miles finds occurring ten times in a hundred lines of *The Task.* The only other of Cowper's favorite nouns directly associated with visual perception is *eye.* More characteristic are abstract or generalized terms: *art, beauty, god, life, nature, world.* Cowper's typical verbs include both *see* and *seem.* His vocabulary, as statistically recorded, seems closer to Johnson's poetic vocabulary than to that of any of his other contemporaries. See Josephine Miles, *Renaissance, Eighteenth-Century, and Modern Language in English Poetry* (Berkeley: University of California Press, 1960), p. 23.

26. 30 October 1784; *Correspondence,* II, 258-259.

27. Davie, "The Critical Principles of William Cowper," p. 182

28. James A. Ray, *Cowper and His Poetry* (London: George G. Harrap, [1914]), p. 84.

29. Leon Boucher, *William Cowper, Sa Correspondance et ses Poésies* (Paris, 1874) p. 186.

30. Walter Bagehot, "William Cowper," *Estimates of Some Englishmen and Scotchmen* (London, 1858), p. 89.

31. Hugh Fausset, *William Cowper,* p. 235.

32. *Monthly Review,* LXVII (October, 1782), 265; quoted in Maurice J. Quinlan, *William Cowper, A Critical Life* (Minneapolis: University of Minnesota Press, 1953) p. 117.

33. John Aikin *Letters to a Young Lady on a Course of English Poetry* (London, 1804), p. 292.

34. W. P. Ker, *Form and Style in Poetry* (London: Macmillan, 1928), p. 170

35. Thomas Quayle, *Poetic Diction* (London: Methuen, 1924), p. 49.

36. Coleridge, *Biographia Literaria; or Biographical Sketches of My Literary Life and Opinions,* 2 vols. (London, 1817) I, 22.

37. Warton, "Three Essays on Pastoral, Didactic, and Epic Poetry," in *The Works of Virgil,* 3rd ed., 4 vols. (London, 1778), I, 401. [First edition 1753].

38. John Constable, *Reflections Upon Accuracy of Style,* 2nd ed. (London 1738), p. 59. [First edition 1731.]

39. Blair, *Lectures on Rhetoric,* I, 390.

John D. Baird (essay date 1978)

SOURCE: Baird, John D. "Cowper's Conception of Truth." *Studies in Eighteenth-Century Culture* 7 (1978): 367-73.

[In the following essay, Baird clarifies Cowper's representation of divine truth in the poems "The Progress of Error" and "Truth."]

William Cowper's poetical activity extended over half a century, from **"Verses written at Bath on finding the heel of a shoe,"** composed in 1748 when he was sixteen, to a scrap of translation from Homer written a few months before his death on April 25, 1800. His contemporary fame, and his present reputation, rest upon the two volumes he published in his early fifties: *Poems by William Cowper, of the Inner Temple, Esq.,* published in 1782, and his masterpiece, *The Task,* published in 1785. While a knowledge of Cowper's concept of truth—more strictly, religious truth—is necessary to a full understanding of all his mature poetry, its importance is most obvious in connection with the first two poems of what may be called Cowper's "major phase," namely, **"The Progress of Error"** and **"Truth,"** both of which were included in *Poems,* 1782. As an example of the misunderstanding to which they are liable, one may quote Canon Benham, who, in the introduction to his edition of the poems, objects that **"The Progress of Error"** is a misnomer; we are led, he says, "to expect a philosophical disquisition, whereas we find that the sum of this poem is that operas, card-playing, intemperance, gluttony, reading of bad novels, are the causes of Error; that they who hate truth shall be the dupe of lies. Quite true, of course; but who supposes that this is an adequate account of the progress of Error?"[1] Well, presumably Cowper did, for one. Consideration of the circumstances in which the poem came to be written may help us to understand why.

In 1763 Cowper suffered a complete nervous breakdown (signalized by an unsuccessful suicide attempt), and left London for ever. In the course of his recovery, under the influence of his physician, Dr. Cotton of St. Albans, he became a convinced Evangelical Christian. Nine years later, in 1773, he suffered a yet more drastic collapse. At the height of the seizure he had a dream which haunted him for the rest of his life. Henceforth he believed that God had condemned his soul not to eternal punishment but to annihilation immediately after the physical death of his body; further, that it was God's wish that he should make away with himself at the first opportunity.

This grim conviction weighed upon Cowper's mind every minute of every day. He could obtain relief only by occupying himself with some activity. First his famous pet hares, then gardening, then drawing provided this necessary diversion. Then in 1778 and 1779 he began to write verse again. These little poems are neither gentlemanly love lyrics such as he had written as a young man-about-town in the 1750s, nor are they hymns such as he had composed in the enthusiastic aftermath of his conversion. Instead, they fall for the most part into two groups: moral fables like **"The Pine-Apple and the Bee"** (always a favourite form with Cowper), or topical poems inspired by the course of the American War. These are loudly patriotic, contemptuous of the Americans and violent against the

French. Most of them were not published during his lifetime—he had to suppress two during the preparation of the 1782 volume when it became clear that their confidence had been misplaced—and two were so strident and abusive that they did not appear in print until 1959.[2]

By the spring of 1780, the writing of verse was providing more and more of Cowper's daily "amusement." In May or early June he started to collect his little poems in a manuscript book, and included poems and translations more frequently in letters to his close friends. At the same time, as luck would have it, a new topic of public interest arose to attract his attention.

This was a book called *Thelyphthora or, A Treatise on Female Ruin . . . Considered on the Basis of the Divine Law.*[3] It was written by a leading Evangelical clergyman, Martin Madan, who happened to be Cowper's cousin. Madan was Chaplain of the Lock Hospital, which had been established to care for "fallen women," and he was acutely conscious of the economic and social pressures which brought "ruin" and disease to thousands of unfortunate young women. The thesis advanced in his two thick volumes is reducible to very simple terms: the man who takes a woman's virginity has, by God's law revealed in the Old Testament, married her, and is consequently responsible for her economic support thereafter. *Thelyphthora* was published at the end of May 1780, just before the outbreak of the Gordon Riots—a coincidence deemed significant by some—and set off a controversy which boiled for a full year and was not soon forgotten.

Cowper, although he never read the book through, knew all about it. His friend and spiritual adviser, John Newton, had told him of it long before it appeared, and he kept Cowper informed of his efforts, and those of other Evangelical clergy, to persuade Madan not to publish.[4] (Newton had a few months before moved from Olney to London, as Rector of St. Mary Woolnoth.) But Madan did not listen to them, and so many of his colleagues, in the autumn of 1780, felt compelled to answer him in print. Madan's very real humanitarian concern passed largely unnoticed; he was accused of having advocated polygamy; he found scarcely any defenders, and in the end retired disappointed to the country, where he solaced himself by translating Juvenal and advocating the more frequent imposition of the death penalty.[5]

For his opponents, however, there was one little difficulty. While of course everyone could see at once that *Thelyphthora* was an evil book—for did it not advocate polygamy?—it was by no means clear that anyone could prove its arguments to be false. Madan was not only a learned man; before his conversion he had been a rising young lawyer; he was experienced in controversy, and he knew how to make out his case. Among the fears of Newton and his colleagues not the least, one suspects, was the horrid apprehension that Mr. Madan could not be refuted.

By November the crisis was past. A reviewer called Samuel Badcock published a lengthy refutation of Madan's views which was understood to answer all the points of learning involved.[6] And Cowper, who had written three or four short poems against his cousin's book, was moved to write his allegorical narrative poem *Anti-Thelyphthora.* This marks the beginning of a year of intense poetic activity on Cowper's part.[7]

As soon as *Anti-Thelyphthora* had been despatched to Newton, who undertook to have it published anonymously, Cowper set to work on another poem, to be called **"The Progress of Error."** Madan is again attacked, this time among a crowd of evil exemplars. This poem was finished in the middle of December 1780, and was at once followed by another, called **"Truth,"** which took about a month to complete. Early in February Cowper added a third long poem, **"Table Talk."** This was designed to be read as a kind of preface to its predecessors; it concludes with Cowper's declaration of intent as a poet. Religion, he says, has never had a "skilful guide into poetic ground," and the poetic ground itself is well-nigh exhausted:

> And 'tis the sad complaint, and almost true,
> Whate'er we write, we bring forth nothing new.
> 'Twere new indeed to see a bard all fire,
> Touch'd with a coal from heav'n, assume the lyre,
> And tell the world, still kindling as he sung,
> With more than mortal music on his tongue,
> That He, who died below and reigns above,
> Inspires the song, and that his name is love.
>
> (732-39)[8]

When we turn, however, to **"The Progress of Error"** and **"Truth"** we are liable, like Canon Benham, to be puzzled. The two poems are clearly a pair, intended as the contrast of night with day. But they do not offer any definitions of error and truth; the doctrinal element suggested by these terms is absent. **"The Progress of Error"** shows us various moral offenders, and shows how their example may corrupt others; **"Truth"** tells us that those who will be saved—and the hideous alternative is never long out of view—trust in faith, not works, have thankful hearts, and read the Bible. From this they gain a knowledge of "Heav'n's easy, artless, unincumber'd plan" (22), which is so easy, artless, and unincumbered that it can be summed up in just three words: "BELIEVE AND LIVE!" (31). But what it is they believe, and the relation of this belief to virtuous conduct—these things are not explained.

Cowper himself was apprehensive about the way this poem might strike the general reader, one not already Evangelical in outlook, and he asked Newton to write a preface that might coat the pill.[9] In his preface, Newton explains that Cowper's poems commend an *"experimental"* religion. He uses the word "experimental" with obvious caution, and the precise signification which it had for him is not certain; however, it seems to mean both a religion in which personal religious experience is the predominating element, and a religion *proved* by experiment. He writes:

> From this state [of misery] the Bible relieved us—
> When we were led to read it with attention, we found
> *ourselves* described.—We learnt the causes of our

inquietude—we were directed to a method of relief—we tried, and we were not disappointed.

Deus nobis haec otia fecit.

We are now certain that the gospel of Christ is the power of God unto salvation, to every one that believeth. It has reconciled us to God, and to ourselves, to our duty, and our situation. It is the balm and cordial of the present life, and a sovereign antidote against the fear of death.[10]

It is helpful at this point to turn to a later poem, **"Conversation,"** written in the summer of 1781. Tell the world, Cowper writes,

> That while she dotes, and dreams that she believes,
> She mocks her Maker, and herself deceives,
> Her utmost reach, historical assent,
> The doctrines warpt to what they never meant;
> That truth itself is in her head as dull,
> And useless, as a candle in a scull,
> And all her love of God a groundless claim,
> A trick upon the canvas, painted flame.
>
> (775-82)

The distinction between "historical assent" and a "lively faith" to which Cowper here refers is of course a common one. It is neatly illustrated by the contrast between Tillotson and Whitefield. Tillotson argues that since we believe in the former existence and deeds of Alexander the Great and Julius Caesar on the basis of written records, so, "if we have the doctrine and history of the gospel, and all the evidence of our Saviour's divine authority, conveyed down to us, in as credible a manner, as any of these ancient matters of fact are, which mankind do firmly believe, then we have sufficient ground to be assured of it."[11] The Calvinist Whitefield, on the other hand, preaching at Bexley on Whitsunday 1739, remarks that ". . . many now read the Life, Sufferings, Death and Resurrection of Jesus Christ, in the same Manner as learned Men read *Caesar's Commentaries,* or *The Conquests of Alexander.* As Things rather intended to afford Matter for Speculation, than to be acted over again in and by us."[12] Salvation depends not on rational assent but on a personal, subjective, unique experience. And when the truth has been made operative by being "acted over again in and by us," it will be manifest to others in the virtuous life which is the outward sign of a lively faith.

In light of these beliefs, which may reasonably be imputed to Cowper, the problems raised by **"Truth"** and **"The Progress of Error"** become less puzzling. They are directed not toward rational conviction but to the creation of a state of mind on the part of the reader. He expounds not what the true believers believe, but the happy results of their believing it—what Newton calls "experimental" religion. And the element of progress in **"The Progress of Error"** is supplied by the constant emphasis on the spread of moral corruption (evidence of lack of true belief) from a single evil example throughout the nation.

It will be clear, however, that the historical and doctrinal elements of the Christian faith have in these poems, and elsewhere in Cowper's poetry, been so far subordinated as almost to disappear, while the inward experience to which these elements should give rise has grown correspondingly in importance. From this follow two notable consequences.

First, from a biographical point of view, it serves to link the insane, suicidal Cowper with the apparently sane author of the great bulk of Cowper's poetry. Newton argued again and again with Cowper that he could not have committed the unforgivable sin; that God could not wish him to destroy himself; that there was no Scriptural warrant for believing that God would ever condemn a soul to annihilation. Cowper remained unshaken in his conviction, based on his unique experience, that his was a unique case and that God's dealings with the rest of His Creation had no bearing upon it. He had made himself immune to rational argument on this point, no doubt by a perversion of Calvinist theology, but a perversion very hard for Calvinism to correct.

Second, to cultivate the religious affections while emptying them of content is to tend to make them transferable. We can see this process at work in **The Task**: the Olney countryside and its rural life begin to usurp the place of revealed truth as the object of deep emotional commitment and the foundation of moral fervor. And from **The Task** the line of influence is clear to Wordsworth and Coleridge.

Notes

1. *The Poetical Works of William Cowper,* ed. E. C. Benham (London, 1870), p. xlviii.

2. *The Correspondence of William Cowper,* ed. Thomas Wright (London, 1904), I, 397-98; Charles Ryskamp, *William Cowper of the Inner Temple, Esq.* (Cambridge, 1959), pp. 237-38.

3. *Thelyphthora; or, a Treatise on Female Ruin, in its Causes, Effects, Consequences, Prevention, and Remedy; Considered on the Basis of the Divine Law: under the Following Heads, viz. Marriage, Whoredom, and Fornication, Adultery, Polygamy, Divorce; With many other Incidental Matters,* 3 vols. (London, 1780-81). The third volume (1781) was issued in an attempt to answer criticisms of the first two.

4. I draw here, and in later discussion of Newton's relations with Cowper, on material which will appear in the new edition of Cowper's letters now being prepared by Charles Ryskamp and James King, and shortly to be published by the Clarendon Press.

5. The best account of Martin Madan's career is that given by Falconer Madan, *The Madan Family* (Oxford, 1933), which also includes an extensive bibliography of the *Thelyphthora* controversy.

6. *Monthly Review,* 63 (1780), 273-87; 321-39.

7. The importance of *Thelyphthora* in stimulating Cowper's poetic output is treated (with different emphases) by Lodwick Hartley, "Cowper and the Polygamous Parson," *Modern Language Quarterly,*

16 (1955), 137-41, and by Norma Russell, *A Bibliography of William Cowper to 1837* (Oxford, 1963), pp. 33-36, 38-40.

8. All quotations from Cowper's poetry follow the text of William Cowper, *Poetical Works,* ed. H. S. Milford, with corrections and additions by Norma Russell (London, 1971).

9. Cowper to Newton, 8 April 1781 (*Correspondence,* I, 289-90).

10. *Poetical Works* (see n. 8 above), pp. 650-51.

11. Sermon CCXLII, *Sermons on Several Subjects and Occasions* (London, 1757), XII, 72.

12. "The Indwelling of the Spirit, the common Privilege of all Believers," in *Discourses on the Following Subjects* (London, 1739), not continuously paged.

Richard Feingold (essay date 1978)

SOURCE: Feingold, Richard. "William Cowper: State, Society, and Countryside." In *Nature and Society: Later Eighteenth-Century Uses of the Pastoral and Georgic,* pp. 121-53. New Brunswick: Rutgers University Press, 1978.

[*In the following excerpt, Feingold evaluates* The Task *as a public poem, examining the work's principal themes and the dynamics of its social critique.*]

The idiosyncrasies of William Cowper's poetic career create an obvious difficulty for a study dealing with his work in a context wider than that provided by the man's life and work themselves. Cowper's life was tormented by a set of symptoms, habits, and fears which his poetry in many places reflects. It seems perfectly reasonable to maintain that whatever can be explained about Cowper's poetry will need to be carefully qualified by referring to his peculiar biography, particularly when we consider that Cowper turned to poetry for reasons intimately connected with the torment his life at times became for him.

The importance of Cowper's biography cannot be denied, but its significance diminishes when we take for our subject those segments of his poetry which are avowedly public in their expression and intention. I am concerned not with Cowper's personal needs or peculiarities as they are reflected in his writing of **The Task,** but with the stance and purpose that shape the public form of the poem. And an insistent note in **The Task** is the poet's claim that he is a normal man who can speak meaningfully to other men about public issues.

> 'T were well, says one sage erudite, profound . . .
> 'T were well, could you permit the world to live
> As the world pleases. What's the world to you?—
> Much. I was born of woman, and drew milk,
> As sweet as charity, from human breasts.
> I think, articulate, I laugh and weep,

And exercise all functions of a man.
How then should I and any man that lives
Be strangers to each other?

[3:191, 194-201][1]

Furthermore, in *The Task,* the chief subject of this [essay],
we can perceive a shift in emphasis away from those
religious fears which so devastated Cowper's mind, and
have so often served as the focal point upon which critical
discussion of Cowper's work has turned. For Hoxie N.
Fairchild, Cowper was the "laureate of Evangelicalism,"
and from this source Fairchild sees springing, in the
ruminative poems and satires preceding *The Task,* the
scolding and threatening vein which is Cowper's mode of
expostulation. But between these poems and *The Task*
Fairchild perceived a shift in tone—wit and urbanity
replacing scolding and threatening—a shift which, without
indicating any radical transformation in Cowper, nevertheless indicated that he was looking out on the world as
would a poet, not a preacher.[2] Moreover, the peculiar terrors with which Cowper invested his communication with
his God, terrors stemming from his conviction that he was
singled out by God as an "object of special detestation,"
are in general not to be found in *The Task.* In other places
Cowper frequently expressed his religious fears in poems
about castaways, about the terrible manifestations of God
in the awful motions of the natural world, and about the
arbitrary cruelty of the rulers of the world, but little of all
this is in his manner in *The Task.*

To be sure, Cowper in reflecting upon the devastation
caused by the volcano in Sicily (2:75-160), can attribute
that fearful event to the anger of God at a corrupt race, but
the poet chooses to draw from the event a moral for all of
England, and does not interpret the catastrophe as a sign
of the wrath specifically intended for himself. Indeed, the
God that reveals himself in the world of nature in this
poem is a God whose major mode is his gentler one, whose
daily miracles are more impressive than his occasional,
sublime spectacles:

What prodigies can pow'r divine perform
More grand than it produces year by year,
And all in sight of inattentive man?
Familiar with th' effect we slight the cause,
And, in the constancy of nature's course,
The regular return of genial months,
And renovation of a faded world,
See nought to wonder at. Should God again,
As once in Gibeon, interrupt the race
Of the undeviating and punctual sun,
How would the world admire! but speaks it less
An agency divine, to make him know
His moment when to sink and when to rise,
Age after age, than to arrest his course?
All we behold is miracle; but seen
So duly, all is miracle in vain.

[6:118-33]

And as for the uneasiness which Cowper often expressed
towards figures of earthly authority—an uneasiness which
some have seen as another reflection of the poet's peculiar

relation with his God—certainly we see that in *The Task*
the princes, kings, and queens of the world come in for
their share of the poet's mistrust and anger; but again, as
the following passage on paternal authority would seem to
indicate, Cowper is making an effort to temper impulses
which are peculiar to him in order to speak to the common
experience of mankind:

How readily we wish time spent revok'd,
That we might try the ground again, where once
(Through inexperience, as we now perceive)
We miss'd that happiness we might have found!
Some friend is gone, perhaps his son's best friend,
A father, whose authority in show
When most severe, and must'ring all its force,
Was but the graver countenance of love;
Whose favour, like the clouds of spring, might low'r,
And utter now and then an awful voice,
But had a blessing in its darkest frown,
Threat'ning at once and nourishing the plant.
We lov'd, but not enough, the gentle hand
That rear'd us.

[6:25-38]

Because much of the best Cowper scholarship has been
biographical, *The Task* has not often received close
analytical scrutiny. Even so fine a critical biography of
Cowper as Maurice Quinlan's offers only rather general
descriptions of *The Task*;[3] Quinlan's criticism of the
hymns and the shorter poems is more successful because
these more personal compositions can be fruitfully approached in terms suggested by Cowper's life. But *The
Task* is composed in a public voice and needs to be studied
as a public poem. Morris Golden's study does indeed
recognize the public nature of the poem, but proceeds to
interpret Cowper's treatment of public themes in the light
of the poet's well-known maladies.[4] Despite some interesting observations about Cowper's attitude toward civilization, and despite his devotion of a full-length book to *The
Task,* Golden adds rather little to previous sketches of that
poem because he refers his observations on the poem's
public concerns back to the story of Cowper's nervous
disorders. The poem, once more, is treated as the peculiar
product of a tortured life.

In his brief introduction to his selections from Cowper in
The Late Augustans, Donald Davie acknowledges how
significant Cowper's biography is to our understanding of
his poetry, but adds a needed corrective to the biographical
emphasis of much Cowper scholarship, and also to the
commonplaces about the poet's pre-romanticism. Davie
writes that in Cowper's "very conservative and late Augustan expressions of Horatian urbanity . . . he resolutely
turns his eye away from his private world, and we go to
him for the fullest image in poetry of the public life of his
times." Lodwick Hartley's excellent study of Cowper has
made sufficiently clear how deeply the man was concerned
with many of the pressing social and political issues of his
time, but Hartley's work does not deal with Cowper's
poetry as art.[5] Norman Nicholson's fine study begins to
combine an awareness of the public nature of *The Task*

with a recognition of that poem's roots in the classics. But Nicholson takes a fairly superficial view of Cowper's treatment of public matters, emphasizing the ideal of retirement as a simple criticism of London life.[6] To date the best study of Cowper's art seems to me to be Patricia M. Spacks's essay in *The Poetry of Vision* (1967), and though her study only touches on Cowper's attitudes towards public experience, focusing instead upon the character of Cowper's visual imagination. . . .

My purpose in this [essay] . . . is to examine *The Task* critically as a public poem—to study its complex judgments of the public world in relation to the bucolic art of the poem. This [essay] will discuss some of the leading themes of Cowper's social outlook. . . .

. . . . .

Probably no line of *The Task* stays more firmly in the reader's mind than the curt and simple formula: "God made the country, and man made the town." It is, of course, a commonplace in Cowper scholarship that the poet's total attitude towards the proper life for man is somewhat more complex than that formula would seem to allow. That the polarities of urbanity and rusticity were not, perhaps, so absolute in the poet's mind as the well-known formula would imply, is clear from an apparent qualification made in another section of the poem: "The town has ting'd the country: and the stain / Appears a spot upon a vestal's robe, / The worse for what it soils" (4:553-55). The onus remains with the town, but Cowper evidently intends to see clearly, to avoid sentimental simplicity. He will use bucolic themes, but he will not indulge in pastoral sentimentality. Furthermore, *The Task* skirts every fashion of contemporary rural sentimentalism, and yet avoids the total plunge; it is an extensive and serious treatment of public problems; its perspective and norms owe much to bucolic tradition. Yet, if it refuses to risk sentimentalizing the country, by avoiding the risk, the poem also fails to raise the country into that symbolic and imaginative fact which it must become in order to evoke from its bucolic elements the full richness of metaphoric statement. We see in *The Task* the elements of bucolic tradition used in a way which marks a crisis in that tradition. My object in this [essay] . . . is to determine how Cowper's ideas about the nature of the social bond affected his intention to work with the bucolic topics of retirement, nature, and art—topics which he used to organize his criticism of contemporary English life.

About two years before he began to write *The Task,* Cowper composed a poem of ninety lines to which he sardonically gave the title **"Heroism."** Touching upon the poem in his study of Cowper, Lodwick Hartley sees it as an expression of some of the poet's thoughts on the enterprise of war. As such, the poem appears to bring in an indictment against the monarchs of the earth, who are likened to the volcano in Sicily, erupting periodically to ravage their unsuspecting and industrious neighboring states in order to plunder their riches. Hartley mentions in passing the presence in the poem of a realistic insight into the economic

motives of aggression, motives regularly camouflaged by such rubrics as national honor and justice, which help to blow the shrill trumpets.[7] The poem ends with a breath of praise blown in the direction of the English king, who, according to the poet, manages to keep both himself and his island innocent of such barbarism.

This much is an adequate summary of the poem, but a closer investigation yields some interesting questions about the evaluation of the nature and purposes of the social and political community implied in the poem. The arrangement of the poem is symmetrical; the first forty lines are devoted to an account of the eruption of Aetna's once "silent fire" and its disastrous effects upon the cultivated fields that had lain on "the mountains sloping sides." The second half of the poem develops a moral from that catastrophic event, showing how an envious monarch whose appetite is excited by the rich harvests of his neighboring state erupts in war against his neighbor in order to plunder his wealth. Of particular note is the poet's use of pastoral language to depict the unsuspecting fields on the mountainside and the similarly unsuspecting lands to be invaded by the greedy king: the mountain "tow'r'd a cloud capt pyramid of snow."

> No thunders shook with deep intestine sound
> The blooming groves that girdled her around.
> Her unctuous olives, and her purple vines,
> (Unfelt the fury of those bursting mines) . . .
>
> [5-8]

until the eruption, when

> In dazzling streaks, the vivid lightnings play.
> But, oh! what muse, and in what pow'rs of song,
> Can trace the torrent as it burns along?
> Havoc and devastation in the van,
> It marches o'er the prostrate works of man—
> Vines, olives, herbage, forest, disappear,
> And all the charms of a Sicilian year.
>
> [18-24]

Similarly, in the peaceful neighboring kingdom, "Earth seems a garden in its loveliest dress" in front of the invading army, but in the army's train it is "a wilderness" where "Famine, and pestilence, her first born son, / Attend to finish what the sword begun." There is nothing remarkable in this definition of the landscape to express moral as well as natural states of being, but the contrast between the cultivated fields and the wilderness serves at least to show that, for Cowper, as for many others, it is the landscape of cultivated nature—the emblem of nature's harmony with art in optimal civilization—that defines the moral center of his span of vision. There is only one instance in all of his work in which he momentarily adopts the more radical norms implicit in the primitivist rather than the cultivated landscape; it is in the opening lines of book two of *The Task,* a moment of special stress when the poet reacts to the crueler facts of human life:[8]

> Oh for a lodge in some vast wilderness,
> Some boundless contiguity of shade,

Where rumour of oppression and deceit,
Of unsuccessful or successful war,
Might never reach me more.

[2:1-5]

But if the moral landscape of **"Heroism"** includes the vision of the wilderness, it is centered, nevertheless, in the little picture of the cultivated country, the emblem of civilization. Cowper never begins with the intention of judging human civilization as irredeemable, and it is only after considerable struggle that his posture as a public poet relaxes in disillusionment with civilization into the acceptance of God's peace in retirement. His initial effort is to judge the works of man on the basis of the norms implicit in the cultivated landscape, not the wilderness. And the cultivated landscape suggests that human civilization can create itself, with the resources and powers God has given to man, as a harmonious resolution of nature and art.

In likening the depredations of warlike monarchs to the periodic eruptions of Aetna, the poem expresses the familiar theory of history as a cyclical process which witnesses the growth, decay, and subsequent rebirth of civilizations. Thus, following the eruption of the volcano, the cultivated landscape is in time restored; Cowper associates the process of restoration with pastoral feelings, here evoked by mention of the myrtle, the shade, the flocks. Time, not work, is emphasized as the agent of restoration, making us think of the process as nature's own, wholly consonant with pastoral expectations:

Yet time at length (what will not time achieve?)
Clothes it with earth, and bids the produce live.
Once more the spiry myrtle crowns the glade,
And ruminating flocks enjoy the shade.

[29-32]

A similar process takes place in the restoration of the conquered and plundered lands; the poetry here, however, is cast in a georgic vein, thus acknowledging, without hardening, the distinction between the restorative processes of nature (suggested in the passage above) and those of human work. Time was the agent of restoration in the first passage; the volcano was the destroyer. Here it is human work that restores, warfare that destroys. But the poem in these two passages works to link these two kinds of positive energy, time and work, to affirm that characteristic eighteenth-century blend of pastoral and georgic understanding:

Yet man, laborious man, by slow degrees,
(Such is his thirst of opulence and ease)
Plies all the sinews of industrious toil,
Gleans up the refuse of the gen'ral spoil,
Rebuilds the tow'rs that smok'd upon the plain,
And the sun gilds the shining spires again.

Increasing commerce and reviving art
Renew the quarrel on the conq'rors' part;
And the sad lesson must be learn'd once more,
That wealth within is ruin at the door.

[67-77]

Yet, in this last account of the reestablishment of civilized industry in the once plundered lands, certain problems suggest themselves. At the center of the poem Cowper concluded his account of the eruption of Aetna by introducing the subject of war as an evil to be understood with the help of the example of "Aetna's emblematic fires" (45)—emblematic, that is, of the havoc caused by the ambitious pride of kings (46). However, a subtle shift in emphasis considerably complicates the problem in those lines which describe the renewal of the cycle of war (73-77). A portion of the burden of guilt is shifted from the shoulders of the ambitious and proud monarchs and comes to rest upon their victims. This sad lesson that must be learned once more is not the schoolwork of the predator; clearly it is the victim who needs the new instruction—and what he is to learn is that "wealth within is ruin at the door." Certainly, the victimized state is not responsible for the greed of its rapacious neighbor, but here there is a suggestion of a more problematic connection between the internal and external causes of international violence than had perhaps been implied earlier in the poem. Thus, in his account of the renewal of the once plundered region, Cowper attributes the georgic energy that "plies all the sinews of industrious toil" to man's "thirst of opulence and ease." Although in Cowper's thought industrious toil is always a virtue, opulence is often depicted as vicious in itself and in its effects. However, as these lines associate the pastoral quality of ease with the vicious condition of opulence, a measure of ambiguity slips into this apparently straightforward poem, disturbing its effort to link the pastoral and georgic ambiences. We perceive that the land of industrious toil, whose wealth invites the aggression of its neighbors, harbors within itself some of the seeds of evil: "wealth within is ruin at the door." The volcano, which had hitherto been a somewhat unsatisfactory emblem for external aggression, takes on added significance as we see that the real issue is not aggressive greed by itself, but aggressive greed as it is provoked by a less obvious, but nonetheless festering, fault within the victim of that aggression: his thirst for opulence and ease. Luxury once again is the vicious mole of nature, festering within, realistically and uncomfortably associated with the pastoral virtue of ease. More—unlike Dyer, Cowper fitfully perceives that industrious toil, too, is somehow implicated with ruinous luxury, and both with war.

"Heroism" is not a perfect poem. Its central device, the volcano, is not a very precise emblem for external aggression; furthermore, the poem raises a problem it fails to resolve by suggesting that the victim of greed is in some measure responsible for the devastation he suffers, because the very wealth which invites attack upon him is the product of his own morally ambiguous industry. The hint arises that the volcano is perhaps more appropriately the emblem of the lurking evil of wealth within the victimized nation than it is of the aggressive depredations of his neighbor state. But Cowper concludes the poem without developing that possibility.

What are ye, monarchs, laurel'd heroes, say—
But Aetnas of the suff'ring world ye sway?

Sweet nature, stripp'd of her embroider'd robe,
Deplores the wasted regions of her globe;
And stands a witness at truth's awful bar,
To prove you, there, destroyers as ye are.

[78-82]

In these lines he returns to his original position, overlooks the subtle qualifications of that position which had crept into his verse, and repeats the essential polarity between the cultivated landscape of peace (sweet nature's embroidered robe) and the wilderness created by warlike greed.

The poem concludes with a curious burst of patriotism:

Oh, place me in some heav'n protected isle,
Where peace, and equity, and freedom smile;
Where no volcano pours his fiery flood,
No crested warrior dips his plume in blood;
Where pow'r secures what industry has won;
Where to succeed is not to be undone;
A land that distant tyrants hate in vain,
In Britain's isle, beneath a George's reign.

[83-90]

As patriotic rhetoric these lines are not especially noteworthy; but considered within the context of bucolic reference they raise some fundamental questions. For example, is the wish for refuge in "some heav'n protected isle" merely an example of easy, unthinking rhetoric, or does it express the poet's longing to escape the vicious cycle of a politics which has failed to function healthily within the moral possibilities defined by the domains of nature (the pastoral fields, the volcano) and civilization (increasing commerce, war)—to escape, that is, to some "heav'n protected isle" where the functioning of nature and civilization is controlled within the overarching and protective dominion of grace? Furthermore, the fact that the conclusion tempers its patriotism with the yearning for retreat suggests that the important aspect of the haven is not so much that it is England but that it is an island. This aspect of England's geography becomes significant in the context of the moral geography of the poem, so to speak, when we consider the earlier lines about the relations between neighboring states. Cowper addresses the warring monarch, about to pounce upon the pastoral domains of his neighbor:

Fast by the stream that bounds your just domain,
And tells you where ye have a right to reign,
A nation dwells, not envious of your throne,
Studious of peace, their neighbours', and their own.
Ill-fated race! how deeply must they rue
Their only crime, vicinity to you!

[47-52]

These lines recall others from the opening section of book two of *The Task,* where again Cowper contemplates the ironies and cruelties of power:

Lands intersected by a narrow firth
Abhor each other. Mountains interpos'd

Make enemies of nations, who had else,
Like kindred drops, been mingled into one.

[16-19]

In each instance the fact of power generates its own realities, makes its own influence felt, in ways that challenge the limits implied by nature. Power makes a mockery of the idea of proper bounds and just domains. The worlds of nature and power conflict with each other, so that the only haven is an island, the only peace is in isolation. To the moral geography defined by the wilderness on the one side and the cultivated landscape on the other, Cowper has added in his poem **"Heroism"** a third ground, the island; but this addition to the landscape is not a place where the political experience of man is manageable and comprehensible within the dialectic of nature and civilization; it is a heavenly isle, and in its isolation from the vicious drama of power, the domains of nature and civilization are successfully harmonized only under the dominion of grace. It is as if civilization is helpless to find within its own proper resources the power to preserve itself. Not surprisingly, this uncomfortable possibility has been expressed in disruptions within the poem's system of bucolic allusion.

· · · · ·

If the curiously unresolved ambiguities of **"Heroism"** stem in part from the poet's serious reservations about the value of society's foremost activity, industry, we can see in *The Task* Cowper wrestling with similar difficulties in his attempt to understand the general nature of the social bond. The perspective finally asserted is that of rural retirement, which, in Cowper's treatment, takes on a meaning significantly different from its metaphorical substance as a topic of pastoral. In Cowper's work retirement is presented finally as an option, not as the emblem of a psychological moment of positive political significance, as, for example, in Pope's *Epistle to Burlington,* where the experience of rural pleasure is intrinsically linked to the poem's vision of a good public and political order. It is the development of the concept of retirement from an emblem to a simple life option that I am concerned with here, together with the implications this process entails for the expression, in bucolic themes, of serious social criticism. I have begun with a consideration of **"Heroism"** because that poem, in its establishment of the isolated island as an alternative source of norms to the cultivated middle landscape, prefigures a similar development of the concept of retirement in *The Task.* In *The Task* retirement is no longer a poetical idea working as a catalyst to resolve the strains between nature and art inside a poem and inside the mind experiencing the poem. Instead, it serves as a suburban option signifying a failure to resolve the antinomy between nature and art in a poem, and of the poet's need to escape, to isolate himself from the battleground of nature and art in life in order to comprehend nature morally as a creature of grace. The world of art is, in the end, left outside of the realm of redemption.

The Task is structured like a rondo; we can enter the poem at almost any point and before long find ourselves at its thematic center, the virtues of rural retirement. The topics that alternate with the central theme either arise from it or lead back to it. The narrative progress in itself embodies no observable climactic direction. The six separate books of *The Task* are not easily distinguishable in terms of their concerns: each major division is about retirement; whatever distinctions exist are noticeable not in the treatment of that central theme, but in the subsidiary themes which alternate with it. Thus, book two weaves its way about the thematic center through the subsidiary topics of clerical corruption and educational abuses; book four defines the virtues of retirement by engaging the problem of the nature of the social bond; book five works its way around a discussion of political liberty, only to return at the end to the praise of retirement as the seat of the only trustworthy freedom, spiritual rest; and book six amplifies the discussion of God's peace as it is experienced in the retired life. Book one serves to introduce the theme of retirement by establishing the polarity between country and town; book three deals with the activities that make retirement useful and valuable.

In book four, **"The Winter Evening,"** the life of retirement is studied in symmetrical juxtaposition with the active life, the thrust of the poet's thought pointing towards a theory of the social bond upon which can be founded an apology for the life of retirement. Book four aims at a balanced statement of the worth of retirement, an evaluation arrived at by a fair consideration of the active life, which is, in the end, renounced. The work begins with the arrival of the eagerly anticipated post, carrying with it the news from the outside world; the early sections of the work describe the retired man's relations with the outside world by depicting his use of the weekly news sheet: he prepares for it with relish, careful at the same time to define his delight as the pleasure arising from the distance separating him from the objects of his interest:

> The grand debate,
> The popular harangue, the tart reply,
> The logic, and the wisdom, and the wit,
> And the loud laugh—I long to know them all;
> I burn to set th' imprison'd wranglers free,
> And give them voice and utt'rance once again.
>
> . . . . .
>
> 'Tis pleasant through the loop-holes of retreat
> To peep at such a world; to see the stir
> Of the great Babel, and not feel the crowd;
> To hear the roar she sends through all her gates
> At a safe distance, where the dying sound
> Falls a soft murmur on th' uninjur'd ear.
>
> [4:30-35, 88-93]

The vicarious pleasure, however, is a complex one. The narrator can imitate in his eager anticipation of the news the very motions of the souls who make the news. He "*longs* to know them all" ; he "*burns* to set th' imprison'd wranglers free" (italics added). At the same time, he has the advantage of a critical perspective, the advantage of distance. Although he speaks of his almost intemperate eagerness to hear the news of the world, nevertheless

"Thus sitting, and surveying thus at ease / The globe and its concerns, I seem advanc'd / To some secure and more than mortal height, / That lib'rates and exempts me from them all" (4:94-97). In this way he defines a middle ground. Unlike the postboy, "the light-hearted wretch, / Cold and yet cheerful" who brings the news and yet is incapable of being touched by it, he nevertheless avoids the lack of consciousness of the other sort, of those who do not understand what they do precisely because of their involvement. Retirement is thus a middle ground, psychologically and morally: it is, in fact, proper participation, since the only alternatives depicted are frenetic involvement or cloddish insensibility. "I behold the tumult, and am still" (4:99-101). Cowper does not, at first, present the picture of retirement as a kind of isolation. It is "with a kindred heart" that the narrator suffers the woes and shares the escapes of the active man (4:116-17).

Still, the perspective of retirement is not productive merely of sympathetic motions; one of its fruits is criticism. Indeed, criticism is the very process which helps to locate and define the moral ground which the happy man of the country inhabits, as the following passage makes clear:

> Now stir the fire, and close the shutters fast,
> Let fall the curtains, wheel the sofa round,
> And, while the bubbling and loud-hissing urn
> Throws up a steamy column, and the cups,
> That cheer but not inebriate, wait on each,
> So let us welcome peaceful ev'ning in.
> Not such his ev'ning, who with shining face
> Sweats in the crowded theatre, and, squeezed
> And bor'd with elbow-points through both his sides,
> Out-scolds the ranting actor on the stage. . . .
>
> [4:36-45]

The country pleasures define and are defined by the urban irritations. This passage is typical of the manner in which the theme of retirement is woven into the fabric of the poem; it arises from, and gives rise to, reflections on the outer, active world. Critical perspective is created by the constant juxtaposition of the two options. Another passage from book four substantiates this point. The narrator launches into a description of one of the pleasures of retirement, the delight to be had from the exercise of the fancy. He writes of a fireside reverie, inspired by the glowing of the red cinders in the hearth; we cannot miss here the note of pastoral *otium*:

> Me oft has fancy, ludicrous and wild,
> Sooth'd with a waking dream of houses, tow'rs,
> Trees, churches, and strange visages, express'd
> In the red cinders, while with poring eye
> I gaz'd, myself creating what I saw.
>
> [4:286-90]

These lines, however, are not their own justification; they are introduced by a glancing thrust at those for whom so simple a pleasure is contemptible:

> Laugh ye, who boast your more mercurial pow'rs,
> That never feel a stupor, know no pause,

Nor need one; I am conscious, and confess,
Fearless, a soul that does not always think.

[4:282-85]

The larger section of the poem to which these lines belong is itself built upon two sets of juxtaposed images: on the one hand, there is the dim, but suggestive light of the glowing rural hearth, on the other is the brilliant light of the fashionable urban salons from which the narrator is measuring his moral as well as physical distance. The entire passage on the happy enjoyment of the pleasures of the imagination, some forty lines long, is introduced by six lines depicting the activities of the corresponding hour in the fashionable world.

Just when our drawing-rooms begin to blaze
With lights, by clear reflection multiplied
From many a mirror, in which he of Gath,
Goliath, might have seen his giant bulk
Whole, without stooping, tow'ring crest and all,
My pleasures, too, begin.

[4:267-72]

Here the lighting is brilliant, not glowing, and multiplied in the outsized mirrors of the salon, it produces its own phantasmagoric effects. The reference to Goliath is significant. Although the idea is not thoroughly worked out in the verse, the narrator seems to have in mind a contrast between two kinds of imaginative experience: the one is restful and restorative, the other is deceptive and irritating, deceptive as was the size and apparent strength of Goliath, whose bulk could easily be contained within the dimensions of the blazing mirrors of the fashionable drawing rooms. In contrast, the retired man's otiose fancy is not merely a reflection of a delusion, as is clear to him when his revery is abruptly ended by the banging of a shutter:

'Tis thus the understanding takes repose
In indolent vacuity of thought,
And sleeps, and is refresh'd . . .
Thus oft, reclin'd at ease, I lose an hour
At ev'ning, till at length the freezing blast,
That sweeps the bolted shutter, summons home
The recollected pow'rs: and, snapping short
The glassy threads, with which the fancy weaves
Her brittle ties, restores me to myself,
How calm is my recess; and how the frost,
Raging abroad, and the rough wind, endear
The silence and the warmth enjoy'd within!

[4:296-98, 302-10]

He calls attention here to the healthful effect of his revery: his understanding refreshed, the man is restored to himself, and the abrupt ending of the revery does not leave his mind a poor shrunken thing, the product of pleasing delusions, but rather creates in him a serene appreciation of his happy situation as he is aroused into awareness of the silence and the warmth he enjoys inside the house. The retired life is contrasted with the fashionable life in terms of the health and heightened awareness of reality available to the one, and denied to the other. The cottage is a kind of pleasance.

This is Cowper's manner—to define the nature and virtues of retirement by constantly juxtaposing with it the corresponding activities of the larger world. In its treatment, therefore, of its central theme, retirement, the poem accomplishes a corollary purpose, the criticism of the active world. It is his judgment of the active world, the milieu of society at large, that concerns us here, because in the end, Cowper's concept of retirement is developed in response to his sense of the nature of social experience, and grows into something rather more like alienation and not the emblematic opportunity for the experience of *otium*—either the Epicurean or Horatian kind.

In book four Cowper presents a panoramic picture of the various elements of English society: we have touched upon (and will return later to) the life of the retired man, and its counterpart, active involvement, seen so far in two of its aspects, the world reflected in the newspaper and the world of the drawing rooms. The experiences of involvement and of retirement are the poles upon which much of book four turns. There appears, also, a third set of experiences in this section of the poem, represented by such figures as the postboy, the laborer, and the industrious poor. These figures do not come into focus as subjects of the poet's attention when it is turned towards the criticism of society: the laborer, like the postboy, represents that order of life which is committed neither to active involvement nor retirement, but connected to nature in the simplest of ways: rugged nerves.

Oh happy; and, in my account denied
That sensibility of pain with which
Refinement is endued, thrice happy thou!
Thy frame, robust and hardy, feels indeed
The piercing cold, but feels it unimpair'd.

[4:357-61]

The teamster of these lines shares with the postboy that low metabolism whose chief blessing is insensibility, a quality which distinguishes these figures from both the fashionable and the retired.[9] Insensibility is not, however, the blessing of the industrious poor. They suffer, and the narrator extends to them his compassion and charity. Nevertheless, their poverty is not one of the narrator's *social* concerns: it does not enter into the system of concerns which structure his indictment of society. It is rather the "undeserving poor" who open for Cowper an entrance into the arena of social criticism, and it is interesting to see the route he takes. The industrious poor he praises for preferring honest poverty to the degradation of beggarship, often, as the narrator says, a well-rewarded beggarship, since knaves in office are "lib'ral of their aid / To clam'rous importunity in rags, / But oft-times deaf to suppliants, who would blush / To wear a tatter'd garb however coarse . . ." (4:413-16). But Cowper has no explanation for the suffering of the industrious poor: nowhere does he suggest which fault or flaw in the economic organization of society bears the responsibility for their plight. And thus their only appeal is to private charity and the hopefully fortunate changes that may come with time.

These figures—the postboy, the teamster, the industrious poor—people the landscape of *The Task* and suggest the presence of modes of experience that Cowper wishes to acknowledge although his real attention is elsewhere, as is clear from his treatment of the undeserving poor. The narrator may be at a loss to explain the suffering of the worthy poor, but the plight of the unworthy is a different matter: gin. The narrator's analysis of the poverty of the rural thief and drunkard leads him abruptly away from the contemplation of the happy insensibility of the teamster and the grinding poverty of the decent poor and back into his central subject—the corruption of the world at large and the contrasting virtues of retirement.

Cowper's study of the rural thief is not an impressive achievement: it supports Donald Davie's assertion that no poet understood what was happening in the English countryside during these years of momentous change in the practice of agriculture. We are presented with a caricature—the chicken stealing wastrel whose sole concern is not to feed his wretched family but rather to raise money for drink. This poverty, the narrator asserts, is the "effect of laziness or sottish waste" (4:431), and to see their results we are ushered into a neighborhood tavern where sitting or reeling in debauch is, not only the nightly thief, but also the lackey, groom, smith, cobbler, joiner, shepherd, and baker, virtually the entire range of rural employment.

Once we are taken inside the tavern, however, the range of the narrator's perspective widens and the spectacle of rural debauchery is placed within a wider context:

> Dire is the frequent curse, and its twin sound
> The cheek-distending oath, not to be prais'd
> As ornamental, musical, polite,
> Like those which modern senators employ,
> Whose oath is rhet'ric, and who swear for fame!
> Behold the schools in which plebeian minds,
> Once simple, are initiated in arts
> Which some may practise with politer grace,
> But none with readier skill!—'tis here they learn
> The road that leads, from competence and peace,
> To indigence and rapine; till at last
> Society, grown weary of the load,
> Shakes her encumber'd lap, and casts them out.
>
> [4:487-99]

These lines depict the tavern scene as a kind of rural analogue to the activities of the great world without: what distinguishes the swearing of the boors from the rhetoric of senators is merely style, and to Cowper's mind style does not redeem. If, as Empson suggests, the pastoral form is one way of expressing the possibility that a beautiful relation exists between noble and peasant so that the noble can celebrate himself in shepherd's dress, the preceding passage can be read as a kind of parody of that idea: the vices of each class are precisely mirrored in their respective styles of debauchery, the rhetoric of senators and the drunken oaths of boors. The passage continues with a crucial elaboration of the manner in which the country louts, in their debauchery, live in harmony with the interests of a corrupt state:

> But censure profits little: vain th' attempt
> To advertise in verse a public pest,
> That, like the filth with which the peasant feeds
> His hungry acres, stinks, and is of use.
> Th' excise is fatten'd with the rich result
> Of all this riot; and ten thousand casks,
> For ever dribbling out their base contents,
> Touch'd by the Midas finger of the state,
> Bleed gold for ministers to sport away.
> Drink and be mad, then; 'tis your country bids!
>
> [4:500-509]

We come back, in these lines, to the unresolved antinomies of Pope's *Epistle to Bathurst,* in which the Mandevillian formula for the relation between private vices and public benefits is examined. Cowper's tone here is caustic and sarcastic, and his point is a serious one, for he can see only a perverse harmony between the larger purposes of the English nation and the private vices which support those purposes. Cowper's recognition of the country's participation in national corruption is expressed in a striking simile likening the manuring of the fields to the fattening of the treasury. The evil of drink, a "public pest . . . like the filth with which the peasant feeds / His hungry acres, stinks, and is of use." The simile concentrates its vituperation into the metaphor identifying the "hungry acres" of the farmer with the excise, "fatten'd with the rich result / Of all this riot." In this crucial passage we have clear evidence of Cowper's unsentimental observations of the countryside, of his sophisticated recognition of its participation in the economy of the nation. The rural fields themselves become an emblem, for the moment, of the treasury, and share in its corruption. Cowper's striking use of the manured fields as a simile for the corrupted treasury is a thoroughly antipastoral apprehension. It indicates how realistic observation and appraisal begin to hamper full imaginative commitment to bucolic habits of expression, and may be usefully contrasted with Pope's richer figure in *The Epistle to Bathurst,* a poem whose social realism has not thoroughly disrupted its thematic and figurative bucolic system:[10]

> Wealth in the gross is death, but life diffus'd,
> As Poison heals, in just proportion us'd:
> In heaps, like Ambergrise, a stink it lies,
> But well-dispers'd, is Incense to the Skies.
>
> [233-36]

Yet Cowper was a patriotic Englishman. *The Task* reflects in many places the poet's effort to discover "public virtue," and to praise it. In these passages of caustic observation, he has not yet expressed that complete disaffection from the national life which later in book four places him clearly apart from it, driving him to accept rural retirement in its most radical form as a totally critical stance. In these realistic passages on the countryside Cowper still asserts the presence of forces which oppose the drift toward corruption. The drunken louts of the country taverns, whom he has compared with "modern senators," continue in the debauchery until "Society, grown weary of the load, / Shakes her encumber'd lap, and casts them out" (4:498-

99). This observation reflects the narrator's fundamental sense of the possibility of public virtue; underlying his criticism of the national corruption is his sense that the corrupt are yet "outcasts" of society, so that the drunkard may be said to be one of the "signatories" of a kind of unspoken pact; he tacitly rejects the community of the virtuous sober who accept his rejection. This community of virtue Cowper labels as "society," and society is the term he often uses to describe that good union of men within the environment of optimal civilization. But the passages we have been considering include within the range of their criticism more than the merely antisocial habits of the drunkards. Cowper is studying, and attacking, the relation between the vices of the antisocial and the political institutions which are the formal expression of social union. Thus, if it is society which casts out its drunken load, it nevertheless is "the Midas finger of the state" (4:507) which creates revenue, through the excise, from the vicious habit. "Drink and be mad, then; 'tis your country bids!" At this point in the poem the narrator seems to distinguish between the state, the power that levies the excise tax and benefits from private debauchery, and society, that community of virtue which seems to have no clear connection to the state, and seems, indeed, to function in opposition to it. The excise tax, the swearing ministers, the drunken louts—all of these are sanctioned by, or at least clearly and formally connected with the political body, the state. But in what relationship does "society" exist with the state? By which mechanism does society rid itself of its dangerous and useless members, who are yet so useful to the state, and who, indeed, are among its senators? Certainly the narrator seems to distinguish between society and the state, locating virtue in the one and vice in the other. The result is that the criticism of corruption is never assimilated to a vision of the essential virtue of the English polity. Virtue is the characteristic of society (a term never clearly defined); vice is the business of the state. The implication is that virtue cannot be an element of the political order. And this, of course, suggests that, for all of his patriotism, Cowper will find no way to express his public themes in a celebrative mode.

Following immediately the section on the drunkenness of the country workmen is a passage lamenting the loss of the pastoral dream of an innocent countryside, a loss accompanied by the disappearance of an age that favored such a dream, "in days like these / Impossible, when virtue is so scarce" (4:529-31). "The town has ting'd the country" (4:553), laments the narrator, and he proceeds to examine the reasons for this unhappy change. The first approach to the problem is the familiar analysis of luxury. Indeed, the evils of luxury are never far from Cowper's thought; thus, in book two, where the poet's attention turns to the collapse of discipline in the schools, the source of even that plague is traced back to luxury: "Profusion breeds them; and the cause itself / Of that calamitous mischief has been found: Found, too, where most offensive in the skirts / Of the rob'd pedagogue!" (2:820-23). And, in book four, where Cowper's subject is not the schools, but the nation in general, this same familiar analysis of social decay is the explanation. However, although luxury is presented here as the chief symptom of a corrupt polity, the cycle of decay begins first with power: "Increase of pow'r begets increase of wealth; / Wealth luxury, and luxury excess" (4:580-81). It is, then, the unhappy confluence of power and wealth that the narrator suggests as the root of England's plight. The first victim of these subversive forces is order:

> The rich, and they that have an arm to check
> The license of the lowest in degree
> Desert their office; and themselves, intent
> On pleasure, haunt the capital, and thus
> To all the violence of lawless hands
> Resign the scenes their presence might protect.
> Authority herself not seldom sleeps,
> Though resident, and witness of the wrong.
>
> [4:586-94]

The argument here is complex; we may notice that "authority" is, in this passage, a term of value. It seems to represent power exerted properly, because exerted by the proper guardians of social order. But in England's present plight "authority herself not seldom sleeps." This is because the rich have themselves become lost in England's new world of power, wealth, luxury, and excess. The power that may be properly used "to check / The license of the lowest in degree" is thus something different from the power that generates wealth, luxury, and excess. This new form of power, Cowper implies, is utterly unlike the power emanating from the proper authority of the formerly virtuous polity. And the passage clearly suggests that the once virtuous polity was characterized by a social order based upon subordination. In this virtuous polity the social order reflected, indeed maintained, the political order. Society and state were inextricably involved with each other. But in the new polity of power and wealth, the polity of the aggrandized state, the moral basis of politics is destroyed along with the old order of society because the former guardians also now join in the new riot of luxury. So that in Cowper's analysis of the effects of the power of the aggrandized state, the very growth of that state destroys that system of human communal identity, society, which had been the basis of the state's legitimacy. In the new England, this moral order, which Cowper calls society, exists with no formal connection to the new apparatus of power, the state, so that the power of England is real but illegitimate. Cowper's social thought does not, any more than that of earlier figures like Pope and Swift, conceive of the possibility that the organization of society creates, rather than reflects, the purposes of the state. A certain kind of order, therefore, Cowper assumes as a good, and this order he understands as a creature of moral rather than political desiderata, though under the right conditions moral and political order can be linked. But power and order can also come to cross purposes, as have the new state and that other, now unpolitical entity, society. In the new state "society" is an undefined mechanism (though it is a term of value), and the power which now emanates from the state is not linked with "society" in a necessary relation. So that private vices like the drunkenness that fills the treasury through the excise tax are not simply public benefits, because Cowper implies a distinction between the political institutions of the state and the moral structure of society.

These points are substantiated by the poet's attack on universal soldiership, which immediately follows the passage on power and luxury. In the narrator's search for the causes of the debauchery of the countryside, the attack on power and luxury is the prelude to his discussion of what seems to him to be the major cause of the countryside's fall from grace.

> But faster far, and more than all the rest,
> A noble cause, which none who bears a spark
> Of public virtue ever wish'd remov'd,
> Works the deplor'd and mischievous effect,
> 'Tis universal soldiership has stabb'd
> The heart of merit in the meaner class,
> Arms, through the vanity and brainless rage
> Of those that bear them, in whatever cause,
> Seem most at variance with all moral good . . .
>
> [4:613-21]

The thought here is peculiar, attributing to an instrument of the state's power, the military, the major responsibility for the state's contribution to the decline of rural order. This shift of emphasis from cause to apparent symptom permits Cowper to invent a short narrative detailing the progress of the country bumpkin from a simple, useful member of the rural order to a superfluous though gorgeous adjunct of the state—a soldier. The narrative is based upon the poet's critical treatment of such ideas as heroism and the nobility of arms, and echoes the poem **"Heroism"** in its revaluation of those ceremonial standards of worth—a revaluation marked by the narrator's awareness of the intimate connection between such traditional measures of value and the corrupt purposes of power which, in fact, they simultaneously serve and disguise. Thus, we find the "noble cause" of soldiership (4:614) to be at odds with "public virtue" (4:615), even as the military splendor of the recruit is at odds with his former rural identity, the recruit who,

> his three years of heroship expir'd,
> Returns indignant to the slighted plough,
> He hates the field, in which no fife or drum
> Attends him . . .
> To be a pest where he was useful once;
> [Is] his sole aim, and all his glory now!
>
> [4:644-47, 657-58]

Nobility, heroism, and glory are the terms which emerge unfavorably from Cowper's scrutiny here, but the important point is that his scrutiny is in the name of public virtue (4:615), whose traditional emblems are nobility, heroism, and glory. Once again, however, public virtue, like that undefined mechanism by which society casts out the rural drunkards, is a quality whose place in the public order is not clear. The state, armed with power, is corrupted by

power; nobility, glory, heroism do not survive Cowper's analysis of their connection with power. How then, and through which public mode of action, does public virtue express itself, removed as it necessarily is from the seat of power which is the state?

The Task supplies no answer to this question; the only virtuous life portrayed is the life of retirement, and this option, as it is developed in the poem, can hardly be understood as the stage for the exercise of public virtue. But public virtue, like that undefined entity, society, is a crucial aspect of Cowper's thought, just as society is a more complex idea in *The Task* than we might be led to believe from the poet's habit of citing the vices of society in order to define the virtues of retirement.

The desire to strike a balance between retirement and involvement is in evidence throughout the poem, although the effort, finally, is not successful because of the poet's inability to discover that aspect of the world at large in which he might move. Thus, in the opening lines of book four, where the narrator described the eager anticipation with which he awaits the post, among the several objects of his curiosity about the doings of the world are the success of the war effort in the American colonies and the condition of India:

> But oh th' important budget! usher'd in
> With such heart-shaking music, who can say
> What are its tidings? have our troops awak'd
> Or do they still, as if with opium drugg'd,
> Snore to the murmurs of th' Atlantic wave?
> Is India free? and does she wear her plum'd
> And jewell'd turban with a smile of peace,
> Or do we grind her still?
>
> [4:23-30]

These are curious thoughts, particularly when considered in the light of the later section on the evils of soldiership and power. Here the retired man expresses, on the one hand, his patriotic disgust for the failure of the English war in the American colonies, a subject which receives more extended consideration in a passage of bitter sarcasm in book five, where the failure of English power at war is attributed to English weakness and moral decline at home; on the other hand, the imperial adventure in India is here the object of a different kind of censure: it is an example of power ruthlessly applied. The whole passage is incompletely realized; no measured indictment or justification of the use of power emerges: more vigor from the troops in the colonies, less from those in India, are equally desirable alternatives. The passage seems to rest on the assumption that there is such a thing as English honor, for that is what is degraded by the drugged behavior of the troops in the colonies (and, as the passage in book five makes clear, by the shameful failure of that war); but the implication here is that English honor would be reflected in the success of English power, a position inconsistent with the concern for India's freedom, and with those passages in *The Task* attacking the brutality of war and conscription, and those others which attack commercial enterprise and luxury for their intimate connection with power and empire. It would seem that the poet is not thinking seriously or systematically here about the problems of power as it is wielded by the English state, but rather that his attention is focused on that portion of honor belonging to English society. The troops in America and the troops in India seem, then, emblems in these lines not of English power, but of English honor, not of the state, but of the society, the term that Cowper does not define but which, in his usage, seems to stand for the communal and moral identity of the English people. It thus becomes possible for the narrator to despise warfare and soldiership as activities of the state, and to praise them as emblems or metaphors of the social identity of the English nation. And it is only with this vague concept of the social order as opposed to the political, that the retired man admits some personal connection.

The troubled distinction between society and state is not a subject of systematic discussion in *The Task,* but it is central to the poet's attempt to define a perspective for himself as a judge of English life. Book four concludes with an assertion of the perspective of retirement, but not before the narrator makes a final attempt to clarify his position on the moral nature of society. In this attempt the following passage is crucial, placed as it is immediately after the attack on the military as the corrupter of the rural order and immediately before a long concluding passage defining the virtues of retirement:

> Man in society is like a flow'r
> Blown in its native bed: 'tis there alone
> His faculties, expanded in full bloom,
> Shine out; there only reach their proper use.
> But man, associated and leagu'd with man
> By regal warrant, or self-join'd by bond
> For int'rest sake, or swarming into clans
> Beneath one head for purposes of war,
> Like flow'rs selected from the rest, and bound
> And bundled close to fill some crowded vase,
> Fades rapidly, and, by compression marr'd,
> Contracts defilement not to be endur'd.
> Hence charter'd boroughs are such public plagues;
> And burghers, men immaculate perhaps
> In all their private functions, once combin'd,
> Become a loathsome body, only fit
> For dissolution, hurtful to the main.
> Hence merchants, unimpeachable of sin
> Against the charities of domestic life,
> Incorporated, seem at once to lose
> Their nature; and, disclaiming all regard
> For mercy and the common rights of man,
> Build factories with blood, conducting trade
> At the sword's point, and dyeing the white robe
> Of innocent commercial justice red.
> Hence, too, the field of glory, as the world
> Misdeems it, dazzled by its bright array,
> With all its majesty of thund'ring pomp,
> Enchanting music, and immortal wreaths,
> Is but a school where thoughtlessness is taught
> On principle, where foppery atones
> For folly, gallantry for ev'ry vice.

[4:659-90]

The passage repeats Cowper's implied distinction between society and state, and proposes a more radical criticism of man's political life than has hitherto appeared in the poem. To this point in the poem there have been many criticisms of the corruptions of the English body politic; what we see here is a destructive analysis of union itself in all the forms it takes when sanctioned by the state: political, mercantile, military.

The first third of the passage (4:569-670) is based upon a simile which suggests a harmonious resolution of the forces of nature and art: man, like the flower growing in its native bed, grows to his fulfillment in society: he "blooms" there. Here again we see that society to Cowper is not merely the object of his criticism, though in general the larger world has served as the foil for the retired life. But as the passage continues with a consideration of the purposes served by the different forms of union within human society, the simile shifts from man as the flower in its native bed (man in society) to man as the flower plucked and arranged for ornament (man leagued with man in politics, in business, in war). The possibility of harmonizing the forces of nature and art thus vanishes in the new vision of the ornamental vase, with its plucked flowers, fading rapidly, stunted in their growth, ("by compression marr'd," 4:669), defiling their neighbors. The ornamental vase, the image of art, represents not man in society, but man leagued with man to exercise power in its various forms. The passage, coming as it does immediately after the attack on soldiership, compares a state-sanctioned organization like the military to the kind of bond typified by the rotting flowers of art in the ornamental vase (although the figures here are not carefully managed, since the precise metaphor for the military is that of swarming insects [4:666], so that man joined with man in war is like a "clan" of swarming insects, which are like the bundled flowers of the crowded vase). All kinds of formal human organization sanctioned by the state are the objects of the poet's attack here: associations created by regal warrant, or by mutual consent "for int'rest sake." The passage, indeed, goes on to include within its attack such forms of political and commercial organization as the chartered borough and the commercial corporation, whose members "lose their nature" though "unimpeachable of sin / Against the charities of domestic life." It is "incorporated man" whom Cowper attacks for such abuses as factories built with blood and the conduct of trade at the sword's point. Indeed, if by "politics" we mean the systematic organization of men into groups that can exert power and respond to it, then what emerges from this passage is a radical criticism of the political impulse itself, in all of the forms it assumes, from state to corporation.

But it is an incomplete criticism. Cowper insists upon the essential decency of human nature in its private mode: the incorporated merchant at home with his family is quite another fellow from the same merchant in league with his business associates. Nothing in the passage evokes the satirical tone which would suggest that the private and inner intensities of the merchant are implicated in his public, corporate behavior. Similarly we are told that there is such a thing as "innocent commercial justice" (4:683): its robe is white; but we are not told on what political power innocent commercial justice might be founded and by which private energies it may be sustained. We *do* learn which political process stains its robe, but Cowper does not say by which political institutions innocent commercial justice might be supported. In short, we see in this passage the epitome of the poem's failure as a document of consistent social thought: there is no theory to explain, no central emblem to express, the relations between power and justice, between state and society. Cowper demands the fruits of justice but rejects every source of political power, every type of political organization, for it is in the very process of political incorporation that he locates the source of injustice and corruption. What we have is a forthright recognition of the corruptions of the social order set forth in a way that precludes the discovery within politics of a remedy for those corruptions. When Cowper proposes retirement in book four, therefore, it is not man he withdraws from, only the institutions, inexplicably evil, created by men who are in themselves good.

Nevertheless, we must keep in mind the complexities of Cowper's outlook on the public world. His social criticism does not involve him in sentimentalizing the rural life as a scene removed from the corruptions of the larger life of the nation. Furthermore, despite his critical insight into the meaning of such terms as honor, nobility, and glory—an insight arising from his awareness of their often intimate connection with the brutal realities of power—they still remain for him terms of value, as we have seen in his concern for English honor as it is exemplified in English military success. But by the end of book four, it has become impossible for him to identify his sense of virtuous community with any of the institutions formally sanctioned by the state. Yet Cowper draws back: at the end of book four, instead of pursuing his critical thoughts as far as they might go, he chooses the option of retirement as a personal solution to the public dilemma he has defined.

> Some must be great. Great offices will have
> Great talents. And God gives to ev'ry man
> The virtue, temper, understanding, taste,
> That lifts him into life; and lets him fall
> Just in the niche he was ordain'd to fill.
> To the deliv'rer of an injur'd land
> He gives a tongue t' enlarge upon, an heart
> To feel, and courage to redress her wrongs;
> To monarch's dignity; to judges sense;
> To artists ingenuity and skill;
> To me an unambitious mind, content
> In the low vale of life, that early felt
> A wish for ease and leisure, and ere long
> Found here that leisure and that ease I wish'd.

[4:788-801]

In these concluding lines to book four, Cowper retreats to a position which, in fact, his analysis of political union ought to have precluded. Once again he admits the pos-

sibility of a virtuous politics, though he removes himself from any participation in it. Once again he speaks of the dignity of monarchs, the sense of judges and the eloquence of freedom fighters, all filling the places ordained for them in the order of things by God. But it is an unsatisfactory conclusion, a private wish parading as a cosmic vision.[11] These lines indicate, at least, that despite his choice of rural retirement, it was not without great effort that Cowper relinquished the posture of the public poet. **The Task** needs to be understood, not as a simple and sentimental statement of the pleasures of retirement, but as a tortured, and often self-contradictory attempt to speak in a public voice . . .

Notes

1. All extracts of Cowper's poetry are from *The Poetical Works of William Cowper,* ed. H. S. Milford, 3d ed. (London: Oxford University Press, 1926). References to "Heroism" are to line numbers; extracts from *The Task* are cited by book and line numbers.

2. Hoxie N. Fairchild, *Religious Trends in English Poetry,* 5 vols. (New York: Columbia University Press, 1939-62), 2:184.

3. Maurice Quinlan, *William Cowper: A Critical Life* (Minneapolis: University of Minnesota Press, 1953).

4. Morris Golden, *In Search of Stability: The Poetry of William Cowper* (New York: Bookman Associates, 1960). For a balanced discussion of the personal and public elements of *The Task* see William N. Free, *William Cowper* (New York: Twayne Publishers, 1970), pp. 104-12.

5. Lodwick Hartley, *William Cowper, Humanitarian* (Chapel Hill: University of North Carolina Press, 1938).

6. Norman Nicholson, *William Cowper* (London: Longmans, Green, 1960).

7. Hartley, *William Cowper, Humanitarian,* p. 151.

8. Quinlan, *William Cowper,* pp. 205-6.

9. Cowper's lack of interest in these figures—he simply does not develop them beyond this acknowledgment of their existence—illustrates, as does the social and psychological distinction he immediately asserts between them and him, how difficult it was for an eighteenth-century poet to imagine a world of Theocritean tranquility and song. Yet Cowper's interest in the psychological experience of *otium* is obvious; to embody it in a metaphoric idea with social implications was nevertheless inconceivable to him.

10. I owe this point to Paul Alpers.

11. "Superficially, the conventional praise of rural life balances the satire of the town. But the shift in tone and argument, from vituperation of man's institutionalized greed to an affirmation that society reflects the divine order of things, is as strikingly unusual as the

conjunction in this passage of the generalization 'everything has its place' with the personalized rejection of ambition. . . . What happens in the final lines is that personal feeling takes the place of moral concern" (Free, *William Cowper,* p. 109).

W. Gerald Marshall (essay date 1987)

SOURCE: Marshall, W. Gerald. "The Presence of 'the Word' in Cowper's *The Task." Studies in English Literature 1500-1900* 27, no. 3 (summer 1987): 475-87.

[*In the following essay, Marshall argues that the loss of contact with the Word of God in the modern city is the central and unifying theme of* The Task.]

Throughout his poetic career, William Cowper maintained a strong Christian faith, one rooted in the Evangelicalism of eighteenth-century England.[1] A major aspect of that faith involves Cowper's understanding of the *Logos,* a concept which influences a number of his works. In his commentary on the Gospel of St. John, a fragmentary composition which, to my knowledge, has been totally ignored in Cowper studies, the poet asserts his belief in Christ as the Word of God, and he stresses the creative function of the *Logos:* "By the Word is to be understood the Son of God; Christ was that Word . . . the Word of God . . . the same Word created all things . . . Christ, therefore, is God the Creator . . . in Him dwelleth the fulness of the Godhead bodily."[2] Christ, then, is "the efficacious Word, the fiat," as Walter Ong expresses it,[3] who creates light out of darkness, order and harmony from the original chaos. Cowper also suggests that the Word is the sustaining force of the natural creation. He writes in his brief commentary that "the Word" is actively present "in all things created."[4]

Cowper places greatest emphasis, however, upon the written Word of God. The poet suggests in his remarks on St. John's Gospel that man should continually "feed" upon the "Word" in Scripture.[5] Indeed, it is the written Word to which a troubled poet could turn for peace: "O How I love thy holy word," Cowper writes in his hymn, **"Afflictions Sanctified by the Word,"** for "It guides me in the peaceful way / I think upon it all the day."[6] And in his hymn, **"The Light and Glory of the Word,"** Cowper uses images of brillant light to convey his belief in the inspired word of scripture:

> The Spirit breathes upon the Word,
>   And brings the truth to sight
>   . . . . .
> A glory gilds the sacred page
>   Majestic like the sun;
> It gives a light to ev'ry age.[7]

These brief, representative statements bring us to the Cowper of *The Task,* who develops with depth and complexity these fundamental concepts of the *Logos. The Task,* of course, is often seen as a rambling, disunified piece,[8] but the theme of the Word, as we shall see, unites at least the poem's main topics: Nature, horticulture, the value of meditative reading in the rural environment, city life and the concomitant discussion of public education, the press, and sermons. This approach to the poem is in keeping with Cowper's own statement regarding the overall intent of *The Task:* "to discountenance the modern enthusiasm after a London life, and to recommend rural ease and leisure as friendly to the cause of piety and virtue."[9] For the poem ultimately asserts that country life is to be preferred to city life because of its closeness to the Word as revealed in the "book" of Nature and in quiet reflection upon Scripture. The city, on the other hand, is depicted as a modern Babylon which has so neglected and abused the Word that it has lost touch with the efficacious source of all life and meaning. Or, as Cowper writes in *The Task:*

> Their only point of rest, eternal Word!
> From thee departing, they are lost, and rove
>   . . . . .
> From thee is all that sooths the life of man.[10]

The important nature scenes in the poem certainly emphasize the essential and primary link between the "eternal Word" just referred to and the natural creation, for all of Nature is presented as the wondrous fruit of the engendering Word, the fiat. The English countryside "leaps forth at once" to the command of God's Word which "calls for things that are not, and they come" (V, 686-87). Beautiful, harmonious nature is "worthy of the word / That, finding an interminable space / Unoccupied, has fill'd the void so well" (IV, 551, 57). The poem also speaks of that "voice, / Which winds and waves obey" (II, 113-14).

Not only is nature created by the Word, but also it is sustained by the *Logos* which speaks to man in and through the creation. The poem opens with a variety of sounds such as "Wintry torrents roaring loud," and "rural sounds" which speak to "the spirit" and restore "the Tone of languid Nature" (I, 181-53). Cowper asserts that all such sounds merge to create a "voice . . . to sooth" (I, 191 and 199). This voice becomes the natural "word." Indeed, nature becomes, metaphorically, God's great *book,*[11] for in his works God "Commands us [as] in his word / To seek *him,*" and in nature man may "read his wonders" (III, 228; V, 798). Through contemplating nature, man may have a deeply spiritual epiphany, an existential experience of the living Word just behind the surface: "Nature [throws] wide / Her veil opaque, discloses with a smile, the author of her beauties . . . eternal Word" (V, 892-97). And the poem concludes, "So *reads* he nature whom the laws of truth / Illuminate. Thy laws, mysterious Word!" (V, 845-46, my emphasis). The poem thus adopts a sacramental view of Nature as providing tangible phenomena which contain the Word as the mysterious, spiritual force which speaks to man of its own order, harmony, and beauty.

We can now see how Cowper begins to develop more deeply the poem's sense of the Word in relationship to the country environment. The poem suggests that one way man may imitate and even participate in the creative expression of the fiat is through the art of gardening. Martin Battestin, summarizing a commonplace aesthetic position of Neoclassical England, suggests that for the poet of the eighteenth century the paradigmatic act of history, to be emulated both in works of art and in the moral life, is the "Logos, whose fiat first brought order out of chaos."[12] The essential creative principle inherent in the Word is, of course, that of *concordia discors*: "harmony and proportion, symmetry and balance" which arise from variety or apparent discord. Such aesthetic principles, Battestin demonstrates, often were applied to the "art" of gardening in the eighteenth century. Samuel Clark, for example, writes that the "true" gardener creates "a work infinitely various, but formally ordered."[13]

Similarly, in Cowper's poem, the true gardener creates not only a literal garden, but a microcosm of the universal order; once again, the fiat becomes the paradigmatic act of history to be imitated, even in the art of gardening. Note the planetary imagery, the imagery of universal wholeness and harmony reflected in the simple, rural garden. The gardener

> Has made a heav'n on earth; with suns and moons
> Of close-ramm'd stones has charg'd th' encumber'd
>   soil,
> And fairly laid the zodiac in the dust.
> He, therefore, who would see his flow'rs dispos'd
> Sightly and in just order, ere he gives
> The beds the trusted treasure of their seeds,
> Forecasts the future whole; that, when the scene
> Shall break into its preconceiv'd display,
> Each for itself, and all as with *one voice*
> Conspiring, may attest his bright design.
>
>   (III, 645-54, my emphasis)

Like the fiat, the gardener creates upon the principle of *concordia discors*. The separate and various elements of the landscape garden ("each for itself") harmonize, as with "one voice," to create a sense of unity in the "future whole." Therein they echo that single "voice" heard at creation which brought forth God's "preconceived" design.

Such is the natural, moral use of the art of gardening. Indeed, Cowper reminisces about a time when rural land was passed down from father to son, when "landscapes" were not simply "gazed upon awhile / then advertised, and auctioneer'd away" (III, 750-56). But now, Cowper suggests, rich landowners from the city destroy the "venerable" homes and land of "our forefathers" in order to make highly expensive, gaudy gardens. Though the older landscape gardens were not as elegant as those created by the wealthy, they were, at least, adhering to the natural contours of the land. The landscape gardener, "Brown" (Lancelot Brown), is hired by the wealthy to create new and elegant gardens in the country, but his creations come at the expense of the poor who must lose their land so that his lavish and, indeed, unnatural gardens can appear. In order to satirize such uses of gardening, Cowper presents Brown as engaging in a devastating parody of the original

creation rendered by fiat. In doing so, Cowper establishes a crucially important pattern for the entire poem, in which there are satires on "uncreating words" which stand in contradistinction to the "creating" Word of God. Indeed, Brown *calls* a garden into existence:

> He speaks. The lake in front becomes a lawn;
> Woods vanish, hills subside, and vallies rise:
> And streams, as if created for his use,
> Pursue the track of his directing wand,
>   . . . . .
> Ev'n as he bids! Th' enraptur'd owner smiles.
>
>   (III, 774-82)

Like the fiat which calls nature into being, Brown's word generates a garden, but unlike creation, Brown's garden violates natural order and perspective: what should be land is water, what should rise falls, what should be deep is elevated. Certainly, Brown's garden lacks "a grace" (III, 82), for there is no harmonious blending of various elements, only increasing disorder, as Brown assumes that nature can be perverted "for his use." Brown's garden is thus presented as the unnatural trickery of a "magician" who parodies the "omnipotent" God (III, 756). Indeed, Brown is presented in much the same manner that Pope presents the goddess, "Dulness," in *The Dunciad*. Pope suggests that Dulness is the "uncreating word" whose voice *uncreates* the natural order of things; what Aubrey Williams says of Pope's poem applies here, for Brown would return the rural harmony to its original "chaos," thus becoming a parody of the Word which generates order from chaos.[14] The Word and its creation thus serve as the standard, the paradigm of gardening, a model clearly imitated by the true gardener. Brown and others who would pervert nature, however, are not welcome in Cowper's rural paradise, and they must return to "London" where "Ambition . . . and vice [and] vanity . . . engulf them all!" (III, 817).

Cowper now suggests yet another way of experiencing the Word which is fostered by the rural environment: quiet meditation upon the written Word. We have presented to us, in various sections of the poem, the poet/narrator alone in his rural retreat, reading works of history (III, 140), or poetry (III, 255)—but especially, "His word" that teaches man "To seek him" (III, 224); "his word sagacious" (III, 254); "His most holy book" (VI, 650). It is, perhaps, scriptural prophecy which offers the greatest hope for the narrator and modern man, for "Sweet is the harp of prophecy" which gives assurance that "all Must be at length" reunited to God (VI, 747 and 819).

In the country, then, the Word may be experienced as: 1) the fundamental reality, the ground of being for the natural creation; 2) the primary aesthetic principle, as symbolized in the art of gardening; 3) intellectual and spiritual nourishment that is discovered in quiet, meditative reading of the Word of Scripture.

We can now shift emphasis and begin to see how the poem depicts city life—a major topic of *The Task*. A central element of London life is the press. The daily paper which is received by the poet/narrator is depicted as the mirror of London, the modern Babylon: through the reading of the paper, the poet is permitted a "peep" at "the great Babel" (IV, 90-91). At the outset of *The Task,* we were presented with an array of delightful, natural sounds. In contradistinction, the newspaper, which provides an overview of the city and its values, is "the herald of a noisy world," and the delivery boy comes "with twanging horn o'er yonder ridge" (IV, 5 and 1). Already, the paper is associated with abuses of "sound."

Moreover, it is of crucial importance to see that the "word" of the press ultimately is depicted as a parody of the Divine Word, the fiat. Once again, then, we have uncreating words, but now the poem has shifted its vision from the garden to the city. The writer of the news has a potent pen, a "fluent quill" which senselessly lumps together "words" about "Houses in ashes, and the fall of stocks, / Births, deaths, and marriages, epistles" (IV, 16-19). And the press, with one "voice" (IV, 35), reports political debate concerning Britain's treatment of India: "The grand debate, / The popular harangue" (IV, 30-31). Since it seems painfully obvious to the poet that the people of India, like all people, should be free, he finds such debate to be a "loud laugh" (IV, 33). He goes on to show that the actual words of the press—prideful political speeches, gossip, and trivial reports—are presented as a microcosm (as a *world* which springs from *words*) which parodies the fiat and its creation. The words of the London press are a "map of busy life," which often reports the ambition of city politicians (IV, 55). Indeed, the words metaphorically create an inky world:

Here runs the mountainous and craggy ridge
That tempts ambition. On the summit see
The seals of office glitter in his [the politician's] eyes;
He climbs, he pants, he grasps at them! At his heels,
Close at his heels, a demagogue ascends,
. . . . .
Here rills of oily eloquence in soft
Meanders lubricate the course they take.

(IV, 57-65)

These politicians thus manage to get their speeches and activity recorded in the press. But this is all "trivial" and represents a "dearth of information and good sense" (IV, 56-71). Thus, the London press contains meaningless "Cat'racts of declamation [which] thunder here" and "forests of meaning [which] spread the page, / In which all comprehension wanders, lost" (IV, 73-75). The rest of the paper "appears a wilderness of strange / But gay confusion . . . Heav'n, earth, and ocean, plunder'd of their seats" (IV, 78-82). Lumped together in this chaos are "Sermons, and city feasts, and fav'rite airs, Aethereal journies, submarine exploits, / And Katterfelto, with his hair on end" (IV, 84-86). The writer's quill, which generates the news, is a parody of the divine, generative principle, as it gives "voice and utt'rance" to a "noisy" world. For the *world* created in the press, with its *ridges* of prideful statements, *summits* of power, *rills* of false eloquence, and *cataracts* of meaningless words represents

an uncreation of order. It is a bathetic world of thunderous declamation with no content, of mountains of words built on illusions of grandeur, of words separated from meaning. The press, finally, is a sterile world, a "wilderness"— the ultimate travesty of a world teeming with life which is engendered by the *Logos.* The words of the press thus create a world of language which is a parody of *the Word* itself and the world it has generated, a world of harmony, order, and substantial meaning. The London press thus stands condemned in its own triviality by the Divine Word to which it is compared through the technique of allusion. An abuse of words is an abuse of *the Word.*

Similar abuses appear in the city's educational system. Cowper asserts that "in ancient days" (II, 699) English public education upheld high principles. Education was, metaphorically, presided over by a "sage call'd Discipline" whose *word* was sacred and "*Bespoke* him past the bounds of freakish youth" (II, 704, my emphasis). Just as the *Logos,* itself, speaks with wisdom, righteousness, love, and truth, so Discipline speaks forth his word: "in his speech was heard / Paternal sweetness, dignity, and love," along with "learning, virtue, piety, and truth" (II, 706-707; 700). His "voice" (II, 721), like the fiat itself, creates order from the potential chaos of classrooms, for he "held" the "passions," and his words "shook the delinquent with . . . fits of awe." Under the *efficacious* power of his word, there grew a little "garden" of learning: "Learning grew, / Beneath his care, a thriv'ng, vig'rous plant" (II, 715, 722, 713-14).

But modern London has lost such educational values, Cowper suggests, and abuses the word of education. Discipline has now lost his *voice* in the public schools: "his voice, unstrung, / Grew tremulous, and mov'd derision more / Than rev'rence in perverse rebellious youth" (II, 728-29). In the cities, Discipline has been replaced by "Ignorance," who is also directly associated with words and voices: "With parrot tongue," Ignorance "perform'd the scholars' part, / Proceeding soon a graduated dunce" (II, 738-39). The parrot metaphor suggests that the word of Ignorance is highly uncreative, that it merely repeats and reflects the thoughts expressed by other dunces, and it can hardly be said to be inherently generative as is the *Logos.* Indeed, this parrot tongue becomes an uncreating word that would transform the once orderly world of public education into chaos:

A dissolution of all bonds ensued;
The curbs, invented for the mulish mouth
Of head-strong youth, were broken . . .
. . . . .
A mock'ry of the world!

(II, 743-50)

The uncreating word of Ignorance and its resultant chaos are a parody of the orderly creation of God.

A central hope in the poem for some sort of reform lies in the *preaching* of the Word of God to the people of "Babylon." To Cowper's thinking, sermons are inspired by "His most holy book" of scripture (VI, 650) and are a most important means of communicating God's Word to man. Hence, the true preacher should hold his office as "sacred," for his sermon is the earthly expression of the eternal Word: he is the "legate of the skies" (II, 337-38). The minister's sermon, like the sacred text, itself, should be filled with power when the homilist *speaks out* [my emphasis]" against violations of divine law and "thunders" forth his sermons (II, 340-41). At the same time, the effective sermon must bring the soothing, peaceful message of the Gospel—the expression of the incarnate Word, Himself; the minister must remember that "the gospel *whispers* peace [my emphasis]" and that, like the redeeming Word of Christ, his word "restores the weak" (II, 342-43). The minister should display an eloquence and skill which carry with them the very heart of the Word of scripture: "[the preacher] in strains . . . sweet . . . Reclaims the wand'rer, binds the broken heart" (II, 341-43).

Unfortunately, the poem suggests, such ministers have all but vanished in the modern city and have been replaced by abusers of words. Such preachers use language which contains no inherent meaning and they preach sermons void of the efficacious power of the Word upon which they base their text. These false preachers, these "things that mount the rostrum with a skip," simply

> pronounce a text;
> Cry-hem: and, reading what they never wrote
> Just fifteen minutes, huddle up their work,
> And with a well-bred whisper close the scene!
>
> (III, 409-13)

Such an abuse of words parodies the creation by fiat, for these ministers symbolically have descended the chain of being to the level of a "thing," thus speaking themselves out of their own humanity. Moreover, such a minister makes a mere show of words: "He seek[s] to dazzle me with his tropes . . . and play his brilliant parts before my eyes" (II, 423-25). His word, unlike the *reality* of *the Word,* is a mere show or illusion. Not allowing his listeners to "feed" upon the Word of scripture, he "starves his flock!" (II, 429). To misuse words in sermons is, in the world of *The Task,* to parody God himself; and, again, to abuse words is to abuse the Word: "He [the preacher] mocks his Maker, prostitutes and shames / His noble office" (II, 427-28). Little wonder these abuses in speech exist, since the fake minister has been taught by a false Doctor or teacher of ministers, whose "voice" (II, 351) is one which:

> sells accent, tone,
> And emphasis in score, and gives to pray'r
> Th' *adagio* and *andante* it demands.
> He grinds divinity of other days
> Down into modern use; transforms old print
> To zig-zag manuscript, and cheats the eyes.
>
> (II, 359-64)

These are clearly abuses of words: selling homiletical skills for profit, using form and eloquence with no spiritual

content, depriving words of those qualities which Cowper, Pope, and other Augustan writers would see as essential. For here, words have lost their efficacious, redeeming and enlightening aspects. The "word" of the "Doctor," unlike the Word of scripture, uses form with no substantial content, words severed from truth and meaning.

It is within the general context of scripture and preaching that we now find a final rendering of the Word. Cowper certainly implies that pulpits have failed to transform modern London. As an alternative, he suggests that literature—indeed, his own poem—can be an important means of providing scriptural teaching and the homiletic force that seem to be lacking elsewhere. Occasionally, *The Task* closely mirrors—in tone, imagery, and theme— scriptural passages.[15] Let us first note such activity in the poetic text and then examine further implications as regards the central theme of the Word.

Cowper closely follows well-known scriptural passages when he asserts that "all below" is vanity, that "Nothing is proof against the gen'ral curse / Of vanity, that seizes all below" (III, 266-67). The source for the passage is, of course, the Book of Ecclesiastes: "All is vanity . . . I have seen all the works that are done under the sun; and, behold, all *is* vanity" (Eccles. 1:3 and 14, KJV). Emphasizing the transitoriness of life, the poet writes in the same passage: "All flesh is grass, and all its glory fades" (III, 261). Here are precisely the same words in the Book of Isaiah: "All flesh is grass . . . the grass withereth, the flower fadeth" (Isa. 40:6-7).

But the poem also offers a vision of hope and, again, Cowper turns to the prophet Isaiah and his vision of the millennium:

> Rivers of gladness water all the earth,
> The various seasons woven into one,
> And that one season an eternal spring,
>
>   . . . . .
>
> The lion, and the libbard, and the bear
> Graze with fearless flocks; all bask at noon
>
>   . . . . .
>
> Antipathies are none. No foe to man
> Lurks in the serpent now: the mother sees,
> And smiles to see, her infant's playful hand
> Stretch'd forth to dally with the crested worm,
>
>   . . . . .
>
> All creatures worship man, and all mankind
> One Lord, one Father.
>
> (VI, 763-84)

Here is Isaiah's scriptural account of the millennium: "the wolf also shall dwell with the lamb . . . and a little child shall lead them. . . . And the sucking child shall play on the hole of the asp . . . for the earth shall be full of the knowledge of the lord, as the waters cover the sea. . . . And in that day [all] shall say, praise the Lord" (Isa. 11:5-9; 12:4).

This is immediately followed by further direct parallels with biblical prophecy, this time elements of the vision of St. John in the Book of Revelation. A prophetic voice describes the end-time, when

One song employs all nations; and all cry,
"Worthy the Lamb, for he was slain for us!"

. . . . .

Till, nation after nation taught the strain,

. . . . .

All kingdoms and all princes of the earth
Flock to that light.

(VI, 791-802)

Paralleling the poem are these lines in Revelation: "And I beheld, and I heard the voice of many angels . . . Saying with a loud voice, Worthy is the Lamb that was slain . . . And every creature which is in heaven, and on the earth . . . [said] Blessing . . . to Him who sitteth on the throne, and unto the Lamb" (Rev., 5:11-13). Immediately after these passages, the poem offers a brief *commentary* on the scriptural "text" which has just ended: "Thus heav'n-ward all things tend. For all were once / Perfect, and all must be at length restor'd" (VI, 818-19). This brief commentary certainly heightens the scriptural nature of the prophetic passages, since, of course, biblical passages would receive such analysis in popular commentaries of the period.

The chief way in which the passages we have examined relate to the theme of the Word is that they emphasize the value of Scripture, the written Word of God; these sections of the poem are, then, meant to stand in direct contrast to the abuses of the Word revealed by the false preachers and teachers of London who were discussed earlier. The sections which so closely mirror biblical writings are certainly among the most eloquent and memorable in *The Task,* and it is through them that Cowper has chosen to provide the reader with the most all-encompassing vision, both of human weakness and of man's possibility for renewal. With the power of the Word itself, the passages suggest that city life, with its neglect and abuse of the Word, is a world of vanity and empty dreams much like the world described by "the preacher" in Ecclesiastes; but modern man, after realizing his situation, can participate in the vision of a future which is immersed in the presence of the living Word in the heavenly Jerusalem, a vision found in Scripture. When Cowper wishes to make his point this far-reaching, even visionary, he turns to the Word of Scripture to provide depth and persuasive expression. The poet/narrator thus becomes much like the true preacher who uses the Word in proper ways.

Moreover, there is a somewhat deeper element here. In the sections of the poem which are modeled after biblical passages, the reader has a poetic text which he is invited to read as though it were a Scriptural text, and he has a narrative voice that he is now asked to "hear" as though it were a biblical voice. Ultimately, this technique becomes an important *symbolic* element of the poem: it suggests that the poetic text gives priority to the scriptural text which it has, essentially, become; that the poem speaks with greater force and dignity when it permits *the Word* to consume the mere poet's words with its own holy presence. The poem, like the book of nature, thus becomes *sacramental*: the visible phenomenon of the poetic text oc-

casionally parts or symbolically vanishes to reveal *the Word* as fundamental ground of its own "being," just as it is for Nature itself.

We can, then, perceive that *The Task* has a central, unifying statement: the modern city has abused and lost contact with the Word, the source and meaning of life and the source and meaning of all significant uses of words themselves. This Word may best be experienced in a peaceful, rural environment through contemplation of the "book" of Nature, and through reflection upon Scripture and literary works, such as *The Task,* which speak to "noisy" (IV, 5) Babylon of a Word beyond sound.

Notes

1. For an excellent discussion of Cowper's religion, see Norman Nicholson, *William Cowper* (London: John Lehmann, 1951), pp. 26-45.

2. I am deeply indebted to Mr. Joseph Bourneau of Widener Library, Harvard University, for invaluable assistance in locating this work. Cowper's "Notes on St. John's Gospel" is printed in the Reverend Josiah Bull's *John Newton: An Autobiography and Narrative* (London: The Religious Tract Society, 1868), pp. 373-77. This passage covers pp. 373-75.

3. Walter J. Ong, S. J., *The Presence of the Word* (New Haven: Yale Univ. Press, 1967), p. 288. Obviously, I am indebted to Father Ong for the title of my own essay.

4. "Notes on St. John's Gospel," p. 374.

5. "Notes on St. John's Gospel," p. 377.

6. *The Poetical Works of William Cowper,* ed. H. S. Milford (London: Oxford Univ. Press, 1934), pp. 456-57, hereafter referred to as *Poetical Works.*

7. *Poetical Works,* p. 452.

8. For studies of the poem see Gilbert Thomas, *William Cowper and the Eighteenth Century* (London: George, Allen and Unwin, 1948), pp. 256-97; Roderick Huang, *William Cowper, Nature Poet* (Oxford: Oxford Univ. Press, 1957), pp. 67-92; Hoosag K. Gregory, "Cowper's Love of Subhuman Nature: A Psychoanalytic Approach," *PQ* 46, 1 (January 1967):42-57; William N. Free, *William Cowper* (New York: Twayne, 1970); Vincent Newey, "Cowper and the Description of Nature," *EIC* 23, 1 (January 1973):102-108, and *Cowper's Poetry* (Totowa, N.J.: Barnes and Noble, 1982), pp. 16-42, 93-207; David Boyd, "Satire and Pastoral in The Task," *PLL* 10, 4 (Fall 1974): 363-77; Dustin Griffin, "Cowper, Milton, and the Recovery of Paradise," *EIC* 31, 1 (January 1981):15-26; P. M. S. Dawson, "Cowper's Equivocations," *EIC* 33, 1 (January 1983):19-35; and Martin Priestman, *Cowper's 'Task': Structure and Influence* (London and New York: Cambridge Univ. Press, 1983). Priestman deals with the idea of Cow-

per's "self-recreation in the shape of the truly exemplary figure" in the poem (p. 5). The study thus sees the poem as an attempt by the poet to define himself.

The most serious attempt to establish unity in the poem, other than my own, is that of Thomas E. Blom, "The Structure and Meaning of *The Task*," *PCP* 5 (1970):12-18. This essay emphasizes the theme of the "fall" and redemption as being central to the poem. But this theme is much too commonplace, even inherent, in retirement literature to bear the weight Blom assigns it. Rather, the inherent concern with fall and redemption, as we shall see, becomes only a part of the poem's much larger discussion of the Word. Blom also points out some passages in the poem which echo Biblical prophecy. My own work offers more extensive uses of scriptural allusions in the poem and relates such elements to the theme of the Word, which Blom does not mention.

9. The passage is found in Cowper's letter of 10 October 1784 to the Rev. William Unwin. Cited in Nicholson's *William Cowper,* pp. 89-90. See note 1.

10. *Poetical Works,* V, 897-98, p. 219. Hereafter, references to the poem are to this edition and are cited by book and line.

11. The idea that Nature is God's "book" is commonplace in seventeenth and eighteenth-century English theology. For example, Bishop Peter Browne (whose works appear in Cowper's personal library), asserts that the world is a "book to be read," a book which contains the "living Word." See *Things Divine and Supernatural* (London, 1733), p. 9. Cowper's library holdings appear in Thomas Wright, *The Life of William Cowper* (London: T. Fisher Unwin, 1892), pp. 659-65.

12. Martin C. Battestin, *The Providence of Wit* (Oxford: Clarendon Press, 1974), p. 56.

13. Cited in Battestin, pp. 79-80, 46-57.

14. *Pope's Dunciad: A Study of its Meaning* (New Haven: Yale Univ. Press, 1967), pp. 143 and 139. Williams refers to the goddess, Dulness, as an "anti-*Logos*" (p. 154). Williams also points out that in Pope's poem abuses of *words* in literary art, in the press, and in public speaking represent abuses of *the Word* itself, the *Logos*. Similar ideas are expressed by other writers of the Neoclassical period. For example, in Dryden's "MacFlecknoe," Shadwell, through his abuses of writing, is presented as a parody of Christ, the Word. See Michael Wilding, "*MacFlecknoe*," *EIC* 19, 4 (1969):355-70.

15. Blom has noted some of the poem's prophetic allusions, but his use of this material differs greatly from my own. See note 8.

Andrew Elfenbein (essay date 1989)

SOURCE: Elfenbein, Andrew. "Cowper's *Task* and the Anxieties of Femininity." *Eighteenth-Century Life* 13, no. 3 (November 1989): 1-17.

[*In the following essay, Elfenbein follows Cowper's "revalorization of the feminine" in* The Task, *a process of poetically elevating femininity from a subordinate position relative to masculinity.*]

The poetry of William Cowper, especially his most famous poem, *The Task,* both encapsulates the developments of eighteenth-century poetry from Popean satire to the doctrine of sensibility and anticipates the achievements of the early romantics. *The Task,* more than any other poem of the later eighteenth century, functions as a turning point in literary history because of its radical redefinition of possibilities for the poetic subject. Critics, however, have rarely paid close attention to Cowper's powerful manipulation of ideology, and locating precisely his innovations can help us comprehend the peculiar complexities of the position of the poet in relation to society during this era.

I will argue that Cowper's particular power reveals itself most strikingly in his treatment of femininity, a quality that nineteenth-century critics persistently associated with him. Lord Jeffrey, for instance, mentions Cowper's "feminine gentleness and delicacy of nature, that shrank from all that was boisterous, presumptuous, or rude."[1] Hazlitt condemns the "effeminacy about him, which shrinks from and repels common and hearty sympathy."[2] Sainte-Beuve associates him with the private, feminine world of the home.[3] Metaphors of femininity underlie much modern commentary on Cowper as well: "Discounting his innate modesty and a tendency to apologize for his authorship, such remarks [about the necessity of amusement] seem appropriate to the leisurely pace and comparatively mild emotional drive of much of his verse."[4] Though commonplace now, this association was not made by his earliest reviewers.[5] Rather, it appeared after his poetry was published in editions that contained his biography, such as those of Hayley, Southey, and Grimshawe. When his poetry was read in a biographical light, critics saw the femininity of his life reflected in his poetry and vice versa. Some, like Hazlitt, claimed that Cowper's femininity lessened the value of his poetry. For Evangelists like Grimshawe, who associated the feminine with moral virtue, the femininity of Cowper's life reinforced the exemplary character of his poetry.[6] Sainte-Beuve found him to be the supreme poet of family life (p. 182). For these early critics, Cowper's femininity was a central issue in reading and evaluating him.

The trap that Cowper's femininity has posed so often for his critics is that of condescension, and more recent critics like Martin Priestman and Bill Hutchings have tried to divorce Cowper's art and life to escape the trap.[7] Yet the earlier critics sensed an issue of vital importance to his poetry, and *The Task* in particular, when they discussed his femininity. Cowper's femininity must be understood in relation to the attitudes, expectations, and activities that were associated, either literally or figuratively, with women in eighteenth-century England.[8] As is now familiar, the opposition between the social categories of masculine and feminine was expressed through polarities that implied the subordination of the feminine to the masculine, such as passive-active, weak-strong, private-public, leisure-work, dependent-independent, feeling-reason, beautiful-sublime, child-adult, and chastity-sexuality. Katherine Rogers has noted that

> the qualities considered feminine were those appropriate to a subordinate class. Steele casually remarked that modesty is "the chief Ornament" of women, integrity of men. Both are virtues, of course, but the first is self-effacing; the second, self-assertive. Women were credited with wit, but this quality was supposed to predispose them to vanity and in any case was constantly made subordinate to the masculine faculty of judgment. Men argued, in a neat circle, that since men are the lawgivers, God must have qualified them with greater strength and reason than women; being better endowed, they should of course rule.[9]

The construction of polarized masculine and feminine attributes was hardly unique to eighteenth-century England. Then, as today, perceptions of the validity of these polarities varied widely, and writers such as Sterne, Wollstonecraft, and Richardson were constantly manipulating, reformulating, and challenging them. Nevertheless, the fundamental separation of masculine and feminine was well established and pervasive enough in eighteenth-century England to permit us to evaluate Cowper's life and art in terms of it.

Before his first breakdown in 1763, Cowper tried to cope with the pressures of the public, masculine world of London. His breakdown stemmed largely from his terror of the public; he wrote in his memoir *Adelphi* that he was among those "to whom a public examination of themselves on any occasion is mortal poison" (*Letters,* 1:15). In 1765 when he chose not to return to London after having left St. Alban's hospital, where he had stayed while recovering from his insanity, he signified his inability to sustain himself in a traditional masculine role as a money-earner. Specifically, he resigned his position as Commissioner of Bankrupts:

> I had still one piece of preferment left which seemed to bind me under a necessity of returning thither [to London] again. But I resolved to break the band, and chiefly because my peace of conscience was in question. I had for some years held the office of Commissioner of Bankrupts worth about £60 per annum. Conscious of my ignorance in the law I could now no longer be contented to swear that I would do my duty faithfully in every commission, according to my ability, while I knew that I had no ability to perform it at all. I resigned it therefore and by so doing released myself from an occasion of great sin, and from every obligation to return to London. By this means, indeed, I reduced myself to an income scarcely sufficient for my

> maintenance, but I would rather have been starved in reality than have deliberately offended against my Saviour.

> (*Letters,* 1:41)

He portrays the position of a money-earner as a prison, emphasized in the imagery of bondage, and it seems an overdetermined coincidence that his position should be that of a Commissioner of Bankrupts. In escaping this prison, he left the aggressive, public, masculine world for a private, feminine one of retreat. His characteristic diffidence took over to the point where he was completely dependent. Cowper wrote that he could not be left alone without feeling utterly helpless:

> My brother who attended me hither [to Huntingdon] had no sooner left me than, finding myself surrounded by strangers in a place with which I was utterly unacquainted, my spirits began to sink and I felt . . . like a traveller in the midst of an inhospitable desert, without a friend to comfort or a guide to direct him.

> (*Letters,* 1:43)

His most recent biographer emphasizes his "habitual shyness" and "extraordinary passivity," both feminine attributes (King, pp. 32, 84). All his life and particularly after his first breakdown he needed mother and father surrogates to care for him: Mrs. Unwin, his brother, Dr. Cotton, John Newton, Lady Hesketh, and Margaret Perowne. Constantly, he put himself into the feminine position of submissiveness, passivity, and dependence. His madness only increased the degree to which he needed the support of others to live. Such attitudes related him to real and fictional eighteenth-century "men of feeling," such as Sterne's Yorick, Mackenzie's Harley, and James Boswell, who thought Cowper's melancholy even worse than his own.[10] What distinguished Cowper from them was his chastity, a trait that further reinforced his femininity. His early courtship of his cousin Theadora led to nothing, his semiflirtatious relation with Lady Austen ended in a complete separation, and the prospect of marrying Mrs. Unwin brought on another mental breakdown. Whether his sexual dysfunction was physical, mental, or both is still unknown; he almost certainly did not have sex after his first breakdown, whether or not he had had it before.[11]

Not only his inner psyche but also his external daily existence was femininized. In the 1780s, when he wrote **The Task,** he lived far from the glare of London in retirement at Olney and spent most of his time in the company of Mrs. Unwin and Lady Austen. The Evangelism he devoutly followed was associated with women, partly because Evangelists valued women as upholders of morality and partly because the movement opened up new opportunities for women in the public sphere. His daily activities, gardening, tending pets, writing letters, were all stereotypically associated with women, as Reynolds's paintings suggest.[12] Although Hutchings has emphasized Cowper's skill as a poetic craftsman, Cowper often presented himself as an amateur (Quinlan, p. 113). He described his poetry as a whim, a therapy to escape painful feelings, and women's writing was associated with amateurism in the eighteenth century (Rogers, p. 23). While none of these traits individually would be distinctively feminine, together they suggest that Cowper not only followed but also intensified patterns of behavior associated with femininity.

Yet Cowper was not comfortable with his position, and his personal conflicts appear as textual ones in his poetry. His simultaneous identification with and struggle against femininity surface most powerfully in his masterpiece, *The Task.* Sexual distinctions are fundamental to the poem because Cowper imagines moral issues in these terms. The town, specifically London, is the bad woman. Her crimes are laxness and profusion:

> It is not seemly, nor of good report,
> That she is slack in discipline; more prompt
> T'avenge than to prevent the breach of law:
> That she is rigid in denouncing death
> On petty robbers, and indulges life
> And liberty, and oft-times honour too,
> To peculators of the public gold.
>
>   (1.729-35)[13]

Cowper has some praise for London, particularly for her artists Reynolds and Bacon (both male), but, as Patricia Spacks notes, his condemnation of her is more powerful than his praise.[14] He recalls the biblical tradition of the town as the bad woman, a painted Whore of Babylon who hides her corruption underneath a beautiful exterior. The hypocritical hostess and her friends provide a concrete example of the town's wicked superficiality:

>   She, that asks
> Her dear five hundred friends, contemns them all,
> And hates their coming. They (what can they less?)
> Make just reprisals; and, with cringe and shrug,
> And bow obsequious, hide their hate of her.
>
>   (2.642-46)

The hyperbole of her "five hundred friends" suggests how profusion collapses into emptiness. The hostess surrounds herself with friends as hypocritical as she. The conventions of the town do not govern amicable human relations, but replace them. Related to the town as bad woman is the university as bad nurse:

> Now, blame we most the nurslings or the nurse?
>   . . . . .
> The nurse no doubt. Regardless of her charge,
> She needs herself correction; needs to learn,
> That it is dang'rous sporting with the world,
> With things so sacred as a nation's trust,
> The nurture of her youth, her dearest pledge.
>
>   (2.771, 775-79)

The university is an extension of the town because both share the same faults, laxness and profusion. As a nurse, the university seems to offer education and discipline, but really promotes idleness. The wicked students are like bad children, "nurslings," who ruin themselves because they do not have a mother on whom they can depend for correction.

The bad woman appears both as personification, the town and the university, and as particular human type, the hypocritical hostess. Effeminate men are another type of the feminine gone awry. Throughout *The Task,* Cowper manifests anxiety about possible deviations from a feminine ideal. Although he lived a life of leisure, did not have sex, and conformed to feminine modes of behavior, no one could condemn more harshly than he effeminate soldiers and preachers:

> But, loose in morals, and in manners vain,
> In conversation frivolous, in dress
> Extreme, at once rapacious and profuse;
> Frequent in park with lady at his side,
> Ambling and prattling scandal as he goes;
> But rare at home, and never at his books,
> Or with his pen, save when he scrawls a card;
> Constant at routs, familiar with a round
> Of ladyships—a stranger to the poor;
> Ambitious of preferment for its gold,
> And well-prepar'd, by ignorance and sloth,
> By infidelity and love of world,
> To make God's work a sinecure; a slave
> To his own pleasures and his patron's pride:
> From such apostles, oh, ye mitred heads,
> Preserve the church!
>
>   (2.378-93)

These effeminates exhibit the same laxness and profusion as London and the university; they are "rapacious and profuse" and Cowper emphasizes their association with feminine company. He was hardly the only author to inveigh against effeminacy in the eighteenth century, but the unusual length and indignation of this passage and a previous one on effeminate soldiers (2.221-32) indicate his deep uneasiness about this type and almost hysterical need to distinguish himself from it. He lingers in mixed fascination and revulsion over a type that suggests the dangers for a male taking on feminine characteristics. One goal of his poem is to convince us and himself that his femininity is not theirs.

Though "man" for Cowper is a far less concrete concept than "woman," he often associates at least one aspect of "man" with abuse of power and insensitivity to emotional ties; the slave trade epitomizes this facet of Cowper's "man":

> There is no flesh in man's obdurate heart,
> It does not feel for man; the nat'ral bond
> Of brotherhood is sever'd as the flax
> That falls asunder at the touch of fire.
> \He finds his fellow guilty of a skin
> Not colour'd like his own; and, having pow'r
> T'enforce the wrong, for such a worthy cause
> Dooms and devotes him as his lawful prey.
>
>   (2.8-15)

The imagery of bondage, in which the natural bond of brotherhood is replaced by the man-made bond of slavery, recalls both Cowper's memoir and the poem's earlier simile of the "unwholesome dungeon" (1.437) as an image of the town; it looks forward to his pessimistic presentation of "this prison-house the world" (2.661), where "the world" is the public world. His abhorrence of slavery is fired by his description in the poem of his own past as an escape from the bondage of public life. Only once he is safely away from the masculine domination of the town has he the courage to write, "I had much rather be myself the slave, / And wear the bonds, than fasten them on him" (2.35-36).

Not all men in the poem are wicked. Cowper pays tribute to artists, but his personal ideal is the good preacher:

> He 'stablishes the strong, restores the weak,
> Reclaims the wand'rer, binds the broken heart,
> And, arm'd himself in panoply complete
> Of heav'nly temper, furnishes with arms,
> Bright as his own, and trains, by ev'ry rule
> Of holy discipline, to glorious war,
> The sacramental host of God's elect!
>
> (2.343-49)

He elevates preaching to a superhuman office and transfers to the preacher Christ's attributes as doctor and warrior. The preacher is a specifically masculine ideal, one who can be powerful and active because he is sustained by divine authority. The other good man of **The Task** is his brother John at Cambridge. John is a perfect combination of feminine ideals, "manners sweet" and "gay good-nature," and masculine discipline; while he was at Cambridge, "order yet / Was sacred" (2.783-86). Like the preacher, he uses his power for benevolent ends. Yet this exemplary figure is dead, inaccessible in the hostile present. Cowper monumentalizes both the good preacher and his brother until the ideals they represent appear hopelessly unattainable. In the context of the poem, both are overwhelmed by concrete, present evils, effeminate preachers and lax students. Cowper's good man is in an imaginative limbo, powerless against the combined forces of the bad woman and the bad man.

In contrast, Cowper pictures the good woman vividly when he personifies nature and the rural life. For him, nature is never a sublime, masculine force, but a civil woman, "nature in her cultivated trim" (3.357). He opposes art, associated here and elsewhere with man, to the superior, nurturing beauty of female nature:

> The air salubrious of her lofty hills,
> The cheering fragrance of her dewy vales,
> And music of her woods—no works of man
> May rival these; these all bespeak a pow'r
> Peculiar, and exclusively her own.
> Beneath the open sky she spreads the feast;
> 'Tis free to all—'tis ev'ry day renew'd;
> Who scorns it starves deservedly at home.
>
> (1.428-35)

The metaphor of the feast suggests that nature is always mother nature; the good woman is the good mother. Nature is an extension of his peaceful, domestic life in the country. Her mere presence creates a superior moral atmosphere:

> The spleen is seldom felt where Flora reigns;
> The low'ring eye, the petulance, the frown,
> And sullen sadness, that o'ershade, distort,
> And mar the face of beauty, when no cause
> For such immeasurable woe appears,
> These Flora banishes, and gives the fair
> Sweet smiles, and bloom less transient than her own.
>
> (1.455-61)

His desire to portray the healing powers of mother nature draws him to identify himself with a woman; he, like "the fair," is cheered by Flora out of "immeasurable woe." His decision to describe a woman cheered by nature rather than a man suggests that his sensitivity to nature is a feminine rather than a masculine trait. Life surrounded by nature is not uncivilized, but civilization freed from the dangers of the town. Although Cowper seems at times to praise all society, he has a limited ideal of virtuous, rural society in mind. Spacks notes that "Cowper insists on a distinction between the 'civilization' of cities—characterized by 'refinement'—and that of the country" (p. 185). This distinction surfaces in the passage, ostensibly about Omai, that describes Cowper's move from the bad civilization of the city, a refined barbarism, to the good civilization of country:

> Blest he, though undistinguish'd from the crowd
> By wealth or dignity, who dwells secure,
> Where man, by nature fierce, has laid aside
> His fierceness, having learnt, though slow to learn,
> The manners and the arts of civil life.
> His wants, indeed, are many; but supply
> Is obvious, plac'd within the easy reach
> Of temp'rate wishes and industrious hands.
> Here virtue thrives as in her proper soil;
> Not rude and surly, and beset with thorns,
> And terrible to sight, as when she springs
> (If e'er she spring spontaneous) in remote
> And barb'rous climes, where violence prevails,
> And strength is lord of all; but gentle, kind,
> By culture tam'd, by liberty refresh'd,
> And all her fruits by radiant truth matur'd.
>
> (1.592-607)

Cowper's move from London to Olney was a move from a place where violence prevailed to one that was "gentle, kind / By culture tam'd." The civilization praised here is another aspect of the nourishing mother, the rural life. In his essay "Mother, Memory, Muse, and Poetry after Pope," John E. Sitter has noted "the tendency through much of the century to associate the muse with the mother and the poet with the faithful son" ; here, the rural life has become the muse.[15] In relation to this mother, Cowper is a feminized good child.

Having associated the town with the bad woman and man, and the country with the good woman, he turns in Book 3 to develop his self-portrait more concretely. As in his memoir, he describes himself in feminine terms as a powerless, ineffectual, solitary being:

> Since pulpits fail, and sounding-boards reflect
> Most part an empty ineffectual sound,

What chance that I, to fame so little known,
Nor conversant with men or manners much,
Should speak to purpose, or with better hope
Crack the satiric thong? 'Twere wiser far
For me, enamour'd of sequester'd scenes,
And charm'd with rural beauty, to repose,
Where chance may throw me. . . .

                                                    (3.21-29)

He refuses a major voice for a minor one by claiming that all his earlier social satire in the poem is as much "empty ineffectual sound" as that reflected by the sounding boards. Faced with his powerlessness to affect society, he concludes that "to fly is safe" (3.688) because he believes emphatically in a fugitive and cloistered virtue. In the famous "stricken deer" passage, he again pictures himself as a weak creature utterly dependent on the male "one," Christ, who rescues him. As Hutchings notes, "[The passage] gives his own retirement a personal force, to add to the moral force accorded by his reaction to evil in Book 2" (p. 214). The male sex of his rescuer implicitly puts him in a feminine position, and the arrows "deep infixt" are tinged with phallic overtones. Identifications with feminine powerlessness continue throughout Book 3. His gardening does not require "robust tough sinews, bred to toil" because it is only an amateur employment, work "such as may amuse, / Not tire, demanding rather skill than force" (3.405-07). Later, he describes the need to sweep leaves from the floor "with a woman's neatness" (3.616). His description of crazy Kate in Book 1 assumes a retrospective significance from these passages. It is puzzling there because it does not fit comfortably with the book's predominant theme of distinguishing the town from the country. In light of Book 3, Kate comes to represent a dark side of the feminine, one more threatening to Cowper than the bad woman of the town because her insanity in some measure figures his own. Because her powerlessness and dependence lead to her madness, she raises the haunting fear that femininity may not be an escape from madness but a path to it. Like the effeminate soldiers and preachers, Kate suggests potential dangers in femininity that Cowper must exorcise.

He quiets the threat of crazy Kate by locating his feminized persona firmly in a space governed by the good woman. Books 3 and 4 present in concrete detail what the "blest he" passage presented figuratively. They contain many vignettes of happy rural life, but his most sustained portrait of "domestic happiness, thou only bliss / Of Paradise that has surviv'd the fall" (3.41-42) occurs near the opening of Book 4:

But here the needle plies its busy task,
The pattern grows, the well-depicted flow'r,
Wrought patiently into the snowy lawn,
Unfolds its bosom; buds, and leaves, and sprigs,
And curling tendrils, gracefully dispos'd,
Follow the nimble finger of the fair;
A wreath that cannot fade, of flow'rs that blow
With most success when all besides decay.
The poet's or historian's page, by one

Made vocal for th'amusement of the rest;
The sprightly lyre, whose treasure of sweet sounds
The touch from many a trembling chord shakes out;
And the clear voice symphonious, yet distinct,
And in the charming strife triumphant still;
Beguile the night, and set a keener edge
On female industry: the threaded steel
Flies swifly, and, unfelt, the task proceeds.

                                                    (4.150-66)

This passage has many implications for Cowper, but his equation between "female industry" and "the task"—*The Task* is particularly striking. "Nature in her cultivated trim" is brought indoors through the embroidery, and the power struggles of the town are tamed to "charming strife" and "threaded steel." This female industry is Cowper's ideal, not a paradise within, but a paradise within doors. While his earlier self-presentation emphasized the weakness of the feminine, the domestic scenes suggest its sustained bliss. If he cannot have masculine power and assertiveness, he can at least have feminine virtue and industry.

He goes on to disrupt the town-country polarity, somewhat surprisingly since it has been the major structural principle organizing the poem. The country is not as pure as we thought: "The town has ting'd the country" (4.553). Cowper predictably images the country's corruption as a change from the good woman to the bad:

          The rural lass,
Whom once her virgin modesty and grace,
Her artless manners, and her neat attire,
So dignified, that she was hardly less
Than the fair shepherdess of old romance,
Is seen no more. The character is lost!
Her head, adorn'd with lappets pinn'd aloft,
And ribbands streaming gay, superbly rais'd,
And magnified beyond all human size,
Indebted to some smart wig-weaver's hand
For more than half the tresses it sustains.

                                                    (4.534-44)

The transformation of her wardrobe reverses the decay of crazy Kate's clothes. The profusion and laxness of the bad woman, the town, has ruined the type of the virtuous good woman of rural life. The male version of this decline is the peasant who becomes a soldier and returns having "lost / His ignorance and harmless manners too" (4.650-51). Like the university students, he has given up discipline and become a bad child, "crook'd, and twisted, and deform'd" (2.772), as opposed to Cowper, the good child. The falls of the rural lass and peasant bring out Cowper's distrust of sexuality: the lass loses her "virgin modesty" and the soldier is ready "to break some maiden's and his mother's heart" (4.656). His condemnation of their sexuality reflects how he associates chastity with virtue to bolster his moral character. Unlike them, he remains immune to the sexual temptations of the town, which are synecdoches for all its vices.

Surprising as the breakdown of the town-country polarity at first seems, it concludes a subtle but decisive shift in the middle books. If virtue versus vice cannot correspond to country versus town, then it must correspond to William Cowper versus everyone else. His little domestic paradise is not typical of rural life; it is unique. His solitary, feminine existence is the *only* bastion of virtue in a world rank with corruption. He is no longer just a type of the happy domestic man, but a special, privileged being whose superior virtue allows him to comment authoritatively on the rest of humanity. The difference between two passages about his authority as a poet dramatizes this shift:

> What's the world to you?—
> Much. I was born of woman, and drew milk,
> As sweet as charity, from human breasts.
> I think, articulate, I laugh and weep,
> And exercise all functions of a man.
> How then should I and any man that lives
> Be strangers to each other?
>
> . . . . .
>
> I cannot analyse the air, nor catch
> The parallax of yonder luminous point,
> That seems half quench'd in the immense abyss:
> Such pow'rs I boast not—neither can I rest
> A silent witness of the headlong rage
> Or heedless folly by which thousands die,
> Bone of my bone, and kindred souls to mine.
>
> (3.195-201, 214-20)

> Thus sitting, and surveying thus at ease
> The globe and its concerns, I seem advanc'd
> To some secure and more than mortal height,
> That lib'rates and exempts me from them all.
> It turns submitted to my view, turns round
> With all its generations; I behold
> The tumult, and am still.
>
> (4.94-100)

In the first passage, Cowper justifies himself, as does Pope in "Dialogue II" of the *Epilogue to the Satires,* by claiming that he is typical, no different from other men. This stance dominates the early books, in which he writes satire as a concerned individual, but not one who is necessarily special. In the second passage, he has become special and superior. His position is the same as Johnson's "observation" in *The Vanity of Human Wishes,* a superhuman, prophetic stance. It has authority because the observer distanced from society can see its flaws better than those enmeshed in it. As Cowper knows, his stance is more rhetorical fiction than truth, and he treats his claim to it with some irony in Book 4. Nevertheless, to occupy a superior moral position is more powerful than to be in the same position as everyone else. In the last two books, Cowper grows more serious about his right to this position, and the authoritative power of his voice increases dramatically.

He licenses this increase by seeing himself in relation to God rather than to society. In relation to God, his marginalized, feminized existence is not a proof of ineffectuality but of prophetic power. He becomes the voice of one crying in the wilderness, the prophet in exile. Like Milton, because he is cut off from an ordinary vision, he claims he has access to a divine vision; because he is isolated from the power of man, he becomes a vessel for the power of God. Satire, which he admits is ineffectual, is the major poetic stance available to him when he sees himself in relation to society. When he sees himself in relation to God, satire fades before the superior force of religious indignation:

> But there is yet a liberty, unsung
> By poets, and by senators unprais'd,
> Which monarchs cannot grant, nor all the pow'rs
> Of earth and hell confed'rate take away:
> A liberty, which persecution, fraud,
> Oppression, prisons, have no power to bind;
> Which whoso tastes can be enslav'd no more.
> 'Tis liberty of heart, deriv'd from heav'n;
> Bought with HIS blood who gave it to mankind,
> And seal'd with the same token!
>
> (5.538-47)

Cowper now inveighs against slavery not because he feels compassion for slaves but because he possesses special insight, "unsung / By poets, and by senators unprais'd." His use of Christian imagery might seem to imply a larger Christian community, but he never imagines himself in such a community; he speaks as the only virtuous Christian in the world. As a result, he infuses conventional Christian images with considerable personal passion:

> Chains are the portion of revolted man,
> Stripes and a dungeon; and his body serves
> The triple purpose. In that sickly, foul,
> Opprobrious residence, he finds them all.
> Propense his heart to idols, he is held
> In silly dotage on created things,
> Careless of their Creator.
>
> (5.581-87)

Cowper's prophetic stance here leads him to transform the prison images that before expressed his terrified view of the town into a divine vision of original sin. He reveals that his passions have been throughout the poem in the service of a voice greater than his:

> The STILL SMALL VOICE is wanted. He must speak,
> Whose word leaps forth at once to its effect;
> Who calls for things that are not, and they come.
>
> (5.685-87)

While he imagines that Deists obfuscate their prose with "poetic trappings," Cowper hears and to an extent reproduces the biblical "STILL SMALL VOICE" of God's grace. His poetry becomes more than mere trappings. The capital letters suggest the power latent in the voice that seems feeble and powerless; they are a paradigm for the poet.

The "STILL SMALL VOICE" is a feminine image given masculine authority, and it underlines how radically Cowper has revalorized his feminine position. The man who earlier presented himself as passive and feeble, incapable "from heights sublime / Of patriot eloquence to flash down fire" (2.216-17), now flashes down from his "more than mortal height" the fires of religion. Because Cowper has left the prison-house of the world and ascended to religious heights, he claims that his vision is purer than that of those who cannot see beyond the everyday:

> Knowledge dwells
> In heads replete with thoughts of other men;
> Wisdom in minds attentive to their own.
> Knowledge, a rude unprofitable mass
> The mere materials with which wisdom builds,
> Till smooth'd and squar'd and fitted to its place,
> Does but encumber whom it seems t'enrich.
> Knowledge is proud that he has learn'd so much;
> Wisdom is humble that he knows no more.
>
> (6.89-97)

Knowledge is masculine, proud, and public; wisdom is feminine, humble, and private. The stricken deer, made wise through solitude, turns to judge those who cast him out. He never doubts his religious voice the way he doubts his satiric one; as a prophet, he can be sure of the power of his words.

His revalorization of femininity becomes more pronounced in the final book when he recalls the activities and affections that earlier associated him with domesticity and re-presents them in a prophetic light. Nature and gardening now become pathways to God. He is no longer like "the fair" whom Flora coaxed out of immeasurable woe. Rather, by perceiving nature, he worships the divine: "Nature is but a name for an effect, / Whose cause is God" (6.223-24). As Spacks notes, "The 'lecture' nature offers is the revelation that there is no separation, finally, between the visual glory (or, for that matter, the visual barrenness) of the natural world and its theological meaning. The vibrant 'soul in all things' need only be recognized; perception of its energy is part of Cowper's direct relation-seeking poetic perception of the imagined scene itself" (p. 205). His close-ness to nature is transformed from a relation to a benevolent mother to one with a powerful father, God. He is still the child, but one bolstered by masculine rather than feminine authority. The contrast between his physical walk through nature in Books 1 and 6 plays out in miniature his growth in spiritual power:

> Descending now (but cautious, lest too fast)
> A sudden steep, upon a rustic bridge,
> We pass a gulph, in which the willows dip
> Their pendent boughs, stooping as if to drink.
> Hence, ancle deep in moss and flow'ry thyme,
> We mount again, and feel at ev'ry step
> Our foot half sunk in hillocks green and soft,
> Raised by the mole, the miner of the soil.
>
> (1.266-73)

> Here, unmolested, through whatever sign
> The sun proceeds, I wander. Neither mist,
> Nor freezing sky nor sultry, checking me,
> Nor stranger intermeddling with my joy.
>
> (6.295-98)

In his joyous wandering he comes upon "the tim'rous hare" and "the stock-dove, unalarm'd." His love for them is no longer a feminine indentification with "harmless nature, dumb" (3.329) but a proof of his ability to share his "universal Father's love" (6.449). Those critics who poke fun at Cowper for attacking cruelty to animals twice, in Books 3 and 6, have missed the point. The difference between the two passages demonstrates how the power of Cowper's voice has grown through his relation to God. Even his chastity is no longer a sign of virtuous femininity or mere unmanliness, but an indication of ostracized yet enduring truth:

> Oh for a world in principle as chaste
> As this is gross and selfish! over which
> Custom and prejudice shall bear no sway,
> That govern all things here, should'ring aside
> The meek and modest truth, and forcing her
> To seek a refuge from the tongue of strife
> In nooks obscure, far from the ways of men.
>
> (6.836-42)

Triumphantly, he pictures himself not as unfit for society but as too good for it. Cowper draws on the femininity of Christ to justify his prophetic position; the "meek and modest truth" describes them both. This passage is perhaps the clearest example of how, by using his femininity as a pathway to the divine, he guarantees his prophetic author-ity. Having brought himself into a loving relation with God the Father, he can see in himself attributes of God the Son. He also pointedly omits Eve from his version of the Fall story to avoid the traditional association of the feminine with original sin. The good child has taken on divine dimensions.

The poetry that results from his revalorization falls into two modes. The first is the paradoxical feminized sublime of the holy city:

> Behold the measure of the promise fill'd;
> See Salem built, the labour of a God!
> Bright as a sun the sacred city shines;
> All kingdoms and all princes of the earth
> Flock to that light; the glory of all lands
> Flows into her; unbounded is her joy,
> And endless her increase.
>
> (6.798-804)

Cowper's rhetoric stems from the Bible, but the role of the feminine in his poem underlines the climactic significance of personifying Salem as a good woman, the antitype of London or of Sicily, whose devastation by an earthquake he vividly describes in Book 2 as an evil that "sin has wrought" (2.133). Martin Price describes the status of the poet in Cowper's feminine sublime: "The poet has transcended the world. He must struggle constantly to regain that transcendence, but he disdains any show of power. His unsuspected mildness is as much instinct with energy as the lark's song; it serves only to protect the other self within."[16] Unfortunately, "unsuspected mildness" is not always aesthetically compelling. The vision of Salem is disappointingly feeble after the vigor his voice has attained in the poem's second half. It fails because the holy city as good woman is too easy a solution to the problematic of the feminine that Cowper develops. He does not infuse the description with the personal tensions peculiar to *The Task,* only with millenialist verbiage.

He takes a much greater risk in the passage immediately following, the only time in the poem he approaches a deeper sublimity:

> Perhaps the self-approving haughty world,
> That as she sweeps him with her whistling silks
> Scarce deigns to notice him, or, if she see,
> Deems him a cypher in the works of God,
> Receives advantage from his noiseless hours,
> Of which she little dreams. Perhaps she owes
> Her sunshine and her rain, her blooming spring
> And plenteous harvest, to the pray'r he makes,
> When, Isaac like, the solitary saint
> Walks forth to meditate at even tide,
> And think on her, who thinks not for herself.

> (6.940-50)

Cowper's "unsuspected mildness" becomes heroic. In these extraordinary lines, the man who presented himself in his memoir as being so dependent on others that he could not be left alone for a few hours imagines that the lives of thousands depend on him because he influences the weather. The moment of greatest sublimity is the moment of greatest silliness. Johnson's mad astronomer is reborn and taken with absolute seriousness. Cowper ventures briefly to imagine himself in a position of power and his poetic triumph is that we want to believe him.

Even in this moment of egotistical sublimity, his "perhaps" signals a reluctance to commit himself fully. As if repenting having given himself too much power, he afterwards presents himself with none:

> So glide my life away! and so at last,
> My share of duties decently fulfill'd,
> May some disease, not tardy to perform
> Its destin'd office, yet with gentle stroke,
> Dismiss me, weary, to a safe retreat,
> Beneath the turf that I have often trod.

> (6.1000-05)

His fear of having transgressed is so great that he strikes himself down before God can. But the moment of sublimity is not entirely without effect, because it confirms a conviction of his adult masculinity that has been hinted at in images throughout the last two books, such as that of the free man who casts off his chains "with as much ease as Samson his green wyths" (5.737). He imagines the female "haughty world" to be dependent on him, and he differentiates himself from the bad woman:

> She judges of refinement by the eye,
> He by the test of conscience, and a heart
> Not soon deceiv'd; aware that what is base
> No polish can make sterling; and that vice,

> Though well perfum'd and elegantly dress'd,
> Like an unburied carcase trick'd with flow'rs,
> Is but a garnish'd nuisance, fitter far
> For cleanly riddance than for fair attire.

> (6.987-94)

He has distinguished himself from the bad woman throughout the poem, but he distinguishes between "he" and "she" more resolutely here than anywhere else. In criticizing the bad woman, he takes on an uncompromisingly masculine role. In his closing tribute to Lady Austen, he proudly says that he was "obedient to the fair" only as long as he pleased before asserting his own poetic will to "please her more" (6.1008-09). God, not Lady Austen, is his chosen audience. Cowper has recuperated his masculine ego ideal of the preacher outlined in Book 2 by becoming the "messenger of truth" and "legate of the skies" (2.337-38). The preacher is the most acceptable masculine role he can imagine, and it is as such that he ends *The Task.*

For clarity's sake, I have presented as a linear progression what is actually a complex and dialectical development. Nonetheless, it is accurate to say that the revalorization of the feminine is an overall goal in this notoriously circular poem, and much of the greatness of *The Task* comes from Cowper's ability to manipulate the cultural commonplaces of sexual distinction into a source of poetic strength. The poem is difficult for modern readers because it has few passages of radiant poetic beauty; much of the verse, particularly when seen out of context, is second rate. Its power does not reveal itself in short excerpts (as it is often read) but in the movement of the whole, in which Cowper discards the Popean satiric vein that he knows to be ineffectual and re-invents the Miltonic stance of the inspired prophet.

For the romantics, *The Task* opened up new possibilities for the poetic voice. Cowper is not a romantic; he never asserted the value of his own personality apart from God and his prophecy is conservative, not radical. Instead, he empowered the figure of the recluse by developing the progress of the inner life into a prophetic subject. The challenge he posed for Blake and Wordsworth was how to achieve such power without paying the terrible price of isolation and madness. Rather than revalorizing femininity as Cowper had, they need to transform it. Blake's conception of mental fight and the banners militant of Wordsworth's Imagination hearken back to Cowper's belief that the true prophet's "warfare is within" (6.935). Yet even as the romantics make the prophetic position more masculine and powerful, they are haunted by the ideal of Cowperian femininity. Wordsworth's *Prelude* is indebted throughout to Cowper, and the lines in which Wordsworth epitomizes his ideal of the loving man suggest his deep awareness of what had Cowper accomplished in *The Task:*

> And he whose soul hath risen
> Up to the height of feeling intellect
> Shall want no humbler tenderness, his heart
> Be tender as a nursing mother's heart;
> Of female softness shall his life be full,

Of little loves and delicate desires,
Mild interests and gentlest sympathies.[17]

Notes

1. Quoted in the intro. to James Robert Boyd's edn. of *The Task, Table Talk, and Other Poems of William Cowper* (N.Y.: A. S. Barnes, 1857), p. 12.

2. *Lectures on the English Poets,* in *The Complete Works of William Hazlitt,* ed. P. P. Howe, 21 vols. (N.Y.: AMS, 1967), 5:91.

3. "William Cowper ou de la poésie domestique," *Causeries du lundi* 11 (1854): 139-97.

4. D. J. Enright, "William Cowper," in *The Pelican Guide to English Literature,* ed. Boris Ford, 7 vols. (Baltimore: Penguin, 1966), 4:392.

5. See the comments of James King in his *William Cowper: A Biography* (Durham, N.C.: Duke Univ., 1986), pp. 154-55.

6. See his comments on Cowper's character in Boyd, pp. 7-20. For a discussion of the relation of Evangelism to women, see Barbara B. Schnorrenberg and Jean E. Hunter, "The Eighteenth-Century Englishwoman," in *The Women of England: From Anglo-Saxon Times to the Present,* ed. Barbara Kanner (Hamden, Conn.: Archon, 1979), pp. 199-201. Ann Douglas's *The Feminization of American Culture* (N.Y.: Avon, 1977) provides an interesting parallel to some of the issues raised by Cowper's *Task.*

7. See Priestman, *Cowper's Task: Structure and Influence* (Cambridge: Cambridge Univ., 1983) and Hutchings, *The Poetry of William Cowper* (London: Croom Helm, 1983).

8. Cowper himself rarely, if ever, used the words "feminine" or "femininity" to describe himself; the terms themselves are mine, not his. He often did just the opposite by insisting on his masculinity, as in his letter to Mrs. King: "There was a time . . . when I amused myself in a way somewhat similar to yours; allowing, I mean, for the difference between masculine and female operations" (*The Letters and Prose Writings of William Cowper,* ed. James King & Charles Ryskamp, 5 vols. [Oxford: Clarendon, 1979-86], 3:221; subsequent refs. in text). His anxiety about femininity surfaces as early as 1756 in his essay for *The Connoiseur,* no. 111, about the mamma's boy Billy Suckling (*Letters,* 5:4-7).

9. *Feminism in Eighteenth-Century England* (Urbana: Univ. of Illinois, 1982), p. 38. Rogers's book, particularly the 1st chap., is the source of most of the information in this paragraph. Wollstonecraft still provides the best overview of the typical 18th-c. idea of the feminine in chap. 5, "Animadversions on Some of the Writers Who Have Rendered Women Objects of Pity, Bordering on Contempt," of *Vindication of the Rights of Woman,* a chap. in which she quotes Cowper. Schnorrenberg and Hunter have an excellent bibliography of works concerning women in 18th-c. England.

10. See Boswell's comment, "I was quite shocked to hear of such a state of mind. My own was good by comparison" (*Boswell: The Great Biographer, 1789-1795,* ed. Marlies K. Danziger & Frank Brady [N.Y.: McGraw-Hill, 1989], p. 129).

11. On Cowper's problematic sexuality, see King, p. 28, and Maurice J. Quinlan, *William Cowper: A Critical Life* (Minneapolis: Univ. of Minnesota, 1953), pp. 42-44.

12. There are many such paintings by Reynolds, but a sample would include *Elizabeth (Widdrington), Mrs. Thomas Riddell* (41), *Lady Cockburn and her Three Eldest Sons* (70), *The Honorable Mary Monckton* (77), *Mrs. Pelham Feeding Poultry* (91), *Master Henry Hoare as* The Young Gardener (112), and *The Cottagers: Mrs. and Miss Macklin and Miss Potts* (118); numbers refer to plates in Ellis Waterhouse's *Reynolds* (London: Phaidon, 1973).

13. All quotations from *The Task* are from *Poetical Works,* ed. H. S. Milford, 4th edn. (London: Oxford, 1971). Refs. refer to book and line numbers.

14. "William Cowper: The Heightened Perception," in *The Poetry of Vision: Five Eighteenth-Century Poets* (Cambridge, Mass.: Harvard Univ., 1967), p. 185.

15. *ELH* 44 (1977): 331. Even when Cowper describes the pleasures of leaving behind for brief periods the familiar, feminine "shelter'd vale" for "forests, or the savage rock" (1.513, 518), he somewhat tames what could have been a move into a more masculine view of the wild by describing the "savage rock" as a place that "hides the sea-mew in his hollow clefts / Above the reach of man" (1.518-19). The rock becomes a protection for the sea–mew against the intrusion of man, and the rock's "hollow clefts" have feminine overtones.

16. "The Sublime Poem: Pictures and Powers," *Yale Review* 58 (1969): 212.

17. 1805 *Prelude,* 13.204-10; quoted from *The Prelude: 1799, 1805, 1850,* ed. Jonathan Wordsworth et al. (N.Y.: Norton, 1979).

W. B. Hutchings (essay date 1989)

SOURCE: Hutchings, W. B. "William Cowper and 1789." *Yearbook of English Studies* 19 (1989): 71-93.

[*In the following essay, Hutchings evaluates Cowper as a political poet, especially in his responses to the French Revolution.*]

If a reader hopes that William Cowper's poem, **'Annus Mirabilis, 1789',** will provide welcome evidence that the English literary world responded with alacrity to the events in Paris, he or she will be rapidly disabused:

The spring of eighty-nine shall be
An aera cherish'd long by me,
Which joyful I will oft record,
And thankful at my frugal board;
For then the clouds of eighty-eight,
That threaten'd England's trembling state
With loss of what she least could spare,
Her sov'reign's tutelary care,
One breath of Heav'n, that cry'd—Restore!
Chas'd, never to assemble more,
And far the richest crown on Earth,
If valued by its wearer's worth,
The symbol of a righteous reign,
Sat fast on George's brows again.[1]

(l. 32)

Cowper's choice of his favourite octosyllabics, 'dear Mat Prior's easy jingle',[2] may be seen as setting an appropriately low tone for such a disappointing answer to a promising title. Even the terms of Cowper's praise of George III, as moral guardian of the nation and—in the rest of the poem—husband to a much-loved queen, may strike us as insular and inward-looking. We are culturally and politically as far from Paris as, well, Weston Underwood, where Cowper wrote the poem, together with others on similar topics[3] (**'On the Queen's Visit to London'**, **'On the Benefit Received by His Majesty from Sea-Bathing'** and an earlier, now lost poem anticipating George's recovery). Yet these are all designed for public popularity. Cowper sent **'Annus Mirabilis'** in March 1789 to his cousin, Lady Hesketh, who, he well knew would find the sentiments highly congenial, and within a week he was reporting, with a touch of venial disingenuousness, that it was to be presented to the Queen herself 'by some kind body or another, I know not whom'.[4] (Cowper was less of a shrinking violet where poetic honour was concerned than his general reputation would suggest.) The poem then appeared in the *Morning Herald* in April; while **'The Queen's Visit'** was printed in *The Times* of 15 June, and the stanzas claiming that the waves had restored the strength of the sovereign of the nation whose navies rule those waves were published in the *Whitehall Evening Post* and the *Public Advertiser* in July, following George's visit to Weymouth in June. No such public display of Cowper's awareness of more historically significant happenings abroad emerged from the age's leading poet.

Here, then, is a clear example of English parochialism and self-satisfaction: press, poet, people and monarchy linked together in mutual and self-enclosed support. 'History has given an air of ludicrous irony to Cowper's estimate of the event for which 1789 was to be memorable'.[5] If we are to rescue Cowper from such an accusation, then perhaps we have to present the argument that a poem on the subject of George's recovery from 'a depressed and violent insanity'[6] must be a form of 'disguised autobiography'.[7] The poet who would later write in **'The Castaway'** that 'misery still delights to trace / Its semblance in another's case' (ll. 59-60) might be equally prepared to relate his experiences to George's: public expression of joy would be the national equivalent of private, unutterable feelings. Such an interpretation has the comforting advantage of fitting another of the common stereotypes which beset discussion of Cowper, that everything he wrote must, in some way, reflect personal agony and an inner world. Such egocentricity would naturally find a reason for applauding George's renewed health, but would find no echo in foreign revolutions. It is just unfortunate that none of these poems betrays any private concern; and that, far from rejoicing in the recovery of a royal alter ego, Cowper wrote the poems convinced of his own damnation. It would be going a bit far to attribute the perception of such a semblance to the mind of a loyal subject: such ideas are best left to a Byron.

If the theory of 'another's case' is open to interpretative doubt, then the charge of parochialism is simply untenable. From the perspective of hindsight the king's illness during the winter of 1788-89 might be a minor matter when compared with the upheavals in France in the late 1780s and 1790s, but it was potentially a major matter and one which might have profoundly changed the state of Britain and affected British reception of events abroad. From November 1788 George was 'on the brink of death and passed through many weeks of oblivion and alienation'.[8] It seemed that the Prince of Wales would need to become Regent. The familiar Hanoverian pattern of animosity between the generations was given political importance by the polarization of politics between Pitt and Fox, a polarization which had already aligned the parties with the king on one side and the Prince of Wales on the other. During the Fox-North coalition of 1783, 'there are signs that Fox attempted to manipulate the Prince for direct political purposes'[9] and, as we shall see, George III intervened equally directly to ensure the downfall of the ministry and its replacement by a Pitt administration. George's hatred of Fox, exacerbated by his belief that he had led the Prince astray morally (Fox's gambling and womanizing were notorious and dogged him throughout his career), developed into a very clear political division between a monarchist, old 'Tory', attitude to the constitution and that professed by the Whigs as inheritors of the Glorious Revolution. That Fox and the Whigs generally mishandled the issue[10] should not obscure the potential effects of the Regency crisis. Had Fox been in power when a response to the French Revolution was demanded, who knows what might have occurred? It is still possible, of course, that the gradual break-up of the Whig consensus which took place when they were in opposition would have happened, more or less gradually, if they were in office; but power can work strange effects.

Now this is to speculate. But the potential importance of events in England during the winter of 1788-89 should make us re-think our reaction to Cowper's poems of the time. Far from proving that he was a reclusive, self-obsessed poet, out of touch with the large movements of the public world, they indicate his sharp perception of that world. His implied stance in these poems is as a Pitt supporter; but his letters of the time qualify this slightly. His expressions are sometimes openly pro-George and thus implicitly pro-Pitt; and are based upon a fear of the political opposition, of 'the worst men in the nation' who might form a 'vicious government'. His pleasure at the king's recovery is accompanied by a sardonic estimation of an opposition forced to feign delight: 'Sheridan, I expect, will soar in rhetorical exstasies; Burk [*sic*] will say his prayers are answer'd, and Fox will term it the happiest event that he has ever witness'd; and while they thus speak, they will gnash their teeth and curse inwardly. Oh they are a blessed Junto; may opposition to ministry be their business while they live!'[11] But it is noteworthy that these strongly-worded letters are all to his Pittite cousin, Lady Hesketh. His letters to others express sympathy for the king, but not this degree of political antagonism to the opposition. He makes it clear (for example in his letters for 20 December 1788 and 29 January 1789) that, at this time, he trusts Pitt more than he does any other power-group, but desists from the extremes of language he uses in writing to Lady Hesketh.

We should remember this qualification as we begin to trace Cowper's political views as expressed at various points of his life, culminating in his responses to the French Revolution. For he did indeed react strongly to events in France, though in his letters rather than in poetry. At the time when news began to filter through, Cowper's role as a published poet had effectively moved from original poetry to translation. His major task, the translation of Homer, was published in July 1791, and he began the process of translating Milton's Italian and Latin poems as part of a projected edition later that year. Mary Unwin's first debilitating paralytic stroke occurred in December, followed the next year by Cowper's own renewed depressions of 1792 and 1794. His production of poetry during these years was understandably slight, and equally understandably tended to concentrate on private events for a private audience (e.g. '**To Mary**' of 1793).

But the mind as revealed by his correspondence continued to show interest in public events and a readiness to subject them to the scrutiny of his political views. It is a mistake to see Cowper as uninterested in the world. His account at the beginning of the fourth book of ***The Task*** of the arrival of the post delivered by 'the herald of a noisy world' concludes with the poet's eagerness to hear of news from the newspaper. A reading of Cowper's own letters reveals an apparently contradictory attitude to news from the outside world: at one moment (8 February 1783) he will say, defensively, 'You will suppose me a Politician; but in truth I am nothing less. These are the thoughts that occur to me while I read the News paper, and when I have laid it down, I feel myself more interested in the success of my early Cucumbers, than in any part of this great and important Subject', while at another (31 January 1782) he will insist, 'Suppose not however that I am perfectly an unconcerned Spectator, or that I take no interest at all in the affairs of my country. Far from it—I read the News—I see that things go wrong in every quarter'. The clue once again lies in considering the recipients of the letters. His protestations of unconcern are invariably addressed to John Newton, while his other correspondents (in this case

Joseph Hill) receive the full weight of his fascination with events both at home and abroad. The situation is analogous to Cowper's apparent nervousness in communicating with Newton about ***The Task***. Whereas Newton had been very much involved in the preparations of Cowper's 1782 volume of moral satires, poems with a distinctly evangelical flavour (Newton even wrote a preface for the volume of so stern a character that Joseph Johnson, his publisher, persuaded Cowper to cancel it),[12] Cowper left him in the dark about his writing of ***The Task*** until the last minute. It is almost by way of an aside that he says in a letter written on 30 October 1784,

> I am again at Johnson's; in the shape of a Poem in blank verse; consisting of Six books, and called ***The Task***. I began it about this time Twelvemonth, and writing sometimes an hour in a day, sometimes half a one, and sometimes two hours, have lately finished it. I mentioned it not sooner, because almost to the last I was doubtfull whether I should ever bring it to a conclusion.

Such doubts had not prevented him from eagerly discussing the poem earlier with other correspondents. Newton was not amused.[13]

It is certainly true that Cowper's early letters, up to his breakdown of 1773, adopt the kind of evangelical tone of which Newton would approve. But after this time, when he experienced the dream which, he thought, committed him to eternal damnation, his interest in worldly matters grows: it is as if expulsion from the world of God turns his attention to the world of humanity. When, in later letters, he adopts a religious contempt for mere politics, it is only because the events upon which he is commenting are such as to make him despair of a propitious outcome. It is not true to say as Philip Anthony Brown does in *The French Revolution in English History* (1918) that Cowper's interest in the French Revolution was an exception to his normal attitude as 'an elderly evangelical, profoundly convinced that the times were evil, but also that "man never was reformed by man, nor ever will be"'; nor that 'Reform agitations in the past had moved him only to pity at wasted pains, with some passing dread of civil commotions' (p. 31). The letter cited here—written on 17 August 1779 to another clergyman, William Unwin—is actually one of a series concerning the Petitioning Movement, in the course of which Cowper can interestingly be seen to be working out a not negligible political philosophy. In this letter he simply remarks that the 'Kentish Petitioners . . . mean well, but the Case is hopeless, & consequently the Attempt (may I venture to say it?) idle'; but his reasons for such defeatism are thought out. Any reform of Parliament, he says, must be effected by Parliament itself. Will any petition be strong enough to persuade those entrenched in privileges to forgo them? The king, meanwhile, is helpless: 'No Measure of Government can proceed without a majority on its Side, a Majority cannot be had unless it be bought, then what answer can his Majesty possibly return to the Petition?' Historians might question Cowper's apparent faith in the good intentions, as well as powerlessness, of George III, but his analysis of the problems facing reform movements within an ossified constitutional establishment is shrewd enough, as nineteenth- as well as eighteenth-century history shows.

The Petitioning Movement of 1779 and 1780 was part of the developing debate about the rights of electors, in this sense a continuation of the controversy surrounding Wilkes and the Middlesex election in the 1760s. The Yorkshire movement of freeholders, organized by Christopher Wyvill, initially aimed its protest against high taxes and alleged waste of public money, but, as it developed, it became in effect an attack upon excessive executive power. As such, it was allied with the general stance of the Rockingham group of Whigs. Sir George Savile, who presented the Yorkshire petition to the Commons on 8 February 1780, was a Yorkshire MP and a friend of Rockingham. Although there were no direct ties between the Yorkshire movement and the Rockingham group in parliament, its effect was to consolidate the forces of reform around Rockingham, Shelburne, and Fox, out of a shared desire to establish power structures more representative, as they saw it, of the British people.[14] Cowper refers to Savile's speech in a letter shortly afterwards (13 February 1780), and provides an analysis of the issue which makes us qualify any conclusion that he was blindly pro-George. He compares the present reign with that of Charles I (later reading of Hume's history leads him to reconsider this in a letter of 8 May 1780—as well it might—but the analysis of the present situation remains constant):

> The undue Extension of the Influence of the Crown, the Discountenancing and Displacing of Men obnoxious to the Court, though otherwise men of unexceptionable Conduct & Character, the Waste of the Public Money, & especially the Suspicion that obtains of a fixt Design in Government to favor the Cause of Popery are Features common to both Faces. Again, these Causes have begun to produce the same Effects now as they did in the Reign of that unhappy Monarch.

This belief in the tendency of the reign of George III to seek to extend its own prerogatives at the expense of the parliamentary rights established in 1689 is very much a Whig, Rockinghamite position. We should balance these sympathies, however, by Cowper's fear of the consequences of the Yorkshire movement: Savile's speech, he says, reminds him of Horace's description, borrowed from Ennius, of the opening of the temple of Janus, discord leading the way to war. He sees radical movements as anarchic; but he puts the blame for their existence squarely on the administration.

This kind of balance is, indeed, the most striking aspect of much of Cowper's political commentary, whether explicitly in the letters or implicitly (as is usually the case) in the poetry. A small example of this is provided by his celebratory verses **'On the Promotion of Edward Thurlow, Esq. to the Lord High Chancellorship of England'**:

> Round Thurlow's head in early youth,
>   And in his sportive days,

> Fair science pour'd the light of truth,
>   And genius shed his rays.[15]

(l. 1)

Thurlow had come to prominence as a parliamentarian when he had defended the ministry's action in the Wilkes affair, and George's appointment of him as Lord Chancellor in 1778 was an attempt to strengthen the besieged administration of Lord North. As such, Thurlow proved to be one of the toughest antagonists of the growing Rockinghamite opposition. He later played a key role in George's intervention in Fox's India Bill, the cause of a major constitutional crisis at whose centre was the very issue of the limits and extensions of royal prerogatives.[16] So Cowper can praise a man whose political position is very different from his own. We should not make too much of this even-handedness, since Cowper writes as an old, though increasingly former, friend of Thurlow. Cowper had met Thurlow when studying legal practice as a clerk in London in 1751.[17] The capacity for even-handedness is, none the less, characteristic.

A particularly striking example of this is afforded by Cowper's response to the Admiral Keppel affair. This arose from 'an indecisive battle off Ushant'[18] in which the Channel fleet under Keppel met inconclusively with a French fleet in July 1778. Public dissatisfaction led to the thoroughly British desire to sacrifice an admiral 'pour encourager les autres'; but the first candidate, Sir Hugh Palliser, accused of ignoring Keppel's orders, wrote a letter to the *Morning Post* laying all the blame on Keppel. Political spice was given to the argument by the protagonists' contrary loyalties: while Palliser's sympathies were with the Court faction, Keppel was a member of the Rockingham group (later, indeed, Keppel was First Lord of the Admiralty in the second Rockingham administration of 1782 when Fox was Foreign Secretary, and held the same post again in the Fox-North coalition of 1783). The outcome of the Commons debate was the court-martial of Keppel, which took place in early 1779. The antigovernment press saw political animus in the decision to try Keppel; and his acquittal was hailed by the Whigs as a blow to the ministry.[19] Cowper's stanzas on Keppel's trial are patently Whig in their praise of Keppel, their imputation of ill motives to his accusers, and their reference to the solidarity of the fleet in Keppel's cause (many of the serving officers being also associated with the Rockinghamites):

> Keppel Returning from afar
>   With Laurels on his Brow,
> Comes Home to Wage a Sharper War
>   And with a fiercer Foe.
>
> The Blow was rais'd with cruel Aim,
>   And meant to pierce his Heart,
> But Lighting on his well-earn'd Fame,
>   Struck an Immortal Part.
>
> Slander and Envy strive to tear
>   His wreath so justly won,

But Truth, who made his Cause her Care,
   Has bound it faster On.

The Charge that was design'd to Sound
   The Signal of Disgrace,
Has only call'd a Navy round
   To praise him to his Face.

But on the night of Keppel's acquittal a celebrating crowd broke into Sir Hugh Palliser's house in Pall Mall, looting it and later burning his effigy on Tower Hill.[20] Cowper's poem on this part of the affair attacks the behaviour of the rioters. Palliser, too, is 'a Warrior staunch and true', and, although he has made 'One false Step', for which he is now ashamed, he deserves his due respect. Their hero has given them the lead:

Yet Keppel with deserv'd Applause,
Proclaims him Bold in Britain's Cause
And to his well known Courage pays
The Tribute of Heroic Praise.

                          (l. 15)

The pattern here reminds us of Cowper's letter to Unwin on Sir George Savile: the source of corruption is unambiguously George's government, but public disorder is under no circumstances to be tolerated.

A similar fear of the mob underlies Cowper's poems provoked by the Gordon Riots of June 1780, that most violent expression of anti-Catholic populism. A Latin poem, **'In Seditionem Horrendam',** rather naively, if understandably given the anti-French paranoia so common in eighteenth-century England, propagates a rumour which Cowper had read in *The General Evening Post* that French influence lay behind the riots.[21] Nobler in instinct, though, are his stanzas **'On the Burning of Lord Mansfield's Library'.** Mansfield, the Lord Chief Justice, was known to favour the Catholic Relief Act, and his house in Bloomsbury Square came in for particularly destructive attention from the mob on the fifth night of the riots, he and his wife having only just made their escape to their country home, Caen Wood.[22] Cowper's poem laments the loss of Mansfield's library in terms of a new Vandalism:

So then—the Vandals of our isle,
   Sworn foes to sense and law,
Have burnt to dust a nobler pile
   Than ever Roman saw!

                          (l. 1)

A pendant poem, **'On the Same',** reflects gratefully on the safety of Mansfield himself, while repeating the Roman parallel:

When wit and genius meet their doom
   In all devouring flame,
They tell us of the fate of Rome,
   And bid us fear the same.

                          (l. 1)

The poems concentrate solely on Mansfield as a man of learning; and the anarchy theme is enough to make them consistent with Cowper's attitudes. But Cowper would, of course, know of Mansfield's record to date, which again suggests his willingness to seek balanced judgements. William Murray had been one of the 'old Whigs' under Newcastle, but made his name after his elevation to Lord Chief Justice as Lord Mansfield. As such, he was brought into the Wilkes case as someone thought to be sympathetic to the government. Mansfield's closeness to the ministry is indicated by the way in which he was viewed by the Rockinghamite opposition, like the Earl of Bute, as a conspirator in schemes to re-establish arbitrary government.[23] In the course of the trial, in which Wilkes's conviction for seditious libel was upheld, Mansfield 'laid it down that the decision as to what constituted a seditious libel was a matter for the judge. The jury could only decide as to its printing and publication'.[24] But four years later, in 1772, Mansfield delivered his celebrated judgement in the Somersett case to which Cowper refers in *The Task*:

Slaves cannot breathe in England; if their lungs
Receive our air, that moment they are free;
They touch our country, and their shackles fall.

                        (II, l. 40)

Thus Mansfield seems, curiously, to have both extended and diminished the rights of the individual: 'His exposition of the law about seditious libel in the cases of Wilkes, Junius, and the dean of St. Asaph aroused great anger because it so severely limited the responsibility of juries. Amid general applause, on the other hand, he established the doctrine (in Somersett's case) that slaves enjoyed the benefits of freedom while they stood on English soil.[25]

Cowper's other lines on the Gordon Riots appear in *Table Talk,* published with the Mansfield poems in his 1782 volume. The greater length of this poem and its discussion format allow Cowper to develop more fully the relationship between his libertarian principles and his abhorrence of mob-rule. Freedom is the essential basis for all civilization, creating the necessary conditions for the individual's intellectual and spiritual development. Freedom, though, can 'Grow freakish, and o'er leaping ev'ry mound / Spread anarchy and terror all around' (ll. 302-03). Our response to this should not be to do away with freedom altogether, but to ensure that it is properly guarded by wholesome laws responsibly applied. This is the only way to prevent the pattern of action and reaction, of extreme answering extreme, which we have seen Cowper deploring, from the opposite angle, in his remarks on the dangers of government's tendency to arbitrary rule:

Let active laws apply the needful curb
To guard the peace that riot would disturb,
And liberty preserv'd from wild excess,
Shall raise no feuds for armies to suppress.

                        (l. 314)

Thus the Gordon Riots, which Cowper goes on to describe, are as much an assault upon liberty as is arbitrary government:

When the rude rabble's watch-word was, destroy,
And blazing London seem'd a second Troy,
Liberty blush'd and hung her drooping head.

(l. 322)

Here is a classic Whig position: the rule of law exists to preserve the individual's freedom from any kind of group force.

In his commentary on political affairs, Cowper consistently sees that liberty as under threat from both sides, from excessive executive power and blindly destructive popular agitation. The Gordon Riots are a particularly dangerous example of the latter. Cowper makes his attitude to the chief instigator of the riots, Lord George Gordon, quite clear in the stanzas, **'Cum Ratione Insanire'**, which he puts into Gordon's mouth on the occasion of his imprisonment in Newgate.[26]

When London blazed then I was warm,
    Association-drunk,
And hoped in that illustrious storm
    Britannia should have sunk.

Two themes I chose, Popery one,
    Prerogative the other,
And Tag and Rag by canting won
    And Bob-tail and his brother.

(l. 5)

This picks up Cowper's sentiments expressed to John Newton at the time of the riots. After describing his relief that Newton is safe (Newton had moved from Olney to London earlier that year as rector of St Mary Woolnoth), Cowper writes (12 June 1780) of the lasting impression which must have been made on him by a 'Metropolis in flames, and a Nation in Ruins', and goes on to congratulate Newton on his wisdom in not himself becoming a member of the Protestant Association. Cowper's immediate linking of physical conflagration with national destruction remains constant in letter and poem; and his depth of feeling on the matter is shown by his daring, for once, to express firm views to Newton. Newton was actually, as one might expect, sympathetic to the principles of the Protestant Association as a group whose aim was the safeguarding of the Protestant religion: his letter to which Cowper's is a reply describes how the original members of the Association are unhappy about the way that things have turned out. Cowper's own clear statements show how his basic political fears are stronger than the sectarian commitments expected of a disciple of Newton.

Gordon was presenting a petition to Parliament in protest at the projected removal of restrictions from Catholics. In that sense his actions were part of the climate of petitioning which dominated political affairs in the first half of 1780. That Cowper perceived similarities between the potential dangers of the Savile movement and those realized in the Gordon movement is indicated by his composition in 1780 of two poems called **'The Modern Patriot'.** The first he intended to send to William Unwin with his

letter of 13 February, in which he balances fear of the anarchic consequences of Savile's speech with comments on 'undue Extension of the Influence of the Crown'. He changed his mind because, as he says in a letter of 27 February 1780, he was 'not quite pleased with a Line or two which I found difficult to mend', but then, he goes on to say, his views too had altered after reading Burke's speech in the newspaper and being 'so well pleased with his Proposals for a Reformation, & with the Temper in which he made them, that I began to think better of his Cause and burnt my Verses'. The surviving poem of the same title probably dates from later in the year, the time of the Gordon Riots. It may be that Cowper adapted some of the original poem to the new circumstances. Like that of **'Cum Ratione Insanire',** the tone is sarcastic:

Rebellion is my theme all day,
    I only wish 'twould come
(As who knows but perhaps it may)
    A little nearer home . . .

When lawless mobs insult the court,
    That man shall be my toast,
If breaking windows be the sport
    Who bravely breaks the most.

But oh! for him my fancy culls
    The choicest flow'rs she bears,
Who constitutionally pulls
    Your house about your ears.

(ll. 1, 9)

If there is a textual overlap (the question is, of course, 'unanswerable',)[27] then initial criticism of those who are over-zealous in their assaults on an administration which has among its suspected faults 'a fixt Design . . . to favour the Cause of Popery' is effortlessly transformed into an attack on those who seek to bring down that government violently in the name of protestant reaction.

It is perhaps significant that it was reading Burke's speech which changed Cowper's mind about the motives of the parliamentary opposition. As we have seen from Cowper's reaction to the Regency crisis, he was by no means an uncritical admirer of Burke, so that any praise must be seen as carefully thought out. It was in the context of the Petitioning Movement that Burke headed the Rockingham Whigs' attempt to move economic reforms in the administrative organization of government. His speech of 11 February—almost certainly the one to which Cowper refers—was an extended exposure of the economic confusion by which the king was 'entitled to separate households and separate officials, all of them, it was implied, merely burdening the kingdom unnecessarily and providing the means of corruption'.[28] In the weeks following, Burke introduced a bill for 'the better Regulation of his Majesty's Civil Establishments', whose clauses were debated with predictable fervour in committee stage. Burke's general object was to secure 'the independence of Parliament and the economic reformation of the civil and other establishments'[29] and, as far as that went, he gained considerable support from the Commons: his proposal to abolish the Board of Trade was carried by 207 to 199 on 13 March, and that to abolish the third Secretary of State was only narrowly defeated, 208 to 201. But when it came to motions rather nearer the monarchical bone, he could not take Parliament with him: the proposal to abolish the Treasurer of the Chamber, a member of the king's own establishment, was convincingly defeated, 211 to 158, Burke's support diminishing drastically while his opponents' held firm. The conclusion would seem to be that it was one thing to operate proper economies within government, but another to risk 'an insult to the King and a usurpation of power'.[30] Thus, although there remained considerable feeling in some quarters that the royal prerogative was dangerously extended, there was also no majority for anything which might be interpreted as a converse assault upon that prerogative.

'Prerogative' is Gordon's second theme, according to **'Cum Ratione Insanire'.** Cowper's position, as evidenced by his close monitoring of the events of 1780, seems to share the uncertain attitude born of fear of both extremes, reflective of the wider constitutional uncertainties, which surfaced during the controversial reign of George III. On 16 March 1780 he is definitive in his libertarian statements:

> I did not know, (for I know nothing but what I learn from the General Evening) that there was a deliberate Purpose on the part of Government to set up the Throne of Despotism. If that is the Case, no doubt but the Standard of Opposition will flame against it, till it has consumed to Ashes the Devisers of a Project that in this Country, is sure to terminate in the Ruin of them that form it! Alas! Of what Use is History, & why should Kings be taught to Read, if they Read to so little Purpose.

This strong response aligns Cowper with the Burke-Fox side of the current parliamentary disputes, testifying to his fundamental principles. But two months later on 6 May 1780, after Burke's proposals had been defeated, he is much more cautious, saying that, although the patriots (Cowper here used the word without its sarcastic implication in **'The Modern Patriot'**) have an aim which 'is desirable & highly reasonable', any further pursuit of them at present would only serve to 'kindle the Flames of Civil War' and be counter-productive. So that fear of violence, rendered in the same language as in **'Cum Ratione Insanire'**, places an uneasy stop to the pursuit of principle: a conclusion which is an uncertainty, not a compromise. Another letter, written on 18 March 1780, sums up Cowper's position most clearly:

> I am sorry to learn, not from the Newspaper, but by a Letter from a very intelligent Person in London, that arbitrary power is the aim of the Court, & Rebellion upon the point of breaking out against it. The love of Power seems as natural to Kings, as the desire of Liberty to their Subjects; the excess of either is vicious, & tends to the ruin of both. But when excess is found on both sides, & nothing but despotism will content the one & anarchy the other, it needs no great political discernment to foresee the consequence.

Cowper's informant was Joseph Hill, to whom he addressed both the libertarian flourish of 16 March and the cautious concern of 6 May; and it looks as if Hill's own political enthusiasms have led him to exaggerate the situation somewhat (it perhaps says a lot about Cowper that he can talk politics to both Hill and, later on, the ardently Pittite Lady Hesketh). The actuality of the position corresponds more to the classic Whig view as stated here by Lord John Cavendish in a letter to Burke after Burke had sent him a copy of his *Reflections on the Revolution in France*: 'Though some of our allies have now and then run wild; our original sett have allways contended for that temperate resistance to the abuse of power, as should not endanger the publick peace, or put all good order into hazard.'[31] Citing this definition, Ian R. Christie in *Stress and Stability* goes on to claim that it sums up the Rockinghamite position: 'Although these men saw themselves as defending the constitutional settlement of 1689 against renewed attack, they never contemplated an appeal to force, or a violent or extensive alteration of the political system. Their practical programme was confined to "economical reform", which was little enough; parliamentary reform they shunned' (p. 42). Whatever may be the rights or wrongs of such a summary of Whig opposition thought in the late eighteenth century (the writer is concerned to argue that such elements of the British context as a marked degree of social stability, in addition to economic wealth and a distinctive and persuasive 'conservative' intellectual lobby, meant that the conditions of British society were fundamentally different from those of French society at the time, and consequently far less amenable to violent revolution on the French model), it does seem to define a position close to that of Cowper.

A balance between patriotism (in the modern sense), a belief in the primacy of the rights of his own country, and a fundamental adherence to the principle of freedom of thought and action within the limits of public order is the mark of Cowper's not unsophisticated political thought. This balance, indeed, he maintains even in contexts where important elements of parliamentary Whig opinion differ from him: more 'Whig' than the Whigs? The American Revolution provides a convenient example of this, and a telling one in view of the sharp differences of opinion within the Whig camp—then as now—about whether the principles behind that event were the same, or at any rate similar enough in their fundamentals, as those operating in the later French Revolution.

Some of Cowper's poems of the period declare a militant patriotism of a common enough kind. **'A Present for the Queen of France'**, written towards the end of 1779, reflects the same pro-British sentiments which inform **'ΕΠΙΝΙΚΙΟΝ'**, a 'victory song' on French losses in India and the West Indies, **'To Sir Joshua Reynolds'**, which proposes 'French Disappointment, British Glory' as fit subjects for the painter's palette, and **'On the Victory Gained by Sir George Rodney'**, a celebration of the Admiral's defeat of a Spanish fleet off Cape St Vincent in January 1780. These are poems which reflect Cowper's distinctly robust attitudes; but attitudes which are not automatic responses devoid of principles. The address to the Queen of France concludes by exhorting her to consider that

> *Great* and *Good* belong
> Not to the King that does the Wrong;
> Those Titles he Asserts alone,
> Who Just and Equal on his Throne,
> Manfully Vindicates his own:
> Yet will not, dares not, Use his Might
> To Violate another's Right.

(l. 42)

As is clear from a number of letters of the period, Cowper's main reason for seeing the war as right and wishing it to be pursued rigorously lay in his belief that Britain's traditional enemies were using the American issue as an excuse for pursuing their own territorial ambitions and desire for British abasement. They were thus involved in violating the rights of others. The British, however, were engaged in defending their rights in America against what, in a letter of 18 June 1780, he unambiguously dubs a 'rebellion'. Such an attitude allies Cowper with George III and his administration, against the elements of Whig thought which were sympathetic to the Americans' cause. On 4 December 1781, he defends his opinions on the grounds that they are the natural responses of 'the Son of a staunch Whig and a man that loved his country', and goes as far as to link what he perceives as the decline of Britain with the loss of the colonies: 'I consider the loss of America as the ruin of England', he declares on 9 December 1781, after Yorktown has put an end to the bullish sentiments of the poems. Hereafter, his poetic statements on the war reflect this sense of the defeat of that for which Britain once stood. While the war was in progress Cowper wrote a passage of **'Table Talk'** which sets the Dunkirk spirit of the present into the context of the triumphal age of the Elder Pitt:

> Poor England! thou art a devoted deer,
> Beset with ev'ry ill but that of fear.
> The nations hunt thee, and thou standst at bay.
> Undaunted still, though wearied and perplex'd,
> Once Chatham sav'd thee, but who saves thee next?

(l. 362)

And after the war Cowper's assertive but not uncritical praise for his country in the second book of *The Task* ('England, with all thy faults, I love thee still') again uses the time of Chatham and Wolfe as a point of reference by which the present must be harshly judged: **'Table Talk'**'s question is still unanswered. This growing pessimism is reflected in the letters of the time, for example in one of 31 January 1782, where he talks of the way in which that proper sentiment of patriotism which had been activated by the events of 1759 was still with him although 'the course of public events has of late afforded me no opportunity to exert it'.

But it is not just this patriotism which Cowper sees as being truly 'Whig'. The last-quoted letter goes on to talk glowingly, as part of its past versus present theme, of 'the men whose integrity, courage, and Wisdom broke the bands of tyranny, established our constitution upon its true basis'. This essentially moral and libertarian basis for legitimate revolutionary activity—Cowper had been reading Catherine Macaulay's *History of England from the Accession of James I to the Elevation of the House of Hanover* and is probably referring to the state of England after the Civil War[32]—makes it clear that Cowper is not unthinkingly anti-revolution. The praise of Chatham in **'Table Talk'** is similarly founded upon a perception of him as a moral defender of liberty:

> In him, Demosthenes was heard again,
> Liberty taught him her Athenian strain;
> She cloath'd him with authority and awe,
> Spoke from his lips, and in his looks, gave law.
> His speech, his form, his action, full of grace,
> And all his country beaming in his face,
> He stood, as some inimitable hand
> Would strive to make a Paul or Tully stand.
> No sycophant or slave that dar'd oppose
> Her sacred cause, but trembl'd when he rose,
> And every venal stickler for the yoke,
> Felt himself crush'd at the first word he spoke.

(l. 342)

These lines follow on from the account of the Gordon Riots quoted earlier: morally-based liberty is perceived as very different from mob-rule, which is really another form of slavery. And it is in these terms that Cowper saw the American revolution. Looking back on the conduct of the war, Cowper is quite prepared to be critical of Britain's role: 'England, more perhaps through the fault of her Generals than her Councils, has in some instances acted with a spirit of cruel animosity', he tells Newton in a letter of 26 January 1783; while 'the Americans, who if they had contented themselves with a struggle for lawfull Liberty would have deserved applause, seem to me to have incurred the guilt of parricide, by renouncing their parent, by making her ruin their favorite object, and by associating themselves with her worst Enemy for the accomplishment of their purpose'. Cowper thus accepts that the colonists had rightful grievances, but insists that their method of pursuing their demands took them into morally indefensible activity. It is clear elsewhere, for example in a letter of 16 March 1780, that Cowper sees the Americans' association with Britain's European enemies as committing the former to far worse despotism than that from which they sought to escape: in an image of much weight for Cowper, he describes the Americans as emancipating themselves 'from one Master, only to serve a Score'. He later (on 13 October 1783) repeats this argument to Newton: 'A revolt can hardly be said to have been successful that has exchanged only an apprehended tyranny for a real one, and has shaken off the restraints of a well order'd Government, merely to give room and opportunity for the jarring opinions and interests of its abettors to throw all into a state of anarchy'. Again, Cowper openly accepts that the Americans were right to fear George's despotism—we have seen that Cowper was quite prepared to attack George for extension of his prerogative—but perceives the result of the methods employed as a lapse into an equally tyrannical anarchy of contesting powers:

> Their fears of arbitrary imposition were certainly well founded, a struggle therefore might be necessary in order to prevent it, and this end might surely have been answer'd without a renunciation of dependence. But the passions of a whole people once put in motion are not soon quieted, contest begets aversion, a little success inspires more ambitious hopes, and thus a slight quarrel terminates at last in a breach never to be healed, and perhaps in the ruin of both parties.

The language of 'anarchy' and 'ruin' is consistent with a basic principle running through Cowper's political thought, that disorder constitutes its own tyranny; but his language also connects him with another strain of Whig belief. Talk of 'parricide', of 'renouncing their parent' is of a piece with the nation-as-family interpretation of the 1689 settlement which enshrined central Whig tenets. The sovereignty of parliament was the central guarantor of the integrity of the nation and the freedom of the people since it both acted as a guardian against excessive powers of the executive and the judiciary and served to ensure stability because of 'the predominance in parliament of one of the major groups with a vested interest in freedom from interference, the landed gentry',[33] a group, that is, whose interests were identified with those of the nation, Rockingham Whigs alongside traditional Tories. The strain of Whig thought which perceived the American Revolution as founded upon the principles of the Glorious Revolution, a strain most notably represented by Fox, was thus at odds in its interpretation with another, equally valid, Whig concept of history and the nation. The Burke of his conciliation speech of 1775, in which he both accepted the ultimate sovereignty of parliament and the need for flexibility of approach, provides an instance of an attitude more like Cowper's: Burke 'contended that the empire was like a family in which the father, no doubt, had legal authority but which was ruled and held together not by law but by a union of hearts, the unconscious give and take of daily action together'.[34] Here we see the potential divisions in Whig thought which the French Revolution would realize and demonstrate publicly.

As we approach the events of 1789 and estimate Cowper's response to them, only a careful and all-round consideration of his place within the cross-currents of eighteenth-century political opinion can lead us to a measured conclusion. He remained a loyal subject of his king, no matter what degree of justified criticism he felt the need to express at times. He grew to distrust the role of the opposition, or parts of the opposition, during the American war as being motivated more by factionalism than by principle,[35] and this is clearly reflected in his attitudes during the Regency crisis. This also explains why, quite properly, he should consider the recovery of George as an event of major significance. But, underlying all his comments on individual events there is a constant devotion to the idea of liberty. This is a liberty which must be distinguished from

anarchy and which has to be defined very much in terms of eighteenth-century Whig constitutional thought, rather than any twentieth-century democratic notions. It is, nevertheless, an impulse within Cowper which is highly recognizable to us, especially when it manifests itself in such a public issue as that of slavery.

This was an issue close to Cowper's heart throughout his life. A large section of **'Charity'** in the 1782 volume is dedicated to an impassioned attack on the slave trade, perceived as an especially degrading attack upon natural human freedom; and *The Task* takes up the issue in ringing tones:

> I would not have a slave to till my ground,
> To carry me, to fan me while I sleep,
> And tremble when I wake, for all the wealth
> That sinews bought and sold have ever earn'd.
> No: dear as freedom is, and in my heart's
> Just estimation priz'd above all price,
> I had much rather be myself the slave,
> And wear the bonds, than fasten them on him.
>
> (II, l. 29)

As the issue came to a head in political discussion in the late 1780s—Pitt was directly involved in encouraging William Wilberforce in his crusade from 1787 and was a supporter of Wilberforce's bill 'to prevent the farther importation of slaves into the British Colonies in the West Indies' which was defeated in the Commons in 1791[36]—so Cowper's writing against slavery took increasingly public form, **'Pity for Poor Africans'** appearing in the *Northampton Mercury* in August 1788, **'The Morning Dream'** in *The Gentleman's Magazine* in November, **'The Negro's Complaint'** in *Stuart's Star* in 1789 (there were other parts of the world than France that year), and a sonnet addressed to Wilberforce in the *Northampton Mercury* in 1792.

Human rights within the terms of the British constitution were, however, just as important to Cowper: indeed, opposition to slavery was simply a logical extension of those rights. We thus find that, despite his loyalty to the crown, his response to the constitutional crisis of 1783-84 was clear and unambiguous. George's hostility to the Fox-North coalition was extreme and well-known; but his actions over Fox's India Bill took that hostility to unacceptable lengths. This bill sought to control the activities of the East Indian Company by means of commissioners in London. It passed through the Commons, but George then let it be known, through the medium of Lord Temple and with the connivance of Pitt, Thurlow, and others, that, in the words used by Fox in the Commons, 'whoever voted for the India Bill were not only not his friends, but he should consider them as his enemies'.[37] The bill was defeated in the Lords on 17 December 1783, and George ordered the resignation of Fox and North the next day. In effect, the king had intervened in parliamentary processes in order to dismiss his ministers; and 'no constitutional defence of the king's action is possible, nor was any attempted at the time by his supporters'.[38]

Cowper was among those who saw the activities of the East India Company as exploitation and who therefore agreed with Fox that regulation was urgently needed. In **'Expostulation'** he had inveighed against the export of 'slav'ry to the conquer'd East' (l. 365), seeing British action as a form of despotism, and he will ask rhetorically in *The Task,*

> Is India free? and does she wear her plum'd
> And jewell'd turban with a smile of peace,
> Or do we grind her still?
>
> (IV, l. 28)

Later, at the time of the impeachment of Warren Hastings in 1788, despite his sympathies for Hastings as a fellow-pupil of Westminster (sympathies which, presumably, account for his lines addressed to Hastings written in 1792), he is equally clear about how the British have been, as he puts it in a letter of 16 February 1788, 'Tyrants in the East', and a week later on 22 February he defends Burke's rhetoric against Hastings. On the specific issue of George's interference in the affairs of parliament, Cowper is similarly clear: in a letter of 27 December 1783 he wrote 'It is not a time of day for a King to take liberties with the people': and on 4 February 1784 he wrote 'of all follies, that of an English Monarch who at this time of day has need to be taught the true limits of his prerogative, and the danger of exceeding them, is the greatest': 'Stuartism in my mind,' he wrote on about 22 February 1784, 'has been the characteristic of the present reign. And being, and having always been somewhat of an Enthusiast on the subject of British liberty, I am not able to withold my reverence and good wishes from the man whoever he be, that exerts himself in a constitutional way to oppose it'. That phrase, 'in a constitutional way', is crucial here in explaining Cowper's earlier attitude towards the American rebels and his continued loyalty to the king whom he so clearly criticizes: even as he writes, as here on 25 January 1784, against George, he declares himself 'the King's most loyal Subject', one who holds 'his prerogative sacred' and would 'never wish prosperity to a party that invades it'. Real liberty can only lie in the balance of prerogatives: the Whig position is defined anew even as its delicate balance is under threat from both royal interference and opposition extremism. As he writes in the letter just quoted from: 'I distrust the Court, I suspect the Patriots'.

Cowper's reactions to the French Revolution—for, even in old age and under pressure of renewed illness, such a public event inevitably fascinates him—follow with a logic not always evident in writers whose response to 1789 took a more public form. Reactions within the ranks of the Whig political hierarchy ranged, of course, from Burke's conservative development of his view of an organic society to Fox's spontaneous welcome for the fall of the Bastille: 'How much the greatest event it is that ever happened in the world! and how much the best!'.[39] At issue was the inheritance of the old Whig values. Burke made his main tasks those of discriminating between the Glorious Revolution and the events in France and of persuading his readers

that 'he and the Whigs who remained true to the ideals of the Rockingham party were the true heirs of 1688, not the radical societies'.[40] Whether one takes a cynical view of Fox's behaviour in the years after 1789 ('Fox was prepared to shade over into obscurity his views on the French Revolution and to use them as a political means of composing dissensions within his own party')[41] or whether one is prepared to acknowledge some fundamental principle to which he remained faithful ('deeper than any political theory, was a kind of instinct for liberty, which . . . tended to make him impetuously anti-government'),[42] his differences from Burke, and eventually Portland and others, led to the break-up of the Whig 'party' and thus assured the kind of government Britain would have under Pitt and his successors.[43]

Within this range of opinion, Cowper traces a path very much in accord with his established principles. His immediate reaction, expressed in a letter of around 18 December 1781, is optimistic, almost as ecstatic as Fox's: 'On the whole . . . the present appears to me a wonderful period in the history of mankind. That nations so long contentedly slaves, should on a sudden become enamour'd of liberty and understand as suddenly their own natural right to it, feeling themselves at the same time inspired with resolution to assert it, seems difficult to account for from natural causes.' To the establishment of a Constituent Assembly and the assertion of a Declaration of Rights, such responses appear perfectly justified, qualified as they are by Cowper's futile warning that the French must add to their newly-found love of liberty an equivalent love of peace and the word of God. But the events of 1790 and 1791 begin to cast doubt on such optimism. Cowper does not however renege on the essential principles: in 1791, he still insists in a letter of 26 February, that France 'will never be enslaved again', and repeats his earlier opinion (see letter for 7 July 1790) that some extremism is inevitable in the early days of such a major transformation of society when people make 'their first escape from tyrannic shackles'. When he comments (for example in a letter of 22 July 1791) on the Birmingham riots of July 1791, his criticism is aimed not at those celebrating the anniversary of the fall of the Bastille, but at the violence of loyalists' 'horrid zeal for the church' and 'horrid Loyalty to Government'. (He is careful, however, to declare, on 30 August 1791, his support for Elizabeth Carter's loyalist sympathies to the like-minded Lady Hesketh.) Although on 11 July 1791 he expressed pity for the King and Queen on hearing the news of the flight to Varennes the month before, it is not until the next year on 15 July 1792, after the violent revolutionary atmosphere had been intensified by the summoning to Paris of the National Guards (the fédérés), that fear becomes a dominant element in Cowper's comments: 'I wait with trembling ears for the News from Paris. The Crisis is terrible and the upshot most important. As a well-wisher to mankind I cannot but wish the affairs of that miserably distracted country settled, and am happy in the hope that it will not be in the power of any Malecontents fatally to disturb our own'. By now, then, that belief that liberty is as much endangered by anarchic excesses as by despotism has begun to qualify Cowper's willingness to give the Revolution time to come to order. The situation would be made more dramatic by the fact that his friends, the Throckmortons, were in Paris until two days before the events of 'the terrible 10th of August', when the Tuileries was sacked and the King and Queen taken prisoner.[44]

Later news, such as that of the execution of Louis in January 1793, confirms Cowper's growing antipathy to the violence. On 29 January 1793 he wrote: 'Alas poor Louis! I will tell you what the French have done. They have made me weep for a King of France, which I never thought to do, and they have made me sick of the very name of liberty, which I never thought to be. Oh how I detest them'. He writes like this to William Hayley, while confirming his opinion to more Tory-inclined correspondents, such as Walter Bagot as here in a letter of 4 March 1793: 'Though you are Tory I believe, and I am Whig, our sentiments concerning the mad-caps of France are much the same. They are a terrible race, and I have a horror both of them and their principles'. These principles now, of course, have long since departed from those of Cowper's constitutional Whiggism: it is as if the fears expressed on such occasions as the Gordon Riots have been realized on the streets of Paris, and Cowper expresses himself fervently in the wish that such events may not happen in London (the letter to Hayley quoted above, for example, talks significantly of 'spirits' in England who wish to enact the same kind of tragedy experienced in France 'on the stage of England').

Yet this is only one part of Cowper's developing response. Despite everything, violence in France, its potential spreading to England and its actual spreading to the battlefields of Europe, Cowper continues to perceive and adhere to initial, fundamental principles. 'We are here all of one mind respecting the cause in which the Parisians are engaged', he tells one correspondent on 10 September 1792, 'wish them a free people and as happy as they can wish themselves' (Mrs. Unwin, he teasingly tells Lady Hesketh on 18 December 1792, 'all Foxite as she is, loves you dearly'). It is the conduct of the people of France, he goes on, which is shocking and unacceptable; their method, that is, of pursuing those basic rights. This becomes the main tenor of his remarks: they 'had a good cause', he declares to Lady Hesketh in the same letter, 'but have spoil'd it by their excessive folly, and disgraced it indelibly by their unexampled barbarity'. It is the French who have departed from their initial true principles, allowing their justified desire for freedom to lapse into excess of disorder. That balance which is essential to true liberty had been disrupted as violently in the one direction as the *ancien régime* had distorted it in the other.

But this does not mean that the basic principles are devalued, and Cowper at this late stage of his life is eager to declare those principles. Here in a letter of 1 December 1792, he writes:

> All nations have a right to chuse their own mode of government, and the sovereignty of the people is a doctrine that evinces itself; for whenever the people chuse to be masters they always are so, and none can hinder them. God grant that we may have no revolution here, but unless we have a Reform we certainly shall. Depend upon it . . . the hour is come when power founded in patronage and corrupt majorities must govern this land no longer. Concessions too must be made to Dissenters of every denomination. They have a right to them, a right to all the privileges of Englishmen, and sooner or later, by fair means or by force, they will have them.

For it is ultimately the lesson of the French Revolution for Britain which concerns Cowper. He is aware throughout his life of the failures within the English system, be it an opposition which replaces principle by faction or a king who intervenes in the parliamentary process. So strong is his feeling about the government under Pitt (whose good qualities he is quite capable of perceiving), that he calls it a 'diseased Government' in a letter written on 16 December 1792 to Joseph Hill. He fears on one side the forces of court and administration which are responsible for the illness, and the consequences of a reaction against that illness which he sees as inevitable if left to itself in England, as surely as it has arisen in France. Only a sensible course of parliamentary and religious reform will ensure that a path will be traced between the two excesses; and this path is the path of constitutional liberty. In a letter written on 7 May 1793 to the Tory Lady Hesketh he defines his Whiggism:

> There is no *true* Whig who wishes all the power in the hands of his own party. The division of it which the lawyers call tripartite is exactly what he desires, and he would have neither King, Lords nor Commons unequally trusted, or in the smallest degree predominant. Such a Whig am I, and such Whigs are the real friends of the Constitution.

Whether or not Cowper was being prescient when he wrote his lengthy discrimination between arbitrary and constitutional monarchy in book five of *The Task,* his choice of contrast was indeed a happy one. We love, he declares, the king who

> loves the law, respects his bounds,
> And reigns content within them: him we serve
> Freely and with delight, who leaves us free:
> But recollecting still that he is man,
> We trust him not too far. King though he be,
> And king in England too, he may be weak,
> And vain enough to be ambitious still;
> May exercise amiss his proper pow'rs,
> Or covet more than freemen choose to grant:
> Beyond that mark is treason. He is our's,
> T'administer, to guard, t'adorn the state,
> But not to warp or change it. We are his
> To serve him nobly in the common cause,
> True to the death, but not to be his slaves.

(l. 332)

Cowper's symbol of the failure to sustain such balance of powers within the state under the banner of freedom serves as both a testimony to the consequences of inflexible monarchy and a warning to Britain:

Then shame to manhood, and opprobrious more
To France than all her losses and defeats,
Old or of later date, by sea or land,
Her house of bondage, worse than that of old
Which God aveng'd on Pharaoh—the Bastile!

(l. 379)

Notes

1. *Cowper: Poetical Works,* edited by H. S. Milford, fourth edition, with corrections and additions by Norma Russell (London, 1967).

2. 'An Epistle to Robert Lloyd, Esq.', l. 4, in *The Poems of William Cowper,* edited by John D. Baird and Charles Ryskamp, vol. 1 (Oxford, 1980): the edition cited for poems up to 1782.

3. James King, *William Cowper: a Biography* (Durham, N. Carolina, 1986), p. 184. Vincent Newey, *Cowper's Poetry* (Liverpool, 1982), pp. 238-40, is the best discussion of the poems.

4. *The Letters and Prose Writings of William Cowper,* edited by James King and Charles Ryskamp, 5 vols (Oxford, 1979-86), 5 March 1789; 12 March 1789.

5. Philip Anthony Brown, *The French Revolution in English History* (London, 1918), p. 27.

6. J. Steven Watson, *The Reign of George III* (Oxford, 1960), p. 304. Ida Macalpine and Richard Hunter, *George III and the Mad-Business* (London, 1969), pp. 172-75, diagnose George's illness as porphyria. John Brooke, *King George III* (London, 1972), p. 339, agrees with this judgement.

7. King, p. 184.

8. Macalpine and Hunter, p. 24.

9. F. O'Gorman, *The Whig Party and the French Revolution* (London, 1967), p. 8.

10. O'Gorman, pp. 34-39.

11. *Letters,* 15 February 1789; 4 February 1789; 25 February 1789.

12. King, pp. 105-07.

13. King, pp. 147-48.

14. Dorothy Marshall, *Eighteenth-Century England,* second edition (London, 1974), p. 462; Watson, pp. 228-31; I. R. Christie, *Wilkes, Wyvill and Reform* (London, 1962).

15. In *Poems* edited by Baird and Ryskamp, p. 405.

16. Marshall, pp. 441, 447; Watson, pp. 266-67; Robert Gore-Browne, *Chancellor Thurlow. The Life and Times of an Eighteenth-Century Lawyer* (London, 1953), pp. 39-44, 214-19.

17. Charles Ryskamp, *William Cowper of the Inner Temple, Esq.* (Cambridge, 1959), pp. 60-63.

18. Watson, p. 213.

19. Marshall, p. 448; Watson, p. 213; Thomas Keppel, *Life of Augustus Viscount Keppel,* 2 vols (London, 1842), II, 75-187.

20. Keppel, II, 190-91.

21. *Letters,* 18 June 1780.

22. Marshall, p. 471; J. Paul de Castro, *The Gordon Riots* (London, 1926), pp. 6, 98-99.

23. Ian R. Christie, *Stress and Stability in Late Eighteenth-Century Britain* (Oxford, 1984), p. 39.

24. Marshall, p. 401.

25. Watson, p. 57.

26. For dating of the poem, see *Poetical Works,* edited by Milford, p. 690.

27. *Poems,* edited by Baird and Ryskamp, p. 546.

28. Marshall, p. 465.

29. Watson, p. 231.

30. Watson, p. 232.

31. *The Correspondence of Edmund Burke,* edited by Thomas W. Copeland *et al.,* 10 vols (Cambridge, 1958-78), VI, 161.

32. *Letters,* 31 January 1782, p. 13, n. 6.

33. Watson, p. 55.

34. Watson, p. 200.

35. e.g. his defence of the Earl of Sandwich, first Lord of the Admiralty, *Letters,* 24 February 1782.

36. John Ehrman, *The Younger Pitt* (London, 1969), pp. 391-99.

37. John Cannon, *The Fox-North Coalition* (Cambridge, 1969), pp. 133; Ehrman, *The Younger Pitt,* pp. 126-27.

38. Cannon, p. 142.

39. Letter to Richard Fitzpatrick, 30 July 1789: *Memorials and Correspondence of Charles James Fox,* edited by Lord John Russell, 4 vols (London, 1853-57), II, 361.

40. F. P. Lock, *Burke's Reflections on the Revolution in France* (London, 1985), p. 51.

41. O'Gorman, p. 45.

42. Sir Herbert Butterfield, 'Charles James Fox and the Whig Opposition in 1792', *Cambridge Historical Journal,* IX (1949), 298.

43. O'Gorman, passim; L. G. Mitchell, *Charles James Fox and the Disintegration of the Whig Party* (Oxford, 1971), passim.

44. *Letters,* 9 September 1792.

Dustin Griffin (essay date 1990)

SOURCE: Griffin, Dustin. "Redefining Georgic: Cowper's *Task.*" *ELH* 57, no. 4 (winter 1990): 865-79.

[*In the following essay, Griffin views* The Task *as an eighteenth-century modification of the classical Georgic poetic form, while arguing that it depicts a more privatized and spiritualized conception of labor and its relation to the divine order than its predecessors.*]

Cowper's *Task* strikes most readers as a long and meandering discursive poem, divided rather arbitrarily into six books, and unified by little more than its concern with rural pleasures. Does the poem in fact have any clearer focus, any generic principle of order? My suggestion is that while the poem does not display the kind of unity or coherence one finds in a narrative long poem like *Paradise Lost,* or in an expository theodicy like *An Essay On Man,* it nonetheless possesses more than just the single "tendency" that Cowper claimed for it in a famous letter.[1]

While Pope's poem moves from proposition to proposition in a progression accurately summarized in the poem's prose arguments, Cowper's—four times longer—deliberately follows a roundabout way, and seems to take up scenes and subjects as he happens upon them, in the course of a leisurely mental excursion. Certain central topics recur frequently in opposed pairs—town and country, God's works and man's works, simplicity and luxury, leisure and work—and Cowper works on these topics a series of variations not always consistent with each other, revealing what may be his own ambivalence, or else acknowledging that the mind is typically various and varying from itself. Indeed, the poem seems to assume and embrace the fluidity of mental life, in which "fleeting images . . . fill / The mirror of the mind" (2.290-91), in which "the mind / Of desultory man" (curiously fitted to the variousness of the earth), "studious of change, / And pleas'd with novelty" (1.506-10), may be indulged and gratified by the poet, much as the observer's eye is conducted along its "sinuous course, / Delighted" by the "slow winding Ouse" (1.163-66).[2]

The danger of such a sinuous style, open as it is to shifts and turns in mood and subject, yielding to the slightest pressure, is that the poet's meditative river will lose itself in an endless plain. To provide himself some sense of direction, Cowper establishes several large thematic or narrative frames. The end of his wandering walk—both its conclusion and its purpose—is a vision not of God's works but of God himself. In traditional fashion, this poem long loved for its natural description leads to an epiphany of nature's creator. At the end of book 5 Cowper bids his reader "Acquaint thyself with God, if thou would'st taste / His works" (5.779-80). One can read in nature "the unambiguous footsteps" of God (5.812), and can vividly imagine that mystical moment when Nature throws wide "her veil opaque" and "discloses . . . / The author of her beauties" (5.891-93).

Cowper reminds himself and his reader that though as narrator he rambles, he is always ultimately homeward bound. In book 3 the narrator (ironically resembling Milton's Satan) winds his "devious course uncertain" but is always "seeking home" (3.3). In book 5, like a foreign traveler panting to return to his own country, Cowper looks to the stars to guide him "home / From toilsome life to never-ending rest" (5.837-41). Rest after labor is one of the most common biblical images of comfort, and the promise made to the faithful. Cowper may here also recall that in *Paradise Lost,* another poem about homecoming, fallen man is destined to wander until Christ at last "bring[s] back / Through the world's wilderness long wandered man / Safe to eternal paradise of rest."[3]

For Cowper home means—in very traditional fashion—the final release from toil. But until that release mortal man must be a day-laborer, must work for his bread in the sweat of his face. And yet work for Cowper is not a curse; it is instead the means whereby man establishes his dignity, occupies his time productively, and serves his God. Ultimately it is through work that man earns his eternal rest: "let us labor therefore," says Paul to the Hebrews, "to enter into that rest" (Heb. 4:11). Traditionally, the poetic form devoted to the celebration of labor (as Cowper knew) is the georgic. My argument is that Cowper found in the generic resources of georgic a means of focusing his long poem, and further that Cowper redefined the meaning of labor and thus redefined the georgic for his generation.

Reading Cowper's poem as a georgic will in fact help us sharpen our sense of a genre that we have defined rather casually. Georgic, we customarily say, means a poem that is discursive, didactic, concerned with the agricultural foundation of a great nation, even concerned with providing instruction in a rural art. Its locus classicus is Virgil's four-book poem (and we rarely look outside of Virgil for georgic topics). If a poem bears its Virgilian model closely in mind, and centers on a didactic purpose, we call it "formal georgic"—Phillips's *Cyder,* Dyer's *Fleece,* Smart's *Hop-Garden*—which, like Virgil's poem, links the strength of rural arts to the health of a nation. It is clear that *The Task* is not a formal georgic. Except for the section in book 3 on the growing of cucumbers, *The Task* devotes very little of its attention to agricultural practice, and when it does so makes clear that the growing of cucumbers is of little benefit to anybody but the gardener himself.

In recent years we have also used the term "georgic" to refer to a number of well-known poems in the eighteenth century that display the major characteristics of the genre in a less rigorous way. Denham's *Cooper's Hill,* Pope's *Windsor Forest,* even Dryden's *Annus Mirabilis* have been said to be shaped by georgic conventions, by which we usually mean not much more than that the poems are governed by a flexible decorum that permits the poet to range widely: the poems are discursive and didactic, they use the materials of rural nature as a means of dealing ultimately with larger political themes, and they may (or may not) touch on a rural art (or sport). By this looser conception of the genre, *The Task* might well be considered a georgic.

But the definition is so elastic that many quite different poems might gather under this large umbrella—Jonson's "To Penshurst," Dryden's epistle "To my Honour'd Kinsman, John Driden, of Chesterton," Thomson's *Seasons,* even some of Pope's Horatian epistles. We can recognize that eighteenth-century poets did not feel obliged to preserve the purity of the traditional genres, and that many poems in the period seem to be shaped by several different generic frames at once. But we should also recognize that in modifying or in combining genres, those poets were probably more aware of the conventions they were violating and the boundaries they were crossing than we are.

One traditional boundary, for example, is that which separates georgic from pastoral. For Virgil there was a clear distinction between the two forms, and we can be reasonably certain that the distinction survived among Renaissance English pastoralists, and among the translators of Virgil, including Dryden. Some modern critics, however, have assumed that the distinction lost clarity in the eighteenth century, perhaps because the narrow stream of classically-inspired pastoral seems to lose itself in the great flood of poetry of natural description. Richard Feingold, for example, has examined *The Task* within what he calls the "bucolic tradition" and what he sees as that tradition's recurrent concern with the relation of art and nature.[4] His key term—"bucolic tradition"—tends to blur some important traditional distinctions between the two bucolic forms, the pastoral and the georgic. But there is some reason to believe that English poets of the seventeenth and eighteenth centuries, who knew their Virgil very well, retained a sense of the two genres that had as much to do with spirit as form. Pastoral traditionally concerns the relatively carefree world of shepherds, exemplars of the world of leisure or *otium.* The pastoral figure's object is pleasure, and this essentially pagan element has to be de-emphasized when the form is taken over by Christian writers. Georgic, on the other hand, concerns the more active world of farming, and the life of negotium, employment, occupation, work. In some respects georgic lends itself better than pastoral to Christian uses, since it shares with Christianity a high valuation of purposive labor. The Bible indeed is a far greater source of georgic imagery than pastoral: laborers in the vineyard outnumber scriptural shepherds. Because *The Task* does not emphasize instruction in any rural art, Feingold and most other critics have assumed that the poem contains at most a georgic episode, perhaps no more than a mock-georgic interlude, in book 3, entitled **"The Garden."**[5] But if we think of georgic since Virgil as a poem concerned above all with the value of work, we may have a useful way of seeing the wholeness of a poem that Cowper tellingly entitled *The Task.*

A recent book by Anthony Low, *The Georgic Revolution,* shows how the English poets of the seventeenth century concerned themselves, far more than we have realized, with a world in which labor—even physical labor—was not simply the curse of Adam, or the fate of servants and rustic clowns—but was a basis of human dignity and the foundation for a strong society.[6] Milton is perhaps the poet of that century who most clearly reorients the attention of the English gentleman from an aristocratic code of honor and heroic deeds to an alternative ethic of painstaking dedication to one's duties and responsibilities, religious, domestic, and civil. The epic virtues are those of a magistrate—boldness and courage, ambition, decisive leadership. The georgic virtues are less spectacular: steadiness, application, endurance, what Adam must learn in *Paradise Lost* and what Jesus displays in *Paradise Regained.* Cowper was of course a deep admirer of Milton, and though I would not claim that Cowper consciously set out to write a Miltonic georgic, and indeed cannot claim that he ever used the term "georgic" in describing *The Task,* I argue that the georgic spirit is the presiding principle of his poem. I suggest further that Cowper went back to Virgil's own *Georgics,* though his use of the poem is critical rather than reverential, and in some cases even corrective. One means of correcting Virgil is to look to a higher authority—the Bible—and to draw into his poem, by means of subtle allusion, the Christianized georgic world of Milton.

Cowper of course knew Virgil's *Georgics,* and often quoted from them (presumably by memory) in his letters. More significant is that Cowper seems to have understood what Virgil meant by *labor improbus*—the unrelenting toil which ultimately conquers all (1.145).[7] Cowper too knows how "slow / The growth of what is excellent; so hard / T'attain perfection in this nether world" (*Task,* 1.83-85). "Perfection" may indeed be beyond reach, especially for Cowper, who feared that regardless of his performance in this "nether world," his ultimate fate was sealed, and would not be altered by deeds no matter how perfect. But unremitting labor might serve the lesser function of occupying the mind. As James King's recent biography suggests, Cowper himself was never so happy, so free from mental anguish, as when he was working steadily, absorbing himself wholly in the task of translating Homer: "My task that I assign myself," he wrote in 1785 (the year *The Task* was published), "is to translate forty lines a day. . . . Perhaps I am occupied an hour and a half, perhaps three hours. . . . This, you see, is labour that can hurt no man."[8] Indeed, given Cowper's religious mania, it is perhaps not unreasonable to speculate that entitling his poem *The Task* obliquely invoked a world, like Milton's, where God, a severe "task-master," laid tasks on the poet.[9] God had (so it seemed) assigned Cowper no task, no necessary work, in this life. The poet longed for a task to be performed, that he might work and thereby satisfy the just demands made upon him. For Milton the word "task" had strongly literary associations—the "noble task" of defending liberty ("To Mr. Cyriack Skinner," 11), the "sad task" of narrating the fall of man (*Paradise Lost,* 9.13), the "sad task and hard" of narrating the war in heaven (5.564). Such tasks are heroic; more important, they constitute service and obedience to God's will, and are thus part of what Pope (another important predecessor to Cowper) called "that task, which as we follow, or despise, / The eldest is a fool, the youngest wise."[10]

Cowper's *Task* begins with an oblique allusion to the end of Virgil's own *Georgics* and the pseudo-Virgilian proem at the beginning of the *Aeneid*. Virgil had concluded his *Georgics* with an implicitly mock-heroic contrast between his own leisurely singing of rural pleasures and great Caesar's thundering wars: "Thus I sang of the care of fields, of cattle, and of trees, while great Caesar thundered in war by deep Euphrates" (4.559-61). In the rejected proem to the *Aeneid*—lines that may be spurious—Virgil puts pastoral and georgic behind him and turns to epic wars: "Ille ego, qui quondam gracili modulatus avena / carmen, et egressus silvis vicina coegi / ut quamvis avido parerent arva colono, / gratum opus agricolis; at nunc horrentia Martis" [I am he who once turned my song on a slender reed, then, leaving the woodland, constrained the neighbouring fields to serve the husbandmen, however grasping—work welcome to farmers: but now of Mars' bristling]. Cowper reverses the progress, and turns from great themes to small.

> I sing the Sofa. I, who lately sang
> Truth, Hope, and Charity, and touch'd with awe
> The solemn chords, and with a trembling hand,
> Escap'd with pain from that advent'rous flight,
> Now seek repose upon an humbler theme;
> The theme though humble, yet august and proud
> Th' occasion—for the Fair commands the song.
>
>   (1.1-7)

Cowper descends from the high moral strains of his 1782 *Poems* to an apparently humbler song of a sofa, "commanded" to his task by the mighty "Fair." After Miltonic "advent'rous flight" he seeks "repose" (equally Miltonic, in fact), and hints perhaps that this will be a task that he can accomplish lying down, in literal "repose" upon the sofa.[11] While Milton has "escaped the Stygian Pool" of hell on "bolder wing" to sing of heaven (*Paradise Lost,* 3.13-14), Cowper inverts the direction, and ironically resembles Milton's devils, who seek "repose" in "abject posture" after their dangerous flight (1.319-22). The parodic beginning of *The Task,* with its facetious tone, should not mislead us into thinking that Cowper is ironically subverting a georgic tradition characterized by earnestness and sobriety. The poem is not simply the result of the task, assigned him by Lady Austen, of writing about her sofa. It quickly moves beyond this genteel domestic assignment to consider the importance of labor, occupation, and employment (all three words recurrent in the poem). At its close Cowper surveys how far he has come. He had begun playfully with a "light task," dressing the sofa with flowers, "obedient to the fair" (6.1008-1009). But he went on to a more georgic task, from flowers to better fruits, "wholesome, well-digested; grateful some / To palates that can taste immortal truth" (6.1014-15). And his real audience, it becomes plain, is not Lady Austen, or even "the world" (1020) at large, but God, "whose eye is on the heart" (6.1022). His real taskmaster (and model) is

not "the Fair" but "the First and Only Fair" (5.675), by whose work the world and man were made, and by whose "labours of love" (5.570) man is transformed "from fool to wise, from earthly to divine" (5.697).

Cowper's georgic poem of course celebrates the life of retirement and "repose." He is aware of the implicit paradox and, perhaps somewhat defensively, takes pains to assert that the retired life is in fact a life of activity:

> How various his employments whom the world
> Calls idle; and who justly, in return,
> Esteems that busy world an idler too!
> Friends, books, a garden, and perhaps his pen,
> Delightful industry enjoy'd at home,
> And nature in her cultivated trim
> Dress'd to his taste, inviting him abroad—
> Can he want occupation who has these?
> Will he be idle who has much t'enjoy?
> Me, therefore, studious of laborious ease,
> Not slothful; happy to deceive the time,
> Not waste it; and aware that human life
> Is but a loan to be repaid with use,
> When he shall call his debtors to account
> From whom are all our blessings; bus'ness finds
> Ev'n here.
>
>   (3.352-367)

The passage is thematically central to the pattern I am describing. Employments, industry, occupation, business— this cluster of georgic terms asserts, against the suspicions of the great world, that retirement is not idleness. Time may be deceived or beguiled, but at the same time it must be used, not wasted. Cowper's pompous Miltonism—"Me, therefore, studious of laborious ease"—is a deliberate self-mocking touch, but it sustains Cowper's design of correcting the world's mistaken impressions. Poets are traditionally devoted to ease, otium rather than negotium. Cowper wants to insist that poets are laborers too. At the end of the *Georgics* Virgil speaks of "flourishing in the arts of inglorious ease" (4.564), a line Cowper knew well, and used as the epigraph for his own poem, **"Retirement,"** in 1782. Through a kind of bilingual pun, Virgil's *studiis florentem ignobilis oti* becomes Cowper's "studious of laborious ease, / Not slothful": an ease not inglorious but laborious, not pastoral but georgic. The emphatic "not slothful" (362) perhaps fends off the fear that "ease" is a sign of moral lapse. Cowper is explicitly *not* like Milton's Belial, who counsels "ignoble ease, and peaceful sloth" in hell (*Paradise Lost,* 2.227). And Cowper's seriousness is underlined by the glancing allusion to the Parable of the Talents: life is only loaned to us, and must be repaid "with use" (Cowper puns here on the old term for "interest").

The employments of the retired life include the tasks performed in the drawing room, from writing poems to "weaving nets for bird-alluring fruit" or "twining silken threads round iv'ry reels" (4.263-64). Though the tasks require little strenuous effort, and the end results may seem more ornamental than useful, Cowper stresses that he sees them as responsibilities laid upon him by those "whom man was born to please" (265). Even the embroidering of a cushion with a floral pattern is a "task," patiently performed. The pleasing result of "female industry" is "a wreath that cannot fade" (4.156, 165). Cowper's tone is difficult to catch here. On the one hand he is wittily aware of making great things of small; on the other, his appropriation of Isaiah and Peter hints at his hope that those who lead a quiet and decent domestic life are on their way toward receiving a greater wreath, "a crown of glory that fadeth not away" (1 Peter 5:4).

Other employments include the famous labors of the gentleman gardener. These tasks require "skill" rather than "force." Like the classical husbandman he bears responsibility for the success or failure of the enterprise. The "many cares" of the garden are ultimately his. But he serves primarily as planner and supervisor, making sure that "the hand / Of lubbard labour"—the servants who do the hard work—does not loiter or misapply its "unskilful strength" (3.397-407). Brute force, he says, "may turn the clod, and wheel the compost home," but "elegance, chief grace the garden shows / . . . is the fair result / Of thought, the creature of a polish'd mind" (3.637-40). Cowper clearly retains some of the aristocratic prejudice against manual labor that compromises the pure georgic spirit. (I will come back to this point.) When the gentleman retires from his gardening labors, he repairs to the parlor for tea and conversation with his friend and patroness, Mrs. Unwin; his hired hands join the village artisans to drown their weariness in the local alehouse:

> the craftsman there
> Takes a Lethean leave of all his toil;
> Smith, cobbler, joiner, he that plies the shears,
> And he that kneads the dough; all loud alike,
> All learned, and all drunk!
>
> (4.474-78)

The gentleman's delights are finer. Because "lubbard labour" is unable to feel a keen pleasure in a well-espaliered fruit tree, the gentleman himself takes personal charge of pruning, and acts the Calvinist role of merciless judge, dooming the weak, distempered, and barren shoots.

More important are the "occupations of the poet's mind" (2.298). Again, poetry is both a difficult task and (for that reason) a source of pleasure. "There is a pleasure in poetic pains / Which only poets know" (2.285-86). Though "retired" and "stretch'd at ease in Chertsey's silent bowers," the poet Cowley (like his admirer, Cowper) was "not unemploy'd" (4.727-29). Calm evening's "gentle hours" are gladly devoted to "the poet's toil" (4.262). Whether as gardener or as poet the retired man is engaged in what Cowper (using a venerable European pun) calls "cultivation" (6.189)—of the rural garden, of those arts which make up "cultivated life" (1.679), and finally of himself. His primary task, indeed, is to cultivate, to "improve," and at least not to leave "unemploy'd" the mind that God gave him (3.368). And when the laboring poet finds a great task, "lights at last / On some fair theme, some theme

divinely fair" (6.753-54), such as might be imposed by (and might please) "the First and Only Fair," then it is less "arduous" to write than not to write. The great theme of book 6, as Cowper's headnote puts it, is "the Restoration of all Things." "Not t'attempt it, arduous as he deems / The labour, were a task more arduous still" (6.757-58).

Such labors are no curse, or if so, they are "soften'd into mercy" (1.364-65). "The employs of rural life" (3.625) for Cowper are in fact repeatedly associated with health: they bring sound sleep (1.365) as "strenuous toil" brings "sweetest ease" (1.388). Ease is not just the effect of a grateful vicissitude, a pause from labor. The labor itself, as in Milton's Eden, is almost refreshing. The laborer's "spirits" are "prompt to undertake, / And not soon spent, though in an arduous task" (1.400-401). Just as all creation subsists by "ceaseless action" (1.367), so man subsists by labor. "Absence of occupation," Cowper says in another poem, "is not rest; / A mind quite vacant is a mind distress'd" (**"Retirement"**, 623-24). Work is "pleasant" (3.656), industry is "delightful" (3.356). A life of "constant occupation" is a life "without care" (3.693). Such labor recalls not only the innocent gardening of Adam and Eve in Eden; it is an image of God's own work. The account of growing cucumbers is broken, like God's original labors, into stages. When the greenhouse is completed, "the first labour ends" (3.489), perhaps a subsurface allusion to the refrain in Genesis: "And the evening and the morning were the first day" (1:5). Man's "constant occupation" is an image too of the "ceaseless force" that sustains the universe, God "Whose work is without labour" (6.219, 228).

The end of man's labor is not the traditional georgic end of nation-building. As Feingold has well shown, Cowper has no faith in corporate life.[12] His occupations are self-directed: they can build some order in his own life, or at least keep off despair, and secure "the mind / From all assaults of evil" (3.679-80). The devil, after all, finds work for idle hands and minds. His efforts to gain "triumphs o'er himself" (6.937) win him no epic laurels. This is a Miltonic better fortitude. "His warfare is within" (6.935), and the victory—as in traditional georgic—comes only through the fervent labors of an unfatigued spirit:

> There unfatigu'd
> His fervent spirit labours. There he fights,
> And there obtains fresh triumphs o'er himself,
> And never with'ring wreaths, compar'd with which
> The laurels that a Caesar reaps are weeds.
>
> (6.935-39)

With guidance from Milton, Cowper here returns to correct his georgic ancestor, Virgil, whose *Georgics* began and ended with a tribute to Caesar, wreathed with myrtle (1.28), and the subject of an extravagant "triumph" at the beginning of book 3. Cowper's wreath, once more, is the crown of glory that fadeth not away. By an ironic reversal the unfatigued georgic laborer is the true epic warrior; the military chief is a mere reaper in the fields, and his labor is fruitless, for the laurels he "reaps are weeds."

To say that Cowper corrects Virgil is perhaps to put it too strongly. For the *Georgics* as a whole are deeply ambivalent about the world of Caesar that the poem in part celebrates. Virgil presents more than one view of the relation between country virtue and Roman greatness. In the words of one recent critic, rustic life may be seen either as the "source" of Roman strength and virtue, or as an "alternative" to it.[13] Particularly in the famous passage that concludes the second book, "O fortunatos nimium . . ." (2.458), Virgil—like Cowper after him—finds in the security and contemplative pleasures of the country a world exempt from the flashing display and furor of the capital. It is to this side of Virgil's *Georgics*—not the celebration of Roman power—that Cowper is attracted. But where Virgil makes of rustic life what Gary Miles calls an "uncertain ideal," and finally associates it with a "remote and inaccessible past" in the long-gone Golden Age, Cowper displays some confidence (if not for himself, then for others) that a life of quiet virtue, "more golden than that age of fabled gold / Renown'd in ancient song" (6.996-97), can still be led in Pitt's imperial England.[14]

And yet by the end of *The Task* Cowper even claims—perhaps because he does not wish to sever the traditional georgic link between the sturdy farmer and the health of the state—that the retired man, by doing good works within his humble sphere, "serves his country, recompenses well / The state," and "in the scale of life / Holds no ignoble, though a slighted, place" (6.968-71). Cowper's implicit claim that as poet he "serves . . . the state" springs from his grafting of Horace onto Virgil's georgic. Horace in the *Epistle to Augustus* had argued that the poet "serves the state" [*utilis urbi*].[15] In Cowper's hands Horace's poet, the retired man (from Horatian tradition), and Virgil's farmer blend into one exemplary figure. But the link between private labor and public good is far less realized than in Virgil. Cowper's retired man is not a producer of food, a dispenser of laws, or a guarantor of liberty. He may indeed appear to others to be only an "incumbrance on the state, / Receiving benefits, and rend'ring none" (6.958-59). Yet the retired' man serves his country. Not because the country "stand[s]" by the "skill" of its sturdy farmer-soldiers (6.975), but because the retired man can at least claim that "his follies have not wrought her fall" (6.975-76). And the "state" which Cowper's retired man "recompenses" turns out not to be the civil power at all.[16] It is a higher power, "the state, beneath the shadow of whose vine / He sits secure" (6.969-70). Cowper invokes another georgic metaphor (Tityrus sits under the cover or protective shade of a beech tree at the end of the *Georgics*), but its strongest associations are biblical rather than Virgilian.

To sit under the shadow of a vine is a common image of comfort or security in the Bible (1 Kings 4:25; compare Song of Sol. 2:3; Jon. 4:5). But Cowper probably has in mind the famous prophecy in Micah of the last days, when God "shall be established in the top of the mountains." After the familiar words about beating swords into plowshares and spears into pruning hooks, Micah foretells

the days when "they shall sit every man under his vine and under his fig tree; and none shall make them afraid: for the mouth of the LORD of hosts hath spoken it" (4:1-4). Whose "state" can Cowper refer to but that of God, who hides his faithful under the shadow of his wings (Ps. 17:8, cf. Ps. 57:1)? Though far from the world of the court, ministry, and place-men, the retired man too (as the quiet pun brings out) has a "place" in the "scale of life" more important (because by gradual steps it reaches up to God) than any in the great world.[17] "Ignoble" may be one more memory and correction of Virgil's *ignobilis oti*. For Virgil *ignobilis* also suggested humble or obscure, for which a poet need not apologize. By Cowper's time the English equivalent "ignoble" was more likely to suggest "worthless" than "humble." Virgil's retired poet is *ignobilis*—out of the limelight that properly belongs to Caesar. Cowper won't render that much to the Caesars of the world. His poet is emphatically not "ignoble"—but unjustly "slighted" by the great world, just as the "homely . . . shepherd's trade" (i. e., the poet's) is "slighted" in Milton's "Lycidas" (65). Indeed, Cowper's line and his image of the ultimately rewarded retired man seems a reworking—with details from Virgil and the Bible—of a famous apostrophe in "Lycidas." Milton asks a painful question about the uncertainty of earthly fame: "Alas! what boots it with uncessant care [itself a georgic image] / To tend the homely slighted shepherd's trade" (64-65). He is answered with reassurance that true fame "is no plant that grows on mortal soil" (78).

The Task emerges from Feingold's analysis as a poem which finds bucolic topics unable to express and apprehend the modern state, almost an anti-georgic.[18] I have tried to suggest, on the other hand, that the poem has a clear georgic design. By redefining labor—with help from the Bible and from Milton—as a virtually spiritual activity, and shifting his attention from the public sphere to the private, Cowper reaffirms, though he significantly modifies, the traditional georgic values of steady dedication to a homely and unspectacular task. And his poetry—quietly allusive, soberly witty, temperately fervent—embodies those values.

Cowper would perhaps be happy if we concluded here, and adopted his perspective on spiritual labor in the private sphere. But it is worth remembering his distinction between such labor and real physical labor, and worth noting what Cowper's spiritual georgic leaves out of account. As a barometer of late eighteenth-century English culture, Cowper registers the power of rural evangelicalism. But he tells us little of the incipient concern for the real laborers in England's fields whose pinched lives begin to be visible in a contemporary poem like Crabbe's *The Village* (1784) or in the recently rediscovered work of poets like Ann Yearsley.[19]

What is more, Cowper's redefined idea of georgic almost conceals the economic base that makes possible the life of retired leisure/labor that he celebrates. Occasionally we glimpse the hand of "lubbard labour." But for the most part Cowper prefers to look at physical labor from afar. The "clinking hammers" and "grinding wheels" in the village and town are "unpleasing sounds" (1.229-31) which he prefers to escape. He takes more pleasure in beholding the plowman as part of the picturesque scenery, "the distant plough slow-moving, and beside / His lab'ring team that swerv'd not from the track, / The sturdy swain diminish'd to a boy!" (1.160-62). Labor goes on all around him, and makes possible the gentleman-farmer's quiet life, produces and delivers the bread promptly (1.244-45), and supplies his many wants. The "industrious hands" that satisfy his "temp'rate wishes" (1.597-99) are not—for the most part—his own. He is freed for leisurely walks. Thanks to the largesse of a neighboring squire, he has access to a private park (we can be sure its "folded gates" [1.330] do not open to admit the peasant). Even if "Nature's works" are "free to all" (1.434), the finer delights that Cowper praises are not really available to the man who works until sundown. The "pensive wanderer" (1.761) in noontide groves is not, so to speak, a field laborer on his lunch break.

To be fair to Cowper, it must be granted that his rural landscape is not utterly unpeopled (a charge that Collins, Gray, and even Wordsworth do not always escape). The "foddering of cattle" is accomplished not by an unseen hand but by a laborer who carves hay from the stack, "deep-plunging and again deep-plunging oft / His broad keen knife into the solid mass" (5.33-35), and Cowper shows real appreciation for his skill. The "woodman" is observed leaving "the cheerful haunts of men" to wield his axe in "yonder forest drear," but Cowper is as much interested in the woodman's scampering dog as in the "sturdy churl" himself (5.41-53). The archaism both distances the woodman and places him as a member of a distinctly lower order, equipped by nature to bear his burdens. Indeed, Cowper's "compassion" (4.374) with the industrious poor is checked by the assurance that the rural laborers are "form'd to bear" hard weather (350) and—lucky for them—are "denied / That sensibility of pain with which / Refinement is endu'd" (357-58). So the wagoner feels cold "unimpair'd" (361), and "plods on" (353) with "half-shut eyes, and pucker'd cheeks" (352), more like the beasts that drag the wagon than the sympathizing poet.[20] It would be unfair to demand that Cowper find a way to include the world of Crabbe's *Village* within the georgic confines of **The Task**. (Crabbe is in fact selective in other ways). But it is worth remembering that Cowper's world of spiritual labor—despite the universalist claims of his evangelicalism—is limited to the few (whether happy few or anxious few is beside the point). The physical laborer is capable at best of the virtues of industry, patience, and resignation, but Cowper's woodman, wagoner, and fodderer do not raise their eyes to a higher state. In this respect Cowper is very much a man of his age and of its dominant conservative ideology. Just as it is the independent landed gentleman who, freed from the limits of an occupation and the lure of the court and city, is qualified to govern and to survey society with authority,[21] so it is the man of "refinement"—education, leisure, and a comfortable income— who rises through spiritual georgic to an apprehension of divine order.

Notes

1. To William Unwin, 10 October 1784, in *Letters and Prose Writings of William Cowper,* ed. James King and Charles Ryskamp, 5 vols. (Oxford: Clarendon Press, 1981), 2:285.

2. Cowper's poems are cited from his *Poetical Works,* ed. H. S. Mitford, 4th ed. (London: Oxford Univ. Press, 1934). All further references will be cited parenthetically in the text.

3. *Paradise Lost,* 12.312-14, cited from *The Poems of John Milton,* ed. John Carey and Alastair Fowler (London: Longmans, 1964). All subsequent references to Milton's poetry will be cited from this edition by book and/or line number parenthetically in the text.

4. Richard Feingold, *Nature and Art: Later Eighteenth-Century Uses of the Pastoral and Georgic* (New Brunswick: Rutgers Univ. Press, 1978).

5. Feingold, 159. See also Vincent Newey, *Cowper's Poetry* (Totowa: Barnes and Noble, 1982), 184-85; and John Chalker, *The English Georgic* (London: Routledge and Kegan Paul, 1969), 203.

6. Anthony Low, *The Georgic Revolution* (Princeton: Princeton Univ. Press, 1985).

7. I cite the *Georgics* from the Loeb Library edition, Virgil, *Eclogues, Georgics, Aenied 1-6* (London: Heineman, rev. ed. 1967). All further references to Virgil will be cited parenthetically in the text. For Cowper's quotations from the *Georgics,* see *Letters and Prose Writing* (note 1), 1:297, 324; 2:240; 3:198, 4:440.

8. Quoted in James King, *William Cowper* (Durham: Duke Univ. Press, 1986), 208. Cf. "Cowper may well have felt that as long as there was Homer there was life for him. Certainly the prospect of future labors on the project seemed to revive and refresh him at this time" (214).

9. Sonnet 7 ("How soon hath time"), 14. A "task," as Johnson notes in his *Dictionary,* is not simply work; it is "imposed by another."

10. *Imitations of Horace,* Ep. 1.1.43-44, quoted from *The Poems of Alexander Pope,* ed. John Butt (New Haven: Yale Univ. Press, 1963).

11. The word "repose" is especially associated by Milton with prelapsarian Eden.

12. Feingold, esp. 155-92.

13. Gary Miles, *Virgil's "Georgics": A New Interpretation* (Berkeley: Univ. of California Press, 1980), xi.

14. Miles, 160.

15. Horace, Epistle 2.1 ("To Augustus"), line 124, cited from the Loeb Library edition, *Satires, Epistles, and Ars Poetica* (Cambridge: Harvard, 1970).

16. The word "recompense" seems odd here. In Cowper's day it was strongly associated with biblical reward and retribution. Is Cowper unconsciously hoping that the retired man—or that he himself—will one day be "recompensed"? Cf. 3.430-31, where the gardner's summer labors are recompensed with fruits in winter.

17. Cowper perhaps here recalls Milton's "scale of nature" (*Paradise Lost,* 5.509), where, as Raphael says, "in contemplation of created things / By steps we may ascend to God" (511-12).

18. Feingold, 191-92.

19. Yearsley's *Poems on Several Occasions,* sponsored by Hannah More, appeared in 1785, and her *Poems on Various Subjects* in 1787.

20. Even syntax assimilates man to beast. "Forth goes the woodman, . . . / From morn to eve his solitary task. / Shaggy and lean and shrew'd . . ." We assume Cowper still refers to the woodman, until he continues: ". . . with pointed ears / And tail cropp'd short . . . / His dog attends him" (5.41-47).

21. On this theme, see John Barrell, *English Literature in History, 1730-1780* (New York: St. Martin's, 1983), 33-40.

Peter Faulkner (essay date 1991)

SOURCE: Faulkner, Peter. "William Cowper and the Poetry of Empire." *Durham University Journal* (July 1991): 165-73.

[*In the following essay, Faulkner focuses on Cowper's expressions of British Imperialist ideology—and its inherent ambivalence—in his poetic works.*]

Cowper's **'Boadicea. An Ode'** must be one of the most forceful and effective Imperialist poems of the late eighteenth century. The regular rhythm of its trochaic quatrains gives weight to the prophecy it announces through the movement back and forth in history. The "British warrior Queen" is presented in heroic terms in her resistance to the invading Romans; Boadicea was already a potent symbol of Englishness (one of the long line of representatives of victory-in-defeat). She goes for advice to "the Druid, hoary chief", again a respected symbolic figure, sitting sagaciously under "the spreading oak"—a neat emblem of his 'natural' authority. The Druid's only comfort for her is in predicting the eventual fall of Rome:

> Rome shall perish—write that word
> In the blood that she has spilt;
> Perish, hopeless and abhorr'd,
> Deep in ruin as in guilt.

Then a new Empire will be created:

> Other Romans shall arise,
> Heedless of a soldier's name;
> Sounds, not arms, shall win the prize,
> Harmony the path to fame.
>
> Then the progeny that springs
> From the forests of our land,
> Arm'd with thunder, clad with wings,
> Shall a wider world command.
>
> Regions Caesar never knew
> Thy posterity shall sway;
> Where his eagles never flew,
> None invincible as they.

The imagery of these stanzas is far from clear. At first it seems as if the Empire prophesied is to be one of peace and, perhaps, the arts. But the references to 'thunder', 'wings' and 'command' suggest warfare, and the last stanza is certainly Imperialistic in its claim: only Britain's forces shall prove truly invincible. Boadicea is inspired by these words, and hurls them at the Romans as she dies in battle; and the poetic voice ends by contrasting the futures of the two nations:

> Ruffians, pitiless as proud,
> Heaven awards the vengeance due:
> Empire is on us bestow'd,
> Shame and ruin wait for you.

Whereas Victorian schoolmasters encouraged their pupils to see the Roman Empire as a forerunner of the British, Cowper offers the sharpest of contrasts: the ruffianly Romans doomed to failure, shame and ruin, the deserving British to imperial power awarded by Providence.

The rhetorical force and formal neatness of the poem, together with its straightforward sentiments, no doubt account for its popularity in the nineteenth century, and its inclusion by W. E. Henley in his *Lyra Heroica* in 1891. There would indeed be nothing surprising about such a poem coming from the pen of an eighteenth-century Henley. But it is far more surprising coming from a leading Evangelical moralist and proponent of withdrawal from the active life, whose other poems include vigorous denunciations of the Slave Trade, a flourishing though seldom emphasised part of the Empire so celebrated. The rest of this essay will attempt to provide a fuller account of Cowper's political attitudes in order to provide a context for the poem, and to raise some questions about its relation to the poet's overall ideological position.

The volume of poetry in which **'Boadicea'** appeared, in 1782, was Cowper's first, although the poet was already fifty-one. It also included several longer, mainly satirical, poems in rhyming couplets, from which the poet's political outlook can be gauged. As Maurice Quinlan puts it, "Cowper's family were Whigs, and he himself was ever a lover of liberty, but a liberty within the framework of traditional British institutions".[1] He presented a Whig belief in constitutional monarchy, embodied in the often criticised figure of George III, but was pessimistic about the contemporary situation. He saw signs of impending chaos, foreshadowed by the loss of the American colonies, which he attributed to French interference, and disturbingly represented by the Gordon Riots of 1780.

The poem **'Table-Talk'** is a dialogue in which many social issues are considered, including the responsibilities of the monarch. The couplet which concludes this part of the poem—

> Blest country! where these kingly glories shine;
> Blest England! if this happiness be thine—

balances the reader on the word 'if' in a way that suggests that the present prosperity of the country is precarious. Although the poet can praise British Liberty in true Whig fashion, he also warns that John Brown's *Estimate* of 1757, which foretold the decline of Britain, may have been wrong then but appropriate in the present. God may be about to send Britain along the path of "Nineveh, Babylon and ancient Rome". **'Expostulation'** similarly warns that Britain could follow the course of Israel, a nation once blessed by Providence but disastrously fallen since. And God's possible anger is related to British conduct in India:

> Hast thou, though suckled at fair Freedom's breast,
> Exported slavery to the conquer'd East?
> Pull'd down the tyrants India served with dread,
> And raised thyself, a greater, in their stead?
> Gone thither arm'd and hungry, return'd full,
> Fed from the richer veins of the Mogul . . . ?

Such questions show that Cowper was no uncritical admirer of what the British were doing abroad. He shared the widespread suspicion of the actions of the East India Company, and expressed his doubts with effective sarcasm here. Interestingly, in view of the arguments of **'Boadicea',** the poem goes on to praise the Roman contribution to British civilization:

> He brought the land a blessing when he came,
> He found thee savage and he left thee tame.
> Taught thee to clothe thy pink'd and painted hide,
> And grac'd thy figure with a soldier's pride . . .

By contrast the Druids in this poem represent a barbaric paganism:

> Thy Druids struck the well-strung harps they bore
> With fingers deeply dyed in human gore;
> And while the victim slowly bled to death,
> Upon the tolling chorus rung out his dying breath.

The poem rather inconsistently then asserts that England is in a much better condition than it had once been, because of Providence's care—"Peculiar is thy grace by thee possess'd / Thy foes implacable, thy land at rest"—but warns of the need for a return to the true faith.

Finally, **'Charity'** reflects at some length on the economic and commercial developments of the age. The first part contrasts Captain Cook with the conquistador Cortez. Cook

had been killed in Hawaii on his third voyage to the Pacific in 1779. Cowper presents him as an agent of Charity, approaching all men in terms of equality:

> Wherever he found man, to nature true,
> The rights of man were sacred in his view;
> He soothed with gifts, and greeted with a smile,
> The simple native of the new-found isle . . .
> Nor would endure that any should control
> Her freeborn brethren of the southern pole.

By contrast, Cortez is "odious for a world enslaved", having conquered and subjugated the "ancient Incas". This is followed immediately by a passage celebrating Commerce in the Whig fashion of Thomson's *Seasons*:

> Again—the band of commerce was design'd
> To associate all the branches of mankind;
> And if a boundless plenty by the robe,
> Trade is the golden girdle of the globe.

The celebration is poetically effective in its confident sweep of assertion, but is suddenly checked:

> But ah! what wish can prosper, or what prayer,
> For merchants rich in cargoes of despair,
> Who drive a loathsome traffic, gauge and span
> And buy the muscles and the bones of man?

Cowper's indignation about the Slave Trade is powerfully conveyed. He was aware of its appalling inhumanity from his contact with the Reverend John Newton, who had been a slave-trader before his conversion to Evangelical Christianity and his friendship with Cowper. The passage then, however, develops surprisingly by arguing that, if slavery is unavoidable, it should at least be conducted without violence. The section concludes, disturbingly to the modern reader, with a speech of gratitude from an emancipated slave, thanking his master for having brought him from "Africa's once loved, benighted shore" to the service of a Christian benefactor. If this seems anti-climactic today, it must be remembered that the Slave Trade would not be abolished until 1807, and slavery itself in the British Empire not until 1833.

Martin Priestman has written interestingly on **'Charity'** in his book on *The Task*,[2] as evidence of Cowper's political views:

> Cowper was an eighteenth-century Whig, and there is no doubt that the basis of his political outlook was eighteenth-century Whig mercantilism: that is, that the interests of trade were the fundamental interests of the country.
>
> (p.35)

He goes on to suggest that in this poem "the cardinal Christian virtue is located first and foremost in trade, with Captain Cook more or less as its patron saint" (p.36). It is certainly striking that Cook should be the first figure that we encounter in a poem devoted to Charity, but it must be said that the description of Cook's activities makes no reference to trading; it is difficult from the passage to see what Cook *is* doing in Hawaii—he seems to be a kind of ambassador for internationalism, making men aware of their common humanity. And certainly the contrast with Cortez has nothing to do with their comparative success as traders, everything to do with morality: an emphasis that is continued in Cowper's attack on the Slave Trade. It could of course be argued that the failure to make explicit Cook's commercial associations is evidence of Cowper's own self-deception, and this could be seen as representative of a general wish in Britain to see the expansion of the Empire as a humanistic rather than a commercial enterprise. What it certainly suggests is that Cowper's thinking in these areas is not always very precise or consistent.

Three years were to pass before the publication of *The Task* in 1785. Letters from this period provide evidence of Cowper's continuing concern with these issues. A particularly striking letter of 1783 refers to Omai, who was brought from Tahiti in 1774 to England where he became something of a social success as well as a curiosity, and was painted by Reynolds in the turban and robe of an Arab prince.[3] Cowper's letter tells of his pleasure in reading accounts of travels like those of Cook, but comments sceptically on their value:

> The principal fruits of these circuits, that have been made around the globe, seem likely to be the amusement of those that staid at home. Discoveries have been made, but such discoveries as will hardly satisfy the expense of such undertakings. We brought away an Indian, and having debauched him, we sent him home again to communicate the infection to his country—fine sport to be sure, but such as will not defray the costs. Nations that live upon bread-fruit, and have no mines to make them worthy of our acquaintance, will be but little visited for the future. So much the better for them; their poverty is indeed their mercy.[4]

These are hardly the sentiments of an enthusiast for either Commerce or Imperialism.

This also applies to Cowper's attitude to India, as expressed in letters in 1784. He explained his view at some length to John Newton in January; he could sympathise with none of the protagonists in the dispute over the East India Company:

> I distrust the Court, I suspect the patriots. I put the Company entirely aside, as having forfeited all claim to competence in such a business, and see no remedy of course, but in the annihilation, if that could be accomplished, of the very existence of our authority in the East Indies.[5]

Cowper returned to the question in April (in a letter in which he nevertheless asserted that "It is hardly possible for a man to interest himself less than I do in what passes in the political world").[6] He argued that the conflict was between the Crown and the Commons, and that the only hope for the country was "that we may one day be disencumber'd of our ruinous possessions in the East".[7]

Not surprisingly, this subject-matter made its way into *The Task,* published with some other poems in 1785. Book I, dedicated to 'The Sofa', takes the reader to the Pacific and to Omai. He is presented as a victim of Western curiosity and the object of the poet's pity:

> But far beyond the rest, and with most cause,
> Thee, gentle savage! whom no love of thee
> Or thine, but curiosity perhaps,
> Or else vain-glory, prompted us to draw
> Forth from thy native bowers, to show thee here
> With what superior skill we can abuse
> The gifts of Providence, and squander life.

Omai has now been returned to his island, but he must be missing "Sweets tasted here, and left as soon as known". Cowper pictures Omai walking along the beach and looking for a sail, aware of his own country's "Forlorn and abject state"—there is no idealization of primitive culture here. But no English ship is to be expected because—and the reason given is a striking recognition of colonialist values—the island is not commercially exploitable:

> We found no bait
> To tempt us in thy country. Doing good,
> Disinterested good, is not our trade.
> We travel far, 'tis true, but not for nought;
> And must be bribed to compass earth again
> By other hopes and richer fruits than yours.

The tone is a great deal more pessimistic than in the earlier account of Captain Cook in **'Charity',** and commercial values are no longer celebrated. The Book goes on to warn, in Evangelical terms, of the danger to England of its current moral laxities, focussed in the inhabitants of the city—"God made the country, and man made the town"—whose 'folly':

> Has made, what enemies could ne'er have done,
> Our arch of empire, steadfast but for you,
> A mutilated structure, soon to fall.

This formulation brings out the contradiction, often felt in *The Task,* between Cowper's patriotism and his religion. The "arch of empire", mutilated by the loss of America, may be about to fall: the implied pathos of this, and the moral critique of those held to be responsible, distracts attention from what at other times are felt to be the questionable attributes of that Empire itself.

These are emphasized immediately at the opening of Book II, **'The Time Piece'**, in another indignant passage about Slavery:

> We have no slaves at home—Why then abroad? . . .
> Slaves cannot breathe in England . . .
> That's noble, and bespeaks a nation proud
> And jealous of the blessing. Spread it then,
> And let it circulate through every vein
> Of all your empire; that where Britain's power
> Is felt, mankind may feel her mercy too.

Here Britain is being challenged to extend its professed commitment to liberty to all those in its colonies. The

Somerset case of 1772 was believed to have asserted that slavery could not exist in Britain; it was logical as well as moral to argue for the extension of the principle beyond this country.

Cowper then moves on, through a series of warnings about the present state of the world, to his most sustained piece of patriotic writing:

> England, with all thy faults, I love thee still,
> My country! and while yet a nook is left
> Where English minds and manners may be found,
> Shall be constrain'd to love thee . . .

Cowper effectively employs one of the central *topoi* of English patriotic discourse, the nostalgic suggestion of a long-established people persisting in conditions of some unexplained challenge ("while yet a nook *is left*"). There is strong suggestion of decline in the passage, with blame for it directed at "effeminates":

> How, in the name of soldiership and sense,
> Should England prosper, when such things, as smooth
> And tender as a girl, all essenced o'er
> With odours, and as profligate as sweet,
> Who sell their laurel for a myrtle wreath,
> And love when they should fight; when such as these
> Presume to lay their hands upon the ark
> Of her magnificent and awful cause?

Here the idea of racial degeneracy conveys a strong sense of distress over contemporary affairs, although the imagery is so generalized that it is difficult to see its exact target. What coherence there is is supplied by Cowper's persistent hostility to the superficial values he attributes to city life, associated with his distaste for French culture. But there is a good deal of irony in finding the peace-loving Cowper employing the joint criteria of "soldiership and sense". He becomes more specific in his references when he contrasts the present with the recent past, when it was:

> praise enough,
> To fill the ambition of a private man,
> That Chatham's language was his mother tongue,
> And Wolfe's great name compatriot with his own.

These two great heroes of empire had recently died:

> Each in his field of glory: one in arms
> And one in council—Wolfe upon the lap
> Of smiling Victory that moment won,
> And Chatham, heart-sick of his country's shame!

These two deaths had already been transformed into Imperialist icons: in Benjamin West's painting 'The Death of Wolfe' (1771), showing the hero dying at the moment of victory, surrounded by, among others, "a philosophical Cherokee",[8] and in John Singleton Copley's 'The Death of Chatham' (1780) in which the man who had led Britain to victory in the Seven Years War collapses denouncing the feebleness of British policy in the American colonies. James Sambrook comments on the great popularity of both these pictures as engravings, and adds:

In both paintings a modern scene is imbued with the heroic grandeur normally reserved for an antique hero or a Christian saint, so that what is created by poses, expression, and lighting is an ideal beyond the mere historical fact.[9]

Cowper is here working in the equivalent literary mode:

> Oh, rise some other such!
> Or all that we have left is empty talk
> Of old achievements, and despair of new.

On the whole, it is that sense of past glory that pervades the rest of *The Task,* especially in Book III, with its attack on the "crowded coop" of London with its "Hordes / Of fluttering, loitering, cringing, begging, loose / And wanton vagrants", and in Book IV, with its denunciation of taverns as places of drunken debauchery (the Evangelical Cowper at his most puritanical), of the unsettling effects on young men of service in the militia, and of all forms of social 'combination':

> Hence merchants, unimpeachable of sin
> Against the charities of domestic life,
> Incorporated, seem at once to lose
> Their nature, and, disclaiming all regard
> For mercy and the common rights of man,
> Build factories with blood, conducting trade
> At the sword's point, and dyeing the white blood
> Of innocent commercial justice red.

Again, the exact target of this criticism is not immediately clear. However, the reference to "trade / At the sword's point" suggests the operations of the East India Company, and the word 'incorporated' points forward to Blake's 'London' with its "chartered streets" and "chartered Thames". Vincent Newey suggests that "mercantile corporations are seen . . . as the source—and emblem—of rampant institutionalized greed; private and domestic virtue . . . ceases to influence men once they are associated . . ."[10] Cowper is becoming presciently aware, we might suggest, of the ethos of the emergent bourgeoisie as a class whose values are distinct from those of the individual tradesmen composing it.

Such political insights persist in the last two Books, though seldom related to Imperialism. Book V denounces absolute monarchy, associated with Russia and France, and praises constitutional monarchy within the rhetoric of British Freedom:

> He [the King] is ours,
> To administer, to guard, to adorn the state
> But not to warp or change it. We are his,
> To serve him nobly in the common cause,
> True to the death, but not to be his slaves.

But the praise of English Freedom is succeeded by pessimistic forebodings: "the age of virtuous politics is past, / And we are deep in that of cold pretence". Even the "loud declaimers on the part / Of liberty [are] themselves the slaves of lust". Newey identifies Fox, "a notable profligate", as the referent here.[11] True Liberty, in fact, is not political at all, but spiritual:

'Tis liberty of heart, derived from Heaven,
Bought with His blood who gave it to mankind,
And sealed with the same token.

This is the direction taken in the last part of the poem, which helps to account for its great popularity in Evangelical circles in the early nineteenth century. Book VI denounces human cruelty to animals, and human self-importance ("Man praises man"), and moves towards its conclusion on two levels, neither of which has any link with Imperialism. Firstly, there is an eloquent prophecy of the Second Coming in which all the nations will be united in praise of God:

> From every clime they come
> To see thy beauty, and to share thy joy,
> O Sion! an assembly such as earth
> Saw never, such as heaven stoops down to see.

Nationality is transcended in this religious vision. The second level of the conclusion focusses on the poet himself in this world:

> He is the happy man whose life even now
> Shews somewhat of that happier life to come . . .

The aspiration is to become this "happy man" whose virtue shows itself in humility and unselfishness and whose "warfare is within". Far from any kind of Imperialist vision, we have an emphasis on small-scale charities; his 'influence' is 'spent'

> In soothing sorrow and in quenching strife,
> In aiding helpless indigence, in works
> From which at least a grateful few derive
> Some taste of comfort in a world of woe.

Cowper's horizons now extend to heaven, but their England is a modest rural sphere; a Little England indeed, at some distance from the earlier nostalgic celebration of Chatham and Wolfe.

The Task is of course Cowper's major poem, but his later writings continue to show differing aspects of his political outlook. The opening of the trial of Warren Hastings (with whom Cowper had been at school at Westminster) in February 1788 brought a strong expression of opinion in a letter to Lady Hesketh:

> I recommend it to you, my Dear, by all means to embrace the fair occasion, and to put yourself in the way of being squeezed and incommoded a few hours, for the sake of hearing and seeing what you will never have opportunity to see and hear hereafter, the trial of a man who has been greater and more feared than the Mogul himself, and of his Myrmidon Sir Elijah [Impey]. Whatever we are at home, we have certainly been Tyrants in the East; and if these men have, as they are charged, rioted in the miseries of the innocent, and dealt death to the guiltless with an unsparing hand, may they receive a retribution that shall make all future Governors and Judges of ours in those distant regions

tremble. While I speak thus, I equally wish them acquitted. They were both my Schoolfellows and for Hastings I had a particular value.[12]

Later in 1788 Cowper received via John Newton a request from "some Gentleman employed about the abolition of the Slave-trade" for "some good Ballads to be sung about the streets on that subject, which they mean to print and distribute, and think they might be of use to the cause".[13] He complied with the request, at first sending two pieces:

> One a serious Ballad to the Tune of Hosier's Ghost, called **'The Negro's Complaint'**—The other in a different strain and entitled—**'Sweet meat has sower Sauce, or the Slave-trader in the dumps.'**[14]

He went on to write **'Pity for Poor Africans'** and **'The Morning Dream'** in the ballad form, and an associated **'Epigram'**. Quinlan notes: "Of the four ballads that Cowper is known to have composed, **'The Negro's Complaint'** enjoyed the greatest popularity. Thousands of copies were printed by the London abolitionists".[15] Today, **'The Negro's Complaint'** is unimpressive. Cowper quite rightly avoided using any form of pidgin English, but the language put into the mouth of the Negro is too formal to be vivid, and his attitude is improbably high-minded. The last stanza runs:

> Deem our nation brutes no longer,
>   Till some reason ye shall find
> Worthier of regard and stronger
>   Than the colour of our kind.
> Slaves of gold, whose sordid dealings
>   Tarnish all your boasted powers,
> Prove that you have human feelings
>   Ere you proudly question ours!

Similarly, **'The Morning Dream'** projects its optimistic vision in all-too-easy terms. The woman in the boat who cries, "I go to make freemen of slaves" no sooner confronts personified Oppression on the "slave-cultured island" than he immediately falls and dies. The poet explains the dream to himself:

> That Britannia, renown'd o'er the waves
>   For the hatred she ever has shown
> To the black-sceptred rulers of slaves,
>   Resolves to have none of her own.

Britannia's rule was far less pure, and the prophecy nearly twenty years too early. The other two poems, though probably less successful at the time, are more interesting now. **'Sweet Meat has Sour Sauce'** is put into the mouth of a British slaver who has heard that the trade is to be abolished and is consequently disposing of the instruments of its practice. The jaunty tone is effectively juxtaposed with the grim subject-matter:

> Here's padlocks and bolts, and screws for the thumbs,
> That squeeze them so lovingly till the blood comes;
> They sweeten the temper like comfits or plums,
>   Which nobody can deny, deny,
>   Which nobody can deny.

When a negro his head from his victuals withdraws,
And clenches his teeth and thrusts out his paws,
Here's a notable engine to open his jaws.
    Which nobody, etc.

Twould do your heart good to see 'em below
Lie flat on their backs all the way as we go,
Like sprats on a gridiron, scores in a row,
    Which nobody, etc.

This is powerful denunciatory writing which makes the white reader distinctly uncomfortable, particularly because "nobody can deny" its factual basis. Equally effective is **'Pity for Poor Africans',** this time put into the mouth of an Englishman:

I own I am shocked at the purchase of slaves,
And fear those who buy them and sell them are
    knaves;
What I hear of their hardships, their tortures, and
    groans,
Is almost enough to draw pity from stones.

At this point the speaker takes an unexpected line—though one all-too-familiar in our more recent experience of boycotts:

I pity them greatly, but I must be mum
For how could we do without sugar and rum?
Especially sugar, so needful we see:
What, give up our desserts, our coffee, and tea!

Besides, if we do, the French, Dutch and Danes
Will heartily thank us, no doubt, for our pains;
If we do not buy the poor creatures, they will;
And tortures and groans will be multiplied still.

Until foreigners give up the trade, why should the English? The speaker clinches his argument by telling a story of a boy whose friends want to rob a poor man's orchard. At first the boy is reluctant, but he is persuaded that the others will go in any case; so he may as well join them. The poem concludes:

His scruples thus silenced, Tom felt more at ease,
And went with his comrades the apples to seize;
He blamed and protested, but join'd in the plan;
He shared in the plunder, but pitied the man.

The final couplet constitutes a succinct and witty critique of the whole ethos of 'liberal' Imperialism in which Cowper was himself to some extent implicated.

This is brought out in some of Cowper's 'occasional' poems for the following year, 1789—written just before the French Revolution: **'Annus Mirabilis', 'On the Queen's Visit to London'** and **'On the Benefit Received by His Majesty from Sea-bathing in the Year 1789'.** In the first of these, the poet celebrates George III's recovery from serious illness in extravagant terms.

And for the richest crown on earth
If valued by its wearer's worth,

The symbol of a righteous reign
Sat fast on George's brows again.

The second poem celebrates the Queen's visit to London on the night of 17th March 1789 to witness the celebrations of her husband's recovery:

Pleased she beheld aloft portray'd
    On many a splendid wall
Emblems of health and heavenly aid,
    And George the theme of all.

In both poems, the form produces a tone which seems too light for the implied emotions, as Newey suggests.[16] He also points out that the poems embody "'bourgeois' assumptions . . . not least in the fact that the king actually figures less as a political force than as a husband". The poems appeared respectively in the *Morning Herald* and *The Times.* The third poem, with its somewhat bathetic lengthy title, was published in both the *Whitehall Evening Post* and the *Public Advertiser*; it consists of two stanzas:

O Sovereign of an isle renown'd
    For undisputed sway,
Wherever o'er yon gulf profound,
    Her navies wing their way.

With juster claims she builds at length
    Her empire on the sea,
And well may boast the waves her strength,
    Which strength restored to Thee.

This is neatly managed, if not without a certain vagueness: there is no explanation of the comparison suggested by 'juster', or of the exact implications of Britannia's empire being built "on the sea". But it is clearly important for Cowper to associate the idea of justice with the kind of monarchical values here praised. Newey comments well on the political attitude informing this group of poems:

. . . although Cowper was so out of sympathy in ***The Task*** with the consumerist and commercial spirit of eighteenth-century England, yet he was altogether in favour of the armed imperialism in which that spirit in fact found its strongest outlet and, through trade, its basic means of practical realization. This expansionist patriotism—which is declaimed with greater zeal in Boadicea's prophecy of how her British progeny 'Arm'd with thunder, clad with wings, / Shall a wider world command'—and the thoroughgoing preoccupation with domestic virtues are the twin emphases of Cowper's representative Whig and bourgeois position . . . the end of a process which had begun exactly a century before in the Act of Settlement, or 'Glorious Revolution', of 1689 . . .[17]

My only reservation about this account is to suggest that "expansionist imperialism" and "the thoroughgoing preoccupation with domestic virtues" are not, and cannot be, brought into ideological harmony, as our whole account of Cowper's writings in this area has suggested. The tensions within Cowper's own attitudes may be seen as symptomatic of problems within British Imperialist ideology itself, with its uneasy combination of moral and economic elements, its love of England and its claims to wider authority. In Cowper's case it is appropriate to record that his praise of the monarchy in 1789 did not imply any moderating of his detestation of the Slave Trade. In 1792 rumours were spread to the effect that he had changed his mind on the issue; he replied with a letter to the local *Northampton Mercury*:

> Sirs,
>
> Having lately learned that it is pretty generally reported both in your county and this, that my present opinion concerning the Slave Trade differs totally from that which I have heretofore given to the public, and that I am no longer an Enemy, but a Friend to that horrid traffic, I entreat you to take an early opportunity to insert in your paper the following lines, written no longer since than this very morning, expressly for the two purposes of doing just honour to the gentleman with whose name they are inscribed, and of vindicating myself from an aspersion so injurious.
>
> I am etc.
> Wm. COWPER
> Weston Underwood, April 16, 1792.

Sonnet

> Addressed to William Wilberforce Esq.
> I praise thee, WILBERFORCE! and with disdain
> Hear thee by cruel men and impious call'd
> Fanatic, for thy zeal to loose th'enthralled
> From exile, public sale, and slav'ry's chain.
> Friend of the poor, the scourg'd, the fetter-gall'd,
> Fear not lest labour such as thine be vain.
>
> Thou hast achiev'd a part, hast won the ear
> Of Britain's Senate to thy glorious cause;
> Hope smiles, joy springs, and though cold caution draws
> Delay between, the better hour is near
> That shall remunerate all thy pains severe
> By peace to Afric, fenced with British laws.
>
> Then let them scoff—two prizes thou has won—
> Freedom for Captives, and thy God's—WELL DONE.[18]

Cowper, for all his genuine patriotism, and his evident belief in an ideal British Empire, could never reconcile himself to the "horrid traffic" which constituted an unignorable part of its reality, like the exploitation of India. For this reason the poetry exhibits an inconsistency of attitude which demands the modern reader's constant alertness, and perhaps also wins his respect.

Notes

1. Maurice J. Quinlan, *William Cowper. A Critical Life.* Greenwood Press, Westport, Connecticut, 1953; p.106.

2. *Cowper's 'Task'. Structure and Influence.* Cambridge University Press, Cambridge, 1983.

3. James Sambrook, *The Eighteenth Century,* Longmans, London, 1986, p. 194.

4. *Letters,* ed. J. King and C. Ryskamp, Clarendon Press, Oxford, (1979)—II, (1981) 168 (6 October 1783).

5. *Letters,* II, (1981), 207 (25 January 1784).

6. *Letters,* II, (1981), 234 (11 April 1784).

7. ibid. 235.

8. Sambrook, op.cit., p. 192.

9. ibid. pp. 153-4.

10. Newey, op.cit. p. 178.

11. Newey, ibid, p. 141.

12. *Letters,* III, (1982), 104 (16 February 1788).

13. *Letters,* III, (1982), 130 (21 March 1788).

14. Ibid. p.131.

15. Op.cit. p.165; for a full discussion, see V. Mtubani, 'Poetry and the Slave Trade', Ph.D. thesis, Exeter University, 1979.

16. Op.cit. p.239.

17. Newey, op.cit., pp.239-40.

18. *The Letters and Prose Writings,* IV, (1984), pp.59-60.

Richard Terry (essay date 1994)

SOURCE: Terry, Richard. "'Meaner Themes': Mock-Heroic and Providentialism in Cowper's Poetry." *Studies in English Literature 1500-1900* 34, no. 3 (summer 1994): 617-34.

[*In the following essay, Terry analyzes the sources, technique, subject matter, and style of Cowper's mock-heroic poetry, linking these with the poet's belief in Evangelical providentialism.*]

I

William Cowper's poetry has traditionally been seen in two opposite ways: either as a late relic of English Augustanism or as a harbinger of a newer romantic aesthetic.[1] This ambivalence is nowhere more evident than in his handling of one particular form: mock-heroic. While Cowper's adoption of the form affiliates him superficially with the earlier poetic era of Dryden and Pope, his use of it generates a range of moral sympathies that are very different from those in Augustan poems of the same kind. Cowper's mock-heroic, unlike that of earlier practitioners, has also tended to be seen as the projection of a troubled personality, and, for a writer so prone to temperamental gloom, it easily invites criticism as a rather strained attempt at cheerfulness and whimsy. This accusation has been cogently made by Claude Rawson, who has also produced the sternest general reading of Cowper's mock-heroic against the tenets of Augustan exponents of the same form. He accuses Cowper's practice of having no "meaningful relation to a primary heroic idiom, none of Pope's assured loyalty to the grandeurs he subverts, and none of Swift's assurance in the debunking of grandeurs."[2] Apparently, Cowper's mock-heroic is seen either as psychologically driven (a thin whistling in the dark) or as a mere exercise in stylization, with all the gestural emptiness of a party-piece. How, then, do we read Cowperian mock-heroic? And must any reading inevitably be curtailed by the twin dilemmas identified by Rawson? This essay aims to place Cowper's mock-heroic in the context of his providentialist faith and, by doing so, to argue for both the magnitude and the *gravitas* of his achievement.

II

It is useful to begin by mapping out the main occasions of Cowper's mock-heroic writing. Cowper's practice essentially falls into two parts, the distinction being whether its formal register is drawn from Homer or Milton, the poets whose work, taken together, was mainly responsible for the repertoire of understood mock-heroic effects. The details of his creative association with Milton are well known, and reflect an attachment on Cowper's part so strong as to be called literary filiation.[3] He steeped himself in Milton's poetry from an early age, the first stirring of his enthusiasm being recorded in *The Task,* 4.709-17.[4] In later life, he defended Milton against Johnson's churlish (as Cowper saw it) "Life" and wrote a poem expressing outrage at the exhumation of Milton's supposed remains on 3 August 1790.[5] In 1793 Milton appeared to him in a dream and expressed a vague approbation for his poetical endeavors (*Letters,* 24 February, 4:297-98). Two years before the dream, he had accepted a commission to undertake a lavish edition of Milton's verse, involving the production of a corrected text as well as a translation of Milton's Latin and Italian poetry. Shortly after receiving the commission he wrote to Clotworthy Rowley, pluming himself on the strength of his credentials: "Few people have studied Milton more, or are more familiar with his poetry than [mys]elf" (*Letters,* 22 October 1791, 3:579). But this early buoyancy was mistaken, for the project came to pall on him and was never completed. Cowper's relationship with Homer, equally, was cemented by the undertaking of a professional labor. Shortly after composing *The Task* (1785), he embarked on a translation of the *Iliad* and *Odyssey,* a project that saw publication in July 1791. Moreover, the translation conflated Cowper's two areas of expertise, for he ill-advisedly cast his translation in Miltonics in the belief, set down in the "Preface," that the two styles had a fundamental affinity: "no person, familiar with both, can read either without being reminded of the other" (*Letters,* 5:65).

Cowper's Homeric translation and the experimental and unfinished poem **"Yardley Oak"** (1791) are the two principal occasions where his application of Miltonics

seems "straight," serving neither an ironic or comic impulse nor demonstrating a stylistic verve purely for its own sake. Elsewhere, Miltonic imitation for the most part entails mock-heroic, and Cowper's poetic career appropriately begins with a Miltonic mock-heroic poem, **"Verses written at Bath on Finding the Heel of a Shoe"** (1748). The poet, stumbling on the discarded heel of a shoe, praises this humble gift granted him by Fortune and speculates on the heel's former owner ("some rude peasant clown"). The incident is then read for "illustrious hints," glimmerings of moral insight contained within it, these being set down at the poem's close:

> Thus fares it oft with other than the feet
> Of humble villager:—the statesman thus,
> Up the steep road, where proud ambition leads,
> Aspiring first uninterrupted winds
> His prosp'rous way; nor fears miscarriage foul,
> While policy prevails, and friends prove true:
> But that support soon failing, by him left
> On whom he most depended, basely left,
> Betray'd, deserted, from his airy height
> Head-long he falls; and thro' the rest of life
> Drags the dull load of disappointment on.

(p. 264)

Already Cowper had developed a gamut of techniques for mimicking the grand style. There is the gradual unraveling of the sense from the folds of a complex syntax; a penchant for verbal mimesis, evident in the use of monosyllables to convey strenuous motion: "Up the steep road . . . Drags the dull load of disappointment on" ; and an assortment of stylistic devices culled from *Paradise Lost,* such as participial listing ("Betray'd deserted") and reversal of word order ("miscarriage foul"). Yet Cowper's adherence to Milton transcends style alone and bears witness to larger mutualities of temperament and religious background. This early Miltonic mock-heroic has a vein of seriousness, for example, in its employment of lexical terms crucial to Milton's vision of human fall and redemption: "proud," "ambition," "foul," "support," "height," and "falls."

For other examples of Miltonic mock-heroic, we have to turn to *The Task,* which contains several Miltonically stylized passages, some with an obvious burlesque intent. The vogue for comic Miltonics seems to have been pioneered by John Philips's parody *The Splendid Shilling* (1701); and Philips's easy migration from parodying Milton's style to imitating it respectfully in poems such as *Cyder* (1708) set a precedent for Cowper's equal flexibility in moving between comic and straight Miltonics. *The Task* reflects a phase in the gradual attenuation and diffusion of mock-heroic as a literary form. The mock-heroic poem was prolific in the early Augustan era, and its finest examples have obviously become canonical within neoclassical verse: Dryden's *MacFlecknoe* (1682), Pope's *The Rape of the Lock* (1712), and *The Dunciad* (1727). Many mock-epics were designated as "heroi-comical" poems, as on the title-page of the *Rape,* and the authors of the major mock-epics often made reference to earlier works in the same form. As the century progressed, however, mock-heroic was sustained less by single poems than by the introjection of mock-heroic sections within longer noncomic poems. This trend is already evident in James Thomson's *The Seasons* (1730), which occasionally lurches into mock-epic set-pieces, and is reflected later by *The Task*.[6] The process is one in which mock-heroic persists, sometimes luckily in the hands of the finest talents, but by which it is eventually enfeebled.

The Task is composed, for the most part, in limpid blank verse, but at several points it veers upwards into Miltonics. It begins with the "Historical deduction of seats" (1.88), charting the genealogy of the modern sofa, where Miltonic style comes together with a conventional georgic interest in the genesis of an invention. Book 2, **"The Time-Piece,"** incorporates a digressive description of an earthquake recorded in Sicily on 18 August 1783, rendered in comically inflated Miltonics: "the fixt and rooted earth, / Tormented into billows . . . with vortiginous and hideous whirl / Sucks down its prey insatiable" (2.100-103). Inverted word order, latinism, and the general clamor of the verse all suggest parody of Milton. Book 3, **"The Garden,"** opens with a Miltonic exordium, taking stock of the poem's progress to date and introducing a more personal voice: "I feel myself at large, / Courageous, and refresh'd for future toil" (3.18-19). The use of a personalized exordium is itself reminiscent of Milton (as in *Paradise Lost* 1, 3, 7, 9), but the first ten lines of Cowper's book are also dense with Miltonic echoes. Finally, there is the well-known and eccentric passage on the cultivation of cucumbers (to which I will return), where comic Miltonics are combined with a set of georgic instructions on a horticultural technique.

These examples detail where Cowper's practice of mock-heroic is affiliated with Milton. Where his mock-heroic instead takes its source from Homer, it often seems more ephemeral and casually manneristic, lacking the larger complexities entailed by stylistic allusion to Milton. During the period when he was translating Homer, Cowper's letters are marked by the regular appearance of Homeric spoofs. A letter written to Samuel Rose in 1789, for example, contains eight lines of mock-Homeric verse describing the unpacking of a hamper, beginning "The straw-stuff'd hamper with his ruthless steel / He open'd, cutting sheer th'inserted cords" (*Letters,* 4 October 1789, 3:313). The element of Homeric style most vigorously exploited in Cowper's parodies is the compound epithet (as "straw-stuff'd"), and this device is also foregrounded in some mock-heroic poems, such as **"On the Death of Mrs. Throckmorton's Bulfinch"**:

> A beast forth-sallied on the scout,
> Long-back'd, long-tail'd, with whisker'd snout,
> And badger-colour'd hide.
>
> (p. 384)

The presence of compound epithets provides a litmus test for where Cowper's mock-heroic mainly derives from Homer as opposed to being mock-Miltonic.[7]

III

Cowper's poetry, like Milton's, grants a special status to "mean themes." Milton's challenge to the ethical system of traditional epic leads to his promotion of countervalues of love, faith, and sacrifice that are seen as being not merely more pious but more unassuming and humble than heroic values. To assert "the better fortitude / Of patience and heroic martyrdom" undercuts the epic morality, subjecting it to a polarizing irony that is incipiently mock-heroic.[8] Similarly, in Book 12, when Adam articulates a regimen for spiritual living in the post-Edenic world, his morality is calculatedly downbeat:

> Henceforth I learn, that to obey is best,
> And love with fear the only God, to walk
> As in his presence, ever to observe
> His providence, and on him sole depend,
> Merciful over all his works, with good
> Still overcoming evil, and by small
> Accomplishing great things, by things deemed weak
> Subverting worldly strong.
>
> (12.561-68)

Adam's paradoxical optimism ("by things deemed weak / Subverting worldly strong") is modeled on the nine beatitudes of the Gospel of Matthew (5:3-11), with their transvaluing promise of an extraworldly reward for the "meek" and "poor in spirit."[9] Milton's own moral rhetoric, like that of the beatitudes, habitually expresses a preference for the small over the great. A related sort of recuperation of the small is evident throughout Cowper's oeuvre. George Eliot remarked, for example, that Cowper "is alive to small objects, not because his mind is narrow, but because his . . . heart is large."[10] *The Task*'s constant edginess about the diminutiveness of its topics also suggests awareness of Miltonic parallels. The poem begins by announcing "The theme though humble, yet august and proud / Th'occasion" (1.6-7); and there are further nervous protestations: "meaner theme," "humbler theme," "humble theme" (5.729; 1.5; 6.719).

I want to suggest that Cowper's mock-heroic poems habitually attempt to rehabilitate and valorize small things, an intention deriving in part from an awareness of how Milton counterpointed great and small in order to urge a Christian morality. Cowper also understood how mock-heroic ironies of disproportion could be tied into a moralizing and religious discourse. Before advancing this argument, though, I should say something about the nature of eighteenth-century mock-heroic itself.[11] Mock-heroic involves bringing together a poetic form and content that are at cross-purposes to each other. The trademark of eighteenth-century mock-heroic, as opposed to the contemporary poetic travesty, was that it intermeshed a high style and low content. Granted that mock-heroic entailed the bringing together of antithetical elements, the principal aesthetic issue concerned the unitary effect wrought by this dialogic technique. Eighteenth-century mock-heroic was not understood to involve mere counterpoint, but was seen more as an aesthetic tug-of-war: the issue being whether style presided over content (and ennobled it) or content presided over style (and demeaned it). Edmund Smith, for example, applauded the mock-heroic over and above the travesty on the grounds that "It is much easier to make a great thing appear little, than a little one great": in other words, the effect of the mock-heroic conflation of high style and low subject-matter was, in his view, that the former acts upon, and elevates, the latter.[12] Although most critics concurred with this view, it was still countered by the gloomier one that the mock-heroic formula could allow content sway over style. This would mean that a poem's formal dignities would be tarnished by its low content, the whole work being subject to an aesthetic downward mobility.

Augustan poetry is distinguished both by being prepared to broach trivial or humble subjects and by stylistic strategies that allow it to retain polish while doing so. Accordingly, those genres that are most conspicuous for entertaining lowly subjects (such as mock-heroic and georgic) are ones where this lowliness is offset by calculated heightening of expression. Mock-heroic, then, had a necessary role within Augustan poetics not just because it allowed the exercising of a singular form of comic irony, but also because it provided a format in which low and mean things could be mentioned while being at the same time subdued within a cordon of refined style. One example of this is provided by Henry Fielding's poem "A Description of U—n G—[Upton Grey]," a comic poem written to a city belle by a frustrated suitor pent up in the country. Much of the poem consists of an exaggerated description of the *longueurs* of the country environment:

> On the House-Side a Garden may be seen,
> Which Docks and Nettles keep for ever green.
> Weeds on the Ground, instead of Flow'rs, we see,
> And Snails alone adorn the barren Tree.
> Happy for us, had *Eve*'s this Garden been;
> She'd found no Fruit, and therefore known no Sin.
> Nor meaner Ornament the Shed-Side decks,
> With Hay-Stacks, Faggot Piles, and Bottle-Ricks;
> The Horses Stalls, the Coach a Barn contains;
> For purling Streams, we've Puddles fill'd with Rains.
> What can our Orchard without Trees surpass?
> What, but our dusty Meadow without Grass?
> I've thought (so strong with me Burlesque prevails,)
> This Place design'd to ridicule *Versailles*;
> Or meant, like that, Art's utmost Pow'r to shew,
> That tells how high it reaches, this how low.[13]

What the beau takes to be the unsalubrious nature of his country dwelling is made evident less by stylistic description than by the counterpointing of its details against images of rustic refinement. The "puddles," for example, jar against "purling streams"—a traditional component of stylized pastoral landscaping; and at the passage's close, the narrator rests his aversion to his "Place" on its being a direct antithesis to the splendor of Versailles: the gardens at Versailles being the finest among imaginable landscapes, Upton Grey the worst. The whole passage is quintessentially Augustan: although its emphasis is on the meanness and parochialism of the rural dwelling, this dwelling is

still mediated to the reader through a series of urbane antitheses: country vs. city, real countryside vs. pastoral ideal, Upton Grey vs. Versailles.[14] These antitheses suggest two intentions: to contain the "humble" within a governing irony that dictates how the reader should respond to it; and to ensure that the intrusion of the humble is offset by simultaneous diversions at the levels of style and allusion. In this use of mock-heroic, the humble is both satirized for being humble while also being made palatable for readerly consumption. Fielding's poem typifies a set of pressures that are active in early-eighteenth-century mock-heroic, and from which Cowper's own practice of mock-heroic represents such a striking departure.

IV

Many of Cowper's poems address mean subjects, a paradigmatic poem in this context being **"On Observing Some Names of Little Note in the Biographia Britannica"** (1782). Cowper sent it to William Unwin in a letter of 1780 and expressed delight at the diversity of the *Biographia*'s entrants, thinking this more desirable than had it "admitted none but those who had in some way or other Entitled themselves to Immortality" (*Letters*, 3 September 1780, 1:386). This respect for lives of unspoken achievement buried in the register of history has some affinity with the rewards promised in the beatitudes for spiritual lives founded on humility and meekness. **"On Observing Some Names,"** though, is not fully representative of Cowper's poems self-consciously addressing humdrum subjects, simply because the vast majority of these are devoted to animals, many of them also being mock-heroic. Cowper's interest in stylized descriptions of animal behavior was expansive, embracing as well as mock-heroics a clutch of conventional fables such as **"A Fable"** (1780), **"The Poet, the Oyster and Sensitive Plant"** (1782), **"The Nightingale and Glow-worm"** (1782), and **"Pairing Time Anticipated"** (1795). Cowper tended to interpret the behavior and misfortunes of animals as indicative of his own spiritual distresses. His spiritual journal *Adelphi*, for example, records several incidents in which encounters with animals act as a cue for self-analysis and new spiritual awareness.[15]

Cowper's mock-heroic cannot be understood in isolation from what he believed about the creational status of animals' lives. Keith Thomas has taken the turn of the eighteenth century as a watershed in attitudes to the keeping of animals, after which the possession of domesticated pets became increasingly fashionable.[16] Cowper himself kept dogs, cats, and domesticated hares, and was prepared to turn his pen to posthumous tributes to animals owned by friends. Elegiac poems written on the deaths of animals were a curious but prodigious side line in the broader sentimental vogue, and the existence of such satiric imitations as Chatterton's mock-elegy on the death of a cat (1769) and Walpole's parodic "Epitaph on Two Piping Bullfinches," suggests the extent of the fashion.[17] Cowper's concern for animals, however, was not shaped by the sentimental cult so much as by traditional providentialist assumptions about man's responsibility towards the natural world. These stressed that man's position regarding his fellow creatures was that of an appointed steward; animals were placed at his disposal, but he had no right to exercise claims on their lives beyond those of necessary subsistence. Cowper elaborates these opinions, especially an opposition to the gratuitous taking of animal lives, in a passage in Book 6 of *The Task,* his beliefs being broadly consistent with those enunciated fifty years previously in James Thomson's *The Seasons* (1730) and Pope's *Essay on Man* (1733-1734).[18] Their foundation is an understanding of creation as a hierarchical order (a "chain of being") in which man's relation to animals (as a higher being to a lower one) was seen as analogous to God's relation to man.

Cowper's sensitivity to the travails of animals, then, was not extraordinary, but distinctive for its strong providentialism and inspired by the belief that animals' lives were consequential and demanded respect from humans, because those lives were ultimately held in fee to God. One mock-heroic poem that embodies these beliefs is the curious **"To the Immortal Memory of the Halibut on which I Dined This Day."** The poem details the spawning, embryonic life and maturation of a halibut. Its habitat is the "unexplor'd abyss" of the world's oceans, where the fish:

> wast a voyager on many coasts,
> Grazing at large in meadows submarine,
> Where flat Batavia just emerging peeps
> Above the brine,—where Caledonia's rocks
> Beat back the surge,—and where Hibernia shoots
> Her wondrous causeway far into the main.
> —Wherever thou hast fed, thou little thought'st,
> And I not more, that I should feed on thee.
> Peace therefore, and good health, and much good fish,
> To him who sent thee! and success as oft
> As it descends into the billowy gulph,
> To the same drag that caught thee!—Fare thee well!
> Thy lot thy brethren of the slimy fin
> Would envy, could they know that thou wast doom'd
> To feed a bard, and to be prais'd in verse.

(p. 360)

Though a piece of flummery, the poem demonstrates how Cowper's trivial delights invariably grade into more serious reflections. What takes the poem into mock-heroic is the prevalence of Miltonic traits of syntax and diction, as well as specific allusions, such as, in line 19, a somber reminiscence of Satan's baleful meditation on spying Adam and Eve: "Ah gentle pair, ye little think how nigh / Your change approaches" (*Paradise Lost* 4.366-67). The precise sensibility towards animals encoded within the poem can easily confound the modern reader: not only does the feat of imaginative empathy seem excessive, but also Cowper's sympathy for the living fish passing so fluidly into a celebration of its harvesting and of its arrival at his own table is bemusing. But Cowper's sympathetic impulses toward animals were predicated on a strict understanding of their creational status and role, and this allowed him to see the halibut's death and consumption as a happy fulfillment of its purpose.

Coming together here are ingredients common to many of Cowper's mock-heroic poems: a humble object (usually an animal), a stylistic gusto taken to the point of burlesque, and a providentialist construction of the thing or incident being described. Several poems detail instances of animal behavior that proved readily susceptible to spiritual extrapolation. One such is the self-consciously mock-heroic poem **"The Colubriad,"** which describes how the poet killed a snake that appeared in one of his outhouses and menaced his pet cats. The word "Colubriad" derives rather archly from the Latin for snake, and the "-iad" suffix had long acted as a titular specification of mock-heroic.[19] The episode is rendered in the style of an epic combat: the poet is "well arm'd" and "Fill'd with heroic ardour," and the decapitation of the snake is likened to the slaying of a mythical beast (p. 341). Cowper had earlier reported the event, in an embryonically mock-heroic manner, in a letter to William Unwin (3 August 1782), and the letter—though not the poem—contains a moral extracted from the incident: "We are never more in danger than when we think ourselves most secure, nor in reality more secure than when we seem perhaps to be most in danger" (*Letters,* 2:68). The existence of twin versions of the incident, epistolary and poetical, suggests that the pretext for mock-heroic was to point the moral, to celebrate the providentialist insight vouchsafed by the event. In the case of **"The Colubriad,"** the moral is eclipsed from the poem, but in other poems, the statement of just such a moral constitutes the climax. For example, in a letter to Lady Hesketh on 27 June 1788, Cowper recounted an incident concerning his dog, Ben. The two had been walking by a riverside, when Cowper tried unsuccessfully to pluck a water lily floating near the bank. Having walked on, he was surprised to see his pet plunge into the stream and retrieve the flower for its master. The episode yielded a poem entitled **"The Dog and the Water-Lily: No Fable."** The stylization is subduedly mock-heroic, the last stanza running as follows:

> But, chief, myself I will enjoin,
>   Awake at duty's call,
> To show a love as prompt as thine
>   To Him who gives me all.

(p. 383)

The dog's ready compliance with the unvoiced desire of its master provided an image of a spiritual biddability that Cowper was keen to emulate himself. Mock-heroic again comes together both with some foibles of animal behavior and with a conviction that God speaks and signals his purposes through animals' actions. A poem that might appear merely an exercise in mawkish sentimentality doubles as a paean of thanksgiving to God.

The plight of animals was nowhere so redolent of Cowper's own spiritual insecurities as when they died. The letters show the deaths of animals as the frequent stimulus for excursions into mock-heroic. A letter, for example, to John Johnson included a comically militarized rendering of the killing of one of Cowper's turkey hens by another:

"we have had a terrible battle in our Orchard" (*Letters,* 17 April 1790, 3:367). Although this is only a stylistic quip, Cowper's single finest mock-heroic poem is one in which an animal's death looms portentously as an allegory of his own spiritual trepidation: **"On the Death of Mrs. Throckmorton's Bulfinch."** The poem begins

> YE nymphs! if e'er your eyes were red
> With tears o'er hapless fav'rites shed,
>   O share Maria's grief!
> Her fav'rite, even in his cage,
> (What will not hunger's cruel rage?)
>   Assassin'd by a thief.
> Where Rhenus strays his vines among,
> The egg was laid from which he sprung,
>   And though by nature mute,
> Or only with a whistle blest,
> Well-taught, he all the sounds express'd
>   Of flagelet or flute.

> (p. 383)

The opening is fervid, with a flurry of punctuation marks. Cowper's poem, similar in subject-matter to Gray's "Ode on the Death of a Favourite Cat," also manifests the trait of Gray's poem that aroused Johnson's dislike: its disconcerting slither between literalism and allegory.[20] So Cowper wants to foster the allegorical image of the bird's being "Assassin'd by a thief" while attributing to the rat the realistic, but unthieflike, motive of hunger. As well as striking a comically doleful note, the opening also establishes the parameters of literary reference and mock-heroic parallel. The songster's tragedy, for example, mimics both that of Orpheus and, perhaps more pertinently, of Lycidas, who also knew "to sing, and build the lofty rhyme," and whose death is equally a loss of song.[21]

The literary and mythical resonances, the inflated emotion and hyperbolical style—all suggest mock-heroic. The event comes to a climax between lines 43 and 54:

> Just then, by adverse fate impress'd,
> A dream disturb'd poor Bully's rest;
>   In sleep he seem'd to view
> A rat, fast-clinging to the cage,
> And, screaming at the sad presage,
>   Awoke and found it true.

> For, aided both by ear and scent,
> Right to his mark the monster went—
>   Ah, Muse! forbear to speak
> Minute the horrors that ensued;
> His teeth were strong, the cage was wood—
>   He left poor Bully's beak.

> (p. 384)

The denouement is presaged by a wittily cruel echo of *Paradise Lost* 8.309-11, where Adam, sent into a stupor, dreams of being conveyed to his new home of Eden, only to find that he

>   waked, and found
> Before mine eyes all real, as the dream
> ad lively shadowed.

The bird's premonition proves sinisterly accurate, yet running counter to the dark irony of the episode is a strong vein of spiritual consolation. Cowper wrote three poems on caged birds (the others being **"On a Goldfinch Starved to Death in His Cage"** [1782] and **"The Faithful Friend"** [1795]), and birds in captive state clearly presented him with an emotive image of the plight and pathos of the human soul immured within its physical body. It is an obvious truism of the Christian contemplation of death that the decease of the body liberates the spirit. In both Cowper's poems that deal with the deaths of caged birds (eaten and starved), the trauma of death undergone in captivity view with the uplifting tidings of a soul's release. **"On a Goldfinch,"** for instance, is spoken (presumably) by the bird's soul, remembering the death of its material body, a death which has restored it to a liberty akin to that which it once enjoyed in the wild. Lines 11-12 report how:

> In dying sighs my little breath
>   Soon pass'd the wiry grate,

where the last falterings of respiration are compounded with a Christian intimation of the exhalation of the soul at the point of death (p. 305). Although this upbeat message of the soul's delivery from the toils of mortal existence is more emphatic in the poem on the goldfinch, the repetition in **"Mrs. Throckmorton's Bulfinch"** of a death that both occurs in imprisonment and cheats imprisonment makes for a definite consolatory logic.

There are other grounds on which to see Cowper's poem as seriously religious. There is, for example, a broad parallel of predicament between the bereft bullfinch and the drowning man in **"The Castaway"** as well as localized consistencies of imagery. A presage of the bird's death is given by the meteorological fact that "Night veil'd the pole" and **"The Castaway"** opens on an equally somber note of spiritual darkness: "OBSCUREST night involv'd the sky" (p. 431). That **"On the Death of Mrs. Throckmorton's Bulfinch"** is a Christian poem is not in spite of, or at variance with, its also being a mock-heroic one. For there is no kind of poem in which Cowper is more likely to be scrutinizing Christian salvation or contemplating the perils of his own soul than in mock-heroic. Just *why* this should be the case, I now want to address.

V

Animals bulk so large in Cowper's writing partly because he regarded their lowliness in the creational order as a metaphor for the spiritual dejection of the unpardonably sinful. The "Spiritual Diary," to which he applied himself during his traumatic summer of 1795, shows him figuring his spiritual anxieties in terms of the poignancy of animals: "It is I who have been the hunted hare. . . . I have been a poor Fly entangled in a thousand webs from the beginning" (*Letters,* 4:468-69). The hunted hare and ensnared fly are minor types of Cowper's doomed bullfinch, and all three images suggest his emphatic sense of personal reprobation. The predicament of animals, though, does not always appear as confirmation of the sealed fate of damnation, for their example sometimes holds out the possibility of a saving admonition. For example, Cowper's belief that animals' lives had only a circumscribed worth, albeit a genuine one, sounded a useful note of caution for human beings. His own view of God was one that conceded the expendability of all human life:

> Stand now and judge thyself.—Hast thou incurr'd
> His anger, who can waste thee with a word,
> Who poises and proportions sea and land,
> Weighing them in the hollow of his hand,
> And in whose awful sight all nations seem
> As grasshoppers, as dust, a drop, a dream?

> (**"Expostulation,"** p. 51)

The gradual obliteration of humanity in the last line accorded with a pronounced aspect of Cowper's religious temperament. He believed that true Christian belief should assimilate a strong sense of creational disproportions, especially the crushing disproportion of God to man. Indeed, Cowper's sensitivity to the ironically imbalanced relation of God to all created life dictates that mock-heroic should be the poetic form in which he so often chooses to convey his religious experience.

Cowper, himself, had an accentuated sense of what it was to suffer slight or oversight, and many of his poems champion the merit of entities that might seem prone to being disregarded—especially animals. His interest in humble things is also reflected in the much-used word "worth," which occurs with cognates nearly fifteen times in *The Task* alone. One common collocation is "true worth," a phrase that carries the force of paradox: intimating that worthiness often reveals itself in places where it might least be suspected. Cowper conceived *The Task* as being, in some part, an encomium on "If not the virtues, yet the worth, of brutes" (6.724); having elected to entitle the first book **"The Sofa,"** he professed hope that the artifact should be "very worthily advanced to the titular honor it enjoys" (*Letters,* 11 December 1784, 2:309); and Book 6 also contains a passage outlining the poet's sense of responsibility toward worthy things:

> when a poet, or when one like me,
> Happy to rove among poetic flow'rs,
> Though poor in skill to rear them, lights at last
> On some fair theme, some theme divinely fair,
> Such is the impulse and the spur he feels
> To give it praise proportion'd to its worth,
> That not t'attempt it, arduous as he deems
> The labour, were a task more arduous still.

> (4.751-58)

"Praise proportion'd to its worth": this formulation could stand as the keynote of Cowper's mock-heroic. For the rationale of such poems is to postulate "worth," especially in connection with entities that might seem worthless. The trajectory of his mock-heroic is invariably upwards: the aggrandizements of style lend dignity to the subject, rather than being incriminated downwards by association with content that is trivial and banal. The implication of what I am saying is that Cowper's mock-epics are "self-consuming artifacts." To read, say, **"On the Death of Mrs. Throckmorton's Bulfinch"** is to suppose initially that the poem's style is out of kilter with its subject, that the exaggerations of treatment only serve to highlight the triviality of the event being described. Yet the poem is committed to confounding just such a supposition, and replacing it with a recognition of the true creational status of the bullfinch and of the true solemnity of its death. Once this has been grasped, the poem's ostensible "irony" simply disappears. This, then, seems to be the heuristic function of Cowper's mock-heroic poems and set-pieces, to intimate an irony and then to disabuse us of it.

Cowper's mock-heroic runs so much counter to the Augustans' association of mock-epic with satire that he frequently glosses his practice as a form of panegyric. For example, in a letter to Samuel Rose, he referred to the recently composed mock-heroic **"The Dog and the Water-Lily"** as "my little dog's eulogium" (*Letters,* 11 September 1788, 3:211). Similarly, in Book 3 of *The Task,* Cowper reformulates the poem's original artistic brief as being "T'adorn the Sofa with eulogium due" (line 12), yet the object's actual "adornment" at the start of the poem is heavy with mock-heroic overtones. The suspicion that the word "eulogium" provides an "official" label for tendencies that are, in reality, more ambiguously mock-heroic also arises from the cucumber episode in the same book. The cucumber is situated within a literary genealogy by the assurance that "gnats have had, and frogs and mice, long since / Their eulogy" (3.452-53), referring to the Homeric *Batrachomyomachia* and the Virgilian *Culex*. Yet both these works were treasured in the eighteenth century as instances of classical burlesque. That Cowper refers both to them and to his own cucumber set-piece as "eulogies" suggests the curiously magnanimous tone of his mock-heroic.

The challenge that Cowper's mock-heroic poems make to the world's adverse estimations is sometimes far-reaching. The oddest comes with the homily to the cucumber in Book 3 of *The Task,* a homily founded on a cruel pathos intrinsic to the cucumber's experience: "when rare / So coveted, else base and disesteem'd" (3.447-48). The cucumber's ignominy and its quirky commemoration in Cowper's poem have a precise antecedent in an earlier poem, **"Charity"** (1782). A paean on Christ's glorification is ushered in with the following couplet:

> look at him, who form'd us and redeem'd;
> So glorious now, though once so disesteem'd.

> (p. 88)

The triumph over disesteem of both Christ and the humble cucumber, triumphs that Cowper's poems both reflect and enact, intimates how intently he hoped for recovery from the dead weight of his own spiritual pessimism. When he did imagine Christian redemption, he imagined it as founded on the fact

That, thron'd above all height, [Christ] condescends
To call the few that trust in him his friends.

(p. 88)

The miracle of redemption consists of a divine condescension that refuses to accept disproportion, enacting instead a gravitation of high to low that is strictly unmerited. This miraculous disdain of "merit" is precisely how Cowper explains the nature of divine grace in his *Adelphi*: "The grace and mercy of God are His own, and He dispenses them in what measure and manner He pleases, not regarding the merit of the object (which is infinitely less than nothing in the best of us) but His own glory" (*Letters* 1:12). God's charitable dipensation, "not regarding the merit of the object," dovetails at a literary level with impulses that are most naturally embodied in mock-heroic. Those facets of Cowper's mock-epic poetry that have sometimes been found consistent only with a failure of purpose and execution are the very same that make them feats of human condescension and "grace." As such, they show him visiting on others in art what he hoped to have visited on himself in the travails of his soul.

Notes

1. See Donald Davie, "The Critical Principles of William Cowper," *The Cambridge Journal* 7 (December 1953): 182-88: "Such criticism as there is has labeled Cowper 'Romantic precursor'; and it seems that we read his poems only to discover in them things that have been better done since. . . . No one will deny that the Wordsworthian and other potentialities are there but . . . [his] work is far more the consummation of one tradition than the prelude to another" (p. 182).

2. Claude Rawson, *Order from Confusion Sprung: Studies in Eighteenth-Century Literature from Swift to Cowper* (London: Allen and Unwin, 1985), p. 370.

3. See Dustin Griffin, "Cowper, Milton and the Recovery of Paradise," *EIC* 31, 1 (January 1981): 15-26, esp. 15-17.

4. Cowper's poetry is cited everywhere from *Poetical Works,* ed. H. Milford, 4th edn. (rprt.), corrected by N. Russell (London: Oxford Univ. Press, 1967). References to *The Task* are by book and line number; for all other poems, references are by page number.

5. Letter of 31 October 1779, in *The Letters and Prose Writings of William Cowper,* ed. James King and Charles Ryskamp, 5 vols. (Oxford: Clarendon Press, 1979-86), 1:306-308. References to the *Letters* are henceforth given in text.

6. This phenomenon owes much to principles of construction operative in long eighteenth-century poems. See my article "Transitions and Digressions in the Eighteenth-Century Long Poem," *SEL* 32, 3 (Summer 1992): 495-510.

7. Cowper's Homeric mockery owes much to his involvement in the "Nonsense Club," formed with colleagues from Westminster. See Lance Bertelsen, *The Nonsense Club: Literature and Popular Culture, 1749-1764* (Oxford: Clarendon Press, 1986).

8. Cited from Milton, *Paradise Lost,* ed. Alastair Fowler (London: Longman, 1971), 9.31-32. Subsequent references to *Paradise Lost* are from this edition.

9. Cited from the *Revised Standard Version.*

10. George Eliot, "Worldliness and Other-Worldliness: The Poet Young," *Westminster Review* 67 (January 1857), rprt. in *Essays of George Eliot,* ed. Thomas Pinney (New York: Columbia Univ. Press, 1963), pp. 335-85, 382.

11. Still the most generally useful study of mock-heroic is R. P. Bond, *English Burlesque Poetry, 1700-1750* (Cambridge, MA: Harvard Univ. Press, 1932). See also Ulrich Broich, *The Eighteenth-Century Mock-Heroic Poem* (Cambridge: Cambridge Univ. Press, 1990).

12. Quoted in Samuel Johnson, "Life of Philips," in *Lives of the English Poets,* ed. G. B. Hill, 3 vols. (Oxford: Clarendon Press, 1905), 1:323.

13. *Miscellanies of Henry Fielding, Esq; Volume One,* ed. Henry Knight Miller (Oxford: Clarendon Press, 1972), pp. 54-55.

14. Some useful remarks on the tendency of Augustan poems to incorporate lowly material only in the vicinity of controlled ironic antitheses are provided in D. H. Burden, "Crabbe and the Augustan Tradition," in *Essays and Poems Presented to Lord David Cecil,* ed. W. W. Robson (London: Constable, 1970), pp. 77-92.

15. See *Letters,* 1:12-13, for an incident involving a dog and a flock of sheep, the occurrence of which Cowper ascribes to "supernatural agency."

16. Keith Thomas, *Man and the Natural World: Changing Attitudes in England 1500-1800* (London: Allen Lane, 1983), pp. 92-191.

17. See "Elegy [I]," in *The Complete Works of Thomas Chatterton,* ed. Donald S. Taylor and Benjamin B. Hoover, 2 vols. (Oxford: Clarendon Press, 1971), 1:270-71; Horace Walpole, "Epitaph on Two Piping-Bullfinches of Lady Ossory's, Buried under a Rose-Bush in her Garden," in *The New Oxford Book of Eighteenth Century Verse,* ed. Roger Lonsdale (Oxford: Oxford Univ. Press, 1984), p. 588.

18. See *An Essay on Man,* 3.43-70, in *The Poems of Alexander Pope,* ed. J. Butt et al., 11 vols. (London: Methuen, 1939-69), 3,1; and *The Seasons* (1746 edn.), ed. James Sambrook (Oxford: Clarendon Press, 1981), "Spring," 336-78. Cowper discusses the behavioral habits of his three hares in the *Gentleman's Magazine* (June 1784), rprt. in *Letters* 5:40-

44. His attitudes towards animals are considered in Lodwick Hartley, *William Cowper: Humanitarian* (Chapel Hill: Univ. of North Carolina Press, 1938).

19. See R. P. Bond, "-IAD: a Progeny of the *Dunciad*," *PMLA* 44 (December 1929): 1099-1105.

20. See Johnson, "Life of Gray," in *Lives*, 3:434.

21. Milton, *The Complete Shorter Poems*, ed. John Carey (London: Longman, 1971), p. 240.

Deborah Heller (essay date 1995)

SOURCE: Heller, Deborah. "Cowper's *Task* and the Writing of a Poet's Salvation." *Studies in English Literature 1500-1900* 35, no. 3 (summer 1995): 575-98.

[*In the following essay, Heller interprets* The Task *as Cowper's effort to sublimate his personal belief that he was spiritually condemned into a poetic manifestation of God's approval.*]

I

In the summer of 1764, while a patient at St. Albans Asylum for the Insane, William Cowper underwent a conversion to Calvinist Evangelicalism. During an intense bout of paranoia and self-contempt, he found a faith to save him from despair, a revivalist brand of Calvinism which stressed the absolute efficacy of faith and the uselessness or "filthy rags" of human effort. The keynotes of this theology are sounded in the *Memoir* Cowper wrote several years later, in which he describes the precise moment of his conversion. He recalls searching the scriptures for "comfort and instruction" and discovering some apt verses in Romans: "Immediately I received strength to believe it. Immediately the full beams of the sun of righteousness shone upon me. I saw the sufficiency of the atonement He had made, my pardon sealed in His blood, and all the fullness and completeness of my justification. In a moment I believed and received the Gospel."[1] In this episode Cowper emphasizes the miraculous and instantaneous nature of salvation by conversion—the only mode of salvation the Calvinists recognized and an event upon which they placed great importance because a sinner received his full pardon through Christ's blood at this moment. The faith that the sinner receives comes not from his own will or desire, but from outside agency. This faith ("strength to believe") brings the inner conviction of acceptance by God, which for Calvinists means conviction of election. As long as one maintains this felt conviction, election remains sure; but if the feeling of faith ever falters, the entire edifice of Calvinist salvation may come tumbling down.

In the case of William Cowper, it did indeed come tumbling down. We know from any number of good biographies—and from his letters themselves—that Cowper never renounced belief in the truth of Calvinism, but

that he did lose faith in his own election. He had a "fateful dream" in 1773 during a second bout of madness, in which he heard God pronouncing his reprobation (*actum est de te, periisti*: "It is all over with thee, thou hast perished"). These Latin words may have been nothing more than an unconscious recollection of some Roman comedy Cowper had been reading or knew by heart.[2] Yet they were not at all amusing to him when he awoke into consciousness and pondered their meaning; indeed, he took them as his spiritual death sentence.[3]

Thus in 1773 Cowper had stripped from him the spiritual identity he had been given through his conversion some years earlier. Though once he had been saved by amazing grace, his salvation had been somehow revoked. And given the absolute dualism of the Calvinist system, which claims that one is *either* elected or reprobated, this loss of election amounted necessarily to proof of his reprobation—a state of permanent rejection by God that the tormented self can do nothing to redress. In letters written throughout his life, Cowper will persist in declaring himself a reprobate and in feebly lamenting the powerlessness and pathos of his fallen state. Cowper's Calvinist advisor, John Newton, could not help to free Cowper from the bondage in which Calvinism had tied him, for that would require rejecting Calvinism itself. As long as Cowper subscribed to Calvinism, he was bound inextricably in a psychic knot. He had been denied his Christian salvation, and he was powerless to bend the will of the Father who had withdrawn his blessing.

Yet the salvation that Cowper was not granted in life he seized for himself in his art. It is the thesis of this essay that *The Task* was Cowper's means to a *poetic* salvation, poetic in the sense that Cowper *made* or *effected* by artistic efforts at least an imaginary bestowal of God's gift of approval. Theologically it was impossible to force God's hand, but poetically Cowper was able to rewrite his life as a chosen "Servant of God," an Old Testament type which forms and transforms the poetic persona of *The Task. The Task* tells the story of Cowper's own experience of retirement at Olney, focusing on the development of the poet's employments during his rural seclusion. But Cowper's own life experiences merely supply the materials for writing the persona of *The Task.* Through the use of typological allusions to the Old Testament and other devices, Cowper constitutes his persona as a man whose works follow a salvific path, leading ultimately to a blessed state, a state prospered by God. The close parallel between Cowper's own life and that of the persona in *The Task* allows a transference of the persona's success onto Cowper: salvation is bestowed upon the poet at last, if only through poetic wish fulfillment.

James King and others speak of *The Task* as "spiritual autobiography,"[4] and I myself used similar language when I stated that *The Task* "tells the story" of Cowper's life. I have, however, also stated that Cowper fashions spiritual achievements for his persona in *The Task* that go infinitely beyond the somber facts of Cowper's own spiritual life. In order to maintain simultaneously these two seemingly contradictory ways of speaking, we must precisely define the sense in which *The Task* is spiritual autobiography. If autobiography means the "writing of one's own life," where ought we to let the emphasis fall? Is autobiography the writing of one's own *life*? or is it the *writing* of one's own life? In *The Task* the emphasis indeed falls on the writing or poetic shaping of the persona's life out of the raw materials of Cowper's life.

The scriptive or poetic achievement of *The Task* is best perceived against the backdrop of Cowper's biography, specifically his search for work after his spiritual crisis. As Cowper writes in a letter of winter 1784, he feels that his usefulness, in the church at least, has been rendered null by his reprobation: "Why am I thus? Why crippled and made useless in the church just at that time of life when my judgement and experience being matured, I might be most usefull. Why cashiered and turn'd out of service, 'till . . . there is no reasonable hope left that the fruit can ever pay the expence of the fallow?" (2:200). In another letter, written about a year after finishing *The Task,* Cowper catalogues the occupations that he had used to assuage his feelings of uselessness: "I have been emerging gradually from this pit [of despair]. As soon as I became capable of action, I commenced carpenter, made cupboards, boxes, stools. I grew weary of this in about a twelvemonth, and addressed myself to the making of bird-cages. To this employment succeeded that of gardening, which I inter-mingled with that of drawing . . . I renounced it, and commenced poet" (2:455). In the poem **"Retirement"**, written several years before *The Task,* Cowper again enumerates some of the occupations that exercised him during his rural seclusion. These "pleasures harmlessly pursued" (line 784) are mentioned in a sequence including gardening, landscape painting, and poetry—occupations which, as John Baird has noted, "were all, at one time or another, Cowper's."[5] *The Task* shows Cowper's persona engaged in many of the same occupations as those named in **"Retirement"** and the letters. The difference, however, is that *The Task* weaves these activities into a shaping narrative that culminates in the persona's salvational triumph. In order to appreciate how the poem achieves this triumph, it is helpful to imagine two axes running through it, one horizontally, and one vertically. Along the horizontal axis Cowper charts his persona's search for useful work: the speaker's employments begin, as we shall see, in relative purposelessness, bog down in failure and frustration midway, and reach assurance and, indeed, exalted status at the end. As the speaker's labors evolve from aimlessness to exalted service, the poem itself develops from the frivolous to the sublime, from mock-heroic to millennial prophecy. Thus what I call the horizontal axis is really a narrating of two histories: that of the poet in retirement and that of the poem he writes. But the ultimate achieve-ment of the poem is due not to these dual narrative lines alone so much as to the vertical line of typological allu-sion that Cowper cuts through them; for these allusions

transfigure the persona into a Servant of God, whose pursuit of tasks becomes his progress through the stages of a life of blessedness.

II

THE TASK: a sign on the title page pointing to what? pointing in what direction? First of all a name, *THE TASK* is juxtaposed on the title page with *A POEM, IN SIX BOOKS. BY WILLIAM COWPER, OF THE INNER TEMPLE, ESQ.*[6] A name, then, without semantic depth, referring to the poem before us, a useful label for the volume in our hands. Yet *THE TASK* is more than a detachable label like the *titulus* or tag hanging from a papyrus roll. It is also a signifier with its place at the head of, and forming a part of, the chain of signifiers. Delimited by the definite article, it is at first, perhaps, the specific task imposed upon the poet by Lady Austen: to "sing the sofa." But the meaning of the signifier slides as the poem unrolls. As the motto on the title page tells us, the task will evolve; it will develop through time: *Fit surculus arbor* ("the shoot becomes a tree"). Cowper's "Advertise-ment" further explains how the task of singing the sofa becomes, eventually, the whole poem, the "Volume" bear-ing Cowper's name on the title page:

ADVERTISEMENT

The history of the following production is briefly this:—A lady, fond of blank verse, demanded a poem of that kind from the author, and gave him the SOFA for a subject. He obeyed; and, having much leisure, connected another subject with it; and, pursuing the train of thought to which his situation and turn of mind led him, brought forth at length, instead of the trifle which he at first intended, a serious affair—a Volume!

The vector drawn from the "trifle" to the "serious affair" is but little weakened by Cowper's self-deprecating gloss on "serious affair"—"a Volume!" nuanced by the exclamation point. The poem enacts this transformation from trifle to serious affair along what I have called its "horizontal axis." Though the "Advertisement" claims that only the loosest of methods governs the composition of *The Task,* merely a fortuitously connected "train of thought," the poem is in fact a carefully contrived *apologia* for Cowper's life. As the reader pursues the linear chain of the poem's move-ment—its syntax, as it were, or perhaps "syn-Task"—he may watch, if he looks closely, the subtle shifting of the signifier "task" in its reference to poetic work: from the task of **"The Sofa,"** through some intermediate tasks, to the high task of Miltonic religious verse, to the culmina-tion of Cowper's lifework—*The Task* itself. Meanwhile, however, the reader is aware of the progressive develop-ment of the persona's depicted life tasks, tasks drawn from and particularized by Cowper's own occupations in retire-ment. At the poem's conclusion, poetic task and life task converge, as Cowper deftly reasserts his authorial pres-ence, reidentifying his life with the depicted life of his persona:

It shall not grieve me, then, that once, when call'd
To dress a Sofa with the flow'rs of verse,

> I play'd awhile, obedient to the fair,
> With that light task; but soon, to please her more,
> Whom flow'rs alone I knew would little please,
> Let fall th' unfinish'd wreath, and rov'd for fruit.
>
> (6.1006-11)

The task of the poem is here represented simply—too simply—as poetic performance, as a roving from "flow'rs" to "fruit." In truth, the narrative of the task is paralleled by a narrative of tasks, which I have called "life tasks," and which are represented in addition to the task of writing the poem itself. Thus as we proceed through the poem we have the parallel of a developing life with a developing poem.

To speak, as I have done, of two parallel lines of tasks, is perhaps somewhat misleading, since there is often a mixing of the two species of tasks. The semantic fields of poetic process (the poem's unfolding) and that of life labor (the persona's life evolving) interpenetrate each other promiscuously throughout the poem, and metaphor is usually the tool that permits the shift of registers from poem to life and vice versa. We see such a shift at the beginning of book 3, where Cowper uses an extended simile of traveling not only to describe the progress of the poem but to suggest generally the progress of a life with its vagaries and assumed goals ("His devious course uncertain, seeking home"):

> As one who, long in thickets and in brakes
> Entangled, winds now this way and now that
> His devious course uncertain, seeking home;
> Or, having long in miry ways been foil'd
> And sore discomfited, from slough to slough
> Plunging, and half despairing of escape;
> If chance at length he find a greensward smooth
> And faithful to the foot, his spirits rise,
> He chirrups brisk his ear-erecting steed,
> And winds his way with pleasure and with ease;
> So I, designing other themes, and call'd
> T' adorn the Sofa with eulogium due,
> To tell its slumbers, and to paint its dreams,
> Have rambled wide. In country, city, seat
> Of academic fame (howe'er deserv'd),
> Long held, and scarcely disengag'd at last.
> But now, with pleasant pace, a cleanlier road
> I mean to tread. I feel myself at large,
> Courageous, and refresh'd for future toil,
> If toil await me, or if dangers new.
>
> (3.1-20)

The simile of wandering is here more than a mere vehicle for describing the progress of poetic style. It exists in excess of its metaphoric function and produces the supplementary notion of a wayfarer "seeking home," suggesting, in addition to poetic progress, the career of a life, even a life-as-pilgrimage. At the same time, the notion of "task" has been shifted, via the travail of the road, from a single task—to sing the Sofa—to a more generalized notion of work ("future toil, / If toil await me") or search for work. Work and wandering have been conjoined, appearing both as a metaphor for the poem's progress and,

subsisting as metaphorical supplement, inscribing the narrative of the persona's life development.

The themes of work and wandering, shuttling back and forth between the register of poetry and the register of life, provide a kind of motive force in the poem—a mimesis of temporal structure simulating not only one-thing-after-another but also "project" or expectation of the future. As the persona strides across the poem, pausing occasionally to assess his position (e.g., "But truce with censure. Roving as I rove, / Where shall I find an end, or how proceed?" [4.232-4]), or as he takes up task after task, discarding one activity and beginning another, we get the impression of time passing and a life unfolding. The reader has the illusion of witnessing the persona's life unfold, so to speak, from the inside, viewing the process from within the lived flow of time. He does not view that developing life from the great height of omniscience, nor look back on it from the privilege of retrospect; instead, he has the illusion of watching the persona proceed through the minutiae of everyday life, working and wandering and resting—and constantly commenting on and appraising his activities.

Allowing, then, for the interpenetration and mixing of registers, the reader may follow the speaker traveling through the diachronic movement of the poem—its horizontal axis, as I have called it. After the speaker concludes in book 1 that the Sofa best suits "the gouty limb" (line 107) and the "relaxation of the languid frame" (line 81), he begins walking and does not cease his constant motion until the end of *The Task.* In book 1 he strides randomly across landscapes, taking the reader with him as companion: "Descending now (but cautious, lest too fast)" (line 266); "We mount again, and feel at ev'ry step / Our foot half sunk in hillocks green and soft" (lines 271-2); "The summit gain'd, behold the proud alcove / That crowns it!" (lines 278-9); "And now, with nerves new-brac'd and spirits cheer'd, / We tread the wilderness" (lines 350-1). A great walker—as was Cowper himself—the speaker enjoys the sheer freedom of muscular movement, that most primitive exertion of the will. Philosophizing, he rationalizes his practice:

> By ceaseless action all that is subsists.
> Constant rotation of th' unwearied wheel
> That nature rides upon maintains her health,
> Her beauty, her fertility.
>
> (lines 367-70)

But here begins a critical meditation linking motion, activity, and work that will accompany us throughout the horizontal movement of the poem. In the lines just preceding, the speaker has been describing "the thresher at his task" and concludes:

> see him sweating o'er his bread
> Before he eats it.—'Tis the primal curse,
> But soften'd into mercy; made the pledge
> Of cheerful days, and nights without a groan.
>
> (lines 363-6)

Work, the merciful "primal curse," is thus conjoined with the concept travel/activity (both are examples of the "ceaseless action" that provides the health of the universe), and so begins the persona's discursive discussion of work and the consequent hierarchization of tasks culminating in the writing of religious poetry in book 6.

The persona's "discursive" meditation on work helps produce the poem's reality effect of a life-being-lived: we seem to witness the speaker reasoning about the relative value of different tasks. Just as importantly, the meditation contributes to one of the major themes of the whole poem—the persona's concern to vindicate the usefulness of his life and tasks. Thus, as the discursive meditation on work proceeds, "ceaseless action" alone appears not good enough: an activity must be weighed for its usefulness. Even the poet's favorite activity—walking—must be scrutinized. As the discussion of work develops, so the description of the poet's walking takes on additional nuances. In book 1 he walked for sheer pleasure, without goal or purpose. He is indeed still walking in books 5 and 6 (entitled, respectively, **"The Winter Morning Walk"** and **"The Winter Walk at Noon"**), but the physical activity is no longer its own sufficient justification. Walking for health might now be described by the persona's exclamation as he watches the lengthened shadows of his legs move along a wall in the early morning of book 5: "Prepost'rous sight! the legs without the man" (line 20). A pair of legs moving unattached through space are indeed as preposterous as the proverbial decapitated chicken. It is the man who should be the object of our judgment, and the use he makes of his walking the basis of our evaluation. By book 6 the concept "walking" has been transformed into one of meditative, "sheltered walk" (6.Argument):

> I again perceive
> The soothing influence of the wafted strains,
> And settle in soft musings as I tread
> The walk . . .
>   . . . . .
> No noise is here, or none that hinders thought.
>
>   (lines 67-76)

At the close of book 6, the walking poet will have been assimilated to the "solitary saint," who "Isaac like" "Walks forth to meditate at even tide" (lines 948-9). Thus the favored activity of the persona, walking, will be welded to his special task—meditation and its product, meditative poetry.

Cowper's primary challenge was to "vindicate" "the retired man . . . from the charge of uselessness," as he puts it in the Argument of book 6. Between books 1 and 6, he presents all the activities of the retired man—even the most trivial ones—as steps on his persona's life journey, stages in the realization of his hero's destiny. At first the persona is wandering aimlessly, not in pursuit of any obvious goals. Eventually, in book 2, he settles on the work of writing satire. But while he finds delight in the process of

writing satiric verse ("There is a pleasure in poetic pains / Which only poets know" [2.285-6]), he realizes also that poetry, unless useful, is vanity ("But is amusement all? Studious of song, / And yet ambitious not to sing in vain, / I would not trifle merely" [2.311-3]). The problem with satire is that it can subdue no vices (2.320); it can only treat superficial foibles. Therefore, although it has been a stage in the persona's journey, it is not an adequate activity in itself and so is rejected. At the beginning of book 3, Cowper's persona represents himself as one about to make a new beginning, free and striding on the open road, ready to introduce a new and more congenial poetic theme. He portrays himself as energetic, refreshed, ready for labor:

> I feel myself at large,
> Courageous, and refresh'd for future toil,
> If toil awaits me, or if dangers new.
>
>   (3.18-20)

Since book 3 illustrates so well the persona's discursive argumentation about work and displays in such detail the issues involved in his self-vindication, it will be worthwhile to examine the argument of that book more closely.

The poet's personal bliss in rural retreat, the personal paradise to be found in the Garden, is the ostensible subject of book 3. But there is more. The burden of the book's argument is to prove that God ordained rural retirement to be the setting most conducive to "the cause of piety, and sacred truth, / And virtue" (lines 707-8). Thus, expatiating on the charms of "domestic happiness," the speaker declares, "Thou art the nurse of virtue" (line 48). The troubling question, however, will be, in what does virtue consist? Is it simply Candidean cultivation of one's own garden, or does it require a turning outward toward the uses of mankind? He enumerates the advantages of retirement repeatedly, almost compulsively—

> O, friendly to the best pursuits of man,
> Friendly to thought, to virtue, and to peace,
> Domestic life in rural leisure pass'd!
>
>   (3.290-2)

But after a defensive description of such advantages (3.352-60), he is reminded of a question he had asked himself in book 2: "But is amusement all?" (line 311). The enjoyments he enumerates—friends, books, gardening, writing, work around the home, excursions in nature—may indeed invite the accusation of idleness, if idleness can mean "lack of meaningful activity."

The requirement of meaningful work must therefore be answered when the poet turns to his own case. Lines 361-78 of book 3 reveal the twists and turns of the persona's rationalizations. He is anxious to prove, first, that country retirement does not mean idleness or sloth: "Me, therefore, studious of laborious ease . . . bus'ness finds / Ev'n here" (lines 361-7). He further knows that God has entrusted each of his servants with talents from which he expects rich returns (lines 363-6). The poet's peculiar talents lie in the use of his mind ("sedulous I seek t'improve . . . The mind he gave me" [3.367-9]). He must drive it "To its just point—the service of mankind" (3.372). Here, then, is the crux: he must reconcile his turn inward to the inner garden with the impetus outward to the service of mankind. He appears to accomplish this in lines 373-8, but his success is only a rhetorical victory. The poet has sensibility ("interior self" and "heart"); he has "mind" and uses it; and he seeks "a social, not a dissipated life": therefore, he concludes, he has "business" ; he "feels himself engag'd t'achieve . . . a silent task." But what is this "silent" task? It cannot be the sounds of his poetry. It turns out instead to be the search for pearls of wisdom, "sought in still water, and beneath clear skies" (3.382). The poet, in his turnings, has not really progressed beyond the self-centered enclosure of his garden. Nor do the following lines (386-675), describing the activities of "the self-sequester'd man," bring him beyond his trivial gardening pursuits. He prunes trees, sows flowers, and—in a mock-heroic account—grows laborious cucumbers. Defending his literary effort against unfriendly critics, he mocks those who would call his song, like the cucumbers, "the fruit / Of too much labour, worthless when produc'd" (3.564-5). Defensive, indeed, is the best description of the poet at this stage in the poem. He has not succeeded in proving the usefulness of his retirement; instead, it is a mere retreat from the world, a silent reveling in the joys of peace and quiet.

Nowhere in book 3 does Cowper's poet name a positive usefulness which the retired man extends to mankind. His only contribution is to "draw a picture of that bliss" (3.694) for mankind, even though he knows they will not take advantage of the blessings of the countryside. He furthermore asserts that God himself ordained the country as the scene of virtue, truth, and piety:

> I therefore recommend, though at the risk
> Of popular disgust, yet boldly still,
> The cause of piety, and sacred truth,
> And virtue, and those scenes which God ordain'd
> Should best secure them and promote them most.
>
> (3.705-9)

This is to win his point by fiat. He has brought in *deus ex machina* to justify his rural retreat. Still, we remember his earlier motions toward claiming the ultimate social usefulness of his life in the country. The proof of such usefulness will have to await the developments of book 6, where meditative walking forth in solitude will coincide with the supremely praiseworthy work of writing prophetic verse. But the ultimate resolution of the tension between social usefulness and rural retirement will not be the result of a dialectical argument. It will not be the syllogistic conclusion of discursive reasoning. Instead, it will be *imposed* on the horizontal argument of the poem by the crossfiber of the vertical dimension. (Let us use the metaphor of the warp and woof of a text.) As the poetic shuttle shoots the filling yarn through the growing web, and as the fabric of the poem grows line by line, eventually a pattern emerges

as the whole is completed. The vertical threads, as I have already suggested, are provided by the transformative powers of biblical typology, specifically the "Servant of God" type that Cowper imposes on his persona. Meanwhile, the horizontal threads of the poem present a succession of tasks and a hierarchical evaluation of those tasks. As it would take too long to summarize this horizontal argument book by book, we must let our discussion of book 3 suffice as illustration. Let me merely emphasize that the discursive argument does not effect the salvational triumph of the poem. It serves rather as a means to unfold the persona's life (and Cowper's) in all its quotidian particulars while giving at the same time the impression of progress. Traveling, movement, succession of tasks, temporal progress of the poem: these all convey the impression of a life unfolding through time. What is required for the final salvific achievement of the poem is some device for showing the holiness of that life in its everyday, homely detail. That device is provided by the vertical strands of the web, the typological crossweave.

III

The metaphor of a vertical dimension to the poem opposed to a horizontal dimension finds its utility in its suggestion that one chain of signifiers—the "horizontal" one—can be given added depth or be shifted in meaning by the insertion of certain "vertical" elements into it. Perhaps the metaphor of the loom is still the most apt: vertical threads provide essential elements of a pattern that grows to completion as horizontal line is added to horizontal line. Such "vertical threads" are woven into the fabric of *The Task* in the form of typological markers. Though their influence extends throughout *The Task,* two main insertion points anchor the pattern: 3.108-33 and 6.747-1024. These two strategically placed passages superimpose on the persona's life the identity of Servant of God.

The first insertion point occurs at 3.108, where an abrupt utterance of personal confession jars the reader after some sixty lines of diatribe against the corruption of contemporary mores:

> I was a stricken deer, that left the herd
> Long since; with many an arrow deep infixt
> My panting side was charg'd, when I withdrew
> To seek a tranquil death in distant shades.
> There was I found by one who had himself
> Been hurt by th'archers. In his side he bore,
> And in his hands and feet, the cruel scars.
> With gentle force soliciting the darts,
> He drew them forth, and heal'd, and bade me live.
> Since then, with few associates, in remote
> And silent woods I wander, far from those
> My former partners of the peopled scene;
> With few associates, and not wishing more.
> Here much I ruminate, as much I may,
> With other views of men and manners now
> Than once, and others of a life to come.
> I see that all are wand'rers, gone astray
> Each in his own delusions; they are lost

In chase of fancied happiness, still woo'd
And never won.

(3.108-27)

Many critics have noted the intensely personal tone of this passage, even choosing, like me, the word "confession" to describe its contents.[7] Vincent Newey speaks of the "transparency of its 'confession,'" seeing in the passage one example of the "immediate presence . . . of authorial consciousness and self-consciousness" that he believes informs the poem as a whole.[8] There is more than a grain of truth to this. The passage does evoke the impression of authorial confession, of the "real" author dropping his mask and revealing an element in his personal history. However, I must insist that this impression of "transparency" and "immediate presence" is above all a textual construct—albeit an extremely complex one. Whether or not Cowper did in fact use *The Task* as a fetishized and easily manipulated embodiment of his own life—as I believe he did—it is nevertheless too simple to speak of "Cowper's [direct] identification with the stricken deer," as Newey does.[9] The very definition of a literary text requires that the poet be absent in his poem. His "presence" in that absence, which I concede exists as impression, is indeed a mysterious epiphenomenon that needs to be discussed in terms of textual effects.

What makes the Stricken Deer passage stand out as the "personal" confession of the author is its abrupt shift of tone away from the satiric voice that immediately precedes it to a sudden and unexpected voice of pathos. This new voice appears as a dropping of the Horatian, satiric mask that immediately precedes it and as a deviation from the tradition-laden Virgilian voice with which the poem begins: "I sing the Sofa. I, who lately sang / Truth, Hope, and Charity," etc. (1.1-2).[10] But besides the pathetic tone, the passage appears to roll away the stage props of the poet-in-retirement-singing-his-song and to reveal something about the condition of the author before the performance began. The real reason for retirement is that the author has been wounded by the world; and the real nature of the retirement may be best explained by comparing it with a state of exilic sacrifice.

Readers often identify the Stricken Deer passage as autobiographical because the satiric mask is almost immediately resumed in a deliberate gesture, as the poem takes up again a tone of diatribe, this time against "men of science." The brief glimpse behind the scenes lets us believe that we have seen the real Cowper out of costume, and it leads us to posit an autobiographical dimension, albeit a concealed one, for the entire poem. But this posited autobiography is but half of the significance of the Stricken Deer passage. The special power of these lines lies in their use of typology to transform the entire poem. Over against the "life" revealed in the passage stands the "writing" of that life—or its "rewriting"—in biblical types. As I shall show, the Servant of God type, which is inserted here, has the power to shift our interpretation of the persona's evolving life to a higher register, thus leading to a "transcendent"

view of the poet-in-retirement which effectively reveals him as the chosen of God.

Paul Korshin, the only writer I have found who even addresses the matter of typology in *The Task,* cites Psalms 42:1 as the probable source of Cowper's imagery here; and he emphasizes the "personal typology" of these lines,[11] thus stressing the autobiographical dimension. An allusion to that passage in Psalms ("As the hart panteth after the waterbrooks, so panteth my soul after thee, O God"), with the use of the deer or hart as a type of Christ, is surely to be found here. We can go a step further, however, by recognizing that the passage actually evokes the more general type of the Servant of God, of which the deer or hart symbol is itself a species. The defining characteristic of the deer in the poem and his common feature with Christ is his quality as "stricken." This, I believe, alludes to a different biblical context (the Servant Song at Isa. 52:13-53:12) and evokes the typology of the Servant of God found there. I quote the portion of the Servant Song that Cowper makes verbal and conceptual allusion to:

> He is despised and rejected of men; a man of sorrows, and acquainted with grief: and we hid as it were our faces from him; he was despised, and we esteemed him not. Surely he hath borne our griefs, and carried our sorrows: yet we did esteem him *stricken,* smitten of God, and afflicted . . . *All* we like sheep have *gone astray; we have turned every one to his own way*; and the Lord hath laid on him the iniquity of us all . . . for he was cut off out of the land of the living: for the transgression of my people was he *stricken.*

Isa. 53:3-8 (my italics)

Cowper uses certain keywords and paraphrases to evoke the Isaianic passage as a whole: "stricken," "all gone astray," and, as a distributive gloss on "all gone astray," "each in his own delusions." Add to this his use in the passage of the typology of the suffering Christ (who is the supreme antitype of the Servant of God), and we may confidently read in Cowper's lines a literary application of Servant of God typology. Furthermore, as we shall see, the use of the Servant type at 3.108-27 is but the left-hand bracket of a set of parentheses that is closed in book 6, where we find extensive echoes of Isaiah at 6.759-816, and where the entire Servant Song at Isaiah 52:13-53:12 is reiterated structurally at 6.906-50.

The Servant of God is an Old Testament type who finds his greatest antitype in the person of Christ. Some of his important characteristics are as follows:

(1) He resembles the sacrificial victim or scapegoat, in that he suffers for the sins of the people. (Under this aspect he is sometimes referred to as the "Suffering Servant.")

(2) He has redemptive powers, though they are often for a time hidden.

(3) He is despised by the very people whom he has been sent to save.

(4) He is God's chosen and will be glorified in the end.

Though the Servant type is fulfilled by many biblical figures (the patriarchs, the prophets, Moses, David, and Job have all been designated as the Servant of God),[12] the most important—and, indeed, defining—instance occurs at Isaiah 52:13-53:12, which is the longest and most elaborate of the four "Servant Songs" found in the Book of Isaiah.[13] Knowledge of the type—with the characteristics I have listed above—is so deeply embedded in Western consciousness, that we are quite familiar with the type, even if we do not happen to know the name scholars have attached to it. It is this implicit knowledge of the typological code that Cowper was relying on to bring home to his readers the significance of the Stricken Deer passage. Indeed, it is this implicit knowledge of the code that makes readers attribute to the passage the pathos that, by the code, informs it. Even readers not familiar with the Isaianic passage in question would be able to read Cowper's lines correctly, just by virtue of their cultural "competence."

The suffering aspect of Cowper's speaker ("I was a stricken deer," etc.) and the comparison with the suffering Christ mark him as the type of the Servant of God. As yet, however, only the aspect of the *suffering* Servant has been applied to him. The redemptive powers (like Christ's: "With gentle force soliciting the darts, / He drew them forth, and heal'd and bade me live" [3.115-6]) have not yet been applied. The effect, then, of the Stricken Deer within its context, is to suggest a reinterpretation of the persona's retirement as a life of exile, occasioned by some unnamed wound. The ones who wounded him are, however, the same ones who wounded Christ: "There was I found by one who had *himself* / Been hurt by th'archers" (3.112-3, my italics). The archers are the "world," the "many" in their unremitting wickedness, the ones whom Cowper's speaker rebukes in his satiric diatribe. It is their wickedness that has occasioned the rural retreat. Cowper's persona has therefore been excused for his retirement, but he has not yet been justified by his redemptive work. As we have seen, his satiric labors are useless for redeeming the world; yet it is just these satiric labors that he resumes after the interruption occasioned by the Stricken Deer passage.

When viewed as one link in the horizontal chain of the poem, this passage can be read as merely one more attempt to prove to the world the acceptability of rural seclusion. Read this way, the Stricken Deer confession appears of a piece with the various other argumentative tactics undertaken by the speaker to vindicate himself in the face of a world he presumes to be hostile to him. The persona announces his identity metaphorically to give a special spiritual luster to his retired life.[14] However, to see only the local function of the Stricken Deer is to miss its special role as a colorful vertical thread constituting an essential part of the text's pattern as a whole. As is often the case with typology, the use of the Servant type here establishes not merely a relationship of similarity in this or that respect between two compared things; rather, other qualities of identity besides the immediate point of comparison are transferred from the type to the antitype. In the case of

Cowper's Stricken Deer, the point of contact between the persona (the antitype) and the Servant of God (the type) is the aspect of suffering. However, all the other aspects exist in the antitype *in potentia,* awaiting future realization. When these other aspects are in fact realized in book 6, we have the luxury of seeing in retrospect the expectation that was set up, but remained unfulfilled, at 3.108-27.

Though, as I have said, we need not refer Cowper's passage back to the Isaianic text in order to appreciate his use of Servant of God typology, there is no better place to contemplate the type in all its features than Isaiah 52:13-53:12. There we find the other features besides suffering that I have already mentioned in my list above: redemptive powers, chosenness, and glorification. The future glorification of the Servant is the point on which the Servant Song at Isaiah 52:13-53:12 begins: "Behold, my servant shall deal prudently [RSV: *"prosper"*], he shall be exalted and extolled, and be very high." Gerhard von Rad comments on the passage as follows: "The unusual aspect of this great poem is that it begins with what is really the end of the whole story, the Servant's glorification and the recognition of his significance for the world. This indicates, however, one of the most important factors in the whole song—the events centring on the Servant can in principle only be understood in the light of their end. It is only thus that all the preceding action can be seen in its true colours."[15] As von Rad's remarks suggest, the type of the Servant of God is more than simply an individual with more or less static characteristics; he is rather hero of a story (*histoire*) with certain elements that can be rearranged in any particular telling of the story (*discours*). The end of the story—glorification—is essential for understanding all other events of the story. In fact we might say that this promise for the future is a necessary constituent of the type of Servant of God. The suffering servant will be vindicated by his future glorification: it will be proved that he is really the chosen Servant of God. The proof is projected into the future. In any application of the Servant typology, therefore, the vindication of the suffering servant must eventually be realized, or the type remains incomplete. This necessity can produce, as it were, the narrative tension of unfulfilled prophecy. In the case of **The Task,** we might say that Cowper's persona has been handed, at the "stricken deer" passage, one half of a *symbolon,* or broken coin, but must produce the other half in order to prove that he is truly God's chosen servant. The "stricken deer" typology implies both halves of the story: exaltation and glory as well as lowliness and suffering. The reinterpretation of the humble Servant as chosen of God thus not only exists *in potentia* at this stage of the poem, but it begins to color our reading of the "horizontal" progress of the poet's humble life in retirement. Already at this stage, the reader is being schooled to reinterpret the life and travails of the persona as resembling the unappreciated—even despised—life of the Servant of God, whose humble life conceals his real glory as God's chosen instrument. The informed reader will even begin to see traits of the to-be-exalted Isaianic prophet: compare, for example, 3.261-2 ("All flesh is grass, and all its glory fades / Like the fair flow'r dishevell'd in the wind") with Isaiah 40:6-7. Yet, as I have suggested, the growing pattern supplies first hint, then ambiguous interpretation, then completed picture.

The "tension of unfulfilled prophecy," as I have called it, is built into the typology of the Servant of God in the aspect of hiddenness.[16] The servant's name was named before he was born (Isa. 49:1); then God hid him "in the shadow of his hand" (Isa. 49:2), and those whom he was sent to redeem despised him and "esteemed him not" (Isa. 53:3); yet God has pledged his glorification in the future (Isa. 49:3: "Thou art my servant, O Israel, in whom I will be glorified"), when the Servant shall fulfill his prophetic mission (Isa. 49:6: "I will also give thee for a light to the Gentiles, that thou mayest be my salvation unto the end of the earth"). In short, the Servant must be humbled, even despised; he must for a time be unrecognized as the chosen of God: such is the hiddenness built into his character.

The true identity of the Servant must, however, be revealed. Cowper's persona, who appeared as a Suffering Servant in book 3, is finally revealed in book 6 to have the other characteristics of the Servant of God: redemptive powers and glorification by God. The first evidence of his true identity is met at 6.759-817, where the poet erupts into full-blown prophetic utterance. His song of the New Jerusalem (6.759-817) echoes the prophetic Book of Isaiah in so many particulars that it might, indeed, be called a New Isaiah.[17] This is a fitting fulfillment of the Servant's redemptive potential, for the Servant in Deutero-Isaiah, as suffering mediator and prophet,[18] was destined both to proclaim and to help bring in the renewed Jerusalem. Yet we must look to the poetic use that Cowper makes of his Isaianic intertext. He uses typology to suggest not that his persona is a second Isaiah, or an Isaiah *redivivus*, but that he is like Isaiah. Just as Isaiah in his office as prophet fulfilled his special service to God, so Cowper's poet, in translating Isaiah's prophecy into millennial terms, is also serving God by writing the New Isaiah. But, while this prophetic display provides a specimen of the persona's poetic powers, we still have not been given a "proof" that the humble retired man is really, in all particulars, the blessed and chosen of God. That occurs at 6.906-50.

Cowper's poet has argued ceaselessly for the usefulness of his tasks, mundane as they seem. Yet no amount of discursive argument has succeeded. It is only through typology that Cowper manages to prove his persona's identity as God's chosen servant. As Paul Korshin puts it, typology can be used as an "evidentiary technique" in secular literature "for purposes of proof, demonstration, and convincing . . . [T]he writer who introduces typological figuralism into a work of literature is proving something, but he or she is not going about it in a direct way."[19] Cowper's "proof" is indeed indirect. After suggesting the climactic fulfillment of the Isaianic prophecy with his song of the New Jerusalem, Cowper comes back down to this premillennial "shatter'd world" (6.823). He calls for

Christ to return and to rule over this fallen world. Then all things will be renewed:

> Custom and prejudice shall bear no sway,
> That govern all things here, should'ring aside
> The meek and modest truth, and forcing her
> To seek a refuge from the tongue of strife
> In nooks obscure, far from the ways of men.

> (6.838-42)

In this fallen world the Truth, like Cowper's persona, must "seek a refuge . . . / In nooks obscure, far from the ways of men." This is a message expounded already in book 3—that rural retirement is the best setting for virtuous works of contemplation. Yet what we have here in book 6 is more than mere repetition of the sentiment, "God made the country, and man made the town" (1.749). The retired man is here vindicated through typological "proof" as his hiddenness is shown to conceal the blessed life of the Servant of God. The "proof" begins at 6.906:

(1) 6.906-7: He is the happy man, whose life ev'n now
> Shows somewhat of that happier life to come.

(2) 6.915-8: The world o'erlooks him in her busy search
> Of objects, more illustrious in her view;
> And, occupied as earnestly as she,
> Though more sublimely, he o'erlooks the world.

(3) 6.924-9: Therefore in contemplation is his bliss,
> Whose pow'r is such, that whom she lifts from earth
> She makes familiar with a heav'n unseen,
> And shows him glories yet to be reveal'd.
> Not slothful he, though seeming unemploy'd,
> And censur'd oft as useless.

(4) 6.940-50: Perhaps the self-approving haughty world,
> That as she sweeps him with her whistling silks
> Scarce deigns to notice him, or, if she see,
> Deems him a cypher in the works of God,
> Receives advantage from his noiseless hours,
> Of which she little dreams. Perhaps she owes
> Her sunshine and her rain, her blooming spring
> And plenteous harvest, to the pray'r he makes,
> When, Isaac like, the solitary saint
> Walks forth to meditate at even tide,
> And think on her, who thinks not for herself.

In the course of this passage, the Christianized *beatus ille* of country retreat is transformed into a "solitary saint" who intercedes for the sinners of the world. He has indeed become the Servant of God, fulfilled in his glorious work. Even the structure of this passage resembles that of the Servant Song at Isaiah 52:13-53:12:

(1) The presentation of the Servant (6.906-7) = Isaiah 52:13 ("Behold, my servant shall deal prudently, he shall be exalted and extolled, and be very high").

(2) The hiddenness and neglect of the Servant (6.915-8) = Isaiah 53:3 ("and we hid as it were our faces from him; he was despised, and we esteemed him not").

(3) The prophetic powers and knowledge of the Servant justify many (6.924-9) = Isaiah 53:11 ("by his knowledge shall my righteous servant justify many").

(4) The Servant's intercession for the sins of many (6.940-50) = Isaiah 53:12 ("and he bare the sin of many, and made intercession for the transgressors").[20]

I would not want to push this structural parallel too far. It shows, however, the analogy—in all essential features—between the Servant of God and Cowper's "happy man" (who, though presented in the third person, is precisely a representative of the persona and, by extension, of Cowper). The final step in Cowper's typological "proof" is the curious "Isaac like, the solitary saint / Walks forth to meditate at even tide" (6.958-9). This allusion to the language of the KJV Genesis 24:63 ("And Isaac went out to meditate in the field at the eventide: and he lifted up his eyes, and saw, and, behold, the camels were coming") is a very complex application of typological as well as linguistic detail. Isaac is in fact a type of the Servant of God, but Cowper uses him here for a very particular purpose. It is Isaac's specificity as obscure figure, who is also carrier of the blessing, that recommends him for Cowper's use here.

The narrative of Genesis 24:1-67, in which the verse Cowper alludes to is embedded, tells the story of Abraham sending his servant to find a wife for his son Isaac. The remarkable feature of the narrative, according to Gerhard von Rad, is the way the trivial, seemingly unimportant details of the story are shown to be managed in all their particularity by the providence of God.[21] Similarly, Isaac's actions in the narrative, though slight and seemingly commonplace, also take their place in the chain of God's providence. Isaac does not appear as actor in the story until the verse I have cited above (Gen. 24:63), and then his actions are strangely unmotivated and arbitrary: he goes out to meditate at eventide and happens to see the caravan bringing his future wife, Rebekah. The circumstantial character of these details can be explained philologically by the assumption that the entire narrative was written as a "connecting piece" to fill a gap in the already existing patriarchal stories.[22] Be that as it may, it was precisely the haecceity of Isaac's walking forth to meditate at eventide and happening to meet his destiny (in the form

of Rebekah, future carrier of the seed of Abraham) that recommended this passage of the KJV to Cowper. Isaac's walking forth, his meditation—these are the details which tie him to the ambulatory, contemplative poet-in-retirement; but his blessedness, hidden in seeming blandness—this is the detail that is especially relevant to Cowper's persona and completes the proof of his special status as Servant of God. Thus the persona of *The Task* has been handed the second half of the *symbolon* promised in book 3, and the typological "proof" is complete.

In conclusion, I argue that, just as the persona is in many ways Cowper's poetic double, so the blessed status imputed to him has also been imputed to Cowper by means of the poem. Cowper's dilemma in real life was that his lot—so he was unalterably convinced—was reprobation. No amount of work, no amount of arguing about work, could secure him God's approval. Yet his imaginative double is shown, from the omniscient perspective of the completed poem, to have been God's chosen from before his birth. Through the device of paralleling life and poem, of paralleling task and *Task,* Cowper has been able to present a God's-eye view—*sub specie aeternitatis*—of his persona's life as a whole, completed as the poem is completed. From that perspective, we are able to see the parts *in uno* and thus realize what we were unable to discern from the horizontal, "temporal" progress of the poem—that the retired poet-persona is in fact one of God's elect. As Cowper reinserts himself into the *Task*'s close as the poem's author, we learn that his real goal has been to reverse God's sentence of reprobation and to create a poem—and a life—prospered by his maker's approbation:

> But all is in his hand whose praise I seek.
> In vain the poet sings, and the world hears,
> If he regard not, though divine the theme.
> 'Tis not in artful measures, in the chime
> And idle tinkling of a minstrel's lyre,
> To charm his ear, whose eye is on the heart;
> Whose frown can disappoint the proudest strain,
> Whose approbation—prosper even mine.

(6.1017-24)

Notes

1. *The Letters and Prose Writings of William Cowper,* ed. James King and Charles Ryskamp, 5 vols. (Oxford: Clarendon Press, 1979-84), 1:39. All references to Cowper's prose and letters hereafter will be to this edition, by volume and page, and will appear in the text parenthetically.

2. This combination of the passive perfect participle of *ago,* meaning "finished, all up with" (see *Oxford Latin Dictionary: ago,* 21c), and a form of the perfect of *pereo* used as hyperbolic exclamation meaning "to be ruined, done for" (see *OLD: pereo,* 5) is frequent in Roman comedy: e.g., Terence *Ad.* 324, *periimus; actumst*; Terence *Heaut.* 564, *acta haec res est: perii*; Terence *Eun.* 54, *actumst, ilicet, peristi.* Concordances to the Vulgate show no instances of *actum* (in any number, case, or gender) with this meaning.

3. This was the dream, Cowper explained later to John Newton, "before the recollection of which, all consolation vanishes, and, as it seems to me, must always vanish" (2:385). In another letter Cowper comments enigmatically to Newton: "That a Calvinist in principle, should know himself to have been Elected, and yet believe that he is lost, is indeed a Riddle, and so obscure that it Sounds like a Solecism in terms, and may bring the assertor of it under the Suspicion of Insanity. But it is not so, and it will not be found to be so" (1:341).

4. James King, *William Cowper: A Biography* (Durham NC: Duke Univ. Press, 1986), pp. 155-6. See also Vincent Newey's second chapter (pp. 24-49) in *Cowper's Poetry: A Critical Study and Reassessment* (Liverpool: Liverpool Univ. Press, 1982), where Newey analyzes the confessional and psychodramatic elements of Cowper's poetry.

5. *The Poems of William Cowper,* ed. John D. Baird and Charles Ryskamp, vol. 1:1748-1782 (Oxford: Oxford Univ. Press, 1980), p. 543. I use this edition when quoting poems written before 1782.

6. From a facsimile of the title page of the 1785 edition, reproduced in William Cowper, *Poetical Works,* ed. H. S. Milford, 4th edn. (London: Oxford Univ. Press, 1967), p. 128. All references to Cowper's *The Task* appear parenthetically in the text, by book and line number, and refer to Milford's edition.

7. See Newey, p. 96. Also see Martin Priestman, *Cowper's "Task": Structure and Influence* (Cambridge: Cambridge Univ. Press, 1983), p. 92.

8. Newey, p. 96.

9. Newey, p. 95, alludes here directly to Northrop Frye's seminal article on the Age of Sensibility, where Frye would see the Stricken Deer as an instance of "metaphor . . . conceived as part of an oracular and half-ecstatic process, [where] there is a direct identification in which the poet himself is involved" (Frye, "Towards Defining an Age of Sensibility," in *Fables of Identity: Studies in Poetic Mythology* [New York: Harcourt, Brace, and World, 1963], p. 137; first published in *ELH* 23, 2 [June 1956]: 144-52).

10. Dustin Griffin has pointed out that "Cowper's *Task* begins with an oblique allusion to the end of Virgil's own *Georgics* and the pseudo-Virgilian proem at the beginning of the *Aeneid*": see his article "Redefining Georgic: Cowper's *Task*," *ELH* 57, 4 (Winter 1990): 865-79, 869.

11. Paul J. Korshin, *Typologies in England, 1650-1820* (Princeton: Princeton Univ. Press, 1982), p. 360.

12. Gerhard von Rad notes this fact in his *Old Testament Theology* (hereafter *OTT*), vol. 2: *The Theology of Israel's Prophetic Traditions,* trans. D. M. G. Stalker (New York: Harper and Row, 1965), p. 258 n. 35.

13. Most scholars identify Isa. 42:1-4, Isa. 49:1-6, Isa. 50:4-9, and Isa. 52:13-53:12 as Servant Songs and attribute them to a writer they designate as Deutero-Isaiah. For a good account, see von Rad, *OTT,* 2:250-62. A more exhaustive discussion is available in W. Zimmerli and J. Jeremias, *The Servant of God,* trans. H. Knight et al., rev. edn., Studies in Biblical Theology 20 (Naperville IL: Alec R. Allenson, 1965).

14. This is the reading Martin Priestman makes of the passage: "Here the growing move to establish a 'humble man' persona is justified in terms of the Christian conversion of weakness into strength, and the old conflict between labour and ease begins to be resolved in the paradoxical 'gentle force' of the Christian experience" (pp. 92-3). Priestman's notion of the "humble man" persona shows that he has responded to the Servant of God typology, even though he has not recognized it.

15. Von Rad, *OTT,* 2:256.

16. On the idea of hiddenness of the Servant of God, consult Zimmerli and Jeremias, p. 60.

17. Some echoes are the following: (1) There will be no violence. Animals lose their enmity to each other and to man: 6.773-7 ("The lion, and the libbard, and the bear / Graze with the fearless flocks"); cf. Isa. 11:6, Isa. 66:25. The mother watches unconcerned as the infant plays with the serpent: 6.777-82; cf. Isa. 11:8. (2) The mountain-tops sing and shout: 6.793-5; cf. Isa. 42:11, Isa. 55:12. (3) The brightness of the New Jerusalem, to which kings and gentiles will come: 6.800-2; cf. Isa. 60:1-5 and Isa. 60:19-20. (4) Gentiles will serve the people of Israel: 6.804-17, esp. 804-5 ("Thy rams are there, / Nebaioth, and the flocks of Kedar there"); cf. Isa. 60:7 ("All the flocks of Kedar shall be gathered together unto thee, the rams of Nebaioth shall minister unto thee") and Isa. 60:3-16. (5) Walls of Salvation and gates of Praise: 6.808-10; cf. Isa. 60:18. (6) The end of barrenness and a new fruitfulness: 6.764-8; cf. Isa. 54:1-3.

18. On the Servant as prophet, see von Rad, *OTT,* 2:259.

19. Korshin, p. 391.

20. It is interesting that Talmudic interpretation understands the "intercession" named in this verse as prayer: *B. Sotah* 14a: "'He interceded for the transgressors' (Isa. 53:12): for he implored mercy for the transgressors of Israel that they might return in penitence; by this 'intercession' is meant nothing other than prayer" (cited in Zimmerli and Jeremias, p. 65 n. 283).

21. See Gerhard von Rad, *Genesis: A Commentary,* rev. edn. (Philadelphia: Westminster Press, 1972), pp. 259-60: "Characteristic [of the narrative of Gen. 24:1-67] is the dispensing with external miracles. The story does not say, 'God smote Pharaoh,' 'he opened Hagar's eyes,' 'he visited Abraham,' 'rained fire from heaven,' 'called to Abraham from heaven,'

etc. Here no causal connection is broken, but the miracle takes place in a concealed, quite unsensational management of the events. For in our narrative the actual field of activity for this guidance is less the external, spatial world of things, but rather the inner realm of the human heart in which God works, mysteriously directing, evening, and removing resistance."

22. Von Rad, *Genesis,* p. 259. That would explain the circumstantiality and blandness of Isaac's role in the narrative.

Karen O'Brien (essay date 1998)

SOURCE: O'Brien, Karen. "'Still at Home': Cowper's Domestic Empires." In *Early Romantics: Perspectives in British Poetry from Pope to Wordsworth,* edited by Thomas Woodman, pp. 134-47. London: Macmillan, 1998.

[*In the following essay, O'Brien probes Cowper's juxtaposition of private and public concerns, and his moral focus on the still, small, quiet and humble in* The Task.]

Questions of William Cowper's sense of empire are like those of his 'pre-romanticism': more interesting in the details. The British Empire raises difficulties of style and poetic mode of address in Cowper's poetry which force him to a final reckoning with the traditions of eighteenth-century poetry, if not, ultimately, to the invention of anything we would conventionally describe as 'romanticism' or 'romantic ideology'. Although he was later sentimentalized by the Victorians as the voice of hearth and heart, Cowper displayed in his poetry a robust interest in the politics of imperial expansion. For Cowper, as less obtrusively for Wordsworth and Coleridge, the empire defined the outer limits for a poetic sensibility centred in but not enclosed by the rural home. In particular, Cowper's major achievement, his georgic-descriptive poem *The Task* (1785), is immersed in the turbulent imperial events of the early 1780s. Written from a vantage point in the countryside, the poem takes as its earthly horizon British imperial territories past and future; these range from the newly discovered Pacific islands to India (whose administration by the East India Company was, at the time of writing, the occasion of scandal and constitutional crisis) and to North America, only two years before ignominiously ceded to the rebellious American colonists. Critics have drawn up the balance sheet of Cowper's imperial opinions—for the retaining, by force if necessary, of the American colonies, against slavery, for and then decisively against British rule in India, and so on—although most have resisted the temptation to rummage through his poems for imperialist prejudices or congratulate them for their bouts of anti-colonialism.[1] Cowper was an intelligent but straightforward political thinker whose opinions had the consistency of the evangelical Protestantism against which he measured them, and his specifically political ideas about empire need no further elucidation here.[2] Of more interest is the special quality of Cowper's imperial awareness which permeates and modifies his sense of what it means to be 'still at home' in the country, just as, in turn, the homely stillness at the centre of *The Task* resists the generic pressure of georgic towards an easy confluence of rural, national and imperial vistas.[3]

For the poem begins with the words 'I sing the Sofa'— with, in other words, an eastern and exotic word and a mock-classical formula awkwardly at home in an English country setting. Sofas, Cowper reveals a few lines later, were originally made of Indian cane, and, like most private persons of his day, his main point of contact with the empire was, indeed, through the consumption of furniture, tea and sugar (I: 39). Cowper's mock-epic history of sofas collapses abruptly into a long prelude on his love of rural life, and his new task becomes how to establish a domestic position of poetic address which can incorporate, without appearing diminished by, a responsible sense of the wider life of politics and empires. In many of the earlier eighteenth-century descriptive poems which influenced Cowper's work, such as John Philips's *Cyder,* Thomson's *Seasons,* Dyer's *The Fleece* or Jago's *Edge Hill,* the mode of rural poetic address to an expanding nation is drawn from the traditional resources of georgic; the description of the aesthetic and productive qualities of the British landscape is itself an act of *pietas* to the sources of the nation's metropolitan and imperial greatness. From the prospect vantage points, adopted in these poems at moments of emotional elevation, the poets see, with an eye which coordinates rural, national and providential visions, the moral enlargement of the countryside in the imperial sphere. Thomson's *Seasons,* in particular, is, obsessively, a poem about boundlessness which begins with a dizzying prescription to 'generous Britons' to pour 'Nature's better Blessings [. . .] / O'er every Land, the naked Nations cloath, / And be th' exhaustless Granary of a World!'[4] *The Task* has none of these imperial prospects. The global sensibility of Cowper's earlier poem **'Charity'** (1782), in which trade is eulogized as the 'boundless plenty' and 'golden girdle of the globe' bringing the world into a divine order of economic reciprocity, becomes, in *The Task,* the lonely gaze of Omai, the Pacific islander who once visited England and who now yearns to return.[5] Cowper imagines Omai back at home in Tahiti on a mountain top 'with eager eye / Exploring far and wide the wat'ry waste / For sight of ship from England' (I: 664-6). Omai's prospect of the British Empire is doomed to disappointment since, as Cowper explains, the English have no economic interest in Pacific territories 'inclosed', as he puts it, 'in boundless oceans never to be pass'd' (I: 628-9). Thomsonian boundlessness reappears here in a fable of imperial isolation. The story of Omai also appears to recapitulate Pope's striking inversion of the colonial gaze at the end of *Windsor-Forest* when 'naked [Indian] youths and painted chiefs' come to England to 'admire / Our Speech, our Colour, and our Strange Attire!'[6]

Although deeply imbued with *The Seasons,* then, *The Task* eschews or inverts its imperial vistas, and the moral value of Cowper's landscape is not, as it is for Thomson, guaranteed by labour. Cowper describes little hard work of any kind, although a good deal of energy is inefficiently expended on the rearing of season-defying cucumbers and hot-house fruits (III: 447-623). The distinctive achievement of *The Task* is its disengagement of the rural home, peasant cottages, gentry piles and all from the simultaneously bucolic and mercantile vision of previous eighteenth-century georgic poems. The poem separates the pre-lapsarian idyll of the rural environment, most fully expressed in the third book, from its satirical and moralizing political voices. In the process, however, Cowper sacrifices the rich metaphorical congruities available to earlier poets of garden, nation and empire, and he concedes that the political awareness upon which he bases his praise and blame of England and its empires comes from a mediated, second-hand vision of the world. 'They love the country', Cowper remarks with deliberate artlessness and revisionist emphasis, 'and none else, who seek / For their own sake its silence and its shade' (III: 320-1). This is an apparently romantic sentiment. Wordsworth, perhaps echoing this line at the close of 'Tintern Abbey', declares that, in the presence of Dorothy, the 'steep woods and lofty cliffs, / And this green pastoral landscape / [. . .]' become 'More dear, both for themselves, and for thy sake!'[7] An additional rhythmic stress loiters over the word 'thy' as if to emphasize that Dorothy is a more vivid companionable presence than, say, Mary Unwin, Cowper's quiet companion in *The Task.* Unlike Wordsworth, however, Cowper's choice of the country makes visible a process of conscious poetic disinvestment of its 'silence and its shade' from the public life of the town. This public life is, Cowper repeatedly tells us, the realm of 'Custom and prejudice' (VI: 838), and is part of the whole fabric of history and social assumption against which he erects a 'faithful barrier not o'erleap'd', as Milton's Satan o'erleaped the walls of paradise, 'with ease' (III: 681). Inside the barrier, the poet has evolved day-to-day customs and rituals of his own for their own sake, merely to allow his life to 'glide away' agreeably (VI: 1000). Wordsworth explains that the pleasurable 'feelings' which a 'good man' takes from the countryside to the town have exerted 'no trivial influence' on the conduct of his life.[8] Cowper undertakes a more risky imaginative juxtaposition between the acknowledged trivialities of country life and the mercantile and political world of the town without feeling obliged to forge a connection between them in terms of morally regenerative continuity.

These points are best illustrated by a detailed examination of the texture of Cowper's verse in relation to his inward and international concerns, and, in particular, by a passage in which he reflects directly upon his seclusion from the public domain. This passage occurs a short way into the fourth book of *The Task,* entitled **'The Winter Evening'**, and opens with the eagerly awaited arrival of the post boy, with 'news from all nations lumb'ring at his back' (IV: 7). The boy is, like the poet, cheerfully indifferent to the good or bad news he brings in the letters and papers. Even so,

the poet confesses to an irrepressible, sensationalist appetite for any news of the empire which might emerge from the boy's leather sack:

> who can say
> What are its tidings? have our troops awak'd?
> Or do they still, as if with opium drugg'd
> Snore to the murmurs of th'Atlantic wave?
> Is India free? and does she wear her plum'd
> And Jewell'd turban with a smile of peace,
> Or do we grind her still? the grand debate,
> The popular harangue, the tart reply,
> The logic and the wisdom and the wit
> And the loud laugh—I long to know them all:
> I burn to set th'imprison'd wranglers free,
> And give them voice and utt'rance once again.
>
> (IV: 24-35)

All Cowper's attitudes to empire, elsewhere articulated in this poem, in the 1782 volume of poems and in the letters, are here condensed. The snoring British troops are those defeated some years before in America who, in Cowper's opinion, had lacked the courage and the political support to keep the 13 British colonies out of the incapable hands of the Americans.[9] We are also reminded of Pope's attack on Walpole's failure to protect British imperial interests in the Americas, and the 'Chiefless Armies' who 'dozed out the Campaign' at the end of *The Dunciad.*[10] Indeed, Cowper was throughout the 1770s and 1780s something of a hawk on the American question, despite the fact that his political idol Chatham had, until the moment of his death, passionately urged conciliation with the colonies. Cowper attributed the loss of the colonies to a domestic failure of patriotic nerve and, after the British capitulation to peace, predicted worse to come: 'I consider the loss of America', he wrote in 1781, 'as the ruin of England.'[11] The 'grand debate' alludes to the tumultuous passage of Fox's India Bill in the Commons and its defeat, after royal intervention, in the Lords, and, particularly perhaps, to Burke's great speech of 1783 in favour of crown regulation of the East India Company. Cowper was consistently anti imperial on the Indian question and, after the failure of Fox's India Bill which he earnestly supported, he wrote in a letter that he 'would abandon all territorial interest in a country to which we can have no right'.[12] Cowper was simultaneously enthralled and horrified by Burke's torrent of Ciceronian invective against both the Company and his old school friend, the Governor-General, Warren Hastings.[13] The word 'grind' catches the bitter and concrete satirical style of Burke's speech, as earlier in *The Task* Cowper's attack on those 'peculators of public gold', the nabobs, with their 'overgorg'd and bloated' purses, recalls Burke's harangue against the 'peculating despotism' of the Company in India, and his depiction of the young nabobs as 'birds of prey and passage, with appetites continually renewing for a food that is continually wasting' (I: 735-7).[14]

This portion of **'The Winter Evening'** combines Cowper's already familiar imperial opinions with a witty consideration of the medium of print. Print, as the first person plurals in the passage imply, constructs its own complicities and communities of readers. Reading brings guilt by association but also a pleasing sense of moral exoneration from the mimic life of a nation known only through the papers. The poet draws the sofa up to the fire, pours himself a cup of tea and starts to read. A jumble of parliamentary news, anecdotes of popular entertainers and adverts for makeup and false teeth transfers itself from the page to the poet's imagination where the city world is miniaturized like a peep show.[15] Cowper is then prompted to reflect on this process of print mediation:

> 'Tis pleasant through the loop-holes of retreat
> To peep at such a world. To see the stir
> Of the great Babel and not feel the crowd.
> To hear the roar she sends through all her gates
> At a safe distance, where the dying sound
> Falls a soft murmur on th'uninjured ear.
> Thus sitting and surveying thus at ease
> The globe and its concerns, I seem advanced
> To some secure and more than mortal height,
> That lib'rates and exempts me from them all.
> It turns submitted to my view, turns round
> With all its generations; I behold
> The tumult and am still. The sound of war
> Has lost its terrors 'ere it reaches me;
> Grieves but alarms me not. I mourn the pride
> And av'rice that makes man a wolf to man,
> Hear the faint echo of those brazen throats
> By which he speaks the language of his heart,
> And sigh, but never tremble at the sound.
> He travels and expatiates, as the bee
> From flow'r to flow'r, so he from land to land;
> The manners, customs, policy of all
> Pay contribution to the store he gleans,
> He sucks intelligence in ev'ry clime,
> And spreads the honey of his deep research
> At his return, a rich repast for me.
> He travels and I too. I tread his deck,
> Ascend his topmast, through his peering eyes
> Discover countries, with a kindred heart
> Suffer his woes and share in his escapes,
> While fancy, like the finger of a clock,
> Runs the great circuit, and is still at home

(IV: 88-119)

The syntactic and lexical simplicity achieved in this transparent passage of verse is typical of those moments in *The Task* when Cowper relieves the winding seriality of his reflections with moments of heightened awareness. Other eighteenth-century writers of blank verse, such as Thomson, Dyer or Akenside, simulate visual prospect through an accelerated syntactic momentum which carries their imaginations forward to an enticing or terrifying horizon. Akenside, for example, dramatizes the almost physical propulsion of the man whose 'lab'ring eye / Shoots round the wide horizon, to survey / Nilus or Ganges rowling his bright wave / Thro' mountains, plains, thro' empires black with shade, And continents of sand'.[16] Cowper does admit to a surveying 'relish of fair prospect', and confesses how his 'eye / [. . .] posted' on 'speculative height / Exults in its command', although he never speculates and his verse never transports him as far as the

Nile or the Ganges (I: 141, 288-90). The survey in the above passage of *The Task* comes, not from the eye, but from an indirect apprehension of the great Babel outside, and brings an untroubled admission of emotional and political disengagement from the public world. It is tempting to read this passage as an ironic commentary on the poet's domestic insulation from the 'globe and its concerns', both here and in the poem as a whole.[17] However, Cowper is one step ahead of these incipient ironies, and there is, for example, a self-knowingness in the overtly imperious phrase 'it turns submitted to my view'.

In a broader way, these ironies are contained by Cowper's moral valuation of stillness. The passage borrows some of its philosophic seriousness from the section of Lucretius' *De Rerum Natura* upon which it is based. The second book *De Rerum* opens with a meditation on the pleasures of philosophical detachment: 'Suave [. . .] magnum alterius spectare laborem' ('it is pleasant to survey the great tribulation of another man'). Lucretius imagines himself looking down (the verb is 'despicere') from a great philosophic eminence upon others wandering without purpose in the world. Cowper, too, knows that he is, in both figurative senses, looking down on the world ('despiciens'). He does not say whether his claim to 'exemption' from the world with its wars and empires derives from a higher commitment to Christian duty or from the epicurean sufficiency of pleasure. The affirmation of special insight comes, rather, from the limpid quality of the verse itself, particularly the words, 'I behold / The tumult and am still'. Only at moments of personal revelation and Christian self-dedication does Cowper's verse risk this kind of baldness. We are reminded of the 'stricken deer' passage in **'The Garden'** when Christ removes the arrows of sin and misery from the poet's side: 'He drew them forth, and heal'd and bade me live' (III: 116). The same reverential parataxis is employed later in the same book to describe a man engaged in the 'silent task' of daily piety:

> He that attends to his interior self
> That has a heart, and keeps it; has a mind
> That hungers, and supplies it; and who seeks
> A social, not a dissipated life,
> Has business.

(III: 373-7)

Such moments of extreme verbal simplicity symbolize the conjoining of Christ with the inner self. In his prose conversion narrative, *Adelphi*, Cowper had told how Christ spoke to the soul of his younger self in a voice which he represents as simple, still and small. During much of his suicidal depression before the conversion, Cowper claims that he heard Satan urging him with a Miltonic voice to make evil his good, but, on conviction of sin, he recalls that the Lord told him plainly, 'Think what you are doing; consider, and live.'[18] Later, when Cowper describes being reborn in Christ, he says that he heard the divine words, 'Peace, be still'. When, in *The Task*, Cowper beholds the tumult and is still, he once again performs an act of verbal quietism in the evangelical faith that the moral core of the self needs no Miltonic rhetoric and no ornamental language to speak and be heard.[19]

The moral satires of Cowper's 1782 volume of poetry are all in couplets, and the switch in *The Task* to blank verse was, in part, a quest for this kind of clarity. The question of clarity in relation to the technicalities of poetry is much discussed in Cowper's letters and acquires particular urgency after his reading of Samuel Johnson's *Lives of the Poets*. Cowper was furious with Johnson for his ruling on 'the unfitness of the English Language for Blank Verse', indignant at his treatment of Milton, and apoplectic at his condescension to Prior.[20] Cowper's defence of Prior's 'familiar style' in a letter to William Unwin reads like an idealized description of his own:

> To make verse speak the language of prose, without being prosaic, to marshall the words of it in such an order, as they might naturally take in falling from the lips of an extemporary speaker, yet without meanness; harmoniously, elegantly, and without seeming to displace a syllable for the sake of the rhyme, is one of the most arduous tasks a poet can undertake.[21]

This letter was written in 1782, and soon after, Cowper would abandon the relaxed rhymed couplets of his current work for the 'arduous task' of extemporary-seeming blank verse. The letter implies that, even at this stage, Cowper saw rhyme as ultimately superfluous to his style, not so much a discipline as something to be discreetly tucked into the unaffected syntactic ordering of the verse.[22] Even so, as *The Task* progressed, he became mindful of the dangers of diffuseness entailed by this new unrhymed form of poetry. He may have remembered Johnson's alarming diagnosis of the symptoms of intellectual and moral laxity in the blank verse of Akenside ('The exemption which blank verse affords from the necessity of closing the sense with the couplet . . .').[23] Cowper's blank verse claims no enthusiastic 'exemption' from grammatical and moral intelligibility; even when he reaches a meditative stake 'that lib'rates and exempts' him from the bustle of the world, he observes a more than usually strict duty to clarity.

'The words are multiplied till the sense is hardly perceived', Johnson further complained of Akenside's verse, 'attention deserts the mind, and settles in the ear'.[24] It is amusing to note that T. S. Eliot's more measured reservations about Milton's aural style have the same flavour of Anglican disdain for the verbal indiscipline of poetic nonconformity: 'a dislocation takes place, through the hypertrophy of the auditory imagination at the expense of the visual and the tactile, so that the inner meaning is separated from the surface . . .'[25] Cowper, it must be said, has nothing to say on behalf of Akenside, but in his letters and annotations, he defends Milton as a poet uniquely capable of integrating aural surface and inner meaning.[26] He also, by a curious metonymy, later repeated in 'The Garden', links clarity in blank verse to moral self-discipline (III: 684-93). Here he writes to William Unwin again shortly before the publication of *The Task*:

> Blank verse [. . .] cannot be chargeable with much Obscurity, must rather be singularly perspicuous to be so easily comprehended. It is my labour and my principal one, to be as clear as possible. You do not mistake me when you suppose that I have a great respect for the virtue that flies temptation. It is that sort of prowess which the whole strain of Scripture calls upon us to manifest when assailed by sensual Evil.[27]

The passage from 'The Winter Evening' respects the kind of linguistic clarity and moral withdrawal advocated in this letter. In many other descriptive poems of the eighteenth century, the moral benefits of survey are differently conceived. Akenside speaks of 'exhibiting the most ingaging prospects of nature, to enlarge and harmonize the imagination, and by that means insensibly dispose the minds of men to a similar taste and habit of thinking in religion, morals and civil life'.[28] He is like one of the expatiators described in the 'Winter Evening' passage, travelling imaginatively from land to land, and, like Thomson and Dyer, correlating in his poetry an expansive sensibility, style and vision of the world. Cowper's poetry has the opposite tendency, electing to curb the range of vision and to disaggregate nature into its component details. As he explains to his interlocutor in 'Table Talk', he sees the world with the restricted view of a humble man: 'An ell or two of prospect we command, / But never peep beyond the thorny bound / Or oaken fence that hems the paddock round'.[29]

In the passages of natural description in *The Task,* Cowper dissolves the rural sights and sounds into detail by means of a restless verse in which caesurae at unexpected points in the lines fall in behind small and varied units of syntax, and Miltonic vocabulary and elastic enjambement are carefully rationed to a few conspicuous occasions. This minute variousness in the verse is, as Cowper explained in a letter of 1786, deliberately and highly wrought: 'I give as much variety in my measure as I can, I believe I may say as in ten syllables it is possible to give, shifting perpetually the pause and cadence.'[30] Cowper's chosen style of blank verse differs significantly from the forward thrust of Wordsworth's more Miltonic periods not least because it enables him to position delicately within the line the detailed and trivial things which Wordsworth prefers to absorb into a wider aural texture. *The Task* is, for many critics, a poem of the merely trivial, a work written, in Hazlitt's view, 'with the finicalness of the private gentleman', and nowhere more notoriously so than in the comic georgic passages about greenhouses and cucumber growing.[31] In the passage from 'The Winter Evening', Cowper voluntarily indicates, with words such as 'loopholes', 'peep' and 'peering eyes', his own awareness that a world known at second hand is a world inevitably trivialized, but accepts this with a kind of wise passiveness which he invites his newspaper-reading audience to share. Yet, in the long section of 'The Garden' given over to the raising of cucumbers and other greenhouse fruits, Cowper's elaborate georgic comedy and brazenly mock-Miltonic verse force us to a reckoning with the quaint inconsequence of his life of rural ease. Here, Cowper indulges in the polysyllabic vocabulary, heavy enjambement and inverted syntax which he so strenuously denies himself in plain text passages elsewhere.

Claude Rawson has found in these passages a 'stylistic loss of nerve'. Their 'ceaseless twitchings of mock-heroic impulse are designed to make an amiable fuss around the very absence' of the kind of 'decisive position' capable of generating a genuinely mock-heroic perspective.[32] However, these passages can be read in exactly the opposite way as evidence for a stylistic *gaining* of nerve elsewhere in *The Task,* and this reading is possible if we pay attention, once again, to the tradition of imperial georgic to which this poem obliquely relates. Cowper's greenhouse concentrates in miniature the exotic natural products of the world 'warm and snug' under a single roof (III: 568): oranges and limes, the 'golden boast / Of Portugal and western India', peppers, geraniums and ice-plants crowd together in defiance of the natural seasons (III: 571-2). Cowper's description of these exotic items recalls those lavish tributes of fruits and spices which Baroque panegyrists of empire, such as Waller or Dryden, imagined sailing in from the British Empire towards the feet of Cromwell and Charles II. In *Windsor-Forest,* Pope used similar images when he prophesied that the 'Balm shall bleed, and Amber flow, / The Coral redden, and the Ruby glow' as part of the world's spontaneous tribute to the Thames's universal British Empire of peace.[33] In *The Task,* it is the poet who plays the role of petty emperor receiving his tribute of fruits and flowers, and who possesses orphic power, like that of Denham's or Pope's Thames, over the world's exotic produce:

> th'Azores send
> Their jessamine, her jessamine remote
> Caffraia; foreigners from many lands
> They form one social shade, as if conven'd
> By magic summons of th'Orphean lyre
>
> (III: 583-7)

As well as making a witty sally against the imperial poetics of the Augustans, Cowper is poking fun at Thomson's rather solemn eulogium in 'Summer' to that symbol of imperial consumption, the pineapple:

> Oft in humble Station dwells
> Unboastful Worth, above fastidious Pomp.
> Witness, thou best Anana, thou the Pride
> Of vegetable Life, beyond what'er
> The Poets imag'd in the golden Age.[34]

Thomson's epideictic is delivered with a straight face, and the exotic note sounded by 'Anana' leads him directly to his great prospect of the uncolonized lands of the tropics. Cowper, as we can now perhaps more clearly see, has engaged not so much in mock-Miltonics as mock-Thomsonics, by investing ordinary plants with portentous moral, national and imperial meaning.

Elsewhere in *The Task,* Cowper has the stylistic nerve to endow the plants, animals and people of Britain with independent, trivial life. This seems to me the opposite of

romantic ideology, a withholding from metaphor of the essential components of God's creation and a conservation of their trivial rather than transcendent being. National and international concerns, and all the affairs of the world created by man, are approached in *The Task* by a more direct route. Cowper creates in this work a poetry of political disinvestment the better to sustain, over long passages of overt political concern, an uncontaminated, antithetical voice of social prophecy. This curiously disembodied voice, so prominent in all the books of *The Task,* speaks from the stillness and personal exemption which Cowper claims in **'The Winter Evening'** passage: 'Folly such as your's', he inveighs against the urban rich, 'Has made [. . .] / Our arch of empire, stedfast but for you, / A mutilated structure, soon to fall' (I: 770-4). The 'great Babel' he mentions in the passage becomes elsewhere in the poem a picture of London as a 'boundless' and seething mercantile metropolis, and is intensified as a vision of the sinful *civitas terrena* from which only the global empire of the New Jerusalem in the last book can rescue mankind: 'Eastern Java there / Kneels with the native of the farthest West, / And Aethiopia spreads abroad the hand / And worships' (VI: 810-13). The closing pages of *The Task* engage in a moral revaluation of Protestant spirituality as a man's best service to his country. Cowper proclaims the social usefulness of the obscure, quiet man: as the saying goes, 'Stillest streams / Oft water fairest meadows' (VI: 929-30). This is, for Cowper at the end of his task, both a species of quietism and the moral axis along which to build a more just and devout Protestant nation and empire.

Notes

1. On Cowper's attitude to empire, see Vincent Newey, *Cowper's Poetry: A Critical Study and Reassessment* (Liverpool: Liverpool University Press, 1982), pp. 239-40 and *passim.* Also Peter Faulkner, 'William Cowper and the Poetry of Empire', *Durham University Journal,* 83 (1991), 165-73.

2. On Cowper's political views, see also Newey, 'William Cowper and the Condition of England', in *Literature and Nationalism,* eds Newey and Ann Thompson (Liverpool: Liverpool University Press, 1991) and Bill Hutchings, 'William Cowper and 1789', *The Yearbook of English Studies,* 19 (1989), 71-93 (in fact, a general article on Cowper's politics).

3. *The Task, A Poem, in Six Books,* IV: 119, in *The Poems of William Cowper,* eds, John D. Baird and Charles Ryskamp (3 vols) (Oxford: Clarendon Press 1980-95), II. Citations will be taken from this edition, although much important information can also be found in the edition by James Sambrook, *The Task and Selected Other Poems* (London: Oxford University Press, 1994).

4. *The Seasons,* ed. James Sambrook (Oxford: Clarendon Press, 1981), ll. 68-77. On georgic and empire, see my 'Imperial Georgic, 1660-1789', in *The Country and the City Revisited,* eds Donna Landry

and Gerald Maclean (Cambridge: Cambridge University Press, forthcoming 1998).

5. *The Poems of William Cowper,* I: l. 86.

6. *The Twickenham Edition of the Poems of Alexander Pope,* eds John Butt et al. (11 vols) (London and New Haven, NH: Methuen, 1939-69), I: ll. 405-6.

7. *Lyrical Ballads and Other Poems,* eds James Butler and Karen Green (Ithaca, NY: Cornell University Press, 1992), 1798 text, ll. 158-60.

8. *Lyrical Ballads,* 1798 text, ll. 31-4.

9. See *The Letters and Prose Writings of William Cowper,* eds James King and Charles Ryscamp (5 vols) (Oxford: Clarendon Press, 1979-86), I: 570.

10. *Twickenham Edition,* V: ll. 617-18. This allusion is not mentioned by Cowper's editors.

11. *Letters,* I: 555.

12. *Letters,* II: 235. See also 'Expostulation' (1782) in *Poems,* I: ll. 364-71.

13. *Letters,* IV: 72-3.

14. 'Speech on Fox's India Bill' (1783) in *The Writings and Speeches of Edmund Burke,* vol. V, ed. Peter Marshall (Oxford: Clarendon Press, 1992), pp. 430 and 402 respectively. This speech was published as a pamphlet in 1784.

15. Baird and Ryskamp's edition traces many of Cowper's observations to his daily newspaper, *The Morning Chronicle.*

16. 'The Pleasures of Imagination' (1744 version), in *The Poetical Works of Mark Akenside,* ed. Robin Dix (Madison, NJ: Fairleigh Dickinson University Press; London: Associated University Presses, 1996), I ll. 176-9.

17. For a somewhat different but subtle and illuminating reading of this passage, see Martin Priestman, *Cowper's 'Task': Structure and Influence* (Cambridge: Cambridge University Press, 1983), pp. 112-14.

18. *Adelphi: A Sketch of the Character . . . of the Late Rev. John Cowper* (published 1802), in *Letters,* I: 21.

19. *Letters,* I: 41 (echoing Mark 4: 39). Cowper's particular interest in Catholic Quietism was revealed by the publication, in 1801, of his translation of the poems of Mme Guyon. See *Poems,* II.

20. *Letters,* I: 307; II: 10.

21. *Letters,* II: 10.

22. On Cowper's use of the couplet, see Wallace C. Brown, *The Triumph of Form: A Study of the Later Masters of the Heroic Couplet* (Chapel Hill: University of North Carolina Press, 1948), pp. 132-41.

23. *Lives of the Poets,* ed. G. B. Hill (3 vols) (Oxford: Clarendon Press, 1905), III: 417.

24. *Lives of the Poets,* III: 412.

25. *On Poetry and Poets* (London: Faber, 1951), p. 143.

26. *Letters,* II: 500.

27. *Letters,* II: 288.

28. 'The Pleasures of Imagination' (1744 text), Preface, in *The Poetical Works,* p. 88.

29. *Poems,* I: ll. 581-3.

30. *Letters,* II: 586.

31. *The Collected Works of William Hazlitt,* eds Arnold Glover and A. R. Waller (12 vols) (London: J. M. Dent, 1902), V: 91.

32. *Order from Confusion Sprung: Studies in Eighteenth-Century Literature from Swift to Cowper* (London: Humanities Press, 1985), p. 371.

33. *Twickenham Edition,* I: ll. 393-4.

34. *The Seasons,* II: ll. 683-7.

FURTHER READING

Criticism

Cecil, David. Prologue to *The Stricken Deer, or the Life of Cowper,* pp. 13-29. Indianapolis: Bobbs-Merrill Company, 1930.

> Comments on the poet's relation to eighteenth-century literature and the duality of madness and the mundane in his life.

Ellison, Julie. "News, Blues, and Cowper's Busy World." *Modern Language Quarterly* 62, no. 3 (2001): 219-37.

> Evaluates Cowper as "the earliest and most influential adapter of the newspaper to reflective poetry" in Britain, focusing on his long poem *The Task.*

Kroitor, Harry P. "The Influence of Popular Science on William Cowper." *Modern Philology* 61, no. 4 (May 1964): 281-87.

> Considers Cowper's detailed and factual treatment of natural phenomena in his poetry.

Newey, Vincent. "William Cowper and the Condition of England." In *Literature and Nationalism,* edited by Vincent Newey and Ann Thompson, pp. 120-39. Liverpool: Liverpool University Press, 1991.

> Explores Cowper's poetic reflections on current events and historical circumstances, particularly as they relate to a social awareness of England and the British Empire.

———. "Cowper, William (1731-1800)." In *A Handbook to English Romanticism,* edited by Jean Raimond and J. R. Watson, pp. 83-91. New York: St. Martin's Press, 1992.
    Contains a summary of Cowper's life and thematic commentary on his poems "The Castaway" and *The Task.*

Nicholson, Norman. *William Cowper.* Harlow, Essex: Longman Group, 1960, 39 p.
    Sympathetic survey of Cowper's life and works, including critical analysis devoted to the *The Task* and a select bibliography.

Paxman, David. "Failure as Authority: Poetic Voices and the Muse of Grace in William Cowper's *The Task.*" In *1650-1850: Ideas, Aesthetics, and Inquiries in the Early Modern Era,* Vol. 5, edited by Kevin L. Cope, pp. 203-42. New York: AMS Press, 2000.

Probes the satirical and rhetorical contexts of Cowper's multiple narrative personae in *The Task* as they reflect on received poetic and moral authority in the eighteenth century.

Perkins, David. "Cowper's Hares." *Eighteenth-Century Life* 20, no. 2 (1996): 57-69.
    Psychological and literary examination of Cowper's identification and sympathy with animals.

Spacks, Patricia Meyer. "The Soul's Imaginings: Daniel Defoe, William Cowper." *PMLA* 91, no. 3 (May 1976): 420-35.
    Compares Cowper's poem "The Castaway" and Defoe's novel *Robinson Crusoe* as representations of spiritual autobiography.

Additional coverage of Cowper's life and career is contained in the following sources published by the Gale Group: *British Writers,* **Vol. 3;** *Dictionary of Literary Biography,* **Vols. 104, 109;** *DISCovering Authors Modules: Poets; DISCovering Authors 3.0; Literature Resource Center; Nineteenth-Century Literature Criticism,* **Vols. 8, 94; and** *Reference Guide to English Literature.*

James Dickey
1923-1997

(Full name James Lafayette Dickey) American poet, novelist, critic, essayist, scriptwriter, and author of children's books.

INTRODUCTION

A prominent figure in late twentieth-century American literature, Dickey is noted for his intense exploration of primal, irrational, and creative forces in poetry and prose. Often classified as a visionary neo-romantic in the tradition of Walt Whitman, Dylan Thomas, and Theodore Roethke, Dickey emphasized the primacy of imagination and examined the relationship between humanity and nature. He frequently described the confrontations of war, sports, and the natural world as a means of probing such issues as violence, mortality, artistic inspiration, and social values. In his poetry, Dickey rejected formalism, artifice, and confession, favoring instead a narrative mode featuring energetic rhythms and charged emotions. In addition to his verse, Dickey authored the acclaimed novel *Deliverance* (1970), a symbolic work that portrays extremes of human behavior outside the confines of contemporary civilization.

BIOGRAPHICAL INFORMATION

Dickey was born in Buckhead, Georgia, to Eugene Dickey, a lawyer, and Maibelle Swift Dickey, and was their second son, conceived after his older sibling, Eugene Jr., died of meningitis. Dickey attended North Fulton High School in Georgia, where he was a devoted member of the track and football teams. He later entered Clemson College in 1941, but enlisted in the U.S. Army Air Corps the following year, subsequently serving as a radar officer in the Pacific during World War II. (Biographers also note that during his lifetime Dickey maintained he was a U.S. fighter pilot who flew approximately 100 combat missions over Japan and Korea; however, these claims are unsubstantiated and likely false.) Returning to the United States after Japan's defeat, Dickey attended Vanderbilt University, graduating in 1949 with a B.A. and in 1950 with an M.A. in English. After teaching English at the Rice Institute in Houston, Texas, for only four months, Dickey was recalled to active duty by the U.S. Air Force during the Korean War. He returned to Rice for the period between 1952 to 1954 and later became an instructor at the University of Florida in Gainesville. Meanwhile, Dickey had begun compiling notes for his novel *Alnilam* (not completed and published until 1987) and continued writing and publishing poetry. The recipient of a Sewanee Review Fellowship in 1954,

Dickey moved to Europe to focus on poetic composition. Having returned to the United States by 1955, he entered the advertising industry as a copywriter located first in New York City and later in Atlanta, Georgia. The well-received publication of his first collection of poetry, *Into the Stone and Other Poems* in 1960 marked the beginning of a period of dramatic growth in Dickey's literary career, which would shortly make him one of the most recognized writers on the American scene. A 1961–62 Guggenheim Fellowship took him to Positano, Italy, where he wrote the collection *Drowning With Others* (1962). As a poet in residence at a succession of colleges and universities during the 1960s, Dickey continued to produce esteemed volumes of poetry, including *Buckdancer's Choice* (1965). He later settled into a teaching position at the University of South Carolina in Columbia in 1969, which he maintained for the rest of his life. Dickey achieved national prominence in 1970 as the author of the novel *Deliverance* (he also wrote the script for the popular 1972 film adaptation and enacted a small part). While he continued to produce poetry, Dickey kept a high public profile through the 1970s and devoted more of his time to fiction, television and film scripts, literary criticism, journals, and children's books. Still, he considered himself foremost a poet, significantly reading his piece "The Strength of Fields" at President Jimmy Carter's 1977 inauguration. The 1980s and 1990s witnessed the publication of several more volumes of his verse, two novels, and some additions to his substantial body of critical writing. Dickey died January 19, 1997, of complications related to lung disease.

MAJOR WORKS

Throughout his writing career, Dickey drew upon crucial events in his life for subject matter, turning a tendency toward intense personal introspection into source material for his poetry and fiction. Notably, his early verse—featured in the three collections *Into the Stone and Other Poems, Drowning With Others,* and *Helmets* (1964)—draws on his feelings of guilt for his role in World War II and the Korean War, ruminations on his older brother's death, and reflections upon his Southern heritage. In these volumes, Dickey explores such topics as family, love, war, death, spiritual rebirth, nature, and survival—a range of themes that reappear in his subsequent body of work. Stylistically, Dickey's early verse relies upon traditional stanzaic units and generally manifests his expansive and affirmatory tone, even as it frequently depicts tragic or near-tragic circumstances. Additionally, these volumes contain several poems concerned with the wilderness in which Dickey stresses the importance of maintaining the primal physical and imaginative powers that he believed are suppressed by civilization. Dickey's next poetic collection, *Buckdancer's Choice,* signaled a shift toward more open and complex verse forms. Featuring internal monologues, varied spacing between words and phrases in place of punctuation, and subtle rhythms, *Buckdancer's Choice* probes human suffering in its myriad forms. A representative work from the collection, and one of his most-studied and controversial poems, "The Firebombing" demonstrates Dickey's ambivalence toward violence as it juxtaposes the thoughts of a fighter pilot as he flies over Japan and his memories twenty years later. In his poetry of the 1970s, Dickey began to employ what he termed "country surrealism," a technique by which he obscures distinctions between dreams and reality to accommodate the irrational. Throughout his later poetry, Dickey laments the loss of youth, expresses a profound fear of mortality, and explores visionary qualities and creative energies. For example, "The Eye-Beaters," published in *The Eye-Beaters, Blood, Victory, Madness, Buckhead and Mercy* (1970), concerns blindness, artistic vision, and the pursuit of truth. A thorough reworking of a poem by the Dutch writer Hendrik Marsman, *The Zodiac* (1976), is a long, self-referential piece about an intensely visionary alcoholic poet and his tormented process of artistic creation. In the title poem of *The Strength of Fields* (1979), Dickey affirms his faith in humanity while addressing various moral dilemmas. *Puella*

(1982) blends myth and reality to portray the imagined maturation of Dickey's young wife, Deborah, from adolescence to adulthood. A final collection of original verse, *The Eagle's Mile* (1990), reaffirms Dickey's exploration of imaginative vistas and symbolically evokes the liberating powers of flight. Among Dickey's fictional works, the novel *Deliverance* reiterates several themes prevalent in his poetry, primarily the rejuvenation of human life through interaction with nature. The work focuses on four suburban men who seek diversion from their unfulfilling lives by canoeing down a remote and dangerous river. The characters encounter human violence and natural threats, forcing them to rely on primordial instincts in order to survive. In his second novel, *Alnilam* (1987), an ambitious experimental work centering on a blind man's attempts to uncover the mysterious circumstances of his son's death, Dickey denounces corruption and abuse of power. A third novel, *To The White Sea* (1993), recounts in vivid detail a downed American airman's trek from Tokyo through Japan's northern wilderness during World War II. In addition to such works of fiction, Dickey was an esteemed poetry critic and produced several volumes of essays and journals, including *The Suspect in Poetry* (1964), *Babel to Byzantium: Poets and Poetry Now* (1968), and *Sorties: Journals and New Essays* (1971), in which he offers subjective viewpoints on poetry and asserts his preference for artistic intensity and intuition.

CRITICAL RECEPTION

While many of Dickey's individual poems had begun to appear in literary journals during the late 1940 and 1950s, the publication of *Into the Stone and Other Poems* in 1960 launched his swift rise to national literary prominence. The honoring of *Buckdancer's Choice* with a National Book Award for poetry in 1966 solidified Dickey's reputation as premier American poet. Indeed, *Poems 1957-1967* (1967), which encapsulates the earliest phase of Dickey's poetic output, was well-received upon its appearance and, according to many, continues to be representative of his strongest work in verse. While the significance of *The Eye-Beaters, Blood, Victory, Madness, Buckhead and Mercy* was outshined by the dramatic success of Dickey's novel *Deliverance* of the same year, commentators continue to value the collection for the complex and impassioned poetic expressions it contains. Dickey's twelve-part poem *The Zodiac,* however, elicited largely negative responses, and some have suggested that it indicates a general decline in the quality of his poetic efforts as the author concentrated his creative energies elsewhere. The lyrical reflections of Dickey's subsequent volume, *Puella,* while more favorably received than the poetry of *The Zodiac,* perplexed some critics by its dramatic departure in subject and style from the poet's earlier verse. And, although Dickey himself excised many of these poems from his retrospective volume *The Whole Motion: Collected Poems, 1945-1992* (1992), the work has attracted the interest of critics for the insights it gives into Dickey's view and representation of women. A final offering of original poetic material, *The Eagle's Mile* made a relatively smaller impression on critics, though a few have since maintained that it includes some of his most visionary and creative verse. The release of *The Whole Motion* and the posthumously published *James Dickey: The Selected Poems* in 1998 presented commentators with the opportunity to reflect on Dickey's considerable literary talents and accomplishments, as well as his engaging poetic voice, one of the most noteworthy and distinct in contemporary American literature.

PRINCIPAL WORKS

Poetry

Into the Stone and Other Poems 1960
Drowning With Others 1962
Helmets 1964
Two Poems of the Air 1964
Buckdancer's Choice 1965
Poems 1957-1967 1967
The Eye-Beaters, Blood, Victory, Madness, Buckhead and Mercy 1970
The Zodiac [based on Hendrik Marsman's poem of the same title] 1976
Tucky the Hunter [illustrations by Marie Angel] (children's poetry) 1978
Veteran Birth: The Gadfly Poems 1947-1949 1978
The Strength of Fields 1979
Scion 1980
The Early Motion 1981
Falling, May Day Sermon, and Other Poems 1981
Puella 1982
The Central Motion: Poems, 1968-1979 1983
Bronwen, the Traw, and the Shape-Shifter [illustrations by Richard Jesse Watson] (children's poetry) 1986
The Eagle's Mile 1990
The Whole Motion: Collected Poems, 1945-1992 1992
James Dickey: The Selected Poems 1998

Other Major Works

The Suspect in Poetry (criticism) 1964
Babel to Byzantium: Poets and Poetry Now (criticism) 1968
Deliverance (novel) 1970
Self-Interviews (conversations) 1970
Sorties: Journals and New Essays (essays) 1971
Night Hurdling: Poems, Essays, Conversations, Commencements, and Afterwords (poetry and prose) 1983
Alnilam (novel) 1987
To the White Sea (novel) 1993
Striking In: The Early Notebooks of James Dickey (notebooks) 1996

CRITICISM

Howard Nemerov (review date 1963)

SOURCE: Nemerov, Howard. "Poems of Darkness and a Specialized Light." *Sewanee Review* 71, no. 1 (winter 1963): 99-104.

[*In the following review of* Drowning With Others, *Nemerov offers an impressionistic, then critical, assessment of Dickey's second volume of poetry.*]

Coming to know an unfamiliar poetry is an odd and not so simple experience. Reviewing it—conducting one's education in public, as usual—helps, by concentrating the attention; perhaps, though it is a gloomy thought, we understand nothing, respond to nothing, until we are forced to return it actively in teaching or writing. It is so fatally easy to have opinions, and if we stop here we never reach the more problematic, hence more interesting, point of examining our sensations in the presence of the new object.

The following notes have to do with coming to know, with the parallel development of sympathy and knowledge. Undoubtedly they raise more questions than they can answer; and they may strike the reader not only as tentative but as fumbling and disorganized also, for the intention is to record not only what happened but something as well of how such things happen.

The situation of reviewing is a special case, narrower than merely reading, and nastier, certainly at first, where one's response is automatically that of a jealous cruelty. Hmm, one says, and again, Hmm. The meaning of that is: How dare anyone else have a vision! One picks out odds and ends, with the object of making remarks that will guarantee one is A Critic. Little hairs rise on the back of the neck. One is nothing if not critical. For instance:

> I spooned out light
> Upon a candle thread . . .

Triumphant sneer. Surely this is too ingenious by far? Has he no self-control?

But already I have suspicions of my behavior. I am afraid that a great deal of literary criticism amounts to saying that mobled queen is good, or bad.

Despite myself, I observe that I quite like Mr. Dickey's characteristic way of going: a line usually of three beats, the unaccented syllables not reckoned, or not very closely reckoned; it offers an order definite but not rigidly coercive, allowing an easy flexibility and variation. Although the line so measured will tend to the anapest often, it doesn't lollop along as that measure usually does, maybe because the poet is shrewd enough not to insist on it by riming:

The beast in the water, in love
With the palest and gentlest of children,
Whom the years have turned deadly with knowledge
. . .

All the same—give a little, take a little—an indulgence in riming makes hash of this procedure. Mr. Dickey once indulges, in (mostly) couplets:

With the sun on their faces through sand
And the polyps a-building the land . . .

And so on. Awful. Enough about that.

2.

At a second stage, perhaps a trifle less superficial, I find myself thinking how very strange is the poetry of meditation musing on inwardness, where the images of the world are spells whose repetition designs to invoke—sometimes, alas, only in the poet—a state of extraordinary perceptions, of dreaming lucidities sometimes too relaxed. This poetry has not much to do with the clean-cut, muscular, metaphysical way of coming to conclusions; probably in English Wordsworth is the inventor of those landscapes most closely corresponding to certain withdrawn states of the mind, reveries, day-dreams—the style that Keats, with a sarcasm in which there seems all the same a proper respect, calls the Wordsworthian, or Egotistical Sublime.

One of the qualities of such a poetry—or of Mr. Dickey's poetry, to come off the high horse—is a slight over-insistence on the mysteriousness of everything, especially itself:

A *perfect, irrelevant* music
In which we *profoundly* moved,
I in the *innermost* shining
Of my blazing, *invented* eyes,
And he in the *total* of dark. . . .

This is the language of a willed mysticism, and it is hard to see any of the words I have underlined as performing a more than atmospheric function—the poet wants the experience to be like profound, perfect, innermost, etc., and incants accordingly.

Another quality, which I take to be related also to the tonal intention of a grave continuousness, is the often proceeding by participles, as though nothing in the world of the poem ever quite happened but just went on happening, e.g. (from the same poem):

With my claws growing deep into wood
And my sight going slowly out
Inch by inch, as into a stone,
Disclosing the rabbits running
Beneath my bent, growing throne,
And the foxes lighting their hair,
And the serpent taking the shape
Of the stream of life as it slept.

The objections of this stage have a perfectly reasonable air of being right: you describe a characteristic, and present evidence to show that this characteristic *is* in the poetry.

Surely this is How To Do Literary Criticism? All the same, I am still suspicious, and even beginning to get annoyed, because by this time, in order to say what I have said, I have had to read many of the poems a number of times, and have realized that I care for some of them a good deal. In particular, **"The Owl King,"** from which I have quoted the two passages, looks to me like a moving and thoroughly accomplished performance. Even more in particular, the two passages themselves, when read in their places, look appropriate to what is going forward. I have a residual feeling of being cantankerously right in my objection to the first passage quoted, but would incline to say now that the passage is a weak place in the poet's process, but not destructive of the poem.

3.

There does come a further stage, where one begins to understand something of the poet's individuality and what it decrees for him in the way of necessities, his own way of putting together the bones and oceans of this world.

Mr. Dickey's materials have a noble simplicity, a constancy extending through many poems. Merely to catalogue them is no use; to project in a single relation their somewhat delicate developments is perhaps impossible, but I shall have to make some more or less compromised try at it.

My impression of the process of his poetry is that it runs something like this: water—stone—the life of animals—of children—of the hunter, who is also the poet. It is rarely or never so simple as this, yet the intention seems often enough this, a feeling one's way down the chain of being, a becoming the voice which shall make dumb things respond, sometimes to their hurt or death; a sensing of alien modes of experience, mostly in darkness or in an unfamiliar light; reason accepting its animality; a poetry whose transcendences come of its reconciliations. Salvation is this: apprehending the continuousness of forms, the flowing of one energy through everything. There is one other persistently dramatized relation, that of the child to his father; and one that is more autobiographical, that of the poet to a brother who died before he was born. And now to particularize this matter.

These are poems of darkness, darkness and a specialized light. Practically everything in them happens at night, by moonlight, starlight, firelight; or else in other conditions that will make ordinary daytime perception impossible: underwater, in thick fog, in a dream—I note especially a dream of being in a suit of armor—, inside a tent, in a salt marsh where because of the height of the grass you "no longer know where you are."

Another term for this situation is blindness: the blind child whose totem, or Other, is the owl king who cannot see by day but for whom, at night, "the still wood glowed like a brain." In another poem the owl's gaze "most slowly begins to create / Its sight from the death of the sun." For this power of creation from within, and for being a hunter, the owl is the magician-poet of an intellectual and "holy" song; in **"The Owl King"** it is he who for the lost, blind child incarnates the mighty powers of sight, growth, belief, resulting in reconciliation and understanding:

> Far off, the owl king
> Sings like my father, growing
> In power. Father, I touch
> Your face. I have not seen
> My own, but it is yours.
> I come, I advance,
> I believe everything, I am here.

The power of poetry, which is to perceive all the facts of the world as relation, belongs in these poems equally to both parties: to the hunter and his victim; to the child and the father he is trying to become; to the father and the child he was, whom he has lost and is trying to find again. The paradoxical continuousness of all disparate forms one with another, in this generated world, is what Mr. Dickey's poems concentrate on representing, often by the traditional lore of the four elements, as in **"Facing Africa,"** where the speaker and his son look out over the ocean from stone jetties (hence "the buttressed water"), where:

> The harbor mouth opens
> Much as you might believe
> A human mouth would open
> To say that all things are a darkness.

Thence they look toward an Africa imagined to "bloom," to be "like a lamp" glowing with flashes "like glimpses of lightning," giving off through the darkness "a green and glowing light." In the crisis of the poem this serial relation of the elements is fused in the imagined perception of the other continent, the alien life:

> What life have we entered by this?
> Here, where our bodies are,
> With a green and gold light on his face,
> My staring child's hand is in mine,
> And in the stone
> Fear like a dancing of peoples.

Perhaps it is central to Mr. Dickey's vision that stone and water are one, the reflected form of one another.

Possible to continue for a long time describing these complex articulations of simple things. Very little use, though, to a reader who has not the poems to hand. Besides, it must be about time for someone to ask, Well, is it great poetry or isn't it? and someone else to ask, What about objective, universal standards for judging poetry?

About all that I shall say to the reader: If you believe you care for poetry you should read these poems with a deep attention. They may not work for you, probably they cannot work for you in just the way that they do for me, but I quite fail to see how you are going to find out by listening to me.

Probably the reviewer's job goes no further than that. Not to be thought of as malingering, though, I shall make a couple of other remarks.

I have attended to Mr. Dickey's poems, and they have brought me round from the normal resentment of any new experience, through a stage of high-literary snippishness with all its fiddle about "technique," to a condition of sympathetic interest and, largely, assent. There are some brilliant accomplishments here: among them, apart from the ones I have partly described, **"Armor," "The Life-guard," "The Summons."** There are also some that sound dead, or (what is effectively the same thing) that I do not much respond to, including some that I don't understand. Where his poems fail for me, it is most often because he rises, reconciles, transcends, a touch too easily, so that his conclusions fail of being altogether decisive; that near irresistibly beautiful gesture, "I believe everything, I am here," may represent a species of resolution that comes to his aid more often than it should. Perhaps he is so much at home among the figures I sort out with such difficulty that he now and then assumes the effect is made when it isn't, quite.

There is this major virtue in Mr. Dickey's poetry, that it responds to attention; the trying to understand does actually produce harmonious resonances from the poems; it seems as though his voyage of exploration is actually going somewhere not yet filled with tourists: may he prosper on the way.

Laurence Lieberman (review date 1967)

SOURCE: Lieberman, Laurence. "James Dickey: The Worldly Mystic." In *Beyond the Muse of Memory: Essays on Contemporary American Poets,* pp. 73-82. Columbia: University of Missouri Press, 1995.

[*In the following review of Dickey's* Poems: 1957-1967, *originally published in 1967, Lieberman remarks on Dickey's poetic vision and its mixture of the comic and the serious.*]

The persona in James Dickey's new poems, those that appear in the final section, "Falling," of his book ***Poems: 1957-1967,*** is a unique human personality. He is a worldly mystic. On the one hand, a joyous, expansive personality—all candor, laughter, and charm—in love with his fully conscious gestures, the grace and surety of moves of his body. An outgoing man. An extrovert. On the other hand, a chosen man. A man who has been picked by some mysterious, intelligent agent in the universe to act out a secret destiny:

> . . . something was given a life-
> mission to say to me hungrily over
>
> And over and over *your moves are exactly right*
> *For a few things in this world: we know you*
> *When you come, Green Eyes, Green Eyes.*
>
> from **"Encounter in the Cage Country"**

How does a man reconnect with common, unchosen humanity when he has just returned from the abyss of nonhuman, chosen otherness? That is the chief problem to which the final volume addresses itself. How to be a man who feels perfectly at home, and at his ease, in both worlds—inner and outer. A man who can make of himself and his art a medium, a perfect conductor, through which the opposed worlds—both charged with intensity—can meet and connect, flow into each other. The worldly mystic. It is the vision of a man who for years has been just as committed to developing his potential for creative existence as for creative art. All discoveries and earnings, spiritual or worldly, must carry over from one universe to the other.

In the best poems of the previous volume, *Buckdancer's Choice,* the self is frustrated, paralyzed, helplessly unable to establish liberating connections with the world. The chief obstacle to self-liberation is a sense of moral guilt. In **"The Firebombing," "The Fiend,"** and **"Slave Quarters,"** the self is pitilessly subjected to encounters with life that induce feelings of criminality. Clearly, the writer has deliberately trapped the persona in predicaments of contemporary American life that automatically create an aura of grave moral jeopardy. In all three poems, the conflict between the worldly-mindedness of modern life and the inner life of the spirit is dramatized. Materialism of a kind that blocks the persona in its struggle to connect with the world is embodied in the indulgences of suburban middle-class home life of **"The Firebombing"**; in the businesslike exterior of **"The Fiend,"** his guise of normalcy and ordinariness; and in the catalog of inferior occupational stereotypes, earmarked for African Americans by our society, in **"Slave Quarters."**

Wherever being is trapped in oneself or in others, the existential self must work, either through art or directly in life, to make lifesaving connections—all those connections that create the free interchange of spirit between being and being. The word *connect* is the central one in Dickey's new poetry. His spirit must connect with the world, with "all worlds the growing encounters." In the best poems, all the connections are good. "I am a man who turns on," and when he turns on, all worlds he connects with turn on, since wherever he connects, he creates personal intimacy, injects intensity: "People are calling each other weeping with a hundred thousand / Volts."

The one poem that perfectly reconciles the contradictions between worldliness and the inner life of the spirit is **"Power and Light."** The happiness of power and light heals all broken connections, "even the one / With my wife." For the artist, the hardest connections to "turn good" may be the home connections, the ones thorny with daily ritual and sameness: "Thorns! Thorns! I am bursting / Into the kitchen, into the sad way station / Of my home. . . ." But if the connections are good, all worlds flow into each other, the good healing, cleansing the bad. There is woe in the worldly side of marriage, but it is good in its spiritual and sexual dimensions, in the "deep sway of underground."

"Power and Light" dramatizes the secret life of a pole climber, a technician who works for the power company.

Through the disguise of the persona, Dickey explores symbolically the ideal relationship between the artist and his audience, the poet and his readers:

> . . . I feel the wires running
> Like the life-force along the limed rafters   and all
>   connections
> With poles   with the tarred naked belly-buckled black
> Trees I hook to my heels   with the shrill phone calls
>   leaping
> Long distance   long distances through my hands   all
>   connections
>
> Even the one
> With my wife, turn good . . . Never think I don't
>   know my profession
> Will lift me: why, all over hell the lights burn in your
>   eyes,
> People are calling each other   weeping with a
>   hundred thousand
> Volts   making deals   pleading   laughing like fate,
> Far off, invulnerable   or with the right word pierced
> To the heart
> By wires I held, shooting off their ghosty mouths,
> In my gloves.

The pole climber's spirit raises the spirits of the dead and damned from Hell—marriage, too, being a kind of hell. The "ghostly mouths" of the spirits can all reconnect through the power lines—lines of the poem—and save themselves. The poet is blessed with such an access, a surplus, of lifesaving joy, that he can afford to let it—the flood of power and light—overflow into the grave, into Hell. He doesn't so much give life to the damned as open them up to hidden resources of life, newly accessible in themselves, by making connections. "Long distance," an eerie experience to begin with, becomes more haunting still when Dickey extends it to include connections between living and dead spirits.

Dickey proceeds in his vision to a point "far under the grass of my grave." No matter how deep he travels, even to Hell, in the fuller mastery of his art he is confident that "my profession / Will lift me," and in lifting him, it will lift thousands of others from Hell, his readers all over the world, symbolically making long-distance phone calls all night, connecting, all the connections good. He feels the same power, whether in the basement of his home, "or flung up on towers walking / Over mountains my charged hair standing on end." The spirit that pervades and dominates this poem, finally, can be identified as the spirit of laughter, a laughter closely akin to that of Malachi the stilt jack in Yeats's "High Talk," or the mad dancer of "A Drunken Man's Praise of Sobriety." Like these poems, **"Power and Light"** verges on self-parody in its hyperbolic imagery and rhetoric: "And I laugh / Like my own fate watching over me night and day."

The comic spirit of **"Power and Light"** recovers the ground lost by the tragic spirit in the moral dilemmas of **"The Firebombing"** and **"Slave Quarters."** If modern man feels helpless before the massive political nightmare of his time, he finds he can retreat into "pure fires of the Self" for spiritual sustenance. This is the artist's escape and salvation. If he can't connect with the tragic people of this world's hell in daylight, by direct political action, he must reach them in "the dark, / deep sway of underground." The artist's night is the "night before Resurrection Day." He will resurrect the imagination, the spiritual life, of his age. He performs these wonders, ironically, drunk in his suburban basement. A general in disguise. An unacknowledged legislator of the world. Regrettably, the philosophy *if I turn on everyone turns on with me* may offer small comfort in the political world.

If the worldly mystic spends a good portion of his day-to-day existence reconnecting with the world, at other times we find him searching for the pure moment in solitude, waiting to receive messages from the unseen beyond and to answer the call. If he is receptive enough, he may pick up clues to learning his being from a wide range of sources: a rattlesnake, a blind old woman, a caged leopard. In all such poems Dickey himself would seem to be the protagonist, the poem being a kind of reportage of an event from the author's life, in contrast with poems such as **"Power and Light"** and **"Falling,"** in which the persona and the author are completely separate, on the surface level.

"The Flash" is a weak poem, hardly more than a fragment of verse, but it gives the key to understanding the revelatory moments in the other poems in the group:

> Something far off   buried deep and free
> In the country   can always strike you dead
> Center of the brain. There is never anything
> It could be   but you go dazzled . . .

You can't explain the flash logically, or fasten hold of it with your senses, but what is felt when "you go dazzled" is instantly recognizable, and can be distinguished, unerringly, from other events of the spirit. The flash is a spiritual fact that registers in the poet's intelligence with the same cold, tough certainty as a snakebite. It is a guarantee of the inner life, but also insists on the inner life of the Other, of others "far off buried deep and free."

In **"Snakebite,"** the encounter with the Other seems fated. "The one chosen" finds "there is no way not / To be me." There is no way out, or through the experience, except saving oneself:

> . . . It is the role
> I have been cast in;
>
> It calls for blood.
>
> Act it out before the wind
> Blows: unspilt blood
>
> Will kill you. Open
> The new-footed tingling. Cut.
> Cut deep, as a brother would.
> Cut to save it. Me.

One must act out the roles that are thrust upon one by the Other, inescapably, as by the rattlesnake's poison. Art must invade those moments in life when failure to perform the correct self-saving gesture is to die. Art is a strange kind of intimacy, a blood brotherhood, between the artist and himself. The poem must be an act of bloodletting. In saving the poem, as in saving one's life from snakebite, a man must be his own brother. No one else can help.

Midway through the action, the speaker shifts from the mortal necessity of lancing the wound to a moment of comic staging. At this point in Dickey's art, it seems appropriate and convincing for the comic spirit to interrupt the most serious human act of self-preservation. The laughter of self-dramatization parallels similar moments in **"Encounter in the Cage Country,"** in which comic relief enhances the seriousness of the exchange between man and leopard:

> . . . at one brilliant move
>
> I made as though drawing a gun from my hip-
> bone, the bite-sized children broke
> Up   changing their concept of laughter,
>
> But none of this changed his eyes, or changed
> My green glasses. Alert, attentive,
> He waited for what I could give him;
> My moves   my throat my wildest love,
> The eyes behind my eyes.

In **"False Youth II,"** the blind grandmother's message, like the word of an oracle, is delivered with absolute certitude: "You must laugh a lot / Or be in the sun." Her advice strikes a reader as being a deeply personal and literal truth in the author's life at the time he wrote the poem, and this hunch is borne out by the relevance her words have to many of the best poems of the new volume. A comic spirit pervades poems such as **"Power and Light," "Encounter in the Cage Country,"** and **"Sun"** that one had not met or foreseen in Dickey's earlier work.

Dickey presents an experience from life in **"False Youth II"** that taught him to see deeply into the shifting sands of his own personality as he slid, imperceptibly, from youth into middle age. Youth is a "lifetime search" for the human role, or roles, that, when acted out, will serve as a spiritual passport of entry into middle age. The necessary role may take the form of a physical gesture that perfectly corresponds to deep moves of the spirit: "My face froze . . . in a smile / That has never left me since my thirty-eighth year."

The old blind woman unknowingly assumes the role of a fortuneteller. She has developed a superhumanly receptive sense of touch. Her life is contracted intensely into her hands, her fingertips having grown fantastically sensitive and alive. As she runs her fingers over his eyes and forehead, the poetic images envision a scientific and quasi-scientific composite of data linking electromagnetism, finger painting, astronomy, genetics, and fortune-telling:

. . . I closed my eyes as she put her fingertips lightly
On them   and saw, behind sight   something in me-
    fire
Swirl in a great shape like a fingerprint   like none
    other
In the history of the earth   looping   holding its wild
    lines
Of human force. Her forefinger   then her keen nail
Went all the way along the deep middle line of my
    brow
Not guessing but knowing   quivering   deepening
Whatever I showed by it.

The wisdom of the old woman has a primeval quality about it. Her acutely sharpened instincts and sense of touch precede the scientific age and surpass recorded modern science in a revelation of human personality that draws on the learning of many sciences, but goes beyond each in its ability to *connect* them all, which is not to say this literally happens in life. It happens, rather, in the images of the poem's vision.

She leads him to discover that he has come to a crossroads in his life and art. He must learn his life, as his art, and each stage of existence—in both worlds—concludes with a search for the blueprint to the next stage. The blueprint cannot simply be willed into existence. It is contained as a deeply true, hidden map of possibility within his developing self. If there are alternative paths latent and waiting to be journeyed in the self at any particular spiritual crossroads (as in Frost's poem "The Road Not Taken"), there is one best route available at each crucial juncture. It is discoverable, and, once discovered, it has an unmistakable ring of truth: "Not guessing but knowing quivering deepening." Although the answer waits inside him to be released, he cannot find his way to it by himself. He arrives in himself through a deep conjunction with another being, in faith, "some kind of song may have passed / Between our closed mouths as I headed into the ice." There must be communion with the Other. Connection.

If one of the major new themes in Dickey's fifth volume is comic dramatization of his own personality, another is sexual realism. In both, he parallels the later Yeats. If we compare the vision in **"The Fiend"** with that in **"Falling"** and **"The Sheep Child,"** we can get an idea of how far Dickey's art has traveled between the first major poem dealing with the theme of sexual realism and the last. In **"The Fiend,"** the free-flowing form and the split line are fully exploited. This technique is well suited to sustained psychological realism. Also, the fiend is a thoroughly convincing persona. The encounter between him and life experience, though voyeuristic and "abnormal," is presented as final, incisive, fulfilling.

But somehow, the center of the poem's vision is too far from tragedy and believable danger: the poem lacks risk, the emotional pitch of a cosmos of love/beauty stretching to contain and transform a brutal agony of being. The sexual transcendence the persona unknowingly achieves is almost too evident, preordained. Equipoise is not felt to be

the outcome of a fierce yoking together of oppositely charged beings, as in the act of coitus between the farm boy and the mother ewe of **"The Sheep Child"**:

    . . . *It was something like love*
From another world that seized her
From behind, and she gave, not lifting her head
Out of dew, without ever looking, her best
Self to that great need. . . .

The stench of evil in **"The Fiend"** is smothered under the catalogs of domestic inanities. There is no trace of the searing terror of **"The Sheep Child,"** the terror of our settled scheme of things being ripped apart. It is too easy to dismiss the fiend as a genial saint—spiritually, if not bodily, harmless. **"The Sheep Child"** and **"Falling"** threaten us with glimpses into a world of becoming that is grimly near to us, a mere hand's reach away from those extensions of being into the beyond that we all easily attain in moments of emotional intensity. And yet, that farther reach somehow eludes us, staying just out of our ken. The secret of uncompromised being is just a spiritual stone's throw away, but we are cut off. These poems soar into that further beyond with a sense of effortlessness and inevitability.

"The Fiend" was a breakthrough into the hinterland of sexual transcendence, but what begins as a reader's sympathetic identification ends as a comfortably removed appreciation of the poem's novelities. **"The Sheep Child"** and **"Falling"** trap the reader in a haunting, if inexpressible, certainty that a much larger, grander, demonic world—compounded of Heaven and Hell—lies just the other side of the limits of his known, calculable existence. And it waits, like the dead, for him to step inside:

    I woke, dying,

    In the summer sun of the hillside, with my eyes
    Far more than human. I saw for a blazing moment
    The great grassy world from both sides,
    Man and beast in the round of their need,
    And the hill wind stirred in my wool,
    My hoof and my hand clasped each other,
    I ate my one meal
    Of milk, and died
    Staring . . .

The reader must be willing to drown, fly, burn with a flame that sets all dreams on fire, and be the fire.

From **"The Fiend"** to **"Falling,"** Dickey has been trying to find a medium that would enable him to *use* the maximum of his creative intelligence in poetry. To this end, he has chosen in **"Falling"** exactly the right subject and form. Both are moving toward a rhythm of experience that can sweep away all obstacles to realizing the fullest human potential:

    "One cannot just fall   just tumble screaming all that
        time   one must use / It."

When a woman's life space has suddenly contracted into a few seconds, the necessity to conquer mental waste, to salvage every hidden but discoverable shred of mental possibility, becomes absolute.

The opening sections of the poem stress the extent to which the girl's will, intention, participates in her experience. Her body and mind are both forced initially into reactions of powerful self-protective resistance, a mere reflex response to shock. But her will and creative imagination take on a larger and larger quotient of control. The female style of control is mixed with passivity, but the dynamic passivity of girding the body, sensually, as she "waits for something great to take / Control of her." The beauty of healthy, fulfilled physical life is Dickey's momentary stay against the chaos of the poem's life-crushing void. Within a moment of perfectly fulfilled physical being, her spirit lives an eternity.

The girl is strangely mated to air. The first half of her long, erotic air embrace is a turning inward. She is learning how to be, to be "in her / Self." She masters "one after another of all the positions for love / Making," and each position corresponds to a new tone or motion of being. The second half of her adventure is a going outward. She is no longer waiting to be taken hold of, but now *she* is the aggressor, who "must take up her body / And fly." The shifts in her body cycle—falling, floating, flying, falling—stand for consecutive stages in a being cycle, rising, as she falls to her death, to a pinnacle of total self-realization. It is a movement from extreme self-love to extreme beyond-self love, a movement from being to becoming, from becoming to going beyond. Although her fall concludes with an autoerotic orgasm, she connects, at the moment of climax, with the spirits of farm boys and girls below; there is a profound flow of being between them. This unobstructable river of feeling between the self and the world is the life process to which Dickey ascribes ultimacy in his vision.

If ideas of rebirth and reincarnation are among the most compelling and pervasive in Dickey's art, the idea of resurrection by air—not water, earth, or fire—is the one that rises, finally, into apocalypse. A cursory glance at Dickey's biography might well support my hypothesis that, since the gravest spiritual losses to his manhood were incurred in air—via the incineration of women and children in the napalm bombing of Japan—he could be expected to seek compensatory gains to redeem himself, paradoxically, through that medium. In fact, he does achieve his most sustaining spiritual and poetic gains through the vision of air genesis. It is my hope that in the years to come Dickey will return to the perplexing questions of war and race dealt with in **"The Firebombing"** and **"Slave Quarters,"** and bring to his renewed treatment of those themes—surely the most troubling specters of our day—the larger generosity of spirit we find in the vision of **"Falling"** and **"Power and Light."** If there is a passion today that can counterbalance all the hell in us, it is the ardor that fills these poems.

Ralph J. Mills Jr. (review date 1968)

SOURCE: Mills, Ralph J., Jr. Review of *Poems 1957-1967,* by James Dickey. *TriQuarterly,* no. 11 (winter 1968): 231-42.

[*In the following review, Mills explores Dickey's almost mystical poetic process and his characteristic themes—including the spiritual interpenetration of the living and the dead—but criticizes his lack of imagination in works like "The Firebombing," and observes a diminishing intensity in his later poems.*]

As various poets and critics have been remarking over the past few years, both the mood and the means of much of the important new American poetry has been noticeably changing. While it is difficult in the midst of such movement to predict with anything like accuracy the final course of contemporary poetry's drift and flow, there are certain characteristics which have become rather evident. In a recent essay, "Dead Horses and Live Issues," (*The Nation,* April 24, 1967), the poet Louis Simpson discusses some of them and also indicates the kind of poetry which is currently being rejected. "There is," he says, "an accelerating movement away from rationalistic verse toward poetry that releases the unconscious, the irrational, or, if your mind runs that way, magic. Surrealism was buried by the critics of the thirties and forties as somehow irrelevant; today it is one of the most commonly used techniques of verse." Simpson goes on to specify some of the likely influences to come into play under these circumstances and the dangers of particular sorts of Surrealism, especially the dogmatic irrationalism of André Breton. Then he adds, affirmatively: "Contrary to Breton, poetry represents not unreason but the total mind, including both reason and unreason . . . Poetic creation has been described by some poets—Wordsworth and Keats come to mind—as a heightened state of consciousness brought about, curiously, by an infusion of the unconscious . . . The images are connected in a dream; and the deeper the dream, the stronger, the more logical, are the connections."

If these excerpts from Simpson's essay will not do to describe all the tendencies apparent in American poetry at present (and they were not intended to do so), they have a genuine applicability to Simpson's own recent work, to the poetry of Robert Bly, James Wright, W. S. Merwin, Donald Hall, and James Dickey—though one must say at once that these poets differ distinctly from one another too. Open this new volume of Dickey's poems [*Poems 1957-1967*] (which gathers together the larger part of his four previous books and concludes with a book-length section of recent pieces) at any page and you find the artistic realization of Simpson's statement: a poetry which indeed seems composed of "images . . . connected in a dream." Night and sleep, dominated by moonlight (as in Wallace Stevens), moreover, take a prominent place in many of the poems, from **"Sleeping Out at Easter"** from *Into the Stone* (his first book) to **"The Birthday Dream"** from the new section entitled *Falling.* But even when he is not directly treating sleep Dickey has a power of imagination that fulfills itself in dreamlike effects. Take, for instance, the initial stanza of **"A Screened Porch in the Country."** The situation is so ordinary—a group of people sitting inside a lighted porch on a summer night, their enlarged, distended shadows cast outward onto the surrounding grass—and the imaginative rendering of its implications so extraordinary that the reader's habitual way of looking at things, as with Rilke's "Archaic Torso of Apollo," is profoundly shaken. Here, too, one must "change [his] life," or at least his conception of it:

> All of them are sitting
> Inside a lamp of coarse wire
> And being in all directions
> Shed upon darkness,
> Their bodies softening to shadow, until
> They come to rest out in the yard
> In a kind of blurred golden country
> In which they more deeply lie
> Than if they were being created
> Of Heavenly light.

Dickey's imaginative processes free the body of its earthly ties and permit it a kind of infinite capacity for extension. In the passage above a transformation occurs within the poet's vision which locates human bodies in an entirely different dimension; their shadows come to possess their spiritual being or constitute its reflection. The ingredients of the external occasion, as already noted, are commonplace, but Dickey's sudden intense visualization stuns us with the revelation of a hidden metaphysical or religious insight. For the poem proceeds to describe a species of metempsychosis—although, of course, no literal death is involved and the inhabitants of the screened porch are not even consciously aware of the curious spiritual transmigration in which they are participating with their shadow selves—that brings the "souls" of these people into communion with the world of small night creatures and insects who come only to the edge of "the golden shadow / Where the people are lying." The reader finally gets the haunting feeling of having shared deeply in the life of creation and so loosened the boundaries of the selfish ego. Here are the other three stanzas that complete the poem.

> Where they are floating beyond
> Themselves, in peace,
> Where they have laid down
> Their souls and not known it,
> The smallest creatures,
> As every night they do,
> Come to the edge of them
> And sing, if they can,
> Or, if they can't, simply shine
> Their eyes back, sitting on haunches,
>
> Pulsating and thinking of music.
> Occasionally, something weightless
> Touches the screen
> With its body, dies,
> Or is unmurmuringly hurt,
> But mainly nothing happens
> Except that a family continues

> To be laid down
> In the midst of its nightly creatures,
> Not one of which openly comes
>
> Into the golden shadow
> Where the people are lying,
> Emitted by their own house
> So humanly that they become
> More than human, and enter the place
> Of small, blindly singing things,
> Seeming to rejoice
> Perpetually, without effort,
> Without knowing why
> Or how they do it.

This poem provides merely one example—and that not so obvious as might be—of what H. L. Weatherby has called "the way of exchange" and Robert Bly terms "spiritual struggle" in Dickey's poems.[1] Most evident at first in his pieces about animals and hunting, where the poet almost miraculously divides his intuitive powers so as to depict his own inner state in the role of human perceiver or hunter and the sensations of the animal who knows he is pursued, the notion of exchange has far-reaching effects, which include an interpenetration of the worlds of the living and the dead in such poems as **"In the Tree House at Night," "The Owl King," "Hunting Civil War Relics at Nimblewill Creek," "Drinking from a Helmet," "Reincarnation (I),"** and **"Sled Burial, Dream Ceremony."** It also, more generally, encompasses the imaginative devices of bodily and spiritual extension, metamorphosis, and metempsychosis of which I have spoken. All of these characteristics, and in addition a preoccupation (strong in his first three books and still present in more recent work) with ritual and archetypal modes of experience, confirm Dickey as a poet who possesses an imagination of a primitive, magical type. Obviously, he is at the same time a modern man of considerable sophistication; but the fact that he hunts with bow and arrow and that he has been a decorated fighter pilot in both World War II and the Korean War indicates something of the broad spectrum of his experience.

The themes of Dickey's best poetry, however, have a timeless aura about them; and while contemporary material and various objects of modern technology necessarily appear in places in his writing, they are simply appropriated and subordinated to the larger concerns at hand. (At any rate, this seems a fair account until we come to some of the poems from *Buckdancer's Choice*—**"The Firebombing,"** for example.) Thus in **"Hunting Civil War Relics at Nimblewill Creek"** the poet and his brother, who has a mine detector to locate buried metal, "mess tin or bullet," find that this mechanical instrument becomes the means for entering into a state of near-mystical communion with the soldiers who died on this battle ground. As his brother listens through the ear-phones of the detector, Dickey sees his face transformed by a new awareness, strange and awesome, of the way of communication he has unwittingly opened up with the past and the dead; and the brother's expression, in turn, communicates that awareness in all its uncanny force to the poet until he, too, has been captured by the same experience:

> We climb the bank;
> A faint light glows
> On my brother's mouth.
> I listen, as two birds fight
> For a single voice, but he
> Must be hearing the grave,
> In pieces, all singing
> To his clamped head,
> For he smiles as if
> He rose from the dead within
> Green Nimblewill
> And stood in his grandson's shape.

Here we are close to the idea of exchange between the dead and the living or a transmigration of souls, though it is viewed in this instance not as a literal fact but an unforgettable moment of perception among the living—the poet and his brother. The end of the poem finds Dickey arrived at the threshold of a profoundly moving recovery of his (and our) human ancestry:

> I choke the handle
> Of the pick, and fall to my knees
> To dig wherever he points,
> To bring up mess tin or bullet,
> To go underground
> Still singing, myself,
> Without a sound,
> Like a man who renounces war,
> Or one who shall lift up the past,
> Not breathing "Father,"
> At Nimblewill,
> But saying, "Fathers! Fathers!"

The details of this passage are enormously evocative. His kneeling posture and his careful excavation of relics imply a reverential attitude towards the dead, who are resurrected, as it were, in the poet's inwardness, in feeling and imagination, to enlarge his own humanity so that it knows no limits but flows outward to merge with the being of every creature and thing, and, beyond them, to touch at times the realm of the supernatural. The act of digging, as the stanza discloses, takes on the aspect of a descent into the kingdom of the dead, and the poet returns with his new knowledge upon him: the revelation which becomes his poem. In his well-known study *The Poetic Image* C. Day Lewis notes that a whole poem may be an image composed of smaller contributing images; and of that larger image he offers a general definition which is surely applicable to the poem we have been discussing and also to a fundamental impulse running through Dickey's finest pieces. "The poetic image," he remarks, "is the human mind claiming kinship with everything that lives or has lived, and making good its claim."

A little further on, to stay with Day Lewis, he says that the poet is "in the world . . . to bear witness to the principle of love, since love is as good a word as any for that hu-

man reaching-out of hands towards the warmth in all things, which is the source and passion of his song." Plainly enough, this statement elaborates what its author said about the poetic image, only in this instance he looks behind the work for its underlying (whether conscious or not) intention. James Dickey's poems are truly remarkable in just this respect. **"The Owl King,"** which is too long for discussion here, can be read as a mythic poem of initiation and exchange between human life and the rest of creation basic to Dickey's imaginative sympathies. In **"The Salt Marsh"** and **"Inside the River"** the poet submits himself to two different experiences in which his own being is altered by elements of the natural world. The concluding lines of **"Inside the River"** have again the ritual symbolic significance we grow familiar with in Dickey's work:

> Move with the world
> As the deep dead move,
> Opposed to nothing.
> Release. Enter the sea
> Like a winding wind.
> No. Rise. Draw breath.
> Sing. See no one.

The beautiful poem **"Drinking from a Helmet"** describes the incredible changes that occur when a soldier on some Pacific island (presumably some version of the poet himself, as most of Dickey's speakers appear to be) picks up the helmet of a dead countryman to hold his water ration. First, he sees his own reflection on the water's surface framed by the helmet's edges, so he seems to be wearing, in this mirror-image, with safety what another was killed in. As he continues to drink and then to contemplate what remains of the water, his own reflection is replaced by other sorts of details which in their suggestiveness point the direction the speaker's experience now takes:

> At the middle of water
> Bright circles dawned inward and outward
> Like oak rings surviving the tree
> As its soul, or like
> The concentric gold spirit of time.
> I kept trembling forward through something
> Just born of me.

The next two stanzas are devoted to an evocation of the dead ("I fought with a word in the water / To call on the dead to strain / Their muscles and get up . . ."), but we are told that "the dead cannot rise up" though "their last thought hovers somewhere / For whoever finds it." Dickey does find it; and in the eight stanzas that follow there is an elaboration and intensification of the kind of experience rendered in **"Hunting Civil War Relics at Nimblewill Creek."** The speaker feels himself "possessed," filled out from within by something "swallowed whole" from the helmet, and attains to a sense of rebirth and immortality: he has absorbed and revivified in some mystical fashion the person of the dead soldier and has obviously been transformed himself in the process. Subsequently, he discards his own helmet and puts on the one he has found:

Warmed water ran over my face.
My last thought changed, and I knew
I inherited one of the dead.

That is to say, the speaker's own thoughts die with his
cast-off helmet; he assumes the dead soldier's final thought
with his headgear and seems to be baptized with the last
of the water into a new life. The inherited thought is really
a vision drawn from the deceased's past, apparently the
final flash of memory across his dying mind, and shows
two boys talking in a forest of gigantic redwood trees. The
two closing sections of the poem envisage the speaker's
destiny: he will survive the war and journey afterwards in
search of the dead soldier's brother to carry to him the
experience of possession and the life-concluding memory
which the helmet has conveyed:

XVIII

I would survive and go there,
Stepping off the train in a helmet
That held a man's last thought,
Which showed him his older brother
Showing him trees.
I would ride through all
California upon two wheels
Until I came to the white
Dirt road where they had been,
Hoping to meet his blond brother,
And to walk with him into the wood
Until we were lost,
Then take off the helmet
And tell him where I had stood,
What poured, what spilled, what swallowed:

XIX

And tell him I was the man.

The claim of kinship mentioned by C. Day Lewis is powerfully realized in this poem, and the speaker provides a link
between the dead and the living, between the lost soldier
and his brother, that lengthens out the pattern of relations
beyond those of **"Hunting Civil War Relics at Nimblewill Creek"** by reaching from time past toward time
future. (The conditional tense of the final portion, like the
significance of the poem's last line, makes for a certain
ambiguity with regard to the speaker's actual location in
time and his identity, but such indefiniteness does not
detract from the reader's impression of temporal
movement.) Yet the very strength of the human bonds
Dickey creates in this poem leads one to wonder all the
more at the moral abyss which separates it from the piece
that begins his next volume, *Buckdancer's Choice.*

"The Firebombing," clearly based on the poet's experiences as a night-fighter pilot on bombing missions in Asia
during World War II, starts off with nocturnal recollec-
tions, entertained years later in the seemingly secure
American suburbs, of what he has done to others—burned
them alive with napalm, destroyed their property, killed
their animals—and the attempt (not very strenuous, I fear,
at least in the context of the poem) to project himself into
their place, to suffer and understand, and so in part at any
rate to expiate his actions. But in spite of an epigraph
from the *Book of Job* ("Or has thou an arm like God?")
and another one from the contemporary German poet
Günter Eich (untranslated as epigraph, but in Vernon Watkins' version from Michael Hamburger and Christopher
Middleton's *Modern German Poetry 1910-1960* it reads:
"Think of this, after the great destructions / Everyone will
prove that he was innocent"), some lines near the beginning already imply that the effort to awaken such emotions
is doomed to failure:

All families lie together, though some are burned alive.
The others try to feel
For them. Some can, it is often said.

The flat, impersonal tone of that last sentence is rather
indicative of the results of Dickey's attempt—which
purportedly comprises the substance of the poem—to "feel
for" his deeds, his victims, because close to the end he can
tell us that he is "still unable / To get down there or see /
What really happened." We cannot quarrel with the apparent honesty of this statement. If the poet is incapable of
entering the experience of his victims, there is little to be
done about it—though we may recall, with a start, his
amazing imaginative sympathies with the animals he hunts.
Yet in a bizarre, contradictory way the bulk of the poem
concentrates on the re-creation of its author's feelings and
perceptions during a night raid with napalm bombs on
Japanese civilian, rather than military, objectives. Again,
as in some of the hunting poems, we see the poet dividing
himself in imagination between his own consciousness and
a simultaneous intuition of the existence of the hunted; but
it is here precisely in **"The Firebombing"** that Dickey's
imaginative gift collapses at the moral level. While he offers us dramatic impressions of his flight and weaponry
(the headiness of power becomes quite plain—and
terrifying) and of the imagined horror and destruction
wrought upon the land below and its inhabitants by his attack, he expends poetic energy on the creation of images
through which these events and details are dramatized
without ever arousing a commensurate moral—which is to
say, human—awareness. In other words, the poet would
appear to be re-living this segment of his past more for
aesthetic than for any other reasons, for the pain and terror
of his victims are dwelt on and vividly presented (though
without sympathy) even when we are going to be told at
the conclusion that he "can imagine / At the threshold
nothing / With its ears crackling off / Like powdery leaves,
/ Nothing with children of ashes . . ." Perhaps I am
misjudging Dickey's underlying impulse, but if I am the
poem still holds puzzling inconsistencies. Robert Bly, who
has written a second essay on Dickey's work, a sharp but
not quite just criticism of *Buckdancer's Choice,*[2] notes
some instances of rather weak irony and self-criticism in
the poem, of "complaint" about the pilot-speaker who can
feel no remorse for his actions, but certainly such qualifications are almost unnoticeable. Here is a passage which
describes the moment the pilot releases his napalm and the
holocaust that follows (something Dickey has no difficulty
in imagining). References to "anti-morale" raids, "Chi-

cago" fire, and "all American" fire, while they may be intended to serve an ironical-critical function in their context, are feeble by comparison with the overall effect of a fascinated exulting in destructive force, in the superiority of flight and the malevolent artistry of bombing:

> The ship shakes bucks
> Fire hangs not yet fire
> In the air above Beppu
> For I am fulfilling
>
> An "anti-morale" raid upon it.
> All leashes of dogs
> Break under the first bomb, around those
> In bed, or late in the public baths: around those
> Who inch forward on their hands
> Into medicinal waters.
> Their heads come up with a roar
> Of Chicago fire:
> Come up with the carp pond showing
> The bathouse upside down,
> Standing stiller to show it more
> As I sail artistically over
> The resort town followed by farms,
> Singing and twisting all the handles in heaven kicking
> The small cattle off their feet
> In a red costly blast
> Flinging jelly over the walls
> As in a chemical war-
> fare field demonstration.
> With fire of mine like a cat
>
> Holding onto another man's walls,
> My hat should crawl on my head
> In streetcars, thinking of it,
> The fat on my body should pale.

The self-reproach of the last stanza above is hollow and meaningless next to the fierce delight of re-living that period of godlike superiority. Perhaps Dickey will not try to prove himself innocent, as Günter Eich's poem suggests men do, and that is fine. But Dickey also departs sharply from the spirit of Eich's conclusion, which states: "Think of this, that you are responsible for every atrocity / Enacted far from you." Further on, he makes other gestures aimed toward compassion and feeling; he remarks that "detachment" and "the greatest sense of power in one's life" should be "shed" (apparently by either one or the other odd means of getting drunk or adopting a severe diet), though in the course of the poem these statements again amount to very little. What is strong, vivid, and passionate in **"The Firebombing"** springs directly from the occasion which gave the poem its title and from the poet's participation in it; any real concern for the terrible fate imposed upon others seems secondary.

A similar failing is evident in such poems as **"The Fiend"** and **"Slave Quarters,"** both of which employ speakers whose chief desire is the fulfillment, through a warped masculine sexual power, of their own sick fantasies. The knife-carrying, middle-aged voyeur of the first poem and the lustful slave-owner (whose ghostly body the poet enters

and joins with) of the second are victims of their private delusions: neither can escape from his diseased view and both are determined to realize their fantasies as fact, though the realization must inevitably do violence to others. In these poems, then, one finds a sort of lyricism of the perverse with little else to be said for it. But Dickey demonstrates here, as in **"The Firebombing,"** an obsession with power and the imposition of will—and a total insensitivity to the persons who are the objects of its indulgence. Admittedly, **"Slave Quarters"** is the more ambitious poem and attempts in some ways a more difficult feat of understanding; still it is, for me, imaginatively deficient.

Among the recent poems from the lengthy section entitled *Falling,* I believe we must find notable instances of a diminishing of Dickey's poetic intensity, though such a comment does not everywhere apply. Nonetheless, a regrettable straining after material and effect—perhaps really after novelty—seems to me fatally injurious to most of the longer pieces: **"May Day Sermon . . ." "Falling," "Sun," "Reincarnation (II),"** and **"Coming Back to America."** Faults frequently pointed out by Dickey's critics are painfully evident in **"Falling"** and **"May Day Sermon . . .":** these poems are drawn out, repetitive, overwritten, blurred, and diffuse; the 'ideas' behind them are contrived, and in the case of **"Falling,"** cannot be sustained even by Coleridge's "willing suspension of disbelief." Finally, except for striking passages or images, these poems become boring.

This verdict should not be taken as wholly negative, however, for Dickey can still write poems with the energy and imagination which distinguishes his finest work from *Drowning with Others* and *Helmets* (by far his best books). **"The Birthday Dream," "The Leap," "Snakebite," "Sustainment," "The Head-Aim,"** and **"Deer Among Cattle,"** as well as others, are examples of good Dickey poems. I quote **"Deer Among Cattle":**

> Here and there in the searing beam
> Of my hand going through the night meadow
> They all are grazing
>
> With pins of human light in their eyes.
> A wild one also is eating
> The human grass,
>
> Slender, graceful, domesticated
> By darkness, among the bred-
> for-slaughter,
>
> Having bounded their paralyzed fence
> And inclined his branched forehead onto
> Their green frosted table,
>
> The only live thing in this flashlight
> Who can leave whenever he wishes,
> Turn grass into forest,
>
> Foreclose inhuman brightness from his eyes
> But stands here still, unperturbed,
> In their wide-open country,

The sparks from my hand in his pupils
Unmatched anywhere among cattle,
Grazing with them the night of the hammer
As one of their own who shall rise.

At the top of his form Dickey does reveal a large capacity for feeling, for steeping his spirit in the being of others and in the very life of creation; and we think of the poets with whom his most authentic poems have their affinity: Whitman, Lawrence, Roethke; and among the younger: James Wright, Jon Silkin, Robert Bly, Donald Hall, W. S. Merwin; perhaps some European poets as well. But these affinities are broken in the poems which are morally insensate.

Dickey is a prolific writer, to judge from the size of a decade's production, and he has won sudden fame and publicity. Large reputations—we know it as a commonplace—can be exceedingly dangerous in the pressures they bring always to be new and inventive (the blight of the contemporary painter and sculptor) in order to maintain one's laurels, especially in a culture dedicated to the modish and to consumer consumption of artistic goods; and a poet of Dickey's strengths can be damaged as easily as can a lesser one. I hope that will not happen, for he is, defects aside, a very gifted, truly imaginative poet who has already given us excellent pieces. No doubt his work must alter and grow toward full maturity,[3] but its developments need to derive from inner necessity and not in answer to the external demands of reputation or public role. In any event, this collection of Dickey's poetry is an important book; it merits attentive reading—and its readers will be far from unrewarded.

Notes

1. "The Way of Exchange in James Dickey's Poetry," *Sewanee Review,* Summer 1966, and "The Poetry of James Dickey," *The Sixties,* Winter 1964, respectively. Readers should also see Norman Friedman: "The Wesleyan Poets, II" *Chicago Review,* 19, 1, 1966; and Michael Goldman: "Inventing the American Heart," *The Nation,* April 24, 1967.

2. In *The Sixties,* 9, 1967.

3. Dickey has written an interesting account of his history and aims as a poet in "The Poet Turns on Himself," included in *Poets on Poetry,* edited by Howard Nemerov (New York: Basic Books, 1966), which I had not seen at the time of writing this essay. He offers there some important comments on his more recent poetry.

Laurence Lieberman (essay date 1968)

SOURCE: Lieberman, Laurence. "Notes on James Dickey's Style." In *James Dickey: The Expansive Imagination,* edited by Richard J. Calhoun, pp. 195-201. DeLand, FL: Everett/Edwards, Inc., 1973.

[*In the following essay, originally published in 1968, Lieberman presents commentary on Dickey's innovative and varied use of poetic symbolism and form.*]

In *The Suspect in Poetry,* a first collection of James Dickey's criticism, he eliminates from his canon of taste, one by one, those writers of reputation he finds suspect. Similarly, the development of his art, from book to book, is a conscious stripping away of those techniques of style and mental strategies which have grown suspect after repeated use. In the poems themselves he may leave the explicit record of steps in a willed metamorphosis of style; moreover, each conversion of manner bolsters a corresponding conversion of imagination.

To begin, Dickey's handling of figurative language suggests a basic distrust of the remoteness from human experience of traditional figures of speech. In the early war poem, **"The Performance,"** the speech figures are so closely wedded, annexed, to the human events, it would be a mistake to think of them as being metaphors or figurative at all, in the usual sense. They are elements of style and expression which are an extension of meaning that is felt to have been already inherent in the experience itself, waiting to be released, or to emerge from the living receptacle as a photo emerges from a negative. The phrases have all the mystery and suggestiveness of metaphor, but reduce decorative and artificial qualities to a minimum: "blood turned his face inside out," "he toppled his head off," "the head rolled over upon its wide-eyed face," "sun poured up from the sea." Style takes the reader deeply into the experience, intensifying the being in the poem without literary self-consciousness. The poet is telling a story, and if the way he tells the story is as remarkable as the story itself, the *way* of telling remains dutifully subordinate to *what* is told—imparts urgency and intensity to the story.

In the later war poem **"Drinking From a Helmet,"** as in **"The Performance,"** metaphor and personification are so well anchored to harrowing sense impressions that they heighten physical realism:

(1) I climbed out, tired of waiting
    For my foxhole to turn in the earth
    On its side or its back for a grave.
(2) In the middle of combat, a graveyard
    Was advancing after the troops . . .
(3) Where somebody else may have come
    Loose from the steel of his head.
(4) Keeping the foxhole doubled
    In my body and begging . . .
(5) I drew water out of the truckside
    As if dreaming the helmet full.

So far are these images from creating the usual remove, the abstracting from literal experience, we expect from figures of speech, these figures seem to carry us into a more intense and immediate literal-ness than literal description could possibly afford. The figures suggest a mind stretching its natural limits of perception to assimilate experience of pain and anguish that can only be apprehended accurately through hallucination. Excruciating mental experience is translated into exact physical correlatives. There is no question of a straining after clever or original images—rather, these queer transpositions of qualities between beings and things are the mind's last resort to keep a hold on its sanity, to stay in touch with its physical environs.

Dickey's use of symbolism is as innovatory as his language. Quite often, the least fully realized poems reveal, in a raw lucidity, ideas and symbols that become the subtly hidden mainstay in the best poems. He draws on the arcane system of thought and symbology in these poems, much as Yeats drew on *A Vision,* in crystallizing the structure of ideas in his most achieved art. We can turn to these poems, as to a skeleton key, for clues that can often be found nowhere else.

Perhaps the first poem of this type is **"Dust."** In Whitman's vision of reincarnation, traditional worms feed on corpses and bring them back to life through the soil and grassroots. In *Helmets,* Dickey's third volume of poems, his vision is largely confined to that view. However, in **"Dust"**—a poem in the fourth volume *Buckdancer's Choice*—he moves toward a new vision of reincarnation through worm-like dust motes, "spirochetes boring into the very body of light," a rebirth through sunlight and air. He conceives dust as a middle condition, a mediating form between organic and inorganic matter, life and death, much as scientists conceive the virus as a sort of intermediate limbo—a twilight zone—between plant and animal life. Dust motes seem to embody a partial being, or intelligence, as they wait in air and sunlight for spirits just arisen from the newly dead to whirl through them, changing them into "forms of fire," into "incandescent worms," and finally, amassing them into a shape, "a cone of sunlight." That shape of dust is pervaded by being, and becomes a human. The left-overs, "extra motes," are unable to get into a human form at this time, but ready. They wait.

In **"Dust,"** as in many poems of the later volume *Falling,* Dickey seems to be formulating his symbology into a coherent system of thought, a metaphysics of being. A formal theosophy begins to take shape, if these poems are read conjointly. Subsequently, to trace the development of these symbols in Dickey's cosmos is to find that he has been consistent and scrupulous in carrying them through successive stages of his art. Though particular symbols deepen in meaning and intensity in poems which treat them as primary subjects—**"Dust," "The Flash," "Snakebite," "Sun"**—their basic identity is consistent with their meanings in other poems. Dickey seems to have deliberately extracted recurring components of his art for specialized treatment, each in a separate poem. Partly, he seems to be trying to find out for the first time why each of these symbols, or symbolic events, has such a powerful hold over his poetic imagination. Also, he is codifying the symbols into a systematized philosophy.

To turn from symbolism to a discussion of the management of line and form, in Dickey's early work the long sentence, often extended over several stanzas, is the chief

unit of measure. This type of verse movement served Dickey well for three volumes of work, though in some poems the line falls into artificiality and rhythmic straining when the technique becomes self-imitative, and lacks complete absorption in the subject (**"The Island"** and **"The Scratch"**).

In **"Drinking From a Helmet,"** Dickey breaks away from the line and stanza units he has grown so attached to. But he stays confined to many of the old sentence rhythms until he begins to evolve the split line of *Buckdancer's Choice.* The form in **"Drinking From a Helmet"** operates like a film strip. Each frame/stanza focuses on an event, physical or spiritual, separate in time from the others. The movement is that of a film strip, rather than a motion picture, since the pauses or silences between frames are as functional in the poem's rhythmic structure as are the stanzas themselves. This form is an extremely important development for Dickey, since it readily achieves effects exactly opposite to the unbroken flow and rhythmic sweep of most of the previous work. Any such innovation in Dickey's form is accompanied by equivalent modifications in the handling of line and pacing of action.

In the poems of *Buckdancer's Choice* and *Falling,* the chief unit of measure is the phrase, a breath unit (or breathing unit), as opposed to a grammatical unit. The sentence, as a unit of measure, is all but lost, though occasionally a sentence beginning or ending does seem to punctuate a larger compartment of verse, and more important, a reader usually keeps the illusion that he is moving within the extremeties of a rather free-floating sentence (an illusion that is completely lost, say, in parts of the stream-of-consciousness flow of Joyce and Faulkner). This form adapts perfectly to a welter of experience in flux. The rhetoric keeps drawing more and more live matter into the poem, as from a boundless supply. The entire poem maintains a single unbroken flow of motion. In this respect, the medium owes more to the moving picture, to film technique, than to other poetry. The verse paragraph break is never a true interruption to the rhythmic sweep of the phrase-chain. It merely suggests a shift in perspective, a slowing down and speeding up of the unstoppable momentum, an occasional amplification of the breath-spaces that already separate every phrase from phrase.

Dickey's new form, incorporating the split line, is most successfully managed in the poem **"Falling."** The triumph of the split line technique in **"Falling"** is principally the net result of the ingenious variety of effects Dickey is able to achieve by playing off the phrase-unit against the hexameter line unit. The length of the breath-phrases ranges from a single word to a couple of lines. A single line frequently affords as many as five separate phrases:

> Do something with water   fly to it   fall in it
>   drink it   rise
> From it   but there is none left upon earth   the clouds
> have
>   drunk it back
> The plants have sucked it down   there are standing

>   toward her only
> The common fields of death   she comes back from
>   flying to falling

The enjambments between lines are nearly always consciously functional, whether they interrupt a single breath unit and break up the phrase, or connect breath units:

>   . . . My God it is good
> And evil   lying in one after another
>   of all the positions for love
> Making   dancing   sleeping . . .

The astonishing variety of rhythms is mainly induced by balancing caesuras within the line, and varying the patterns of balance in successive lines:

> She is watching her country lose its evoked master
>   shape
>   watching it lose
> And gain   get back its houses and people   watching
>   it bring up
> Its local lights   single homes   lamps on barn roofs
>   if she fell
> Into the water she might live   like a diver   cleaving
>   perfect   plunge
> Into another   heavy silver   unbreathable   slowing
>   saving
> Element: there is water   there is time to perfect
>   all the fine
> Points of diving . . .

The new form makes available to Dickey avenues of sensibility and resources of language and subject that were not accessible in earlier poems. For the poet, what it is possible to say is mainly a matter of versatility of technique. In many of the best poems of Dickey's most recent collection, he is moving toward a more direct engagement with life-experience than ever before. In **"Power and Light"** and **"Encounter in the Cage Country,"** the art is less in the writing than in the uniquely comic personality of the persona, who treats his life as a medium for realizing hidden possibilities for creative existence. There is a strange new departure here in Dickey's work. The poem hardly seems like literature. **"Encounter"** is perhaps the most personally explicit of all his poems. Usually, Dickey's poems reporting true personal experience combine explicit concrete reportage with a revelation of meaning, as in **"The Hospital Window"** and **"Cherrylog Road."** A reader senses that the poem's discovery is a dimension of the experience that came to the poet as an imagined afterthought, even though the symbolic language and imagery of the poem suggest the experience and the meaning that informs it occurred simultaneously in life. But then, it is the business of poetic art to create that illusion.

"Encounter in the Cage Country" drops the usual barriers between Dickey's life and art. It is as though the writer has reached that stage of his life when the skills of his artistry—comic staging, search for identity, haunting intensification of being—must spill over into his life-experience:

> . . . I knew the stage was set, and I began
> To perform   first saunt'ring   then stalking
> Back and forth like a sentry   faked
> As if to run . . .

Life itself becomes the instrument for creative becoming. It is no longer necessary for the poem to add the dimension of mystery to the experience through consciously willed art, since the personal event itself contains more magic, a sharper ring of truth, than the most subtly imagined poems can afford. The poem creates the illusion, if illusion it is, of being merely a sort of heightened reportage, and it may well stand in the same relation to Dickey's poetic art as *The Sacred Fount* assumes in the canon of Henry James' fictive art. It is a poem that will probably be examined by critics as a key to understanding the fascinating relation between Dickey's art and life. In **"Encounter in the Cage Country,"** Dickey holds up a mirror to himself.

Raymond Smith (essay date 1972)

SOURCE: Smith, Raymond. "The Poetic Faith of James Dickey." *Modern Poetry Studies* 2, no. 1 (1972): 259-72.

[*In the following essay, Smith describes Dickey's "poetic faith" as a sense of belief in nature illustrated most clearly in his hunting poems and in the mystic visions of his 1970 volume* Eye-Beaters, Blood, Victory, Madness, Buckhead and Mercy.]

Dissociating himself from the contemporary mode of cultivated cynicism, James Dickey refers to himself in *Self-Interviews* (1970) as a "born believer." It is this capacity for belief that is a dominant characteristic of his poetry. It is a poetry of acceptance and celebration in the manner of Whitman. Dickey's faith is rooted in nature: nature is teacher and life-giver, and his reverence for nature is manifest in a primitive, almost totemic treatment of animals. The poet finds a brother in the owl, the deer, the bull. Hunting, once necessary for human survival, has become for him a ritual, a means of entering into a kind of communion with the hunted animal. Yet, while his faith is rooted in nature, it flowers in myth.

A good introduction to the poetic faith of Dickey is his **"The Heaven of Animals."** This paradoxically entitled poem evinces a latitudinarian attitude, accepting in the realm of immortality these soulless, mindless creatures: "Having no souls, they have come, / Anyway, beyond their knowing." It is not the knowledge of the animals but their instinct, a natural force which he subscribes to wholeheartedly, that raises them into heaven; this state of life after death appears as the ultimate flowering of the instinct: "Their instincts wholly bloom / And they rise. / The soft eyes open." The animal heaven does not exclude the violence of the hunt. Rather than tamper with the instinct of the carnivore, the poet perfects its tooth and claw:

For some of these,
It could not be the place
It is, without blood.
These hunt, as they have done,
But with claws and teeth grown perfect,

More deadly than they can believe.

"The lion would not really be a lion," Dickey explains in *Self Interviews,* "if, as the Bible says, the lion lies down with the lamb. It would be the form of the lion but not the spirit." In heaven, the carnivore's instinctual spring, its most characteristic and fulfilling action, is blissfully extended: "their descent / Upon the bright backs of their prey / May take years / In a sovereign floating of joy." The victims in Dickey's animal heaven fulfill themselves as victims. The poet does modify nature here to the extent that he eliminates the fear and pain that earthly prey would feel:

And those that are hunted
Know this as their life,
Their reward: to walk

Under such trees in full knowledge
Of what is in glory above them,
And to feel no fear,
But acceptance, compliance.
Fulfilling themselves without pain
At the cycle's center,
They tremble, they walk
Under the tree,
They fall, they are torn,
They rise, they walk again.

Calling upon the cyclical nature of life, the poet is able to maintain his vision. The poem ends with an emphasis upon nature's unceasing movement toward renewal.

The relationship between nature and faith is better illustrated by the poem **"Trees and Cattle,"** in which Dickey successfully attempts to integrate man with nature to achieve that precious "feeling of wholeness" referred to in *Self Interviews.* "What I want more than anything else," he explains, "is to have a feeling of wholeness. Specialization has produced some extremely important things, like penicillin and heart transplants. But I don't know how much they compensate for the loss of a sense of intimacy with the natural process. I think you would be very hard-put, for example, to find a more harmonious relationship to an environment than the American Indians had. We can't return to a primitive society; surely this is obvious. But there is a property of the mind which, if encouraged, could have this personally animistic relationship to things." In the dreamlike **"Trees and Cattle,"** the poet finds himself standing in a sun-soaked autumn pasture, where he realizes his bond with other living things; in a scene shimmering with potential, he is suddenly aware of immortality.

The poem opens with a view of the trees, emphasizing unshaded sunlight and golden leaves—an image so intense that it threatens to evaporate:

Many trees can stand unshaded
In this place where the sun is alone,
But some may break out.
They may be taken to Heaven,
So gold is my only sight.

A sense of wonder, of infinite value, of potentiality has been introduced into the poem. Identifying with the trees, the poet lets two slowly moving cows step into the picture: "Through me, two red cows walk; / From a crowning glory / Of slowness they are not taken." The red cows share the potentiality of the golden trees in that the ambling cattle may paradoxically turn the dried-up field into a conflagration: "Let one hoof knock on a stone, / And off it a spark jump quickly, / And fire may sweep these fields, / And all outburn the blind sun." There is a potential brilliance here akin to that of Hopkins' embers that "gash gold-vermilion."

The light imagery, with light as a metaphor for life, is continued in terms of a briefly burning flame. The poet, caught up in the same cyclic process as the trees, identifies with them as he suggests the sacred nature of the life-death cycle:

Like a new light I enter my life,
And hover, not yet consumed,
With the trees in holy alliance,
About to be offered up,
About to get wings where we stand.

The introduction of "wings," prepared for in the first stanza, transforms an idea of imminent death into one of imminent rebirth. The potentiality of the autumn scene is emphasized further before it is actualized in the form of a bull emerging from the sunlight. Identifying with the bull, the poet has a new sense of the immediacy of existence:

The whole field stammers with gold,
No leaf but is actively still;
There is no quiet or noise;

Continually out of a fire
A bull walks forth,
And makes of my mind a red beast
At each step feeling how
The sun more deeply is burning

Because trees and cattle exist.

The poet is more aware of the sun, more aware of his own vitality, because he is aware of the trees and the cattle, because he has identified his light with theirs.

The poem concludes with the poet leaving the field of light and losing his potency, his vision, his very life; for he was given his heart "in some earthly way": "I go away, in the end. / In the shade, my bull's horns die / From my head; in some earthly way / I have been given my heart." But there is a sudden reversal in the final stanza as the poet proceeds to amplify the statement about his "earthly" nature:

Behind my back, a tree leaps up
On wings that could save me from death.
Its branches dance over my head.
Its flight strikes a root in me.
A cow beneath it lies down.

The image of the tree rising up with life suggests, as it did earlier in the poem, the idea of rebirth. The imminent renewal of the tree will save the poet who is of the same earth. The fact of renewal "strikes a root" in him as he identifies once more with the trees and cattle.

Dickey's identification with the life-renewing bull in **"Trees and Cattle"** looks forward to his hunting poems, where the primitive, totemic relationship between man and animal emerges more clearly. Hunting, for Dickey, is a way of achieving "rapport with the animal." In *Self-Interviews,* he explains: "the main thing is to re-enter the cycle of the man who hunts for his food. Now this may be playacting at being a primitive man, but it's better than not having any rapport with the animal at all. . . . I have a great sense of renewal when I am able to go into the woods and hunt with a bow and arrow, to enter into the animal's world in this way." In **"Springer Mountain,"** the hunter not only goes into the woods but also rids himself of civilization in the form of his clothing to run naked with a deer, which has moved down the mountain "in step with the sun." When the hunter removes his clothes, "the world catches fire." With the "green of excess" upon him, he moves with the buck toward the stream of renewal— "Winding down to the waters of life / Where they stand petrified in a creek bed / Yet melt and flow from the hills / At the touch of an animal visage." The nature of the renewal is suggested when the hunter speaks of being "For a few steps deep in the dance / Of what I most am and should be / And can be only once in this life."

In **"Approaching Prayer,"** the poet carries his identification with the hunted animal to the point of taking upon himself the consciousness of a boar, fatally wounded by the hunter's arrow. The projection begins on a literal level, as the poet covers his head with a hollow boar's head, donning the trophy like a primitive priest. The poet advances to a more spiritual level of projection as he imagines the last sensations of the hog:

The man is still; he is stiller; still
                    . . . . .
Something comes out of him
Like a shaft of sunlight or starlight.
I go forward toward him.
                    . . . . .
With light standing through me,
Covered with dogs, but the water
Tilts to the sound of the bowstring
                    . . . . .
The sound from his fingers,
Like a plucked word, quickly pierces
Me again, the trees try to dance
Clumsily out of the wood.

(An interesting note to this poem is unintentionally provided by Geoffrey Norman in "The Stuff of Poetry" (*Playboy,* 1971). Commenting on Dickey's "fine mimetic flair," Norman writes that "his crowd stopper is . . . a razorback hog. He can draw his big shoulders into a tight droop, thrust his broad forehead out and begin bobbing and snorting until he actually does resemble an old razorback.")

Another one of Dickey's "totems" is the owl, winged hunter and seer, which dominates the forest of the night. The owl looms larger than life in Dickey's recent novel, *Deliverance* (1970), where it perches on the tent of the canoeists during their first night in the woods. An omen of the man-hunting to come, the owl spends the night seeking out prey. The narrator hunts with him in his imagination: "I imagined what he was doing while he was gone, floating through the trees, seeing everything. I hunted with him as well as I could, there in my weightlessness. The woods burned in my head. Toward morning I could reach up and touch the claw without turning on the light." In the poem **"The Owl King,"** there is another, more obviously ritualistic encounter between man and owl in the dark woods: an owl teaches a blind child to see.

The first part of this long, three-part poem is from the point of view of the blind child's father. The child has been lost in the woods and, as Dickey explains in *Self-Interviews,* the father is "trying to furnish his blind son with an audible point of reference toward which the child can come, some kind of continuous sound." The father describes his call as "a sound I cannot remember. / It whispers like straw in my ear, / And shakes like a stone under water. / My bones stand on tiptoe inside it." Drifting into the forest, the sound forms a kind of magical ring "Round a child with a bird gravely dancing." The father's cry is echoed by the owl king's song, which comes back out of the woods "touching every tree upon the hill." Entranced by the strange music that he has produced, the father instructs the blind child: "Come, son, and find me here, / In love with the sound of my voice. / Come calling the same soft song, / And touching every tree upon the hill." The child will be led out of the forest to the father by ritualistically touching each tree as the song did.

In the second part of the poem, the point of view shifts from the father to the totemic owl. In *Self-Interviews,* Dickey describes the bird as "the quintessential owl, the immortal owl . . . kind of a Nietzschean owl who is able to see in the dark by an act of will over a long period of time. . . . He eventually controls the night forest completely because he's the only one who can see and fly." The owl king's story begins:

I swore to myself I would see
When all but my seeing had failed.
Every light was too feeble to show
My world as I knew it must be.
At the top of the staring night
I sat on the oak in my shape
With my claws growing deep into wood
And my sight going slowly out
Inch by inch, as into a stone . . .

The owl's vision is similar to that set forth in **"The Heaven of Animals"**; it juxtaposes the hunter-victim ecology with the idea of the continuity of life. The owl sees "rabbits running / Beneath my bent growing throne, / And the foxes lighting their hair, / And the serpent taking the shape / Of the stream of life as it slept." The interior nature of the vision, similar in its archetypal aspect to that of **"The Eye-Beaters"**—another poem about blind children—is emphasized as the speaker elaborates upon his act of will: "That night I parted my lids / . . . and saw dark burn / Greater than sunlight or moonlight, / For it burned from deep within me." This return to the primitive, instinctual past is emphasized later when the child, having regained his sight, utters the Roethke-like paradox: "I see as the owl kings sees, / By going in deeper than darkness."

The encounter between the owl king and the blind child, touched upon in the first part of the poem, is elaborated here from the owl's point of view:

> Through trees at his light touch trembling
> The blind child drifted to meet me,
> His blue eyes shining like mine.
> In a ragged clearing he stopped,
> And I circled, beating above him,
> Then fell to the ground and hopped
> Forward, taking his hand in my claw.
> Every tree's life lived in his fingers.

Life moves from the trees through the child's fingers into the claw of the owl. The unitary character of life, apparent in these lines, is made even more explicit in the dance of the creatures that follows: "Gravely we trod with each other / As beasts at their own wedding, dance." The music to which they dance is the song of the father, described "As though the one voice of us both." The ritual-like dance performed, the owl teaches the blind boy to see; the child's vision is similar to that of his teacher: "The mouse in its bundle of terror, / The fox in the flame of its hair, / And the snake in the form of all life." Part two concludes with the expression of the speaker's will that "All dark shall come to light."

The action of the poem is given its fullest and most exquisite expression in the third and final part—the child's story. It begins with the child's movement into the forest, a journey beautifully expressed in terms of motor and tactile perceptions:

> I am playing going down
> In my weight lightly,
> Down, down the hill.
>
>   . . . . .
>
> A leaf falls on me,
> It must be a leaf I hear it
> Be thin against me, and now
> The ground is level
> It moves it is not ground,
> My feet flow cold
> And wet, and water rushes
> Past as I climb out.

Having crossed the barrier between the human and animal worlds, the child enters the forest. He is suddenly aware of

the presence of the owl in the tree overhead before it floats to the earth to take him by the hand. To the music of the sighing father, the dance begins:

> The huge bird bows and returns,
> For I, too, have done the same
> As he leads me, rustling,
> A pile of leaves in my hands;
> The dry feathers shuffle like cards
> On his dusty shoulders.

Like the brothers in Dickey's poem **"In the Tree House at Night,"** the owl and the child climb into the branches of a living tree, where in the light of the moon the child will learn to see: "I learn from the master of sight / What to do when the sun is dead, / How to make the great darkness work / As it wants of itself to work." The boy's eyes open to nature—to the coiled snake, to the hunting fox:

> A creature is burning itself
> In a smoke of hair through the bushes.
> The fox moves; a small thing
> Being caught, cries out,
> And I understand
> How beings and sounds go together;
> I understand
> The voice of my singing father.
> I shall be king of the wood.

The vision leads to understanding; understanding, to power—control. Crossing the symbolic creek again ("a religious fire / Streaming my ankles away"), the child returns to his home. His father, under the spell of "the endless beauty / Of his grief-stricken singing and calling" is baying to the moon: "He is singing simply to moonlight, / Like a dog howling, / And it is holy song / Out of his mouth." The father's singing has become a mindless, instinctive, natural act—in Dickey's view "holy." The poem concludes with the son identifying with his father and confessing his faith:

>   Father, I touch
> Your face. I have not seen
> My own, but it is yours.
> I come, I advance,
> I believe everything, I am here.

The conclusion of the poem, as Dickey put it in *Self-Interviews,* is "an act of total acceptance of the world through the figure of the child." The child, like Dickey, is a "born believer."

Dickey's statement of faith in **"The Owl King"** has a certain mythic quality. The poem resembles the medieval dream vision, where a bird or animal often acts as a guide for the dreamer. There is a cyclical pattern involved, with the child moving away from his father, into the woods, and back to his father again. The child's experience can be seen, on one level at least, as a form of renewal in the manner of **"Springer Mountain."** The father, involved with loss and expression, can be seen as the poet. Dickey is clearly not dealing with any of the traditional myths as he was in **"The Vegetable King,"** which treats the theme of renewal in terms of the death and resurrection of a sacrificial king. He is working with something new. As Joseph Campbell has observed, with the decay of the traditional myths or religions, it is the creative artist who must provide us with a new mythology. In "Man & Myth" (*Psychology Today*, 1971) Campbell explains: "In traditional societies the symbols and myths that were the vehicles of social values were presented in socially maintained rites that the individual was required to experience. All the meaning was in the group, none in the self expressive individual. The creative mythology of the modern artist arises when the individual has an experience of his own—of order, or horror, or beauty—that he tries to communicate by creating a private mythology. So it is the creative individual who must give us a totally new type of nontheological revelation, who must be the new spiritual guide." Although Campbell did not have him in mind, Dickey is one of those modern artists who is creating a new mythology.

The first of the title poems of Dickey's latest collection of poems, *The Eye-Beaters, Blood, Victory, Madness, Buckhead and Mercy* (1970) is another, ultimately more successful mythic vision. Confronted by the horror of blindness among children, the poet creates a mitigating fiction: the children in their darkness tap the collective unconscious, the repository of vital images of the primitive past. The poem opens with an account of an arrival at a children's home, where the visitor is met by a group of young people who have gone blind. The children, whose arms are tied to their sides, fight to free themselves: "they holler howl till they can shred / Their gentle ropes whirl and come loose." Their arms free, the blind children "smash their eyeballs" with their fists to generate the only light available to them—"sparks." With the help of the visitor's imagination, these sparks are transformed into images from the collective unconscious: "In the asylum, children turn to go back / Into the race: turn their heads without comment into the black magic / Migraine of caves." Returning to the cave of their Stone Age fathers, the blind children watch a primitive artist draw:

> There, quiet children stand watching
> A man striped and heavy with pigment, lift his hand with color coming
> From him. Bestial, working like God, he moves on stone he is drawing
> A half-cloud of beasts on the wall. They crane closer, helping, beating
> Harder, light blazing inward from their fists and see see leap
> From the shocked head-nerves, great herds of deer
> . . .

Opening his eyes for a moment to the afternoon sun, the visitor sees it as a "painfully blazing fist of a ball of fire / God struck from His one eye." The outer world is immediately negated by the inner, which is presented in lines that wonderfully suggest the desperate frenzy of creativity:

> No; you see only dead beasts playing
> In the bloody handprint on the stone where God gropes like a man
> Like a child, for animals where the artist hunts and slashes, glowing
> Like entrail-blood, tracking the wounded game across the limestone
> As it is conceived. The spoor leads   his hand changes   grows
> Hair like a bison horns like an elk unshapes in a deer-leap emerges
> From the spear-pitted rock, becoming what it can make unrolling
> Not sparing itself clenching re-forming rising   beating
> For life.

God striking the sun becomes the cave man drawing in blood becomes the blind child beating its eyes. All are engaged in a desperate magic.

The visitor is interrupted at this point by his reason, which tells him that what he sees "in the half-inner sight / Of squinting, are only . . . children whose hands are tied away / From them for their own good children waiting to smash their dead / Eyes, live faces, to see nothing." Admitting to his fiction, the visitor explains that he is trying to "Re-invent the vision of the race knowing the blind must see / By magic or nothing." He admits further that the fiction is necessary for his own survival:

> . . . it helps me to think
> That they can give themselves, like God from their scabby fists, the original
> Images of mankind: that when they beat their eyes, I witness how
> I survive in my sun-blinded mind: that the beasts are calling to God
> And man for art, when the blind open wide and strike their incurable eyes.

The visitor's predicament is that of modern man: rationalism (the sun) has blinded him to the art, or myths, of his ancestors; to survive, he needs new art.

Reason, interrupting, insists that there is "For the blind nothing but blackness forever nothing but a new bruise / Risen upon the old." The visitor stresses again the indispensable nature of vision: "In the palm of the hand the color red is calling / For blood the forest-fire roars on the cook-stone, smoke smothered and lightning- / born and the race hangs on meat and illusion hangs on nothing / But a magical art." Creating a myth to secure psychological sustenance, the visitor is working with magic as the Stone Age artist worked with magic in painting pictures of animals on the cave wall to secure success in the hunt.

The poem ends as the visitor, deliberately rejecting reality for illusion, enters the cave to assume the persona of the Stone Age hunter-artist. The vague "you" of the preceding part of the poem is now "I":

It is time for the night
Hunt, and the wild meat of survival. The wall glim-
 mers that God and man
Never forgot. I have put history out. An innocent eye,
 it is closed
Off, outside in the sun. Wind moans like an artist. The
 tribal children lie
On their rocks in their animal skins seeing in spurts of
 eye-beating
Dream, the deer, still wet with creation, open its im-
 age to the heart's
Blood, as I step forward, as I move through the beast-
 paint of the stone,
Taken over, submitting, brain-weeping.

Not stopping here, the visitor steps back further into darkness as he projects into the animals that he is creating as
hunter-artist. It is the totemic deer of **"Springer Mountain"** that he identifies with specifically:

Beast, get in
My way. Your body opens onto the plain. Deer, take
 me into your life-
lined form. I merge, I pass beyond in secret in
 perversity and the sheer
Despair of invention   my double-clear bifocals
 off   my reason gone
Like eyes . . . Give me my spear.

With the call for a spear, the magical identification with
the primitive hunter-artist is completed—and in a daringly
literal way as usual.

On a certain level of abstraction, **"The Eye-Beaters"** can
be read as a statement about art, or more specifically
poetry. The poet-visitor himself is the "eye-beater"; blinded
by the sun, he beats his eyes for the chance spark that may
leap through his brain. Modern rationalism has cut him off
from the healing, life-sustaining roots of his past. His only
salvation is a journey down the years, into the darkness of
the collective unconscious, the cave—to enter into the
"life- / lined form" of the deer "still wet with creation."
Dickey's stance is directly opposed to any art for-art's-
sake aesthetic; art for him is a bloody business—"the artist
hunts and slashes" in "the sheer / Despair of invention."
Art is as vital to life as eating. The poem is a wonderful
statement of Dickey's faith in the primitive, mythmaking
power of man.

An important constant, then, in Dickey's work is his poetic
faith, which is manifest throughout—from *Into the Stone*
(1957) to *The Eye-Beaters, Blood, Victory, Madness,
Buckhead and Mercy* (1970). This faith, however, has not
prevented the emergence of a growing sense of man's
mortality, which is particularly evident in the latest collection of poems. This darkening of Dickey's vision is
especially evident when **"The Owl King"** is compared to
"The Eye-Beaters." The blind child who blesses the trees
as he moves with confidence through the forest is replaced
by the institutionalized child who has to be restrained
from striking his blind eyes. The singing of the one poem
is reduced to the moaning of the other. The vision comes

easily, naturally in **"The Owl King"**; painfully in **"The
Eye-Beaters."** Despite these differences, both poems
reflect a fundamental trust in the basic instincts of man.
The most important of these natural forces, which man
shares with other living things, is the power of self-
renewal. "There is a wing-growing motion / Half-alive in
every creature," Dickey has written in **"Reincarnation
(II),"** and it is this motion that is dealt with in one way or
another in many of his poems.

Robert W. Hill (essay date 1973)

SOURCE: Hill, Robert W. "James Dickey: Comic Poet."
In *James Dickey: The Expansive Imagination,* edited by
Richard J. Calhoun, pp. 143-55. DeLand, FL: Everett/
Edwards, Inc., 1973.

[*In the following essay, Hill highlights Dickey's comic
poetic vision, even as it frequently manifests amidst tragic
circumstances.*]

Sometimes James Dickey talks too much, as in **"May Day
Sermon"** or **"Looking for the Buckhead Boys,"** but this
fault comes directly out of what is good in him. For
Dickey, life is moving and absolutely uncapturable; stasis
is tragedy. One thinks of the copius and flowing Falstaff,
whose life goes on forever in the power of effusive
relationships; and when his love is abruptly fronted by
rigid confinement of it, he dies, tragically. The comic Wife
of Bath is pathetic in her declining years, but the going
on, her pilgrimaging and wiving forever, is comic. In
Anatomy of Criticism, Northrop Frye says that comic
fortune often results in a new society precipitated by the
comic hero and formed around him. Constance Rourke's
American Humor suggests that the integration of cultures
into a single culture is what is seen and recorded by comic
writers. I suggest that comedy is more that which promises
to go on; marriages are made, and fruitful continuance is
implied.

Tragedies are about fatal containment. Despite such future-
oriented resolutions as the establishment of Fortinbras at
the end of *Hamlet,* that play is about Hamlet and the royal
family's disaster, the disaster of the state in them. But it is
a unique thing ended with them. There may be other
tragedies, as those implied to come after the death of Be-
owulf, for example, but they are themselves. It is the sense
of finality, delimitation of human activity, not just the matter of declining fortune, that is tragedy; it may not even
concern society as a whole. Comedy is optimistic, openly
affirming, not necessarily taking place within the societal
framework noted by Frye, but within the individual. Thus
we may talk of tragic poetry and comic poetry apart from
their dramatic or moral qualities, or their societal relationships. Dickey is primarily a comic poet because he affirms
copious and on-going life.

Paradoxically, Dickey has three poems about death that
may be useful in trying to understand his comic vision:
"The Lifeguard" (p. 51),[1] **"The Performance"** (p. 30),

and **"Falling"** (p. 293). The first of these is about a lifeguard who tried but failed to save a drowning child. Late at night, solitary in a boathouse, he speaks of the other children who trusted him as they watched him dive again and again. The poem ends with a vision of the dead child out of the killing lake:

> He is one I do not remember
> Having ever seen in his life. . . .
>
> I wash the black mud from my hands.
> On a light given off by the grave
> I kneel in the quick of the moon
> At the heart of a distant forest
> And hold in my arms a child
> Of water, water, water.

This poem offers no expansive vision for its persona. One might claim that the lifeguard's life-sense has expanded in his new consciousness of death and guilt, but that would be to overlook the finality of the last two lines of the poem. The lifeguard is forever caught in that death-guilty moment, and the poem is tragic for its stasis in futility.

The other two death poems are of a different thematic order; they move in the direction of comic vision rather than tragic. **"The Performance"** tells the story of an amateur gymnast, a pilot in World War II's Pacific, who was captured by the Japanese and beheaded. Before his death, however, he "amazed" his "small captors" with "all his lean tricks." The climax of his performance was:

> . . . the stand on his hands,
> Perfect, with his feet together,
> His head down, evenly breathing,
> As the sun poured up from the sea
>
> And the headsman broke down
> In a blaze of tears, in that light
> Of the thin, long human frame
> Upside down in its own strange joy,
> And, if some other one had not told him,
> Would have cut off the feet
>
> Instead of the head,
> And if Armstrong had not presently risen
> In kingly, round-shouldered attendance,
> And then knelt down in himself
> Beside his hacked, glittering grave, having done
> All things in this life that he could.

This is a poem about a man of good-will and free spirit who is decapitated. Yet I have had students to laugh, albeit nervously, when it was read aloud to them. Something of the finality of death is negated by Donald Armstrong's comic vision. His life is cut short, shall we pun, and we care very much that he is lost; but his story is one of abundant life, the excess that makes laughter and art. For Dickey it is particularly significant that Armstrong's affirmation is in terms of physical acts, and that by inverting his own body he inverts the fears of death into joys of life and the tragic into the comic.

From all that we know of him, Donald Armstrong always had the comic vision which allowed him to perform for

his executioners, but this is not the case with the stewardess in **"Falling."** The process of her fortune might be graphed like this: (1) She is in relatively good fortune, alive and functioning in her tightly uniformed way; (2) her fortune suddenly collapses as she is blown out the door of the airplane; (3) she gradually, then more rapidly, grows aware of life, encompassing everything of her human world in recollection and hope—love, T.V.'s, lakes, skydiving, fields, fertility, mystery—rising infinitely beyond whatever "life" she had known before; and (4) she dies as a poetic fertility sacrifice and goddess, a tragic downturn which nonetheless maintains the girl on a higher plane of fortune than her former stiff existence: she becomes a life symbol.

"Falling" is an especially important poem because it exemplifies the integrative consciousness that Dickey identifies as good, and that we have designated as comic. In the epigraph we read that the stewardess is twenty-nine, the cruelest loss-of-youth age, and the poem plays on her being bound up, lacking the freedom and effusiveness of youth. She "moves in her slim tailored / Uniform," and when she falls, "Still neat lipsticked stockinged girdled by regulation her hat / Still on . . . ," we are set up by the poet for the loosening of garments that indicates her return to good natural things later in the poem. She soon finds that her body is "maneuverable," and we are told of "her / Self in low body-whistling wrapped intensely in all her dark dance-weight / Coming down from a marvellous leap. . . ." But the acute physical sense of her falling quickly fuses with the symbolic structuring of the theme of fertility. She falls "with the delaying, dumfounding ease / Of a dream of being drawn like endless moonlight to the harvest soil. . . ." As she hurtles toward the death that earth holds for her, her mind fills with life images: birds, woods, fields, water. She even comes to believe that if she could soar to a lake and hit it just right ("there is time to perfect all the fine / Points of diving"), she would emerge "healthily dripping / And be handed a Coca-Cola. . . ." She has already been linked symbolically with the crescent fertility moon, and this slant reference to Coca-Cola's exploitation of Astarte foreshadows the sacrifice to the fields that the stewardess will become.

By the time she must face death without hope, the stewardess has attained a sense of life's breadth that would make her an integrative, comic visionary, if she were to live. But she cannot, and in her new knowledge of nature she escapes the unassailable single terror of hysteria; she chooses the ritual of her death:

> Do something with water fly to it fall in it drink it rise
> From it but there is none left upon earth the clouds
>   have drunk it back
> The plants have sucked it down there are standing
>   toward her only
> The common fields of death she comes back from fly-
>   ing to falling
> Returns to a powerful cry the silent scream with which
>   she blew down
> The coupled door of the airliner nearly nearly losing
>   hold

Of what she has done remembers remembers the shape
  at the heart
Of cloud fashionably swirling remembers she still has
  time to die
Beyond explanation. . . .

She removes her clothes, desiring to strike the earth with
as much of its naturalness as she can will to herself. The
poem reverberates with the union of her, the earth, and the
blood-mystical farmers on the ground who await "the
greatest thing that ever came to Kansas":

Her last superhuman act the last slow careful passing
  of her hands
All over her unharmed body desired by every sleeper
  in his dream:
Boys finding for the first time their loins filled with
  heart's blood
Widowed farmers whose hands float under light covers to find themselves
Arisen at sunrise the splendid position of blood
  unearthly drawn
Toward clouds. . . .

She is almost apotheosized at this moment, the falling
goddess of fertility come to astound her cult with her
death:

            . . . All those who find her impressed
In the soft loam gone down driven well into the image
  of her body
The furrows for miles flowing in upon her where she
  lies very deep
In her mortal outline in the earth as it is in cloud can
  tell nothing
But that she is there inexplicable unquestionable and
  remember
That something broke in them as well and began to
  live and die more
When they walked for no reason into their fields to
  where the whole earth
Caught her. . . .

Obviously, **"Falling"** is not a completely comic poem, but
in the stewardess' expansive vision—her creative identity
with the natural world—we can see Dickey's comic
impulse at work. In this poem he counterposes an inherently tragic narrative and the comic sense of fertile
continuance. The stewardess is ultimately important to us,
not because she dies so strangely, but because she comes
alive as she falls.

Up to this point, we have not discussed the essential quality—joy—that distinguishes Dickey's unadulteratedly
comic poems. Works like **"The Heaven of Animals"** (p.
59), **"Encounter in the Cage Country"** (p. 274), **"Cherrylog Road"** (p. 134), and **"Power and Light"** (p. 256)
are fully optimistic, effusive with natural potentials, joyous.

The Dantean comic end, a heaven for people, does not
enter into Dickey's poetry. It might be that it carries for
him (out of a Southern Bible Belt culture) connotations of

spiritual fixedness—a tragedy for human creatures.
Besides, what he has called his "religion of sticks and
stones" would be antithetical to any traditional Christian
notions of immortality and divine reward. So he writes of
"The Heaven of Animals," a cyclical living and dying
that allows ideal participation of the living individual in
the most profound processes of nature. Joy for the physical creature is to fulfill his sensuous natural self:

Here they are. The soft eyes open.
If they have lived in a wood
It is a wood.
If they have lived on plains
It is grass rolling
Under their feet forever. . . .

One suspects that Dickey is much more sensitive to the
savage bliss of the predatory cats in this poem than to the
fearless acquiescence of the hunted. But because of the
restrictions of the *tour de force,* he does portrary a kind of
saintly victimage at the end:

Their reward: to walk

Under such trees in full knowledge
Of what is in glory above them,
And to feel no fear,
But acceptance, compliance.
Fulfilling themselves without pain

At the cycle's center,
They tremble, they walk
Under the tree,
They fall, they are torn,
They rise, they walk again.

There is, nonetheless a fakery about this poem that seems
to come from Dickey's discomfort in the presence of the
Ideal. He is a poet of process, of the imperfection of human and non-human nature; he believes in an ongoing life
force that "seems to promise immortality to life, but
destruction to beings," as Melville has put it (*Mardi,*
LXIX). Dickey sees joy in the animals' heaven, and he
wants the poem to show his belief in integrative nature;
but he deserts his position on the side of nature when he
removes pain from the prey's experience. This is a very
neat poem; however, in straining after its point it misses
the profundity of real experience.

A much more real thing happens in **"Encounter in the
Cage Country."**[2] Dickey (it is difficult to speak of "the
persona," since it is so plainly Dickey himself) explores a
very complex set of responses. At one level he is
egocentric, asserting his human superiority over this beast:

Among the crowd, he found me
Out and dropped his bloody snack. . . .

. . . we saw he was watching only
Me. I knew the stage was set, and I began
To perform. . . .

He is playing a role, but not so much for the cat as for the
spectators who have gathered for his display of American

tourism: ". . . at one brilliant move / I made as though drawing a gun from my hip- / bone. . . ." He imagines having great power over the crowd as well as over the panther: ". . . the bite-sized children broke / Up changing their concept of laughter. . . ." At another level, however, he believes that he is communicating with the animal, thus affirming their kinship. Unlike the "sophisticated," superior human being before him, the black panther is not fooling:

> But none of this changed his eyes, or changed
> My green glasses. Alert, attentive,
> He waited for what I could give him:
>
> My moves my throat my wildest love,
> The eyes behind my eyes. . . .

The man has found confirmation for his instinctual life in the eyes of a caged beast; he has drawn power that is deeply known and inexplicably communicable: ". . . the crowd / Quailed from me and I was inside and out / of myself. . . ."

The poem is comic in two ways: it asserts the natural union of human beings and other animals, and it is funny. Laurence Lieberman makes reference to the latter, saying, "While the humor enhances the seriousness of the exchange between man and beast, it also balances the terror as the poem rises to a peak of spiritual transcendence." With regard to the former, he notes a shift in attitude from Dickey's earlier animal poems: ". . . he no longer transforms into a new, wholly other being; instead, he intensifies and deepens the human self by adding animal powers to it."[3] These two observations are of the essence of Dickey's comic vision. It cannot merely exclude the terrible; an expansive vision must have room for the sprawling human potential and the fatal constrictions of circumstance. And it all must end in affirmation—joy at being alive. **"Encounter in the Cage Country"** ends with the poet's knowing that he is uniquely human, separate, and yet not unknown to the almost mystical life force:

> . . . something was given a life-
> mission to say to me hungrily over
>
> And over and over *your moves are exactly right*
> *For a few things in this world: we know you*
> *When you come, Green Eyes, Green Eyes.*

"Cherrylog Road" and **"Power and Light"** are more exclusively human poems. Especially in **"Cherrylog Road,"** Dickey relies on the vitality of common people to approach the comic vision. The nature-force that he writes about is the sexual urge of youngsters from the country. The occasion of the plot is a lovers' tryst in a junkyard. The girl has to slip away from her frightening father on the pretext of stealing parts off the junked cars:

> I popped with sweat as I thought
> I heard Doris Holbrook scrape
> Like a mouse in the southern-state sun
> That was eating the paint in blisters
> From a hundred car tops and hoods.

> She was tapping like code,
> Loosening the screws,
> Carrying off headlights,
> Sparkplugs, bumpers
> Cracked mirrors and gear-knobs,
> Getting ready, already,
> To go back with something to show
>
> Other than her lips' new trembling. . . .

The quality of Dickey's humor here is not strained; the funny things in this poem come from exuberance—extravagant images that might very well have occurred to a boy who could rendezvous in such a wildly imaginative place. His fear of Doris' father is funny with the fears of youth, although there is no reason to doubt that the red-haired man might wait:

> In a bootlegger's roasting car
> With a string-triggered 12-gauge shotgun
> To blast the breath from the air. . . .

The scene intrudes upon the youthfully serious passion with an irreverence that does not slow the two lovers at all:

> . . . we clung, glued together,
> With the hooks of the seat springs
> Working through to catch us red-handed
> Amidst the gray breathless batting
>
> That burst from the seat at our backs. . . .

When the sexual experience is over, the boy, parted from his girl and flushed with success, goes to his motorcycle. Dickey's description reproduces perfectly the happy haste of kinds who got away with it:

> . . . she down Cherrylog Road
> And I to my motorcycle
> Parked like the soul of the junkyard
> Restored, a bicycle fleshed
> With power, and tore off
> Up Highway 106, continually
> Drunk on the wind in my mouth,
> Wringing the handlebar for speed,
> Wild to be wreckage forever.

This poem's greatest accomplishment is in its depiction of youthful passion and resourcefulness, not in its portrait of true love. Doris Holbrook is never as important as an individual woman as she is as the catalyst for the boy's excitement. In this poem we are not confronted with moral sensitivity and complex psychology. Nor is there mystical interaction of the human with the non-human, although Dickey does make some gestures in the direction of pathetic fallacy in order to tie the young lovers symbolically to natural processes:

> So the blacksnake, stiff
> With inaction, curved back
> Into life, and hunted the mouse
>
> With deadly overexcitement. . . .

This is a story of the finding and fulfilling of humanity in natural instincts without regret. These young do not ponder consequences; they act from their energies, and they affirm the wild freedom of having done what was wanted and having freely joined with another human being. There is only a distant fear of reprisal, and that vanishes from the moment "I held her and held her and held her. . . ." The poem is comic partly because the reader believes that this rendezvous might very well take place again, equally without guilt, equally breathlessly, with the young motorcyclist tearing off again, drunk again on the wind.

The repetition of experience implied in **"Power and Light"** is, from one point of view, tragic. It is a poem about a telephone lineman who feels fully alive only in terms of his work. His wife and children are trouble to him, and at the beginning of the poem he has gone away from them into the basement to drink after work. For most of the poem he is drunk, and he tells how his personal power and light come from his work and his liquor: one satisfies him when he is away from home, and the other lifts him out of the darkness of the basement into the light of his upper house, inured to his unpleasant domestic situation. Insofar as he is trapped by an unchangingly bad home life, the man is tragic; but insofar as he is able to find renewal within himself, and new optimism, he is comic.

This man loves the work of his hands; he is optimistic in turning to physical action for his inspiration, and when that work time is done, he turns inward with drink, to find the "pure fires of the Self." He has comic vitality in seeing the extensions of himself multiplied and spreading world-wide into expression, nothing blocked, everything reaching out and fulfilling the needs of language and emotion:

>   . . . all connections
> Even the one
> With my wife, turn good turn better than good turn
>   good
> Not quite, but in the deep sway of underground among
>   the roots
> That bend like branches all things connect and stream
> Toward light and speech. . . .

He talks like a ring-tailed roarer, and his courage rises until he cannot simply talk anymore:

>   . . . I strap crampons to my shoes
> To climb the basement stairs, sinking my heels in the
>   tree-
> life of the boards. Thorns! Thorns! I am bursting
> Into the kitchen, into the sad way-station
> Of my home, holding a double handful of wires
>
> Spitting like sparklers
> On the Fourth of July. . . .

This kind of going ahead with bluster and stomp makes the lineman one of a long line of comic extroverts: *miles gloriosus*, Falstaff, Pecos Bill, Paul Bunyan, etc. Constance Rourke calls this type the frontiersman, or back-

woodsman, but Dickey's interest is not so much in the lineman's word-flinging comic forebears. He sees the man as one who is profoundly conscious of fate and the grave in the midst of his imaginative palaver:

> And I laugh
> Like my own fate watching over me night and day at
>   home
> Underground or flung up on towers walking
> Over mountains my charged hair standing on end
>   crossing
> The sickled, slaughtered alleys of timber
> Where the lines loop and crackle on their gallows.
> Far under the grass of my grave, I drink like a man
>
> The night before
> Resurrection Day. . . .

For Dickey, the comic vision is essentially inclusive of all life—people and things, terror and exaltation. One of the differences between Dickey and that other great garrulous includer, Walt Whitman, is that Dickey is more consistent in keeping both the good and evil in mind—unblended, intrinsic—throughout his poetry. The comic vision is a balanced one, enabling men to go on despite deaths and nagging wives, but the deaths and wives are not forgotten. To tramp through the kitchen with Thor's bolts in hand and terrible spikes at heel is not to forget that there is opposition, but it *is* to say to that opposition, ". . . I am a man / Who turns on. I am a man."

Notes

1. *Poems 1957-1967* (Middletown, Connecticut, 1967). All page references will be to this edition.

2. At public readings, Dickey likes to tell of how he actually met the black panther at the London Zoo; the experience is obviously dear to him.

3. Laurence Lieberman, intro. *The Achievement of James Dickey* (Glenview, Illinois: Scott, Foresman, 1968), p. 21.

Joan Bobbitt (essay date 1978)

SOURCE: Bobbitt, Joan. "Unnatural Order in the Poetry of James Dickey." *Concerning Poetry* 11, no. 1 (spring 1978): 39-44.

[*In the following essay, Bobbitt focuses on Dickey's often grotesque poetic juxtaposition of the world of nature and the world of man.*]

Neither James Dickey's reverence for nature nor his fear that "we have lost the cosmos" while constructing our technological society marks him as unique. Yet, by his own admission, Dickey is no ordinary "stick and stone" pantheist. His avowed interest in the relationship between the "man-made world" and the "universe-made world" may bear some resemblance to Wordsworth, Emerson, or even Lawrence, but his expression of it is hardly typical.[1] Throughout his poetry, Dickey employs shockingly bizarre or ludicrous images to communicate the alien position of nature in the "civilized" world. Indeed, the juxtaposition of the world of nature and the world of man often leads to grotesque incongruities. Things seem severely twisted by comparison. In the sea, the shark finds a natural home: in the parlor, its presence becomes unnatural. The poet sees civilization as so far removed from nature, its primal antecedent, that only such aberrations can aptly depict their relationship and, as he implies, possibly restore them to harmony and order.

Dickey makes it clear, however, that what seems to be unnatural is only so because of its context in a civilized world, and that these deviations actually possess a vitality which modern man has lost. In **"Kudzu,"** for example, nature's power flows from the plant to the speaker, who needs its strength even though his civilized character dictates that he must destroy the giver. As early as the first line, kudzu is associated with something alien and menacing. A "far Eastern vine," it refuses to stay within the bounds set for it by man, "the clay banks it is supposed to keep from eroding" (11. 2-3). Ironically, man has acknowledged his dependency by introducing it to the land himself. He cannot control nature alone; he must use nature to control nature. Yet nature is not easily harnessed to do man's bidding. Instead, the kudzu grows past the artificial limits imposed on it. In line 6, the vines crawl up telephone poles, which take on human characteristics as they shriek to avoid being smothered. As nature twisted and distorted by man, they resist these "ghosts," reminders of what they once were, who have come now to reclaim them.

Nature's uncanny power becomes even more evident in the second section of the poem, lines 9-31. Here the kudzu seems to be endowed with an almost super-human strength of will. With determination it encroaches upon the domain of man, casting a spell over all it touches. As the tendrils crawl snake-like across the fields and toward the windows, "you sleep like the dead" (1. 15). In this "silence," grown "Oriental" (1. 16), civilized man has no place. He cannot step upon this parody of a hallowed ground for his leg will plunge even deeper into a mystery where "it should not, it never should be" (1. 19). Nature is denying man even as man is denying nature. Though the speaker recognizes rationally that the movement of the kudzu is mindless, not purposive, he nonetheless stands in awe of and fears its power. Indeed, it is this very mindlessness, so alien to anything he knows, which frightens him most. The danger which he fears, moreover, is not imaginary, but quite real. Through some mysterious transformation, the vines appear almost to have become serpents, the traditional symbol of evil. Regardless of how they came to be there, the snakes which twine themselves among the kudzu pose a definite threat. They seem to grow "in earthly power" because they cannot safely be contained by man. Under the "huge circumstance of concealment," they are ready to destroy. The cows, products of man's paltry at-

tempts to domesticate nature, prove no match for them. So pervasive is their power that all nature seems to respond: even the dead wood of the stalls "strain[s] to break into leaf" (1. 31), as the dying cows look on.

When the kudzu taps, Raven-like, at the window, civilized man realizes that he must stop cowering in fear and assume control of nature. To do so, he once again relies on nature to fight nature. Though he failed before, this time he employs the aid, not of an alien plant which may easily become uncontrollable, but of a domestic animal, the hog. With the fat which diminishes their vulnerability, these "meaty troops" thrash out the snakes. Just as the snakes are linked to the kudzu, the hogs are likened to their owners. In the leaves, "the sound is intense, nearly human with purposive rage" (1. 45). The animals seem to absorb the will of their masters as they trample and destroy the enemy. Appropriately, it is the hog that can most successfully do man's bidding and fight his battles. Alone, he proves inadequate to the task of confronting and subduing nature. With the death of the snakes, the kudzu loses its power and withers away "Leaving a mass of brown strings / Like the wires of a gigantic switchboard" (1. 59). Like the telephone pole, it is but a ghost of what it once was and bears more resemblance to a man-made thing than to its true nature. Yet the telephone poles and the stalls still exist, though admittedly in a different state, while the kudzu, robbed of its power, ceases to live. In "restoring the lightning to the sky" (1. 61), man has put nature in its place and can sleep safely.

Still, civilized man seems diminished by his own victory. In his "frail" house, he muses on "the surface of things and its terrors" (1. 65) and comes to the recognition that his own nature has indeed been enhanced by the kudzu and that its loss is also his. Just as the vines send "great powers" into the bodies of the snakes, "energy also flowed / . . . from the knee-high meadow" (11. 72-3) to him. The kudzu provides a kind of transfusion of nature's power into a human body that is somehow deficient, what H. L. Weatherby terms "the way of exchange," a mysterious regenerative process which may take place between man and his opposites."[2] With the "green sword twined among / the veins" (11. 75-6) the arm grows and takes on new strength. Such vigor does not come from "proper shaved fields" or "safe cows" (11. 75-6), nature which has been tampered with by man, but only from nature which refuses to be harnessed by man. While he sleeps, the power comes to him despite the closed windows, and in him it prospers. His waking self, however, finds it necessary to root the invader out or risk destruction by an irrational force. Yet the alien plant has made an impact on the civilized world, and in remembering, man is acknowledging his own need of a power which only nature can provide.

In **"The Sheep Child,"** Dickey once again depicts the relationship between rational man and irrational nature through a bizarre image. Though Georgia farm boys admit the masturbatory function of nature in their wild need "to couple with anything" (1. 12), their fear of the product of complete irrationality in man, the sheep child, forces them to be civilized. Like the legend of the kudzu, the story of the "woolly baby pickled in alcohol" (11. 17-18) in an Atlanta museum serves as a grim reminder of what happens when the irrational takes control. Such "things can't live" (1. 13) because man and nature pose two extremes which are seemingly irreconcilable. Yet Dickey frequently "focuses on the earth's beasts as a means to the angels."[3] Though the creature's eyes are open, no one is able to face that vacant stare. To do so would be to acknowledge the possibility of the animal in man. Such demonstrations of irrationality, however imaginary, are best left to dusty corners. In fact, the civilized urban society momentarily forgets as the boys take "their own true wives in the city" (1. 19). But the poet remembers and wonders if the story is merely fiction.

In the figure of the sheep child, Dickey credits himself with having created the most unique persona in literature.[4] This grotesque combination of two worlds, the world of nature and the world of man, speaks "merely with his eyes" (1. 25), perhaps a Platonic reference to the dwelling place of the soul. In describing his conception and birth, the sheep child stresses harmony in nature. His mother stands "like moonlight" in the pasture, an image which implies union among all things. Indeed, Dickey calls the female sheep a heroine "who accepts the monstrous conjunction and bears the monstrous child because in some animal way she recognizes the need it is born from."[5] Despite its mindlessness and irrationality, nature willingly serves man. When she is seized from behind, the sheep child's mother gives "her best / self to that great need" (11. 34-5). Having conceived, she assumes human qualities and sobs "at what she must do" (1. 38).

In the dying moments of his birth, the sheep child looks with "eyes more than human" (11. 40-1). A part of both worlds, he can momentarily know their truths, and in viewing "man and beast in the round of their need" (1. 43), he senses a fullness, an overall completeness not apparent to the merely human. According to George Lensing, Dickey actually believes "that animal life, in its natural and instinctive wisdom, is one to which humans may aspire and in which they may find their own heightened identity."[6] Yet, despite his knowledge, the sheep child cannot live, and with his death, those truths become only faintly detectible behind staring eyes.

From the harmony of the pasture, the dead sheep child is brought to his "father's house" (1. 49), a dusty, unvisited museum. In contrast with the world of nature, the world of man seems empty and sterile. Pickled in his "immortal waters" (1. 52) the sheep child's eyes confide his truths to the "sun's grains," the only visitors to his "hellish-mild corner" (1. 51). Unlike a two-headed kitten or some other freak of nature, he does not attract the curious for whom his existence would bear testimony that man is also fallible. Such unnatural creatures seem to parody a world which, in his delusion, man believes he controls rationally and absolutely. Consequently, the lesson which the sheep

child teaches is resisted. Like the kudzu, however, he is remembered and in the memory there is an admission of need. Dickey uses the imaginary sheep child to represent nature denied and man diminished as a consequence: "What I intended was that this *contra naturum* creature born from this monstrous clandestine marriage between a human being and an animal is not *contra naturum* but very much *naturum*."[7] The fear which keeps farm boys from coupling with animals and forces them "deep into their known right hands" (1. 60) is civilized man's rejection of the irrational within himself. The memory of the sheep child drives man to marry and to raise his kind, and, in doing so, it becomes a civilizing tool. Yet as Laurence Liberman points out in "The Worldly Mystic," he is now ever-conscious, caught "in a haunting, if inexpressible certainty that a much larger, grander, demonic world— compounded of Heaven and Hell—lies just the other side of the limits of his known, calculable existence."[8]

In **"The Fiend,"** Dickey employs the unnatural in the same manner and for the same purpose as in **"Kudzu"** and **"The Sheep Child,"** bringing the power of nature to the civilized, normal world. The fiend specifically embodies the sexual power in nature which becomes grotesque when concentrated in this one unlikely man. A Jekyll and Hyde figure, by day he is the most ordinary of people, a worried accountant who somehow epitomizes the tedium and mediocrity of civilized existence. At night, however, he transcends this dreary state, though he never quite discards its trappings, the straightened tie and pocketful of pens given him by salesmen. When he assumes the role of voyeur, the accountant loses many of his human characteristics and as a consequence becomes in harmony with nature. As fiend, he is able to "swarm" and "glide up the underside light of leaves" (1. 3). When he masturbates, all nature seems to be moving with him. At such moments "he holds in his awkward, subtle limbs / the limbs of a hundred understanding trees" (11. 39-40). In providing him with cover and protection, nature seems to give approval. Indeed, in his lust it is nature in the form of the wind that sets him in motion. Through the fiend, Dickey stresses this inter-dependence between man and nature. When he coughs, "the smallest root responds" (1. 86). When he sees a naked girl, the wind "quits in mid-tree" and "birds / freeze to their perches" (11. 21-2). In no instance does nature oppose him. Even watchdogs are quieted by his hand which, like Christ's could "calm sparrows and rivers" (1. 63). Instinctively, they sense in him a kindred spirit. Like the sheep child, the fiend views the truths of both worlds, and his eyes and the dogs' are "the same pure beast's / Comprehending the same essentials" (11. 65-6). Lieberman rightly observes that the "encounter between him and life-experience, though voyeuristic and 'abnormal,' is presented as final, incisive, fulfilling."[9]

Against this natural harmony, Dickey poses the sterility of civilized existence. What the fiend witnesses is a form of death in life symbolized by the soundless TV shows. "Gesturing savagely" (1. 48) the actors act out their parts. Yet reading their lips is like "reading the lips of the dead"

(1. 49). Sound isn't even necessary, for nothing is being said. This same lifelessness is a reflection of the lives of the apartment dwellers. The effect of watching them through closed windows is much the same as watching a meaningless TV show. Without even the pretense of vitality, "indifferent men drift in or out of the rooms" (11. 70-1) or doze over the newspaper. Almost omniscient, the fiend is always "near them when they are weeping without sound" (1. 95). From his vantage point in the trees, he watches as "doctors, looking oddly / Like himself worm a medical arm up under the cringing covers" (11. 100-102). No-where does he see any evidence of happiness or contentment: civilization seems to be synonymous with impotence.

The fiend, however, is a mediator between man and nature, and its power is invested in him. A grotesque parody of the saviour, he can transform even a "sullen shopgirl" (1. 19) into something more than human. His watching affects man-made things: the TV screen sputters with wormy static as though it senses an alien presence. Similarly, the girl herself changes. The fiend sends his power to her in a ray of light, and she no longer moves herself, but is moved by an invisible force, "some all-seeing eye of God" (11. 27-28). Even her "stressed nipples" have a life of their own as they "rise like things about to crawl off her" (1. 25). As she is carried by "some hand come up out of roots" (1. 28) to the shower, she shares with the fiend the distinction of being one with the natural world. Time seems to stop. Civilization itself passes away as the other apartments sink to ground level, "burying their sleepers in the soil" (1. 18). In this isolation, the "sullen shopgirl" takes on mythological characteristics. The steamed shower becomes her "cloud chamber," and she sings as if "come up from river-fog" (11. 31-32, 34). With her hair in "rigid curlers" (1. 20), she seems an unlikely goddess. Yet even apartment-dwellers can be transfigured by the fiend's light and become "saints" (1. 24).

In his role as saviour, the fiend fulfills a definite, though only faintly acknowledged, need in man. The unhappy women whom he views are especially aware of their emptiness. Because they are women, they are instinctively close to nature. Their bodies respond with "moon-summoned blood" (1. 84) and are nature's receptacles in the sexual act. Sensing the impotence of the civilized world, they fill their beds with teddy bears and "overstuffed beasts" (1. 99) in a vain attempt to capture some of nature's vitality: "for what / women want / Dwells in bushes and trees" (11. 72-3). Lacking this sexual power, they "must save their lives / By taking off their clothes" (11. 53-4). Only by returning, at least spiritually, to his natural state can man find fulfillment. In his abnormality, the fiend saves by his "beholding" (1. 54) and thereby confers on deficient man a type of "immortality" (1. 68).

Like the kudzu, however, the "worried accountant" poses a potential threat to the civilized world. In denying the natural or irrational in himself, man has forced its power into concealment. For the apartment-dwellers, natural instincts are relegated to their proper place under cringing covers. The work of the fiend too must be done by stealth in the night. Such denial though can never be a permanent state. Already, the fiend has difficulty uncurling his toes from branches; his bird movements die hard. The "solid citizen" (1. 62) is little more than a figment of the imagination. Too many pulled shades have undermined his solidity. Ultimately, nature will assert itself, perhaps, as Dickey implies, violently. When the fiend comes down from his tree to make a "final declaration" (1. 118), the irrational which has been denied will make an irrecoverable intrusion into the civilized world.

In these representative poems, Dickey attempts to fulfill his professed poetic aim of charging "the world with vitality, with the vitality that it already has, if we could rise to it."[10] The kudzu is a product of the natural world introduced into the world of man, while the fiend is a product of the civilized world that seeks to return to nature. Though unable to live in either, the sheep child is the offspring of both worlds. In all instances, these aberrations function by either the consent or action of man who acknowledges a need for nature's power, if only at the unconscious level. Indeed Dickey seems to be suggesting here, as in his novel, *Deliverance,* that "survival might depend upon an ability to shed the veneer of civilization and call forth the monster within us, to meet our buried selves face to face. . . ."[11] In his poetry, the unnatural provides a means of satisfying this need and establishing order between man and nature.

Notes

1. James Dickey, *Self-Interviews* (Garden City, NY: Doubleday, 1970), p. 67.

2. H. L. Weatherby, "The Way of Exchange in James Dickey's Poetry," in *James Dickey: The Expansive Imagination,* ed. Richard J. Calhoun (Deland, Fla.: Everett/Edwards, 1973), p. 54.

3. Eileen Glancy, *James Dickey: The Critic as Poet* (Troy, NY: Whitson, 1971), p. 24.

4. Lecture delivered at Loyola University in New Orleans, 1967.

5. Dickey, p. 165.

6. George Lensing, "James Dickey and the Movements of Imagination," in *James Dickey: The Expansive Imagination,* p. 164.

7. Dickey, p. 165.

8. Laurence Lieberman, "The Worldly Mystic," in *James Dickey: The Expansive Imagination,* p. 74.

9. Lieberman, p. 73.

10. James Dickey, *Sorties* (Garden City, NY: Doubleday, 1971), p. 5.

11. Donald J. Greiner, "The Harmony of Bestiality in James Dickey's *Deliverance,*" *South Carolina Review,* 5, No. 1 (December 1972), 44.

James M. French (review date 1978)

SOURCE: French, James M. Review of *The Zodiac,* by James Dickey. *Prairie Schooner* 52, no. 1 (spring 1978): 113-15.

[*In the following review of* The Zodiac, *French notes that Dickey's ambitious poem is deeply flawed and improperly realized.*]

James Dickey's reputation as a writer has grown in the past ten years. In fact, Dickey has lately become a highly visible public figure as well. Within the past two years his poetic productivity and presence has not diminished. In that period he has published **The Zodiac,** written the text to *In God's Image,* and graced the ritual occasion of Jimmy Carter's inauguration. As a poet, James Dickey is not undeserving of the recognition he has now achieved. Yet at least one of Dickey's latest offerings, **The Zodiac,** does not demonstrate the strength of much of the earlier verse.

The Zodiac is by far Dickey's most ambitious effort to compose a long and major poem. In the headnote he describes **Zodiac** as a poem "based on another by the same title" (p. 7) by the Dutch poet, Hendrik Marsman. Dickey discounts his work as translation; instead, "it is a story of a drunken and perhaps dying Dutch poet who returns to his home . . . and tries desperately to relate himself to the universe." It is in this mode that Dickey presents Marsman and transforms him into a symbolic vehicle. One is not surprised, then, to see Marsman's tragic life in terms of a self-conscious examination of the poetic process.

The Zodiac ends with a proclamation that the generative "tuning fork" of the universe:

> shall vibrate through the western world
> So long as the hand can hold its island
> Of blazing paper, and bleed for its images:
> Make what it can of what is:
>
> So long as the spirit hurls on space
> The star-beasts of intellect and madness.
>
> [P. 62]

For a poem that rarely breaks free of the tortured syntax of Dickey's insane and drunken protagonist, these last lines are amazingly coherent. It seems to be Dickey's point that while "bleeding . . . for images" one can gain eloquence as well as grace. The basic concept is a familiar one—the poet is akin to outcast, madman, or prophet. Ever since Coleridge, the literary world has seen an array of sensitive and suffering wanderers. Dickey maintains the image of the Mariner through Marsman, substitutes a "tuning fork" for the animating force of the Aeolian Harp, and an ambiguous sexual tragedy in Marsman's past takes the place of the murdered albatross (sec. 9). It would be unfair to condemn Dickey for the display of what may indeed be central mythic elements, but his use of Romantic themes and images is often cloyingly obvious. For example,

Dickey represents Marsman's alcoholism and obsession with death in a descent motif. While Marsman is suffering from delirium tremens, the narrator states:

> —god-*damn* it, he *can't* quit,
> But—*listen* to me—how can he *rise*
>   When he's *digging?* Digging through the smoke
> Of distance, throwing columns around to find . . .
>
> He's drunk again.
>
> [P. 40]

This passage demonstrates the extent to which the "bleeding" poet can be reduced to cliché. For Dickey, Marsman's message was that one shouldn't "shack up with the intellect," yet to "conceive with meat / Alone" is to doom the "child" (p. 47). Thus the struggle for the marriage of heaven and hell, mind and heart continues. This modern sense of alienation is brought to a climax when, in the face of the "expanding Universe," Marsman "can't tell Europe / From his own Death" (p. 39). Like these examples, the language repeatedly strikes one as banal and unimaginative.

Obviously, Dickey had great ambitions in the creation of the poem. But for this reviewer the goals of the poem are never successfully realized. One is never sure whether the erratic syntax and abrupt alterations in speaker, time, and voice simply parallel and reflect the mental state of Marsman. There is the temptation to judge Dickey's verse as haphazardly constructed or flawed. It is also difficult to determine the correlation between the Zodiac and the structure of the poem. The poem's twelve sections seem more convenient than functional. As a type, **The Zodiac** does have precedents. Don Finkel's *Adequate Earth,* Warren's *Audubon: A Vision,* and Berryman's *Homage to Mistress Bradstreet* are all examples of successful mixtures of the historical, psychological, and mythic. Dickey's predicament in **The Zodiac,** though, may be a result of his own poetic theorizing. In *Babel to Byzantium,* Dickey wrote that he was gaining interest "in the conclusionless poem, the open or ungeneralizing poem, the un-well-made poem." While **The Zodiac** is neither "conclusionless" or "ungeneralizing," it is certainly "un-well-made."

If Dickey is now at the popular zenith of his career, his audience can expect his publishers to capitalize on the marketability of his name. I hope, though, that our unofficial poet laureate does not allow more works like **The Zodiac** to reach the public in third-rate condition.

Richard J. Calhoun and Robert W. Hill (essay date 1983)

SOURCE: Calhoun, Richard J., and Robert W. Hill. "Reaching Out to Others." In *James Dickey,* pp. 25-53. Boston: Twayne Publishers, 1983.

[In the following essay, Calhoun and Hill undertake a thematic and stylistic survey of the poetry in Dickey's second collection, Drowning With Others, *occasionally comparing the volume with his earlier* Into the Stone.*]*

To speak of the poet's stance, his personality, in the second book is perhaps abstract and inexact, but Dickey becomes a more self-accepted, assertive actor instead of the relatively passive observer. Repeatedly, in *Into the Stone,* with poems like **"The Call," "The Vegetable King," "The Sprinter's Sleep,"** and **"The Other,"** Dickey's narrator is overwhelmed by Something Out Yonder. *Drowning with Others* (1962) proceeds with more confidence, less mincing (probably too strong a word) than that first book. It is as though the poet found his calling, to transliterate the experiences of the physical world into the physical symbols of poetry.

THE SOLITARY SELF IS NOT ENOUGH

In *Drowning with Others,* Dickey extends and develops the themes of *Into the Stone,* but one consideration emerges with particular emphasis: social interconnection. With the first poem of the book, **"The Lifeguard,"** mutual responsibility is made clear: the familiar guilt motif is made a social affair. Having lost a child to the dark lake, the fallen hero retreats from the silent accusation of the children who once saw him as godlike and who consequently felt utterly safe while he was on duty. Like the protagonist in a later poem, **"Power and Light,"** this lifeguard feels that he must escape from people and try to recover in solitude when things have gone wrong. His self-esteem prior to his failure seems to have depended much upon his responsibility to society. During his retreat, at night, he envisions a mystical child arising from the lake, smiling. At the end, however, reality asserts itself, and the lifeguard is left hopelessly to "hold in my arms a child / Of water, water, water."

Dickey pursues his nature theme in the society of hunters in **"Listening to Foxhounds,"** which begins in the full fellowship of the hunt. The men sit around campfires, listening to their "brothers," the hounds. Then the focus draws down to one man whose dog has made his own remarkable sound. The omniscient-seeming point of view is unusual for Dickey, but the voice gradually shifts to the second person: "You know which chosen man has heard." The poem's most wondrous effect is in merging the social group of fox-hunters with the singular narrator (who obfuscates himself in the second person) and with the almost spiritual identity of men with hounds, who, in their pursuit, have their own identity with the foxes. The men strain emotionally together, competitively hoping to recognize their own hounds even as they try to conceal unmanly enthusiasm. This reticent single-mindedness about one's own dog redoubles the tension when, "if one should do so," the narrator "might" imagine the fox. Fully aware of his comrades' social pressure, the speaker must be even more self-contained than in awaiting public joy over his dog: "Who runs with the fox / Must sit here like

his own image, / Giving nothing of himself. . . ." He imagines that his private musings are more energized, more intense, and more mysterious than those of the other hunters; but their society is essential to his imaginative experience.

"Between Two Prisoners" allows for a social connection like the hunter's with the victimized fox, but its ambiguity as to who the prisoners are plays out Dickey's preference for narration that intermingles what is inside with what is outside the speaker of the poem. As with **"The Performance,"** the narrator takes into account not only the American prisoners and their feelings but also the condition (and eventual death) of at least one of the Japanese guards. The schoolroom setting is significant as the prisoners and their captors are separated by force in a building where society normally teaches how to connect through civilized traditions. With prisoners immobilized, "A belief in words grew upon them / That the unbound, who walk, cannot know." Once, in this place, children communicated by "deep, hacked hieroglyphics" in their school desks, or through "the luminous chalks of all colors" with which they adorned the classroom; but now "The guard . . . leaned close / . . . To hear in a foreign tongue, / All things which cannot be said." Later, as the small guard is hanged "In a closed horse stall in Manila . . . / No one knows what language he spoke / As his face changed into all colors." The villain, as in **"The Enclosure,"** is war itself, whose villainy includes the perversion of the high social virtue of language: "Speaking words that can never be spoken / Except in a foreign tongue, / In the end, at the end of a war."

"A View of Fujiyama After the War" also depicts unanticipated connections among military enemies. The poem shows, with only moderate success, the ambiguities inherent in defeat and victory. Foreshadowing **"The Firebombing,"** Dickey's social theme here is ironic, since the poem tells what the poet has *not* had to suffer—the indignity of being (figuratively) alive again only because the enemy lives and can write poems on foreign soil. The poet's guilt is partly for his cannibalism of his and others' lives.

BROTHERS: LIVING AND DEAD

Although its role is much reduced, Dickey's brother-ghost persists in *Drowning with Others.* **"In the Tree House at Night"** deals both with Dickey's older, deceased brother, Eugene, and with his younger, surviving one; while **"Armor"** concentrates on the brother-ghost, so vividly construed earlier in **"The Underground Stream," "The String,"** and **"The Other."**

In portraying the brother-guilt, **"Armor"** comes to more mature resolution than some earlier poems. Its main image—the speaker's donning armor—corresponds to Dickey's putting on a boar's head in **"Approaching Prayer"** (1964), to having a life-mask made and suffering eye-burn and temporary blindness just prior to writing the

"Cahill Is Blind" section of *Alnilam* (Dickey's novel in progress), and perhaps even to playing helmeted football in high school and college. Dickey is a willful mind-mover: he likes imposing environmental (or apparel) changes to enhance his imagination. In **"Falling,"** the stewardess, thrown suddenly out of a plane's door, removes her clothes as she descends, thus intentionally to alter herself "beyond explanation" before she hits the ground. Conversely altering himself by putting armor on—which normally makes a person less vulnerable—Dickey's speaker becomes strangely more vulnerable. He imagines the shell as having "the power of the crab and the insect," suggesting that he is better able to survive certain physical onslaughts. But he chiefly turns the armor into a self-reflexive mirror. It forces him inward and causes him to call up the encompassing spirit of his dead brother, "whose features I knew // By the feel of their strength on my face / And whose limbs by the shining of mine." It is the brother again, but with a somewhat different mission than before. In this poem he merges spiritually with the narrator, becoming a sort of infused sponsor for his entry into Heaven. There is no guilt, only opportunity. When this poem is done, the speaker no longer feels that his life will be constantly enthralled by the memory or spirit of his brother. Now, by abandoning the armor to stand by itself in the woods as a symbol of his brother, waiting separate and apart from the speaker, this more reconciled man comes to the place in his life where he is able to imagine meeting his brother, taking on his shell again as a glowing energy-field in the woods—but only after death, only at the time of eternal union. Enabled by this armorial vision, the narrator can put the brother aside, live his own life to its end, rejoin his brother (if their immortality should prove to commingle), and investigate the mystical armor to see "What man is within to live with me / When I begin living forever."

"In the Tree House at Night" is an effort to expunge brother-guilt by acting out the spirit's commands, of play-fully indulging useful, constructive energies. But the play confirms serious relations both with the ghostly dead and with nature. It calls for the poet to make full contact with society other than the wandering spirits. The poet's preoccupation with mere survivorship has here been much diverted, and the poem's almost blatant sexuality (stanzas 6-8) would indicate that the poet is less guilt-ridden than gratified by his brother.

The narrator assumes sensual but vegetative traits:

> My green graceful bones fill the air
> With sleeping birds. Alone, alone
> And with them I move gently.
> I move at the heart of the world.

As in **"The Vegetable King,"** Dickey keeps his plant imagery vague, thus leaving himself free to use his trees as media for sporadic returns. Dickey appears to want his trees primarily to bear a message rather than to be specific, real things. As in **"Fog Envelops the Animals,"** trees are subject to transformation, whereas animals in early poems

are rarely so altered. Later, in **"The Sheep Child," "Madness"** (1969), **"For the Last Wolverine,"** and the two **"Reincarnation"** poems, as he stretches for extraordinary insights, his creatures also become extraordinary, even to the limit of creating a *delirium tremens* lobster for *The Zodiac* (1976).

In resorting to images of trees rather than people, or even animals, Dickey runs a risk of losing contact with his readers, but his formidable rhetoric compensates. To begin with "And" solicits the reader's assent that he was already somehow with the poet before he began. But even with a solicitous beginning, Dickey's first line draws the reader up short: "And now the green household is dark." Having been enticed into the *a priori* narrative, then brought abruptly to a halt by a one-line opening sentence, the subjugated reader is chastened to accept a deliberate, meditative description, as though the reader himself had rustled about and settled in to spend the night in a tree house. Dickey attends closely to the details of nature ("The half-moon completely is shining / On the earth-lighted tops of the trees"), and the reader is seduced to the narrator's physical perspective, there to accept the speaker's isolation even as the brothers are paradoxically also present:

> We lie here like angels in bodies,
> My brothers and I, one dead,
> The other asleep from much living,
>
> In mid-air huddled beside me.

"Hunting Civil War Relics at Nimblewill Creek" also portrays a brother-companion, but this one is alive and helping the narrator search old battlefields with a metal-detector. Both youngsters are descendants and therefore survivors of the men in the terrible war almost a century before. Their closeness is important because it is partly through seeing his brother's face transmit the influence of the dead that the speaker gains insight into the battle-ground. The spirits rise from within the dormant things buried in the earth and integrate with living society. The speaker feels communion with his "one brother," but he also senses that the brother is a spiritual conduit, a human analogue to the metal-detector: the machine identifies and reveals the lost "mess tin or bullet" while the living instrument—the brother—rears up the ancestral spirits.

FATHERS AND CHILDREN

There are many more poems about father-child than about sibling relationships in *Drowning with Others*: **"The Owl King," "Dover: Believing in Kings," "To His Children in Darkness," "The Hospital Window," "The Magus," "Antipolis,"** and **"Facing Africa."** The trend represents a broadening, if not a maturing, of the poet's concerns. The responsibility of a parent for his or her child is highly significant to Dickey's growing social concerns.

"The Call," of *Into the Stone,* builds upon three major images: the father—who speaks these lines—the blind son, and the owl king. Obviously unsatisfied with his treatment of the subject in one poem, Dickey came later to include **"The Call"** as Part I of **"The Owl King,"** in *Drowning with Others*. The poem is technically interesting for its dislocation of everyday reality and its entry into a mythical, magical world not seen in Dickey's work anywhere else. With the father calling after his son, who is lost in the woods of the owl king, Dickey misdirects the reader not so much to castigate the father's wrongheadedness as to indicate the vastness and difficulty of mystical knowledge. The reader is in awe of what surrounds the speaker, not pitying or condescending. The father's (and the reader's) inklings here are of the see-through-a-glass-darkly sort, later to be fully known through the owl and the son. **"The Call"** moves like a question, with the father wondering as to the source and composition of his own calling sound. Dickey could not let such ambiguities rest, later enlisting the owl king and finally the son for substantial clarification in two additional sections to the poem.

However it might first have begun to stir in his mind as an exploration of parental responsibility, **"The Owl King"** is one of Dickey's most completely spiritualistic and animistic poems. Although its finished three parts are specifically assigned to father, son, and owl king (echoes of Father, Son, and Holy Ghost are deafening), the poem is actually about the interlocking—even the interchangeability—of the myriad spirits of the world. Seeking the blind child, the father is not only immersed in his own sounds but also attuned to nature. He knows that true knowledge proceeds from feeling: "I feel the deep dead turn / My blind child round toward my calling."

Dickey sets reader and father on a mystical journey by the illogicality of the setting: "Through the trees, with the moon underfoot, / More soft than I can, I call." The search for something spiritual, in artistic terms, is nearly allegorical, a mode Dickey returns to later, with **"The Eye-Beaters"** (1968) and *The Zodiac* (1976). And so the owl king, no regular bird, is somewhat like Plato's philosopher who has left the cave to peer painfully at the sun and then to return with unimagined truths to persuade his benighted (and hostile) fellows. But this excursion into sunlight has a different effect:

> At last I opened my eyes
> In the sun, and saw nothing there.
> That night I parted my lids
> Once more, and saw dark burn
> Greater than sunlight or moonlight,
> For it burned from deep within me.

With claws tight upon the limbs, embedded and needing to be "prised up," the owl king is plugged into nature, empowered by it from within.

More than the human father, the owl king is an active creator: "I swore to myself," he says, and "Every light was too feeble to show / My world as I knew it must be." He must make the world according to his own vision: "I heard what I listened to hear." Since the owl is not human, his

voice, creative though it be, is inadequate to the clear expression of his own insights. But his vision ("all but my seeing had failed") leads him to the child, who, when found, becomes unified with the owl in their response to the father's searching call. The blind child learns, by some mystical apprehension, the action of the owl's "blazing, invented eyes." He learns to constitute—or reconstitute—each living thing by its own special quality, "Each waiting alive in its own / Peculiar light to be found."

Part II signals that Dickey has no illusions that it is better to be an owl. The blind son is described by the owl himself as possessing great powers: "Every tree's life lived in his fingers." But the owl king at the end of Part II asserts his superiority as the creative fulcrum of the poem, while the human beings play off the steady center of the owl. The father calls for the son; the owl king mediates; and the son assimilates it all. The conclusion of Part II makes it clear that the child's mind is imaginatively bound and directed by the owl king, but it is compelled to the end of regaining his father. The owl king is a dream, however much he may be the willful and "ruling passion."

Part III, **"The Blind Child's Story,"** is consistently different in diction and rhythm from Parts I and II, which more closely resemble each other. Part III opens with emphasis on the youth of the speaker: "I am playing going down / In my weight lightly, / Down, down the hill." Here Dickey is able to reexperience the senses in a way that we often associate with a child's startlingly fresh outlook: "A leaf falls on me, / It must be a leaf I hear it / Be thin against me." The lines rush on, as if the poet were to imagine the constant flow of sensual messages through the body of a blind child; and the unconventional syntax, comma-spliced, fused, and enjambed, helps to convey the image movement.

> . . . and now
> The ground is level,
> It moves it is not ground,
> My feet flow cold
> And wet, and water rushes
> Past as I climb out.

When the first stanza concludes, "I own the entire world," the reader's assent is virtually assured because the child is not able to visualize the limits and demarcations in which sighted persons continuously acquiesce: "It closes a little: the sky / Must be cold, must be giving off / Creatures that stand here." The child senses the constellations which so entice Dickey's interest in other poems, the celestial influences that generate things in this fleshly world; and the boy becomes assertive: "I say they shine one way." He confirms the phenomenological substance of the things he can sense: "Trees they are trees around me, / Leaves branch and bark." But the child's apprehension of himself is more than as a receptor of sensations to confirm worldly objects. He is said by "someone," he tells us, to "seem to be blessing them."

As the boy recounts his claw-in-hand greeting of the owl, he says what perhaps only a child might believably say in such extraordinary circumstances: "Nothing is strange where we are." That is, as the child is deprived of his "highest" sense—sight—he is also set loose from many adult limitations as to how the world impinges upon him. Touch and hearing, for instance, are more immediate, primitive, less mediated avenues between the Me and the Not-Me.

The owl is acknowledged as Mentor: "I learn from the master of sight / What to do when the sun is dead." But the real energies originate within the things perceived: ". . . to make the great darkness work / As it wants of itself to work." The child envisions a fox and a shining serpent, earlier described by the owl as "the snake in the form of all life." Another lesson comes as the fox strikes, and "a small thing / Being caught, cries out. . . ." This sudden shock of violent death in the woods enables the child to make another essential connection: "How beings and sounds go together; / I understand / The voice of my singing father." The mortal cry of the "small thing" is enough for the boy to grasp the grief of his father, too. The human child's assimilative mind prevails, and he descends to regain the real world, now transformed to some extent by his new insights. After such transcendence and descent, some residual insight remains: "The wood comes back in a light / It did not know it withheld." The boy's understanding has deepened; he has perceived the source of perception to be within the things perceived. He has learned to interact with the real world by practicing the imaginative dream-magic of the owl king. The child is able to connect at last with his father, caught up now in that natural world newly and brilliantly seen by the blind son. Even the owl, now, has been assimilated by the child to some degree of identity with the father: "Far off, the owl king / Sings like my father, growing / In power." And the child, newfound—but mostly to and by himself—closes the poem affirmatively, confidently, having inherited some energies of the father as well as the owl king.

"To His Children in Darkness" foreshadows another projection of Dickey's imagination into the dark: **"The Eye-Beaters."** In both poems, the narrator imagines what someone else knows in darkness: in the early poem, his children's dreams are invented; in **"The Eye-Beaters,"** the institutionalized blind children's primordial visions are imagined. The blind children (in their kind of darkness) strike and bruise their faces in hopes of rendering some sensation of light, some optic glimmer by the force of blows. It is the adults—the father and the visitor—who create the images and attribute them to the children. From their inspiration, each adult narrator then can probe his own imagination to make sense of the finite human condition and thus can extend its limits through imaginative effort.

The father and the son in **"Facing Africa"** have no such high aesthetic or archetypally loaded experience together. The poem is somewhat like **"A Dog Sleeping on My Feet"** as the speaker draws some natural, connective energy from the ocean near his feet. Not even physically touching the water or the boats lying "at rest," the man and his son are linked to them by the "long, / Warm, dangling shadows" of their legs as they are seated on the "stone jetties." The son's presence is important in this poem because it provides a handle of social and familial behavior to allow the narrator a check on his poetic enthusiasm, his seeking after knowledge without the brake of social scrutiny. The son also gives the father social affirmation, a necessary balance here as it is in **"A Dog Sleeping on My Feet"** and, later, in **"Slave Quarters."** Responsibility and true hopefulness are embodied in the offspring, and, in this case, the son has even come to participate in the imagining, the new knowing, of the father.

"Antipolis" is of an almost equally exotic context as Africa, for this American poet. The poem is of the "Guggenheim" variety, *de rigueur* for those who have traveled expressly for the purpose of becoming authors. The Greek city, the "powder-blue ocean," the son reading Greek, and the poet's self-image as multi-spirited, all are elements to play on the foreignness of the scene to jar the naive American loose to hold more sophisticated concepts and imagery: "I hear in my voice two children, / My son and my soul, / Sing to each other through ages." The poem delves briefly into the theme of potentiality when, at the beginning, the poet feels himself looked "clear through" by the things around him, particularly the market-place squids, hanging for purchase, whose eyes "deepen" and "hold me brightly." The poet is surrounded by perceptions and perceivers, by the ancient dead and the living son, all focused upon and invigorated by his own singing self. His sense of potentiality is incorporated in the son with him: his hope of continuance is at least in part embodied in that vibrant son of his flesh.

A much longer work than most of Dickey's early poems, **"Dover: Believing in Kings,"** uses the persons of father and mother; but the mother is yet only pregnant, and the son is imagined as the son of a king, the father a king, all participating in the mythically accoutred place imagined by the narrator at Dover Beach. This elaborate poem, a glowing rather than a blazing thing, allows, by its length and its simply beautiful tones, the poet to draw together several of his major themes.

The first line sets us hard upon the earth with the speaker and his wife driving off the boat to settle firmly upon land after having crossed the English Channel. The minor mythology of greased swimmers, a mythology particularly fondly held after the exploits of the World War II underwater demolition teams, clamoring like lemmings through the waters, sets the tone for exploring other, more profound myths. As with many of Dickey's speakers, this one's recollection of, or longing for, the marathon swimmer points up a kind of deficiency in himself, a recognition by the person who had crossed in a car on a boat, very unheroically. But such is only a hint, for the speaker learns that his own strengths are more in his sensitive intelligence (Dickey says, "If my poetry has done anything, it has resulted in an increase of both sensitivity and drama in American poetry," *S,* 90) than in his physical stamina and courage: "Within a wind, a wind sprang slowly up."

Dickey's speaker ultimately turns to tell of himself as a king. The weathering gray of Dover merges with the birds and sea, shifting at last to royal images. The grandeur and majesty of the scene produce associations of the stern, gray effort of birds casting themselves (like Hopkins's windhover) against the "airstream of the cliffs," their breasts bearing the gray assault, and then, almost miraculously, the king emerges to the overwhelming awe even of the birds: *In a moment you cannot imagine / Of air, the gulls fall, shaken.*" With this imagery of royalty and his wife pregnant with a son imagined to be Arthur, the narrator makes a poem to be a call to high intellectual and spiritual refinement, to displace the clunking tourism of the opening lines. As birds move along the line of the cliffs, the people below follow along, feeling majestic enough to comprehend "the balancement of light / *The king wears newly, in singing.*" The poem is much of joy but also of solemnity; its measured, alternating iambs and anapests recall the rhythms of high-eloquent speech, of oratory without bombast.

As finely tuned as **"Dover: Believing in Kings"** is, its solemnity strikes the serious pose of the poet whose skills are there but whose idea of poetry has not yet matured to the unforced idiosyncrasy of the distinctive James Dickey. **"The Magus,"** published two years after **"Dover,"** invokes by its very title those austere magi-makers of the twentieth century—T. S. Eliot and W. B. Yeats. But Dickey's poem wants to work in two directions at once: to dispel the conventional magi-mystery and to call up the natural mystery of all human life. "This child," he concludes, "is no more than a child." But by this twentieth and last line, the poem has practiced an hypnotic two-line stanza form whose lines are almost all heavily end-stopped, and whose parallel structures of various kinds all work to the benefit of ritual sounds, of almost liturgical pace, and of the puzzlement that any parent may feel at the claim of one Holy Child to be more holy than one's own. The "two / long-lost other men [who] shall be drawn / Slowly up to the brink of the house," recall, of course, the two other magi. But they also, in this poem, reintroduce the ghostly dead imagery, our shadowy close and infinitely distant ancestors. The poem is less powerful than it seems to want to be, and its cautious understatement, even with the late peak of three rhetorical questions, succumbs to paralysis. It is just not enough for the poet to say to himself, "An event more miraculous yet // Is the thing I am shining to tell you." The shining is never bright enough to break the shell of controlled intellect in this poem: the child never quite ascends to his own glory. So the father's allegations are hollow.

As much as he accomplishes by projecting imagined dreams into children, by symbolically journeying with his son over shadowy seas to Africa, by drinking and roaring his way through Antipolis for his son's enrichment, by meditating through a verbal symphony at Dover, or by starkly undercutting the high religious ambience of the magi, Dickey comes in these poems about fathers and children to speak most plainly and most effectively in

"The Hospital Window." An anomaly like **"The Performance"** among the war poems of *Into the Stone,* **"The Hospital Window"** reiterates the theme of survivorship— not, as with Donald Armstrong, through some heroic gesture—this time to survive, with a mixture of grief and joy, one's own father. As is common in early Dickey poems, this one begins with a momentarily puzzling dislocation. The speaker's descent in an elevator is deliberately obscured to assure the author the purest sort of control over the reader's expectations and observations: "I have just come down from my father. / Higher and higher he lies / Above me. . . ." The second stanza begins with the repetition, "Still feeling my father ascend," and thus the poet creates the illusion of the father's impending death, his rising away, as into heaven, as the son sinks away from him.

With all the exterior windows glazed by sunlight for the son's view from out in the street, he moves around to catch sight of his father and thus moves almost obliviously into the automobile traffic. The clamorous near-death of the street, the horn-blowing and the outrage, serve to emphasize the vitality of the son, who has only the hope of a silent fatherly wave from a hospital window, a wave punctuated and accentuated by the visible "grinning" of the father, whom the son judges to be "not afraid for my life, either, / As the wild engines stand at my knees." To recognize imminent death—upward in the person of his father, downward in the descent of the son, and all around in the ferocious traffic—is one of the chief lessons of poetry. Except for the somewhat overdone concluding stanza, with an exact repetition of the poem's first line, **"The Hospital Window"** is a "pin-tingling hand" of a poem. Its life is in its perception and imagination of death, and the grown son here is in control of the meaning of his father's mortal precedent for his own human life.

DROWNING WITH OTHERS: NONE SHALL SURVIVE

"The Hospital Window" sets forth in gentler terms than **"The String"** or some of the war poems Dickey's preoccupation with survivorship. The idea seems on the surface to be a selfish one, but in fact it turns on the point of the poet's recognition of his part in the human race; he sees and fully comprehends the interrelationship of all people, especially when it comes to mortality. **"Drowning with Others"** functions for Dickey to pluralize his recurrent ghostly brother-figure.

The elements of water and light are enough to transform the physical appearance, the mass, the weight, of the people involved in swimming for their lives; and the poet himself is led to drifting syntax and mystic-sounding images. Hanging on the edge of willful obscurity, Dickey allows just enough hard detail to seduce us back into the pursuit of the poem's meanings. The figures in the water reach and touch and appear to fly with wingbones of the shoulderblades. The people become participants in the elements: "If I opened my arms, I could hear // Every shell in the sea find the word / It has tried to put into my mouth."

The sea's overwhelming power has translated into the speaker's belief that the sea is trying to communicate. As much as its title suggests a communion of humanity, this poem is actually more self-indulgent, more falsely sensation-seeking, than most of Dickey's more mature works. Like **"Into the Stone"** for its mysticism and its singular, abstracted vision, **"Drowning with Others"** might have gone well in Dickey's first book, whose **"The Underground Stream"** it also recalls. Dickey himself somewhat derogates the poem in *Self-Interviews*: "I wanted to call the book *Drowning with Others,* so I decided I'd better write a poem by the same title to give some status to the book's title. I don't think it's a very strong poem; it seems awfully obscure to me" (*SI,* 116).

Perhaps the strongest case for the poem's value is in its representation of the survivorship theme, with a bizarre turn of mind given by the narrator, who, whether he actually, finally drowns or not, is a survivor for a long enough time that he may tell the experience. Additionally, with the reference to the merging of meaning with the elements of nature, the poet emphasizes his theme from **"The Owl King"** and elsewhere that *things* have the power to emanate meaning and energy from themselves, not entirely to be the inventions—the fictions—of the human observers, and yet those emanations become incorporated with and help to define the personality of the participants in those experiences.

Part of this survivorship effect is to come to the edge of mortal mergence, to enter a region of potential oblivion and the most intense self-awareness. In **"The Lifeguard,"** the young man who has failed at his job feels guilt which is heightened by his own approximation to death. He has been submerged, with the frenzy of feeling his breath waste away, in the cold, lightless lake where he feels the black mud in his hands. To have failed in his responsibility is one thing, but to have lived instead of his ward, to have been left unable even for that futile cry, "Let me die in his place!" is to multiply the mortal despair. The child comes to the lifeguard alone, after dark, in the moonlight, after all have gone to bed; and even though the lifeguard has for a moment the bright moon-child from the heart of the forest in his arms, the final despair is devastating—the illusion is insistently illusory. Despite all signs of recognition and regeneration, the lifeguard's own survival comes to the terrible futility of water spilling through his helpless fingers. The comfort Dickey sometimes perceives in nature is absent, as in general **"The Lifeguard"** is less overt in calling for powers to come from nature. The images are more naturally blended in the consciousness of the lifeguard. It is not as though he pursues meanings so much as he is tragically caught by them. The natural images— moon, water, forest, mud, human faces—reinforce and embody the experience he has had during the fateful day.

One consequence of being a survivor is to have perspective upon destruction no one else can have. One of Dickey's most unusual survivor poems is **"The Dream Flood,"** in which the narrator has achieved to such a state of detachment as to gain the perspective of the Deluge, the destroyer of biblical proportions, which gives the poet the occasion to imagine truly overwhelming force. Distance can become, in poems, a dream; thus the poet can reach into his psyche in ways that so-called realism will not allow.

"The Dream Flood" begins with the speaker's invocation, oddly, to "ask and receive / The secret of falling unharmed / Forty nights from the darkness of Heaven." Conspicuously, Dickey alludes to the forty days' rain of Noah's Flood, but he also (perhaps unwittingly) calls to mind the fall of the angels. The poem, being a "dream flood" by designation, sets about immediately to dislocate somewhat surrealistically the actual cosmography: "descend to the moon / Where it lies on the ground." Dickey, of course, is using a phenomenon he often employs, the appearance of the moon in some reflecting surface, usually, and in this case, in water. Earlier, in the first poem of *Drowning with Others,* **"The Lifeguard,"** Dickey uses the floating moon as a prefiguration of the lifeguard's imagined ability to walk on the water. In **"The Dream Flood,"** the reality of the moon's light, as it is indeed "sunlight transmitted by stone," is eerily accurate even as it sets our reason on edge—but no more than the concept of world-wide flood would do. Once on the earth, however, the rainwaters (now personified and accommodated with poetic intelligence) move more realistically, building and seeping with mind-boggling dimensions, but without the arch diversion of sense and common sense that the poet practices upon us in the first two stanzas.

Dickey's skillful selectivity in the catastrophe—he talks repetitively of the horses and trees—allows the readers to supply to such understatement their own intensity for the truest comprehension of disaster. The dreamlike floating of things is as eerie as the moon's inversion. The horses float contained in their stalls: "Their bodies in cell blocks of wood / Hang like a dust that has taken / Their shape without knowing of horses."

Later, the Flood-Poet says, "I withdraw, in feeling the cloud / Of Heaven call dazzlingly to me / To drop off my horses and forests," and the poem turns its attention from "grasses and fence wire of glory / That have burned together like a coral with depth" to the effect of the Flood upon human beings. But the Flood recalls only women, no men, as its victim-lovers—no surprise, after closely reading **"The Enclosure."** When the last three stanzas lean so heavily upon the female victims, the reader is justifiably driven back to see that the rain, flood, and sun images are standard images of maleness, of the dominating, fructifying principles that can turn destructive, as Coleridge's Ancient Mariner testifies. The male principle is almost omnipotent, until the time comes at the end to bring life again to the dead. The poem conveys an immense sadness at such paradox, and one wonders why Dickey chose to exclude this imperfect but affecting poem from *Poems 1957-1967.* The Flood-Poet is called "impotent waters," and the evaporating "sunlight / Straining in vain / With her lost, dead weight" cannot restore life. The last line ("Lift. I am dreaming. Lift.") is what each woman "shall implore," but the chief impact of this dream flood is one of more general destruction for the world and terrible enlightenment for the Flood-Poet, who is the ultimate survivor, the destroyer of all things besides itself.

ART, AND THE BODY IN THE GRASP OF THE WORLD

While **"The Dream Flood"** represents an extreme effort by the poet to distance himself from the physical action of his poem, **"The Scratch"** drives the poet back into the body. But, like **"The War Wound"** (1964) and earlier war poems, it functions as an emblem. The poet speculates that the scratch on his wrist was "once hid in a fiery twist / Of brier," evoking the theme of potentiality seen in **"The Owl King."** But intellect dominates the poem, not the thing-ness of things: "I watchfully sit down / to lift it wisely, and see / Blood come, as at play." The intellectual speculation does not allow us to accept passionately the Victorian resolve and quasi-heroic posture at the end: "I shall dream of a crown till I do."

For all its aesthetic straining, **"The Scratch"** reiterates Dickey's interest in beginning his poems with images that stick in the mind. His poem-making generally proceeds directly out of the things of the natural world. **"A Birth"** shows how the poet makes life within his own imagination and then gives it free rein. Art is thus an illusion in the service of perceiving the most independent, vital conditions, the most natural: "Inventing a story with grass," says Dickey, "I find a young horse deep inside it."

With its particular attention to mother and child, **"A Birth"** signifies the creation of things in art which then generate other, seemingly independent things—like one's own children. The four-stanza poem breaks cleanly midway, with the narrator's contemplation of his "inventing a story" in the first half; and, his "mind freed of its own creature," he turns "to find [himself] deep in [his] life." The interlocking of life-forces and art is directly reminiscent of **"A Dog Sleeping on My Feet"** and **"Trees and Cattle,"** as well as the family-conscious poems of *Into the Stone.* **"A Birth"** clearly identifies the poet as the central figure, not the other subjects (or objects) in it. The poet is, of course, in charge of the poem—the whole thing is an act of his imagination. But within the third stanza, the language is notably passive (in fact, it is relatively passive from line two, after "Inventing a story"). The speaker's creative effort immediately gives way to the story's own almost magical volition: "I find a young horse deep inside it." The second stanza begins, "And he is free, strangely, without me," so the poet's story turns over to become "his story"—the horse's—which then melds with the sun in the story. At the end, when the poet has presumably returned to his own real world, with his child and his mother in the room, the return of the real-world sun generates yet another horse, another story.

The affirmation of art in the poem is that it has a reality that lies beyond the conscious control of the artist. The imagination is able to construct images and stories that take off in whatever direction they "naturally" go, rather than following some line that the artist feels he may absolutely manipulate. **"A Birth"** begins as a pastoral emblem-poem, but it begins to breathe without the conscious volition of the poet. As is often the case in later Dickey poems, the landscape is taken over, given vitality, specifically by an animal. Dickey does not normally write poems about art—his best aesthetic statements are in his poems as poems and in his prose criticism—but these earlier works of aesthetic intention do foreshadow such extensive explorations of the subject as **"The Eye-Beaters"** and *The Zodiac.*

"In the Lupanar at Pompeii" is made with style and diction more like later Dickey poems (or like those early exceptions, **"The Performance"** and **"The Hospital Window"**), with their force of simple declarative sentences, without, for the most part, poetical rhetoric and sententiousness. The tourist-poet is loose among the ruins of a glorious past civilization, seeking significance and longing for some universality by virtue of the references to other cultures in other, faraway places. But here Dickey has elected to write about the destruction of Pompeii from the point of view of a man who wants mainly to know about the ancient whorehouses.

The poem's specific lesson, however, given out of the mouths of the "painted, unchanging women" and those of "the desperate dead," is "Passion. Before we die / Let us hope for no longer / But truly know it." The lesson is easily said, and one receives it with a touch of humor; but, as with "Beauty is truth, truth beauty," told by Keats's Grecian Urn, a suspect orator, the final utterance of Dickey's poem is equally suspect, with the dusty, incinerated dead, mouthing of passion, where theirs was found in the heat of their deaths, more than in the carnal heat of whores. Perhaps the strongest section of the poem is in Dickey's statement about the nature of lust:

> I think of the marvel of lust
> Which can always, at any moment,
> Become more than it believed,
> And almost always is less:
> I think of its possible passing
> Beyond, into tender awareness,
> Into helplessness, weeping, and death:
> It must be like the first
> Soft floating of ash. . . .

Almost nowhere until he gets to **"Sun"** and **"Adultery,"** both in the "Falling" section of *Poems 1957-1967,* does Dickey touch so sensitively upon the frayed nerves of human sexuality.

"In the Lupanar at Pompeii" is a good poem but not a great one. It combines Dickey's emblematic technique, taking the figures fixed in stone to devise meaning from them, as well as from Dickey's continuing interest in the ghostly dead. Here, though, the dead are less truly immanent. They function as mere voices of the petrified emblems; their passion is only wispily evoked, and the poet himself is left as a half-humorous, mildly nervous man intelligent enough to take the serious occasion of Pompeii to think on things as important as lust and death. Like "Ode on a Grecian Urn," it reminds us of the terrible gap between the dead and their stony immortality in art.

"Snow on a Southern State" is another of those poems that begins with physical dislocation, with the poet purposefully disrupting the readers' expectations of geography, balance, and direction. Using the word "labor" to indicate in the first line how his effort is conscious, the poet describes his movement on a train. The sense of reflection, the ghostlike apprehension of himself as some floating creature outside the self, the feeling of odd directions and inverted expectations, all contribute to the poem's efforts to create the otherworldliness so often conjured up by snowfall. The alteration and concealment of familiar physical forms, the muffling of sounds, the tactile gray of the cold snowy days help the poet bring his narrator to new insights about himself and the world around him. The poignancy of one's return to home country is more to be adjusted for the speaker's coming to unfamiliar sights now that the snow, so infrequent in the South, is visiting at the same time. In a manner recalling **"A Screened Porch in the Country,"** the chief early impact of the snow leads the narrator "dumbly" to address the denizens outside the train beyond his voice, to tell them comfortingly of the snow's transience, that it is clearly passing, as he is, through their town like a harmless ghost of themselves.

The most peculiar effect of the snow comes later to the speaker. As memory alters the past and thus renews it, this snow alters the place, all its sensuousness, and obscures but also renews its covered land for the narrator. The poem turns in its later stanzas to speak ominously of "weddings opposed by the world," "A dead cotton field," and "the equilibrium / Of bones . . . falling, falling." Such retreat into vague, even obscurantist, incidents, away from the long, relatively secure description of the scene, somewhat dislocated but secure, is perhaps too much for the poem to bear. Mostly it suggests the power of the mind in art to alter the past and the present, as snow can alter even the familiar scenes of our homes.

As Dickey's effort to deal in poems about the poetic enterprise may be seen to dwindle away (neither **"Snow on a Southern State"** nor **"To Landrum Guy, Beginning to Write at Sixty"** saw publication before *Drowning with Others,* and Dickey omitted both from *Poems 1957-1967*), it is exciting to look once again at **"A Dog Sleeping on My Feet,"** which follows as though the poet has burst out to acknowledge what he so intensely held within himself in **"Listening to Foxhounds."** He abandons the consideration of the group's judgment upon a man who would imagine himself in union with the quarry—the fox. He openly writes of himself as a writer, in close physical contact with his dog, who in turn has been dreaming (the poet imagines) of chasing the fox.

The poem strains somewhat in lines that discourse upon the problem of verbalizing natural, spiritual experiences:

> . . . my hand, which speaks in a daze
> The hypnotized language of beasts,
> Shall falter, and fail

> Back into the human tongue. . . .

But it is a plain statement of Dickey's view that the truest power of language is sensual and the truest source of inspiration is a physical apprehension of nature. The poem ends with a return to reality, wife and sons: "From the dream of an animal." Like Frost's "Stopping by Woods on a Snowy Evening," Dickey's poem resumes the world of social necessity ("Assembling the self I must wake to") with all the residue he can sustain of "the scent of the fox" upon his waking. He must sleep "to grow back [his] legs," to return fully to the human world; but there is a certain amount of duplicity in the poet's speaking throughout as a poet, a writer who is conscious of using his material. Nonetheless, it is instructive as to Dickey's attitudes toward nature and art. It reemphasizes the importance to Dickey's art of animals—dog and fox—as the best guides to human participation in nature.

ANIMATE CREATURES—SIGNS

It is unusual for Dickey to conclude in so palpably didactic a manner as the final three lines of **"The Movement of Fish"**: "One must think of this to understand / The instinct of fear and trembling, / And, of its one movement, the depth." In a direct line of fish-in-the-stream images from Faulkner and Hemingway, Dickey displays a minor turn of Kierkegaardian existentialism. The image is memorable, if not entirely original, and the poem begins with a startlingly simple truth: "No water is still, on top. / Without wind, even, it is full / Of a chill, superficial agitation." Dickey equates, one supposes, the surface of everyday human things with "The trivial, quivering / Surface," under which the fish have True Being. The implications are (1) that the human being who makes his feeble breaths and sounds, barely rippling the water, is not in touch with the profundity of the waters or of the fish's experience; (2) that fish are instinctually attuned since they are literally immersed in the medium of their sustenance; (3) that fish are threatened from above (the people in boats) and from below (whatever fatal pursuers are out of sight in the dark depths), a nameless threat that is also connected, at least for the poet, with the fact that fish swim suddenly, as in terror, "picking up speed, still shooting // Through half-gold, / Going nowhere." The emptiness of that observation is most unusual in Dickey's work, as it implies that nothing really can be done to save our souls. Tragic experience is deep, but mere survival is of dubious value since meaning and direction are left void at the end of this poem. Such starkness in Dickey's poems, as rarely as it occurs, stands as a challenge to the discovery of meaning in the simple vitality of living things.

Richard Howard has said of *Drowning with Others,* "James Dickey is still a poet of process rather than of particular presences, and of presences rather than persons, in his apprehension of nature as of selfhood."[1] Surely one of Dickey's finest poems is **"The Heaven of Animals,"** a work that glorifies process and, at the same time, as Howard calls it, "pure recurrence."[2]

"The Heaven of Animals" resembles **"The Performance"** in its clean, persuasive narrative line, as though pure description is not the real point. Temporal flow in the timeless setting of heaven is the paradoxical focus of our experience through the poem. **"The Performance"** echoes again in the depiction of stoic necessity relieved by an oddly unexpected joy, a curious sense of ecstasy in the midst of sanctioned carnage. The carnage is necessary in this Heaven; it is the course of heavenly order. But there is also relief that one might feel in knowing—absolutely knowing—what one's role is, even if one is the victim. It is the animal world's version of Plato's Republic, in which justice is defined as each man's doing his job. The astonishment of the animals is emphasized, perhaps to avoid suspicion of their being bored with eternal certainty: ". . . claws and teeth grown perfect, / More deadly than they can believe." (It is like lust in Pompeii.)

The poet seems to want heaven's perfection to extend to all the animals, but his own sympathies—his best satisfactions—lie clearly with the predators (who are not themselves portrayed as prey of other predators). The passive prey are "fulfilling themselves without pain," but "They tremble." The poet's effort to make a heaven of (for?) animals is not nearly so democratic as it may at first appear. The pleasantest of all worlds is one in which the strong have willing (and trembling) prey; it is the fulfillment of the predator's sadistic desire for fear in his quarry that we see most of. The poem is about the perfection of the law of the jungle, without the horrid cycle at its fullest—no vultures to rip away the flesh of lions and leopards. That would be too disquieting for a poet who seizes the opportunity to make a world in which the strong prevail without guilt, without compunction, only to savor joy and flight, the savagery of killing without the obligations of consequence.

Such a poem would not be possible without a fallen world; as Richard Howard says, "when this world is called a fallen world, what is meant is that our soul, our aspirations, our hungers have collapsed into our present body, our present landscape, and that the instruments of our transcendence are at the same time the tools of undoing: *resurrection for a little while,* as Dickey laments and exults."[3] Survivorship subsides as a theme, for here all survive. if that is the ultimate goal. But what of the emptiness of purpose? The prospect of heaven is shaky enough in terms of Dickey's poems; such perfect order and conditions are beyond comprehension, even aspiration, in such poems as **"The Performance," "The Owl King," "Dover: Believing in Kings,"** and, later, **"The Eye-Beaters," "May Day Sermon,"** and *The Zodiac.* **"The Heaven of Animals"** is a chilling poem, however perfected and articulated; it is of a world entirely different from the humane vision of **"The Sheep Child"** or **"Madness,"** in which the poet writes of animal aberrations but has not abandoned his basic compassion for some cold dream of domination.

Perhaps the fixed and predictable carnage of **"The Heaven of Animals"** is one way of Dickey's handling metaphysically based fear. Earlier in his life, prior to the influence of his Vanderbilt University astronomy professor, Carl Siefert, Dickey "had always been like Pascal, frightened by the silence of the infinite spaces" (*SI,* 37). But later, as a poet, his fears in nature are most often when animals are present or are thought to be. With **"Fog Envelops the Animals"** fear is a major emotion, especially as it is unmanageable, unaccountably exuded as a vibration or overtone of the natural world as a whole. In this respect, the poem is like **"The Shark's Parlor," "Pursuit from Under,"** and other late Dickey poems. The imagery associated with fog is also something that recurs later, particularly in **"May Day Sermon."** However, the fear Dickey's narrators feel has less to do with the fog than with what might come or go in it. No doubt the fog-enshrouded creatures are symbolic of some more fearful thing—death itself, probably—but the beasts are there, waiting as images of the dreadful abstraction. (It is in this aspect that, once again, **"The Heaven of Animals"** proves the exception. Heaven is where death and sensation are present but fear is not. However much the prey may tremble, oblivion is abjured, and fear is therefore abated.) To the narrator of **"Fog Envelops the Animals,"** the fog is not only a monolithic threat, but he also personifies it at the same time as he discriminates among his own "selves": "Soundlessly whiteness is eating / My visible self alive." Then the speaker moves suppositiously into some version of foggish ecstasy:

> I shall enter this world like the dead,
> Floating through tree trunks on currents
> And streams of untouchable pureness
>
> That shine without thinking of light.

Even as he takes on qualities of the fog, he comes to feel that some of those were originally his: "I feel my own long-hidden, / Long-sought invisibility / Come forth from my solid body."

MAN THE PRECARIOUS
INTRUDER—TRANSCENDENCE DESIRED

"Fog Envelops the Animals" deals with an important poetic act for Dickey—not the same as an aesthetic act—that is, the assimilation of some profound emotional insight by willfully imagining oneself in extraordinary relation with the ordinary. The speaker of this poem is present—the hunter—and he is actively imagining the experience of being foglike. For instance, he not only envelops animals; he also penetrates and interfuses with trees: "Floating through tree trunks" and "Through the hearts of the curdling oak trees." It is this additional aspect of transcendence at which Dickey is boldest, and perhaps most vulnerable: ". . . I don't think you can get to sublimity without courting the ridiculous. Therefore, a good many of my poems deal with farfetched situations. . . . [Critics] give you the impression that we belong to a generation whose catch-word is 'Aw, come off it! You don't really feel anything like that!' I don't want to come off it! I want to go *with* it! . . . I think that cynicism is probably the easiest, least profitable, and least valuable human emotion. . . . I'm a born believer and not a disbeliever. This doubtless has its dangers. But such as it is, there it is" (*SI*, 65-66). He is willing to accept the insights of the human creature who has imagined himself one with nature, and then he improves on nature. He reapplies the human ability to imagine and experience vicariously things that no one, no creature human or nonhuman, has ever experienced, thus probing further the limits of the human mind and body.

More specifically, by imagining the extraordinary condition, by this stretching the limits of conscious human experience, Dickey is able to probe—as poets should, as great poets do—the areas of human experience laid over by familiarity or dullness or timidity. Especially as Dickey reaches deep to examine fear, as in **"Fog Envelops the Animals,"** do we find him most pressurized, most persuasive, not, as with many other poets, when he is faced with tragic circumstances, with pity. Dickey responds to terror. The Melvillean strain of "Silence. Whiteness. Hunting," with which Dickey ends this poem, is homiletic only in its paraphrase. For the poet, it is experiential. In his best poems, the reader is also allowed. It is mythic activity, to reimagine the world in terms that move humankind even without their quite knowing why. And the process is infinitely variable: "If sensations turn into soul—into an ineffable quality that can never be accounted for by the sensations themselves—it is because the sensations reach an ever-changing mind that transforms them, as a merely passive receiver, the sort of mind Locke likens to blank paper, could not."[4]

Sometimes the action of the mind upon nature is morally unsettling, as in **"The Summons,"** in which the narrator raises a call which is truly evil. Unlike **"The Call,"** of *Into the Stone,* which is made by a desperate father who seeks his son lost in the woods, **"The Summons"** presents a speaker who is almost morally condescending to himself. There are even signs that the speaker is deceiving himself. At the very outset he says, "For something out of sight, / I cup a grass-blade in my hands, / Tasting the root, and blow." It seems obvious, although at least three other times the poet speaks too generally of the "beast" he hunts ("some being," "something"), that the true-life hunter would certainly know what beast he called and what sort of fairly specific response to expect. What is most curious, and most directly incriminating, is that the hunter uses a love-call to draw the beast to death at the same time as he tries to preempt moral censure by alluding to his lost innocence as the poem closes:

> . . . I pluck my longbow off the limb
> Where it shines with a musical light,
> And crouch within death, awaiting
> The beast in water, in love
> With the palest and gentlest of children,
> Whom the years have turned deadly with knowledge:
> Who summons him forth, and now
> Pulls wide the great, thoughtful arrow.

The duplicity of the act, of the quarry's being enticed by a self-consciously ironic human being, is emphasized by the self-satisfied coldness of the hunter's "great, thoughtful arrow." It is prefigurative of **"The Firebombing,"** in which the aesthetic distance of a bomber-pilot allows him to feel both aware and absolved. Even though the word "beast" is used to denominate the hunter's target, not enough can be done to exonerate the poet for his "summons" to death of the natural creature who seeks love. Whereas **"Fog Envelops the Animals"** insists upon the presence of fear as a crucial ingredient to meaningful hunting, this poem is entirely fearless—a strike from ambush—entirely invulnerable to the compassionating influences of nature, entirely demonstrative of the poet whose human reason has allowed him to seduce and kill with impunity some grand beast who comes to the call of love. Unlike the kind of love Dickey shows in **"Madness"** (1969), whose frenetic passion also leads to death, there is no threat here to the hunter, no true participation or identification.

A similar distance from nature is evident in **"For the Nightly Ascent of the Hunter Orion Over a Forest Clearing,"** which foreshadows *The Zodiac* and raises the question of why Dickey is so taken with the far-distant constellations. He has been a pilot-navigator in wartime, and he has studied astronomy as a college student and as an amateur astronomer; but it seems especially pertinent that these constellations, as they are named for earth-forms, imaginings of poets and artists, stand as projections outward of the human intellect and imagination.

"For the Nightly Ascent" ends with the speaker, after "ambiguous undulations" (to crib from Wallace Stevens's "Sunday Morning"), finding himself somehow not only a mortal hunter who might want to be a tree even as he wants stealthy mobility, but also "a man of stars." In the final lines a paradox emerges. Dickey's narrator has consciously sought the cosmic, unconscious knowledge of the heavens. Granted, the transformation of the mortal man into the starry Orion is only by analogy ("Unless he rises // As does the hunter Orion"), but the effort is real. The man is aware that he stands with one foot "longing to tiptoe / And the other to take the live / Stand of a tree that belongs here." In some ways it recalls the curious mixture of vegetation and animal-spirits in **"The Other,"** or the beast and angel figures in **"To His Children in Darkness,"** but this poem signals an even more expansive Dickey aspiration, to contact and to use the powers of infinite, starry space.

Dickey's transcendent leap in this poem, however, does not allow him to fly utterly away. The speaker begins, "Now secretness dies of the open," and the reader recalls those occasional experiences of openness and exaltation from which the closed-off human creature more often than not has prevented himself. But this poem is strange in its human-nonhuman straddling; the beasts and birds of the night awaken, gain power from their various nocturnal sources—"the owl's gaze // Most slowly begins to create / Its sight from the death of the sun"; the mouse is invigorated by knowing of the owl; and the fox comes out of the ground as though recharged by earth's magnetism or something equally vibrant—and the speaker, moving through the creaturely activity, emerges into openness and then aspires upward, away from the magnetic living in which he is immersed. The paradox is extended as Orion (and the man, one presumes) is illuminated by his own self-light, perhaps as each night creature has its own special illumination and source of vitality (as **"The Owl King"** also depicts). In **"Fog Envelops the Animals"** the speaker's invisibility comes from within to help him identify with the fog: in **"For the Nightly Ascent"** what is left *behind* is invisibility, and what is come to is "the light / Of himself."

In **"The Rib,"** Dickey alludes slightly to Adam and Eve, as one might anticipate from the title, but mainly the poet uses his own body as meaningful object, as emblem, through which he may perceive and empower himself anew. Somewhat as he does in **"The Summons,"** Dickey begins with an effort to mystify by using the general "Something." The mysterious thing in this case is quickly shown to be the decayed carcass of an indistinguishable animal. Dickey captures squarely the feeling of threat which surrounds such discoveries (survivorship may sometimes result in sudden paranoia): a casual walker never knows exactly how such deaths happened, if the bones are the only remains. Then the person may well grow apprehensive that the unknown killer—be it disease, enemy, or simply amorphous death—still lurks about. The rib in hand causes the speaker to attribute death to all his surroundings.

As the hunter contemplates "the wounds of beasts," he is forced to consider his own fleshly package of mortality: "A rib in my right side speaks / To me more softly // Than Eve. . . ." This reaching into the self because of having touched some external emblem is reminiscent of the poems in *Into the Stone,* especially the "War" section, but the embodiment of the narrator's mortal condition into himself is more persuasive than the lurking presence of the dead brother in **"The Underground Stream"** and other poems.

Unhappily, **"The Rib"** suffers from weak language and a trite-sounding ending: "I rise, going moonward toward better / And better sleep." But Dickey's decision to exclude **"The Rib"** from *Poems 1957-1967* seems less defensible than most of his other such decisions. The most justifiable reason may be that a reversion to "love" as a purportedly major part of the poem, after only one casual reference to Eve in the final three stanzas, suggests that Dickey is trying for more universal significance than this poem will bear. Perhaps more interestingly, this poem speaks of a conjunction of violence and love which comes to have more emphasis as Dickey's career progresses.

However much Dickey strives for transcendent experience in them, emblematic poems such as **"The Rib"** allow him to get in and out of meanings with minimal emotional stress; they stand ultimately as clever foci of consider-

ations. Sometimes the poet's efforts at empowering vision extend to images of his family. **"A Screened Porch in the Country"** stands more daringly on the edge of family and nature, waiting there for glowing insights, if not sparks to fly. It is notable for the poet's detachment from the objects—family, in this case—of his contemplation, a detachment similar to that in **"The Hospital Window"** and **"The Celebration,"** also family poems.

When Dickey describes the people on the porch by calling them "bodies softening to shadow," he summons the reader to accept something of what Conrad meant when he wrote in *Heart of Darkness* that, to Marlow, "the meaning of an episode was not inside like a kernel but outside, enveloping the tale which brought it out only as a glow brings out a haze, in the likeness of one of these misty halos that sometimes are made visible by the spectral illumination of moonshine."[5] Dickey's people are seen only as projections of themselves, their own shadows from their lamplike house:

> . . . until
> They come to rest out in the yard
> In a kind of blurred golden country
> In which they more deeply lie
> Than if they were being created
> Of Heavenly light.

The distinction that Dickey makes is important, for in most of his poems, it is clear that human beings are superior. Here, though, he elevates some nonspecific, nonrational essence of the people to absolute prominence. The second stanza explicitly relegates "The smallest creatures"—animals—to unconsciousness, or at least wordlessness, although their own essence is somehow accessible to the poet, if not to the people on the porch. In this aspect— the primacy of the poetic act—this poem is like **"Listening to Foxhounds."** Dickey allows to these mysterious edge-of-night-light creatures the experience of music: "Sing, if they can, / Or, if they can't, simply shine . . . , / Pulsating and thinking of music." The claim for humanity, though, is that it can

> . . . become
> More than human, and enter the place
> Of small, blindly singing things,
> Seeming to rejoice
> Perpetually, without effort,
> Without knowing why
> Or how they do it.

The natural creatures are fine, and people are fine; but the best is when people turn almost passive, "Emitted by their own house," projected into nature by their very humanness. The poem is notably romantic in its depiction of the excellence of nonrational knowledge, the highway to transcendence it provides. But Dickey's firm hold on physical reality, the actual scene, allows the reader to stop short of the loosest, flabbiest magico-mystical qualities of such poetry. Perhaps the deftest touch is that Dickey draws up the reins of supposition right at the end of the poem:

"Seeming to rejoice," only "seeming," he says. The human encounter with nonhuman nature must always be slightly suspect, slightly tenuous, for the connection is always susceptible to peculiarly human rationality and imagination.

"The Change" reiterates Dickey's interest in the primordial essence of all natural things, thus the essence of humanity. Here he finds it in a hammerhead shark, a brother who can never evolve, as the poet says, "No millions of years shall yet turn him // From himself to a man in love." Yet the poet finds in the creature the living spark that has somehow persisted and produced humankind over those same eons. The poet speculates what he would be if he could somehow embody both the shark and the person, to become:

> . . . what I would make of myself
> In ten millions years, if I could,
>
> And arise from my brute of a body
> To a thing the world never thought of
> In a place as apparent as Heaven.

This poet's pursuit is for something at "the heart of [his] brain," not to discount what the human intellect perceives and constructs, but to include with those powers something of the brute force and the instinctual knowing of creatures so mysteriously long-existing as the shark.

"The Change" also recalls more obliquely the theme of brotherhood, the unknown companion of Dickey's youth and of his prebirth. The sense of brotherhood that Dickey feels with the natural world, especially with beasts of prey, is tied intimately with his sense of survivorship in a predominantly hostile universe, a place in which such a brotherhood and such combinations of power as he aspires to in this poem are the prerequisites for immortality.

Nonetheless, in the searching for transcendent power, as risky as it may be, the poet does not forget the needs of beauty and gentleness, the fine perceptions and creations of people:

> . . . the heart of my brain has spoken . . .
> Gently of ends and beginnings,
> Gently of sources and outcomes,
> Impossible, brighter than sunlight.

The words of the poet have been subsumed in the radiant knowledge of suprarational powers of insight, of ways to know that only the universe as a whole may possess but which Dickey desires. The shark is to remain one of his most potent images of essence, most conspicuously in "The Shark's Parlor" (1965). Ironically, as he calls the poem "The Change," Dickey's overwhelming sense of the unchangingness of the shark over the centuries is the major source of interest of the poem. It is only his speculation, his wild imaginative flight, not even very convincing, that suggests that any change is possible in people, much less in the shark.

In most of his poems, though, Dickey believes firmly in the efficacy of thinking, in the power of the human imagination to penetrate the physical world to perceive and even to affect the spiritual world, even to affect the creatures of the nonhuman natural world. In "Autumn" the poet infers that trees somehow tune into the capacity of human beings, that they may think themselves through the fall changes, to turn leaves, perhaps, then, even to prepare for their own mortal conclusions: "I see the tree think it will turn / Brown, and tomorrow at dawn / It will change as it thinks it will change."

The subtlety of Dickey's poem goes beyond easy personification. The poet observes that the changes will come faster than the trees believe; even as human beings, even those who become aware of their mortality, always come to death sooner than they know and almost certainly sooner than they wish. The trees come to their deaths, their falls, as they recall the glorious greens of their fruitful time, just as a dying man may recall something of his own rich life.

The apparition of an angel allows the poet cheaply to reestablish the religious concerns that run throughout the poem, but it also raises doubts about the integrity of the poet's vision, as though he changes key and departs his original nature imagery as the burden of his song.

The last poem in the book, "In the Mountain Tent," allows the narrator access to both animate and inanimate nature. He gives in to the "profound, unspeakable law" which then allows him the state of mind which admits him into the natural arena, the world of the essences of things, the world of the truest light on nature, the best insights of human and nonhuman nature. The spirit of creation appears to be intelligent and purposeful, as Dickey describes the "thought-out leaves of the wood," suggesting that the leaves are the manifestations of the thought-creation of trees and ultimately of some spirit-force behind and beyond them. The minds of animals, then, become the ground for the poet's contemplations, the power source as well as the subject matter of his spiritual exercises. And the ultimate word for the man seems to be poetry which emerges as though from the mind and quality of nature's creatures, not something that could merely be manufactured by the rational, distilled creature—man: "I am there like the dead, or the beast / Itself, which thinks of a poem." But a poem is a made thing, the creation-again of the spirit of the natural world:

Czeslaw Milosz, the 1980 Nobel laureate, writes in "Ars Poetica?"—

> . . . poetry is rightly said to be dictated by a daimonion,
> though it's an exaggeration to maintain that he must be an angel . . .
> . . . poems should be written rarely and reluctantly,
> under unbearable duress and only with the hope
> that good spirits, not evil ones, choose us for their instruments.[6]

Dickey's American rather than East European mentality, buoyed with some senseless optimism in a hard world, almost invariably leads him to believe that no matter what comes as poetry, the spirit must be good. He does not seem so much to screen out as to expect that to let oneself have "free-falling" access to the minds of the beasts is to have access to the immanent spirit of creation and therefore of good—not evil—daimonions.

It is fitting that the last poem in Dickey's second book so wholly and enthusiastically embrace the natural world and exclaim its present right of poetry, but one must remember that the voice of the poet here is only as mediator: "From holes in the ground comes my voice / In the God-silenced tongue of the beasts. / 'I shall rise from the dead,' I am saying." These last lines recall **"To His Children in Darkness,"** in which the poet sees himself in forms both beastly and angelic, his voice somehow miraculous, in dreamlike authority, to tell the truths of the human soul by synthesizing (in that earlier case, for his sons) the forces of the natural and supranatural world as it comes to glory in a human being's self-consciousness and his ability to be conscious of the external world as well. It is a risky, threatening business, this transcendence. We must be bold.

Notes

1. Richard Howard, *Alone with America* (New York: Atheneum, 1980), p. 99.

2. Ibid., p. 102.

3. Ibid., p. 119.

4. Robert Langbaum, *The Modern Spirit: Essays on the Continuity of Nineteenth- and Twentieth-Century Literature* (New York: Oxford University Press, 1970), p. 19.

5. Joseph Conrad, *The Heart of Darkness,* ed. Robert Kimbrough (New York: W. W. Norton, 1963), p. 5.

6. Czeslaw Milosz, "Ars Poetica?" *Antaeus* 30/31 (Spring 1978): 148-49.

Joyce Carol Oates (essay date 1984)

SOURCE: Oates, Joyce Carol. "Out of Stone, into Flesh: The Imagination of James Dickey, 1960-1970." In *The Imagination as Glory: The Poetry of James Dickey,* edited by Bruce Weigl and T. R. Hummer, pp. 64-107. Urbana: University of Illinois Press, 1984.

[*In the following essay, Oates studies Dickey's collections from* Into the Stone, *to* Eye-Beaters, Blood, Victory, Madness, Buckhead and Mercy, *addressing his development and principal poetic themes, and highlighting Dickey's unique expression of man's instinctual savagery.*]

> Despair and exultation
> Lie down together and thrash
> In the hot grass, no blade moving. . . .
>
> Dickey, **"Turning Away"**

> A man cannot pay as much attention to himself as I do without living in Hell all the time.
>
> Dickey, *Sorties*

The remarkable poetic achievement of James Dickey is characterized by a restless concern with the poet's "personality" in its relationships to the worlds of nature and of experience. His work is rarely confessional in the sense of the term as we have come to know it, yet it is always personal—at times contemplative, at times dramatic. Because Dickey has become so controversial in recent years, his incredible lyric and dramatic talent has not been adequately recognized, and his ceaseless, often monomaniacal questioning of identity, of the self, of that mysterious and elusive concept we call the personality, has not been investigated.

Yet this is only natural: it is always the fate of individuals who give voice to an era's hidden, atavistic desires, its "taboos," to be controversial and therefore misunderstood. Dickey's poetry is important not only because it is so skillful, but because it expresses, at times unintentionally, a great deal about the American imagination in its response to an increasingly complex and "unnatural" phase of civilization. (To Dickey mental processes have come to seem "unnatural" in contrast to physical acts: hence the "Hell" of the quote from his journal, *Sorties*.) He has said, quite seriously, that "the world, the human mind, is dying of subtlety. What it needs is force" (*Sorties,* Garden City, New York, 1971; p. 85). His imagination requires the heroic. But the world cannot and will not always accommodate the hero, no matter how passionately he believes he has identified himself with the fundamental, secret rhythms of nature itself. One comes to loathe the very self that voices its hopeless demands, the "I" that will not be satisfied and will never be silent. *I myself am hell* is a philosophical statement, though it is expressed in the poetic language of personal emotion.

The volumes of poetry Dickey has published so far—***Into the Stone*** (1960), ***Drowning with Others*** (1962), ***Helmets*** (1964), ***Buckdancer's Choice*** (1965), ***The Eye-Beaters, Blood, Victory, Madness, Buckhead and Mercy*** (1970)—present a number of hypothetical or experimental personae, each a kind of reincarnation of an earlier consciousness through which the "self" of the poet endures. He moves, he grows, he suffers, he changes, yet he is still the same—the voice is a singular one, unmistakable. It asks why, knowing the soul heroic, the man himself is so trapped, so helpless? Dickey's central theme is the frustration that characterizes modern man, confronted with an increasingly depersonalized and intellectualized society—the frustration and its necessary corollary, murderous rage. Dickey is not popular with liberals. Yet one can learn from him, as from no other serious writer, what it is like to have been born into one world and to have survived into another. It might be argued that Dickey is our era's Whitman, but a Whitman subdued, no longer innocent, baptized by American violence into the role of a "killer/victim" who cannot locate within his society any standards by which his actions may be judged. A personality eager to identify itself with the collective, whether nature or other men, can survive only when the exterior world supports that mystical union of subject and object. Dickey speaks from the inside of our fallen, contaminated, guilt-obsessed era, and he speaks its language.

This was not always so: his earliest poems are lyric and meditative. They present a near-anonymous sensitivity, one hypnotized by forms, by Being in which dramatic and ostensibly intolerable truths are resolved by a formal, ritualistic—essentially magical—imagination into coherent and well-defined unities; his later poems submit this sensitivity to a broken, overheated, emotionally and intellectually turbulent world. The "stoneness" of the first volume undergoes an astonishing variety of metamorphoses until, in **"The Eye-Beaters"** and **"Turning Away: Variations on Estrangement,"** it emerges as stark, isolated, combative self-consciousness, in which "A deadly, dramatic compression / Is made of the normal brow. . . ." The poet begins as Prospero, knowing all and forgiving all, and, through a series of sharply tested modes of perception, comes to seem like Hamlet of the great, tragic soliloquies.

Who can tell us more about ourselves?—about our "American," "masculine," most dangerous selves? Even more than Whitman, Dickey contains multitudes; he cannot be reproached for the fact that some of these aspects of a vast, complex self are at war with the others. He experiments with the art of poetry and with the external world and the relationships it offers him (will he be lover?—murderer?—observer?), but what is most moving about his work is his relentless honesty in regard to his own evolving perception of himself, the mystery of his "personality." He refuses to remain in any explored or conquered territory, either in his art or in his personality. Obsessed with the need to seek and to define, he speaks for those who know that the universe is rich with meaning but are not always able to relate the intellectual, conscious aspect of their natures to it. Thus, the need to reject the "conscious" mind and its public expression, civilization itself, which is so disturbing in Dickey. Indeed, *Sorties* is very nearly a confession of despair—the poet seems unable to integrate the various aspects of his nature, conceiving of the world of the intellect and art as "Hell." "Believe me, it is better to be stupid and ordinary," Dickey tells us early in the book. What such a temperament requires, however, is not less intelligence, but more.

Dickey has not always expressed himself in such extreme terms, and he has been, all along, a careful craftsman, knowing that meaning in poetry must be expressed through language, through a system of mental constructs. In fact, it must be invented anew with each poem; it must be rigorously contracted, abbreviated, made less explosive and less primitive. In an excellent essay in *The Suspect in Poetry* he cautions young poets against abandoning

themselves to their unconscious "song," which he defines as "only a kind of monstrousness that has to be understood and ordered according to some principle to be meaningful."[1] The unrestrained and unimagined self must be related syntactically to the external world in order to achieve meaning.

Yet the phenomenal world changes; language shifts, evolves, breaks free of its referents; and the human ego, mysteriously linked to both, is forced to undergo continuous alterations in order simply to survive. In the poem **"Snakebite"** (1967) the "stage of pine logs" and the "role / I have been cast in" give way suddenly and horribly to the dramatic transition from the pronoun "it" to the pronoun "me" as the poet realizes he is confined in his living, breathing, existential body: he is not playing a role after all. If he wants to survive he will have to drain that poison out of his blood stream. Therefore, one of the burdens of the poet's higher awareness is to discover if there is any metamorphosis, any possible reincarnation, that is ultimately more than a mode of perception, *a way of arranging words.* Otherwise we begin to imagine ourselves as totally "estranged." To deny that estrangement we must deny our very framework of perception— language and sanity and logic—as if, by annihilating the mental construct of incarnation, we might somehow experience it on a level far below consciousness. Certainly Dickey has emphasized the poem as physical experience; he has set up opposing pseudocategories of the poetry of "participation" and the poetry of "reflection" (*Sorties,* p. 59). Such an estrangement rests, however, upon the metaphysical assumption that man's intellect is an intruder in the universe and that the language systems he has devised are not utterly natural, natural to his species. Surely the human invention or creation of language is our species' highest achievement; some psycholinguists speculate that human beings are born with a genetic endowment for recognizing and formulating language, that they "possess genes for all kinds of information, with strands of special, peculiarly human DNA for the discernment of meaning in syntax."[2] Failing to accept the intellect as triumphantly human, rather than somehow unnatural, the poet is doomed to endless struggles with the self. The "variations on estrangement" at the end of *The Eye-Beaters* deal with countless battles and meadows strewn "with inner lives," concluding with the hope that the poet's life may be seen "as a thing / That can be learned, / As those earnest young heroes learned theirs, / Later, much later on."

An objective assessment of one's situation must be experienced apart from life itself, then. And only "much later on." To use a critical term Dickey appropriated from Wordsworth, he is a poet of the "Second Birth," not one who, like Rimbaud or Dylan Thomas, possessed a natural instrument for poetry but one who eventually reduces the distinction between "born" and "made" poets only by hard work, by the "ultimate moral habit of trying each poem, each line, each word, against the shifting but finally constant standards of inner necessity" (*The Suspect in*

Poetry, pp. 55-57). Contrary to his instinct for direct, undiluted self-expression, the poet has tried to define and develop his own personality as a "writing instrument"; he has pared back, reduced, restrained the chaotic "monstrousness" of raw emotion in order to relate his unique experience to common experience. He contradicts Eliot's ideal of an impersonal poetry, yet paradoxically refuses to endorse what he would call the monstrousness of confessional verse: "The belief in the value of one's personality has all but disappeared. . . ."

But what is personality, that a belief in it might save us?

Not a multileveled phenomenon, Dickey's sense of "personality," but rather a series of imagined dramas, sometimes no more than flashes of rapport, kinships with beasts or ancient ancestors—as in the apocalyptic **"The Eye-Beaters,"** in which personality is gained only when "Reason" is rejected in favor of primitive action. The process of increasing self-consciousness, as image after image is explored, held up like a mask to the poet's face,[3] absorbed, and finally discarded, comes to seem a tragic movement, as every existential role in the universe must ultimately be abandoned.

"Intact and Incredible Love"

Dickey has said that the century's greatest phrase is Albert Schweitzer's "reverence for life." This conviction runs through his work but is strongest in the earliest volumes. *Into the Stone* consists of contemplative, almost dreamlike poems that investigate the poet's many forms of love: beginning with the mythical, incantatory dissolution of the individual personality into both "dark" and "light" and concluding with the book's title poem, which emphasizes the poet's confident "knowing" and his being "known" through his relationship with a woman.

"Sleeping Out at Easter" is terse, restrained, as the "Word rising out of darkness" seems to act without the deliberate involvement of the poet. As dawn arrives in the forest, the "Presences" of night turn into trees and "One eye opens slowly without me." Everything moves in its own placid, nonpersonalized pattern, out of darkness and into the sunlight, and the world is "made good" by the springing together of wood and sun. The metamorphosis of Presences into daytime trees is one that could occur without the poet's song, yet the poet voices a total acceptance, as if he knew himself uniquely absorbed in the cycle of night/day, his "magical shepherd's cloak . . . not yet alive on [his] flesh." In other, similarly incantatory poems, the poet lies at the edge of a well, contemplating himself and his smile and the "grave face" of his dead brother, or lies "in ritual down" in a small unconsecrated grove of suburban pines—trying to get back, to get down, beneath both gods and animals, to "being part of the acclaimed rebirth" of spring (**"The Vegetable King"**). (Years later, when his poetry has undergone tremendous changes, Dickey will deal again with the transformation of a human being into a tree, in **"The Fiend,"** one of his most eccentric poems).

Into the Stone contains a number of war poems, but in spite of their subject they absorb the poet's personality much as the nature poems do, locating in confusion and panic certain centers of imagination, of decision, that the poet is able to recall years later, when "at peace." **"The Enclosure"** is the first of Dickey's many poems that "enclose" and idealize women: a group of war nurses on a Philippine island are protected by a compound with a wire fence, but the poet imagines them whispering to the soldiers outside "to deliver them out / Of the circle of impotence. . . ." In lines of curious, ceremonial calm the poet declares how, after the war, this vision led him to "fall / On the enemy's women / With intact and incredible love." Of the war poems, the most vivid is **"The Performance,"** which celebrates the paradox of pain and triumph in the memory of David Armstrong, executed by the Japanese; Dickey remembers Armstrong doing a handstand against the sun, and his death by decapitation is seen as another kind of "performance." Even here there is a sense of acquiescence, finality, as if the cycle of nature could absorb this violent death as easily as it could absorb the shapes of trees back into primordial Presences.

The reverential awe of **"Trees and Cattle"** places the poet's consciousness in a "holy alliance" with trees, cattle, and sunlight, making his mind a "red beast"—his head gifted with ghostly bull's horns by the same magic that allowed Lawrence to imagine his head "hard-balanced, antlered" in **"A Doe at Evening"**; the sun itself burns more deeply because trees and cattle exist. A miracle of some kind has occurred, though it cannot be explained, and the poet half believes he may be saved from death; as, in a later poem, **"Fog Envelops the Animals,"** the poet-hunter is somehow transformed into the "long-sought invisibility" of pure things or events or processes: "Silence. Whiteness. Hunting." But *Into the Stone* is characterized by passivity and no hint of the guilty, pleasurable agitation of physical life, whether hunting or love; the title poem describes the poet "on the way to a woman," preoccupied with a mystical absorption into the "stone" of the moon. The woman is outside the concern of the poem, undefined, not even mythologized; the poet is not vividly portrayed, as in **"Cherrylog Road"**; he could be any man, any lover, believing that "the dead have their chance in my body." All is still, mysterious, calm. The poet "knows" his place and his love, quite unlike the moon-drawn men of a later poem, **"Apollo,"** who are seen as floating "on nothing / But procedure alone" and who symbolize "all humanity in the name / Of a new life. . . ." This later poem makes the "stone" of the moon into "stones," breaks up a seamless cosmology into a universe of "craters" and "mountains the animal / Eye has not seen since the earth split" (the earth-moon split an ancient and honored moon theory, of obvious symbolic, if not scientific, value)—not the Platonic oneness of stone, but stones:

> . . . We stare into the moon
> dust, the earth-blazing ground. We laugh, with the
> beautiful craze
> Of Static. We bend, we pick up stones.
>
> (**"Apollo"**)

A more dramatic sense of self is evident in Dickey's second book, *Drowning with Others.* Here he imagines the torturous memories of a lifeguard who failed to save a drowning child; he imagines himself inside the hunting dream of a dog sleeping on his feet; he contemplates fish in **"The Movement of Fish"** with the alert, awed scrutiny of Lawrence himself, making a judgment, like Lawrence's, that arises from the distant Otherness of the fish's world, where its sudden movement has the power to "convulse the whole ocean" and teach man the Kierkegaardian terror of the leap, the "fear and trembling" of great depths that are totally still, far beneath the superficial agitation that men see or float upon in their boats.

Yet the hunted/hunting animals of **"The Heaven of Animals"** are poetic constructions, Platonic essences of beasts wholly absorbed in a mythical cycle of life-death-rebirth: at the very center of nature these beasts "tremble," "fall," "are torn," "rise," and "walk again," like Emerson's red slayer and his perpetual victim. "The Heaven of Animals" is all but unique in Dickey's poetry because the poet himself has no clear position in it, as if its unity of Being somehow excluded an active intellectual consciousness; if we look back at the poem from **"Fog Envelops the Animals"** and other hunting poems and from Dickey's statements in *Self-Interviews* (Garden City, New York, 1970) about the mysterious "renewal" he experiences when hunting, we can assume that his deepest sympathies are with the predators, but this is not evident from the poem itself, which is one of his finest, most delicate achievements. The owl of **"The Owl King"** is another poetic (and not naturalistic) creature, a form of the poet himself who sits "in my shape / With my claws growing deep into wood / And my sight going slowly out, / Inch by inch. . . ." Superior forces belong to those who, like the owl, can see in the dark; or to those who, like Dickey himself, possess extraordinary powers of vision[4] that set them apart from other, average men. But the forces are benevolent, godly, and restrained—the owl king participates in a mysterious ceremony with the blind child "as beasts at their own wedding, dance" and is not the symbol of cold, savage violence of the owl perched upon the tent in *Deliverance,* just as the poet-narrator of the volume *Drowning with Others* is not the helplessly eager murderer of *Deliverance.* Here, in the owl king's Roethkian kingdom, all nature is transformed by mind, its brutal contingencies and dreams suppressed, the possible "monstrousness" of its song made into a childlike lyric. Its final stanzas link it to earlier poems of Dickey's in which tension has been resolved by an act of impersonal, godly will:

> Far off, the owl king
> Sings like my father, growing
> In power. Father, I touch
> Your face. I have not seen
> My own, but it is yours.
> I come, I advance,
> I believe everything, I am here.

Through the child's (blind) acceptance, Dickey accepts the world; just as, in the anguished **"The Eye-Beaters,"** he rejects the world of normal, rational vision, having been shaken by the experience of seeing blind children beat at their eyes in order to "see." In **"The Owl King"** the transcendent, paternal bird withdraws into the darkness of his own vision, while the lost child's father emerges, "In love with the sound of my voice," to claim his child; both aspects of the poetic consciousness are required if the child is to be saved, cherished, and yet both are dependent upon the child's acquiescence. (Just as, for the hunter, the imagined "acquiescence" of the hunted—the slain—is a ritualistic necessity; see Dickey's attempted justification of his love of hunting in *Self-Interviews*). This poem is a "song of innocence" whose unearthly simplicity—the child moves from tree to tree as if blessing them—will be transformed, years later, into the nightmarish "song of experience" of the crazed blind children in **"The Eye-Beaters."** Then, the objects of the poet's pity being, in themselves, hopeless, not even human children, beyond all love or language, the poet himself will narrowly escape madness. But this is years later, years deeper into flesh.

ENTERING HISTORY

In his third book, *Helmets,* Dickey begins to move out of the perfected world of eternal recurrence, no longer the awed, alert, but essentially passive observer, now ready to experience history. It is clear that Dickey desires to take on "his" own personal history as an analogue to or a microcosmic exploration of twentieth-century American history, which is one of the reasons he is so important a poet. In his inspired, witty, and ingeniously balanced essay on Randall Jarrell in *The Suspect in Poetry,* Dickey says he can discover in Jarrell's poetry very little excellence of technique, but he insists that Jarrell's contribution—"that of writing about real things, rather than playing games with words"—is a valuable one. Dickey indicates implicitly that *he* will take on both the challenge of being an artist and a historian of our era, which he has, applying a superior poetic talent to Jarrell's "realm . . . of pity and terror . . . a kind of non-understanding understanding, and above all of helplessness."[5]

Once he is released from the sacred but bloodless cycle of nature, Dickey is concerned with giving life to this "non-understanding understanding" of creatures simpler than himself, or of an earlier form of himself, as in the beautiful, perfect poem, **"Drinking from a Helmet."** In **"The Dusk of Horses"** the emphasis has shifted from acceptance to a sharper awareness of distinctions between self and object, the need for the human participant in an action to judge it:

> No beast ever lived who understood
>
> What happened among the sun's fields,
> Or cared why the color of grass
> Fled over the hill while he stumbled,
>
> Led by the halter to sleep
> On his four taxed, worthy legs. . . .

> (**"The Dusk of Horses"**)

In this and similar poems in *Helmets* the graceful fluidity of the lines is like the fluidity of the earlier poems: the god's-eye vision set to music. As the theme of "helplessness" grows, however, Dickey loses interest in well-made and sweetly sounding poetry and pours his remarkable energies into such extravaganzas of shouts and shrieks as **"May Day Sermon."** And where death might once have been resolved by a mystical affirmation of unity, in the recent poem **"Diabetes"** it is resolved by a surreptitious drink of beer; in **"The Cancer Match,"** by whiskey.

Throughout *Helmets* there is an increasing growth, as if the subjects long loved by the poet are now shifting out of the hypnosis of love itself, beginning to elude his incantatory powers: coming alive and separate. In a poem reminiscent of Wallace Stevens' "Anecdote of the Jar," Dickey stands by a fence with his palm on the top wire and experiences a vision or a nervous hallucination of the disorder that would result if the tension of the wire were broken:

> If the wire were cut anywhere
> All his blood would fall to the ground
> And leave him standing and staring
> With a face as white as a Hereford's. . . .
>
> ("Fence Wire")

The "top tense strand" is like a guitar string "tuned to an E," whose humming sound arranges the acres of the farm and holds them "highstrung and enthralled." Suddenly the poet in his human role must accept a position in nature which is superior to that of trees and cattle, an intellectual responsibility that will involve both exultation and the risk of despair. But because of Dickey's hand on this fence wire,

> The dead corn is more
> Balanced in death than it was,
> The animals more aware
>
> Within the huge human embrace
> Held up and borne out of sight
> Upon short, unbreakable poles
> Where through the ruled land intones
> Like a psalm. . . .

Because of the sensational aspects of some of his later poems, Dickey is not usually known to have concerned himself so seriously, and so perceptively, with the metaphysics behind aesthetic action; it is characteristic of his energy and his pursuit of new challenges that a very few poems about "poetry" are enough for him. If read in its proper chronological place in Dickey's work, **"Fence Wire"** is a moving as well as a significant poem; it is the first clear statement of the poet's sense of himself as involved responsibly in history. In his most powerful poems the tension between that "top thread tuned to an E" and the abandonment to one's own possible, probable "monstrousness" provides a dramatic excitement generally lacking in these early, though entirely admirable poems, and less content with lyric verse itself, Dickey will experiment with wildly imaginative monologues in which words float and leap all over the page.

In *Helmets* there is also a new sense of exploration into an "Otherness," not a declaring of unities, analogues, "correspondences" between all phenomena in nature: Dickey stands **"At Darien Bridge"** and muses upon the chain-gang workers who built the bridge many years ago, when he was a child; he hopes to see a bird, the one bird "no one has looked for," and the scratched wedding band on his finger recalls the convicts' chains—like them, he longs for freedom, or even death, or at least the ability to believe again in "the unchanging, hopeless look / Out of which all miracles leap." (In contrast to the miraculous vision of **"Trees and Cattle."**) In **"Chenille"** he encounters another kind of poet, an old woman who darns quilts endlessly, not ordinary bedspreads of the kind made by machine and sold in the normal world but quilts decorated with red whales, unicorns, winged elephants, crowned ants— "Beasts that cannot be thought of / By the wholly sane." Increasingly, the surreal intrudes into what should be the real, or sane; in **"On the Cosawattee"** Dickey and his companion on a canoeing trip are shocked to see how the water has been defiled by a poultry-processing plant upstream:

> All morning we floated on feathers
> Among the drawn heads which appeared
> Everywhere, from under the logs
>
> Of feathers, from upstream behind us,
> Lounging back to us from ahead,
> Until we believed ourselves doomed
> And the planet corrupted forever. . . .

Though the two men shoot the rapids and finally escape this horror, the canoeists of *Deliverance* return to experience the river's mysterious dangers and the unhuman ground-bass of sound that becomes "deeper and more massively frantic and authoritative" as they continue—and this time not all will survive, and none will get back to civilization with anything like this poem's triumphant declaration of the human ability to escape other human defilement. In the blaze of noon the canoeists on the Coosawattee River feel:

> The quickening pulse of the rapids
> And entered upon it like men
> Who sense that the world can be cleansed
>
> Among rocks pallid only with water,
> And plunged there like the unborn
> Who see earthly streams without taint
> Flow beneath them. . . .

"Cherrylog Road" is the first of the unmistakable Dickeyesque poems: nostalgic and comic simultaneously, demystifying the love so laboriously mystified elsewhere, even naming names ("Doris Holbrook") and giving directions:

> Off Highway 106
> At Cherrylog Road I entered
> The '34 Ford without wheels,
> Smothered in kudzu,

With a seat pulled out to run
Corn whiskey down from the hills. . . .

And in this automobile graveyard the boy moves from car to car, delighted to be naming, placing, experiencing, without the need to make anything sacred or even essentially important: from the Ford to an Essex to a blue Chevrolet to a Pierce-Arrow, "as in a wild stock-car race / In the parking lot of the dead. . . ." He hopes his girl friend will come to him from her father's farm "And . . . get back there / With no trace of me on her face"; when she does arrive and they embrace, their love-making takes place in the same "stalled, dreaming traffic" as the hunting of mice by blacksnakes, and beetles soon reclaim the field of the car's seat springs. The narrator leaves on his motorcycle, which is unglamorized, "Like the soul of the junkyard / Restored, a bicycle fleshed / With power"—an earlier, more convincing version of the spectacular **"May Day Sermon."**

"The Poisoned Man" deals with the same situation explored in a later poem, **"Snakebite"** (from *Falling*, in *Poems 1957-1967*) in which the victim of a poisonous snake is forced to cut himself with a knife in order to drain out the poison. In the earlier poem a formal, almost allegorical meaning evolves from the terrifying experience; the poet has a kind of vision, feeling that his heart's blood could flow "Unendingly out of the mountain. . . ." **"Snakebite"** reduces this visionary abstraction to "I have a problem with / My right foot and my life." Aging, the poet is urgently concerned with survival itself; he has called himself a poet of "survival." In another poem about snakes, **"Goodbye to Serpents,"** Dickey and his son observe snakes in a Parisian zoo, and Dickey tries to concentrate on them as he never has in the past. His meditation is so complete that he seems to pass into them, seeing the human world of towers and churches and streets "All old, all cold with my gaze. . . ." and he longs to believe that he has somehow retained, at the same time, his own human presence, the human miracles of "self" and "love." But it is a failure:

And I know I have not been moved
Enough by the things I have moved through,
And I have seen what I have seen

Unchanged, hypnotized, and perceptive. . . .

Unchanged, hypnotized, and perceptive: a strange combination of words. But in the first of Dickey's "reincarnation" poems in a later volume, *Buckdancer's Choice,* he becomes a snake with head "poisonous and poised." Perhaps he is suggesting that the very awe of nature that mesmerized him has prevented his being "moved" humanly by the things he has experienced. The mystic's world of total acceptance has always contrasted sharply with the world of human suffering.

Helmets concludes with one of Dickey's most remarkable poems, the little-discussed **"Drinking from a Helmet."** The young narrator, in wartime, drinks from a helmet he picked up near his foxhole and sways "as if kissed in the brain," standing

. . . as though I possessed
A cool, trembling man
Exactly my size, swallowed whole.

He throws down his own helmet and puts on the one he has found, an inheritance from the dead. Then he seems to "see" in his own brain the dying man's last thought—a memory of two boys, the soldier and his older brother in a setting of tremendous trees "That would grow on the sun if they could. . . ." Where **"Approaching Prayer"** traced what seemed to be the poet's conscious effort to imagine a dying hog's experience, **"Drinking from a Helmet"** seems sheer unwilled vision:

I saw a fence
And two boys facing each other,
Quietly talking,
Looking in at the gigantic redwoods,
The rings in the trunks turning slowly
To raise up stupendous green.
I would survive and go there,
Stepping off the train in a helmet
That held a man's last thought,
Which showed him his older brother
Showing him trees.
I would ride through all
California upon two wheels
Until I came to the white
Dirt road where they had been,
Hoping to meet his blond brother,
And to walk with him into the wood
Until we were lost,
Then take off the helmet
And tell him where I had stood,
What poured, what spilled, what swallowed:

And tell him I was the man.

The relationship between the two brothers is interesting, because it reverses the relationship of Dickey and his own older brother, who evidently died before Dickey was born. (See **"The Underground Stream," "The String,"** and other poems in which the "tall cadaver" of the brother is summoned up by the poet, who believes himself conceived by his parents "out of grief" and brought to life "To replace the incredible child" who had died. The psychologically disastrous results of such a belief, if sincere, hardly need to be examined; one is always a "survivor," always "guilty," and always conscious of being an inferior substitute for some superior being.) Here, the younger brother has died and Dickey himself will go to visit the surviving older brother, as if, somehow, both he and his older brother were living and able to speak to each other; a life-affirming magic, in spite of a young soldier's death.

MONSTERS

After *Helmets* Dickey's poetry changes considerably. The colloquial tone and unserious rhythms of **"Cherrylog Road"** are used for deadly serious purposes as Dickey explores hypothetical selves and the possibility of values outside the human sphere. Where in an early poem like **"The Performance"** a mystical placidity rendered even a brutal execution into something observed, now most actions, most states of being, are examined bluntly, brutally, emotionally, as the poet subjects himself to raw life without the sustaining rituals of Being.

Dickey has many extraordinary poems, fusions of "genius" and "art," but the central poem of his work seems to be **"The Firebombing,"** from ***Buckdancer's Choice.*** No reader, adjusted to the high, measured art of Dickey's first three volumes, can be ready for this particular poem; it is unforgettable, and seems to me an important achievement in our contemporary literature, a masterpiece that could only have been written by an American, and only by Dickey.

"The Firebombing" is an eight-page poem of irregular lines, abrupt transitions and leaps, stanzas of varying length, connected by suburban-surreal images, a terrifying visionary experience endured in a "well-stocked pantry." Its effort is to realize, to *feel,* what the poet did twenty years before as a participant in an "anti-morale raid" over Japan during the closing months of World War II. Its larger effort is to feel guilt and finally to feel anything. One of the epigraphs to the poem is from the Book of Job: "Or hast thou an arm like God?" This is Dickey's ironic self-directed question, for it is he, Dickey, the homeowner / killer, the Job / God, who has tried on the strength of vast powers and has not been able to survive them. Irony is something altogether new in Dickey:

> Homeowners unite.
>
> All families lie together, though some are burned alive.
> The others try to feel
> For them. Some can, it is often said.

The detachment is not godly, but despairing. Though he is now Job, he was at one time the "arm of God," and being both man and God is an impossibility. Dickey's earlier war poems always show him a survivor, grateful to survive, rather boyish and stunned by the mystery of a strange rightness beneath disorder; it seems to have taken him many years to get to this particular poem, though its meaning in his life must have been central. Now the survivor is also a killer. What of this, what of killing?—What is a release from the sin of killing? Confession, but, most of all, guilt; if the poet cannot make himself feel guilt even for the deaths of children, how will it be possible for him to feel anything human at all?—

> . . . some technical-minded stranger with my hands
> Is sitting in a glass treasure-hole of blue light,
> Having potential fire under the undeodorized arms
> Of his wings, on thin bomb-shackles,
> The "tear-drop-shaped" 300-gallon drop-tanks
> Filled with napalm and gasoline.

This stranger is, or was, Dickey himself, who flew one hundred combat missions through the South Pacific, the Philippines, and Okinawa and participated in B-29 raids over Japan; but he is only a memory now, an eerily aesthetic memory. He exists in the mind of a suburban husband and father, worrying about his weight and the half-paid-for pantry that is part of his homeowning and his present "treasure-hole":

> Where the lawn mower rests on its laurels
> Where the diet exists
> For my own good   where I try to drop
> Twenty years. . . .

So many years after the event, what remains? He is now a civilian, a citizen, an American who understands himself in ironic, secret charge of all the necessary trivia of unaesthetic life—the purchasing of golf carts and tennis shoes, new automobiles, Christmas decorations—that he knows as the "glue inspired / By love of country," the means by which the possibly atomistic or death-bound ego is held fast in its identity. Though the wonder remains, he is far from the moon-hypnotized, somnambulistic rhythms of the past; **"The Firebombing"** is what Dickey would call an "open poem," one in which a certain compulsiveness in the presentation of the subject matter precludes or makes peripheral an aesthetic response,[6] and the poet's own recollection of his action is mocked, if it must be assessed in stylized terms:

> As I sail artistically over
> The resort town followed by farms,
> Singing and twisting
> All the handles in heaven   kicking
> The small cattle off their feet
> In a red costly blast
> Flinging jelly over the walls
> As in a chemical war-
> fare field demonstration.

Remembering this, he knows that "my hat should crawl on my head" and "the fat on my body should pale"—but one of the horrors of this bombing raid is that it has somehow destroyed a normal human response, as if the "arm of God" the pilot had assumed had also annihilated him. Having shown us so convincingly in his poetry how natural, how inevitable, is man's love for all things, Dickey now shows us what happens when man is forced to destroy, forced to step down into history and be an American ("and proud of it"). In so doing he enters a tragic dimension in which few poets indeed have operated. Could Whitman's affirmation hold out if he were forced to affirm not just the violence of others, but his own? If war is necessary, warriors are necessary; someone must sacrifice his cosmic love; and not only is the traditional life-praising song of the poet savagely mocked by his performance as a patriot in wartime, but the poet cannot even experience his own deeds, for he has acted as a machine inside a machine. In **"The Firebombing"** everything must remain remote and abstract, not experienced in any vital way. The Machine Age splits man irreparably from his instinctive need to see, to feel, to *know* through the senses. The Whitmanesque affirmation of man is difficult to sustain if the poet can see the objects of his love only from a great height, through an intellectual telescope. When Whitman feels he is "on the verge of a usual mistake" ("Song of Myself," stanza 38), it is only an emotional mistake; he could never have considered the nihilism of a self without emotions, in which his inventiveness could really attach itself to nothing because it could experience nothing.

After this dreamlike unleashing of "all American fire," the poet states flatly that *death will not be what it should*—a counterstatement, perhaps, to Schweitzer's *reverence for life.* This is the poet's unique vision:

> Ah, under one's dark arms
> Something strange-scented falls—when those on earth
> Die, there is not even sound;
> One is cool and enthralled in the cockpit,
> Turned blue by the power of beauty,
> In a pale treasure-hole of soft light
> Deep in aesthetic contemplation,
> Seeing the ponds catch fire
> And cast it through ring after ring
> Of land. . . .
>
> . . . . .
>
> It is this detachment,
> The honored aesthetic evil,
> The greatest sense of power in one's life,
> That must be shed in bars, or by whatever
> Means, by starvation
> Visions in well-stocked pantries. . . .

These "visions" will inspire in the poet wilder and wilder imaginings in his own creative life and an abandonment of the ego as "homeowner" in favor of the ego as "hunter" or "primitive." The mechanized State tempts one to an aesthetic evil, and so perhaps salvation may be found in a pre-aesthetic, prehistorical animality that will seize upon possible rites (the structural basis of *Deliverance*) in order to exorcise the despairing and suicidal violence of the animal self. Whether Dickey's themes are explorative rather than absolute, whether his work traces an autobiographical query or a record, the function of his poetry seems to be the demonstration of the failure of such a vision. And yet it is certainly tempting to take on the viciousness—and the innocence—of the animal, to take for our totems owls, snakes, foxes, wolverines, and to reject forever the possibilities of detachment and evil that are inherent in civilization.

Like Dostoyevsky, Dickey considers the helplessness of the *killer.* But, unlike Dostoyevsky, he cannot imagine a transformation of the killer into a higher form of himself: the mysterious process by which Raskolnikov grows and by which Smerdyakov can be seen as a rudimentary form of Father Zossima. But Dickey cannot operate through metaphor, as Dostoyevsky did, for he was the man, he did these things, *he* and no one else. Though his poetry charts a process of wonders, a changing of selves, finally he is only himself, a particular man, trapped in a finite and aging body with memories that belong to him and not to the rest of us, not to any liberalized concept of the guilt we all "share." (Like Marcuse, Dickey could probably feel no more than scorn for the "repressive tolerance" of some aspects of liberalism.) If made general and universal, in order to be shared, is guilt itself not made an aesthetic event?—a luxury?—a perversion?

But the narrator of the poem cannot concern himself with such abstractions:

> All this, and I am still hungry,
> Still twenty years overweight, still unable
> To get down there or see
> What really happened.
>
> . . . . .
>   . . . It is that I can imagine
> At the threshold nothing
> With its ears crackling off
> Like powdery leaves,
> Nothing with children of ashes, nothing not
> Amiable, gentle, well-meaning. . . .

A poetry of Being can move to perfect resolutions, but this poetry of anguished Becoming cannot. ("Some can, it is often said," Dickey has remarked, ironically and sadly.) The narrative and confessional elements of **"The Firebombing"** demand a totally different aesthetic: the aesthetic-denying open form. No reconciliation of opposites is possible here because the poet cannot reconcile himself to his earlier self. And so what of "Absolution? Sentence?" These do not matter for "The thing itself is in that."

"The Firebombing" is central to an understanding of Dickey's work. It could not have been prophesied on the basis of the earlier, Roethke-inspired poems; but once it appears, unsuppressed, it is so powerful an illumination that it helps to explain a great deal that might remain mysterious and puzzling. *Buckdancer's Choice, Falling,* and, above all, *The Eye-Beaters* deal with mortality, decay, disease, perhaps attributable in part to the poet's actual aging, but only in part, for the descent into a physically combative and increasingly unaesthetic world is not the usual pattern our finest poets follow, as both Roethke and Yeats, and other poets of the "Second Birth," suggest. Yet the emphasis Dickey places upon mortality, his self-consciousness about it, is a motif that begins to appear even in his literary criticism. How is it possible that the man who believes in nature—in natural processes—should feel uneasy about the natural process of aging? It is a paradox in Hemingway also, but perhaps it is to be understood in Rilke's terms: our fear is not of death, but of life unlived. In an introduction to Paul Carroll's *The Young American Poets* (Chicago, 1968), Dickey makes a statement that totally contradicts the contemplative, balanced criticism of *The Suspect in Poetry* of only four years previous:

> The aging process almost always brings to the poet the secret conviction that he has settled for far too little. . . . The nearer he gets to his end the more he yearns for the caves: for a wild, shaggy, all-out, all-involving way of speaking where language and he (or, now, someone: some new poet) engage each other at primitive levels, on ground where the issues are not those of literary fashion but are quite literally those of life and

death. All his lifelong struggle with "craft" seems a tragic and ludicrous waste of time. . . .

(p. 7)

One would imagine, from such remarks, that the speaker is far older than forty-five; "the nearer he gets to his end . . ." is a visionary statement that might be comprehensible in the Yeats of *Last Poems,* but astonishing in a poet who is the same age as the Yeats of *The Green Helmet.* But if a denial of "craft" (or civilization) is needed in order to release spontaneous energy, then one can see why, for Dickey, it must be attempted.

ENTROPY

Buckdancer's Choice received the National Book Award in 1965, and in 1967 Dickey put together his *Poems 1957-1967* for Wesleyan University Press. The *Poems* do not observe strict chronological order, however, beginning with the demonic **"May Day Sermon to the Women of Gilmer County, Georgia, by a Woman Preacher Leaving the Baptist Church,"** one of Dickey's most flamboyant poems. Clearly, Dickey does not want the reader to enter the world of *Into the Stone* with the innocence he himself had entered it; that celebration of forms is all but outshouted by the eleven-page sermon, which is about violence done to and by a young girl in Georgia, and about her escape with her motorcycle-riding lover, "stoned out of their minds on the white / Lightning of fog"—

> singing   the saddlebags full of her clothes
> Flying   snagging   shoes hurling away   stockings grabbed-off
> Unwinding and furling on twigs: all we know   all we could follow
> Them by was her underwear   was stocking after stocking where it tore
> Away, and a long slip stretched on a thorn   all these few gave
> Out. Children, you know it: that place was where they took
> Off into the air   died   disappeared   entered my mouth your mind

It is an incredible achievement, with the intonations of a mad, inspired sermon, the flesh elevated beyond the spirit, but both elevated into myth. It is a myth that transforms everything into it: everything turns into everything else, through passion. The intellect exercises very little control in this "wild, shaggy, all-out, all-involving" work, and though Dickey has expressed doubt over the value of Allen Ginsberg's poetry,[7] one is forced to think of certain works of Ginsberg's and of how, under ether sniffing or morphine injection, Ginsberg wrote all of *Ankor Wat* and that extravaganza "Aether," in which a preaching voice proclaims certain truths to us: "we are the sweeping of the moon / we're what's *left over* from perfection"—"(my) Madness is intelligible reactions to / Unintelligible phenomena"—

And—

> What *can* be possible
> in a minor universe
> in which you can see
> God by sniffing the
> gas in a cotton?

("Aether," in *Reality Sandwiches*)

Dickey is much more violent, more heartless than Ginsberg, of course, since he is driven by energies more archaic than is Ginsberg, who is a philosopher with a respect for the syntax of the imagination if not of superficial grammar; the **"May Day Sermon"** is at once revenge for and repetition of the helplessness of the bomber pilot, a mythic annihilation of a punishing, near-invisible father, and an escape off into space, the girl's clothing cast off behind her like the airline stewardess' clothing in **"Falling."** In all the exuberant spurts of language there is violence, but especially here:

> And she comes down   putting her back into
> The hatchet   often   often   he is brought down-laid out
> Lashing   smoking   sucking wind: Children, each year at this time
> A girl will tend to take an ice pick in both hands   a long pine
> Needle   will hover   hover: Children, each year at this time
> Things happen quickly   and it is easy for a needle to pass
> Through the eye of a man bound for Heaven   she leaves it naked goes
> Without further sin through the house

After countless readings, **"May Day Sermon"** still has the power to shock: consider the "needle-eye-Heaven" joke. The maniacal repetitions make one wince ("get up . . . up in your socks and rise"), and the Dylan Thomas-surreal touches sometimes seem forced ("Dancing with God in a mule's eye"), but the poem's shrieking transmutation of murder, nakedness, eroticism, fertility, and poetry into a single event has an irresistible strength: "everything is more *more* MORE." Nature itself becomes active in the process of transmutation as even "peanuts and beans exchange / Shells in joy," and in a poetic sleight of hand reminiscent of Thomas's *Ballad of the Long-Legged Bait* at its apocalyptic conclusion, "the barn falls in / Like Jericho." The countryside itself is speaking through the woman preacher "as beasts speak to themselves / Of holiness learned in the barn." It is mysticism, but existential and ribald, noisy, filled with the humming of gnats and strange prophecies:

> Each May you will crouch like a sawhorse to make yourself
> More here   you will be cow chips   chicken croaking . . .
>
> . . . . .
>   and every last one of you
> will groan
> Like nails barely holding   and your hair be full of the gray

Glints of stump chains.   Children, each year at this
   time you will have
Back-pain, but also heaven

In **"May Day Sermon"** Dickey creates a patchwork of
images that go beyond the "not wholly sane" images of
"Chenille."

However, *Buckdancer's Choice* contains several very
personal and moving poems dealing with mortality, the
title poem and **"Angina"** (which deal with Dickey's
mother, an invalid "dying of breathless angina"), **"Them,
Crying," "The Escape,"** and one that reasserts the mystical possibility of transcending death, its certainties
expressed in a steady three-beat line:

All ages of mankind unite
Where it is dark enough.
. . . . .
All creatures tumbled together
Get back in their wildest arms
No single thing but each other. . . .

(**"The Common Grave"**)

But the most passionate poems are counterstatements
concerned with developing images adequate to express
horror; in **"Pursuit from Under"** the poet summons up a
terrifying image that does not have its place in his own
experience, or even in his probable experience, but is a
conscious re-creation of a memory. He is standing in a
meadow, in August, and imagines he hears the "bark of
seals" and feels "the cold of a personal ice age. . . ."
Then he recalls having once read an account of Arctic
explorers who died of starvation and whose journal
contained a single entry of unforgettable horror:

. . . under the ice,

The killer whale darts and distorts,
Cut down by the flawing glass

To a weasel's shadow,
And when, through his ceiling, he sees
Anything darker than snow
He falls away
To gather more and more force
                      . . . then charges
Straight up, looms up at the ice and smashes
Into it with his forehead. . . .

And so the killer whale pursues the poet, even in this
familiar meadow in the South, and he thinks of "how the
downed dead pursue us"—"not only in the snow / But in
the family field." It is interesting to note that Norman
Mailer's nihilistic and very deliberately "literary" novel
Why Are We in Vietnam? also transports its protagonist/
victim to the Arctic in order to allow him a vision of God-
as-beast; this "vision" is then imposed upon all of
American (universal?) experience and can allow for no
possibilities of transcendence. If God is a beast (as Dickey
concludes in **"The Eye-Beaters"**), then the beast is God,
and one must either acquiesce to Him and experience the

helplessness of terror in an ordinary southern meadow, or
imitate Him, taking on some of His powers. But, increasingly, the poet reaches out beyond his own geographical
and historical territory to appropriate this vision. It
demands a distortion or a rejection of naturalistic life; at
times, as he admits, a kind of necessary theatricality, as he
explains in *Self-Interviews* why hunting is so important to
him: ". . . the main thing is to re-enter the cycle of the
man who hunts for his food. Now this may be playacting
at being a primitive man, but it's better than not having
any rapport with the animal at all . . . I have a great sense
of renewal when I am able to go into the woods and hunt
with a bow and arrow, to enter into the animal's world in
this way." And, in *Deliverance,* the experience of
"renewal" or deliverance itself is stimulated by a hunt for
other men; simple animals are no longer enough, and the
whole of the novel is constructed around those several
intensely dramatic moments in which the narrator sights
his target—a human and usually forbidden target—and
kills him with an arrow from his powerful bow. The arrow
is at least real; the napalm and gasoline bomb are not,
since they are dropped upon abstractions. And, too, the
necessary intimacy of the besieged men in *Deliverance* approximates a primitive brotherliness, excluding the confusion that women bring to a world of simple, clear, direct
actions. For women, while mysterious and unfathomable,
are also "civilization."

But if women are objects, goddess objects, they too can be
assimilated into the mystique of primitive power-worship.
One of the most striking poems in all of Dickey's work is
"The Fiend," which magically transforms a voyeur/lover
into a tree, into an omnipotent observer, back into a voyeur
again, while throughout he is the poet who loves and
desires and despairs of truly knowing his subject; the poem
is a long, hushed, reverential overture to murder. Yet the
equation of the voyeur with the poet is obvious, and the
poem concludes ominously by remarking how "the light /
Of a hundred favored windows" has "gone wrong somewhere in his glasses. . . ." Dickey is remarkably honest in
acknowledging the value he puts upon his own fantasies,
in contrast to the less interesting world of reality. What is
important is *his* imaginative creation, *his* powers of seeing. In praise of what a Jungian would call the "anima,"
Dickey has said in *Sorties* that "poor mortal perishable
women are as dust before these powerful and sensual
creatures of the depths of one's being" (p. 4). A dangerous
overestimation of the individual's self-sufficiency, one
might think, especially since there is always the possibility
of that interior light going "wrong somewhere in his
glasses."

In fact, in Dickey's later poems eyesight becomes crucial,
aligned with the mysterious grace of masculinity itself.
When one's vision begins to weaken, there is an immediate danger of loss of control; conversely, "sight" itself can
be rejected, denied, as a prelude to glorious savagery. Or
the denial of vision can facilitate a more formal, sinister
betrayal, as Dickey imagines himself as, simultaneously, a
slave owner on a southern plantation and the white father

of an illegitimate black son and the father-who-denies-his-son, a master driven to madness by his role as an owner, in the poem **"Slave Quarters."** Dickey's question concerns itself with many forms of paternal betrayal, a betrayal of the eyes of others:

> What it is to look once a day
> Into an only
> Son's brown, waiting, wholly possessed
> Amazing eye, and not
> Acknowledge, but own. . . .

How take on the guilt . . . ? is the poem's central question.

In the section *Falling* in *Poems 1957-1967,* Dickey explores further extensions of life, beginning with **"Reincarnation (II),"** in which the poet has taken on the form of a bird. His first reincarnation was into a snake, which we leave waiting in an old wheel not for food but for the first man to walk by—minute by minute the head of the snake becoming "more poisonous and poised." But as a bird the poet undergoes a long, eerie, metaphysical flight that takes him out of mortality altogether—

> to be dead
> In one life is to enter
> Another   to break out   to rise above   the clouds

But **"Reincarnation (II)"** is extremely abstract and does not seem to have engaged the poet's imaginative energies as deeply as **"Reincarnation (I)"** of *Buckdancer's Choice.* It is balanced by the long **"Falling,"** an astonishing poetic feat that dramatizes the accidental fall of an airline stewardess from a plane to her death in a corn field. "The greatest thing that ever came to Kansas" undergoes a number of swift metamorphoses—owl, hawk, goddess—stripping herself naked as she falls. She imagines the possibility of falling into water, turning her fall into a dive so that she can "come out healthily dripping / And be handed a Coca-Cola," but ultimately she is helpless to save herself; she is a human being, not a bird like the spiritual power of **"Reincarnation (II),"** and she comes to know how "the body will assume without effort any position / Except the one that will sustain it enable it to rise live / Not die." She dies, "driven well into the image of her body," inexplicable and unquestionable, and her clothes begin to come down all over Kansas; a kind of mortal goddess, given as much immortality by this strange poem as poetry is capable of giving its subjects.

The starkly confessional poem **"Adultery"** tells of the poet's need for life-affirming moments, though they are furtive and evidently depend upon a belief that the guilt caused by an act of adultery is magical—"We have done it again we are / Still living." The poem's subject is really not adultery or any exploration of the connections between people; it is about the desperate need to prove that life is still possible. *We are still living*: that guilty, triumphant cry. In this poem and several others, Dickey seems to share Norman Mailer's sentiment that sex would be

meaningless if divorced from "guilt." What role does the woman play in this male scenario? She is evidently real enough, since she is driven to tears by the impossibility of the adulterous situation; but in a more important sense she does not really exist, for she is one of those "poor mortal perishable women" temporarily illuminated by the man's anima-projection, and she is "as dust" compared to the fantasy that arises from the depths of the lover's being. Descartes' *I doubt, hence I think; I think, hence I am* has become, for those who despair of the Cartesian logic of salvation, *I love, hence I exist; I am loved, hence I must exist. . . .*

With Dickey this fear is closely related to the fundamental helplessness he feels as a man trapped in a puzzling technological civilization he cannot totally comprehend. Even the passionate love of women and the guilt of adultery will not be sufficient, ultimately, to convince the poet that he will continue to exist. He identifies with the wolverine, that "small, filthy, unwinged" creature whose species is in danger of extinction, in the poem **"For the Last Wolverine."** The wolverine is an animal capable of "mindless rage," enslaved by the "glutton's internal fire," but Dickey recognizes a kinship with it in the creature's hopeless desire to "eat / The world. . . ."

Yet, for all its bloodthirsty frenzy, the wolverine is in danger of dying out. It is a "nonsurvivor" after all. The poet's mystical identification with this beast is, paradoxically, an identification with death, and death driven, indeed, is the impulse behind his musing: "How much the timid poem needs / The mindless explosion of your rage. . . ." Like Sylvia Plath and innumerable others, the poet imagines a division between himself as a human being and the rest of the world—the universe itself—symbolized by the fact that his consciousness allows him to see and to judge his position, while the rest of nature is more or less mute. It is doubtful, incidentally, that nature is really so mute, so unintelligent, as alienated personalities seem to think; it is certainly doubtful that the human ego, the "I," is in any significant way isolated from the vast, living totality of which it is a part. However, granted for the moment that the poet is "timid" when he compares himself to the most vicious of animals, it is still questionable whether such viciousness, such "mindless explosion" of rage, is superior to the poem, to the human activity of creating and organizing language in a coherent, original structure. The prayer of the poem is very moving, but it is not the wolverine's consciousness that is speaking to us: "Lord, let me die but not die / Out."

Dickey has dramatized from the inside the terrors of the personality that fears it may not be immortal after all; its control of itself and of other people and of the environment seems to be more and more illusory, fading, failing. "Entropy"—a much-used and misused term—refers to the phenomenon of energy loss and increasing disorder as a system begins to falter, and is always a threat, a terror, to those who assume that the system to which they belong or which they have themselves organized was meant to be infinite. There is no space here to consider the psychological reasons for the shift from man's assumption of immortality as an abstraction (the "immortal" soul was expected to survive, but not the "mortal" man—the personality or ego) to his frantic and futile hope for immortality in the flesh. There are cultural, political, economic reasons, certainly, but they cannot entirely account for the naïveté of the wish: *I want to live forever.* Because this wish is so extraordinarily naïve, even childish, it is never allowed in that form into the consciousness of most intelligent people. When it emerges, it is always disguised. It sometimes takes the form of a vague, disappointed despair; or rage without any appropriate object; or a hopeless and even sentimental envy of those human beings (or animals) who strike the despairing one as too stupid to know how unhappy they should be. The excessive admiration of animals and birds and other manifestations of "unconscious" nature is, in some people, a screen for their own self-loathing. They are in "hell" because the activity of their consciousness is mainly self-concerned, self-questioning, self-doubting. The rest of the world, however, seems quite content. As entropy is irrationally feared by some, it is as irrationally welcomed by others. Disorganization—chaos—the "mindless explosion" of repressed rage: all are welcomed, mistaken for a liberating of the deepest soul.

MYSTICISM: EVOLUTION, DISSOLUTION

Mysticism is generally considered in the light of its highest religious and spiritual achievements. Most literature on the subject deals exclusively with saintly human beings, some of whom have experienced not only a powerful emotional enlightenment but an intellectual enlightenment as well. These mystics are the ones who have, in a sense, created our world: it is unnecessary to mention their names, since in a way those of us who live now have always lived, unconsciously, involuntarily, within the scope of their imaginations—as a writer lives, when he is writing, within the vast but finite universe of his language. There is an existence beyond that, surely; but he cannot quite imagine it. That I exist at this moment—that I am a writer, a woman, a surviving human being—has very little to do with accident, but is a direct, though remote, consequence of someone's thinking: *Let us value life. Let us enhance life. Let us imagine a New World, a democracy.* . . . It is not true, as Auden so famously stated, that poetry makes nothing happen. On the contrary, poetry, or the poetic imagination, has made everything happen.

Yet "mysticism" can swing in other directions. Essentially, it is a loss of "ego," but it may result in a loss of "ego control" as well. A mysterious, unfathomable revolution seems to be taking place in our civilization, and like all upheavals in history it is neither knowable nor governable; like inexplicable branchings in the flow of life, in evolution, it goes its way quite apart from the wishes of entire species, let alone individuals. However, it seems to be characterized by loss of ego, by experiences of transcendence among more and more people, especially younger

people. Yet one brings to that other world of mysticism only the equipment, the conscious moral intelligence, that one has developed through the activities of the ego: the experience of oneness with the divine, the knowledge of *That Art Thou,* gives us in its benevolent expression Jesus Christ, Gautama Buddha, and other founders of great religions, and in its malignant and grotesque expression a Hitler, a Stalin, a Charles Manson. The most important study of this subject still remains William James's *Varieties of Religious Experience,* since it was written by a man who did experience a sense of his ego's dissolution but who had not a ready-made religious structure into which he might leap. The mystic breaks free of human codes of morality, of all restraints, of "civilization," of normality itself. Useless to argue with him, for he *knows.* When D. H. Lawrence declares that he is allied with the sun and not with men, he is speaking out of the certainty of his religious knowledge that he *is* a form of energy and derives his finite being only from a higher, external form of energy. Literary critics may concern themselves with metaphors, symbols, and allusion, but most writers are writing out of their deepest experience; the playful organization of words into structures, the aesthetic impulse, is always a secondary activity. And so is social action. And so is that social being, the "ego."

But when the conscious ego has despaired of discovering values in the social world or in the world of spirit, the dissolution of that ego will probably not result in a higher wisdom, in an elevation of the moral sense so passionately required for survival. Instead, the mystic may plunge into his own ancestral past, into his own "animal" nature. This is especially tempting in an era characterized by superficiality, bad thinking, and outright inhumanity, for these abnormalities are considered "normal" and therefore "human." Something must be valued—some god must be worshiped. Where is he? Where is it? *Who has experienced him?*

So it is not surprising that many people value the "animal" over the "human," as if animals were not extraordinarily intelligent in their own contexts. In any case animals are not valued for what they are, but for their evidently uncivilized qualities; perhaps even for their cunning and savagery, their "innocence." Should it be argued that animals live and die within strict codes of behavior (which in our species is "morality"), the romantic will not listen; he is certain that *his* animals are free, wild, even immortal in their own way. They always do all the things he has wished to do, but has not dared. They are not so obviously and embarrassingly his own creation as a cartoonist's animals are his, but they share, often with the female sex, that special numinous grace of being the image bearers of men. If it is a question of mere survival, the ideal will be a predator who cannot not survive, because he demands so little of his environment. Ted Hughes's *Crow* poems, for instance, are concerned with a minimal consciousness that is always human, though reduced to beak and claws and uncanny keenness of vision. But the poems are, upon examination, oddly abstract, even rhetorical and argumentative; they have very little of the slashing emotional immediacy of Dickey's best poems. What to Ted Hughes is an allegorical possibility is for Dickey an existential fact.

As the poet wakes from his dream of "stone," enters the turbulent contests of "flesh," he will no longer be able, even, to "sail artistically over" the wars of his civilization. He must participate in them as a man; if they will not come to him, he must seek them out.

The horror of Dickey's novel *Deliverance* grows out of its ordinary, suburban framework, the assimilation of brutal events by ordinary men; not near-Biblical figures like Crow, or men trapped in a distant and hostile world, but four middle-aged, middle-class men who want to canoe along a dangerous but attractive river not far from their homes. The novel is about our deep, instinctive needs to get back to nature, to establish some kind of rapport with primitive energies, but it is also about the need of some men to do violence, to be delivered out of their banal lives by a violence so irreparable that it can never be confessed. It is a fantasy of a highly civilized and affluent society, which imagines physical violence to be transforming in a mystical—and therefore permanent—sense, a society in which rites of initiation no longer exist. This society asks its men: *How do you know you are men?* But there is no answer except in terms of an earlier society, where the male is distinguished from the female, so far as behavior is concerned, by his physical strength and his willingnes to risk life. But killing other men can be made into a ritual, a proof of one's manhood; *Deliverance* is about this ritual. It is like Mailer's short novel *Why Are We in Vietnam?* in its consideration of homosexuality, though for Mailer homosexuality evokes terror and for Dickey it evokes loathing. The boys in the Mailer novel tremble on the verge of becoming lovers in their Arctic camp, but they draw back from each other, terrified, and are then given tremendous energies as "killer brothers" now united to go fight the war in Vietnam. Both novels demonstrate not any extraordinary fear of homosexuality but, what is more disturbing, a fear of affection. Dickey has so created his backwoods degenerates as to be beyond all human sympathy, so that most readers are compelled to become "killers" along with the narrator. The murder of the homosexual threat, whether an exterior force or an inner impulse, results in an apparent increase in animal spirits and appetite, and the narrator is able to return to civilization and to his wife, a man with a profound secret, in touch with an illicit, demonic mystery, delivered. Violence has been his salvation—his deliverance from ordinary life.

The Eye-Beaters, Blood, Victory, Madness, Buckhead and Mercy is as crammed and various as its title suggests. A few poems are bluntly confessional, the **"Apollo"** poem is linked to a historic event, and all are in the same tone of musing, sometimes cynical, sometimes tender contemplation. The volume ends with **"Turning Away: Variations on Estrangement,"** a complex, abstract work of philosophical inquiry; but most of its poems are linked firmly to domestic things, and even the difficult subjects of disease and death are made "livable," in Dickey's words.

The book is disturbing because it asks so many questions but refuses to answer them. It is filled with questions: *What did I say? Or do? Am I still drunk? Who is this woman? Where? Can you see me? Can the five fingers / Of the hand still show against / anything? Have they come for us?* It is also disturbing because of its attitude toward certain subjects: men suffering from diabetes and cancer are not treated solemnly, and in Dickey's fantasy of dying from a heart attack (or love) he and the nurse/prostitute flicker downward together "Like television like Arthur Godfrey's face / Coming on huge happy." The book's seventeen poems are of widely varying length and seem to make up a dialogue or combat among their various themes, as if the poet were entering into a battle with aspects of his soul—the word "battle" used deliberately here, because Dickey declares in **"Turning Away"** how it is necessary to turn "From an old peaceful love / To a helmet of silent war / Against the universe."

Many of the poems are about diseased emotions or diseased forms of hope, such as the futility of seeking out one's youth by "going home" decades later; but several deal with specific disorders—**"Diabetes," "The Cancer Match," "Madness,"** and **"The Eye-Beaters"** (which is about both blindness and insanity). **"Diabetes"** is a brutally frank, sardonic confessional poem in two parts which begins with the poet's gigantic thirst: "One night I thirsted like a prince / Then like a king / Then like an empire like a world / On fire." But the thirst is not a thirst for life, it is not a metaphor; it is clinically real. After the illness is diagnosed, the poet sees sugar as "gangrene in white," and his routine of exercise is attended by an ironic counting, a parody of his earlier poetic themes:

> Each time the barbell
> Rose each time a foot fell
> Jogging, it counted itself
> One death two death three death and resurrection
> For a little while. Not bad! . . .

He will endure a "livable death," scaled down and presided over by a nice young physician. The second half of the poem, "Under Buzzards," has Dickey imagining in heavy summer the "birds of death" attracted by the "rotten, nervous sweetness" of his blood, the "city sugar" of his life. In a final, defiant gesture, the poet deliberately summons the birds of death, but he does it in a curiously unheroic way, by taking a forbidden drink of beer:

> Red sugar of my eyeballs
> Feels them [the buzzards] turn blindly
> In the fire rising turning turning
> Back to Hogback Ridge, and it is all
> Delicious, brother: my body is turning is flashing
> unbalanced
> Sweetness everywhere, and I am calling my birds.

Characteristic of this volume is a repeated use of terms to link the reader with the poet: "my friend," "brother," "companion," "my son," "you." The whole of **"Venom"** is a kind of prayer, the poet and his listener joined as brothers who must "turn the poison / Round," back on itself, the venom that comes "from the head" of man and corrupts his life blood. **"Madness"** is about a domestic dog that contracts rabies and must be killed, but it is also a call for "Help help madness help."

Balancing the poems of disease are several about Dickey's sons and the *Life*-commissioned double poem, **"Apollo,"** placed near the physical center of the magazine and divided by a black page—a symbol of the black featureless depths of space in which our planet, "the blue planet steeped in its dream," has a minute existence. The poems to or about Dickey's sons are all excellent, though there is an air of sorrow about them. **"The Lord in the Air"** is prefaced by a quotation from Blake: ". . . If the spectator could . . . make a friend & companion of one of these Images of wonder . . . then would he meet the Lord in the air & . . . be happy." Dickey seems to be reimagining an earlier role of his own as he describes a son's performance with a crow whistle, so deceiving the crows that they come to him from miles away, "meeting the Lord / Of their stolen voice in the air." The crows have but one word, a syllable that means everything to them, and in gaining control of it the boy becomes a kind of poet. A "new / Power over birds and beasts" has been achieved by man, but "not for betrayal, or to call / Up death or desire, but only to give" a unique tone "never struck in the egg." *O Chris come in, drop off now* is the language Dickey allots to himself; magic has become the property of his boy.

"Messages" deals with images of life (butterflies with "ragged, brave wings")—and death (a cow's skeleton), and matches the father's protectiveness with his wisdom, which his sleeping son cannot yet be told: that life is a gamble, a play "in bones and in wings and in light." The poem is also about the necessity of a father's surrendering his son to life—"to the sea"—with the reminder that human love exists in its own world, unchallenged by the nihilistic depths of the ocean or the speechless primitive world. The love evident in the "message" poems is totally lacking in the disease poems, as if the speakers were angrily fighting self-pity; **"The Cancer Match"** imagines cancer and whiskey fighting together, in the drunken mind of a dying man who has "cancer and whiskey / In a lovely relation": "I watch them struggle / All around the room, inside and out / Of the house, as they battle / Near the mailbox. . . ." No dignity here, even in dying; the poem refuses to mourn the body's decay.

Addressing himself to the Apollo moon shot, Dickey synthesizes the diverse emotions of awe, suspicion, cynicism, and acquiescence; like Mailer in *Of a Fire on the Moon,* he cannot help but wonder if some catastrophe will be unleashed ("Will the moonplague kill our children . . . ?"), and just as Mailer contemplated photographs of the moon's surface and thought of Cézanne, Dickey, in the imagined consciousness of one of the moon explorers, hears lines from Gray's Elegy "helplessly coming / From my heart. . . ." A triumph of technology is seen in terms of aesthetic triumphs of the past. Both men express doubt

about the future, but both accept its inevitable direction, though Dickey is characteristically more emotionally involved:

> My eyes blind
> With unreachable tears   my breath goes all over
>   Me and cannot escape. . . .
> Our clothes embrace we cannot touch we cannot
>   Kneel. We stare into the moon
> dust, the earth-blazing ground. We laugh, with the
> beautiful craze
>   Of static. We bend, we pick up stones.

The future is explorable, however, only through one's imaginative identification with other men. The most powerful poems in *The Eye-Beaters* are those that refuse to deal with the future at all and explore old obsessions with the past. The pathetic double poem **"Going Home"** takes the poet ("the Keeper") back to his own lost childhood, where he encounters his Old Self like a "younger brother, like a son," in a confusion of homes, times, places, rooms that live "only / In my head." His childhood is distant from the adulthood he now inhabits, in which he is a Keeper of rooms "growing intolerable," through which he walks like a stranger, "as though I belonged there." The riddle of *Identities! Identities!* the younger Dickey puzzled over (in the poem **"Mangham"** of *Buckdancer's Choice*) still taunts him, as past and present contend, and the Keeper fears he will go mad with his questions:

> And tell me for the Lord God
> 's sake, where are all our old
> Dogs?
>   Home?
>   Which way is that?
> Is it this vacant lot? . . .

In a final admission of defeat, the "mad, weeping Keeper" realizes that he cannot keep anything alive: none of his rooms, his people, his past, his youth, himself. Yet he cannot let them die either, and he will call them "for a little while, sons." In **"Looking for the Buckhead Boys,"** a poem on the verge of turning into a short story, the futile search for one's youth in the past is given a specific location, and the poet returns to his home town to look for his old friends; if he can find one of them, just one, he believes his youth will once again "walk / Inside me like a king." But his friends are gone, or changed, or paralyzed or, like Charlie Gates at the filling station, not really the person for whom the poet has a secret "that has to be put in code." The poem ends with a flat anticlimatic imperative: "Fill 'er up, Charlie." Encountering one's past, in the form of an old friend, underscores the impossibility of "keeping" the past.

"The Eye-Beaters" is an extravagant, curious fantasy, supposedly set in a home for children in Indiana. In this home some children have gone blind, evidently since admission; not just blind, but mad, so that their arms must be tied at their sides to prevent their beating their eyeballs in order to stimulate the optic nerves. By no naturalistic set of facts can one determine how this "home" can be real, and so the reader concludes that the entire poem is an explorative fantasy, like **"The Owl King,"** which dealt with a child's blindness. The blindness of the children and their pathetic response to it is so distressing that the Visitor must create a fiction in order to save himself from madness. He tries to imagine what they see:

> Lord, when they slug
> Their blue cheeks blacker, can it be that they do not
>   see the wings
> And green of insects   or the therapist suffering kind-
>   ly   but
>   a tribal light old
> Enough to be seen without sight?

The vision he imagines for them is prehistoric; a caveman artist, "Bestial, working like God," is drawing beasts on a cave wall: deer, antelope, elk, ibex, quagga, rhinoceros of wool-gathering smoke, cave bear, mammoth, "beings that appear / Only in the memory of caves." The niches of the children's middle brain, "where the race is young," are filled not with images of the Virgin but with squat shapes of the Mother or with the bloody hand print on the stone "where God gropes like a man" and where the artist "hunts and slashes" his wounded game. Then the Visitor's rational, skeptical nature argues with him, addressing him as "Stranger"; perhaps the children want to smash their eyes in order to see nothing, and the Visitor's invention of the cave-man artist is an expression of his own blindness, his hope for magic that might "re-invent the vision of the race." He admits his desire to believe that the world calls out for art, for the magical life-renewal of art, and not for the blankness of nothing save physical pain. Otherwise it is possible that he will go mad. Otherwise what can he value in his own poetry? The artist must be a therapist to the race, and not simply to himself; but Dickey concludes this complex poem by acquiescing to his own self-defined "fiction," a kind of lie that enables him to identify himself with the cave-man artist and to escape the deadening truths of his Reason by choosing "madness, / Perversity." He projects himself back into a dim racial memory, a hideous vision that excludes history. No salvation, except by way of a total surrender to the irrational and uninventive:

> Beast, get in
> My way. Your body opens onto the plain. Deer, take
>   me into your life-
> lined form. I merge, I pass beyond in secret   in
>   perversity and the sheer
> Despair of invention   my double-clear bifocals off
>   my reason gone
> Like eyes. Therapist, farewell at the living end. Give
>   me my spear.

The prayer, addressed to a "Beast," necessarily involves the poet in a transformation downward, into a kind of human beast whose "despair of invention" forces him to inarticulate, violent action. It is possible that the conclusion is an ambiguous one—the artist denying his art through a self-conscious work of art—or, as Raymond Smith has seen it, in an essay called "The Poetic Faith of James Dickey,"[8] the poet rejecting any art-for-art's-sake

aesthetic. However, the final words of the poem seem the expression of a suicidal loss of faith in anything but action, and that action primitive and bloody.

Dickey had diagnosed this action as **"Perversity,"** and the poem has a passionate, religious feel about it, the testament of a loss of faith in one religion (Art) and the tentative commitment to another (the "Beast"). This is the mystical leap that Dickey's imagination has yearned for, the defiance of his higher, artistic, moral self, experienced in middle age as a banality from which he must—somehow—be delivered.

The forms of Dickey's "heroism" are anachronistic, perhaps, but his despair may be prophetic.

In these later poems, the poems of "flesh," there is a dramatic ferocity that goes beyond even the shimmering walls of words he created for **"Falling"** and **"May Day Sermon."** Dickey is there, inside the poem; reading it, we are inside his head. He is willing to tell everything, anything; he is willing to become transparent, in war now against his own exquisite sensibility. *Help help madness help*: the book's shameless cry.

Society did not always shy away from the self-expression of its most sensitive and eccentric members. Much has been written about the relationship of so-called primitive people with their priests and shamans: these societies benefited from their leaders' ecstasies and bizarre revelations and did not destroy them as heretics or castrate them by interpreting their visions as "only poetry." What value can the visionary give to his own experience if, returning to the world with it, he is at the very most congratulated for having invented some fascinating, original metaphors? Dickey, so disturbing to many of us, must be seen in a larger context, as a kind of "shaman," a man necessarily at war with his civilization because that civilization will not, cannot, understand what he is saying. Mircea Eliade defines the shaman as a "specialist in ecstasy": traditionally, he excites himself into a frenzy, enters a trancelike state, and receives the power of understanding and imitating the language of birds and animals. He is not a "normal" personality, at least in these times. He participates in what is believed to be divine.

If the shaman, or the man with similar magical powers, has no social structure in which to interpret himself, and if he is obviously not normal in the restrictive sense of that word, his instincts will lead him into a rebellion against that world; at his most serene, he can manage a cynical compromise with it. Irony can be a genteel form of savagery, no less savage than physical brutality. In some intellectuals, irony is the expression of disappointed hopes; in others, it is a substitute for violence. It *is* violent. If the release offered by words no longer satisfies the intense need of the sufferer, he will certainly fall into despair, estrangement. Hence a preoccupation, in Dickey, with physical risk, a courting of the primitive in art and in life (in carefully restricted areas, of course), and a frantic, even masochistic need to continually test and "prove" himself.[9] The ritual of hunting cannot ultimately work, because it is so obviously a "ritual"—a game—and bears no relationship at all to what hunting was, and is, to people who must hunt for their food. It is just another organized adventure, another "timid poem." Consciousness is split on a number of levels: the sensual keenness inspired by adultery and guilt, the excitement inspired by near death, the mindless rage of the beast who fears extinction, the plight of the overweight suburban homeowner, the husband, the father, the poet . . . and yet the truest self seems somehow detached, uninvolved. **"Turning Away,"** the last poem in *The Eye-Beaters,* deals with aspects of estrangement not simply in terms of marriage but in terms of the self, which hopes to see "Later, much later on" how it may make sense—perhaps as a fictional creation, in a book.

If regression cannot be justified by calling it "ritual"— hunting, fighting, excessively brutal sports—it must be abandoned. If the poet can no longer evoke the "primitive," since his body cannot keep pace with the demands of his imagination, the primitive ideal must be abandoned. Physical prowess—extraordinary keenness of eyesight—can be undermined by that baffling human problem, mortality and disease. Death awaits. Yet one is not always prepared for it. If it is seen as an embarrassment, another obscure defeat, it will never be accepted at all; better to pray for the Apocalypse, so that everyone can die at once, with no one left to think about it afterward. The stasis celebrated in much of contemporary literature, the erecting of gigantic paranoid-delusion systems that are self-enclosed and self-destructing, argues for a simple failure of reasoning: the human ego has too long imagined itself the supreme form of consciousness in the universe. When that delusion is taken from it, it suffers. Suffering, it projects its emotions outward onto everything, everyone, into the universe itself. Our imaginative literature has largely refused to integrate ever-increasing subtleties of intuitive experience with those of intellectual experience; it will not acknowledge the fact that the dynamism of our species has become largely a dynamism of the brain, not the body. Old loves die slowly. But they die.

The concluding poem in *The Eye-Beaters* differs from the rest in many ways. It is primarily a meditation. It is almost entirely speculative, an abstract seventeen-stanza work dealing with the mystery of the soul. The familiar theme of battle and certain specific images involved (helmets, meadows of "intensified grass") are used in a way new to Dickey; its tone of hard, impassive detachment contrasts with the despairing ferocity of **"The Eye-Beaters"** and the poems of disease.

The immediate occasion for the poem is evidently dissatisfaction with an "old peaceful love." Another person, nearby, is "suddenly / Also free . . . weeping her body away." But the confessional quality of the poem is not very important; the poet's detachment approaches that of Eliot's in "Four Quarters." Dickey could very well be

writing about himself—his relationship with his "soul" (which in mystical literature is usually identified with the feminine, though that interpretation is probably not necessary). The poet's problem is how, as a "normal" man, to relate his predicament with the human condition generally. As in **"Reincarnation (II),"** the poet discovers himself released from one life and projected into another where he feels himself "Like a king starting out on a journey / Away from all things that he knows." Outside the "simple-minded window" is a world of ordinary sights from which one may take his face; yet this world is one of danger and "iron-masked silence." In utter stillness the poet stands with his palm on the window sill (as he once stood with his palm on the fence wire) and feels the "secret passivity" and "unquestionable Silence" of existence: man wears the reason for his own existence as he stands and, in such a confrontation, the "tongue grows solid also."

Imagined then as a kind of Caesar (Dickey would like to "see with / the eyes of a very great general," here as elsewhere), he realizes he has nothing to do in his own life with his military yearnings and his hope for himself to be utterly free of any finite time or place, an omni-potent life force released from identity to "breed / With the farthest women / And the farthest also in time: breed / Through bees, like flowers and bushes: / Breed Greeks, Egyptians and Romans hoplites / Peasants caged kings clairvoyant bastards. . . ." His desire is so vast as to exclude the personal entirely; he must turn away, at least in imagination, from the domesticity of his life, so that his soul can achieve the release it demands. It is nothing less than the wide universe that is the object of its desire; like the wolverine, the poet's soul hungers to "eat the world." This desire is in itself a kind of miracle or reincarnation:

> Turning away, seeing fearful
> Ordinary ground, boys' eyes manlike go,
> The middle-aged man's like a desperate
> Boy's, the old man's like a new angel's. . . .

Dreaming, the poet sees horses, a "cloud / That is their oversoul," and armed men who may spring from his teeth. He must speak of battles that do not stain the meadow with blood but release "inner lives"—as if through a pure concentration of will, of artistic creation, the poet realizes:

> So many things stand wide
> Open!   Distance is helplessly deep
> On all sides   and you can enter, alone,
>   Anything   anything can go
> On wherever it wishes   anywhere in the world or in
>   time
>   But here and now.

What must be resisted is the "alien sobbing" nearby; the poet's attachment to a finite self, a domestic existence, must be overcome, as if he were a guard on his duty to prevent the desertion of the higher yearnings of his soul. The most abstract charge of all is his sense that he might be, even, a hero in a book—his life might be "a thing / That can be learned, / As those earnest young heroes learned theirs, / Later, much later on."

"Turning Away" is a tentative reply to the despairing vision of **"The Eye-Beaters,"** and it concludes a collection of widely varying poems with a statement about the need to transcend the physical life by an identification with the timeless, "physical life" having been examined frankly and unsparingly and found to be generally diseased. The poem's immediate occasion is marital discord, but Dickey's imagery of battle is a very generalized one—"So many battles / Fought in cow pastures fought back / And forth over anybody's farm / With men or only / With wounded eyes—" Dickey's most inclusive metaphor for life is life-as-battle; for man, man-as-combatant.

The emphasis Dickey places in his later poems upon decay, disease, regression, and estrangement suggests that they may constitute a terminal group of poems: terminal in the sense that the poet may be about to take on newer challenges. Having developed from the mysticism of Stone into and through the mysticism of Flesh, having explored variations on unity and variations on dissolution, he seems suspended—between the formal abstractions of **"Turning Away"** and the jagged primitive-heroic music of **"The Eye-Beaters,"** perhaps still seeking what Blake calls the "Image of wonder" that allows man to "meet the Lord in the Air & . . . be happy."

In any case, Dickey's work is significant in its expression of the savagery that always threatens to become an ideal, when faith in human values is difficult to come by—or when a culture cannot accommodate man's most basic instincts, forcing them backward, downward, away from the conscious imagination and back into the body as if into the body of an ancient ancestor: into the past, that is, forbidding intelligent entry into the future.

Notes

1. *The Suspect in Poetry* (Madison, Minnesota: The Sixties Press, 1964), p. 47.

2. Lewis Thomas, M.D., "Information," in the *New England Journal of Medicine,* December 14, 1972, pp. 1238-39.

3. Dickey either literally or figuratively puts on masks in any number of poems—notably "Armor," "Drinking from a Helmet," and "Approaching Prayer" (in which he puts on a "hollow hog's head").

4. Dickey's perfect vision singled him out for training in night fighters in the Army Air Corps. Throughout his poetry there is a concern, not just imagistic or metaphorical, with vision—eyesight—that makes doubly poignant his conclusion in "False Youth: Two Seasons" (from *Falling*) that his youth was "a lifetime search / For the Blind." Also, the conclusion of "The Eye-Beaters" shows us the poet "in perversity and the sheer / Despair of invention" taking his "Double-clear bifocals off"—then succumbing to a fantasy of regressive madness.

5. *The Suspect in Poetry,* p. 77. The word "helplessness" is repeated several times in connection with Jarrell, and in an essay on Howard Nemerov (a review of Nemerov's *Selected Poems,* 1960), Dickey praises Nemerov for what seem to me the wrong reasons: ". . . the enveloping emotion that arises from his writing is helplessness: the helplessness we all feel in the face of the events of our time, and of life itself: the helplessness one feels as one's legitimate but chronically unfair portion of all the things that can't be assuaged or explained" (p. 67). Throughout *Self-Interviews,* which seems the work of a different James Dickey, one who cannot do justice to the excellence of the essential Dickey, there is a reliance upon an inner, moral helplessness, as if certain emotional prejudices were *there,* in human nature, and one might as well acquiesce to them; though elsewhere does Dickey take on as rigorously combative a tone as Nietzsche in feeling that the true artist would not tolerate the world as it is even for one instant.

6. From Dickey's account of his growth as a poet, in *Poets on Poetry,* edited by Howard Nemerov (New York, 1966), pp. 225-38. It is ironic that Dickey should so distrust and mock his own reflective, intellectual nature, since he knows himself a poet of the "Second Birth"—one who has worked hard at his craft. Yet his finest poems give the impression of having been written very quickly; one feels the strange compulsion to read them quickly, as if to keep pace with the language. Dickey's poems are structures that barely contain the energies they deal with. That "agent" in the poem known as the "I" is unpredictable, at times frightening, for he may lead us anywhere. Dickey might have written extraordinary short stories had he not chosen to develop himself as a poet almost exclusively. In an excellent essay, "The Self as Agent," from *Sorties,* Dickey says that the chief glory and excitement of writing poetry is the chance it gives the poet to "confront and dramatize parts of himself that otherwise would not have surfaced. The poem is a window opening not on truth but on possibility . . ." (p. 161).

7. Dickey's reviews of *Howl* and *Kaddish* are both negative. He says that Ginsberg's principal state of mind is "hallucination" and that the poetry is really "strewn, mishmash prose." Yet Dickey allows that, somewhere, in the Babel of undisciplined contemporary poets, "there might one day appear a writer to supply the in-touch-with-living authenticity which current American poetry so badly needs, grown as it has genteel and almost suffocatingly proper." From *The Suspect in Poetry,* pp. 16-19. When a poet-critic speaks in these terms, one may always assume he is talking about himself, whether he knows it or not.

8. Raymond Smith, "The Poetic Faith of James Dickey," *Modern Poetry Studies,* Vol. 2, No. 6, pp. 259-72. Masculine response to Dickey's poetry probably differs inevitably from a woman's response.

9. Dickey has granted a number of interviews, all of them characterized by an extraordinary frankness. In a recent one, the poet William Heyen asks him to

discuss the violent "morality" of *Deliverance,* and Dickey states that there is a kind of "absolutism" about country people in his part of the world: "Life and death . . . are very basic gut-type things, and if somebody does something that violates your code, you *kill* him, and you don't think twice about it. . . . the foremost fear of our time, especially with the growing crime rate, crime in the cities and so on, . . . the thing that we're most terrified of is being set upon by malicious strangers. . . ." He therefore agrees with the decisions his characters make in the novel, and it is clear from his discussion of Ed Gentry's decision to kill and Gentry's growing realization that he is a "born killer" (Dickey's words) that the novel, like much of the poetry, is an attempt to deal with an essentially mystical experience. That it is also brutal and dehumanizing is not Dickey's concern. Murder is "a quietly transfiguring influence" on the novel's hero. "A Conversation with James Dickey," ed. by William Heyen, *The Southern Review* (Winter, 1973) IX, 1, pp. 135-56.

Harold Bloom (essay date 1985)

SOURCE: Bloom, Harold. "James Dickey: From 'The Other' through the *The Early Motion.*" *Southern Review* 21, no. 1 (winter 1985): 63-78.

[*In the following essay, Bloom assesses Dickey's pre-1965 poetry, commenting on such pieces as "The Other," "Drowning With Others," "In the Mountain Tent," "Approaching Prayer," and "Drinking from a Helmet."*]

I first read James Dickey's early poem, **"The Other,"** some twenty years ago. Having admired his recently published book, ***Drowning With Others,*** I went back to his first book, ***Into the Stone,*** at the recommendation of a close friend, the poet Alvin Feinman. Though very moved by several of the earlier poems, I was affected most strongly by the one called **"The Other."** It has taken me twenty years to understand why the poem still will not let me go, and so I begin with it here. I don't think of Dickey as a poet primarily of otherness, but rather as a heroic celebrator of what Emerson called "the great and crescive self," indeed of the American self proper, which demands victory and disdains even great defeats. Dickey, as I read him, is like what Vico called the Magic Formalists or Blake named the Giant Forms. He is a throwback to those mythic hypotheses out of which strong poetry first broke forth, the bards of divination whose heroic vitalism demanded a literal immortality for themselves as poets. But even a Magic Formalist learns that he is at best a mortal god.

The pain of that learning is the central story of Dickey's poetry, and I choose to evade that pain here in order to emphasize Dickey's countersong of otherness. Since I will take him scarcely into his middle years, I will be ignoring all of his most ambitious poetry, "the later motion," as he has called it. Though his work from 1965 to the present clearly is more problematic than the poems I will discuss, its achievement quite possibly is of a higher order. But it is too soon to prophesy Dickey's final stature, and criticism must discourse on what it loves before it broods upon the limits of the canonical. What I know and love best, so far, in Dickey's poetry is "the early motion," and the counter-song of otherness in that motion moves me most. I have circled back to that poem, **"The Other,"** and turn to it now to locate an origin of Dickey's quest as a poet.

That origin is guilt, and guilt ostensibly of being a substitute or replacement for a brother dead before one was born. Freud, I think, would have judged such guilt to be a screen memory, and I am Freudian enough to look or surmise elsewhere for the source of guilt in the poems of ***Into the Stone.*** From the beginning of his poetic career, Dickey was a poet of Sublime longings, and those who court the Sublime are particularly subject to changeling fantasies. The poem he titled **"The Other"** is manifestly Yeatsian, whether directly or through the mediation of Roethke, but the argument already is Dickey's own, and in all respects it is the meter-making argument, and not the derived diction and metric, that gives this poem its great distinction. Indeed Dickey, an instinctive Emersonian from the start, despite his southern heritage, literalizes Emerson's trope of a meter-making argument by the extraordinary device of packing the seventy-seven lines of this lyrical reverie into what has always felt to me like a single sentence. How could there be a second sentence in a poem that identifies itself so completely with the changeling's will to be the other, when the other ultimately is the god Apollo?

Somewhere, Dickey identified his triad of literary heroes as the unlikely combination of Keats, Malcolm Lowry, and James Agee, presumably associated because of their early or relatively early deaths, and because of their shared intensity of belief in what could be called the salvation history of the literary art. But Dickey is very much a poet of Sensibility, in the mode that Frye once defined as *the Age of Sensibility,* the mode of Christopher Smart and of William Collins, among other doomed poets whose threshold stance destroyed them upon the verge of High Romanticism. The Keats who moves Dickey most, the Keats of the letters, is the culmination of the major theme of the poets of Sensibility, the theme that, following Collins, I have called the Incarnation of the Poetical Character. Lowry and Agee, though I don't recall Dickey mentioning this, were curiously allied as verse writers by the overwhelming influence that Hart Crane exerted upon both of them. Dickey seems to prefer Crane's letters to his poems, which oddly parallels his preference of Keats's letters. But Keats and Crane, like Lowry and Agee in their verse, represent fully in their poems the Incarnation of the Poetical Character, where the poet, in the guise of a young man, is reborn as the young god of the sun. That is clearly the genre of Dickey's **"The Other,"** but the clarity is shadowed by Dickey's early guilt concerning what the poem accurately names as "my lust of self."

What self can that be except the magic and occult self, ontological rather than empirical, and in Yeatsian or Whitmanian terms, self rather than soul? The guilt that shadows Dickey's marvelous seventy-seven-line utterance is the guilt induced by what Freud came to call the above-I or the over-I (the superego), a rather more daunting though no less fictive entity than Emerson's Oversoul. Emerson had the shrewdest of eyes for anxiety, but Freud's eye, as Wallace Stevens once wrote, was the microscope of potency. The guilt of family betrayal must ensue from the changeling fantasy of the family romance, and for Freud (as for Kenneth Burke), all romance is family romance. But the family romance of the poet *as* poet tends to depart from the domain of the merely biographical family. Dickey's assertion of self as person was the desire to rise from the "strength-haunted body" of a "rack-ribbed child" to the Herculean figure he has been since, a titanic form among contemporary poets. But since poems can attempt the truth only through fictions or tropes, the poem of **"The Other"** is compelled to treat the child's aspiration as the drive towards becoming Apollo, poetry itself. The youthful Henry James, reviewing *Drum-Taps,* scorned Whitman as an essentially prosaic temperament trying to lift itself by muscular exertion into poetry. The elderly Henry James, weeping over the great *Lilacs* elegy, scorned his own youthful review; but, properly modified, it can give us a critical trope for reading Dickey: an essentially poetic temperament lifting itself by muscular exertion into poetry.

Dickey's most curious characteristic, from **"The Other"** through ***Puella,*** is his involuntary but striking dualism, curious because so heroic a vitalist ought not to exemplify (as he does) so Pauline and Cartesian a mind-body split, or even so prevalent a sense of what Stevens termed the dumb-foundering abyss between ourselves and the object. What the poem surprisingly shows for and to Dickey is that his own body becomes his brother, or Apollo, or "the other." If the body is the divine other, then pathos becomes both sublime and grotesque, because the body must change, and the final form of that change is death. **"The Other"** is almost the first of Dickey's poems, and in some ways he has never surpassed it, not because he has failed to develop, but because it is unsurpassable. The whole of Dickey is in it already, as the whole of Shelley is in *Alastor,* or the whole of Yeats is in *The Wanderings of Oisin.* I repeat that this does not mean that Dickey simply has unfolded; so restless and reckless an experimentalist is outrageously metamorphic. But all his changes quest hopelessly for a disjunctiveness his temperament refuses to allow him. The "holes" that space out the poems of his major phase never represent discursive gaps or even crossings from one kind of figuration to another. Instead, they impressively mark or punctuate the exquisite desperation of the will to live, the lust of self that is not to be railed at, because it does represent what Keats called "a sickness not ignoble": the sickness unto death of heroic poetry.

"The Other," like so much of Dickey's best work, is very clearly a Southern American poem, and yet its Incarnation of the Poetical Character is necessarily universal in its imagery and argument. This is the universal purchased at the high cost of what was to be a permanent guilt, the guilt of a poet who as poet greatly desired *not* to be egocentric, despite the demands of the mythology that found him from the start. Those demands are felt even in the opening movement of **"The Other"**:

> Holding onto myself by the hand,
> I change places into the spirit
> I had as a rack-ribbed child,
> And walk slowly out through my mind
> To the wood, as into a falling fire
> Where I turned from that strength-haunted body
> Half-way to bronze, as I wished to.

Dickey's natural religion always has been Mithraism, the traditional faith of soldiers, and certainly the most masculine and fierce of all Western beliefs. Despite the Persian origins of Mithra, Rome assimilated him to Apollo, and Dickey's major alteration is to make the Incarnation of the Poetical Character into a Mithraic ritual. The "bronze" of this first stanza will be revealed, later in the poem, as both the statue of Apollo and the body of the sacrificial bull slain by Mithra. As the boy Dickey slings up the too-heavy ax-head, he prays:

> To another, unlike me, beside me:
> To a brother or king-sized shadow
> Who looked at me, burned, and believed me:
> Who believed I would rise like Apollo
>
> With armor-cast shoulders upon me:
> Whose voice, whistling back through my teeth,
> Counted strokes with the hiss of a serpent.
> Where the sun through the bright wood drove
> Him, mute, and floating strangely, to the ground,
> He led me into his house, and sat
> Upright, with a face I could never imagine,
>
> With a great harp leant on his shoulder,
> And began in deep handfuls to play it.

"Burned" is the crucial trope here, since the brother, as god of the sun, leads only into the heat and light that is the house of the sun. The oracular hiss is Pythian, though the voice truly becomes Dickey's own. What Dickey, *in the poem,* develops most brilliantly is the figure of downward movement, which is introduced in the second stanza as the combined fall of sweat and leaves, and further invoked in the fall of light. Later in the poem, music falls, followed in the final line by the casting down of foliage. All these fallings substitute for the hidden ritual in which the bull's blood falls upon the Mithraic adept, the warrior in the act of becoming Apollo:

> My brother rose beside me from the earth,
>
> With the wing-bone of music on his back
> Trembling strongly with heartfelt gold,
> And ascended like a bird into the tree,

And music fell in a comb, as I stood
In a bull's heavy, bronze-bodied shape
As it mixed with a god's, on the ground,
And leaned on the helve of the ax.

The "great, dead tree" of the poem's second stanza might be called Dickey's first major fiction of duration, the origin of his quarrel with time. Being Dickey's, it is the liveliest of dead trees, yet it cannot propitiate this poet's poignant longing for a literal immortality:

Now, owing my arms to the dead
Tree, and the leaf-loosing, mortal wood,
Still hearing that music amaze me,
I walk through the time-stricken forest,
And wish another body for my life,
Knowing that none is given
By the giant, unusable tree

And the leaf-shapen lightning of sun,
And rail at my lust of self
With an effort like chopping through root-stocks:
Yet the light, looming brother but more
Brightly above me is blazing,
In that music come down from the branches
In utter, unseasonable glory,

Telling nothing but how I made
By hand, a creature to keep me dying
Years longer, and coming to sing in the wood
Of what love still might give,
Could I turn wholly mortal in my mind,
My body-building angel give me rest,
This tree cast down its foliage with the years.

"This tree" is at last Dickey himself as fiction of duration, the poet become his own poem, indeed "made / By hand," and so a house made by hands, a mortal body. When desire can turn monistic, for Dickey, it can become only a mortal turn, a trope knowing it is only trope. The other is divine, but only as Apollo or Mithra was divine, rather than as Jesus or Jehovah. A poem "about" a body-building child has transformed itself into the Sublime, into the body-building angel who has never since given Dickey any rest.

Retrospectively, I suppose that the poem **"The Other"** first moved me because so few American poems of twenty years ago had anything like Dickey's remarkable ability to be so humanly direct and yet so trustingly given to the potential of figurative language. The Dickey of the early motion seemed to have found his way back, almost effortlessly, to the secrets of poetry. I remember that the first poem by Dickey that I read was the title poem of *Drowning With Others,* a title that is itself an unforgettable trope, worthy of Emily Dickinson's apprehension that an acute consciousness, even when aware of neighbors and the sun, of other selves and outward nature, still died quite alone, except for its own identity, a totemic single hound. What is Sublime in the self finally is capable only of "drowning with others," but that is only part of what is central in what remains one of Dickey's most singular and enduring poems.

If I remember aright, Dickey himself doesn't much like this poem, and thinks it obscure rather than strong. Indeed, I recall his insistence that he wrote the poem only so as to give status to his book's title. His account of the poem's referential aspect was strangely literal, but I think this is one of his poems that sneaked by him, as it were:

There are moments a man turns from us
Whom we have all known until now.
Upgathered, we watch him grow,
Unshipping his shoulder bones

Like human, everyday wings
That he has not ever used,
Releasing his hair from his brain,
A kingfisher's crest, confused

By the God-tilted light of Heaven.
His deep, window-watching smile
Comes closely upon us in waves,
And spreads, and now we are

At last within it, dancing.
Slowly we turn and shine
Upon what is holding us,
As under our feet he soars,

Struck dumb as the angel of Eden,
In wide, eye-opening rings.
Yet the hand on my shoulder fears
To feel my own wingblades spring,

To feel me sink slowly away
In my hair turned loose like a thought
Of a fisherbird dying in flight.
If I opened my arms, I could hear

Every shell in the sea find the word
It has tried to put into my mouth.
Broad flight would become of my dancing,
And I would obsess the whole sea,

But I keep rising and singing
With my last breath. Upon my back,
With his hand on my unborn wing,
A man rests easy as sunlight

Who has kept himself free of the forms
Of the deaf, down-soaring dead,
And me laid out and alive
For nothing at all, in his arms.

I read this as another lyric of poetic incarnation, a rather less willing assumption of the divine other, perhaps even a defense against the Orphic predicament, but still a revision of the poem **"The Other."** Indeed, I wonder if one way of characterizing Dickey's obsessive strength as a poet is to say that he cannot stop rewriting that essential early poem. For the man who turns from us in the opening line of **"Drowning With Others"** is the Orphic Dickey, poet and divine other. Like the richhaired youth of Collins, or Coleridge's youth with flashing eyes and floating hair, or Stevens' figure of the youth as virile poet in "Mrs. Alfred Uruguay," this other Dickey has hair released into "a kingfisher's crest, confused / By the God-tilted light of Heaven." Apollo is reborn again, but as Orphic drowning man, fit version of the poet of Sensibility in America, be he Hart Crane or Roethke or Agee or Dickey. But if the man turning from us in this poem is Dickey in the act of Sublime apotheosis, then whoever is that "I" rather desperately chanting this hieratic spell? Perhaps that is why Dickey as commentator judged this grand lyric too obscure, despite its palpable strength.

Our poet is weird in the true sense, one of the Fates (as Richard Howard, lexicographer among bards, might remind us), and his natural mode is the uncanny. What he has done here may be obscure to his spectral self, but his magic or occult self gathers his spectral self, until even that "I" keeps "rising and singing / With my last breath." And so truly neither self dies, or can die, in this soaring lyric of divination. Perhaps there is a touch, not indeliberate, of Dylan Thomas in the metric here, and even allusive overtones of Thomas at moments in the diction. That resemblance may even be a hidden cause of Dickey's distaste for his poem, but I remark upon it to note the difference between the poets, rather than their shared qualities. On mortality, the warrior Dickey cannot deceive himself, but a poet whose totem seems to be the albatross does not fear death by water. Few lines are as characteristic of Dickey as "And I would obsess the whole sea."

I take it that "drowning with others" is a trope for "winging with others," and that the dominant image here is flight, and not going under. Flight of course is Freud's true trope for repression, and an Orphic sensibility never ceases to forget, involuntarily but on purpose, that its vocation is mortal godhood, or not dying *as a poet*. Drowning with others, then, as a trope, must mean something like dying only as the immortal precursor dies or writing poems that men will not let die. Though its scale is small, this is Dickey's *Lycidas*, even as **The Zodiac** will be his cosmological elegy for the self. The child building up a Mithra-like body is still here in this poem, but he is here more reluctantly, caught up in the moments of discovering that a too-closely-shared immortality becomes mortality again, the stronger the sharing is known.

Dickey, being one of our authentic avatars of the American Sublime, exemplifies its two grand stigmata: not to feel free unless he is alone, and finally to know that what is oldest in him is no part of the Creation. After two poems wrestling with otherness, I need to restore his sense of solitude, his Emersonian self-reliance, and the great poem for this in his early motion is **"In the Mountain Tent,"** which appropriately concludes the book ***Drowning With Others***. I remember that Dickey contrasts this with the more famous **"The Heaven of Animals,"** a lovely poem, but not one with the power of this meditation:

> I am hearing the shape of the rain
> Take the shape of the tent and believe it,
> Laying down all around where I lie
> A profound, unspeakable law.
> I obey, and am free-falling slowly

> Through the thought-out leaves of the wood
> Into the minds of animals.
> I am there in the shining of water
> Like dark, like light, out of Heaven.

> I am there like the dead, or the beast
> Itself, which thinks of a poem—
> Green, plausible, living, and holy—
> And cannot speak, but hears,
> Called forth from the waiting of things,

> A vast, proper, reinforced crying
> With the sifted, harmonious pause,
> The sustained intake of all breath
> Before the first word of the Bible.

> At midnight water dawns
> Upon the held skulls of the foxes
> And weasels and touseled hares
> On the eastern side of the mountain.
> Their light is the image I make

> As I wait as if recently killed,
> Receptive, fragile, half-smiling,
> My brow watermarked with the mark
> On the wing of a moth

> And the tent taking shape on my body
> Like ill-fitting, Heavenly clothes.
> From holes in the ground comes my voice
> In the God-silenced tongue of the beasts.
> "I shall rise from the dead," I am saying.

Whether a Christian or not, this speaker appears to entertain a belief in the resurrection of the body. Even in this solitude of spirit, the uncanny in Dickey, his *daimon*, enters with the poem's implicit question: Whose body, mine or that of the other? Is it every man who shall rise in the body, or is it not a more Gnostic persuasion that is at work here? The Gnostic lives already in the resurrected body, which is the body of a Primal Man who preceded the Creation. What a Gnostic called the Pleroma, the Fullness, Dickey calls beautifully "the waiting of things." The dead, the animals, and Dickey as the poem's speaker, all hear together the Gnostic Call, a vast crying out of the waiting of things. Without knowing any esoteric Gnosticism, Dickey by poetic intuition arrives at the trope of the Kabbalistic holding in of the divine breath that precedes the rupture of Creation. What Dickey celebrates therefore is "The sustained intake of all breath / Before the first word of the Bible." That word in Hebrew is *Beresit,* and so the vision of this poem is set before the Beginning. At midnight, not at dawn, and so only in the light of a rain image reflected from the beasts, Dickey speaks forth for the beasts, who have been silenced by the Demiurge called God by Genesis. In Dickey's own interpretation, the man experiences both a kinship with the beasts and a fundamental difference, since he alone will rise from the dead. But I think the poet is stronger than the poet-as-interpreter here. To rise from the dead, in this poem's context, is merely to be one's own magical or pneumatic self, a self that precedes the first word of the Bible.

It isn't very startling to see and say that Dickey, as poet, is not a Christian poet, but rather an Emersonian, an American Orphic and Gnostic. This is only to repeat Richard Howard's fine wordplay upon what could be called the Native Strain in our literature. What startles me, a little, is to see and say just how doctrinal, even programmatic, Dickey's early Orphism now seems. The Orphism has persisted, emerging with tumultuous force in the superbly mad female preacher of Dickey's **"May Day Sermon,"** which I recommend we all read directly after each time we read Jonathan Edwards' rather contrary sermon, "Sinners in the Hands of an Angry God." Rhetorically, though, that is a very different Dickey than the poet of *The Early Motion,* whose Orphism perhaps is the more persuasive for being almost overheard, rather than so emphatically heard.

I turn my charting of the early motion to Dickey's next book, *Helmets,* which so far may be his most distinguished single volume, a judgment in which I would neither want nor expect him to concur. "Helmet," as a word, ultimately goes back to an Indo-European root that means both "to cover and conceal," but also "to save," which explains why "helm" and "helmet" are related to those two antithetical primal names, Hell and Valhalla. Dickey's book, of course, knows all this, Dickey being a preternaturally implicit knower, both as a poet and as a warrior—or, combining both modes, as an archer and hunter. Had I time and space, I would want to comment on every poem in *Helmets,* but I will confine myself to its two most ambitious meditations, **"Approaching Prayer"** and the final **"Drinking from a Helmet."** Certain thematic and agonistic strains that I have glanced at already can be said not to culminate but to achieve definitive expression in these major poems. I qualify my statement because what is most problematic about Dickey's poetry is that nothing ever is allowed to culminate, not even in *The Zodiac,* or **"Falling,"** or **"May Day Sermon."** So obsessive a poet generally would not remain also so tentative, but Dickey's is a cunning imagination, metamorphic enough to evade its exegetes.

As a critic himself obsessed with the issue of belatedness, I am particularly impressed by the originality of **"Approaching Prayer,"** which Dickey rightly called "the most complicated and far-fetched poem I've written." I should add that Dickey said that some fifteen years ago, but it is good enough for me that his observation was true up to then. The far-fetcher was the good, rough English term that the Elizabethan rhetorician Puttenham used to translate the ancient trope called metalepsis or transumption, and **"Approaching Prayer"** is certainly an instance of the kind of poem that I have learned to call transumptive. Such a poem swallows up an ever-early freshness as its own, and spits out all sense of belatedness, as belonging only to others. **"Approaching Prayer"** is at moments Yeatsian in its stance and diction, but what overwhelmingly matters most in it can only be called "originality." I know no poem remotely like it. If it shares a magic vitalism with Yeats and D. H. Lawrence, its curious kind of

wordless, almost undirected prayer has nothing Yeatsian or Lawrentian in its vision. And it is less like Dickey's true precursor, Roethke, than it is like Robert Penn Warren's masterful "Red-Tailed Hawk and Pyre of Youth," which, however, was written long after it and perhaps may even owe something to it.

Originality in poetry, despite Northrop Frye's eloquent assertions, has little to do with the renewal of an archetype. Instead, it has to do with what I would call a struggle against facticity, where "facticity" means being so incarcerated by an author, a tradition, or a mode that neither author nor reader is aware of the incarceration. Dickey calls his poem **"Approaching Prayer,"** but as his revisionist or critic, I will retitle it "Approaching Poetry" or even "Approaching Otherness." I grant that Dickey has said, "In this poem I tried to imagine how a rather prosaic person would prepare himself for the miraculous event which will be the prayer he's going to try to pray," but surely that "rather prosaic person" is a transparent enough defense for the not exactly prosaic Dickey. No one has ever stood in Dickey's presence and felt that he was encountering prose. The poem's speaker is "inside the hair *helmet*" (my emphasis), and this helmet too both conceals and saves. At the poem's visionary center, the boar's voice, speaking through the helmet, gives us the essential trope as he describes his murder by the archer: *"The sound from his fingers / Like a plucked word, quickly pierces / Me again."* The bow, then, is poetic language, and each figuration is a wounding arrow. Who then is slaying whom?

Like any strong poet, Dickey puts on the body of his dead father, for him, let us say, the composite precursor Yeats/Roethke. Shall we say that the strong poet, in Dickey's savage version, reverses the fate of Adonis, and slays the boar of facticity? I hear the accent of another reversal, when Dickey writes:

> My father's sweater
> Swarms over me in the dark.
> I see nothing, but for a second
>
> Something goes through me
> Like an accident, a negligent glance.

Emerson, in his famous epiphany of transmutation into a Transparent Eyeball, chanted: "I am nothing; I see all; the currents of the Universal Being circulate through me; I am part or particle of God." Dickey's surrogate sees nothing, but for a second is all, since that something going through him, glancingly negligent, accidental, also makes him part or particle of God. Addressing beasts and angels, this not so very prosaic personage speaks both as beast and as angel. But to whom? To part or particle of what is oldest, earliest in him, to the beyond that comes straight down at the point of the acceptable time. But acceptable to whom? The God of the hunt is hardly Yahweh Elohim. Dickey's closing chant salutes the God through the trope of "enough": a violent enough stillness, a brain having enough blood, love enough from the dead father, lift enough from the acuity of slaughter—all enough to slay reason in the name of something being, something that need not be heard, if only "it may have been somehow said." The apocalyptic Lawrence of the last poems and *The Man Who Died,* and the Yeats of the final phase, celebrated and so would have understood that "enough." As an American Orphic, as pilot and as archer, Dickey is less theoretic, more pragmatic, in having known just that "enough."

If I were writing of the later Dickey, the poet of **"The Firebombing," "Slave Quarters," "Falling,"** and *The Zodiac,* then I would invoke Blake's Proverbs of Hell on the dialectics of knowing enough by knowing more than enough. But I am going to conclude where Dickey himself ends *The Early Motion,* with the gracious approach to otherness that characterizes the nineteen fragments that constitute **"Drinking from a Helmet."** Dickey remarks that the fragments are set between the battlefield and the graveyard, which I suspect is no inaccurate motto for the entire cosmos of what will prove to be the Whole Motion, when we have it all. Though it is a suite of war poems, **"Drinking from a Helmet,"** even in its title, moves toward meaning both of Dickey's major imaginative obsessions: divination through finding the right cover of otherness, and salvation from the body of this death through finding the magic body of the poet.

A survivor climbs out of his foxhole to wait on line at a green water-truck, picking up another's helmet to serve as a drinking vessel. Behind him, the graves registration people are laying out the graveyard for those still fighting. The literal force of this is almost too strong, and conceals the trope of divination, defined by Vico as the process of evasion by which the poet of Magic Formalism achieves godhood—a kind of mortal godhood, but immortality enough. Drinking from a helmet becomes the magic act of substitution, fully introduced in the luminous intensity of fragment VIII:

> At the middle of water
> Bright circles dawned inward and outward
> Like oak rings surviving the tree
> As its soul, or like
> The concentric gold spirit of time.
> I kept trembling forward through something
> Just born of me.

The "something" is prayer, but again in the peculiar sense adumbrated in the poem **"Approaching Prayer."** Dickey always has been strongest at *invention* (which Dr. Johnson thought the essence of poetry) and his invention is triumphant throughout the subsequent progression of fragments. We apprehend an almost Blakean audacity of pure vision, as the speaker struggles to raise the dead:

> I swayed, as if kissed in the brain.
> Above the shelled palm-stumps I saw
> How the tops of huge trees might be moved
> In a place in my own country
> I never had seen in my life.
> In the closed dazzle of my mouth

> I fought with a word in the water
> To call on the dead to strain
> Their muscles to get up and go there.
> I felt the difference between
> Sweat and tears when they rise,
> Both trying to melt the brow down.

I think one would have to go back to Whitman's *Drum-Taps* to find an American war poetry this nobly wrought. Vision moves from Okinawa to rural America, to the place of the slain other whose helmet has served as the vessel of the water of life:

> On even the first day of death
> The dead cannot rise up,
> But their last thought hovers somewhere
> For whoever finds it.
> My uninjured face floated strangely
> In the rings of a bodiless tree.
> Among them, also, a final
> Idea lived, waiting
> As in Ariel's limbed, growing jail.

Ariel, imprisoned by the witch before Prospero's advent, then becomes the spirit of freedom, but not in this poem, where only to "be no more killed" becomes freedom enough. "Not dying wherever you are" is the new mode of otherness, as vision yields to action:

> Enough
> Shining, I picked up my carbine and said.
> I threw my old helmet down
> And put the wet one on.
> Warmed water ran over my face.
> My last thought changed, and I knew
> I inherited one of the dead.

Dickey at last, though only through surrogate or trope, is at once self and other. What was vision becomes domesticated, touchingly American:

> I saw tremendous trees
> That would grow on the sun if they could,
> Towering. I saw a fence
> And two boys facing each other,
> Quietly talking,
> Looking in at the gigantic redwoods,
> The rings in the trunks turning slowly
> To raise up stupendous green.
> They went away, one turning
> The wheels of a blue bicycle,
> The smaller one curled catercornered
> In the handlebar basket.

The dead soldier's last thought is of his older brother, as Dickey's longing always has been for his own older brother, dead before the poet was born. Fragment XVIII, following, is the gentlest pathos in all of Dickey:

> I would survive and go there,
> Stepping off the train in a helmet
> That held a man's last thought,
> Which showed him his older brother
> Showing him trees.
> I would ride through all

California upon two wheels
Until I came to the white
Dirt road where they had been,
Hoping to meet his blond brother,
And to walk with him into the wood
Until we were lost,
Then take off the helmet
And tell him where I had stood,
What poured, what spilled, what swallowed:

That "what" is the magic of substitution, and the final fragment is Whitmanian and unforgettable, being the word of the survivor who suffered and was there:

And tell him I was the man.

The ritual magic of a soldier's survival has been made one with the Incarnation of the Poetical Character. Of all Dickey's poems, it is the one I am persuaded that Walt Whitman would have admired most. Whitman too would have said with Dickey: "I never have been able to disassociate the poem from the poet, and I hope I never will." What Whitman and Dickey alike show is that "the poet" is both an empirical self, and more problematically a real me or me myself, an ontological self, and yet a divine other. Both poets are hermetic and esoteric while making populist gestures. There the resemblance ends, and to pursue it further would be unfair to Dickey or any contemporary; it would have been unfair even for Stevens or for Hart Crane. The Dickey of the later motion is no Whitmanian; if one wants an American analogue, one would have to imagine Theodore Roethke as an astronaut, which defeats imagination. But I end by citing Whitman because his final gestures are the largest contrast I know to James Dickey's ongoing motions in his life's work. Whitman is up ahead of us somewhere; he is perpetually early, warning us: "Will you speak before I am gone? will you prove already too late?" The burden of belatedness is upon us, but if we hurry, we will catch up to him:

Failing to fetch me at first keep encouraged,
Missing me one place search another,
I stop somewhere waiting for you.

Not Dickey; he cannot stop, yet he has taken up part of the burden for us. Whitman is larger, but then no one is larger, and that largeness is a final comfort, like Stevens' "Large Red Man Reading." Dickey speaks only to and for part of us, but that part is or wants to be the survivor; wants no more dying. Words alone, alas, are not certain good, though the young Yeats, like the young Dickey, wanted them to be. But they can help us to make "a creature to keep me dying / Years longer," as Dickey wrote in the poem of **"The Other."** I conclude by going full circle, by returning to the poem with the tribute that it could prove to contain the whole motion within it. Dickey cannot "turn wholly mortal in [his] mind," and that touch of "utter, unseasonable glory" will be his legacy.

James Applewhite (review date 1985)

SOURCE: Applewhite, James. "Reflections on *Puella*." *Southern Review* 21, no. 1 (winter 1985): 214-19.

[In the following review of Puella, *Applewhite admires the diversity and taut clarity of this poetic collection.]*

In considering the relation between these poems from the point of view of a girl growing into a woman, and those poems of adventurous experience from a masculine point of view which make up the bulk of the poet's work, we should remember that the nature of the speaker, of his or her status in the poem, has always been a crucial issue in the work of James Dickey. Dickey helped resurrect the poetic persona from the crippling self-directed irony of Modernism. His macho stance was not itself a problem except insofar as it may have seemed to make Hemingwayesque claims reaching outside the poems to a base in some grandiosely daring lifestyle. The point lies in how often, from the beginning, Dickey avoided this danger, gave one the impression of universal experiences encountered by a set of eyes and ears and muscles representative of everyone capable of being excited by the climb, the hunt, the stream. There was not so much the exposition of known abilities and manly accomplishments, as of surprised discovery, as the speaker of the poem encountered again a part of personality which had already somehow fused with a like current in the surround of woodland or war situation or crowded fairground. The excitement of Dickey has always resided in how provisionally, at the outset, the poem's speaker has been identified, how blindly and inevitably he has been called to by a deeper-lying stratum of his being. Like Lear "he hath ever but slenderly known himself" because the poet is in a sense all men (and all women), and thus knowledge of the self can never be complete, must wait upon the compulsion outside the ego toward that energetic ground the poet shares with trout and his parents and all other riders on the crowded Ferris wheel and the fiend waiting in darkness in the tree.

Apollo is all light, technical means, sun-clarity, but the image of blindness haunts the Dickean universe, and the poetic transaction takes place often in darkness, even underwater. To find himself the poet must lose himself. "For I is another," said Rimbaud. Thus to take the identity of a woman (or girl) is only to enter more completely that voyage into the terra incognita the poet must always traverse in his "given" poems. If the daughter in **"Root Light"** in her numinous birth caul of bubbles is part of the quick heart of the river, then entering that other thing more completely would be to feel through her senses, wake in her psyche. This the poet has done in *Puella*. In a poem such as **"Veer-Voices: Two Sisters Under Crows"** the author's single male identity is transformed, split, mirrored, and redoubled. One sister, the speaker, verges toward the identity of the other, and both represent the human tensions from "the night-mass of families . . . our stifled folk" as they are given tongue by the veering, dividing cries of crows. These alien voices, tight strung and barbed like the wire underneath them, fill the sisters' "surround," bisect it from all angles and make a multi-tongued "cry of unfathomable hordes," into which the sisters' tight unexpressed human individuality is fused and expressed.

In the face of the many problems caused in the West by the restrictive masculine sensibility, it is particularly interesting that now Dickey devotes a whole book to another point of view. Though I don't think it quite convincing to translate **"The Surround"** (originally published in the *Atlantic* as James Dickey's tribute to James Wright) into a Deborah-poem simply by the inclusion of a subtitle, that title itself *is* of interest: "Imagining Herself as the Environment, / She speaks to James Wright at Sundown." One part of the Hemingway persona tells of shooting the lion like a boast. It is not that aspect of the male self that *knows* the lion, feels from his arteries. That is a Hemingway (or Dickey) not locked in a uniform of male courage and will, but part of the hunting/hunted, terrified and terrifying frieze of animals and jungle. Part of the environment. If Dickey views this identification with the environment as feminine, then it is all the more appropriate that he take on the persona of Deborah, because at his best he is more among the animals than with the hunter; he is beyond any known identity, as simply the keenest edge of being alive in salt marsh or zoo, heartbeat and sinew.

Loss of self in the discovery of a more essential and continuous ground of perception is central to Romantic poetry. Keats thought of children just come into the world as atoms of perception, sparks of an original light of seeing that was from God. Whitman in "There Was a Child Went Forth Each Day" is delivered from knowing only the self of intentions, business, willed projects by seeing the father as "self-sufficient, manly, mean, anger'd, unjust"; the child's identification with him has been foiled by "the blow, the quick loud word, the tight bargain, the crafty lure," and expands like a spirit denied any single body to possess a partial residence in everything it sees. In his sight of the "fish suspending themselves so curiously below there" the word *curiously* reminds us of just how wonderfully strange are all the not-selves becoming partial selves for the poet, as his never completed, blind identity finds temporary home in mare's foal or old drunkard staggering home from the outhouse—as, for Dickey, in sheep child or in the awakening of a girl/woman growing toward self-knowledge among crows and cornfields.

Though *Puella* in its diversity (including, along with poems of nature identification, others dealing with piano playing, dancing, and the art of tapestry) resists simplification into a single developmental sequence, there is, for me at least, a core of psychological process. Poems early on in the book reveal Deborah waking to her individual identity, once with the aid of a mirror (**"Deborah, Moon, Mirror, Right Hand Rising"**). This regarding of the self by the self, in a circle shining with the moon, begins the relation between the psyche and the world. But Dickey knows, and feels through Deborah, the child's apocalyptic tendency to oppose this world (which opposes its wishes), and has dramatized a holocaust of this location in time and space in the initial poem: **"Deborah Burning a Doll Made of House-Wood."** Yet the love of carpenters here, of their "God-balanced bubbles" (in carpenters' levels) suggests an adaptation toward the structure of houses, of adulthood, which is developing, along with the child's blazing ability to negate the world about it, the "power to see / Pure loss. . . ." So as the sequence moves on into later poems such as **"Veer-Voices"** a dialectic is entered upon, and the psyche learns to express itself through identification with things about it—as with these voices of crows. After poems of horseback riding and first onset of menses, there is the lyrically mysterious **"Ray-Flowers."** I am reminded of Blake's "The Book of Thel." The essential metaphor of Dickey's poem is of a down-light drifting fall, and I suspect that at bottom this fall is into the world we know, and *from* some center of self-contained spiritual identity which still, as in the opening poem, opposes the limiting holds of gravity and time. The image of a feather holds the "whole mingling oversouling loom / Of this generation," and the persona, probably now an adolescent, grows "Akin to it, down-haired, like the near side of smoke. . . ." I take this to suggest a consoling poetic vision of lightness, of potential imaginative flight, which helps compensate for "where we fall, or fell."

If my reading of **"Ray-Flowers"** as a poem of resistance to involvement with the physical facts, yet of final acceptance, is correct, then **"Deborah as Scion,"** next, makes a great deal of sense. At the family cemetery Deborah sees her dead ancestors in a moment of vision, "Gravedirt exploding like powder / Into sunlit lace. . . ." From the "green mines" of the family plot, the lives and labor of these earlier women, their "dark dazzle of needles," are unearthed. Deborah, having discovered her single self in the world, having accepted this "fall," now feels pressing upon her the sequence of mothers before who have stamped her with their "eyebrows, / Breasts, breath and butt. . . ." She feels herself alive for a moment in their whalebone corsets, "closed bones" which suggest the body she has inherited as well as the restrictions of dress. These corsets are perhaps the epitome of confinement, the final indication of being trapped in a condition and a time. What I find hard to make sense of in the latter part of this two-section poem is the transition to a vision of whales and whaling. Are the whales, sounding and breaching, an image of sexuality? Is this a further compensatory freedom? I am not sure.

Dickey's tendency to use sensory illusion, (as when his father's hospital room keeps ascending toward "Heaven" with the momentum of an elevator ride in **"The Hospital Window,"** *Drowning with Others*), seems related to his sense of awakening to the world and its curiousness. In **"Heraldic: Deborah and Horse in Morning Forest"** we get once again this immersion through motion in a phenomenal flux which is complexly, physically *present*: for the horse and rider, "twigs from all sprung angles" speed toward the eyeball, as these two race toward "the wildly hidden log prowling upward. . . ." World as process, as flow, as danger, seeks to engulf the perceiving identity. As when Wordsworth in Book I of *The Prelude* sees the mountain rising through optical illusion to stride after him in his purloined rowboat, so the Dickean self feels Dionysian nature looming over in a tidal wave that threatens the small boat of ego and its limited capacity for identification. The confrontation is terrifying yet fruitful. If the poet or his persona rides out the surge, part of the blind world is given sight.

As "All Presences change into trees" (**"Sleeping Out at Easter,"** *Into the Stone*), the one eye that opens slowly is the sun's, but also the poet's; and *"All dark is now no more"* because of his reawakened, world-creating consciousness. When the poet makes the rain "Take the shape of the tent and believe it" (**"In the Mountain Tent,"** *Drowning with Others*), he is creating definitions, asserting order. These seeings, these comings back to the surface, counterpoint the blindnesses, the divings under. Dickey, like the paradigm of the poet as second Creator, is romantic, and therefore the balance may seem sometimes to incline more toward the flood than toward the Ark. But finally he is a poet who rides it out, whose reassertions of order evoke (and investigate) a crucial boundary: between the light of the farmhouse with screened porch and the dark with its nightly creatures, that the shadows of the figures on the porch stretch out toward. Like the poet, these figures in **"A Screened Porch in the Country"** (*Drowning with Others*) are extended into a world beyond the consciously human, there to be touched by the soft bodies usually repelled by the boundary of wire.

I can't help feeling Dickey one of our most poignant literary enigmas. When we first met in the sixties, he the arm-waving windmill of energy, the eye of a hurricane of gossip and rumor, he sat quietly in my house for hours, watching the Masters on TV and holding my two-year-old daughter in his lap. Influenced, perhaps, by that memory, I have since felt an edge of delicacy in both man and poet that others apparently did not always feel. Now here in *Puella* the fight between warrior male psyche and "the enemy women" has been resolved in favor of a wider self-capacious enough to include sensitivities that the aggressive personal identity may in some respects have offended. I see Dickey sometimes as a figure wandering a giant landscape, the hurt, lush South of our unconscious inheritance. The conscious, male poet, bearing his baggage of wound, prejudice, ego-limitation, is sometimes transfixed by magnetic lines arising from pasture, salt marsh, or Civil War battle-ground, to be made momentarily a voice expressive of the great life beyond him. "Birds speak, their voices beyond them" (**"Sleeping Out at Easter"**), just as the voice of the poet is beyond mere will, intention, personality of which a person might boast. The experiences which matter don't belong to anyone, man or woman. They are gifts to the species from its past, to the eye from its landscape. The anonymous, blind son reveals the light of the man's mind, of which he is father. Trees are resurrected from dawn mist within the eyes which create them. The historical personage and its burdens have been used by a larger self.

Not that any of this is easy or automatic. Dickey has devoted enormous labor to finding himself in his craft. It is just that he has had the final good fortune to lose that

self in words as only the greatest have done: falling from a jet liner, undressing, or leaving the Baptist Church, a woman preacher, or here, now, waking to consciousness and womanhood as Deborah. We see in *Puella* that the powerful Dickey of old is still at work, and that he has succeeded in adding at least a handful of these new poems to the central canon. I am impressed by the singularity of taut, musical phrases, remembering Dickey the musician, composer of "Dueling Banjos" for the movie *Deliverance*. The influence of Hopkins in these poems brings a tenser rhythmic and imagistic organization, pulls the rigging shipshape. At least **"Deborah Burning a Doll Made of House-Wood," "Deborah, Moon, Mirror, Right Hand Rising," "Veer-Voices: Two Sisters Under Crows," "Ray-Flowers,"** and the first section of **"Deborah as Scion"** will join the other great central Dickey poems we remember and reread.

Ronald Baughman (essay date 1985)

SOURCE: Baughman, Ronald. *"Buckdancer's Choice."* In *Understanding James Dickey*, pp. 62-77. Columbia: University of South Carolina Press, 1985.

[*In the following essay, Baughman examines the principal poems of* Buckdancer's Choice, *illuminating significant themes and mentioning Dickey's sustained evocation of human ambivalence and equivocation.*]

In *Buckdancer's Choice* Dickey achieves full maturity as a poet. These are exciting poems, many of them discernibly longer, less constricted in form, more "open" than his previous works. In his essay "The Poet Turns on Himself," Dickey defines his concept of the "un-well-made" or "open" poem: "It would have none of the neatness of most of those poems we call 'works of art' but would have the capacity to involve the reader in it, in all its imperfections and impurities, rather than offering him a (supposedly) perfected and perfect work for contemplation, judgment, and evaluation."[1] The "open," or more conclusionless, poem not only creates the visual excitement of unexpected spatial arrangement upon the page but also invites psychological complexity, narrative power.

The poet in *Buckdancer's Choice* strips away the protecting and concealing masks employed in *Helmets* and openly addresses the questions haunting him throughout his work. In **"The Firebombing,"** the war poem which begins the volume, he asks whether he should seek absolution or sentence for his Air Force bombing activities. The speaker can find no easy answer; but that he is asking the question reveals his desire to move from self-laceration toward potential renewal. This question of absolution or sentence also underlies the writer's exploration of his other key subjects. In the family poems Dickey focuses on the mother-child relationship that has given him life but also produced a guilt about being alive. **"Slave Quarters,"** an important social poem, probes the moral quandary generated by the master and slave love-hate relationship so much a part of Southern history. **"The Fiend,"** one of his unique love poems, dramatizes another form of socially disapproved and yet curiously elevating passion. In nature, too, the writer illustrates, through **"The Shark's Parlor,"** how a boy's victory over a shark creates both a moment of youthful glory and a lifelong haunting memory. Dickey directly treats, in the major works of this collection, the ambiguities caught in survivor's guilt.

The volume's first poem, **"The Firebombing,"**[2] dramatically reveals the difficulties the speaker has in bringing himself back to life after combat. Looking back on his actions during World War II, he realizes that he has had no choice about what he has done—firebombing was, after all, his duty; yet he also concedes that through his bombing missions he has caused horrifying deaths to innocent populations. Dickey has declared that the poem treats "a very complex state of mind, guilt at the inability to feel guilt."[3] His statement suggests at least some of the ambiguities that permeate the poem and its speaker's mind.

As Dickey says of the protagonist in "The Jewel," the central figure in **"The Firebombing"** is a man "doubled strangely in time." Riding in the streetcars, sitting in bars, checking his well-stocked pantry, or shining flashlights on his palm trees in present-day America, he envisions his enemies' world which in the past he has helped to destroy. That the ordinary details of his present life persistently recall that other locale suggests the extent to which he is haunted by his past experiences, by questions about his own guilt or innocence in causing the deaths of Japanese civilians. To come to some answer he engages in a series of imaginative re-creations of his experience.

First he examines his own role during the war. As a pilot he became, like his plane, a kind of machine. He learned not to feel concern for his victims or to apply moral judgments to his actions; instead, he measured only how well he performed his task. He became "some technical-minded stranger with my hands" who flew artistically accomplished missions. As a pilot he had the power of life and death over others, but

>   . . . when those on
>   earth
>   Die, there is not even sound;
>   One is cool and enthralled in the cockpit,
>   Turned blue by the power of beauty, . . .

Such detachment has allowed him to be a successful pilot and to perform his duty without remorse.

Yet because his actions now haunt him, he also feels compelled to envision the scenes of destruction that he has caused. As a pilot he had been "unable / To get down there or see / What really happened." Since he could not witness, could not be there, he uses his imagination to portray what he could not see in actuality:

>   All leashes of dogs
>   Break under the first bomb, around those

>   In bed, or late in the public baths: around those
>   Who inch forward on their hands
>   Into medicinal waters.
>   Their heads come up with a roar
>   Of Chicago fire:
>   As I sail artistically over
>   The resort town followed by farms,
>   Singing and twisting
>   All the handles in heaven   kicking
>   The small cattle off their feet
>   In a red costly blast
>   Flinging jelly over the walls
>   With fire of mine like a cat

>   Holding onto another man's walls. . . .

Through these horrifying images which have held him for twenty years, he shows that "With this in the dark of the mind, / Death will not be what it should."

Finally, to get to the truth of his experience, the speaker tries to put himself in the place of his victims. He commands himself to

>   Think of this   think of this
>
>   I did not think of my house
>   But think of my house now. . . .

As a homeowner seemingly in league with other homeowners, both American and Japanese, he wants to feel a sense of unity with his victims:

>   All families lie together, though some are burned alive.
>   The others try to feel
>   For them. Some can, it is often said.

Yet the protagonist is not among those who can—simply and automatically—"feel" for these victims. Rather, his response is more complex.

He has been involved in the destruction of families hauntingly like his own; that he was just doing his duty does not, he knows, expiate him. Uncertain finally about the extent of his own moral responsibility, he will not attempt to simplify it, either for himself or others. Instead, he can only pose yet another question: "Absolution? Sentence? No matter; / The thing itself is in that." What Dickey suggests here is that the question of guilt or innocence is too complicated to be easily stated or resolved. If he wishes honestly to treat the question, he must acknowledge all the ambiguities it does, in fact, contain. Thus his speaker finally comes to no certain conclusion but instead continues to grope with the ambivalence implicit in his situation.

A similar emotional quandary is dramatized in **"Buck-dancer's Choice"**[4] and **"Angina,"** two family poems that focus on the mother-child relationship. Although the poet expresses great affection and admiration for his mother in these works, his feelings are also influenced by guilt. He realizes that he has been born only because an older child has died and that his birth has endangered the life of his mother, a heart patient. Thus their relationship contains profound emotional ambiguities.

In the title poem Dickey's mother serves as a model of courage in the face of death. To counter her agony she whistles "The thousand variations of one song; / It is called Buckdancer's Choice." Through her music the child-speaker envisions the dying art of a black buck-and-wing dancer who flaps his elbows in a futile attempt to transform them into wings. Together these two performers merge in the child's mind as emblems of human refusal to give in to death:

> Through stratum after stratum of a tone
> Proclaiming what choices there are
> For the last dancers of their kind,
>
> For ill women and for all slaves
> Of death, and children enchanted at walls
> . . . . .
>
> Not dancing but nearly risen
> Through barnlike, theatrelike houses
> On the wings of the buck and wing.

The personal, private arts of the two performers, which are caught in the three-beat anapestic lines, inspire the child, another slave of death, to pursue his own art years later.

Again, in **"Angina,"**[5] the speaker asserts that "when I think of love" it embodies itself in "an old woman" who "takes her appalling risks." Though doctors had warned her that to bear children would cause her death, she nonetheless has had four; to this woman "Existence is family," although "Her children and her children's children fail / In school, marriage, abstinence, business." Aware of her agony, the speaker stands at her bedside and hears death "saying slowly / to itself."

> I must be still and not worry,
> Not worry, not worry, to hold
> My peace, my poor place, my own.

Here the voice of death and that of the son fuse. Measured against the woman's courage, death does indeed hold a "poor place"; so too does the grown child who is conscious that he, like his siblings, has imperiled his mother's life, has caused her enormous disappointments. He thus feels a mixture of love and guilt in his relationship with her, an ambiguity that he cannot resolve but must explore.

Dickey's honesty in facing emotional truths about himself extends as well to the larger social context. Although he feels strong affection for the South, he acknowledges the guilt implicit in his region's history. In **"Slave Quarters,"**[6] Dickey records a contemporary white Southerner's responses to his ancestors' sexual domination of black slave women. In many respects **"Slave Quarters"** is about a special kind of love, but one that accommodates an active indifference which is a form of hate as well. The sexual encounters between slave owner and slave are always described as "love" in the poem, yet the owner's attitude suggests his arrogance, his complete freedom to take possession whenever he chooses and then to feel no sense of obligation or concern afterward.

Like the protagonist of **"The Firebombing,"** Dickey's speaker is a man who bridges the present and the past, fusing the two periods in his own imagination. His dilemma, as a contemporary Southerner, involves how to acknowledge his own place within the legacy he knows was wrong:

> How take on the guilt
>
> Of slavers? How shudder like one who made
> Money from buying a people
> To work as ghosts
> In this blowing solitude?

Although he knows that the master-slave relationship was wrong, he also feels drawn to it and to the social system it implies.

While visiting the site of a former plantation, the speaker re-creates in his mind the life established in "the great house" of the South. In the daytime house of social order and decorum the plantation owner has led an aristocratic life. Like the protagonist in **"The Firebombing"** who surveys his well-stocked pantry and suburban home, the planter records his affluence: he is

> proud of his grounds,
> His dogs, his spinet
> From Savannah, his pale daughters,
> His war with the sawgrass, pushed back into
> The sea it crawled from.

His taming of the wilderness into a fruitful, cultivated environment sparks the contemporary Southerner's pride. But only the plantation dogs decipher what is true of both the owner and the speaker, "what I totally am"—a creature of lust and sexual power. In one sense the slave master has the same kind of power over others' lives that the pilot does in **"The Firebombing."**

At night, in the moonlight—the light associated in Dickey's work with madness and a special inner vision—the plantation owner leaves his house and his "thin wife" and "seeks the other color of his body." The speaker recognizes the very real passion in the relationship between the white man and the black woman, whether in the past or in the present:

> My body has a color not yet freed:
> In that ruined house let me throw
> Obsessive gentility off;
> Let Africa rise upon me like a man
> Whose instincts are delivered from their chains. . . .

Such passion is good, alive; yet it grows out of power over other human beings.

Furthermore, when in his ancestor's time this passion creates "A child who belongs in no world," the slave master responds with indifference. For the present-day speaker this uncaring attitude is his region's greatest sin. He cannot imagine heartlessly confining a child to a life as a doorman, waiter, parking lot attendant, or member of a road gang simply because the father will not acknowledge his son. In *Self-Interviews,* Dickey states that "the main thing I characterize as the emotion of love is the wish to protect the other person."[7] Since the slave owner ignores the requirement to protect the black woman and their child, his guilt is profound.

In **"Slave Quarters"** Dickey evaluates the extremely ambivalent feelings he has about his region's history. As he states in his essay "Notes on the Decline of Outrage," every white Southerner must appraise the attitudes that he retains from his past: "Not for a moment does he entertain the notion that these prejudices are just, fitting, or reasonable. But neither can he deny that they belong to him by inheritance, as they belong to other Southerners. Yet this does not mean that they cannot be seen for what they are, that they cannot be appraised and understood."[8] However, as in **"The Firebombing,"** the appraisal in order to be honest must convey all the ambiguities that remain.

"Them, Crying"[9] clearly embodies the wound motif that operates throughout Dickey's poetry, and, like **"Slave Quarters,"** it emphasizes the writer's unconditional compassion for children who suffer. About this subject he feels no ambivalence. In his portrait of a truck driver who spends his nights in hospitals comforting sick and dying children, he therefore describes a man who does not scrutinize his motives—a desire for absolution or sentence—but instead simply acts.

Dickey writes, "I've always had the most complete horror of hospitals. . . . I view hospitals as charnel houses. . . . I hold it against doctors that they're not miracle workers; they're helpless in so many ways. . . . To me, the voice of a child who is alone, frightened, and in pain is an appeal so powerful that it can go through any barrier and be heard anywhere."[10] His own feelings about children in pain become those of his protagonist, an outsider who is "Unmarried, unchildlike, / Half-bearded and foul-mouthed" but who at night is "called to by something beyond / His life," the appeal of hospitalized children. The trucker's personal characteristics make him seem one unlikely to feel concern for others; in fact, Dickey purposely has selected a figure who is ordinarily thought of as insensitive and boorish. Acutely aware that he does not belong within the medical and family groups in the hospital, the truck driver nonetheless consoles children in ways doctors cannot;

> *For our children lie there beyond us*
> *In the still, foreign city of pain*
>
> *Singing backward into the world*
> *To those never seen before,*

> *Old cool-handed doctors and young ones,*
> *Capped girls bearing vessels of glucose,*
> *Ginger ward boys, pan handlers, technicians,*
> *Thieves, nightwalkers, truckers, and drunkards*
> *Who must hear, not listening, them:*
> *Them, crying: for they rise only unto*
>
> *Those few who transcend themselves,*
> *The superhuman tenderness of strangers.*

Unlike most of those who gather in the hospital, the trucker "transcends" himself in agonizing for a small child's return to life. And his unselfish, unambivalent response provides the miracle that helps the child "rise," either to health and life or to heaven as an angel.

Returning to a more ambiguous figure in **"The Fiend,"**[11] Dickey reasserts the tone dominating much of *Buckdancer's Choice.* Here his protagonist is both evil and good: the conventional view of the voyeur is mirrored by the poem's title; yet in its course the fiend also becomes a source for love. Fusing the potential for violent death with the possibility for transforming love, the beholder bestows a rare gift—both threatening and promising—upon those he watches:

>   Not one of these
>   beheld would
>   ever give
>   Him a second look   but he gives them all a first
>   look that goes
>   On and on   conferring immortality while it lasts

As he watches people through their apartment windows, he sees and participates in the familiar dramas of their lives:

>   In some guise or other he is near them when they are
>   weeping without sound
>   When the teen-age son has quit school   when the
>   girl has broken up
>   With the basketball star   when the banker walks
>   out on his wife.
>   He sees mothers counsel desperately with pulsing girls
>   face down
>   On beds full of overstuffed beasts   sees men dress
>   as women
>   In ante-bellum costumes with bonnets   sees doc
>   tors come, looking oddly
>   Like himself. . . .

He learns to read their lives as he reads their lips, "like reading the lips of the dead." And as he crouches in tree limbs, calming dogs and connecting with birds and other creatures of nature's night, he observes people who involve themselves only with the artificial, lifeless images reflected by their television screens. His is a passionate connection; theirs is passive and empty.

Yet his greatest gift and greatest threat goes to those lonely, too often unnoticed women whose husbands and lovers do not provide the intensity of emotion the fiend offers. When he watches "a sullen shopgirl" undress to shower, for example,

> She touches one button at her throat, and rigor
> mortis
> Slithers into his pockets, making everything there—
> keys, pen
> and secret love—stand up.

The thematic fusion of love and death is dramatically suggested through the rigor mortis image. However, when he "gets / A hold on himself" sexually, the shopgirl senses a connection with her unseen admirer, and she is transformed:

> With that clasp she changes-
> senses   something
>
> Some breath through the fragile walls   some all-
> seeing eye
> Of God   some touch that enfolds her body
> some hand come up
> out of roots

Once she is "beheld" she becomes "a saint" and "moves in a cloud." She sings, "As if singing to him, come up from river-fog," and is changed into an ideal of womanhood, into a goddess. For this girl as well as for all the other people he observes, "It is his beholding that saves them."

On the other hand, to those who close their shades and refuse disclosure to him, he harbors an implicit threat of danger, of possible death. Such harm will, he knows, finally emerge when he moves from his hidden existence into an open declaration of who and what he is. He will follow a closed-shade shopgirl home and into her apartment to behold her directly. And once he abandons his secret life for an open disclosure, the fusion of love and death will probably culminate in his raping and killing the one he beholds.

With the figure of the voyeur as his protagonist the poet ventures far from the conventional bounds of morality. **"The Fiend,"** like **"Slave Quarters,"** formulates a complex vision of human passions and their potential, a vision far removed from traditional concepts of love. And because this vision is complex, it underlines the ambiguities Dickey perceives in his world.

"The Shark's Parlor"[12] portrays one of nature's fiends, the shark—a creature who, like the snake, represents for the poet the power of indifferent, inexorable destruction. Yet like its human counterpoint in **"The Fiend,"** the shark in this work also has transforming powers for the human being who confronts it. Dickey says the poem recounts a coming-of-age experience.[13] Clearly, however, what the protagonist learns through his struggle with the shark is that victories over the powers of death are bound to be transitory.

As the poem begins, the adult speaker invokes "Memory" to recall the time in his youth when he and his friend, Payton Ford, had fished for a shark from the porch of a beach house. Fortified by their "first brassy taste of / beer" and their nightly dreams of "the great fin circling / Under

the bedroom floor," the two spread blood upon the sea to lure the creature to their hook. The struggle between the caught shark and the boys, helped by other "men and boys," is a monumental one. Although they finally drag him onto the porch and into the house, he nearly destroys their "vacation paradise":

> cutting all four legs from
> under the dinner table
> With one deep-water move   he unwove the rugs in
> a moment throwing pints
> Of blood over everything we owned   knocked the
> buck teeth out of my picture
> His odd head full of crushed jelly-glass splinters and
> radio tubes thrashing
> Among the pages of fan magazines   all the movie
> stars drenched in sea-blood.

And as the protagonist says:

> Each time we thought he was dead   he struggled
> back and smashed
> One more thing   in all coming back to die
> three or four more times after death.

By triumphing over this creature of the deep, the speaker seems to have attained manhood, seems to have defeated the mindless powers of death and destruction. Yet, as he reveals at the end of the poem, he has felt compelled to buy the beach house under which the shark still symbolically swims and which he can still symbolically wreck. The narrator thus concedes that his youthful struggle with death has been—and will continue to be—forced upon him: he feels "with age / . . . in all worlds the growing / encounters." His triumph therefore remains equivocal; the initiation experience contains real ambivalence for him.

Throughout **Buckdancer's Choice** Dickey raises difficult questions about his own and his speakers' roles in relationship to the events and people in their lives. That he comes up with no clear answers—no clear verdicts of absolution or sentence—may at first suggest that he is avoiding his responsibility as an artist. However, his stance in fact reveals his honesty, his integrity, his refusal to reduce complex issues through simple answers. By probing and finally accepting the ambiguities of his situation, Dickey opens the way to renewal, for which he continues to strive in the succeeding collections.

Notes

1. *Babel to Byzantium* 291.

2. *Buckdancer's Choice* (Middletown, CT: Wesleyan University Press, 1965) 11-20; *Poems 1957-1967* 181-88.

3. *Self-Interviews* 137.

4. *Buckdancer's Choice* 21-22; *Poems 1957-1967* 189-90.

5. *Buckdancer's Choice* 63-65; *Poems 1957-1967* 226-27.

6. *Buckdancer's Choice* 73-79; *Poems 1957-1967* 234-39.

7. *Self-Interviews* 148.

8. *Babel to Byzantium* 274-75.

9. *Buckdancer's Choice* 31-33; *Poems 1957-1967* 198-200.

10. *Self-Interviews* 141-42.

11. *Buckdancer's Choice* 68-72; *Poems 1957-1967* 230-33.

12. *Buckdancer's Choice* 39-42; *Poems 1957-1967* 205-08.

13. *Self-Interviews* 146.

Paul Christensen (review date 1986)

SOURCE: Christensen, Paul. "Toward the Abyss: James Dickey at Middle Age." *Parnassus* 13, no. 2 (spring-summer 1986): 202-19.

[*In the following review of* The Central Motion: Poems, 1968-1979, *Christensen considers Dickey's Southerness and evaluates his poetry of middle age from the collections* Eye-Beaters, Blood, Victory, Madness, Buckhead and Mercy *(1970),* The Zodiac *(1976), and* The Strength of Fields *(1979).*]

> "The secret is that on whiteness you can release
> The blackness . . ."
>
> —*The Zodiac,*

The psychological geography of America is familiar by now: the East and West form a significant polarity in culture—the one old and resolute, fixed by time; the other fluid and novel, sending back its innovations which ruffle and reconstitute American identity. East and West make up a sort of tectonic plate of crumbling and emerging reality. The Midwest is that drab emptiness no one can fill except with a certain malevolence of humor: it is the only place in America that never tempered its reality with a threatening frontier. As in the case of Indiana, the heartland of America until the 1950s, where no Indians (despite its name!) confronted the whites who settled it. Almost at the moment it was occupied, there ensued in the Midwest its tedious image of a placid, almost rancid domesticity, from which artists and thinkers of each generation have longed for and immortalized their dreams of escape—either to the East or to the West, depending on the sensibility of the escape. But the South remains a puzzle, even to the most ardent Southern historians. The South is difficult from almost any perspective, but interesting in its opaqueness and mystique. It was an anomaly from the outset: half its states are named after English kings and queens, the other half have Indian names; its culture was derived from medieval Western Europe, and its aristocratic ways were cultivated in the teeth of a democratized, industrial North. The Civil War was, in some respects, a replay of the French Revolution, in which sans-culotte Yankees destroyed an intransigent nobility. The emergence of a national corporate economy in America following the Civil War parallels the development of an industrial republic from the smoking buckets of the guillotine.

The identity of the South does not lie in its opposition to the North but in its opposition to itself, within itself, a whirligig of polarities that in their fury and violence forged the essential nature of the region. "Love-hate," James Dickey wrote, "is stronger than love or hate." The kudzu vine that conquers numberless pastures and meadows, barns and electric poles of the Deep South is a metaphor of the voluptuous fertility of the ground; but it is countered in the classic antebellum South by a sedate and exacting symmetry of nature on the plantation estates—a willful control of the green world brought over from neoclassical Europe. The image we have of the South, nationally, is of an unsynthesized state somewhere between kudzu and Monticello, between cypress swamps and lynch mobs and the pristine whiteness of a Greek-styled manor house, columned and domed, an emblem of human triumph over the powerful counterthrust of tropical abundance. The original polarity between human symmetry and nature's fertility has undergone constant revision, but it remains the key point of the South's psychic bearings. The vestiges of an old order's will are embodied in Blanche DuBois and in Stanley Kowalski's dark fertility, which longs to overtake her. The polarities within the Southern psyche are myriad, a Zen universe of poised and equal adversaries that constitute the yin and yang of its sensibility.

In a way, the South is the burial ground of the Western mind. The South was formed in the closing decades of the European Renaissance, in the era in which a state culture was being wrested from a sacred one, dooming Europe to decline from a civilization to an economic system. The Western mind, as Charles Olson has argued, began somewhere far back in time in a feud with nature. The axis of Western thought ever since had been toward the control of the realms of growth and decay, the domination of the natural order. It sought to protect itself from mutability through a faith in a heaven of immortal things, each perfect and unchanging; so long as it was able to aspire to such a realm of static bliss, the Western mind thrived in its conflict with all its earthly adversaries. But when the sacred and mundane were separated politically in the Protestant Reformation, the aspirations of the Western mind were thwarted and redirected to nurturing a secular state, with all its mundane responsibilities and repairs. The loss of heaven, as Georg Lukacs observed, was the loss of reality in European art and philosophy. The Renaissance separation of essence from substance closed the routes to heaven in Western ideology and aesthetics, and a kind of sorrowful dream was vented and driven off to the new Eden of the Southern United States. The South glowed like a dream for two centuries: wide fields of symmetrical cultivation, a code of chivalrous conduct, the naming of cities after those of Rome and Greece. The South was an ersatz European country, with the Negro essential to its pretensions: his servile role in the social order was the fulfillment of an old Western ambition: for the Negro was supremely the human extension of Africa's wild, undiluted nature.

The moment the South grasped its role as the inheritor of Europe's humanism, its mind was forged and its psychological conflicts were set in motion. It was an old order in a new country; it was a civilization thrust upon a wilderness; it was a regime of whites ruling over blacks. It was a culture of refinements that soon learned savage ways of punishment and internecine feuding. In every way, the South grappled with opposition and conflict, and its culture was oddly mute to the rest of the nation and the world. Its silence for two centuries was secretive, a brooding within itself that resembled the hard silence of a schizophrenic patient. The South had no way to grow or develop, no way to traffic with the world; it was captive to its own profound conflict and contradiction. In "Notes on the Decline of Outrage" (1961), Dickey describes the feelings of a white Southern male who has boarded a bus with blacks:

> At this moment he is very much aware of himself as a Southerner, and that he is in some way betraying someone or something, even though the impulse which brought him to his present seat on the bus may have been completely laudable, *sub specie aeternitatis.* Oddly enough, he cannot help feeling also a sharp upswing of defiant joy at remembering that he *is* a Southerner, a joy that in no way wishes to distinguish approval from disapproval, right from wrong, good from evil.

His memories of a Southern grandfather are "now intolerably confused," for his grandfather's life was "inextricably entangled with attitudes which, rightly seen, are and have always been indefensible, inhuman, corrupt, and corrupting."

> The young man understands himself as the victim of a cruel and fathomless paradox, a dilemma between the horns of which only a god could survive and still retain his identity.

Dickey has tried to make a poetry of that "mixed state" of mind which he argues, here and elsewhere in essays, *is* the Southern mind. In "The Poet Turns on Himself," published in 1966, he set out this goal for himself:

> I should like now to develop a writing instrument which would be capable of embodying these [inseparably bound] moments and their attendant states of mind, and I would be most pleased if readers came away from my poems not at all sure as to where the danger and the repose separate, where joy ends and longing begins. Strongly mixed emotions are what I usually have and what I usually remember from the events of my life. Strongly mixed, but giving the impression of being one emotion—that is the condition I am seeking to impose on my readers, whoever they may be.

The South is where the European mind unraveled; the brittle culture that kept alive its separatist vision of things collapsed under the tread of another culture. What whelmed up from its ruins and smoking cinders is the *afterlife* of the Western mind—the imagination entangled in oppositions and paradoxes. The literal and material experience of Southern life is only a surface under which the depths of myth and mystery glitter; the Southern character is a mosaic of contending elements, bestial and human, dark and light, irrational and rational. Poe's voice rises out of the region to declare the start of this imagination, its erased borders and maze-like patterns of thought, its lurid and brilliant perceptions. He was the first anticipation of the breakdown of categorical logic; what rose to replace it was an odd fusion of Indian, African, and European dispositions, the slow and inexorable mixing of elements to create the jointed processes of Southern awareness—felt in its dialects, its rural architecture, its peculiar and contradictory jurisprudence, its paradoxic masculinity, which compresses myriad conflicting images of boy-men in the same youth; its sacred and desecrating values of the female, and so on. The Western mind thinned out into a delta here, a swampy mixture of elements that dissolved its original binary character. This Southern fusion is the point of Twain's *Huckleberry Finn,* whose plot shows the creation of the Southern mind—as tutored by a black surrogate father, whose spiritual advice is opposed to the literal, skeptical outlook Huck has inherited from Europe. Huck cannot affect the reality of the river settlements with mere logical powers; he learns to accept the paradoxes of human character through repeated trial and error, until he has achieved double-sightedness and can sympathize with the entangled elements composing human nature.

The writer who approaches the subject of the South must look for a graspable aspect of its paradox. For Faulkner, as for George Washington Cable and Kate Chopin, the essential paradox was time itself: the lingering insistence of a high European culture, the steady erosion of it by the present, between which dangled the helpless Southern soul. When Dickey emerged in the 1960s, he had been well schooled in the literature of the region. He had the good fortune to be born in Atlanta, perhaps the center of Southern paradox—destroyed by Sherman, rebuilt as the capital of the new South, it became the emblem of urban industrialism surrounded by the primitive culture thriving in its hills and river valleys. It is the seat of Emory University and of the Coca-Cola Company; it was to become in Dickey's mind the citadel of urban drudgery, from which the average Atlantan longed to escape—into the hillsides, where he could drink at the springs of its primitive counterpart once more. Dickey attended Clemson briefly, and after the war took degrees from Vanderbilt, where an aging fringe of the original agrarians still lingered on its faculty. Their work obliquely enters into Dickey's style and attitudes, but it was the paradox of Southern life itself that shaped even the earliest lyrics of Dickey's canon.

The rites of passage of Southern boyhood have been explored by every major writer of the region; they differ remarkably from female rites, particularly as noted in Eudora Welty's fiction, as in "Moon Lake," where mock intercourse is performed on a nearly drowned girl by a wiry, primal lifeguard. A Negro pushed her into the lake from her perch, and in her rescue, all the girls of the camp watch as a male ritually matures the frail form beneath his legs. But where the Southern female receives her lessons in life and life-bearing, the Southern male is taught the mysteries of death and violence, of the role of hunter in nature. He is raised to see himself as the destroyer of Otherness, a conqueror of the primal realm. But to kill the enemy requires that one perceive his affinity and kinship with the lower world. The growing up of the Southern boy requires a rebirth in nature, from which he emerges only after he has killed an animal and rubbed his face in the blood of his victory, as does "the boy" in Faulkner's "The Old People." Only then can he return to the city and accede to adulthood, from which, periodically, Dickey warns, one must escape and re-enter the green realm to be rejuvenated.

Dickey's adult characters are uncomfortable with age, unwilling to lose their primal powers. They point up the underlying dilemma of the Southern vision of the male—he is imagined a little past puberty and no further. There is a limit to the range of virile identity in the Southern mind—it includes the warrior in combat, the young heir, the suitor and husband in the flush of his first marriage, but beyond a void begins and a hollow honor descends upon those who are middle-aged. The "colonel" is a stereotype of mock-seriousness, stiffly attired in white in his mansion retreat, a kind of fisher-king waiting to be overtaken by a youthful suitor of his daughter's. He is a figure of wisdom but of dwindling authority; power can be held only by repeated challenges of nature: the hunt, battle, expeditions, rescues.

The problem besetting Dickey's *The Central Motion: Poems, 1968-1979* is that he has tried to deal with middle age, his own, and fails to perceive in it value or meaning. It is only negative—a loss against which he loudly and dramatically declaims. The collection reprints three books of the 1970s: *The Eye-Beaters* (1970), *The Zodiac* (1976), and *The Strength of Fields* (1979). The poems span his middle years from his mid-forties to the age of fifty-six. Hence the title, the central motion, with its insinuation of a central *e*-motion. There is a centering drive in much of the work: the lines of most poems are balanced on an axis, "hung," Dickey remarked to me some years ago, "as if on a string, like a mobile." Sometimes the enjambments are awkward, with lines broken at random to make them fit his expanding and contracting shapes, his balances. The poems spread out like Rorschach blotches, or balloon up and down like a breathing bulb. In their conscious shapings, they express the craftsmanship, if not the vision Dickey struggles to impose here. To center anything thus is a nerve-racking act of precision, and there is a good deal of trembling and frustration in the tone of these poems. The lyrics are often shrill, at times agonized to find a dramatic finale to essentially uneventful experience.

The exaggerated tension in the book suggests Dickey's dread of his subject, as if growing older were a terrible curse with grim consequences. The opening poem, **"Diabetes,"** is nearly frantic with fear of debility and death. The persona lugs his ailing body around at night full of "self- / Made night water." His doctor has made him swear off booze and all his other vices, or else he can look forward / To gangrene and kidney // Failure boils blindness infection skin trouble falling / Teeth coma and death." It is not a promising start for a book about the wisdom years. Instead, it begins with a dark threat against one's desire to remain recklessly young under one's soft chin and sagging belly. This pitch of rhetoric is sustained throughout all three books, into the final poems, which are Dickey's loose renderings of fourteen foreign-language poems, also about old age, dying, illness, and a serene final resignation to it all.

Dickey cannot find a justification for his own mortality; the loss of youthful powers is irreplaceable by wisdom or any nourishing vision of the remainder of life. There are no rituals or rites of passage for the mid-life adult to undertake to redeem himself. He can only dread the further loss of his powers, or remember with poignance the range of his youthful passions. The figure stumbling around in **"Diabetes"** has lost his bearings: everything he believed in had to do with strength and courage. This is where the Southern dream of manhood aborts—when older age becomes the waking nightmare. Now it is upon him, and a terrible throe ensues in operatic, shrilly pitched lyric thrashings. The language is anguished, distorted, the syntax skewered into Lear-like raging soliloquies. Dickey means to play out to the end his own final curtain as a Southern male; but the passions running through the poems are very toxic, the potent confusions that drove Hemingway to suicide. Missing here are the resourceful and cunning self-rescues in Saul Bellow's mid-life novels, *Henderson the Rain King* (1959) and *Herzog* (1964).

But for Dickey there is no going forward; to dwindle in strength and courage is unthinkable. He plies his theme with melodramatic hyperbole, but keeps an eye on the effect he is having on his audience. Dickey knows when he is hamming his emotions and when they cause him genuine *angst*; but the poems merge candor and bombast into one lyric keen. He can change his act on a nod; some of the poems take an abrupt turn from self-pity to show us his fatherly affections, as in two poems on his sons, **"Messages,"** with their tender words from an otherwise hard-boiled parent. Soon after, he is off once more, raging in his ambulance on the way to the emergency room, having collapsed in the street, shouting his fustian and gesturing like an old tragedian in the poem **"Mercy,"** arms outstretched as he delivers this close:

> My lips　 hold them down don't let them cry
> With the cry　 close　 closer　 eyeball to eyeball
> 　　In my arms, O queen of death
> 　　Alive, and with me at the end.

This peroration is intended for his favorite nurse, who has rushed down to find her old warrior dying again. The tone of this poem is murky—a mixture of pathetic sincerity and self-mocking irony. It turns over its own psychological ruse by minimizing and clowning in a serious crisis.

"Mercy" is at least a coping strategy—a satire on the failing body; another is in **"Two Poems of Going Home,"** perhaps the most often-sought escape from middle age: to look up one's youthful haunts, which Dickey does with good humor in **"Looking for the Buckhead Boys,"** where he wanders around in an imaginary Tyree's Pool Hall, finding his old gang shooting pool around the table—but "it's a shoe store now," and even this vivid fantasy fades out on the middle-aged speaker. Alas. Both poems of "return" offer trite plots; Dickey tries to compensate by rhetorical extravagance, by a sprawling typography that strews phrases across the page, winds in inner voices, ghosts, and all the rest of lyric gothic machinery. But they remain the maunderings of mid-life; try as he might, Dickey has only produced a few sentimental journeys at dramatic pitch:

> Let me go pull my car out
>   Of the parking lot in back
> Of Wender and Roberts'. Do I need gas? No; let me
>   drive around the block
>   Let me drive around Buckhead
>   A few dozen times   turning   turning in my
> foreign
>   Car till the town spins   whirls till the chrome
> vanishes
>   From Wender and Roberts'   the spittoons are
> remade
> From the sun itself   the dead pages flutter the hearts
>   rise up, that lie
>   In the ground, and Bobby Laster's back-
> breaking fingers
>   Pick up a cue-stick   Tommy Nichols and I
> rack the balls . . .

The poem **"Apollo"** celebrates the first manned lunar mission and appeared originally in *Life* magazine with a big spread; it is cleverly deployed in ***The Eye-Beaters*** as a variation on the dread of mortality. The moon is the bleak planet of death, hanging in its dark void above. Dickey relives the experience of going behind it, where all communication with the living ceases, and of coming round again to a sight of earth. A full black page dramatizes the silent phase of the trip, the "hysterical void," but Dickey jubilates as the ship floats back to light:

> Almighty! To come back! To complete the curve   to
>   come back
>   Singing with procedure   back through the last
> dark
>   Of the moon, past the dim ritual
>   Random stones of oblivion, and through the blind
> edge
>   Of moonlight into the sun
>
>   And behold
>
> The blue planet steeped in its dream

Of reality, its calculated vision shaking with

The only love.

Death is nothing; life is everything, but exactly what life is remains unspoken. It is merely a continuation of the struggle. But this undimensional imperative counters all thoughts of death but the fear of it. Dickey is at an impasse in this book—he has gone from youth to age, only to dread the progress. The poems do not penetrate experience; instead, they build up a wall of extravagant evasions to it. The forays back to youth and wartime memories are brief escapes from torment; the illness poems are full of self-mocking humor. The obsession with death fears is everywhere; he transforms all his experience into it, but this momentary fiat of imagination is then blocked by an unwillingness to argue for relief or consolation. That is why the sudden appearance of **"The Eye-Beaters"** is so extraordinary in the stagnant relation of the other poems. It suddenly leaps off in a new direction, alien to the other poems.

The eye-beaters of the poem are blind children in an asylum who beat on their eyes to experience visions; they beat them till they bleed and turn black. An older man narrates his visit to them and sympathizes with, almost approves of their tortuous behavior—he, too, is blind and has no vision of his own. The poem seems to acknowledge the intellectual catch of all the preceding poems—the aging persona who cannot drink, smoke, or womanize must now preserve what health remains, even as he dreams of youth and escape from his ailing body. The children are in a similar intellectual paralysis, prisoners of their own malfunctioning organisms who also need to be consoled and delivered. As they beat on their eyes, visions form, he imagines, that are nothing more than hemorrhages, but to the inner eye are like the scrawls of cave walls—the figures etched in feces and vegetable dyes by primordial man, who was also "blind" and desperate to create a consoling vision for his life. The children re-create for themselves the same archetypal images that were first seen thirty thousand years ago in the corridors of the Dordogne caves. In a way, history is static in this poem—a suspended state of desire in which the same archetypes appear across the whole human era, from beginning to now. There is considerable merit to the thesis, and other poets have recently been exploring the notion of such archetypal patterning in the deep imagination—in the work of Robert Bly and even more recently in Clayton Eshleman. Eshleman's thesis is that the cave drawings "narrate" the emergence of the human mind from the animal continuum, the lonely vigil of which is both mourned and celebrated. He suggests in *Hades in Manganese* (1981) and in *Fracture* (1983) that the dancing figures of the caves are half man, half animal, lonely misbegotten things in exile from the edenic continuum of other life forms. This thesis vaguely circulates in **"The Eye-Beaters"** as the basis of the primordial mind, which the children and the adult visitor both return to in their own different states of desperation. Somehow their human identities are inadequate, unfulfilling, isolating—and in disease or older age, to be human is to be cast off into the hopeless void. The "collective consciousness" hinted at in this poem encloses the children, the speaker, and the primate hominids of the Paleolithic era. Each goes about in his cave, physical or psychological, etching those primitive but vitalizing formations from his spiritual hunger for companionship.

It is a good poem, and its roots go far back into earlier work—into other poems touching on the human relation to the animal world, as in **"The Sheep-Child"** and **"The Shark's Parlor."** In its dread of life and loneliness, it bears relation to other classic poems in the vein, among them Yeats's "Among School Children" and Dylan Thomas's "I See the Boys of Summer." But personal solace is not forthcoming in Dickey's poem; it ends on a note of indeterminacy. The goal of the poem was the agony, not the relief. It is a grotesque poem in the original sense of the word, from grotto, the cave, the dark soul. It bears pointing out that Dickey, like few others in American poetry, is a grotesque writer—from the tradition of Bosch, Goya, Céline, Burroughs—whose energies have always been directed at the hidden depths of pain and distortion in life. Its negative tradition is a running commentary through the centuries on different notions of the Sublime, the Beautiful—but in reverse. Solace for Dickey is not in escape from the pain but in finding commiseration through others also in pain, the exploration of pain itself, its myriad volatile images and fused emotions.

The line of reasoning in **"The Eye-Beaters"** prompted the ambitious, failed effort called *The Zodiac,* which appeared six years later, in 1976. The poem is about another eye-beater, a Dutch poet whose "triangular eyes" look into the cold Christian heaven and alter all its abstractions with animal totems of his own invention. Reordering the zodiac and paganizing the lifeless divinity of the Christian view somehow consoles his besotted mind, though how is never clear or persuasive. The book-length piece is a dark, sweaty, booze-laden sequence, monotonous in pace, raspy-voiced in its slangy lyric climaxes and repeated epithets. It is disheveled in every way—with a laundry-line typographic scheme that drapes the onrush of phrases over the whole page space. Dickey is at sea trying to make up a new mythology through the guise of his deranged persona.

Both **"The Eye-Beaters"** and *The Zodiac* bear much in common—they constitute Dickey's forays into the speculative realms of Charles Olson. By 1970, Dickey was played out on the themes of youth and heroism. Olson died the same year and left behind a contentious canon and a bevy of admiring young intellectuals to spread its heady gospels. Dickey was not amused by Olson's brief spate of publications, but he paid attention to them through the years, as did other major figures who frequently took aim at Olson in the journals. The real bone of contention was Olson's attack of Western beliefs—he dismissed them out of hand as alienating and delusory; his argument was for a reconception of nature as an autonomous, harmonious order that Western metaphysics had distorted and maligned for millennia. Olson saw nature through the eyes of primi-

tive cultures, through the language systems and other texts of Mayan, Sumerian, and other non-Western cultures, and found their view more nearly exact and welcoming of this "other" order in the universe. It was the basis of a truth about life, and was covered up and nearly obliterated by the false humanism of Western tradition. This seemed to throw too much in doubt at once, but it was arresting and intriguing even to Olson's angriest detractors. Dickey tries out the notion of a valid primordial "sight" in **"The Eye-Beaters,"** but in *The Zodiac* he seems to be writing a *Maximus Poems* in miniature, under flamboyant disguises and with disclaimers posted at the outset. This may seem an awkward thesis to put forward in the light of the harsh words Dickey wrote in *Babel to Byzantium* (1968, 1981), but he could turn around even there and say, "Yet I have a weakness for long poems of this kind." "His mind," he wrote, "seems to me a capable one," and his *Maximus* poems, though "unsuccessful," contain a "few moderately interesting sections . . . worth reading."

By 1966, in "The Poet Turns on Himself," he wrote: "I began to conceive of something I called—doubtless misleadingly—the 'open' poem: a poem which would have none of the neatness of most of the poems we call 'works of art' but would have the capacity to involve the reader in it, in all its imperfections and impurities, rather than offering him a (supposedly) perfected and perfect work for contemplation, judgment, and evaluation." But this is precisely what Dickey complained of in 1961 in Olson's "structure of fortuitous association," which five years later is grafted onto Dickey's poetic, since he is now "interested most of all in getting an optimum 'presentational immediacy,' a compulsiveness in the presentation of the matter of the poem that would cause the reader to forget literary judgments entirely and simply experience." This is a slight rephrasing of poetic statements both Williams and Olson had made in the 1950s, the poem as vehicle for conveying the undiluted perceptual force of a poet to his reader.

The turn to Olson, however veiled or half-conscious, is curious and problematic: the Southern poet regarded himself as a force of conservation of certain Western values, which in Olson are under attack. Olson had specified a disorder that released creative energies; the Southern legacy put a value on controlling one's materials as a siphoning off of essences in the poetic act. Even Poe retained the graces of lyric and its sturdiest conventions of the European tradition. With few exceptions, Southern writers, though of perplexed emotion, held out for order over materials as an imperative of art. One must wonder if it is the *Zeitgeist* of the mid-century or the disarming arrogance of Olson that made Dickey question his own rules and conventions and throw them out.

But one affinity between Olson and Dickey is always just under the surface of Dickey's poetry: his "permanent interest . . . in the forfeited animal grace of human beings, occasionally redeemed by athletes . . . and the hunter's sense of understanding with the hunted animal." Both

Americans expressed attitudes toward the natural world previously articulated by D. H. Lawrence, which sets them apart in the distinctive, rebellious direction of recent poetry. Whereas poets like Theodore Roethke and James Wright admired the grace and peace of certain animals, Dickey, Olson, and Lawrence longed for the violent, untamable animal realm that would overpower the frailties of human awareness. They wanted reunion with a primal world of violence and instinct, which they glimpsed in certain primordial images. All three writers expressed an intense masculinity and dreaded the loss of their animal powers through the refinements of human evolution.

The drama of these uneven poems of middle life is of a Southern poet moving out of the boundaries of his literary heritage into a great uncertainty of composition and idea, which he deals with by incorporating principles of his most suspect contemporary. Olson at least asked big questions and wondered aloud in his messy compositions, and sought no firm conclusions to his arguments. It was more important to be lost in one's creative confusion, which Dickey now wanted for himself—the "conclusionless poem," with its language at once "open" and "ungeneralizing," the poem "un-well-made." If Faulkner exploded the sentence to lay bare the paradoxical content of his own feelings, it is not until Dickey that the line of Southern poetry is finally broken open to allow a disorderly subjectivity to tumble out of it. The "tradition" of Southern writing, rich as it is, eccentric and volatile as it may seem, was bridled by its inherited European aesthetic. The line from Faulkner to Wolfe to Barthelme is a dissent and an opening out of the prose structure of fiction; it cannot be traced in poetry much before the wild, disordering tendencies of Dickey's poems in the mid-1960s.

For all that, *The Zodiac* is not very good. As a long poem, it lacks the mosaic infrastructure required for suspense and rapid, jagged movement forward; it rarely achieves the fortuitousness desired; and it labors to show a mind liberated from old assumptions, which comes and goes in a boozy haze of imprecision and feigned madness. The long poem is essentially a ritual, a "dark game" which, when carried out well, shows a Western poet seated among the fragments of his own culture and of others, which he sorts through and reassembles in order to bring off his own eccentric perspective on life. Dickey's persona can't do that; the poet behind him is not speculative by nature but sure-handed and too exacting. The kind of mind Dickey wants to invent—the Olsonian speculator of lofty, difficult notions—is simply too foreign to him. Instead, he falls back on his old maunderings and bellyachings through his speaker—whose alcoholism threatens his life and whose desire to bring "God's crazy beasts" back into metaphysics simply fades out. Olsonianisms are rife in the poem: in things like "He can't tell Europe / from his own death," to such Black Mountain tropes as "Don't shack up with the intellect: / Don't put your prick in a cold womb." The poem wants to conceive a "human universe," Olson's phrase, to replace the one prescribed through centuries of desultory metaphysics. Dickey's instinct is correct in the

poem—to seize upon some scheme for heaven that rekindles the Western passion to mine essence from substance, to put spirit back into its coils of flesh once more, but the means and the conceptual process are missing. Dickey can only record the sweating melodrama of the effort, not its steps of mental progress. Sadly, his poem becomes a Hollywood treatment of the long poem—scenes and dialogue, little of the essential substance of its subject.

The Zodiac obscures Dickey's merits. His early poems quickly showed his genius in probing the unspoken bond between urban and wilderness realms that still nourished Southern identity. In a sense Dickey is another Dickens, a tale-teller of dazzling, hallucinatory powers who could break into the latent consciousness of his audience and reconstruct its content in poetry. The South was losing its green world at the time, becoming an urbanized, diluted sprawl of industrial culture, which Dickey spoke directly to, with dread, anger, outrage, and with dreamscapes and mythical characters which spoke to one's longings for some past world of inseparable relations to nature. His rescuers and daredevils are all figments of the Southern dream of transcendence and immersion—the paradox of having and lacking one's place in nature. He perplexed his critics at the start, but roused his audience and commanded it with a series of short, powerful books through the 1960s that established him at once as the premier voice of his times—the mixed fate of Southern culture. But by middle age, the direction of those shrewd powers to articulate the spirit of the region was shifted to his own situation, to his concerns as an aging, virile male whose image was now to be catered to. Half invented by his own dramatic poems, he was now partly captive of it and required in his own mind lyrics to sustain it—to portray himself as a lion in old age. Even the eye-beater in *The Zodiac* is virile as well as pathetic, a hunter in armchair with a pen for a rifle, his prey all the wilderness of his imagination, which he imposes upon the night sky. The long poem fell apart, into the pieces of his own confused intentions—dead-end speculations of uninspired language; a breast-beating drunken hero, whose pains are monotonous, and a concern for failing health and an aging mind, at which he is vivid and dramatic.

The Strength of Fields (1979), the third and last book of *The Central Motion,* is a slight but fluid collection of original poems, with an appendix of fourteen translations. Dickey has made some adjustments to style in it—an emphasis on sound and the musically enriched phrase, and away from a crisp narrative focus. The poems seem reluctant to tell anything—an image will do, as in **"Root-Light, or the Lawyer's Daughter,"** with its rush of baroque imagery, its subject withheld until the final lines, when a naked girl dives from a bridge into a river as a lasting memory of youth and beauty. **"The Strength of Fields"** was commissioned for Carter's inauguration, and it is an elegant tribute to a new President. It explores the delicate sense of fealty between one isolated self and the lives that fill the surrounding cosmos as a low, baleful train whistle is heard in the distance to remind one of change and mortality. The poem's elegant sophistications of language are tempered a bit by the form they construct—an open-ended variation on the blues ballad of freight trains and lonely travel. **"The Rain Guitar"** is a silly bit of mythmaking, with Dickey as magic minstrel again, playing his regional music as an English fisherman helplessly dances in excitement. It is a throwback to the magical realism Dickey produced earlier, but its self-glorifications hardly seem naïve any longer.

Especially interesting is the poem **"For the Death of Lombardi,"** which is Dickey at his vintage best. In Lombardi Dickey finds a mystical Southern father—someone who drove the boys to manhood, who died and is lamented self-consciously in mythical terms as a source of Dickey's own manhood. His death by cancer is metaphorical of a terrible inexorability, which Dickey fears now that he is "middle-aged and gray." Other fathers are listed in the lament: Paul Hornung, who "has withdrawn from me," and George Patton, "who created armies" the way Lombardi "created us." Lombardi is the archetypal coach. His death spells death for all he raised—"We're with you all the way / You're going forever, Vince." It is followed, a bit too neatly, with **"False Youth: Autumn: Clothes of the Age,"** in which Dickey gets a haircut and is scorned by the barber as a "middle-aged hippie." Upon leaving, he notices a youth wearing an embroidered jacket with a portentous figure on it:

> eagle riding on his claws with a ban-
> ner
> Outstretched as the wings of my shoulders
> Coming after me with his flag
> Disintegrating, his one eye raveling
> Out, filthy strings flying
> From the white feathers, one wing nearly gone:
> Blind eagle but flying
> Where I walk, where I stop with my fox
> Head at the glass to let the row of chairs spell it
> out
> And get a lifetime look at my bird's
> One word, raggedly blazing with extinction and soar-
> ing loose
> In red threads burning up white until I am shot
> in the back
> Through my wings or ripped apart
> For rags:
>
> *Poetry.*

Mortality, old age, and death are the terms of this poetry, but Dickey seems to have found peace with himself. The poems are less shrill and frenzied; they balance once more on their plumb lines, the lines tapering and expanding as he packs all the music he can into their lumpy, jarring phrases. Some of the language reads like tongue-twisting elocution drills, but there are also somber themes that buoy up the dizzying lyric spells. In the closing poem of Part One, **"Exchanges,"** Dickey merges his words with lines from Joseph Trumbull Stickney, as both describe the California coast. The Stickney lines are romantic and reverent, while Dickey's are sober and realistic: together they merge the two halves of history—the beautiful wilderness, the gloomy sea of oil rigs and pollution. It ends on Dickey's most persistent theme: the human curse upon nature:

> Nothing for me
> Was solved. I wandered the beach
> Mumbling to a dead poet
> In the key of A, looking for the rainbow
> Of oil, and the doomed
> Among fish.
>
> *—Let us speak softly of living.*

The group of translations which closes *The Central Motion* bears the nervous title "Head-Deep in Strange Sounds: Free-Flight Improvisations from the un-English," and offers some loose renderings of various poems. "I chose them nearly at random," he tells us in his preface, but most are about old age, fate, a serene resignation to the way of things:

> I am of shadow and of sun of the sun
> Returning always,
>
> And I laugh, silently.

"O death so dear to me" opens another poem. Beyond the theme of aging, there is another, more subliminal one: a longing for the animal realm:

> I am tired of existing
> As an animal of intelligence—
> . . . Let us go back into the immense and soft-handed,
> double
> Fire-bringing ignorance.

But Dickey is clever by half. *He* hasn't made his peace; he has found it through others and only cosigns their counsels through his own boisterous, rowdy American versions. His tone almost contradicts *their* emotions: "I play the hell-game / That dances on the horizon," or "Raging with discovery like a prow / Into the oncoming Never." He tells us through a Yevtushenko poem, "I'm not a damn thing but old," but that "It's *horrible* to live / And even more horrible / not to live."

The Central Motion is the waffling poetry of a major writer of the 1970s. It's a slim volume with a few very good poems in it; the rest is confusion and ramblings, awkward experiments and grim failures. It comes after a decade of remarkable successes and awards and was perhaps an inevitable falling off. The seventies were themselves unheroic and inward-looking, and their atmosphere wears off in this work. The view is almost always within, at failing health and waning convictions; it is a book about struggle and grief, arguments with the self, a desire to go on as the feet grow leaden. It is partly about being caught in one's own confected image, the duties that it imposes, which are false and wearying. Americans took to Dickey, even non-readers, who flocked to his readings. Sporting-goods manufacturers plied him with canoes and power bows, hoping for his endorsements. The book seems to sigh under the load of that publicity and vanity, as real things ensue—mortality, death of loved ones, illnesses, qualms, and fears. It is a book of thrashings and throes by a man who cannot easily face his aging. Unlike Lear, who reached an epiphany of sorts—that man is a bare, forked animal gripped by change—Dickey's voice keeps arguing alone in the dark, in thickets of confusion and ill humor, trying to find the drama and the lyric ebullience to somehow get through it. But all Dickey can argue here is that youth is everything—and to lose it is the only tragedy.

Gordon Van Ness (essay date 1989)

SOURCE: Van Ness, Gordon. "'Stand Waiting, My Love, Where You Are': Women in James Dickey's Early Poetry." *James Dickey Newsletter* 6, no. 1 (fall 1989): 2-11.

[*In the following essay, Van Ness traces Dickey's use of the mythic archetype of the "Queen Goddess" and idealization of women in such works as "Adultery," "The Fiend,"* Puella, *and other less well known poems.*]

In assessing James Dickey's poetry, critics have often focused on his wide-ranging variety of thematic concerns, recognizing the interrelation of the topics themselves and their often biographical connection to the artist. Ronald Baughman, for example, states that as Dickey "treats his major subjects—war, family, love, social man, and nature—the writer is working out his constantly evolving perspective as a survivor" (8). Richard Calhoun and Robert Hill have written of his "emotional primitivism," which Dickey himself defines only as that "condition where we can connect with whatever draws us" (136). Critics have felt, in other words, that attempts to confront narrow aspects within Dickey's poetry invariably risk distortion and oversimplification. As Robert Kirschten in the most recently published book on the poetry admits: "Indeed, his subject matter is as mixed as his emotional effects," a realization which necessitates four "hypotheses" to scrutinize Dickey's "lyric universe" (3).

Yet, if examination of a single subject within Dickey's poetry invites misconception because of its specialized focus, it nevertheless may offer large insights, the possibility of identifying some unified field theory, as it were, by which to understand Dickey's "universe." As Dickey himself notes regarding the whole question of identity, "one must work with such misconceptions for whatever hint of insight—the making of a truth—they may contain: that fragment of existence which could not be seen in any other way and may with great good luck, as in the best poetry, be better than the truth" (*Night Hurdling* xi). I wish to suggest, therefore, that in his early poetic treatment of women, Dickey consciously used mythic archetypes to depict what Joseph Campbell in *The Hero With A Thousand Faces* calls the Queen Goddess of the World. My discussion primarily centers on certain short, overlooked, or un-

examined poems, both published and unpublished, in that longer works such as **"Falling"** and **"May Day Sermon"** have been numerously examined by critics and that, in any event, these poems also support my contention. In narrowing my topic and making this assertion, I am conscious that Dickey's image as macho or Byronic, what Calhoun and Hill refer to as his "sexual legendry" and "nearly Rabelaisian experiences" (138, 2), has influenced previous criticism and renders debatable any interpretation of, say, **"The Earth Drum"** or **"A Morning,"** two unpublished poems discussed below that are dominated by a distinctly male perspective.[1]

In an overlooked essay entitled "Complicity" and published in *Night Hurdling* (1983), Dickey notes the poet Paul Claudel's view of Woman as "the promise that cannot be kept," and he then declares: "From going to and fro in the earth, and from walking up and down in it—the real earth, and not just the enchanted fragment of it that blazes in the longing mind to furnish her setting—she becomes a hidden archetype to the beholder rendered god-like by her presence: his possession and promise, soulless and soulful at the same time, receding, flashing up with a terrible certainty at the most inopportune times that she then makes opportune" (217). Such a view of women as mythic incarnations of the female principle receives earlier attention in Dickey's discussion of his poem **"The Enclosure."** Referring to the nurses the airmen saw in World War II as they were trucked to the awaiting planes, Dickey states: "they were unmistakenly women. They had the inaccessibility I've always deemed such an important part of the man-woman relationship: the idealization of woman. You can see this idea in many places, not just in my poems" (*Self-Interviews* 91). Dickey's comments suggest that he, and by extension all men, views women as idealized figures whose possibilities offer fulfillment, the end of male isolation and inadequacy and the completion of the self.

Dickey's years at Vanderbilt had exposed him to the works of such mythologists and anthropologists as Joseph Campbell, Sir James George Frazer, Jane Ellen Harrison, and W.H.R. River. Following his unrestricted readings of many of their books, he consciously began using myth as the basis of his poetry. Indeed, the bound, unpublished notebooks Dickey kept in the early Fifties, in which he sought to determine his poetic method, suggest the conscious employment of this perspective and, specifically, the idealization of mortal women into an archetype who promises larger, life-fulfilling knowledge. One entry, for example, asserts: "it is part of my job to show that physical sex-fulfillment is only the prelude to a greater hunger which is unappeasable, but which is related to the idealized *image* of sex." Another notation states: "the inviolable virgin one longs for." Another asks: "—are the mythic and the 'true-to-experience' irreconcilable? Are the archetypal + the 'true-to-experience'?"[2]

In *The Hero With A Thousand Faces* Campbell characterizes the hero's rites of passage, the ultimate adventure of which occurs as "a mystical marriage of the hero-soul with the Queen Goddess of the World." Campbell describes her as "mother, sister, mistress, bride. Whatever in the world has lured, whatever has seemed to promise joy, has been premonitory of her existence—in the deep of sleep, if not in the cities and forests of the world. For she is the incarnation of the promise of perfection; the soul's assurance that, at the conclusion of its exile in a world of shared inadequacies, the bliss that once was known will be known again" (111). Frazer in *The Golden Bough* refers to this incarnate female principle as the "great Mother Goddess, the personification of all the reproductive energies of nature" (385). Always associated with her is a lover who is divine yet mortal and with whom she unites. The Queen Goddess, however, as Campbell further details, soon becomes temptress: "The mystical marriage . . . represents the hero's total mastery of life; for the woman is life, the hero its knower and master. And the testings of the hero, which were preliminary to his ultimate experience and deed, were symbolical of those crises of realization by means of which his consciousness came to be amplified and made capable of enduring the full possession of the mother-destroyer, his inevitable bride" (120-121). Through her promise, in other words, the hero becomes fully actualized, his consciousness freed of all limitations; yet in the very process of uniting with the world, he experiences revulsion. Campbell asserts: "life, the acts of life, the organs of life, woman in particular as the great symbol of life, become intolerable to the pure, the pure, pure soul" (122). Woman transforms him into something greater than he was, but in doing so the hero becomes disillusioned that the real does not sustain his previous idealized image. Dickey himself perhaps best acknowledges this disparity when he asserts in *Sorties*: "The phantom women of the mind—I speak from the man's standpoint only—are a great deal more important than any real women could ever possibly be. They represent the Ideal, and as such are indestructible. It is quite arguable that poor mortal perishable women are as dust before these powerful and sensual creatures of the depths of one's being. I believe that no one can understand what it is to live a human life without understanding this, at least to some small degree" (4). For Dickey women are actualizing agents without whom men remain unfulfilled and for whom they seek because as ideal figures they offer larger possibilities.

First published in *Poetry* in 1959, **"Into the Stone"** suggests this mythic view of what Woman can effect. Dickey notes that the poem depicts "the quality of a love relationship" as the speaker approaches "the love object, the woman," and that "not only the world of the person in love is changed by the new love relationship, but the whole universe is changed" (*Self-Interviews* 98). Calhoun and Hill assert that the poem shows love as "almost a naturalistic sacrament" (21), while Baughman states that love becomes "a principal means of countering death" (26). None of the criticism centers specifically on the woman, whose presence informs the poem though she herself never literally appears. Nor should she, for **"Into the Stone"** concerns itself with the liberating results of union on the hero. Cambell alludes to these effects when

he describes the hero's approach to the Queen Goddess: "Woman, in the picture language of mythology, represents the totality of what can be known. The hero is the one who comes to know. As he progresses in the slow initiation which is life, the form of the goddess undergoes for him a series of transfigurations: she can never be greater than himself, though she can always promise more than he is capable of comprehending. She lures, she guides, she bids him burst his fetters. And if he can match her import, the two, the knower and the known, will be released from every limitation" (116). As he journeys "On the way to a woman," the speaker in Dickey's poem comes "through the land between." Their union has affected the natural world: "The moon turns around in the fix / Of its light." But it has also transformed the hero: "Like the dead, I have newly arisen, / Amazed by the light I can throw. / Stand waiting, my love, where you are." Possessed with new and larger powers, he knows "No thing that shall die as I step / May fall, or not sing of rebirth." His quest has taken him "Very far from myself," but as a consequence, "I am he who I should have become." Amazed by his initiation into innate mysteries, the speaker knows that "The dead have their chance in my body." The woman's complicity has transformed him, for "I am known; I know my love." However, Dickey clearly wishes to suggest that the Queen Goddess throughout her series of transfigurations creates the speaker's greater awareness: "Each time, the moon has burned backward. / Each time, my heart has gone from me / And shaken the sun from the moonlight. / Each time, a woman has called." The poem reveals Woman as a creature whose powerful attraction promises the man larger knowledge and initiation into natural mysteries.

Occasionally in his early poetry Dickey deliberately employs Christian myth to depict the archetypal Woman. Published in *Drowning With Others* (1962), **"The Rib,"** for example, though its focus is on kinship with the natural world, alludes to Adam and Eve: "A rib in my right side speaks / To me more softly / Than Eve," whom the poet describes as "the bidden, unfreeable shape / Of my own unfinished desire / For life, for death and the Other." Here Woman becomes the means through which the speaker figuratively dies and whose symbolic rebirth promises larger understanding of those processes, specifically death, which govern the world. Another poem, **"Eden,"** an unpublished manuscript in the Washington University Special Collections, also focuses on the Genesis myth. Fifteen typed pages long in its last-completed draft, it concerns creativity generally; however, the poem specifically presents the story of a painter of pornographic pictures dying of encephalitis who decides to combine sex and religion into one final portrait of Eden. Dickey's notes for the poem read in part: "We should start with Adam himself, coming into being color by color. Eve is also coming. What is gradually revealed is their relationship to the man who is conceiving them—somewhat like God may be supposed to have conceived them—out of sickness and chance and death." Dickey writes of Eve's appearance on the canvas, "a woman this time / Taking form, her whole body / Weeping-red, as if skinned alive, / Just born of her man. The one in all time / Equal to his desire." Later, her form complete, she "quivers / With affirmation of being" and then "Eden is accomplished in this room." Again, it is the archetypal woman, Eve, whose presence signifies wholeness.

In what is Dickey's only published poem whose title is a woman's name, **"Mary Sheffield,"** first published in *Shenandoah* in 1964, provides another example of how Dickey attributes larger, life-sustaining qualities to a woman; through her, the man realizes new knowledge. The poem depicts a speaker who, "Forever at war news," stands thinking in the "low green of water" by the river's bank. It is "the last day but one before world war," and he is conscious of the water's running, "quietly carving / red rocks," and of time's passage which in retrospect will soon reveal a cataclysm of violence and death. Nearby Mary Sheffield sings, "sustained in the poured forms of live oaks / taking root." Both she and her song belong to nature: "When the slight wind dies / each leaf still has two places / such music touched alive." Her singing suddenly, intimately, involves the physical world: "all things spread sail sounds gather / on blunt stone streaming white / E minor gently running." Discovering himself involved with her, "loving Mary Sheffield / for her chord changes," the speaker figuratively joins with her by sitting down in the river. His transformation happens quickly; he is freed from time: "anywhere water flows the breastplate of time / rusts off me sounds green forms low voice / new music long long / past." Mary Sheffield's singing becomes the means by which the narrator achieves a heightened understanding of the unchanging processes inherent in the natural world.

Dickey's idealization of Woman does not ignore the reality lived by mortal females. Behind the archetype, he declares, are "real women, giving to the ideal the substance it requires from the lived world, and serving to make more powerful and imperious those all-powerful creatures of the depths of our being, the slaves of our needs who enslave us" (*Night Hurdling* 217). That "lived world," however, is not only one dominated by unrealizable male expectations but also by death and suffering. Both **"The Leap"** and **"The Scarred Girl"** reflect Dickey's awareness that "taking on the mortal and identifying flesh without which all ideals die" (*Night Hurdling* 217) necessitates confronting finitude. First published in *Poems 1957-1967* (1967), **"The Leap"** concerns a woman who "married a man whom she didn't get along with, had his children, and eventually committed suicide because of it" (*Self-Interviews* 172). Obviously affected by what he states was an actual situation, Dickey uses her suicide to suggest a previous leap in the seventh grade, "when boys were beginning / To be as big as the girls." Then, Jane MacNaughton before a dance jumped up and "touched the end / Of one of the paper-ring decorations / To see if she could reach it. She could." Now, years later, having seen pictured in the paper the body of Jane MacNaughton Hill on the top of a taxi, "lying cradled / In that papery steel as though lying in the grass," the speaker realizes she has "reached me now as well." Caught and betrayed by "some boy who did not

depend / On speed of foot," the speaker's classmate has reached through the years with "her light, earth-spurning feet" to show him at last the nature of relationships, what Dickey himself calls "the results of her being a woman" (*Self-Interviews* 172). Humbled by the fact that "My feet are nailed to the ground," the narrator, now with larger understanding, knows "Whatever it proves when you leap / In a new dress, a new womanhood, among the boys." The poem, while it idealizes a woman, also displays an awareness of the reality of an ephemeral world.

Similarly, **"The Scarred Girl,"** published in *New Yorker* in 1963, reflects Dickey's awareness of what being a woman means, in this instance this culture's worship of physical beauty. Interpreting an incident that happened while he attended North Fulton High School, Dickey depicts "a girl who was the prettiest girl in Atlanta, by far. She was not pretty in a sexy way, but she had a Madonna-like beauty" (*Self-Interviews* 130). In an automobile accident her face shattered the windshield and, despite years of plastic surgery, "She never looked anything like she had before" (*Self-Interviews* 131). In the poem the girl worries that "the bright, fractured world," momentarily whole before her face breaks the glass, now "Burns and pulls and weeps / To come together again." She desires to have "The pastures of earth and heaven / Restored and undamaged, the cattle / Risen out of their jagged graves / To walk in the seamless sunlight / And a newborn countenance / Put upon everything." Her selflessness and her inner, spiritual beauty elevate her and provide the narrator with a new knowledge of what womanhood should be. In his explanation of the poem, Dickey declares: "I had been reading in Plato about the Good, the True, and the Beautiful. This girl was true—although she seemed almost too good to be true—and good and beautiful she surely had been. It struck me that when a woman who is only beautiful loses her beauty through an accident or through age, she has had literally everything taken away from her. But she had this marvelous resource of being good, too. So . . . as I say at the end of the poem, that is now 'the only way'" (*Self-Interviews* 131). With "good no nearer, but plainly / In sight," the girl with her final transfiguration assumes the transcendent quality of Campbell's Queen Goddess.

Dickey's concern with relationships, manifested in such otherwise unrelated works as **"In the Treehouse at Night"** and **"Hunting Civil War Relics at Nimblewill Creek,"** also appears in poems focusing specifically on men and women, among them **"Adultery"** and **"The Fiend."** Incautious critics have particularly attacked these latter poems, which sexually idealize women. Commenting on **"Adultery,"** which was published in *Nation* in 1966, Dickey writes: "As I get older I write more and more about sex. Adultery seems to me to be the most potentially beautiful and fruitful relationship between men and women, and also the most calamitous and destructive. . . . Not love with responsibility, but love without responsibility; just sex and being together like it is in the movies and in the popular songs of the forties where it's all lovely and there are no troubles connected with it. This is not an unworthy ideal, nor is it contemptible. It can result in some bad human situations and has, doubtless, many times, and will again. But if you are willing to pay the price of anxiety and possible disgrace, an adulterous situation is frequently, for a very short period of time, absolutely glorious" (*Self-Interviews* 166). Calhoun and Hill blatantly declare: "Although '**Adultery**' makes an effort to portray evenhandedly the anxious passions of the man and the woman, [it is] powerfully male-dominant" (32). While told from the male perspective, however, the poem neither celebrates nor condemns adultery. Rather it shows its human dimension, the fact that "Gigantic forepleasure lives / Among such scenes, and we are alone with it," that "we would not give / It up, for death is beaten," and that "Guilt is magical." Dickey's intent centers on the momentary enhancement of the act for both the man and the woman, not on its ethics. The poem manifests his belief that even in an illicit affair, the nature of which is usually transitory, women become elevated to a status that renders them life-enhancing. Dickey's narrator recognizes that despite his guilt, he will not end the relationship because "One could never die here." While the male voice dominates, it is the woman's unspoken presence that informs the poem, rendering the speaker more conscious of himself, the setting, and others.

Regarding "**The Fiend,**" first published in the *Partisan Review* in 1965, Dickey observes: "I think the idealization of women is indigenous to men. There are various ways of idealizing women, especially sexually, based in almost every case on their inaccessibility. . . . But when a woman functions as an unobtainable love object, then she takes on a mythological quality" (*Self-Interviews* 153). Exploring a deviant aspect of the male tendency to view a woman as transcendent, the poem depicts a voyeur who climbs a tree by an apartment house to watch secretly while a woman undresses and then showers. It suggests that, continually frustrated at not being able to behold her, the voyeur will eventually enter her room and knife her to death. Commenting on the fiend himself, Dickey asserts: "It's important to the voyeur to have an invisibility that enables him to function in kind of a God-like way, as though he could be present at any scene, sexually or otherwise, that he wished to be present at" (*Self-Interviews* 153). Dickey's poetic intent also included the idea "that women, with their great hunger to be idealized, might feel something of this extreme, concentrated idealism coming in from the night where the voyeur in the tree would be having his transports of ecstasy. The woman would feel that she was on a kind of stage, and it would be a wonderful sexual experience for her. Because she's not being just looked at; she's being *beheld,* which is different" (*Self-Interviews* 154). Specifically, "**The Fiend**" examines the positions of power from which men and women view each other: the ability or need of the former to control events, whom he sees and when, while maintaining invisibly "some all-seeing eye / Of God"; and the desire of the latter to demand that attention, to stand and "move like a saint," "Uncontrollable," a "blaze of uncompromised being." The poem should not be viewed principally, as Calhoun and Hill do, for its "ability to teeter on the brink of perversity and yet hold balance enough to maintain readers' interest and empathy" (71). The woman becomes Campbell's Queen Goddess whose "movement can restore the green eyes / Of middle age looking renewed." That Dickey's concerns are inaccessibility, idealization, and fantasy, and not sexual degradation, are shown not only by the poem's title but also by his statement that "I'm fighting very hard, as I think everybody else ought to be fighting, against the notion of sex as mere meat" (*Self-Interviews* 168).

Two other early poems, "**The Earth Drum**" and "**A Morning,**" both unpublished, illustrate that Dickey's portrayal of women should almost always be viewed within the larger context of myth and myth-making: the idealization of mortal females into an archetype and the hero's subsequent view that the woman, symbol of life and source of the hero's power, finally "falls" because her own flesh, her own desires, condemn her as unworthy. Written in the late 1940s after Dickey had graduated from Vanderbilt and was teaching at Rice University in Houston, Texas, "**The Earth Drum**" is clearly an apprentice work. It depicts the marriage ceremony of an unnamed protagonist, seemingly Tarzan, to a woman who "solely merits gleam / Glenned and mooned." As Dickey searched for a technique and style to deliver best certain aspects of myth, his language sometimes became imitative and inflated, even abstract, but it nevertheless retained the influence of his readings in mythology and anthropology. Exhorting the animals to "Rise ever . . . to his carnal coming," the speaker urges that they "warp him to the ritual where / Lyricks on diamond joints beyond his muddy thumbing / The chaste and frost-cut queller." With his "unsubtle, shagged and plexus-dweller / Brow," Tarzan approaches the one who "curvets the void / Bequeathed by the latest girl his hands misplace / Upon bedevilled dark." Here the woman promises an understanding presently beyond the "Evangel anthropoid" because previous incarnations of the Queen Goddess have failed to sustain him.

Focusing on the hero's enlightenment as a consequence of the woman's inability, finally, to maintain her ideality, "**A Morning,**" presently in the Washington University Special Collections, presents a speaker who is walking on the beach and whose nearby dog "surroundingly howls." The dog senses change and reacts to it: "Painfully he is changing / His voice from a voice for the moon / To the voice he has for the sun." The sun's more glaring reality implies that for the man new knowledge has come reluctantly, a lessening of possibilities inherent in the moon's more suggestive light. The speaker reaches into the water and picks up "a piece of the sea / To feel how a tall girl has swum / Yesterday in it too deeply." Because she was "below the light," the woman has become "More naked than Eve in the Garden." The speaker's physical connection to and emotional participation with the sea links him again to this lost woman such that his "hands are shining with fever." Yet the memory of the girl and the knowledge she has brought him provide the speaker with an understanding of what change means. He realizes the "long, changing word of the dog" and "the pain when the sun came up / For the first time on angel-shut gates / In its rays set closer than teeth." The poem does not specify the nature of the narrator's relationship to the woman or what actually happened to her, whether she drowned or whether her death was figurative. Rather, **"A Morning"** presents Dickey's imaginative attempt to understand an archetypal situation in which the hero's fulfillment requires the loss of the woman.

This idealization of mortal women pervades Dickey's early poetry and noticeably appears in all his volumes, including *Puella* (1982), his full statement on this theme. The book's pointed epigraph, T. Sturge Moore's lines, "I lived in thee, and dreamed, and waked / Twice what I had been," suggests Dickey's continuing belief in Woman as a source of life-enhancing possibilities. More important, however, *Puella* attempts to present Deborah's girlhood "male-imagined." Taken together, the poems trace her maturation and reveal her heightened consciousness of the world, including her kinship with the elements of fire, air, earth, and water, and her growing knowledge of human relationships. The first-person point of view, in lyric poems that only in composite yield any real sense of "story," along with a technique that offers reality through simultaneous, intuited images or associations, gives the book a psychological depth and richness not derived from Dickey's previous narrative methods.

The involved technique is important, for the images Deborah conveys evoke an emotional complex inherent in certain narrative points in time that increasingly seem timeless, that is to say, mythical, presenting the simultaneous penetration of worlds—male and female, present and past, transcendent and physical. Deborah understands, as she reflects in **"The Lyric Beasts,"** that Woman is "a body out-believing existence: / The shining of perfection, the myth-chill" and that "One form may live from another." She enjoins the men who "witness" her to "Rise and on faith / Follow. It is better that I should be; / Be what I am not, and I am." Given the reality of mortal men and women, Deborah knows that "Controlled, illusory fire is best / For us." In the imaginations of men, who are "Young outriders of the Absolute," she is "hurled and buried." Yet if men require idealized women, mortal females also need men to achieve completion, for Deborah in **"The Lode"** recognizes her inherent inadequacy: "Teach me / And learn me, wanderer: every man-jack rain-soaked and vital / To the bone." Male sexual potency releases her yet confirms her own heightened role. She thinks in **"Deborah in Mountain Sound: Bell, Glacier, Rose"**: "With one glance, one instant / Crystallization / Of an eyelash she is set, the mason's rose / Of ice sculpture in her fist, / Her image flash-frozen, unmerited / And radiant in the making-fluid of men." At the end of *Puella,* having undergone a series of transfigurations, Deborah finally becomes the Surround, and "With half of my first child, / With invention unending," she achieves mythic dimensions, a creature more her creation than that of men. The book's concluding

poem, **"Summons,"** using an italicized refrain reminiscent of Dickey's earliest works, offers her vision both of herself and her world and a pronouncement whose utter simplicity suggests intuitive knowledge: "*Have someone be nearing.*"

In his early notebooks written almost forty years ago, Dickey declares: "It is the task of poetry to find and articulate the archetypal individual (or, possibly, racial) vision, examine it, determine (or arrive at a tentative, or even assign one) its meaning, + make this meaning available." His poetry has done just that, presenting the inherent male tendency to mythologize Woman, to render her transcendent, the source of possibility and the means through which he fully realizes his potential in a world whose larger mysteries have been revealed. Only by means of the Queen Goddess can the mythic hero finally complete his rites of passage.

Notes

1. I am indebted to Professor Calhoun Winton of the University of Maryland and Professor Joyce Pair, editor of the *James Dickey Newsletter,* for making a copy of "The Earth Drum" known and accessible. Professor Winton states Dickey gave him sometime during or shortly before 1949. "A Morning" presently resides in Washington University Special Collections.

2. The unpublished early notebooks are on deposit at the South Caroliniana Library of the University of South Carolina. Access is restricted. Material from James Dickey's notebooks may not be reprinted without his permission.

Works Cited

Baughman, Ronald. *Understanding James Dickey.* Columbia, SC.: U of South Carolina P, 1985.

Calhoun, Richard J., and Robert W. Hill. *James Dickey.* Boston: Twayne, 1983.

Campbell, Joseph. *The Hero With a Thousand Faces.* Princeton: Princeton UP, 1968.

Dickey, James. *Drowning With Others.* Middletown, CT: Wesleyan University Press, 1962.

———. *Night Hurdling.* Columbia, SC and Bloomfield Hills, MI: Bruccoli Clark, 1983.

———. *Poems 1957-1967.* Middletown, CT: Wesleyan University Press, 1967.

———. *Puella.* Garden City, NY: Doubleday, 1982.

———. *Self-Interviews.* Ed. Barbara and James Reiss. Garden City, NY: Doubleday, 1970.

———. *Sorties.* Baton Rouge: LSU Press, 1982.

Frazer, Sir James George. *The Golden Bough.* 1 Vol. Abridged Edition. New York: Macmillan, 1951.

Kirschten, Robert. *James Dickey and the Gentle Ecstasy of Earth: A Reading of the Poems.* Baton Rouge: Lousiana State UP, 1988.

Richard Tillinghast (review date 1992)

SOURCE: Tillinghast, Richard. "James Dickey: The Whole Motion." *Southern Review* 28, no. 4 (autumn 1992): 971-80.

[*In the following review, Tillinghast provides a laudatory overview of Dickey's poetic career.*]

The publication this summer of James Dickey's *The Whole Motion* finally makes available under one cover the poems he has published during a career that has spanned more than four decades. The extravagant imagination of the man who has given us such titles as *The Eye-Beaters, Blood, Victory, Madness, Buckhead and Mercy* couldn't be content with something as drab as "collected poems," though the book's subtitle identifies it as such. Dickey came of age during a cultural moment when poets' reputations were often founded as much on the excesses of their personal lives as on the quality of their work. When one surveys the lives of Robert Lowell, Sylvia Plath, John Berryman, Allen Ginsberg, Randall Jarrell, Elizabeth Bishop, Theodore Roethke, and Anne Sexton, one gets the impression that mid-century American poetry somehow, with great difficulty, managed to get written between gin-fueled one-night stands in motel rooms and recovery periods in mental hospitals and drying-out spas, in an atmosphere of extreme emotional and mental states and strikingly unconventional behavior.

In the lifestyle arena, James Dickey has not disappointed. Stories about the man have become a thriving perennial in the field of literary gossip. I could without straining my memory probably tell you a dozen of these stories—most of them really funny, and many of them bearing at least some relation to the truth—and so, I imagine, could many readers of this review. But his lifestyle is not the only reason Dickey has become the most visible southern writer of his day. His interests in the backcountry survivalist movement, in whitewater canoeing, and in bow hunting have dovetailed with regional and national rediscovery of the wilderness.

The enormously popular movie made from his novel *Deliverance* made Dickey visible to all sorts of people who don't read contemporary poetry—as well as to people who don't read much of anything other than *People* magazine, Stephen King, and *TV Guide*. When Jimmy Carter, a president who in retrospect looks better and better all the time, chose his fellow Georgian to deliver a poem at his inauguration, Dickey took on the ceremonial role in Washington that Robert Frost played in John F. Kennedy's presidency. By the mid-seventies Dickey had become so much of a legend that we tended to forget he was, before

anything else, a superb and stunningly original poet. Few poets who began writing in the sixties—certainly few southern poets—can credibly claim not to have been influenced by James Dickey. I gladly include myself as someone who has read, loved, and probably unconsciously imitated his poetry ever since I came under its spell over thirty years ago.

A delightful and unexpected feature of *The Whole Motion* is the inclusion of almost fifty pages of uncollected poetry written before Dickey's first book, *Into the Stone.* Here we see a less flamboyant poet than the one we would come to know later, but the general outlines of his style and his ruling preoccupations are already recognizable. One of these early poems, **"The Sprinter at Forty,"** introduces a figure Dickey would return to throughout his work: the over-the-hill athlete. Sports, competitive sports in particular, are emblematic of life and youth for this poet who has often spoken proudly of his college football days at Clemson University, and has written about them notably in **"The Bee"** from *Falling, May Day Sermon, and Other Poems.* In **"The Sprinter at Forty,"** the speaker states, "I receive the wish to live more / Which nothing but motion can answer" (a formulation that resonates with the word "motion" in the title of the entire collection). In an intellectual climate where football has been thought of as a "proto-fascist" activity, Dickey's identification with the sport has allowed him to put his finger on the pulse of our culture, because the competitive athlete is the American male's favorite fantasy hero. Dickey turns the superannuated athlete into a quintessentially American figure of pathos.

Yet Dickey avoids glorifying the athlete, presenting him instead as put-upon, often injured, under attack, as in **"In the Pocket,"** subtitled "NFL", from *Eye-Beaters*: "hit move scramble," goes the quarterback's interior monologue, "Before death and the ground / Come up LEAP STAND KILL DIE STRIKE / Now." **"For the Death of Lombardi,"** from *The Strength of Fields,* shows how fully—in contrast to other poets, some of whom have tended to detach themselves from commercialized American culture—Dickey has operated within that culture. He has provided a point of intersection for the hero and the victim, one whose voice often enough is the American football fan's. Speaking for them, "those who entered the bodies / of Bart Starr, Donny Anderson, Ray Nitschke, Jerry Kramer / Through the snowing tube on Sunday afternoon," Dickey mourns the Green Bay Packers' legendary coach:

> . . . We stand here among
> Discarded TV commercials:
> Among beer-cans and razor-blades and hair-tonic bottles,
> Stinking with male deodorants: we stand here
> Among teeth and filthy miles
> Of unwound tapes, novocaine needles, contracts, champagne
> Mixed with shower-water, unraveling elastic, bloody faceguards . . .

In *The Eagle's Mile,* Dickey's most recent book, the celebration of **"False Youth"** is replayed in an overblown Whitmanian romp called **"The Olympian,"** where, after an afternoon spent drinking Olympia beer, Dickey spoofs his own fantasy, imagining a race between himself, in his "hilarious, pizza-fed fury," and an Olympic champion:

> . . . O hot, just hurdlable
> gates
>   Of deck-chairs! Lounges! A measured universe
> Of exhilarating laws! Here I had come   there I'd
> gone
>   Laying it down confusing, staggering
>   The fast lane and the slow, on and over
> And over recliners, sun-cots, cleaning-poles and
> beach-balls . . .

In his early poems Dickey did not throw himself into the seductive punch bowl of contemporary American culture. He lived and wrote at one remove from all that, in the world of his own vision. In the very first poem in the collection, **"The Baggage King,"** where the pile of soldiers' luggage on an island in the Pacific rises "Like the hill of a dead king," Dickey's predisposition to see experience in terms of ritual announces itself. The mythic dimension in his poetry has always exercised a strong attraction for me, and it shows both his continuity with and his break from older poets such as T. S. Eliot and Allen Tate and even poets closer to his own age such as Robert Lowell. These poets were drawn explicitly to religious conversion, and tried to adumbrate their sense of larger significances behind everyday events by reference to classical mythology. Their evocations of the Greek and Roman myths could take the form, in Donald Hall's parodic account of the period, "of long poems in iambics called 'Herakles: A Double Sestina'"; or they could be subtle and exquisite, as in the last two quatrains of John Crowe Ransom's "Vision by Sweetwater":

> Let them alone, dear Aunt, just for one minute
> Till I go fishing in the dark of my mind:
> Where have I seen before, against the wind,
> These bright virgins, robed and bare of bonnet,
>
> Flowing with music of their strange quick tongue
> And adventuring with delicate paces by the stream,—
> Myself a child, old suddenly at the scream
> From one of the white throats it hid among?

The early Dickey has more in common with Ransom than meets the eye—especially since the similarities of vision are obscured by strong differences not only of diction and versification, but of intent. (Ransom was, by the way, a Cleveland Browns fan, but a poem by him on professional football is unthinkable.) Dickey has never wanted to write just for the highly educated elite whom Ransom appealed to, but for the mass American audience.

But the personal myths of which I was speaking came to Dickey, it would seem, either from reading about pantheistic religions and fertility cults or simply from an intuitive sense of how well their way of seeing things triggered his own imagination. Watching the movie *Black Robe* recently, I was reminded by a simplified description of the Algonquian version of the afterlife—"At night in the woods the souls of dead people hunt the souls of dead animals"—of Dickey's **"Heaven of the Animals,"** where not human hunters but animals hunt other animals: "These hunt, as they have done, / But with claws and teeth grown perfect, // More deadly than they can believe." Dickey's treatment of the fate of the victims might suggest a certain callousness toward others' pain, but I think it is more accurately seen as a mystical view of the world wherein predation and suffering are subsumed within an all-inclusive unity, where:

> . . . those that are hunted
> Know this as their life,
> Their reward: to walk
>
> Under such trees in full knowledge
> Of what is in glory above them,
> And to feel no fear,
> But acceptance, compliance.
> Fulfilling themselves without pain
>
> At the cycle's center . . .

"The Owl King," one of the first Dickey poems I read, sublimates the predatory instinct in a similar way: "I felt the hooked tufts on my head / Enlarge, and dream like a crown." Here Dickey may be very close to intuiting how the raw power of feudal overlords became ritualized into the institution of kingship.

The Owl King must have represented at the same time a version of himself. I first met Dickey at the home of Monroe and Betty Spears in Sewanee, Tennessee, in about 1960, roughly the time this poem would have been written. Spears, who introduced me to modern poetry at Sewanee, was the professor at Vanderbilt whom Dickey credits with firing his enthusiasm for poetry when he entered graduate school after being discharged from the Air Force after World War II. In 1960 Dickey was still writing advertising copy in Atlanta for Coca-Cola—selling his soul to the devil by day, as he liked to put it, and buying it back at night by writing at the kitchen table of his suburban house, inventing himself as a poet. I can picture him there: "I in the innermost shining / Of my blazing, invented eyes." In **"The Vegetable King,"** from *Into the Stone,* the poet explicitly becomes a king—the king of fertility cults, who dies with the dying year to be reborn with the spring. Here, "From my house and my silent folk / I step, and lay me in ritual down," the poet writes, "One night each April." He wills himself into ritual death and renewal, "And begin to believe a dream / I never once have had / Of being part of the acclaimed rebirth / Of the ruined, calm world, in spring . . ."

Many of the poems from this period celebrate the act of willed possession, wherein the self is overtaken by the dream of kingship seen in **"The Vegetable King,"** or where the blind child in **"The Owl King"** from *Drowning* *with Others* receives his summons, delivered in the incantatory three- and four-beat anapestic line that Dickey wrote so beautifully in his early books:

> Through the trees, with the moon underfoot,
> More soft than I can, I call.
> I hear the king of the owls sing
> Where he moves with my son in the gloom.
> My tongue floats off in the darkness . . .

This call, this summons to a transformed reality, is always, in addition to whatever else it might be, the poem's summons, the siren song of the Muse or White Goddess. Dickey makes it quite clear that the call to poetic ecstasy, like the annunciation of kingship in the fertility rite, brings with it the threat of extinction, just as the Vegetable King, returning to his wife and family, "bears you home / Magnificent pardon" but also "dread, impending crime." **"A Dog Sleeping on My Feet,"** from *Drowning with Others,* recounts the summons specifically in terms of possession by the poem, and in an image of the crucifixion and a glancing echo of the rhetoric of the King James Bible ("Marvelous is the pursuit"), evokes the psychic peril of inspiration:

> The poem is beginning to move
> Up through my pine-prickling legs
> Out of the night wood,
>
> Taking hold of the pen by my fingers.
> Before me the fox floats lightly,
> On fire with his holy scent.
> All, all are running.
> Marvelous is the pursuit,
> Like a dazzle of nails through the ankles . . .

It may be that Dickey's greatest work still lay ahead of him at this point, but I wonder if he ever again achieved the exquisite purity, the Botticelli-like sense of sanctity, of the poems he wrote in the late-night isolation of the Atlanta suburbs.

The inclusion of the uncollected early poems makes clear how essential this kind of psychic self-immolation (I feel uncomfortable with my own ponderous language here, but it's hard to put it more simply) was to Dickey in the early days. **"Drifting,"** a marvelous poem I had never seen before, dramatizes the process of leaving the self behind—using a metaphor perhaps borrowed from Rimbaud's "*Le Bateau Ivre*":

> It is worth it to get
> Down there under the seats, stretched believingly out
> With your feet together,
> Thinking of nothing but the smell of bait and the sky
> And the bow coming
> To a point and the stern squared off until doomsday.

The metaphor may be Rimbaud's, but the details are very southern, with the idiomatic overkill of prepositions in "get / Down there under the seats" and the grandeur of the viewed sky undermined by the "smell of bait." Rimbaud in a bass boat!

If you can imagine this poem in the *oeuvre* of one of his contemporaries—Sylvia Plath, John Berryman, or Anne Sexton, to construct an implausible "for instance"—then this voyage would suggest suicide:

> Once in a lifetime a man must empty his pockets
>   On the bank of a river,
> Take out two monogrammed handkerchiefs and tie
>   them
>
>   To the oars stuck in the sand:
> These mark the edge of the known . . .

This represents no death wish, however, but rather the poet's wish to leave his personality behind, and to float as Keats does—"Not charioted by Bacchus and his pards, / But on the viewless wings of Poesy."

If one thinks of Dickey's suburban pastoral as an idyll he entered gladly, gratefully, after the war, still the war continued to haunt him—a process that is especially clear in *Helmets* (1964). In the poem **"Drinking from a Helmet,"** the GI poet, by drinking from the helmet of a man he imagines to have been killed, takes on that man's identity: "I stood as though I possessed / A cool, trembling man / Exactly my size, swallowed whole." This is an image of the warrior who must go back to his peace-time world and live the life of the civilian, all the time carrying within him the man who has fought, has managed to avoid being killed, has himself perhaps killed.

In *Buckdancer's Choice,* winner of the National Book Award in 1965 and the third of the astonishing trio of books that began in 1962 with *Drowning with Others,* Dickey addressed the dilemma of the returned warrior in one of his most controversial poems, eight pages long, **"The Firebombing."** The speaker in the poem, a comfortable yet uneasy suburbanite, tries in the midst of a typical middle-class life spent paying bills, mowing the lawn, and fretting about his receding hairline to come to terms with his experiences as a fighter pilot who carried out "anti-morale" napalm bombing runs against Japanese civilian targets. Memories of the firebombings intrude themselves just at the edges of quotidian concerns, cropping up as "fire" in the word "firewood" does in a broken line in this passage that describes his suburban home: "Where the lawn mower rests on its laurels"—the clichéd wording hinting at its owner's less than acute state of mind:

> Where the diet exists
> For my own good   where I try to drop
> Twenty years, eating figs in the pantry
> Blinded by each and all
> Of the eye-catching cans that gladly have caught my
>   wife's eye
> Until I cannot say
> Where the screwdriver is where the children
> Get off the bus where the fly
> Hones his front legs   where the hammock folds
> Its erotic daydreams   where the Sunday
> School text for the day has been put   where the fire
> Wood is   where the payments

For everything under the sun
Pile peacefully up . . .

In 1967 Robert Bly, speaking from the pulpit of his influential magazine, *The Sixties,* castigated the poem in a vitriolic essay called "The Collapse of James Dickey." His main contention was that "'**Firebombing**'" (note how leaving "The" out of the title changes its meaning) "makes no real criticism of the American habit of firebombing Asians." Bly was demanding that the poem's subject should be not the ambivalence felt by one particular pilot toward his own actions, but rather that the poem should become a kind of editorial against all American military action in Asia, with the premise that the war in the South Pacific against the Japanese was identical to the war against North Vietnam. Dickey once wrote that we live "in the age of the moral putdown," and after attacks like Bly's, he was in a position to know. In abandoning any notion of aesthetic evaluation of poetry and insisting it become propaganda for the critic's political beliefs, Bly was ahead of his time—since his approach has become dogma among the Politically Correct theorists who now dominate academia. Bly condemns the poem because it displays "no real anguish. If the anguish were real, we would feel terrible remorse as we read, we would stop what we were doing, we would break the television set with an ax, we would throw ourselves on the ground sobbing."

I have addressed myself mainly to poems from the first part of Dickey's *Whole Motion*—the first 240 pages of a 475-page collection—because these are the poems that speak to me most strongly. While writing this piece I have reached for my original Wesleyan Poetry Series paperbacks of *Drowning with Others, Helmets,* and *Buckdancer's Choice* to remind me of the sense of discovery I got reading these books almost thirty years ago. Even the atrocious cover art of these books bespeaks an awkward sincerity, reminiscent of Baptist Sunday School teachers' instruction manuals. I have never been as enthusiastic about Dickey's work from *Falling, May Day Sermon, and Other Poems* on. In his introduction to *Falling, May Day Sermon, and Other Poems,* Dickey writes of designing "an on-end block or wall of words, solid or almost solid, black with massed ink, through which a little light from behind would come at intermittent places." And that for me is part of the problem. The wall of words, like the famous "wall of sound" introduced into Top 40 music by Phil Spector, seems to sacrifice some of the quieter, more subtle effects Dickey achieved in his earlier writings.

In poems like "**Falling,**" Dickey tries to imitate a motion whose sweep outruns the ability of his language to keep up with it. "**The Sheep Child,**" one of his most notorious (I use the word in its original, not its *People* magazine sense) poems, narrated by a dead half-human, half-sheep fetus pickled in alcohol in a museum in Atlanta, strikes me as southern grotesquerie gone over the limit. "**Adultery,**" on the other hand, dares to treat the same fine line between originality and questionable taste (or am I sounding like Robert Bly?); yet it succeeds, because one thing that

Dickey is not is a hypocrite. "**Encounter in the Cage Country**" continues this remarkable poet's intuitive interaction with the natural world, but I prefer the poems where Dickey goes out to meet the animals on their own turf, not in the London Zoo. Maybe I heard too many sermons when I was a boy, but I flip the pages of "**May Day Sermon to the Women of Gilmer County, Georgia, by a Woman Preacher Leaving the Baptist Church**" just as I flip my car radio dial past the Sunday morning sermons. *The Zodiac* may capture with perfect verisimilitude the drunken ravings of a poet with an unusual imagination; but I've been there myself sufficiently often to know that a little drunken raving goes a long way.

Having said that, and not having even ventured a glance in the direction of Dickey's achievements as a literary critic and novelist, I think there are many fine things in the later parts of *The Whole Motion.* Dickey's elegy for Vince Lombardi I have already cited. "**The Rain Guitar**" from *The Strength of Fields,* where Dickey sits in the rain by an English stream near Winchester Cathedral playing the guitar (he is of course a virtuoso picker) while an Englishman with a wooden leg casts for trout, is as tight, as inspired, as jaunty as anything he has ever written. The poem ends:

> I was Air Force,
> I said. So was I; I picked
> This up in Burma, he said, tapping his gone leg
> With his fly rod, as Burma and the South
> west Pacific and North Georgia reeled,
> Rapped, cast, chimed, darkened and drew down
> Cathedral water, and improved.

The reeling (of the fly reel, and the reel Dickey is playing on the guitar), the rapping (on the wooden leg, as well as the word in its sixties sense), the chiming (of the two men's war experiences, along with the Cathedral bells) synchronize magically.

"A good poet," Randall Jarrell wrote in a much-quoted passage on Wallace Stevens from *Poetry and the Age,* "is someone who manages, in a lifetime of standing out in thunderstorms, to be struck by lightning five or six times; a dozen or two dozen times and he is a great." Less often quoted is the way the paragraph begins: "Some of my readers may feel about all this [Jarrell's remarks on Stevens' *Auroras of Autumn*] . . . 'Shouldn't the Mature poet be producing late masterpieces even better than the early ones?'. . . . All such questions show how necessary it is to think of the poet as somebody who has prepared himself to be visited by a daemon, as a sort of accident-prone worker to whom poems happen. . . ." Dickey is, in this sense, surpassingly, sublimely accident-prone. May he continue to stand out in thunderstorms, wearing his famous denim jacket with the eagle embroidered on it, so that we, like the barbershop rednecks in "**False Youth: Autumn: Clothes of the Age,**" can:

> get a lifetime look at my bird's
> One word, raggedly blazing with extinction and soar-
> ing loose

In red threads burning up white until I am shot in
the back

Through my wings   or ripped apart
For rags:

Poetry

Gordon Van Ness (essay date 1992)

SOURCE: Van Ness, Gordon. "The Children's Poetry." In
*Outbelieving Existence: The Measured Motion of James
Dickey,* pp. 71-74. Columbia, SC: Camden House, 1992.

[*In the following essay, Van Ness summarizes the critical
reception of Dickey's two volumes of children's poetry.*]

Dickey's two children's books, *Tucky the Hunter* (1978)
and *Bronwen, the Traw, and the Shape-Shifter* (1986),
have received almost no critical study, perhaps because he
has devoted so little published effort in this regard
compared to other major twentieth-century poets like Randall Jarrell and Anne Sexton. Reviews are sparse, mostly
superficial, and generally mixed. Both books concern the
exploits of a family member, the former involving
Dickey's grandson, James Bayard Tuckerman Dickey, and
the latter, his daughter Bronwen Elaine. In addition, both
works mythologize the adventure the protagonist undergoes, a larger-than-life confrontation with real or imagined
creatures.

Good children's poetry possesses a singing quality, a
melody and motion. If the poem is mysterious, meditative,
or nostalgic, the lines move slowly and the words become
subtle. Language is exact and descriptive as well as
sensory and connotative. While such poetry displays a
strong emotional resonance, its foundation lies in ideas;
therefore, it also appeals to the intellect, often taking
everyday facts of life and giving them new meaning or
showing the strange and extraordinary as safe and even
life-enhancing. Whatever the experience presented, it must
exhibit an arresting significance. Illustrations are not only
comprehensible but also evoke emotional identification, allowing for the large exercise of the reader's imagination
and an intense personal response. Like the text, they
provide a vital, wholesome perspective by which to
understand life. Taken together, words and pictures
constitute an integrated, complex work of visual art, with
each aspect creating conditions of dependence and
interdependence. The text and the illustrations cohere and
complement one another such that the book's format and
layout are, finally, an aesthetic, psychological, and intellectual consideration.

Tucky the Hunter and *Bronwen, the Traw, and the
Shape-Shifter* exhibit certain of these qualities, but each is
flawed. *Bronwen,* which Dickey labels "A Poem in Four
Parts," is the more complex in character and plot, the
more dramatic, and the more likely to intrigue both adults
and children. However, while the black-and-white draw-

ings by Richard Jesse Watson are intricately detailed, they
not so much complement the poem as establish a counter-
claim to the reader's interest. By contrast, the pastel
sketches by Marie Angel in *Tucky the Hunter* more
delicately cohere with the text rather than confront it, but
the plot is simple and the protagonist's adventure mostly
static. With both books, reviewers failed to offer substan-
tive analysis, their commentary often revealing only the
most general knowledge of Dickey's poetic themes. Logue
(1979), for instance, declares that *Tucky the Hunter*
celebrates the imagination of Dickey's grandson, his "oneness with the animal kingdom and his popgun" (68), as he
hunts and shoots in his bed the world's wild creatures.
Angel's paintings thoroughly detail the natural world, and
the collaboration of poem and paintings seems "arrested in
mid-flight of fantasy" (68). Johnston (1978) considers the
work another successful example of Dickey's collaborative efforts with visual artists, which has produced such
books as *Jericho: The South Beheld* (1974) and *God's Images* (1977). The rhymes "trip along drolly" (88), and the
water colors display "imagination and sensitivity" (88).
Kirkus Reviews (1978) provides the most condemnatory
overview, calling the verses "forgettable" (917). Unlike
other critics, the reviewer compares *Tucky* with works by
authors of noted children's literature, including Maurice
Sendak and A. A. Milne. Dickey's subject is "suburban
nighttime exploits" (917), but the book lacks Sendak's
poise and the conclusion is too obvious and reassuring.
Tucky is "kind of slippery for children, too slight for
adults" (917). Angel's delicate illustrations, while striking,
overwhelm the meager text, which, unlike Milne, is
"mismatched to the mock-serious tone of the poem" (917).
In their later bio-critical study, Calhoun and Hill (1983)
discern familiar Dickey themes of hunting and a spiritual
exchange with nature, citing the line, "They sang in mystic
double-tongue, the tongue of man and beast." Also evident
from Dickey's mature poetry is the presence of the
suburbs. Because *Tucky the Hunter* offers nothing poetically innovative, Calhoun and Hill declare only that the
book "seems to work" (101) with its limitations, but they
neither analyze these themes nor attempt to compare their
use with the mature poems.

Skinner (1979) remains the only critical essay focusing on
Dickey's first children's book, though its brevity is indicative of the academic response to Dickey's efforts in this
area. Tucky matures as a result of his experiences, which
includes imaginary visits not only to places like Alaska,
the Philippines, and Africa, but also to "the suburbs of the
sun" and "the suburbs of Venus and of Mars." When
Susan, Tucky's mother, comes to check on her sleeping
son, he gives her the song of the meadow lark, his hunting
trophy, so that she, too, participates in his adventure. The
poem's "fun" (56) derives from Dickey's ability to merge
into the narrative delightful sounds with periodic nonsense.
Endeavoring to involve the reader, he also includes
suspense: "Tucky hunted EVERYTHING / but I hope not
YOU and ME!" The music, set by quatrains with an *abcb*
rhyme scheme, enhances the text. Yet because each
quatrain consists of two separate couplets, the poem's

pace speeds up, and the rhymes become expected. Most of the first and third lines have four accented syllables; the second and fourth, three. Alliterative phrases like "At Samarkand the whirling stars all whistle wild and pale" and "he slew it for its song" contribute to the poem's musical quality. Additionally, Skinner notes Dickey's use of onomatopoeia ("snapping wolverine" and "bumbling Kodiak") and his vivid verbs that render improbable events both realistic and musically pleasing ("a grinning crocodile in the Ganges thick and brown, / gobbled up a newsboy in the middle of the town"). Such qualities broaden the poem's appeal to include adults as well as children. *Tucky the Hunter* enables children to share a boy's imaginative dreams as he discovers "his oneness with the universe and its inhabitants" (58), but adults respond to the musical qualities in the language.

The reviews of *Bronwen, the Traw, and the Shape-Shifter* are primarily negative. *Kirkus* (1986), while advising that adults would share Dickey's enjoyment in elevating his daughter into myth, also states that the poem is awkward if read aloud. The meter is "complex" and the diction "uneven" (1289), occasionally simple and childlike and at other times extended into complex images. The text's "poetic fantasy" (1289), however, is effectively portrayed by Watson's illustrations, which capture the "dark romantic tone" (1289) reminiscent of Sendak but are longer and more complicated than the latter. Whalin (1986) also criticizes the book's language. Bronwen's adventures appear in "excruciatingly lengthy detail" (173). The large, black-and-white drawings are "strong" (173) but do not mitigate the "plodding language" and "dragging action" (173). Though intended as an epic, which should have a quickened pace, *Bronwen* more often remains stationary.

Macaulay's (1987) essay-review details his objections in order to determine where specific fault lies for a work not so much an epic as "an endless poem" (31). Book one succeeds, introducing Bronwen and the All-Dark as the heroine and villain, respectively, as well as her magical traw, and moving from the sunlight and safety of the garden to the menacing shadows of Bronwen's bedroom as the All-Dark awakens. However, as the story progresses, it "flattens" (31) because imagination yields to mere acceptance. "Conventional fantasy" replaces the "power of suggestion" (31). The images that present Bronwen's battle with the All-Dark must be viewed not only in their format but also with the illustrations, and Watson's pictures reveal "the dangers of illustrating a text that already illustrates itself" (31). The drawings possess a sense of darkness but no mystery; having texture, they lack feeling. Moreover, the pictures struggle against themselves. The "star-warsian double-page spread" (31) that depicts Bronwen's battle with fire, wind, and water conflicts with the illustrations that portray the empowering of the traw. Macaulay asserts, however, that "the real battle is between words and pictures, between the imagined and the unavoidable, the suggested and the concrete" (31). Behind any successful picture book lies the integration of these opposites, but *Bronwen* becomes two books, one of words and the other

of pictures, which share only the common packaging. Suggesting that its failure lies with an agent or editor who saw "a sure thing" (31) in Dickey's name and Watson's pictures, Macaulay then concludes by declaring the book "an over-designed, ill-conceived, pretentious product" (31) that undercuts the abilities of both artists.

Sporborg's (1987) lengthy review sees *Bronwen* positively, declaring that the "timeless fear of the dark" (25) inspires the book's "powerful echoic verses" (25). Bronwen's "vision-quest" (26) involves confronting the elements of fire, wind, and water; success in each instance costs her the magic in one of the traw's tines. Only when she battles "the endless black deep of the earth" and wins because the traw's handle blazes with magic power is the All-Dark finally defeated. Sporborg observes the changes in tone and poetic cadence that reflect a deepening despair as the narrative becomes more threatening. While the literal interpretation of the subject matter, together with the dedication ("To Bronwen and Her Mother in the Elements"), suggests an autobiographical content, the book speaks more openly to all readers.

Bibliography

Calhoun, Richard J., and Robert W. Hill. *James Dickey.* Boston: Twayne, 1983.

De La Fuente, Patricia, ed. *James Dickey: Splintered Sunlight.* Edinburg, TX: Pan American University, 1979.

Johnston, Albert H. "Tucky the Hunter." *Publisher's Weekly* 214 (31 July 1978): 88.

Kirkus. "Bronwen, the Traw, and the Shape-Shifter." 54 (15 August 1986): 1289-90.

Kirkus. "Tucky the Hunter." 46 (15 August 1978): 917.

Logue, J. D. "Books About the South." *Southern Living* 14 (January 1979): 68.

Macaulay, David. "*Bronwen, the Traw, and the Shape-Shifter.*" *New York Times Book Review.* 8 March 1987. 31.

Skinner, Izora. "A Fun Poem by James Dickey." In De La Fuente 56-58.

Sporborg, Ann. "*Bronwen, the Traw, and the Shape-Shifter.*" *James Dickey Newsletter* 4 (Fall 1987): 25-28.

Whalin, Kathleen D. "*Bronwen, the Traw, and the Shape-Shifter.*" *School Library Journal* 33 (October 1986): 173.

Patricia Laurence (essay date 1994)

SOURCE: Laurence, Patricia. "James Dickey's *Puella* in Flight." *South Carolina Review* 26, no. 2 (spring 1994): 61-71.

[*In the following essay, Laurence analyzes the volume* Puella, *emphasizing a movement toward the aesthetic "possession" of its female subject and a balancing stylistic quality of "lightness" in the poems.*]

James Dickey's collection of poems, *Puella,* begins with the dedication, "To Deborah—her girlhood, male-imagined." The nineteen difficult poems published in only one edition by Doubleday in 1982, and a small private printing by Pyracantha Press in 1985, limn a poet's changing imaginings of his young wife as a girl coming of age. The poems illumine Dickey's epigraph:

> I lived in thee, and dreamed, and waked
> Twice what I had been.
>
> > T. Sturge Moore

Coming to these poems from the masculine wilds of Dickey's novel, *Deliverance,* the work that looms largest in the American imagination, we veer in this collection into another kind of male voyage, this time into womanhood. Male imaginings of women have been under review since Virginia Woolf in her graceful polemic, *A Room of One's Own,* attempted to explain, in part, the imaginative necessity that women so often are to men. She describes "the looking glass vision," how "women have served all these centuries as looking-glasses possessing the magic and delicious power of reflecting the figure of man at twice its natural size" (35). Dickey is no exception: he awakes from his imagined encounter with Deborah's girlhood at least "twice" what he had been.

Feminist critics continue in the spirit of Virginia Woolf to observe the male voicing of womanhood as they take new critical turns into the historical and social inscriptions of language that bind women to certain roles or images. Amidst this scholarly activity, however, women continue to wonder why women poets do not write collections of poems about the boyhood of their lovers or husbands, and why male poets and novelists are so intrigued by the idea of possessing with the pen, the girlhoods or womanhoods of the women with whom they are engaged. The obsession to recover her past, particularly her sexual relationships, and to know and record them jealously leads to a terrifying conclusion. What such works share with Dickey's more innocent *Puella* is the author's desire to possess his woman, "before she met him."

Through the centuries, a reader might identify this impulse to "possess" as peculiarly male; women more often are "possessed" than "possessing." As Emily Dickinson states:

> I am afraid to own a Body
> I am afraid to own a soul
> Profound-precarious property
> Possession.

Women are often afraid to own their own souls, bodies and voices, let alone anyone else's. And when they do seek to possess, as does the energetic Maud Bailey in A. S. Byatt's recent novel, *Possession,* it is, astonishingly, Victorian love letters. Since this critical consideration of Dickey takes place at a time when such social paradigms are being questioned—when women are less patient with male fictionalization of women's experience and are struggling to possess their own voices in literature—we pause. . . . Dickey has, after all, presented us, in his previous works, with a certain vision of the "masculine."

Acknowledging then that "possession" is Dickey's drive in these poems, "lightness" is the quality that holds. "Puellae" in various kinds of personal and cultural flight are, somehow, levitated by the quality of Dickey's writing. He breathes what he has lived and dreamed of the sensuous life of his "puella"—in her Southern landscape—into her voice in these poems. We, in the meantime, rehearse in our heads the current declension of "correctness." Puella: We must remain in our own skins. Puellae: We must remain in our own bodies. Puellae: We must remain in our own gender. Fixed identities. Dickey, despite his glorification of male initiations and macho stances—the hunter, the ex-combat pilot—resists such fixity of identity and admirably pits his imagination against social naming. As James Applewhite perceptively says of the poem, Dickey seeks "to feel through her senses, wake in her psyche" (150). I would broaden the field of "being" or "non-being" even further to suggest that he also attempts to awaken the consciousness of a doll, trees, rain, a whale, an environment or the sounds of crows. Dickey's *Puella* attempts what Gerard Genette ascribes to literature in general: "[I]t breathes new life into the world, freeing it from the pressure of social meaning, which is named meaning, and therefore dead meaning, maintaining as long as possible that opening, the uncertainty of signs which allows one to breathe" (41).

Acknowledging the "uncertainty of signs," we make the critical turn from identity politics with its delineation of "identity" as fixed, toward a more complex view of the relation between gender, the imagination, and literature. Defend we must Dickey's exploration of the "I" and the "not I" as dimensions of being, and his imaginative rights to live in Deborah. He places a female speaker in a mythical and Southern landscape, breathing into her his voice: classical images of Athena springing from the head of Zeus come to mind. But note that he voices not only the dissolving line between male and female, but also girlhood and womanhood, past and present, the animate and inanimate, human and nature, and the actual and mythical. Deborah, somehow, always in motion, always "veering" into being something else, is a vector, Ungraspable. The challenge then of reading these subtle difficult poems is, "who is speaking?" And as Virginia Woolf further queries in one of her short stories, "when the self speaks to the self, who is speaking?" Is it Deborah? The male poet? Or is it an androgynous voice, both the "male" and "female" self of Dickey in dialogue? And what about the various animate and inanimate voicings that are also part of this speaker?

Different aspects of Deborah, ostensibly the changing, growing speaker, are presented in this collection. Each poem "veers" in another direction, some of them clustering about certain themes like magnetic filings. Dickey imagines Deborah in mythical and cultural relation to her body (menses, sex, death); to her family (mothers, grandmothers); to the house (civilization); to nature (Southern landscape, moon, rain, woods / flowers, animals); to sounds (the piano, crows); to the past (heraldry); and to fantasies. In **"From Time,"** Deborah imagines "for Years at the Piano"; in **"The Lode,"** we experience "Deborah's Rain Longing"; in **"Tapestry and Sail,"** "She Imagines Herself a Figure Upon Them"; in **"The Surround,"** "Imagining Herself as the Environment, She Speaks to James Wright at Sundown."

The formalist Russian critic Mikhail Bakhtin warns that, resist as we might, social namings are in us, and inscribed in our experience and language. We find in the opaque language of these poems a male presence or sensibility, at times, making it difficult to assess whose "experience" is being represented. In the first poem in the collection, **"Deborah Burning a Doll Made of House-Wood,"** Deborah burns her childhood self symbolized by a doll. She begins,

> I set you level,
> Your eyes like the twin beasts of a wall.
>
> As a child I believed I had grown you,
>   And I hummed as I mixed the blind nails
> Of this house with the light wood of Heaven—
>   The rootless trees there—falling in love
> With carpenters—their painted, pure clothes, their flawless
>   Baggies, their God-balanced bubbles, their levels.

Through Deborah's voice, we encounter metaphors of carpentry. The tools of Deborah's perception that take the measure of the "doll," also her childhood self, are the "level" with its "God-balanced bubble," "the blind nails," "the light wood of Heaven," and "the squared mess of an indoor wood-yard." The poet has breathed language that is gender-marked into Deborah's voice as she watches the dust of her doll, indeed her childhood, bodying "into smoke." This leaves us with a sense that both the male speaker and Deborah intertwine in perception, language and voice. Deborah continues, and we visually observe a balance in the spacing of the first line below to match Deborah's perception—"levelling" throughout the poem— and then in the fifth line, we observe the step-like lines of the "rungs," the "climbing," and the "domestic ascent" of the doll-child:

>   I am leaving: I have freed the shelves
>
>   So that you may burn cleanly, in sheer degrees
>   of domestic ascent, unfolding
>   Boards one after the other, like a fireman
>   His rungs out of Hell
>   or some holocaust
>   whelmed   and
>   climbing:

Both the spaces and the words speak and mean in a Dickey poem. Deborah, after this ascent, this levitation of the doll-self, has "the power to see / Pure," and moves on to

another aspect of the self in **"Deborah, Moon, Mirror, Right Hand Rising."** In this poem she observes in a mirror "the moon coming up in my face," and she experiences,

> New Being angled with thresholds.
>   Woman of the child
>
>   I was, I am shone through now
> In circles, as though the moon in my hand were fall-
>   ing
>
>   Concentrically, on the spirit of a tree
> . . .

Here Deborah is absorbed into both a natural and mythical world through her mirror; comically, "All pores cold with cream." She is moon; she is human, she is tree, even dryad; she is stone. Transparent,

> A woman's live playing of the universe
>   As inner light, stands clear,
>   And is, where I last was.

All kinds of identities are mystically traversed in her "new being." The poet imagines Deborah in "a body out-believing existence, . . . set going by imaginative laws, emblem eyes, degenerate with symbols" ("The Lyric Beasts"). The landscape of dream and myth, juxtaposed with Dickey's familiar terrain of woods and animals and the physical pleasure of being, leads us to appreciate the deeply felt connection between the man and the changing woman in these poems.

Again, the quality of the writing and perception that one experiences in these poems is "lightness," the feeling that one falls through them sensuously, somehow balanced in flight: and, at times, levitating, rather than just reading them. Italo Calvino in *Six Essays for the Next Millennium,* discusses the virtue that the quality of "lightness" that removes "weight from the structure of stories and from language" (3) will have, as he projects this quality into the future of literature. He predicts that "The lightness is also something arising from the writing itself, from the poet's own linguistic power, quite independent of whatever philosophic doctrine the poet claims to be following" (10). In choosing an image for the new millennium, he selects one that might well apply to some of Dickey's poetry: "The sudden agile leap of the poet-philosopher who raises himself above the weight of the world showing that with all his gravity he has the secret of lightness" (12).

This lightness is present in even the darkest of Dickey's poems. In one of the most intriguing poems of the collection, **"Veer Voices: Two Sisters Under Crows,"** Dickey's voice splinters into the voice of Deborah, her sister as well as the screeches of the crows—somehow to be heard all through this poem, with "their spirit-shifting splits / Of tongue." Again, we observe the poet traversing different dimensions of "being," not localized in the human, but located mid-way between nature and the human in sound

and image. The screech of crows "veer-crying and straining like wire" shadows this poem, the sisters psychically
placed under the screeching of the "night-mass of
families":

> Sometimes are living those who have been seen
>   Together   those farthest leaning
>   With some dark birds and fielded
> Below them   counter crying and hawing in savage
>   openness
>   For every reason. Such are as we, to come out
>   And under and balance-cruise,

The spaces of varying length and the placement of words
in this description of the dark birds, sisters, together, create a visual veering or change of direction to match the
veer-voices of the sisters:

> A crossroads and passing out
> One kind of voice in skinned speeches
> All over the place   leaning and flying
>   Passing into
>   flying in and out
> Of each other
>
>   with nothing to tell of
> But the angles of light-sensitive dust
>   Between fences leaded with dew,
>   You might say back,
>
>   Come with me
> Into the high-tension carry

We both see and hear the voices of the sisters and the
crows "flying" in and out, identities blurring in the tense
visual field of words and spaces on the page. It is almost
as if the "countercrying" crows who "surround" the sisters
in nature teach a voice or a knowledge of no human tone,
"unfathomable" to human ears. Again Dickey explores the
"I" and the "not I": sisters in relation to one another, a
man in relation to women, humans in relation to birds and
their sounds in nature. Dickey bids the sisters to listen and
move into the "high-tension carry" of this other world.
Despite the Poe-like ominousness of the invitation, this
poem, nevertheless, has a quality of lightness.

"Turning" not only his poetic lines but the dark parable of
the two sisters into "lightness," Dickey again reminds us
of the paradoxical "lightness" to be found in "gravity."
This "lightness" arising from the gravity of the dark intuitions about Deborah's relations, about the relation between
the human and natural worlds, then becomes a principle
for reading *Puella*. Dickey, the poet, navigating the space
of the page as Dickey, the air force pilot, navigated the
space of sky in World War II and the Korean War.

In the poem, **"Deborah in Ancient Lingerie, in Thin
Oak Over Creek,"** Deborah asserts all that she can "do"
but again the stances and the language somehow suggest a
male mirroring. The poet captures the "lightness" of the
erotic acrobatics of a man and a woman with the imagery
of the aerial beam and heron-veins in a landscape of
mythic and actual outdoors. The poem and the reader
levitate:

> I can do
>   gently, just over you:
>   balance-beam disdain
>   Like heron-veins over the forest
>   When my spirit is branching, when I
>   Catch it and don't spend it, I can do:
>   All kinds of caused shade
> I can do, and unparalleled being
>   I can do, snake-screaming
>   Withering, foster-parenting for animals
> I can do
>   very gently from just about
>
>   Right over you, I can do
>   at no great height I can do
>   and bear
> And counter-balance and do
>   and half-sway and do
>   and sway
>   and outsway and
>   do.

We catch the sensuous rhythm of the erotic from the visual
patterning of word and space, as well as the wildness of
the sound of "snake screaming." And in the macho tones
of words and movements, the repetition of "do" and
"gently . . . over you" and "balance-beam disdain" and
"catch" and not "spend" and repeated swayings, we sense
this is a man—not Deborah—complicating again our notion of the experience and the speaker represented in these
poems. Nevertheless, in the "move" and "do" and "bear"
and "sway" and "half-sway" and "outsway," we, as readers, move across the visual space of the page in a
choreography of eye and sense, creating a special relationship between the poet and the reader. The spaces of varying length to mark pauses and even a full black page in an
earlier poem, **"Apollo,"** for the first manned moon orbit,
suggest conceptual, visual, and auditory play in Dickey's
poetry. The spaces and blackness are a place, just as Laurence Sterne offered in *Tristam Shandy,* for the participation of the reader.

The "female" companion piece to **"Deborah in Ancient
Lingerie, in Thin Oak Over Creek"** may be the glorious
poem, **"RayFlowers."** Though it feels like a violation to
quote only part of this poem or any of the other poems in
this collection because of the importance of Dickey's
choreography of space, a part of it will supply the feeling
of lightness, and falling, and "consent":

> As when we all fell all day
>   Consenting
>   Sight-softening   space-massing
>   Time-thickening   time-floating more
>   Light

The repetition of words such as "consenting" (somehow
echoing Molly Bloom's "yes, she said yes . . ."), "sown,"
"fall" and lines such as:

>   Come:
>   Muffle   splinter   increase   fill

suggest something, I think, closer to female sensibility.
But then we might ask why Deborah says later,

Super-nerved with weightlessness:

All girls of cloud and ego in your time,
      Smoked-out millennial air-space
         Empowered with blurr, lie down
With bindweed force   with angelic clutter and stillness
            As I hold out and for you unfold
            This feather-frond of a bird . . .

Though straining for Deborah's own sexual dawning in this poem, it is, nevertheless, intertwined with the male speaker's prowess, unfolding his "feather-frond of a bird." We shift in different lines to different aspects of sexual experience.

One poem where Dickey crosses over more successfully into female and animal experience and voice is **"Deborah as Scion."** Deborah at the family cemetery connects with her mothers and grandmothers, traversing the line between the past and the present. In this passage, which is beautiful in its movement and too long to quote, Deborah moves "back, from mother to mother" and is "totally them in the / Breasts, breath and butt." But she is also curiously alive and in touch with whales whose bones have served for the corsets of confinement for them and Deborah:

            I stand now in your closed bones,
   Sucked-in, in your magic tackle, taking whatever,
         From the stark freedom under the land,
   From under the sea, from the bones of the deepest
   beast,
         Shaped now entirely by me, by whatever
         Breath I draw.

Identifying with the whales, crossing over from the human to the animal, Deborah and the whales are "paired bones of the deep" joined by the confinement and violation of their bodies. Whatever her own bodily confinements, her being grows as she identifies with and feels the ripping-up and boiling down of the whale "for animal oil." She hears "the weird mammalian bleating of bled creatures" and thinks,

               This animal
   This animal   I stand and think

Its feed   its feel   its whole lifetime on one air:
   In lightning-strikes I watch it leap . . .

Anyone who has ever watched a "volcanic" whale leaping in the deep knows Deborah's visceral sense of the primeval, and of the mythic proportions of these creatures. Perhaps the "volcanic," unconscious structuring of a girl's sexuality into the poem reminds us of Deborah's moving out from cultural restriction into her own experience of sexuality as a woman. "Out-believing" her existence as a woman, entering into the experience of a whale, we again move into a "deepening sense of being" that Laurence Lieberman writes of in a Dickey poem. And we hear, hear, the "weird mammalian bleating of bled creatures" just as we heard the "snake screaming" and the screeching of the

crows in earlier poems. And in the penultimate poem, **"The Surround,"** where Deborah imagines herself as the environment speaking to James Wright at Sundown, she is no longer even human but mythically dissolved as a presence in the environment—spiritually sprinkled in nature—to surround and protect the male poet, James Wright, as a beneficent spirit:

               Stay with me
            And without me, hearing
      Your hearing come back in a circle. After midnight no
      ax
            Shall be harmful to your whole-
      ness,
      No blood-loss give life. You are in your rings, and
      growing
            In darkness. I quell and thicken
            Away. I am

The surround, and you are your own.

In this collection then, Dickey, the male poet, blurs easy distinctions between male and female, man and woman and nature, the animate and the inanimate, the human and the animal, the past and the present, the actual and the mythic, and the landscape of mind and place and page. What is most important is that Dickey attempts (with mixed results) to present a girl-woman, not solely in relationship to other people, but in relation with her girl-hood, womanhood, body, life, death, and nature. She does not exist in traditional relation to man, though she is "themed" to meet the male poet. We find her, imperfectly mixed in voice with male sensibility, in relation to the universe. Entering into many dimensions of being and non-being, not just the **Puella** of the title, Dickey attempts to breathe new and strange life into poetry. He invites the reader into the generous space and dance of words on the page—his puella, somehow, in flight.

Works Cited

Applewhite, James. "Reflections on *Puella*." *Southern Review* 21, (January 1985): 214-19.

Bakhtin, Mikhail. *The Dialogic Imagination*. Trans. Michael Holquist. Austin: U of Texas P, 1981.

Calvino, Italo. *Six Essays for the Next Millennium*. Trans. Patrick Creagh. Cambridge, Mass.: Harvard UP, 1988.

Dickey, James. *Deliverance*. Boston: Houghton Mifflin, 1970.

———*The Eye-Beaters, Blood, Victory, Madness, Buckhead and Mercy*. Garden City, New York: Doubleday, 1970.

———*Poems, 1957-67*. Middletown, Conn.: Wesleyan UP, 1967.

Genette, Gerard. *Figures of Literary Discourse*. Trans. Alan Sheridan. New York: Columbia UP, 1982.

Lieberman, Laurence. *The Achievement of James Dickey*. Glenview, Ill.: Scott, Foresman, 1968.

Woolf, Virginia. *A Room of One's Own.* New York: Harcourt Brace Jovanovich, 1929.

Robert Kirschten (essay date 1995)

SOURCE: Kirschten, Robert. "The Momentum of Word-Magic in James Dickey's *The Eye-Beaters, Blood, Victory, Madness, Buckhead and Mercy.*" *Contemporary Literature* 36, no. 1 (spring 1995): 130-63.

[*In the following essay, Kirschten expresses the magical, mythopoeic mode of Dickey's verse.*]

In the late sixties, when he collected his first five books of poetry into one volume, James Dickey had reached such a considerable level of literary success that Louis Untermeyer claimed that ***Poems 1957-1967*** "is the poetry book of the year, and I have little doubt that it will prove to be the outstanding collection of one man's poems to appear in this decade." While Peter Davison and James Tulip ranked Dickey and Robert Lowell as the two major poets in the country, John Simon was even more enthusiastic when he declared, "I place Dickey squarely above Lowell." However, in 1968, with the appearance of Dickey's very next book, ***The Eye-Beaters, Bloos, Victory, Madness, Buckhead and Mercy,*** critics seemed annoyed, even dismayed, at the new direction of his highly experimental collection of verse. Herbert Leibowitz noted that the "balance of pure abandon and meticulous observation breaks apart in Dickey's latest volume," and further, that a "stagy, unpleasant hysteria enters the poems." Benjamin DeMott charged that the "poet runs on unrestrainedly," giving "no shapely object to delight in, little refinement of feeling or subtlety of judgment, no intellectual distinction, no hint of wisdom." Even as staunch an early supporter as Richard Howard lamented that "The look of these poems on the page is disconcerting: forms are sundered, wrenched apart rather than wrought together." Howard then concludes with a statement of considerable strength: "The cost to [Dickey's] poetry is tremendous, for it has cost him poems themselves—there are not poems here . . . only—only!—poetry."

Despite the severity of these appraisals, *Eye-Beaters* contains at least seven of Dickey's major poems and constitutes one of the central transitional texts in Dickey's poetic canon.[1] During this period, Dickey's experiments in two basic areas, form and diction, opened a number of technical, poetic doors that propelled him through his remarkable and controversial book-length poem ***The Zodiac*** in 1976 to major achievements in the eighties in ***Puella*** and ***The Eagle's Mile,*** two of his best volumes of verse. In ***The Eye-Beaters,*** Dickey still kept his eye at times on a classical sense of narrative—the story-based poem on which he built such a wide following of readers; however, he also began to highlight word groups that radically altered his techniques of telling and gained him especially dramatic entrance to the world of darkness and

terror that strongly unsettled Leibowitz, DeMott, and Howard. These word groups reveal fundamental methods in Dickey's word-magic and the subsequent momentum of his poetic thought, which, to my mind, has been misrepresented by many of his negative critics. These critics look for intellectual or discursive thinking in a poet who is not understandable only to the rational mind, and, as a result, they find Dickey's poems lacking in elements that are completely irrelevant to his poetic program.[2] Dickey's best poems in this book are not hysterical, unrestrained, unshaped, unsubtle, or wrenched apart but are intricately constructed forms generated by a mode of thinking that is rooted in anthropological and mythopoeic criticism, namely, contagious magic.

Presupposing an ancient, universal law of contact between animate and inanimate objects, even those which are geographically distant such as the moon and stars, contagious magic seems, at first, primitive, simple, or scientifically mistaken. However, when developed through the complex combinations within his extraordinary diction, Dickey's version of this practical causal principle allows him to reinvent a world in which magic not only seems plausible but natural and even necessary. For out of his animated series of "natural" connections, Dickey constructs a diverse range of rituals, ranging from sacrificial rites to linguistic acts of creation, which, reflexively, depend on his magical ontology for their effectiveness. When properly constructed, these rites reveal special, therapeutic powers designed to bring some measure of human control to the catastrophic, real worlds of "blood" and "madness." The plausibility of Dickey's word-magic takes its authority from its appeal to deeper reaches of the human mind that are closed to more discursive modes of lyric action. Not "deep-image poetry" exactly, his poetry operates through archetypal images within a deeply appealing and personal mode that also engages and alters the social self, especially the self traumatized by war. While his verbal and formal magic has distinguished precedents in the work of Hart Crane, Dylan Thomas, Theodore Roethke, and even Samuel Taylor Coleridge, critics often fail to judge Dickey by those principles that have been used to canonize these writers. To establish critical criteria—especially those in a mythopoeic mode—more accurately attuned to Dickey's true poetic vision in ***The Eye-Beaters,*** we need to focus on a number of issues that preoccupied the poet at this point in his career: his construction of poetic form in relation to word-magic, the subsequent shift of formal momentum in his poetry from action to image, and the shaping elements in at least one of the historical genres in which he was writing.

. . . . .

To initiate his keynote speech to the South Atlantic Modern Language Association in November 1982, Dickey borrowed a distinction from the *Notebooks* of poet Winfield Townley Scott.[3] Centering on two kinds of poetry, or, rather, two kinds of poetic diction, this distinction is simple enough yet reveals much about Dickey's own poetic practice. The first type of poetry is, according to Scott, literalistic and marked by its capacity for moving, external reference. It is "a commentary on human life so concentrated as to give off considerable pressure." Two of its central practitioners are Wordsworth and Hardy, and it "is represented by [Edwin Arlington] Robinson's [line]: 'And he was all alone there when he died.'" The second and opposite type, less literal and more evocative in character, "is a magic gesture of language" (*Night Hurdling* 125), among whose proponents are Poe and Rimbaud; this second type is illustrated by lines from Hart Crane's poem "Voyages":

> O minstrel galleons of Carib fire,
> Bequeath us to no earthly shore until
> Is answered in the vortex of our grave
> The seal's wide spindrift gaze toward paradise.

> (*Poems* 36)

For Dickey, the key word in these lines is "spindrift," whose peculiar qualities place Crane among what Dickey calls, following Scott, the "Magic-Language exemplars" of poetry. Instead of a literal or essential component of the seal's manner of seeing, "spindrift" belongs less to the "reality-world" of animal vision than to the "word-world" (126) of verbal association (or what Crane calls, in his well-known phrase, the "logic of metaphor" [221]). Dickey explains that "'Spindrift' is sea-foam, wave-foam, usually wind-blown along beaches, and, though the seal's eyes may be wide, and his gaze toward Paradise, 'spindrift' is really not, cannot be, part of his vision: the word is word only, associational word, and in its way beautiful, but word" (126).[4]

Instead of inventing poems characterized by statements that have an empirical or external referential direction, the poets of word-magic work from inside a reverberating, self-generating world of linguistic interplay. According to Dickey, these writers are less interested in realistic narratives or personal anecdotes which convey maxims about the world of human action and ideas than in the evocative powers and suggestions of words themselves. This wordplay may be further understood by considering its opposite, namely, that kind of diction that belongs to poets whom Dickey calls "the literalists." Unlike the "magic-language practitioners," "literal-minded poets" believe "in words as agents which illuminate events and situations that are part of an already given continuum" (*Night Hurdling* 131). For example,

> The Robinson line . . . is simply factual. There are only plain words in it: a statement. Plain words in ordinary order; nothing unusual, much less exotic. The line puts the reader into contemplation of something that happened to someone, and the condition of the happening: it is the clear pane of glass that does not call attention to itself, but gives clearly and cleanly on a circumstance.

> (126)

On the other hand, word-magicians do not give primacy to plot or to the discursive revelations of character, but to a dream mode or some kind of surrealistic space in which the powers of reason have little importance. Although Dickey's remarks were made with *Puella* (1982) in mind, the book with his fullest use of word-magic and to which this article is a preliminary study, these observations reveal much about his own magical approach throughout his poetry. This approach is evident as far back in Dickey's work as the opening poem, the magical chant **"Sleeping Out at Easter,"** in his first collection of poems, *Into the Stone* (1960). Of word-magicians, Dickey said in 1982:

> For the Magicians, language itself must be paramount: language and the connotative aura it gives off. . . . The words are seen as illuminations mainly of one another; their light of meaning plays back and forth between them, and, though it must by nature refer beyond, outside itself, shimmers back off the external world in a way whereby the world—or objective reality, or just Reality—serves as a kind of secondary necessity, a non-verbal backdrop to highlight the dance of words and their bemused interplay.

> (*Night Hurdling* 126-27)

However magical Dickey's interests became at this point, he never fully divorced himself from his commitment to literal-mindedness or his belief in the necessity of basic storytelling. For in the same essay, he criticizes purely magical poetry for its considerable limitations. In magical poetry divorced from public concerns, Dickey says, "the *world* is lacking, and the buzz of language and hit-or-miss-metaphor-generation is everything; the poem itself is nothing; or only a collection of fragments" (*Night Hurdling* 138). Although he admits to being "profoundly interested" in "the absolute freedom" that the magical making of metaphors offers the poet, Dickey also wants lyrics "bound into one poetic situation, one scene, one event after the other" (139). A further problem with the magical method, especially in the surrealistic school, is that it invents without discovering, as Wallace Stevens noted. It does not reveal the contents of the unconscious but mere phantasms. Nor does it have "*drama*," for it "cannot *build*." Of poems in this style, Dickey observes that they have no narrative, no logic, no idea development, no transformation, no "publicly available" themes (137).

If one wonders in which camp Dickey places his own poetic language, he provides what appears to be a decisive response earlier in his address. Although he greatly admires the best of them, he claims, "I am not of the party of the magic-language practitioners" (*Night Hurdling* 129). At first glance, this self-classification seems true. Because so much of Dickey's early poetry depends on anecdotal narrative and extrinsic reference to topics and events from his own life (world war, family, animals, even a Southern Baptist preacher), he seems justified in placing himself among those poets whom he calls "literal-minded" (129), for example, Robert Frost, Edgar Lee Masters, and Randall Jarrell. From a stylistic or linguistic point of view, however, Dickey's poetry also suggests an extremely strong magical orientation. In the mid and late sixties in particular, Dickey began to experiment with word groups bunched together by means of techniques such as the "block format" (**Central Motion** v) and the "split line" (*Self-Interviews* 184-85). At this time, words themselves and their "connotative aura" (*Night Hurdling* 127) became singularly featured on the pages of his lyrics. In **"May Day Sermon," "Falling," "The Shark's Parlor," "The Fiend,"** and to some extent in **"The Firebombing,"** he built "wall[s] of words" (116) out of distinctive visual and semantic combinations that were not only striking to behold but, more importantly, approximated, as Dickey says, "the real way of the mind as it associates verbally. . . . in bursts of words, in jumps" (*Self-Interviews* 184).

One major effect of the method (or "real way") of these mental word "bursts" and "jumps" is the construction of an emotionally immediate, if not obsessive, universe in which the magical contiguity of natural forms of life and death is conveyed by Dickey's imagistic contiguities. Dickey calls the semantic aspect of this magical contact "apparently unjustifiable juxtapositions" and "shifts of meaning or consciousness" (*Self-Interviews* 185). These juxtapositions may be rationally "unjustifiable" but, from a poetic and emotional point of view, they enable the objects inside his visually bracketed word groups to exchange (or share) properties in an especially dramatic and vivid manner. These stylistically fused traits build scenes so rich in texture that they constitute the animating ground of the poem's action and thus possibility for Dickey's characters. **"May Day Sermon"** provides an especially vivid example of how the poet's word-magic "jumps" across the page with a stunning momentum that energizes the woman preacher who delivers the lines. This momentum also animates the objects of nature in Dickey's universe and reveals how he thinks magically through them:

>   Sisters, understand about men
> and sheaths:
>
> About nakedness: understand how butterflies, amazed,
>   pass out
> Of their natal silks how the tight snake takes a great
>   breath   bursts
> Through himself and leaves himself behind   how a
>   man casts finally
> Off everything that shields him from another   be-
>   holds his loins
> Shine with his children forever   burn with the very
>   juice
> Of resurrection
>
>   (*Poems* 7)

In this section, Dickey's word-magic builds the poem's (and nature's) momentum by means of his striking grammatical strategies of predication, strategies that, as we will see, are also central to his magical method in **"Pine."** In the arrangement of word blocks in **"May Day Sermon,"** nouns such as "butterflies," "the tight snake," "man," and "his children" share the ejaculatory, universal motion of sheaths and nakedness which "pass out," breathe, burst, "shield," behold, "[s]hine," and "burn with . . . resurrection." This sharing is effected by an elaborate series of delayed predicates in parallel constructions in which the

poet omits punctuation and connectives in favor of breath spaces. By keeping mechanical interrupters and conjunctions to a minimum, Dickey creates an oratorical and ontological momentum marked by "fluidity and flux" (*Voiced Connections* 155) that is his own specification of William James's famous stream of consciousness.[5] Dickey's poetic flow—more like a tidal wave in this poem—makes objects exchange attributes by making the mind "jump" between nouns and predicates such that a verb (and its textural traits) in one clause may be plausibly predicated of two or more preceding subjects. In the lines cited above, the subject of "burn" is "loins" but may as well be "children," for both "loins" and "children"—albeit in different modes—"burn with the very juice / Of resurrection." Dickey does not use this technique only for single terms. Because he begins his word blocks with dynamic verbs, gerunds, and present participles, he drives these blocks forward in a stream of sexual, natural, and grammatical motion while simultaneously allowing the eye to linger upon visually separated word groups so that entire groups of words appear to serve as nouns for several series of subsequent verbals. Several lines later in **"May Day Sermon,"** it is a trout which flows and slides upstream, but Dickey's spatial arrangement of his word groups makes it appear that the trout's "cold / Mountain of his birth" does the same, for the trout "heads upstream, breathing mist like water, for the cold / Mountain of his birth flowing sliding in and through the ego- / maniacal sleep of gamecocks" (*Poems* 7). The metaphysical mechanism behind these shared predicates is a mode of connection that Sir James Frazer calls "contagious magic" in *The Golden Bough,* namely, "that things which have once been in contact with each other are always in contact" (13). In Dickey's poetic universe, these grammatical and ontological connections produce a magical animism, in which, to use Joseph Campbell's phrasing, "there is no such thing as absolute death, only a passing of individuals back and forth, as it were, through a veil or screen of visibility, until—for one reason or another—they dissolve into an undifferentiated ground that is not of death, but of potential life, out of which new individuals appear" (*Sacrifice* 9).

Not only objects and groups of objects are animated by mental word-magic in Dickey's world. Dickey's word-magic also drives the emotionally animating end of **"May Day Sermon,"** which is nothing less than the resurrection in springtime of nature, sexual instinct, and the vocalized anima (or soul) of the victimized daughter, all under the aegis of the oratorical triad of energized women: preacher, audience, and subject of the sermon (the daughter). The daughter of the abusive, backwoods, Bible-reading father is able to return from the dead each year precisely because, in Dickey's lyric universe, "there is," in Campbell's words, "no such thing as absolute death." Dickey's is a world in which life and death cyclically and magically dissolve into and out of each other and in which the animating power of the woman preacher's eternal logos—like "men" and "nakedness"—also "bursts," "[s]hine[s]," and "burn[s] with the very juice / Of resurrection." The daughter does not die for her sexual freedom but dies as a fertility goddess who transcends death each spring, like the earth itself, by riding the eternal continuum of decay, regeneration, and rebirth, empowered in Dickey's world-view by the words of women and the poet's magical modes of "resurrection." The very possibility of the daughter's archetypal transcendence is thus rooted in a magically empowered and conceived setting which eternally energizes her.

If the ritualized methods and the ground of action in Dickey's lyrics take on a special primitive power in the mid sixties, the effects of his word-magic and its reverberating linguistic momentum become even more pronounced in the late sixties and the early seventies. His magical diction is primarily effected through catalogues of tactile, concrete metaphors, hypenated word combinations, and explosive, staggered groups of action-packed gerundives. When working in a distinctively surrealistic or hallucinatory dream mode, Dickey distances himself even further from his earlier formal strategies, realistic anecdotes, and the relatively sober revelations of romantic perception, in favor of an exuberant emphasis on magical imagery. For instance, in **"The Eye-Beaters,"** the narrator does not go inside the minds of blind children for internal revelation when he visits a home for the children in Indiana, but instead externalizes his imagined vision of what they see as he addresses himself:

> Smudge-eyed, wide-eyed, gouged,
> horned, caved-
> in, they are silent: it is for you to guess what they
> hold back inside
> The brown and hazel   inside the failed green   the
> vacant
>   blue-
> eyed floating of the soul.
>
> (*Eye-Beaters* 50)

At first, there appears to be little here of what could be traditionally called a complicated plot which changes the fortunes of its characters. Neither the children nor the narrator can change. Try as he may, the speaker cannot alter the condition of the blind children who beat their eyes in frustration. In a sense, then, the animating end of this poem is the realistic failure of the poet's magical, elaborate techniques of animation. This failure, however, is only half the equation. After acknowledging the therapeutic limits of his poetry, the speaker frantically continues to build his fictional wall of mythic images for his own sake and for that of the real "vision" of the children. He argues rationally that in spite of their blindness, these children are still important, and that "what they see must be crucial / To the human race." Despite his claim to reason, Dickey's magic produces nothing more than a semihysterical nightmare of his own darkness and rage as the poet tries to see what is "under their pummeled lids" (54).

His word-magic is thus closer to word-madness than magic. Yet this madness has its own peculiar visioning power. In **"May Day Sermon,"** while partially maddened by her belief system, by abuse to the farmer's daughter, and by Dickey's inflamed rhetoric, the woman preacher

nonetheless effects an optimistic, mythopoeic reincarnation of the victimized girl. In *The Eye-Beaters,* Dickey's word-madness seeks a magic that at first appears ineffective. This magic is built out of nothing but the "sheer / Despair of invention" (55) in the real world where the narrator's poetic powers cannot heal. However, what comes most alive in this world—even more than plot and character—is the poet's mental cave of magical images, that is, the cave of "perversity" and "madness," constituted by Dickey's wall of words. It is as if he has taken us inside Plato's cave of illusions or inside one of the Paleolithic caves at Montesquieu-Avantes in the Pyrenees and left us in the dark. In such a world, "Half-broken light flickers" briefly and shows us partial images of "ibex quagga . . . cave bear aurochs [and] mammoth" (54, 51). However, this is a mental world which is even darker and more claustrophobic, where the poet's "reason" has "gone / Like eyes" (55), and only his primal images offer him solace. We thus come closer to experiencing the dark world of these children than we ever would have without Dickey's disturbing and dazzling poem, at the heart of which is yet another of his extraordinary, primitivistic exchanges. This exchange transforms speaker and reader by linking sighted readers to blind children, even though the mode of shared "vision" is only—or, to use Richard Howard's exclamation, "only!"—poetic.

As we trace the evolution of Dickey's use of magical language, what is important to note in **"The Eye-Beaters"**—as well as in **"Mercy," "Victory,"** and **"Pine"** in the same volume—is that Dickey's walls of words are so powerful that their contagious, magical energy appears to displace plot, character, and revelation as emotionally central parts of his poetic action. These traditional shaping elements are, of course, still prominent in his work of this period. However, we may well be able to claim—using Dickey's own description of poetic word-magicians—that, in these boldly experimental poems, he has gone further than ever toward giving primacy to "language and the connotative aura it gives off." This new primacy of parts enables him to invent a new poetic "Reality [which] serves as a . . . backdrop to highlight the dance of words and their bemused interplay" (*Night Hurdling* 127). To put it another way, Dickey's radically magical walls of reality establish settings which not so much displace thought and character as they take on the functions of character, revelation, and the solution (or opposition) to the protagonist's driving needs. In **"May Day Sermon,"** magical word groups not only create the physical setting but also the animating ground of change and motivation for the woman preacher. Yet they also constitute a formal revolution, what would in contemporary criticism be called a "deconstruction," in which Dickey's word-magic achieves a parity of power with the classic, Aristotelian elements of thought and action, and even becomes the central pattern of thought and action. By focusing on "[the] action of words upon each other, for whatever meaning or sensation they may throw off, evoke" (131), Dickey uses these networks of "meaning or sensation" not to remain mired in sensation but to invent what is for him a new kind of poetic form.

Insofar as his new diction produces a "connotative aura" that radically alters his speaker's fundamental mode of perception while also shaping and guiding the reader's point of view, Dickey's mythical language becomes both his poetic action *and* his basic method of representation. This collapse—or fusion—of analytic distinctions is true for all poetry insofar as poetry's shaping causes are synthesized within its verbal materials. But for Dickey, his distinctive change in emphasis yields especially vivid insights into a new way of thinking through words which themselves revolutionize his poetry.

. . . . .

If, in this middle period of his career, Dickey begins to think in a radically mytho-magical mode while quite consciously moving away from ancedote and narrative, we see yet another reason why his poetry upsets the Aristotelian causal hierarchy which privileges plot the way Dickey did in his early work. The very nature of thought manifested in Dickey's word-magic demands this formal shift. For, as Ernst Cassirer notes, "mythical consciousness . . . knows nothing of certain distinctions. . . . it lacks any fixed dividing line between mere 'representation' and 'real' perception, between wish and fulfillment, between image and thing" (*Mythical Thought* 36). Further, by using a mode of thought which burkes classical logical axioms and assumes instead magical principles—such as "the part not only *stands for* the whole but positively *is* the whole" (64)—Dickey confounded many critics in the late sixties and early seventies by inventing an "aura" that baffled them when they applied discursive or meditative criteria. For when Dickey's linguistic "aura" became a dominant force, it produced a dreamworld like that of the undifferentiated reality of primitive consciousness; thus many readers dismissed the poems in *The Eye-Beaters* as formless or poorly constructed. On the contrary, these poems are intricately constructed, and further, they are designed to convey the atmosphere of nightmares or dream consciousness, the very nature of which is cloudy or phantasmic.

One magical mode, the conversion of properties or attributes of objects into bodies, appears in the scenic imagery of **"Mercy,"** a nightmare poem about the narrator's lover Fay, a nurse at a hospital in "slum Atlanta," whom he picks up at the nurses' dormitory called "Mercy Manor." By mixing hypostatized, imagistic traits of love, mortality, blood, and banal pop culture in a dazzling scene of surrealistic transformation, Dickey converts Fay into a contemporary Persephone, macabre yet heroic. While "perfume and disinfectant battle / In her armpits" (*Eye-Beaters* 15), she straddles the worlds of life and death, goddess-like, when, in the poem's conclusion, the speaker imagines himself "Collapsed on the street," having a kind of heart (or love) attack: "I nearly am dead / In love" (16). Herself a stark contrast in the colors of healing and of death, Fay leans over him as he calls for her kiss to silence the cry of mortality from his lips and to bear him safely from the world of darkness into the "mercy" of St. Joseph's hospital:

> She would bend
>   Over me like this   sink down
>   With me in her white dress
>   Changing to black   we sink
>   Down flickering
> Like television   like Arthur Godfrey's face
>   Coming on   huge   happy
>   About us   happy
>   About everything   O bring up
> My lips   hold them down don't let them cry
> With the   cry   close   closer   eyeball to
>   eyeball
>   In my arms, O queen of death
>   Alive, and with me at the end.

(16)

If Fay, like Persephone, possesses a goddess-like power of healing and renewal, she does so because the poet rescues her from a convincing technical, pop cultural hell that enervates yet simultaneously animates her. As he does in **"The Eye-Beaters,"** Dickey builds another dynamic wall of words—this time, down the middle of the page—that makes the night world of hospitals come alive in a sensuously dark dream scene. This scene is not static. As the drama develops, the setting not only gains emotional power by means of the affective accumulation of Dickey's detail; it propels the action forward by providing an overwhelming opponent of "night" and "mortality" against which the speaker battles for "care" and "love." In the night world of this hospital, "love," if not life, has never felt more vulnerable. One cause of this vulnerability is the massive sense of indifference that the setting, indeed, the world, evinces toward the speaker. This anomie is reflected in Dickey's magical, imagistic hypostatization of Arthur Godfrey's smiling television face, whose mind-numbing, "happy" countenance benignly smiles over the night world of pain and death with the comic indifference of a plastic Halloween mask. Ernst Cassirer says that in magical thought, "The 'image' does not represent the 'thing'; it *is* the thing; it does not merely stand for the object, but has the same actuality, so that it replaces the thing's immediate presence" (*Mythical Thought* 38). We do not confuse Arthur Godfrey with his image. Rather, Dickey so animates the banality of the image that its preposterous happiness becomes an oppressive, real, actual body. In this animated, surrealistic space, the poet turns a complex of cultural and technological relations into "a pre-existing material substance" in which, in Cassirer's words, "all mere properties or attributes . . . become *bodies*" (55). By magically making banality a substance, Dickey provides one element in the poisoned substratum of a contemporary, urban scene against which the energized passion of a goddess-woman offers temporary redemption from the speaker's hysterical "wail" and the dark, cold world of mortality and indifference.

In this stage of Dickey's poetic career—which may be labeled a magical period in which he makes a radical move from action to image—voice, points of view (reader's and speaker's), and plot seem less like specific, separable literary devices than undifferentiated aspects of the dreamy aura of his word selection. These strategically constructed word groups reveal the movement of his mind from linguistic block to block in modes of nondiscursive, non-analytical thought that Cassirer discusses in his chapter "Word Magic" in *Language and Myth*:

> mythic ideation and primitive verbal conception. . . . [involve] a process of almost violent separation and individuation. Only when this intense individuation has been consummated, when the immediate intuition has been focused and . . . reduced to a single point, does the mythic or linguistic form emerge, and the word or the momentary god is created. . . . the process of apprehension aims not at an expansion, extension, universalizing of the content, but rather at its highest intensification. . . . The conscious experience is not merely wedded to the word, but is consumed by it. Whatever has been fixed by a name, henceforth is not only real, but is Reality.
>
> (57-58)

In the momentum of Dickey's thought in the best poems from *The Eye-Beaters,* objects and events are individuated through narratives that antagonize and separate agents. Things and acts are also individuated through strategic spatial separations (different from the split line but an offshoot of it) and through emphases of the arrangement of words on the page. Dickey's word blocks isolate images in focused impressions that, when grouped in his distinctive series of sequences, give the sense that a name and its referent are magically connected—indeed, that reality is built out of momentary bursts of tangible, tactile names. These names not only share the properties of what they signify but feel as if they are some essential part (or the whole) of their referents while simultaneously amplifying the emotional impact of those parts. At times, Dickey's focused images give us an animal's surrealistic, enlarged perspective of heads and eyes in word groups that themselves enlarge the objects represented. For example, in **"Madness,"** a family hound is bitten by a rabid female fox, and the experience of sound and pain is conveyed and enlarged in a poetic form marked by the isolation of intensified moments from the story:

she bit down
Hard on a great yell
To the house being eaten alive
By April's leaves. Bawled; they came and found.
The children cried

Helping tote to the full moon
Of the kitchen   "I carried the head"   O full of
eyes
Heads kept coming across, and friends and family
         Hurt   hurt
   The spirit of the household, on the kitchen
Table being thick-sewed

(*Eye-Beaters* 48)

To no small degree, the basic representational device in this poem progressively becomes the form of the poem. That is, the strategic isolation of the names of fragments

of events results in a magic pointillism that fixes as its primary patterned reality the surrealistic aspects of the core event that pattern depicts. Summarized under the title of **"Madness,"** the basic narrative is simple: a family dog is bitten, becomes rapid, is hunted down, then beheaded. However, the stylized, magical story is considerably more complex, primarily because of the way it is told: the conversion of a family hound into an energized, manic god of the hunt and kill, who, through a narrative of hallucinatory frenzy marked by the contagious, explosive escalation of sexuality and violence, dies a divine death as a nonretaliatory scapegoat; the humans in the poem project their own mimetic desire for violence upon this sacrificial monster who is expelled from the circle of domestic safety and then closes the poem's process of overflowing violence with his own execution. Dickey's verbal methods of separation, individuation, and amplification are essential to the monster-making process because they amplify the dog's bizarre and dangerous traits into monstrous proportions, so that his sacrificial death, dramatically mandated, purges the stable world that he himself has infected and threatened. One instance of this amplification process occurs after the dog is bitten. It is carried into the family kitchen, and the phrase "O full of eyes" floods the moment with what Dickey construes to be the animal's vision, yet also isolates that moment with an image in which eyes seem disembodied and bizarre, as would befit a being which is in the process of transgressing normal social boundaries. That the poem is so effectively disturbing and dark reveals that Dickey's vibrant word-magic makes fully tangible the traits of surrealistic monstrosity which the poem requires for its sacred drama.[6]

Although there is none of the archetypal pairing of the intensely dramatic mythopoeic opposites of sex and violence in the three-page lyric **"Pine,"** this poem reveals several other aspects of Dickey's remarkable—and difficult—mode of magical meditation.[7] Cast in a sequence of "successive apprehensions" (or "four ways / Of being"), with a fifth, concluding, single-word section ("Glory"), **"Pine"** examines a pine tree by means of four senses: hearing, smell, taste, and touch. At first glance, the poem's process of thought appears to be built out of compounds—or, to use Dickey's own term, "a dark / Flood"—of traits which the speaker is "Opening one by one." Each section features, though not exclusively, one sense which Dickey examines by means of a series of percepts, analogies, intuitions, and visceral experiences of the body. This flood of synesthetic experience combines to form a whole of some kind, when, at the end, Dickey claims:

A final form
And color at last comes out
Of you alone putting it all
Together like nothing
Here like almighty

V

Glory.

(*Eye-Beaters* 46)

To some extent, Dickey's mode of perception resembles the kind of accumulation that, according to Denis Donoghue, constitutes "the self" in Walt Whitman's lengthy catalogues:

> he begins by saying, Let *x* equal the self. Then *x* equals *A* plus *B* plus *C* plus *D* plus *E* . . . where each letter stands for a new experience contained and possessed, and the self is the sum of its possessions. This is the law of Whitman's lists. If you say that the self—*x*—is the sum of its possessions . . . then the more you add to the right-hand side of the equation, the more you enrich the left, and you do this without bothering about the "nature" of the *x*. You assume, as most Romantic poets did, that the self is not at any moment fixed, complete, or predetermined, and then you are free to develop or enlarge it at any time by adding to its experience.
>
> (964)

The Romantic aspect of Dickey's poetic identity certainly coincides with the latter part of Donoghue's observation about flow and indeterminacy. However, Dickey's mental method of accumulation—and, consequently, his conception of his poetic "self"—does not depend on a mere unity that is the "sum of its possessions." Dickey does not build his perceptual objects out of discrete properties only, but, instead, conceives a different kind of whole constituted by an empathic mode of consubstantiality. One may best see the method in his word-magic in the Melanesian concept of "mana," which is a general, undifferentiated power that appears in different forms and different objects in a sacred, rather than a profane, world. In such a realm, not every animate thing possesses "mana," only certain objects that evoke a sense of wonder and delight. Sacred wonder and delight in the world of physical sensation and magical things (especially animals and natural objects in motion) are constants in Dickey's lyric universe, the various elements of which are bound together by a principle of shared power that Cassirer calls the "law" of "concrescence or coincidence" (*Mythical Thought* 64):

> Mythical thinking . . . knows such a unity neither of combination nor of separation. Even where it seems to divide an action into a number of stages, it considers the action in an entirely substantial form. It explains any attribute of the action by a specific material quality which passes from one thing in which it is inherent to other things. Even what in empirical and scientific thought appears to be a mere dependent attribute or momentary property here obtains a character of complete substantiality and hence of transferability.
>
> (55)

Even though the major parts of **"Pine"** are divided by individual sense, Dickey builds the poem's progression out of a fluid "merging of properties" (*Mythical Thought* 77) which is effected by collections of hyphenated compounds and jammed fragments of thoughts and feelings. These compounds—especially Dickey's phrase "sift-softening"—and his fragmented, syntactic shorthand recall the opening lines from the fourth stanza of Gerard Manley Hopkins's "The Wreck of the Deutschland":

> I am soft sift
> In an hourglass—at the wall
> Fast, but mined with a motion, a drift,
> And it crowds and it combs to the fall[.]
>
> (13)

Hopkins's "soft sift / In an hourglass" serves to remind him that his body decays with time and that he can achieve redemption only by "Christ's gift" of eternal salvation, "proffer[ed]" in the gospel (13). In **"Pine,"** Dickey's "sift-softening" does not stand for the "motion" and "drift" of a heightened sense of personal mortality. Rather, "sift-softening" is one stage in his poetic process of rendering both sensible and transferable the motion of the wind through pine needles. If yet another mark of magical thinking is that substance and force are not sharply distinguished, then Dickey's fusion of force and thing demonstrates even more fully his mythopoeic mode of transforming relations between objects into tactile, living presences which he offers to perception. For instance, here is Dickey's flow of compounded properties that he unifies—or, in his own word, "assign[s]"—as he makes the force of the sound of pine sensuous and, therefore, substantial:

> Low-cloudly it whistles, changing heads
> On you. How hard to hold and shape head-round.
> So any hard hold
> Now loses; form breathes near. Close to forest-
> form
> By ear. . . .
> . . . . .
> Overhead assign the bright
> and dark
> Heels distance-running from all　　　overdrawing the
> only sound
> Of this sound　　　sound of a life-mass
> Drawn　　in　　long　　lines　　in　　the
> air　　unbroken　　brother-saving
> Sound merely soft
> And loudly soft just in time　　　then nothing and
> then
> Soft　　　soft and a little caring-for　　　sift-
> softening
> And soared-to.
>
> (***Eye-Beaters*** 44)

Because the form of the sound of pine is difficult to grasp—as Dickey says, "any hard hold / Now loses"—he hypostatizes the pine's "sound of a life-mass" by inventing a sequence of modes of motion, each of which is assigned a distinctive trait such as sifting, soaring, and whistling. By giving even the softest sound a tangibility, Dickey makes his own poetic process of perception—and thus his poetic form—substantial. What was "hard to hold" now has elements that can be held, and can be held in a discernible sequence or form. Further, by making sound a mode of motion shared among the fragments of his "apprehension," Dickey also makes these substantial traits transferable from one part of the apprehension to another, and thus to the whole percept. The form of the stanza is the flow of the traits of felt motion commingling and building toward a whole. This process of substantiation and consubstantiation begins to culminate in the phrase "O ankle-wings lightening and fleeing" (44), which represents the magical fusion of the substantiated properties of the "sound" of pine; these properties include speed, lightness, evanescence, alternation, and texture. A few lines later, in its conclusion, the stanza reveals one whole, unified aspect of pine in terms of hearing. Pine's basic properties merge in the figure of "footless flight," which the reader understands can be heard yet is difficult to hear—like the sound of pine—for it is "coming and fleeing / From ear-you and pine, and all pine" (44).

Another way to examine the poem's formal momentum is to think of Dickey's cataloguing and combining of properties as a mythopoeic mode of predication, that is, as a preliminary process of naming—and thus dividing—an undifferentiated subject into specific predicates from which he builds a differentiated reality. As an analogue of this preliminary, linguistic stage of cognition, Dickey's poem makes pine feel like "mana," in that it emerges through his word groups with what feels like its own mysterious energy and power. Like the Sioux conception of Wakanda ("Great Spirit," or world creator, or mystery, or grandeur, or sacredness—the term is nearly untranslatable in English), the spirit-force of pine grows magically through animated substances and, in Dickey's case, toward an ultimate, imaginatively conceived unity that differentiates it from its ground of perception. In his primitive predication of properties and in his conception of an animated whole, Dickey's poetic method is radically perspectival. As Cassirer notes, "for mythical thinking[,] the attribute is not one defining the aspect of the thing; rather, it expresses and contains within it the whole of the thing, seen from a different angle" (*Mythical Thought* 65). Not only is each perceptual sense in each major part of **"Pine"** "a different angle"; each tangible attribute of each sense is also "a different angle." Further, as we saw, each "angle" reveals and incorporates the whole by means of Dickey's complex movement of concrete imagery. These new angles are themselves new views, new names of aspects of pine rendered plausible, determinate, and separable from the preconscious welter of sensation out of which pine reveals itself to consciousness.

In his verbal act of distinguishing perspectives, Dickey calls pine into being through the magical power of naming. With regard to this constitutive, predicative dimension, Dickey's perspectival form is a linguistic act of creation. Like the narrative thrust in many primitive creation myths, the direction of Dickey's mythic speech moves a differentiating human preconsciousness away from the chaotic condition of heaven and earth before things had names and thus could be verbally distinguished. What is magical and sacred about this naming is that, in Dickey's poem, names do not merely signify but convey the potential powers of the things named and thus symbolically created. In **"Pine,"** Dickey's series of imagistic potencies—for example, "Your skull like clover lung-swimming in rosin" (*Eye-Beaters* 45)—literally become

the poetic essence of the identity of pine as the speaker's whole being, not just the rational component of the human mind, engages the world of nature and its emerging objects through his nascent language. No better description of the epistemological implications of Dickey's unity-effecting word-magic can be found than in an analogy between the primitive process of object formation and its relation to language, taken from the biblical narrative of creation. Cassirer recalls that after the word of God separated darkness from light to produce heaven and earth, the distinctively human element then entered the linguistic process of genesis:

> the names of earthly creatures are no longer directly given by the Creator, but have to wait their assignment by Man. . . . In this act of appellation, man takes possession of the world both physically and intellectually—subjects it to his knowledge and his rule. . . . This unity, however, cannot be discovered except as it reveals itself in outward form by virtue of the concrete structures of language and myth, in which it is embodied, and from which it is afterward regained by the process of logical reflection.
>
> (83)

Dickey's one-word conclusion to **"Pine"** thus signals his sacred finale to the linguistic process of inventing a "momentary god." In this kind of "holy" and "mythico-religious" atmosphere, the unity-effecting name and the god's nature (or power) are thus felt, however evanescently, to be one: "Glory."

. . . . .

Another formal achievement derived from the momentum of word-magic and magical thinking in *The Eye-Beaters* is the most dramatic aspect of Dickey's neo-Romanticism, namely, his reinvention of the ode of terror. To be sure, Dickey has explored the world of nightmares and dream consciousness from the very beginning of his work in poems such as **"The Vegetable King"** (1960) and **"The Firebombing"** (1964). However, in **"Mercy"** and **"Madness,"** his word-magic in this volume signals his fullest and most frightening contribution to a genre of poetry that was extremely popular in the late eighteenth and early nineteenth centuries. Represented on Coleridge's dark side by "The Rime of the Ancient Mariner" and "Dejection: An Ode," this genre took its criteria for excellence from Longinus's classic treatise "On the Sublime," especially that aspect of the sublime that focuses on "the most striking and vehement circumstances of passion" (16). Because, in Edmund Burke's opinion, the sublime produces "the strongest emotion which the mind is capable of feeling" (cited in Ronald Crane 446), and because terror was felt to be an emotional corollary of the feeling of religious dread occasioned by nothing less in importance than "the supreme evil" (447), the ode of terror was held by many to be the highest form of lyric. Although there is no explicit theodicean component in **"Victory,"** this historic genre—"so wildly awful, so gloomily terrific" (447), as the eighteenth-century critic Nathan Drake enthusiastically put it—combined a number of traits that bear directly on Dickey:

To excel in this species of Ode demands a felicity and strength of genius that has seldom been attained; all the higher beauties of poetry, vastness of conception, brilliancy of colouring, grandeur of sentiment, the terrible and the appalling, must combine, and with mysterious energy alarm and elevate the imagination. A lightning of phrase should pervade the more empassioned parts, and an awful and even dreadful obscurity, from prophetic, or superhuman agency, diffuse its influence over the whole.

(447)

"Terrible" and "appalling," with a "mysterious energy" that appears to issue from a "superhuman agency," **"Victory"** is Dickey's striking nightmare poem about one of the most "supreme evil[s]" of human experience: world war. The poem recounts the story of a GI in the Pacific theater who anticipates the surrender of the Japanese on V-J Day (September 2, 1945) two years before the actual fact. "[T]wo birthdays // Back, in the jungle, before [he] sailed high on the rainbow / Waters of victory" (38), the soldier drinks whiskey sent by his mother as a present, then explains to her—apparently, in a letter—how he later found himself drunk in a tattoo parlor in Yokahama, with "four / Men . . . bent over me," who tattoo his entire torso with a brightly colored snake that follows the contours of his body:

> it was at my throat
> Beginning with its tail, . . .
> moving under
> My armpit like a sailor's, scale
> By scale. . . .
> . . . . .
> I retched but choked
> It back, for he had crossed my breast. . . .
> . . . . .
> Oh yes and now he lay low
> On my belly, and gathered together the rainbow
> Ships of Buckner Bay. I slumbered deep and he crossed the small
> Of my back   increased
> His patchwork hold on my hip   passed through the V between
> My legs, and came
> Around once more   all but the head   then I was turning   the snake
> Coiled round my right thigh and crossed
> Me with light hands

(*Eye-Beaters* 40-41)

The soldier's experience with this all-devouring, demonic snake warrants immediate comparison with two turbulent moments from Coleridge's odes of terror. Dickey's snake-filled, nightmare world in **"Victory"**—especially "the dark side / Of the mind" (*Eye-Beaters* 40)—recalls Coleridge's "viper thoughts, that coil around my mind, / Reality's dark dream!" from "Dejection: An Ode" (419). When Coleridge turns from these viperous thoughts to "listen to the wind," he hears, with greater terror, the "groans, of trampled men, with smarting wounds—/ At once they groan with pain,

and shudder with the cold!" Likewise, Dickey's world of war is filled with the pain of men, that of his living "buddies," "ready," as he is, "to sail . . . toward life / After death," along with the memories of "others long buried / At sea" (38). Even more important, the retching and choking of Dickey's soldier in a time of war suggest the sixth stanza from "Ode to the Departing Year," which records Coleridge's rage and shock at human slaughter carried out in the name of liberty during the French Revolution and at the massacre of Ismail in 1770. After experiencing, "on no earthly shore," a nightmare vision of the Departing Year, whose past events and "robe [are] inscrib'd with gore" (388), this Romantic poet awakes to find that his predatory dream continues to flood traumatically through his soul, to the same degree that World War II traumatically pervades Dickey's and fiction (even half a century later in Dickey's best and most recent novel, *To the White Sea*). One has only to place sections from **"Victory"** and "Ode to the Departing Year" side by side to note the emotional frenzy and and pain shared by the two writers.[8] Here are Coleridge's words, still striking after two hundred years:

> Yet still I gasp'd and reel'd with dread.
> And ever, when the dream of night
> Renews the phantom to my sight,
> Cold sweat-drops gather on my limbs;
>   My ears throb hot; my eye-balls start;
> My brain with horrid tumult swims;
>   Wild is the tempest of my heart;
> And my thick and struggling breath
> Imitates the toil of death!
> No stranger agony confounds
>   The Soldier on the war-field spread,
> When all foredone with toil and wounds,
> Death-like he dozes among heaps of dead!

(389)

While terror signals the presence of an emotionally animating form in both poems and indicates the genre to which they belong, the method of closure in each differs considerably, and this difference sheds further light on the momentum of Dickey's word-magic. To be sure, both poems close with a suffocating terror that demands release. Each poet has worked his way through considerable psychological pain; however, to remain in a state of such dread is emotional, moral, and political paralysis. In short, the pervasive terror in the body of each ode demands the poet's return to action in his conclusion, lest the momentum in each piece remain mired in pathetic tragedy.[9] This two-step process—stasis and renewal—occurs in Coleridge's ending when he warns England that it has been protected from the political terrors of the Departing Year primarily because of the military value of its geographic isolation. Threatened even as he closes, Coleridge hears "the Birds of warning sing," then personally resolves to be "unpartaking of the evil thing" (389) and to remain alert, "Cleans'd from the vaporous passions that bedim / God's Image" (390).

Dickey, also acutely aware of catastrophic evil in human nature, needs to be "Cleans'd" from his exposure to the atrocities of war, which, like Coleridge, he personifies in animal form.[10] Although both poets subscribe to a harmonious pantheism that incorporates historical calamity as fully realistic material for the poetic imagination, Dickey postulates nothing like a divine providence—as does Coleridge when he "recentre[s]" his "immortal mind" (390)—as a subsumptive or unifying principle to which he can appeal for relief. Instead, on a personal level, Dickey dramatizes an inferred, magical animism in which life and death are not exclusive opposites but shared moments in a cycle of perpetual motion. In a world in which life and death constantly emerge into and out of each other, Dickey's snake—unlike Coleridge's birds, "the famish'd brood of prey"—has a double nature. First, the boa constrictor-like coiling and physical mutilation of the snake constitute a "confrontation" or "death encounter" for the speaker, a poetic event that has an emotional analogy with his vast experience of death from war and simultaneously stands for his desire for the symbolic death of his mutilated war self. With what appears at first to be an "appalling" movement, the snake then enters its subject from behind, and an opposite movement begins, namely, the renewal of the soldier that is initiated in the poem's final line. Strangely enough, the motion of the snake alters—indeed, redeems—both serpent and host, for the snake acquires, in Drake's terms, a "mysterious energy" that transforms the soldier, Christ-like, into "the new prince of peace":

>   I   felt   myself
> opened
> Just enough, where the serpent staggered on his last
> Colors   needles gasping for air   jack-
> hammering
>   My right haunch burned by the hundreds
> Of holes, as the snake shone on me complete   es-
> caping
>   Forever   surviving   crushing   going
> home
>   To the bowels of the living,
>   His master, and the new prince of peace.
>
>   (*Eye-Beaters* 41)

As is the case with Dickey's animals in many of his poems, such as **"Approaching Prayer," "Eagles," "Reincarnation I and II,"** and **"The Sheep Child,"** the snake now functions redemptively by assuming the role of what is a shamanic commonplace in anthropological literature, namely, a power animal. In keeping with the classical, mythological character of a power animal, Dickey's snake acquires a "mysterious power" that is both malign and benign. On the one hand, as a cross-cultural symbol of the range of human evil (including war), the snake is a traditional object of terror. Joseph Campbell says, "in its threatening character, as a traveling aesophagus, the serpent is . . . an image of the consuming power of the . . . will [in nature], foreboding death to all that lives" (*Mythologies* 378). On the other hand, Campbell notes, "The ability of the serpent to shed its skin and thus to renew itself, as the moon is renewed by sloughing its shadow, has recommended it, throughout the world, as an obvious image of the mystery of the [same] will in nature, which is ever self-renewing in its generation of living be-

ings" (378). This ancient mythological connection between snake and moon thus enables the serpent to play its double role by providing it with the "self-renewing" power that is passed on to the soldier. In **"Victory,"** as in **"May Day Sermon"** and **"The Eye-Beaters,"** Dickey establishes yet another magical setting in which his poetic agent is energized as he tries to overcome overwhelming odds. On the road of this momentous psychic journey, Dickey's soldier struggles forward to rid himself of war by acquiring traits of natural objects which are really rhetorical, self-animating aspects of his own mind.[11] That nature should seem beneficent and helpful, rather than another debilitating oppressor, adds considerably to the momentum of the healing process.

Consequently, in Dickey's ritual scene, the moon is not static but carries with it a renewing, ancient, magical light. For example, in **"Victory,"** "two birthdays / Ago," when the soldier got drunk—drunkenness being another variation of the hallucinatory state of shamanic transition—he did so at night when "the moon burned with the light it had when it split // From the earth" (*Eye-Beaters* 39). Dickey's soldier, like this moon, has been "split" by war from the human and emotional ground that he desperately requires. However, this moon retains the "light" or energizing possibility to split, then become something different and uniquely powerful, a possibility and process that bear direct analogy to the soldier's ritual journey of healing and self-empowerment. While expressing a dynamic relation between life and death, metaphors throughout the poem further bind the motions of snake and moon, suggesting once more that, in Dickey's world, there operates something analogous to Frazer's principle of a power-exchanging, contagious magic. When the soldier says, "I reached for the bottle. It was dying and the moon / Writhed closer to be free," the dying energy of whiskey's liberating hallucination gives rise to the snakelike motion of the moon, which sheds its animating light on the soldier's "smile of foreknowledge" that he will survive the war. Similarly, just before the visionary snake emerges from the bottle, the speaker indicates another, closer connection between snake and moon that images the archetypal movement of life out of death: "Had the Form in the moon come from the dead soldier / Of your bottle, Mother?" (39). Finally, even during the tattooing process, the passive host gives himself over to the animating, magical motion of the snake. Earlier, he described the snake by saying, "the angel / Of peace is limbless" (39-40). Yet as the snake covers his body, the soldier identifies with the shape and motion of this "dreadful . . . superhuman agency" (Drake's terms) and so takes on its sustaining and renewing moon-energy as he notes, "limbless I fell and moved like moonlight / On the needles" (40).

Even though Dickey's poem suggests that the "Form in the moon" (which I read to be an incipient image of the "snakehead") comes from a masculine source (albeit from his mother: "the dead soldier / Of your bottle"), and though the form's shape suggests a phallocentric image, the serpent is, by no means, a universal sign of masculine power. As an instrument of self-revelation and transformation, the serpent is conceived in many cultures as a feminine totem that symbolizes modes of coming to consciousness that bear directly on central religious components in Dickey's poem. For example, Campbell notes that in "India's Kundalini Yoga . . . the energy of life—all life—is symbolized as . . . a female serpent." In this sect,

> The aim of the yoga is to wake this Serpent Maiden, coiled in upon herself, and bring her up the spine to full consciousness, both of herself and of the spiritual nature of all things. She is awakened by the sound of the energy of the light of consciousness (the sound of the syllable "om"), which is brought to her first on the rhythm of the breath, but fully heard only when she has uncoiled and ascended to the center of the heart.
>
> (*Mythologies* 291)

As it does in this Indian ritual initiated through feminine power, the snake in **"Victory"** covers the soldier's body with a motion that constitutes a hypnotic, somatic meditation, a meditation that, like Dickey's poem, involves the total transformation and awareness of its participant. Examples of the movement of Dickey's snake warrant repeating here to confirm this striking analogy: "the snake . . . was at my throat / Beginning with its tail . . . moving under / My armpit. . . . He coiled around me . . . I turned with him side / To side . . . he grew. . . . I lay and it lay / Now over my heart. . . . and I knew that many- / colored snakeskin was living with my heart our hearts / Beat as one" (40-41).

In Campbell's citation, the symbolic purpose of the Indian snake is to unify all human emotional and psychic centers, whether at the lowest point in the genitals or at the higher reaches of the heart. This somatic concordance then leads each center along the "One Way Trail" to full consciousness at "the crown of the head" (*Mythologies* 291). To carry the whole man—sensory and cognitive, conscious and unconscious—through a comprehensive healing process, Dickey's serpent enters the soldier's bowels with the ritual motion of the mythical ouraboros, the serpent eating its own tail in the eternally circular process of separation and return to an energizing source. When Dickey's serpent passes the navel (that part of the body that Campbell interprets as a mythological symbol of "[the] will to power, aggression" [291]) and enters the soldier, we may read this event as the poem's climactic moment, a culmination of the fully conscious, circular transformation of the aggressive, wartorn, and exhausted phallus into an instrument of peace and renewal. Thinking through the physical imagery of the male body, Dickey transcends the merely physical by concluding in the mystical tradition of T. S. Eliot in "East Coker." While we may see a pun equal to Kenneth Burke's wordplay in his essay on the bodily tropes, we also see a standard, religious oxymoron in Eliot's words that locates Dickey's poetic attitude in a well-documented series of theological traditions, namely, that "In my end is my beginning" (129).[12]

If one thinks that this kind of closural magic (or, indeed, the formal, snakelike movement of Dickey's poem down

the page) is trivial or may be reduced to static, sensory experience, one needs only to examine similar forms of "religious" meditation in other cultures, ranging from that of the Hopi Indians to certain Oriental religions.[13] Consistent with the world-views in many of these beliefs, Dickey's magical method in **"Victory"** is not a form of escapism but rather a nondualistic way of clearing the ego of earthly pain in order to stand outside dominating sensation and emotion, and thus to free oneself from their tyranny. In many ways, the animating emotional form of **"Victory"** is analogous to the utterance of the mythic syllable *om*, which carries its practitioner through levels of consciousness, beyond myriad mental opposites, to the infernal and celestial vision deep within one's own soul. Dickey's magical, religious method of closure is thus both ancient and cross-cultural; it is directed to an external narrative of traumatic historical events, yet also inner-directed to the most sensitive reaction to these events by the human body. That this method should involve a sexual component becomes even more intelligible when related to certain basic religious principles, shared by Buddhist and Hindu sects. As Campbell notes of the Sahajiya cult in the Pala dynasty from Bengal, between A.D. 700 and 1200:

> it was held that the only true experience of the pure rapture of the void was the rapture of sexual union, wherein "each is both." This was the natural path . . . to the innate nature (*sahaja*) of oneself, and therewith of the universe: the path along which nature itself leads the way.
>
> So we read . . . "This sahaja is to be intuited within." "It is free from all sounds, colors, and qualities; can be neither spoken of nor known." "Where the mind dies out and the vital breath is gone, there is the Great Delight supreme: it neither stands steady nor fluctuates; nor is it expressible in words." "In that state the individual mind joins sahaja as water water." "There is no duality in sahaja. It is perfect, like the sky."
>
> . . . One knows then: "I am the universe: I am the Buddha: I am perfect purity: I am non-cognition: I the annihilator of the cycle of existence."
>
> (*Masks of God: Oriental Mythology* 351)

"Victory" originally appeared in the *Atlantic Monthly* in 1968. Twenty-five years later, in fall 1993, Dickey dramatized yet again his paramount interest in mystical momentum by using word-magic to conclude his novel *To the White Sea*. Here, his hero-predator, the American tail gunner Muldrow, shot down over war-torn Japan, is killed by Japanese soldiers. As their bullets go through him, he does not exactly die but rather enters a desireless, objectless, bodiless world, like the Sahajiyaian realm of supreme rapture, in which "the mind dies out and the vital breath is gone," which "neither stands steady nor fluctuates," and in which there is "no duality," for "the individual mind joins [nature] as water water." This absolute, circular flow—the union of life and death, waking and dreaming, pain and the absence of sensation—then hypnotically transports him to a kind of waking trance beyond even these harmonious opposites. In the novel's final lines, Muldrow's predatory quest ends when he closes his eyes and the individuality of his speaking voice dissolves into a darkened silence, which Campbell calls the "fourth element" of *om,* "the sphere of bliss," described in the Mandukya Upanishad as "neither inward- nor outward-turned consciousness, nor the two together . . . neither knowing nor unknowing . . . the coming to peaceful rest of all differentiated, relative existence: utterly quiet: peaceful-blissful" (*Masks of God: Creative Mythology* 666). In the purity of his motionless motion, this soldier, like the soldier in **"Victory,"** is propelled by the momentum of Dickey's extraordinary word-magic into the ecstatic silence that is his and its own final form:

> When I tell you this, just say that it came from a voice in the wind: a voice without a voice, which doesn't make a sound. You can pick it up any time it snows, where you are, or even just when the wind is from the north, from anywhere north of east or west. I was in the place I tried to get to. I had made it in exactly the shape I wanted to be in, though maybe just a little beat up. But the main thing was that I had got to the landscape and the weather, and you can remember me standing there with the bullets going through, and me not feeling a thing. There it was. A red wall blazed. For a second there was a terrific heat, like somebody had opened a furnace door, the most terrible heat, something that could have burned up the world, and I was sure I was gone. But the cold and the snow came back. The wind mixed the flakes, and I knew I had it. I was in it, and part of it. I matched it all. And I will be everywhere in it from now on. You will be able to hear me, just like you're hearing me now. Everywhere in it, for the first time and the last, as soon as I close my eyes.

(274-75)

Notes

1. Poems that I should like to nominate as major in this collection are "Under Buzzards" (part 2 of "Diabetes"), "Mercy," "Victory," "Pine," "Madness," "The Eye-Beaters," and "Turning Away."

2. For example, "the stagy, unpleasant hysteria" with which Leibowitz faults Dickey may, in fact, be an emotional sign that Dickey has formally achieved exactly the kind of poem he intended to produce, with "hysterical" effects totally appropriate to its genre. See my discussion of "Madness," "Mercy," and "Victory" below. Ernest Suarez deals perceptively with the considerable critical misperception of Dickey, especially in chapter 4. See also Romy Heylen's valuable distinction between "reflection poetry" and "a participation poem or performance poem that quite simply must be experienced," with Dickey falling under the latter heading.

3. Dickey's speech, titled "The G.I. Can of Beets, The Fox in the Wave, and The Hammers Over Open Ground," is collected in *Night Hurdling* (124-40).

4. Whether or not we agree that "spindrift" cannot be part of this seal's vision—one recalls Crane's own, vigorous defense of his language in a famous letter to Harriet Monroe (*Poems* 234-40)—Dickey's comments on Crane's word selection lead to further considerations about magical wordplay in poetry which are relevant for the beginning of our inquiry.

5. For Dickey's view of William James, see Baughman, *Voiced Connections* 155.

6. Dickey calls this mode of lyric "country surrealism" (*Sorties* 100).

7. My own reading of "Pine" differs from yet is indebted to Ernest Suarez's analysis (134-36).

8. If we apply Drake's criteria as well as conventional standards of the ode to "Victory" and "Ode to the Departing Year," we find that both poems qualify as singular representatives in the genre of terror. First, both poems are long—Dickey's at 131 lines, Coleridge's at 161—which enables each to develop a considerable vastness of conception regarding war and the toll it takes on human emotion. Further, both possess an occasional reference of considerable, if not ceremonial, importance, Dickey's to V-J Day, Coleridge's to the year 1796 and a preceding, tragic history; each occasional reference produces the feeling of an elevated status of public utterance, even though each poem is represented in a profoundly personal mode of address. Both poems entail elaborate stanzaic organization, exquisite detail and coloring, and a somewhat similar style of indentation, although Dickey's is more pronounced and much less regular than Coleridge's. While Dickey uses no rhyme and his tone is less heightened, both lyrics convey a considerable seriousness that slowly alters and transports the reader into a state of impassioned dread. Rhetorically, this dread aids the political position of each poet by giving him a vulnerable sincerity that makes him sympathetic and morally convincing.

9. Arguing for the value of "poetic" rather than merely "semantic" meaning, Kenneth Burke puts the issue in a poignant statement that could well represent Dickey's poetic stand against certain self-indulgent aspects of confessional poetry: "I wonder how long it has been since a poet has asked himself . . . Suppose I did not simply wish to load upon the broad shoulders of the public medium my own ungainly appetites and ambitions? Suppose that, gnarled as I am, I did not consider it enough simply to seek payment for my gnarledness, the establishment of communion through evils held in common? Suppose I would also erect a structure of encouragement, for all of us? How should I go about it, in the sequence of imagery, not merely to bring us most poignantly *into* hell, but also *out* again? . . . Must there not, for every flight, be also a return, before my work can be called complete as a moral act?" (*Philosophy* 138-39).

10. As critic Ronald Baughman poignantly points out in "James Dickey's War Poetry: A 'Saved, Shaken Life,'" it is not just the snake that terrorizes Dickey,

but also a veteran's residual terror of surviving the war. It is a well known biographical fact that Dickey spent the formative years of his young adulthood (1942-46) serving in the Army Air Force in the South Pacific. After Dickey flew nearly one hundred missions with the 418th Night Fighters, after he saw his American colleagues killed and mutilated by the enemy, and after he was an integral part of the killing mechanism of war, it is little wonder that so much of Dickey's poetry is driven by his internal need to deal emotionally with the shock of combat.

11. This self-enabling rhetoric is extremely important, especially on a personal and emotional level. The reader has only to ask how many times he or she has had to fight back from psychological or physical attack, whether in a major social arena such as world war or in the wars conducted on the battlegrounds of one's profession, family, or love life, where the threat of failure is the constant enemy. For a similar rhetoric, though presented in a more explicit mode of direct address, see Whitman's "A Noiseless Patient Spider" (Whitman 450). See also "Rhetoric and Primitive Magic" and the "Realistic Function of Rhetoric" in Kenneth Burke's *A Rhetoric of Motives* (40-46).

12. See Kenneth Burke, "The Thinking of the Body" and "Somnia ad Urinandnum," *Language as Symbolic Action* 308-58. See also William James's famous chapter "Mysticism" in *The Varieties of Religious Experience* 299-336.

13. See Joseph Campbell's description of the Hopi Indian Snake Dance, which occurs in late August in the lunar month called "the Big Feast Moon," in *Mythologies* 290.

Works Cited

Baughman, Ronald. "James Dickey's War Poetry: A 'Saved, Shaken Life.'" *South Carolina Review* 10 (Apr. 1983): 38-48.

———, ed. *The Voiced Connections of James Dickey: Interviews and Conversations.* Columbia: U of South Carolina P, 1989.

Burke, Kenneth. *Language as Symbolic Action: Essays on Life, Literature, and Method.* Berkeley: U of California P, 1966.

———. *The Philosophy of Literary Form: Studies in Symbolic Action.* New York: Vintage, 1957.

———. *A Rhetoric of Motives.* Berkeley: U of California P, 1969.

Campbell, Joseph. *The Masks of God: Creative Mythology.* New York: Viking, 1968.

———. *The Masks of God: Oriental Mythology.* New York: Viking, 1962.

———. *Mythologies of the Primitive Planters: The Middle and Southern Americas.* Part 3 of *The Way of the Seeded Earth.* Vol. 2 of *Historical Atlas of World Mythology.* New York: Harper, 1989.

———. *The Sacrifice.* Part 1 of *The Way of the Seeded Earth.* Vol. 2 of *Historical Atlas of World Mythology.* New York: Harper, 1988.

Cassirer, Ernst. *Language and Myth.* Trans. Susanne K. Langer. New York: Dover, 1946.

———. *Mythical Thought.* Vol. 2 of *The Philosophy of Symbolic Forms.* Trans. Ralph Manheim. New Haven: Yale UP, 1955.

Coleridge, Samuel Taylor. Poems and prose. *English Romantic Poetry and Prose.* Ed. Russell Noyes. New York: Oxford UP, 1956. 373-447.

Crane, Hart. *The Complete Poems and Selected Letters and Prose of Hart Crane.* Ed. Brom Weber. Garden City, NY: Anchor, 1966.

Crane, Ronald, ed. *Critics and Criticism: Ancient and Modern.* Chicago: U of Chicago P, 1952.

Davison, Peter. "The Difficulties of Being Major: The Poetry of Robert Lowell and James Dickey." *Atlantic Monthly* Oct. 1967: 223-30.

DeMott, Benjamin. "The 'More' Life School and James Dickey." *Saturday Review* 28 Mar. 1970: 38.

Dickey, James. *The Central Motion: Poems, 1968-1979.* Middletown, CT: Wesleyan UP, 1983.

———. *The Eagle's Mile.* Hanover: Wesleyan UP, 1990.

———. *The Eye-Beaters, Blood, Victory, Madness, Buckhead and Mercy.* Garden City, NY: Doubleday, 1970.

———. *Night Hurdling: Poems, Essays, Conversations, Commencements, and Afterwords.* Columbia, SC, and Bloomfield Hills, MI: Bruccoli Clark, 1983.

———. *Poems 1957-1967.* Middletown, CT: Wesleyan UP, 1967.

———. *Puella.* Garden City, NY: Doubleday, 1982.

———. *Self-Interviews.* New York: Dell, 1970.

———. *Sorties.* Baton Rouge: Louisiana State UP, 1984.

———. *To the White Sea.* New York: Houghton, 1993.

Donoghue, Denis. "Walt Whitman." *Leaves of Grass.* Ed. Sculley Bradley and Harold W. Blodgett. New York: Norton, 1973. 962-72.

Eliot, T. S. "East Coker." *The Complete Poems and Plays: 1909-1950.* New York: Harcourt, 1952. 123-29.

Frazer, Sir James George. *The Golden Bough.* New York: Macmillan, 1963.

Heylen, Romy. "James Dickey's The Zodiac: A Self-Translation?" *James Dickey Newsletter* 6.2 (1990): 2-17.

Hopkins, Gerard Manley. *Poems and Prose of Gerard Manley Hopkins.* Ed. W. H. Gardner. Baltimore: Penguin, 1953.

Howard, Richard. "Resurrection for a Little While." *Nation* 23 Mar. 1970: 341-42.

James, William. *The Varieties of Religious Experience.* London: Collier, 1961.

Leibowitz, Herbert. "The Moiling of Secret Forces: *The Eye-Beaters, Blood, Victory, Madness, Buckhead and Mercy.*" *The Imagination as Glory: The Poetry of James Dickey.* Ed. Bruce Weigl and T. R. Hummer. Urbana: U of Illinois P, 1984. 130.

Longinus. "On the Sublime." Ed. Mark Schorer, Josephine Miles, and Gordon McKenzie. *Criticism: The Foundations of Modern Literary Judgment.* New York: Harcourt, 1948. 10-24.

Simon, John. Rev. of *Poems 1957-1967,* by James Dickey. *Commonweal* 1 Dec. 1967: 315.

Suarez, Ernest. *James Dickey and the Politics of Canon: Assessing the Savage Ideal.* Columbia: U of Missouri P, 1993.

Tulip, James. "Robert Lowell and James Dickey." *Poetry Australia* 24 (Oct. 1968): 39-47.

Untermeyer, Louis. "A Way of Seeing and Saying." *Saturday Review* 6 May 1967: 55.

Susanna Rich (essay date 1996)

SOURCE: Rich, Susanna. "Dickey's 'The Firebombing'." *Explicator* 54, no. 2 (winter 1996): 110-13.

[*In the following essay, Rich construes Dickey's poem "The Firebombing" as implicating the reader in its speaker's guilt.*]

Jacques-Louis David originally displayed his painting *The Sabines* facing a cartouched oval mirror. When patrons turned their backs to the painting to look into the mirror, they saw themselves flattened two-dimensionally into the midst of the battle of the Sabines against the Romans—either imprinted over the central figure of the woman with arms outstretched as if on a crucifix, or standing under her arms, as if under protective wings. With a slight shift, the viewer became imprinted over the figure of the naked invading Roman who has his back to us, a round shield covering him. David's unusual orchestration made a political statement at the time of the French Revolution: We are all involved and implicated in the struggle over freedom. The spectator may turn a back to it only to find herself or himself more fully reflected in it.

What David did with *The Sabines,* James Dickey does with his perhaps most controversial poem **"The Firebombing."** This poem, written sympathetically from the point of view of an ex-bomber pilot in World War II, has been described by Robert Bly as "gloating over power over others." He calls Dickey a "Georgia Cracker Kipling" for writing what Bly characterizes as "new critical

brainwashing that doesn't wash." But **"The Firebombing"** can be shown to implicate the reader in the blame for the firebombing of Japan during World War II. Bearing out the experiences of many war veterans, this reading is sound on several levels. First, politically, by sanctioning a government that, in war, sends people into battle, Americans sanction the bloodshed that ensues. Soldiers follow orders that are, "on behalf of the American people." Second, psychologically, when the weight of guilt is too hard to bear, we pass it on to others to share it with us. Dickey, through the mirror of his craft, deftly reflects back into the picture those of us who deny complicity and disagree with the poem's message.

The poem begins with a rousing imperative, much like a pep talk given by a sergeant to his soldiers: "Homeowners unite"—a one-line, two-word stanza that looms larger because of the frame of white space around it. Dickey uses five of these one-line stanzas in the first three pages, and then, just when we become accustomed to them, stops. His stanzas vary in length, organization, and line length. Sometimes he begins the next line at the visual point where the previous line ends. We feel dropped. All this variation is unsettling, inviting us to grasp onto some comforting structure, impose it ourselves, just as a government imposes orders onto its military in the chaos of battle.

Unsettling, as well, is his shift to triple spacing between words, dividing verbs from adverbs, prepositions from their objects, verbs from their objects, nouns from their verbs. This invites the reader to try, albeit unconsciously, to pull the words back to comfortable regularity, thus including the reader in the shaping of the words on the page and, by implication, closing the distance between us as passive listeners and the speaker as active creator. In some places this spacing invites us to punctuate, as for example in these lines:

> Grocery baskets   toy fire engines
> New Buicks stalled by the half-moon
> Shining at midnight on crossroads   green paint
> Of jolly garden tools   red Christmas ribbons:

This invitation to punctuate is a haunting move, for dropping punctuation into written discourse as an afterthought, done by someone other than the author, is visually, and metaphorically, like dropping bombs into a landscape.

Dickey further unsettles us with stutterings:

> In a dark dream   that   that is
> That is like flying inside someone's head
> Think of this   this of this
>   . . . . .
> Letting go   letting go

As with any stutterer, we are tempted to say it for him just to stop the halting, get closure, be finished with it. And so we are drawn into the bombing, for these lines stutter the way a machine gun would. We want the words to empty out, the bombs to leave the bomb bay. With these and other unsettling moves Dickey makes us vulnerable, forcing us to look for some structure into which we can settle.

Dickey also draws us in with patterns such as anagramatic alliteration. For example, he often starts a series of lines with the same letters, as in stanza 3:

> There are cowl flaps . . .
> The shovel-marked . . .
> The enemy . . .

or later:

> Forever I do sleep . . .
> For home that breaks . . .
> From my wingtips . . .

Even his capitalization of first words offers the safety of return, and so we grab for the next line, and the next line, and are driven along to read more of the bomber's rapturous ode. Then there are visual and aural alliterations that link words in lines and across lines: the *b*'s in,

> Break under the first bomb, around those
> In bed, or late in public baths . . .

and the look and sound of *c*'s in,

> Of Chicago fire:
> Come up with the carp pond showing . . .

Whitmanesque catalogues of the landscape viewed from the cockpit name the elements of what is being bombed, like Adam's first naming and thus making conscious the parts of Paradise. We are drawn to this voice by its exuberance and power. We want to be part of a power that is not affected by moral strictures that seem, like the Japanese villages seen from the distance of an airplane, mere abstractions.

It would be easy for us to blame the pilot-speaker, to unburden ourselves of the guilt of having enjoyed this poem and of feeling the power of destruction. But there is the "Catch 22": If we blame the firebomber, we destroy what we have co-created, and if we do not, then we are co-pilots and guilty as well.

Dickey begins **"The Firebombing"** with an epigram taken from the Book of Job, "Or hast thou an arm like God?" Dickey offers us two alternatives: to be blameworthy by blaming the firebomber for his lack of guilt, or to be forgiven by forgiving; to damn like the devil, or to forgive with the sweep of God's arm, and thus, like David's spectator, become the Christlike Sabine with outstretched arms—the one taken in violence.

Work Cited

Dickey, James. "The Firebombing." *Buckdancer's Choice.* Middletown: Wesleyan UP, 1965. 181-88.

Russell Fraser (essay date 1998)

SOURCE: Fraser, Russell. "James Dickey's Dear God of the Wildness of Poetry." *Southern Review* 34, no. 1 (winter 1998): 112-24.

[*In the following essay, Fraser records his impressions of Dickey's poetic voice and style.*]

Dickey invokes this "Dear God of the wildness of poetry" in a poem of the '60s, **"For the Last Wolverine."** He liked poems about animals, the wilder the better. Doomed to extinction, the wolverine gnaws its prey and looks straight at eternity, dimly aware of being the last of its kind. The poet doesn't mind if the reader thinks of him. Omnivorous and insatiable, he is like Thoreau devouring the woodchuck, all of it, hooves, hair, and hide.

When Dickey died at the beginning of 1997, he had dwindled, said his friend Lance Morrow, to a seventy-three-year-old ruin, "his flesh slack over the armature of bone, the lungs and liver a disaster." *Life* magazine, introducing the pop icon thirty years before, didn't script an ending like this. The "bare-chested bard" it celebrated "looks, acts and often talks exactly like a professional football coach." Standing six feet three inches and weighing 205 pounds, he has a paunch and huge biceps, incidentally a fresh literary voice. The biceps, etcetera, get into the voice in an elegy **"For the Death of Lombardi,"** the Green Bay Packers coach who thought winning was "the only thing." In the poem he is dying of cancer, and his boys, Paul Hornung, Ray Nitschke, and Jerry Kramer, storied names, stand around him. "We're with you," they say, having to believe there's such a thing as winning. "We're with you all the way / You're going forever, Vince."

This sounds like the stuff of "the Sunday spirit-screen," but the tricky thing is to hear what the lines are actually saying. They don't all speak for Dickey, a former football star at Clemson. The boy in the poem, sobbing into his jersey, is drawn by Norman Rockwell, whose art of half-truths misses life's bleakness, so stints on its glory. Dickey sees how the glory is contingent on loss. Not all of us win; on the contrary, everybody loses. Once golden like the poet—in his fantasy life a dead ringer for Hornung, the Packers' great running back—we subside into gray middle age. The poem's last lines tell us, when we look at them again, that we and the dying man are going the same way. Forever. But this isn't a poem that sets up expectations only to overthrow them, and the emotion it brims with is real.

Football gives Dickey his taking-off point for considering some home truths, incident to living. Life hangs by a hair, but the bruises it prints on us, "as from / Scrimmage with the varsity," are man-creating and help us survive. **"The Bee,"** dedicated to the football coaches of Clemson, acts out this proposition and is meanwhile an ode to the game. Putting the old wingback through his paces again, knee action high as it was in his youth, fat man's body exploding through the five-hole over tackle, it bids him dig hard, for something must be saved. His son, stung by a bee that won't let go, is running in panic into the murderous traffic of the highway. Racing to save him, the poet hears his dead coaches, their voices still quick on the air. "Get the lead out," they scream, and Dickey, leaving his feet at the last possible moment, brings his son down "where / He lives." At the end of this marvelous poem, he salutes the dead instructor who taught him: "Coach Norton, I am your boy."

But no modern poet is easier to poke fun at. More about football, **"In the Pocket"** is fun, except that the joke is on him. In the grasp of pursuers—"enemies," he calls them—he reaches inside himself, as sports-writers say:

> hit move scramble
> Before death and the ground
> Come up   LEAP STAND KILL DIE STRIKE
>
> Now.

That is what the writers mean when they liken football to life, and the only possible response is dismay. Dickey had genius, many poems attesting it, but critical talent wasn't his. He wrote too much, twenty volumes in thirty years, and the failures he left unchallenged drag his large output earthward.

He has a sappy, portentous side, and his young man's silliness doesn't go away. In prose reflections (*Sorties*) he should have kept to himself, he considers masturbation, "one of the most profound forms of self-communication." The best "abdominal exercise" was fucking. His wrinkled skin prompts this observation: "You can look at your foot . . . and it is not the foot you ever had before." Well, yes. In his late forties, he wondered how he would spend the rest of his life. A whirlwind, it was. "But is it the *right* whirlwind?" He goes on about sex, but "phantom women of the mind" got to him more than real ones. The confusion introduces a wistful Platonist, one who believes (according to Robert Frost) that "what we have here is an imperfect copy of what is in heaven. The woman you have is an imperfect copy of some woman in heaven or in someone else's bed." That is Dickey's idea. For better or worse, his poetry is restless, always looking over the fence. I'll come to the better part of this later.

He offers a target as broad as a barn, and critics who don't like him have a field day. He wouldn't keep his head down. That made him highly vulnerable, said Monroe Spears, a sympathetic critic. But this was lucky, for without the vulnerability, good things in his poetry wouldn't happen. In his novel *Deliverance,* he is Lewis, he told himself, a great white hunter more talkative than Hemingway's. His ideal society is peopled by "survivors" who live in the woods, hunting, fishing, and strumming guitars. Surprising us, Dickey had the nerve to sneer at Robert Bly. But I vote Yes to the novel's big idea. Thinking of how it would be in the wild, the hero says: "You'd die early, and you'd suffer, and your children would suffer, but you'd be in touch."

The nature lover owed a lot to art. Evaluating an artist friend ("somewhat derivative"), Dickey draws his own portrait, ecstatic as he bends to the work. Surely, some "original inscape" must be coming. But "[i]nstead, when it comes, it comes out looking like Graham Sutherland or Van Gogh." The word "inscape" is a tipoff, and much of him comes out like Gerard Manley Hopkins—"hoe blade buckle bifocal," and so on. Dickey's first-person pronoun harks back to Whitman's, and trying out the high rhetorical wire, he tilts toward Hart Crane: "O claspable / Symbol the unforeseen on home ground The thing that sustains us forever" (**"Coming Back to America"**). Dylan Thomas was one of his heroes, "the only predecessor." These are dangerous masters.

Dickey isn't a discursive poet, his unit being the line, not the verse paragraph. Many lines are catenae, multicolored beads on a string. As in **"The Shark's Parlor"**:

> crabs scuttling from under the floor . . .
> An almighty fin in trouble   a moiling of secret forc-
>   es   a false start
> Of water   a round wave growing . . .

His apprehension of things is paratactic, circumscribing what he can do. A psychologist like him finds it hard to sustain interest, and his long poems gleam only sporadically "like the flashing of a shield," a phrase from Wordsworth's *Prelude*. In between the gleams, the matter, as with Wordsworth, inclines to the turgid. Wordsworth's blank verse isn't part of Dickey's equipment, though, nor is Stevens's, in some great poems that harness the mind.

But his catenae are crystalline, at least enough of them to compel attention. In **"The Escape"** they fuse, creating a structure like the windowpanes in the poem, fitting the noon sun together:

> An enormous glass-fronted hospital
> Rises across the street, the traffic
> Roars equally from all four sides,
> And often, from a textile mill,
> A teen-age girl wanders by,
> Her head in a singing cloth
> Still humming with bobbins and looms.

Structure remains a problem—following his metaphor, the sun reflecting off the glass is apt to blind the eye—and Dickey's poems aren't easy going. The difficulty they give isn't the kind that arises from complex meanings but from a built-in liability of oracular poetry. W. B. Yeats on Hopkins (in the *Oxford Book of Modern Verse*) seems on the point or near it: "His meaning is like some faint sound that strains the ear, comes out of words, passes to and fro between them, goes back into words, his manner a last development of poetical diction." "Poetical diction" here means an arresting but florid vocabulary, language disoriented to quicken perception. Change the content, "never the form," said a cynical English statesman—good advice, but Dickey ignores it. Like Hopkins and the other masters he emulates, he defeats expectation in diction and syntax, as in **"Paestum"**:

> Snakes under the cloud live more
> In their curves to move. Rain falls
> With the instant, conclusive chill

Of a gnat flying into the eye.
Crows fall to the temple roof;
An American feels with his shoulders
Their new flightless weight be born . . .

The fracturing of normal usage irritates more than enlightens, and seems a modern affectation that will pass.

Dickey's self-conscious style approximates the condition of music, the big Romantic kind that aims to pin you to the wall. The other side of this is a paucity of nice discriminations. Declaimed poetry grows monotonous, and the bard is a windbag in long poems like **"Reincarnation (II)."** He hoped for language that "has a kind of unbridled frenzy about it," becoming (as he acknowledged) inevitably more obscure. Like Mark Rothko, to whom he compared himself, Dickey loved colors, "just colors," and wanted to build up "great shimmering walls of words." It seems they went up at command or by magic, like the walls that obeyed Amphion's lyre. His best poems say he knew better, but his aesthetic is slippery, befitting the man who was drunk (if you believe him) for his last twenty-five years. This was boasting, but of a piece with his advice to his students at the University of South Carolina. Tune into the "celestial wireless," he told them—the worst advice you can give to the young.

He wants so much, like a Thomas Wolfe in poetry, and the strain and cupidity tell. Everything is pristine and worth wonder. Compared to frivolous city fellers, he's awfully down to earth. In poetry, it's "the real, deep thing" that engages him, and he is "sure sick to death" of literary sophists. No misguided Platonist (the moralist now, not the lover of ideal women) put more stress on content, a great poem's "first prerequisite." Of course he didn't cotton to John Berryman, all that intolerable *playing* (his italics). T. S. Eliot's subtleties went by him, and Eliot's having-us-on definition of poetry as "superior amusement" was like a red flag to Dickey's bull. To forfeit this side of poetry and/or Eliot's breezy view of it seems too bad, a loss for poetry in general, in particular Dickey's.

"Learned treatises" on poetry made his thumbs prick, as did learned poetry, Eliot's or Ezra Pound's. He said "intelligence always leads to overrefinement"; and against "palaver, and analysis," he posed "large basic emotions." I think we take his point while deploring its tendency. Our age of criticism has had its revenge on a poet who looked skeptically at academic critics pecking away at their laptops. Being a critic, I have a laptop, but have had to lean on a friend who knows how to "access" the library's outsize computer. Punching up the poet's name, my friend makes learned titles appear on the screen—in this case of Dickey, upwards of three hundred. Though he was vain enough, that would have appalled him.

Poetry struck him with the force of revelation, and he never got off the road to Damascus. Reading Theodore Roethke, "the greatest poet this country has yet produced," Dickey realized with astonishment that he wasn't dead. Hyperbole is his element, but the second term at least is true, his poetry bearing it out. One way or another he wriggled free of mortality, getting beyond or outside himself. When he pronounces on life, his voice seems to know something he didn't.

In **"May Day Sermon to the Women of Gilmer County, Georgia, by a Woman Preacher Leaving the Baptist Church,"** Dickey brings us to the place where God speaks from the burning bush:

> About nakedness: understand how butterflies, amazed,
>   pass out
> Of their natal silks   how the tight snake takes a great
>   breath bursts
> Through himself and leaves himself behind   how a
>   man casts finally
> Off everything that shields him from another   be-
>   holds his loins
> Shine with his children forever   burn with the very
>   juice
> Of resurrection: such shining is how the spring creek
>   comes
> Forth from its sunken rocks   it is how the trout foams
>   and turns on
> Himself   heads upstream, breathing mist like water,
>   for the cold
> Mountain of his birth. . . .

Thanks to an enabling poet, down-and-outers, not out of pocket but evacuated in spirit, burst through the imprisoning bounds of the city into a bed of roses (**"Bums, on Waking"**). If we say that poetry is an act of generosity, Dickey's illustrates what this means.

He sought to re-create the world; and oxymoron, the conceit of the contraries, is a means to his end. "I want to work with extremely crazy, apparently unjustifiable juxtapositions," he said, opening as great a division as possible between his comparative terms. Sometimes he fails to bridge them or is only showing off. When this happens, he is like Icarus falling into the sea, a failure but the splash makes you notice. Napalm and high-octane fuel pair with good bourbon and GI juice in **"The Firebombing,"** and the plane carries a monstrous burden "under the undeodorized arms" of its wings. I'd rate these pairings only so-so. In **"Power and Light,"** however, he straps crampons onto his shoes to climb the basement stairs, smiling when he says this—an improvement.

All poets are oxymoronic, and really good poets make ill-assorted things complicitous. Seeing them together, we find not strangeness but congruity we hadn't noticed before. Eugenio Montale, a modern master—Dickey does variations on him in his "Free-Flight Improvisations"—has an antipoetic sun like drippings on chimney tops, and iridescent words like the scales on a dying mullet. Many grudge this mordant phrasing, but Montale wills us to endorse it as right for the milieu he works in. Reshuffling old bones, Dickey is like that.

Except that comparing him to Montale needs a "Yes, but" reservation. Though Dickey plays with standard grammar and the way words reticulate, violating as he does this conventional notions of form, his poetry is old-fashioned, an honorable word, and in its attitudes toward life more *pro* than *anti.* It struts its stuff, frowned on by approved moderns—Eliot, his great antagonist, heading the list. Whatever the subject, it lights up "Like a bonfire seen through an eyelid" (**"A Folk Singer of the Thirties"**). The eyelid is the delimiting form.

A poem for a dying lady, **"Angina"** is highly formal—try counting the beats per line and estimating the kind of poetic foot your ear seems to hear. Emotion that might be mawkish wells up in this poem, but the controlling form makes it supportable. Thinking of love, the poet imagines taking a chairlift:

> Up a staircase burning with dust
>
> In the afternoon sun slanted also
> Like stairs without steps
> To a room where an old woman lies. . . .

From the pink radio comes "helplessly bad music," paradoxically her only help; and death,

> A chastened, respectful presence
> Forced by years of excessive quiet
> To be stiller than wallpaper roses,
>
> Waits, twined in the roses, saying slowly
> To itself, as sprier and sprier
> Generations of disc jockeys chatter,
> I must be still and not worry,
> Not worry, not worry, to hold
> My peace, my poor place, my own.

Macabre and tender, this ending is like Emily Dickinson a hundred years later, not least in its spareness of line.

Conceiving of poetry as "part of the Heraclitean flux," Dickey rejected "marmoreal, closed forms." Alexander Pope is no doubt marmoreal, and so are epigrammatists like Walter Savage Landor. But all form is closed, decisions having been taken, and this sounds suspiciously modern—worse yet, postmodern. Still, he jibbed at the role assigned him, "a kind of spokesman for spontaneity," and said "nothing can exist without form." Dickey's distinguishing thing—after you notice the sensibility, vigor, knack for invention, and so on—is that he is a formalist in an age of slapdash. His style is gerundival (*moving, unfurling, keeping, covering, living, watching*), and favors parallel constructions:

> In some guise or other he is near them when they are
>   weeping without sound
> When the teen-age son has quit school   when the girl
>   has broken up
> With the basketball star   when the banker walks out
>   on his wife.

(Both quotations are from **"The Fiend,"** a.k.a. The Poet.) Walt Whitman, famous for breaking the mold, is such another, both needing a centripetal pull.

Or the pull is away from the ego. Too much *I* is a problem in Dickey, and knowing that, he took measures. He didn't want to be the failed writer of **The Zodiac** who "can't get rid of himself enough / To write poetry." He gets rid of himself by hitching on to public events (like the inaugural of the president, or of the governor of South Carolina), or by preferring narrative forms to lyric, where the danger of drenching the poem in the self is much greater. **"The Eye-Beaters"** tells a story, glossed in the margins à la "The Ancient Mariner"; and **"Falling,"** taking off from a clipping in the New York *Times,* reclaims territory that used to be fiction's. Doing what he can to slough the tyranny of self, Dickey imagines his way into a woman's life, or joins his voice to other voices, one that of a Chinese poet who died more than a millennium earlier. "The dead at their work-bench altars" tutor his ego, letting him know there's nothing new beneath the sun.

One of Dickey's permanent poems, **"The Rain Guitar,"** shows the opportunist, always a good role for a poet. Traveling England in the rain, he has his guitar with him, and it prompts the question: "With what I had, what could I do?" Winchester is the scene, but where is the cathedral? "Out of sight, but somewhere around," like the War in the Pacific, North Georgia railroad tracks, British marching songs, and a buck dance. Harmonizing, they make a tune all its own, affecting, also comic, also "improved"— Dickey's word—by lumping discrete things together, then fishing for a common term.

He has a gift for comedy, seen to best advantage in **"Daughter."** Powerful stuff comes our way in this poem— "Roll, real God. Roll through us"—and we might end up stranded in the land of rodomontade. But humor, toning things down, retrieves them. Its function is more than expedient, however—true of all the great comic turns, beginning with the drunken porter in *Macbeth.* Not chastely classical but deliberately impure, Dickey mixes tears and laughter, making a compound tougher than its unadulterated parts.

A poet in the modern idiom, he mostly frees himself of old constraints like rhyme and meter. But no good verse is free, an invidious word for poetry, and conventional forms are vestigial in Dickey, like the ghost of iambic pentameter in *The Waste Land.* He likes writing in stanzas, for example septets:

> And now the green household is dark.
> The half-moon completely is shining
> On the earth-lighted tops of the trees.
> To be dead, a house must be still.
> The floor and the walls wave me slowly;
> I am deep in them over my head.
> The needles and pine cones about me . . .
>
>   (**"In the Tree House at Night"**)

This sounds to my ear like a sestina, structure being firmly linear and feeling intensely focused but at the same time dispersed. Each stanza—there are eight altogether—walls itself off from the others, and such unity as you get comes from the anapestic rhythm, Dickey's hallmark. After seven lines, his poem wants to break off, but the beat, impelling us forward, won't let it.

Dickey feels at home in short lines, and if his metric were old-style, it would often be trimeter. The short line suits and helps generate his uncomplicated male truths, simple but not simpleminded. Familiar protagonists keep turning up, as in a repertory theater: stonecutters, hunters, fishermen, soldiers, and aviators—men of action, not introspection. "Therapist, farewell," he writes in **"The Eye-Beaters"**: "Give me my spear." Don't call him "macho," however, but a man who has his hands on the ropes. His competent heroes reflect him. "I have had my time," he says in **"Summer,"** and we believe it.

"The Lifeguard," stamped with the seal of the *Norton Anthology of Poetry,* is a tale of balked purpose and young life cut short; but an emphatic rhythm, both at ease and powerful, asserts continuities. Words recur, half a dozen of them, as in a sestina, and feminine endings heighten the disciplined run of the lines. At the end of each six-line stanza, exhaustion supervenes, the three-beat line reducing to two, and the poem seems to die on us. But then, a breath taken, it gets going again. This isn't dogged or defiant, like Samuel Beckett's "I can't go on, I'll go on," only natural, the way spring follows winter.

Form is the hero in **"Fence Wire,"** from *Helmets,* the volume where Dickey comes into his own. "Arranging" the fenced-in acres of a farm, the humming sound of electric current defines the life of its animals too. It does this the way Stevens's jar on a hill in Tennessee takes dominion over the world that surrounds it. A war poem from the same volume, **"Horses and Prisoners,"** has a figure that suggests Dickey's special achievement, formal but incandescent. Growing flowers pound like hooves in the grassy infield where the horses used to be, and the dead men are enclosed by the poet's mind, "a fence on fire."

Dickey's commitment to form isn't generally acknowledged. Howard Nemerov, in a 1963 review of *Drowning with Others,* sees "a willed mysticism"—damaging, if true. Nemerov's poet wills himself "to sink out of sight," like the man who speaks in **"The Driver,"** eluding the shape (or form) that declares him. But this version of Dickey misses the mark. Form in his poetry is the condition of life, and the "fence," always there, prevents it from leaking away.

Two poems worth revisiting clarify his conservatism, the kind that holds fast to dear life. In **"The Driver,"** he swims down to a submerged half-track and sits where the dead driver of the title sat before him. Wanting to cross over to the undiscovered country, he says, or tries to say: "I am become pure spirit." But only the dead, who no longer hear life's high requiem, can say that. At last he swims back to the surface and, leaping for the sky just before darkness claims him, fills his lungs with the breath of life.

Opting for life, he opts for a purview of truth. Religious cranks and political ideologues are, like willfully mystic poets, avid of the whole truth. First, though, they have to kill their truth, impaling it like a specimen. No poet aspires more than Dickey, but he settles for our human condition, necessarily a privation. He does this again in **"A Dog Sleeping on My Feet."** Taking his cue from the sleeping animal, he yearns to speak "The hypnotized language of beasts." This may be worth doing but doesn't go with what we are, and at the end he breaks off, faltering and failing "Back into the human tongue."

In the wolverine poem I began with, Dickey seems to exalt a "mindless" way of being, "beyond reason," and it wouldn't be hard to fellow these quotations with others. But it isn't intellect he takes aim at. The butt of his wrath is the desiccated and goal-oriented man whose instinct is for decapitation. John Crowe Ransom puts it that way in his poem "Painted Head," where the mind, floating free, leaves "the body bush" behind. Dickey's poems explore what happens when the mind is independent of the body. Finding out what happens, he quit his advertising job, sold his house, and headed for the territories.

"The Salt Marsh," another keeper from the volume Nemerov looked at, locates Dickey amid stalks of sawgrass, swallowed up in a growing field that offers no promise of harvest. His body tingles like salt crystals, and the sun directly above him destroys all four points of the compass. But losing himself, he finds himself, and as the grass bends before the wind, he bends with it. "Supple" is the word for this, for the poetry too, not stately but quick with motion, often musical, and by its nature communicating repose.

Music isn't prized much in modern poetry, going all the way back to Pound's animadversions on the "swishiness and slushiness" of the post-Swinburnian line. Poets and their critics, canonizing anti-poetry, equate dissonance and truth, and the bulk of Montale will illustrate nicely. Music resonates in Dickey, though, setting him apart in his time. He knew what poetry ought to offer—not finding it in Charles Olson, dismissed for his lack of "personal rhythm," or in William Carlos Williams's "tiresome and predictable prosiness," and still less in Mark Strand, whose "deliberate eccentricity" seemed merely silly. Never mind if these judgments meet your agreement: all the words are chosen with malice aforethought. Thinking them over gets you closer to Dickey's intention.

The rhythm he heard had to be "characteristic of the writer." Also it had to be syncopated, *i.e.,* off the beat. His ear is cocked for the beat, however, absolutely the sine qua non. The critical thing was to *move* on the song without losing the music. In the *Buckdancer* poems, the key changes often, but not so often that it baffles the ear. Prosiness was tameness, when the poem stops swinging or its claws are blunted or drawn.

The "timid poem" needed wildness, Dickey said in **"For the Last Wolverine."** But he wasn't a primitive, flinging about the bedclothes or burning down the house, and his lines for Richard Wilbur declare an un-Beat-like poet:

the great wild thing is not seeing
All the way in to the center,
But holding yourself at the edge,
Alive, where one can get a look.

"Holding yourself," as if walking a tightrope: this poet is poised, like a bow-and-arrow man, like a musician, two roles Dickey excelled in. The other term to key on is "alive," evidently equated with wildness. It doesn't mean abandon, though, but the abandoning of self that goes with complete involvement. The hero in *Deliverance* makes this meaning vivid.

But writing about writers, especially poets, one tends to straighten them out—a mistake. I mustn't discover too much order in Dickey, who had his crazy side, like Ancient Pistol when he sang of Africa and golden joys. The wildness he commends to us is partly itself, hair-raising when it gets into the music. Some examples:

on August week ends the cold of a personal ice
age
Comes up through my bare feet.

("**Pursuit from Under**")

My life belongs to the world. I will do what I can.

("**The Strength of Fields**")

Or this reminiscence of an old man in a terminal ward, lying back,

his eyes filmed, unappeased,
As all of them, clucking, pillow-patting,
Come to help his best savagery blaze, doomed, dead-
game, demanding, unreasonably
Battling to the death for what is his.

("**Gamecock**")

This recognizable voice of Dickey's sounds in an early poem, "**The Performance**," remembering Donald Armstrong, a fellow airman, beheaded by the Japanese. About to die, he rises, kingly, round-shouldered, then kneels

down in himself
Beside his hacked, glittering grave, having done
All things in this life that he could.

That is the voice we want in poetry, suitable for life's occasions, the kind we must get through alone.

R. S. Gwynn (review date 1999)

SOURCE: Gwynn, R. S. Review of *The Selected Poems*, by James Dickey. *Hudson Review* 52 (summer 1999): 323-28.

[*In the following excerpted review of Dickey's* The Selected Poems, *Gwynn acknowledges the energy of the poet's early verse, unfortunately underrepresented in this collection.*]

If James Dickey, whose selected poems[1] have recently appeared, is to have any lasting legacy, it strikes me that it will lie in the way he was able to infuse our suburban humdrum with an energy that is well nigh sacramental. Rereading early poems like "**Sleeping Out on Easter**," "**The Vegetable King**" or "**The Mountain Tent**," I *know* that this is just Everyguy camping out in a state park on the fringes of urban Atlanta, but a palpable shiver still comes with lines like:

I am hearing the shape of the rain
Take the shape of the tent and believe it,
Laying down all around where I lie
A profound, unspeakable law.

Those incantatory trimeters contribute to the effect, true, but I can never hear them without feeling a little smaller and weaker, without wishing my inadequate sleeping bag could hide me completely. As stagey and predictable as many of Dickey's performances seem when we revisit them, they were, and *are,* capable of generating an awe that none of his contemporaries ever quite managed. If I am not quite struck with it on reading "**Falling**" for the umpteenth time, I can at least honestly recall that I *was* the first five or six.

Rupert Brooke's reputation has declined mightily, but that falling off seems less precipitous than the collapse of Dickey's, the fault less of the poems that made his name than of the noisy celebrity and weak books of his last two decades. His work has all but disappeared from the anthologies of American literature, and even in Norton's recent *The Literature of the American South* he is allotted only the same number of pages as nikki giovanni! His son's widely read memoir and the inevitable biographies will doubtless spur reassessments; thus, it is good to have Robert Kirschten's portable volume at hand. That said, I can't help but have several regrets about the editor's initial assumptions and the choices that result. In an attempt to define Dickey's best qualities, Kirschten outlines Dickey's "four major poetic modes": his natural mysticism, his Pythagorean reverence for music, his romanticism, and his primitivism. These are valid enough, perhaps, but they ignore the solid grounding in his generation's realities that gave Dickey's early work such resonance. First, there are the war poems. Kirschten includes "**The Performance**," with its curious syntax brilliantly mimicking the unsteady acrobatics of its doomed protagonist, but he excludes "**Between Two Prisoners**," in which two captured Americans await execution in an island schoolroom, and the spooky "**The Driver**," where Dickey (as always, a problematical assumption) dives into a Pacific lagoon and sits in the driver's seat of a sunken half-track.

Further, I miss many of Dickey's best poems of postwar civilized discontent: "**The Leap**," a narrative about the suicide of a woman remembered from childhood; "**On the Coosawattee**," which contains the probable (and certainly less melodramatic) genesis of *Deliverance*; "**Power and Light**," a brutal blue-collar dramatic monologue; and "**Adultery**," which is bracketed by the best opening and closing lines of any Dickey poem: "We have all been in rooms / We cannot die in, and they are odd places, and sad" and

> We have done it again   we are
> Still living. Sit up and smile,
> God bless you. Guilt is magical.

I would have preferred more guilty magic like this (and where is the marvelous **"Kudzu"**?) to reprinting the ten-page **"Reincarnation (II)"** or more than the briefest sample from Dickey's last book, the inscrutable ***The Eagle's Mile.***

Kirschten states that his aim is "to gather and showcase [Dickey's] very best material" and in doing so has to admit that Dickey's collected poems, ***The Whole Motion,*** is a bit *too* whole for most tastes (even Dickey excluded portions of the slack ***Puella***). Kirschten does get a fair portion of the best ones in his limited space (the book is over a hundred pages shorter than ***Poems 1957-1967***), but it is probably a sign of the times that in introducing Dickey's four "politically controversial" poems—**"Slave Quarters," "The Fiend," "The Sheep Child,"** and **"The Firebombing"**—he feels it necessary to attach a disclaimer (his italics): "Further, *representation is not recommendation.*" Now we can all sleep better. One wonders how this editor would preface a selection from the works of Robert Browning.

Note

1. *The Selected Poems,* by James Dickey. Ed. by *Robert Kirschten.* Wesleyan University Press.

Denis Donoghue (essay date 1999)

SOURCE: Donoghue, Denis. "Lives of a Poet." *New York Review of Books* 46 (18 November 1999): 55-57.

[*In the following essay, Donoghue chronicles Dickey's life and career, his poetic development and influences, and his popular success combined with literary decline.*]

In November 1968 James Dickey told readers of the *Atlantic Monthly* that Theodore Roethke (1908-1963) was "in my opinion the greatest poet this country has yet produced." He also took the opportunity to rebuke Beatrice Roethke for allegedly setting a limit on Allan Seager's disclosures in *The Glass House,* his biography of her husband:

> It may be that she has come to regard herself as the sole repository of the "truth" of Roethke, which is understandable as a human—particularly a wifely—attitude, but is not pardonable in one who commissions a biography from a serious writer.

In the December issue of the magazine several prominent poets and critics replied to Dickey's essay. While they rejected his nomination of Roethke as the greatest

American poet, none of them wondered aloud how he had disposed of Whitman, Dickinson, Frost, and Stevens before awarding the prize. Nor did any of them remark that Dickey seemed to be claiming Roethke for himself and fending off rival suitors, even the poet's widow. That the Consultant in Poetry to the Library of Congress should be handing out the grand rosette to Roethke or any other poet didn't strike the poets and critics as inappropriate. In the December issue, too, Beatrice Roethke corrected Dickey's factual errors and said that "with one exception, a matter in which I had no selfish interest, Seager was free to say anything he could substantiate with honest evidence." There the matter ended, so far as I know.

It was a minor episode, but it marked a new, vulgar phase of Dickey's career, the years in which, not content to be a mere poet, he turned himself by force of will into a public presence, a mythic figure, laureate of John Wayne's America.

James Lafayette Dickey was born on February 2, 1923, to Eugene Dickey and Maibelle Swift Dickey in Buckhead, a neighborhood of Atlanta, Georgia. His mother came from an established and well-to-do family. His father was, as the poet's son Christopher describes him in his memoir, a "dilettante lawyer and devoted gambler who took his son with him to cockfights, or to watch raccoons chained to floating logs fighting off packs of hounds, or to just about anything else where blood and death had money riding on them."[1] James Dickey read indiscriminately—pulp fiction, Southern novels, bits of philosophy—and gave his spare hours to weightlifting and bodybuilding, inspired by Mr. Universe, Charles Atlas. In 1942 he enrolled at Clemson Agricultural College, did pretty well in football there, and enlisted in the Army Air Corps. In February 1943 he started basic training as a pilot, but failed the course and had to settle for the smaller thrill of becoming a radar observer, an "intercept officer."

After the war, he entered Vanderbilt University and started writing poems and critical essays, some of which were published in *Sewanee Review.* In 1950 he took a teaching job at Rice Institute in Houston, Texas, until he was called up during the Korean War and assigned to teach radar at bases in Mississippi and Texas. Returned to civilian life, he set about making a career in poetry, reviewing, and teaching, helped along by the novelist Andrew Nelson Lytle and the critic Monroe K. Spears.

Dickey's early work in criticism, collected in *The Suspect in Poetry* (1964) and *Babel to Byzantium* (1968), was remarkably pugnacious. He was willing to praise a few English poets, especially dead ones—Christopher Smart, Blake, Hopkins—and with reservations a few living ones, including Dylan Thomas, W. S. Graham, Philip Larkin, Jon Silkin, and Geoffrey Hill. European poets sent him into hyperboles: Char, Supervielle ("the best poet of the twentieth century," "my all-time favorite poet in any and all languages"), and Montale, "in my opinion the greatest living poet." But he dismissed nearly every American poet who might appear to be a competitor. He derided "the overrefined, university-pale subtleties" of the genteel tradition of American poetry, which was content with the "well-meaning, mannered management of nothing." He regarded Ginsberg's *Howl* as "the conventional maunderings of one type of American adolescent, who has discovered that machine civilization has no interest in his having read Blake." William Carlos Williams was "a poet of no merit whatsoever." Charles Olson was "congenitally unable to say one memorable thing." Dickey deplored the influence of Wallace Stevens, "whose mannered artificiality and poetry-about-writing-poetry-about-poetry have driven large numbers of writers delightedly back into their shimmering, wordy sensibilities and buried them there." He sympathized with Anne Sexton and other "confessional" poets in their tragic lives, but could not take their poems seriously. He told Donald Hall:

> I want a poetry that illuminates my experience. I want a poetry that gives me some of my life, over again; that restores something to me, or creates a need for more life, more feeling; something that gets me closer to the world: that gets me *inside* the world, in a new way, or in a way older than the world.

Roethke and Robert Penn Warren were the American poets Dickey praised most consistently:

> The powerful, almost somnambulistic statements of [Roethke's] observations and accountings come to us as from the bottom of the "deep well of unconscious cerebration" itself, from a Delphic trance where everything one says is the right, undreamed-of, and known-by-the-gods-all-the-time thing that should be and never is said.

Warren was of the true visionary company, because his poetry was "so deeply and compellingly linked to man's ageless, age-old drive toward self-discovery, self-determination." "I think of you as the best of all of us," Dickey told him.

But Warren was an exception in one respect. He was a visionary in the sense that his poems gave feelings and intimations every privilege over the authority of mere events, but he was also sane. Most of the writers Dickey cared about were post-Romantic figures, men ruined in their lives but recovered in their Orphic, Delphic words—Hart Crane, James Agee, Malcolm Lowry, Roethke. In a note on Smart's "A Song to David," Dickey asked:

> How shall we deal with the mad in their perfect disguises? From the beginning we have suspected them of magic and have wanted what they have, the revelations. But how may we come by these and still retain our own sanity? What must *we* do in order to connect safety with the insane at their clairvoyant and dangerous levels?

"What we have always wanted from the insane," he said, is "the life-extending, life-deepening insight, the ultimate symbolic sanity."

In this respect, Roethke was Dickey's exemplar: he had manic phases, and then he could not write, but when he was sane, he remained at one with his visions, and spoke with their authority. Before and after the manic episodes, he was the strange, childlike poet whom Kenneth Burke described in "The Vegetal Radicalism of Theodore Roethke." In an early notebook Dickey transcribed sentences from Burke's essay. Examining Roethke's *The Lost Son* and "The Visitant," Burke said that this poet "goes as far as is humanly possible in quest of a speech wholly devoid of abstractions." Using Kant's distinction, in the *Critique of Pure Reason,* between the three phases of knowledge—intuitions of sensibility, concepts of the understanding, and ideas of reason—Burke asked:

> Do not these distinctions of Kant's indicate the direction which poetry might take, in looking for a notable purification of language? If one could avoid the terms for "ideas," and could use "concepts" only insofar as they are needed to unify the manifold of "intuitions," the resultant vocabulary would move toward childlike simplicity.

Roethke's aesthetic, and Dickey's to a degree, could then be summed up as a minimum of "ideas," and a maximum of "intuitions," "concepts" being admitted as a regrettable necessity. But Dickey was more willing than Roethke to add conceptual notes to his intuitions, as in **"Power and Light"** he refers to "the red-veined eyeball of a bulb," and in **"False Youth: Two Seasons"** he writes of "the tight belt of time." Roethke would have stopped at "eyeball" and "belt"; he would not have added the conceptual explanations.

In "The Visitant," to stay with Burke's instance, Roethke begins with a natural scene, conveyed as fully as possible by intuitions of sensibility:

> A cloud moved close. The bulk of the wind shifted.
> A tree swayed over water.
> A voice said:
> Stay. Stay by the slip-ooze. Stay.
>
> Dearest tree, I said, may I rest here?
> A ripple made a soft reply.
> I waited, alert as a dog.
> The leech clinging to a stone waited;
> And the crab, the quiet breather.

It is "such a natural scene," Burke said, "as would require a local deity, a *genius loci,* to make it complete." Hence as the poem begins, "the place described is infused with a *numen* or *pneuma,* a concentration of spirit just on the verge of apparition." Dickey's note reads:

> K. Burke: "begins with such a natural scene as would require a genius loci to make it complete." Idea of a "completing" or "fulfilling" presence. "As would require" here the suggestive phrase. Scene which you set up during which the audience waits for an unknown

inevitability to be fulfilled, to complete the scene which requires it. Sense of presence. Might be fruitful. Can be terribly hammed up.

It is a sensitive note, up to a point, indicating that Dickey started out as an artist, however careless he became in that capacity during the later years. The *genius loci,* the spirit of the place, is implicit in the way its different parts cohere; it has nothing to do with an audience waiting for something to happen. But Dickey saw in Roethke's poems, and clearly in Burke's account of them, a direction of energy eminently congenial to his own talent: to endow a landscape, a scene, with the spirit of the place, and to constitute himself as that spirit. Corresponding to the imagery of Roethke's "vegetal radicalism," which features roses, orchids, and weeds, Dickey had his own geological and animal images of rivers, mountains, forests, deer, snakes, wolves. He becomes the *genius loci* by being attentive to the peremptory radiance of the natural world.

One of the poems in *Helmets* (1964), **"In the Marble Quarry,"** has Dickey descending to a quarry in North Georgia and rising with a block of marble on a pulley:

> To feel sadness fall off as though
>   I myself
>   Were rising from stone
>
>   Held by a thread in midair,
> Badly cut, local-looking, and
>   totally uninspired,
>   Not a masterwork
>
>   *Or even worth seeing at all
> But the spirit of this place just the same,
>   Felt here as joy.*

"As joy," because if Dickey feels himself to be the spirit of the place, nothing more is needed to authenticate the experience. If he wants to round out the experience further, he appeals to astronomy, the largest natural perspective that displaces metaphysics as the grammar of Being.

This explains, I think, why Dickey's poems take their bearings from the natural world to the extent of regarding the acculturated world as an aberration, however insistent. As a young man he read Alfred North Whitehead's *Process and Reality* and was impressed by Whitehead's emphasis on "presentational immediacy"—"our perception of the contemporary world by means of the senses"—and on the assumption that "actual entities in the contemporary universe are causally independent of each other." That seemed as close to the beginnings of knowledge as Dickey could come. Until forced by circumstances, he gave little credence to the world in its "later" cultural, domestic, social, political, and moral manifestations—the world in which each thing seems rigid to him and resists being transformed. "The natural world seems infinitely more important to me than the manmade world," Dickey said. "There's a part of me that has never heard of a telephone." His chosen poetic place is the natural scene, mostly

Georgia, the back woods, and South Carolina, where some terrain, even yet, is untamed, and therefore susceptible to his mythic desires, processes of transfiguration. In return for such attention, the natural world gives him the conviction that he is flying upon wings other than his own; it seems to take the harm out of dying by assimilating it to larger sequences and continuities.

But Dickey did not long remain content with the decorum of poetry and the *genius loci.* He got going as a writer after the war and started being noticed in 1954. He published his best poems in *Into the Stone and Other Poems* (1960), *Drowning with Others* (1962), *Helmets* (1964), and *Buckdancer's Choice* (1965). When Roethke died on August 1, 1963, Dickey thought that he was now king of the cats and should step forward to claim the privilege. When he took up his appointment as Consultant in Poetry to the Library of Congress in September 1966 and moved to Washington, he entered on a period of his life and work that was to be personally and poetically disastrous, though it must have seemed, in a material sense, a triumph. Sounding off on the poetry circuit, money, fast cars, women, drunkenness—"I like it like Patton liked war," he told Gordon Lish—added up to his becoming a star.

Crux: The Letters of James Dickey tells the wretched story, mainly because the editors decided to make the letters annotate Dickey's career:

> The letters assembled in this volume represent perhaps twenty percent of James Dickey's located correspondence. The double rationale for selection was first to document the growth of a major writer—how a scarcely educated jock discovered that he possessed genius and that writing was the only thing that counted—then, second, to document the ways he fulfilled his genius and advanced his career. Jim was unabashedly a careerist. He had a clear understanding of the odds against any poet, no matter how gifted, and he recognized that his poetry did not exist if it was not read. He deliberately promoted and exaggerated his several reputations—genius, drinker, woodsman, athlete—until the legends took over after *Deliverance.*

Most of the letters were written to other writers, and there are memorable details, as in a letter to Robert Fagles:

> Poetry makes plenty happen; it can change your life. My whole existence has proceeded from one *word* in a poem, which I read in an anthology on Okinawa during the last weeks of the second War.

The editors of *Crux* tell us that the word was "shivered," in these lines from Trumbull Stickney's "Live Blindly and Upon the Hour":

> Thou art divine, thou livest,—as of old
> Apollo springing naked to the light,
> And all his island shivered into flowers.

But what many of the letters reveal is Dickey's myth-making vanity. The materials include true statements, bombast, improprieties, and lies. I suppose it is true that he hunted deer with bow and arrow and diamondbacks with a blowgun. He canoed the rapids of the Coosawattee River. Did he, at the age of eighteen, marry a woman in Australia, as he claimed, before he married Maxine Syerson? No. In a letter to John Berryman he referred to meeting someone in Waco, Texas, "where I was in the Air Force for the second time, and just back from Korea." He was never in Korea. Nor was he a fighter pilot, though he allowed Bill Moyers to say on WNET on January 25, 1976, that he was, and he let the *Atlantic Monthly* call him "a former star athlete, fighter pilot with more than 100 missions on his record in World War II and the Korean conflict." Did he really attend a lecture by Camus at the Sorbonne—"and he was talking about the Existentialist proposition that we no longer have any supernatural sanctions"? I don't believe it.

The letters indicate that Dickey's life from 1967 on belongs to the history of publicity and legend-making. "I am at a stage now," he told Richard Wilbur on September 16, 1968, "where I can reach a really *mass* audience." The only thing he could not do was stay quiet. He was so compulsively accessible that an editor at *Esquire* thought he would pose nude for the magazine. He had the grace to decline: "Please tell Jill Goldstein that I have decided not to pose nude; that, really, is not for me." *Deliverance* appeared on March 23, 1970, and became a best seller, second to Erich Segal's *Love Story*. The book was Dickey's dream of immortality, man and the natural world, two forces nearly equal. His hero Lewis Medlock "could do with his life exactly what he wanted to," challenging the river, the rocks and falls: "My God, those falls must have been something, back there," Lewis says to Ed Gentry.

Dickey's career was now a triumph of visibility. "I am shaking the great man's throne," Dickey said of Robert Lowell on November 19, 1970. Filming of *Deliverance* started in May 1971, and Dickey had a minor part as Sheriff Bullard. Meanwhile he abandoned scruple and delicacy. He was out of control. *Sorties,* a ragbag of critical pieces, was one of the ten books nominated in the Arts and Letters section of the National Book Award in 1971. In a string of calumnies, Dickey urged Stanley Burnshaw, one of the three judges for the award, not to give it to Edmund Wilson, "the most over-rated literary critic I have ever read":

> His work is one long tissue of self-indulgent clichés and self-aggrandizement. And when I read the Lowells in the *New York Review of Books* talk about what a "great writer" he is, I feel the sudden cold touch which indicates the prevalence of literary log-rolling in this country. Edmund Wilson is a great writer to the Lowells and to the *New York Review of Books* simply because he endorses Lowell as a poet.

The award went to Charles Rosen for *The Classical Style.*

The Selected Poems and *The James Dickey Reader* serve different purposes. The *Reader* gives samples of every phase of his work, good and bad. It is niggardly on the early poems, but it includes nine pages of *The Zodiac* (1976), a poem I could barely force myself to read. It is ostensibly the soliloquy of a drunken Dutch poet, Hendrik Marsman, forcing the stars to deliver the meaning of life:

> You son of a bitch, you!
> Don't try to get away from yourself!
> I won't have it! You know God-damned well I mean you! And you too,
> Pythagoras! Put down that guitar, lyre, whatever it is!

The poems account for less than half of the *Reader,* the rest is taken up with excerpts from the novels *Deliverance, Alnilam* (1987), *To the White Sea* (1993), and *Crux,* an unpublished and indeed barely begun novel. (Crux is a constellation in the southern hemisphere near Centaurus and Musca; it is also called the Southern Cross.) The *Reader* also includes essays from *Babel to Byzantium, Sorties* (1971), and *Night Hurdling* (1983). **The Selected Poems** does not cover the scene; it intends to present the best of Dickey and to draw poems from all the books except **The Zodiac.** But again the early books, which contain his best work, get short measure; only three poems from **Into the Stone,** five from **Drowning with Others,** six from **Helmets,** and seven from **Buckdancer's Choice.**

Comparing both books with **The Whole Motion: Collected Poems 1945-1992,**[2] I find that the editors, while often disagreeing in their selections, are at one in emphasizing the social, domestic poems at the expense of the visionary or planetary ones. Most of the chosen poems are those in which an actual event has taken place and seized Dickey's attention, and he makes the most of it. **"The Hospital Window"**—it's in the *Reader,* not in *The Selected Poems*—begins, "I have just come down from my father," and I assume it started from such a visit. It may be that the visionary poems have not attracted many readers, and that the circumstantial poems are easier to hold in mind. But it is unfortunate that the poems of natural magic, such as **"Inside the River,"** have not been selected from *The Whole Motion.* Only a determined reader will go to that book now that the *Reader* and *The Selected Poems* are available. Here is a passage from **"Inside the River":**

> Let flowing create
> A new, inner being:
> As the source in the mountain
> Gives water in pulses,
> These can be felt at
> The heart of the current.
> And here it is only
> One wandering step
> Forth, to the sea.
> Your freed hair floating
> Out of your brain.

Here, as throughout the poem, intuitions of sensibility survive their passage through the imperative phrases. The poem is unlikely to win as many readers as **"The Hospital Visit," "The Fiend,"** and the celebrated piece of magical realism, **"Falling,"** do, but it embodies a distinctive part of Dickey's talent, the neo-Roethkean part, which produced some of his finest and least flamboyant work.

Notes

1. Christopher Dickey, *Summer of Deliverance: A Memoir of Father and Son* (Simon and Schuster, 1998), p. 30.

2. Wesleyan University Press/University Press of New England, 1992.

FURTHER READING

Bibliography

Glancy, Eileen. *James Dickey, The Critic as Poet: An Annotated Bibliography With An Introductory Essay.* Troy, NY: Whitston Publishing Company, 1971, 107 p.

> Compilation of primary and secondary sources until 1971, preceded by a summary introduction to Dickey's literary career.

Criticism

Berry, David C. "Harmony with the Dead: James Dickey's Descent into the Underworld." *Southern Quarterly* 12, no. 3 (April 1974): 233-44.

> Probes Dickey's theme of the connection between the living and the dead and the possibilities it offers for renewal.

Cassity, Turner. Reviews of *The Strength of Fields* and *The Zodiac,* by James Dickey. *Parnassus* 8, no. 2 (summer 1980): 177-93.

> Derisive reviews of *The Strength of Fields* and *The Zodiac* that generally deprecate the former, while calling the latter Dickey's magnum opus.

Corrington, John William. "James Dickey's *Poems 1957-1967*: A Personal Appraisal." *Georgia Review* 22, no. 1 (spring 1968): 12-23.

> Review of Dickey's *Poems 1957-1967* that sees the work as a record of "the growth of the poet's mind." Includes readings of the poems *"Adultery"* and *"A Folk-Singer of the Thirties"* as representative works.

Davis, Will. "James Dickey: An Interview." In *James Dickey: Splintered Sunlight: Interviews, Essays, and Bibliography,* edited by Patricia De La Fuente, pp. 6-23. Edinburg, TX: Pan American University School of Humanities, 1979.

> Dickey explains his views on poetic form and expression, comments on numerous American writers, and makes observations on the necessity and future of poetry.

Davison, Peter. "The Great Grassy World from Both Sides: The Poetry of Robert Lowell and James Dickey." In *James Dickey: The Expansive Imagination,* edited by Richard J. Calhoun, pp. 35-51. DeLand, FL: Everett/Edwards, Inc., 1973.

> Comments on the searching quality of Dickey's verse, its thematic complexity, the poet's skilled use of narrative, and his "explosive" poetic development between the years 1957 and 1967.

Friedman, Peggy, and Betty Bedell. "A Conversation with James Dickey." *Kalliope* 1 (February 1979): 30-35.

> Dickey discusses his thoughts on narrative, poetic revision, and contemporary American poetry.

Korges, James. Review of *Drowning With Others,* by James Dickey. *Minnesota Review* 3, no. 4 (summer 1963): 473-491.

> Includes a highly laudatory assessment of *Drowning With Others,* which only takes exception to Dickey's seemingly arbitrary use of poetic form in his second collection of verse.

Lensing, George S. "The Neo-Romanticism of James Dickey." *South Carolina Review* 10, no. 2 (April 1978): 20-32.

> Interprets Dickey's writing in terms of an emergent tradition of American neo-romanticism, while concentrating on his "poetry of the unrepressed ego" and use of "audacious metaphor."

Morris, Harry. Review of *Poems 1957-1967,* by James Dickey. *Sewanee Review* 77, no. 2 (spring 1969): 318-25.

> Criticizes Dickey's logic, prosody, lack of precision, and limited poetic development in his *Poems 1957-1967.*

Plumly, Stanley. Review of *The Zodiac,* by James Dickey. *American Poetry Review* 6, no. 4 (July-August 1977): 42-43.

> Calls Dickey's twelve-part poem *The Zodiac* "a mistake in conception and execution."

Silverstein, Norman. "James Dickey's Muscular Eschatology." *Salmagundi,* nos. 22-23 (spring-summer 1973): 258-68.

> Reverential sketch of Dickey's life, poetic vision, and technique.

Wright, James. Review of *Into the Stone and Other Poems,* by James Dickey. *Poetry* 99, no. 3 (December 1961): 178-83.

> Praises the clear and evocative poems of Dickey's *Into the Stone and Other Poems,* commenting briefly on a representative piece, "The Performance."

Additional coverage of Dickey's life and career is contained in the following sources published by the Gale Group: *American Writers Supplement,* Vol. 4; *Authors in the News,* Vols. 1, 2; *Beacham's Encyclopedia of Popular Fiction: Biography & Resources,* Vol. 1; *Concise Dictionary of American Literary Biography, 1968-1988; Contemporary Authors,* Vols. 9–12R, 156; *Contemporary Authors Bibliographical Series,* Vol. 2; *Contemporary Authors New Revision Series,* Vols. 10, 48, 61; *Contemporary Literary Criticism,* Vols. 1, 2, 4, 7, 10, 15, 47, 109; *Contemporary Poets; Contemporary Popular Writers; Contemporary Southern Writers; Dictionary of Literary Biography,* Vols. 5, 193; *Dictionary of Literary Biography Documentary Series,* Vol. 7; *Dictionary of Literary Biography Yearbook,* 1982, 1993, 1996, 1997, 1998; *DISCovering Authors Modules: Novelists, Poets, Popular Fiction and Genre Authors; DIS-Covering Authors 3.0; Literature Resource Center; Major 20th-Century Writers,* Eds. 1, 2; *Novels for Students,* Vol. 9; *Poetry for Students,* Vols. 6, 11; and *Reference Guide to American Literature.*

Katherine Philips
1632-1664

English poet and translator.

INTRODUCTION

At the time of her death, Philips was considered the first British woman poet of high regard. Her verses on friendship and royalist politics earned her the respect and admiration of such contemporaries as Sir Charles Cotterell and Jeremy Taylor. Having no model of prescribed women's poetry, Philips borrowed ideas popular among male poets of the time, such as platonic love, but soon shifted her focus to an unconventional theme: love between women friends. Scholars' regard for her declined in the late eighteenth century as critics dismissed her significance. However, modern feminist scholars have reinvigorated an interest in her poetry, particularly her verse regarding love among women.

BIOGRAPHICAL INFORMATION

Philips was born in London in 1632, the daughter of a prosperous cloth merchant, John Fowler. Her maternal uncle, John Oxenbridge, befriended poets John Milton and Andrew Marvell. Evidence indicates that Philips was a talented child, reading the Bible in its entirety by age four and committing sermons to memory when she was ten years old. She is reputed to have started writing poetry at an early age although no evidence of this survives. Philips attended Mrs. Salmon's Presbyterian boarding school in Hackney. Following her widowed mother's marriage to Sir Richard Philips, fifteen-year-old Philips joined her mother in rural Wales. A year later, she married the widowed son of her stepfather. John Philips was a fifty-four-year-old Parliamentarian. Despite their age difference and conflicting political views, they appear to have enjoyed an amicable marriage, producing one son, who died in childhood, and a daughter. Philips formed intense friendships with both men and women, giving them fanciful pseudonyms and referring to them as her "Society of Friendship." Whether the society was mostly a figment of Philips's imagination or if it ever met is a subject of debate. Many of her poems are written to and in honor of these figures with the purpose of being circulated among her friends. In 1660, following the Restoration, Philips's husband began to experience career difficulties, which his wife endeavored to improve via her field of influence. While in Dublin seeing to his affairs, Philips was encouraged by Roger Boyle, the Earl of Orrery, to complete a translation of Corneille's *La Mort de Pompee*. In addition,

she began writing politically based poetry advocating the Royalist position. In 1664, Philips went to London to attempt to suppress a pirated publication of her poetry from appearing; publication by a gentlewoman could have resulted in social scandal and ruin. While there, she succumbed to smallpox.

MAJOR WORKS

Because of the brevity of Philips's life, she left a small volume of poetry. In the first part of her writing career, Philips focused on the theme of love among friends. Specifically, she advocated a true form of friendship between women, a philosophical concept unaccepted among men at the time. Her best known and most highly regarded works consist of odes to her female friends, such as "Friendship in Emblem, or the Seale, to my dearest Lucasia." She wrote most of her verse in rhyming couplets with attention to regular meter. As she grew older, Philips wrote more about the political events of the day. In her later poems honoring public figures and events such as the coronation, she promoted a Royalist view. In addition, Philips completed the translation of Corneille's play *La Mort de Pompee* and left a translation of his *Horace* unfinished at her death.

CRITICAL RECEPTION

At the time of her death, Philips was one of the most highly regarded women writers in Britain. John Keats and John Dryden paid tribute to her. But Philips's reputation as a first-rate poet and pioneer of the genre faltered, primarily due to unflattering reviews in the late eighteenth century. Literary critics agree that Philips was generally viewed as a minor figure in British literature during the next two centuries. However, by the end of the twentieth century, Philips was garnering renewed interest. Paula Loscocco (1993) argues that Philips had declined in popularity when critics began to ignore the masculine aspects of her writing, focusing entirely on her femininity and then dismissing her as therefore insignificant. Scholars such as Kathleen M. Swaim (1997) and Lucy Brashear (1979) have questioned how a woman of Philips's social position and geographic isolation could have established herself as a prominent national poet. Through their research, they stress that Philips self-consciously created her reputation as a reluctant poet who merely circulated verse among her friends in order to promote her position and secure a popular standing. They warn readers to remember that Philips could only operate within the boundaries of the social confines of her day. Literary critics link Philips with Aphra Behn because of their shared interest in love among women and their groundbreaking work as British women writers. Debate continues over the nature of Philips's prescribed love between women, with some scholars arguing that she is advocating lesbian relationships, and others claiming that Philips referred to a type of intense friendship. Travis Dupriest (1992) maintains that both readings of her work are credible.

PRINCIPAL WORKS

Poetry

Poems. By the Incomparable Mrs. K. P. 1664
Poems. By the Most Deservedly Admired Mrs. Katherine Philips, the Matchless Orinda. To which is Added, Monsieur Corneille's Pompey and Horace, Tragedies. with Several Other Translations out of French 1667

Other Major Works

Pompey: A Tragedy [translator] (play) 1663
Horace [translator; completed by John Denham] (play) 1668
letters from Orinda to Poliarchus (letters) 1705

CRITICISM

Elinor M. Buckingham (essay date 1902)

SOURCE: Buckingham, Elinor M. "The Matchless Orinda." *Sewanee Review* 10 (1902): 269-84.

[*In the following essay, Buckingham relates the significance of Philips's contributions to English poetry.*]

Every age has its little lights that burn for a time with more or less brilliancy and then go out. Possibly a memory of them lingers on into the next age or to succeeding generations; but for the most part the memory is dwindled to a mere name, and few stop to inquire what gave the name its meaning. Among the names that have come down to us from the time of Charles II. is that of "The Matchless Orinda," so called, a lady who passed for a great poetess in her day, and who attracted to her side some of the best and most distinguished men of the Restoration period; whose poetry was read and admired well on into the eighteenth century, but who is remembered now chiefly because Dryden mentioned her in his ode on Mrs. Anne Killigrew, or because Keats praised her in a letter to his friend Reynolds. Yet she was a woman of strong individuality and sprightly wit, the first English woman to make a name for herself in poetry. Her letters and her poems give abundant evidence of the charm which made her so honored in her own day, and well repay a little study in the present time.

Katherine Fowler was born in London January 1, 1631, the daughter of a prosperous merchant. Her mother was Katherine Oxenbridge, daughter of a president of the Plysicians' College, and Aubrey says that her grandmother, a friend of Francis Quarles, was in her day given to poetry. Her family was Presbyterian, evidently of the well-to-do middle class.

She must have been considered especially gifted by her family; for a cousin, who had charge of her until she was eight years old, tells how she had "read the Bible through before she was full four years old." In those days a boy's training was first the Psalter, then reading the Bible, then his accidence—that is, the Latin grammar—and it was thought worthy of note that Alexander Broome was in his accidence at four years old and a quarter; while Anthony Wood, the antiquarian and scholar, born in 1632, was not put to school even to learn the Psalter till 1637, and only when he was seven years old was he ready to go into his accidence.

Little Miss Fowler had also a remarkable memory. She could repeat whole passages from Scripture, and "enjoyed hearing sermons which she could bring away verbatim, when she was ten years old." Evidently she was somewhat vain of her precocity. Being brought up in the Presbyterian faith, "she was much against the bishops, and used to pray to God to take them to himself." She was accustomed to pray aloud by the hour together, "as the hypocritical fashion in those days was," apparently in the hope of being overheard. Tradition says she wrote verses early, but there is no certain record.

At the age of eight years, she was sent to Hackney, to a fashionable Presbyterian school, kept by a Mrs. Salmon, where presumably she learned dancing, painting, and music, as well as French, in which she became really proficient.

As she grew up, the civil war came on, and as soon as she began to think for herself, which must have been before she was seventeen years old, she adopted the tenets of the Church of England, and became an ardent adherent of the royal family. At seventeen she married, as a second wife, James Philips, Esq., of the Priory, Cardigan, her mother having previously married the father of James Philips.

Whether religious differences made any separation between her and her family, as some writers suppose, is doubtful. She never mentions them in the letters that are preserved, nor in her poems, and none of them apparently belonged to the circle of friends she gathered about her. There is record of a debt contracted by Mr. Philips in 1653, for which her uncle, J. Oxenbridge, was bound, and for which the uncle was thrown into Fleet Prison twenty-eight years later; so that there must have been pretty close friendship with some members of her family.

From the time of her marriage, when she became mistress of a household, it is evident that she began to manage her husband and her acquaintance not domineeringly but capably.

The portrait prefixed to her poems shows a rather pretty, exceedingly intelligent face, with a good deal of mild but persistent will force, eminently practical and sensible. Mr. Gosse calls her "a bustling little Welsh lady." Aubrey says she was "very good-natured, not at all high-minded; pretty fat; not tall, reddish-faced." If she was like the women of to-day who resemble her portrait, she was probably the most efficient member of the household, with an ability for conducting clubs, reading circles, and evening card parties, an aptitude for drawing about her the best and most aristocratic society of the neighborhood, and for making herself beloved as well as quietly humored in her fads.

One of her fads was Friendship, of the conscious and demonstrative sort. As early as 1651 she had gathered about her a circle of friends, both men and women, who took fanciful names, Calanthe, Lucasia, Regina, etc., by which they were always known among themselves. One imagines her husband, a man older than herself and, if accounts do not misrepresent, a trifle sluggish of temperament, as good-naturedly allowing himself to be dubbed Antenor; but there were other men, men of note, who did not belong to her immediate neighborhood, who also joined the mystic circle. Jeremy Taylor, who was living in

Wales, when she went there, became the noble Palæmon; Sir Charles Cotterel was the most generous Poliarchus, and so on. She herself became Orinda the Matchless.

Whether the other members thought so highly as she of this bond of friendship is a question. One after another the ladies married and moved away; but it is quite plain that a large part of her thoughts were devoted to Friendship, friendship in the abstract made concrete in the persons of her neighbors. She was troubled by the sentiment some one expressed that women are incapable of true friendship, and asked the opinion of her friend Palæmon on that and three other points concerning friendship: How far is a dear and perfect friendship authorized by Christianity? How far may it extend? and, How are friendships to be conducted? To which he replied with a most satisfactory and complimentary "Discourse on Friendship," concluding with the assurance that, though a woman may not assist a friend in just the same way as a man, yet her friendship is as real and comforting.

All these magnanimous and magniloquent sentiments were intended for her private delectation, unless she thought fit that they should pass further than her eye and closet, in which case she was entreated to consign them to Dr. Wedderburne, to whose guidance Dr. Taylor committed himself. This called out an effusion from Mrs. Philips, **"To the most noble Palæmon, on his incomparable Discourse on Friendship:"**

> We had been still undone, wrapt in disguise;
> Secure, not happy; cunning, and not wise;
> War had been our design, int'rest our trade;
> We had not dwelt in safety, but in shade,
> Hadst thou not hung out light, more welcome far
> Than wand'ring seamen think the northern star.

Apart from these interests she had plenty to occupy her mind in her husband's affairs. As Aubrey says in his succinct note-taking fashion, "He had a good estate, but bought crown lands; he mortgaged," etc., with all that etc. implies. "His brother Hector took off the mortgages and has the lands." Mrs. Philips set herself resolutely to disencumbering his estate, and the few letters of hers that are preserved are taken up alternately with poetry, her friends, and the account of how the business prospers. In 1662 she crossed the channel to Ireland, partly to accompany her dear friend, Lucasia, who had just committed the much-to-be-lamented act of marrying. Orinda was sure she would be eternally unhappy. She wrote to Poliarchus: "When I have tarried here awhile, I shall return home with a heavy heart, but with the satisfaction, nevertheless, that I have discharged my duty to my friend, whose loss I shall eternally regret. She tells all of us she is extremely happy, and that all that love her ought to take part in her happiness. If you have written anything to me to Cardigan relating to this affair, pray write again to me to Dublin in Italian, for I know not when I shall receive the letters that will come to Cardigan the latter end of this week, and I am very desirous to know your thoughts on this matter, that, since I cannot bring relief to your sorrows, I may at least share them with you."

Poliarchus himself had aspired to the hand of the fair Lucasia, who goes by the name of Calanthe in this part of the correspondence; and the good Orinda must have enjoyed to the uttermost her own perspicacity in divining the future wretchedness of Calanthe and the value of her own friendship for Sir Charles in condoling with him, and, if need be, receiving his sighs in Italian, safe from the prying curiosity of others. Bustling, as Gosse imagines her, I do not think she should be called, but active-minded and eager to exert her abilities in all directions she certainly was.

All this time she was taking an interest in the affairs of the world, writing verses on **"His Majesty at His Passage into England," "On the Fair Weather Just at the Coronation," "To Her Royal Highness, the Duchess of York, on Her Commanding Me to Send Her Some Things I Had Written," "To Mr. Henry Lawes,"** besides many poems to her personal friends in varied meters. At the same time she was learning Italian, and in the course of a few months fitting herself not only to understand the Italian postscripts of Poliarchus, but to insert bits of information in that language in her own letters.

Once in Ireland and with Lucasia determined to be happy, she was turning to her husband's affairs, when she was distracted by a new interest. She had already translated a scene from Corneille's "Pompée," and, "by some accident or other," this scene having fallen into the hands of the Earl of Orrery, "he was pleased to like it so well," she writes, "that he sent me the French original, and the next time I saw him so earnestly importuned me to pursue that translation that, to avoid the shame of seeing him, who had so lately commanded a kingdom, become petitioner to me for such a trifle, I obliged him so far as to finish the act in which that scene is."

From this auspicious beginning she went on to what was probably the most exciting and happiest year of her life. She was introduced by the Earl of Orrery to the various members of his family in Dublin—the Duke and Duchess of Ormond, the Countess of Cork, and to the Earl of Roscommon, and others. Apparently she stayed with the Countess of Cork. It is the period of her life which we know best, because it was now that she was constantly writing to Sir Charles Cotterel for advice and criticism of her *Pompey,* which she undertook to translate entire. Not only so, but when it was finished the Earl of Orrery insisted upon having it acted, and "advanced one hundred pounds toward buying Egyptian and Roman habits." To increase the length of the performance, and add to the brilliancy of the occasion, she wrote five songs to be sung in the intervals of the acts, and was "promised that they should be set by the greatest masters in England."

One would think that she would have little time for anything else. No sooner was the play acted than it was necessary to publish an edition in Dublin. Then Sir Charles must be commissioned to present a copy to the Duchess of York, but His Majesty having asked for it, the original copy was given to him. Then a dedication to the Countess of Cork must be written. Meanwhile it was publishing in London, under the supervision of Sir Charles, and the poor lady was distracted between the fear that she should not preserve a proper decorum and that something should go astray or amiss.

But at last she had leisure to write about her husband's affairs, and we must suppose that she had not forgotten them all this time. Two or three trials for the possession of lands were coming off, and she was in a great state of mind because her witnesses were not forthcoming and she lost one suit.

In the end, and it was at the end of a full year, she departed from Ireland, having succeeded better than she might have hoped in Antenor's business. One wonders a trifle what he was doing all this while, though we do hear of his carrying Cardigan for Sir Charles in the parliamentary elections. And we wonder still more what was become of the little daughter five years old, whom Mrs. Philips never intrudes upon Poliarchus in her brilliant correspondence. Doubtless she engineered from a distance both the elections and the little girl's education.

No wonder that when she was finally at home in Wales she longed for a more active existence. She apologizes thus for a set of verses sent to Poliarchus: "All I desire is that when you read this poem you will not condemn me for a dullness that you will find growing upon me; but consider that my absence from all the conversation that can refine my wit, the employments of a country life, and the uneasiness of my fortune, are able to blunt a much finer pen than ever I was mistress of. And indeed I find the weight of my misfortunes sink me down so low, that unless I am quickly restored to the refreshing charms of your company, I shall be past recovery and incapable of enjoying it."

Even here, however, she found opportunities to distract her mind into some degree of activity. To her deep dismay, she had found after translating *Pompey,* that Waller had set his heart on doing the same thing, and that he and Sir Charles Sedley and their friends had been translating an act apiece, while her version was acting on the boards in Dublin, and the world was crying for an edition. This was sufficiently alarming to the lady, who was thus set up without intention as the rival of the most correct and most venerable poet of the day; but again in England, in this copy of verses which she sent to Poliarchus, and which he presented to the King and Queen, she found that a second time she had chosen a subject which Waller was treating. She was in great agitation. Not so much, however, as to lose command of her pen to turn pretty phrases. She wrote: "And indeed Mr. Waller has, it may be, contributed not a little to encourage me in this vanity, by writing on the same subject the worst verse that ever fell from his pen. But sure he, who is so civil to ladies, had heard that I designed such an address, and, contenting himself with having got so much the advantage of me in *Pompey,* was willing to yield me this mate in chess, and to write ill on purpose to keep me in countenance."

But a more serious disturbance was the surreptitious publication under her own name of her occasional poems, which by this time were numerous, and being passed from hand to hand, inquired for at court, the product, moreover, of a woman who had just achieved so great success in Dublin, had become well known and were worth publishing. This was a terrible blow to her. Naturally the book might have many errors in it, and various disasters rose in her mind. The mishap threw her into an illness from which she was slow to recover.

The accident brings out a juster view of her character and of the times than we should otherwise have had. While she was in Ireland evidently her head was a little turned; but when she understood what her success meant, and how prominent she had become, that she was entering in public upon a career hitherto sacred to men, she probably was genuinely scared. She was the first and almost the only woman who dared to write poetry. Lady Newcastle might compose poetry and essays, but Lady Newcastle was a woman of rank and could afford to be eccentric. Aphra Behn had not begun to write, and would not have been recognized by Mrs. Philips in any case. Poor Orinda was a respectable middle-class female with a turn for scribbling and a penchant for royalty and aristocracy. Moreover she had sense and ability, but to be dragged before a public whom she did not know was too much for her conservative modesty. Only after Poliarchus had offered to see a new edition through the press, and revise it if need be with his own pen, did she recover her peace of mind.

She had tasted the sweets of popularity, however, as well as the bitter, and she could not resign herself to her quiet country life. At last all things were in train for her start for the city, and her last letter but one is full of the expected journey. In May, 1664, she was in London, where she must have been some six or eight weeks, and we are sure from her friends, her favor at court, and her own sprightliness and wit, that they must have been happy.

Smallpox was rife nearly all the time in those days, however. The highest as well as the lowest succumbed to it. She was seized when her life seemed only half run, and on July 22, 1664, when she was little more than thirty-three years old, she was in her grave.

Had she lived, her poems might have appeared very soon; as it was, the plague; the fire, and the war with the Dutch delayed this monument to her fame, which was not licensed till 1667, and apparently waited for printing till 1678. The poems made a goodly quarto, prefaced by laudatory effusions by the Earls of Orrery and Roscommon, Abraham Cowley, James Tyrrell, and others.

That she was held in high esteem by these persons is clear, though it is hard to believe that Lord Roscommon was quite in earnest when he borrowed Horace's lions in the desert, and wrote:

> The magic of Orinda's name
> Not only can their fierceness tame;

> But if that mighty name I once rehearse,
> They seem submissively to roar in verse.

The most remarkable tribute of all is contained in the preface, which we may suppose was written by Poliarchus himself: "As for her virtues, they as much surpassed those of Sappho as the theological do the moral."

In the midst of all this extravagance, however, it is evident that the men were trying to say something that they really felt. Even in the next century the Duke of Wharton wrote, without any motive for flattery: "And 'tis not the first time I have been wonderfully pleased with her solid masculine thoughts, in no feminine expression. Her refined and rational thoughts of friendship, which is a subject she very much delights in, show a soul much above the common level of mankind, and mightily raise my desire of practicing what she so nobly describes." And in the early part of the nineteenth century her poems were picked up in a second-hand bookstall, inscribed with verses of praise and love, written and signed by successive members of a family named Bonner, showing that she came home to the hearts of readers of the eighteenth century.

Probably most of this intimate love was due to her many poems on friendship, most of which are in one way or another devoted to her dearest Lucasia. They began as early as December 28, 1651, when the excellent Mrs. Anne Owen was adopted into the society and received the name of Lucasia; and they continue to the end. Then there are poems on the marriage and death of friends, a poem on **"Country Life,"** one on **"Retirement,"** and so on, nearly all of them coming home in subject, if not always in treatment, to the most intimate relations of our lives.

This personal note is especially prominent in Mrs. Philips's poetry, when we compare it with the poems of other writers of the period, and on the whole it seems that she was best in this vein, which flowed spontaneously. Here is a specimen taken almost at haphazard:

> Come, my Lucasia, since we see
>   That miracles men's faith do move,
> By wonder and by prodigy,
>   To the dull angry world let's prove
>   There's a religion in our love.
>
> For though we were designed t' agree
>   That fate no liberty destroys,
> But our election is as free
>   As angels, who with greedy choice
>   Are yet determined to their joys—
>
> We court our own captivity,
>   Than thrones more great and innocent.
> 'Twere banishment to be set free
>   Since we wear fetters whose intent
>   Not bondage is but ornament.

Many of these poems are songs, and some were set to music. Almost all of this class are in stanza form, and in these the movement is pretty and the thought more succinctly expressed than in the more ambitious poems, which were written in heroic couplets. They show a surprising variety of cadence and of rhythm, too. There was still something of the Elizabethan lyric power in Mrs. Philips, which did not leave her entirely even after she had long practiced the rhymed pentameter; and for the ideas, it seems that the quatrain or any set stanza forced her to express more definite thought in given space than the couplet, which could be multiplied indefinitely.

Here are a few specimens of the variety of her stanzas:

> 'Tis true, our life is but a long disease
> Made up of real pain and seeming ease;
>   Yon stars, who these entangled fortunes give,
>   O tell me why
>   It is so hard to die,
>   Yet such a task to live.
>   Content, the false world's best disguise,
>   The search and faction of the wise
>   Is so abstruse and hid in night
>   That, like that fairy red-cross knight,
> Who treacherous falsehood for clear truth had got,
> Men think they have it when they have it not.
>   I did not live until this time
>   Crowned my felicity,
> When I could say without a crime:
>   I am not thine, but thee.

One thing is noticeable: she refrains almost altogether from the Pindaric ode. In one poem, **"Upon Mr. Abraham Cowley's Retirement,"** she is in duty bound to write something that looks irregular like Cowley's masterpieces, but it sounds more like Wordsworth than like Cowley. The Elizabethan cadences were too strong on her ear to allow of any monstrous irregularity. Then, too, it seems that a woman's love of orderliness and neatness and a woman's care for details entered into all her poetry. Moreover from the first she had been conscious of the roughness into which English poetry had fallen. Her earliest printed poem, which heads the list of fifty-three complimentary pieces, prefixed to the 1651 edition of Cartwright's "Comedies, Tragi-Comedies, and Other Poems," indicates her attitude toward poetry in general:

> Stay, prince of phansie, stay, we are not fit
> To welcome or admire thy raptures yet.
>
> Unsequester our phansies and create
> A worth that may upon thy glories walt;
> Then we shall understand thee and descry
> The splendor of restored poetry.

Her ear did not tolerate certain liberties which her reason did not approve, as it was also quite incapable of insisting upon the more subtle cadences and harmonies which neither she nor her age had studied. Mrs. Philips had a knack at rhyming rather than any real poetic gift; and so, though her taste forbade harsh sounds, it is not infrequently the case that both sense and true harmony suffer. Clearly, however, she went at her art with conscientiousness as well as love. By the time she came to the translation of

Pompey if not earlier, she was a student of versification as well as of translation, and probably her attitude is a fair specimen of the temper of the times.

In a letter to Poliarchus, December 11, 1662, she wrote: "I had it once in my mind to tell you that I was loath to use the word *effort,* but not having language enough to find any other rhyme without losing all the spirit and force of the next line, and knowing that it has been naturalized at least these twelve years, besides that it was not used in that place in the French, I ventured to let it pass." And in criticism of the lines in Act V., Scene 2,

> If Heaven, which does persecute me still,
> Had made my power equal to my will,

she said, "My objection to them is, that the words *heaven* and *power* are used as two syllables each." Elsewhere she had already written, "As for the words *heaven* and *power,* I am of your opinion, too, especially as to the latter; for the other may, I think, be sometimes so placed as not to offend the ear when it is used in two syllables."

In another letter criticising the translation of *Pompey* by Waller, Sedley, Lord Buckhurst, and Filmore, she discants on the liberties the translators have taken with their original, and goes on: "But what chiefly disgusts me is that the sense most commonly languishes through three or four lines, and then ends in the middle of the fifth, for I am of opinion that the sense ought always to be confined to the couplet; otherwise the lines must needs be spiritless and dull." This concerning the correct Waller!

It is certain that her own poetry grew smoother and more regular during the fifteen years or more that she was writing, and that she cultivated the heroic couplet. All her ambitious poems are in that meter, from the **"Lines to Mr. Henry Vaughan, Silurist, on His Poems,"** which, though not printed till 1678, deal with the subject of his first volume published in 1646, and are probably her earliest known verses, down to the address **"To His Grace, Gilbert, Lord Archbishop of Canterbury, July 10, 1664,"** only twelve days before her burial. She succeeded in polishing her couplet much more carefully as she went on, and followed her rule for stopping the sense with the couplet more closely in *Pompey* than in most of her earlier works. She studied her art to some purpose, also, for the whole structure of the sentence and of the couplet is more dignified and closer knit than at first.

It must be remembered that she was really a pioneer in the new school, for men as well as women. She died at the age of thirty-three, in 1664, before Dryden, who was only eight months her junior, had accomplished anything even as good as her poetry. From 1643, the royalist poets, Davenant, Cowley, Shirley, and the Duke of Newcastle, Lady Margaret Lucas (afterwards Duchess of Newcastle), Hobbes, Killigrew, and others gathered about Henrietta Maria in France, and could learn whatever French literature and literary men had to teach them at first hand. By that time the Hotel Rambouillet had done its work, and the time of the Precieuses Ridicules had not yet come. The society of the Hotel had purified and dignified conversation and cultivated correct diction in writing, and men on the spot must gain something from the atmosphere to the benefit of their language. But the classic influence had not yet begun; nor had Mme. de la Fayette yet declared that a sentence struck out of a book was worth a louis d'or, and a word worth twenty francs. Mlle. de Scudéry, in the height of her popularity, was writing her interminable romances, built somewhat on "The Arabian Nights" pattern, which supplied Dryden with material for his dramas a generation later.

Katherine Philips did not have the advantage of even this French influence at first hand. Born in London, a girl of the middle class, going only to a fashionable school in the suburbs, growing up amid the tumult of the civil war, a Presbyterian in Puritan England, she showed considerable vigor of mind when, at seventeen years, she had thrown off the Presbyterian faith, was an ardent advocate of King Charles and his religion, and had married a gentleman a good many years her senior. Whatever French ideas she received she adapted rather than adopted. She must have been familiar with the ways of the Precieux, for she chose fanciful names for the members of her society, but so did nearly every one else. Undoubtedly she knew Mlle. de Scudéry by heart, probably in French. But once married and settled in Wales, she could not mingle much in the polite society of literature. Henry Vaughan was one of her dearest friends and admirers, but he did not belong to the new French school. Jeremy Taylor was another friend, but he was not a "new" poet. Sir Henry Deering and Mr. Henry Lawes she knew; at one time she visited Cowley; in 1661 she was in full possession of the friendship and esteem of Sir Charles Cotterel, who lent her French books and taught her Italian; but most of her work must have been done for herself, and her theories must have been the result of her own studies and meditation, with an occasional impetus from outside.

As was usually the case in that age, her improvement came rather in style than in matter. Indeed, one of her earliest poems, the first in the volume, has as much vigor as any. It is **"Upon the Double Murther of King Charles I. in Answer to a Libellous Copy of Rhimes by Vavasor Powell:"**

I think not on the state nor am concerned
Which way soever the great helm is turned,
But as that son, whose father's danger nigh
Did force his native dumbness, and untie
The fettered organs; so this is a cause
That will excuse the breach of nature's laws,
Has Charles so broke God's laws he must not have
A quiet crown, nor yet a quiet grave?
Tombs have been sanctuaries; thieves lie there
Secure from all their penalty and fear.

For the next ten years she was sequestered in the country; her circle of friends was mostly women, who served as objects for her anxiety, her eager friendship, her lavish

praise, and as subjects of numerous lyrics and occasional pieces, but not otherwise as incentives to the cultivation of the poetic art. The pentameters of this period are comparatively infrequent, though the form persists, especially for such subjects as **"Happiness," "A Revery," "Submission,"** etc.

Suddenly, in 1660, she had opportunity to chant a welcome **"To His Majesty at His Passage into England," "On the Fair Weather Just at the Coronation,"** and other addresses, which brought her into court notice. She went to Ireland, where she met Lord Orrery, Lord Roscommon, and the ladies of their families, and between flattery and real inspiration translated Corneille's "Pompée," and wrote a few dedications and songs. Then straightway, after a few months of bustle and importance and the pleasures of society in London, she was snuffed out like a candle.

In 1664 the Restoration period of verse-making was still in its infancy. The old poetry was hopelessly dead, and the new was still to grow. In Mrs. Philips's poems there is scarcely anything so crude or so definitely bad as most of the complimentary verses prefixed to them, though Cowley and Roscommon and Tyrrell were among the men who contributed these poems. If Dryden did not learn directly from her, as he says he did, at least she must have had an indirect influence in helping him to understand the smoothness and the dangers of the couplet. We may not say, as one critic says, that "as our first poetess she at any rate should obtain rank relatively as high as that which we accord to Cædmon, our first poet;" but if Cowley and Sir John Denham and Dryden felt that to know her was a liberal education, she certainly must have given inspiration to the contemporary world.

The fact that French models were more and more studied, and that she threw all the weight of her influence into the same scale, does not detract from her claim to leadership. She was a thorough master of French, but she had devoted herself to pruning English verse according to new models before ever the court removed from Flanders or English poets came back to England. The reaction which was taking place in English poetry had many feminine traits when contrasted with the masculine vigor of the Elizabethans, and a woman of strong intellect and character was just the person to help along the movement toward polish and propriety of diction, which in France itself owed so much to Mme. Rambouillet and her associates.

Lucy Brashear (essay date 1979)

SOURCE: Brashear, Lucy. "The Forgotten Legacy of the 'Matchless Orinda.'" *Anglo-Welsh Review* 65 (1979): 68-76.

[*In the following essay, Brashear documents how Philips's persona as a reluctantly published gentle-lady was contrived to ensure her own success but prohibited future British women from publishing poetry.*]

Virginia Woolf believed that women were "trained" to be novelists rather than poets. In *A Room of One's Own* she described the restricted background of the "common sitting-room" as the most important influence responsible for the training of women writers at the time of Jane Austen in observing and analysing character. While Woolf's theory clarifies the peculiar aptitude of eighteenth and nineteenth century women for the novel genre, it does not explain their reluctance to follow the example of Queen Elizabeth and other "learned ladies" of the English Renaissance, such as the Countess of Pembroke, who was admired as a patron of poets as well as poet herself. Despite the decline of the learned-lady tradition and the discouragement of women from poetry during the period following Elizabeth's reign, the 1667 publication of the poems of Katherine Philips, known better as the "matchless Orinda", dramatically revived the deference accorded women poets. Writing at a time when an aspiring woman poet was socially ostracized and publication virtually closed to her, Orinda's triumph proved that professional recognition for women poets was possible. Curiously, however, her achievement failed to revitalize the lyric strain so admired among the women of the Renaissance. On the contrary, with the exception of the poet Anne Finch, who failed to attain Orinda's popular success, no woman poet of distinction appeared after Orinda for a century and a half. Even though her recognition invested women poets with a new respectability and made it possible for those who followed to publish, paradoxically Orinda was responsible for the fact that women writers refrained from poetry and sought acceptance in prose fiction. An examination of two aspects of Orinda's literary reputation, her circle of friends and her poems on friendship, resolves this enigma.

Traditionally biographers have presented Orinda as the impresario of an elite intellectual society which she memorialised in poetry celebrating the virtue of friendship, but the exact nature of this social circle is uncertain. Based on one of her early poems, **'To the Excellent Mrs. Anne Owen, upon receiving the Name of Lucasia, and Adoption into our Society, December 28, 1651'**, the idea that Orinda presided over a literary coterie, whose members assumed classical pseudonyms, became generally accepted.[1] Orinda, however, made no mention of a fashionable salon in her writings and historical documents do not support this claim.[2] Philip Souers, her most recent biographer, believes her "society" was a limited and private group consisting of her most intimate women friends.[3]

Whether or not a "society" existed is beside the point. Undoubtedly Orinda found a circle of friends useful in her pursuit of literary recognition as an avenue of distribution for her poetry and as a sympathetic audience for her ideas on Platonic friendship. Despite her protestations to the contrary, Orinda's literary "soul", unlike Emily Dickinson's, was not one to "select its own society / Then shut the door". Friends meant readers and circulators of her poems, which, in turn, brought her to the threshold of literary repute, albeit at the backdoor. Even more important, certain of her friends were able to vanquish that last hurdle in the pathway to fame—publication. Rather than shun the "fair guerdon" of fame, Orinda shrewdly solicited "that last infirmity of noble mind" through the support and cooperation of friends.

The ploys Orinda used to become accepted as a friend by so many influential literary men are not documented; all that we know is that her background did not provide the necessary connections to introduce her to this select group. In addition to the handicap of being a woman, she was born to a middle-class London family and educated at Mrs. Salmon's school for girls. At the age of fifteen, she moved to the small community of Cardigan Priory, Wales, and within a few years married. It is remarkable indeed that within sixteen years Katherine Philips—a married woman of limited education, remote from the mainstream of the literary world—became a celebrity, familiarly called Orinda and admired by such notable men as Jeremy Taylor, Henry Lawes, Henry Vaughan, Abraham Cowley, and the Earls of Roscommon and Orrery. Her translation of Corneille's drama, *Pompey,* and its Dublin production were praised and her poems were welcomed at the Restoration Court of Charles II. Orinda was enthusiastically christened "matchless" and celebrated as England's first Sappho. Although other British women had written poetry,[4] she was the first recognized publishing poet: between 1667 and 1710, four editions of her *Poems* appeared, as well as an unauthorized publication in 1664.

From the beginning of Orinda's writing career, her poems and letters reveal that she was fully aware of society's restrictions against a serious woman poet, especially one with an eye toward publication. If she were to see her poetry in print, someone other than herself would have to be responsible. Consequently, Orinda behaved the only way a lady of the seventeenth century could: she would have us believe that she shunned fame and was undeserving of professional recognition. In her poetry she self-effacingly deplores her "feeble hand",[5] but, nonetheless, claims that the respect she feels for venerable people requires her to commemorate their names in poetry. Her letters also make similar statements of her poetic ineptitude[6] as well as betray an almost neurotic fear that people will think her secretly desirous of public acclaim (*Poliarchus*, pp. 128, 220-221, 224-225, 228-237; *Temple*, p. 41). The self-image she projects is that of a gentle and genteel woman who has dedicated her life to the practice of Platonic love as she interpreted it in her poems dealing with friendship. She portrays herself as a woman who yearned for a rural retreat with her friends (*Poliarchus*, pp. 148, 229) but who was reluctantly forced to become a part of the literary world. That she successfully promoted this image is proven by the anonymous tribute in the preface to her poems as a woman who did not desire "the fame of being in print" and "was troubled to be so exposed" (Saintsbury, p. 492).

Orinda's image of herself as a rural recluse who enjoyed only friends and "scribblings" is difficult to reconcile, however, with events she records in her letters: frequent trips to London brought about by manipulated strategies; a two-year stay in Dublin, fêted by the literati while *Pompey* was produced; her delight in the reception of this drama and the subsequent demand for its publication; the launching of a second Corneille translation, *Horace*; her keen interest in the translation of poetry as well as critical opinions on the art of poetry; and social intimacy with many distinguished literary people. These are all activities which suggest a woman vitally interested in the public life of a professional writer.

Despite Orinda's professed distaste for women poets to appear professional, she herself exerted close attention to minute details in the printing of her drama *Pompey* (*Poliarchus*, pp. 127-128). Although her name does not grace the title page—not even her initials—the literary world knew Orinda was the translator-poet, and she was celebrated, indeed, lionized, by society. As she encouraged circulation of the *Pompey* printings, as well as her occasional poems, she enjoyed the acclaim awarded a successful poet, even though she had misgivings in respect to initiating publication of her now sought-after poetry. No acceptable precedent sanctioning a woman's right to publish existed, and she was not of the mettle to call attention to herself by maverick behaviour as did the Duchess of Newcastle and later Aphra Behn.

In 1664, when she learned that an unauthorized printing of her poetry was in process, she wrote in alarm to Dorothy Osborne Temple, expressing anxiety that this publication would result in her social ostracism (p. 41). At the same time Orinda wrote similar letters to her friend Sir Charles Cotterell, deploring this "Accident" (p. 224). She painfully concluded that poetry is "a Diversion so unfit for the Sex to which I belong, that I am about to resolve against it for ever . . ." (p. 234) and reaffirmed that she "never writ a Line . . . with Intention to have it printed . . ." (p. 228). In deference to Orinda's wishes her friends used their influence and halted the fraudulent edition, but not before "many of the books were privately sold", according to the writer of the preface to Orinda's authorized publication (Saintsbury, p. 490). Considering the remarkable excellence of the pirated edition and the advantages it offered to Orinda's career, it is tempting to speculate that she herself engineered the entire incident, but no evidence exists to this effect.

Orinda's apprehension of the damage to her social image were she to undertake publication herself were well founded. Undoubtedly, she vicariously shared the opprobrium accorded the eccentric Duchess of Newcastle. Even the usually generous Dorothy Osborne wrote to her future husband, Sir William Temple, chastising Lady Newcastle: "Sure, the poor woman is a little distracted, she could never be so ridiculous else as to venture at writing books, and in verse too".[7] Orinda, however, was strangely quiet on the subject of Lady Newcastle's poetry. Her single reference to this fantastic but remarkable woman occurs in a letter to Sir Charles in which she tells him of Edmund Waller's contempt for Lady Newcastle's poetry (p. 206).

Orinda's version of this episode suggests that she, a writer like the Duchess, may anticipate similar treatment.

As a publishing poet, Orinda had more to fear than social ostracism. Long before the spurious printing, Orinda recognized that her writing might place her family also in an embarrassing—even shameful social position. In a mystifying poem written to her husband titled **'To Antenor, on a Paper of mine which J. J. threatens to publish to prejudice him'** (p. 535), Orinda suggests that the printing of one of her poems might jeopardize her husband's reputation. She implies that the poem itself contains nothing defamatory, but rather that the sex of the writer herself is sufficient to do injury to her husband.

Thus, because of society's censure of women poets as well as her own apprehensions, Orinda chose to circulate her poems among friends. This procedure is described in several of her letters. To Sir Charles she sent a poem in commendation of the Queen, seeking his critical advice and, at the same time, prodding him to distribute it further (pp. 199-201). Later she sent the same poem to Dorothy Temple, soliciting her approval also (p. 40). In Orinda's last letter to "Worthy Poliarchus" (her name for Sir Charles), she candidly admits that she has freely circulated her poems but that she has been "betray'd" by her "dearest and best friends" (pp. 234-235), who she implies were responsible for permitting her work to reach the wrong hands. Although a self-righteous Orinda professes embarrassment when an unscrupulous printer threatened to publish a miscellany of her poems, she brought about her own literary theft by prodigal handouts.

Thirteen years prior to this last letter to Sir Charles, however, she had already benefited from the strategy of circulating her manuscripts; when she was only twenty, one of her poems appeared among the dedicatory tributes prefixed to the 1651 edition of William Cartwright's poetry. The title of the poem, **'To the Memory of the most Ingenious and Vertuous Gentleman Mr. Will Cartwright, my much valued Friend'**, suggests a close relationship between them, but no record acknowledges their acquaintance. Furthermore, Orinda was still a child of twelve when Cartwright died. Although the truth of this "valued" friendship is still a mystery, the incident reveals that at a tender age Orinda cultivated the practice of expressing her admiration for individuals by writing them flattering lyrice which were then circulated as graceful compliments. Thus, a deluge of circulating lyrics may have been the means of attracting the attention of the compilers of the Cartwright volume, who then invited Orinda to contribute a dedicatory poem in the company of several esteemed contributors, five of whom were Henry Lawes, Henry Vaughan, Francis Finch, John Birkenhead, and Sir Edward Dering. In 1655 these worthies were assembled again to contribute to Henry Lawes's *Second Book of Ayres,* for which Orinda supplied both a prefatory and a friendship poem in her literary name.

This literary group may well have been an extension of her social circle back in Cardigan Priory, composed of her personal friends, who were called by such fictitious names as Lucasia, Rosania, Ardelia, and Charistus. Although none of Orinda's male literary friends are known to have lived close to her home, her writings chart a continuing familiarity with them and their inclusion in her special circle,[8] thus insuring herself a broader circulation for her poetry.

Not only did Orinda's friends help circulate manuscripts but they also acted as a sounding board for her ideas on friendship. Fully half of her poetry is written to personal friends and deals with the subject of friendship.

Just as no precedent existed for the publication of women's poetry, none prescribed acceptable poetic topics for women poets. Had the youthful and inexperienced Orinda written solely for her own amusement, poetic matter would have been of small concern; but with a view toward circulation, she was sorely pressed to find subjects appropriate for a broad and sophisticated audience. Romantic lyrics written to one's husband were without a model; furthermore, they might not circulate. As for her children, only two poems— both elegies—refer to her son Hector. Custom prescribed the right to record her grief over the death of a son, but none to convey her feelings at hs birth. No mention is ever made of her namesake daughter Katherine. One looks vainly for topics that provided the foundation of her life— home, family responsibilities, and personal joys and frustrations.[9] The conclusion is inescapable: finding no literary precedent to direct her, Orinda refused to write about about her own experiences.

Consequently, she turned to the recognized writers of the School of Donne and the Tribe of Ben for literary models. In particular, however, she derived the theme of Platonic love upon which she founded her friendship poems from the poetry of Cavalier England. Since social custom forbade her a counterpart to Waller's Sacharissa, the half-imaginary woman whom Waller memorialized in poetry, Orinda moulded the concept of Platonic friendship to suit her distinctive needs as a woman poet and wrote many of her poems to women friends. In this respect she clearly violated the Renaissance concept restricting friendship to men only,[10] a practice she openly challenged in her poem, **'A Friend'**:

> If souls no sexes have, for men t'exclude
>   Woman from Friendship's vast capacity,
> Is a design injurious or rude,
>   Only maintain'd by partial tyranny.
> Love is allow'd to us and Innocence,
> And noblest friendships do proceed from thence.
>
>   (p. 561, stanza iv)

Orinda may have been criticized for upholding an unorthodox position or perhaps she was troubled by her own iconoclasm. Whatever the reason, she asked the renowned churchman, Jeremy Taylor, to clarify "How far a dear and a perfect friendship is authorized by the principles of Christianity?" In his response[11] Taylor defined friendship primarily as a male virtue, enjoyed by a few

women, usually in their relationships with their husbands (p. 94). Despite his reservations, the good Divine instruction, ten rules governing it (pp. 95-98). Ignoring Taylor's clear condemnation of Platonic friendship as "tinsel dressings" (p. 81), she continued to write friendship poems, elevating friendship to a believable and sincere expression of human virtue. Of even more importance, Orinda was the first recognized English poet to suggest that women could genuinely like and admire each other.

Orinda's final reward of knowing her poems would be published came about as a result of the unauthorizing printing. Although she had succeeded in suppressing this publication, some of the copies were still in existence, a situation which virtually required a corrected edition. Urged by friends to replace the surreptitious edition, melodramatically she put the entire matter into the capable hands of Sir Charles: ". . . if you still judge it absolutely necessary to the Reparation of this Misfortune . . . I shall resolve upon it with the same Reluctancy that I would cut off a Limb to save my Life" (p. 233). Ironically, while Orinda was in London, being urged by friends to publish, she was fatally stricken with small-pox. Nevertheless, within three years her poems were published, followed by three later editions. Her letters to Cotterell were also published in two editions.

Orinda's tenuous position as a serious writer can best be appreciated by reference to a tribute in the preface to her 1667 edition in which an anonymous writer describes her poems as "no disgrace to the name of any Man that amongst us is most esteemed for his excellency in this kind, and there are none that may not pass with favour, when it is remembered that they fell hastily from the pen but of a Woman". In the face of this obstinate attitude toward women poets evident even among her friends, Orinda's elaboration machinations and covert stratagems to attain literary recognition are understandable as well as admirable.

Sweet as Orinda's success story is, her career was an impossible one to follow. The role of "reluctant poetess" who writes lyrics to her friends—and who wasn't her friend?—is an obvious ruse that is good but one time around. Further, lyrics apostrophizing friendship were considered ingenious from the pen of Orinda, but "slavish" from others. Joan Philips, Lady Wharton, Jane Barker, and Elizabeth Singer Rowe all published soon after Orinda,[12] but none were awarded her distinction despite their obvious emulation of both her art and methods.

It is unfortunate that when Orinda opened the door for other women poets, her image became the critical yardstick for measuring their poetry. For example, John Dryden approved of the poems of Elizabeth Thomas because they were "too good to be a Woman's" and reminded him of Orinda's;[13] however, he cautioned Thomas to avoid the "Licenses" of Mrs. Behn (p. 127). Dryden compared his gifted protégée, Anne Killigrew, to Orinda also ('Ode to Mrs. Anne Killigrew', 11, 162-164). Other men of critical discernment admired Orinda and contributed to her deification: John Evelyn, for one, in a letter to the Duchess of Newcastle, included Orinda's name in a list of great women from the ancients to the moderns.[14]

In a poem titled 'Upon the saying that my Verses were made by another', Anne Killigrew complained bitterly of the deference granted Orinda:

> What she did write, not only all allow'd,
> But ev'ry Laurel, to her Laurel, bow'd. . . .[15]

In a similar vein, Anne Finch, Countess of Winchilsea, realistically appraised the impossibility of ever escaping Orinda's shadow.

> Nor shalt thou reatch Orinda's prayse,
> Tho' all thy aim, be fixt on Her.[16]

Lady Winchilsea's friend, Alexander Pope, however, never mentioned Orinda, her poems, or her letters in any extant record. Despite this curious omission, Pope's familiar image, "this long Disease, my Life" ('An Epistle to Dr. Arbuthnot', 1, 132), first appeared as the opening line of a poem by Orinda titled 'Song to the Tune of Adieu, Phillis': "'Tis true our life is but a long disease . . ." (p. 578). In addition to this similarity six other instances are also cited in the Twickenham Edition of Pope.[17] Further, Orinda's experimentation with the philosophical verse essay and the closed heroic couplet indicates another kind of resemblance which, in turn, suggests that Orinda may have exerted an unacknowledged influence on the poetry of Alexander Pope.

Orinda's career, however, had an opposite effect on women writers. Although they continued to pay court to her memory, those of the stature of Aphra Behn, Mary Manley, Lady Mary Wortley Montague, and Mary Wollstonecraft turned to prose, anticipating the women novelists of the nineteenth century. It is significant that a century after Orinda's death Samuel Johnson felt no obligation to include the name of the first recognized woman poet in his *Lives of the Poets*; on the other hand, he enthusiastically supported the young novelist, Fanny Burney. Whether or not women were "trained" to the novel, as Virginia Woolf supposed, they could certainly see that recognition was more accessible in the field of prose fiction.

Lionized in her own time and deified by succeeding generations, Orinda, whose image was truly "matchless," unwittingly but effectively preempted the field of poetry from other women for well over a century and, as a consequence, suppressed the beginnings of a poetic movement among their numbers. Despite her illustrious reputation as a poet, however, she has become a legend associated with the dilettantism of the *Précieuse* school and ironically her real legacy has been forgotten: in the face of the united powers of tradition and authority, Orinda proved that a woman poet was capable of earning professional recognition; just as important, she elevated the position of all women by insisting that they, as well as men, were worthy of sharing and expressing the noble virtue of friendship.

Notes

1. George Saintsbury, ed., *Minor Poets of the Caroline Period* (1905; rpt. Oxford: The Clarendon Press, 1968), I, 487. Subsequent references to the 1667 publication of Katherine Philips's *Poems,* including the preface, will be from this edition and noted in the text. See also George W. Bethune, *The British Female Poets,* Essay Index Reprint Series (1848; facsimile rpt. Freeport, N.Y.: Books for Libraries Press, 1972), p. 28; Edmund Gosse, *Seventeenth Century Studies,* 4th ed. (Londin: William Heinemann, 1913), p. 232.

2. Douglas Bush, *English Literature in the Earlier Seventeenth Century, 1600-1660,* 2nd ed. rev. (Oxford: The Clarendon Press, 1962), p. 129.

3. Philip Webster Souers, *The Matchless Orinda,* Harvard Studies in English, 5 (Cambridge: Harvard University Press, 1931), p. 78. Subsequent biographical details in the life of Katherine Philips will be from this book.

4. Although the Duchess of Newcastle's poetry, *Poems and Fancies* (1653), appeared fourteen years before Orinda's, Lady Newcastle's poems, which were publshed by her husband, did not receive critical approval from the literary community.

5. "To the Countess of Roscommon, with a Copy of Pompey", Saintsbury, p. 592, 1. 30.

6. Philips, *Letters from Orinda to Poliarchus* (London, 1705), pp. 128, 148, 180, 199—202, 219, 234-235. Subsequent references from the letters of Katherine Philips to Sir Charles Cotterell with be from this edition and noted in the text; see also Katherine Philips's letters to Dorothy Temple in the following edition: Julia G. Longe, ed., *Martha, Lady Gifford: Her Life and Correspondence* (London: George Allen and Sons, 1911), p. 40. Subsequent references to this letter will be taken from this book.

7. Dorothy (Osborne) Temple, *Letters from Dorothy Osborne to Sir William Temple, 1652-1654,* ed. Edward Abbott Parry (London, 1888), p. 100.

8. Three of these literary friends were also given pseudonyms: Francis Finch became "Palaemon" (as was Jeremy Taylor also); Birkenhead became "Cratander" (an uncertain identity but supported by Souers); and Dering became "Silvander". Although Orinda wrote congratulatory poems to both Lawes and Vaughan, she did not call them by fictitious names.

9. Orinda wrote three poems to her husband and in one poem celebrates her own birthday, "On the first of January, 1657".

10. Ruth Kelso, *Doctrine for the Lady of the Renaissance* (Urbana: University of Illinois Press, 1956), p. 140: "For the most part love was taken to be an affair between men and momen, and friendship strictly confined to men".

11. Jeremy Taylor, "A Disource of the Nature and Offices of Friendship", *The Whole Works,* ed Reginald Heber (1847-1854; rpt. Nem York: Georg Olms Verlag, 1969), I, 69-98. Subsequent references to this essay will be from this edition.

12. Joan Philips, *Ephelia, Female Poems on Several Occasions* (London, 1679); Lady Anne Wharton, *Verses by the Excellent Poetess, Mrs. Wharton* (London, 1688); Jane Barker, *Poetical Recreations Consisting of Original Poems, Songs, Odes, etc. With Several New Translations. In Two Parts. Part I. Occasionally Written by Mrs. Jane Barker. Part II. By Several Gentlemen of the Universities and Others.* (London, 1688); although Mrs. Rowe revealed an unorthodox feminine militancy in some of the poems, her preoccupation with friendship and purity drew from her admirers a favourable comparison to Orinda. Her works appear in *Ephelia. Female Poems on Several Occasions* (London, 1696).

13. Charles E. Ward, ed., *The Letters of John Dryden* (1942; rpt. New York: AMS Press, 1965), p. 125. Subsequent references to Dryden's letters will be from this book.

14. William Bray, ed., *Diary and Correspondence of John Evelyn* (London: Georpe Routledge & Sons, n. d.), pp. 653-654.

15. Anne Killigrew, *Poems,* introd. Richard Morton (1686; facsimile rpt. Gainesville, Florida: Scholars' Facsimiles & Reprints, 1967), p. 46.

16. Myra Reynolds, ed., "The Preface", *The Poems of Anne Countess of Winchilsea* (1903; rpt. Chicago: University of Chicago Press, 1974), p. 7.

17. John Butt, ed., *Twickenham Edition of the Poems of Alexander Pope,* 2nd ed. (London: Methuen & Co., 1938-1962), II, 307, 321n, 325n, 341n; III, 1. 45n 60n; and IV, 105n.

Claudia Limbert (essay date 1986)

SOURCE: Limbert, Claudia. "Two Poems and a Prose Receipt: The Unpublished Juvenalia of Katherine Philips." *English Literary Renaissance* 16, no. 2 (spring 1986): 383-90.

[*In the following essay, Limbert describes a manuscript purported to be the earliest examples of Philips's poetry.*]

In his brief biography of the Royalist poet Katherine Philips (1632-1664), known in her time as "The Matchless Orinda," John Aubrey (the cousin of Philips' lifelong friend and schoolmate, Mary Aubrey Montague) claims that, having been influenced as a small child by her grandmother Oxenbridge's interest in writing poetry, Katherine Philips had "Loved poetry at schoole, and made verses there."[1] While no poetry from these early school years seems to have survived, a hitherto unpublished manuscript in the uncatalogued Orielton Collection of the National Library of Wales[2] reveals Philips as a practicing poet, possibly as early as her fourteenth year.

The daughter of a prominent London merchant, John Fowler,[3] Philips was brought up in a family with strong Puritan connections.[4] A precocious child who could read the Bible at four and who "Took sermons down verbatim when she was but 10 years old," Philips was known to pray for an hour at a time and was, as a child, "much against the bishops, and prayed to God to take them to him."[5] At eight, she was enrolled at Mrs. Salmon's School in Hackney.[6] Obviously, the school climate was hospitable to Royalists as well as to Puritans, for Philips' two best friends at school—Mary Harvey (who later married Sir Edward Dering, a man devoted to the interests of the Crown) and Mary Aubrey—were both Royalists.

From the incomplete records available, it would seem that Orinda remained in London until she was approximately fourteen, when her widowed mother married Sir Richard Phillips [sic] of Picton Castle, Wales, and took her daughter along to her new home. At sixteen, Katherine married Colonel James Philips,[7] a prominent Puritan Parliamentarian and widower of fifty-four who had been married to Sir Richard's deceased daughter Frances by whom he had a small daughter. Orinda then moved to her new husband's home in Cardigan where James was active in politics, variously serving as a Commissioner of the Sequestration Committee, as a Commissioner of the Propagation of the Gospel Committee, and as High Sheriff, Justice of the Peace, councilman, and mayor.[8]

Shortly after her marriage, Philips' reputation as a poet began to grow; her poems were widely circulated by the friends who were also her poetic subject matter. In particular, Philips' best work may be her graceful Platonic friendship poems to and about her women friends whom she elevates to the status of goddesses with symbolic trappings of fire, water, and twinned spirits. There is no evidence that the women involved responded in kind.

Besides writing poetry, Philips translated Corneille's *Pompée*[9] which was enthusiastically received in 1663 at the new Theatre Royal in Dublin[10] before being published both in Ireland[11] and in London.[12] It was at about this same time that a group of her poems fell into the hands of Richard Marriott, a London publisher, who filed to print a pirated edition on 25 November 1663.[13] While Philips was in London, partly to take care of business for her husband and partly to make certain that her friends had been successful in suppressing this pirated edition, she succumbed to smallpox on 22 June 1664. She left behind her a partial translation of Corneille's Horace (which was completed by Sir John Denham and which became a favorite with the court of Charles II)[14] as well as a considerable literary reputation. Her work was praised by Cowley, Tyrell, Flatman, and the Earls of Orrery and Roscommon in a posthumous edition of her poems,[15] and later by Keats.[16]

Philips' mature creative life is well documented by these commendatory poems and some contemporary accounts as well as by Philips' letters and poetry but, until recently, Aubrey's claim that Philips had written poetry while at school was the only evidence of any writing activity before her marriage. Now, however, the Orielton manuscript, composed of two poems and a short prose receipt that are relatively unformed and unpolished compared to her later work, yields a great deal of useful information about this poet's early years.

The envelope holding the manuscript bears the inscription "Emma Owen / Ode to her dog Sancho."[17] Just below, in a different ink, is written: "Also verses by C. Fowler"— Katherine Philips' maiden name. Folded within is the ode to the dead Sancho, plus a sheet of paper in another hand. On one side of this sheet is a poem beginning "No blooming youth shall ever make me erre." Under the poem appears "Humbly dedicated too M[rs] Anne Barlow" and the poem is signed "C. Fowler." On the reverse is both a poem beginning "A marry[d] state affords but little ease" and, in prose, "A receipt to cure a Love sick Person who can't obtain the Party desired."

The manuscript itself, written in a slightly less sure, more childish hand than Philips' later copybook,[18] can be fairly well dated. Since the poems concern marriage, they would have been written sometime after 1 December 1646, when Orinda's mother married Sir Richard, but before late August of 1648 when Orinda herself married. Thus, Philips was between fourteen and sixteen years of age.

It is not surprising to find such a manuscript among the materials from Orielton. Located three miles southwest of Pembroke, Wales, and now a nature study center,[19] Orielton was once the home of Anne Lewis Owen (called "Lucasia" by Philips), who was the object of Philips' most intense friendship. Besides Orielton, the Owen family also owned Llandshipping, just across the East Cleddau River and to the southeast of Picton Castle where Philips lived with her mother and step-father before her own marriage. The Anne Barlow of the manuscript can be identified as one of the Barlows living at the manor house of Slebech (pronounced Slebets),[20] less than two miles northeast of Picton Castle. Thus, all three young women lived within a short distance of one another.

Anne Barlow was one of nine children, two of her sisters becoming lady abbesses in France. Anne's first husband was Nicholas Lewis of Hean Castle and her second was Lewis Wogan of Wiston.[21] Genealogical information shows that she was approximately the same age as Philips and Owen. Anne's father John Barlow, a Royalist and "a church papist," is listed among the commanders captured in 1642 by Parliamentary forces at Fort Pill.[22] His extensive and personal estate was finally sequestered on 13 May, 1651.[23] Thus, the records would indicate that the Barlows most likely were at Slebech during the period before Philips' marriage in 1648.

As one reads the manuscript, it soon becomes clear that this is the earliest known evidence of Orinda's break from Puritanism and her subsequent commitment to the Royalist cause, a change most likely made while still at school. Here, Philips establishes herself as seeking an ideal Royalist husband: literate, of "good estate," and possessing beauty of mind. But Fate dealt Philips something quite different. James Philips, while instrumental in the formation of a local free school,[24] was never recorded as being a man of books. He was recorded, however, as having made many enemies and was seen by some to be an enthusiastic sequestrator.[25]

Additionally, the manuscript provides a glimpse of Philips' early creative life, demonstrating that she was already familiar with the mechanics of composition and was approaching mastery of the heroic couplet. This manuscript also signals Philips' interest in communicating with other women through poetry, although the absence of her subsequent use of pseudonyms for her friends is noticeable since the work is dedicated directly to Anne Barlow. However, by at least 15 February 1651/2, Philips was employing pseudonyms, as in her "Philoclea's Parting."[26] Perhaps even more significant than the absence of a pseudonym for Barlow is the absence of the Orinda persona, so obvious later in her copybook.

Finally, in these pieces, Philips deals, as so many beginning poets do, with the topic of romance, but her voice is that of a pragmatic young woman of good humor voicing clearly anti-romantic expectations about love and marriage. The sentiments are hardly original, yet the perspective and voice are not so common in English literature. One thinks of Shakespeare's Beatrice or Congreve's Millamant, but the witty sophistication of such characters is very distant from Philips' tone. That distance might in some measure be related to the fact that Philips does not speak as a character imagined by a male author but as herself, a woman who would go on to transform herself into "the Matchless Orinda," the celebrator of the Platonic love of one woman for another.

[Text]

> No blooming youth shall ever make me err
> I will the beauty of the mind prefer
> If himans rites shall call me hence
> It shall be with some man of sence
> 5 Nott with the great butt with a good estate
> Nott too well read nor yet illetterate
> In all his actions moderate grave & wise
> Redyer to bear than offer injuries
> And in good works a constant doer
> 10 Faithfull in promise & liberall to the poor
> He thus being quallified is allways seen
> Ready to serve his friend his country & his king
> Such men as these yout say there are but few
> Their hard to find & I must grant it too
> 15 Butt if I [ever] hap to change my life
> Its only such a man shall call me wife.
>
> Humbly Dedicated too M[rs] Anne Barlow C. Fowler
> A marry[d] state affords but little Ease
> The best of husbands are so hard to please
> This in wifes Carefull faces you may spell
> Tho they desemble their misfortunes well

5 A virgin state is crownd with much content
  Its allways happy as its inocent
  No Blustering husbands to create y^r fears
  No pangs of child birth to extort y^r tears
  No childrens crys for to offend your ears
10 Few worldly crosses to distract y^r prayers
  Thus are you freed from all the cares that do
  Attend on matrymony & a husband too
  Therefore Mad^m be advised by me
  Turn turn apostate to loves Levity
15 Supress wild nature if she dare rebell
  Theres no such thing as leading Apes in hell

A RECEIPT TO CURE A LOVE SICK PERSON WHO
CANT OBTAIN THE PARTY DESIRED

Take two oz: of the spirits of reason three oz:
of the Powder of experiance five drams of the Juce
of Discretion three oz: of the Powder of good advise
& a spoonfull of the Cooling watter of consideration
make these all up into Pills & besure to drink a
little content affter y^m & then the head will be
clear of maggotts & whimsies & you restored to y^r
right sences but the persons that wont be ruld must
become a sacrifise to cupid & dye for love for all
the Doctors in the world cant cure y^m

if this wont do apply the plaister & if that wont
do itts out of my power to find out what will

Notes

1. John Aubrey, *Aubrey's Brief Lives,* ed. Andrew Clark (Oxford, 1898), II, p. 153.

2. Orielton Collection, Parcel 24. National Library of Wales. Having found the manuscript under discussion, I discovered that I had been anticipated by two others: Ronald Lockley who gives excerpts in his *Orielton: The Human and Natural History of a Welsh Manor* (London, 1977), pp. 19-20, and Patrick Thomas who quotes the MS in full in "An Edition of the Poems and Letters of Katherine Philips," Diss. Univ. of Wales, 1982, III, pp. 129-30. However, Lockley confuses Anne Barlow with Anne Lewis Owen and does not identify "C. Fowler." Thomas, by the generic limitations imposed upon an edition, is unable to devote space to the implications of the manuscript. Additionally, since neither author's work is readily available, the Orielton MS is presented here for consideration.

3. John Fowler belonged to the Clothworkers' Guild, having paid his 29d. fee to join the guild on 18 July 1612. Between 1615-16, he became wealthy enough to set up his own workshop and to hire employees. By 1623, he had been elected as fourth of the four Wardens of the Yeomanry for 1624. He appears in annual lists of the Livery until his death in 1642. Joshua, his son by his first wife and Katherine's half-brother, became a member in 1645. (Letter received from D. E. Wickham, Archivist for the Clothworkers' Guild, 4 July 1984.)

4. An uncle, John Oxenbridge, became pastor of the First Church of Boston, Massachusetts. See *The Records of the First Church in Boston, 1630-1868,* ed. Richard D. Pierce (Boston, 1961), XXXIX, p. xxxiv. An aunt, Elizabeth Oxenbridge Cockcroft, in 1645 took as her second husband Oliver St. John, Cromwell's Chief Justice of the Common Pleas from 1648-60 who had been married formerly to Cromwell's cousin Elizabeth. See William Durrant Cooper, *The Oxenbridges of Brede Place, Sussex and Boston, Massachusetts* (London, 1860), p. 6. Additionally, Katherine Philips' own mother lived to marry three times, her last husband being the famous Puritan military leader and writer of devotional books for his troops, Philip Skippon, Cromwell's major-general of London. See "The Will of Phillip Skippon, Major-General," Prob. 11/300, pr. 25 October 1660, by his son Phillip. Public Records Office, London.

5. Aubrey, II, p. 153.

6. Little is known of Mrs. Salmon's School and nothing of its curriculum. Indeed, its very existence can no longer be documented since none of the ratebooks for the period have survived. (Letter received from David Mander, Archivist for Library Services of Hackney, 15 January 1985.)

7. An intent to marry was filed in London 23 August 1648. See *Marriage License Allegations in the Registry of the Bishop of London, 1597-1648,* ed. Reginald M. Glencross (London, 1937), XXV, p. 256.

8. Basil Henning, *The History of Parliament: The House of Commons, 1660-1690* (London, 1983), III, p. 239.

9. The National Library of Wales has lately purchased another manuscript copy of *Pompey* (NLW 21867B—General Collection), their first copy being NLW 776B. The more recent acquisition is believed to date from the second half of the seventeenth century. It appears to have been originally part of a larger volume, coming to the library with the remains of raised bands and gold-tooled calf on its spine.

10. W. R. Chetwood, *A General History of the Stage* (London, 1749), p. 52 and Katherine Philips, *Letters from Orinda to Poliarchus* (London, 1705), letter no. xxvi, dated 8 April 1663, p. 124.

11. *Letters,* p. 122.

12. *A Transcript of the Registers of the Worshipful Company of Stationers, 1640-1708 A. D.* (London, 1913; rpt. New York, 1950), p. 339.

13. *Stationer's Register,* p. 334. The edition concerned is *Poems By the Incomparable Mrs. K. P.* (London, 1664).

14. Records indicate one performance where Lady Castlemaine took a part, wearing the Crown Jewels taken from the Tower of London for the occasion. See *The London Stage, 1660-1800,* ed. William Van Lennep (Carbondale, Ill., 1965), I, pp. 128-29.

15. Katherine Philips, *Poems By the most deservedly Admired Mrs Katherine Philips, The Matchless Orinda To which is added Monsieur Corneille's Pompey and Horace, Tragedies* (London, 1667).

16. John Keats, *The Letters of John Keats,* ed. Maurice Buxton Forman, 3rd ed. (London, 1947), letter no. 22, dated 21 September 1817, p. 45.

17. Emma Owen, who lived during the early eighteenth century, was the eleventh of twelve children of Sir Arthur Owen and Emma Owen of Orielton. Dying childless, she was married to William Bowen of Williamston, Pembrokeshire, one of the Bowens of Upton Castle. Ronald Lockley documents this information and the existence of her dog Sancho whose grave he found in a little cemetery for three pets located just behind Orielton manor on the other side of a lily pond. See Lockley, pp. 23-24.

18. Katherine Philips, "Poems: Orinda," NLW 775B, National Library of Wales.

19. Letter received from J. D. Owen, Curator of the Ceredigion Museum, Cardiagan, Wales, 5 July 1984.

20. *Bartholomew Gazeteer of Britain,* comp. Oliver Mason (Edinburgh, 1977), p. 224. All mileages are drawn from a map in this volume on p. 22.

21. Francis Green, "The Barlows of Slebech" in *West Wales Historical Records* (Carmarthen, Wales, 1913), p. 144.

22. John Roland Phillips, *Memoirs of the Civil War in Wales and the Marches, 1642-1649* (London, 1874), II, p. 153.

23. Green, p. 142. John Barlow "of Slebitch" is also mentioned as one being investigated under "An Act concerning the Sequestration of South-Wales and County of Monmouth 23 Feb. 1648/9" in *Acts and Ordinances of the Interregnum, 1642-1660,* ed. C. H. Firth and R. S. Rait (London, 1911), II, p. 14. However, nothing seems to have been done until the date mentioned by Green. As Green states, Barlow's son John did not petition to regain one-fifth of the property for himself and the other children until 13 November 1651. Yet, when their request was granted, arrears were also awarded dating from 24 December 1649. This then would indicate an earlier sequestration date, but a date still well within the period considered here.

24. John Roland Phillips, *A List of the Sheriffs of Cardiganshire from A. D. 1539 to A. D. 1868 with Genealogical and Historical Notes* (Carmarthen, Wales, 1868), p. 17 and W. A. L. Vincent, *The State and School: Education, 1640-1660 in England and Wales* (London, 1950), p. 54.

25. W. R. Williams, *The Parliamentary History of the Principality of Wales, 1541-1895* (Brecknock, Wales, 1895), p. 30.

26. Philoclea, so far unidentified, can now be named by means of Philips' copybook, NLW 775B, p. 37, as being "Mrs. M. Stedman" who was probably Mallet Stedman of Strata Florida, Cardiganshire, less than forty miles northeast of Cardigan. Mallet was one of four children of John Stedman and Jane Vaughan. Mallet's eldest brother, James, married Margaret, daughter of Richard Owen of Rhiwsaeson, Montgomery. Upon James Stedman's death in 1672, Margaret married Hector Philips, the brother of James Philips. See Francis Green, "Stedman of Strata Florida" in *West Wales Historical Records* (Carmarthen, Wales, 1921), pp. 100-01.

Harriette Andreadis (essay date 1989)

SOURCE: Andreadis, Harriette. "The Sapphic-Platonics of Katherine Philips, 1632-1664." *Signs: Journal of Women in Culture and Society* 15, no. 1 (autumn 1989): 34-60.

[*In the following essay, Andreadis traces Philips's conscious use of male Platonic friendships as a model for her homoerotic poetry about friendships between women.*]

Katherine Philips, known as "The Matchless Orinda," was the first English female poet to achieve a considerable reputation in her own time. She was extravagantly praised, indeed lionized, by her male contemporaries: Abraham Cowley, the earl of Roscommon (Wentworth Dillon), Jeremy Taylor, John Dryden, and much later, even John Keats referred to her as the female standard of excellence toward which all other women ought to aspire.[1] Andrew Marvell may have been influenced by some of her poetic language and Henry Lawes set a number of her poems to music.[2] Laudatory references continue into the eighteenth century, particularly by women writers who, responding to male commentary on the proper female poetic persona, saw in Philips a model of success to be emulated.[3] In her own time, despite her bourgeois background, her great charm and cultivated feminine modesty gained her admittance, after the Restoration, to the best literary and court circles. The nobility, some of whom were literati, welcomed her presence and felt graced by her genius.

The acclaim of her contemporaries has by now, however, worn very thin: she is seen as having "wielded persistently her all too fluent pen," as having had friendships with women "florid in their intensity," or as having "wanted to take on, by cajolery rather than by assault, an artistic role generally reserved for men."[4] In works of literary history, she is listed generally as a minor Caroline poet who kept alive the traditions of the cavalier poets through the years of the Interregnum. For the most part, she has been studied as a member of male literary circles, for the sake of her distinguished literary connections or for her literary influence.[5] In works dealing with women writers, she is most often described as a minor example of *préciosité* or, conversely, as an example of "the growing influence of neoclassicism,"[6] and, thus, she is given a perfunctory place in anthologies.[7] At best, she is regarded as the poetic model for a later, female "school of Orinda" or as an influence on certain male poets. At worst, she is accused of versifying gossip.[8] Even such a recent, and sympathetic, critic as Lillian Faderman does little to alter the view of Philips's 1931 biographer, Philip Webster Souers, that "her greatest claim to attention is that she was among the few who kept alive in the teeth of Puritan scorn and persecution the old court tradition, and handed it over ready for use to the returning wits of the Restoration."[9]

Her production was small since her life was short. It includes a single volume of poems written for her friends, published in an unauthorized edition in the year of her death, and then reedited, expanded, and reprinted posthumously by her friend and literary executor, Sir Charles Cotterell; a translation of Pierre Corneille's *Pompey* and a partial translation of *Horace* completed by Robert Denham; a volume of her letters to Sir Charles, dubbed Poliarchus in *précieuse* fashion, edited and published posthumously by him in 1705; and four letters to "Berenice," an anonymous noblewoman, published with the *Familiar Letters* of John Wilmot, earl of Rochester, in 1697. In all, five editions of her work appeared after the unauthorized 1664 folio edition of her **Poems,** the final one being the 1710 octavo of her **Works.**[10] Her reputation during the seventeenth century was based on a privately circulated group of poems addressed to her intimate women friends and chronicling in some detail her emotional relations with them. Her other poems were mostly occasional or moral-philosophical exercises in what we now consider the traditional, and rather undistinguished, mode of the seventeenth century; elegies, encomia, political poems, verse essays on friendship, poems of personal retirement and contemplation, and a journey poem are characteristic. Philips's real contribution to English letters, however, though acknowledged by her contemporaries and by the women writers who succeeded her, has been either overlooked or trivialized by students of English literature since the late eighteenth century. It is remarkable that, as a woman, she could have achieved the considerable reputation she enjoyed among her contemporaries. That her contribution was acknowledged by them is without question. We must then ask what that contribution really was and why it was so highly esteemed.

An examination of the materials of Philips's life and work reveals a woman whose emotional focus was primarily on other women and whose passionate involvement with them guided much of her life and inspired her most esteemed poems. Philips's original and unusual use of literary conventions accounts for the acclaim she was accorded by her contemporaries, and her unique manipulation of the conventions of male poetic discourse, of the argumentative texture of John Donne, of the language of the cavaliers, and of the tradition of platonic love became the means by which she expressed in an acceptable form her homoerotic impulses. Philips's contribution was to appropriate the cavalier conventions of platonic heterosexual love, with

their originally platonic and male homoerotic feeling, and to use those conventions and that discourse to describe her relations with women. While homoerotic male poetic discourse in the form of male friendship poetry was by no means unusual during the Renaissance and early seventeenth century, Philips's is the earliest printed example of a woman's poetic expression in English of intense same-sex love between women.

The poems that brought her acclaim, and that still are considered her best work, established a "society of friendship" that used, superficially, the rhetorical conventions of the cavalier poets and of French *préciosité*. In her attempt to create an ideal "society" of friends, in her use of pastoral nicknames for her friends, in her reading of Italian and French romances, and in her attraction to the idea of platonic love, Philips embraced current literary and courtly fashions.[11] To see her work merely as an example of *préciosité* does not, however, do justice to the breadth of interests and influences her work reveals. Moreover, though she uses its superficial trappings, her poetic language does not fit the *précieux* prescription for periphrasis, tortured hyperbole, or excessive imagery. Instead, a disinterested reading of Philips's works suggests a more judicious view than has been offered by literary critics: like others among her contemporaries, most notably Abraham Cowley, one of her admirers, she moved in the course of her literary career—as did a number of male poets—from the private, contemplative, metaphysical mode of her poetry during the Interregnum to a more public neoclassical style during the Restoration.[12] Her earlier work is composed for the most part of the platonic love lyrics to her female friends that initially won her praise; but later, during and after the Restoration, she turned to longer poems on public themes and to the translations of Corneille. Certainly Philips was ambitious and certainly her work was embedded in the traditions, culture, and fashions of her time. Yet it would be more accurate to say that the forms she used coincided with and appropriated literary fashion rather than that she wrote as she did only because she courted poetic success. The evidence of her life indicates that the forms she used also fulfilled important personal needs.

Philips used the conventions of her time to express in her own poetry a desexualized—though passionate and eroticized—version of platonic love in the love of same-sex friendship. In Philips's poetry friendship between women is infused with the passionate intensity and rhetoric of heterosexual love as it was understood by seventeenth-century male poets. The major influence on her friendship poems may not be the cavaliers or *préciosité* but John Donne and the metaphysical conceit, for the intensity of her friendship feelings is expressed through echoes of Donne's early seduction poems.[13]

An attentive reading of her poems addressed to Rosania, her pseudo-classical name for her school friend Mary Aubrey, and to Lucasia, Anne Owen, who replaced Rosania in Philips's affections after Rosania's marriage, reveals the intensity of Philips's emotions and her unique use of convention as a vehicle to express her intimate feelings. ***To my Lucasia, in defence of declared friendship,*** one of Philips's best-known and most admired poems, is typical of her work: she appropriates both the sentiments of metaphysical platonism and the form of male poetic discourse to shape her passion. Stanzas 8 through 12 are especially clear in illustrating her rhetorical strategies:

> Although we know we love, yet while our soule
>   Is thus imprison'd by the flesh we wear,
> There's no way left that bondage to controule,
>   But to convey transactions through the Eare.
>
> Nay, though we read our passions in the Ey,
>   It will obleige and please to tell them too:
> Such joys as these by motion multiply,
>   Were't but to find that our souls told us true.
>
> Believe not then, that being now secure
>   Of either's heart, we have no more to doe:
> The Sphaeres themselves by motion do endure,
>   And they move on by Circulation too.
>
> And as a River, when it once has pay'd
>   The tribute which it to the Ocean ow's,
> Stops not, but turns, and having curl'd and play'd
>   On its own waves, the shore it overflows:
>
> So the Soul's motion does not end in bliss,
>   But on her self she scatters and dilates,
> And on the Object doubles, till by this
>   She finds new Joys, which that reflux creates.[14]

Evident here is the manner in which Philips channels a passionate emotional intensity into acceptable metaphysical images and argument. The platonic union of souls, the eyes as vehicles of the spirit, and the analogy between the movement of human hearts and the circulation of the spheres were stocks in trade of the male discourse of metaphysical passion for women. Here, a female poetic voice uses these conventional images to address her intensely beloved female friend. In her invocation to her beloved to speak their love, she adds to these images the particularly female and subliminally erotic analogy of a river's flow, which captures the rhythms of female sexual passion.

Philips's use of Donne, rather than the lesser cavalier poets, for her model is apparent not only in the echoes of his particular images but more precisely in the force of her argumentative stance, in the relentless development of thought through the manipulation of conceit. ***To My excellent Lucasia, on our Friendship,*** again echoes Donne:

> I did not live untill this time
>   Crown'd my felicity,
> When I could say without a crime,
>   I am not Thine, but Thee.
> This Carkasse breath'd, and walk'd, and slept,
>   So that the world believ'd
> There was a soule the motions kept;
>   But they were all deceiv'd.

> For as a watch by art is wound
>   To motion, such was mine:
> But never had Orinda found
>   A Soule till she found thine;
> Which now inspires, cures and supply's,
>   And guides my darken'd brest:
> For thou art all that I can prize,
>   My Joy, my Life, my rest.
> Nor Bridegroomes nor crown'd conqu'rour's mirth
>   To mine compar'd can be:
> They have but pieces of this Earth,
>   I've all the world in thee.
> Then let our flame still light and shine,
>   (And no bold feare controule)
> As innocent as our design,
>   Immortall as our Soule.

[No. 36, 176]

Except that these poems are addressed to a woman, they could have been written by a man to his (female) lover. Clearly, the discourse used by Philips is both male and heterosexual. And, in this poem, it reaches beyond the merely conventional image of "two friends 'mingling souls'" in the extravagant intensity of the conceit of the watch.[15]

"To My excellent Lucasia" adumbrates Donne's imagery as well as the intellectual form of his metaphysical poetic. The union of lover and beloved, the soullessness of the "Carkasse" before discovery of the beloved, the negative comparison of the condition of the beloved to more worldly joys ("Nor Bridegroomes nor crown'd conqu'rour's mirth") to enforce the sacredness of the relation, and the insistence on the "innocent . . . design" of their love, are also integral to Donne's love poetry.

"Friendship in Emblem, or the Seale, to my dearest Lucasia" perhaps most obviously draws on Donne in its use of the compass image from *A Valediction: Forbidding Mourning.* Here again, the crucial element that distinguishes her source as Donne rather than the cavaliers is the sustained force of her intellectual argument in developing the conceit. Stanzas 6 through 13 illustrate this clearly:

> The compasses that stand above
> Express this great immortall Love;
> For friends, like them, can prove this true,
> They are, and yet they are not, two.
>
> And in their posture is express'd
> Friendship's exalted interest:
> Each follows where the other Leanes,
> And what each does, the other meanes.
>
> And as when one foot does stand fast,
> And t'other circles seeks to cast,
> The steddy part does regulate
> And make the wanderer's motion streight:
>
> So friends are onely Two in this,
> T'reclaime each other when they misse:
> For whosoe're will grossely fall,
> Can never be a friend at all.

And as that usefull instrument
For even lines was ever meant;
So friendship from good = angells springs,
To teach the world heroique things.

As these are found out in design
To rule and measure every line;
So friendship governs actions best,
Prescribing Law to all the rest.

And as in nature nothing's set
So Just as lines and numbers mett;
So compasses for these being made,
Doe friendship's harmony perswade.

And like to them, so friends may own
Extension, not division:
Their points, like bodys, separate;
But head, like soules, knows no such fate.

[No. 29, 132-35]

The conceit of the compass, an emblem of constancy, as used by Donne to explore the meaning of his approaching absence from his wife is here present as subtext in Philips's poem.[16] Her use of the same conceit—and it is her most obvious echo of Donne—to describe her passionate friendship for Lucasia is played against the silent text of Donne's poem, which reverberates through it and underlines its platonism as well as its eroticism.

These are only a few examples of Philips's appropriation of Donne and the metaphysical mode of argument. A reading of all of her poems to her female intimates yields others. It is the intense, passionate quality of her feeling, the emotional tension inherent in the argument of the conceit, that distinguishes these poems from her other poetic efforts. She appropriated a male heterosexual poetic discourse, with its platonism, its implicit eroticism, and its impassioned argument via conceits, rather than the less intense, more distant tone of the male friendship poetry of her contemporaries because this discourse suited the deeply intimate nature of the emotions she sought to chart and for which she sought a vehicle.

Though Philips's expression may bear some resemblance to the platonism of some earlier male friendship literature, such as Michel de Montaigne's essay, "On Friendship," she probably was not acquainted with earlier renaissance models.[17] Most of her reading was limited to her near contemporaries, whose friendship poetry employs, instead of a renaissance platonic ideal, the Horatian ideal of civilized life and the Aristotelian notion of friendship as the bond of the state to defend against the "cavalier winter."[18] These contemporaries are more concerned to place friendship in the context of retirement to nature as an escape from the turmoil of the times than to explore the ecstasies and trials of intimacy through the language of platonism. Theirs is a generalized approach to the subject that is in contrast to Philips's impassioned use of direct address and metaphysical conceit.

That these poems were not merely clever exercises in courtly convention by a woman seeking reputation and patronage (as were, perhaps, some of her Restoration poems addressed to royalty) is confirmed by the circumstances of Philips's life and letters. Born Katherine Fowler, the daughter of a prosperous London cloth merchant, in 1648 she married James Philips, whom she was to call Antenor in keeping with her penchant for devising pseudo-classical names for her intimates. She was sixteen; he was fifty-four. Clearly, in this marriage, probably arranged by her mother, she loved and respected her husband as she was socially and morally bound to do. Yet, clearly also, there was much distance between them in addition to their respective ages. He lived on the remote west coast of Wales at Cardigan Priory, while she was attached to the intellectual and social amenities of London and took, or created, every opportunity to return to literary and court circles. Her politics were also different from his: she remained a royalist like her friends and courtly admirers, while he and her family were parliamentarians. This publicly recognized political difference at least once threatened his political career.[19]

Antenor's absence never evoked the same metaphysical anguish in Philips as did that of Rosania or Lucasia; she wrote of him most often in terms of her "duty." A telling contrast is that between the frequently unrestrained emotion in her many poems lamenting the absence of a female friend[20] and the relative coolness of her single poem to Antenor upon his absence and of her descriptions of her "duty" to Sir Charles. On her immanent departure from Ireland and Lucasia, she wrote: "I have now no longer any pretence of Business to detain me, and a Storm must not keep me from ANTENOR and my Duty, lest I raise a greater within. But oh! that there were no Tempests but those of the Sea for me to suffer in parting with my dear LUCASIA!" (Letter 19, 631). This passage succinctly points to a contrast that is apparent throughout Philips's writing; it juxtaposes, on the one hand, her feelings of obligation to her husband and, on the other, her passion for Lucasia. As to the rest of her immediate family, her son is mentioned only twice in her writings, both times in poems, one of them a particularly dull one about his death at the age of forty-one days; her daughter, who survived her, is never mentioned at all, either in her poems or in her letters.[21]

Having endured, in 1652, Mary Aubrey's (Rosania's) defection from their friendship into marriage, Philips wrote at least one poem on her "apostasy," and quickly replaced her with Anne Owen (Lucasia).[22] In 1662, Anne Owen, too, married, and Orinda despised Owen's new husband, Marcus Trevor, which added to her grief. Nevertheless, she accompanied the newlyweds to Dublin and stayed on for a year, ostensibly to conduct her husband's business (he was now in some financial and political distress owing to his parliamentarianism) and to finish *Pompey* and see it played at the Theatre Royal, Smock Alley, Dublin. She had also begun to develop aristocratic connections: the earl of Orrery offered her encouragement, she frequented the duke of Ormonde's salon, and she was becoming friendly with the countess of Cork.

She described her feelings to Sir Charles, whose suit to Anne Owen she had unsuccessfully encouraged, presumably in an attempt to keep Anne within her immediate social circle and in close geographical proximity: "I am much surpriz'd that she, who is so well-bred, and her Conversation every way so agreeable, can be so happy with him as she seems to be: for indeed she is nothing but Joy, and never so well pleas'd as in his Company; which makes me conclude, that she is either extremely chang'd, or has more of the dissembling Cunning of our Sex than I thought she had" (Letter 13, 603).[23] She wrote repeatedly to Sir Charles of her grief and disappointment, not unmixed with bitterness, at the loss of her bond with Anne Owen. Her grief in these letters is as acute as the passion in the earlier poems is intense. From Dublin on July 30, 1662, she wrote:

> I now see by Experience that one may love too much, and offend more by a too fond Sincerity, than by a careless Indifference, provided it be but handsomly varnish'd over with civil Respect. I find too there are few Friendships in the World Marriage-proof. . . . We may generally conclude the Marriage of a Friend to be the Funeral of a Friendship. . . . Sometimes I think it is because we are in truth more ill-natur'd than we really take our selves to be; and more forgetful of past Offices of Friendship, when they are superseded by others of a fresher Date, which carrying with them the Plausibility of more Duty and Religion in the Knot that ties them, we persuade our selves will excuse us if the Heat and Zeal of our former Friendships decline and wear off into Lukewarmness and Indifferency: whereas there is indeed a certain secret Meanness in our Souls, which mercenarily inclines our Affections to those with whom we must necessarily be oblig'd for the most part to converse, and from whom we expect the chiefest outward Conveniencies. And thus we are apt to flatter our selves that we are constant and unchang'd in our Friendship, tho' we insensibly fall into Coldness and Estrangement.

[Letter 13, 601-2]

Her letters to Sir Charles during this period are full of disappointed idealism, of highmindedness scorned. The scale of values Philips holds dear in these letters, and in her poetry, places the noble feelings of disinterested friendship far above the frequently compromised and banal motives of marriage and duty. Nevertheless, her notion of disinterested friendship is driven by intensely passionate commitment to the individual woman in question, so that when, in the usual course of things, her friend marries, she responds as a lover scorned. The feelings she expressed in her letters to Sir Charles concerning the defection of Anne Owen reverberate from the poems she had written ten years earlier on the apostasy of Mary Aubrey:

> Lovely apostate! what was my offence?
> Or am I punish'd for obedience?
>
> . . . . .
>
> For our twin-spirits did so long agree,
> You must undoe your self to ruine me.
>
> . . . . .

> . . . Glorious Friendship, whence your honour
>   springs,
> Ly's gasping in the croud of common things;
>
> . . . . .

> For from my passion your last rigours grew,
> And you kill me, because I worshipp'd you.

[*Injuria amici,* no. 38, 182-83]

Thus Philips reveals a covert, innate rebelliousness; she protests with chagrin Mary Aubrey's and Anne Owen's replacement of such romantic sentiments with ones more suitable to the exigencies of social and economic life.

Her last known passionate attachment seems to have been to "Berenice," whom she knew at least since 1658, when she wrote begging her to come to Cardigan and console her for Lucasia's absence.[24] Philips evidently continued her correspondence with "Berenice" after returning from Ireland to her home at Cardigan Priory in Wales because the last letter is dated from there a month before her death in London. The tone of the four letters to "Berenice" is a combination of nearly fawning supplication to a social superior and breathless passion, the two inextricably fused:

> All that I can tell you of my Desires to see your Ladiship will be repetition, for I had with as much earnestness as I was capable of, Begg'd it then, and yet have so much of the Beggar in me, that I must redouble that importunity now, and tell you, That I Gasp for you with an impatience that is not to be imagin'd by any Soul wound up to a less concern in Friendship then yours is, and therefore I cannot hope to make others sensible of my vast desires to enjoy you, but I can safely appeal to your own Illustrious Heart, where I am sure of a Court of Equity to relieve me in all the Complaints and Suplications my Friendship can put up.

[Letter 51, 773][25]

It is impossible to disentangle the elements of Orinda's passion for "Berenice," complicated as their relationship was by social inequality and as our understanding of it is by an absence of any information external to the four letters. However, Philips's tone in these letters seems desperate beyond any conventional courtliness; she yearns to fill the void left by Lucasia's absence and, later, rejection.

After her success with *Pompey* on the Dublin stage, Philips found it difficult to remain immured at the Priory and finally was able to solicit an invitation from her friends, and her husband's permission, to return to London, where she died of smallpox at the age of thirty-one. A major change had taken place in Philips's life when the loss of her friendship with Lucasia was coincidentally accompanied by the foundering fortunes of her husband, which she attempted to remedy through her well-placed friends. That she had not succeeded in doing so when she died suggests that the double blow she had suffered left her depressed (as the anxiety in her last letters to Sir Charles shows), weakened, and vulnerable to disease.

After the defection of Lucasia, she wrote no more of the poetry that had won her such high praise; instead, she poured her energies into using her court connections to gain patronage for herself and, probably unsuccessfully, preferment for Antenor. She wrote numerous poems to royalty, self-consciously addressing public themes, and increasingly fewer intimate poems to particular friends. Also, she vied with the male wits for recognition of her theatrical translations, which are still considered the best English versions of Corneille.[26] Philips's immersion in Corneille and the adoption of a more neoclassical style may have been politically expedient in the early 1660s, but at this time in Philips's life, Corneille's subordination of personal passion to duty and patriotism in the long speeches that she translated also must have appealed to her own need to control her disordered emotions.[27]

Her royalist sympathies throughout the Interregnum no doubt now enabled her to advance the interests of her parliamentarian husband as well as her own literary ambitions. Souers comments on the notable change in her poems and in her stance toward literary circles: "The Cult of Friendship may be said to have died with the marriage of its inspirer. All that remained was the empty shell, which, in this case, means the names, so that when, later, poems addressed to new friends appear, it must be kept in mind that the old fire is gone."[28] Souers's judgment is borne out by the poems Philips addressed to the Boyle sisters, daughters of the countess of Cork, a patron during Philips's stay in Ireland. Though she attempts to continue, or perhaps to revivify, the traditions of her cult of friendship by bestowing pastoral nicknames, Philips reveals in her later poems the conflict and ambivalence with which more intimate approaches to her social superiors are fraught. She confronts this problem of friendship with aristocratic women directly in **"To Celimena"** (1662-64), addressed to Lady Elizabeth Boyle; the eight-line poem concludes: "Wouldst thou depose thy Saint into thy Friend? / Equality in friendship is requir'd, / Which here were criminal to be desir'd" (no. 107, 472). Her earlier passionate avowals of friendship have become reverential.[29]

The poems that made Orinda famous depended for their creation on Philips's personal affections. When the person to whom those affections were directed removed herself permanently from the sphere of Philips's life, the well of her unique creativity dried up, though she continued to refine her craft. Orinda may have sought other muses, such as "Berenice," but if indeed she did, the quest seems to have been fruitless, or even half-hearted, given the severity of her loss and the need to turn her attention to the matter of her husband's (and her own) livelihood and economic well-being. That Philips was aware of the change in her interests and, indeed, undertook it deliberately, is poignantly obvious in her comments to Sir Charles from Dublin on May 2, 1663: "I have us'd all the Arts that Diversion could afford me, to divide and cure a Passion that has met with so ill a Return, and am not a little oblig'd to my Lady Cork's Family for assisting me in that Intention: But oh! I begin already to dread what will become of

me, when I return home, and am restor'd to the sight of those Places, where I have been so often blest with the Enjoyment of a Conversation in which I took so much Delight, and is now for ever ravish'd from me" (Letter 29, 672). She needed, however, to keep up appearances and, as Souers notes, did so in a perfunctory manner—conscious that impassioned friendship was incompatible with social advancement—by continuing to write poems to women that retained the form, if not the passion, of her earlier work.

An examination of Philips's life in conjunction with the poems that initially won her praise thus reveals that her friendship poems to Rosania and Lucasia were an unvarnished expression of her love channeled into the already acceptable, even fashionable, mode of male heterosexual poetic discourse. Once we understand that the feelings in these poems are "real" and that they are confirmed by her letters to Sir Charles and "Berenice," it becomes clear that they are also homoerotic and have a place beside the long classical tradition of the literature of male love.

Male friendship literature written in English before the 1580s, according to Stephen Latt, relies heavily on classical precedent and "tends to be unoriginal or, at best, a rehearsal of old commonplaces—without originality, without personal application."[30] In the 1580s, however, male friendship literature exhibited a movement "towards a more emotional expression of friendship,"[31] which appropriated the civilities of Horatian and Aristotelian ideals and which continued into the seventeenth century with the poems of Thomas Carew, James Howell, Richard Lovelace, and Henry Vaughan (who was also part of Orinda's circle of male literary friends). In describing the friendship literature of the years 1620-64, Latt notes a "gradual movement away from the public level of experience. With the pressures of the times, writers turned increasingly inward. The turmoil of dissension, the chaos of rebellion, and the catastrophe of regicide freed loyal monarchists to desert the public scene."[32] Philips's poetry paralleled rather than emulated this male tradition, and it is distinguished from the poetry of her contemporaries in its personal intensity and in the metaphysical platonism she used to address female friendship.

Philips's awareness of the connection between her own feelings and the male tradition of friendship is manifest to some extent in her attempts to assure herself of the acceptability of her attachments by writing to Jeremy Taylor concerning the religious nature and limits of friendship. His answer to her, in "A Discourse of the Nature, Offices, and Measures, of Friendship, with Rules of Conducting It, in a Letter to the Most Ingenious and Excellent Mrs. Katharine Philips" (1657), cannot have been very satisfactory; his view is, as one might expect, rigorously androcentric in its treatment of women as friends only in relation to men: "A man is the best friend in trouble, but a woman may be equal to him in the days of joy: a woman can as well increase our comforts, but cannot so well lessen our sorrows."[33] Reaffirming traditional views, Taylor denied women's capacity for true friendship with men and ignored friendship between women. Perhaps more satisfying to Philips was the opening of Francis Finch's treatise *Friendship* (1653-54), dedicated to Anne Owen, "D. Noble *Lucasia-Orinda*," in which Finch publicly acknowledged and graciously complimented the relationship so important to Philips.[34]

She turned her fluent control of contemporary seventeenth-century male poetic idiom to her own particular uses, thus placing herself uniquely in a tradition whose only previous female exponent was the classical poet Sappho. That this daring manipulation of convention caused admiration for her work is quite apparent in the commendatory poems that introduce her poetry and in other contemporary comments that repeatedly praise her likeness to Sappho. Philips seems to have been the first English poet to have evoked that classical comparison. Until it later became a more conventional literary compliment, toward the end of the century, this comparison seems to have been somewhat problematic because of Sappho's presumed sexual transgressions. Sappho's work was recognized as the highest literary achievement in lyric poetry by a woman; although her subject matter was regarded as questionable by contemporary writers, it was echoed by Orinda. Sir Charles wrote in the preface to the 1667 edition of Philips's poems which he edited: "We might well have call'd her the English *Sappho*, she of all the female Poets of former Ages, being for her Verses and her Vertues both, the most highly to be valued. . . . And for her Vertues, they as much surpass'd those of *Sappho* as the Theological do the Moral, (wherein yet *Orinda* was not her inferior)."[35] One Philo-Philippa, the anonymous author of one of the commendatory poems for this volume, writes:

> Ingage us unto Books, *Sappho* comes forth,
> Though not of *Hesiod's* age, of *Hesiod's* worth,
> If Souls no Sexes have, as 'tis confest,
> 'Tis not the he or she makes Poems best:
> Nor can men call these Verses Feminine,
> Be the sense vigorous and Masculine.[36]

Abraham Cowley, the author of *Davideis,* which contains at least one homoerotic passage, describes Philips's poetic art:

> 'Tis solid, and 'tis manly all,
> Or rather, 'tis Angelical:
>   For, as in Angels, we
>   Do in thy verses see
> Both improv'd Sexes eminently meet;
> They are than Man more strong, and
>   more than Woman sweet.

Moreover, in the following he is at pains to describe Philips as a more virtuous Sappho, to distinguish her exemplary modesty and purity from the manners of her model:

> They talk of *Sappho,* but, alas! the shame
> Ill Manners soil the lustre of her fame.
> Orinda's inward Vertue is so bright,

> That, like a Lantern's fair enclosed light,
> It through the Paper shines where she doth write.
> Honour and Friendship, and the gen'rous scorn
>   Of things for which we were not born,
> (Things that can only by a fond disease,
> Like that of Girles our vicious stomacks please)
> Are the instructive subjects of her Pen.[37]

Praise of Philips as the standard of female excellence and poetic skill continued through the seventeenth century and into the mid-eighteenth century. Her name is linked with those of Aphra Behn ("Astrea") and Sappho in many of the commendatory poems and epistles written by women that preface plays written by women for the London stage of Queen Anne; she became a model to be emulated and replaced. In 1696, Mary Pix addressed Delariviere Manley on "her Tragedy call'd *The Royal Mischief*": "Like *Sappho* Charming, like *Afra* Eloquent, / Like Chast *Orinda* sweetly Innocent."[38]

Nancy Cotton and Jane Spencer point out that Orinda and Astrea became the two ideals in a female tradition to which later women writers aspired.[39] Yet Sappho continued to provide the second figure in a separate dyad and continued to be linked with Orinda when the issue was female poetic genius, so that the comparison of Orinda to Sappho became increasingly conventional.[40] The persistence of this association is apparent in these lines from John Duncombe's 1754 *The Feminiad: A Poem,* which echo very clearly the sentiments expressed by Cowley almost a century earlier:

> Nor need we now from our own Britain rove
> In search of genius, to the Lesbian grove,
> Tho' Sappho there her tuneful lyre has strung,
> And amorous griefs in sweetest accents sung,
> Since her, in Charles's days, amidst a train
> Of shameless bards, licentious and profane,
> The chaste ORINDA rose; with purer light,
> Like modest Cynthia, beaming thro' the night:
> Fair Friendship's lustre, undisguis'd by art,
> Glows in her lines, and animates her heart;
> Friendship, that jewel, which, tho' all confess
> Its peerless value, yet how few possess![41]

Though, after this, Orinda's reputation seems to have declined, its particular characteristics were reclaimed intact when, in 1905, George Saintsbury wittily introduced her poetry as "her Sapphic-Platonics."[42]

These comparisons with Sappho are important because they refer to the great classical female model of lyric poetry, but they are also important because they explicitly indicate a similarity of subject matter. Even though Cowley and Duncombe acknowledged this similarity of subject matter, they were also, paradoxically, eager to dispel the erotic content implicit in the comparison by emphasizing Orinda's purity. What we would now call the bisexuality of Sappho, to which Cowley and Duncombe allude, was also part of Sappho's legend for Orinda's contemporaries. Sappho's reputation for erotic involvement with women, as well as with men, was conveyed to the seventeenth century primarily by certain passages in Ovid's *Heroides*

("No more the *Lesbian* Dames my passion move, / Once the dear Objects of my guilty Love"), by Horace's references to *mascula Sappho* and to Sappho's complaints about the young women of Lesbos, and by the ode preserved by Longinus from Sappho to a female lover.[43] Donne himself wrote the explicitly sexual poem *Sapho to Philaenis*:

> And betweene us all sweetnesse may be had;
>   All, all that *Nature* yields, or *Art* can adde.
> My two lips, eyes, thighs, differ from thy two,
>   But so, as thine from one another doe;
> And, oh, no more; the likenesse being such,
>   Why should they not alike in all parts touch?
> Hand to strange hand, lippe to lippe none denies;
>   Why should they brest to brest, or thighs to thighs?[44]

Bayle's *Dictionary* (1710), though somewhat later, also is unequivocal in its view of Sappho's erotic activities ("her Amorous Passion extended even to the Persons of her own Sex" and "*Sappho* always passed for a Famous *Tribas*," or tribade), citing evidence that had been available since the Renaissance.[45] We can infer, then, that the writers of contemporary encomia to Orinda understood the nature of allusions to Sappho but were eager to dispel any suggestions of unnatural sexuality. They wished to pay her the high compliment of comparing her to the great classical lyricist not only for her poetical voice, but also for the uniqueness of her subject matter, at the same time that they wished to reconfirm her platonic purity. The encomium was appropriate and perhaps inevitable, if somewhat uncomfortable. Eventually, as it became more conventional, the comparison to Sappho was often used to suggest only literary accomplishment until Saintsbury recalled its original significance. Since Saintsbury, readers of Philips's work have simply neglected or trivialized her contribution to the history of poetic ideas: the recovery of the homoeroticism of platonic ideals in their classical lesbian context.

It was Philips's use of the conventions of male poetic discourse, particularly of the metaphysicals and the cavaliers, and her echoing of the literary tradition of male friendship, that sanctioned her unconventional subject and, in fact, made it a novelty in her time. Because her discourse was familiar her subject was acceptable. Without those conventions, and without Philips's modest and feminine demeanor in court circles, and her exemplary personal virtuousness, it seems unlikely that her poetry would have been praised as it was. Her literary example initiated a tradition of published female friendship poetry whose parameters have yet to be defined. The men who were her contemporaries accepted her ideals of passionate friendship between women and were persuaded to regard them as ennobling because they could recognize in their rhetorical strategies a parallel or analogue to their own ideals of heterosexual platonism and male friendship. That her poetic model was Donne, with his unquestioned heterosexual eroticism, only emphasizes the erotic nature of her passions.

The aspect of homosexuality that is pertinent to this study of Philips is a curious one. The poetic use of classical pastoral and friendship conventions in renaissance and seventeenth-century literature tells us next to nothing about the actual circumstances of people's lives. But in the case of Katherine Philips, external sources in the form of her letters and her highly unusual use of convention indicate that the feelings expressed in her poems were more than conventional or courtly gestures. This fact calls for an inquiry into the history of homosexuality in England.

We still know very little about the private erotic relations between women in seventeenth-century England. Lesbianism was not named as a reason for prosecuting women and few private documents have come to light that describe lesbian activities during this period.[46] The appearance, not too long after Philips's death, of literary documents by English women that portray explicitly lesbian activity—such as the duchess of Newcastle's play, *The Convent of Pleasure* (1668), Anne Killigrew's poem of erotic flagellation, "Upon a Little Lady Under the Discipline of an Excellent Person" (1686), Aphra Behn's poem "To the Fair Clarinda, Who Made Love to Me, Imagined More than Woman" (1688), and Delariviere Manley's "new *Cabal*" in her roman à clef *The New Atlantis* (1709)—surely is suggestive. However, these documents stand in an at best ambiguous relation to actual intimate behaviors, although they do indicate clearly that lesbian activities, as the twentieth century understands them, had been publicly articulated by women by the late 1660s and were regarded as scandalous infractions of the laws of nature.[47] In English cultural mythology, tribades were classed with pederasts, and probably papists, but we do not today have more reliable documentation of their activities, as we do about those of male homosexuals.

Alan Bray has described the change that took place in male homosexual life in England from 1650 to 1700. According to his research into court records and other documents, it was at this time that "molly" houses came into being as a symptom of the increasing isolation of practicing homosexuals from traditional institutions. This was the beginning of what we now call a homosexual subculture that evidently did not include women, though the appearance of explicitly lesbian literary subject matter might suggest the existence of an analogous female subculture. Of course, as Bray suggests, at the point of emergence of a subculture, the dominant culture officially recognizes that such individuals do indeed exist. Bray hypothesizes, on substantial grounds, that before 1650, and before the official acknowledgment of the existence of homosexual behavior, "the conflict between individual desire and the values of society as a whole" was resolved by a "cleavage . . . between an individual's behaviour and his awareness of its significance."[48] Before 1650, that is, there was a happy collusion between the individual and his culture to deny the meaning of his behavior, since pederasts were considered monstrous. Thus, male homosexuality was an unacknowledged, but hardly unusual, activity in such respectable institutions as the public schools and the apprentice/master system.

What is known as lesbianism to the twentieth century, though frequently unacknowledged or trivialized by patriarchal culture, always has existed as a sexual behavior. On the one hand, social construction theory suggests that expressions of lesbian behavior, as well as definitions of and discourse about that behavior, vary from one era and culture to another since sexuality is a cultural construct rather than—as has been traditionally claimed in patriarchal culture—determined by nature.[49] On the other hand, current debates about an appropriate definition of lesbianism do not offer a satisfactory method for describing the erotic experience or self-understanding of women before the mid-eighteenth century, when acknowledgment of female sexuality was severely inhibited in English-speaking and other Western cultures. Bonnie Zimmerman summarizes the attempts by Adrienne Rich, Catharine Stimpson, and Lillian Faderman to establish a useful working definition of lesbianism for historical scholarship; she cautions us to avoid the "simplistic universalism" that results when we use the overly inclusive "lesbian continuum" described by Rich as well as the exclusive genital sexuality of Stimpson's definition, which may have political utility in the twentieth century but inhibits attempts to reconstruct female eroticism in earlier historical periods.[50] Faderman's work mediates between the definitions proposed by Rich and Stimpson by using the convention of "romantic friendship" to describe the erotic relations between women from the mid-eighteenth century to the historical moment in the twentieth century in which lesbians became self-identified. Yet Faderman's use of this convention, like Carroll Smith-Rosenberg's reading of the language of nineteenth-century American women, leaves much to be desired: it evades the nature of the erotic content of much of the earlier literature she discusses and defuses its implications.[51]

To describe the historical consistency of erotic experience in women's friendship as it is expressed in literature and to identify a particular stance toward other women that partakes of the erotic, whether or not it is known actually to have culminated in behavior now described as sexual, we must revise Faderman's definition so that it includes the earlier periods and initiates a revaluation of earlier texts that does not diminish their possible erotic dimensions. We can begin this redefinition of lesbianism by reassessing earlier texts and reconsidering erotic relations between women as a possible dimension of their meaning. Because "the historical relationship between genital sexuality and lesbianism remains unclear," we must first accept certain earlier *texts* as lesbian insofar as they convey an experience of passion or eroticism that expresses "libidinous energy," whether or not it includes verifiable experience of genital activity.[52] Second, we must be willing to acknowledge that the *writers* of these texts may have been lesbians insofar as they apparently understood and were able to convey "libidinous energy" between women, even though it may never be possible to know the precise nature of their sexual activities.[53] In this way, we do justice to the nature of their contents and perhaps also avoid a Procrustean distortion of the writer's experiences.

Although the validity of social construction theory is difficult to dispute, it is also true that earlier women writers lived and wrote in a patriarchal culture that obscured the nature of female sexuality and the contexts of women's writing. That being so, it is necessary to put aside heterosexist bias and homophobia in order to recognize the ways in which lesbian eroticism does indeed manifest itself.

Given this perspective, there is no question that Katherine Philips produced lesbian texts, that is, texts that are amenable to lesbian reading in the twentieth century. It is also possible that contemporary female readers of Philips's texts found in them those qualities that we call lesbian echoed in their own feelings and that this contributed to their popularity and influential status among later women writers, as well as to their neglect and/or disparagement by some twentieth-century female critics.[54] Whether, and to what extent, Philips might have expressed her homoerotic feelings genitally is impossible to assess without the availability of further biographical evidence and must remain for now a moot—and perhaps irrelevant—question.[55] However, the evidence surveyed here confirms that Philips's was indeed a lesbian experience. The passion Philips expressed in her poetry and in her letters, and the absence of its expression in other areas of her life (i.e., toward husband or children), indicates a fervor in her feelings for women that would not have been acceptable either to herself or to others *except* as given shape in conventional form. To name this experience "romantic friendship," in conformity with the euphemizing language of the eighteenth century, would dilute the power of her poetry and deny her the full dimensions of her experience by perpetuating the trivialization of lesbianism. Therefore, we must acknowledge that her manipulations of the conventions of male poetic discourse constitute a form of lesbian writing.

We might argue, then, by analogy, that erotic behavior among respectable women was, until the last third of the nineteenth century, carried on in the same way as was male homoeroticism before 1650—that there was a "cleavage" between consciousness and behavior that allowed the individual and her society to evade naming the behavior—and that such erotic behavior was, in fact, later institutionalized and made acceptable by the convention of "female romantic friendship." The work and life of Katherine Philips furnished an example that made possible the later acceptance of eroticized friendships between women as a respectable alternative to the specter of unnatural vice. Her example may also suggest that it is appropriate to reassess, from this perspective, the language and conventions through which "romantic friendship" has been expressed and to examine the extent to which we may have misread its erotic content.

Notes

I am indebted to Kathryn M. Kendall for suggesting that I write this essay; to my colleagues in the Medieval and Renaissance Seminar at Texas A&M University for their useful comments on an early draft; to the anonymous *Signs* reviewers and associate editors for their judicious suggestions; and to Quincy Spurlin and Melanie Hawthorne for helpful discussions. A version of this essay was presented at the National Women's Studies Association meetings, Rutgers University, June 1984. Research was made possible by grants from Texas A& M University, for which I am grateful.

1. See Philip Webster Souers, *The Matchless Orinda* (Cambridge, Mass.: Harvard University Press, 1931); and the most recent edition of her work, Patrick H. B. Thomas, "An Edition of the Poems and Letters of Katherine Philips, 1632-1664" (Ph.D. diss., University College of Wales, 1982), xxviii-lviii, on Philips's reputation. Fidelis Morgan, *The Female Wits: Women Playwrights of the Restoration* (London: Virago, 1981), 3-11, esp. 3-4, quotes Keats's letter to John Hamilton Reynolds (September 21, 1817) distinguishing "one beautiful Mrs Philips" from other poets of her sex.

2. See Allan Pritchard, "Marvell's 'The Garden': A Restoration Poem?" *Studies in English Literature, 1500-1900* 23, no. 3 (1983): 371-88; Souers, 57-79; and Thomas, 74.

3. See Nancy Cotton, *Women Playwrights in England: 1363-1750* (Lewisburg, Pa.: Bucknell University Press, 1980), 194-212.

4. Kathleen M. Lynch, *The Social Mode of Restoration Comedy* (New York: Macmillan, 1926), 113-23, esp. 114; Morgan, 6; and Hilda L. Smith, *Reason's Disciples: Seventeenth-Century English Feminists* (Urbana: University of Illinois Press, 1982), 152-56, esp. 154.

5. See Allan Pritchard and Patrick Thomas, "Orinda, Vaughan and Watkyns: Anglo-Welsh Literary Relationships during the Interregnum," *Anglo-Welsh Review* 26, no. 57 (1976): 96-102.

6. Jennifer R. Waller, "'My Hand a Needle Better Fits': Anne Bradstreet and Women Poets in the Renaissance," *Dalhousie Review* 54 (Autumn 1974): 436-50, esp. 441.

7. See, e.g., Sandra Gilbert and Susan Gubar, eds., *The Norton Anthology of Literature by Women* (New York and London: Norton, 1985), 81-82; Moira Ferguson, ed., *First Feminists: British Women Writers, 1578-1799* (Bloomington: Indiana University Press, 1985), 102-13; Angeline Goreau, *The Whole Duty of a Woman: Female Writers in Seventeenth-Century England* (Garden City, N.Y.: Dial Press, 1987), 15-16, 193-205; and Katharine M. Rogers and William Mc-Carthy, eds., *The Meridian Anthology of Early Women Writers* (New York: Penguin, 1987), 373-75. An exception is Elizabeth H. Hageman's presentation of nineteen poems ("Katherine Philips: The Matchless Orinda," in *Women Writers of the Renaissance and Reformation,* ed. Katharina M. Wilson [Athens and London: University of Georgia Press, 1987], 566-608).

8. Waller, 444.

9. See Lillian Faderman, *Surpassing the Love of Men: Romantic Friendship and Love between Women from the Renaissance to the Present* (New York: Morrow, 1981), 68-71; and Souers, 276-77.

10. Sir Charles, in editing the 1667 edition, expanded the unauthorized 1664 quarto by including a letter he had received from Philips before her death; his own introduction; commendatory poems and eulogies by the earls of Orrery and Roscommon, Abraham Cowley, the anonymous Philo-Philippa, and others; some additional poems by Philips, including short translations from the French; and her *Pompey* and *Horace.* The editions of 1669, 1678, and 1710 are essentially reprints of the one edited by Sir Charles. The poems were not available again until George Saintsbury edited them, using the 1678 edition; see his *Minor Poets of the Caroline Period* (Oxford: Clarendon, 1905), 486-612. The two modern editions of Philips are those of Thomas (n. 1 above), which includes the *Letters to Poliarchus* (1705), the letters to "Berenice," and a previously unpublished, unedited letter; and Catherine Cole Mambretti, "A Critical Edition of the Poetry of Katherine Philips" (Ph.D. diss., University of Chicago, 1979). I have consulted the copies of the 1664 and 1667 editions, as well as the manuscript poems in the hand of Sir Edward Dering and the 1705 *Letters,* all of which are located in the Humanities Research Center, University of Texas, Austin.

11. *Préciosité* was a fashionable style associated with the literary salon at the Hôtel de Rambouillet in Paris during the first half of the seventeenth century; it was originally characterized by "the pursuit of elegance and distinction in manners, style, and language, devising new and metaphorical expressions, avoiding low or barbarous words, and pursuing clearness and precision" (Sir Paul Harvey and J. E. Heseltine, eds., *The Oxford Companion to French Literature* [Oxford: Clarendon, 1959], 568). These qualities lent themselves to excess and, eventually, to parody by those not associated with the salon. Thomas accepts the view of Philips as a *précieux* poet on the grounds that *préciosité* is a form of coterie poetry particularly appropriate to the English Interregnum (xviii-xxi). Despite Henrietta Maria's introduction of this French literary and intellectual fashion into England in the 1630s, however, the cavalier poets (and Philips) do not conform to the closed society Odette de Mourgues finds necessary for *préciosité* to flourish: "What characterized English court lyricists (and the seventeenth-century Cavalier poets are a good illustration) is that they were more ready to absorb than to reject" (*Metaphysical, Baroque, and Précieux Poetry* [Oxford: Clarendon, 1953], 102-42, esp. 141). See Thomas (xxi-xxv) on Philips's so-called society of friendship. Though Thomas is critical of earlier attempts to reconstruct this society, his own account of its nature

is also speculative. It remains unclear, for instance, to what extent the persons included by Philips in her society at various times knew each other, whether or not they ever met as an organized group, or whether, instead, inclusion might not have been used by Philips as a means of flattering and drawing closer to herself those whose friendship she sought. The degree of slippage between the possibly fictive ideal attributed to Orinda by her friend Sir Edward Dering and the reality may have been considerable (see letter to Anne Owen [Lucasia], written shortly after Philips's death, eulogizing Orinda's ideal society [quoted by Thomas, xxii]). An apparently similar slippage occurs in Philips's use of classical names, both for herself and for others. She seems to have used these in her social life as well as in her poetry: almost all her surviving letters are signed "Orinda," and Sir Edward Dering uses the names familiar from her poetry in his letters both to her and to their mutual acquaintances (Letterbook, 1661-1665 [Ohio Historical Society microfilm, Philips MS. 14932]). This suggests that, for Philips and perhaps for a few of her friends, there was some conflation between the literary personae she created and the actual persons they were meant to represent. I have attempted to retain the quality of this ambiguity in the discussion that follows.

12. On Cowley, see Bruce King, *Seventeenth-Century English Literature* (New York: Schocken, 1982), 144; and Nicholas Jose, *Ideas of the Restoration in English Literature* (Cambridge, Mass.: Harvard University Press, 1984), 67-96.

13. Faderman (n. 9 above), 69-70; and Hageman (n. 7 above), 572-73, have also noted Philips's use of Donne.

14. Thomas, no. 59, 270-74. The text of Philips's works used here is that established by Thomas; all further references in my essay, as well as subsequent citations to Thomas, refer to his "An Edition of the Poems and Letters of Katherine Philips, 1632-1664." Saintsbury's 1905 text, however, is the most readily available.

15. Thomas also notes the unusual intensity of this conceit but fails to locate its model in Donne (177).

16. Thomas quotes Rosemary Freeman (*English Emblem Books* [London: Chatto & Windus, 1948], 148) on the significance of the compasses in Donne as "an accepted emblem of constancy" (136-37).

17. See Faderman (n. 9 above), 65-68, for pertinent examples of earlier male friendship literature.

18. Earl Miner, *The Cavalier Mode from Jonson to Cotton* (Princeton, N.J.: Princeton University Press, 1971), 256-59. Miner uses the term "cavalier winter" to describe the exclusion of royalists, among whom were the cavalier poets, from social and political power during the Interregnum.

19. See Souers (n. 1 above), 79-92; and Thomas, v, 3-4, 158-59, and 163-64. *Upon the double murther of K. Charles, in answer to a libellous rime made by V.P.* (1650-51), Philips's royalist reply to Vavasor Powell's poem attacking the memory of Charles I, seems to have become a useful tool in the hands of James Philips's political enemies, though he seems not to have attempted to restrain her expression of her sympathies. After the Restoration, her poems addressed to the newly restored royal family not only reflected the change in atmosphere which meant that poets could once again address the court, but they also reflected her concern for her husband's political situation and their mutual need for patronage.

20. See, e.g., *Orinda to Lucasia parting, October 1661. at London* (Thomas, [n. 1 above], no. 93, 430).

21. Lucy Brashear ("The Forgotten Legacy of the 'Matchless Orinda,'" *Anglo-Welch Review,* no. 65 [1979], 68-76, esp. 72) also observes this omission: "One looks vainly for topics that provided the foundation of her life—home, family responsibilities, and personal joys and frustrations"; but her conclusion, that "finding no literary precedent to direct her, Orinda refused to write about her own experiences," overlooks the important possibility that Philips was indeed writing about those experiences that "provided the foundation of her life" in writing about the emotional friendships that compensated for a less than absorbing domestic experience.

22. See *On Rosania's Apostacy, and Lucasia's Friendship* (Thomas, no. 68, 332-33), and *Injuria amici* (Thomas, no. 38, 182-83), probably also addressed to Rosania on the occasion of her marriage. Compare these with the more formal and perfunctory *Rosania's private marriage* (Thomas, no. 37, 178-79).

23. Letters 1-12 to Sir Charles (Thomas, 554-600) describe Philips's activities on behalf of his suit to Lucasia. Souers (123-27, and 132) has identified the "Calanthe" of these letters as Anne Owen (see also Thomas, viii and lxi). Orinda's relationship with Sir Charles was one of mutual benefit: as he sought to advance her husband and her career, so she encouraged his courting of Lucasia, though she seems to have had the additional motive of wanting to keep Lucasia nearby. Philips refers to the Italian postscripts inquiring after "Calanthe" in Sir Charles's letters, which she answers in English, apologizing that she can read but not write Italian. The enterprise thus had a rather clandestine air because "Calanthe" often asked after, and even seems to have read, some of Sir Charles's correspondence.

24. Thomas identifies "Berenice" as Lady Elizabeth Ker (or Carre), one of the daughters of Robert Ker, first earl of Ancram (216), but his argument for doing so is not entirely convincing. Philips had addressed her in *To the Rt. Hono: the Lady E.C.* (no. 45, 207-12), which is, like the letters to "Berenice," full of breathless admiration.

25. The letters to "Berenice" were published in T. Brown, ed., *Familiar Letters written by the late Earl of Rochester, with letters written by Mr. Thomas Otway and Mrs. K. Philips* (London, 1697), sigs. K7ᵛ-L8, esp. L4. The erotic tone of the letters to "Berenice" is even more striking when compared with that in the letters to Sir Charles or in the one surviving letter to Lady Temple (Thomas, Letter 53, 781-86), also aristocrats whose friendship and good will Philips was eager to propitiate but with whom she was clearly not intimate in the same way.

26. See "Pierre Corneille" in Harvey and Heseltine, eds. (n. 11 above), 170.

27. Thomas implies that *Pompey* is political allegory (723), while Jacqueline Pearson points out its contemporary relevance (*The Prostituted Muse: Images of Women and Women Dramatists 1642-1737*) [New York: St. Martin's, 1988], 122). Jose (n. 12 above, 131) observes that "the word 'restore' runs like a *leitmotif*" throughout the play, which was performed in 1663.

28. Souers (n. 1 above), 148; Thomas concurs (vii-viii).

29. See also *To the Lady E. Boyl* (Thomas, no. 102, 455-56), *To my Lady Ann Boyle's saying I look'd angrily upon her* (Thomas, no. 85, 403), and *To my Lady M. Cavendish, choosing the name of Policrite* (Thomas, no. 95, 436-37), all written between 1662 and 1664, after the defection of Lucasia, and all exhibiting Orinda's consciousness of the difficulties of friendship with social superiors. Ann Boyle was known as "Valeria"; Mary Cavendish, whose maiden name was Butler, was a daughter of the duke of Ormonde. This dispersal of Philips's poetic affections among three different women is telling in light of the philosophy she had expounded in *A Dialogue of Friendship multiplyed* (Thomas, no. 97, 440-41): "The purity of friendship's flame" requires "that the hearts so close do knit, / They no third partner can admit."

30. Stephen Latt, "The Progress of Friendship: The Topoi for Society and the Ideal Experience in the Poetry and Prose of Seventeenth-Century England" (Ph.D. diss., University of California, Los Angeles, 1971), 74.

31. Ibid., 187.

32. Ibid., 184.

33. Reginald Heber, ed., *The Whole Works of the Right Rev. Jeremy Taylor,* 15 vols. (London, 1822), 11:299-335, esp. 331. Philips takes up this issue in *A Friend* (Thomas, no. 64, 304*a*): "If soules no sexes have, for men 't' exclude / Women from friendship's vast capacity, / Is a design injurious and rude, / Onely maintain'd by partiall tyranny."

34. Thomas, 56-57 and 263. See *To the noble Palaemon on his incomparable discourse of Friendship* (Thomas, no. 12, 53-54) and *Friendship* (Thomas, no. 57, 260-62).

35. Katherine Philips, *Poems* (London, 1667), sigs. a1ᵛ-a2 (also Saintsbury [n. 10 above], 493).

36. Ibid., sig. d1 (also Saintsbury, 498). Philo-Philippa's poem was one of the many verses and letters sent to Philips following the performance of *Pompey.* Philips's interest in Philo-Philippa no doubt contributed to Sir Charles's decision to include the latter's verses in his edition: "One of them, who pretends to be a woman, writes very well, but I cannot imagine who the Author is, nor by any Inquiry I can make, have hitherto been able to discover. I intend to keep that Copy by me, to shew it you when next we meet" (Letter 26, 658).

37. Philips, sigs. c1-c1ᵛ (also Saintsbury, 496).

38. Delariviere Manley, *The Royal Mischief* (London, 1696), sig. A3ᵛ· Similar references in the prefatory material to plays by women, chiefly linking Orinda and Astrea as precursors, continue through the 1690s into the beginning of the eighteenth century. See, e.g., the commendatory poems to Catherine Trotter that preface her plays, *Agnes de Castro* (1696), *Fatal Friendship* (1698), and *The Unhappy Penitent* (1701).

39. See "Orinda and Astrea" in Cotton (n. 3 above), 194-212; and Jane Spencer, *The Rise of the Woman Novelist* (Oxford and New York: Basil Blackwell, 1986), 22-33. While female writers continued to admire the two divergent traditions fostered by the very different personal and literary styles of Philips and Aphra Behn, male writers disparaged the flamboyance of "Astrea's" behavior and writing.

40. Spencer also notes the persistent use of the comparison to Sappho, emphasizing its literary aspect (27-32). Gerard Langbaine, *An Account of the English Dramatick Poets* (Oxford, 1691; reprint, New York and London: Garland, 1973), sig. Cc2-Cc3ᵛ· provides an example of the perpetuation of the literary strain of this compliment in the late seventeenth century.

41. John Duncombe, *The Feminiad* (London, 1754), sig. B2ᵛ· lines 104-15.

42. Saintsbury, 488.

43. See Ovid, *Heroides* (Sappho to Phaon) 15.15-20, 201-2; Horace, *Epistles* 1.19.61, and *Odes* 2.13.24-25; and Longinus, *On the Sublime* 10.2. The translation from Ovid given here is Pope's 1707 version (*The Poems of Alexander Pope,* ed. John Butt [New Haven, Conn.: Yale University Press, 1963], 29, lines 17-18).

44. Lines 44-50. See Sir Herbert Grierson, *The Poems of John Donne* (London: Oxford University Press, 1960), 110-12, for the complete text of this poem.

45. See "Sappho" in Pierre Bayle, *An Historical and Critical Dictionary,* 4 vols. (London, 1710), vol. 4, sigs. Rrr3-Rrr4, esp. Rrr3. Marie-Jo Bonnet, *Un choix*

sans équivoque: Recherches historiques sur les relations amoureuses entre les femmes XVIe-XXe siècle (Paris: Editions Denoël, 1981), 23-34, gives a history of Sappho and of the use of *tribade* in French literature from the sixteenth through the nineteenth centuries. The term itself comes from the Greek τριβειν, used to identify a woman who engaged with other women in acts considered unnatural. The contemporary debate about Sappho's presumed lesbianism, which Bayle describes in his notes, still continues in the twentieth century. See Howard Jacobson, *Ovid's "Heroides"* (Princeton, N.J.: Princeton University Press, 1974), 290-99; and Judith P. Hallett, "Sappho and Her Social Context: Sense and Sensuality," and Eva Stehle Stigers, "Romantic Sensuality, Poetic Sense: A Response to Hallett on Sappho," both in *Signs: Journal of Women in Culture and Society* 4, no. 3 (Spring 1979): 447-64 and 465-71, respectively, for an exposition of the arguments concerning the nature of Sappho's relations with women. *Lesbian* is of course a modern word, not in the *Oxford English Dictionary* in its present, sexualized meaning, and in the Victorian *Century Cyclopedia* only as a prim "amatory" or "erotic."

46. Though the preponderance of studies address lesbianism in the late nineteenth and early twentieth centuries (e.g., Jane Rule, *Lesbian Images* [New York: Pocket Books, 1976]; Estelle B. Freedman, Barbara Charlesworth Gelpi, Susan L. Johnson, and Kathleen M. Weston, eds., "Special Issue: The Lesbian Issue," *Signs* 9, no. 4 [Summer 1984]); and MarieJo Bonnet, Lillian Faderman, and Jeanette Foster (*Sex Variant Women in Literature* [1956; reprint, Tallahassee, Fla.: Naiad Press, 1985], 17-50) survey the evidence, written almost entirely by men, for female homoeroticism in earlier periods; and Judith C. Brown presents an extensively documented example of behavior in *Immodest Acts: The Life of a Lesbian Nun in Renaissance Italy* (New York: Oxford University Press, 1985). See also Ferguson, ed. (n. 7 above), 31-36, for a survey of early women's writing on love and friendship; and Ruth Perry, *The Celebrated Mary Astell* (Chicago: University of Chicago Press, 1986), esp. 120-48, for an account of late seventeeth-century female attitudes toward sexuality.

47. Margaret Cavendish, duchess of Newcastle, Aphra Behn, and Delariviere Manley were considered less than acceptable in polite society, and at least the duchess of Newcastle and Delariviere Manley may have been playing in these works to the libertinism of their audiences. The last three poems in Anne Killigrew's book, all three concerning passion between women, *Upon a Little Lady* . . . being the last, are preceded by a disclaimer denying her authorship (Anne Messenger, *His and Hers: Essays in Restoration and Eighteenth-Century Literature* [Lexington: University Press of Kentucky, 1986], 29-36, esp. 29).

48. Alan Bray, *Homosexuality in Renaissance England* (London: Gay Men's Press, 1982), 67-68.

49. Bonnet (n. 45 above, 11-190, passim) gives numerous examples of male definitions of "unnatural" activity between women before 1900 in France.

50. Bonnie Zimmerman, "What Has Never Been: An Overview of Lesbian Feminist Criticism," in *Making a Difference: Feminist Literary Criticism,* ed. Gayle Greene and Coppelia Kahn (London and New York: Methuen, 1985), 177-210, esp. 183-88. See also Catharine Stimpson, "Zero Degree Deviancy: The Lesbian Novel in English," in *Writing and Sexual Difference,* ed. Elizabeth Abel (Chicago: University of Chicago Press, 1982), 243-59; and Adrienne Rich, "Compulsory Heterosexuality and Lesbian Existence," *Signs* 5, no. 4 (Summer 1980): 631-60. Rich's views have been the occasion of considerable discussion concerning their usefulness for historical scholarship: see Ann Ferguson, Jacquelyn N. Zita, and Kathryn Pyne Addelson, "On 'Compulsory Heterosexuality and Lesbian Existence': Defining the Issues," in *Feminist Theory: A Critique of Ideology,* ed. Nannerl O. Keohane, Michelle Z. Rosaldo, and Barbara C. Gelpi (Chicago and London: University of Chicago Press, 1982), 147-88.

51. Zimmerman addresses the difficulties inherent in Faderman's definition, as does Martha Vicinus in "Sexuality and Power: A Review of Current Work in the History of Sexuality," *Feminist Studies* 8, no. 1 (Spring 1982): 133-56, esp. 147-51. Martin Bauml Duberman ("'I Am Not Contented': Female Masochism and Lesbianism in Early Twentieth-Century New England," *Signs* 5, no. 4 [Summer 1980]: 825-41, esp. 831, n. 5) comments on the sometimes tenuous distinction between sensuality and sexuality made by Carroll Smith-Rosenberg in her classic study, "The Female World of Love and Ritual: Relations between Women in Nineteenth-Century America," *Signs* 1, no. 1 (Autumn 1975): 1-29.

52. Zimmerman, 186. While Zimmerman cautions critics to exercise judiciousness in reading texts by presumably heterosexual women, she points out that "if a text lends itself to a lesbian reading, then no amount of biographical 'proof' ought to be necessary to establish it as a lesbian text" (185). A further elaboration of this view can be found in Barbara Smith's 1977 reading of Toni Morrison's *Sula*, "Toward a Black Feminist Criticism," in *The New Feminist Criticism: Essays on Women, Literature, and Theory,* ed. Elaine Showalter (New York: Pantheon, 1985), 168-85; and Jean E. Kennard's reader-response theory, "Ourself behind Ourself: A Theory for Lesbian Readers," *Signs* 9, no. 4 (Summer 1984): 647-62. Perry (n. 46 above) uses the phrase "libidinous energy" to describe Mary Astell's expression of her feelings toward women but to deny Astell's lesbianism (141).

53. Lillian Faderman discusses the "techniques of bowdlerization" used by biographers to avoid recognizing erotic relations between women, and

Francis Doughty asks, "Why are there different standards of evidence in establishing heterosexuality as opposed to homosexuality?" ("Who Hid Lesbian History?" and "Lesbian Biography, Biography of Lesbians," respectively, both in *Lesbian Studies: Present and Future,* ed. Margaret Cruikshank [Old Westbury, N.Y.: Feminist Press, 1982], 115-21 and 122-27, esp. 123).

54. See, e.g., Lynch (n. 4 above), Morgan (n. 1 above), and H. Smith (n. 4 above). Kennard's theory (n. 52 above) is helpful in understanding their responses as those of resisting readers who sense an unacceptable eroticism in Philips and "seek to affirm themselves by a denial of 'the other' rather than through a full recognition of it" (658).

55. Stigers's account of Sappho (n. 45 above) bears consideration in relation to Philips: "Such love was separate from daily domestic life with a husband. . . . Sappho must have known enough of both the romantic yearning for transcendent union and the different quality of lesbian intimacy from heterosexual intimacy to create a romantic, alternate female world" (467).

Travis DuPriest (essay date 1992)

SOURCE: DuPriest, Travis. Introduction to *Poems: 1667,* by Katherine Philips, pp. 3-25. Delmar, New York: Scholars' Facsimilies & Reprints, 1992.

[*In the following essay, DuPriest provides an overview of Philips's career and life, probing the issue of her lack of posthumous popularity.*]

With the emergence of feminist criticism has come the reconstruction of history; and with this reconstruction, the awareness that many women writers and thinkers have been forgotten in a largely male canon—some purposefully suppressed; others, consistently allowed, perhaps encouraged, to drop out of the sweep of recorded history and out of the anthologies of intellectual and literary ideas.[1] Opponents of feminist criticism in literature, history, and religion, often point out that important women have held high places in society and have been honored by their peers—Sappho, Queen Elizabeth, Julian of Norwich, Hilda of Whitby and the like. But these same critics point less enthusiastically to bright women once admired but now largely neglected. Such women in the latter category are the eighteenth-century poet, Elizabeth Singer Rowe[2] (1674-1737) and our present study in this reprint, the seventeenth-century poet, Katherine Philips[3] (1631-1664).

Playing what she considered the proper role of a lady, perhaps participating in something of a genteel literary tradition, Katherine Philips was self-deprecating, as Louise Bernikow, editor of *The World Split Open,* notes when citing Philips' own comment: "She who never writ any line

in my life with an intention to have it printed. . . ."[4] She was apparently horrified that her poems had been published in 1664 without her permission and had the publisher recall the book. It is, though, difficult to assess from this distance Philips' self-expressed modesty—whether it be aristocratic convention, genuine humility, or a necessary protection of her own femininity. An interesting footnote to the episode is that several of her more satirical and feminist poems were not among those included in the 1664 edition.

The editor of *The Whole Duty of a Woman* cites this passage:

". . . sometimes I think that to make verses is so much above my reach, and a diversion so unfit for the sex to which I belong, that I am about to resolve against it forever."[5]

Why, though, would one so retiring allow her translation of a Corneille play to be produced in Ireland to large audiences and public notoriety? She is largely removed from the political world of her day, though she does write on several political issues, one of which was the murder of King Charles I, an interesting feminist issue in itself given her husband's M.P. status while she remained a royalist during the Interregnum.

She was close to influential men of the times and was destined, as it were, for publication. While her subject matter is not largely public, her literary world is nonetheless a real one—the real world of tenderness among friends, some men, mostly women, and the hushed world of love between women. The literary world which Katherine Philips creates and herself as Orinda inhabits—is a vastly interesting one, and one not so free of questions and controversy as one might imagine of a "private" woman poet whose primary topic is the seemingly neutral topic of friendship.

HER LIFE

Katherine Fowler, born New Year's Day, 1631, was the daughter of a London merchant named John Fowler and his wife Katherine Oxenbridge, herself the daughter of Dr. John Oxenbridge, a Presbyterian and Fellow of the Royal College of Physicians.[6] Like Janus, namesake of the month of her birth, Katherine was herself to look both backwards and forwards—backwards to a world dominated by male education and letters; forward to her own considerable notoriety as a well-educated woman, poet, translator, and serious friend. A student at the well-known boarding school at Hackeny, Katherine was apparently a child prodigy who was encouraged and well educated. Numerous sources mention her interest in scripture, languages, and writing from an early age.

After the death of her father, Katherine's mother married Hector Philips, the father of James Philips. In 1647 Katherine would become, at seventeen, the second wife of James, a member of parliament; hence Katherine spent part of her time in London and part in Wales at the Philips' home, at the Old Priory, Cardigan. At Hackney school, Katherine probably began to write her verses as apparently her grandmother Oxenbridge had done as a youth, but it was at her pastoral home in Cardigan where she wrote and intellectually, if not physically, presided over her Society of Friendship, in part a coterie of actual friends and in part a literary convention modeled on classical rules of friendship.

Besides her interest in writing, she was also keenly interested in religion. Born into a Presbyterian family, she seriously studied scripture and ecclesiastical affairs, often seeking discussion and debate on theological issues. John Aubrey, that purveyor of noteworthy lives, records that "When a child, she was mighty apt to learn . . . she had an excellent memory and could have brought away a sermon in her memory."[7] Eventually, despite her background, she herself came to appreciate the Church of England and was moved to consult one of its most eminent divines: in the 1650s, she wrote a query to Jeremy Taylor, sometime resident in Wales during the Interregnum, who had been chaplain to King Charles I and who, after the Restoration of King Charles II, was named Bishop of Down and Connor in Ireland. She also knew Dr. Henry Vaughan, Silurist and poet, of Breconshire, Wales.[8]

Her inquiry to Taylor is enshrined—I trust close to her own words—in Taylor's "Discourse on the Nature and Offices of Friendship," first published in 1657.[9] Mrs. Philips' question, as we have it in Taylor's "Discourse," is, "How far a dear and perfect friendship is authorized by the principles of Christianity?"[10] This question alone, we are led to believe, occasioned Taylor's long and lovely essay on friendship in which he argues as a Christian humanist for the virtues of particular friendships, that is, friendships between close personal friends, as opposed to the more generally applied concept of friendliness toward all which one might deduce from reading the New Testament. Taylor, in his casuistic, moderately latitudinarian manner, assures Mrs. Philips, and other readers, that it is not against Christian teachings for people to have, hold, and nurture particular friendships such as the ancients extolled. His eloquent response must have delighted Katherine Philips, and no doubt countless others who read it after publication.[11]

Through her Society of Friends and through her manuscripts, which no doubt circulated among friends, Philips became well known, widely read, and eventually praised by noted literary contemporaries. Her successful translations of Corneille's plays and acclaimed productions in Dublin, as well as the popularity of a number of poems, brought her attention and endorsement, but unfortunately this talented, interesting woman died of smallpox at the age of thirty-three while in London.

Her son, only forty days old, had died in 1647 and is memorialized in one of her loveliest poems, a sonnet, **"Orinda Upon Little Hector Philips."** Her daughter, Katherine, born in 1656, lived and later married Lewis

Wogan of Pembrokeshire. Mrs. Katherine Philips was buried in St. Benet's, Sherehog, London, as was her baby son Hector. The church, formerly dedicated to St. Osyth's, was burned during the Great Fire of 1666.

A SEVENTEENTH-CENTURY TRADITION OF FRIENDSHIP

In ancient Greece and Rome, friendship was seriously studied and practiced as a primary virtue and was often seen as the true end of philosophy, the love of wisdom, the love of the good. Writers and thinkers such as Plato, Aristotle, and Epicurus wrote extensively on the topic of friendship, but these thinkers saw friendship as a relationship, often intellectual, to be enjoyed and practiced between men. It was a question whether a woman was fit to be a friend or a fit recipient of friendship, at least in the elevated context of philosophy. Authentic friendship was the province of men.

In the more strictly-defined literary tradition, Homer shows numerous examples of male friendship, Patroclus and Achilles, for example, from the *Iliad,* and in the *Odyssey.* Louise Bernikow, in her section on friends in *Among Women* traces a male tradition of friendship in the context of war and competition and compares that tradition with a tradition of female friendship in Sappho and Katherine Philips.[12]

During the Middle Ages and Renaissance in Europe, much the same positions held among those who wrote on friendship—that high or philosophical friendship was a masculine enterprise, though in the Renaissance, the intelligence and role of women in society was increasingly acknowledged by such writers as Castiglione and Thomas More. Indeed, the great international scholar and Christian humanist, Erasmus, satirizes the decadence of male intelligence and governance and by implication other conventions of society—in his "Abbot and the Learned Woman."[13]

Interestingly, during the English Renaissance of the sixteenth and seventeenth centuries, friendship again emerges as a serious philosophical study and practice. Although Aelred of Rivaulx had written his book, *Spiritual Friendship,* in the Middle Ages,[14] his work was for friends within the monastic community. In the sixteenth and seventeenth centuries, however, we see the concern with friendship as both intellectual idea and human relationship: Writers such a Montaigne[15] on the continent and Bacon[16] in England wrote essays on the subject; and friendship was a favorite topic of biblical commentators of the day (citing the Old Testament David and the New Testament Christ, and others as examples of those who fostered particular friendship), as well as popular writers on morals and manners. Richard Allessee, for example, devotes several pages in the best-selling *Whole Duty of a Man*[17] to friendship and its rightful exercise. Jeremy Taylor's lengthy essay extends the metaphor of friendship as foundation for all human relations, even civilization itself.

Devoting both her life and her writing to friendship, Katherine Philips begins a quiet intellectual revolution in her Welsh country home: as a woman she not only invades the male world of letters but the male subject matter of serious, virtuous, philosophical friendship. In so doing, she shows considerable talent as a poet and knowledge of the classics and of scripture, creating both her own neo-classical world of ideas and a new spiritually based on classical and Christian precepts.

Her inquiry to Jeremy Taylor showed to what extent she took Christianity seriously, and it showed as well her high seriousness over particular, that is personal, friendships. Furthermore, her poems focus almost exclusively on female friendship, showing that women make worthy friends and are worthy recipients of friendship. As Bernikow puts it, she picks up where Sappho left off: this high estate of female friendship becomes love in many poems. It is also its own religion.

Just as Philips' stance of humility is open to debate and interpretation, so is the sexuality expressed in her poetry. *The World Split Open* maintains that her expression of love of woman for woman is as threatening to some critics as was Shakespeare's expression of love for the young boy in his sonnets. Harriette Andreadis argues for a Lesbian interpretation,[18] while Angeline Goreau of *The Whole Duty of a Woman* sees Philips as an intellectual who has digested her classics and shows women to be subjects of philosophical virtue.

Both readings are credible; the poems are indeed sensual, tender, and affectionate, yet they are definitely intellectual exercises as well. However the reader responds, the point not to be forgotten is that Philips, the "English Sappho," has broken convention and has challenged the male hold on serious, virtuous friendship. As Goreau points out, for Philips "friendship was a platonic ideal, a sacred connection between persons, far removed from the sphere of the merely sexual. Katherine Philips defined it as 'love refin'd and purg'd from all its dross.' The rejection of the possibility of sex frees Philips to express her feelings far more passionately than she might otherwise have done."[19] Others with differing sensibilities will obviously disagree and perhaps even see her sexuality and passion as that which engages her in the equally passionate intellectual celebration of women.

While we do not know for sure which of the ancients—Aristotle, Epicurus, Cicero—she may have read or was sharply aware of, we can assume that she knew platonic or neo-platonic ideas: her uses of classical names, allusions, and Latin phrases shows us her love of the classical world. Though her poetry is more abstract and less physical and concrete than Sappho's, she nonetheless echoes the classical world of Sappho, especially the world of female affections.

She may also have been well read in what I would call the seventeenth-century neo-classical school of friendship. Many people wrote on friendship, as was noted above, and Katherine Philips may have known Montaigne's essay, "Of Friendship," which had been translated into English by John Florio in 1603, though as a translator of Corneille's plays, Mrs. Philips had no need of Englished versions of French writers. She may well have read the considerable section on friendship in the popular handbook of the day, *Whole Duty of a Man* (1655); or, given her interest in scripture, she may have read any one of numerous and widely-available biblical glosses and commentaries on "friends" and "friendship." Her letter to Jeremy Taylor occasioned one of the greatest contributions to the neo-classical school of friendship, and her own poetry provides the single-most consistent devotion to the topic in the seventeenth century.

The delightful outcome of her learning we find in her considerable volume of poetry, running to two hundred forty-two pages in the small, handbook-sized 1664 edition and to one hundred ninety-eight pages in the larger, folio-sized 1667 edition which also included another one hundred twelve pages of Corneille translations. The poems, in both "first" editions, the unauthorized 1664 and the posthumous 1667, are largely on the classical theme of friendship and on the Society of Friendship which has assured her place in literary history.

HER SOCIETY OF FRIENDSHIP

There has been much controversy over the exact nature and meaning of Philips' Society of Friendship. Was it an actual gathering, salon perhaps, of friends? Was the Society all female, or were males allowed? Was the Society an intellectualization, an imagined, classical "school" of the poet's mind?

As Philip Souers, her biographer says, we have not really much more evidence than that which Katherine Philips herself gives us; therefore, many questions still tickle us. The best guess seems to be that the Society was largely imaginary, though partially a coterie of actual friends. Some see in it a projection of repressed, or perhaps fulfilled, Lesbian desires.

An older generation of literary historians, in particular George Saintsbury, saw the Society of Friendship as the whim of a harmless woman: "the whole thing (the classical names and Society of Friendship) is a sort of 'side show' to the Heroic entertainment which is one of the reasons it does not appear that 'Antenor' [Katherine's husband] objected, or that he had any reason to object."[20] Indeed, the use of classical names is playful; however, the scorn of 'side show' is excessive. As Louise Bernikow points out, Katherine Philips is the first woman since Sappho who wrote of love of women and who used classical themes; her writings are, therefore, a true treasure of literary history and of women's history and philosophy.

Philip Souers is himself doubtful about the reality of the Society as a salon holding meetings; however, he correctly sees Orinda's (Katherine's name for herself in the poems) classical penchant in its more serious philosophical setting in the history of ideas: "For Orinda friendship had a peculiar meaning. It was the Platonic mingling of souls; it had about it a certain mysticism, which made it a kind of religion to be realized only by initiation into its esoteric knowledge. Such a friendship, limited as it was in Orinda's eyes to persons of the same sex, was an ideal which lent itself easily to the inspiration of a society."[21] Souers cites her poem, "Friendship in Embleme, or the Seal. To my Dearest Lucasia." (29) and concludes, along with the poem's conclusion that the Society was that which "will transmit to Fame / *Lucasia* and *Orinda's* Name."

In Chapter III, "Friends and Friendship" of his book, Souers cites Edmund Gosse and George Bethune who gave credence to Orinda's "Society" in the 1800s, but he himself has many doubts that any real salon or society could have functioned given Katherine Philips' youth (in her 20s), place (living great distances from the women she mentions, in Wales), and times. Hence, Souers affirms the Society as an "official order of Friendship in the kingdom of feminine sensibility."[22]

Scant evidence hinders our interpretation of Orinda's Society, but clearly it is a serious idea within the classical and philosophical world of her poetry. Just as she would seem to have a heightened use of the word *friendship,* so, I believe, she may very well use *society* as a metaphor for the like-minded, as she uses *friendship* as an extended metaphor for intimacy.

Her poetry mentions a Society, a seal, and members. Men are also given classical names and epithets in the poems and would seem, at times, to be part of her classical coterie. It is uncertain whether men could "belong" to her Society; Souers thinks not, but cites several male inhabitants of her poetry: Antenor (James Philips), Silvander (Sir Edward Dering), Palaemon (Francis Finch; later, after Finch's death, Jeremy Taylor), and others. Souers is more certain that Ardelia, Philoclea, Regina, and Rosania were actual "members" of Orinda's Society, Regina being most likely Regina Collier, wife of John Collier, friend of John Fowler. Rosania, Souer asserts, was Mary Aubrey, Katherine's oldest friend from school days. Lucasia was Anne Owen, whom most agree was most certainly a member of the Society. Other critics assume male, as well as female membership, in Orinda's Society of Friendship.

No doubt feminist and historical critics will continue to revise the interpretation of the Society: Katherine's attitudes certainly show an aversion to marriages which remove her friends from single-minded attention and affection. Like Sappho, the "English Sappho" waxes both hot and cold in her expressions of affection. Orinda is the mistress who "expels" "members" out of favor and who "initiates" neophytes into the mysteries of the cult of feminine friendship—its own religion, its own laboratory of love.

HER POETRY OF FRIENDSHIP

Along with her colonial counterpart, Anne Bradstreet, Katherine Philips was one of the first women writers in English to have a book of her poetry published. She prob-

ably began writing poetic imitations, as was the habit of all schoolchildren of her day. Fond of Henry Vaughan (1622-1695), a native Welshman, she wrote any number of verses after his poetry; in fact her first published works appeared as part of a volume of Vaughan's poetry in 1651 and later that same year, in a collection by Cartwright. She circulated her own poetry in manuscript and became known among the literati in the 1650s and early 1660s.

When she went to Dublin in 1662 she was asked by the Earl of Orrery, later one of the commendors of her unauthorized volume of *Poems* of 1664, to complete a translation of the playwright Corneille's "Pompee." She did, and the play, produced in 1662, was successful and was printed the next year, 1663, in Dublin and in London. An unauthorized edition of *Poems* was brought out in 1664 but was suppressed by Marriott, the publisher, at the request of the author. As we noted earlier, despite her deference, she gained in popularity, and at the time of her death in 1664 was a well-known writer. Her verse was collected and published under the direction of Sir Charles Cotterel. This edition of *Poems* also contained her translation of Corneille's "Horace" as well as "Pompee," both included for textual integrity in this reprint.

Her subject matter is almost exclusively that of personal, particular friends, or that of the concept of friendships. There were seventy-four poems in the unauthorized 1664 edition; some one hundred twenty-three poems, translations, and the plays in the posthumous 1667 edition, of which one hundred sixteen were original poems. Of her one hundred sixteen poems, some twenty are occasional; several are on royal subjects, and several are specifically about religion, though the categories of her poems usually hover between the secular and the theological. Some concern contemporary writers and musicians, such as Henry Vaughan, Henry Lawes, Cartwright, Abraham Cowley, Roger L'Estrange and Jeremy Taylor. Others concern abstract emotions, but the vast majority are on love and its higher manifestation—friendship. She writes in a variety of forms—epistles, prayers, songs, and apostrophes and displays a range of voices, tones, and techniques. Her idiosyncrasies include a love of capitalizations in mid-line and contractions (such as "w'are") not unlike those found in the poems of Thomas Traherne.

When she writes on weather conditions in **"On Fair Weather Just at the Coronation,"** (4) she uses a simile alluding to Israel. In **"To Her Royal Highness the Duchess of York,"** (9) she writes about her own writing. But friendship is a sub-text even when it is not the text of her poetry, as she shows in a variety of cases how the qualities issuing from friendship, or the want of friendship, affect circumstances. For Katherine Philips, wisdom and friendship are one, yet friendship lightens life, as it does in **"A Retir'd Friendship, To Ardelia"** (22): "Come, my *Ardelia* to this Bower, / Where kindly mingling Souls Awhile / Let's innocently spend an hour / And at all serious follies smile" (*1667*, p. 28, *1664,* p. 56). The thesis for her poetry might be found in **"Lucasia"** (27): "Wisdom and Friendship have one single Throne / And make another Friendship of Their own" (*1667*, p. 35; *1664*, p. 67).

Philips' voice has an impressive tonal range. Working primarily in rhymed couplets, she can, as literary historian George Saintsbury said, be uninspiring, certainly to the modern ear, yet at times she sings with an electric vigor that awakens the reader. With echoes of John Donne, she says in **"Injuria Anicitiae"** (38): "lovely Apostate! What was my offense? or am I punish'ed for Obedience?" (*1667*, p. 53; *1664*, p. 109).

While she may indeed tend toward the poetic of the Restoration period, she is at ease in the world of seventeenth-century philosophical poetry; and at her best exploring what her epistolary friend, Jeremy Taylor, explored with her—the nature and offices of friendship. Regretting, as many a philosopher and essayist has, the poor estate friendship holds in society, Philips writes, in **"The Enquiry"** (58):

> Why are the bonds of Friendship tied
> With so remis a knot,
> That by the most it is defied
> And by the rest forgot?
> Why do we step with so light sense
> From Friendship to Indifference.
>
> (*1667*, p. 81; *1664*, p. 164)

For Philips, friendship is the highest calling, the noblest office, higher even than marriage—she speaks of the "bonds of friendship" even as Jeremy Taylor in his "Discourse" sees marriage as the epitome of friendship. Philips does not simply examine friendship, she exalts it among human relationships, particularly among women.

Her most frequently cited poems have been **"Orinda Upon little Hector Philips"** (101) and the one John Keats particularly admired, **"To M. A. at parting"** (53), and both for good reason. The latter begins with an especially metaphysical zestiness:

> I Have examin'd and do find,
> Of all that favour me
> There's none I grieve to leave behind
> But only only Thee.
> To part with Thee I needs must die,
> Could parting sep'rate Thee and I.
>
> (*1667*, p. 74; *1664*, pp. 150-51)

And reaches a crescendo in stanza 9:

> Thus our twin-souls in one shall grow
> And teach the World new Love,
> Redeem the Age and Sex, and show
> A Flame Fate dares not move:
> And courting Death to be our friend,
> Our Lives together shall end.
>
> (*1667*, p. 76; *1664*, p. 154)

Here she joins Platonic intellect with heartfelt, physical emotion—love of the mind and love of woman for woman.

Her deep affection for her husband and her male friends are seen in such poems as **"To the noble Palaemon . . ."** (12), **"To Sir Edward Dering (the noble Silvander) . . ."** (14), **"To Mr. Henry Lawes"** (15), **"To Mr. Henry Vaughan, Silurist . . ."** (21), **"Mr. Francis Finch . . ."** (52), and **"To my dearest Antenor . . ."** (54) which develops a lonely metaphysical image of a mirror. And the sorrowful love of her baby son who died is beautifully expressed in "And now (sweet Babe) what can my trembling heart / Suggest to right my doleful fate or thee, / Tears are my Nurse and sorrow all my Art . . ." (*1667*, p. 148), as it is, I think even more poignantly, in **"Epitaph on her Son H. P. at St. Syth's Church"** (88) which ends

> And so the Sun if it arise
> Half so glorious as his Eyes,
> Like this Infant, take a shroud
> Buried in a morning Cloud.
>
> (*1667*, p. 134)

HER FEMINISM

Though not always, Philips often writes as a woman to other women about women's issues, at least in many of her poems. Her repeated theme is love elevated to high or serious friendship among women.

Others have or will have to answer questions about her sexuality, about Lesbianism. What is clear is that she champions friendship—of men and women and affection between women, that she does not see marriage as the panacea for women or even the opportunity for happiness, and that she has serious criticism of men mixed in with her high praise of individual men and women.

She champions female bonding in **"To the honoured Lady E. C."** (45):

> You are so much above your Sex, that we
> Believe your Life your greatest courtesie:
> For Women boast, They have you while you live
> A Pattern and a Representative.
>
> (*1667*, p. 64; *1664*, p. 130)

From **"Friendship's Mystery . . ."** (17) we learn that friendly love between women is not prosaic and mundane, is not the ordinary friendship of men, but rather elevated to a cult of love. Again echoing John Donne she writes:

> Come, my *Lucasia,* since we see
> That Miracles, Men's faith do more,
> By wonders and by prodigy,
> To the dull angry world let's prove
> There's a Religion in our Love.
>
> (*1667*, p. 21; *1664*, p. 43)

The bonding and the sacredness of female friendship is, moreover, vivifying and nutritive. In actuality, this female bonding is recreative of the individual psyche; it is, in contemporary parlance, self-actualizing. Her poem entitled **"Friendship"** (57) ends:

United More than Spirits Faculties,
Higher in thought than are the Eagle's eyes;
What shall I say? When we true friends are grown,
W'are alike—Alas, w'are like ourselves alone.

(*1667*, p. 79; *1664*, p. 161)

Her understanding of friendship's role in the process of individuation echoes Aristotle's theories of selflessness among friends and looks forward to modern theories in psychology.[23]

As a philosopher, Philips asks the eternal questions concerning human happiness. And like Plato, she finds ultimate satisfaction in the realm of thought and ideas. In a poem to her sister on the occasion of her marriage, Philips issues a caution against the assumption that marriage will make a woman happy. In stanza two of **"To My Dear Sister Mrs. C. P. on her Marriage"** (20) she writes:

But these shall be my great Solemnities,
Orinda's wishes for *Cassandra's* bliss.
May her context be as unmix'd and pure
As my Affection, and like that endure.
And that strong Happiness may she still find
Not Owning to her Fortune, but her Mind.

(*1667*, p. 26; *1664*, pp. 52-53)

Philips clearly sees and bluntly states that the intellect is the quality which produces long-lasting happiness, not the fortune of being married. She again celebrates "serious things" (*1667*, p. 28; *1664*, p. 56) in her tribute, **"To Mr. Henry Vaughan, Silurist, *on his Poems*"** (21) and in her tribute **"To Mr. Henry Lawes"** (15) whom she congratulates for "Music to th'Ear, or to the Intellect" and in which she cleverly honors the musician with a musical definition of "Friendship the Unison of well-tun'd Hearts" (*1667*, p. 18; *1664*, p. 37).

She is openly critical of marriage and of the condition marriage reduces women to. She is again quick-witted and sure, perhaps uttering her own experienced wisdom as a woman intellectual in a "man's world"? From **"An Answer to another persuading a Lady to Marriage"** (108):

Forbear hold Youth, all Heaven here,
And what you do over,
To others Courtship may appear
'Tis Sacrilege to her.
She is a publick Deity,
And were't not very odd
She should depose herself to be
A petty Houshold God?

(*1667*, p. 155)

In a stinging statement such as this, Philips heightens her literary ingenuity, here alluding to the gods of the temples and the lesser gods of the home in Roman mythology. Seeing the young bride as a goddess, Philips, though, presents her potential marriage as the deposition of a figure worthy of public worship, to become a "petty" god in a domestic niche.

Her criticism of men in general is most caustic (and playful) in **"Upon the graving of her Name upon a Tree in Barnelmes Walks"** (91):

Trees are More generous Then Men,
Who by a Nobleness so pure
Can first oblige and Then endure

(*1667*, p. 137).

She can be quick and witty, and humorously ironic. Is **"The Virgin"** (90) delivered tongue in check?: "A Beauty, not to Art in debt, Rather agreeable than great" (*1667*, p. 136). One wonders.

As a feminist, Philips' primary poetic aim is the celebration of female affectionate ties, yet she does often contrast the feminine and masculine condition, as in the line from **"Content, to my dearest Lucasia"** (18): "Men think they have it when they have it not" (*1667*, p. 22; *1664*, p. 45). Paralleling her criticism of men is her exoneration of Eve, the original woman, in the story of the fall from Genesis. Here she delightfully combines a radical reading of Adam and Eve with a blunt condemnation of a person suing her husband. **"To Antenor, on a Paper of mine . . ."** (33):

Must then my Crimes, become thy Scandal too? . . .
For *Eve's* Rebellion did not *Adam* blast,
Until himself forbidden Fruit did taste?

(*1667*, p. 147; *1664*, á31, p. 91)

As her "crime" has no reality for her husband, so Eve's rebellion against God was solely her own, until Adam decided, on his own, to become involved. Clearly this woman, in her own "June-December" marriage, has strong criticisms of men and the institution of marriage. Her poems are most productively read in the context of the long-standing tradition of friendship as well as the context of her feminism. And yet a third important context emerges.

HER SPIRITUALITY

The exalted nature of friendship in Philips' poetic vocabulary derives from her classical savvy, from neoplatonic idealized love in particular; from her obvious affection—physical or imagined—of her close friends; but also from her Christianity. She firmly believes friendship to be both the high virtue of the ancients as well as a blessing from God. For her, friendship is the essential metaphor for expressing God's relation to the created world, to humanity, a metaphor for divine intimacy and an inner life of close, affectionate relationship with God and others.

For Philips, God's miracle of miracles, the Incarnation, is an act of friendship. And throughout her poetry she develops a spirituality of friendship whereby she talks at once about Christian doctrine in a vocabulary of friendship and, then again, of friendship in a decidedly Christian (biblical and doctrinal) vocabulary.

Overlooked by almost all of her critics—historical, literary, and feminist alike—her knowledge and use of Christianity shows Katherine Philips to be a sophisticated theologian in her poetry, focusing as she does time and again on central Christian concerns of harmony in creation and charity in life. As such, she also takes her place with seventeenth-century Christian humanists who see mutual service between the Christian religion and classical wisdom.

In **"A Sea-voyage from Tenby to Bristol . . ."** (16), Philips links the fall of humanity with the theme of friendship:

> Behold the fate that all our Glories sweep,
> Writ in the dangerous wonders of the Deep;
> And yet behold Man's easie folly more,
> How soon we curse what erst we did adore.

> (*1667,* p. 20; *1664,* p. 41)

Her homage herein to friendship is total; like Taylor in his "Discourse," Philips reckons friends to be as God to her in a given situation. She continues:

> My Voyage taught me so much tediousness.
> In short, the Heav'ns must needs propitious be,
> Because *Lucasia* was concern'd in me.

> (*1667,* p. 21; *1664,* p. 42)

Moreover, she likens friendship to the tensions between fate and free will; she parallels this theological discussion with a charming angelic analogy, in **"Friendship's Mystery . . ."** (17): "For though we were design'd to' agree, / That Fate no liberty destroys, / But our Election is as free . . ." (*1667,* p. 21; *1664,* p. 43). Continuing in stanza four, she writes, "we court our own captivity . . . / 'T were banishment to be set free, . . ." (*1667,* p. 22; *1664,* p. 44) and concludes in stanza six:

> Our Hearts are mutual Victims laid,
> While they (such power in Friendship lies)
> Are Altars, Priests, and Off'rings made;
> And each Heart which thus kindly dies,
> Grown deathless by the Sacrifice.

> (*1667,* p. 22; *1664,* p. 45)

One of her loveliest and most moving poems, **"Friendship's Mystery,"** explores in stunning imagery of sacrifice the mutuality of friendship. Her piercing sixth stanza, echoing Herbert's "Altar" and Donne's playful admixture of religion and lust in "The Canonization," shows Philips at her metaphysical best. The whole uses the Christian doctrine of election (she was born into a Presbyterian family) and a theology of paradox ("doubled by the loss"; "each Heart which Thus kindly dies, / Grown deathless by the Sacrifice") as overlay and underpinning for its exploration of the mysteries of friendship, subtly alluding to St. Paul's paradoxical "service which is perfect freedom."

Further, in poem 71, **"2 Cor.: 5.19 God was in Christ reconciling the World to himself,"** she shows God's very nature to be that of Friend. The essence of Christianity is

God's friendship with that which he created. Here she aligns herself with a tradition of English writers from Aelred of Rivaulx to her contemporary, Jeremy Taylor, who uses friendship as the essential metaphor for understanding God's creative power and sustaining care: "Then God took stand in Christ, studying a way / How to repair the Ruin'd World's decay . . . / Felicity? . . . / And what still are we, when our King in vain / Begs his lost Rebels to be Friends again? . . . What God himself hath made he cannot hate / For 'tis one act to Love and to Create . . ." (*1667,* p. 110; *1664,* pp. 214-15).

Humanity's Friendship with God was created—the act of creation and love are one—man rebelled, but God reinitiates the friendship with humanity: "As God with open Arms the World does woe . . ." (*1667,* p. 111; *1664,* p. 216) There can be little doubt that for Katherine Philips human friendships are a "type" of this divine relationship. Little doubt that her theology is a strong drive in her affections. In "L'Accord du Bien" (65), her theme is the harmony of creation, another subtext throughout most of her poems: "And hence it is we Friendship call / Not by one Virtue's name but all. / Nor is it when bad things agree / Thought Union, but conspiracy" (*1667,* p. 99; *1664,* p. 197).

For her, friendship takes on Platonic qualities, but that is not the whole picture; friendship is a Christian endeavor as well. Like John Donne, she quite easily treats love and friendship in the terms and language of religion, and she naturally yokes Platonic and Christian ideas. Reiterating harmony of beings once more—a particularly feminine theme?—she begins with this blunt conjecture in **"A Friend"** (64):

> Friendship's an Abstract of this noble Flame,
> 'Tis Love refin'd and purg'd from all its dross,
> The next to Angel's Love, if not the same,
> As strong in passion is, though not so gross:
> It antedates a glad Eternity
> And is an Heaven in Epitome.

> (*1667,* p. 94; *1664,* p. 189)

If until recently the love of woman for woman in Philips' poetry has escaped analysis, so has the intellectually religious inner dimensions of her poetry. Whatever her School of Friendship is exactly—coterie, salon, or philosophical ideal—it must also be seen as a spiritual school. She takes her inquiries into friendship seriously and as well, her inquiries into religion.

Notice that in commenting on the private marriage of a friend, Philips excerpts the spiritual truth of "lack" and silence classic themes of the contemplative tradition. Whatever her motive in penning these lines, the spiritual insight is keen in **"Rosania's private marriage"** (37):

> The greatest Actions pass without noise,
> And Tumults but prophane diviner Joys
> Silence with things transcendent nearest suits . . .
> The greatest Emperours are serv'd by Mutes.

> (*1667,* p. 52; *1664,* p. 106)

Philips' sensitivity to the inner life, the imagination, and to human and divine relationships give her work a true spiritual depth. We have experienced a revival of the spirituality of Julian of Norwich in recent years; we yet await the discovery of Katherine Philips' poetic spirituality.

HER FATE

Why has someone so greatly admired in her own day, with a modest following throughout successive generations— John Keats, for example, greatly admired one of Philips' poems—remained but a "footnote" in seventeenth-century literature anthologies until very recently when she has been included in anthologies of women writers, though quite modestly represented in even most feminist anthologies?

There are no doubt numerous reasons. On a purely literary, historical level, an analogy to the seventeenth-century poet Edmund Waller is perhaps not unfair. Waller, though a man, has not stood the tests of time and taste. Like Waller, Philips was a good poet, a careful crafter, sensitive to versification and meter and conceit; yet in breadth of subject matter and poetic texture not as dynamic as say an Anne Bradstreet.

Yet one wonders, along with Bernikow and others, if Philips' "friendship become love" from woman to woman may not have negatively influenced anthologizers, most of whom were men? One wonders even more why she has been scorned by literary historians who seem to go out of their way to find something negative rather than to highlight her uniqueness in English literary history, her learning, her poetics, and her humor and satire? One still wonders, though, at her relatively "minor" status among womanist and feminist anthologies.

True, she has never dropped totally through the cracks, having been treated in the late 1800s by Edmund Gosse and having received a substantial biography by Philip Souer in 1931, and having made it into the *DNB* as well as Saintsbury's *Minor Poets of the Seventeenth Century.* Yet time and again, subtle indictments surface, as though "damn'd with faint praise," her efforts kept in the back hallway, as it were, of literary history. As one feminist critic has put it when men write about love it is serious business; when women do the same thing, it is called "sentimental."

The Witherspoon anthology of seventeenth-century literature gives her a couple of paragraphs of introduction and a page of text. The *Dictionary of National Biography* article on her cites her as a "verse-writer"; interestingly, the equally "minor" Edmund Waller is termed a poet. The entry from the *DNB* concludes by saying of Katherine Philips that her "fame as a poet [was] always considerably in excess of her merits" and that her fame "did not long survive her. . . ."[24] George Saintsbury, in the Introduction to her work in his collection at the turn of the century, *Minor Poets of the Caroline Period* is even less kind:

The poems of 'The Matchless Orinda' are better suited to stand the test on which Joe Gargery apologized for his indulgence at the public house than that on which William Taylor of Norwich judged poetry and was laughed at by Carlyle for judging it. They 'do not overstimulate': On the division of "Quotidian and Stimulant" they approach nearer than to the latter.[25]

In much the same vein of pomposity, Mr. Saintsbury will allow her entrance into his volumes: "But this is no reason for excluding them from such a collection as this, where some at least of the constituents are rather too much than too little heady." In all fairness, Saintsbury did recognize some of her talents, and he did wish, as I do now, to reintroduce Philips to contemporary readers. He saw her poems as "the settling down of poetry to its more prosaic kinds and expressions about the period of the Restoration."[26] Nevertheless, the condescending tone of his Introduction is unnecessary and offensive.

Compare for example these notes from the "Orinda Pamphlet," published in 1904 in Hull which also recognizes Philips' limitations to those comments above of Saintsbury on her poetics:

From "Orinda Pamphlet":

> Theory and habit were one with Katherine Philips . . . Her plain lyre was one of the newest pattern, in time with Waller's, Denham's and Cowley's almost anticipating the Augustan precisions . . . the borderlands or prose. But we must take 'Orinda' as she is, with her somewhat amateur energy, her rough contractions and elisions, her pretty and effective artistic bravado.[27]

HER PUBLISHING HISTORY

"The Matchless Orinda," Katherine Philips, as we have noted, eschewed publication. The first edition of her poetry, an unauthorized and no doubt hastily printed one, came out the same year as her death, *Poems* 1664: the second edition (the first authorized), in 1667, "to which is added . . . Corneille's Pompey and Horace, tragedies with several other translations out of French," edited by Sir Charles Cotterell, M.P. from Cardigan. The imprimatur of the first authorized edition is under the signature of Roger L'Estrange, August 20, 1667; the commendatory poems are by Abraham Cowley. From the 1667 preface: "We might well have called her the English *SAPPHO,* she of all the female Poets of former ages, being for her Verses and Vertues both, the most highly to be valued; but she has called herself *ORINDA,* a name that deserves to be added to the number of the muses, and to live with honor as long as they." The edition is commended by the literati of the day, a rather impressive list: the Earl of Orrery, the Earl of Roscommon, Abraham Cowley, Philo-Philippa, James Tyrell, and Thomas Flatman, M.A. There also follows a commendatory poem, "On the Death of Mrs. Katherine Philips" by Abraham Cowley, whose name alone gives the edition serious contemporary literary credibility.

After the 1664 and 1667 editions of her poems followed numerous editions of her work. Often under her own pen name, "Orinda," Katherine Philips, like Edmund Waller, was admired, and for some time following her death, editions of her **Poems** continued to be reprinted. After the 1664 and 1667 editions came others in 1669, 1678, and 1710; selections in Poems by *Eminent Ladies,* 1755 and 1757, and inclusion in collections such as *A Collection of Divine Hymns and Poems* by the Earl of Roscommon . . . Mrs. Katherine Philips, etc., of 1709. She is also the subject of *The Poetical Remains of the Duke of Buckingham, Madam Philips, etc.,* 1698. She was later included in G. E. B. Saintsbury's *Minor Poets of the Caroline Period,* vol. 1, 1905 and **Selected Poems** were reprinted in Cottingham, near Hull, by J. R. Tutin in 1904 and as well in the "Orinda Booklets," no. 1, 1903. J. R. Tutin also printed *Four Early English Poetesses* as a "Hull Booklet," no. 7, in 1908.

As late as Keats (1795-1821) we find that the "Matchless Orinda" was read and admired by the best of English poets, who wrote admiringly of her poem **"Mrs. M.A. at parting"** in an 1817 letter to J.H. Reynolds. More recently, she has become widely anthologized in collections of women writers, notably *The World Split Open,* the *Penguin Book of Women Poets, The whole Duty of a Woman,* and the *Norton Anthology of Literature by Women,* and other collections focusing on women's issues and literature. She has also begun to receive attention from a younger generation of feminist scholars and has been the subject of scholarly papers at literary and women's studies conferences.

KATHERINE PHILIPS IN THE BRITISH LIBRARY

Poems . . . to which is added . . . Jacob Tonson: London, 1710.

Poems . . . to which is added . . . London, 1710.

Poems, etc. G.E.B. Saintsbury. *Minor Poets of the Caroline Period,* vol. 1, 1905.

Poems by eminent ladies, etc., 1755 (vol. 2).

Poems by eminent ladies, etc., 1775 (vol. 2, pp. 179-94).

Selected Poems. Katherine Philips, "The Matchless Orinda." Cottingham, near Hull, 1904.

Selected Poems [With an "appreciatory note" by L. I. G., i.e., L. I. Guiney], p. 48, 1904. *The Orinda Booklets,* no. 1, 1903.

From Early English Poetesses. J.R. Tutin. Hull Booklets, no. 7, 1908.

The Poetic Remains of the Duke of Buckingham, Madam Philips, 1698.

A Collection of divine Hymns and Poems . . . by the E. of Roscommon . . . Mrs. Katherine Philips, etc., 1709.

Letters. Wilmot. Earl of Rochester. *Familiar Letters,* etc., 1697.

Letters from Orinda to Poliarchus [Sir Charles Catherell], 1705.

This facsimile is the 1667 edition of **Poems,** from Yale University Library.

CONCLUSION

Katherine Philips' subject matter, limited though it may be by comparison to some poets, may have been her downfall in literary history, yet it is this very subject matter which challenges us to consider her anew today. Philips' merits rest not solely on her sex but on her unique treatment of subjects such as friendship, especially among women, and her occasional poems on marriage, departures, deaths, and admirations.

As it turns out, Katherine Philips has a broader range of subjects than has heretofore been acknowledged. In what I take to be her appreciation of Taylor's "Discourse," **"To the noble Palaemon [Jeremy Taylor], on his incomparable Discourse on Friendship"** (12), she notes that Taylor too reckons friendship "Means and Angels bliss" and she asks of Taylor, "Whether we owe more to thy Brain or Heart" (*1667,* p. 15; *1664,* p. 31). Surely we may ask the same of her poetry. In his *Discourse,* Taylor had argued that women could most certainly be friends—in the high and serious sense of Philips' inquiry and of his own essay. Isn't at least a part of the irony of Katherine Philips' fate in the anthologies and in English literary history that she indeed had anticipated Taylor, treating friendship as a metaphor for intimacy and a muse for her own form of Christian humanism?

Notes

1. For a good general statement on this subject, see Toni M. Frank, "Women's History Takes Giant Strides," Kathryn Kisk Sklar (Interview); *University of California Clip Sheet* (Berkeley, Cal.), vol. 57, no. 21 (February 23, 1981), n.p. For specific interpretations of Katherine Philips, see Bernikow, Gilbert and Guber, Goreau, Andreadis, and others cited below.

2. *The Miscellaneous Works in prose and verse of Mrs. Elizabeth Rowe.* . . . 2 vols. (London, 1739).

3. *Poems By the incomparable Mrs. K. P.* (J. G. for R. Marriott, 1664). See also *Poems* . . . to which is added . . . Corneille's Pompey and Horace, tragedies. With several other translations out of French. (J. M. for H. Herringham: London, 1867).

4. Louise Bernikow, *The World Split Open: Four Centuries of Women Poets in England and America, 1552-1950.* (New York: Vintage, 1974), p. 22.

5. Angeline Goreau, *The Whole Duty of a Woman* (Garden City, N.J.: Doubleday, 1985), p. 15.

6. See "Philips, Katherine," *Dictionary of National Biography.* Edited by Sir Leslie Stephen and Sir Sidney Lee. Vol. XV. (London: Oxford University Press, 1973), pp. 1063-1064. (*DNB* in later references.)

7. John Aubrey, *Brief Lives* (Oxford, 1989), 2:153-54, in Goreau, p. 193.

8. See my series of articles on Dr. Henry Vaughan in *The Living Church*: "Henry Vaughan, Nature Poet," "Henry Vaughan, Silurist," "Henry Vaughan, Mystic Correspondent," "Poet of the Second Race," and "Henry Vaughan, Christian Poet," vol. 199, nos. 10, 11, 12, 13 and 14 (Sept. 3, 10, 17, 24, and Oct. 1, 1989).

9. See *The Measures and Offices of Friendship* (1662) by Jeremy Taylor. A Facsimile Reproduction with an Introduction by Travis DuPriest. Delmar, N.Y.: Scholars' Facsimiles and Reprints, 1985.

10. Jeremy Taylor, *A Discourse of the Nature, offices, and Measures of Friendship,* with rules of conducting it. Written in answer to a letter from M. K. P., 1657. See also *The Measures and Offices of Friendship . . .*

11. Contemporary feminist critic Louise Bernikow, however, sees in Taylor's essay a distasteful use of male imagery: Louise Bernikow, "Friends," in *Among Women* (New York: Harper & Row, 1980), pp. 122-23, citing the use of knife imagery with its attendant phallicism. Harriette Andreadis also sees Taylor's response as unsatisfactory; see footnote 18.

12. See Louise Bernikow, "Friends," *Among Women* (New York: Harper & Row, 1980), pp. 116-25. Bernikow briefly traces the tradition of masculine literary friendship from the *Iliad* to modern times, showing links between war and honor and male friendship. While the discussion is helpful in placing Katherine Philips in the literary tradition of female friendship going back to Sappho, her point about Taylor's phallicism (knife imagery), though certainly true, is deflecting, in that Taylor was quite supportive of Philips and of the importance, even religious nature, of friendship. Nor does she cite male writers from antiquity, like Aristophanes who satirizes males and war, or Archilichus who shows us a very different picture from Homer of men in the ancient world. Nevertheless, this overview is interesting and helpful, particularly in tracing a literary tradition of female friendship.

13. Erasmus, Omnia Opera D. Erasmi. Froben Basileae, 1540. See also "The Abbott and the Learned Lady" as presented in *The Humanities,* vol. I (New York: D. C. Heath, 1985).

14. Aelred of Rivaulx, *Opera Omnia, ope studio,* R.P., 1618.

15. Michael Montaigne, *Essais de Messire Montaigne.* 2 vols. S. Millanges: Bourdeaux, 1580. See also *The Essayes of Michael Lord of Montaigne,* trans. by John Florio. G. Routledge: London, 1886 and *The Essays. . . .* V. Sims: London, 1603.

16. Francis Bacon, *The Essaies of Sir Francis Bacon Knight, the Kings Solliciter Generall,* John Beale: London, 1612.

17. Richard Allessee, *The Whole Duty of a Man,* 1655. See *The Whole Duty of a Man.* Dublin, 1812.

18. Harriette Andreadis, "The Sapphic-Platonics of Katherine Philips, 1632-1664," *Signs: Journal of Women in Culture and Society,* 1989, vol. 15, no. 11, pp. 34-60.

19. Goreau, p. 201.

20. George Saintsbury, *Minor Poets of the Caroline Period* (Oxford: Clarendon Press, 1905), p. 487.

21. Philip W. Souers, *The Matchless Orinda* (Cambridge: Harvard University Press, 1931), p. 41.

22. Souers, p. 44. See also Edmund Gosse, *Seventeenth-Century Studies* (London, 1914), pp. 208 and 229-58 and *Among Women,* p. 121 and L. I. G., "Appreciatory Note," "Katherine Philips, The Matchless Orinda," *The Orinda Booklets,* No. 1 (Hull, 1904), p. 5. Souers, pp. 44-45.

23. See Louise Bernikow, *Among Women,* pp. 116-25 for a discussion of female friendship. See footnote 12.

24. *DNB,* p. 1064.

25. Saintsbury, p. 486.

26. Saintsbury, p. 487.

27. "Appreciatory Note," *The Orinda Booklets,* p. 8.

Paula Loscocco (essay date 1993)

SOURCE: Loscocco, Paula. "Manly Sweetness: Katherine Philips among the Neoclassicals." *Huntington Library Quarterly* 56, no. 3 (summer 1993): 259-79.

[*In the following essay, Loscocco links the decline in popularity of Philip's poetry with changes in gender viewpoints and neoclassicism.*]

When Katherine Philips's posthumous ***Poems*** appeared in 1667, the volume included prefatory verses by Abraham Cowley celebrating her as England's esteemed "Woman Laureat."[1] Few at the time dissented from Cowley's assessment, and many—some of them prominent writers—agreed.[2] By now, however, as critic Harriette Andreadis remarked in 1989, the "acclaim of [Philips's] contemporaries has . . . worn very thin": at best she has a poem or two in anthologies, representing a minor link between metaphysical and neoclassical poetry; at worst, critics disparage her work as "florid," "cajoling," or overly "fluent."[3]

No one has yet adequately accounted for the decline in Philips's literary fortunes.[4] When did this decline occur? What was the nature of her original reception? What were subsequent views of her work like?[5] How did different senses of her poetry evolve? My essay attempts to answer these kinds of questions. I locate the decline in Philips's reputation in the eighteenth century, and I account for it by charting the interplay between changes in the reception of her poetry and changes—especially as these involve questions of gender—in neoclassical literary aesthetics of the seventeenth and eighteenth centuries.[6]

In the course of my discussion, I identify three major phases in Philips's reception. The first spanned the 1650s and 1660s. The many writers who applauded Philips's works during these years did so in the gendered terms provided by contemporary neoclassical literary aesthetics, paying particular attention to what they described as the "masculine" strength and "feminine" sweetness of her verses. The second phase occurred in the late seventeenth and early eighteenth centuries. Though enthusiasm for Philips's poetry continued to be expressed during these years, a reworking of the central concepts of neoclassical poetics dramatically altered the gender-configurations of the terms used to describe her poems. As a consequence, readers who praised her writings at this time did so by focusing exclusively on what they perceived to be the masculine qualities of her writing. The third phase began while the second was still in progress. At the height of the laudatory and "masculine" period in Philips's reputation, a certain Thomas Newcomb used the prevailing preference for literary masculinity against her and condemned her poetry as being irredeemably feminine. Arising from and speaking to an aesthetics hostile to what a contemporary characterized as "Feminine Expression" of any kind,[7] Newcomb's critique appears to have tipped the balance of opinion against Philips: after his attack of 1712, no edition of her works was printed for the rest of the century, and when individual poems were reprinted, they invariably appeared in specialized collections devoted to the works of "lady poetesses."[8] With scattered exceptions, it is only in recent years that scholars have argued for broader recognition of Philips's literary skills and merits.[9]

I

We can most readily gauge the nature of Philips's mid-seventeenth-century reception if we examine the commendatory verses prefacing her 1667 *Poems.* All of these verses follow the same general progression. A poem begins by addressing the fact of Philips's sex and its presence in her poetry; it goes on to discuss her poems in traditionally neoclassical terms. In this way, I would suggest, the commendatory poems portray Philips not only as a woman writer, but also—perhaps even primarily—as a neoclassical poet.

In her study of the conventions of seventeenth-century commendatory poems on women writers, Joanna Lipking comes to just the opposite conclusion.[10] She agrees that men praise these women for their ability to excel (like men) as poets, but she also finds that this praise tends to revert to the fact that these poets are women. A "characteristic feature of men's commendations" of a woman writer, she notes, is "their ineluctable drift toward the feminine side of her identity" (p. 59). Lipking focuses exclusively on the gender-content of poems about women writers. At least in the case of Philips, however, mid-seventeenth-

century readers did not limit themselves to issues connected with her gender. Rather, they repeatedly and pointedly broadened their discussions to include other aspects of her poetry. If we likewise expand our discussion, we can discover the ways in which Philips's contemporaries paid serious attention to her not only as a woman, or a woman poet, but also as a poet writing successfully within the neoclassical idiom of her day.

The central statement of the literary tastes of the era, John Dryden's 1668 *An Essay of Dramatick Poesie,* serves as a yardstick against which to measure the neoclassical content of the encomia on Philips.[11] Dryden begins by setting the ancients against the moderns. Eugenius, spokesman for the moderns, takes the upper hand immediately: "'I cannot think so contemptibly of the Age in which I live, or so dishonourably of my own Countrey, as not to judge we equal the Ancients in most kinds of Poesie, and in some surpass them'" (p. 12). Roger Boyle, in "The Earl of Orrery to Mrs. Philips," takes a similar if somewhat hyperbolic stand when he sets her achievements against those of the Greeks and Romans:

> Past ages could not think those things you do,
> For their Hill was their basis and height too:
> So that 'tis truth, not compliment, to tell,
> Your lowest height their highest did excel.

> (Saintsbury, ed., *Minor Poets of the
> Caroline Period,* p. 494)

We have, of course, no way of determining Orrery's sincerity in these lines. But comparison of his words with those of Dryden suggests that Orrery's terms of praise are consistent with those of Restoration literary discussion generally, and are not specific to encomia on women poets.

Dryden also contrasts French and English dramatic poetry, arguing in favor of the latter. "'[O]ur errours are so few, and little,'" states Neander, the proponent of English poetry, "'and those things wherein we excel them [the French] so considerable, that we ought of right to be prefer'd before them'" (p. 51). Philips's translations of Corneille's plays made her work a natural focus for this kind of critical discussion. Orrery's praise of her translations remains pointedly within the terms of nationalist debate and does not refer to her gender:

> You English Corneil[le]'s Pompey with such flame,
> That you both raise our wonder and his fame;
> If he could read it, he like us would call
> The copy greater than th'original. . . .
> The French to learn our language now will seek,
> To hear their greatest Wit more nobly speak.

> (P. 494)

Philo-Philippa, in **"To the excellent Orinda,"** similarly claims in traditionally neoclassical fashion that Philips's translations "Refin'd and stamp'd" the French original, transforming its "ore" into English gold (p. 499).

Most centrally, Dryden's *Essay* and the encomia to Philips share a definition of literature as "sweet" yet "correct," "easy" yet "significant," a definition highly prized by neoclassical poetics. The writers of the "'last Age'" (p. 13), Dryden, in the person of Eugenius, notes,

> "can produce nothing so courtly writ, or which expresses so much the Conversation of a Gentleman, as Sir *John Suckling*; nothing so even, sweet, and flowing as Mr. *Waller*; nothing so Majestique, so correct as Sir *John Denham*; nothing so elevated, so copious, and full of spirit, as Mr. *Cowley*. . . ."
>
> All of them were thus far of *Eugenius* his opinion, that the sweetness of *English* Verse was never understood or practis'd by our Fathers . . . : and every one was willing to acknowledge how much our Poesie is improv'd, by the happiness of some Writers yet living; who first taught us to mould our thoughts into easie and significant words.
>
> (P. 14)

Dryden's pairings of terms here, "sweet" and "easie" with "Majestique" and "significant," strikingly recall the single most common feature of the commendatory poems on Philips: the attention paid to her synthesis of "masculine" and "feminine" poetic qualities. In this context, the encomia's terms of gender, though deriving from and specific to the poems' female subject, also participate in general poetic discourse in ways separate from the sex of the poet. "Feminine" does refer to Philips's gender; it also refers to the qualities of "smoothness" and "sweetness" valued by contemporary literary aesthetics. "Masculine" suggests the anomalous achievement of poetry by a woman; it also suggests the qualities of "wit" and "strength" that were understood to ground and steady the mellifluousness of neoclassical verse.

Stanza 3 of Cowley's "Upon Mrs. Philips her Poems" provides a clear example of the dual allegiances that terms like "strength" and "sweetness" have in the commendatory poems:

> Where'er I see an excellence,
> I must admire to see thy well-knit sense,
> Thy numbers gentle, and thy fancies high,
> Those as thy forehead smooth, these sparkling as thine eye.
> 　'Tis solid, and 'tis manly all,
> 　Or rather, 'tis angelical:
> 　For, as in Angels, we
> 　Do in thy verses see
> Both improv'd sexes eminently meet;
> They are than Man more strong, and more than Woman sweet.
>
> (P. 496)

Lipking focuses on Cowley's reference to Philips's forehead and eyes as evidence of a male poet's inability to see beyond gender (p. 61). It is perhaps more to the point, however, to note that Cowley's mixed-sex "angelical" is an almost perfect analogue to Dryden's ideal of poetry that is both "strong" and "sweet." All that Cowley has done to the terms here is to make explicit, as suits his occasion, the gender-markings of the two adjectives.

Philo-Philippa is even more revealing. Her poem describes Philips's translation of *Pompey* as that play's ultimate point of development, mixing as it does Philips's feminine "fancy" and Corneille's masculine "sense" (p. 499). She then offers one of the encomia's most neoclassical critiques of Philips's poetry:

> A gliding sea of crystal doth best show
> How smooth, clear, full, and rich your verse doth flow:
> Your words are chosen, cull'd, not by chance writ,
> To make the sense, as anagrams do hit.
> Your rich becoming words on the sense wait,
> As Maids of Honour on a Queen of State.
> 'Tis not white satin makes a verse more white,
> Or soft; Iron is both, write you on it.
>
> (P. 499)

Smooth sense, soft iron: Philo-Philippa's terms dovetail with Dryden's, exemplifying the ways in which the commendatory verses prefacing Philips's 1667 **Poems** portray her as a successful poet according to the literary standards of her day.[12]

As the poems by Philo-Philippa and especially Cowley suggest, the reputation of Philips's poetry was bolstered by the fact that neoclassical literary discourse in mid-seventeenth-century England was itself gendered: commentators regularly used terms of gender to describe and praise poetic achievement. Lipking notes that the encomia on women poets compliment women for combining masculine strength and wit with feminine beauty and softness, but she downplays the crucial fact that these qualities were held up as ideals for writers of both sexes (p. 58). Men as well as women found their writings praised for being, in Cowley's words, "than Man more strong, and more than Woman sweet." Cowley, in fact, perhaps the single most applauded mid-century poet,[13] was himself frequently described in this manner.

On the occasion of Cowley's death in 1667, John Denham wrote of his poetry:

> His fancy and his judgment such,
> Each to the other seem'd too much,
> His severe judgment (giving Law)
> His modest fancy kept in awe:
> As rigid Husbands jealous are,
> When they believe their Wives too fair.
>
> (*Works of Denham*, ed. Banks, p. 151)

Critical discourse had by 1667 established as conventional the proposition that (implicitly feminine) fancy required the counterpoising weight of (implicitly masculine) judgment. Denham's description of Cowley modifies this convention in several ways. First, he emphasizes the equality of fancy and judgment, noting that "Each to the other seem'd too much." He extends this perception into the following lines, where ambiguity as to whether "fancy" or "judgment" is the subject of the verb subtly undermines the traditional priority given "severe judgment." In addition, his reference to "Husbands" and "Wives" is unusually explicit in its gendering of judgment and fancy. By characterizing husbands / judgment as "severe," "rigid," "jealous," and apt as a consequence to "believe" their "modest" wives / fancy "too fair," moreover, Denham alters conventional emphasis. Instead of virtuous judgment holding licentious fancy in check, virtuous fancy is presented as the faultless equal of a judgment that tends to over-censoriousness and misperception.

If Denham locates in Cowley's writing a marriage of gendered fancy and judgment, Thomas Sprat goes considerably further, praising Cowley's poetry for its ability to embrace what he calls a "variety of Sexes in Poetry."[14] He begins his discussion of Cowley's literary achievement neutrally enough, noting that "[i]n his life he join'd the innocence and sincerity of the Scholar with the humanity and good behaviour of the Courtier. In his Poems he united the Solidity and Art of the one with the Gentility and Gracefulness of the other" (pp. 128-29). Almost immediately, however, he brings to the surface the gender-markings of scholarly "solidity" and courtly "gracefulness." Certain readers might argue that Cowley's verses were far from uniformly "graceful"; this, Sprat argues, was Cowley's "choice, not his fault":

> Where the matter required it, he was as gentle as any man. But where higher Virtues were chiefly to be regarded, an exact numerosity was not then his main care. This may serve to answer those who upbraid some of his Pieces with roughness, and with more contractions than they are willing to allow. But these Admirers of gentlenesse without sinews should know that different Arguments must have different Colours of Speech: that there is a kind of variety of Sexes in Poetry as well as in Mankind: that as the peculiar excellence of the Feminine Kind is smoothnesse and beauty, so strength is the chief praise of the Masculine.

> (P. 129)

Though Sprat here promotes "strong" or "masculine" poetry, he does so only in defiance of critics who require unrelievedly "smooth" or "Feminine" verse. The ideal is gendered "variety": he applauds Cowley for choosing a style that is, as he sees it, alternately sweetly "Feminine" or strongly "Masculine," as the content requires. Because he describes literary style through metaphors of gender, Sprat also distances his discussion (though perhaps inadvertently) from any reference to a writer's actual sex. "Masculine" and "Feminine" describe styles appropriate to the material being written, not to the sex of the person doing the writing.

Cowley's writing was portrayed by others, then, in much the same terms that he himself used to portray Philips's. Not coincidentally, in the years following the deaths of Philips (1664) and Cowley (1667), a number of writers joined the two poets together in the kind of literary union of the sexes perceived to be at the heart of their respective poetics. James Tyrrell's poem prefacing Philips's 1667 *Poems* notes that Cowley—"the great Pindar's greater Son"—has "retir'd" to Heaven, leaving the world bereft:

"He, and Orinda from us gone, / What Name, like theirs, shall we now call upon?" (p. 500). Francis Bernard, commending his friend, Thomas Flatman, on his 1674 *Poems and Songs,* argues that anyone "who e're did hear, / Of *Cowley* or *Orinda*'s fame" would appreciate Flatman's poems.[15] In her 1688 *Poetical Recreations,* Jane Barker, warning her friends against the now debauched Muses, cites Cowley and Philips as the twin poets of chaste love:

> Though to *Orinda* they [the Muses] were ty'd,
> That nought their Friendship cou'd divide:
> And *Cowley*'s Mistress had a Flame
> As pure and lasting as his *Fame*:
> Yet now they're all grown *Prostitutes*.[16]

Perhaps the definitive pairing occurs in James Gardiner's prefatory poem to Samuel Woodford's 1667 *A Paraphrase Upon The Psalms of David.*[17] Gardiner understands English letters to have restored drooping poesy to its original glory, and he cites Philips and Cowley as beacons of a new poetic golden age in which "pure spirit[s]" mix with "manly Theam[s]":

> One of each Sex this fruitful Age has shown,
>   (And fruitful had she been, if none
>   But that immortal Paire were known;)
>   Though she has many more to boast,
> *Cowley,* and bright *Orinda* do adorn it most.

> (Sig. (d)v)

The frequency with which writers like Gardiner cite Philips and Cowley as their age's "immortal Paire" in poetry makes it clear that Philips was praised by her contemporaries as the peer of a writer like Cowley. The extraordinary pairing of a man and a woman poet also reinforces the idea that mid-seventeenth-century literary culture understood "variety of the Sexes," an even blend of masculine and feminine literary attributes, as a constitutive element of its poetry.

When Cowley described Philips's poems as "than Man more strong, and more than Woman sweet," then, he was speaking within what was to his contemporaries an established literary aesthetic. By explicitly gendering "strength" as masculine and "sweetness" (or "softness") as feminine, Cowley used neoclassical terms in ways common to the authors of his era. And by positing an ideal balance between these terms, Cowley joined other writers in assigning equal value to contemporary concepts of literary masculinity and femininity.

II

The aesthetic Cowley described, however, did not last. As early as the 1670s, there appeared what seems to have been a backlash against the notion of a literary aesthetic based on positive attributes linked to both genders.[18] Though "sweet" and (especially) "strong" remained critical terms of choice from the mid-seventeenth century to the mid-eighteenth, articulating central neoclassical literary values, the concepts of gender associated with the two terms changed dramatically in the late seventeenth century. Mid-seventeenth-century writers, as I have shown, linked the terms "strong" and "sweet" to contemporary concepts of masculinity and femininity. By the end of the century, however, these terms had acquired an entirely different set of gender-associations: "strong" and "sweet" had come to be attached *only* to masculinity; femininity had been removed from encomiastic critical vocabulary altogether. By the end of the century, literary femininity—frequently but not always signaled by the term "softness"—had in fact become a potent tool of critical dispraise. I describe this shift in gender-associations in order to provide a context in which to understand the vicissitudes of Philips's literary reputation.

Wentworth Dillon, the earl of Roscommon, provides a trenchant example of the ways in which terms of praise previously associated with femininity could be re-gendered as masculine. In 1657, James Howell had proposed a marriage between "[m]ale" English and implicitly "feminine" romance languages like French.[19] Twenty-seven years later, in his 1684 *An Essay on Translated Verse,* Roscommon redefined the relationship between the two languages as a competition in which the English tortoise overtakes the French hare:

> But now *We* [English] shew the world a nobler way,
> And in *Translated Verse* do more than *They* [French],
> Serene and clear, Harmonious *Horace* flows,
> With sweetness not to be exprest in *Prose.*

English "sweetness" here is not simply a question of verse as opposed to prose. Rather, Roscommon states,

> The *Fault* is more their *Languages* than theirs:
> 'Tis courtly, florid, and abounds in words,
> Of softer sound than ours perhaps affords;
> But who did ever in *French Authors see*
> The comprehensive *English Energy?*
> . . . I'l Recant, when *France* can shew me *Wit,*
> As strong as *Ours,* and as *succinctly Writ.*

> (Spingarn, ed., *Critical Essays,* 2:298)

The superior "serene and clear . . . sweetness" that Roscommon hears in English, then, is a function not only of versification but also of the language's native energy, succinctness, and strength. French, on the other hand, owes its "courtly" and "florid" nature to its inherently "softer sound." Though Roscommon distinguishes between admirable sweetness and unfortunate softness, however, he does not explicitly attach gender to either quality.[20] He leaves this for John Dryden to do, in the commendatory poem which prefaces Roscommon's work.

In his 1668 *Essay* (written 1665), Dryden had spoken for his time when he had embraced a literary aesthetic based on "feminine" sweetness and "masculine" strength. Twenty years later, he spoke for a different time when he articulated an altered understanding of these two key neoclassical concepts. In his 1684 poem, *"To the Earl of Roscommon, on his Excellent Essay on Translated Verse,"*

Dryden nimbly repatriates "sweetness" into masculine critical territory.[21] He recounts how in medieval times "barb'rous Nations, and more barb'rous Times / Debas'd the majesty of Verse to Rhymes," but how, later, Italy and France resuscitated poetry by showing "What Rhyme improv'd in all its height can be; / At best a pleasing Sound, and fair barbarity" (p. 172). It was up to the English, however, to complete the restoration of poetry, by transforming "fair" and implicitly feminine "Rhyme" into explicitly masculine "Verse." *"Brittain,* last," Dryden notes, "In Manly sweetness all the rest surpass'd" (p. 172). Manly sweetness: the phrase is remarkable, given the precision with which poets twenty years earlier had repeatedly characterized "sweetness" as "like a *woman.*" It is possible that Dryden here has simply condensed the traditional pairing, distilling masculine strength and feminine sweetness into "manly sweetness." But his unusual way of formulating the convention suggests that the phrase instead represents a self-conscious attempt to legislate the way in which the term "sweetness" is to be understood. Used in this way, the adjective "manly" not only prevents the almost automatic association of "sweetness" with femininity, but it also replaces femininity with the opposing idea of manliness. The phrase "manly sweetness" works to redefine a central neoclassical literary term away from femininity and toward masculinity.

My reading of "manly sweetness" is supported by the remarkable fact that in the ode, *"To the Pious Memory of the Accomplisht Young Lady Mrs Anne Killigrew,"* written two years later, Dryden scrupulously avoids characterizing her virtues and achievements as sweet or feminine in any way.[22] In his portrayal of Killigrew's literary and moral lineage, for example, Dryden never once mentions a female relation. Instead, her "Father was transfus'd into [her] Blood" (p. 110); she acquired her "Morals" and "Noble Vigour" by reading "the best of Books, her Fathers Life" (p. 111). At her birth, her "Brother-Angels" played their harps (p. 110), and "all the Blest Fraternity of Love" rejoiced (p. 111). Dryden draws deliberate attention to the ways in which he separates Killigrew from her natural gender, as comparison of his poem on Killigrew with Cowley's on Philips makes clear. Philips, Cowley states, is "than Man more strong, and more than Woman sweet." Killigrew's "Wit," Dryden declares, "was more than Man, her Innocence a Child!" (p. 111). A child: Dryden here degenders what had once been understood as the feminine quality of "Innocence," while at the same time he preserves the paired symmetry of Cowley's neoclassical formulation. His efforts suggest the degree of opprobrium that seems by the mid-1680s to have attached to literary terms associated in any way with women or femininity.

The recoil away from femininity in neoclassical poetics was in full force by the mid-1680s, but we can find evidence of its existence before then. As early as the 1670s, individual male writers began to lash out at poetry that could be characterized as either feminine or sweet. In 1670, for example, Samuel Woodford, in a poem prefacing Izaak Walton's *Life of Herbert,* declares that *"Sacred Poesie"*

No longer shall a Virgin reckoned be,
    (What ere with others 'tis) by me,
    A Female Muse, as were the Nine:
    But (full of Vigor Masculine)
An Essence Male, with Angels his Companions shine.[23]

Woodford banishes femininity from the realm of sacred poetry altogether, insisting that the spirit of such poetry is essentially male. His vision of poetry (and later of Herbert) as a male angel anticipates Dryden's description of Killigrew's "Brother-Angels" and contrasts sharply with Cowley's angels, in whom "Both improv'd sexes eminently meet." In 1677, the writer "A. B." similarly defends the masculine *"Vigour"* of John Cleveland's muse against *"smooth, weak Rhymer*[s].*"*[24] *"Let such to Women write,"* he sneers, spelling out the thinly veiled gender-markings behind his comments, *"you write to Men"* (sig. a4v).

The generation of women poets who came of age after the mid-seventeenth century offered eloquent testimony concerning changes in attitudes toward gender in the neoclassical literary environment. A number of these writers identified the mid-century as the Age of Orinda, and bemoaned the fact that, by the mid-1680s, that age had come and gone. They were acutely aware that an aesthetic that welcomed literary values identified with women, like sweetness or softness, had represented an encouraging environment for actual women writers. They were equally aware that an aesthetic that scorned what it conceived of as feminine literary values, or appropriated terms traditionally linked to femininity as "male," would almost certainly prove to be inhospitable to women writers.

Perhaps the clearest statement of the effect on women poets of the shift in critical values appears in Anne Killigrew's poem *"Upon the saying that my VERSES were made by another,"* published in 1686.[25] Killigrew compares her circumstances with those of Philips, and finds not only that Philips was admired apart from the fact of her sex but also that she lived in an age that singled out for particular applause the kinds of writing that it associated with women:

    Orinda, (*Albions* and her Sexes Grace)
Ow'd not her Glory to a Beauteous Face,
It was her Radiant Soul that shon With-in. . . .
Nor did her Sex at all obstruct her Fame,
But higher 'mong the Stars it fixt her Name;
What she did write, not only all allow'd,
But ev'ry Laurel, to her Laurel, bow'd!

                    (P. 46)

What a woman of Philips's day wrote, Killigrew remarks with revealing astonishment, was not only "allow'd"—it was actually *preferred.* In contrast, Killigrew describes her own era as an "Envious Age" (p. 47) in which readers unjustly accuse her of plagiarism and scorn her person. The comparison with Philips suggests that Killigrew's "Sex" has indeed "obstruct[ed] her Fame." And though she claims that the hostility she has encountered is directed "only to Me alone" (p. 47), her decision to compare her

situation with that of a poet who had been dead for almost two decades implies a contrast more of eras than of persons.

Other writers corroborate Killigrew's sense that a female "golden age" of literature lies in the mid-century past. Among the poems prefacing Jane Barker's 1688 *Poetical Recreations* is one by "Philaster" which begins,

    Soon as some envious *Angel's* willing hand
    Snatch'd Great *Orinda* from our happy Land . . .
    Then our Male-*Poets* modestly thought fit,
    To claim the honour'd *Primacy* in *Wit.*

                    (Sig. A5)

A "Young Lady of Quality," writing on the occasion of Aphra Behn's death in 1689, voices similar sentiments.[26] Tracing a poetical lineage from Philips to Behn (p. 55), she now finds the line broken:

    Let all our Hopes despair and dye,
    Our Sex for ever shall neglected lye;
    Aspiring Man has now regain'd the Sway,
    To them we've lost the Dismal Day.

                    (P. 56)

As the examples of Philaster and the "Young Lady of Quality" suggest, expressing fears that "Man has now regain'd the Sway" was by the 1680s a conventional means to flatter[27] or mourn a woman poet. Nevertheless, receptiveness to writing by women and to literary qualities associated with femininity did decline dramatically in the late seventeenth century, and this lends some poignancy to conventional tributes to the Age of Orinda. As Margaret Newcastle warned with astonishing prescience in 1653, eras like her own, in which things associated with femininity were welcomed and encouraged, were fleeting:

    if it be an Age when the effeminate spirits rule, as most
    visible they doe in every Kingdome, let us take the
    advantage, and make the best . . . in witty Poetry, or
    any thing that may bring honour to our Sex.[28]

An age in which "effeminate spirits" rule: Newcastle's phrase, suggesting as it does both actual women and "feminine" values, almost perfectly expressed the mid-century literary situation. Within thirty years, her warning about the future proved equally accurate.

The change in critical values that women writers in the 1680s describe—away from a literary aesthetic that held femininity and masculinity in equal esteem—gained considerable momentum in the early eighteenth century. Perhaps the clearest expression of this fact appears in critical discussion about an ostensibly unrelated issue: the increasing professionalization of literature. Such discussion has a bearing on an analysis of the gender-configurations of neoclassical poetics because it characterizes the difference between amateur and professional writing as a difference between a feminine (or effeminate) worse and a masculine better.

Alexander Pope, in a 1710 letter to Henry Cromwell, distinguishes between two kinds of poets.[29] The first includes those who, writing "to establish a reputation" (p. 109), at times produce an "extreamly majestic" poetry (p. 110); Pope clearly imagines himself to be among this group of writers. He cites Richard Crashaw as an example of the second kind of poet. Crashaw, states Pope, "writ like a Gentleman, that is, at leisure hours, and . . . to keep out of idleness" (p. 109). Pope refers to writers like him as "*Versifiers* and *witty Men,* rather than as *Poets,*" and associates them with "*Miscellan*[y]" or amateur writing (p. 110).

In the imitation of Horace's *First Epistle of the Second Book* (1637), Pope attaches gender to the two kinds of writing he described to Cromwell.[30] He links "Gentlemen" poets with amateur writing (p. 203) and locates the heyday of such poets at the Restoration:

> In Days of Ease, when now the weary Sword
> Was sheath'd, and *Luxury* with *Charles* restor'd; . . .
> The Soldier breath'd the Gallantries of France,
> And ev'ry flow'ry Courtier writ Romance. . . .
> No wonder then, when all was Love and Sport,
> The willing Muses were debauch'd at Court;
> On each enervate string they taught the Note
> To pant, or tremble thro' an Eunuch's throat.
>
> (P. 207-9)

Pope could not be clearer: the age of amateur versifying was an age in which "flow'ry" romance and "debauch'd" Muses emasculated poetry, "soften[ing]" (p. 207) the "Soldier" into a lisping "Eunuch." His own age, he acknowledges, continues in this tradition of effeminate amateurism: "Sons, Sires, and Grandsires, all will wear the Bays, / Our Wives read Milton, and our Daughters Plays" (p. 209). Pope nostalgically depicts a vague but distinctly masculine "Time was," a mythic past that contrasts with both the Restoration and his own age, when a "sober Englishman" could govern "his servants," "his Wife," and "his Son," imitating "his Fathers" and instructing "his Heir" (p. 209). Pope then attaches "true" poetry to this patriarchal idyll. The "Poet," he declares, is not a playful "Man of Rymes" (p. 225), but rather "a Poet's of some weight, / And (tho' no Soldier) useful to the State" (p. 211). A true poet is like a "Soldier" before the Restoration "soften'd" him: like Horace, he has "*a manly Regard to his own Character*" (p. 192).

The identification by 1700 of good or serious poetry with masculinity and poor or amateur versifying with femininity had significant impact on early eighteenth-century characterizations of previous poets. A critic who wished to commend a seventeenth-century poet resorted to eighteenth-century encomiastic terms and concepts that proved, in terms of gender, to be the inverse of the ones chosen by that poet's contemporary admirers. In 1697, for example, in an anthology entitled *Miscellany Poems,* the editor distinguishes between past and present poetry:

> *I was considering how much this* Art [Poetry] *was esteemed amongst our* Forefathers, *and how Venerable, nay, almost Sacred, the* Name *of a Poet was then. . . .*

> *I think the great Difference* [between then and now] *lies here, That Poetry is now no longer the* Fountain of Wisdom, *the* School of Virtue.[31]

In the poem that follows, he notes that the works of the "Ancients" (p. 32) which he so admires are "more *Masculine*" than those of modern writers, who, he complains, are mere "*Womens* Fools" (p. 38). When he praises "our Forefathers" and the "Ancients" as pillars of poetry, however, he does not mean to commend only classical writers like Homer or Sophocles or Virgil. Rather, the final exemplar of "ancient" masculinity is, in his view, the writer who had for decades been singled out as the "sweetest" of the early neoclassical poets, Edmund Waller:

> But if you wou'd Respect or Love express,
> And shew your Passion in a Comely Dress,
> Learn how from Courtly *Waller*'s Deathless Layes
> Chastly to Love, with Modesty to Praise.
>
> (P. 42)

The terms of commendation available to a writer in 1697 simply did not include the words traditionally applied to Waller, like "sweet" or "soft," marked as these were by their prior association with femininity. The closest a writer in that year could come to describing Waller's "Courtly" poetry was to describe his purity of style and content as "Comely"—in a "Masculine" sort of way.

As with Waller, so with Philips: by the late seventeenth and early eighteenth centuries, the critical vocabulary available to commend a woman poet like Philips was almost entirely masculine in its orientation. This situation accounts for the curious fact that several early eighteenth-century writers praise her poetry only for its manly strength—and not, as Cowley did, also for its womanly sweetness. Theophilus Cibber echoes other critics when he discusses her poetry:

> Mrs. Philips's poetry has not harmony of versification, or amorous tenderness to recommend it, but it has a force of thinking, which few poets of the other sex can exceed, and if it is without graces, it has yet a great deal of strength.[32]

Dryden's 1699 epistolary comments to Elizabeth Thomas on Philips demonstrate that praise of Philips's "strength" means praise of literary qualities identified with masculinity.[33] "'Tis not over gallant, I must confess," he begins,

> to say this of the fair Sex; but most certain it is, that they generally write with more Softness than Strength. On the contrary, you want neither Vigour in your Thoughts, nor force in your Expressions, nor Harmony in your Numbers, and methinks I find much of Orinda in your Manner (to whom I had the Honour to be related, and also to be Known).
>
> (P. 125)

Dryden's remarks are extraordinary in a number of ways. First, he links writers of "the fair Sex" with literary "Softness"—and he makes it clear that it is far from complimentary to women to do so. He also describes Thomas's "Manner" as implicitly masculine, characterized as it is by a "Strength" not "generally" seen in writings by women. Most strikingly, however, he identifies this admirably masculine style, possessing as it does both "Vigour" and "force," as the "Orinda" in Thomas's writing.

Richard Gwinnet, also writing to Elizabeth Thomas, singles out the "masculine" qualities of Philips's poems for praise as well. Philips's "Country Life," Gwinnet writes,

> is so sweet a *Poem,* and sprinkled with such profound Philosophical Thoughts, expressed in easy Poetical Language, . . . that though I have read several Poems, in more Tongues than One, upon the same Subject, yet I do not know where to find a better.[34]

Gwinnet describes Philips's poetry as "sweet," "profound," and "easy," neoclassical terms which, he goes on to suggest, are fundamentally "Masculine." "I have looked a little into Mrs. *Philips,*" Gwinnet writes, "and it is not the first Time I have been wonderfully pleased with her solid Masculine Thoughts, in no Feminine Expression" (p. 38). Like Dryden on Roscommon, Gwinnet commends the "sweet[ness]" of Philips's poem as one of the qualities that identifies and places her work within the masculine literary universe. By suggesting that her poems have "no Feminine Expression," Gwinnet also pays Philips one of the highest compliments available to a reader—especially a reader of women's verses—in the early eighteenth century. A far cry from Cowley's "than Man more strong, and more than Woman sweet," Gwinnet's phrase nevertheless matches Cowley's in its attempt to praise Philips's poems in terms that reflect the gender-configurations reigning in contemporary neoclassical discourse.

III

A markedly different response to Philips appeared in 1712. In that year, the Reverend Thomas Newcomb published a versified lampoon on "modern" writers entitled *Bibliotheca.*[35] The poem's mock-hero is a befuddled old "Doctor" who happily fondles a series of books; Newcomb inserts his critiques of individual writers as the Doctor moves from volume to volume. Women poets come in for particular attack. "One day," writes Newcomb, the Doctor "Does to the Female World repair, / To please himself among the Fair, / (Where if no Sense was to be found, / He's sure to be oblig'd with Sound)" (p. 28). Newcomb is especially biting in regard to Philips. "ORINDA next demands his view / For Titles fam'd and Rhiming too; / And had been read, but that her Song, / To be admir'd, was quite too long" (p. 30). If the Doctor never actually reads Philips, however, Newcomb does, and he describes her poetry in damningly gendered terms:

> Their Mistress['s] want of Pride to shew,
> Her Numbers glide but wondrous low,
> Instead of Rapture, give us Sleep,
> And striving to be humble, creep. . . .

> Softness her Want of Sense supplies,
> She faints in every line and dyes.

> (Pp. 30-31)

Comparison with Alexander Pope's 1711 *An Essay on Criticism* brings Newcomb's agenda out into the open:

> If *Chrystal Streams* with pleasing *Murmurs creep,*
> The Reader's threaten'd (not in vain) with *Sleep*:
> Then, at the *last,* and *only* Couplet fraught
> With some *unmeaning* Thing they call a *Thought,*
> A *needless Alexandrine* ends the Song,
> That like a wounded Snake, drags its slow length along.[36]

What Newcomb adds to Pope's lines is simply the association of poor verse with women and femininity. The punning phrase, "want of pride to shew," implies that a woman's attempt to express her modesty serves only to reveal her immodesty. Substituting "sense" with "Softness" suggests that her poetry is feminine in the specific sense of being weak. And Newcomb's last line adds a sly sexual innuendo that obliterates the passage's nominal focus on Philips's poetry itself.

Newcomb must substantially misrepresent both Philips and her poetry in order to depict them in the feminized way that he does. He refers to the poet, for example, as a "Virgin" and an "Unhappy Maid," and claims that she wielded her poetry (in vain) to charm some "Youth" into "Wedlock" (pp. 30-31). In fact, Philips was married at age sixteen, before she wrote almost any of the extant poetry; she also never wrote courtship verses of any kind. Newcomb's claims to the contrary suggest a willful misreading of her poems in the service of blasting Philips as a failed—because female—poet.[37]

Newcomb, seeking to censure Philips, is as careful to paint her with her sex as Cibber, Dryden, and Gwinnet, aiming at praise, are to circumvent it. In so doing, he takes what is for his time a highly idiosyncratic negative position on the seventeenth-century poet.[38] Unfortunately for Philips, however, Newcomb's lone denunciation of her poetry, supported as it was by a neoclassical aesthetic profoundly antagonistic to "Feminine Expression," seems to have carried considerable weight: as noted earlier, the last eighteenth-century edition of Philips's *Poems* appeared in 1710, just two years before Newcomb published the *Bibliotheca.*[39]

We can explain Newcomb's influence in part by pointing to the fact that multiple editions of the *Bibliotheca* kept Newcomb's censure of Philips before the reading public throughout the eighteenth century. Critic William Roberts notes that John Nichols, manager of *Gentleman's Magazine,* included Newcomb's poem in the third volume of his *Select Collection of Poems,* and that John Bell's 1781 and 1807 reprints of the works of William King also included the *Bibliotheca.*[40] As Roberts notes, enthusiasm for Philips's works may have been "offset to some degree by the cleverly derogatory comments of Thomas Newcomb's *Bib-*

liotheca" (p. 194); by the mid-eighteenth century, the sustained exposure of readers to his negative assessment of her poetry may have helped to obscure it from neoclassical view altogether.

Multiple editions of the *Bibliotheca,* however, do not in themselves adequately account for the kind of critical clout Newcomb's rather obscure poem seems to have carried. A more significant factor behind the poem's effect on Philips's literary reputation lies in Newcomb's manipulation of a critical climate in which the highest praise was to refer to a poet's work as "manly" strong and the lowest censure was to call it womanly "soft." Like Cowley's, Philips's poems would surely have gone out of fashion in the eighteenth century without Newcomb's help.[41] But Newcomb hurried Philips's decline, and insured its persistence, by branding her poetry with her sex— something which had not previously been done to this particular poet. The means of censuring Philips as a feminine writer had existed from the 1670s; few critics before Newcomb, however, had cared to censure Philips, and thus few if any had described her in this way. Once Newcomb's damaging charges of the feminine nature of Philips's poetry were made, however, only a readership willing to take on the daunting task of defending a woman's writing from her sex could have saved Philips's reputation. In the world of eighteenth-century neoclassicism, where a woman's writing and her sex were, as in Newcomb, increasingly linked and jointly censured, this kind of readership simply did not exist. As a consequence, and according to Newcomb's wishes, Philips's poems "faint[ed] in every line, and dye[d]."

Notes

1. "On the Death of Mrs. Katherine Philips," in *Poems By the most deservedly Admired Mrs. Katherine Philips The matchless Orinda* (London, 1667), sig. gv. The complete 1678 edition of Philips's *Poems* is reprinted in George Saintsbury, ed., *Minor Poets of the Caroline Period,* vol. 1. (Oxford, 1905), 485-612. Cowley's poem appears on 502-3. Subsequent discussion of the encomia on Philips's *Poems* provides page references to Saintsbury's edition.

2. John Dryden, Henry Vaughan, Sir William Temple, Wentworth Dillon, the earl of Roscommon, and Roger Boyle, the earl of Orrery, are among the many who wrote poems of tribute to Philips.

3. Harriette Andreadis, "The Sapphic-Platonics of Katherine Philips, 1632-1664," *Signs* 15 (1989): 35. Disparagement of Philips and her writing persists, sometimes even among scholars committed to focusing serious attention on her work. In the introduction to his recent edition of Philips's poems, for example, Patrick Thomas derides her efforts to cultivate a sophisticated audience of readers and fellow-writers, accusing her of "weaving a web of Frenchified literary friendships" (Katherine Philips, *The Poems,* vol. 1 of *The Collected Works of Katherine Philips, The Matchless Orinda,* ed. Patrick Thomas [Stump Cross,

England, 1990], 10). He also mocks her "deluded belief in unanimity between friends," noting that when she heard of a friend's marriage, she "cried herself nearly blind" (p. 16). The blurring of poetry and biography implicit in Thomas's comments recurs in other negative critiques.

4. Andreadis's explanation is not entirely satisfactory. The conventional nature of Philips's poetry renders Andreadis's sense of her work as a quasi-autobiographical revelation of her sexuality problematic. And negative reaction to Philips began in the eighteenth century—not in the nineteenth, as Andreadis states.

5. Patrick Thomas provides an invaluable compilation of the history of Philips's reception to 1800 in his edition (pp. 22-39).

6. As the title indicates, this essay focuses on Philips's place within the critical tradition of neoclassicism, where her reputation declined. It glances only briefly at the different and later issue of Philips's place within the critical tradition of women's literary history, where her work was regarded favorably throughout the eighteenth and nineteenth centuries. See note 8 below.

7. Richard Gwinnet, in *Pylades and Corinna; or, Memoirs of the Lives, Amours, and Writings of Richard Gwinnet . . . and Mrs. Elizabeth Thomas,* 2 vols. (London, 1731-32), 2:38-39.

8. The last eighteenth-century edition of Philips's *Poems* appeared in 1710, just two years before Newcomb's *Bibliotheca.* The last edition of her *Letters* appeared in 1729. The first modern edition of her poems was brought out by Saintsbury in 1905; the most recent is Thomas's 1990 *Poems.* Her letters have not been reprinted. Some eighteenth- and nineteenth-century collections that include and discuss Philips's poems include George Ballard, *Memoirs of several ladies of Great Britain* (Oxford, 1752); George Colman and Bonnell Thornton, eds., *Poems by Eminent Ladies,* 2 vols. (London, 1755); Alexander Dyce, ed., *Specimens of British Poetesses* (London, 1827); Frederic Rowton, ed., *The Female Poets of Great Britain* (London, 1848); George Bethune, ed., *The British Female Poets* (London, 1849); Sarah Josepha Hale, *Women's Record: or, Sketches of all Distinguished Women* (London, 1853); Jane Williams, *The Literary Women of England* (London, 1861); and Julia Kavanagh, *English Women of Letters,* 2 vols. (London, 1863).

9. See Marilyn L. Williamson, *Raising Their Voices: British Women Writers, 1650-1750* (Detroit, 1990), 64-133; Dorothy Mermin, "Women Becoming Poets: Katherine Philips, Aphra Behn, Anne Finch," *ELH* 57 (1990): 335-55; Elaine Hobby, *Virtue of Necessity: English Women's Writing, 1649-88* (Ann Arbor, Mich., 1989), 128-42; Elizabeth H. Hageman, "Katherine Philips: The Matchless Orinda," in

Katharine M. Wilson, ed., *Women Writers of the Renaissance and Reformation* (Athens, Ga., 1987), 566-608; Margaret J. M. Ezell, *The Patriarch's Wife: Literary Evidence and the History of the Family* (Chapel Hill, N.C., 1987), 62-100 (esp. 85-87). Given Philips's reception history, it is somewhat ironic that current efforts to reintroduce the poet into mainstream critical discussion require specialized studies of women writers.

10. Joanna Lipking, "Fair Originals: Women Poets in Male Commendatory Poems," *Eighteenth Century Life,* n.s., 12 (1988): 58-72. Page references are given subsequently in the text.

11. John Dryden, *Prose, 1668-1691,* ed. Samuel Holt Monk, vol. 2 of *The Works of John Dryden* (Berkeley and Los Angeles, 1971), 2-81. Page references are given subsequently in the text.

12. Philo-Philippa's portrayal of Philips's style as a clear, full sea of flowing crystal also corresponds to a central neoclassical passage in John Denham's *Cooper's Hill*: "O could I flow like thee, and make thy stream / My great example, as it is my theme! / Though deep, yet clear, though gentle, yet not dull, / Strong without rage, without ore-flowing full" (*The Poetical Works of Sir John Denham,* ed. Theodore Howard Banks, 2d ed. [Hamden, Conn, 1969], 77). Page references to this edition are given subsequently in the text.

13. Arthur H. Nethercot, *The Reputation of Abraham Cowley (1660-1800)* (Philadelphia, 1923), 5.

14. "An Account of the Life and Writings of Mr. Abraham Cowley: Written to Mr. M. Clifford," in J. E. Spingarn, ed., *Critical Essays of the Seventeenth Century,* 3 vols. (Bloomington, Ind., 1963), 2:119-46. Page references to this edition are given subsequently in the text.

15. Thomas Flatman, *Poems and Songs* (London, 1674), sig. (a8).

16. Jane Barker, *Poetical Recreations: Consisting of Original Poems, Songs, Odes, & c* (London, 1688), 95.

17. *"To my dear Friend Mr.* Samuel Woodford, *upon his Paraphrase of the Psalms,"* in Samuel Woodford, *A Paraphrase upon the Psalms of David* (London, 1667), sig. (c3)-(d2). Page references to this edition are given subsequently in the text.

18. Lipking finds that male praise of women writers "went out of fashion" at the turn of the century (p. 66). She ascribes this change to the fact that by the eighteenth century writing by women was less of a novelty (p. 69).

19. *"Of the Original of the English Toung, And her As*sociation *With the Italian, Spanish, and French, &* c.," in [James Howell], *Poems on Several Choice and Various Subjects* (London, 1663), 20-21.

20. He does so implicitly, however. The poem participates in a larger nationalist discourse in which anything associated with France—especially "soft[ness]"—carries connotations of femininity at best and effeminacy at worst.

21. John Dryden, *Poems 1681-1684,* ed. H. T. Swedenberg, Jr., vol. 2 of *The Works of John Dryden* (Berkeley and Los Angeles, 1972), 172-74. Page references to this edition are given subsequently in the text.

22. John Dryden, *Poems 1685-1692,* ed. Earl Miner, vol. 3 of *The Works of John Dryden* (Berkeley and Los Angeles, 1969), 109-15. Page references to this edition are given subsequently in the text.

23. Robert H. Ray, ed., "The Herbert Allusion Book: Allusions to George Herbert in the Seventeenth Century," *Studies in Philology* 83 (1986): 99.

24. John Cleveland, *Clievelandi Vindiciae; Or, Cleveland's Genuine Poems, Orations, Epistles, & c.* (London, 1677), sig. Bv. Page references to this edition are given subsequently in the text.

25. Anne Killigrew, *Poems (1686),* ed. Richard Morton (Gainesville, Fl., 1967), 44-47. Page references to this edition are given subsequently in the text.

26. "AN ELEGY UPON The Death of Mrs. A. BEHN; The Incomparable ASTREA. *By a Young Lady of Quality,"* in G. Thorn-Drury, ed., *A Little Ark Containing Sundry Pieces of Seventeenth-Century Verse* ([London], 1921), 53-57. Page references to this edition are given subsequently in the text.

27. Philaster goes on to suggest that Barker has replaced Philips.

28. Margaret Newcastle, *Poems, And Fancies* (London, 1653), sig. Aa2v (after 160).

29. Alexander Pope, *The Correspondence of Alexander Pope,* ed. George Sherburn, 5 vols. (Oxford, 1956), 1:109-11.

30. Alexander Pope, *Imitations of Horace,* ed. John Butt, vol. 4 of *The Poems of Alexander Pope,* 2d ed. (New Haven, Conn., 1953), 189-231. Page references to this edition are given subsequently in the text.

31. *Miscellany Poems* (Cambridge, 1697), 32-33. Page references to this edition are given subsequently in the text.

32. Theophilus Cibber, *The Lives of the Poets of Great Britain and Ireland* (1753), vol. 2 (Hildesheim, Germany, 1968), 157.

33. *The Letters of John Dryden,* ed. Charles E. Ward (Durham, N.C., 1942), 125.

34. *Pylades and Corinna,* 38-39. Cited in *Poems,* ed. Thomas, 34-35.

35. [Thomas Newcomb], *Bibliotheca: A Poem. Occasion'd by the Sight of A Modern Library* (London, 1712). Cited by R. K. Alspach in "The

Matchless Orinda," *Modern Language Notes* 52 (1937): 116-17. Page references to Newcomb's edition are given subsequently in the text.

36. Alexander Pope, *Pastoral Poetry & An Essay on Criticism,* ed. E. Audra and Aubrey Williams, vol. 1 of *The Poems of Alexander Pope* (New Haven, Conn., 1961), 279-80.

37. Roger D. Lund defends Newcomb against charges of gender-bias, but he admits that Newcomb's "relative even-handedness disappears . . . in Newcomb's condescending satire on Philips's sex" ("*Bibliotheca* and 'the British Dames': An Early Critique of the Female Wits of the Restoration," *Restoration* 12 [1988]: 103).

38. See Thomas, *Poems,* 31-33, for information on Philips's early eighteenth-century reception.

39. Though I am arguing that Newcomb's poem played a significant role in the decline of Philips's reputation, I do not mean to overstate its inherent power or influence. What effect *Bibliotheca* had on Philips's reception derived primarily from the prevailing hostility to literary "femininity," and all that may have been needed to tip the critical scales against a particular woman poet was a single negative critique organized around issues of gender.

40. William Roberts, "Saint-Amant, Orinda, and Dryden's Miscellany," *English Language Notes* 1 (1964): 195.

41. In *Epistles,* II.i, Pope notes: "Who now reads Cowley? if he pleases yet, / His moral pleases, not his pointed wit; / Forgot his Epic, nay Pindaric Art, / But still I love the language of his Heart" (*Imitations,* 201).

Arlene Stiebel (essay date 1993)

SOURCE: Stiebel, Arlene. "Subversive Sexuality: Masking the Erotic in Poems by Katherine Philips and Aphra Behn." In *Renaissance Discourses of Desire,* edited by Claude J. Summers and Ted-Larry Pebworth, pp. 223-36. Columbia: University of Missouri Press, 1993.

[In the following essay, Stiebel argues that Philips and Aphra Behn employed conventions of the day to protect their respectability while professing their homosexuality.]

Although in recent discourses of desire there has been polite acknowledgment of the importance of relationships among women, much contemporary literary theory and criticism ignores the existence of lesbians.[1] Critics tell us that there are women who were "autonomous," or unmarried; women who chose a "professional" or career mode rather than a familial allegiance; women who, because they were married, automatically qualify as heterosexual despite their primary emotional and erotic bonds with other women; and some anomalous women who had a hard time fitting in with societal expectations of their time and so remained celibate. Only in a very few cases, and usually famous ones, such as that of Gertrude Stein, is it openly stated that literary women had sexual relations with other women and wrote about them. Most literary critics, even some who themselves are lesbians, collude in the polite fiction of obscurity that clouds lesbian literary lives. Bonnie Zimmerman confirms Marilyn Frye's analysis that "we are considered to be both naturally and logically impossible."[2]

The tradition of denial extends even to such distinguished works as Lillian Faderman's ground-breaking study and the most recent articles dealing with literature by lesbians. Through various critical representations, emotionally intense relationships between women are asserted to be nonsexual. Faderman insists not only that we do or can not know whether these women had "genital sex," but that even if they did, it is unimportant because historically there was no such thing as a "lesbian." Although it is now fashionable to exploit this notion of the social construction of sexual identity, such semantic hairsplitting seems to beg important questions of sexuality in literature.[3]

Adrienne Rich's theoretical observations in "Compulsory Heterosexuality and Lesbian Existence" lead to the position that choice for women was so restricted by patriarchal coercion that true sexual preference may often have been obscured or invisible, requiring conformity to a social norm in which even the acknowledgment of a sexual preference for a woman was a radical act.[4] Given these circumstances, the marriages of women known to have their primary emotional and sexual attachments to other women effectively provided them with the protection necessary to maintain respectability. Recognizing the historical circumstances of lesbian identity ought not to deprive it of sexuality.

Sandra M. Gilbert and Susan Gubar also relegate lesbians to the sexual sidelines. In their anthology of women's literature, they use every opportunity in footnotes, biographies, and glosses to explain away, where possible, evident same-sex choices in the lives and texts of lesbian authors. An example of how this bias works is evident in the way they distort Katherine Philips's clearly erotic poems. In their analysis, the eroticism is diffused through disembodied generalization into a sterile intellectual bonding. Their approach robs Philips's work of its emotional intensity. Surprisingly, their refusal to acknowledge the erotic in Philips's poems comes more than fifty years after Philip Webster Souers's standard biography, which carefully and clearly presents the succession of women to whom Philips was attached.[5]

Harriette Andreadis, in an article in *Signs,* obscures the issue even further. She describes Philips's poetry as "desexualized—though passionate and eroticized." In Andreadis's argument, eroticism is not sexual, so she can claim for Philips a type of lesbianism that maintains the social respectability she sees as an important aspect of Philips's reputation and life. Andreadis rehearses in detail some recent arguments dealing with gay and lesbian sexuality to attempt a definition of what is "lesbian." According to her definition, Philips had "a lesbian experience," wrote "lesbian texts," but may not have "expressed her homo-erotic feelings genitally." Andreadis's definition does not include women's experiences of physical desire as a component of lesbianism. By writing sensuality out of lesbian literature, Andreadis maintains the tradition of denial, which is perpetuated in Dorothy Mermin's more recent article. Refusing to acknowledge a lesbian sexual-ity, Mermin picks up Andreadis's assertion that Philips's poems "did not give rise to scandal" and were therefore "asexual, respectable." Mermin's characterization of "female homosexuality" as "unseemly" clearly indicates her approach to this literature.[6]

How can contemporary critics continue to overlook, if not deny outright, the lesbian content of poems so clearly erotically charged with the love of women for women? The fact is that they can if they want to, for just as figura-tive language has the power to reveal more than it states, it can also conceal. When Muriel Rukeyser publicly wrote of her lesbianism, she noted in the content and title of her 1971 autobiographical poem "The Poem as Mask," a technique that lesbian writers have used for centuries to express their love for women:

> When I wrote of the women in their dances and wild-
> ness,
>   it was a mask,
> on their mountain, god-hunting, singing in orgy,
> it was a mask; when I wrote of the god,
> fragmented, exiled from himself, his life, the love
>   gone down with song,
> it was myself, split open, unable to speak, in exile
>   from myself.
>
> (1-5)[7]

Stein encoded her work, Amy Lowell sometimes changed pronouns to disguise her speaker's sex, and Willa Cather changed her protagonists' gender. Katherine Philips and Aphra Behn also used masking techniques based in the literary conventions of their time, but although they used the same conventions as their male counterparts did, the effects of their verses were radically different.

Evident in the poems of Philips and Behn is the use of literary conventions we take almost for granted—the courtly love address to the beloved and her response, the idealized pattern of Platonic same-sex friendship, and the hermaphroditic perfection of the beloved who incorporates the best qualities of both sexes. The difference in the use of these conventions by the women poets lies in the significant fact that the voice of the lover is nowhere disguised nor intended to be understood as that of a male. Rather, Philips and Behn exploit the conventions to proclaim to all who would read their poems that the desire of a woman for a woman lover falls well within accept-able literary norms. The very transparency of their mask-ing techniques is what makes them so fascinating.

Their contemporaries recognized the homosexual bias of the two authors. Both women were praised by other, male, poets as "sapphists," that is, women writers in the tradition of Sappho of Lesbos, whose verse fragments clearly celebrate the erotic attachments of women, lament their separation and loss, and generally become the first acknowledged model for female-identified love poems.

Katherine Philips (1632-1664) was known as "The Match-less Orinda" and "The English Sappho" of her day. Privately circulated in manuscript during her lifetime, her *Poems* were first published post-humously in 1664. That incomplete edition was superseded by the *Poems* in 1667, which became the basis for the subsequent edition of 1678. Of the collected poems, more than half deal with Orinda's love for other women. In addition to poems addressed to her beloved "Lucasia" (Anne Owen), there are poems by Philips to "Rosania" (Mary Aubrey), who preceded Luca-sia in her affections, and to "Pastora," whose relationship with "Phillis" is celebrated by Lucasia after her own female lover has gone. In addition to these poems using the names Philips bestowed on members of her "Society of Friendship," which was "limited . . . to persons of the same sex," Philips writes in her own historical voice openly to Anne Owen as well as **"To the Lady E. Boyl"** with declarations of love.[8]

Central to Philips's short life—she died of smallpox at thirty-one—was the romance with Anne Owen, and central to her poetry is the conventional representation of their involvement through the images of classical friendship and courtly love. **"Orinda to Lucasia,"** in a traditional pastoral mode, illustrates the importance of the presence of the female beloved. Lucasia is the sun who will restore the light and energy of day (life) to Orinda, who cries for her "friend" to appear as the birds, flowers, and brooks call for their own renewal at a delayed sunrise. The "sun" is "tardy," so that the "weary birds" must "court their glori-ous planet to appear." The "drooping flowers . . . languish down into their beds: / While brooks . . . Openly murmer and demand" that the sun come (8-12). But Lucasia means *more* to Orinda than the sun to the world, and if Lucasia delays too long, she will come in time not to save Orinda, but to see her die.

> Thou my Lucasia are far more to me,
> Than he to all the under-world can be;
> From thee I've heat and light,
> Thy absence makes my night.
>
> . . . . .
>
>   if too long I wait,
> Ev'n thou may'st come too late,
> And not restore my life, but close my eyes.
>
> (13-16, 22-24)

Traditional lovesickness unto death from a cruel mistress becomes transformed here to an urgent request for the presence of the willing beloved who will grant life if she comes speedily, but will be her chief mourner should the speaker expire.

Conventional oxymoronic terminology permeates the verse—light versus dark, day versus night, presence and absence, life and death—while the elements of nature that reflect the lover's state of being are, in a reversal of the magnitude of traditional signification, portrayed microcosmically in relation to the macrocosm of Orinda's feelings. The true relationship between the lovers is clear, if we allow ourselves to read the text explicitly. But through the lens of customary literary metaphors, the relationship of the two women can be explained away as being only figuratively erotic—a clever reworking of the spiritualized romance tradition combined with idealized classical friendship to de-emphasize the sexual reality inherent in the concrete, physical terminology of the poem. That is, the familiar literary conventions of the poem may mask and diffuse its pervasive eroticism. But to recognize the use of conventions as an elaborate mask is to acknowledge the reality of sexual desire that the poem simultaneously reveals and cloaks.

The relationship between Lucasia and Orinda is further developed and clarified in **"To My Excellent Lucasia, on Our Friendship,"** for which the traditional soul-body dichotomy is the metaphorical basis. In this poem, Orinda's soul is not only given life by Lucasia, but Lucasia's soul actually *becomes* the animating force of her lover's body:

> the world believ'd
> There was a soul the motions kept;
> But they all were deceiv'd.
>
> . . . . .
>
> never had Orinda found
> A soul till she found thine.
>
> (6-8, 11-12)

The lovers are united in one immortal soul, and their relationship grants to the speaker attributes similar to those of a "bridegroom" or "crown-conquerer." But here too, Philips presents the metaphor in hyperbole that extends the more orthodox presentation, "They have but pieces of the earth, / I've all the world in thee" (19-20). The echo of Donne's lines from "The Sun Rising," "She's all states, and all princes I / Nothing else is" (21-22), forces the reader to regard the lovers' relationship as one of traditional courtly desire transformed into the sacramental union with a soul mate through whose agency one participates in the heavenly. Further, their love also remains "innocent" because they are both women. Given their mutually female design, the speaker can "say without a crime, / I am not thine, but thee" (3-4) and encourage their "flames" to "light and shine" without "false fear," since they are "innocent as our design, / Immortal as our soul" (23-24).

The speaker is careful to invoke both spirituality and innocent design as justifications for such language of excess, even though convention would allow her the license to claim another's soul as her own because of their affection alone. But, as female lovers, they need more than a mere statement rejecting what Donne characterizes in "A Valediction: forbidding Mourning" as "Dull, sublunary lovers' love" (13), to make their union acceptable. So Orinda's argument is that she and Lucasia are "innocent."

We may read this assertion as a refutation of the guilt surrounding accusations of unnatural love between women, as an outspoken declaration that lesbianism is not to be maligned. But I read it another way, in the time-honored tradition of irony that finds answers to bigotry in terms of the ignorance of prejudice itself. Orinda can maintain that love between women is "innocent" because, as Queen Victoria much later asked, what could women do? In a phallocentric culture that defines sexual behavior according to penile instrumentality, sex exclusive of men is not merely unthinkable, it is impossible. Which of us is unfamiliar with the characterization of "sex" as "going all the way," and what woman has not at one time or another been reassured that if it did not go in "nothing happened"? In England, although male homosexuality was outlawed, women together could not commit a sexual crime. If the norm is androcentric, eroticism among women is illusionary, female "friendships" are merely spiritual bonds, and lesbians are nonexistent.

As long as the definition of the sex act is inextricably linked to male anatomy and behavior, the question of what can women do is moot. So in order to address the question of sexuality in these poems, we must reexamine what we mean by erotic attraction and sexual activity. If we confuse ejaculation with orgasm, and both of these with sexual satisfaction, and deny the realities of varied sexual responses that are not centered actually or metaphorically in male anatomy, the true nature of lesbian relationships will remain masked. And to the extent that the bias of heterosexual denial and ignorance maintains that intercourse is the sexual norm, then, by definition, activity from which a penis is absent provides women with a love that is "innocent."[9]

In **"To My *Lucasia,* in defence of declared Friendship,"** Orinda openly argues, "O My Lucasia, let us speak our Love, / And think not that impertinent can be" (1-2). Unlike Donne's male speaker in "The Flea," who asserts that "use make you apt to kill me" (16), as women, Orinda and Lucasia "cannot spend our stock by use." Their "spotless passion never tires, / But does increase by repetition still" (27-28). So female "friends" may enact their sexuality on quite different terms than their male counterparts. Sometimes the terminology of Philips's poems, so frequently reminiscent of Donne's, presents a lesbian sexuality only slightly masked, as in her wholesale borrowing of what may be Donne's most celebrated metaphor, that of the "stiff twin compasses" (26) from "A Valediction: forbidding Mourning" in **"Friendship in Embleme, or the Seal. To my dearest Lucasia"**:

> 6.
>
> The Compasses that stand above
> Express this great immortal love;

For Friends, like them, can prove this true,
They are, and yet they are not, two.

7.

And in their posture is exprest
Friendship's exalted Interest:
Each follows where the other leans,
And what each does, this other means.

8.

And as when one foot does stand fast,
And t'other circles seeks to cast,
The steddy part does regulate
And make the wand'rer's motion straight.

(21-32)

Literary and cultural conventions of friendship here only partially mask the eroticism implicit in Donne's famous metaphor. The mask preserves Philips's respectability, while the sexual energy that infuses the women's friendship is highlighted by the use of the formerly heterosexual image.

As a representative of Sappho in the British Isles, Katherine Philips was praised for her poetic skills. Twenty years after her death and the first appearance of her poems in print, the Matchless Orinda was succeeded by the Incomparable Astrea, Aphra Behn (1640-1689), whose poetic reputation was enhanced by favorable comparisons with her well-known predecessor.[10] Behn was known primarily as a scandalous playwright, although she also wrote incidental poems and what is perhaps the first real novel in English, *Love Letters between A Nobleman and His Sister* (1682-1685), which set the generic model (epistolary) and topic (courtship) for future lengthy prose works.[11]

Behn was married and widowed early, and as a mature woman, her primary publicly acknowledged relationship was with a gay male, John Hoyle, himself the subject of much scandal. She celebrates gay male love between the allegorical Philander and Lycidas, as she describes her social circle in a poem called "Our Cabal." Her description of their "friendship" reflects the convention of androgyny, as it becomes the justification for "Tenderness . . . / Too Amorous for a Swain to a Swain" (187-88). Behn was herself apostrophized by her admirers for her androgyny, which was seen as the desirable reconciliation of an arguably masculine mind with her apparently feminine physique. The conventional reconciliation of sexual opposites was expressed in dedicatory poems to her collection *Poems upon Several Occasions: With A Voyage to the Island of Love*.[12] The hermaphroditic paradigm is the basis for so many of these verses that the conventional encomiastic mode itself becomes a masking device to acknowledge the sexuality of her poems. "Such work so gently wrought, so strongly fine, / Cannot be wrought by hands all Masculine," writes J. C., who, along with J. Adams, praises her for "A Female Sweetness and a Manly

Grace." J. Cooper uses the conventional marriage of "*Venus* her sweetness and the force of *Mars* . . . Imbracing . . . in thy due temper'd Verse" to characterize what J. C. terms "the Beauties of both Sexes join'd . . . with a strange power to charm."

But the most complex presentation of the hermaphroditic ideal is Behn's own. "To the fair Clarinda, who made Love to me, imagin'd more than Woman" explicitly states in the title the true relationship between the two women, and the poem develops the concept of a love that is "Innocent" into a full exploration of the safety in loving an androgynous female.

> FAIR, lovely Maid, or if that Title be
> Too weak, too Feminine for Nobler thee,
> Permit a Name that more Approaches Truth:
> And let me call thee, Lovely Charming Youth.
> This last will justifie my soft complaint,
> While that may serve to lessen my constraint;
> And without Blushes I the Youth persue,
> When so much beauteous Woman is in view.
> Against thy Charms we struggle but in vain
> With thy deluding Form thou giv'st us pain,
> While the bright Nymph betrays us to the Swain.
> In pity to our Sex sure thou wer't sent,
> That we might Love, and yet be Innocent:
> For no sure Crime with thee we can commit;
> Or if we shou'd—thy Form excuses it.
> For who, that gathers the fairest Flowers believes
> A Snake lies hid beneath the Fragrant Leaves.
>   Thou beauteous Wonder of a different kind,
> Soft *Cloris* with the dear *Alexis* join'd;
> When e'r the Manly part of thee, wou'd plead
> Thou tempts us with the Image of the Maid,
> While we the noblest Passions do extend
> The love to *Hermes, Aphrodite* the friend.

If Clarinda's "weak" and "feminine" characteristics are insufficiently noble to evoke the superlatives of praise that are more appropriately addressed to a "Youth," then that very appellation lifts the constraints on a woman-loving female in pursuit of her courtship. The beloved's combination of masculine with female characteristics, the Maid and the Youth, the nymph and the swain, confers a sexual freedom on the lover, who can argue that friendship alone is addressed to the woman, while the erotic attraction is reserved for the masculine component of her beloved androgyne. This makes their love "innocent." Further, as we have seen, two women together can commit no "Crime," but *if* they can, Behn argues with sophistical Donnean wit, Clarinda's "Form excuses it." Katherine Philips relies on her lover's "design" as the basis for the love that can be "innocent." But Aphra Behn goes even further. Here Clarinda is not merely observably a female. As the Neoplatonic courtly beloved, her "Form" partakes of the ideal forms of the universe, desire for which refines the erotic to the highest plane of spiritual love, a morally acceptable transformation of mere physical attraction that might otherwise offend.

The serpent among the flowers imagery is a standard allusion to the phallic, with Edenic associations of sin. But the "different kind" who is the beloved in this poem clearly mitigates against any aspects of sinfulness by allowing the speaker (in a multilayered and witty pun) to extend her love to Hermes, and her friendship to Aphrodite in a socially acceptable construction of their passionate attachment. Behn's argument here is reminiscent of Shakespeare's response to the "master mistress" of his "passion" in Sonnet 20, where the speaker distinguishes between the androgynous youth's physical attributes designed "for women's pleasure" and the kind of love that may be appropriately shared between men: "Mine be thy love, and thy love's use their treasure" (14). We can read Behn's poem as the speaker's justification of her own approach to a forbidden beloved. But Clarinda is no traditionally passive maiden fair. She is the one who, the title states, "made love" to the speaker, and, in the last quatrain, her "Manly part . . . wou'd plead" while her "Image of the Maid" tempts. Clarinda, therefore, may also be seen as the initiator of their sexual activity, with the speaker justifying her own response in reaction to the public sexual mores of her time. This reciprocal construction of the poem may suggest the mutuality of a lesbian relationship that rejects the domination and subordination patterns of traditional heterosexual roles.

Behn's verse entertainment, "Selinda and Cloris," portrays a reciprocal relationship between women as unparalleled. It includes both physical and intellectual attraction, friendship and sexuality. Cloris "will sing, in every Grove, / The Greatness of your Mind," to which Selinda responds "And I your Love" (74-76). They trade verses and sing together in a presentation of the traditional pastoral speaker as poet, lover, singer, and shepherd:

> And all the Day,
> With Pride and Joy,
> We'll let the Neighbr'ing Shepherds see,
> That none like us,
> Did e'er Express,
> The heights of Love and Amity.

> (77-82)

This celebration of the female lovers' mutual joy in a variant on the traditional masque of Hymen presents in song and dance a formal dramatic closure that emphasizes the eroticism of the women's relationship in a conventional representation that also may serve to disguise it.

Two other poems addressing women as lovers or potential lovers are also interesting. In each case, the combination of direct statement and literary convention highlights the erotic content of the verse. In "To My Lady Morland at Tunbridge," Behn employs the customary compliment to the beautiful woman, but expresses also a womanly concern for virginity. In a reversal of convention, the speaker's concern is for the chastity of the lover rather than that of the beloved, "A Virgin-Heart you merit, that ne'er found / It could receive, till from your Eyes, the *Wound*" (47-48). Behn was sufficiently interested in the unidentified woman whose eyes struck hers, or in the poem itself, to rewrite it as "To Mrs. Harsenet, on the Report of

a Beauty, which she went to see at Church." Carola Harsnett Morland seems, in this case, to have been Behn's audience rather than the subject of the poem, and Behn writes to her openly of her physical attraction to another woman. In "Verses design'd by Mrs. A. Behn to be sent to a fair Lady, that desir'd she would absent herself to cure her Love. Left Unfinished," the audience is clearly the beloved, and the content of the poem as well as the title indicates that this love is unrequited, "The more I strugl'd to my Grief I found / My self in *Cupid's* Chains more surely bound" (18-19). Eros is clearly a factor in the lack of fulfillment this poem conveys.

The complexity of Behn's verse—its logical argument, pastoral and courtly conventions, biblical and classical allusions, and social comment—epitomizes the disguise that reveals meaning. Such eloquent masking allows the audience to go away satisfied that no breach of decorum has been made. It permits us to deny, dismiss, or marginalize that which we do not wish to acknowledge, and exempts the poet from social condemnation while bestowing critical acclaim for her ingenuity.[13] Just as in society the conventional polite fiction disguises true feeling, in literature conventional representations of friendship, courtly romance, and female androgyny may mask true meaning. In a male-dominated society, with a male-oriented literature, women authors who chose to write honestly about important issues in women's lives (and sexual issues may be at the core of these) needed to convey their experiences in ways that express meaning on more than one level simultaneously. By using conventions as maskings, invoking all the connotations of masquing as play, Katherine Philips and Aphra Behn present alternative views of sexuality that are still considered taboo. It is time for us as readers at least to acknowledge the lesbian content in these works. The real question is not how innocent were they, but how innocent are we?

Notes

1. A version of some of the material in this essay appears in my article "Not Since Sappho: The Erotic in Poems of Katherine Philips and Aphra Behn," in *Homosexuality in Renaissance and Enlightenment England: Literary Representations in Historical Context,* ed. Claude J. Summers (New York: The Haworth Press/Harrington Park Press, 1992), 153-71, also published as a special issue of the *Journal of Homosexuality* 23 (1992).

2. Zimmerman, *The Safe Sea of Women: Lesbian Fiction 1969-1989* (Boston: Beacon Press, 1990), 62.

3. Faderman, *Surpassing the Love of Men: Romantic Friendship and Love Between Women from the Renaissance to the Present* (New York: William Morrow, 1981). For some early examples of this critical approach, see Ellen Moers, *Literary Women* (New York: Doubleday, 1976); and Louise Bernikow, *Among Women* (New York: Harper and Row, 1980). For a contrary and unique appreciation of lesbian writers and themes, see Jane Rule, *Lesbian Images*

(New York: Crossing Press, 1982). For an example of how this current theory relates to the English Renaissance, see Alan Bray, *Homosexuality in Renaissance England* (London: Gay Men's Press, 1982). For a more woman-centered treatment of some similar ideas, see Susan Cavin, *Lesbian Origins* (San Francisco: Ism Press, 1985). In their Introduction to *Hidden from History: Reclaiming the Gay and Lesbian Past* (New York: New American Library, 1989) the editors, Martin Bauml Duberman, Martha Vicinus, and George Chauncey, Jr., note that Faderman has been charged by other historians with denying the importance of sexual activity in lesbian women's lives (7).

4. In Rich, *Blood, Bread, and Poetry* (New York: Norton, 1986), 23-75.

5. Gilbert and Gubar, eds., *The Norton Anthology of Literature by Women* (New York: Norton, 1985), 81; and Souers, *The Matchless Orinda* (Cambridge: Harvard University Press, 1931).

6. Andreadis, "The Sapphic-Platonics of Katherine Philips, 1632-1664," *Signs: Journal of Women in Culture and Society* 15, no. 1 (1989): 34-60 (quotations from 39, 59); Mermin, "Women Becoming Poets: Katherine Philips, Aphra Behn, Anne Finch," *ELH* 57 (1990): 335-56 (quotations from 343). Mermin also derogates Philips's poems for their lack of a particular kind of energy usually associated with heterosexual desire and not part of Philips's clearly lesbian tone: "Her celebrations of love usually lack, however, the dramatic tension between flesh and spirit that imparts nervous urgency to Donne's amatory verse" (343).

7. Quoted in Florence Howe & Ellen Bass, eds., *No More Masks: An Anthology of Poems by Women* (New York: Doubleday, 1973).

8. The texts of Philips's *Poems* in the 1664, 1667, and 1678 editions are identical. See also Philips's *Letters from Orinda* (London, 1705); Souers, *Matchless Orinda*, 41; and Philips, *Poems*, 1664, 149.

9. Much has been written recently by women about female sexuality. See, for example, Shere Hite, *The Hite Report: A Nationwide Study of Female Sexuality* (New York: Macmillan, 1976); as well as two books by Joann Loulan, *Lesbian Sex* (San Francisco: Spinsters, Ink, 1984) and *Lesbian Passion* (San Francisco: Spinsters/Aunt Lute, 1987).

10. "*Greece* in *Sappho*, in *Orinda* knew / Our Isle; though they were but low types to you." From "To the excellent Madam BEHN, on her Poems," J. Adams, in Aphra Behn, *Poems Upon Several Occasions: With A Voyage To The Island Of Love* (London, 1684).

11. Two recent biographies of Behn are Maureen Duffy's *The Passionate Shepherdess* (London: Cape, 1977); and Angeline Goreau's *Reconstructing Aphra: A Social Biography of Aphra Behn* (New York: Dial Press, 1980). Vita Sackville-West's brief life of Behn, *The Incomparable Astrea* (London: Russell & Russell, 1927), remains an interesting historical document. The standard edition of Behn's works is that edited by Montague Summers, *The Works of Aphra Behn,* 6 vols. (1915; repr. New York: Benjamin Blom, 1967).

12. (London, 1684).

13. For a discussion of how Behn employs this technique to create a double perspective on rape and seduction in her most famous poem, "The Disappointment," see my essay, "Not Since Sappho."

Kathleen M. Swaim (essay date 1997)

SOURCE: Swaim, Kathleen M. "Matching the 'Matchless Orinda' to Her Times." In *1650-1850: Ideas, Aesthetics, and Inquiries in the Early Modern Era.* Vol. 3, edited by Kevin L. Cope, pp. 77-108. New York: AMS Press, 1997.

[*In the following essay, Swaim compares Philip's poetry with verse by John Milton and John Donne to analyze her unique contribution to English literature.*]

Among the most prominent names that literary archaeology into England's earliest women writers has brought forward is that of Katherine Philips (1631/2-64), whose engaging sobriquet, "The Matchless Orinda," offers a quick glance into the drawing-rooms of a lost cultural moment. Her contemporaries took Philips very seriously indeed as a poet, a moral model, a pioneer, an inspiration and a nonpareil, the English Sappho, the Muse's darling and equal. Besides adding the claim "matchless" to the "Orinda" she chose for herself, John Oldham (1653-83), for example, includes Philips as one of five poetic worthies along with Chaucer, Milton, Cowley, and Denham.[1] Despite the range of honorifics from contemporary male and female commentary alike, traditional literary history has victimized Philips within what modern feminism identifies as "the politics of benign neglect."[2]

This study seeks to repair some of the neglect of Philips's poetry through a pluralistic or multivalenced inquiry, one of the recognized kinds of feminist criticism. By comparing several of her lyrics with precise analogues from John Milton and John Donne—cherished favorites of the seventeenth-century literary canon—this study supplies some fresh means for historically and aesthetically contextualizing her work. It puts forward some epistemic and cultural grids of the transitional historical moment she self-consciously inhabited. The poetic territory to which Philips chiefly laid claim, woman's friendship, would seem to endorse a non- or even anti-political stance, but, as we shall see, her subject matter and the poetic discourses in which it is couched are themselves cultural and political signifiers.

My contrastive methodology highlights more chronological than gendered difference to discover surprisingly political dimensions to Philips's performance. Section I below contrasts two Philips's lyrics with two nearly contemporaneous sonnets on the same subjects by John Milton to argue that, poetically, Philips's work focuses the contestation of the sixteenth-century's characteristic resemblance and representationalism against the eighteenth-century's empowering of discourses along the lines that Michel Foucault traces in *The Order of Things.* Whatever its ultimate limitations, Foucaultian typology can productively ground the rediscovery of an author like Philips. Section II takes up the intertextualities of Philips's appropriation of John Donne's famous compass conceit from "A Valediction Forbidding Mourning" in order to "explore the multiple paths that lead to the unmasking of cultural artifacts as socially symbolic acts," the task that Fredric Jameson assigns to the political unconscious within his 1981 study of that title. Together these sections attend to the widening frameworks of a text's social grounding that Jameson distinguishes as the text, the social order, and the ideology of form. They annotate Philips's literary texts within a narrowly defined political history of punctual events and chronically sequenced happenings, but also place them within less diachronic and time-bound social history more largely, taking into account the constitutive tension between social classes as well as the larger patterns of history as a succession of modes of production and social formations.[3]

Two of Philips's non-friendship poems precisely parallel two poems by John Milton to differentiate the historical positioning of these authors, their literary generations and cultural contexts. The analogues enact the social and biographical within the formal and aesthetic. The first poem celebrates a particular moment of Philips's biography, her twenty-sixth birthday in 1657/8, and as such it invites comparison with Milton's sonnet acknowledging the passing of his twenty-third year (1632).[4] Philips manifests what Earl Miner describes as the Cowley effect, that is the distancing of the poet from his/her subject matter and situation, attended by a heightened consciousness of the reader.[5] Her second-generation practice assumes a public and political mantle, as Milton's assumes an aesthetic or laureate mode. Keenly aware of inhabiting a world spinning and turning upside down, Philips, like so many other poets of the later seventeenth century, locates herself in the present moment and in immediate historical realities at the expense of transcendence and prophecy.

Milton's birthday sonnet, the seventh out of a lifetime total of twenty-three, confirms his commitment to poetry and piety and anticipates a life of lofty achievement. In form as in content, it aspires to the laureate mode, specifically to that fashioning of an official, ethically exemplary poetic self that Richard Helgerson attaches to seventeenth-century "self-crowned laureates":[6]

> How soon hath Time, the subtle thief of youth,
>   Stol'n on his wing my three and twentieth year!
>   My hasting days fly on with full career,

> But my late spring no bud or blossom show'th.
> Perhaps my semblance might deceive the truth,
>   That I to manhood am arriv'd so near,
>   And inward ripeness doth much less appear,
>   That some more timely-happy spirits endu'th.
> Yet be it less or more, or soon or slow,
>   It shall be still in strictest measure ev'n
>   To that same lot, however mean or high,
> Toward which Time leads me, and the will of Heav'n;
>   All is, if I have grace to use it so,
>   As ever in my great task-Master's eye.[7]

This sonnet assumes Virgilian, Ciceronian, and Christian endorsements of its rhetoric, ethical argument, and poetic aspiration, of its affirmation of divine will and heroic human patience. When it was first published in the collection of Milton's youthful English and Latin verse in 1645, it looked forward specifically to the imminent "brave new world" of Puritan, Republican political hopes in which Milton actively invested, but it enfolds any political assumptions within the laureate tradition's public/private univocality and within Milton's sense of the poet as *vates* (prophet) or spokesman for his culture and his God and of making the whole design of his life "a true poem" (*Poems* 694).

In the absence of any overt statements in her poetry or prose, we cannot know if Katherine Philips ever read this or indeed any of Milton's poems, but a similar poem, **"On the I. of January, 1657,"** likewise commemorates her twenty-sixth birthday in twelve lines of pentameter couplets. This brief, virtually unknown poem looks back upon the history that Milton's poem anticipated:

> Th' Eternal Centre of my life and me,
> Who when I was not, gave me room to be,
> Hath since (my time preserving in his hands)
> By moments numbred out the precious sand[s],
> Till it is swell'd to six and twenty years,
> Checquer'd by Providence with smiles and tears.
> I have observ'd how vain all glories are,
> The change of Empire, and the chance of War:
> Seen Faction with its native venom burst,
> And Treason struck, by what it self had nurs'd:
> Seen useless Crimes, whose Owners but made way
> For future Candidates to wear the Bay.[8]

Like Milton's, Philips's poem views her life *sub specie aeternitatis,* though it otherwise speaks motives and aspirations that differ markedly from Milton's presentation of a self heroicized within classical and biblical discourses. Its first half acknowledges the point in life she is just achieving with a grateful eye to divine cause and preservation. Its second half retrospects not theology but chronology. It reviews the historical categories that have defined life in England during Philips's adult years: Empire, War, Faction, Treason, and "useless crimes" more generally. "The *change* of Empire, and the *chance* of War" (my italics) gives a deft, linguistically balanced formulation to the Civil War, the beheading of a monarch, the Interregnum, the Stuart return—the extraordinary sequence of events that serves as background to her time and awareness. Her more political vision anticipates an era of poetry not for herself alone but for her society generally to displace the chaotic political negotiations she sees as slouching toward oblivion.

We cannot know if Philips was deliberately giving Milton's earlier construct a twist that could contain her differently based sense of life and literary performance, but the poetics and the self of her lyric reflect a distinctly later age. In form as in content, both make theological gestures, but where Milton is personal, Philips is political. Where Milton enfolds his sense of his own destiny in inherited imageries (theft, springtime) and in biblical parable (Matthew 25: 14-30), Philips looks to the later expressional norms of heroic couplet and abstract diction that were to dominate the literary reigns of Dryden and Pope. Like Milton's, Philips's poem concludes on a quietist note.

Philips is political not just by belonging to and being marked by a particular time, place, and self-consciousness, but also by engaging that world and rewriting the experience that power and history have written upon her, by interwriting personal, social, and natural experience.[9] In a quite deliberate choice, political positioning is a matter of status, ambition, and authority for her. It is worth remembering that Philips begins her published volume of *Poems* with titles and subjects that insist upon her political self-presentation and right to comment, such titles as **"Upon the double murther of K.Charles, in answer to a libellous rime made by V.[avasor] P.[owell]"**; **"On the numerous access of the English to waite upon the King in Holland"**; **"Arion on a Dolphin to his Majestie in his passadge into England"**; **"On the faire weather at the Coronacon"**; **"To the Queene on her arrivall at Portsmouth. May. 1662"**; *et cetera.*[10] Where Milton builds his poem and constructs his poetic self by enfolding his education, literary inheritance, and biblical grounding securely within a poetics of the heroicized personal, Philips gives politics full priority, even over the writing self. She aligns her life with history, not, as Milton does, with transcendence.

Besides these similar threshold affirmations of poetic commitments and destinies, Philips and Milton also shared a common friend and collaborator in Henry Lawes (1596-1662), perhaps the most notable of English lyric musicians in this most musical of ages.[11] Both Milton and Philips enjoyed personal as well as professional relationships with Lawes, Milton in spite of Lawes's pronounced Royalist allegiance. Throughout his long career, Lawes set to music poems by both Milton and Philips, and both sang his praises in poems, Milton in Sonnet 13, "To my freind Mr. Hen. Laws Feb. 9. 1645" [= 1646 n.s.][12], and Philips in 40 lines of heroic couplets entitled **"To the truly noble Mr Henry Lawes"** (#15). These comparable poems extend the historical, epistemological, and literary differences glimpsed above.

Milton's tribute was first printed in Henry and William Lawes's *Choice Psalmes put into Musick* (1648) dedicated to the then imprisoned Charles I.

Harry, whose tuneful and well measur'd Song
  First taught our English Music how to span
  Words with just note and accent, not to scan
  With *Midas*' Ears, committing short and long,
Thy worth and skill exempts thee from the throng,
  With praise enough for Envy to look wan;
  To after age thou shalt be writ the man
  That with smooth air couldst humor best our tongue.
Thou honor'st Verse, and Verse must lend her wing
  To honor thee, the Priest of *Phoebus*' Choir
  That tun'st their happiest lines in Hymn, or Story.
Dante shall give Fame leave to set thee higher
  Than his *Casella,* whom he woo'd to sing,
  Met in the milder shades of Purgatory.

(Poems 144)

This sonnet, like the birthday one, is finely executed in the Miltonic appropriation of the Spenserian model, with a strong break between octave and sestet, insistent enjambment, tough content, and a surprisingly muted ending. Its diction and logic defy the simplistic sweetness of the genre as passed down from the Elizabethans, and its strong literary reference, here detailing both classical myth and Italian epic, exploits the reader's literary study, memory, and ingenuity. Milton's Lawes sonnet again claims laureate and vatic "authority." Its personal/public univocality follows the practice of so many of Milton's sonnets in elevating an historic personnage as heroic exemplar of the loftiest principles of character, piety, or in this case art.

Katherine Philips's collaboration and association with Lawes date from at least the 1650s. He was the music teacher to several of her lifelong friends and set to music at least three of her other poems:[13] **"Set by Mr. H. Lawes / A Dialogue between Lucasia and Orinda"** (*Works* 1.94-5); **"On the death of my first and dearest childe, Hector Philipps, borne the 23ᵈ of Aprill, and dy'd the 2ᵈ of May 1655. set by Mr Lawes"** (220), and **"Friendship's Mysterys, to my dearest Lucasia. (set by Mr. H. Lawes.)"** (90-1). The last of these was published in Lawes's *Second Book of Ayres and Dialogues* (1655), a volume Philips's biographer describes as a virtual commentary on Philips's pseudonymous "society."[14]

Despite their differing sizes and formats, Philips's poem joins Milton's not just in claiming Lawes as "friend," but in making him representational of the largest ideas. Neither author exploits the pun in their subject's name, but both celebrate *measure, order,* and *govern* in what are perhaps allied gestures. Calling Lawes "Great soule of nature," Philips like Milton embeds her subject within the cosmos and the layered harmonies that impel it:

Nature, which is the vast creation's soule,
That steady curious agent in the whole,
The art of heav'n, the order of this frame,
Is onely number in another name:
For as some King, conqu'ring what was his own,
Hath choice of severall titles to his crown;
So harmony, on this score now, that then,
Yet still is all that takes and governs men.

(Works 1.87)

Like Milton, Philips views Lawes in relation to preceding and subsequent ages, though for her those ages are not marked as literary.

As with Philips's birthday poem, this one too relies heavily upon the abstract conceptual diction that was so much to dominate the Age of Reason, but her procedure realizes a metaphor even within such constraints. Thus after establishing the cosmic governance of harmony and number, she hinges a series of principles of character and person upon a musical diction:

> Beauty is but *Composure,* and we find
> Content is but the *Concord* of the mind,
> Friendship the *Unison* of *well-tun'd* hearts,
> Honour's the *Chorus* of the noblest parts,
> And all the world on which we can reflect,
> *Musique* to th'Eare, or to the Intellect.

My italics show how, in fact, each poetic line turns upon the same verbal hinge, the final two lines here balancing more largely upon the summational word that comes just at their juncture.

Such dictional exploitation functions much as imagery functions in the earlier poetics. What is now imaged is not some item of experiential reality but a category of discourse. That radical alteration in the base of the poetic—here for Philips as elsewhere for her contemporaries and heirs generally—embodies in a telling miniature the epistemological transformation that Foucault illuminates in *The Order of Things* between the resemblance that dominated the sixteenth century and the classification that came to prevail in the eighteenth. Gone is the profound kinship between language and the world and the shared epistemology of conjuncture, and in its place appear new systems of artificial, arbitrary, man-made signs translating apprehended realities into manipulated discourses.[15]

Several of Philips's tributes to Lawes reconstitute the earlier representationalism, most notably in taking up themes that other works of Milton attach either to Lawes himself or to the Platonic Idea or best earthly practice of music.

> If then each man a little world must be,
> How many worlds are coppy'd out in Thee?
> Who art so richly formed, so compleat,
> T'epitomize all that is good and great;
> Whose stars this brave advantage did impart,
> Thy nature's more harmonious then thy art.

These lines (15-20) cast as a rhetorical question the multilayered roles within which Milton coded Lawes's presentation of himself in *A Mask,* as simultaneously composer, music teacher, Orphean pastoral poet-singer, Thyrsis, Attendant Spirit, and generally—musician layering into Music itself—as mediator between the careful deity and needy, worthy humans. Since Philips's tribute is couched in the resolutely assertive sonorities of heroic couplets rather than the allegorical prophetic poetics of Milton's masque, such layerings are much curtailed in her verse. Indeed where Milton seeks to raise his materials and his audience's vision to the resonating heavens, Philips's concern is to bring down and contain vision and subject within the confidences of a familiar world shorn of numinousness.

In allied Milton works, *ad Patrem* offers a grateful tribute to his musical father and *At a Solemn Music* compounds voice and verse, that is singer and song, within a supralunary vision of the Music of the Spheres and the inability of fallen humans to hear it. Both these early Milton works may be invoked to footnote Philips's next lines:

> Thou dost above the Poets praises live,
> Who fetch from thee th'Eternity they give;
> And as true reason triumphs over sence,
> Yet is subjected to intelligence:
> So Poets on the lower world look down,
> But Lawes on them; his height is all his own.
> For, like divinity it self, his Lyre
> Rewards the wit it did at first inspire:
> And thus by double right Poets allow
> His and their Laurells should adorn his brow.

The conclusion here is very like Milton's neat turn in Sonnet 13: "Thou honorest Verse, and Verse must . . . honor thee." Both authors box themselves into and out of self-referentiality. Both project tributary works, not themselves, as the agency of praise, but where Milton displaces the gesture from himself to Dante and Dante to Casella (*Purgatorio* 2.76-117), Philips projects hierarchies of mental faculties and the arts—Foucaultian discourses—situating herself on high though below the subject of her praise. Where Milton's gaze is prophetically upward, Philips shares with Lawes a downward glance at lesser mortals.

Although we might expect Milton to offer the public poem and Philips the personal one, the opposite proves to be the case in this pairing as in the former one. Her concluding ten lines give Philips's poem not just a public but a political turn, compounding the sort of expectations that the birthday poem conditioned us to expect with the cosmic compass of the present design:

> Live then (Great soule of nature!) to asswage
> The savage dullness of this sullen age;
> Charm us to sence, for though experience faile,
> And reason too, thy numbers will prevaile.
> Then (like those Ancients) strike, and so command
> All nature to obey thy generous hand:
> None can resist, but such who needs will be
> More stupid then a Stone, a Fish, a Tree.
> Be it thy care our Age to new-create:
> What built a world may sure repayre a state.

As before, where Milton insists upon his own inheritance of divine and human literary lines and inspiration—Phoebus and Dante—Philips is deeply conscious of inhabiting and retreating to a particular historical and political place. It is usual to assume female poets' remoteness from politics and power,[16] but this, like the earlier Milton example, demonstrates not just an interest in such matters, but a vision that includes their relation to the writing self and private interests as well.

Philips's concluding lines contain two surprising literary gestures, and both encapsulate the adjustments in governing poetic between, on the one hand, Milton—the first half of the seventeenth century, and Renaissance poetry generally—and, on the other, the Restoration, Enlightenment epistemology, and its modern linguistic and desacramentalized legacy.[17] The first of these represents an Orphean career and destiny. That ultimate poet, when fully empowered by the ancients and the Renaissance, overwhelms all resistance to his combination of poetry and music, wresting responsive order from animals, plants, and stones, even indeed from the god of the underworld himself. As Milton presents such power in *Il Penseroso,* in order to free his bride Eurydice, Orpheus so enchanted that deity that he "made Hell grant what Love did seek" (*Poems,* 108). In Philips's contrast of modernity's savage, sullen dullness with Orpheus' sensual and harmonious charms, we recall too Milton's epithet for Orpheus as the Muse's "enchanting son, / Whom Universal nature did lament" (*Lycidas,* 59-60). Even in its generalized phrasing, Philips's gesture toward such inherited narrative under the category of "those ancients" manifests her age's deliberate displacement of the myths its predecessors reveled in to a fault. She enacts Abraham Cowley's 1656 dismissal of some of his contemporaries' classical borrowings as "the Cold-meats of the *Antients,* new-heated, and sew set forth."[18]

Philips's final ten lines begin by distinguishing between historical eras, its own recognized as "sullen," but available for "new creation" under the harmonious leadership represented by Lawes. The second literary surprise and reward of this conclusion reinvokes the Harmony that at the poem's outset had built the world and nature and served as its soul and agent. Here Harmony's creativity is reaffirmed, but also reassigned within the foregrounded present to the lesser task of "repayr[ing] a state," a phrase deftly balanced against "buil[ding] a World."

That culminating, if anticlimactic, distinction between divinely ordained cosmos and humanly constructed political organization embodies in miniature the radical shift in apprehended power from the Reformation orthodoxy with which the seventeenth century began to the crudely natural, fragile stasis a Hobbesian, indeed a modern, world has to settle for. The earlier model—epitomized, for example, in Philip Sidney's rehearsal of Menenius Agrippa's speech on the "body politic" in *Defense of Poesie* or in Shakespeare's *Coriolanus* 1.1—projects a macro/microcosmic, organic, natural, mutually dependent, analogical society, universe, and epistemology underwritten by the further analogue of the Church as the visible body of Christ. The later model—epitomized in the refigured "body politic" of the famous frontispiece of Hobbes's *Leviathan* (1651)— occurs not as an organic "true" analogy but a static "occasional" metaphor. It presents a human construct, a

controlled and controlling device through which political power manipulates its disciplined population into an instrument to achieve ideological purposes quite distinct from the instrument itself.[19]

Milton is often viewed as the late flowering of Renaissance literary performance because his practice so essentially assumes resemblance as the foundational principle and form of experience and knowing. But Philips inhabits the Cartesian alternative in which orders of thought, not orders of analogy, dominate. The later mode privileges analysis, scientific orders, and proof. It values discriminations of difference not identity; as a corollary, it values too the occasional finite likenesses it can discover, measure, and enumerate. Philips's development of Donne's compass conceit—discussed in Section II below—even more fully extends the Foucaultian typology to a point where signs displace resemblance and self-conscious awareness replaces the earlier divinely inspired language of things. Rather than the discovery of the anterior resonating truths of the older system, the new signs perform an arbitrary, fabricated, and now only certain or probable signifying function. They leave behind a cause/effect relation in favor of a sign/thing-signified one, and a random and circular divination in favor of progressive analyses and fabricated signs within systematized knowledge. What has been lost is both a guaranteed relationship between signs and their contents and the mediating bond of resemblance. In the new mode, a sign not only becomes "the *representativity* of the representation in so far as it is *representable,*" but it also inhabits "the interstices of ideas . . . in a perpetual state of decomposition and recomposition" (Foucault, *Order* 52, 59, 60-61, 63, 65, 67).

At the deepest level, the emerging epistemology thus reenacts the extraordinarily fluid contemporary politics. When the truthful figuration of the world moves out of language and into perception, language necessarily enters a period of transparency and neutrality.[20] Epistemologically and poetically—as politically and culturally—these signatures of seventeenth-century change mark Katherine Philips's literary practice, and this linguistic development—as we shall see in the next section—shows her world writing itself through Philips's poetry in a series of conventions of genre and mode that transcode social needs and social realities ranging well beyond the confining private interests that normatively bound occasional verses.

Fredric Jameson launches *The Political Unconscious* (1981) with the imperative "Always historicize!" an operation that distinguishes between the object and the subject, between the "objective" structures of a cultural text and the historical emergence of the audience's interpretive categories or codes (9). When Katherine Philips's **"Friendship in Emblem, or the Seale, to my dearest Lucasia"** (#29) borrows the famous metaphysical conceit of "stiff twin compasses" from John Donne's "A Valediction Forbidding Mourning," the cross-generational intertextualities again produce new insight into Philips's less familiar texts and contexts, but to discover them we must allow the interpretive act to resurrect some sedimentary master codes. The categories of analysis for these contrasting texts largely leave behind the earlier politics of individual biography in favor of the politics of social class and ideological program. They discover Katherine Philips in the peculiar political position of writing to legitimize a ruling class under temporary contestation.

Philips's subject matters include political affirmations, topographical descriptions, elegies, social and familial tributes, and translations of both lyrics and plays from the French—all established genres of the time—but something more than half of her 116 poems—and the work for which she is best known by far—treat female friendship—that is the "sentimental friendship" that Janet Todd defines as "close, effusive tie[s], revelling in rapture and rhetoric."[21] Since we are relatively unfamiliar with the literary systems—and, of course, the gender systems—that underwrite her subject matter, these poems tend to sound very much alike to our ears. We forget that on first glance virtually all Petrarchan sonnets, invoking the same metaphors and themes, will sound very much alike too, for the authors' deepest intentions honor the conventions they embrace. Practitioners of specialized literary modes measure their originality by increments that the uninitiated may find minute.

A recent commentator generalizes that Philips's celebrations of love lack "the dramatic tension between flesh and spirit that imparts nervous urgency to Donne's amatory verse,"[22] but a close look at the intertextualities of these two poems discovers a female poet not tamely reinscribing a male text, but embracing a female poetic that reaches beyond male discourse to an alternative French female literary tradition. Although her contemporaries understood this as shaping her practice—and despite the manifest political linkage—canonical literary inquiry has nearly always ignored the continental context that could make sense of the priorities of Philips's verse, just as vested academic specialties have drawn rigid barriers between Renaissance and eighteenth-century literatures, in effect assigning a great many English works between 1660 and 1700 to limbo.

The final stanzas of Donne's "Valediction Forbidding Mourning" draw out a justly famous metaphysical conceit likening a pair of lovers to the two feet of a compass, one centered and fixed soul, sometimes leaning after its oblique extension, sometimes drawing it erect. Their love with its compelling "inclination" and firmness achieves the perfection of circularity, ending with its own beginning. The compass image occurs as the final three of a total of nine quatrains.

> If they [our souls] be two, they are two so
>   As stiffe twin compasses are two,
> Thy soule the fixt foot, makes no show
>   To move, but doth, if the'other doe.
>
> And though it in the center sit,
>   Yet when the other far doth rome,

> It leanes, and hearkens after it,
>   And growes erect, as that comes home.
>
> Such wilt thou be to mee, who must
>   Like th'other foot, obliquely runne.
> Thy firmnes makes my circle just,
>   And makes me end, where I begunne.[23]

Ever since Izaak Walton's *Life of Donne,* this image has been singled out for particular notice, and it is often said to encapsulate the unique compounding of imagery and themes that characterize not only Donne's poetry but seventeenth-century metaphysical poetry generally.[24] Although ostensibly addressed to the poet's beloved, in fact this work, like Petrarchan "love" poetry generally, targets a male audience similar to the author in education, wit, and gender conditioning. Such poetry makes "love" the vehicle for meditations upon self, art, and the largest of human and divine truths.

There seems little doubt that Philips was deliberately borrowing the image from an acclaimed master. Her reinscription implies an analogous female poetic and a woman's community to create and receive such works. Tellingly, her poem does directly address its declared interlocutor. In its largest reaches, Philips's borrowing from Donne enfolds a gendered poetic politics within the historical and epistemological changes already noted. Philips takes up the image in stanzas 6-14 of a sixteen-quatrain, tetrameter lyric:

6

> The compasses that stand above
> Express this great immortall love;
> For friends, like them, can prove this true,
> They are, and yet they are not, two.

7

> And in their posture is express'd
> Friendship's exalted interest:
> Each follows where the other Leanes,
> And what each does, this other meanes.

8

> And as when one foot does stand fast,
> And t'other circles seeks to cast,
> The steddy part does regulate
> And make the wanderer's motion streight:

9

> So friends are only Two in this,
> T'reclaime each other when they misse:
> For whoso're will grossely fall,
> Can never be a friend at all.

10

> And as that usefull Instrument
> For even lines was ever meant;

So friendship from good-angells springs,
To teach the world heroique things.

11

As these are found out in design
To rule and measure every line;
So friendship governs actions best,
Prescribing Law to all the rest.

12

And as in nature nothing's set
So Just as lines and number mett;
So compasses for these being made,
Does friendship's harmony perswade.

13

And like to them, so friends may own
Extension, not division:
Their points, like bodys, separate;
But head, like soules, knows no such fate.

14

And as each part so well is knitt,
That their embraces ever fitt:
So friends are such by destiny,
And no Third can the place supply.

15

There needs no motto to the Seale:
But that we may the mine [mind?] reveale
To the dull ey, it was thought fit
That Friendship onely should be writt.

16

But as there is degrees of bliss,
So there's no friendship meant by this,
But such as will transmit to fame
Lucasia and Orinda's name.

(1.107-8)

In borrowing the figure of the compass, Philips recognizes a male society, its central figure Donne, the Platonizing of sexual love he/they so often articulated, and their characteristic superimposition of a metaphysical dimension upon a fully envisioned physical object and the processes appropriate to that object. But where Donne is engaged in an act of discovery, or what every schoolboy of his age would call an act of Invention, Philips performs an act of appropriation and interpretive reading. Where Donne fuses disparates together with striking originality, Philips breaks down, or de-fuses, the constituent parts of a borrowed conceit. Working within quite different literary conventions and epistemological assumptions, Philips at once reconstitutes a metaphysical conceit and de-intensifies its metaphysics into safe, stable assertion. Her form like her content glances as well at the emblem genre.

Philips invokes Donne's precedent as the initiating or ritual embodiment of her poetic "society." Her sixth stanza likens friends to a compass in being both one and two.

Her seventh highlights the compass's "posture," where "leaning" coincides with grasping each other's "meaning" with which it rimes, a compound of "inclination" and perfect understanding. The eighth stanza recasts Donne's chief conceit of one male circling foot and the other fixed female one. Politically, where Donne posits female sympathetic immobility and male freedom, Philips makes the participants interdependent mirroring peers with equal freedom and equal control.[25] Stanza 9 combines the numerical from stanza 6 with the stabilizing from stanza 8 to separate friends only in the ability of one to "reclaim" the other from an error. Donne's metaphysics, thus, transmutes to Philips's ethics.

It transmutes too to physics, and the technological developments of stanza 10 reflect late century prospects. Philips considers the scientific and mathematical processes of her "usefull Instrument" within a contemporaneous Royal Society discourse emphasizing *even lines, design, rule,* and *measure*. She translates number or quantity into equivalence or qualitative extension when the points of the compass, though separate, in fact signify not division but harmony, order, and completeness. Besides articulating the radical epistemological change detailed above, such technological specificity enacts a secular and female-empowering by-product of Puritan meditative traditions that disciplined the mind to careful interpretive scrutiny of the "creatures" and the "occasions" of daily life.[26]

Philips's final stanzas develop the abstract dimensions of her subject. They politicize friendship into the central governor of all actions and proffer it as a just and stable standard against the recognition—new and transforming to the century's thought—that "in Nature nothing's set," a point that Donne elsewhere phrases as "the new Philosophy calls all in doubt" ("The First Anniversary," 205). Moreover, her friendship "springs" from good Angels "To teach the world heroique things." The friendship Philips celebrates in this and similar lyrics compounds mutual feeling and knowledge with full understanding, growth, freedom, aspiration, enlightenment, even heroism, nobility, and divinity.

Philips's **"Friendship in Emblem"** collects and illuminates a congeries of contemporary fact and discourse as a prism does light. At a basic level, it aligns with the emphatically "social" poetry of those contemporary Cavalier writers Alexander Pope described as "the Wits of either Charles's days, / The Mob of Gentlemen who wrote with Ease."[27] Such poets enfold active courtly and military engagement within celebrations of each other and their networks of personal relations. They produce a poetry that mirrors the mannerism of contemporary art, since mannerism too emphasizes the author's sense of himself as an inheritor and a latecomer reconstituting his predecessors' achievements in a poetic characterized by polish, virtuosity, and a seemingly effortless savoir faire. Such poets "often decorat[e] the smaller concerns of life in a style forged to express the greater."[28]

Encoding contemporary attitudes toward originality and literary history, John Dryden rewrote Chaucer's *Canter-*

bury Tales, Shakespeare's *Antony and Cleopatra,* and even Milton's very recent *Paradise Lost,* and Alexander Pope recast Donne's *Satyres* into what he considered ordered, comprehensible clarity and refined expression. In a similar tidying or reclamation operation, Philips's **"Friendship in Emblem"** unties the knots of Donne's excessive *discordia concors* even as she reenvisions his "usefull Instrument" in up-to-date scientific grids. The era of such recastings was also an era of translations, not just Dryden's *Aeneid* and Pope's *Iliad,* but dozens of lesser exercises, including Philips's own. Both kinds of transliteration reflect a sense of cultural displacement, loss, and alienation, and urgently reach for transitioning, for larger meanings, and for reconnections to disrupted cultural continuities.

More largely, Philips's poem does for her age what she said friendship did for the heart. It "(like Moses bush presum'd), / Warm'd and enlighten'd, not consum'd." Where the classically learned Milton might have referred his views on friendship to the calm virtue of Cicero's *De amicitia,* Philips draws hers from a quite different and, of course, modern tradition. For both, friendship rests upon concords of goodness, wisdom, loyalty, and happiness. In the example of Milton's friendship for Lawes, social concord quickly gives a local habitation and a name to universal ordering principles of cosmic harmony. To understand Philips, we must draw upon other kinds of understanding. Milton was the most individualistic of men—the *OED* credits him with several of the earliest uses of the very word *individual*—but Philips was very much a social being, and came of age within a milieu formulating new structures of personal and social interaction. Her poetry draws strength from and popularizes a female version of the emerging conventions.

To understand Philips's insistence upon friendship, we must draw back briefly to a longer view of evidence. Virtually by definition, Calvinism generates what Max Weber describes as the "feeling of unprecedented inner loneliness of the single individual."[29] An imbalance toward individual autonomy will in time necessarily rebound in the direction of social reciprocity, and the seventeenth century acts out such a carom from the Reformation in multiplying new social quasi-institutions with at least skeletal organization—men's interest groups such as the Royal Society, for example, or semi-private gatherings at taverns, coffeehouses, and chocolate houses. Such social intensifications at convenient public sites signal the rise of a diverse gentry, with sufficient leisure for intellectual and social pursuits and ambitions and with new tastes, specializations, discourses. In the second half of the century, the Court itself was a coterie, defiantly defensive against Puritanism and anti-Catholicism, the more so from pre-Restoration confederacy on French soil. The very etymology of CABAL—precisely datable to a pamphlet of 1672—emblematizes the tendency.[30] Conventicle coreligionists translate exclusive associations based on common goals and strict loyalty even to the lower strata of society.

The seventeenth century empowered new ideals of personal friendship. For the young, the new boarding or "public" schools provided isolated environments and generational and academic disciplines that nurtured fellowships based on shared class, tastes, activities, and aspirations. They marked adolescence as an age chronologically prior to marriage during which the young could both define their identities and discover the "other." They fostered friendships grounded in an anthropological "spiritual kinship" modeled on the family that assumed reciprocal obligations, defended its members against external threats, and severely sanctioned failures to follow its rules. Gradually, this sort of extra-familial, voluntary, optional, and flexible society, free of self-interested motives, spread to later age groups. Sometimes *friendship* in the period shares the same vocabulary with *love,* love being "carnal" friendship or "tender" friendship. It can refer not only to everyday social relations, but also to unusually exalted associations.[31] The latter was of course rare, "once in three ages" according to Montaigne who coopts it for males on the grounds that women's souls are not "strong enough to endure the pulling of a knot so hard, so fast, and so durable." In deference to its specific recipient, Jeremy Taylor's 1657 *A Discourse of the Nature and Offices of Friendship, in a Letter to the Most Ingenious and excellent M[rs]. K[atherine]. P[hilips].* partly qualifies this gender exclusion.[32]

Among women, salons in private homes served overlapping purposes, being likewise exclusionary, predominantly single-sex, and with at least rudimentary form. Women's groups, however, organize not around subject matters but around personal styles. At the highest social levels, English female society imported French models of social deportment for defining and representing the self. Specifically, it borrowed the *précieux* discourse that more and more minimized objective content and disregarded data of work, family, practicality, and utility. As filtered socially downward, such cultural transformations were supported by a proliferation of prescriptive texts on proper social behaviors and collections of model conversations and letters.[33]

Many events of Philips's life conspired to ground the "style" of her friendship discourse. During her years at Mrs. Salmon's school for girls at Hackney, Philips formed a particular friendship with a classmate Mary Aubrey, dubbed "Rosania" in Philips's poetic friendship circle, a cousin of the chronicler John Aubrey. After moving with her newly remarried mother to Wales, Philips cited Anne Owen as "Lucasia" in no fewer than 28 poems that interweave celebrations of their friendship with daily occasions.[34] Besides friendship poems to "Ardelia," "Philoclea," "Valeria," and "Celemina," Philips developed a number of (at least) epistolary friendships with such prominent male figures as Jeremy Taylor ("Palaemon"), Sir Edward De[e]ring ("Silvander"), and Sir Charles Cotterell ("Poliarchus"). Her husband as "Antenor" and herself as "the matchless Orinda" also inhabit this apparently imaginary rather than formal society of friendship.[35]

Historically, such discourse reflects the French romances of Philips's reading, but to a modern feminist consciousness, it may also signal women claiming the power to name themselves in gestures at once mimetic and anti-patriarchal.[36]

It is no accident that this social remodelling invokes French romance and précieux traditions. The proudest curricular claim of the new schools for gentlemen's daughters that the young Philips attended was instruction in modern languages with readings in up-to-date French romances.[37] The post-Restoration publication of Philips's *Poems* insists upon her linguistic skills by presenting French texts on verso pages and her translation on matching recto pages.

In the middle decades of seventeenth-century England, allegiance to French literature—to French anything—was a political stance favoring the Stuart family and cause. Before her exile, Queen Henrietta Maria had energetically imported French social practices and ideals onto English soil, including a vogue for her gallant, courtly version of Platonic love modelled on the society of the Hôtel de Rambouillet and its dominant text D'Urfé's L'*Astrée* (1607-27). English versions of the practice are necessarily complexly layered when a French queen, conscious of cultural privilege and opportunity, imports a foreign text itself giving a Renaissance updating to Platonic love and seeks to impose such discourse upon the everyday life and society of its self-consciously different time and place.[38] Further layerings necessarily qualify Philips's late and provincial appropriations of original French sources, Henrietta Maria's influences, and continuously imported new French texts.

French preciosity provides Philips with both a rationale for her society of Platonic friendship and with some features of her poetic. The social and literary précieux movement flourishing in sixteenth- and seventeenth-century France presupposed exclusive and superior language, imagery, and society. Erica Veevers summarizes the style as

> a search for recondite and ingenious comparisons, which at the same time avoided archaic, pedantic, or vulgar expressions; and a dependence on antithesis, allegory, and abstraction, the aim of which was to communicate wittily with the group in ways which avoided obviousness and which often veiled the meaning from outsiders. At its best the style had distinction, at its worst it fell into affectations.[39]

In Odette de Mourgues's provocative summation, précieux literature constitutes "an art not of production but of consumption."[40] Formally, writers sought not originality, accuracy, or vigor of expression, but always to eschew low words, to reduce objects to one or more of their qualities, to take up only what could be contained within acknowledged and well-classified categories, to seek refuge in vagueness and the mechanical workings of formal logic, and in general to reduce the threatening complexity of reality and the contradictions of language to safe absolute assertions. They make considerable use of antitheses and hyperbole, but where antitheses normally provoke witty insight into the familiar, précieux antitheses proffer automatic associations of ideas and the reassuring operations of well-known mechanisms. Alexander Pope's praise of "Nature to advantage dressed, / What oft was thought, but ne'er so well expressed" might well describe the style but for its characteristic prolixity.[41]

Early précieux literary productions featured elaborate imagery and clever conceits—not unlike what students of English literature will know as Elizabethan Petrarchanism, Euphuism, handbook collections of rhetorical tropes and figures, and even metaphysical conceits. But because such poetry does not create new metaphors and in fact tends to kill the metaphors it borrows, its normal evolution is toward the abstract expression that predominates in late seventeenth-century English practice. At a late stage, metaphors are no longer required for expression at all,[42] and as we have seen, Philips often inhabits this stage, the Foucaultian era of linguistic transparency and neutrality noted at the end of Section I above.

To work our way through the formal features of this poetic is to array some characteristics of Philips's Friendship poetry. If the results strike a modern reader as hermetic, exclusionary, and overly circumstantial, it is precisely because they were designed to create these effects. When Philips appropriates Donne's compass image, she aims not to create a fresh metaphor, but to develop a stock comparison within a secure conventional pattern. From her removed vantage, she analyzes the likeness into parts and draws out all its logical consequences. Précieux hyperbole—and this category includes most of Philips's claims for her friendship with "Lucasia"—seeks to escape not just the complexity of reality, but even reality itself, and the interchangeability of their and her hyperbolic metaphors proves the gratuitousness of the device. What in Philips's **"Friendship in Emblem"** at first looks like a metaphysical gesture is merely an exercise in preciosity. We have here not a poetic of disquieting inquiry, not a teasing of reality, but an exercise that minimizes the importance of the feeling or idea it brings forward while deliberately removing it from the realm of actual experience.[43]

Philips's poetry—and précieux poetry in general—should not be dismissed as decadent by-products of excessively decorated and complacent elites. In the examples we have considered, the preciosity of her Donne analogue balances against or even over-balances a heightened awareness of what we saw in the Milton examples, political negotiations and her own and poetry's participation in history. Although précieux poetry may appear escapist, in fact it seeks to "shelter the delicate flowers of civilization from the rough winds of tempestuous times."[44] Précieux poets not only uphold the blessings of culture, they also mobilize in defense of peace, order, and high civilization and thrive by opposing political intrusions and historical chaos.

Such production records the complex nature of Katherine Philips's age, its undertow of relief and hope, its retreat to security and trust—fragile and doomed wishes in what had become a Hobbesian world. "Poliarchus's" introduction to Philips's collected works (1667) shows that from the outset **"Orinda"** was made representational of larger historical designs along these lines. Against the background of the plague and fire of 1666-67 and the preceding Civil War arise her "gentle and tender strains of Friendship"; they will, he hopes, "outlive all these dismal things to see the blessing of Peace, a conjuncture more suitable to their Nature, all compos'd of kindness; so that I hope Time it self shall have as little power against them, as these other storms have had" (*Poems* [1667] a2^{r-v}). In 1675 Milton's nephew, Edward Phillips (no relation), similarly judges her style as "suitable to the humour and Genius of these times."[45]

Against the chaos of the seventeenth-century's radical transformations of faith, knowing, social categories, and material culture, a world literally turned upside down, Katherine Philips bravely proffers what she has found to be true and worthy and transcendent, filtered through French conventions she saw as securing the English future. Her friendship expresses not so much an achieved state as the rather desperate hope that such an achievement might come to pass. For her, friendship can restore coherent virtue, order, and stability to the frenzied flux of the social and political worlds she inhabited.

For a young woman in the early 1660s such hopes might have held promise, but as additional decades marked the advance of the century, such hopes and such strengths seemed less and less realizable in the private and larger worlds. Thus Anne Killigrew (1660-85) speaks for the following generation in idealizing "True Friendship" as "a Rich Cordial" and "the sweet Refection of our toylsome State," and Lady Winchilsea similarly echoes "Orinda" in 1713 in identifying friendship as

> the Support of Human-kind;
> The safe Delight, the useful Bliss,
> The next World's Happiness, and this.[46]

As Killigrew sees it, however, modern friendship mixes ill with good, passes dross for gold, and "for one Grain of Friendship that is found, / Falshood and Interest do the Mass compound."[47] Elsewhere Killigrew—again by contrast with her deteriorated epoch—eulogizes Philips as a "Radiant Soul" and "*Albions* and her Sexes Grace," as one to whose laurel all other laurels once bowed and whose name is now fixed high among the Stars ("Upon the saying that my *Verses* were made by another").[48] Although we may set aside some of the extravagance of contemporary praise of "the matchless Orinda," adjusted understandings of Philips's literary universe, her gendered and generational differentiation, make it possible, I believe, to credit the reverence and wisdom that contemporaries found essentialized in her and that inspired a later generation of female poets with grateful awe.

Notes

1. Earl Miner, *The Restoration Mode from Milton to Dryden* (Princeton: Princeton University Press, 1974), 424.

2. Nancy K. Miller, *Subject to Change: Reading Feminist Writing* (New York: Columbia University Press, 1988), 28. In Earl Miner's exhaustive three-volume analyses of seventeenth-century poetry—to cite just one example—only some fourteen out of a total of 1200 pages so much as mention the names of women poets of the century, and only one poem on one page (*The Cavalier Mode from Jonson to Cotton* [Princeton: Princeton University Press, 1971], 301) by one poet, Katherine Philips, is presented for anything like its own case, and that with carefully couched condescension (*Cavalier* 222, 300, 302, 304). Anne Killigrew's name, it is true, appears on five pages, but only because Dryden (clearly Miner's favorite author) happened to write a famous ode to her. Miner dismisses Killigrew's own poetry damningly with the label "at best a second Katherine Philips" (*Restoration* 520).

3. Fredric Jameson, *The Political Unconscious: Narrative as a Socially Symbolic Act* (Ithaca: Cornell University Press, 1981), 20, 76, 98, 75.

4. Philips was born the year Milton's sonnet was written, 1632, and she had been dead three years when he published *Paradise Lost* (1667). Although Philips was born and died in London, where their paths might have crossed, she spent more than twenty of her thirty-three years in Wales and another in Ireland, where they could not. In the great chasm that divided the English population, Philips's sympathies were Royalist while Milton's were Republican in the extreme. If Philips accompanied her husband to Westminster when he sat with Parliament, she might have met Milton, but in any imaginable circumstances the two would have constituted a most unlikely conversational pairing.

5. Miner, *The Metaphysical Mode from Donne to Cowley* (Princeton: Princeton University Press, 1969), 195; *Restoration* 4, 7.

6. Helgerson, *Self-Crowned Laureates: Spenser, Jonson, Milton, and the Literary System* (Berkeley: University of California Press, 1983), *passim*.

7. *John Milton: Complete Poems and Major Prose*, ed. Merritt Y. Hughes (New York: Odyssey Press, 1957), 76-7. Hereafter cited as *Poems* within the text.

8. *The Collected Works of Katherine Philips, The Matchless Orinda*, ed. Patrick Thomas (Stump Cross, Essex: Stump Cross Books, 1990-93), 1.213, #94. Hereafter cited as *Works* within the text. Philips's original title reads *Poems By the most deservedly Admired, Mrs. Katherine Philips, The matchless Orinda. To which is added Monsieur Corneille's Pompey and Horace, Tragedies. With several other Translations out of French* (London, 1667). Hereafter cited as *Poems*. The heretofore most convenient version of her work is in volume I of *Minor Poets of the Caroline Period*, ed. George Saintsbury (Oxford: Clarendon Press, 1905).

9. Lauro Martines, *Society and History in English Renaissance Verse* (Oxford: Basil Blackwell, 1985), 1-4.

10. Philips, *Works* 1.69-75. See also Dorothy Merwin, "Women Becoming Poets: Katherine Philips, Aphra Behn, Anne Finch," *English Literary History* 57 (1990): 341.

11. Lawes well earned the subtitle of Willa M. Evans's biography, *Henry Lawes: Musician and Friend of Poets* (New York: Modern Language Association of America, 1941), by providing settings for some 80 of the century's poets, some prominent, some obscure (239-40), and it is easy to see why poets praise his shift away from the polyphonic madrigal that foregrounded musical complexity and toward the new fashion of declamatory or recitative song that highlighted their own art.

12. *John Milton: Poems: Reproduced in Facsimile from the Manuscript in Trinity College, Cambridge: With a Transcript* (Menston: Scolar Press, 1970), and similarly, *Poems 1645: Lycidas 1638* (Menston: Scolar Press, 1970).

13. Evans, *Henry Lawes,* 202, 205-6.

14. Philip W. Souers, *The Matchless Orinda* (Cambridge: Harvard University Press, 1931), 60; similarly Evans 202. "A Dialogue betwixt Lucasia & Rosania, Imitating that of Gentle Thirsis" (*Works* 197-8) seems also to glance at Lawes under the name of the role he played in Milton's *A Mask* of 1634 (Souers 57).

15. Michel Foucault, *The Order of Things: An Archaeology of the Human Sciences* (New York: Vintage Books, 1973), 42-3.

16. For example, Merwin, "Women Becoming Poets," 336, 342.

17. Malcolm Mackenzie Ross, *Poetry and Dogma: The Transfiguration of Eucharistic Symbols in Seventeenth Century English Poetry* (New Brunswick: Rutgers University Press, 1954), 18-19, 87, 181-2.

18. Abraham Cowley, "Preface to *Poems,*" in *Critical Essays of the Seventeenth Century,* ed. J. E. Spingarn (Bloomington: Indiana University Press, 1968), 2.89.

19. Michael Walzer, *The Revolution of the Saints: A Study in the Origins of Radical Politics* (Cambridge: Harvard University Press, 1965), 171-83.

20. Foucault, *Order,* 55.

21. Todd, *Women's Friendship in Literature* (New York: Columbia University Press, 1980), 3. See Harriette Andreadis, "The Sapphic-Platonics of Katherine Philips, 1632-1664," *Signs: Journal of Women in Culture and Society*: 15 (1989): 34-60.

22. Merwin, "Women Becoming Poets," 343. Philips borrows from Donne on other "friendship" occasions as well. See, for example, "Friendship's Mysterys, to my dearest Lucasia" (#17); "To the excellent M^rs. A[nne]. O[wen]" (#25); "To My excellent Lucasia, on our friendship" (#36); "To my dearest Antenor on his parting" (#54); and "Friendship" (#57).

23. *The Complete Poetry of John Donne,* ed. John T. Shawcross (Garden City: Anchor Books, 1967), 88.

24. Walton, *The Lives of John Donne, Sir Henry Wotton, Richard Hooker, George Herbert, and Robert Sanderson,* intro. George Saintsbury (London: Oxford University Press, 1966), 42.

25. Elaine Hobby, *Virtue of Necessity: English Women's Writing 1649-88* (Ann Arbor: University of Michigan Press, 1989), 138.

26. U. Milo Kaufmann, *The Pilgrim's Progress and Traditions in Puritan Meditation* (New Haven: Yale University Press, 1966), passim; Hilda L. Smith, *Reason's Disciples: Seventeenth-Century English Feminists* (Urbana: University of Illinois Press, 1982), 62-3.

27. Pope, Horace Imitation, Epistle 2.i.107-8; Miner, *Cavalier,* passim.

28. Helgerson, *Self-Crowned,* 201, 194-5.

29. Weber, *The Protestant Ethic and the Spirit of Capitalism,* trans. Talcott Parsons (New York: Charles Scribner's Sons, 1930), 104.

30. Germaine Greer et al., eds., *Kissing the Rod: An Anthology of Seventeenth-Century Women's Verse* (New York: Noonday Press, 1988), 257.

31. Maurice Aymard, "Friends and Neighbors," in *A History of Private Life,* ed. Philippe Ariès and Georges Duby, vol. 3 of *Passions of the Renaissance,* ed. Roger Chartier, trans. Arthur Goldhammer (Cambridge: Harvard University Press, 1989), 489, 466-7, 450.

32. Michel de Montaigne, *The Essays of Montaigne Done into English by John Florio* (1603), vol. 1, intro. George Saintsbury, *The Tudor Translations,* ed. W. E. Henley (London: David Nutt, 1892), 197, 200; Jeremy Taylor, *The Whole Works of the Right Reverend Jeremy Taylor, D. D.,* ed. Charles P. Eden, volume I (London: Longman, Brown, Green, and Longmans, 1854), especially 94-5.

33. Elizabeth C. Goldsmith, *"Exclusive Conversations": The Art of Interaction in Seventeenth-Century France* (Philadelphia: University of Pennsylvania Press, 1988), [Illegible Text] 47.

34. "Lucasia," like other of her code names, seems to derive from the plays of William Cartwright, a favorite of Queen Henrietta Maria and Royalist sympathizers, an associate of Henry Lawes, and the subject of Katherine Philips's first published poem (Thomas 1.7, #51). Sir Charles Cotterell ["Poliarchus"] was Charles II's master of ceremonies and politically Philips's most famous associate.

35. Souers, *Matchless,* 39.

36. Miller, *Subject to Change,* 29, building on Iragaray.

37. Kenneth Charlton, "The Educational Background," in *The Age of Milton: Backgrounds to Seventeenth-Century Literature,* ed. C. A. Patrides and Raymond B. Waddington (Manchester: Manchester University Press, 1980), 109-12. Students of English literature will understand the basic features of the romance genre from Sir Philip Sidney's *Arcadia.* Later French works extending the genre enjoyed wide popularity in England, and perhaps closest to Philips herself is her friend Cotterell's translation of de la Calprenède's *Cassandre* in 1652 (partial) and 1661 (complete) (Annabel Patterson, *Censorship and Interpretation: The Conditions of Writing and Reading in Early Modern England* [Madison: University of Wisconsin Press, 1984], 189-90, 264). Philips's non-dramatic translations include a 368-line version of one of Georges de Scudéry's pastorals, and the small volume of letters Philips left behind was also—it has been suggested—modelled on his sister Madeleine's epistolary romances (Alfred A. Upham, *The French Influence in English Literature from the Accession of Elizabeth to the Restoration* [New York: Octagon Books, 1965], 446-7).

38. Upham, *French Influence,* 327-31, 344-5, 363; Erica Veevers, *Images of Love and Religion: Queen Henrietta Maria and Court Entertainments* (Cambridge: Cambridge University Press, 1989), 16.

39. Veevers, *Images of Love,* 15.

40. Odette de Mourgues, *Metaphysical, Baroque and Précieux Poetry* (Oxford: Clarendon Press, 1953), 131-2.

41. de Mourgues, *Metaphysical,* 123, 125-7; Pope, *Essay on Criticism,* 297-8; Georges Mongrédien, *Les Précieux et les Précieuses* (n.p.: Mercure de France, 1963), 19.

42. de Mourgues, *Metaphysical,* 139, 125; Mongrédien, *Les Précieux,* 10, 13-15.

43. de Mourgues, *Metaphysical,* 123, 127, 129.

44. de Mourgues, *Metaphysical,* 116-17.

45. Edward Philips, qtd. in K. Philips, *Works,* 1:24.

46. Winchilsea quoted in K. Philips, *Works* 1.33.

47. Killigrew, "The Discontent," quoted in Ann Messenger, *His and Hers: Essays in Restoration and Eighteenth-Century Literature* (Lexington: University of Kentucky Press, 1986), 229.

48. See Greer, *Kissing,* 306.

Stella P. Revard (essay date 1997)

SOURCE: Revard, Stella P. "Katherine Philips, Aphra Behn, and the Female Pindaric." In *Representing Women in Renaissance England,* edited by Claude J. Summers and Ted-Larry Pebworth, pp. 227-41. Columbia: University of Missouri Press, 1997.

[*In the following essay, Revard compares critiques by male contemporaries of Philips and Aphra Behn.*]

In 1683, *Triumphs of Female Wit* appeared on the London scene, a slender volume that contained three Pindaric odes and a "Preface to the Masculine Sex" defending the right of women to pursue learning and most especially to use their wit to compose poetry. The first ode, "The Emulation," purports to be "Written by a Young Lady" and argues the case for female poets, maintaining that "the *Muses* gladly will their aid bestow, / And to their Sex their charming Secrets show" (5).[1] The ode following, ascribed to a Mr. H, challenges not only the rights the Young Lady claims for her sex but also her temerity in claiming these rights in a poetic form reserved, he asserts, for masculine composition.

> What daring *Female* is 't who thus complains,
>   In *Masculine* Pindarick Strains,
>   Of great *Apollo's Salique* Laws,
>   Both breaks it, and pretends that she
> Pleads only for her Native Liberty.
>
> (6)

It is not astonishing that a gentleman-poet of this era should argue against female rights, but it is rather astonishing that he should carry his argument even to the point of denying a specific verse form to females, claiming Pindaric ode and its poet (Pindar) for an all male preserve of pure poetry. We might ask indeed whether Mr. H's words are only an address to the presumptuous Young Lady of the Pindaric or whether in truth he was aiming his objections at one of the most celebrated women poets of the 1680s, a poet who was in fact employing Pindarics for a wide range of her verses, which were on many occasions as diverse as saluting fellow poets on their work to addressing compliments to the king himself. The woman poet was, of course, Aphra Behn, not only the leading poet-playwright of her time but also, following in the footsteps of Abraham Cowley, its leading Pindarist.

With the publication of his *Pindarique Odes* in 1656, Cowley largely invented the genre as it came to be practiced in the seventeenth century. His odes in irregular metrical patterns and irregularly numbered stanzas or sections were free imitations of the ancient Greek poet, and in the posthumous *Works* published in 1668 became his favorite form of address to a poetic subject. Two of his 1668 Pindarics were directed, in fact, to Katherine Philips, the first in commendation of her poems, the second commemorating her death. That both poems use the Pindaric genre to celebrate a woman poet is not without interest to us, for both Pindarics raise many of the same questions about women and poetry that the 1683 volume, *Triumphs of Female Wit,* raises—that is, the acceptability of a woman pursuing learning and contesting in the domain of poetry that had been almost exclusively male.

Katherine Philips's success as a poet is one of the arguments that Mr. F, the writer of the third Pindaric in the collection, uses to assert that women should be permitted access, along with males, to learning since they could be, like Philips—that is, Orinda—successful as poets. Mr. F, adopting a female persona in this Pindaric, pleads: "Did good Apollo e're deny / Charms to *Orinda's* Poetry?" (13). In both his Pindarics Cowley ostensibly takes the same position on Philips and her poetry. He has come, after all, to praise and to use the Pindaric medium to render that praise.[2] But the very questions that he raises about Philips and her poetry illustrate the difficulty that a male poet has in praising a woman who is neither a mistress nor a patron nor a sovereign, but is, rather, a so-called peer in the poetic profession. In assessing the acceptability of a woman as a poetic equal, Cowley faces some of the same stumbling blocks that the three Pindaric poets grapple with in *Triumphs of Female Wit*. A man's view of a "learned" woman almost always involves a man's view of women in general, and assessment of her literary achievement cannot take place without considering the acceptability of her competing "equally" in the domain of poetic performance. At stake is more than the man's monopoly of wit. For if a man and a woman compete in a literary contest and he "loses," as a man he also loses the right to dominate in other areas. This is precisely what the Young Lady of the *Female Wit* volume argues.

> For should we understand as much as they,
>   They fear their Empire might decay.
>   For they know Women heretofore
> Gain'd Victories, and envied Laurels wore:
>   And now they fear we'll once again
>   Ambitious be to reign
> And to invade the Dominions of the Brain.

(2)

I do not doubt Cowley's real admiration for Katherine Philips nor the cordial relations between the two poets. Katherine Philips, after all, visited Cowley in his retirement at Chertsey and addressed a commendatory Pindaric to him, **"Upon Mr. Abraham Cowley's Retirement"** (*Poems* [London, 1667], 122-24). She not only expressed admiration for him as a man and poet but also conferred the additional compliment by addressing her words in a medium—the Pindaric—that Cowley had made his own.[3] In a way Cowley's Pindarics to Philips merely return the compliment in kind. I also recognize that the effusiveness of Cowley's address to Philips is part and parcel of the genre of commendatory poetry in the seventeenth century. In a genre marked by extravagance—a genre practiced by both male and female poets—it is difficult to sift out the sincere from the overweening compliment. But at issue here is not whether Cowley liked Katherine Philips and admired her poetry. Jean Loiseau contends convincingly that Cowley appreciated her virtue, her hatred of vice and ugliness, and her cultivation of pure and disinterested friendship.[4] But did he truly regard her, as both his poems say, as his equal as a poet? For this is the question: How was the female poet accepted vis-à-vis the male poet as a fellow practitioner of poetry? Was there a real equality in the arts? Not only Cowley but also the other poets who address poems to Philips maintain there was. Should we believe them?

Cowley's first Pindaric to Philips was one of two commendatory poems printed in the 1664 edition of Philips's *Poems*; it was reprinted together with the funeral ode in the 1667 edition of *Poems* along with a preface on her works and with other commendations of Philips by the earl of Orrery, the earl of Roscommon, Philo-Philippa, James Tyrrell, and Thomas Flatman—Tyrrell's and Flatman's odes were also in Pindarics.[5] All of the commendatory poems, even that of Philo-Philippa—allegedly the only female voice—remark on Philips's sex as well as her status as a poet. It seems an unavoidable issue. None praise her simply as a poet. Like these other commendatory poems, Cowley's Pindarics begin by looking at the woman first. The issue of sex becomes so important a motif that the assessment of Philips as a poet takes second place. But in this he is representative of most of Philips's male admirers; it was apparently almost impossible in this era to be gender blind. Further, both of Cowley's Pindarics emphasize the rivalry between men and women poets as well as the rivalry between men and women. Beauty and wit are the themes, and they are interconnected.

Almost inevitably involved in any consideration of a literary contest between men poets and women poets is that of the amatory contest between men and women, a contest in which men traditionally award the victory to women. As Cowley noted in his anacreontic "Beauty," when women contest with men in affairs of love, their advantage of beauty allows them to carry the day. No need for them to put on arms in the contest of love; they win without them:

> Who can, alas, their strength express,
> Arm'd, when they themselves undress,
> *Cap-a-pe* with *Nakedness*?

(ll. 21-23)[6]

What happens, however, when women seek to dominate in that other contest too? In his first ode, "On *Orinda's* Poems," Cowley simply extends the amatory to the literary contest, protesting that men who have been constrained to submit to Woman's beauty must now—in the case of Orinda—submit to her wit:

> We allow'd You Beauty, and we did submit
>   To all the Tyrannies of it;
> Ah! Cruel Sex, will you depose us too in Wit?
>   *Orinda* does in that too raign,
> Does Man behind her in Proud Triumph draw,
> And Cancel great *Apollo's* Salick Law.

(1:1-6)[7]

While connecting these two "supposed" contests appears at first to confer a gracious compliment, it actually limits the woman that it seems to praise, linking her wit to her beauty and confining her to a sphere where she is judged as a woman first and a poet second. Throughout this poem and its sequel, "On the Death of Mrs. *Katherine Philips*," Cowley never passes beyond the easy compliment to Philips's beauty and the virtues of her sex to evaluate the quality and substance of her poetry. The funeral Pindaric opens, like the ode "On *Orinda's* Poems," with a reference to Philips's beauty, deploring (as Dryden later deplored in his Pindaric for Anne Killigrew) that the smallpox that killed her assaulted first "The Throne of Empress Beauty, ev'n the Face" (1:8) before it overthrew "th' inward Holiest Holy of her Wit" (1:19). The funeral Pindaric is a lament for Philips's death; the first Pindaric, written when Philips was alive, purports, however, to be on Orinda's poetry, not on Orinda. Some of the other commendatory poems of the 1667 volumes at least mention one or another of Philips's works (often the ambitious translations of Corneille); Cowley makes no direct reference to either Philips's poetry or her translations.

Whereas it is not rare for commendatory poems to focus on the person, rather than on the work, Cowley in his complimentary poems to male writers and artists pays attention to the work also. When he addresses an ode to Thomas Hobbes, it is not Hobbes's virtue and wit that he praises, but Hobbes's accomplishment in having brought philosophy beyond the age of Aristotle into the modern era. Similarly, his Pindaric to Dr. Harvey may begin with an elaborate and showy amatory myth. But Cowley in comparing Harvey to Apollo pursuing Daphne is alluding to Harvey's scientific work, not to his amorous adventures. Like Apollo, Harvey pursued a Daphne-Nature until she revealed "her" secrets to him. The comparison leads us not to the man but to the scientist. In his poem "On the Death of Sir *Anthony Vandike, the famous Painter*" (*Miscellanies*, 9), Cowley is quite specific in applauding Van Dyke's excellence in drawing, considering the artist first, before he comments on the virtue of the man:

> His All-resembling *Pencil* did out-pass
> The mimick *Imag'ry* of *Looking-glass,*
> Nor was his *Life* less perfect than his *Art,*
> Nor was his *Hand* less *erring* than his *Heart*

> (ll. 15-18)

All these complimentary poems to men are extravagant; but all look at the artist, the writer, the scientist first, then at the man. But in his odes to Katherine Philips, he never lets us forget that we are looking at best at a most curious phenomenon—a woman who writes. Both odes dwell therefore on the qualities that most properly characterize woman: above all, beauty and virtue first and then wit—female wit.

In the first Pindaric, Cowley launches a witty protest that women possess an unfair advantage over men merely because they are women; their sex alone confers beauty, virtue, and fecundity—all female qualities. Now, in aspiring to wit, women conspire to take away the weapon that amorous male poets have used in the battlefield of love to secure themselves against women's natural advantages. The contest of the sexes is an antique one—going back at least to Ovid and his taking arms against the all conquering mistress and her artillery of beauty. Cowley tells us that Orinda has turned this contest topsy-turvy, now taking arms against men in the contest of wit too and, winning

that, "she / Turn'd upon Love himself his own Artillery" (1:17). How seriously should we take this poetic sparring? These witty protests are little different from those the beaux of Restoration comedy use against the supposedly triumphant belles; Cowley has only removed the amatory combat to the realm of poetry. The compliments Cowley confers on Philips resemble those that Congreve's Mirabell resigns to Millamant. When Fainall comments, for example, that Millamant has wit, Mirabell retorts, "She has Beauty enough to make any Man think so; and Complaisance enough not to contradict him who shall tell her so" (*The Way of the World,* 1:i).[8] Apropos of this question of beauty and wit (but now on the subject of male and female poets), another quotation of Congreve springs to mind. In his "Notes on Ovid's Art of Love" Congreve once more resorts to an allusion to women's beauty as a measure for her wit, commenting on the rivalry between Pindar and the ancient Greek poetess Corinna, "who as we are told won the Prize of Poetry four or five Times from *Pindar*; however those that say so, own her Beauty contributed much to that Advantage."[9] We must be suspicious, therefore, of any reference to women's wit that couples it with an aside on her beauty. Cowley has done this consistently in the first two sections of the Pindaric. In section 3, when he appears at last to be discussing Philips's poetry—"thy well knit sense, / Thy numbers gentle, and thy Fancies high" (3:4-5)—he gives all away by once more linking Philips's poetic skills to her beauty, as he completes the rhyme: "Those as thy forehead smooth, these sparking as thine eye" (6).[10] This courtly game confers apparent victory on women but reserves real power for men. By the very wit of his own verse, Cowley has demonstrated that neither Orinda nor any other female poet can carry away the laurels in a real contest of wit. Cowley retains supremacy, even as he "says" he gives it away.

Another issue in this contest between men and women is the question of women's "natural" creativity. Should you not be content, Cowley asks Philips, that Mother Cybele has made you fecund of womb (the sex's natural prerogative), but must you aspire to exceed men in being fecund of brain—men's (he would imply) natural prerogative. Again Cowley appears to award Philips supremacy in creative intellect, as in wit, as he comments how easily she brings forth the children of her brain. She has as many literary offspring as the prolific "*Holland* Countess" has children. But is it praise of a poet's prolific production to link it to another female's fecundity in the proper female sphere of reproduction? The comparison of these two kinds of "production" reminds us of one of the basic issues this age and those that follow often pondered: should women exercise creativity beyond the domestic sphere? Nature gave woman creative energy for the procreation of children, which, when employed elsewhere, may threaten that natural creativity. Mr. H in *Triumphs of Female Wit* reminds the Young Lady of Nature's true design for women's creative impulses: "But sure she ne're designed it / To make your Brains prolifick, or your wit" (7). Cowley never directly criticizes Philips's prolific production of poetry; he doesn't have to. Merely raising the question is enough to remind us that a woman's prolificacy can be misplaced.

Cowley reserves, however, as men traditionally do, his greatest praises for Philips's virtue. So preeminent is she in virtue that she wins through it victory not only over male poets but also over all previous female competitors:

> *Orinda's* inward virtue is so bright,
> That like a Lanthorn's fair inclosd Light,
> It through the Paper shines where she do's write.
>
> (4:7-9)

At this point Cowley comes as close as he ever does to commenting on Philips's poetry. He praises her mastery of the themes of "Honour and Friendship"; these are the "instructive Subjects of her pen" (4:14). But even here he is qualifying his praise, for he is suggesting that it is Philips's preeminence in virtue—woman's proper sphere—that makes her acceptable as a poet. In a poetical as well as a societal context, a woman may excel in virtue. In teaching "Arts, and Civility," she may be so successful that "she overcomes, enslaves, and betters Men" (4:16-17). Virtue is the highest thing that any woman poet—indeed any woman—can aspire to. In commending Philips's virtue as her supreme achievement, Cowley is not alone. Thomas Flatman sums Philips up in the last line of his Pindaric: "all that can be said of vertuous Woman was her due" (*Poems*, sig. f.).[11] The best way for a man to deal with a woman competitor in poetry as in life is to deify her—and so remove her from the competition. Effectively, this is what Cowley does in the final section of "On *Orinda's* Poems." He places Philips in the special category of "virtuous" women. Comparing her to Boadicia—the warlike British queen who fought against, but failed to conquer, the Romans—he awards Philips the "Roman" victory in poetic arms that Boadicia coveted in battle. By deferring to yet another kind of contest, Cowley successfully evades the real question of women's place in poetry's and learning's sphere.

Cowley's funeral Pindaric takes up the same issue of Philips's poetic status, without arriving at any more satisfactory conclusion. It substitutes for the contest in arms of the first ode the famous beauty contest of the three goddesses for the apple. Here Apollo takes Paris's place as judge, presiding over a contest of literary merit and awarding Orinda the prize that Sappho and the Muses stand by and covet. Beauty is not ostensibly the issue here, but it can hardly be dismissed from the reader's mind, as Orinda wins the poetic apple, thereby becoming the "goddess of beauty" for the literary world. Cowley has also deftly confined the competition to woman against woman. Just as he had in the final sections of the previous ode when he alludes to Boadicia as the exemplar of the military "female," he allows Philips to excel in competition with other women.

> *Orinda* on the Female coasts of Fame,
> Ingrosses all the Goods of a Poetique Name.
> She does no Partner with her see,

> Does all the business there alone, which we
> Are forc'd to carry on by a whole Company.
>
> (3:16-20)

Any question of comparative talent or achievement or of admitting women poets into a competition with men Cowley simply bypasses. When he allows men into the competition, he couples wit with virtue. Virtue once more serves to assure Orinda the prize in this poem as in the last: "*Orinda* does our boasting Sex out-do, / Not in Wit only, but in Virtue too" (4:8-9). Cowley has so manipulated the terms of the contest that while seeming to award the highest poetic laurels to Philips, he has done no more than concede that she is the best of the *female* poets. By employing the language of courtly compliment for his address to Philips, he announces to his audience that he is engaging in the game of sexual diplomacy. The issue of Philips's status as a poet is never really entertained. Cowley confers only such supremacy in beauty and wit and virtue as men have always conferred on women whom they court poetically, reserving (tacitly) real intellectual superiority for males and male poets.

It is certainly no accident that many of the arguments that Cowley uses when he appears to compliment female wit reappear in *Triumphs of Female Wit*. There, however, Mr. H argues the countercase—women's inferiority in the intellectual sphere. Like Cowley, he is lavish with courtly compliment, graciously granting women supremacy in "captivating hearts." But in return for such supremacy women should be content to remain the object of wit and wisdom and must not dig and delve in "Apollo's mines." The last part of Mr. H's Pindaric takes up an issue that Cowley does not touch on, but one that both the Young Lady in "The Emulation" and Aphra Behn raise: the right of women to the education of the schools. The Young Lady protests:

> But they [men] refuse to let us know
> What sacred Sciences doth impart
> Or the mysteriousness of Art,
> In Learning's pleasing Paths deny'ed to go
> From Knowledge banish'ed, and their Schools;
> We seem design'd alone for useful Fools . . .
>
> (2:4-9)

She takes the view—in fact a Miltonic one—that knowledge is necessary to the confirmation of virtue and the progress of the soul. Women, after all, have souls just as worthy and noble as men. Mr. H counters her arguments fiercely, using in fact another Miltonic argument—Christ's from *Paradise Regained*—that knowledge does not in itself bestow virtue: "'Tis not a studeous life that brings / Knowledge of revealed things" (6:9-10). In fact, he continues, women may be seeking at their soul's peril "that full view of intellectual Light" (7:4-5). We are never far in the seventeenth century from the fatal tree of knowledge and the trespass of mother Eve against it. By seeking to gain the "*Tree of Knowledge*," he cautions, women will surely lose the "*Tree of Life*." With biting sarcasm he commends their would-be quest:

May you walk safe in Learnings milky way,
     Know all that Men and Angels say,
Expand your Souls to Truth as wide as day.

(7:8-10)

But at the same time he warns the lady against ambitious pride—Eve's and Satan's sin. The learned Young Lady is firmly put in her place.

This lively debate over women's education is one in which Aphra Behn—the era's leading female poet after the death of Katherine Philips—also had a stake. In a Pindaric ode that she sent to Thomas Creech, commending the translation of Lucretius that he published in 1682, Behn raises the issue of women's exclusion from the universities. Behn's poem, however, is not per se a feminist protest. The ode is framed as a compliment to the learned Creech, a scholar at Wadham College, Oxford, and Creech published it with other commendatory poems in the reissue of his translation in 1683.[12] Whatever other issues Behn takes up, she is generous in looking first and foremost at Creech as a learned and accomplished translator of Lucretius. Both Behn's poem and the Young Lady's Pindaric appeared in the same year—the protest for women's education was something very much on the tongues of women in this decade. After Behn offers Creech the usual opening compliments on his work, she points out how his translation has brought the classical author, Lucretius, to a new set of readers—women. While she warmly thanks Creech for enlightening women such as herself, she ironically criticizes the system that has withheld classical authors from women by denying them education in Latin and Greek that would have enabled them to read him themselves.

That she chooses Pindaric ode as a verse form both for her compliments to the learned Creech and for her protest against the exclusion of women from the classics is yet another irony. For Behn could not have come to Pindar or the Pindaric ode—just as she could not have read Lucretius—on her own. To do so she needed the help of a learned man—in this case, Abraham Cowley, whom she openly acknowledges as her mentor in this mode.[13] The form of Pindaric ode that she wrote is, of course, the Cowleian Pindaric, whose metrical irregularities differ markedly from the absolute regularities of true Pindaric ode. It is a verse form that Cowley invented to approximate Pindaric ode and that poets of the seventeenth century, who, like Behn, lacked knowledge of Greek, followed, perhaps thinking that they were writing true Pindaric odes.

Behn's ode to Creech is couched in the courtliest of language. She learned not only her Pindarics from Cowley but also the art of playing at the game of courtly compliment. She addresses Creech as Daphnis and in speaking to and of him assumes the attitude of a shepherdess to an admired shepherd. Much of Behn's own verse was pastoral and courtly. Both in her plays and in her commendatory verse, Behn often plays the game of sexual politics, adopting the language of Ovidian love combat for her address

to men and poets alike. In not relinquishing that artillery of love poetry in her poem to Creech, she imitates the tactics of male writers such as Cowley and their use of a smoke screen of overblown compliments. Behn poses in her address to Creech-Daphnis the kind of courtly rivalry that we saw in Cowley's own address to Philips.

Behn is the mistress of this coy game. She knows how to use the so-called advantages of her sex. Sometimes, however, she can be perfectly straightforward—even gender blind, as she addresses a fellow playwright, such as Edward Howard, warmly encouraging him not to forsake playwriting despite the failure of his play. On the other hand, when she addresses Rochester, whom she idolizes, she is all melting female before the superior master. She can be ambiguous also, as she is in her Pindaric ode to Dr. Burnet, and use courtly language not to compliment the man but to maintain a discreet distance from him and his importuning "Pen." Dr. Burnet was trying to persuade Behn to write an ode to welcome William III to the throne. Behn, who was a Jacobite loyal to the overthrown James II, plays the courtly game to refuse Burnet's request. She does this by assuming the part of the love-struck maid resisting the wit of a persuasive seducer. So she overpraises Burnet and underpraises herself as a poor weak female, thus neatly sidestepping Burnet's request and exposing his less than honorable purpose. This is exactly what we would expect from the author of *The Rover* and the love songs to Lysander, a lover whose insincerity and faithlessness she exposes in her own courtly fashion.

Thus, when we look at Behn's fulsome compliments in the Creech poem to the learned Daphnis, we may be just a little suspicious of her ultimate design. Is she criticizing the learned world of Oxford University that excludes women from its portals even as she appears to compliment one of its shining lights? First of all, I do not doubt Behn's basic admiration for Creech and his translation of Lucretius. Her Pindaric goes beyond the easy courtly compliment: throughout she commends Creech's achievements in Englishing Lucretius in a correct and effective manner. However much she may flatter Creech in his persona as the young Daphnis, she pays him the ultimate tribute of dealing with his scholarship first, his pleasing person second. Although we need not suspect the sincerity of her praise, we cannot ignore gender considerations. Can a woman poet set aside the attitudes of the male establishment toward women when she addresses a man on the subject that necessarily involves the male exclusion of women? On the surface Behn deftly plays the part of a woman content to sit at Creech's feet and bask in the afterglow of his brilliance, accepting, as men like Mr. H in his rejoinder to the Young Lady advised, to humbly sup at the table of man's knowledge. "Thou great Young Man!" she begins,

Permit amongst the Crowd
Of those that sing thy mighty Praises lowd,
My humble *Muse* to bring its Tribute too.

(ll. 1-3)[14]

In an almost coquettish way she apologizes for her "Womannish Tenderness" (l. 14); she had intended to write a strong manly verse, but she is overcome by her emotion. Daphnis kindles a fire in admiring souls. Shepherds and nymphs alike "strow Garlands" at Daphnis's feet, for he conquers, not only in the art of verse but also in the arts of love.

> Advance young *Daphnis* then, and mayst thou prove
> Still Sacred in thy Poetry and Love.
> May all the Groves with *Daphnis* Songs be blest,
> Whilst every Bark is with thy Distichs drest.
> May Timerous Maids learn how to Love from thence
> And the Glad Shepherd *Arts of Eloquence.*
>
> (ll. 127-32)

Is it the man or the translator that Behn is praising as she crosses the boundary from the language of compliment to the language of courtship?

Amid her hyperbolic praise of Creech and his translations, Behn includes some comments on classical learning that can hardly reflect favorably on Creech and his Oxford peers. While in context her comments appear laudatory, she adds a personal history that tells us something different.

> Let them admire thee on—Whilst I this newer way
>   Pay thee yet more than they:
> For more I owe, since thou hast taught me more,
> Then all the mighty Bards that went before.
> Others long since have Pal'd the vast delight;
> In duller *Greek* and *Latin* satisfy'd the Appetite:
> But I unlearn'd in Schools, disdain that mine
> Should treated be at any Feast but thine.
>
> (ll. 17-24)

This looks on the surface like a straightforward thank-you from someone ignorant of classical tongues to the translator who has provided her with access to a text in Latin that she could not have read before. But Behn does not stop here. Instead she goes on to criticize a nation and an educational system that denies knowledge to those like her solely on the basis of sex.[15]

> Till now, I curst my Birth, my Education,
> And more the scanted Customes of the Nation:
> Permitting not the Female Sex to tread,
> The Mighty Paths of Learned Heroes dead.
> The God-like *Vergil,* and great *Homers* Verse,
> Like Divine Mysteries are conceal'd from us.
>   We are forbid all grateful Theams,
>   No ravishing thoughts approach our Ear,
>   The Fulsom Gingle of the times,
> Is all we are allow'd to understand or hear.
>
> (ll. 25-34)

Behn is too clever a writer, however, to allow this digressive passage to become the prelude to a peroration on the male-dominated educational system. No, instead she passes on to more praise of the translator who has so benefited the "ignorant" sex. Yet if we read the parable that follows ironically—as, I believe, Behn intended it to be read—we see that she has not at all changed her tune, only her tactics.

In olden times, she begins, the poet was the means by which knowledge of the gods and their laws was brought to men. He not only educated but also civilized men, bringing them from the savage woods to social order.[16] Now, proposes Behn slyly, the poet-translator has conferred a similar benefit on women, not only alleviating their ignorance and civilizing them but granting them "equality" with men as well.

> So thou by this Translation dost advance
> Our Knowledg from the State of Ignorance,
> And equals us to man.
>
> (ll. 41-43)

With her gracious compliment to the divine powers of poet-translator, Behn ironically enlists Creech in the cause of female rights, making him the benefactor of women and the one who will bring them closer to equality with men. Yet not for a moment has she quit her stance as earnest admirer: "Ah how can we, / Enough Adore, or Sacrifice enough to thee!" (ll. 43-44). Reassuming the posture of adoring female before wise instructor male, she lauds Creech for making all this terribly difficult philosophy comprehensible to the inferior sex, decking, as she says, the "Mystick terms of Rough Philosophy" in "so soft and gay a Dress" that "they at once Instruct and Charm the Sense" (ll. 45-49). Behn has learned a tactic from Milton's Eve on how to soothe the ego of an Adamic don explaining "angelic texts." Why, she seems to say, he has explained everything so clearly that even a woman can understand it.

Behn's poem to Creech was read by her time as gracious praise, not as a female's protest. J. W. in a Pindaric on Behn summed it up: "Well has she sung the learned *Daphnis* praise, / And crown'd his Temples with immortal Bays."[17] By imbedding her protest for women's rights in a poem that the male establishment would read as praise of one of their own, Behn has played a rather subtle double game. The Young Lady of "The Emulation" could be dismissed by a gentlemanly wit like Mr. H as merely hysterical and shrill—and her poem forgotten. Behn's more subtle attack could not so easily be shrugged off.

Behn did not, however, escape the fate of Katherine Philips or that of other women poets of her era, as being cited as a "female" poet, rather than as a poet. As the commendatory verses to the 1684 and 1697 editions of her verse attest, she received the same shallow compliments, being dismissed merely as the "wonder of [her] Sex." Often compared, as Philips had been, to the Muses, to Sappho, and even to Orinda, her female predecessor, she could reach no further than combining the "Beauties of both Sexes"—a female sweetness with a manly grace.[18] Cowley had said a similar thing about Philips (assuming that masculinity is a necessary juncture to femininity to produce poetry). She is lauded, also, as Philips was, in masculine Pindaric strains. But she does not rise so high as to be, as Cowley had been called, Pindar's equal. She is permitted to dwell, however, in the company of Virgil's

Shade and Ovid's Ghost and with Cowley, the first of England's poets.[19] Having no Latin and no Greek, Behn rose as high as a woman might in her age—to be included in a literary Elysium as a companion to Pindar's translator, Cowley.

Notes

1. I am grateful to Warren Cherniak for his illuminating discussions on Aphra Behn and her place in the Restoration. See his book: *Sexual Freedom in Restoration England* (Cambridge: Cambridge University Press, 1995). My thanks also to Achsah Guibbory and Robert Hinman, who read an early version of this paper and offered helpful commentary. *Triumphs of Female Wit, In Some Pindarick Odes, or The Emulation. Together with an Answer to an OBJECTOR against Female Ingenuity, and Capacity of Learning. Also, A Preface to the Masculine Sex, by a Young Lady* (London: T. Malthus, 1683). I am indebted to Warren Cherniak for pointing out this collection to me.

2. Robert Hinman describes Cowley's pindarics on Philips as unqualified praise: "his lofty eulogy of the matchless Orinda's verse celebrates the emergence of woman as man's intellectual peer, and his elegy for her includes his view (also held by Milton) of the necessary relationship between successful poetry and virtue." See *Abraham Cowley's World of Order* (Cambridge: Harvard University Press, 1960), 83-84.

3. For a description of the circumstances of Philips's visit, see Philip Webster Souers, *The Matchless Orinda* (Cambridge: Harvard University Press, 1931), 242. See "An ode upon retirement, made upon occasion of Mr. Cowley's on that subject," *The Collected Works of Katherine Philips, The Matchless Orinda,* ed. Patrick Thomas (Stump Cross, Eng.: Stump Cross Books, 1990), 1:193-95.

4. Jean Loiseau, *Abraham Cowley: sa vie, son oeuvre* (Paris: Henri Didier, 1931), 166.

5. A facsimile of Philips's 1667 volume is now available. See *Poems (1667)* (New York: Scholars' Facsimiles and Reprints, 1992).

6. "Anacreontiques," in *Miscellanies, The Works of Mr. Abraham Cowley* (London, 1668), 33.

7. Verses written on several occasions," *Works,* 2-4.

8. *The Way of the World* in *The Complete Works of William Congreve,* ed. Montague Summers (Soho: The Nonesuch Press, 1922), 3:18.

9. Congreve, "Notes to Ovid's Art of Love," *Works,* 4:130.

10. Also see the Earl of Orrery's poem to Philips that links poetry and love:
    > In me it does not the least trouble breed,
    > That your fair Sex does Ours in Verse exceed,
    > Since every Poet this great Truth does prove,

Nothing so much inspires a Muse as Love.
> (*Poems* [London, 1667], sig. b)

11. The Earl of Roscommon links Philips's supremacy in virtue to her supremacy in a virtuous game of love:
    > Vertue (dear Friend) needs no defence,
    > No arms, but its own innocence;
    > Quivers and Bows, and poison'd darts,
    > Are only us'd by guilty hearts.

    > (sig. b2)

    James Tyrell links virtue and wit:
    > Whether her Vertue, or her Wit
    > We chuse for our eternal Theme,
    > What hand can draw the perfect Scheme?

    > (sig. e)

    When Milton published *Paradise Lost* in 1667, how many admirers linked his wit to his virtue and his beauty?

12. "To the Unknown DAPHNIS in his Excellent Translation of Lucretius," in *T. Lucretius Carus, The Epicurean Philosopher, His Six books. De Natura Rerum, Done into English VERSE with NOTES.* The Second Edition, Corrected and Enlarged. (Oxford: L. Lichfield, 1683). Behn's poem is signed and dated London, January 25, 1682. Behn published her own version of the ode in 1684; it was reprinted after her death in the 1697 edition: Mrs. A. Behn, *Poems upon Several Occasions; with a Voyage to the Island of Love* (London, 1697). Also see *The Works of Aphra Behn,* ed. Janet Todd (London: William Pickering, 1992). Todd cites a different version of the Creech ode.

13. In her pindaric to Dr. Burnet, Behn notes that she is following Cowley in the Pindaric mode, but has never ventured as high as he in the mode. *A PINDARIC POEM to the Reverend Doctor Burnet, on the Honour he did me of Enquiring after me and my MUSE* by A. Behn (London: R. Bentley, 1689).

14. I quote from A. Behn, "To Mr. Creech," *Poems upon Several Occasions: With a Voyage to the Island of Love* (London, 1684), 50-57.

15. Behn was fluent in French, if not in Greek and Latin, and two French translations of Pindar from the early seventeenth century would have been available to her, one by Marin in prose published in Paris in 1617, another in prose and verse by Sieur de Lagausie, published in Paris in 1626. On Behn's lack of Latin see Angeline Goreau, *Reconstructing Aphra, a Social Biography of Aphra Behn* (New York: Dial Press, 1980). Although Behn published paraphrases of Ovid and a translation of Cowley's *Plantarum,* she made a point of saying that she did not know Latin. In his preface to Ovid, Dryden compliments Behn on the facility of her translation (despite her lack of direct knowledge of the original), but in his "A Satyr on the Modern Translator," he rebukes her and others for attempting to translate a language they do not know (54).

16. The ode to Creech is interesting not only as an example of commendatory poetry with a subversive aim, but also on its own merits as an example of late seventeenth-century Pindaric verse. Particularly impressive here is Behn's use of Pindaric techniques: her adaptation of the Pindaric myth and her extension of the Pindaric encomium to Creech to other figures connected with Wadham—notably Sprat, and her mentors Rochester and Cowley. The ode sets its criticism of women's exclusion from the classics in a poem that demonstrates an accomplished classical Pindaric technique.

17. "Upon these and other Excellent Works of the Incomparable Astyraea" in Aphra Behn, *Poems upon Several Occasions* (London, 1697), 3.

18. See especially "To the Lovely witty *Astraea*, on her Excellent Poems," "To the excellent *Madam Behn*, on her Poems," "To *ASTRAEA*, on her Poems," in Behn, *Poems* (London, 1684). Even in "The Life and Memoirs of Mrs. Behn," attached to a reprint of *The Histories and Novels of the Late Ingenious Mrs. Behn* (London, 1696), written purportedly by "a Gentlewoman of her Acquaintance," Beauty is not divorced from Wit and Intellect. The Gentlewoman remarks that Behn was "Mistress of uncommon Charms of Body, as well as Mind . . . Wit, Beauty, and Judgment, seldom met in one, especially in Woman, (you may allow this from a Woman) but in her they were Eminent" (n.p.).

19. F.N.W. "To Madam *A Behn* on the publication of her Poems" (8:13-15) in Behn, *Poems* (1684).

FURTHER READING

Criticism

Easton, Celia A. "Excusing the Breach of Nature's Laws: The Discourse of Denial and Disguise in Katherine Philips' Friendship Poetry." *Restoration: Studies in English Literature Culture, 1660–1700,* 14, no. 1 (spring 1990): 1–14.
Associates Philips's strategies of political disguise and sexual repression with her exploration of poetic language.

Evans, Robert C. "Paradox in Poetry and Politics: Katherine Philips in the Interregnum." In *The English Civil Wars in the Literary Imagination,* edited by Claude J. Summers and Ted-Larry Pebworth, pp. 174-85. Columbia: University of Missouri Press, 1999.
Discusses Philips's poetry in the context of pre-Restoration English politics and argues that the period's political complexity contributes to the artistic richness of Philips's poetry.

Gosse, Edmund. "The Matchless Orinda." *In Seventeenth Century Studies: A Contribution to the History of English Poetry,* by William Heinemann, pp. 229–58. London, 1897.
Originally published in *Cornhill Magazine* in 1881. Provides an overview of Philips's writing.

Hageman, Elizabeth H. "The Matchless Orinda: Katherine Philips." In *Women Writers of the Renaissance and Reformation,* edited by Katharina M. Wilson, pp. 566-608. Athens: The University of Georgia Press, 1987.
Provides an overview of Philips's poetry.

Hobby, Elaine. "Romantic Love—Poetry." In *Virtue of Necessity: English Women's Writing, 1649–88,* 99. 128–42. Ann Arbor: University of Michigan Press, 1989.
Examines Philips's persona and her poems celebrating female friendship.

Limbert, Claudia A. "Katherine Philips: Controlling a Life and Reputation" *South Atlantic Review,* 56, no. 2 (May 1991): 24–42.
Questions the relevance of critical preoccupation with Philips's sexual identity and examines the methods by which she protected her literary reputation.

Limbert, Claudia A. "'The Unison of Well-Tun'd Hearts': Katherine Philips' Friendships with Male Writers." *English Language Notes* 29, no. 1 (September 1991): 25-37.
Speculates on Philips's friendships with such writers as Henry Lawes, Andrew Marvell, and John Milton.

Sant, Patricia M., and James N. Brown. "Two Unpublished Poems by Katherine Philips.'" *English Literary Renaissance* 24 no. 1 (winter 1994): 211-28.
Chronicles the establishment of authenticity of five pre-publication poems attributed to Philips.

Thomas, Patrick. *Katherine Philips ('Orinda').* University of Wales Press, 1988, 71 p.
Surveys Philips's life and career.

Yevgeny Yevtushenko
1933-

(Full name Yevgeny Alexandrovich Yevtushenko. Also transliterated as Evgenii Alexkasandrovich Evtushenko, Yevgeniy Yevtushenko, or Evgeny Evtushenko) Russian poet, novelist, essayist, dramatist, screenwriter, actor, and editor.

INTRODUCTION

A remarkably prolific and charismatic writer, Yevtushenko has enjoyed an exceptional degree of artistic and personal freedom for a writer working during the Soviet regime. Foremost among the first post-Stalin generation of Russian poets, Yevtushenko has attracted a large audience and acquired an international reputation with dramatic readings of his poetry. His poetry articulates both civic and personal themes in a politically charged style reminiscent of the poetic forms and passionate language of an earlier period in Soviet history. With the advent of glasnost in the late 1980s, Yevtushenko became a leading activist in the struggle to reform Soviet society. As a briefly elected member of the Soviet Congress, Yevtushenko is credited with originating the governmental policy of perestroika and continues to speak out against political abuses of power in Russia. Although critical and popular reception of Yevtushenko's work has mostly hinged on the Soviet political climate, critics have generally praised the multicultural quality of his writings and regard Yevtushenko as Russia's premiere but unofficial cultural emissary to the world.

BIOGRAPHICAL INFORMATION

Yevtushenko is a fourth-generation descendant of Ukrainians who were exiled to Siberia. He was born in Stanzia Zima, a small town on the Trans-Siberian railway featured in his first important narrative poem, *Stantsiya Zima* (1956; *Winter Station*). As a teenager, Yevtushenko joined his father on geological expeditions in Kazakhstan and later studied world literature at the prestigious Gorky Literary Institute in Moscow, where he published his first book of poems, *Razvedchiki gryaduschego* (1952). As subsequent volumes appeared throughout the late 1950s and early 1960s, Yevtushenko emerged as the voice of Soviet youth and as a leading proponent of the Cold War "thaw" in diplomatic and cultural relations between the Soviet Union and the United States. In 1960 Soviet authorities permitted Yevtushenko to read his poems in Russia, the United States, and Europe. The result initiated a modest cultural exchange between East and West, making Yevtushenko an

international celebrity. Soon afterward, he published and recited some of his best-known political poetry, including "Babi Yar" and "The Heirs of Stalin" (1962), which generated controversy and publicity in Russia and abroad. Yevtushenko independently published *A Precocious Autobiography* in English in 1963. After the publication of *A Precocious Autobiography,* Soviet officials revoked his privileges. But following the publication of *Bratskaya GES* (1965; *New Works: The Bratsk Station*)—considered by many critics to be his finest poetic work—Soviet officials relented.

During the 1970s, when cultural stagnation and political repression prevailed under Leonid Brezhnev, Yevtushenko began to experiment with literary forms other than poetry, including films and audio recordings. His first novel, *Yagodnyye mesta* (1981; *Wild Berries*), was a finalist for the Ritz Paris Hemingway Prize, and another novel, *Ne umira prezhde smerti* (1993; *Don't Die before You're Dead*), hit the Russian bestseller list in 1995. Meanwhile, Yevtushenko continued to write poetry, including *Invisible Threads* (1982) and *Almost at the End* (1987). In 1989, Yevtushenko was elected to the Soviet Congress of People's Deputies, where he led the democratic reform movement and bolstered its momentum by issuing both *The Collected Poems, 1952-1990,* and *Fatal Half Measures* in 1991. During the failed coup attempt in 1991, Yevtushenko remained to defend the Parliament building as tanks circled. During the ordeal, Yevtushenko composed a poem that he later read to Western television journalists. In 1996, Yevtushenko joined the faculty at Queens College.

MAJOR WORKS

As represented in *The Collected Poems,* Yevtushenko's poetry comprises a wide range of forms and themes that reflect his changing literary style and illumine the strong bond between political and poetic expression in Russian culture. Generally personal or declamatory in tone, Yevtushenko's poems blend political and social concerns of contemporary Soviet society with issues of personal morality. His poems also contrast Western values against the legacy of Stalin's regime, while still showing a deep loyalty to Russia. Yevtushenko's first critical success, *Winter Station,* for instance, lyrically describes the poet's return to his birthplace as he struggles with personal doubts regarding Stalin's social programs. "The Heirs of Stalin," published at the height of the Cuban missile crisis, unsparingly attacks the former Russian ruler and his followers, warning against a resurgence of Stalinism. "Babi Yar," a poem lamenting the Nazi slaughter of tens of thousands of Ukrainian Jews in a ravine near Kiev during World War II, implies that the Soviet regime and Russian people generally sanction anti-Semitic sentiment. Yevtushenko's most ambitious cycle of poems, *Bratskaya GES,* draws parallels between modern Russian experiences and historical antecedents. The poems contrast the symbol of a Siberian power plant bringing light to Russia with the symbol of Siberia as a prison throughout Russian history. The title poem compares Russian workers responsible for building the power plant with slaves who built Egyptian pyramids. As the Soviet regime increased restrictions on artistic expression, Yevtushenko's poems began to exhibit a more somber tone to conform to official styles and themes. Although *Stolen Apples* (1971) addresses themes such as love, travel, and history, *The Face behind the Face* (1979) asserts the social relevance of poets and poetry in the Soviet Union. Another work of this period includes *Pod kozhey Statui Svobody* (1972; *Under the Skin of the Statue of Liberty*), a series of dramatic sketches set in the United States that denounce American violence but extol the idealism of its youth. Among his later poetry collections, *Invisible Threads* (1982) focuses on the need for international unity and is alternately optimistic and pessimistic—a theme common to most of Yevtushenko's work. *Almost at the End* (1987) gathers poetry and prose written in the Gorbachev era and examines differences between the East and West, along with effects of restricted personal freedom and censorship. Notable in this work is "Fuku," a long poem that deconstructs various Western historical figures. Yevtushenko's contribution to literature also includes the novel *Wild Berries,* which ostensibly celebrates Russian philosophy and existence but resembles an American-style thriller with action, sex, and exotic locales. Yevtushenko's *Don't Die before You're Dead* is a fast-paced, quasi-fictional account of the 1991 coup attempt and its psychological consequences for ordinary citizens. *Fatal Half Measures* is a collection of Yevtushenko's speeches and essays on themes advocating glasnost and Soviet democratic reform.

CRITICAL RECEPTION

Critics offer disparate views on the credibility and stature of Yevtushenko. Most Western intellectuals and many Russian scholars extol him as the greatest writer of his generation, the voice of Soviet life. They acknowledge that his speaking tours have won him converts among audiences impressed with his dramatic readings and charismatic personality. Tina Tupikina Glaessner (1967) refers to him as "one of the greatest poets of the modern age." She states that "Bratsk Station" offers the greatest insight into Soviet life of any other work in modern Russian literature. Two decades later, in his 1988 article, Michael Pursglove echoes her sentiments referring to Stantisiya Zima as "one of the landmarks of Soviet literature." Other scholars have noted Yevtushenko's unusual and arresting rhyme structure, strong word choice, and vivid characterizations of Soviet life, particularly in Siberia. However, other scholars, notably Russian critics, have not been as kind to Yevtushenko. Patricia Pollock Brodsky (1992) takes issue with the interpretation that Yevtushenko has been persecuted by the Russian government. And most scathing, Tomas Venclova asserts, in his 1991 essay, that few in the Russian literary community "consider his work worthy of serious study."

PRINCIPAL WORKS

Poetry

Razvedchiki gryaduschego 1952
Tretii sneg: Kniga liriki 1955
Shosse entusiastov 1956
Stantsiya Zima [*Winter Station*] 1956; originally published in the journal *Oktiabr*
Obeschanie 1957
Luk i lira: Stikhi o Gruzii 1959
Babi Yar 1960 originally published in the journal *Literaturnaya gazeta*
Yabloko 1960
Nezhnost: Novyii Stikhi 1962
Posie Stalina 1962
Selected Poems 1962

Other Major Works

CRITICISM

George Reavey (essay date 1965)

SOURCE: Reavey, George. "Yevgeny Yevtushenko: Man and Poet." In *The Poetry of Yevgeny Yevtushenko 1953 to 1965,* translated by George Reavey, pp. vii-xxxvii. New York: October House, 1965.

[*In the following essay, Reavey places Yevtushenko in the context of Russian literature and chronicles his work through the mid-1960s.*]

1. RUSSIA AND THE SPECTRE OF THE POET

There is something about the poet and his poetic utterance that has a terrifying effect on some Russians, and especially on the Authorities, be they Tsarist or Soviet. It is as though poetry were an irrational force which must be bridled and subjugated and even destroyed. If the critics cannot do it, then the police must try. History tells us that the lives of Russian poets have been ravaged. One need only mention the tragic fate that befell Pushkin, Lermontov, Blok, Gumilev, Yesenin, Mayakovsky, Mandelshtam and Tsvetayeva. It is as though Russia were frightened by the expanding image of its culture and, feeling threatened by the possible loss of its own simple theoretical identity, must needs shatter anything more complex as something alien to itself. This may be due to an inherent strain of puritanism. Or to the reaction of an archaic form of despotic paternalism. Perhaps, it is just the painful effect of a too sudden transition from a state of serfdom, orthodoxy, and autocracy to that of an ideologically motivated, totalitarian attempt at industrialization. Whether it is any or all of these possibilities or merely a matter of ineluctable destiny, the position of the poet in the Soviet Union, though apparently more secure in the last decade, is still highly precarious. It is still precarious because some of the younger poets and some of the hitherto muzzled older poets have become more critical and vocal, more determined to express their real feelings and to interpret the truth as they saw it. These poets have been not only anxious to voice their new-found feelings and truths, but also to condemn certain injustices and corrupt practices of the recent past when "substituting falsehood for truth, / They represented truth as falsehood," and to prevent their resurgence in the present. But it is not only a question of ideas. These poets have also been trying to rejuvenate or refresh the language of Russian poetry, which had been gravely constipated by an overdose of political clichés and slogans. They have also criticized certain of the "father images," and have made valiant efforts to enlarge their creative and cultural horizon. This, of course, they could not do without absorbing a great many "modern" elements from the West and reassessing some of the Russian writers of the Silver Age, such as Alexander Blok, Andrey Biely, and Ivan Bunin for example.

But the doctrinal purists, the dogmatists and the hacks will naturally tend to resist this healthy and inevitable trend, and maintain that so-called "ideological coexistence" between the Soviet and "bourgeois" worlds is both impossible and undesirable. The proponents of this point of view can marshall a set of propositions, apparently constant but often variable, which all fall under the general appellation of Socialist Realism (literature or art should be Socialist in content, realist in style). For the last thirty years this formula, which was first enunciated by Stalin in 1933, has been followed, bypassed, avoided, and debated. It has proved elastic: sometimes narrower; at other times, broader. But at the same time it has in practice usually served as a convenient yardstick for cutting a writer down to size or for arbitrary judgment and the condemnation of anything that seemed to endanger the closed, exclusive system of Socialist Realism. "Decadent" or "Formalist" were, and still are, the labels usually fastened to any "alien" or "undesirable" elements from outside. However, Soviet society, like any other, is subject to the laws of growth and decay, and Stalinist concepts are as perishable as any others. To interpret a rapidly changing world, a poet or artist must attune his mind and senses in part to the larger world and not merely to a closed segment of it. He must be allowed at least a large degree of artistic autonomy.

In a speech pronounced in 1921,[1] Alexander Blok, the great Russian poet, had argued that "tranquillity and freedom" were "essential to the poet in order to set harmony free." But he went on to say "they also take away our tranquillity and freedom. Not outward but creative tranquillity. Not the childish do-as-you-will, not the freedom to play the liberal, but the creative will—the secret freedom. And the poet is dying, because there is no longer anything to breathe; life has lost its meaning for him." The negative part of this statement could certainly apply to poetry under the Stalin regime. It does not altogether apply in all cases to Soviet poets today; but, if we are to judge by the tone of some well-established Soviet critics of the official variety, it is not beyond the bounds of possibility that it might apply again at some time in the future. This "creative tranquillity" and this "secret freedom" are precisely what the dogmatists cannot tolerate. Boris Pasternak's sequence ("Wind: Some fragments about Blok") includes one poem that obviously refers to the above theme of Blok's, and it opens as follows:

> Who will survive and be accepted,
> Who censured and accounted dead,
> Such is the province of our toadies—
> Of them alone, empowered thus.

Significantly, the poem has been omitted from the cycle of Pasternak's 1956-60 poems included in the posthumous Soviet edition of his *Poetical Works* (1961). Yet, despite much sniping and frequent ambushes, the *avant garde* of recent Soviet poetry has succeeded in considerably expanding the frontiers of the Soviet poetic consciousness. Yevgeny Yevtushenko's **"Prologue"** may be regarded as an early poem of the new persuasion enunciating not only the poet's own aspirations ("I'm different . . ."), but also those of his advanced contemporaries.

It might seem unnecessary and even a pity to involve Yevgeny Yevtushenko prematurely in the theme of the tragedy of the Russian poets. But Yevtushenko has shown himself well aware of this theme. He refers to it in his *A Precocious Autobiography*, touches on it very directly in the poem, **"Poetry,"** and treats of it in a more Aesopian manner in his brutally vivid ballad, **"The Execution of Stenka Razin"** (1964)[2]:

> It's worth suffering it all without tears,
>   being racked,
>   broken on the wheel,

> if—
>   sooner or later—
> FACES
>   will appear
>   growing out upon
> the faces of the faceless.

More recently, on the Day of Poetry in Moscow (December 20, 1964), he read a newly written poem about Mayakovsky, a poet who has undoubtedly influenced him. He seems to imply in it that Mayakovsky (1893-1930) might have ended up in a concentration camp if he had survived until 1937, the year of the big Stalinist purges, the memory of which is still a living nightmare. That the theme of "The Poet and Russia" has also become a preoccupation with other contemporary poets is evidenced by the fact that, on the same Day of Poetry, Vladimir Tsibin also read a poem of his entitled "The Fate of All Russian Poets" in which, according to the report, he argued that, "since the early nineteenth century Russian poets have been at the mercy of the ruling powers in alternating spells of repression and liberalism."[3] In view of the recent recrudescence of this theme, one is tempted to ask what lies behind this anxiety as to the fate of the poet? Is it a mere expression of historical awareness or that of alarm as to the immediate future? It may be a form of premonition or, perhaps, a mode of vatic incantation against the possibility of such a recurrence.

However, one need not be a Cassandra. My main purpose here is to attempt a portrait of Yevtushenko as a man and to evaluate his contribution to the poetry of his day. To write about Yevtushenko is to treat not of a poet "dead and gone" and tucked away in the index files of stubborn history, but rather to discuss a poet very much alive and widely aware; a poet in the process of creating history, in so far as a poet in his work performs a creative act, interprets a mood, voices the yearnings of others, and points a direction by affirming his emotional and intellectual attitude and by using his native language in a personal and distinctive manner. The way Yevtushenko has gone about doing these things is very individual. He cannot help sharing of course a common background and certain traditions in common with some of his fellow poets. Now in his early thirties, he has shown in the last ten years every evidence of a steady and fruitful poetic development. Youthful and enthusiastic by temperament ("Fear not to be young, precocious . . ."), he is likewise aware of the necessity of maturing without losing his enthusiasm. (At least two poems in this book deal with this theme.) His poetry clearly demonstrates that he has moved from simpler and balder poetic statements to more complex and richer lyrical forms in the 1960's. The texture of his language has become richer and more interesting, and his lyrical quality more evident and intense. He is undoubtedly creating a poetic world of his own, a world of increasing resonance, which is the chief *raison d'être* and measure of a poet.

2. THE POET BETWEEN TWO WORLDS

For a Soviet poet of twenty-eight (1961), Yevgeny Yevtushenko had become remarkably well known, and internationally so. His international reputation, so quickly gained, may be attributed to a number of factors, since a poet rarely becomes widely famous in so short time by virtue of the quality of his poetry alone. By 1960, Yevtushenko was, to all intents and purposes, the voice of the new, post-Stalin generation in the Soviet Union. His poetry, expressive of the new aspirations, sounded a fresh and fearless note, a note to which one had become disaccustomed in Soviet poetry:

> *Frontiers are in my way.*
> It is embarrassing
> for me not to know Buenos Aires and New York.
> I want to walk at will through London,
> and talk with everyone . . .

("Prologue," 1953)

By 1961, he had already traveled widely (in Europe, Africa, Cuba and the U.S.A.). In doing so, he had not shut himself off in a suit of Soviet armor, as so many Soviet travelers have done for various reasons. He had absorbed and reflected on his new environment, had gone out to meet it rather than to hold it off at arm's length. He was also prepared to read his poems in public to Western audiences; and here it must be noted that, like Mayakovsky, he has a voice well geared for reading to large audiences. Then, in September 1961, he had published his **"Babii Yar,"** a poem that raised many issues, social, political, and poetic. The most topical one was that of the persistence of anti-Semitism in the Soviet Union. Yevtushenko's direct treatment of the subject was very forthright and brave. It was this poem more than anything else that gave him such immediate worldwide publicity. **"Babii Yar,"** a deeply felt and beautifully expressed poem, is informed with a compassion that harmonizes with its polemical intent. It was certainly a most effective poem, rousing both emotions and passions, stirring many dovecots and thus demonstrating the potential power of the poetic world. It provoked a whole barrage of rather savage attacks, of which D. Starikov's in *Literatura i Zhizn* (September 27, 1961) was perhaps the most virulent. Starikov went so far as to conclude that "what is important is that the source of that intolerable falsity with which his **'Babii Yar'** is permeated lies in his obvious withdrawal from communist ideology to the positions of bourgeois ideology. This is indisputable." Before 1953, such an attack might have led to grave consequences for the poet, but the fact that he was not immediately packed off to a grimmer part of Siberia was evidence not so much of any great liberalism on the part of the ruling powers as of a more reasonable and cautious approach to the phenomena of literary life.

When I saw him in New York together with his fellow poet Andrey Voznesensky, Yevtushenko had just arrived there after a tour of the United States. It was his first visit to America, and he seemed both to enjoy it and to have a keen interest in all there was to see, from the Empire State Building to the Village beatniks. He was in no sense stuffy

or dogmatic. "I was not raised on dogma," he affirms in one of his poems. Curiosity rather than dogma was a guiding trait in him. He has described this trait in another poem:

> Little eyes like narrow slits,
> whence curiosity peeps out
> upon the world.

To look at him, Yevtushenko is a tall young man of handsome, cleancut, athletic appearance, who radiates energy. He impressed me as being frank and direct, as befitted a poet who, in poem after poem, has stressed the necessity of being honest, frank and fearless, and has attacked dishonesty and hypocrisy. In his earlier poems he might even have seemed to overdo this note of challenging bravado and to sound too bombastic and assertive at times. But this youthful assertiveness can be easily forgiven him when it is realized that he was fighting the battle of his generation on the poetic front against those years of mass falsification which had enveloped the Soviet people in the preceding quarter of a century. Here then was Yevtushenko, a Soviet citizen with, surprisingly, a mind of his own and little feeling of constraint. He therefore began to attract as much attention abroad as he had already at home. He was almost too self-confident, and one worried that he might get into unnecessary trouble. One could not help wondering whether he was not sticking his neck out too far. However, he seemed to bear a charmed life, and to shake off the drenching showers of periodic criticism like a duck. It was not until February-March, 1963, that he got into rather hotter water after publishing his *Autobiographie Précoce* (A Precocious Autobiography) in Paris. An article by him, *My Russia,* had already appeared the year before in *The London Observer,* but the effect of the autobiography as a whole was, of course, greater. Yevtushenko had dared, like Boris Pasternak in the case of *Doctor Zhivago,* to publish a work of his abroad without going through the prior ritual of a censor's blessing or official approval. And just as well, because it is doubtful if that work would have appeared at all in this decade in the Soviet Union. "Autobiography" was the preserve of maturer writers, such as Ehrenburg and Paustovsky. In officious eyes, he had exceeded his prerogatives. He must be put in his place. Yevtushenko was on a reading tour at the time in Germany and France, and he was supposed to travel on to Italy and even, it is said, to Israel. He was promptly recalled to Moscow from Paris. He has since remained in Moscow, at least until the beginning of 1965. He therefore was unable to go on his second projected trip to the U.S.A. in April, 1963, when he was expected to read his poems at Princeton and other American universities. No more trips abroad for the moment, fewer Western contacts. The "frontiers," having opened, were now temporarily shut.

But this pattern did not apply to Yevtushenko alone. It also involved Andrey Voznesensky, a poet no less brave in a different fashion, and some novelists and prose writers such as Nekrasov and Aksyonov. Indeed, there was more to it than just the Yevtushenko Autobiography. It looked as if the *avant garde* writers had become too independent and modern, too critical and western-minded. They had to be given some ideological whipping in the "cleansing" vapors of the Russian, marxist, ideological Steam Bath. The ideological reassessment begun in October, 1962, now took on an increasingly sharp form and developed into a running debate which continued hammer and tongs into June, 1963. There had been Khrushchev's crude outburst against the "modern" artists, such as the sculptor Neizvestny, who were exhibiting at the Moscow Manege in December, 1962, and his apparently uncompromising speech of March 8, 1963. There had been speeches by L. F. Ilyichev, who headed the ideological branch of the Central Committee. And there had been a whole plethora of speeches in writers' organizations, as well as a flood of articles in the dailies and periodicals. The substance of the official propositions was much the same. It boiled down to a reassertion of the controlling principles of Socialist Realism, the rejection of the possibility of "ideological coexistence," and sharp criticism of individual writers. The following from a speech by S. P. Pavlov, the first secretary of the Young Communist organizations, will suffice as an example: "There is scum in every flood. It is also present in our young literature. Especially in the work of Yevtushenko, Voznesensky, Okudzhava . . . We're ashamed of their posturing and vanity. We're ashamed that, blinded by their fame, these young people have begun to bite at the most primitive bait. And our ideological enemies are big specialists in the matter of baits . . ." Despite all the thunder and browbeating, the bark proved worse than the final bite. A large enough number of writers put up a show of resistance, and a sort of *modus vivendi* was arrived at for the time being. But the freedom to travel abroad was very definitely curtailed in the case of certain poets and novelists who were being grilled—those who had exhibited too much individual conscience, as Nekrasov had also done in his articles about his trip to the USA. Yevtushenko was even refused permission to travel to Poland, where he was expected to read his poetry. A *Pravda* editorial of January 9, 1965, reissued a warning against "formalism" and "digressions from realism," and asserted that "there cannot be any peaceful coexistence in the ideological field." This renewed insistence on the same point may well be due to the persistence of the so-called "digressions" or "deviations." It may also have been the result of the nature of some of the poems which had been read in December on Poetry Day.

3. Origins, Youth and Early Poetry

Yevgeny Yevtushenko is proud to call himself a Siberian. "I am of Siberian breed," he proclaims in the opening line of a 1954 poem. I have met other Russians who were also proud of their Siberian origins. This claim has a special connotation in Russia. A "Siberian" regards himself as somewhat superior to an ordinary Russian. He likes to think of himself as bigger, tougher and, above all, *freer*. This may strike us as paradoxical, since Siberia has also been notorious for its prisons and concentration camps. But Siberia was also a land of frontiersmen and pioneers, as well as a Tsarist, and then Soviet dumping ground for

political exiles and rebels (the Decembrists and recalcitrant intellectuals; Dostoyevsky, Babel, Mandelshtam). Many of these exiles settled permanently in various parts of Siberia. There is therefore a certain tradition of intellectual liberty in Siberia. Moreover, the Siberian peasant was never a serf as he had been in Muscovy.

Thus, Yevgeny Yevtushenko was born at Stantzia Zima (Winter Station) on July 18, 1933. Zima Station is a settlement or small provincial town situated on the famous Transiberian railway in the Irkutsk region, near Lake Baikal. Yevtushenko has immortalized his birthplace in many poems, and particularly in his **"Zima Station"** (1956). Zima is also the scene of certain other poems, such as **"The Concert," "Babushka,"** and **"Again at Zima Station."** In the latter poem we find the following playful but affectionate description:

> Zima! a station small with palisade,
> half-a-dozen drooping trees,
> and a kholhoz woman with porkers in a sack . . .

Zima might indeed appear to be a "provincial hole" to some chance traveler like the one bitingly described in **"Again at Zima Station,"** but Yevtushenko has shown himself very attached to it. He feels the need to return there from time to time for spiritual refreshment:

> when have I not adored you, Station Zima,
> as Yesenin did his peasant mother?! . . .
>
> Whenever I come back to you, Zima,
> I always feel as though reborn . . .

He still has relatives there—mainly uncles and aunts.

The name Yevtushenko is Ukrainian. His paternal great-grandfather was a peasant from the province of Zhitomir who had been exiled to Siberia for burning a landowner's house, a not infrequent act in the pre-revolutionary days. His grandfather, Yermolay Yevtushenko, was a soldier who during the Revolution and the civil war became a leader in the East Siberian peasant movement. He then rose to the rank of commander in the Red Army. In the light of Yevtushenko's attitude to the Russian Revolution as an ideal and of his hatred for the abuses of Stalinism, it is significant to note that his grandfather was both an early enthusiastic supporter of the Revolution and, later, an innocent victim of the Stalin purges. The arrest, deportation and utter disappearance of his grandfather, though this fact was at first concealed from the young boy, must eventually have been a great shock to Yevtushenko, who had hitherto tended to accept the image of Stalin as something sacrosanct. His disillusion with this aspect of his past was further intensified after Khrushchev's "secret speech" at the famous Twentieth Congress (1953). Soon after he began writing his long poem **"Zima Station,"** in which he reviewed and reassessed the past and present (his own), and tells us something about the Yevtushenkos.

Yevtushenko's father was a more intellectual type. A steady reader of literature and poetry, a geologist by profession, he introduced his son to serious reading at an early age.

The family, however, split up before the end of the war. The father remarried, and pursued his geological work in Kazakhstan. Yevtushenko's mother Zinaida was born (1910) in Siberia of Latvian parents. His Latvian grandfather, Rudolph Gangnus, a mathematician and writer of geometry textbooks, was also arrested as a Latvian spy during the purges on a trumped-up charge. As a result of the divorce of his parents, Yevtushenko was brought up by his mother and, for a time, by relatives. In a number of poems Yevtushenko has testified to his regard and affection for his mother. In **"I Congratulate You, Mamma,"** he writes that she had given him "neither fame, nor riches" but a "hard, proud faith in the Revolution" and "the ability not to fear."

The young Yevgeny or "Zhenia," as he is more familiarly called, did not spend all of his early youth in Zima Station. In the late 1930's his mother took him to live in Moscow. Then came war. In the autumn of 1941, Zhenia was among the many children evacuated from Moscow. At the age of eight he went back to live with his uncles and aunts in Zima Station, and there he stayed for three years. Yevtushenko later recorded the atmosphere of those years, and especially of "the terrible year '41" in Siberia in his poem **"Weddings"** (1955) and certain other poems. He could never forget those one-night weddings of the Siberian recruits who were rushed to the front to save besieged Moscow. From this poem we also learn that the young "Zhenia" was already a "folk dancer of repute," who could "stamp his feet and bend his knees." The moral he draws at the end of the poem, "My heart's not in the dance, / but it's impossible not to go on dancing," would also apply to other difficult moments in life and especially to his more critical days as a poet. Zima Station, besides serving him as a background for country characters, landscape and forest scenes (the famed Siberian Taiga), also proved a rich source of folklore and folk song, in which the poet-to-be developed an early interest. Indeed, he has been able to make good use of the folk element in a number of his poems, as well as in his poetic language. Some of his poems of 1963-64 are very Siberian and show the impact of folklore. Like Sergey Yesenin, the peasant poet from Ryazan, Yevtushenko has preserved a deep feeling for his native soil and landscape. But he is not only a country poet; he is a city poet too. He has, indeed, described himself as half and half peasant and intellectual.

In 1944, before the war ended, he was brought back to Moscow where he continued his rather desultory education which included, as he tells us, a period of close and dangerous contact with the life of the streets. He was belligerent and fought the toadies. He had difficulties at school and was even expelled from one. But he survived the dangers and hardships, and was writing poems in the midst of it all. Life in Moscow was hard during the war years, for his mother made only a marginal living as a singer in a cinema and then a minor employee. At the age of fifteen, Yevtushenko went off and joined his father for a time in Kazakhstan and got a job, first as a handyman and, then, as a collector with a geological expedition in the Alta

region. It is not surprising that he should have entitled his first published volume of poems **"Prospectors of the Future"** (1952).

There was a moment when, on his return to Moscow, Yevtushenko almost decided to become a professional footballer. But after publishing his first poem, in 1949, in *Soviet Sport,* he opted for literature. Soon people, who thought he had a future as a poet, began to encourage him to go on writing. Eventually he was given a chance to study at the Gorky Literary Institute in Moscow, the official training ground for many Soviet poets and novelists. In the early 1950's he began to be published more widely in the established literary papers and magazines. It was during this period that he met and married his first wife, Bella Akhmadullina, a talented poet of Tartar origin. His first book was followed in rapid succession by five others: *Third Snow* (1955), *The Highway of Enthusiasts* (1956), *Promise* (1957), *The Bow and the Lyre,* and the culminating volume of this series, *Poems of Various Years* (1950). *Poems of Various Years* may be said to mark in a sense the completion of Yevtushenko's initial phase as a poet at the age of twenty-five. In the poems of his first creative decade Yevtushenko had shown himself to be a poet of concentrated aim and wide interests. He was still a youthful poet, whose themes and enthusiasm could generate increasing excitement. He had a distinctive and attractive lyrical note of his own. He had studied rhyme and produced original effects. He was a voice, but he had not yet achieved a great deal. His main themes as behoved a lyrical poet were nature ("Nature requires that we love her"), love, and himself. Then, to these he added a belief in poetry, a faith in the Russian people, a love for his native land, and various patriotic motifs. He also reaffirmed his belief in the original ideals of the Revolution, and condemned the corruption of those ideals. Yevtushenko, we find, is always careful to distinguish between the long suffering and much abused "Russian people" and the race of bureaucrats or careerists who swarmed like locusts over the land:

> It seems
>   we are divorced from nature,
> and have unlearnt
>   to breathe in branches.
> But in us love
>   is alive to all that's Russian,
> green,
>   dewy,
>   and fragrant.

The tone and feeling of the new generation of Soviet poets is well expressed in the following lines of Yevtushenko's from **"There's Something I Often Notice"** (1953):

> Let us share our anxieties together,
> discuss between us, tell others too,
> what sort of men we can't be any longer,
> what sort of men we now desire to be.

There is something these poets must share, something they must break away from, and something they must strive for. In **"Zima Station"** (1956), the long poem which Yevtushenko had been writing since 1953, the poet treats not only of himself, his background, the family history and nature, and the early days of the Revolution, but also of the moral consequences of political corruption and of the shocking revelations that followed Stalin's death ("Now that the doctors have proved innocent . . ."). As a result of all this, the poet, who had previously "had no doubts," now "suddenly felt it necessary to answer these questions for myself." The time had come to do some independent thinking rather than to rely on rationalizations and harmonious solutions to all apparent problems.

The year 1953 had helped to transform Yevtushenko. Until then, though a poet of promise, he was still far from realizing in deadly earnest all the implications of the poet's vocation. He had been apt, he admits, to blink an eye on occasion when a careerist editor would insert a line or two in praise of Stalin in a poem and thus connive at the proliferation of what came to be labelled as "the cult of the personality." However, a dawning sense of responsibility made Yevtushenko adopt a firmer attitude, and he began to make a point of insisting on poetic integrity. He also wrote more boldly and touched upon issues which had, until then, been kept under the surface. These issues may be summed up as the necessity of admitting the horrible mistakes of the 1930-40's and insisting on the truth being told. When they were brought out into the open at last, they naturally appeared controversial and, therefore, caused a great deal of displeasure in certain circles:

> It will go hard with me at times,
> and they will say:
>> "He'd better hold his tongue!"

In Soviet conditions these issues could not help but assume at times a sharp political edge even though they were in the circumstances the subject matter of legitimate poetical expression. The issues Yevtushenko began to raise in his poetry were not something purely subjective, though his manner of doing so was individual, but rather reflected the wider longings and aspirations of that younger generation which was fated to apprehend the new "atomic world" of the 1950's. In one of its main aspects this new generation of "sons" represented an inevitable and too-long-delayed revolt against many representatives of the previous bootlicking generation of the "fathers," who had been caught up in and morally devasted by the world of Stalinist machinations. It was a confrontation as poignant and as unavoidable as that depicted by Turgenev in his *Fathers and Sons,* with this difference, that now, a hundred years later, it was the turn of the younger idealists to attack the established generation of the now compromised cynical radicals. The very concept of the Revolution was now at stake. What had been besmirched, was now to be purified, re-defined, and brought up-to-date. The Revolution was something more than the arbitrary will of one man or of a Stalinist-type bureaucracy. This was not the only aspect involved in what was a deep emotional and critical change going on in the psyche of the Russian people. But, as far as the conflict between sons and fathers was concerned, it is not surprising, perhaps, that the "fathers" officially tried to prevent the rift from growing or even showing and being publicly admitted. Khrushchev had laid it down: in Soviet Socialist society there are no contradictions between generations. There is no father-and-son problem in the old sense. In other words, there has been a steady attempt to hush up or to conceal its very existence, even though Yevtushenko, Voznesensky, and other young poets and writers have been constantly criticized for being "immature" and for not listening to their more experienced "elders." ("He's so young . . . There are older men about. What's he after in such a hurry?") The official critics stress this point again and again. On the other hand, Vsevolod Aksyonov, a writer, in an interview printed in the Warsaw *Polytika* (Spring 1963) can state: "The characteristic of the Soviet youth of our days consists in that it rejects the traditions and the manner of life, which had become established in the days of the cult of personality. The young people reject all this both as a whole and in each particular, and this fact disturbs certain representatives of the other generation."

The function of poetry as practiced by Yevtushenko could not be merely negative and critical, social and political, ethical and moralizing ("forgiving no evil even if it does some good"). By its nature, poetry is the language of the emotions and feelings, a form of aesthetical affirmation and ideal statement. The poets of the new generation had therefore to reaffirm a number of beliefs of an emotional and aesthetic kind as well as their social ideals. They had to assert a renewed belief in the integrity and validity of poetry itself, in the value of the word and the possibilities of language and diction, in the right to experiment with form and to adapt it to a new content. In so far as there has been lyrical revival[4] in the past decade, helped on, it is true, by older poets such as Boris Pasternak, Nikolai Zabolotzky, and Leonid Martynov, and in so far as the poets of this revival with Yevtushenko in their van have been both critical and affirmative, it is not surprising that their promise of a new world should have evoked a keen response from an increasing audience. The best indication of the genuine popularity of the new poetry was in the phenomenal jump in the circulation of books of poetry and in large attendance at poetry readings. In the case of Yevtushenko, the rise has been from earlier editions (in 1959), of 20,000 to editions, in 1962, of 100,000 copies; in that of Voznesensky, from 5,000 (in 1960) to an edition of 60,000 copies in 1964.

In Yevtushenko's **"Prologue,"** a sort of youthful, lyrical manifesto poem, there is, besides the theme of the "frontiers," an insistence on a freer, more embracing art and the need for diversity:

> I want art to be
>> as diverse as myself . . .

He also insists on "movement," "ardor," "freshness," and, above all, on the joy of living. This almost Renaissance sense of joy and exuberance is typical of the poet. It is also exemplified in the poem **"Moscow Freight Station."**

In Yevtushenko there is, on the one hand, an all-embracing abundance of spirit; on the other, an undertone of anxiety, strain, and suppressed anguish ("the warring strains in all my moods"). This duality, which has often proved to be the dynamic force of poetry, represents the emergence of a new and more subjective element in later Soviety poetry. This element had always been present in Russian poetry, and had certainly been an integral part of the poetic worlds of Yesenin and Mayakovsky, but diversity and duality have always been considered dangerous elements from the standpoint of the advocates of Socialist Realism. These latter would argue, as Khruschev did, that "Some people are trying to push us on to the road of ideological coexistence and to palm off the rotten idea of absolute freedom." Or, to put it in another way, as Alexander Chakovsky, the new editor of *Literaturnaya Gazeta,* was quoted as saying[5] during his visit to New York: "We are a goal-oriented society; we will not stand by and let these things harm us. We have a definite line in art—not *laisser-faire,* not *laisser-passer.*" But it is also clear that most of these statements are made by party executives and party critics, and that fundamentally they have little or nothing to do with literature. However, since poets will be poets, and party men will be ideologists and politicians, the twain shall never quite meet in the best of worlds. Thus, tension is bound to persist, sometimes less, sometimes more acute; and the presence of this strain must therefore be suffered like some recurring, incurable ache.

4. POET AND TRAVELER 1960-62

In 1960, the year of Boris Pasternak's sudden death, Yevgeny Yevtushenko was already a maturer and more confident poet. He was ready for bigger and more ambitious tasks. He was about to make the acquaintance of Europe and the United States. He was going to enlarge his horizon and to tempt fortune. He was, indeed, about to become internationally known. And he was also about to discover the limitations which would be applied from the outside upon his dynamic will. Yevtushenko's work and activities from 1960 to early 1965 may be divided into two main phases: the first lasted up to March 1963, when, despite much criticism, he seemed comparatively free to move about, travel abroad, and publish some of his most controversial poems, such as **"Babii Yar"** and **"The Heirs of Stalin"** and **"Conversation with an American Writer."** He even published an autobiography in Paris, which had not been previously submitted to the Soviet censors. In addition, he was able to publish in Moscow three volumes of his poetry, and to get printed in a wide range of Soviet papers, periodicals and magazines. The second phase, during which every effort was made to make him less independent and to recant, has continued with a variation of pressures into 1965. This last phase differs from the previous one in that Yevtushenko has now been confined in the Soviet Union and has not published a single book in the past two years. It is true, however, that he has been able to have some of his new cycles of poems printed in the magazines after about a six-month gap in publication.

In his volume *Yabloko* (*Apple*),[6] published at the end of 1960, Yevtushenko had printed such poems as **"Fresh-**

ness," "Our Mothers Depart," "Moscow Freight Station," "Humor," "The Cocks," to mention only five of the forty-two poems included in the book. These poems evidence a wide variety of theme. Some are occasional, others reflective; some more programmatic, others purely lyrical. The poet's moods vary from sheer exuberance to sadness. There are poems about love and loss, work and pleasure, art and politics, Samarkand and the Volga. There are also poems about the young people of his generation, about their loves and personal frustrations. The recurring theme of love and personal relations is a brave new one in the Soviet Union. In **"Humor,"** Yevtushenko touches boldly on a theme with political overtones—the power of humor or wit in the struggle against tyranny or absolute authority.

> They tried to murder humor,
> but he thumbed his nose at them.

He was able to revive this theme in a different context in a later poem, **"Nefertiti"** (1964), written after his encounter at the Manege Art Exhibition, in which the poet argues for the more enduring quality of a work of art (in this case the bust of Nefertiti) as against the more impermanent authority of political power:

> . . . when, in nature, authority comes face to face
> with beauty, its value depreciates.

In **"The Cocks,"** a poem written while Yevtushenko was vacationing in Koktebel in the Crimea, the crowing cocks "summon us to stop from yielding." These cocks therefore become symbols of an "awakening." When the students in his youthful and lively **"Moscow Freight Station"** settle down to talk on the platform, they very significantly discuss "cybernetics, Mars, and Remarque." Nothing could better illustrate the temper of the new Soviet generation. A decade or two ago they would have certainly been discussing Marx rather than Mars. As for Remarque, his appeal to Soviet youth is still regretted by the more orthodox critics. In another poem the poet calls for "freshness" in "music and language" among other things. Such a plea in the West might seem justifiably appropriate and innocuous, but Yevtushenko intends it in dead seriousness as a protest against the weight of the musty past of ideologically congealed art. **"Freshness"** in this context is a battle cry, though very gently and lyrically expressed in this instance. The same point is made in a more direct and militant, though witty, poem, **"Rockets and Carts"** (1960), in which the poet contrasts a need for a new rocket-like art with the persistence of "cart-like" novels and operas and, no doubt, poems. A statement of this sort rings like a challenge and is obviously aimed at "careerist" authors and artists. In an earlier poem, **"A Career"** (1957), Yevtushenko had already made it abundantly clear that he was for Galileo as against any form of Inquisition and the type of careerist who plays it safe, and he was also for Van Gogh as against the *pompier* type of artist. "We need no pedantic light," he says. In this stand Yevtushenko is by no means alone. Andrey Voznesensky, for example, has made the same point in his more complex poem, **"The Parabolic**

Ballad" (1960), in which he uses Gauguin as the symbol of creative unorthodoxy. It is, perhaps, all rather like Victor Hugo attacking the moribund classical establishment of his day. But the Soviet "establishment" has still a lot of bite left, because it controls the greater part of the critical apparatus. In the situation of Soviet poetry, it would seem a creative and healthy sign to have a point to make, especially if that point is concerned with the defense and possibility of being creative. The danger of course is in overdoing the manifesto element at the expense of the magic of poetry. But if Yevtushenko is at times the moralist, he is far from being entirely so; and the lyrical quality of his poetry has been growing richer rather than poorer.

For Yevtushenko, as well as Voznesensky, 1961 was to be a year of venture and adventure. Traveling together, the two poets visited the United States in April for the first time. That the visit had an impact on both of them is evidenced by the fact that they wrote a number of poems on American themes. Voznesensky wrote a whole cycle of poems under the title of *Triangular Pear* (1962), his most interesting effort so far, because he also attempted to develop new forms. Yevtushenko's poetic reactions in some half-a-dozen poems were more occasional. If the two poets are to be compared, one might say that Voznesensky writes less and more concentratedly, progressively paying more attention to the image as a vehicle of modern sensibility. In his language, too, he employs to a greater extent a variety of modern technical words, thus giving his poetry a particularly modern flavor. He is more of an urban poet than Yevtushenko. Yevtushenko has potentially a wider range of interests, greater facility and a more public presence. For all the increasing differences between them, Yevtushenko and Voznesensky have much in common. They complement each other. There seems to be no point in saying, as some people do, that one poet is "better" than the other. Each of them is making a valuable contribution in his own way. Yevtushenko also paid a visit to Cuba, a visit he was to repeat the following year. The result was a body of poems evoking his impressions of that revolutionary island. He returned to the Soviet Union via Paris. The year before, he had already traveled to England, France, Catalonia, Africa, and even Bulgaria. All these trips have been recorded in poems. It was in September, 1961, after his return from abroad, that Yevtushenko published his internationally famous poem **"Babii Yar."** He had at first some difficulty in getting it accepted, but finally, upon appeal to the highest authority, the poem appeared in *Literaturnaya Gazeta*. It was a very brave and bold attempt to bring out into the open many of the festering sores in the Soviet body politic.

The years 1960-61 were of tremendous importance to Yevtushenko both from the standpoint of the development of his poetry and from that of the growth of his popularity. He published his next two volumes in editions of 100,000 each. *A Wave of the Hand* (*Vzmakh Ruki*), which appeared in the spring of 1962, is a volume of 352 pages. Obviously not all of the poems in it were new. The book is divided into three sections: *Poems About Abroad, Let*

Us Be Great! and *Morning Poems.* The latter contains sixty-five poems, representing a selection of his earlier work from 1952 to 1960. They are mainly the sort of poems that have already been discussed. In the twenty-eight *Poems About Abroad* Yevtushenko has collected the poems he wrote about foreign countries—England, France, Catalonia, Bulgaria, Ghana, Liberia, Togo. These poems are, for the most part, the immediate impressions of a traveler, a sort of diary in verse with here and there a moral drawn or an injunction made. Ten of the poems are about Paris or French themes; four on Cuba; and eight on Africa. There is only one poem, and that a satirical one, **"Uriah Heap,"** about England, and in it Yevtushenko describes a brush he had with a customs officer. Two poems are on American themes: one about Hemingway, whom he apparently saw in passing at a restaurant at an airfield in Copenhagen; and the other about his visit to Harvard in 1961, in which, after waxing lyrical about the similar nature of Russian and American nightingales, he makes a plea for friendship between the two countries. Both these poems have, it seems to me, a soldier lyrical strength more than the other pieces. The Hemingway poem is not just accidental. For over a decade Hemingway has been to Yevtushenko not only an heroic figure, but also a model for writing—a model in the sense of compression, terseness and virility. In the middle section of fifty-seven poems, *Let Us Be Great!* Yevtushenko has gathered those poems which have political overtones, such as **"Envy,"** **"A Career,"** **"Rockets and Carts"** and **"Humor,"** which have been discussed or quoted elsewhere. *Let Us Be Great!* is something like a motto for Yevtushenko. It can be interpreted as a sort of heroic challenge—let us try and live on a higher ethical plane—a very necessary ideal after the low level reached during the Stalinist rule of distrust and betrayal.

Yevgeny Yevtushenko's next book, *Tenderness* (*Nezhnost*), followed quickly on *A Wave of the Hand.* This book was published in the autumn of 1962, soon after Voznesensky's *Triangular Pear.* In outward appearance both these books looked very different from any previous book published by their authors. They had abstract jackets of modern geometric design suggesting the art of Mondrian. In fact, a Soviet critic could easily have labelled them "formalistic." They reminded one of the days of Mayakovsky's *Lef* and the experiments of the Soviet 1920's, which had been condemned since the early thirties. These books looked different, modern and challenging. Even more surprising was that 100,000 copies of *Tenderness* had been printed. It should be noted that Yevtushenko had been abroad prior to the publication of this book. He had been to Cuba again, and had also spent almost a month in England in April-May, reading his poems in London, Oxford and Cambridge, and elsewhere. This was the third year in succession that he had spent some months abroad. He was indeed becoming almost a permanent news item in the international press. Inwardly, *Tenderness* is divided into two sections. The last section of twenty-two poems is entirely devoted to Cuban themes. The Cuban poems of *A Wave of the Hand* had now grown into a whole cycle. At least two poems, **"The American Cemetery"** and **"The Heming-way Hero"** also touch on the American theme largely through Hemingway. In the former poem, Yevtushenko opens as follows:

> The American cemetery,
> abandoned by people,
> gazes sadly and sorrowfully,
> as though asking for love.

Having described the atmosphere of the cemetery and having quoted some complaints about the United States voiced by a Cuban woman, Yevtushenko recalls Hemingway:

> He died, but his deathless lines
> teach us to live greatly,
> but have we, America,
> ever called him "gringo"?

> A Russian, I would very much like
> with all my life and all the destiny
> of flights, construction and creation,
> America, to be together with you.

> I wish the word "gringo" to be
> cleanly erased from the dictionary,
> that all nations might respect
> the graves of their sons.

In the second poem, Yevtushenko meets and talks to the old fisherman Anselmo who had served as the prototype for Hemingway's *The Old Man and the Sea*. It should be borne in mind that, to a young Soviet poet of Yevtushenko's generation, revolutionary Cuba exercises great fascination. All the more so for Yevtushenko, who has been so critical of post-revolutionary corruption in his own Soviet motherland. It is very natural for him to seek some source of purer expression of the revolutionary ideal elsewhere:

> Revolution
>   is a harsh business,
> but it's no gloomy thing,
>   the devil take it!
> Revolution,
>   do away with all things
> that are officious and for parade!

The first section of *Tenderness* contains seventy-four poems, almost all of them new. They cover a wide range of subject matter. There are new poems about Paris and New York (**"Girl Beatnik"** and **"Monologue of the Beat-niks,"** which are better poems than the earlier **"Angry Young Men"**), several polemical poems, and a number of poems about women, as well as a variety of others. In the polemical poems, as in **"Honey,"** Yevtushenko directs his attack against the inhumanity of a wartime official figure ("he's still alive"), and in **"Conversation with an American Writer,"** written in New York, he claims to speak "all on my mind" and delivers a very forthright frontal assault on "the cowardice" of certain "colleagues":

> Yes, I defended men of talent,
> branding the hacks, the would-be writers.

No doubt **"Babii Yar"** should have been, and would have been, included in this volume, too, if it had been found possible to reprint it. In certain other poems such as **"Women,"** **"Saleswoman of Ties,"** and **"The Woman and the Sea,"** Yevtushenko is preoccupied with the nature and character of women. In **"The Woman and the Sea,"** he expresses his admiration for a woman who shows herself determined and strong:

> In moments of stress,
> complication and distress,
> when out of cowardice
> we begin to squirm,
> then women
>   of vigor,
> who like to laugh,
> will remind us
> we
>   are men!

There is likewise compassion, as in the earlier poem **"I Don't Understand,"** for women who have to bear with life's miseries:

> A saleswoman with straggly curls,
> with inept but darling hands . . .
> I now stared hard,
>   and pain pinched my heart,
> and pity, you must know,
>   pure pity
> I felt for her clean, exhausted hands . . .

This note of compassion for women is also characteristic of Boris Pasternak—in his poetry and *Doctor Zhivago.* Yevtushenko has always had a sympathetic eye for the ordinary man and the underdog. He has even been reproached for this. But it is his way of saying that he is aware of the suffering of the Russian people as he certainly is in **"Honey."** This note of universal compassion may explain the title of his book—*Tenderness.* In this connection, his attitude may be defined as that of tenderness towards people and harshness towards the selfish bureaucrats. It may, indeed, be recalled that, in answer to a questionnaire, Yevtushenko once wrote in *Voprosy Litera-turi* that there should be only two Ministers in the future ideal Communist State: Tenderness (*Nezhnost*) and Truth (*Pravda*). There are other poems of his such as **"Hail in Kharkov"** and **"The Railing"** which, in their buoyant and boisterous word play, their alliteration and assonance, remind one of the sound and movement of Pasternak's earlier poetry. **"The Railing"** is an elegiac poem that might well refer to Pasternak and his grave in Peredelkino—"His was a large, childlike smile / upon the face of a martyr of this age." And very like Pasternak's, too, is the rushing sound of:

> The peace of ponds,
>   the crump of crashing icefloes,
> the hazard of bazaars,
>   the integrity of temples,
> gardens in full blow, and clumps of cities.

In **"Hail in Kharkov"** Yevtushenko expresses pure delight in the sound of words, the sounds that convey in a sort of staccato dancing rhythm the thrashing sound of hail. By the end of the poem, in the Yevtushenko manner, the hail also becomes the symbol for a certain natural freedom in which those young of heart can exult:

> All who are young
>   are glad of hail.

But the poet also draws attention to another sort of hail through which he has to walk:

> the hail of gibes,
>   of crafty slanders,
> which assail me on every side.

In the end, the poet interprets "hail is / a reward / to those who fear no barriers."

In early 1965, *Tenderness* was still the last volume of Yevtushenko's poetry to have been published in the Soviet Union. As from late 1962, we have available only those new poems of Yevtushenko which have appeared in the dailies, periodicals and magazines. A notable poem of his, **"The Heirs of Stalin,"** was printed only in *Pravda* (October 21, 1962). It obviously required the authority of that daily for the poem to be printed at all, for in it Yevtushenko very openly raised the question of the persistence and survival of a Stalinist mentality and a body of Stalinist supporters who were still eager to seize power. The poem is frankly anti-Stalinist. It also intrudes into the sphere of foreign politics, since it contains a direct reference to Enver Hoxha of Albania and a hidden allusion to the Chinese problem or, rather, to the pro-Stalinist attitude of the Chinese Communist Party, which is a matter of grave concern to the Kremlin. Yevtushenko urges vigilance to prevent any possible resurrection of Stalinism—"stop Stalin from ever rising again. . . ." The political aspect of this poem is clear enough. What is not so clear is why and how a Soviet poet could have intervened in such a delicate matter. The imprimatum of *Pravda* in this case indicates official sanction and perhaps even the backing of Mr. Khrushchev himself. If so, Yevtushenko at that moment seemed to be in an extraordinary position; he spoke out, he was much attacked, yet he could go on speaking out and raising the most provocative issues. It seemed, indeed, as if he could dare anything. He had reached a height of eminence where he could even write in his **"Poetry"**:

> "The poet
>   is like Kutuzov the clearsighted . . .
> They slander him from left
>   and right,
> but he looks down on the liars with contempt."

But **"The Heirs of Stalin"** was more than just a political poem. It also spoke of the hurt and damage that had been done by Stalin—the distrust he had sown, the prison camps he had filled, the youth he had perverted, the people's good he had neglected, the innocent men he had jailed. In this sense Yevtushenko was speaking both to and for his generation. The poem is also interesting from the purely poetical point of view. Its tone is grave and sustained—ironically enough, it is the tone of an elegy which unexpectedly turns into a denunciation. The imagery is often arresting: the surprising image of the telephone in Stalin's coffin is worthy of Mayakovsky. Throughout the poem there is a certain amount of alliteration effectively used:

> Mute was the marble.
>   Mutely glimmered the glass.
> Mute stood the sentries,
>   bronzed by the breeze.

As in **"Babii Yar,"** Yevtushenko here succeeds in writing a powerful and aesthetically satisfactory poem. The poem is about Stalin, but not about Stalin in the old, mechanical, obsequious manner, to which the poet Pavel Antokolsky referred when he wrote in 1956:

> We, laureates of prizes
> given us in his name,
> had all walked in silence
> through a time now dead.

And, finally, it is not really a poem about Stalin, but one about the aspirations of the new generation, who do not want to be trampled upon and betrayed.

5. THE TURN OF THE WHEEL. THE POETS ARE RESTRICTED

But contrary forces were now at work. Certain elements within the Party were perturbed by the independent attitudes and the unbridled directions which the younger writers were taking. By December of 1962, the criticism was mounting and becoming more official. There was even a verbal passage at arms in public between Khrushchev and Yevtushenko. Whatever the outcome was to be, neither Yevtushenko, nor Voznesensky, seemed unduly disturbed as yet. They went off again to the West of Europe. In early February, 1963, Yevtushenko had arrived in West Germany on a reading tour for the first time there. He read his poems in Hamburg and elsewhere to enthusiastic audiences of students. *Stern* magazine featured him largely in its pages. From Germany he proceeded to Paris where he gave a number of readings which were also widely reported. There, on February 18, he read the poem entitled "The Dead Hand of the Past," which opens as follows:

> Someone is still living as of old,
> attempting to knife whatever's new.
> Someone still glares in the Stalin manner,
> looking at young men askance . . .

At the same time he agreed to the publication of his Autobiography in the Paris *L'Express,* where it began appearing serially on February 21. He was supposed to extend his tour and to visit Italy and the United States again. But within a short time, he was suddenly recalled to Moscow to face a barrage of official criticism and vituperation. The Autobiography had probably proved the last straw. It was far too uninhibited. But it has also been held that Yevtushenko's reading of "The Dead Hand" at the Mutualité in Paris had something to do with his recall. The point is that, as from March 8, when Mr. Khrushchev made a speech about the state of the Soviet arts, to the end of June, when the clamor began to die away, Yevtushenko, Voznesensky, and many other writers, young and old, were subjected to a veritable assault on their nerves. But there were no arrests or terror this time. It was expected that the writers would capitulate and make long speeches of apology and adapt themselves to the ideological requirements. Instead, after making a very brief and noncommital statement, Yevtushenko chose to ignore the whole matter and went off in May on a long trip to Zima Station and other parts of Siberia. He stayed for a time in a village at the mouth of the Pechora river, and by August he had completed a new cycle of poems. Part of the cycle was published in the September, 1963, issue of *Yunost*. This was a sign that the worst of the crisis was over. About six months had passed without Yevtushenko being published. But it is also true that the ideological "authorities," in the persons of L. Ilyichev and S. Pavlov, became disturbed by what they came to term "the conspiracy of silence," that is, the tacit refusal of notable writers like Ehrenburg and Paustovsky, Yevtushenko and Voznesensky, to take part in continuous public debates about the state of the arts and their relation to them. The writers had made their silent point and had managed to survive without anything too drastic happening to them.

Yevtushenko's poems in *Yunost* had been written between May and August. Besides **"Again At Zima Station"** and **"People Were Laughing Behind A Wall,"** the cycle contains some lovely lyrical poems such as **"Beautiful Are the Delights of Early Years,"** and also ballads such as **"Olena's Feet."** In this last the poet describes "Babushka Olena," a sturdy and self-sufficient old woman living in the wilds. At the end of the ballad, the poet implies that he, too, has sturdy legs and can stand on his own feet:

> I'm not accustomed to stooping—
> I have preserved my pride,
> and sorrows will not
> knock me off my feet . . .

In a number of these poems, as in **"People Were Laughing,"** an intensification in Yevtushenko's lyrical mood can be detected:

> People were laughing behind a wall.
> They seemed to be making fun of me.
> I was the butt of all their laughter,
> and how dishonestly they laughed.

It was as if the Pechora air had made him breathe more deeply. In these poems he shows a greater command of poetical resources and seems to grow lyrically more powerful. It is also significant that many of the new poems are written in the ballad style which Yevtushenko handles very well. There is still a tradition of oral poetry extant in that part of the North where he had been staying. By contrast,

he appears more superficial in **"Again At Zima Station,"** an almost perfunctory description of his disgrace:

> I have returned in no good standing,
> and after some sharp reprimands,
> which have their use in the final count . . .

This *Yunost* cycle of poems was criticized in the December issue of *Oktyabr*, and Yevtushenko was again accused of "self-admiration," a charge often brought against him. However, on December 13, during Poetry Week, Yevtushenko did make a public appearance, and read a poem entitled "Ballad About the Punitive Battalion," in which he compared himself to a soldier in such a battalion.[7]

In 1964, Yevtushenko published more than in the preceding year—he had poems in the February *Moskva*, in *Literaturnaya Gazeta* of March 3, and in the July *Novy Mir*. There were nine poems in *Moskva*. Among them were **"Nefertiti"** and **"Other Times Have Come,"** both poems with a polemical underlining, and **"Wood-Cock"** and **"How Piaf Departed,"** two impressive lyrics. In March he published a longish poem, **"The Execution of Stenka Razin,"** a few lines of which have already been quoted, and a strange long poem about Lenin and his relation to the Russian people. Both these poems are in the form of lyrical ballads. They are autonomous parts of a very long poem on which the poet had been working for the past year, a poem provisionally entitled **"The Hydro-Power Station at Bratsk."** This rather overpowering title cannot, however, give us any real idea of the poem. It will certainly *not* be anything like one of those Five Year Plan works of the early 1930's. The Stenka Razin part of it demonstrates that. **"The Execution of Stenka Razin"** is a strange poem or ballad, too. The theme is, of course, a defeated rebel—a rebel who had expected to enter Moscow in triumph, but had instead been taken in a cart to the place of execution in Red Square. Yevtushenko's Stenka Razin has no regrets. He is only sorry he had not strung up more "boyars":

> I have sinned because,
>   though a foe of serfdom,
> I was yet part-serf myself.

This ballad breathes a note not only of bitterness and defeat, but also of resolution. One is naturally tempted to ask what connection the defeated rebel Stenka Razin has to Yevtushenko's own position. The first part of the finished **"Bratsk"** poem was supposed to have been printed in the January, 1965, issue of *Yunost*, but the magazine came out without it. This may be a matter of mere delay or something more significant. The next few months will no doubt tell. But to go back to the July *Novy Mir* of 1964—it added six more Yevtushenko poems, including **"Third Memory,"** **"The Excavator,"** **"On the Pechora,"** and **"Beloved, Sleep,"** the latter a long love lyric with a sort of incantatory power about it. In the lyrical poem **"Third Memory,"** as in **"People Were Laughing,"** Yevtushenko conveys a poignant sense of isolation—an isolation which, it is true, he manages to overcome:

We all live through an hour like this,
when anguish sticks to you like glue
and, in all nakedness exposed,
all life appears devoid of meaning.

In **"How Faltering You Are, My Speech,"** Yevtushenko concludes by comparing himself to the legendary Ivan-the-Fool:

nipping into a cauldron of boiling pitch,
to emerge therefrom a cocksure, brawny man,
smiling confidently in a new caftan,
and twitching his shoulder as if to say:
"Well, would you like to test your strength!"

It can certainly be said that Yevtushenko, though he went through a period bordering on despair, has not faded away as a result of his "disgrace" and semi-incarceration. He is still resilient and energetic. His trip to Siberia has, in the end, apparently proved invigorating and stimulating if we are to judge by the quantity and quality of his later poems. There is a whole batch of them that has yet to be printed. He has grown poetically both in depth and breadth. The Yevtushenko of 1965 is certainly a much bigger, better, and more important poet than his namesake of 1959. As a disciple of Whitman, Mayakovsky, and Yesenin ("I feel kin to Yesenin / and Walt Whitman"), he can combine a more intimate lyricism with an ever-present urge to stretch out further and embrace a wide world of possibilities. There is every reason to suppose that he will continue to grow in stature. If at times he could only curb his facility and diminish his tendency to moralize, then he would become an even greater poet. But he would do so all the more rapidly if the tiresome, paternalistic restrictions were removed and if the following injunction in a poem of Bullat Okudzhava's is heeded:

Guard us poets from foolish hands,
from stupid judgments, blind companions.

Yevgeny Yevtushenko has been waging a battle for the freedom of poetry, for the liberty of expression, and if this has necessitated an emphatic statement here and there, it is his privilege. It remains to be seen if, as he himself wrote about his generation:

We're but the preface to a preface,
a prologue to a newer prologue!

Notes

1. *The Poet's Destination*. Speech pronounced on Feb. 11, 1921, on the occasion of the 84th anniversary of Pushkin's death.

2. *Literaturnaya Gazeta*, March 3, 1964.

3. *The New York Times*, December 21, 1964.

4. See *Survey* No. 46, London: January 1963. Pierre Forgues, "The Young Poets." This article gives a general survey of the poetic revival.

5. "Art for Marx's Sake." *N.Y. Times Magazine Section*, December 20, 1964.

6. Also the name of a popular Russian song.

7. During the war Punitive Battalions were under iron discipline and were given the most dangerous military tasks to perform, usually mine-clearing. They were made up of officers and men who had been convicted of military offenses.

Rosh Ireland (essay date 1967)

SOURCE: Ireland, Rosh. Introduction to *Bratsk Station and Other New Poems,* by Yevgeny Yevtushenko, pp. ix-xxii. Garden City, NY: Anchor Books, 1967.

[*In the following excerpt, Ireland surveys Yevtushenko's career and works.*]

Lord, let me be a poet,
Let me not deceive people.

Y. Yevtushenko

The last decade has seen in the Soviet Union a striking revival of poetry. Interest in the great poets of this century has quickened. Accomplished living poets, under constraint in Stalin's time, have once again found access to the reading public. A number of young poets have come forward to write poetry of a recognizably new kind, to create a vast and enthusiastic audience not only for themselves but for the great poets they claim as mentors, and to transform poetry into a vital medium of communication, a vehicle of expression through which not only their own thoughts and emotions, but also those of the great number of people who make up their audience, can be revealed and recognized to be held in common.

The death of Stalin, followed by his subsequent desanctification, left a generation to learn to think for itself in a society in which no one had been taught to doubt. It has been largely through poetry that the resultant shock has been discussed in terms free of cant; through poetry, a generation has tried to come to terms with life.

The leading figure in the movement urging poetry to the forefront has undoubtedly been Yevgeny Yevtushenko, now a man of thirty-three. His poetry and personality have caused him, within the space of a decade, to be alternately lionized and vilified by both East and West, treated as an unofficial ambassador of his country and accused of treason, compared with Mayakovsky and with Judas Iscariot, accepted as the spokesman of his generation and accused of cynical opportunism. The Soviet writer, whether or not under Stalin, indeed the Russian writer of any age, has had to bear a more direct responsibility for what he writes than writers in the English tradition.

Yevtushenko has not been alone. He himself has been quick to point out other poets whom time may show to have been greater than he, to play down his own achievement and constantly to intimate that he is unable to offer that which his generation needs. Yet among the group of young poets he has been the greatest versifier (technical competence being a feature of the new break-through), the one to take (in his colleague Vinokurov's words) "the mad risk of each new step," the widest-ranging, and of course the first public figure.

He is also of them all the most accessible. If one must pick one feature of Yevtushenko's verse to emphasize, it must be accessibility. His verse is meant to communicate, to find a common language with the reader, indeed to enlist the reader's sympathy, belief, and support—the obscure and the esoteric has no part in it.

Therefore, rightly, he has become the first and the best-known Soviet poet in the West.

His debut as a poet was inauspicious. He published in 1949 some anti-American verse in the newspaper *Soviet Sport* and became, as he puts it, "a real newspaper poet," supplying, in the Soviet tradition, occasional verses for anniversaries and holidays. Meanwhile he developed his poetic muscles by working with the technical devices of poetry—rhyme, meter, alliteration, and metaphor. His first book of verse appeared in 1952, but, he relates, left him with the sour conviction that it was the kind of book no one needed.

In order not to misunderstand totally the Yevtushenko who grew out of this "newspaper poet," it is wise to pay serious attention to what he says in his *Autobiography,* published by *L'Express* in Paris ten years later, about the death of Stalin in 1953, which he takes to be crucial in his life and in his poetry. He examines his own previous view of Stalin and reports on the literary situation at the time: the dearth of poets and the cynical careerism which controlled the Writers' Union, a characterization no doubt partly responsible for the viciousness of attacks on him by orthodox writers when the autobiography appeared. Then, in a passage now well-known, he describes the murderous chaos in the streets at the time of Stalin's lying-in-state and his answer to his mother "Yes, I saw Stalin," meaning that he had seen him in the stampeding crowd and the panic aggravated by the lack of orders from above. From this point onward, he sees himself combining and fusing in his work the intimate lyric, which found immediate response and the revival of which was one of the first signs of the "Thaw," and poetry with a social purpose, through which he hoped to indicate the wrongs of his time, yet, at the same time, to counteract nascent disillusion in his generation.

Yevtushenko's inability to answer for himself the questions he felt to be posed by the events of 1953 took him back in search of a reply to Zima, a small Siberian railway town two hundred miles northwest of Irkutsk, where he had been born and where he had spent the war years as an evacuee. The result was **"Zima Junction,"** one of the outstanding poems published in the "Thaw" year 1956, in which he put his unanswered question to Zima, representing childhood, home, and roots. It is a long narrative poem,

splendidly evocative of the small Siberian town, but full of episodes and meetings which indicate that appearances do not correspond to the underlying reality, whether the matter be marriage, youth, the authorities, beliefs, or personal qualities. All demand a re-examination, an affectionate re-examination but one which will reveal the faults and discrepancies of life.

Other poems published in 1956 in the collection *Enthusiasts' Highway* indicate where Yevtushenko is to find his answer.

> Comrades,
> we must give back to words
> their original sound.

Yevtushenko belongs to a family for whom the ultimate value is the Revolution. The importance of this cannot be stressed too much. He sees as the corrective for the confused situation of the fifties a return to the original values and ambitions of the Revolution, which represents for him not only an historical phenomenon, but a source of conviction and belief which he wishes to dissociate from the injustices of his time.

The years 1955-57 were triumphant ones for Yevtushenko, with books of verse published each year, but they were not untroubled. His marriage to the outstanding poetess Bella Akhmadulina broke up, the hardening of the official attitude to literature in 1957 brought him his share of rather pompous criticism, and exclusion for a time both from the Komsomol and the Literary Institute, where he had been studying. Following the pattern of an earlier difficult year, the returned in 1958 to Zima to write another long poem, **"Where Are You From?"** urging that no one should lose touch with his home ground, and declaring his faith in a generation that had demonstrated its solidarity and stood for truth.

By 1959, when a retrospective collection of his verse appeared, the "modern style" of Yevtushenko had become established and found its imitators. Its main features were striking and unusual rhyme schemes, based not on perfect rhymes but on assonance, alliteration, and association by meaning (any reader of Yevtushenko will find some extraordinary rhyme singing in his head for days); irregular meter—including extensive use of Mayakovsky's stepped line; and garish juxtapositions and bold metaphors (one thinks of the militiamen sticking up in their boxes like teaspoons in Russian glass holders). To these one could add a notable liking for antithesis: Yevtushenko, dealing as he does so often with discrepancies and contradictions, frequently makes use of antithesis in the closing lines of his poems.

The "fourth generation" of Soviet writers, those who had been too young to fight in the Second World War and who shared, as the critic Anninsky pointed out, a common background of evacuation and wartime hardship, had entered poetry and was soon to make its mark in prose.

With 1960 then began Yevtushenko's Wanderjahre. In quick succession he visited France, Africa, the United States, England, and Cuba. The span of his poetry widened to include occasional verse about his journeys, although much he published in his books of 1960 and 1962 does little beyond demonstrate his remarkable ability to turn verses on the small occurrences of everyday life. More importantly, he came forward as an interpreter of his generation abroad ("My Russia" in the London *Observer,* 27 May 1962).

To the same period belong the spectacularly successful **"Poetry Days"** and public poetry readings, which attracted huge audiences. These gave to Yevtushenko, himself a splendid, gripping reader of his own verse (he claims to have given 250 public readings in 1961), and to other poets the opportunity to try out their verse before publication (often long delayed), and assured Yevtushenko a community of emotions with his audience.

In 1961 he published **"Babiy Yar,"** a poem on anti-Semitism. The poet's outspokenness on a topic of worldwide importance—a topic nonetheless most dangerous to broach inside the Soviet Union—brought him extremes of praise and condemnation and focused on him the interest of observers abroad. **"Babiy Yar"** was the first of a notable series of poems which includes **"The Heirs of Stalin"** and **"Fears,"** the publication of which in 1962 was authorized within the context of an extension of Khrushchev's de-Stalinization (under the same dispensation, Solzhenitsyn's *A Day in the Life of Ivan Denisovich* was shortly to follow). The most convenient term to describe this series is "publicist," since in it Yevtushenko used verse as a vehicle for social and political commentary, for the poet's clear expression of his own views on the issues of his time. Yevtushenko attaches great importance to this public function of poetry—as in **"Pushkin Pass,"** 1966:

> Poetry is always the border guard
> at the frontier of the country's conscience.

The year 1962 was a startling success for the younger generation of Soviet writers. Yevtushenko's two new volumes of verse, *A Wave of the Hand* and *Tenderness,* came out in editions of one hundred thousand, and he himself was elected to the board of the Moscow branch of the Writers' Union and appointed to the editorial board of the literary magazine *Youth.* It seemed clear by late 1962 that the generation which had entered literature since Stalin's death, despite the disfavor with which they were regarded by a number of their elders, were being accepted into the official literary community under the aegis not only of officials of the Writers' Union and older writers who had encouraged them, but also of Party spokesmen. At the same time, the nature of their contribution to literature began to be seriously discussed. Taking part in this discussion, Yevtushenko was able, along with other new poets, to acknowledge his debt to Boris Pasternak.

Then came the first of a series of events in which Yevtushenko was to play a leading role, and which one must assume to have largely determined the nature of the poem which forms the greater part of this book—**"The Bratsk Hydroelectric Station."**

The details of Khrushchev's visit to the art exhibition in Moscow in November 1962 and the events which followed it are now well documented. It launched a campaign for the removal of abstractionist and modernist elements from the visual arts, a campaign which spread into a general move to restore socialist realist orthodoxy in all the arts, including literature. The new mood culminated in December and the following March in tense meetings between Khrushchev and his officials, on the one hand, and Soviet artists and writers, on the other.

Yevtushenko was drawn into the December exchanges both to defend abstract painters and sculptors and to clash over **"Babiy Yar."** Then, however, while official attention was shifting to literature, to Ilya Ehrenburg and Viktor Nekrasov in particular, he left to visit West Germany and France. In West Germany he spoke on international confidence and understanding, regretted the absence of diplomatic relations between the Federal Republic and the countries of Eastern Europe (except the Soviet Union), and suggested the establishment of an independent Soviet-German society to organize cultural exchange, all of which led to his being taken for a semi-official spokesman for his country. In France, he published in *L'Express* his autobiography,[1] which reveals a man very different from the brash, self-confident, doughty young literary lion of the Soviet and Western press. It is full of the stories lying at the heart of his poems, all episodes which are stages in understanding, revelations of the way of a world in which outward appearance does not necessarily coincide with inner reality. The autobiography is a development of his consciousness of wrong—injustice, falsehood, and corruption (symbolized by the eerie image of Beria's pale face in a car edging along the pavement in search of a woman)—and a decision to oppose it as a poet, to oppose it by presenting the ideals of the generation of revolutionaries which perished under Stalin to a generation which still suffers from the habits of Stalin's time, and, in wider terms, to oppose the same faults in both East and West on the basis of a belief in the essential goodness of people.

It is perhaps unfair to present the complicated development of a poetic consciousness in such bald terms. Yevtushenko may thereby appear to be a person of wild ambitions and woolly ideals. It is, however, essential to be aware of the poet's view of himself, especially where the poet's background is so alien to us, when coming to grips with a poem like **"Bratsk."**

When Khrushchev spoke in March, he said that Yevtushenko had, on the whole, "behaved properly" abroad, and warned him in only mild terms about his political immaturity and aesthetic errors. Then, however, Yevtushenko became the chief target of violent attacks on the young writers made by conservatives at the Fourth Plenum of the Board of the Writers' Union of the U.S.S.R. and a similar

Plenum of the Board of the Writers' Union of the R.S-.F.S.R.[2] Of those attacked at the first of these meetings, only Voznesensky and Yevtushenko replied. The published report of his speech was indicative of what went on:

"Y. Yevtushenko in the first part of his speech attempted to 'dispute' the sharp criticism leveled at him. . . . However, under the influence of the exigent, principled atmosphere of the Plenum, Y. Yevtushenko was nevertheless constrained to speak of his mistakes . . . (there follows a long account by Yevtushenko of the distortion of his *Autobiography* by the French *L'Express*) . . .

"It must be said that Y. Yevtushenko's speech did not satisfy those taking part in the Plenum: his speech clearly contained notes which indicated that Y. Yevtushenko had not recognized the roots of his errors, both in the case of the publication of his *Autobiography* and in certain of his verses."

Every aspect of his poetry and behavior, from his rhyme schemes to his love poetry, from his misunderstanding of Marxism to his flirtation with the "bourgeois enemy," was condemned in most bitter terms, and he and the whole pleiad of poets he had led were rejected and their supporters and patrons jeered at. Yevtushenko was isolated and, despite an obvious relaxation of the tension in the succeeding months and some guarded statements ventured in his defense, his position was acutely dangerous. The poetry readings and the foreign tours ceased, and Yevtushenko's career as a poet could have been ended.

It is possible to look back and minimize the results of the Party's intervention between December 1962 and March 1963. Yevtushenko's most virulent critics have admitted, at the Second Congress of Writers of the R.S.F.S.R., that they may have been unduly sharp in their criticism of processes which they considered wrong—in other words, that they far overstepped the mark in denouncing Yevtushenko and the others. The first authoritative statement in 1965 about the Party's attitude to the writers indicated a return to a position close to that of the end of 1962. It is evident, however, from his poetry that Party criticism had a profound effect upon Yevtushenko. And indeed it was only toward the end of 1965 that his first book of poetry to appear since that time was published. He was left to reconsider his position, and neither the poems he has published in various journals nor **"Bratsk"** provide more than partial evidence of the result of his re-thinking.

It could not have been unexpected that Yevtushenko should have sought first of all to re-establish contact with his audience. In the summer of 1963, he left Moscow to spend some time in the far north and then, as he had done before in similar circumstances, returned to Zima, where he wrote the first poem to appear since his return from France, **"At Zima Junction Once More."** The poem is built round three episodes, each related to a vital factor in rediscovering his role.

The poet returns to Zima, again downcast, covered, he says, by the dust of his foreign travels and by the dust of unpleasant rumors about him. He is urged to read his poetry by members of the Zima Komsomol, apparently unmindful of his disgrace, and he finds himself accepted and encouraged as a "local" (zemlyak):

> The hall understood. The hall was moved.
> And, gulping tears in my throat,
> I felt this as an advance
> against that which I had to do.
> And it seemed to me, little by little,
> that the walls moved apart,
> and there—in lights, in forest green—
> through the sirens of the Volga and the Urals
> the land called me approvingly . . .

His rapport with his audience was established—and here one recalls Khrushchev's injunction to him to pay more attention to the opinion of workers. Then, in the image of a busy transport depot, he sees the land waiting for words from its "Plenipotentiaries," the prose writers and poets—thus re-establishing another article of his faith, that what he has to say is needed. Lastly, a woman standing by the local military commandant's office brings him to a resolution to defend his country

> against wars, all hardships, any
> eyes glinting with ill-will,
> against the repetition of mistakes,
> against far too nimble careerists,
> and patriots on the surface only.

Once he has satisfied himself that his audience is still willing to listen to him and that the country feels a need for the words of the poet, he states again his old belief in publicist verse aimed at both external enemies and internal dangers.

The majority of the poems he has published since 1963 have been about the North. Almost without exception, they are of high poetic density and of very high technical quality, reflecting the range of his poetic accomplishments from exercises in technical conceits to work with the traditional four-footed iambic. Much of his concern is, again, with his roots in the land, coming to terms with himself, and his role as poet. He himself, no doubt, is the drake which lands on the Pechora to draw sustenance from that river. Once again, he sees isolated episodes as the mirror of a general circumstance: in the failure of his shouts to wake a ferryman on the opposite bank of a river, he sees his inability to be heard in peasant huts; in a muddled conversation, he sees not only that people fail to understand each other, but also that they fail to understand themselves. In all these poems, his most striking metaphor of himself is as a communications launch in the far north, carrying mail and therefore conveying the thoughts and emotions of people, early in the season, when ice and wintry conditions made it difficult for the launch to find a passage. When navigation starts, bigger vessels will appear and the communications launch, having done its job, will be forgotten. This metaphor refers, of course, not only to the difficulties of the "season" in Soviet literature, but also to a motive which has recurred throughout his poetry: that Yevtushenko sees himself merely as the pathfinder, the one to break through in mistakes and compromises, ever unsure of his direction, and to be followed by a greater figure.

If the predominant themes of his recent work have been those already expressed in **"At Zima Junction Once More"**—his own position in difficult circumstances, his roots, and communication among people and with himself—he has nonetheless been able to continue his series of publicist poems. **"Nefertiti,"** published early in 1964, suggests the permanence of beauty, and therefore of art, set against the transience of crude temporal power. The one hundred fiftieth anniversary of the birth of Lermontov in the same year gave him the opportunity to publish **"A Ballad about Benkendorf, Chief of Gendarmerie, and Lermontov's Poem 'Death of a Poet,'"** in which he equated a "divine justice," which Lermontov had predicted for the officials indirectly responsible for the death of Pushkin, with a "poet's justice" awaiting all "phonies, gendarmes, and suckers-up." Last year's "Ballad on Poaching," which, in the form of a feuilleton in verse, exposed the chairman of a Pechora fishing collective who depleted fish stocks by using nets of too fine a mesh, could be taken as a parable on too strict censure of young writers.

The power of these verses has been much subdued, if one compares them with, for example, **"The Heirs of Stalin,"** but it is quite clear that Yevtushenko has encountered difficulty over this period in publishing his verse.

Yevtushenko published the first extracts from **"Bratsk"** early in 1964. The whole poem appeared just over a year later. It was written in years which were extremely difficult for Yevtushenko, when, although the charges of disloyalty which had been made against him were quickly dropped, he was in official disfavor and was forced to find a new role for himself in greatly changed circumstances.

"Bratsk" is a long and discursive epic, the five thousand lines of which clearly represent a huge amount of work. It contains, as Yevtushenko explains in his introduction, his thoughts, assembled within the framework of a clash of two opposed themes. The themes are faith and its antithesis, lack of faith. They are further reduced to a contrast of free and slave labor, and they are represented by two symbols, the protagonists in the dispute. An Egyptian Pyramid presents the eternal futility of man's efforts to free himself; the Bratsk hydroelectric station appears as a monument to free labor achieved by the October Revolution and is, in an obvious extension of the symbol, the source of light for mankind. Within this framework there are a number of disparate elements which include invocations to Russia's great poets, a series of historical episodes, a re-creation of Bratsk itself, biographies of some of its builders, and an examination of the importance of poetry. The dialogue of the Pyramid and Bratsk is only an external unifying factor. One has to search for some internal unity.

"Bratsk" goes much deeper than any of the other post-1963 poems in the context of the poet's search for his relationship with his country and its people. He brings in his country's history, treating it as a number of episodes leading up to the October Revolution. He then tries to connect the Revolution, which he sees as the carrier of great ideals and ambitions ("We are not slaves"), with the legacy of Stalin, and in the connection to solve the problem of his own position as a poet anxious to be within the conscience of his people.

With the exception of a few aspects, duly noted by an official Party critic who gave a generally favorable opinion of the poem, Yevtushenko's history is not unorthodox. He is not sufficiently explicit (perhaps he cannot be so) in his reply to the challenge of the Old Bolshevik in the poem to be careful lest the light of Bratsk be turned against its creators. His reply, that one must be loyal to the ideals of Lenin, is not explicit enough, at least for us, to accept his view of history as convincing support for his position. Perhaps he makes his most important political point in his insistence on finding the connection between the events of Stalin's time and the Soviet Union of the present day. Stalin's legacy is too often limited officially to past time.

There is Yevtushenko's usual unevenness in the poem: some brilliant sections, the success of which is largely due to his mastery of a variety of verse forms; a wide range of material; occasional unsuccessful lines and some disappointing sections, including one unbearably banal biography.

"Bratsk" is, however, a second autobiography. Besides Yevtushenko's view of history, it contains endless echoes of his earlier poems, from **"Zima Junction"** to **"Babiy Yar,"** the coalescing of a coherent view of his errors in the past and a determination for the future, the repetition of many postulations from his original *Autobiography*, and a vast amount of evidence on his view of himself and his own generation.

One other aspect of the poem's inner unity should be mentioned. When he writes in his introduction that the characters appearing in the poem are examples of "faith," the poem takes on the aspect of a poet's search for people who share his faith, a need to find people who share his aspirations. Yevtushenko's poetry, inasmuch as it is the poetry of a leader, demands that others be in close support. Otherwise he is isolated, vulnerable, and disoriented.

"Bratsk" may leave the reader with the impression that in Yevtushenko the poet is servant to the publicist. This is not true of his work as a whole, as the selection of recent poems included in this book with **"Bratsk"** will make clear, for it reveals the striking range of response which Yevtushenko possesses.

"Bratsk" must be seen to represent some measure of compromise with the official balance of values and not a full expression of the poet's own ideas. To find the essential element in Yevtushenko's poetry one must go beyond the publicist verve, the technical brilliance, and the vividness of detail to a basic concern with the human condition. Then Yevtushenko comes forward, not as a revealing source of information about the society in which he lives, but as a poet whose value, like his inquiry, extends beyond the boundaries of the Soviet Union, and whose work is properly the concern of all to whom poetry is important.

Notes

1. The circumstances of the publication of the *Autobiography* are examined in detail in Priscilla Johnson: *Khrushchev and the Arts* (Cambridge, Massachusetts: Massachusetts Institute of Technology, 1965).

2. R.S.F.S.R.—The Russian Soviet Federal Socialist Republic, largest of the fifteen Union Republics which make up the Soviet Union; it includes Moscow and Leningrad.

Tina Tupikina Glaessner and Geoffrey Dutton (essay date 1967)

SOURCE: Glaessner, Tina Tupikina, and Geoffrey Dutton. "Translators' Note on 'Bratsk Station'." In *Bratsk Station and Other Poems,* pp. xxiii-xxv. Garden City, NY: Anchor Books, 1967.

[*In the following excerpt, Glaessner and Dutton extol the importance of Yevtushenko as a poet and remark on the problems encountered translating his poetry into English.*]

To understand this poem of Yevtushenko's, it is essential to realize that the word "Bratsk," the name of the gigantic complex of inland sea and hydroelectric station and factories in Siberia, two thirds of the way from Moscow to Vladivostok, also refers to "brotherhood" in Russian, through the adjective "Bratskiy," "brotherly." It is obviously impossible to reproduce this in English with such grotesqueries as "The Brotherly Hydroelectric Station." Therefore, throughout this English translation, only the words **"Bratsk Station"** have been used. But the dual meanings of the name, as also of "light" meaning both "light" and "enlightenment," are basically and intricately linked throughout the whole poem.

Yevtushenko is one of the greatest poets of the modern age. He is important not only because of the intrinsic quality of his poetry, of such masterpieces as **"Zima Junction,"** but for his unique stature as a poetic force in both East and West. A passionately patriotic Russian, he is also a highly sophisticated and much traveled man. Editions of his poems sell by hundreds of thousands in Russia, and millions listen to his readings; but he has also drawn vast crowds on his visits to the United States, England and Italy. He is not a member of the Communist Party, but a fervent believer in the ideals of Lenin, in what he calls throughout **"Bratsk Station"** the "Commune." Giving the word its original French impetus, he demonstrates its workings in Russian history and holds out the ideal of the future commune of mankind, the brotherhood of nations.

"Bratsk Station" gives, as no other work has done, the essence of modern Russia. It gives it all, the great writers and rebels and revolutionaries under the Tsars; Lenin; the Revolution; some of the evils of Stalinism; the corruption of some Stalinist bosses; the priggishness of some examples of modern Soviet man.

Siberia, the ground on which the whole poem lives, is both the endless prison which engulfed intellectuals under the Tsars and political prisoners under Stalin, and today the source of light from Bratsk, built out of the virgin taigá, the Siberian forest, by people who now actually go to Siberia of their own free will, much to the astonishment of those who remember the prison camps.

In **"Bratsk Station"** Yevtushenko speaks in several voices: his own and those of the Bratsk Station and the Egyptian Pyramid, young and old Russians, the Angara River, a Jew. Some are idealistic, some cynical, some wise with suffering or age, some innocent. The flatness of tone and banality of thought in certain sections would seem to be quite deliberate, when seen in the context of the whole poem; it is a poem that must be read as a whole. Yevtushenko is a highly aware writer, and a master of organization. The enthusiasm and rhetoric of some of his idealistic poems may likewise seem naïve to us non-Communists, though God (or rather Lenin) only knows how the grinding pessimism and mincing ironies of some Western poetry must sound to the Russians. But Yevtushenko is desperately anxious to show that "affirming flame" which W. H. Auden begged for in 1939. It would be easier, or more natural perhaps, for a Russian to be a cynic or a nihilist, after the appalling destruction of a civil war and two world wars in thirty years. Even today it does not seem to be generally realized that in the Second World War alone twenty million Russians were killed, as against about half a million in the British Commonwealth, and three hundred thousand in the United States. In **"Bratsk Station"** the voices of the dead sound constantly behind those of the living.

It is extremely difficult to give any true impression in English of the range and quality of Yevtushenko's poetry. He uses every sort of idiom, from classical poetic diction to the colloquialisms of the different times about which he is writing. He uses a very wide variety of forms of versification, and his rhymes are so subtle that it is better not to risk trying to copy them in English, which in any case has different facilities for rhyme from Russian. Yevtushenko also writes in the style of popular songs, and parodies the solemn efforts of amateur poets (which he admires nonetheless, for the genuine feeling behind them). There are many ironical passages. He loves to play with the multiple meaning of words, and indeed, as has been said, the whole poem is based on a play on the words "Bratsk" and "light."

Grateful thanks are due to Igor Mezhakoff-Koriakin and Rosh Ireland for help in checking the translation.

Yevgeni Sidorov (essay date 1983)

SOURCE: Sidorov, Yevgeni. "Yevgeni Yevtushenko's Solo: On His 50th Birthday." *Soviet Literature* 7, no. 424 (1983): 130-37.

[*In the following essay, Sidorov considers the characteristics of Yevtushenko's poetry, praising him for his contributions to Russian literature.*]

Yevgeni Yevtushenko was born in Siberia at Zima Junction near Irkutsk. The poet's father was a geologist and wrote verse all his life. I knew him and heard him recite his poems. They had something to them, no doubt about that, a kind of romanticism à la Siberian Kipling. It was the father who taught the son to love poetry.

Before the war Yevgeni lived for a while with his mother in Moscow. When war broke out he was evacuated back to Zima to his grandmother's.

Yevtushenko's poems about childhood in wartime Siberia were his first serious literary efforts. He wrote these poems after returning to Moscow, while studying in a poetry circle at the local Young Pioneers' House and at the Gorky Literary Institute.

Yevtushenko had good luck in his friends and mentors. Later he would recall many of them with deep gratitude:

"All my life I have been grateful to the poet Andrei Dostal. For over three years he worked with me almost daily as literary consultant at the Molodaya Gvardia Publishing House . . . I had great luck again in 1949, when I met journalist and poet Nikolai Tarasov in the offices of the newspaper *Sovietski Sport*. Not only did he publish my first poems—he also spent many hours with me, patiently explaining which lines were good, which were bad and why . . . My friendship with Vladimir Sokolov proved invaluable; Sokolov, by the way, helped me enroll at the Literary Institute, although I did not have a school-leaving certificate."

Close contacts with Mikhail Lukonin, Yevgeni Vinokurov and Alexander Mezhirov also proved very instructive for the poet at the start of his career. They set the standard for him, these men who had come back from the war front and knew not only the art of poetry but first and foremost the difficult art of living.

He learned a little from everyone and wrote a great deal, a very great deal. He began publishing his verse regularly at sixteen. His first printed poems showed undoubted talent. He was keenly interested in intensely expressive poetic form. There was individuality in his choice of striking detail, turn of phrase, and rhymes.

At that time a galaxy of future major writers were studying at the Literary Institute—you would meet Robert Rozhdestvensky, Bella Akhmadulina, Mikhail Roshchin or Yuri Kazakov in the corridors and lecture-halls of the Institute. This was a new wave in Soviet literature, whose youth coincided with great changes in the life of society.

The stirrings of spring were particularly keenly felt by young people, by students who avidly read the poems of Leonid Martynov, a poet of an older generation:

> The world is astir
> With something new.
> Songs are what people are thirsting for.
>
> (Translated by Peter Tempest)

Yevgeni Yevtushenko was one of the first to sense the possibilities that the times opened before him. As a poet, he was in point of fact the product of the social scene of the mid -'50s. Ever since most topical social and political themes have been part and parcel of his writing. They have been the most powerful stimulus of his poetry.

Yevtushenko entered the literary scene at a fortunate moment when public interest in poetry was growing immensely. The editions of books of poetry published were growing. Poems were being recited in concert halls and in public squares. Thanks to his civic spirit and ability to cut to the quick, Yevtushenko gradually found himself the focus of readers' attention.

He created a generalised image of the urban youth of that time who saw their purpose in life as service to their country:

> Oh, madcap parties of our youth,
> oh, endless wrangles and disputes,
> the get-togethers of those times!
>
>   . . . . .
>
> Here songs are sung to crazy tunes,
> the plates are cracked, the dancing wild,
> and openly are ridiculed
> the clothes of naked kings.
> Millions of views and questions are asked
> about the paths of Russia's past
> and Russia as it is.

Nothing was beyond the young people's power and everything lay ahead. All-powerful youth, optimism and unbounded self-confidence—that was the prologue of his poetic destiny.

The best early poem of Yevtushenko's is **Weddings.** The drama of a people at war is seen through the eyes of a Siberian boy and expressed through his feelings. Each detail of his sad and reckless dance is truthful and expressive. It is hard to say who feels more desperate—the bridegroom going to the front or the boy called in to dance at one wedding after another, weddings which are also farewell parties. Before our very eyes the boy ceases to be a child becoming the equal of any participant in the people's destiny.

> I'm faint with fright,
>   my feet like lead,

        but I shall dance
            till I drop dead.

That boy would be forever peeping from behind his verse, dancing, no matter what roads Yevtushenko travelled at home and abroad, what impressions of life nourished his work and what poetic roles he took on.

How densely and diversely populated the young Yevtushenko's poems are! The whole of Russia is here and, though it may not speak out directly, it is at least named here: city dwellers and country folk, geologists, gold-diggers, Gypsies, barmaids, students, lift operators, shop assistants, ploughmen, drivers, heads of motor depots, jazzmen, film and theatre actors, vagabonds, alcoholics, cashiers, TV announcers, hunters, artists, critics, yard-keepers, accountants, soldiers, housewives, trackmen, fishermen, trappers, excavator operators, old men and women from villages in Siberia and the Far North. Not many of our poets give voice to such vast crowds and such a variety of professions and trades in their poems. With his poems about foreign countries this human mass grew immeasurably, encompassing the full diversity of the world's population—from beatniks to Presidents.

Nearly every chance encounter leaves a trace in the poet's work. The impressions are not controlled by strict artistic selectivity, they are hurriedly poured into stanzas while they are still fresh and vivid, and not yet pushed into the background by new ones. This is not a conscious principle, as the poet would later insist. It is just his temperament, drawing into the creative process everything that lives, everything that surrounds the man, transforming reflected life into a gushing stream of faces and details.

Side by side with this is poetic musing. Poems about his own generation. About human depth. About talent and mediocrity in art. About kindness and malice. About tenderness. About animosity and friendship. About poetry. About popularity. Civic spirit. Simplicity. Humour. Perfection. And so on.

The whole of Yevtushenko's poetry lies in these two coordinates. Its two principal stylistic features are detail and formula. It does not matter much that a great deal was wellknown before. What does matter is that you got at the truth yourself and expressed it in your own words:

    Try to equate the talent, not the age.
    Being young, but lagging behind—that's the trouble!
    Fighting all falsehood fiercely—that is kindness.
    There's more harm in taking friend for foe
    in haste, than taking foe for friend.
    The evil that's strong must first opposed be
    and only after that—the evil that's lesser.
    And when we cease to be exacting to others,
    we are ceasing to be young.
    What matters if someone
                badgers us?
    It matters more to have true followers.

And so on.

Didacticism and rhetoric are Yevtushenko's constant companions. Often they are impediments, but more often they aid him, helping him to swim to safety. That, by the way, is one of the reasons for his popularity with readers. A feeling for the mass of readers, a prompt didactic response to their needs is the very core of his poetic character. His poems frankly await a public response, his poetry is simply inconceivable without it. He is infinitely dependent on the opinions of his readers and listeners and he endlessly seeks their approval. He does not believe anyone but them.

Once he pointed out quite correctly: "The assonance rhyme, which is for some reason referred to as the Yevtushenko rhyme, was first brilliantly used on the basis of Russian folklore by Kirsanov." His enthusiasm for Kirsanov passed, like whooping cough in childhood, but for a long time, if not forever, Yevtushenko retained a firm interest in root rhymes. The young poet was so carried away by his search for such combination of sounds that some of his poems are entirely built on it.

From the very start Yevtushenko's oratorical plastic verse, sensitive to all poetic influences, needed fresh rhymes because it was consciously guided by the living intonations of colloquial or declamatory speech. The search for originality in style proceeded in various directions, but it was most intensive in the field of rhyme.

It was exactly Yevtushenko who grafted root rhyme onto contemporary Russian poetry. From here it spread to numerous collections of verse of his colleagues and imitators. However, no one used it with such natural mastery and virtuosity as the poet himself. It is often so organically fused with the meaning and verbal texture of the verse that you do not seem even to hear it.

Yevtushenko's imprecise rhyme often has the poetic precision of intonational and semantic marksmanship.

Literary critic Vladimir Lakshin recalls how Alexander Tvardovsky instructed young Yevtushenko in a fatherly manner: "You have an improvisator's talent but you lack the ability, so precious in art, to go back to what you once began. You can occupy the enemy's territory but you cannot consolidate your success, strengthening your rear, digging in and so on." But Yevtushenko will never change, profundity and concentration are not for him. He would have very much liked to follow the advice of the older poet, for whom he had a boundless respect, taking his poems to him and listening without a murmur to the harsh, and as a rule quite justified, dressing-down he got. Yet he could do nothing with himself.

Tvardovsky grew indignant: "He's so complacent. The spotlight runs away from him and he chases it, to get back in the limelight." And at the same time he never lost sight of Yevtushenko, because he had faith and hope in him.

There are poets whose stature grows from book to book. This would not be true of Yevtushenko. Instead of growing he seems to be spreading, extending into space, occupying ever new territory. Let others "consolidate their success". His element is pin-pointing, naming, being the first.

Yevtushenko's *Babi Yar* belongs to poems written in response to an event.

This poem will remain in literature thanks to another propitious circumstance. Dmitri Shostakovich wrote his Thirteenth Symphony to Yevtushenko's verse. The poet himself admits being stunned by the fact that the composer, "in this symphony strung together poems that seemingly could not be so combined. The requiem-like *Babi Yar* with the publicist culmination and the touchingly simple intonation of verses about women in a queue, retrospective poems and the bold intonations of 'Humour' and 'Career'. At the first performance of the symphony something very rare happened to the listeners during those fifty minutes: they cried and laughed and smiled and fell into a reverie."

And that's the truth. I myself sat in the Big Hall of the Moscow Conservatoire, enraptured by the music, and the words which helped the music to reach the hearts of its listeners.

In 1963 Yevtushenko went on a long trip down the Pechora and lived for a while in the North.

That trip left a strong mark on his poetry. He wrote a big cycle of poems, displaying the best qualities of his talent and in the first place his passionate civic spirit and maturity.

The poet became utterly absorbed in the world of the hunters' and fishermen's hard toil, constantly aware of brotherly feeling among the people around him and towards himself. Probably for the first time he understood so clearly that the reader believed him and expected Yevtushenko to speak the truth.

The boundless northern landscapes, team work and the life of people bound together by that work came to life in Yevtushenko's poems with rare plasticity. His work at that time brought him closest to the core of his own personality. Expressive verse permeated with a civic spirit and the indissoluble organic unity of the individual and the people were manifested with genuine poetic fervour. Not long afterwards he wrote the poem *The Bratsk Power Station,* where Russia's history and present-day life are brought together in a fullscale epic.

From the very first pages of the poem two states of mind are contrasted. *The Prayer Before the Poem* with its proud finely chiselled lines ("A poet in Russia is more than just a poet") undoubtedly containing an element of self-appraisal, is followed by a prologue which opens with this confession:

> I am past thirty. Fear engulfs me at night.
> My face sunk in the pillow, I weep

> ashamed that I have wasted all my life,
> but in the morning I go on wasting it.

As he continues to ponder over his creative work Yevtushenko sometimes comes upon poetic programmes that precisely suit his own nature and his gift:

> Escaping any masks' tyranny,
> obey just yourself in your art,
> your naturalness uniquely
> and quietly to it impart!

But Yevtushenko's "naturalness" is such that it does not let him rest or carefully weigh up his thoughts. He overtakes himself at every turn of his life and the striking thing is that this quality does not disappear with the years . . . Eternal, swift-footed and light-hearted youth seethes inside him . . .

It would be a mistake, however, to regard this kind of life in art lacking in morality or devoid of a firm spiritual basis. Yevtushenko is often engaged in vain pursuits but, unlike most, he does not try to conceal them and that alone clearly differentiates his standpoint in poetry. He offers, as it were, the rough drafts of his feverish literary activity for the public to judge and for time to select the most worthy among them and find a permanent place for them in poetry. His self-criticism is not intended only for himself, but for all to hear. What is as a rule divided into private life and life in art is inseparable in Yevtushenko, because he has never learned to separate these two aspects of human existence. The poet feels injustice acutely, unfailingly, whatever form it may take, and he immediately reacts to it with anger and compassion. Here are the sources of his civic spirit and the fountainhead of his poetic publicist writings.

The strongest and most touching notes of Yevtushenko's love lyrics are those of leave-taking, parting, the waning of emotion.

Beginning with his famous *Here's What Is Happening to Me . . .* , it is precisely these notes that make the music of his best love poems.

He has written some remarkable love poems enchanting in their sincerity and genuine feeling. He becomes a truly great lyrical poet when he forgets himself, renounces himself, dissolving in his loved one. The drama of love is for the poet a supreme manifestation of spiritual freedom and selflessness.

> "God!" with all my deep pain I cry.
> "What good is Elysium's eternity?
> Don't let me die
>   later than my beloved!
> Do not mete out
>   this punishment to me!"

He cannot be undivided or precise or harmonious. All his life he has been fighting his awareness of the problematical nature of his own poetic phenomenon. His poems jar on professionals and amateurs alike. They cut one to the quick not because their form—metre, rhyme, rhythms—are irregular or classical. Independently of the sounds and letters they convey a hopeless and at the same time uplifting feeling of loss. The subject may be a woman (**Here's What Is Happening to Me**), nostalgia (verses about the idol of his youth, sportsman Vsevolod Bobrov), Soviet history (**Izya Kramer, Inspector of Lights**), or the *corrida* of Hemingway . . .

Not only has he travelled across all the continents in the world, except for the Antarctic, but he has also written poems about each country he visited.

In his "foreign" cycles Yevtushenko uses a reporting style on principle. Here he feels himself to be, first and foremost, a journalist, a special correspondent of Soviet poetry.

At the same time he has a feeling for the whole universe, a feeling of possessing everything that his eye or hand lights upon. Least of all is he a foreigner in this world and in no time at all settles down in any country . . .

The great brotherhood of men—that is what he sings of and that is his real religion, born of the ideals of our Revolution.

In poems about his travels Yevtushenko often uses the form of a monologue by real or imaginary characters. That is how the poems are titled: **Doctor Spock's Monologue, Monologue of a Broadway Actress, Monologue of a Spanish Guide** and even **Monologue of a Silver Fox on a Fur Farm in Alaska.** He creates real portraits, observing many psychological and other aspects of life abroad.

Yevtushenko's name is indeed known throughout the world, many of those who have not read his poems have heard of him.

Yevtushenko's popularity has undoubtedly been enhanced by the way he recites his poetry in public. He developed this style in his youth and it merits some attention. The verse of some young Soviet poets of the 1950's was intended to be recited, regardless of the literary tradition which each of them followed. In very general terms it may be said that that verse of a rhetorical or romantic quality truly fulfils itself, as a rule, during public recitation, being clearly at a disadvantage when read silently in solitude.

The flexibility of intonation, swinging rhythms, daring rhymes, abundant use of alliteration, combined with a topical and always extremely democratic content—all these features of Yevtushenko's style are manifest in the unity of the poet and the actor. His tall, lithe figure, his expressive hands stressing the highlights of each stanza, his well-trained and resounding voice, now rising to an angry shout, now fading to almost a whisper, emphasising the ends of the line when some phonetic echo or semantic detail has

to stand out especially clearly, make him an excellent reciter and those who have seen him on a platform or television will know what I mean.

I admit that I love my hero. For me Yevtushenko is not just a close friend, a poet, publicist, prose writer, critic, film actor, photographer, and so on, he is also a literary character whose life unfolds like a thriller. He annoys many people and he is as counter-indicative to many as hot spices are to the plain dishes prescribed by dietetic norms.

But there must be a feeling of basic justice in any critic, just as in any author, and a feeling of gratitude to every individual who has done something worthy and useful for the art of the written word in his mother tongue.

And Yevgeni Yevtushenko has done much for Soviet poetry.

Pavel Ulyashov (review date 1986)

SOURCE: Ulyashov, Pavel. "Queuing for Hope (About Yevgeni Yevtushenko's Poem 'Fukú!')."*Soviet Literature* 9, no. 462 (1986): 139-42.

[*In the following review, Ulyashov extols the universal theme and important message of the poem "Fuku!"*]

Yevgeni Yevtushenko's poetry has long been part of the Soviet reader's consciousness: we use his more aphoristic lines as headings for articles, quote his verse in speeches from public rostra, and use some of his catch-phrases in our arguments and conversations ("Civic-mindedness is a rare talent", "In Russia a poet is more than just a poet"). All this testifies at once to Yevtushenko's immense reputation and to the fact that he actively responds to the problems of his time and accurately takes the pulse of society.

Yevtushenko is not drawn to the life of quiet introspection. He has visited Cuba, Vietnam, Chile and Nicaragua, where the flames of revolution have been lit and whence the spirit of freedom and justice is spreading far and wide. It is no wonder therefore that in his new poem **"Fukú!"**[1] Yevtushenko appears as a poet with the ability to think in universal and at the same time discrete and concrete terms, because what he looks for before anything else is people, and above all people fighting for a better life, happiness and the affirmation of their dignity. He understands it as his mission to glorify such people. "In our age the poet is the age itself. In him all countries are like wounds. A poet is an ocean-wide cemetery for all, both for those to whom monuments have been erected in bronze and those who remain anonymous . . . The poet is the ambassador plenipotentiary for all who are oppressed; he does not yield to mediaevalism. Those who have won fame by shedding blood do not deserve eternal glory, but eternal scorn."

The last lines convey an approach to the central theme of the poem, already roughly expressed in its title. The idea—though not new, it is original enough—of looking at Christopher Columbus not only as a great discoverer, but also as a cruel conquistador, a pioneer of genocide and a destroyer of the original and unique culture of the American Indians enables Yevtushenko to pose this question: Do those "great men" who—for the sake of ambition—spilled oceans of blood and sowed on the earth "the famine of body and spirit" have the right to gratitude and commemoration from their descendants? And he answers this question uncompromisingly: Their names should be anathematized, forgotten and despised ("Fukú—a taboo against the name that brought misfortune").

The reader must understand that Yevtushenko looks at a personality—that, say, of Columbus—not as a historian, but from, so to speak, a moral and poetic position, first of all affirming good and justice in the world.

Yevtushenko is easily recognised in his new poem. However, his latest poems **"Mummy and the Neutron Bomb"** and **"Fukú!"** seem to me also to reveal a new Yevtushenko; in any case they show us some hitherto unrealised aspects of his many-faceted talent (I think this is partly a result of his work in the cinema). The power and novelty of *Fukú!* lie in its fusion of past and present, the universal and the personal, the social and the specifically individual. And the reason here does not lie in the connection between the different epochs, but in the fact that the poet feels equally at home in the past and the present. For him time is indivisible: "I am a coeval of every age."

Such an approach to the material—universal-historical and at the same time topical—called for a special form. And Yevtushenko was lucky enough to find it. Today a poem, perhaps also a novel, contains everything. In this epoch, when all genres have become confused, nobody will be surprised at a poem in which verse is interspersed with prose. However, while Yevtushenko's attempts at prose writing have not yet been entirely successful, in **"Fukú!"** the prose and verse passages follow each other organically, the expressiveness of the prose fabric sometimes almost exceeding that of the poetry. For, as everyone appreciates, the poetic is not the exclusive property of verse. Some of the verse passages in the poem are too wordy, whereas the prose text is full and expressive. It may be for this reason that occasionally the verse seems merely to be a commentary on the prose, as, for example, in the sections dealing with Somoza, Pinochet and Hitler. In such cases the rhymed lines are often less impressive than the prose "data providing food for thought", i.e. those facts, shocking our reason and our conscience, which Yevtushenko has come across abroad.

"And suddenly I remembered . . ." is a phrase typical of the inner movement and development of the poem. The year 1941, the evacuation of the civil population, and all that Yevtushenko lived through along with his people during the terrible years of the war, provides him with his moral starting-point.

At the end of the poem are mentioned the names of cities, towns and villages in every part of the world—places the poet has visited, and the dates: 1963-1985. They are the landmarks and years of Yevtushenko's formation and creative development. In the short concluding chapter—"Almost the Last Word"—he himself speaks about the overall trend of his work and its place in Time's forward march.

Yevtushenko is not afraid to tell the reader about the most private and innermost things—about his children, for instance. While calling on the reader to love both his own and other people's children, he thereby warns him against both confining himself to family life and developing global irresponsibility. And then everything intermingles in the poem: thoughts about Yevtushenko's own childhood and the disturbing thoughts about how and why children grow into Duces and Führers. The inner development of his thought and of the underlying idea unites the separate sections of the poem into a single whole, and levels out and organises its composition.

"Courage is frankness, when one speaks openly of both other people's shortcomings and one's own . . ." It is no fortuity that these words of Alexander Fadeyev are quoted in the poem. Yevtushenko himself does not give anyone a chance to accuse him of duplicity or of concealing the truth. Moreover, he himself often takes the offensive, as, for example, when he ridicules in sarcastic terms the liberal verbal "tight-rope walking" of the resolution of the "world's most progressive jury", which did not dare condemn a pro-Nazi film at the Venice Film Festival. His monologue on "rattism" as an epitome of the basest and most misanthropic qualities is full of ironic taunts, and the portraits of its exponents are very expressive indeed.

Yevtushenko has the ability either to turn every fact that has attracted his attention or struck his imagination into an image, or to lend it aphoristic colouring. Thus, in what was formerly Somoza's bunker, he came across a plastic plant, and immediately he gave rein to his imagination, turning a specific fact into a generalised, unmasking image, "An anti-popular dictatorship is a plastic garden."

I admit that in such cases Yevtushenko invents things, suiting some of the pictures of the past to his artistic fantasy and correcting them from the vantage-point of his present knowledge. For it is not enough just to describe an event: it should be seen as a link in a chain with other facts of life, and be felt precisely as a link and not as a ring that has been accidentally dropped. Thus, it is natural that the descendants of members of the Bandera gang, who attacked Yevtushenko during his tour of the United States, should have continued in the tradition of their fathers—those accomplices of the Nazis who in 1941 failed to lay hands on the boy from Zima. (Yevtushenko was born at the railway siding of Zima—*Ed.*) And the press photographer who went out of her way to photograph the scene of the beating of the poet becomes an unequivocal symbol of a certain artistic stand: "Her professional instinct proved stronger than the human instinct to help."

However, to be objective, it must be said that some images did not find their proper place in the complex composition of the poem.

To put it briefly, a critic who does not accept Yevtushenko's manner will find a lot to criticise there. However, I believe that the poem can be denied neither topicality nor emotional "infectiousness". It deals with things that are very important for all of us. And this alone makes it a significant event not only in our literary life, but in our social life as well. The words of Pushkin come to mind, ". . . In this respect moral observations are more important than literary ones".

One cannot fail to accept Yevtushenko's universal response: "When I see this all-devouring universal rattism and frustrated dreams, I feel like a man dying of starvation in Ethiopia." One cannot remain indifferent to the sight of the queue made of starving people, which he likens to Siqueiros's *March of Mankind*. It is a genuinely fantastic picture, and it is no fortuity that in Yevtushenko's subconscious there appear both the mediaeval Rat-catcher and Dante with his circles in Hell, from whence stretch out the amputated hands of Comandante Che Guevara.

Yevtushenko calls for mankind to unite in its striving for peace. One cannot help responding to his appeal to join the queue of brotherhood, solidarity and sympathy in which he himself stands, bearing the number "four billion". And we all will stand in this "queue for hope".

Michael Pursglove (essay date 1988)

SOURCE: Pursglove, Michael. "Yevtushenko's *Stantsiya Zima*: A Reassessment." *New Zealand Slavonic Journal*, 2 (1988): 113-27.

[*In the following essay, Pursglove provides a close textual analysis of* Stantsiya Zima, *which he classifies as a landmark in Soviet Literature.*]

Nineteen eighty-six saw the thirtieth anniversary of the publication of one of the landmarks of Soviet literature, Yevgeny Yevtushenko's *Stantsiya Zima.* At the time of its appearance in the journal *Oktyabr'* in October 1956, its twenty-three-year-old author was virtually unknown. This heavily autobiographical *poema* catapulted him to fame. Its narrator was seen as the representative of a generation which had grown up under Stalinism and which now, amid the reverberations of Khruschev's secret speech denouncing Stalin's 'cult of personality' in February 1956, was reassessing all the values it had hitherto accepted unquestioningly. The poem's themes provoked widespread controversy at the time and have remained at the centre of critical attention ever since.[1] Far less attention has been paid to the formal aspects of the poem, no doubt because here, as elsewhere in his work, the sheer brilliance and exuberance of Yevtushenko's verbal pyrotechnics render him somewhat suspect. So, too, does his undoubted ability

as a reciter—one might almost say performer—of his own poetry. It is argued that the power of Yevtushenko's performance blinds the reader to grave deficiencies in his poetic technique. This argument, at least, cannot be used to denigrate *Stantsiya Zima* since, because of its considerable length, Yevtushenko has never recited it. Unlike, for instance, the celebrated *Babiy Yar,* the poem has always had to be judged from the evidence of the printed page alone.

Despite its fame, *Stantsiya Zima* has been published only three times in the Soviet Union. In its original journal form it was 998 lines long:[2] the 1969 version in the collection *Idut belyye snegi* was 979 lines long and in the 1975 *Izbrannyye proizvedeniya* 975 lines long. The latter two versions are very similar, the only difference being an omitted quatrain.[3]

In view of Yevtushenko's expressed preference for the "good old iambic"[4] it is hardly surprising that this metre predominates. The pentameters are arranged in groups of alternating *abab* rhymes with *a* rhymes feminine and the *b* rhymes masculine. Yevtushenko does not, however, allow this conventional form to become repetitive. Deviations from it and variations on it can be found throughout the poem. A significant deviation from the metre occurs at lines 442-5 when a folk song, sung by a middle-aged woman picking berries, is cast in accentual metre (*Gustým lésom bosonógaya*) with alternating dactylic and masculine rhymes (*bosonogaya / idyot / trogayet / beryot*). An earlier example of imitation folk song occurs at lines 57-62 where, although the iambic metre is maintained, the line length is shortened to tetrameter (*Da k solov'yu nema puti*) and the rhyme scheme altered to *abaaaa*. Apart from the Ukrainian folk song, there are two other sustained deviations from the metrical norm. The first can be found in the allegorical episode (lines 570-7) when the Wheat answers the narrator's naive enquiry as to what he should do to ensure universal happiness. The answer is couched in trochaic tetrameters (*Ni plokhoy ty, ni khoroshiy*) although the *abab / fmfm* rhyme scheme is maintained.

The second example of deviation from the metrical norm follows immediately after the enigmatic answer given by the Wheat. Lines 578-609 constitute an alternative answer to the narrator's question, given by a man whose disillusionment with the behaviour of the local kolkhoz chairman, Pankratov, has forced him to leave Zima in search of Truth. The whole episode is written in what is basically anapaestic trimeter (*Bўl ŏn gōlŏdĕn, mŏlŏd ĭ bōos*) with occasional omission of a syllable (*Pŏvstrĕchālsyă mñe chĕlŏvĕk*) and alternating dactylic and masculine rhymes. Not only is this section metrically different from the bulk of the poem; its opening lines show a deviation from the normal *abab* rhyme scheme. In these eight lines the rhyme scheme is *ababacac* (*dorozhen'koy / teleg / khoroshinkoy / chelovek / malen'kiy / bos / rogalike / nyos*). Such variations in the rhyme pattern appear to signal the beginning of each new section of the poem, each coherent grouping of the multitude of episodes that make up this most episodic of works.

It is no easy task to divide the poem up. The typographical breaks in the text are misleading. Half of them (six out of twelve, after lines 402, 441, 705, 919 and 954) simply precede or follow direct speech. Of the remaining six, one (after line 62) follows the interpolated Ukrainian song which is, in effect, direct speech. Of the others, three are signalled by changes in the rhyme pattern. For example, the break after line 321 falls in the middle of an *aabccb* sequence running from lines 319 to 324 (*ile / ive / teni / rovno / bryovna / oni*). The same sequence is found immediately after the break at line 842 (*strannym / derevyannym / doma / mimo / Rimma / uma*). At line 954, on the other hand, the *abab* sequence is maintained but the first rhyme of the quatrain (*blizkikh*) precedes the typographical break.

In the journal version of the poem there were four other typographical breaks: one (at line 669) unmarked by any change in rhyme scheme, one (line 787) preceding direct speech and two (lines 411 and 513) following direct speech and signalled by deviations from the *abab* rhyme pattern. The change in rhyme pattern is quite marked in both cases: the sequence after 411 runs *aabcccbddee* (*kutsykh / kuzov / shiroko / kosilok / kosynok / korzinok / moloko / perepyolki / pereponki / galdel / glyadel*) while after 513 we find *aabccbddeffe* (*korova / kolola / selo / oglokhli / oglobli / sinyo / podlesok / podvesok / suete / manila / malina / koe-gde*).

There are five other major deviations in the poem from the *abab* scheme at points where there are no typographical breaks in any version of the poem. In four cases the sequence is the same *aabccb* as is found at 321; at 143 *dvoyek / dvorik / oki / kopilku / kobylku / kryuchki*; at 610 *utrom / poputnom / provozhal / znali / priezzhali / priezzhal*; at 754 *likhvoyu / khvoyu / retsept / glupyy / klube / kontsert* and at 854 *struzhki / kukushki / tormoznut / khvatkikh / lopatkakh / mazut*. In the remaining instance, an eleven-line sequence beginning with the truncated line 631 (*i byl takov*), runs *ababaccdeef*.

On the basis, therefore, both of the typographical breaks and the deviations from the normal rhyme pattern, the poem can be tentatively divided into twelve sections, as follows:

1. 1-62 introduction; the author's ancestor

2. 63-142 the author's mother and father

3. 143-323 the author's childhood in Zima; dialogue between Childhood and Youth; his return to Zima and conversation with his younger brother Kol'ka.

4. 324-410 the River Oka; the old man's complaints about his nephew

5. 411-577 picking berries; dialogue with the Wheat

6. 578-609 criticism of Pankratov

7. 610-630 departure by lorry; the head of the household

8. 631-753 the author alone with Nature; his uncles; the tea shop; the complaints of the tipsy journalist

9. 754-843 the club; the author's musings on love

10. 844-853 love in Zima

11. 854-931 the railway; Vovka

12. 932-975 the answer given by Zima

The section I have chosen for special discussion (Section 6) needs to be quoted in full:

> 578 И пошел я дорогой-дороженькой
> мимо пахнущих дегтем телег,
> 580 и с веселой и злой хорошинкой
> повстречался мне человек.
> Был он пыльный, курносый, маленький.
> Был он голоден,
> молод и бос.
> На березовом тонком рогалике
> он ботинки хозяйственно нес.
> Говорил он мне с пылом разное -
> что уборочная горит,
> что в колхозе одни безобразия
> председатель Панкратов творит.
> 590 Говорил:
> «Не буду заискивать.
> Я пойду.
> Я правду найду.
> Не поможет начальство зиминское -
> до иркутского я дойду . . .»
> Вдруг машина откуда-то выросла.
> В ней с портфелем -
> символом дел -
> гражданин пару синовый
> в «виллисе»,
> как в президиуме,
> сиделл.
> «Захотелось, чтоб мать поплакала?
> Снарядился,
> герой,
> в Зиму?
> 600 Ты помянешь еще Панкратова,
> ты поймешь еще, что к чему . . .»
> И умчался.
> Но силу трезвую
> оюутил я совсем не в нем,
> а в парнишке с верой железною,
> в безмашинном, босом и злом.
> Мы простились.
> Пошел он, маленький,
> увязая ступнями в пыли,
> и ботинки на тонком рогалике
> 609 долго-долго
> качались вдали . . .

Even a cursory reading of this passage reveals features that are typical of the poem as a whole. These include syntactic parallelism (582/583), word play (*pyl'nyy / s pylom*), alliteration (583, 589) and internal rhyme (583). Such devices are the stock-in-trade of any competent poet and are widespread in Yevtushenko's work as a whole, and in this poem in particular. What Yevtushenko brings to their use is wit and variety. Indeed, one single line (737), a pessimistic view of contemporary writers, illustrates all four devices:

> Он не властитель,

а блюститель дуум.

Syntactic parallelism comes in various guises. The example at lines 582 and 583 is straightforward anaphora, whereas lines 11 and 12, though rhythmically and syntactically parallel, are contrasted semantically:

> что я сказал,
> 　　　　но был сказать не должен
> что не сказал,
> 　　　　но должен был сказать.

These lines are very close in form to the classical chiasmus. This is found in its pure form at lines 47 and 48:

> мол, там простой народ живет по-барски
> (Где и когда по-барски жил народ)

or, within a single line, at 82 (*ne sami eli khleb, a khleb ikh el*). At line 432 there occurs yet another variant: contrasted parallelism within a single line:

> (Мы разгребали сена вороха)
> 　　　　и укрывались . . .
> (попутчица не укрылась только).

However, what constitutes the most interesting feature of lines 578-609 is the appearance of three key word-roots, here represented by *molod, pravda* and *vyrosla,* which signal key concepts in the poem and run as leitmotifs through it. To these may be added a further three represented by the verbs *otkryt'* and *dumat'* and the adjective *prostoy.*

Of the six concepts represented by these words, the most important is youth. Yevtushenko was only twenty-three when he wrote the poem—'very young' (*ochen' molodoy*) as the author is described at lines 573 and 936. It is, however, not only the author who is described thus. The word *molodoy* recurs throughout the poem in a variety of contexts. For example the author's mother, when still a child, only becomes aware of the Civil War when she encounters a *konnik molodoy* (line 96); the milk drunk by the berry-pickers is *molodoye moloko* (line 417) and, in the same episode, the woman, as she sings her song, becomes young again, a fact emphasised by the folksy reduplication of the adjective (*molodoyu-molodoy*) (line 437), a form repeated at 499.[5] At line 623 it is grass adhering to the wheels of a truck which is *molodaya.* No less frequent are derivatives. For example, after meeting his friend Vovka, the author goes out into the dawn (920):

> Светало . . .
> 　　　Все вокруг помолодело.

The verb is aptly chosen; a new day has literally dawned, but, in the metaphorical sense, the author has rediscovered the idealism of youth and is now ready to face the challenge presented by a rejuvenated, post-Stalinist Soviet Union.

One use of a derivative of *molodoy* is particularly pointed. This occurs in Section 4 when, at line 349, the old man's complaint:

> что раньше молодежь была получше

is given additional force by his allusion, in the next line, to an organisation which includes the word *molodyozh'* in its full title:

> что больно скучный нынче комсомол.

This is not the end of the old man's complaint for, a few lines later, in a piece of pure Yevtushenko, combining chiasmus, alliteration, assonance, word-play and wit, he makes a statement which, incidentally, defies translation into English (371):

> Есть молодежь, а молодости нет.

As so often in Yevtushenko, this generalised statement is followed by a specific example, drawn from personal experience, as the old man recalls his nephew (384):

> Какой он молодой, какой там пыл

and ruefully laments his abandonment of youthful pursuits (389):

> Нет, молодежь теперь не та, что раньше.

The other leitmotifs all reinforce this central idea of youth. Truth (*pravda*) is the goal of the young author. To attain it he must discover answers to complex questions, must think for himself, must distinguish the Simple, which is desirable, from the Simplistic, which is not. The total process is one of growth, of self-realisation, of discovery (6-7):

> Мы открываем новое,
> 　　　то значит,
> Оно открылось прежде в нас, в самих.

The verb *otkryvat'* is used twice more in the poem: at line 562, just before his conversation with the Wheat, the narrator opens his eyes, literally and metaphorically, to the world about him, and at line 854 Zima Junction is revealed when a mist, half-literal, half-metaphorical, clears away. Important derivatives of *otkryt'* are *otkroven'ya* (838) and *otkrovennyy,* which occurs in the very first line of the poem:

> Мы, чем взрослей, тем больше откровенны.

Here the word is linked with the concept of growth, a leitmotif whose importance is reflected in its frequency: *vyrastal* (135), *rost* (355), *vozrast* (370), *vyrosla* (594). To this list must be added the etymologically related root *rod-,* which occurs fourteen times in the poem, mainly in the form of the adjective *rodnoy* (73, 173, 218, 227, 496, 671). Zima Junction is, after all, the author's native town and the place to which he was evacuated as an adolescent from 1941 to 1944. There are some other derivatives of the root: *nerodnaya* (42), *rodnya* (252), *rodilis'* (752) and the Ukrainian *ridna* (55), as well as three instances of *narod* (47, 48 and 275), from whom the author sprang and on behalf of whom he claims to seek answers.

It could be argued that the high incidence of these two related roots results from nothing more than Yevtushenko's acute ear for phonetic similarities. On the other hand it could stem from an awareness, hitherto unremarked by critics, of etymological origins. Examination of another set of etymologically related roots which recurs frequently in the poem seems to argue in favour of the latter explanation. This is the adjective *prostoy* and its derivatives. The word clearly has positive associations for the poet. It is used for example to describe his father, in whom (103):

Добротное, простое было что-то.

This kindly, simple man cannot understand what the author, in lines omitted from all but the *Oktyabr'* version, euphemistically terms the "complexities" of Soviet society which make answers so difficult to come by for his son's generation:

Откуда знал он . . .
о том, что нам не так уж просто будет,
о сложностях тяжелых и больших.

In the event, the answers themselves are simple, as two lines from the **Oktyabr'** version of the berry-picking episode (episode 5) illustrate:

Да это ведь она сквозь дождь и ветер
летела с песней, жаркой и простой.

Examples such as this shed new light on the potentially banal cliché *prostoy narod* (47) or the routine adverb in such lines as 536—

Эх, граждане, мне с вами просто юмор

and 684—

Им отвечали коротко и просто.

The adjective *prostoy* is etymologically connected with the verbs *proschat'sya/poproschat'sya* (to take one's leave) and *proschat'/prostit'* (to forgive), both of which express fundamental themes of the poem.

Numerically important though the *prostoy* leitmotif is, there is one other which occurs still more frequently. This is the verb *dumat'* and its derivatives, seen first at line 14, where the author cites a failure to think as one of the main shortcomings in his life to date.

Увисел я, что часто жил с оглядкой,
что мало думал, чувствовал, хотел.

Thinking, however, as Hamlet points out, has its inherent dangers. It can, for instance, kill spontaneous emotion in anyone not blessed with the *nezadumchivost'* (501) of the woman picking berries. Her very inability to kill emotion through an excess of thinking prompts further thoughts in the author (554)

Раздумывал растерянно и смутно

just as a later encounter does, this time with the young man who criticises Pankratov (638 and 640),

. . . мне брелось раздумчивее
. . . о мног ом думал.

The author passes on the thoughts "honest and profound" thus prompted to the disillusioned journalist in the tea house who responds with the aphorism already cited:

А что сейчас писатель?
Он не властитель, а блюститель дум.

In the course of the poem the narrator gropes his way towards an important conclusion about the nature of thought. It is, above all, a painful process (754):

Платил я за раздумия с лихвой

but it is nevertheless a vital process (the formula *davayte dumat'* is twice repeated). Without thought, love is blind, and blind love is useless (814-15):

Нам не слепой любви сегодня надо,
а думающей, пристальной любви.

Thought must now, however, tip over into cynical cerebration (837-8):

Я знаю—
        есть раздумья от неверья
Раздумья наши от большой любви.

The importance of the *dumat'* leitmotif casts some light on the curious noun *pridumschik* used in the original *Oktyabr'* version of the poem to refer to the author's friend Vovka Drobin in episode 11. The qualities for which Vovka is best known are hardly traditional virtues, and the word *pridumschik,* which might be translated as 'fibber' or 'crafty so-and-so', could, in other contexts, have negative connotations. Here, however, the positive connotations associated with the root *dumat'* outweigh the negative. These positive connotations are reinforced a few lines later, when the last use of this root is given to Vovka (911-12):

Ты что, один такой? сказал мне Вовка,—
Сегодня все раздумывают, брат.

Yevtushenko may have realised the contradiction, for in the 1969 and 1975 versions of this poem the word *pridumschik* is dropped.

Episode 6 also illustrates one of the several minor themes in the poem, also designated by key words. This is the adjective *bosoy,* here referring to the narrator's alter ego, the young man at the start of his own search for truth. It is used to refer to him again at 931, and on two further occasions (20, 889). It and the related adverb *bosikom* refer to the Siberian Garden of Eden in which the narrator wandered before falling into the "complexities" of Moscow life. Another related word *bosonogaya* (442) links both these seekers after truth to the woman picking berries who, in her simple, inarticulate way, has found the Truth.

Episode 6, incidentally, also provides a link between the young critic of Pańkratov and the narrator through the adjective *pyl'nyy*. This echoes the verb *pylit'* applied to the narrator at line 20.

In the poem as a whole there are a number of other such minor themes. One is that of change. Both the author and his country are undergoing massive changes of outlook, philosophy and prospects. This is signalled in lines 3 and 4:

и совладают в жизни перемены
с больими переменами в себе

and reinforced by subsequent repetition of the -*men*- root: *izmenil* (379), *smenyalas'* (550), *peremeny* (738) and *razmenyat'* (823). Set against this theme of change is the reassuringly unchanging sight of the River Oka, to which there are four references.

A similar use of counterpointed themes can be seen in the juxtaposition of the major theme of simplicity and the minor theme of complexity (*slozhnost'*). In one place (163) Yevtushenko emphasises the point by using *neslozhnyy* as a synonym for *prostoy*:

Но жизнь,
      больших препятствий не чиня,
      лишь оттого казалась мне несложной,
      что сложное
                  решали за меня.

The theme is taken up elsewhere by *slozhnost'* (170) and, in the *Oktyabr'* version, by *slozhnostyakh*.

An interesting minor theme is that of wandering, expressed by the verb *brodit'/bresti* and its derivatives. The narrator is a wanderer in search of Truth and five of the references allude to him (*brodil* 151, 634, 844, *bryol* 244 and *brelos'* 638). He is the descendant of Ukrainian peasants banished to Siberia in Tsarist times and thus condemned to a wandering life (*breli*, 33, *bresti-ne dobresti*, 54), which brought them finally to this remote spot on the Trans-Siberian Railway.

The town of Zima has provided the inspiration for three other poems by Yevtushenko: *Soyti na tikhoy stantsiy Zima, Otkuda vy?* and *Ziminskaya ballada.* The most recent of these, *Ziminskaya ballada* (1975), is strongly autobiographical. Its 71 lines relate a single episode in Yevtushenko's youth when he was set upon by a band of young toughs and robbed of a rouble. However, its trochaic tetrameter and *aabccb* stanza mean that its formal differences from *Stantsiya Zima* make detailed investigation of it in this context unprofitable. On the other hand *Soyti na tikhoy stantsii Zima,* originally published in 1953, is written in the same iambic pentameter as *Stantsiya Zima.* Its 48 lines, printed without a break, fall naturally into 12 quatrains, the first three of which rhyme *abba* and the last nine *abab.* Both in form and content it reveals itself as a preliminary sketch for *Stantsiya Zima* itself.

Like *Ziminskaya ballada,* it is a piece of pure narrative, devoid of the rather banal philosophising which is the weakest feature of the *poema,* and containing themes which are developed at length in the longer work—notably the River Oka and the theme of berry-picking (*i prokhodit' brusnichnymi mestami*).

If this is a modest prelude to *Stantsiya Zima, Otkuda vy?* (1959) is a much more ambitious sequel. Published only once in the USSR,[6] this is a fully-fledged *poema,* 680 lines in length, divided into 22 sections of unequal length. As in *Stantsiya Zima,* Yevtushenko not only marks these divisions typographically, but deviates from the basic *abab* rhyme scheme. For example, the break between sections 3 and 4 falls after one line of an *abbaa* sequence (*vezlo / khvalili / lili / zlo / razvezlo*), while the break between sections 10 and 11 comes after one line of an *abba* sequence (*ikh / voskresen'e / vesenne / zolotykh*). There is a similar enjambement between sections 13 and 14, although here the *abab* pattern is maintained (*medlim my / lozh' / mednuyu / polozh'*). However, Yevtushenko further emphasises the break by including in the sequence the only pentameter in a poem otherwise written entirely in iambic tetrameters:

Читатель ждет,
      а мы—
            все медлим мы.

This line is emphasised still more by being virtually rhymeless. In a poem which, unlike *Stantsiya Zima,* often has rhymes which are little more than phonetic echoes (*geroy/geolog; prekrasno/bratstva; pridyotsya/primorskiy* and many others), the rhyme *medlim my/mednuyu* is among the most distant. A few pages later, yet another variant occurs, when the end of section 19 is marked by a switch from *rime croisée* to couplets (*lyubyat/lyudi/lyubya/tebya*). Other variants occur in both the first and last sections of the poem, as well as in section 17. In all three sections the entire rhyme pattern deviates from the normal *abab* pattern. The 12 lines of section 1 are arranged 5:4:3, with the rhymes running *ababa ccdd efe.* The 9 lines of the last section, section 22, run *abbacdccd,* while the even shorter section 17 is cast in the form of a sestet, with the same *aabcbc* pattern as is found in *Ziminskaya ballada* (*Vladivostok/strok/podrobno/voiny/podlozhka/glubiny*).

The underlying structure of the poem, however, lies not in the sections indicated by the typographical breaks, but in the basic *abab* rhyme pattern. Interestingly, the fragment that appears in both *Idut belyye snegi* and *Izbrannyye proizvedeniya* is arranged in quatrains, with the single exception of a five-line sequence. This untitled poem begins with lines 13-16 of *Otkuda vy?* and continues with sections 6 and 7 of the original (lines 153-213).

Of the leitmotifs in *Stantsiya Zima,* only two survive in *Otkuda vy?* The theme of simplicity, of the need to avoid over-simplified answers, is announced early in the poem (36-9):

Не разрешил я все вопросы,
все то, что на душу легло,

но стало мне легко и просто,
хоть и ни просто, ни легко.

Here the key word *prosto* is reinforced by a typical piece of Yevtushenkian chiasmus, which is repeated at lines 228-9. The simplicity found by the narrator in Zima contrasts with what is again euphemistically referred to as the "complexity" of Stalinist society. One aspect of this "complexity" was the existence of political prisoners. On seeing a crowd of these, amnestied after the fall of Beria in 1953, the poet notes (32-3):

Как и в Москве, тут сложно было
и многое не решено.

The theme is reinforced by the repetition of the etymological relations of *prosto: proschat'/poproschat'* (237) and *proschat'/prostit'* (68 and 253). In the last example, the poet confesses his sadness at the way his relatives readily forgive his Muscovite ways. The phrase "forgiving love" (*proschayuschaya lyubov'*) is strongly reminiscent of the "thinking love" (*dumayuschaya lyubov'*) which, the narrator asserts in *Stantsiya Zima,* is now needed in Russia.

The second, and more important leitmotif is signalled by the key word *rodnoy* (9 examples) and the closely related words *rozhdennyy, rodimyy, narod* (2 examples each), *rod, rodich, nenarodno* and *priroda* (1 example each). Indeed, this root appears in the opening lines of the poem:

В степи рожденный,
                    помни степь;
тайгу,
    в тайге рожденный,
                    помни

and also in the fragment published in 1969 and 1975:

Откуда родом я?
            Я с некой
сибирской станции Зима.

The incidence of this root is even greater than in *Stantsiya Zima,* especially when the etymologically related derivatives of *rasti* are included (*vyrastal, vyrastayut, vzroslen'ye, vzroslyy, rastut*). Clearly the process of maturing and the search for the poet's roots have now become the dominant themes. The themes of discovery (*otkryt'*), youth (*molodoy*) and thought (*dumat'*), though briefly present in *Otkuda vy?* are now reduced to the level of such secondary themes in both works as change (associated with the root *-men-*) and truth (*pravda*). However, numerically dominant though the *rodnoy/rasti* theme is in *Otkuda vy?,* its effect is diminished by its use in one of the banal clichés from which the poem as a whole suffers. Four times (305, 364, 368, 590) the phrase *kray rodnoy* is used and on a fifth occasion (639) it is only slightly varied to *kraya—rodimy.*

The poem does share some of the more distinctive formal features of *Stantsiya Zima,* such as the use of anaphora (55-6):

Одну лодыжку держит деготь,
другую крепко держит мед

and of characteristically Yevtushenkian contrasted parallelism (71-2):

(. . . поняла ты тонко)
что не тону совсем,
                    а только
играю в то, что я тону.

Even more characteristic is the linking of adjacent unrhymed lines by using grammatically or etymologically related words at the end of each to create a kind of 'false couplet'. There are at least four examples of this in *Stantsiya Zima,* one of which is the *priezzhali/priezzhal* 'rhyme'. Others are *popalsya/popadu* (402-3), *lozhnom/lozh'* (802-3) and *obmanom/obmanut'* (818-19). Examples from *Otkuda vy?* include (411-12):

сбегась к рыжему Амуру,
десятки рыжих амурчат

and (395-6):

припомнят то, что не смогли мы,
забыв о том, что не могли?!

Sometimes these 'false couplets' are achieved merely by using a different form of the same noun at the end of each line (659-60):

стою на лвду одной ног ою
и на цветах—
            другой ног ой.

Elsewhere, Yevtushenko uses the same device to disguise a pair of couplets (559-62):

О город мужества!
            Как любят
тебя твои большие люди,
и, улицы твои любя,
как любят край вокруг тебя.

Overall, however, although the narrative passages of *Otkuda vy?* match anything from *Stantsiya Zima,* and although its occasional lapses into vapid philosophising are no worse, it lacks the great formal variety of the earlier work. Indeed, its relative formal monotony detracts from it as much as formal variety adds to *Stantsiya Zima.*

Throughout his career, Yevtushenko has repeatedly returned to his Siberian roots for inspiration. The lyric *Ya—sibirskoy porody* (1954), the narrative poem *Po Pechore* (1963) and the long cycle of poems *Bratskaya G.E.S.* (1965) are three products of this process, though none mentions Zima specifically. However, in Yevtushenko's first major excursion into prose fiction, the novel *Ya-godnyye mesta* (1981), Zima plays an important role. The novel is set mainly in the desolate countryside around the town which, for the heroine Ksyuta, is the only town she has ever visited. Zima, with its railway sheds, provides one character with the opportunity to join the proletariat; for another, it is the place where a letter in Japanese can be translated. Many of the themes dealt with in *Stantsiya Zima* recur in the novel: berry collecting; youthful idealism confronted by cynicism; the nature of true literature; the discovery of self; the ravages of alcohol; the essence of Russianness. Like *Stantsiya Zima, Yagodnyye mesta* is episodic in structure and, indeed, the novel has many of the strengths and weaknesses of the poem. Its most memorable scenes are those packed with concrete detail (chapter 21 is a good example); its weakest parts are those devoted to abstract philosophical speculation, such as the obscurely pretentious prologue. Yet for all their thematic similarity, the two works are very different: the poem is a coherent, artistically integrated entity, whereas the novel is uneven, confusing and disjointed. To account for this difference, the reader need look no further than the obvious fact that the prose work, by its very nature, lacks most, if not all, of the unifying devices available to the writer of verse. These Yevtushenko exploits to the full in *Stantsiya Zima.* Whether he has been able to sustain this standard is a question to which he may have given an answer by switching to prose. In *Yagodnyye mesta* he puts into the mouth of another *alter ego,* the young poet Kostya Krivtsov, first a dismissive comment about his great contemporary Voznesensky and then the following answer to the question "What about Yevtushenko?" "He's also passé." (*Eto tozhe proydennyy etap.*)

Others have subscribed to the same bleak view of Yevtushenko, most recently Martin Seymour-Smith, who pronounces him "written out".[7] Yet whatever the truth of this, the technical and thematic variety of *Stantsiya Zima* will secure his place in the history of modern Soviet literature.

Notes

This article is based on a paper given to the Anglo-Soviet seminar on Russian language and literature held in the Pushkin Institute, Moscow, 15-24 September, 1986.

1. There is a comprehensive bibliography of Soviet criticism of Yevtushenko in *Russkiye sovetskiye pisateli: poety,* Moscow, 1984, vol. 7, pp. 347-482. There are very few critical studies of Yevtushenko published in the West. Most notable are R. Milner-Gulland's introduction to the volume quoted in note 2 and the same author's article in the *Modern Encyclopedia of Russian and Soviet Literature,* Gulf Breeze, Florida, 1984, vol 7, pp. 115-22.

2. Most easily accessible in R. Milner-Gulland (ed.), *Yevgenii Yevtushenko: Selected Poetry,* Oxford, 1963, pp. 1-35, it is also found in *Kachka,* London, 1966, pp. 157-91.

3. All line references in this article are to the *Izbrannyye proizvedeniya* edition of the poem.

4. In his *Khochu ya stat' nemnozhko staromodnym* (1963).

5. In the *Oktyabr'* version, the adjective here was *prostoy.* Other examples of folks reduplication are *rano-rano* (644) and *ochen'-ochen'* (936).

6. Also in *Oktyabr'* (1958, no. 10, pp. 97-115), it is most accessible in *Kachka* (see note 2), pp. 53-75.

7. M. Seymour-Smith, *Macmillan Guide to Modern World Literature,* London, 1985, p. 1095.

Carol Rumens (review date 1991)

SOURCE: Rumens, Carol. "Half Free." *New Statesman & Society* 4, no. 142 (15 March 1991): 37.

[In the following review, Rumens characterizes Yevtushenko's poetry as high energy.]

"Who the hell is this damned Y Y?," asks Yevtushenko in the forward to *Stolen Apples* (1973), ironically parroting his various critics: "An unofficial diplomat performing secret missions for the Kremlin? . . . A Soviet Beatle? . . . An export item, perhaps, like vodka or black caviar? . . . When is Yevtushenko sincere? When he is writing about Vietnam or Babii Yar?"

Perhaps he has had to be many different people. Yet the *Collected Poems,* for all its variety, is a consistent narrative, dominated by the haunted figure of a Russian poet, as deeply rooted as any of his breed, sent by success and the mid-20th-century publicity machine into dizzy orbit between the two arch-enemies of the cold war, beaming messages first to one, then the other, and emotionally involved in both. A complex character, living in highly complex times, Yevtushenko often likes to picture himself as a skinny, wily Siberian street urchin, living off his wits. Maybe this figure is the clue to the "real" man, who unites the rebel and the opportunist, the cheer-leader and the dissident, the people's poet and the tormented soul-searcher under one skin.

He was born in 1933 in Zima, a largeish town on the Trans-Siberian railway, the grandson of a Ukranian revolutionary exiled to Irkutsk. His first book was published in 1952, but it was the long poem of 1955, *Zima Station* (mistranslated here, as usual, as *Zima Junction*) that first excited attention. A sentimental but fresh, earthy and heartfelt narrative, it gave the young poet the accreditation to set out on more risky projects such as *Babii Yar* and *Stalin's Heirs.* By the time these poems were published, in the early sixties, the leadership was also beginning to ask questions about Stalinism. Yevtushenko's was the right voice at the right time.

Just as quick to catalogue the sins of the bourgeois imperialists, he was able to please the conformists at home and the radicals abroad, and to keep his integrity. At least, unlike some of the more single-minded dissidents, he was not blind to the flaws in our so-called western democracies. If the tone of his righteous anger sometimes jars, it's because he tends to use the big, conscience-words as a form of emotional shorthand. He can colonise My Lai or El Salvador in a moral gesture that still leaves us a million miles from the hurt and shock of those epicentres.

Imaginative detail (which we will never get from politicians or newscasters) is what's required, even when it's of the more inventive kind—as when he takes off on a startling metaphorical flight inspired by what could have been a too-easy Yevtushenkan subject, the neutron bomb: "Pillows will start looting / Neanderthal skulls from museums. / Shirts / all alone / will pull themselves on statues and skeletons / . . . A mass hanging of neckties from trees / will take place."

Yevtushenko is a vividly colloquial writer working for the most part in traditional rhyme and metre (in Russian, writing formally does not mean strutting in period costume). His American translators provide him with a looser garment, but convey the breezy energy and the sometimes *macho* swagger of his tone ("And like a slugger's hook / across the chops of the ages, / a line!").

The mood of many later poems (1986-90) is somewhat darker; the swagger has gone and, whether contemplating himself or his society, the poet sees doom and exhaustion: rust, ghosts, chasms, things smashed. But the energy of the language flows back, bringing a wealth of tender domestic detail, when he writes about his native region, as in **"Siberian Wooing"**.

And in the sombre, flat statements of **"Half Measure"**, the poet shows he is still game for questioning the system: "With every half-effective / half measure / half the people / remain half pleased. / The half sated / are half hungry. / The half free / are half enslaved."

Tomas Venclova (review date 1991)

SOURCE: Venclova, Tomas. "Making It." *New Republic* 204, no. 18 (6 May 1991): 33-37.

[*In the following review, Venclova dismisses Yevtushenko as a Russian writer of merit, refuting Western interpretations of his poetry and politics.*]

An interesting article by Yevgeny Yevtushenko, part essay, part memoir, recently appeared in *Literaturnaya Gazeta* in Moscow, in which the poet dwells at length on his skirmishes with Soviet reactionaries. The title of the article is "Fencing with a Pile of Dung," which is meant to be a bold metaphor. Among other tales, Yevtushenko tells the story of his visit to the pre-perestroika Kremlin, where he was to be honored with the Order of the Red Banner:

> The Order was presented by a vice chairman of the Presidium of the Supreme Soviet, an Azerbaijani whose last name I cannot, for the life of me, recall. Pinning

the order to the lapel of my jacket and inviting me to a hunting party in Azerbaijan, he awkwardly pierced my jacket, my shirt, and even pricked me. It was rather painful. The Kremlin people hurt me often enough. They hurt others, too.

The next story deals with the presentation of a State Prize to Yevtushenko in 1984 for his long poem **"Momma and the Neutron Bomb."** "The censorship office attempted to ban the poem," he writes, "but it did not succeed." Yevtushenko took his medal and his certificate (and his money). According to the requirements of Soviet protocol, he was expected to express his gratitude to the Party at the ceremony. His wrath was so impossible to contain, however, that he neglected etiquette and returned to his seat without breaking his proud silence. His bravery, he tells us, inspired several other recipients of the prize, who also refused to say thanks.

Now, there is something fundamentally wrong about this picture. You are pampered by a totalitarian government, or you are persecuted by it. You are given honors and awards by party functionaries, or you are not. You are invited to their hunting parties, or you are their open enemy. But both cannot happen to you at the same time. Andrei Sakharov received perks similar to Yevtushenko's while he was busy with the Soviet nuclear program; but later his moral rectitude led him to the camp of the dissidents, and the world knows what followed. You see, you cannot fence with a pile of dung. You either sink into it or you leave it. To pretend otherwise requires extraordinary cynicism, extraordinary naïveté, or both. When Yevtushenko implicitly compares the pain caused by that pricking pin to the sufferings of Sakharov, Pasternak, and many, many others, he goes beyond the limits of naïveté, and even of cynicism. He approaches the obscene.

The case of Yevtushenko is one of the most unusual cases of our times. (Stanislaw Baranczak recently listed it, in *Newsday,* among the top ten hoaxes of the twentieth century.) Two large books by Yevtushenko, which just appeared in English, provide an opportunity to study it more closely. The first is a volume of verse put into English by many translators, including some of the masters of the language. The second is a collection of political speeches, essays, travelogues, and divagations on Russian writers. Both books are provided with rapturous introductions and blurbs: the author is "the legendary Russian literary leader," "a people's poet in the tradition of Walt Whitman," "a seeker of Truth like all great writers," and so on. It seems that many members in good standing of the American literary establishment consider these descriptions to be true, or at least partly true. Unfortunately, they are false.

One thing has to be admitted: Yevtushenko is an incredibly prolific writer who is endowed with a buoyant personality. He is not only a versifier and an essayist, but also a scriptwriter, a film director, an actor, a photographer, a novelist, a political figure, and a world traveler—a Soviet cultural emissary in virtually all parts of the globe, which is a function that he inherited from Vladimir Mayakovsky and Ilya Erenburg, who played the same role on a less extensive scale. In his tender years, Yevtushenko was also a goalkeeper and a folk dancer of repute.

The amount of energy, the sheer labor, devoted to all these enterprises cannot fail to impress. Yevtushenko says about himself, without false modesty but not without reason: "my fate is supernatural, / my destiny astonishing." Sixty-four countries visited by 1976 (by now the number is larger) and forty-six books of original poetry so far—this certainly is supernatural, if we recall that permission to travel abroad once or twice was the sweetest dream of almost any Soviet writer before the Gorbachev era, and that many good poets of the USSR considered themselves lucky if they managed to publish a slim and heavily blue-penciled volume once in a decade. On top of all that, we learn (from his editor Antonina W. Bouis) that Yevtush-enko "has been banned, threatened, censored, and punished," though he has not been imprisoned.

The tales of Yevtushenko's tribulations are not totally unfounded. In the beginning, he did not fit snugly into the Procrustean bed of Stalinist literature, and he was attacked by some of the worst hacks of the period, not least by the anti-Semites. (Yevtushenko has no Jewish background, but his Latvian father's last name, Gangnus, looked suspicious.) Yet the controversy about Yevtushenko was always a quarrel *within* the Soviet literary framework. Yevtushenko never displayed the slightest inclination to work outside it.

A fight within the Soviet establishment, even if it is conducted for a liberal cause, is bound to degenerate into a fight for the benevolence of the authorities. In this regard, Yevtushenko happened to be more skillful, and incomparably more successful, than his dull opponents. And so they never forgave him. Yevtushenko is still denounced by the lunatic fringe, by the Pamyat people and their supporters. (Pamyat has done him a great favor: its opposition has been adduced as proof of his credentials as a humanist and a fighter for freedom.) Much less publicized is the fact that democratic and dissident Soviet critics exposed Yev-tushenko's literary weaknesses and moral vacillations long ago and mercilessly. Today hardly anyone in that literary community considers his work worthy of serious study.

He started out, in 1949, at the age of 16, as an average if precocious maker of Soviet-style poems. His first book appeared at the very nadir of Stalinism, in 1952, and suited the time rather nicely: it was optimistic, full of clichés, and boring. But after coming from his native Siberia to the Moscow Literary Institute, Yevtushenko felt the first timid stirrings of the post-Stalin mood and expressed them, too, in his verses. This stage of his poetry is amply represented in the new English collection. In the era of glasnost, it looks antediluvian. Still, there is something attractive in it: youthful sentimentality, straightforward intonation, impetuous imagery.

Yevtushenko was among the first writers of the period to introduce into his work a slice of real Soviet life—of the

so-called *byt,* the daily grind of tedium, hardship, and deprivation. Here and there he mentioned queues, dirty staircases, bedbugs, fences with obscene inscriptions, and so on. (Later even such taboo subjects as condoms and drinking eau de cologne appeared in his lyrics.) He also wrote about love and its betrayals; and though they are essentially Victorian, those poems provoked attacks on Yev-tushenko as an advocate of promiscuity.

His early verses can be read as an anthology of modes and fads of the bygone days. Some of his heroes (including the narrator) were *stilyagas,* the scornful name for a member of the Soviet "golden youth" who were fond of Western clothes, dances, and so on—a sort of mixture of hippie and yuppie; and the message of Yevtushenko's poetry was that they were good Soviet people who would bravely fight for their socialist fatherland. Yevtushenko played up his Siberian heritage, moreover, and employed all the trivial mythology of Siberia—not the land of the Gulag, but the magnificent wilderness inhabited by rough and honest men. And he emphasized his manifestly difficult childhood ("I started out as a lonely wolf cub"). All these traits were at their most obvious in the long poem **"Zima Junction,"** which appeared in 1955. It made Yevtushen-ko's reputation.

"Zima Junction," a narrative poem about Yevtushenko's visit to his native Siberia, very cautiously touched the political sensitivities of its era: the so-called Doctors' Plot, Stalin's death, the fall of Beria. On the whole, it was full of the usual stuff—decent Chekists, naive but nice Red cavalrymen, upright but flawed Russian peasants, and the author himself, a young lad in search of a way to serve his country. It was attacked by literary conservatives, but it was also instrumental in generating strong support for Yevtushenko in some circles of the Party, among people whose background and experience were similar to his own. There is a persistent rumor that Mikhail Gorbachev was one of them.

Today Yevtushenko states that "in 1953 it seemed I was all the dissidents rolled up into one." And "the early poetry of my generation is the cradle of glasnost." Such revelation are less than modest. In addition, they are untrue. There were many thousands of dissidents in 1953. Most of them were in prison camps or in internal exile. Some of them, like Pasternak, Akhmatova, and Nadezhda Man-delshtam, were still at large, but they were totally cut off from their readers and from the general public. Glas-nost—to be more precise, the revolution taking place in the Soviet Union today—was the fruit of their untold suf-fering, and their incredibly stubborn efforts to maintain moral and cultural standards during that era of contempt. Yevtushenko and his ilk, in other words, took the place that rightfully belonged to others. They promoted literature and ideology that was adapted to their totalitarian milieu, into which they introduced a measure of half truth and half decency.

Many Western critics are fond of uncovering the influ-ences of Mayakovsky, Yesenin, Pasternak, and Blok in Yevtushenko's poetry, thereby suggesting that he is a rightful heir to the giants. The poet himself never tires of invoking their shades, although he does not transcend the level of schoolboyish clichés when he talks about their heritage. His real mentors, however, were second-rate, incurably Soviet, and largely obscure poets such as Stepan Shchipachev, Mikhail Svetlov, Aleksandr Mezhirov, and Konstantin Vanshenkin. (Numerous dedications to them can be found throughout **The Collected Poems.**)

For a time their heir Yevtushenko surpassed them, since he became genuinely popular. His popularity might have been owed in part to his great histrionic gifts. As Andrei Sinyavsky has observed, Yevtushenko managed to revive the theatrical concept of a poet's destiny (rejected by Pasternak, but characteristic of Mayakovsky and Tsvetaeva), according to which a poet's biography had to become an integral part, even the principal part, of his or her work. Readers and audiences had to be well acquainted with a poet's personal life, with his or her everyday dramas. For Mayakovsky and Tsvetaeva, the theatrics were genuinely tragic. For Yevtushenko, in accordance with the worn Marxist dictum, they tended to be farcical.

He succeeded in creating an image of a nice guy, an old chap, a macho simpleton who matter-of-factly recounts his family problems, his sexual exploits, his daily chores and daily doubts. Yevtushenko's audience of Soviet youths, immature and disoriented after several decades of Stalinist isolation, longing for a touch of sincerity, hungrily gulped down anything "Western" and "modern," and adopted Yevtushenko (together with Voznesensky and several others) as their idol. This did not last too long; the more sophisticated part of the audience found real, previously suppressed Russian poetry, and the other and larger part became rather apathetic to all poetry, including Yevtushenko's.

I should acknowledge that two early poems by Yevtushenko made history. Politically, if not poetically, they have a lasting place in the annals of Soviet liberalism. **"Babii Yar"** (1961) treated anti-Semitic tendencies in Russian life, and provoked a rabid reaction in fascist and fascistoid circles. It was a noble public act, perhaps the high point of Yevtushenko's personal and political career. And it differs favorably from Voznesensky's poems on the same topic; it is more measured, discreet, and restrained, and it avoids formal experimentation and the homespun surrealism that is decidedly out of place when one speaks about the Holocaust. Still, it is poetically feeble, and full of sentimental clichés ("Anne Frank / transparent as a branch in April"). But perhaps these weaknesses may be overlooked.

The other famous poem is **"The Heirs of Stalin"** (1962). In its case, the situation is different. Most likely **"Babii Yar"** was a spontaneous outpouring. **"The Heirs of Stalin"** was a calculated gamble, a move in the intra-Party game of old-fashioned Stalinists and Khrushchevian liberals. It did not avoid dubious statements, like "prison camps are empty." (In 1962 they were not.) **"The Heirs of Sta-**

lin" impressed Khrushchev and was printed in *Pravda*. Yevtushenko had managed to place his bet on the winning horse. In his memoirs of the time, the poet portrays himself as a virtual outcast, but the scene that follows in his telling leaves the reader a bit doubtful about the depth of his predicament. At a reception in Havana, presumably in Castro's residence, where Mikoyan also is present, Yevtushenko picks up the issue of *Pravda* with his provocative poem. "[Mikoyan] handed Castro the newspaper. Mikoyan apparently thought that I knew all about it and was rather shocked to see me practically tear the newspaper out of Castro's hands." Hardly an episode in the life of a freedom fighter.

Of course the world traveler did not confine himself to Cuba. Travelogues in verse and prose, including long and not terribly interesting poems on Chile, Japan, the United States, and other places, make up a very considerable part of his creative output. The Western establishment, eager for reassuring signs of moral and cultural revival in Russia, was encouraged by the sight of an audacious person who seemed enlightened and tractable compared with the typical Soviet *nyet* people. And the advertising tricks usually reserved for movie stars were trotted out on the poet's behalf, which increased his already appreciable vanity. (Yevtushenko proudly recounts instances when a Western cultural figure called him "Mayakovsky's son.")

Some misunderstandings with the authorities ensued. Some credit must be given to Yevtushenko, since he behaved with dignity even when he was assaulted by Khrushchev himself. (At his famous meeting with the intelligentsia, Khrushchev delivered himself of the Russian proverb that "hunchbacks are corrected by the grave," at which Yevtushenko retorted: "The time when people were corrected by the grave has passed.") Still, it was as clear as the noon sun that he remained totally loyal to the Party, even if he was a bit heterodox in secondary matters. Thus the campaign against him fizzled. In 1964 he expiated his sins by writing the long poem **"Bratsk Hydroelectric Station."** The poem, long selections of which are included in the English volume, marked a new stage in Yevtushenko's development: an era of resourceful compromises, cheating moves, and clever adaptations to existing conditions (which became more and more stifling after Khrushchev's removal in October 1964). The poet himself pictured his rushing about as a wise stratagem serving the liberal cause. But not many Russian and non-Russian intellectuals agreed with him; the dissident movement virtually discarded Yevtushenko as an ally. And that was irreversible.

"Bratsk Hydroelectric Station" is a paean to one of the typical Soviet industrial projects in Siberia. (Today such projects, usually unprofitable and fraught with ecological disasters, are repudiated by public opinion, and even by the government itself.) The central part of the poem consists of an argument between an Egyptian pyramid and the Siberian powerhouse: the former symbolizes all the conservative and enslaving tendencies of history (Stalinism supposedly included), while the latter defends the cause of idealist faith and human emancipation. Yevtushenko overlooked the fact that the opposition is far from perfect: slave labor or near-slave labor played an approximately identical part in building both monuments. And the forces of freedom are represented in the poem by rather dubious figures. One of them is Stenka Razin, leader of a savage peasant revolt in the seventeenth century, whose confessions sound chilling ("No, it is not in this I have sinned, my people, / for hanging boyars from the towers. / I have sinned in my own eyes in this, / that I hanged too few of them"). There is also a scene where young Lenin (never named but perfectly recognizable) guides a drunken woman (supposedly Mother Russia) by the elbow, and she blesses him as her true son. This transformation of Lenin into a Christlike figure insulted equally the followers of Lenin and the followers of Christ.

Virtually the same applies to many of Yevtushenko's later poetic works. The long poem **"Kazan University"** (1970) described czarist Russia with some wit and verve. Reactionary tendencies of the nineteenth century brought to mind Brezhnevian stagnation, and the liberal scholar Lesgaft, harassed by the authorities, might be easily interpreted as a forebear of Sakharov. But the university of Kazan was also the breeding ground for Lenin, who, according to the author (and to the Soviet textbooks), was the crown prince of Russian democracy. Never mind that Lenin was the very opposite of democracy—and that he never attempted to conceal it. Transforming him into a prophet of human rights, of brotherhood and justice, into a Gandhi or a Sakharov *avant la lettre,* is nauseating. (It is also un-Marxist.)

Many of Yevtushenko's poems on Western topics are characterized by the rangues against the "doltish regime" of Salazar, against the Chilean murderers or American bureaucrats (**"Under the Skin of the Statue of Liberty,"** 1968) can be construed as transparent allegories: in fact, the poet is attacking native Soviet deficiencies. But at the same time the attacks perfectly conform to the general tenor of the Party's propaganda; Salazar, Pinochet, the FBI, and the Pentagon always were convenient bugaboos, and in that capacity helped the Party to keep the people silent and loyal. Moreover, the general picture of the West in these poems is usually touristy and superficial. Fascinated by material standards and the ever changing fashions of the First World, Yevtushenko nevertheless mythologizes his role as "the ambassador of all the oppressed" and a Russian (and Soviet) patriot. There are also endless exhortations for peaceful coexistence and friendship of peoples ("Russia and America, / Swim closer!"), essentially noble, but less than irreproachable in the era of détente.

The poet's editors and promoters tend to emphasize his heroic gestures during the crisis periods in the USSR. It is true that he sent a telegram to Brezhnev protesting the Czech invasion. It is also said that he phoned Andropov to express his intention to die on the barricades if Solzhenitsyn were imprisoned. But his protests were incomparably more cautious, and much less resonant, than the protests of real dissenters, who paid with their freedom. And the telegram to Brezhnev has the air of an intimate exchange of views between allies: Yevtushenko speaks in it about "our action," which is a damaging mistake, "a great gift to all the reactionary forces in the world." The poem **"Russian Tanks in Prague,"** moreover, was circulated secretly and reached a very limited circle, so as to avoid doing any harm to the poet's career.

A poet's dubious moral and political stance does not always preclude good poetry. In Yevtushenko's case, though, it does. His verses, as a rule, do not belong to the realm of poetry at all. They are made up of middlebrow journalism and an interminable flow of didactic chatter; they have virtually nothing in common with the true problems of modern (or any) poetics. For all his declarations of ardor and fervor, Yevtushenko is hackneyed, kitschy, and lukewarm. On almost every page you stumble on something like "eyelashes laden / with tears and storms," or "eyes half-shut with ecstasy and pain." Melodramatic effusions ("My love is a demolished church / above the turbid river of memories") alternate with revelations worthy of a sex manual ("When we love, / nothing is base or tasteless. / When we love, / nothing is shameful.").

I am trying not to be unfair. There are some concessions I must make in Yevtushenko's favor. He is usually free of Voznesensky's pretentiousness. You can find in his books good similes, successful vignettes of daily life, touching characters, and hair-raising stories that may, alas, be true. And his weaknesses become more obvious in translation. I would be inclined to praise such poems as **"Handrolled Cigarettes"** or **"The Ballad of the Big Stamp"** (the latter is hilarious, though it suffers in translation since it lacks a factual commentary about Russian religious sects). And of course Yevtushenko is a figure to reckon with because of his inexhaustible energy. But all these attractive traits are deeply tainted by his taste for comfort and accommodation, by his eagerness to play humiliating games with the censors, by the mixture of self-admiration, self-pity, and coquettish self-deprecation that has become his indelible mark.

Today Yevtushenko is a member—by no means the leader—of the liberal wing of the perestroika establishment. His book of journalistic prose, *Fatal Half Measures,* from which I have quoted extensively, traces his political career between 1962, when *A Precocious Autobiography,* published in the West, caused a passing commotion, and 1990, when his speeches resounded, rather hollowly, in several public forums. The book is preceded by a poem in which Yevtushenko seems to be admonishing Gorbachev: "Don't half recoil, / lost in broad daylight, / half rebel, / half suppressor / of the half insurrection / you gave birth to!"

But the book's title perfectly applies to the poet's own style of action. Fatal half measures, indeed. Yevtushenko lags desperately behind events. The gap between his wordy, complacent prose and the Soviet public mood became unbridgeable long ago. In the book, Yevtushenko launches crusades against nuclear war, against the monopoly of the Party, against Russian chauvinism, against cruelty to animals, and lots of other unsavory phenomena. Most of his thoughts on these topics are with the angels. But they are still wrapped in the old Soviet discourse, and that discourse is finally as dead as nails. He strives to improve his fatherland without rejecting the main part of the ideology that makes such a project hopeless. He is what he always was, a man of fatal half truths, of fatal half measures. In this way, he is the counterpart of his presumably avid reader Gorbachev. Both attempt to promote something like totalitarianism with a human face. It never worked. It never will.

Patricia Pollock Brodsky (review date 1992)

SOURCE: Brodsky, Patricia Pollock. Review of *The Collected Poems 1952-1990*, by Yevgeny Yevtushenko. *World Literature Today* 66, no. 1 (winter 1992): 156-57.

[*In the following review, Brodsky praises Yevtushenko's accessibility and the power of visual details in his poetry.*]

The new **Collected Poems 1952-1990** reflects Yevgeny Yevtushenko's poetic career in microcosm: vast and uneven, sometimes irritating, often appealing, and ever astonishing in its variety. The title is somewhat misleading, since the volume offers only a selection from Yevtushenko's extensive oeuvre, and in addition, several long poems are represented in excerpts only. Yevtushenko's allusiveness can be a problem for Western readers; a few names and terms are explained in footnotes, but this practice could profitably have been expanded. A helpful feature is the chronological list of poems with their Russian titles, date and place of first publication, and location, if any, in the 1983 *Sobranie sochineniĭ* (see *WLT* 59:4, p. 614).

Like the poems themselves, the translations by twenty-five translators vary in quality. A few are revisions of earlier versions. Most of Yevtushenko's poems use slant rhyme relying heavily on assonance, a practice so closely associated with him as to be called "Yevtushenkean rhyme" (*evtushenkovskaia rifma*). Russian's rich phonetic structure allows almost limitless use of this kind of rhyme; a master of the form and clearly one of Yevtushenko's teachers was the poet Marina Tsvetaeva. Wisely, few attempts are made to retain this feature in the English translations, or indeed to use rhyme at all.

From the beginning of his prolific career in the early 1950s, Yevtushenko's poetry has been characterized by strong stances on political issues. He praises Allende and Che Guevara, condemns the Vietnam War, and deplores the situation in Northern Ireland. His criticism is not limited to the West, however. A popular and privileged poet whose readings at one time filled football stadiums and who was given unprecedented freedom to travel abroad, he nevertheless warned against abuses at home, castigating militarists, dishonest bureaucrats, and toadies of all kinds. These critical poems range from **"The Heirs of Stalin"** and **"Babi Yar"** in the early 1960s to **"Momma and the Neutron Bomb"** and poems about the dissident Andrei Sakharov and the Afghanistan war in the 1980s. The roots of his ferocious morality are to be found in his love for Russia, and in his stubborn belief in the ideals of the revolution.

Even the semiofficial poet was not immune from censorship, however. Included in the new collection are a number of poems which were written during the sixties but for political reasons could not be published until many years later. Among them are verses to fellow poets Tsvetaeva (1967/1987) and Esenin (1965/1988), **"Russian Tanks in Prague"** (1968/1990), and **"The Ballad of the Big Stamp,"** a bawdy tale about castration for the good of the party (1966/1989).

Yevtushenko is at his best when he is specific and detailed, and this happens most frequently in poems dealing with his native Siberia, its nature and history, its sailors, whalers, berry pickers. These include the long poem **"Zima Junction"** (1955) and a series written in 1964 about life on the northern frontier. Yevtushenko has a strong visual sense (he is an accomplished photographer), and color often plays an important role in his works. In the fairy-tale-like **"Snow in Tokyo: A Japanese Poem"** (1974), for example, a proper and repressed Japanese matron discovers the wonders of painting and finds the courage to rebel against her stultifying life through the world of color.

A thread running through Yevtushenko's work is the importance of poetry and the responsibility of the poet to mankind. He constantly questions his own talent and mission, thus continuing the Russian tradition of metapoetry. Likewise very Russian is the dialogue between writers living and dead which Yevtushenko carries on, in poems addressed to or evoking Pushkin, Pasternak, Neruda, and Jack London, along with numerous others.

Finally, Yevtushenko's poetry is a kind of personal diary which details his extensive travels and especially his many love affairs and marriages. Remarkable love poems follow the poet from first love, to the birth of his sons, to the sadness of falling out of love again. The poems contain a rich fabric of quarrels, memories, farewells, even a conversation with his dog, who shares the poet's grief that his woman has gone. Perhaps the most attractive thing about Yevtushenko is his human breadth, his willingness to lay himself open to our reactions. *The Collected Poems* provides the reader with numerous opportunities to become acquainted with this engaged and engaging poet, one of the important, questioning voices of our age.

FURTHER READING

Criticism

Carlisle, Olga. "The Art of Poetry VII: Yevgeny Yevtushenko." *Paris Review* 9, no. 34 (spring-summer 1965): 97-115.

> Relates developments in Yevtushenko's career based on interviews conducted with him in the early 1960s.

Conquest, Robert. "The Politics of Poetry." *New York Times Magazine* (30 September 1973): 16-17, 56, 58-60, 62-3, 69-70.

> Surveys Yevtushenko's career, focusing on his declining reputation in the West and Russia.

Cotter, James Finn. "The Truth of Poetry." *The Hudson Review* 44, no. 2 (summer 1991): 343-45.

> Favorable review of *The Collected Poems 1952-1990*.

Eberstadt, Fernanda. "Out of the Drawer & Into the West." *Commentary* 80, no. 1 (July 1985): 36-44.

> Discusses Yevtushenko's novel *Wild Berries* and the writer's relationship to the Soviet authorities.

Todd, Albert C. Introduction to *The Collected Poems 1952-1990,* by Yevgeny Yevtushenko, pp. xv-xxiii. New York: Henry Holt and Company, 1991.

> Remarks on the relationship between Yevtushenko's life experiences and his poetry.

Additional coverage of Yevtushenko's life and career is contained in the following sources published by the Gale Group: *Contemporary Authors,* **Vols. 81-84;** *Contemporary Authors New Revision Series,* **Vols. 33, 54;** *Contemporary Literary Criticism,* **Vols. 1, 3, 13, 26, 51, 126;** *Contemporary World Writers,* **Vol. 2;** *DISCovering Authors Modules: Poets*; *Literature Resource Center*; **and** *Major 20th-Century Writers,* **Ed. 1.**

How to Use This Index

The main references

Calvino, Italo
    1923-1985 .... CLC **5, 8, 11, 22, 33, 39,**
                                      73; SSC 3

---

list all author entries in the following Gale Literary Criticism series:

BLC = *Black Literature Criticism*
CLC = *Contemporary Literary Criticism*
CLR = *Children's Literature Review*
CMLC = *Classical and Medieval Literature Criticism*
DA = *DISCovering Authors*
DAB = *DISCovering Authors: British*
DAC = *DISCovering Authors: Canadian*
DAM = *DISCovering Authors: Modules*
        DRAM: *Dramatists Module;* **MST:** *Most-Studied Authors Module;*
        MULT: *Multicultural Authors Module;* **NOV:** *Novelists Module;*
        POET: *Poets Module;* **POP:** *Popular Fiction and Genre Authors Module*
DC = *Drama Criticism*
HLC = *Hispanic Literature Criticism*
LC = *Literature Criticism from 1400 to 1800*
NCLC = *Nineteenth-Century Literature Criticism*
NNAL = *Native North American Literature*
PC = *Poetry Criticism*
SSC = *Short Story Criticism*
TCLC = *Twentieth-Century Literary Criticism*
WLC = *World Literature Criticism, 1500 to the Present*

The cross-references

See also CANR 23; CA 85-88;
obituary CA116

---

list all author entries in the following Gale biographical and literary sources:

AAYA = *Authors & Artists for Young Adults*
AITN = *Authors in the News*
BEST = *Bestsellers*
BW = *Black Writers*
CA = *Contemporary Authors*
CAAS = *Contemporary Authors Autobiography Series*
CABS = *Contemporary Authors Bibliographical Series*
CANR = *Contemporary Authors New Revision Series*
CAP = *Contemporary Authors Permanent Series*
CDALB = *Concise Dictionary of American Literary Biography*
CDBLB = *Concise Dictionary of British Literary Biography*
DLB = *Dictionary of Literary Biography*
DLBD = *Dictionary of Literary Biography Documentary Series*
DLBY = *Dictionary of Literary Biography Yearbook*
HW = *Hispanic Writers*
JRDA = *Junior DISCovering Authors*
MAICYA = *Major Authors and Illustrators for Children and Young Adults*
MTCW = *Major 20th-Century Writers*
SAAS = *Something about the Author Autobiography Series*
SATA = *Something about the Author*
YABC = *Yesterday's Authors of Books for Children*

Literary Criticism Series
Cumulative Author Index

Alta 1942- .... **CLC 19**
See also CA 57-60
Alter, Robert B(ernard) 1935- .... **CLC 34**
See also CA 49-52; CANR 1, 47, 100
Alther, Lisa 1944- .... **CLC 7, 41**
See also BPFB 1; CA 65-68; CAAS 30;
CANR 12, 30, 51; CN 7; CSW; GLL 2;
MTCW 1
Althusser, L.
See Althusser, Louis
Althusser, Louis 1918-1990 .... **CLC 106**
See also CA 131; 132; CANR 102; DLB
242
Altman, Robert 1925- .... **CLC 16, 116**
See also CA 73-76; CANR 43
Alurista
See Urista, Alberto H.
See also DLB 82; HLCS 1
Alvarez, A(lfred) 1929- .... **CLC 5, 13**
See also CA 1-4R; CANR 3, 33, 63, 101;
CN 7; CP 7; DLB 14, 40
Alvarez, Alejandro Rodriguez 1903-1965
See Casona, Alejandro
See also CA 131; 93-96; HW 1
Alvarez, Julia 1950- .... **CLC 93; HLCS 1**
See also AAYA 25; AMWS 7; CA 147;
CANR 69, 101; DA3; MTCW 1; NFS 5,
9; SATA 129; WLIT 1
Alvaro, Corrado 1896-1956 .... **TCLC 60**
See also CA 163
Amado, Jorge 1912-2001 ... **CLC 13, 40, 106;
HLC 1**
See also CA 77-80; CANR 35, 74; DAM
MULT, NOV; DLB 113; HW 2; LAW;
LAWS 1; MTCW 1, 2; RGWL 2; WLIT 1
Ambler, Eric 1909-1998 .... **CLC 4, 6, 9**
See also BRWS 4; CA 9-12R; 171; CANR
7, 38, 74; CMW 4; CN 7; DLB 77; MSW;
MTCW 1
Ambrose, Stephen E(dward)
1936- .... **CLC 145**
See also CA 1-4R; CANR 3, 43, 57, 83,
105; NCFS 2; SATA 40
Amichai, Yehuda 1924-2000 .. **CLC 9, 22, 57,
116; PC 38**
See also CA 85-88; 189; CANR 46, 60, 99;
CWW 2; MTCW 1
Amichai, Yehudah
See Amichai, Yehuda
Amiel, Henri Frederic 1821-1881 .... **NCLC 4**
See also DLB 217
Amis, Kingsley (William)
1922-1995 ...... **CLC 1, 2, 3, 5, 8, 13, 40,
44, 129**
See also AITN 2; BPFB 1; BRWS 2; CA
9-12R; 150; CANR 8, 28, 54; CDBLB
1945-1960; CN 7; CP 7; DA; DA3; DAB;
DAC; DAM MST, NOV; DLB 15, 27,
100, 139; DLBY 1996; HGG; INT
CANR-8; MTCW 1, 2; RGEL 2; RGSF 2;
SFW 4
Amis, Martin (Louis) 1949- ... **CLC 4, 9, 38,
62, 101**
See also BEST 90:3; BRWS 4; CA 65-68;
CANR 8, 27, 54, 73, 95; CN 7; DA3;
DLB 14, 194; INT CANR-27; MTCW 1
Ammons, A(rchie) R(andolph)
1926-2001 ...... **CLC 2, 3, 5, 8, 9, 25, 57,
108; PC 16**
See also AITN 1; AMWS 7; CA 9-12R;
193; CANR 6, 36, 51, 73, 107; CP 7;
CSW; DAM POET; DLB 5, 165; MTCW
1, 2; RGAL 4
Amo, Tauraatua i
See Adams, Henry (Brooks)
Amory, Thomas 1691(?)-1788 .... **LC 48**
See also DLB 39

Anand, Mulk Raj 1905- .... **CLC 23, 93**
See also CA 65-68; CANR 32, 64; CN 7;
DAM NOV; MTCW 1, 2; RGSF 2
Anatol
See Schnitzler, Arthur
Anaximander c. 611B.C.-c.
546B.C. .... **CMLC 22**
Anaya, Rudolfo A(lfonso) 1937- ...... **CLC 23,
148; HLC 1**
See also AAYA 20; BYA 13; CA 45-48;
CAAS 4; CANR 1, 32, 51; CN 7; DAM
MULT, NOV; DLB 82, 206; HW 1; LAIT
4; MTCW 1, 2; NFS 12; RGAL 4; RGSF
2; WLIT 1
Andersen, Hans Christian
1805-1875 ... **NCLC 7, 79; SSC 6; WLC**
See also CLR 6; DA; DA3; DAB; DAC;
DAM MST, POP; EW 6; MAICYA 1;
RGSF 2; RGWL 2; SATA 100; WCH;
YABC 1
Anderson, C. Farley
See Mencken, H(enry) L(ouis); Nathan,
George Jean
Anderson, Jessica (Margaret) Queale
1916- .... **CLC 37**
See also CA 9-12R; CANR 4, 62; CN 7
Anderson, Jon (Victor) 1940- .... **CLC 9**
See also CA 25-28R; CANR 20; DAM
POET
Anderson, Lindsay (Gordon)
1923-1994 .... **CLC 20**
See also CA 125; 128; 146; CANR 77
Anderson, Maxwell 1888-1959 .... **TCLC 2**
See also CA 105; 152; DAM DRAM; DLB
7, 228; MTCW 2; RGAL 4
Anderson, Poul (William)
1926-2001 .... **CLC 15**
See also AAYA 5, 34; BPFB 1; BYA 6, 8,
9; CA 1-4R, 181; 199; CAAE 181; CAAS
2; CANR 2, 15, 34, 64; CLR 58; DLB 8;
FANT; INT CANR-15; MTCW 1, 2;
SATA 90; SATA-Brief 39; SATA-Essay
106; SCFW 2; SFW 4; SUFW
Anderson, Robert (Woodruff)
1917- .... **CLC 23**
See also AITN 1; CA 21-24R; CANR 32;
DAM DRAM; DLB 7; LAIT 5
Anderson, Roberta Joan
See Mitchell, Joni
Anderson, Sherwood 1876-1941 ..... **TCLC 1,
10, 24; SSC 1, 46; WLC**
See also AAYA 30; AMW; BPFB 1; CA
104; 121; CANR 61; CDALB 1917-1929;
DA; DA3; DAB; DAC; DAM MST, NOV;
DLB 4, 9, 86; DLBD 1; EXPS; GLL 2;
MTCW 1, 2; NFS 4; RGAL 4; RGSF 2;
SSFS 4, 10, 11
Andier, Pierre
See Desnos, Robert
Andouard
See Giraudoux, Jean(-Hippolyte)
Andrade, Carlos Drummond de ..... **CLC 18**
See also Drummond de Andrade, Carlos
See also RGWL 2
Andrade, Mario de .... **TCLC 43**
See also de Andrade, Mario
See also LAW; RGWL 2; WLIT 1
Andreae, Johann V(alentin)
1586-1654 .... **LC 32**
See also DLB 164
Andreas Capellanus fl. c. 1185- .... **CMLC 45**
See also DLB 208
Andreas-Salome, Lou 1861-1937 ... **TCLC 56**
See also CA 178; DLB 66
Andress, Lesley
See Sanders, Lawrence
Andrewes, Lancelot 1555-1626 .... **LC 5**
See also DLB 151, 172

Andrews, Cicily Fairfield
See West, Rebecca
Andrews, Elton V.
See Pohl, Frederik
Andreyev, Leonid (Nikolaevich)
1871-1919 .... **TCLC 3**
See also CA 104; 185
Andric, Ivo 1892-1975 .... **CLC 8; SSC 36**
See also CA 81-84; 57-60; CANR 43, 60;
CDWLB 4; DLB 147; EW 11; MTCW 1;
RGSF 2; RGWL 2
Androvar
See Prado (Calvo), Pedro
Angelique, Pierre
See Bataille, Georges
Angell, Roger 1920- .... **CLC 26**
See also CA 57-60; CANR 13, 44, 70; DLB
171, 185
Angelou, Maya 1928- ..... **CLC 12, 35, 64, 77,
155; BLC 1; PC 32; WLCS**
See also AAYA 7, 20; AMWS 4; BPFB 1;
BW 2, 3; BYA 2; CA 65-68; CANR 19,
42, 65; CDALBS; CLR 53; CP 7; CPW;
CSW; CWP; DA; DA3; DAB; DAC;
DAM MST, MULT, POET, POP; DLB 38;
EXPN; EXPP; LAIT 4; MAICYAS 1;
MAWW; MTCW 1, 2; NCFS 2; NFS 2;
PFS 2, 3; RGAL 4; SATA 49; WYA; YAW
Angouleme, Marguerite d'
See de Navarre, Marguerite
Anna Comnena 1083-1153 .... **CMLC 25**
Annensky, Innokenty (Fyodorovich)
1856-1909 .... **TCLC 14**
See also CA 110; 155
Annunzio, Gabriele d'
See D'Annunzio, Gabriele
Anodos
See Coleridge, Mary E(lizabeth)
Anon, Charles Robert
See Pessoa, Fernando (Antonio Nogueira)
Anouilh, Jean (Marie Lucien Pierre)
1910-1987 . **CLC 1, 3, 8, 13, 40, 50; DC
8**
See also CA 17-20R; 123; CANR 32; DAM
DRAM; DFS 9, 10; EW 13; GFL 1789 to
the Present; MTCW 1, 2; RGWL 2
Anthony, Florence
See Ai
Anthony, John
See Ciardi, John (Anthony)
Anthony, Peter
See Shaffer, Anthony (Joshua); Shaffer,
Peter (Levin)
Anthony, Piers 1934- .... **CLC 35**
See also AAYA 11; BYA 7; CA 21-24R;
CANR 28, 56, 73, 102; CPW; DAM POP;
DLB 8; FANT; MAICYA 1; MTCW 1,
2; SAAS 22; SATA 84; SATA-Essay 129;
SFW 4; SUFW; YAW
Anthony, Susan B(rownell)
1820-1906 .... **TCLC 84**
See also FW
Antoine, Marc
See Proust, (Valentin-Louis-George-Eugene-
)Marcel
Antoninus, Brother
See Everson, William (Oliver)
Antonioni, Michelangelo 1912- .... **CLC 20,
144**
See also CA 73-76; CANR 45, 77
Antschel, Paul 1920-1970
See Celan, Paul
See also CA 85-88; CANR 33, 61; MTCW
1
Anwar, Chairil 1922-1949 .... **TCLC 22**
See also CA 121
Anzaldua, Gloria (Evanjelina) 1942-
See also CA 175; CSW; CWP; DLB 122;
FW; HLCS 1; RGAL 4

Bialik, Chaim Nachman
1873-1934 .... **TCLC 25**
See also CA 170

Bickerstaff, Isaac
See Swift, Jonathan

Bidart, Frank 1939- .... **CLC 33**
See also CA 140; CANR 106; CP 7

Bienek, Horst 1930- .... **CLC 7, 11**
See also CA 73-76; DLB 75

Bierce, Ambrose (Gwinett)
1842-1914(?) ..... **TCLC 1, 7, 44; SSC 9;
WLC**
See also AMW; BYA 11; CA 104; 139;
CANR 78; CDALB 1865-1917; DA;
DA3; DAC; DAM MST; DLB 11, 12, 23,
71, 74, 186; EXPS; HGG; LAIT 2; RGAL
4; RGSF 2; SSFS 9; SUFW

Biggers, Earl Derr 1884-1933 .... **TCLC 65**
See also CA 108; 153

Billings, Josh
See Shaw, Henry Wheeler

Billington, (Lady) Rachel (Mary)
1942- .... **CLC 43**
See also AITN 2; CA 33-36R; CANR 44;
CN 7

Binchy, Maeve 1940- .... **CLC 153**
See also BEST 90:1; BPFB 1; CA 127; 134;
CANR 50, 96; CN 7; CPW; DA3; DAM
POP; INT CA-134; MTCW 1; RHW

Binyon, T(imothy) J(ohn) 1936- .... **CLC 34**
See also CA 111; CANR 28

Bion 335B.C.-245B.C. .... **CMLC 39**

Bioy Casares, Adolfo 1914-1999 ... **CLC 4, 8,
13, 88; HLC 1; SSC 17**
See also Casares, Adolfo Bioy; Miranda,
Javier; Sacastru, Martin
See also CA 29-32R; 177; CANR 19, 43,
66; DAM MULT; DLB 113; HW 1, 2;
LAW; MTCW 1, 2

Birch, Allison .... **CLC 65**

Bird, Cordwainer
See Ellison, Harlan (Jay)

Bird, Robert Montgomery
1806-1854 .... **NCLC 1**
See also DLB 202; RGAL 4

Birkerts, Sven 1951- .... **CLC 116**
See also CA 128; 133, 176; CAAE 176;
CAAS 29; INT 133

Birney, (Alfred) Earle 1904-1995 .. **CLC 1, 4,
6, 11**
See also CA 1-4R; CANR 5, 20; CP 7;
DAC; DAM MST, POET; DLB 88;
MTCW 1; PFS 8; RGEL 2

Biruni, al 973-1048(?) .... **CMLC 28**

Bishop, Elizabeth 1911-1979 ..... **CLC 1, 4, 9,
13, 15, 32; PC 3, 34**
See also AMWS 1; CA 5-8R; 89-92; CABS
2; CANR 26, 61, 108; CDALB 1968-
1988; DA; DA3; DAC; DAM MST,
POET; DLB 5, 169; GLL 2; MAWW;
MTCW 1, 2; PAB; PFS 6, 12; RGAL 4;
SATA-Obit 24; WP

Bishop, John 1935- .... **CLC 10**
See also CA 105

Bishop, John Peale 1892-1944 ..... **TCLC 103**
See also CA 107; 155; DLB 4, 9, 45; RGAL
4

Bissett, Bill 1939- .... **CLC 18; PC 14**
See also CA 69-72; CAAS 19; CANR 15;
CCA 1; CP 7; DLB 53; MTCW 1

Bissoondath, Neil (Devindra)
1955- .... **CLC 120**
See also CA 136; CN 7; DAC

Bitov, Andrei (Georgievich) 1937- ... **CLC 57**
See also CA 142

Biyidi, Alexandre 1932-
See Beti, Mongo
See also BW 1, 3; CA 114; 124; CANR 81;
DA3; MTCW 1, 2

Bjarme, Brynjolf
See Ibsen, Henrik (Johan)

Bjoernson, Bjoernstjerne (Martinius)
1832-1910 .... **TCLC 7, 37**
See also CA 104

Black, Robert
See Holdstock, Robert P.

Blackburn, Paul 1926-1971 .... **CLC 9, 43**
See also CA 81-84; 33-36R; CANR 34;
DLB 16; DLBY 1981

Black Elk 1863-1950 .... **TCLC 33**
See also CA 144; DAM MULT; MTCW 1;
NNAL; WP

Black Hobart
See Sanders, (James) Ed(ward)

Blacklin, Malcolm
See Chambers, Aidan

Blackmore, R(ichard) D(oddridge)
1825-1900 .... **TCLC 27**
See also CA 120; DLB 18; RGEL 2

Blackmur, R(ichard) P(almer)
1904-1965 .... **CLC 2, 24**
See also AMWS 2; CA 11-12; 25-28R;
CANR 71; CAP 1; DLB 63

Black Tarantula
See Acker, Kathy

Blackwood, Algernon (Henry)
1869-1951 .... **TCLC 5**
See also CA 105; 150; DLB 153, 156, 178;
HGG; SUFW

Blackwood, Caroline 1931-1996 .... **CLC 6, 9,
100**
See also CA 85-88; 151; CANR 32, 61, 65;
CN 7; DLB 14, 207; HGG; MTCW 1

Blade, Alexander
See Hamilton, Edmond; Silverberg, Robert

Blaga, Lucian 1895-1961 .... **CLC 75**
See also CA 157; DLB 220

Blair, Eric (Arthur) 1903-1950
See Orwell, George
See also CA 104; 132; DA; DA3; DAB;
DAC; DAM MST, NOV; MTCW 1, 2;
SATA 29

Blair, Hugh 1718-1800 .... **NCLC 75**

Blais, Marie-Claire 1939- .... **CLC 2, 4, 6, 13,
22**
See also CA 21-24R; CAAS 4; CANR 38,
75, 93; DAC; DAM MST; DLB 53; FW;
MTCW 1, 2

Blaise, Clark 1940- .... **CLC 29**
See also AITN 2; CA 53-56; CAAS 3;
CANR 5, 66, 106; CN 7; DLB 53; RGSF
2

Blake, Fairley
See De Voto, Bernard (Augustine)

Blake, Nicholas
See Day Lewis, C(ecil)
See also DLB 77; MSW

Blake, William 1757-1827 .... **NCLC 13, 37,
57; PC 12; WLC**
See also BRW 3; BRWR 1; CDBLB 1789-
1832; CLR 52; DA; DA3; DAB; DAC;
DAM MST, POET; DLB 93, 163; EXPP;
MAICYA 1; PAB; PFS 2, 12; SATA 30;
WCH; WLIT 3; WP

Blanchot, Maurice 1907- .... **CLC 135**
See also CA 117; 144; DLB 72

Blasco Ibanez, Vicente 1867-1928 . **TCLC 12**
See also BPFB 1; CA 110; 131; CANR 81;
DA3; DAM NOV; EW 8; HW 1, 2;
MTCW 1

Blatty, William Peter 1928- .... **CLC 2**
See also CA 5-8R; CANR 9; DAM POP;
HGG

Bleeck, Oliver
See Thomas, Ross (Elmore)

Blessing, Lee 1949- .... **CLC 54**
See also CAD; CD 5

Blight, Rose
See Greer, Germaine

Blish, James (Benjamin) 1921-1975 . **CLC 14**
See also BPFB 1; CA 1-4R; 57-60; CANR
3; DLB 8; MTCW 1; SATA 66; SCFW 2;
SFW 4

Bliss, Reginald
See Wells, H(erbert) G(eorge)

Blixen, Karen (Christentze Dinesen)
1885-1962
See Dinesen, Isak
See also CA 25-28; CANR 22, 50; CAP 2;
DA3; DLB 214; MTCW 1, 2; SATA 44

Bloch, Robert (Albert) 1917-1994 .... **CLC 33**
See also AAYA 29; CA 5-8R; 179; 146;
CAAE 179; CAAS 20; CANR 5, 78;
DA3; DLB 44; HGG; INT CANR-5;
MTCW 1; SATA 12; SATA-Obit 82; SFW
4; SUFW

Blok, Alexander (Alexandrovich)
1880-1921 .... **TCLC 5; PC 21**
See also CA 104; 183; EW 9; RGWL 2

Blom, Jan
See Breytenbach, Breyten

Bloom, Harold 1930- .... **CLC 24, 103**
See also CA 13-16R; CANR 39, 75, 92;
DLB 67; MTCW 1; RGAL 4

Bloomfield, Aurelius
See Bourne, Randolph S(illiman)

Blount, Roy (Alton), Jr. 1941- .... **CLC 38**
See also CA 53-56; CANR 10, 28, 61;
CSW; INT CANR-28; MTCW 1, 2

Bloy, Leon 1846-1917 .... **TCLC 22**
See also CA 121; 183; DLB 123; GFL 1789
to the Present

Blume, Judy (Sussman) 1938- .... **CLC 12, 30**
See also AAYA 3, 26; BYA 1, 8, 12; CA 29-
32R; CANR 13, 37, 66; CLR 2, 15, 69;
CPW; DA3; DAM NOV, POP; DLB 52;
JRDA; MAICYA 1; MAICYAS 1; MTCW
1, 2; SATA 2, 31, 79; WYA; YAW

Blunden, Edmund (Charles)
1896-1974 .... **CLC 2, 56**
See also BRW 6; CA 17-18; 45-48; CANR
54; CAP 2; DLB 20, 100, 155; MTCW 1;
PAB

Bly, Robert (Elwood) 1926- .... **CLC 1, 2, 5,
10, 15, 38, 128; PC 39**
See also AMWS 4; CA 5-8R; CANR 41,
73; CP 7; DA3; DAM POET; DLB 5;
MTCW 1, 2; RGAL 4

Boas, Franz 1858-1942 .... **TCLC 56**
See also CA 115; 181

Bobette
See Simenon, Georges (Jacques Christian)

Boccaccio, Giovanni 1313-1375 ... **CMLC 13;
SSC 10**
See also EW 2; RGSF 2; RGWL 2

Bochco, Steven 1943- .... **CLC 35**
See also AAYA 11; CA 124; 138

Bodel, Jean 1167(?)-1210 .... **CMLC 28**

Bodenheim, Maxwell 1892-1954 .... **TCLC 44**
See also CA 110; 187; DLB 9, 45; RGAL 4

Bodker, Cecil 1927- .... **CLC 21**
See also CA 73-76; CANR 13, 44; CLR 23;
MAICYA 1; SATA 14

Boell, Heinrich (Theodor)
1917-1985 ..... **CLC 2, 3, 6, 9, 11, 15, 27,
32, 72; SSC 23; WLC**
See also Boll, Heinrich
See also CA 21-24R; 116; CANR 24; DA;
DA3; DAB; DAC; DAM MST, NOV;
DLB 69; DLBY 1985; MTCW 1, 2

Boerne, Alfred
See Doeblin, Alfred

Boethius c. 480-c. 524 .... **CMLC 15**
See also DLB 115; RGWL 2

Bradley, John Ed(mund, Jr.) 1958- . **CLC 55**
See also CA 139; CANR 99; CN 7; CSW

Bradley, Marion Zimmer
1930-1999 .... **CLC 30**
See also Chapman, Lee; Dexter, John; Gardner, Miriam; Ives, Morgan; Rivers, Elfrida
See also AAYA 40; BPFB 1; CA 57-60; 185; CAAS 10; CANR 7, 31, 51, 75, 107; CPW; DA3; DAM POP; DLB 8; FANT; FW; MTCW 1, 2; SATA 90; SATA-Obit 116; SFW 4; YAW

Bradshaw, John 1933- .... **CLC 70**
See also CA 138; CANR 61

Bradstreet, Anne 1612(?)-1672 ...... **LC 4, 30; PC 10**
See also AMWS 1; CDALB 1640-1865; DA; DA3; DAC; DAM MST, POET; DLB 24; EXPP; FW; PFS 6; RGAL 4; WP

Brady, Joan 1939- .... **CLC 86**
See also CA 141

Bragg, Melvyn 1939- .... **CLC 10**
See also BEST 89:3; CA 57-60; CANR 10, 48, 89; CN 7; DLB 14; RHW

Brahe, Tycho 1546-1601 .... **LC 45**

Braine, John (Gerard) 1922-1986 . **CLC 1, 3, 41**
See also CA 1-4R; 120; CANR 1, 33; CDBLB 1945-1960; DLB 15; DLBY 1986; MTCW 1

Bramah, Ernest 1868-1942 .... **TCLC 72**
See also CA 156; CMW 4; DLB 70; FANT

Brammer, William 1930(?)-1978 ...... **CLC 31**
See also CA 77-80

Brancati, Vitaliano 1907-1954 .... **TCLC 12**
See also CA 109

Brancato, Robin F(idler) 1936- .... **CLC 35**
See also AAYA 9; BYA 6; CA 69-72; CANR 11, 45; CLR 32; JRDA; MAICYAS 1; SAAS 9; SATA 97; WYA; YAW

Brand, Max
See Faust, Frederick (Schiller)
See also BPFB 1; TCWW 2

Brand, Millen 1906-1980 .... **CLC 7**
See also CA 21-24R; 97-100; CANR 72

Branden, Barbara .... **CLC 44**
See also CA 148

Brandes, Georg (Morris Cohen)
1842-1927 .... **TCLC 10**
See also CA 105; 189

Brandys, Kazimierz 1916-2000 .... **CLC 62**

Branley, Franklyn M(ansfield)
1915- .... **CLC 21**
See also CA 33-36R; CANR 14, 39; CLR 13; MAICYA 1; SAAS 16; SATA 4, 68

Brathwaite, Edward (Kamau)
1930- .... **CLC 11; BLCS**
See also BW 2, 3; CA 25-28R; CANR 11, 26, 47; CDWLB 3; CP 7; DAM POET; DLB 125

Brathwaite, Kamau
See Brathwaite, Edward (Kamau)

Brautigan, Richard (Gary)
1935-1984 ..... **CLC 1, 3, 5, 9, 12, 34, 42**
See also BPFB 1; CA 53-56; 113; CANR 34; DA3; DAM NOV; DLB 2, 5, 206; DLBY 1980, 1984; FANT; MTCW 1; RGAL 4; SATA 56

Brave Bird, Mary
See Crow Dog, Mary (Ellen)
See also NNAL

Braverman, Kate 1950- .... **CLC 67**
See also CA 89-92

Brecht, (Eugen) Bertolt (Friedrich)
1898-1956 ..... **TCLC 1, 6, 13, 35; DC 3; WLC**
See also CA 104; 133; CANR 62; CDWLB 2; DA; DA3; DAB; DAC; DAM DRAM, MST; DFS 4, 5, 9; DLB 56, 124; EW 11; IDTP; MTCW 1, 2; RGWL 2

Brecht, Eugen Berthold Friedrich
See Brecht, (Eugen) Bertolt (Friedrich)

Bremer, Fredrika 1801-1865 .... **NCLC 11**
See also DLB 254

Brennan, Christopher John
1870-1932 .... **TCLC 17**
See also CA 117; 188; DLB 230

Brennan, Maeve 1917-1993 .... **CLC 5**
See also CA 81-84; CANR 72, 100

Brent, Linda
See Jacobs, Harriet A(nn)

Brentano, Clemens (Maria)
1778-1842 .... **NCLC 1**
See also DLB 90; RGWL 2

Brent of Bin Bin
See Franklin, (Stella Maria Sarah) Miles (Lampe)

Brenton, Howard 1942- .... **CLC 31**
See also CA 69-72; CANR 33, 67; CBD; CD 5; DLB 13; MTCW 1

Breslin, James 1930-
See Breslin, Jimmy
See also CA 73-76; CANR 31, 75; DAM NOV; MTCW 1, 2

Breslin, Jimmy .... **CLC 4, 43**
See also Breslin, James
See also AITN 1; DLB 185; MTCW 2

Bresson, Robert 1901(?)-1999 .... **CLC 16**
See also CA 110; 187; CANR 49

Breton, Andre 1896-1966 .. **CLC 2, 9, 15, 54; PC 15**
See also CA 19-20; 25-28R; CANR 40, 60; CAP 2; DLB 65, 258; EW 11; GFL 1789 to the Present; MTCW 1, 2; RGWL 2; WP

Breytenbach, Breyten 1939(?)- .. **CLC 23, 37, 126**
See also CA 113; 129; CANR 61; CWW 2; DAM POET; DLB 225

Bridgers, Sue Ellen 1942- .... **CLC 26**
See also AAYA 8; BYA 7, 8; CA 65-68; CANR 11, 36; CLR 18; DLB 52; JRDA; MAICYA 1; SAAS 1; SATA 22, 90; SATA-Essay 109; WYA; YAW

Bridges, Robert (Seymour)
1844-1930 .... **TCLC 1; PC 28**
See also BRW 6; CA 104; 152; CDBLB 1890-1914; DAM POET; DLB 19, 98

Bridie, James .... **TCLC 3**
See also Mavor, Osborne Henry
See also DLB 10

Brin, David 1950- .... **CLC 34**
See also AAYA 21; CA 102; CANR 24, 70; INT CANR-24; SATA 65; SCFW 2; SFW 4

Brink, Andre (Philippus) 1935- . **CLC 18, 36, 106**
See also AFW; BRWS 6; CA 104; CANR 39, 62; CN 7; DLB 225; INT CA-103; MTCW 1, 2; WLIT 2

Brinsmead, H(esba) F(ay) 1922- ...... **CLC 21**
See also CA 21-24R; CANR 10; CLR 47; CWRI 5; MAICYA 1; SAAS 5; SATA 18, 78

Brittain, Vera (Mary) 1893(?)-1970 . **CLC 23**
See also CA 13-16; 25-28R; CANR 58; CAP 1; DLB 191; FW; MTCW 1, 2

Broch, Hermann 1886-1951 .... **TCLC 20**
See also CA 117; CDWLB 2; DLB 85, 124; EW 10; RGWL 2

Brock, Rose
See Hansen, Joseph
See also GLL 1

Brod, Max 1884-1968 .... **TCLC 115**
See also CA 5-8R; 25-28R; CANR 7; DLB 81

Brodkey, Harold (Roy) 1930-1996 ... **CLC 56**
See also CA 111; 151; CANR 71; CN 7; DLB 130

Brodskii, Iosif
See Brodsky, Joseph
See also RGWL 2

Brodsky, Iosif Alexandrovich 1940-1996
See Brodsky, Joseph
See also AITN 1; CA 41-44R; 151; CANR 37, 106; DA3; DAM POET; MTCW 1, 2

Brodsky, Joseph . **CLC 4, 6, 13, 36, 100; PC 9**
See also Brodsky, Iosif Alexandrovich
See also AMWS 8; CWW 2; MTCW 1

Brodsky, Michael (Mark) 1948- .... **CLC 19**
See also CA 102; CANR 18, 41, 58; DLB 244

Brodzki, Bella ed. .... **CLC 65**

Brome, Richard 1590(?)-1652 .... **LC 61**
See also DLB 58

Bromell, Henry 1947- .... **CLC 5**
See also CA 53-56; CANR 9

Bromfield, Louis (Brucker)
1896-1956 .... **TCLC 11**
See also CA 107; 155; DLB 4, 9, 86; RGAL 4; RHW

Broner, E(sther) M(asserman)
1930- .... **CLC 19**
See also CA 17-20R; CANR 8, 25, 72; CN 7; DLB 28

Bronk, William (M.) 1918-1999 .... **CLC 10**
See also CA 89-92; 177; CANR 23; CP 7; DLB 165

Bronstein, Lev Davidovich
See Trotsky, Leon

Bronte, Anne 1820-1849 ..... **NCLC 4, 71, 102**
See also BRW 5; BRWR 1; DA3; DLB 21, 199

Bronte, (Patrick) Branwell
1817-1848 .... **NCLC 109**

Bronte, Charlotte 1816-1855 ...... **NCLC 3, 8, 33, 58, 105; WLC**
See also AAYA 17; BRW 5; BRWR 1; BYA 2; CDBLB 1832-1890; DA; DA3; DAB; DAC; DAM MST, NOV; DLB 21, 159, 199; EXPN; LAIT 2; NFS 4; WLIT 4

Bronte, Emily (Jane) 1818-1848 ... **NCLC 16, 35; PC 8; WLC**
See also AAYA 17; BPFB 1; BRW 5; BRWR 1; BYA 3; CDBLB 1832-1890; DA; DA3; DAB; DAC; DAM MST, NOV, POET; DLB 21, 32, 199; EXPN; LAIT 1; WLIT 3

Brontes
See Bronte, Anne; Bronte, Charlotte; Bronte, Emily (Jane)

Brooke, Frances 1724-1789 .... **LC 6, 48**
See also DLB 39, 99

Brooke, Henry 1703(?)-1783 .... **LC 1**
See also DLB 39

Brooke, Rupert (Chawner)
1887-1915 ..... **TCLC 2, 7; PC 24; WLC**
See also BRWS 3; CA 104; 132; CANR 61; CDBLB 1914-1945; DA; DAB; DAC; DAM MST, POET; DLB 19, 216; EXPP; GLL 2; MTCW 1, 2; PFS 7

Brooke-Haven, P.
See Wodehouse, P(elham) G(renville)

Brooke-Rose, Christine 1926(?)- ...... **CLC 40**
See also BRWS 4; CA 13-16R; CANR 58; CN 7; DLB 14, 231; SFW 4

Brookner, Anita 1928- .. **CLC 32, 34, 51, 136**
See also BRWS 4; CA 114; 120; CANR 37, 56, 87; CN 7; CPW; DA3; DAB; DAM POP; DLB 194; DLBY 1987; MTCW 1, 2

Brooks, Cleanth 1906-1994 . **CLC 24, 86, 110**
See also CA 17-20R; 145; CANR 33, 35; CSW; DLB 63; DLBY 1994; INT CANR-35; MTCW 1, 2

Brooks, George
See Baum, L(yman) Frank

Bunting, Basil 1900-1985 ...... **CLC 10, 39, 47**
See also BRWS 7; CA 53-56; 115; CANR 7; DAM POET; DLB 20; RGEL 2

Bunuel, Luis 1900-1983 ... **CLC 16, 80; HLC 1**
See also CA 101; 110; CANR 32, 77; DAM MULT; HW 1

Bunyan, John 1628-1688 ..... **LC 4, 69; WLC**
See also BRW 2; BYA 5; CDBLB 1660-1789; DA; DAB; DAC; DAM MST; DLB 39; RGEL 2; WCH; WLIT 3

Buravsky, Alexandr .... **CLC 59**

Burckhardt, Jacob (Christoph) 1818-1897 .... **NCLC 49**
See also EW 6

Burford, Eleanor
See Hibbert, Eleanor Alice Burford

Burgess, Anthony . **CLC 1, 2, 4, 5, 8, 10, 13, 15, 22, 40, 62, 81, 94**
See also Wilson, John (Anthony) Burgess
See also AAYA 25; AITN 1; BRWS 1; CD-BLB 1960 to Present; DAB; DLB 14, 194; DLBY 1998; MTCW 1; RGEL 2; RHW; SFW 4; YAW

Burke, Edmund 1729(?)-1797 .... **LC 7, 36; WLC**
See also BRW 3; DA; DA3; DAB; DAC; DAM MST; DLB 104, 252; RGEL 2

Burke, Kenneth (Duva) 1897-1993 ... **CLC 2, 24**
See also AMW; CA 5-8R; 143; CANR 39, 74; DLB 45, 63; MTCW 1, 2; RGAL 4

Burke, Leda
See Garnett, David

Burke, Ralph
See Silverberg, Robert

Burke, Thomas 1886-1945 .... **TCLC 63**
See also CA 113; 155; CMW 4; DLB 197

Burney, Fanny 1752-1840 .... **NCLC 12, 54, 107**
See also BRWS 3; DLB 39; RGEL 2

Burney, Frances
See Burney, Fanny

Burns, Robert 1759-1796 ... **LC 3, 29, 40; PC 6; WLC**
See also BRW 3; CDBLB 1789-1832; DA; DA3; DAB; DAC; DAM MST, POET; DLB 109; EXPP; PAB; RGEL 2; WP

Burns, Tex
See L'Amour, Louis (Dearborn)
See also TCWW 2

Burnshaw, Stanley 1906- .... **CLC 3, 13, 44**
See also CA 9-12R; CP 7; DLB 48; DLBY 1997

Burr, Anne 1937- .... **CLC 6**
See also CA 25-28R

Burroughs, Edgar Rice 1875-1950 . **TCLC 2, 32**
See also AAYA 11; BPFB 1; BYA 4, 9; CA 104; 132; DA3; DAM NOV; DLB 8; FANT; MTCW 1, 2; RGAL 4; SATA 41; SCFW 2; SFW 4; YAW

Burroughs, William S(eward) 1914-1997 .. **CLC 1, 2, 5, 15, 22, 42, 75, 109; WLC**
See also Lee, William; Lee, Willy
See also AITN 2; AMWS 3; BPFB 1; CA 9-12R; 160; CANR 20, 52, 104; CN 7; CPW; DA; DA3; DAB; DAC; DAM MST, NOV, POP; DLB 2, 8, 16, 152, 237; DLBY 1981, 1997; HGG; MTCW 1, 2; RGAL 4; SFW 4

Burton, Sir Richard F(rancis) 1821-1890 .... **NCLC 42**
See also DLB 55, 166, 184

Burton, Robert 1577-1640 .... **LC 74**
See also DLB 151; RGEL 2

Busch, Frederick 1941- .... **CLC 7, 10, 18, 47**
See also CA 33-36R; CAAS 1; CANR 45, 73, 92; CN 7; DLB 6, 218

Bush, Ronald 1946- .... **CLC 34**
See also CA 136

Bustos, F(rancisco)
See Borges, Jorge Luis

Bustos Domecq, H(onorio)
See Bioy Casares, Adolfo; Borges, Jorge Luis

Butler, Octavia E(stelle) 1947- .... **CLC 38, 121; BLCS**
See also AAYA 18; AFAW 2; BPFB 1; BW 2, 3; CA 73-76; CANR 12, 24, 38, 73; CLR 65; CPW; DA3; DAM MULT, POP; DLB 33; MTCW 1, 2; NFS 8; SATA 84; SCFW 2; SFW 4; SSFS 6; YAW

Butler, Robert Olen, (Jr.) 1945- .... **CLC 81**
See also BPFB 1; CA 112; CANR 66; CSW; DAM POP; DLB 173; INT CA-112; MTCW 1; SSFS 11

Butler, Samuel 1612-1680 .... **LC 16, 43**
See also DLB 101, 126; RGEL 2

Butler, Samuel 1835-1902 .... **TCLC 1, 33; WLC**
See also BRWS 2; CA 143; CDBLB 1890-1914; DA; DA3; DAB; DAC; DAM MST, NOV; DLB 18, 57, 174; RGEL 2; SFW 4; TEA

Butler, Walter C.
See Faust, Frederick (Schiller)

Butor, Michel (Marie Francois) 1926- .... **CLC 1, 3, 8, 11, 15**
See also CA 9-12R; CANR 33, 66; DLB 83; EW 13; GFL 1789 to the Present; MTCW 1, 2

Butts, Mary 1890(?)-1937 .... **TCLC 77**
See also CA 148; DLB 240

Buxton, Ralph
See Silverstein, Alvin; Silverstein, Virginia B(arbara Opshelor)

Buzo, Alexander (John) 1944- .... **CLC 61**
See also CA 97-100; CANR 17, 39, 69; CD 5

Buzzati, Dino 1906-1972 .... **CLC 36**
See also CA 160; 33-36R; DLB 177; RGWL 2; SFW 4

Byars, Betsy (Cromer) 1928- .... **CLC 35**
See also AAYA 19; BYA 3; CA 33-36R, 183; CAAE 183; CANR 18, 36, 57, 102; CLR 1, 16, 72; DLB 52; INT CANR-18; JRDA; MAICYA 1; MAICYAS 1; MTCW 1; SAAS 1; SATA 4, 46, 80; SATA-Essay 108; WYA; YAW

Byatt, A(ntonia) S(usan Drabble) 1936- .... **CLC 19, 65, 136**
See also BPFB 1; BRWS 4; CA 13-16R; CANR 13, 33, 50, 75, 96; DA3; DAM NOV, POP; DLB 14, 194; MTCW 1, 2; RGSF 2; RHW

Byrne, David 1952- .... **CLC 26**
See also CA 127

Byrne, John Keyes 1926-
See Leonard, Hugh
See also CA 102; CANR 78; INT CA-102

Byron, George Gordon (Noel) 1788-1824 ..... **NCLC 2, 12, 109; PC 16; WLC**
See also BRW 4; CDBLB 1789-1832; DA; DA3; DAB; DAC; DAM MST, POET; DLB 96, 110; EXPP; PAB; PFS 1, 14; RGEL 2; WLIT 3; WP

Byron, Robert 1905-1941 .... **TCLC 67**
See also CA 160; DLB 195

C. 3. 3.
See Wilde, Oscar (Fingal O'Flahertie Wills)

Caballero, Fernan 1796-1877 .... **NCLC 10**

Cabell, Branch
See Cabell, James Branch

Cabell, James Branch 1879-1958 .... **TCLC 6**
See also CA 105; 152; DLB 9, 78; FANT; MTCW 1; RGAL 4; SUFW

Cabeza de Vaca, Alvar Nunez 1490-1557(?) .... **LC 61**

Cable, George Washington 1844-1925 .... **TCLC 4; SSC 4**
See also CA 104; 155; DLB 12, 74; DLBD 13; RGAL 4

Cabral de Melo Neto, Joao 1920-1999 .... **CLC 76**
See also CA 151; DAM MULT; LAW; LAWS 1

Cabrera Infante, G(uillermo) 1929- . **CLC 5, 25, 45, 120; HLC 1; SSC 39**
See also CA 85-88; CANR 29, 65; CDWLB 3; DA3; DAM MULT; DLB 113; HW 1, 2; LAW; LAWS 1; MTCW 1, 2; RGSF 2; WLIT 1

Cade, Toni
See Bambara, Toni Cade

Cadmus and Harmonia
See Buchan, John

Caedmon fl. 658-680 .... **CMLC 7**
See also DLB 146

Caeiro, Alberto
See Pessoa, Fernando (Antonio Nogueira)

Caesar, Julius .... **CMLC 47**
See also Julius Caesar
See also AW 1; RGWL 2

Cage, John (Milton, Jr.) 1912-1992 . **CLC 41**
See also CA 13-16R; 169; CANR 9, 78; DLB 193; INT CANR-9

Cahan, Abraham 1860-1951 .... **TCLC 71**
See also CA 108; 154; DLB 9, 25, 28; RGAL 4

Cain, G.
See Cabrera Infante, G(uillermo)

Cain, Guillermo
See Cabrera Infante, G(uillermo)

Cain, James M(allahan) 1892-1977 .. **CLC 3, 11, 28**
See also AITN 1; BPFB 1; CA 17-20R; 73-76; CANR 8, 34, 61; CMW 4; DLB 226; MSW; MTCW 1; RGAL 4

Caine, Hall 1853-1931 .... **TCLC 97**
See also RHW

Caine, Mark
See Raphael, Frederic (Michael)

Calasso, Roberto 1941- .... **CLC 81**
See also CA 143; CANR 89

Calderon de la Barca, Pedro 1600-1681 .... **LC 23; DC 3; HLCS 1**
See also EW 2; RGWL 2

Caldwell, Erskine (Preston) 1903-1987 .... **CLC 1, 8, 14, 50, 60; SSC 19**
See also AITN 1; AMW; BPFB 1; CA 1-4R; 121; CAAS 1; CANR 2, 33; DA3; DAM NOV; DLB 9, 86; MTCW 1, 2; RGAL 4; RGSF 2; TCLC 117

Caldwell, (Janet Miriam) Taylor (Holland) 1900-1985 .... **CLC 2, 28, 39**
See also BPFB 1; CA 5-8R; 116; CANR 5; DA3; DAM NOV, POP; DLBD 17; RHW

Calhoun, John Caldwell 1782-1850 .... **NCLC 15**
See also DLB 3, 248

Calisher, Hortense 1911- ..... **CLC 2, 4, 8, 38, 134; SSC 15**
See also CA 1-4R; CANR 1, 22, 67; CN 7; DA3; DAM NOV; DLB 2, 218; INT CANR-22; MTCW 1, 2; RGAL 4; RGSF 2

Callaghan, Morley Edward 1903-1990 .... **CLC 3, 14, 41, 65**
See also CA 9-12R; 132; CANR 33, 73; DAC; DAM MST; DLB 68; MTCW 1, 2; RGEL 2; RGSF 2

Casas, Bartolome de las 1474-1566
See Las Casas, Bartolome de
See also WLIT 1

Casely-Hayford, J(oseph) E(phraim)
1866-1903 .... **TCLC 24; BLC 1**
See also BW 2; CA 123; 152; DAM MULT

Casey, John (Dudley) 1939- .... **CLC 59**
See also BEST 90:2; CA 69-72; CANR 23, 100

Casey, Michael 1947- .... **CLC 2**
See also CA 65-68; DLB 5

Casey, Patrick
See Thurman, Wallace (Henry)

Casey, Warren (Peter) 1935-1988 .... **CLC 12**
See also CA 101; 127; INT 101

Casona, Alejandro .... **CLC 49**
See also Alvarez, Alejandro Rodriguez

Cassavetes, John 1929-1989 .... **CLC 20**
See also CA 85-88; 127; CANR 82

Cassian, Nina 1924- .... **PC 17**
See also CWP; CWW 2

Cassill, R(onald) V(erlin) 1919- ... **CLC 4, 23**
See also CA 9-12R; CAAS 1; CANR 7, 45; CN 7; DLB 6, 218

Cassiodorus, Flavius Magnus c. 490(?)-c. 583(?) .... **CMLC 43**

Cassirer, Ernst 1874-1945 .... **TCLC 61**
See also CA 157

Cassity, (Allen) Turner 1929- .... **CLC 6, 42**
See also CA 17-20R; CAAS 8; CANR 11; CSW; DLB 105

Castaneda, Carlos (Cesar Aranha)
1931(?)-1998 .... **CLC 12, 119**
See also CA 25-28R; CANR 32, 66, 105; DNFS 1; HW 1; MTCW 1

Castedo, Elena 1937- .... **CLC 65**
See also CA 132

Castedo-Ellerman, Elena
See Castedo, Elena

Castellanos, Rosario 1925-1974 .... **CLC 66; HLC 1; SSC 39**
See also CA 131; 53-56; CANR 58; CD-WLB 3; DAM MULT; DLB 113; FW; HW 1; LAW; MTCW 1; RGSF 2; RGWL 2

Castelvetro, Lodovico 1505-1571 .... **LC 12**

Castiglione, Baldassare 1478-1529 ...... **LC 12**
See also Castiglione, Baldesar
See also RGWL 2

Castiglione, Baldesar
See Castiglione, Baldassare
See also EW 2

Castillo, Ana (Hernandez Del)
1953- .... **CLC 151**
See also AAYA 42; CA 131; CANR 51, 86; CWP; DLB 122, 227; DNFS 2; FW; HW 1

Castle, Robert
See Hamilton, Edmond

Castro (Ruz), Fidel 1926(?)-
See also CA 110; 129; CANR 81; DAM MULT; HLC 1; HW 2

Castro, Guillen de 1569-1631 .... **LC 19**

Castro, Rosalia de 1837-1885 .... **NCLC 3, 78**
See also DAM MULT

Cather, Willa (Sibert) 1873-1947 .... **TCLC 1, 11, 31, 99; SSC 2, 50; WLC**
See also AAYA 24; AMW; AMWR 1; BPFB 1; CA 104; 128; CDALB 1865-1917; DA; DA3; DAB; DAC; DAM MST, NOV; DLB 9, 54, 78, 256; DLBD 1; EXPN; EXPS; LAIT 3; MAWW; MTCW 1, 2; NFS 2; RGAL 4; RGSF 2; RHW; SATA 30; SSFS 2, 7; TCWW 2

Catherine II
See Catherine the Great
See also DLB 150

Catherine the Great 1729-1796 .... **LC 69**
See also Catherine II

Cato, Marcus Porcius
234B.C.-149B.C. .... **CMLC 21**
See also Cato the Elder

Cato the Elder
See Cato, Marcus Porcius
See also DLB 211

Catton, (Charles) Bruce 1899-1978 . **CLC 35**
See also AITN 1; CA 5-8R; 81-84; CANR 7, 74; DLB 17; SATA 2; SATA-Obit 24

Catullus c. 84B.C.-54B.C. .... **CMLC 18**
See also AW 2; CDWLB 1; DLB 211; RGWL 2

Cauldwell, Frank
See King, Francis (Henry)

Caunitz, William J. 1933-1996 .... **CLC 34**
See also BEST 89:3; CA 125; 130; 152; CANR 73; INT 130

Causley, Charles (Stanley) 1917- .... **CLC 7**
See also CA 9-12R; CANR 5, 35, 94; CLR 30; CWRI 5; DLB 27; MTCW 1; SATA 3, 66

Caute, (John) David 1936- .... **CLC 29**
See also CA 1-4R; CAAS 4; CANR 1, 33, 64; CBD; CD 5; CN 7; DAM NOV; DLB 14, 231

Cavafy, C(onstantine) P(eter) ... **TCLC 2, 7; PC 36**
See also Kavafis, Konstantinos Petrou
See also CA 148; DA3; DAM POET; EW 8; MTCW 1; RGWL 2; WP

Cavallo, Evelyn
See Spark, Muriel (Sarah)

Cavanna, Betty .... **CLC 12**
See also Harrison, Elizabeth (Allen) Cavanna
See also JRDA; MAICYA 1; SAAS 4; SATA 1, 30

Cavendish, Margaret Lucas
1623-1673 .... **LC 30**
See also DLB 131, 252; RGEL 2

Caxton, William 1421(?)-1491(?) .... **LC 17**
See also DLB 170

Cayer, D. M.
See Duffy, Maureen

Cayrol, Jean 1911- .... **CLC 11**
See also CA 89-92; DLB 83

Cela, Camilo Jose 1916-2002 .... **CLC 4, 13, 59, 122; HLC 1**
See also BEST 90:2; CA 21-24R; CAAS 10; CANR 21, 32, 76; DAM MULT; DLBY 1989; EW 13; HW 1; MTCW 1, 2; RGSF 2; RGWL 2

Celan, Paul -1970 .... **CLC 10, 19, 53, 82; PC 10**
See also Antschel, Paul
See also CDWLB 2; DLB 69; RGWL 2

Celine, Louis-Ferdinand .. **CLC 1, 3, 4, 7, 9, 15, 47, 124**
See also Destouches, Louis-Ferdinand
See also DLB 72; EW 11; GFL 1789 to the Present; RGWL 2

Cellini, Benvenuto 1500-1571 .... **LC 7**

Cendrars, Blaise .... **CLC 18, 106**
See also Sauser-Hall, Frederic
See also DLB 258; GFL 1789 to the Present; RGWL 2; WP

Centlivre, Susanna 1669(?)-1723 .... **LC 65**
See also DLB 84; RGEL 2

Cernuda (y Bidon), Luis 1902-1963 . **CLC 54**
See also CA 131; 89-92; DAM POET; DLB 134; GLL 1; HW 1; RGWL 2

Cervantes, Lorna Dee 1954- .... **PC 35**
See also CA 131; CANR 80; CWP; DLB 82; EXPP; HLCS 1; HW 1

Cervantes (Saavedra), Miguel de
1547-1616 .... **LC 6, 23; HLCS; SSC 12; WLC**
See also BYA 1, 14; DA; DAB; DAC; DAM MST, NOV; EW 2; LAIT 1; NFS 8; RGSF 2; RGWL 2

Cesaire, Aime (Fernand) 1913- . **CLC 19, 32, 112; BLC 1; PC 25**
See also BW 2, 3; CA 65-68; CANR 24, 43, 81; DA3; DAM MULT, POET; GFL 1789 to the Present; MTCW 1, 2; WP

Chabon, Michael 1963- .... **CLC 55, 149**
See also CA 139; CANR 57, 96

Chabrol, Claude 1930- .... **CLC 16**
See also CA 110

Challans, Mary 1905-1983
See Renault, Mary
See also CA 81-84; 111; CANR 74; DA3; MTCW 2; SATA 23; SATA-Obit 36

Challis, George
See Faust, Frederick (Schiller)
See also TCWW 2

Chambers, Aidan 1934- .... **CLC 35**
See also AAYA 27; CA 25-28R; CANR 12, 31, 58; JRDA; MAICYA 1; SAAS 12; SATA 1, 69, 108; WYA; YAW

Chambers, James 1948-
See Cliff, Jimmy
See also CA 124

Chambers, Jessie
See Lawrence, D(avid) H(erbert Richards)
See also GLL 1

Chambers, Robert W(illiam)
1865-1933 .... **TCLC 41**
See also CA 165; DLB 202; HGG; SATA 107; SUFW

Chamisso, Adelbert von
1781-1838 .... **NCLC 82**
See also DLB 90; RGWL 2; SUFW

Chandler, Raymond (Thornton)
1888-1959 .... **TCLC 1, 7; SSC 23**
See also AAYA 25; AMWS 4; BPFB 1; CA 104; 129; CANR 60, 107; CDALB 1929-1941; CMW 4; DA3; DLB 226, 253; DLBD 6; MSW; MTCW 1, 2; RGAL 4

Chang, Eileen 1921-1995 .... **SSC 28**
See also CA 166; CWW 2

Chang, Jung 1952- .... **CLC 71**
See also CA 142

Chang Ai-Ling
See Chang, Eileen

Channing, William Ellery
1780-1842 .... **NCLC 17**
See also DLB 1, 59, 235; RGAL 4

Chao, Patricia 1955- .... **CLC 119**
See also CA 163

Chaplin, Charles Spencer
1889-1977 .... **CLC 16**
See also Chaplin, Charlie
See also CA 81-84; 73-76

Chaplin, Charlie
See Chaplin, Charles Spencer
See also DLB 44

Chapman, George 1559(?)-1634 .... **LC 22**
See also BRW 1; DAM DRAM; DLB 62, 121; RGEL 2

Chapman, Graham 1941-1989 .... **CLC 21**
See also Monty Python
See also CA 116; 129; CANR 35, 95

Chapman, John Jay 1862-1933 .... **TCLC 7**
See also CA 104; 191

Chapman, Lee
See Bradley, Marion Zimmer
See also GLL 1

Chapman, Walker
See Silverberg, Robert

5; DLBY 1986; INT CANR-5; MAICYA
1; MTCW 1, 2; RGAL 4; SAAS 26; SATA
1, 65; SATA-Obit 46

Cibber, Colley 1671-1757 .... **LC 66**
See also DLB 84; RGEL 2

Cicero, Marcus Tullius
106B.C.-43B.C. .... **CMLC 3**
See also AW 1; CDWLB 1; DLB 211;
RGWL 2

Cimino, Michael 1943- .... **CLC 16**
See also CA 105

Cioran, E(mil) M. 1911-1995 .... **CLC 64**
See also CA 25-28R; 149; CANR 91; DLB
220

Cisneros, Sandra 1954- .. **CLC 69, 118; HLC
1; SSC 32**
See also AAYA 9; AMWS 7; CA 131;
CANR 64; CWP; DA3; DAM MULT;
DLB 122, 152; EXPN; FW; HW 1, 2;
LAIT 5; MTCW 2; NFS 2; RGAL 4;
RGSF 2; SSFS 3, 13; WLIT 1; YAW

Cixous, Helene 1937- .... **CLC 92**
See also CA 126; CANR 55; CWW 2; DLB
83, 242; FW; MTCW 1, 2

Clair, Rene .... **CLC 20**
See also Chomette, Rene Lucien

Clampitt, Amy 1920-1994 .... **CLC 32; PC 19**
See also AMWS 7; CA 110; 146; CANR
29, 79; DLB 105

Clancy, Thomas L., Jr. 1947-
See Clancy, Tom
See also CA 125; 131; CANR 62, 105;
DA3; INT CA-131; MTCW 1, 2

Clancy, Tom .... **CLC 45, 112**
See also Clancy, Thomas L., Jr.
See also AAYA 9; BEST 89:1, 90:1; BPFB
1; BYA 10, 11; CMW 4; CPW; DAM
NOV, POP; DLB 227

Clare, John 1793-1864 .. **NCLC 9, 86; PC 23**
See also DAB; DAM POET; DLB 55, 96;
RGEL 2

Clarin
See Alas (y Urena), Leopoldo (Enrique
Garcia)

Clark, Al C.
See Goines, Donald

Clark, (Robert) Brian 1932- .... **CLC 29**
See also CA 41-44R; CANR 67; CBD; CD
5

Clark, Curt
See Westlake, Donald E(dwin)

Clark, Eleanor 1913-1996 .... **CLC 5, 19**
See also CA 9-12R; 151; CANR 41; CN 7;
DLB 6

Clark, J. P.
See Clark Bekederemo, J(ohnson) P(epper)
See also CDWLB 3; DLB 117

Clark, John Pepper
See Clark Bekederemo, J(ohnson) P(epper)
See also AFW; CD 5; CP 7; RGEL 2

Clark, M. R.
See Clark, Mavis Thorpe

Clark, Mavis Thorpe 1909-1999 ...... **CLC 12**
See also CA 57-60; CANR 8, 37, 107; CLR
30; CWRI 5; MAICYA 1; SAAS 5; SATA
8, 74

Clark, Walter Van Tilburg
1909-1971 .... **CLC 28**
See also CA 9-12R; 33-36R; CANR 63;
DLB 9, 206; LAIT 2; RGAL 4; SATA 8

Clark Bekederemo, J(ohnson) P(epper)
1935- .... **CLC 38; BLC 1; DC 5**
See also Clark, J. P.; Clark, John Pepper
See also BW 1; CA 65-68; CANR 16, 72;
DAM DRAM, MULT; DFS 13; MTCW 1

Clarke, Arthur C(harles) 1917- .... **CLC 1, 4,
13, 18, 35, 136; SSC 3**
See also AAYA 4, 33; BPFB 1; BYA 13;
CA 1-4R; CANR 2, 28, 55, 74; CN 7;

CPW; DA3; DAM POP; JRDA; LAIT 5;
MAICYA 1; MTCW 1, 2; SATA 13, 70,
115; SCFW; SFW 4; SSFS 4; YAW

Clarke, Austin 1896-1974 .... **CLC 6, 9**
See also CA 29-32; 49-52; CAP 2; DAM
POET; DLB 10, 20; RGEL 2

Clarke, Austin C(hesterfield) 1934- .. **CLC 8,
53; BLC 1; SSC 45**
See also BW 1; CA 25-28R; CAAS 16;
CANR 14, 32, 68; CN 7; DAC; DAM
MULT; DLB 53, 125; DNFS 2; RGSF 2

Clarke, Gillian 1937- .... **CLC 61**
See also CA 106; CP 7; CWP; DLB 40

Clarke, Marcus (Andrew Hislop)
1846-1881 .... **NCLC 19**
See also DLB 230; RGEL 2; RGSF 2

Clarke, Shirley 1925-1997 .... **CLC 16**
See also CA 189

Clash, The
See Headon, (Nicky) Topper; Jones, Mick;
Simonon, Paul; Strummer, Joe

Claudel, Paul (Louis Charles Marie)
1868-1955 .... **TCLC 2, 10**
See also CA 104; 165; DLB 192; EW 8;
GFL 1789 to the Present; RGWL 2

Claudian 370(?)-404(?) .... **CMLC 46**
See also RGWL 2

Claudius, Matthias 1740-1815 .... **NCLC 75**
See also DLB 97

Clavell, James (duMaresq)
1925-1994 .... **CLC 6, 25, 87**
See also BPFB 1; CA 25-28R; 146; CANR
26, 48; CPW; DA3; DAM NOV, POP;
MTCW 1, 2; NFS 10; RHW

Clayman, Gregory .... **CLC 65**

Cleaver, (Leroy) Eldridge
1935-1998 .... **CLC 30, 119; BLC 1**
See also BW 1, 3; CA 21-24R; 167; CANR
16, 75; DA3; DAM MULT; MTCW 2;
YAW

Cleese, John (Marwood) 1939- .... **CLC 21**
See also Monty Python
See also CA 112; 116; CANR 35; MTCW 1

Cleishbotham, Jebediah
See Scott, Sir Walter

Cleland, John 1710-1789 .... **LC 2, 48**
See also DLB 39; RGEL 2

Clemens, Samuel Langhorne 1835-1910
See Twain, Mark
See also CA 104; 135; CDALB 1865-1917;
DA; DA3; DAB; DAC; DAM MST, NOV;
DLB 12, 23, 64, 74, 186, 189; JRDA;
MAICYA 1; SATA 100; YABC 2

Clement of Alexandria
150(?)-215(?) .... **CMLC 41**

Cleophil
See Congreve, William

Clerihew, E.
See Bentley, E(dmund) C(lerihew)

Clerk, N. W.
See Lewis, C(live) S(taples)

Cliff, Jimmy .... **CLC 21**
See also Chambers, James
See also CA 193

Cliff, Michelle 1946- .... **CLC 120; BLCS**
See also BW 2; CA 116; CANR 39, 72; CD-
WLB 3; DLB 157; FW; GLL 2

Clifford, Lady Anne 1590-1676 .... **LC 76**
See also DLB 151

Clifton, (Thelma) Lucille 1936- .... **CLC 19,
66; BLC 1; PC 17**
See also AFAW 2; BW 2, 3; CA 49-52;
CANR 2, 24, 42, 76, 97; CLR 5; CP 7;
CSW; CWP; CWRI 5; DA3; DAM MULT,
POET; DLB 5, 41; EXPP; MAICYA 1;
MTCW 1, 2; PFS 1, 14; SATA 20, 69,
128; WP

Clinton, Dirk
See Silverberg, Robert

Clough, Arthur Hugh 1819-1861 ... **NCLC 27**
See also BRW 5; DLB 32; RGEL 2

Clutha, Janet Paterson Frame 1924-
See Frame, Janet
See also CA 1-4R; CANR 2, 36, 76; MTCW
1, 2; SATA 119

Clyne, Terence
See Blatty, William Peter

Cobalt, Martin
See Mayne, William (James Carter)

Cobb, Irvin S(hrewsbury)
1876-1944 .... **TCLC 77**
See also CA 175; DLB 11, 25, 86

Cobbett, William 1763-1835 .... **NCLC 49**
See also DLB 43, 107, 158; RGEL 2

Coburn, D(onald) L(ee) 1938- .... **CLC 10**
See also CA 89-92

Cocteau, Jean (Maurice Eugene Clement)
1889-1963 ...... **CLC 1, 8, 15, 16, 43; DC
17; WLC**
See also CA 25-28; CANR 40; CAP 2; DA;
DA3; DAB; DAC; DAM DRAM, MST,
NOV; DLB 65; EW 10; GFL 1789 to the
Present; MTCW 1, 2; RGWL 2; TCLC
119

Codrescu, Andrei 1946- .... **CLC 46, 121**
See also CA 33-36R; CAAS 19; CANR 13,
34, 53, 76; DA3; DAM POET; MTCW 2

Coe, Max
See Bourne, Randolph S(illiman)

Coe, Tucker
See Westlake, Donald E(dwin)

Coen, Ethan 1958- .... **CLC 108**
See also CA 126; CANR 85

Coen, Joel 1955- .... **CLC 108**
See also CA 126

The Coen Brothers
See Coen, Ethan; Coen, Joel

Coetzee, J(ohn) M(ichael) 1940- ...... **CLC 23,
33, 66, 117**
See also AAYA 37; AFW; BRWS 6; CA 77-
80; CANR 41, 54, 74; CN 7; DA3; DAM
NOV; DLB 225; MTCW 1, 2; WLIT 2

Coffey, Brian
See Koontz, Dean R(ay)

Coffin, Robert P(eter) Tristram
1892-1955 .... **TCLC 95**
See also CA 123; 169; DLB 45

Cohan, George M(ichael)
1878-1942 .... **TCLC 60**
See also CA 157; DLB 249; RGAL 4

Cohen, Arthur A(llen) 1928-1986 ...... **CLC 7,
31**
See also CA 1-4R; 120; CANR 1, 17, 42;
DLB 28

Cohen, Leonard (Norman) 1934- ...... **CLC 3,
38**
See also CA 21-24R; CANR 14, 69; CN 7;
CP 7; DAC; DAM MST; DLB 53; MTCW
1

Cohen, Matt(hew) 1942-1999 .... **CLC 19**
See also CA 61-64; 187; CAAS 18; CANR
40; CN 7; DAC; DLB 53

Cohen-Solal, Annie 19(?)- .... **CLC 50**

Colegate, Isabel 1931- .... **CLC 36**
See also CA 17-20R; CANR 8, 22, 74; CN
7; DLB 14, 231; INT CANR-22; MTCW
1

Coleman, Emmett
See Reed, Ishmael

Coleridge, Hartley 1796-1849 .... **NCLC 90**
See also DLB 96

Coleridge, M. E.
See Coleridge, Mary E(lizabeth)

Coleridge, Mary E(lizabeth)
1861-1907 .... **TCLC 73**
See also CA 116; 166; DLB 19, 98

CANR-23; JRDA; LAIT 5; MAICYA 1; MTCW 1, 2; NFS 2; SATA 10, 45, 83; SATA-Obit 122; WYA; YAW

Corn, Alfred (DeWitt III) 1943- .... **CLC 33**
See also CA 179; CAAE 179; CAAS 25; CANR 44; CP 7; CSW; DLB 120; DLBY 1980

Corneille, Pierre 1606-1684 .... **LC 28**
See also DAB; DAM MST; EW 3; GFL Beginnings to 1789; RGWL 2

Cornwell, David (John Moore)
1931- .... **CLC 9, 15**
See also le Carre, John
See also CA 5-8R; CANR 13, 33, 59, 107; DA3; DAM POP; MTCW 1, 2

Cornwell, Patricia (Daniels) 1956- . **CLC 155**
See also AAYA 16; BPFB 1; CA 134; CANR 53; CMW 4; CPW; CSW; DAM POP; MSW; MTCW 1

Corso, (Nunzio) Gregory 1930-2001 . **CLC 1, 11; PC 33**
See also CA 5-8R; 193; CANR 41, 76; CP 7; DA3; DLB 5, 16, 237; MTCW 1, 2; WP

Cortazar, Julio 1914-1984 ... **CLC 2, 3, 5, 10, 13, 15, 33, 34, 92; HLC 1; SSC 7**
See also BPFB 1; CA 21-24R; CANR 12, 32, 81; CDWLB 3; DA3; DAM MULT, NOV; DLB 113; EXPS; HW 1, 2; LAW; MTCW 1, 2; RGSF 2; RGWL 2; SSFS 3; WLIT 1

Cortes, Hernan 1485-1547 .... **LC 31**

Corvinus, Jakob
See Raabe, Wilhelm (Karl)

Corvo, Baron
See Rolfe, Frederick (William Serafino Austin Lewis Mary)
See also GLL 1; RGEL 2

Corwin, Cecil
See Kornbluth, C(yril) M.

Cosic, Dobrica 1921- .... **CLC 14**
See also CA 122; 138; CDWLB 4; CWW 2; DLB 181

Costain, Thomas B(ertram)
1885-1965 .... **CLC 30**
See also BYA 3; CA 5-8R; 25-28R; DLB 9; RHW

Costantini, Humberto 1924(?)-1987 . **CLC 49**
See also CA 131; 122; HW 1

Costello, Elvis 1955- .... **CLC 21**

Costenoble, Philostene 1898-1962
See Ghelderode, Michel de

Costenoble, Philostene 1898-1962
See Ghelderode, Michel de

Cotes, Cecil V.
See Duncan, Sara Jeannette

Cotter, Joseph Seamon Sr.
1861-1949 .... **TCLC 28; BLC 1**
See also BW 1; CA 124; DAM MULT; DLB 50

Couch, Arthur Thomas Quiller
See Quiller-Couch, Sir Arthur (Thomas)

Coulton, James
See Hansen, Joseph

Couperus, Louis (Marie Anne)
1863-1923 .... **TCLC 15**
See also CA 115; RGWL 2

Coupland, Douglas 1961- .... **CLC 85, 133**
See also AAYA 34; CA 142; CANR 57, 90; CCA 1; CPW; DAC; DAM POP

Court, Wesli
See Turco, Lewis (Putnam)

Courtenay, Bryce 1933- .... **CLC 59**
See also CA 138; CPW

Courtney, Robert
See Ellison, Harlan (Jay)

Cousteau, Jacques-Yves 1910-1997 .. **CLC 30**
See also CA 65-68; 159; CANR 15, 67; MTCW 1; SATA 38, 98

Coventry, Francis 1725-1754 .... **LC 46**

Cowan, Peter (Walkinshaw) 1914- .... **SSC 28**
See also CA 21-24R; CANR 9, 25, 50, 83; CN 7; RGSF 2

Coward, Noel (Peirce) 1899-1973 . **CLC 1, 9, 29, 51**
See also AITN 1; BRWS 2; CA 17-18; 41-44R; CANR 35; CAP 2; CDBLB 1914-1945; DA3; DAM DRAM; DFS 3, 6; DLB 10, 245; IDFW 3, 4; MTCW 1, 2; RGEL 2

Cowley, Abraham 1618-1667 .... **LC 43**
See also BRW 2; DLB 131, 151; PAB; RGEL 2

Cowley, Malcolm 1898-1989 .... **CLC 39**
See also AMWS 2; CA 5-8R; 128; CANR 3, 55; DLB 4, 48; DLBY 1981, 1989; MTCW 1, 2

Cowper, William 1731-1800 ..... **NCLC 8, 94; PC 40**
See also BRW 3; DA3; DAM POET; DLB 104, 109; RGEL 2

Cox, William Trevor 1928-
See Trevor, William
See also CA 9-12R; CANR 4, 37, 55, 76, 102; DAM NOV; INT CANR-37; MTCW 1, 2

Coyne, P. J.
See Masters, Hilary

Cozzens, James Gould 1903-1978 . **CLC 1, 4, 11, 92**
See also AMW; BPFB 1; CA 9-12R; 81-84; CANR 19; CDALB 1941-1968; DLB 9; DLBD 2; DLBY 1984, 1997; MTCW 1, 2; RGAL 4

Crabbe, George 1754-1832 .... **NCLC 26**
See also BRW 3; DLB 93; RGEL 2

Crace, Jim 1946- .... **CLC 157**
See also CA 128; 135; CANR 55, 70; CN 7; DLB 231; INT CA-135

Craddock, Charles Egbert
See Murfree, Mary Noailles

Craig, A. A.
See Anderson, Poul (William)

Craik, Mrs.
See Craik, Dinah Maria (Mulock)
See also RGEL 2

Craik, Dinah Maria (Mulock)
1826-1887 .... **NCLC 38**
See also Craik, Mrs.; Mulock, Dinah Maria
See also DLB 35, 163; MAICYA 1; SATA 34

Cram, Ralph Adams 1863-1942 ..... **TCLC 45**
See also CA 160

Crane, (Harold) Hart 1899-1932 .... **TCLC 2, 5, 80; PC 3; WLC**
See also AMW; CA 104; 127; CDALB 1917-1929; DA; DA3; DAB; DAC; DAM MST, POET; DLB 4, 48; MTCW 1, 2; RGAL 4

Crane, R(onald) S(almon)
1886-1967 .... **CLC 27**
See also CA 85-88; DLB 63

Crane, Stephen (Townley)
1871-1900 ...... **TCLC 11, 17, 32; SSC 7; WLC**
See also AAYA 21; AMW; BPFB 1; BYA 3; CA 109; 140; CANR 84; CDALB 1865-1917; DA; DA3; DAB; DAC; DAM MST, NOV, POET; DLB 12, 54, 78; EXPN; EXPS; LAIT 2; NFS 4; PFS 9; RGAL 4; RGSF 2; SSFS 4; WYA; YABC 2

Cranshaw, Stanley
See Fisher, Dorothy (Frances) Canfield

Crase, Douglas 1944- .... **CLC 58**
See also CA 106

Crashaw, Richard 1612(?)-1649 .... **LC 24**
See also BRW 2; DLB 126; PAB; RGEL 2

Craven, Margaret 1901-1980 .... **CLC 17**
See also BYA 2; CA 103; CCA 1; DAC; LAIT 5

Crawford, F(rancis) Marion
1854-1909 .... **TCLC 10**
See also CA 107; 168; DLB 71; HGG; RGAL 4; SUFW

Crawford, Isabella Valancy
1850-1887 .... **NCLC 12**
See also DLB 92; RGEL 2

Crayon, Geoffrey
See Irving, Washington

Creasey, John 1908-1973 .... **CLC 11**
See also Marric, J. J.
See also CA 5-8R; 41-44R; CANR 8, 59; CMW 4; DLB 77; MTCW 1

Crebillon, Claude Prosper Jolyot de (fils)
1707-1777 .... **LC 1, 28**
See also GFL Beginnings to 1789

Credo
See Creasey, John

Credo, Alvaro J. de
See Prado (Calvo), Pedro

Creeley, Robert (White) 1926- .. **CLC 1, 2, 4, 8, 11, 15, 36, 78**
See also AMWS 4; CA 1-4R; CAAS 10; CANR 23, 43, 89; CP 7; DA3; DAM POET; DLB 5, 16, 169; DLBD 17; MTCW 1, 2; RGAL 4; WP

Crevecoeur, Hector St. John de
See Crevecoeur, Michel Guillaume Jean de
See also ANW

Crevecoeur, Michel Guillaume Jean de
1735-1813 .... **NCLC 105**
See also Crevecoeur, Hector St. John de
See also AMWS 1; DLB 37

Crevel, Rene 1900-1935 .... **TCLC 112**
See also GLL 2

Crews, Harry (Eugene) 1935- ..... **CLC 6, 23, 49**
See also AITN 1; BPFB 1; CA 25-28R; CANR 20, 57; CN 7; CSW; DA3; DLB 6, 143, 185; MTCW 1, 2; RGAL 4

Crichton, (John) Michael 1942- .... **CLC 2, 6, 54, 90**
See also AAYA 10; AITN 2; BPFB 1; CA 25-28R; CANR 13, 40, 54, 76; CMW 4; CN 7; CPW; DA3; DAM NOV, POP; DLBY 1981; INT CANR-13; JRDA; MTCW 1, 2; SATA 9, 88; SFW 4; YAW

Crispin, Edmund .... **CLC 22**
See also Montgomery, (Robert) Bruce
See also DLB 87; MSW

Cristofer, Michael 1945(?)- .... **CLC 28**
See also CA 110; 152; CAD; CD 5; DAM DRAM; DLB 7

Croce, Benedetto 1866-1952 .... **TCLC 37**
See also CA 120; 155; EW 8

Crockett, David 1786-1836 .... **NCLC 8**
See also DLB 3, 11, 183, 248

Crockett, Davy
See Crockett, David

Crofts, Freeman Wills 1879-1957 .. **TCLC 55**
See also CA 115; 195; CMW 4; DLB 77; MSW

Croker, John Wilson 1780-1857 .... **NCLC 10**
See also DLB 110

Crommelynck, Fernand 1885-1970 .. **CLC 75**
See also CA 189; 89-92

Cromwell, Oliver 1599-1658 .... **LC 43**

Cronenberg, David 1943- .... **CLC 143**
See also CA 138; CCA 1

Cronin, A(rchibald) J(oseph)
1896-1981 .... **CLC 32**
See also BPFB 1; CA 1-4R; 102; CANR 5; DLB 191; SATA 47; SATA-Obit 25

Cross, Amanda
See Heilbrun, Carolyn G(old)
See also BPFB 1; CMW; CPW; MSW

Dobrolyubov, Nikolai Alexandrovich
1836-1861 .... **NCLC 5**

Dobson, Austin 1840-1921 .... **TCLC 79**
See also DLB 35, 144

Dobyns, Stephen 1941- .... **CLC 37**
See also CA 45-48; CANR 2, 18, 99; CMW
4; CP 7

Doctorow, E(dgar) L(aurence)
1931- .... **CLC 6, 11, 15, 18, 37, 44, 65,**
113
See also AAYA 22; AITN 2; AMWS 4;
BEST 89:3; BPFB 1; CA 45-48; CANR
2, 33, 51, 76, 97; CDALB 1968-1988; CN
7; CPW; DA3; DAM NOV, POP; DLB 2,
28, 173; DLBY 1980; LAIT 3; MTCW 1,
2; NFS 6; RGAL 4; RHW

Dodgson, Charles Lutwidge 1832-1898
See Carroll, Lewis
See also CLR 2; DA; DA3; DAB; DAC;
DAM MST, NOV, POET; MAICYA 1;
SATA 100; YABC 2

Dodson, Owen (Vincent)
1914-1983 .... **CLC 79; BLC 1**
See also BW 1; CA 65-68; 110; CANR 24;
DAM MULT; DLB 76

Doeblin, Alfred 1878-1957 .... **TCLC 13**
See also Doblin, Alfred
See also CA 110; 141; DLB 66

Doerr, Harriet 1910- .... **CLC 34**
See also CA 117; 122; CANR 47; INT 122

Domecq, H(onorio Bustos)
See Bioy Casares, Adolfo

Domecq, H(onorio) Bustos
See Bioy Casares, Adolfo; Borges, Jorge
Luis

Domini, Rey
See Lorde, Audre (Geraldine)
See also GLL 1

Dominique
See Proust, (Valentin-Louis-George-Eugene-
)Marcel

Don, A
See Stephen, Sir Leslie

Donaldson, Stephen R(eeder)
1947- .... **CLC 46, 138**
See also AAYA 36; BPFB 1; CA 89-92;
CANR 13, 55, 99; CPW; DAM POP;
FANT; INT CANR-13; SATA 121; SFW
4; SUFW

Donleavy, J(ames) P(atrick) 1926- .... **CLC 1,**
4, 6, 10, 45
See also AITN 2; BPFB 1; CA 9-12R;
CANR 24, 49, 62, 80; CBD; CD 5; CN 7;
DLB 6, 173; INT CANR-24; MTCW 1,
2; RGAL 4

Donne, John 1572-1631 ..... **LC 10, 24; PC 1;**
WLC
See also BRW 1; BRWR 2; CDBLB Before
1660; DA; DAB; DAC; DAM MST,
POET; DLB 121, 151; EXPP; PAB; PFS
2, 11; RGEL 2; WLIT 3; WP

Donnell, David 1939(?)- .... **CLC 34**
See also CA 197

Donoghue, P. S.
See Hunt, E(verette) Howard, (Jr.)

Donoso (Yanez), Jose 1924-1996 ... **CLC 4, 8,**
11, 32, 99; HLC 1; SSC 34
See also CA 81-84; 155; CANR 32, 73; CD-
WLB 3; DAM MULT; DLB 113; HW 1,
2; LAW; LAWS 1; MTCW 1, 2; RGSF 2;
WLIT 1

Donovan, John 1928-1992 .... **CLC 35**
See also AAYA 20; CA 97-100; 137; CLR
3; MAICYA 1; SATA 72; SATA-Brief 29;
YAW

Don Roberto
See Cunninghame Graham, Robert
(Gallnigad) Bontine

Doolittle, Hilda 1886-1961 . **CLC 3, 8, 14, 31,**
34, 73; PC 5; WLC
See also H. D.
See also AMWS 1; CA 97-100; CANR 35;
DA; DAC; DAM MST, POET; DLB 4,
45; FW; GLL 1; MAWW; MTCW 1, 2;
PFS 6; RGAL 4

Doppo, Kunikida .... **TCLC 99**
See also Kunikida Doppo

Dorfman, Ariel 1942- .... **CLC 48, 77; HLC 1**
See also CA 124; 130; CANR 67, 70; CWW
2; DAM MULT; DFS 4; HW 1, 2; INT
CA-130; WLIT 1

Dorn, Edward (Merton)
1929-1999 .... **CLC 10, 18**
See also CA 93-96; 187; CANR 42, 79; CP
7; DLB 5; INT 93-96; WP

Dor-Ner, Zvi .... **CLC 70**

Dorris, Michael (Anthony)
1945-1997 .... **CLC 109**
See also AAYA 20; BEST 90:1; BYA 12;
CA 102; 157; CANR 19, 46, 75; CLR 58;
DA3; DAM MULT, NOV; DLB 175;
LAIT 5; MTCW 2; NFS 3; NNAL; RGAL
4; SATA 75; SATA-Obit 94; TCWW 2;
YAW

Dorris, Michael A.
See Dorris, Michael (Anthony)

Dorsan, Luc
See Simenon, Georges (Jacques Christian)

Dorsange, Jean
See Simenon, Georges (Jacques Christian)

Dos Passos, John (Roderigo)
1896-1970 ... **CLC 1, 4, 8, 11, 15, 25, 34,**
82; WLC
See also AMW; BPFB 1; CA 1-4R; 29-32R;
CANR 3; CDALB 1929-1941; DA; DA3;
DAB; DAC; DAM MST, NOV; DLB 4,
9; DLBD 1, 15; DLBY 1996; MTCW 1,
2; RGAL 4

Dossage, Jean
See Simenon, Georges (Jacques Christian)

Dostoevsky, Fedor Mikhailovich
1821-1881 . **NCLC 2, 7, 21, 33, 43; SSC**
2, 33, 44; WLC
See also Dostoevsky, Fyodor
See also AAYA 40; DA; DA3; DAB; DAC;
DAM MST, NOV; EW 7; EXPN; NFS 3,
8; RGSF 2; RGWL 2; SSFS 8

Dostoevsky, Fyodor
See Dostoevsky, Fedor Mikhailovich
See also DLB 238

Doughty, Charles M(ontagu)
1843-1926 .... **TCLC 27**
See also CA 115; 178; DLB 19, 57, 174

Douglas, Ellen .... **CLC 73**
See also Haxton, Josephine Ayres; William-
son, Ellen Douglas
See also CN 7; CSW

Douglas, Gavin 1475(?)-1522 .... **LC 20**
See also DLB 132; RGEL 2

Douglas, George
See Brown, George Douglas
See also RGEL 2

Douglas, Keith (Castellain)
1920-1944 .... **TCLC 40**
See also BRW 7; CA 160; DLB 27; PAB;
RGEL 2

Douglas, Leonard
See Bradbury, Ray (Douglas)

Douglas, Michael
See Crichton, (John) Michael

Douglas, (George) Norman
1868-1952 .... **TCLC 68**
See also BRW 6; CA 119; 157; DLB 34,
195; RGEL 2

Douglas, William
See Brown, George Douglas

Douglass, Frederick 1817(?)-1895 .. **NCLC 7,**
55; BLC 1; WLC
See also AFAW 1, 2; AMWS 3; CDALB
1640-1865; DA; DA3; DAC; DAM MST,
MULT; DLB 1, 43, 50, 79, 243; FW;
LAIT 2; NCFS 2; RGAL 4; SATA 29

Dourado, (Waldomiro Freitas) Autran
1926- .... **CLC 23, 60**
See also CA 25-28R; 179; CANR 34, 81;
DLB 145; HW 2

Dourado, Waldomiro Autran
See Dourado, (Waldomiro Freitas) Autran
See also CA 179

Dove, Rita (Frances) 1952- .... **CLC 50, 81;**
BLCS; PC 6
See also AMWS 4; BW 2; CA 109; CAAS
19; CANR 27, 42, 68, 76, 97; CDALBS;
CP 7; CSW; CWP; DA3; DAM MULT,
POET; DLB 120; EXPP; MTCW 1; PFS
1; RGAL 4

Doveglion
See Villa, Jose Garcia

Dowell, Coleman 1925-1985 .... **CLC 60**
See also CA 25-28R; 117; CANR 10; DLB
130; GLL 2

Dowson, Ernest (Christopher)
1867-1900 .... **TCLC 4**
See also CA 105; 150; DLB 19, 135; RGEL
2

Doyle, A. Conan
See Doyle, Sir Arthur Conan

Doyle, Sir Arthur Conan
1859-1930 .... **TCLC 7; SSC 12; WLC**
See also Conan Doyle, Arthur
See also AAYA 14; BRWS 2; CA 104; 122;
CDBLB 1890-1914; CMW 4; DA; DA3;
DAB; DAC; DAM MST, NOV; DLB 18,
70, 156, 178; EXPS; HGG; LAIT 2;
MSW; MTCW 1, 2; RGEL 2; RGSF 2;
RHW; SATA 24; SCFW 2; SFW 4; SSFS
2; WCH; WLIT 4; WYA; YAW

Doyle, Conan
See Doyle, Sir Arthur Conan

Doyle, John
See Graves, Robert (von Ranke)

Doyle, Roddy 1958(?)- .... **CLC 81**
See also AAYA 14; BRWS 5; CA 143;
CANR 73; CN 7; DA3; DLB 194

Doyle, Sir A. Conan
See Doyle, Sir Arthur Conan

Dr. A
See Asimov, Isaac; Silverstein, Alvin; Silverstein, Virginia B(arbara Opshelor)

Drabble, Margaret 1939- ...... **CLC 2, 3, 5, 8,**
10, 22, 53, 129
See also BRWS 4; CA 13-16R; CANR 18,
35, 63; CDBLB 1960 to Present; CN 7;
CPW; DA3; DAB; DAC; DAM MST,
NOV, POP; DLB 14, 155, 231; FW;
MTCW 1, 2; RGEL 2; SATA 48

Drapier, M. B.
See Swift, Jonathan

Drayham, James
See Mencken, H(enry) L(ouis)

Drayton, Michael 1563-1631 .... **LC 8**
See also DAM POET; DLB 121; RGEL 2

Dreadstone, Carl
See Campbell, (John) Ramsey

Dreiser, Theodore (Herman Albert)
1871-1945 .... **TCLC 10, 18, 35, 83; SSC**
30; WLC
See also AMW; CA 106; 132; CDALB
1865-1917; DA; DA3; DAC; DAM MST,
NOV; DLB 9, 12, 102, 137; DLBD 1;
LAIT 2; MTCW 1, 2; NFS 8; RGAL 4

Drexler, Rosalyn 1926- .... **CLC 2, 6**
See also CA 81-84; CAD; CANR 68; CD
5; CWD

Fierstein, Harvey (Forbes) 1954- ..... **CLC 33**
See also CA 123; 129; CAD; CD 5; CPW;
DA3; DAM DRAM, POP; DFS 6; GLL

Figes, Eva 1932- .... **CLC 31**
See also CA 53-56; CANR 4, 44, 83; CN 7;
DLB 14; FW

Finch, Anne 1661-1720 .... **LC 3; PC 21**
See also DLB 95

Finch, Robert (Duer Claydon)
1900-1995 .... **CLC 18**
See also CA 57-60; CANR 9, 24, 49; CP 7;
DLB 88

Findley, Timothy 1930- .... **CLC 27, 102**
See also CA 25-28R; CANR 12, 42, 69;
CCA 1; CN 7; DAC; DAM MST; DLB
53; FANT; RHW

Fink, William
See Mencken, H(enry) L(ouis)

Firbank, Louis 1942-
See Reed, Lou
See also CA 117

Firbank, (Arthur Annesley) Ronald
1886-1926 .... **TCLC 1**
See also BRWS 2; CA 104; 177; DLB 36;
RGEL 2

Fish, Stanley
See Fish, Stanley Eugene

Fish, Stanley E.
See Fish, Stanley Eugene

Fish, Stanley Eugene 1938- .... **CLC 142**
See also CA 112; 132; CANR 90; DLB 67

Fisher, Dorothy (Frances) Canfield
1879-1958 .... **TCLC 87**
See also CA 114; 136; CANR 80; CLR 71,;
CWRI 5; DLB 9, 102; MAICYA 1; YABC
1

Fisher, M(ary) F(rances) K(ennedy)
1908-1992 .... **CLC 76, 87**
See also CA 77-80; 138; CANR 44; MTCW
1

Fisher, Roy 1930- .... **CLC 25**
See also CA 81-84; CAAS 10; CANR 16;
CP 7; DLB 40

Fisher, Rudolph 1897-1934 .. **TCLC 11; BLC
2; SSC 25**
See also BW 1, 3; CA 107; 124; CANR 80;
DAM MULT; DLB 51, 102

Fisher, Vardis (Alvero) 1895-1968 ...... **CLC 7**
See also CA 5-8R; 25-28R; CANR 68; DLB
9, 206; RGAL 4; TCWW 2

Fiske, Tarleton
See Bloch, Robert (Albert)

Fitch, Clarke
See Sinclair, Upton (Beall)

Fitch, John IV
See Cormier, Robert (Edmund)

Fitzgerald, Captain Hugh
See Baum, L(yman) Frank

FitzGerald, Edward 1809-1883 .... **NCLC 9**
See also BRW 4; DLB 32; RGEL 2

Fitzgerald, F(rancis) Scott (Key)
1896-1940 . **TCLC 1, 6, 14, 28, 55; SSC
6, 31; WLC**
See also AAYA 24; AITN 1; AMW; AMWR
1; BPFB 1; CA 110; 123; CDALB 1917-
1929; DA; DA3; DAB; DAC; DAM MST,
NOV; DLB 4, 9, 86, 219; DLBD 1, 15,
16; DLBY 1981, 1996; EXPN; EXPS;
LAIT 3; MTCW 1, 2; NFS 2; RGAL 4;
RGSF 2; SSFS 4

Fitzgerald, Penelope 1916-2000 . **CLC 19, 51,
61, 143**
See also BRWS 5; CA 85-88; 190; CAAS
10; CANR 56, 86; CN 7; DLB 14, 194;
MTCW 2

Fitzgerald, Robert (Stuart)
1910-1985 .... **CLC 39**
See also CA 1-4R; 114; CANR 1; DLBY
1980

FitzGerald, Robert D(avid)
1902-1987 .... **CLC 19**
See also CA 17-20R; RGEL 2

Fitzgerald, Zelda (Sayre)
1900-1948 .... **TCLC 52**
See also AMWS 9; CA 117; 126; DLBY
1984

Flanagan, Thomas (James Bonner)
1923- .... **CLC 25, 52**
See also CA 108; CANR 55; CN 7; DLBY
1980; INT 108; MTCW 1; RHW

Flaubert, Gustave 1821-1880 .... **NCLC 2, 10,
19, 62, 66; SSC 11; WLC**
See also DA; DA3; DAB; DAC; DAM
MST, NOV; DLB 119; EW 7; EXPS; GFL
1789 to the Present; LAIT 2; RGSF 2;
RGWL 2; SSFS 6

Flavius Josephus
See Josephus, Flavius

Flecker, Herman Elroy
See Flecker, (Herman) James Elroy

Flecker, (Herman) James Elroy
1884-1915 .... **TCLC 43**
See also CA 109; 150; DLB 10, 19; RGEL
2

Fleming, Ian (Lancaster) 1908-1964 . **CLC 3,
30**
See also AAYA 26; BPFB 1; CA 5-8R;
CANR 59; CDBLB 1945-1960; CMW 4;
CPW; DA3; DAM POP; DLB 87, 201;
MSW; MTCW 1, 2; RGEL 2; SATA 9;
YAW

Fleming, Thomas (James) 1927- ...... **CLC 37**
See also CA 5-8R; CANR 10, 102; INT
CANR-10; SATA 8

Fletcher, John 1579-1625 .... **LC 33; DC 6**
See also BRW 2; CDBLB Before 1660;
DLB 58; RGEL 2

Fletcher, John Gould 1886-1950 .... **TCLC 35**
See also CA 107; 167; DLB 4, 45; RGAL 4

Fleur, Paul
See Pohl, Frederik

Flooglebuckle, Al
See Spiegelman, Art

Flora, Fletcher 1914-1969
See Queen, Ellery
See also CA 1-4R; CANR 3, 85

Flying Officer X
See Bates, H(erbert) E(rnest)

Fo, Dario 1926- .... **CLC 32, 109; DC 10**
See also CA 116; 128; CANR 68; CWW 2;
DA3; DAM DRAM; DLBY 1997; MTCW
1, 2

Fogarty, Jonathan Titulescu Esq.
See Farrell, James T(homas)

Follett, Ken(neth Martin) 1949- .... **CLC 18**
See also AAYA 6; BEST 89:4; BPFB 1; CA
81-84; CANR 13, 33, 54, 102; CMW 4;
CPW; DA3; DAM NOV, POP; DLB 87;
DLBY 1981; INT CANR-33; MTCW 1

Fontane, Theodor 1819-1898 .... **NCLC 26**
See also CDWLB 2; DLB 129; EW 6;
RGWL 2

Fontenot, Chester .... **CLC 65**

Foote, Horton 1916- .... **CLC 51, 91**
See also CA 73-76; CAD; CANR 34, 51;
CD 5; CSW; DA3; DAM DRAM; DLB
26; INT CANR-34

Foote, Mary Hallock 1847-1938 .. **TCLC 108**
See also DLB 186, 188, 202, 221

Foote, Shelby 1916- .... **CLC 75**
See also AAYA 40; CA 5-8R; CANR 3, 45,
74; CN 7; CPW; CSW; DA3; DAM NOV,
POP; DLB 2, 17; MTCW 2; RHW

Forbes, Esther 1891-1967 .... **CLC 12**
See also AAYA 17; BYA 2; CA 13-14; 25-
28R; CAP 1; CLR 27; DLB 22; JRDA;
MAICYA 1; RHW; SATA 2, 100; YAW

Forche, Carolyn (Louise) 1950- .... **CLC 25,
83, 86; PC 10**
See also CA 109; 117; CANR 50, 74; CP 7;
CWP; DA3; DAM POET; DLB 5, 193;
INT CA-117; MTCW 1; RGAL 4

Ford, Elbur
See Hibbert, Eleanor Alice Burford

Ford, Ford Madox 1873-1939 ... **TCLC 1, 15,
39, 57**
See also BRW 6; CA 104; 132; CANR 74;
CDBLB 1914-1945; DA3; DAM NOV;
DLB 34, 98, 162; MTCW 1, 2; RGEL 2

Ford, Henry 1863-1947 .... **TCLC 73**
See also CA 115; 148

Ford, John 1586-1639 .... **LC 68; DC 8**
See also BRW 2; CDBLB Before 1660;
DA3; DAM DRAM; DFS 7; DLB 58;
IDTP; RGEL 2

Ford, John 1895-1973 .... **CLC 16**
See also CA 187; 45-48

Ford, Richard 1944- .... **CLC 46, 99**
See also AMWS 5; CA 69-72; CANR 11,
47, 86; CN 7; CSW; DLB 227; MTCW 1;
RGAL 4; RGSF 2

Ford, Webster
See Masters, Edgar Lee

Foreman, Richard 1937- .... **CLC 50**
See also CA 65-68; CAD; CANR 32, 63;
CD 5

Forester, C(ecil) S(cott) 1899-1966 ... **CLC 35**
See also CA 73-76; 25-28R; CANR 83;
DLB 191; RGEL 2; RHW; SATA 13

Forez
See Mauriac, Francois (Charles)

Forman, James Douglas 1932- .... **CLC 21**
See also AAYA 17; CA 9-12R; CANR 4,
19, 42; JRDA; MAICYA 1; SATA 8, 70;
YAW

Fornes, Maria Irene 1930- . **CLC 39, 61; DC
10; HLCS 1**
See also CA 25-28R; CAD; CANR 28, 81;
CD 5; CWD; DLB 7; HW 1, 2; INT
CANR-28; MTCW 1; RGAL 4

Forrest, Leon (Richard) 1937-1997 .. **CLC 4;
BLCS**
See also AFAW 2; BW 2; CA 89-92; 162;
CAAS 7; CANR 25, 52, 87; CN 7; DLB
33

Forster, E(dward) M(organ)
1879-1970 ...... **CLC 1, 2, 3, 4, 9, 10, 13,
15, 22, 45, 77; SSC 27; WLC**
See also AAYA 2, 37; BRW 6; BRWR 2;
CA 13-14; 25-28R; CANR 45; CAP 1;
CDBLB 1914-1945; DA; DA3; DAB;
DAC; DAM MST, NOV; DLB 34, 98,
162, 178, 195; DLBD 10; EXPN; LAIT
3; MTCW 1, 2; NCFS 1; NFS 3, 10, 11;
RGEL 2; RGSF 2; SATA 57; SUFW;
WLIT 4

Forster, John 1812-1876 .... **NCLC 11**
See also DLB 144, 184

Forster, Margaret 1938- .... **CLC 149**
See also CA 133; CANR 62; CN 7; DLB
155

Forsyth, Frederick 1938- .... **CLC 2, 5, 36**
See also BEST 89:4; CA 85-88; CANR 38,
62; CMW 4; CN 7; CPW; DAM NOV,
POP; DLB 87; MTCW 1, 2

Forten, Charlotte L. 1837-1914 .... **TCLC 16;
BLC 2**
See also Grimke, Charlotte L(ottie) Forten
See also DLB 50, 239

Foscolo, Ugo 1778-1827 .... **NCLC 8, 97**
See also EW 5

Fosse, Bob .... **CLC 20**
See also Fosse, Robert Louis

Fosse, Robert Louis 1927-1987
See Fosse, Bob
See also CA 110; 123
Foster, Hannah Webster
1758-1840 .... **NCLC 99**
See also DLB 37, 200; RGAL 4
Foster, Stephen Collins
1826-1864 .... **NCLC 26**
See also RGAL 4
Foucault, Michel 1926-1984 . **CLC 31, 34, 69**
See also CA 105; 113; CANR 34; DLB 242;
EW 13; GFL 1789 to the Present; GLL 1;
MTCW 1, 2
**Fouque, Friedrich (Heinrich Karl) de la
Motte** 1777-1843 .... **NCLC 2**
See also DLB 90; RGWL 2; SUFW
Fourier, Charles 1772-1837 .... **NCLC 51**
Fournier, Henri Alban 1886-1914
See Alain-Fournier
See also CA 104; 179
Fournier, Pierre 1916- .... **CLC 11**
See also Gascar, Pierre
See also CA 89-92; CANR 16, 40
Fowles, John (Robert) 1926- . **CLC 1, 2, 3, 4,
6, 9, 10, 15, 33, 87; SSC 33**
See also BPFB 1; BRWS 1; CA 5-8R;
CANR 25, 71, 103; CDBLB 1960 to
Present; CN 7; DA3; DAB; DAC; DAM
MST; DLB 14, 139, 207; HGG; MTCW
1, 2; RGEL 2; RHW; SATA 22; WLIT 4
Fox, Paula 1923- .... **CLC 2, 8, 121**
See also AAYA 3, 37; BYA 3, 8; CA 73-76;
CANR 20, 36, 62, 105; CLR 1, 44; DLB
52; JRDA; MAICYA 1; MTCW 1; NFS
12; SATA 17, 60, 120; WYA; YAW
Fox, William Price (Jr.) 1926- .... **CLC 22**
See also CA 17-20R; CAAS 19; CANR 11;
CSW; DLB 2; DLBY 1981
Foxe, John 1517(?)-1587 .... **LC 14**
See also DLB 132
Frame, Janet .. **CLC 2, 3, 6, 22, 66, 96; SSC
29**
See also Clutha, Janet Paterson Frame
See also CN 7; CWP; RGEL 2; RGSF 2
France, Anatole .... **TCLC 9**
See also Thibault, Jacques Anatole Francois
See also DLB 123; GFL 1789 to the Present;
MTCW 2; RGWL 2; SUFW
Francis, Claude .... **CLC 50**
See also CA 192
Francis, Dick 1920- .... **CLC 2, 22, 42, 102**
See also AAYA 5, 21; BEST 89:3; BPFB 1;
CA 5-8R; CANR 9, 42, 68, 100; CDBLB
1960 to Present; CMW 4; CN 7; DA3;
DAM POP; DLB 87; INT CANR-9;
MSW; MTCW 1, 2
Francis, Robert (Churchill)
1901-1987 .... **CLC 15; PC 34**
See also AMWS 9; CA 1-4R; 123; CANR
1; EXPP; PFS 12
Francis, Lord Jeffrey
See Jeffrey, Francis
See also DLB 107
Frank, Anne(lies Marie)
1929-1945 .... **TCLC 17; WLC**
See also AAYA 12; BYA 1; CA 113; 133;
CANR 68; DA; DA3; DAB; DAC; DAM
MST; LAIT 4; MAICYAS 1; MTCW 1,
2; NCFS 2; SATA 87; SATA-Brief 42;
WYA; YAW
Frank, Bruno 1887-1945 .... **TCLC 81**
See also CA 189; DLB 118
Frank, Elizabeth 1945- .... **CLC 39**
See also CA 121; 126; CANR 78; INT 126
Frankl, Viktor E(mil) 1905-1997 ...... **CLC 93**
See also CA 65-68; 161
Franklin, Benjamin
See Hasek, Jaroslav (Matej Frantisek)

Franklin, Benjamin 1706-1790 .... **LC 25;
WLCS**
See also AMW; CDALB 1640-1865; DA;
DA3; DAB; DAC; DAM MST; DLB 24,
43, 73, 183; LAIT 1; RGAL 4; TUS
**Franklin, (Stella Maria Sarah) Miles
(Lampe)** 1879-1954 .... **TCLC 7**
See also CA 104; 164; DLB 230; FW;
MTCW 2; RGEL 2; TWA
Fraser, George MacDonald 1925- ...... **CLC 7**
See also CA 45-48, 180; CAAE 180; CANR
2, 48, 74; MTCW 1; RHW
Fraser, Sylvia 1935- .... **CLC 64**
See also CA 45-48; CANR 1, 16, 60; CCA
1
Frayn, Michael 1933- .... **CLC 3, 7, 31, 47**
See also BRWS 7; CA 5-8R; CANR 30, 69;
CBD; CD 5; CN 7; DAM DRAM, NOV;
DLB 13, 14, 194, 245; FANT; MTCW 1,
2; SFW 4
Fraze, Candida (Merrill) 1945- .... **CLC 50**
See also CA 126
Frazer, Andrew
See Marlowe, Stephen
Frazer, J(ames) G(eorge)
1854-1941 .... **TCLC 32**
See also BRWS 3; CA 118
Frazer, Robert Caine
See Creasey, John
Frazer, Sir James George
See Frazer, J(ames) G(eorge)
Frazier, Charles 1950- .... **CLC 109**
See also AAYA 34; CA 161; CSW
Frazier, Ian 1951- .... **CLC 46**
See also CA 130; CANR 54, 93
Frederic, Harold 1856-1898 .... **NCLC 10**
See also AMW; DLB 12, 23; DLBD 13;
RGAL 4
Frederick, John
See Faust, Frederick (Schiller)
See also TCWW 2
Frederick the Great 1712-1786 .... **LC 14**
Fredro, Aleksander 1793-1876 .... **NCLC 8**
Freeling, Nicolas 1927- .... **CLC 38**
See also CA 49-52; CAAS 12; CANR 1,
17, 50, 84; CMW 4; CN 7; DLB 87
Freeman, Douglas Southall
1886-1953 .... **TCLC 11**
See also CA 109; 195; DLB 17; DLBD 17
Freeman, Judith 1946- .... **CLC 55**
See also CA 148; DLB 256
Freeman, Mary E(leanor) Wilkins
1852-1930 .... **TCLC 9; SSC 1, 47**
See also CA 106; 177; DLB 12, 78, 221;
EXPS; FW; HGG; MAWW; RGAL 4;
RGSF 2; SSFS 4, 8; SUFW; TUS
Freeman, R(ichard) Austin
1862-1943 .... **TCLC 21**
See also CA 113; CANR 84; CMW 4; DLB
70
French, Albert 1943- .... **CLC 86**
See also BW 3; CA 167
French, Marilyn 1929- .... **CLC 10, 18, 60**
See also BPFB 1; CA 69-72; CANR 3, 31;
CN 7; CPW; DAM DRAM, NOV, POP;
FW; INT CANR-31; MTCW 1, 2
French, Paul
See Asimov, Isaac
Freneau, Philip Morin 1752-1832 .. **NCLC 1,
111**
See also AMWS 2; DLB 37, 43; RGAL 4
Freud, Sigmund 1856-1939 .... **TCLC 52**
See also CA 115; 133; CANR 69; EW 8;
MTCW 1, 2
Freytag, Gustav 1816-1895 .... **NCLC 109**
See also DLB 129
Friedan, Betty (Naomi) 1921- .... **CLC 74**
See also CA 65-68; CANR 18, 45, 74; DLB
246; FW; MTCW 1, 2

Friedlander, Saul 1932- .... **CLC 90**
See also CA 117; 130; CANR 72
Friedman, B(ernard) H(arper)
1926- .... **CLC 7**
See also CA 1-4R; CANR 3, 48
Friedman, Bruce Jay 1930- ...... **CLC 3, 5, 56**
See also CA 9-12R; CAD; CANR 25, 52,
101; CD 5; CN 7; DLB 2, 28, 244; INT
CANR-25
Friel, Brian 1929- .... **CLC 5, 42, 59, 115; DC
8**
See also BRWS 5; CA 21-24R; CANR 33,
69; CBD; CD 5; DFS 11; DLB 13; MTCW
1; RGEL 2
Friis-Baastad, Babbis Ellinor
1921-1970 .... **CLC 12**
See also CA 17-20R; 134; SATA 7
Frisch, Max (Rudolf) 1911-1991 ... **CLC 3, 9,
14, 18, 32, 44**
See also CA 85-88; 134; CANR 32, 74; CD-
WLB 2; DAM DRAM, NOV; DLB 69,
124; EW 13; MTCW 1, 2; RGWL 2
Fromentin, Eugene (Samuel Auguste)
1820-1876 .... **NCLC 10**
See also DLB 123; GFL 1789 to the Present
Frost, Frederick
See Faust, Frederick (Schiller)
See also TCWW 2
Frost, Robert (Lee) 1874-1963 .. **CLC 1, 3, 4,
9, 10, 13, 15, 26, 34, 44; PC 1, 39;
WLC**
See also AAYA 21; AMW; AMWR 1; CA
89-92; CANR 33; CDALB 1917-1929;
CLR 67; DA; DA3; DAB; DAC; DAM
MST, POET; DLB 54; DLBD 7; EXPP;
MTCW 1, 2; PAB; PFS 1, 2, 3, 4, 5, 6, 7,
10, 13; RGAL 4; SATA 14; WP; WYA
Froude, James Anthony
1818-1894 .... **NCLC 43**
See also DLB 18, 57, 144
Froy, Herald
See Waterhouse, Keith (Spencer)
Fry, Christopher 1907- .... **CLC 2, 10, 14**
See also BRWS 3; CA 17-20R; CAAS 23;
CANR 9, 30, 74; CBD; CD 5; CP 7; DAM
DRAM; DLB 13; MTCW 1, 2; RGEL 2;
SATA 66
Frye, (Herman) Northrop
1912-1991 .... **CLC 24, 70**
See also CA 5-8R; 133; CANR 8, 37; DLB
67, 68, 246; MTCW 1, 2; RGAL 4
Fuchs, Daniel 1909-1993 .... **CLC 8, 22**
See also CA 81-84; 142; CAAS 5; CANR
40; DLB 9, 26, 28; DLBY 1993
Fuchs, Daniel 1934- .... **CLC 34**
See also CA 37-40R; CANR 14, 48
Fuentes, Carlos 1928- .. **CLC 3, 8, 10, 13, 22,
41, 60, 113; HLC 1; SSC 24; WLC**
See also AAYA 4; AITN 2; BPFB 1; CA
69-72; CANR 10, 32, 68, 104; CDWLB
3; CWW 2; DA; DA3; DAB; DAC; DAM
MST, MULT, NOV; DLB 113; DNFS 2;
HW 1, 2; LAIT 3; LAW; LAWS 1;
MTCW 1, 2; NFS 8; RGSF 2; RGWL 2;
WLIT 1
Fuentes, Gregorio Lopez y
See Lopez y Fuentes, Gregorio
Fuertes, Gloria 1918-1998 .... **PC 27**
See also CA 178; 180; DLB 108; HW 2;
SATA 115
Fugard, (Harold) Athol 1932- . **CLC 5, 9, 14,
25, 40, 80; DC 3**
See also AAYA 17; AFW; CA 85-88; CANR
32, 54; CD 5; DAM DRAM; DFS 3, 6,
10; DLB 225; DNFS 1, 2; MTCW 1;
RGEL 2; WLIT 2
Fugard, Sheila 1932- .... **CLC 48**
See also CA 125
Fukuyama, Francis 1952- .... **CLC 131**
See also CA 140; CANR 72

Harper, Frances Ellen Watkins
1825-1911 ..... **TCLC 14; BLC 2; PC 21**
See also AFAW 1, 2; BW 1, 3; CA 111; 125;
CANR 79; DAM MULT, POET; DLB 50,
221; MAWW; RGAL 4

Harper, Michael S(teven) 1938- ... **CLC 7, 22**
See also AFAW 2; BW 1; CA 33-36R;
CANR 24, 108; CP 7; DLB 41; RGAL 4

Harper, Mrs. F. E. W.
See Harper, Frances Ellen Watkins

Harris, Christie (Lucy) Irwin
1907- .... **CLC 12**
See also CA 5-8R; CANR 6, 83; CLR 47;
DLB 88; JRDA; MAICYA 1; SAAS 10;
SATA 6, 74; SATA-Essay 116

Harris, Frank 1856-1931 .... **TCLC 24**
See also CA 109; 150; CANR 80; DLB 156,
197; RGEL 2

Harris, George Washington
1814-1869 .... **NCLC 23**
See also DLB 3, 11, 248; RGAL 4

Harris, Joel Chandler 1848-1908 ... **TCLC 2;**
SSC 19
See also CA 104; 137; CANR 80; CLR 49;
DLB 11, 23, 42, 78, 91; LAIT 2; MAI-
CYA 1; RGSF 2; SATA 100; WCH; YABC
1

Harris, John (Wyndham Parkes Lucas)
Beynon 1903-1969
See Wyndham, John
See also CA 102; 89-92; CANR 84; SATA
118; SFW 4

Harris, MacDonald .... **CLC 9**
See Heiney, Donald (William)

Harris, Mark 1922- .... **CLC 19**
See also CA 5-8R; CAAS 3; CANR 2, 55,
83; CN 7; DLB 2; DLBY 1980

Harris, Norman .... **CLC 65**

Harris, (Theodore) Wilson 1921- ..... **CLC 25**
See also BRWS 5; BW 2, 3; CA 65-68;
CAAS 16; CANR 11, 27, 69; CDWLB 3;
CN 7; CP 7; DLB 117; MTCW 1; RGEL
2

Harrison, Barbara Grizzuti 1934- . **CLC 144**
See also CA 77-80; CANR 15, 48; INT
CANR-15

Harrison, Elizabeth (Allen) Cavanna
1909-2001
See Cavanna, Betty
See also CA 9-12R; CANR 6, 27, 85, 104;
YAW

Harrison, Harry (Max) 1925- .... **CLC 42**
See also CA 1-4R; CANR 5, 21, 84; DLB
8; SATA 4; SCFW 2; SFW 4

Harrison, James (Thomas) 1937- ...... **CLC 6,**
14, 33, 66, 143; SSC 19
See also Harrison, Jim
See also CA 13-16R; CANR 8, 51, 79; CN
7; CP 7; DLBY 1982; INT CANR-8

Harrison, Jim
See Harrison, James (Thomas)
See also AMWS 8; RGAL 4; TCWW 2

Harrison, Kathryn 1961- .... **CLC 70, 151**
See also CA 144; CANR 68

Harrison, Tony 1937- .... **CLC 43, 129**
See also BRWS 5; CA 65-68; CANR 44,
98; CBD; CD 5; CP 7; DLB 40, 245;
MTCW 1; RGEL 2

Harriss, Will(ard Irvin) 1922- .... **CLC 34**
See also CA 111

Harson, Sley
See Ellison, Harlan (Jay)

Hart, Ellis
See Ellison, Harlan (Jay)

Hart, Josephine 1942(?)- .... **CLC 70**
See also CA 138; CANR 70; CPW; DAM
POP

Hart, Moss 1904-1961 .... **CLC 66**
See also CA 109; 89-92; CANR 84; DAM
DRAM; DFS 1; DLB 7; RGAL 4

Harte, (Francis) Bret(t)
1836(?)-1902 .... **TCLC 1, 25; SSC 8;**
WLC
See also AMWS 2; CA 104; 140; CANR
80; CDALB 1865-1917; DA; DA3; DAC;
DAM MST; DLB 12, 64, 74, 79, 186;
EXPS; LAIT 2; RGAL 4; RGSF 2; SATA
26; SSFS 3

Hartley, L(eslie) P(oles) 1895-1972 ... **CLC 2,**
22
See also BRWS 7; CA 45-48; 37-40R;
CANR 33; DLB 15, 139; HGG; MTCW
1, 2; RGEL 2; RGSF 2; SUFW

Hartman, Geoffrey H. 1929- .... **CLC 27**
See also CA 117; 125; CANR 79; DLB 67

Hartmann, Sadakichi 1869-1944 ... **TCLC 73**
See also CA 157; DLB 54

Hartmann von Aue c. 1170-c.
1210 .... **CMLC 15**
See also CDWLB 2; DLB 138; RGWL 2

Haruf, Kent 1943- .... **CLC 34**
See also CA 149; CANR 91

Harwood, Ronald 1934- .... **CLC 32**
See also CA 1-4R; CANR 4, 55; CBD; CD
5; DAM DRAM, MST; DLB 13

Hasegawa Tatsunosuke
See Futabatei, Shimei

Hasek, Jaroslav (Matej Frantisek)
1883-1923 .... **TCLC 4**
See also CA 104; 129; CDWLB 4; DLB
215; EW 9; MTCW 1, 2; RGSF 2; RGWL
2

Hass, Robert 1941- ... **CLC 18, 39, 99; PC 16**
See also AMWS 6; CA 111; CANR 30, 50,
71; CP 7; DLB 105, 206; RGAL 4; SATA
94

Hastings, Hudson
See Kuttner, Henry

Hastings, Selina .... **CLC 44**

Hathorne, John 1641-1717 .... **LC 38**

Hatteras, Amelia
See Mencken, H(enry) L(ouis)

Hatteras, Owen .... **TCLC 18**
See also Mencken, H(enry) L(ouis); Nathan,
George Jean

Hauptmann, Gerhart (Johann Robert)
1862-1946 .... **TCLC 4; SSC 37**
See also CA 104; 153; CDWLB 2; DAM
DRAM; DLB 66, 118; EW 8; RGSF 2;
RGWL 2

Havel, Vaclav 1936- ..... **CLC 25, 58, 65, 123;**
DC 6
See also CA 104; CANR 36, 63; CDWLB
4; CWW 2; DA3; DAM DRAM; DFS 10;
DLB 232; MTCW 1, 2

Haviaras, Stratis .... **CLC 33**
See also Chaviaras, Strates

Hawes, Stephen 1475(?)-1529(?) .... **LC 17**
See also DLB 132; RGEL 2

Hawkes, John (Clendennin Burne, Jr.)
1925-1998 .. **CLC 1, 2, 3, 4, 7, 9, 14, 15,**
27, 49
See also BPFB 2; CA 1-4R; 167; CANR 2,
47, 64; CN 7; DLB 2, 7, 227; DLBY
1980, 1998; MTCW 1, 2; RGAL 4

Hawking, S. W.
See Hawking, Stephen W(illiam)

Hawking, Stephen W(illiam) 1942- . **CLC 63,**
105
See also AAYA 13; BEST 89:1; CA 126;
129; CANR 48; CPW; DA3; MTCW 2

Hawkins, Anthony Hope
See Hope, Anthony

Hawthorne, Julian 1846-1934 .... **TCLC 25**
See also CA 165; HGG

Hawthorne, Nathaniel 1804-1864 ... **NCLC 2,**
10, 17, 23, 39, 79, 95; SSC 3, 29, 39;
WLC
See also AAYA 18; AMW; AMWR 1; BPFB
2; BYA 3; CDALB 1640-1865; DA; DA3;
DAB; DAC; DAM MST, NOV; DLB 1,
74, 183, 223; EXPN; EXPS; HGG; LAIT
1; NFS 1; RGAL 4; RGSF 2; SSFS 1, 7,
11; SUFW; WCH; YABC 2

Haxton, Josephine Ayres 1921-
See Douglas, Ellen
See also CA 115; CANR 41, 83

Hayaseca y Eizaguirre, Jorge
See Echegaray (y Eizaguirre), Jose (Maria
Waldo)

Hayashi, Fumiko 1904-1951 .... **TCLC 27**
See Hayashi Fumiko
See also CA 161

Hayashi Fumiko
See Hayashi, Fumiko
See also DLB 180

Haycraft, Anna (Margaret) 1932-
See Ellis, Alice Thomas
See also CA 122; CANR 85, 90; MTCW 2

Hayden, Robert E(arl) 1913-1980 . **CLC 5, 9,**
14, 37; BLC 2; PC 6
See also AFAW 1, 2; AMWS 2; BW 1, 3;
CA 69-72; 97-100; CABS 2; CANR 24,
75, 82; CDALB 1941-1968; DA; DAC;
DAM MST, MULT, POET; DLB 5, 76;
EXPP; MTCW 1, 2; PFS 1; RGAL 4;
SATA 19; SATA-Obit 26; WP

Hayek, F(riedrich) A(ugust von)
1899-1992 .... **TCLC 109**
See also CA 93-96; 137; CANR 20; MTCW
1, 2

Hayford, J(oseph) E(phraim) Casely
See Casely-Hayford, J(oseph) E(phraim)

Hayman, Ronald 1932- .... **CLC 44**
See also CA 25-28R; CANR 18, 50, 88; CD
5; DLB 155

Hayne, Paul Hamilton 1830-1886 . **NCLC 94**
See also DLB 3, 64, 79, 248; RGAL 4

Haywood, Eliza (Fowler)
1693(?)-1756 .... **LC 1, 44**
See also DLB 39; RGEL 2

Hazlitt, William 1778-1830 ...... **NCLC 29, 82**
See also BRW 4; DLB 110, 158; RGEL 2

Hazzard, Shirley 1931- .... **CLC 18**
See also CA 9-12R; CANR 4, 70; CN 7;
DLBY 1982; MTCW 1

Head, Bessie 1937-1986 .... **CLC 25, 67; BLC**
2; SSC 52
See also AFW; BW 2, 3; CA 29-32R; 119;
CANR 25, 82; CDWLB 3; DA3; DAM
MULT; DLB 117, 225; EXPS; FW;
MTCW 1, 2; RGSF 2; SSFS 5, 13; WLIT

Headon, (Nicky) Topper 1956(?)- ..... **CLC 30**

Heaney, Seamus (Justin) 1939- ..... **CLC 5, 7,**
14, 25, 37, 74, 91; PC 18; WLCS
See also BRWR 1; BRWS 2; CA 85-88;
CANR 25, 48, 75, 91; CDBLB 1960 to
Present; CP 7; DA3; DAB; DAM POET;
DLB 40; DLBY 1995; EXPP; MTCW 1,
2; PAB; PFS 2, 5, 8; RGEL 2; WLIT 4

Hearn, (Patricio) Lafcadio (Tessima Carlos)
1850-1904 .... **TCLC 9**
See also CA 105; 166; DLB 12, 78, 189;
HGG; RGAL 4

Hearne, Vicki 1946- .... **CLC 56**
See also CA 139

Hearon, Shelby 1931- .... **CLC 63**
See also AITN 2; AMWS 8; CA 25-28R;
CANR 18, 48, 103; CSW

Heat-Moon, William Least .... **CLC 29**
See also Trogdon, William (Lewis)
See also AAYA 9

Holland, Isabelle 1920- .... **CLC 21**
　　See also AAYA 11; CA 21-24R, 181; CAAE
　　181; CANR 10, 25, 47; CLR 57; CWRI
　　5; JRDA; LAIT 4; MAICYA 1; SATA 8,
　　70; SATA-Essay 103; WYA

Holland, Marcus
　　See Caldwell, (Janet Miriam) Taylor
　　(Holland)

Hollander, John 1929- .... **CLC 2, 5, 8, 14**
　　See also CA 1-4R; CANR 1, 52; CP 7; DLB
　　5; SATA 13

Hollander, Paul
　　See Silverberg, Robert

Holleran, Andrew 1943(?)- .... **CLC 38**
　　See also Garber, Eric
　　See also CA 144; GLL 1

Holley, Marietta 1836(?)-1926 .... **TCLC 99**
　　See also CA 118; DLB 11

Hollinghurst, Alan 1954- .... **CLC 55, 91**
　　See also CA 114; CN 7; DLB 207; GLL 1

Hollis, Jim
　　See Summers, Hollis (Spurgeon, Jr.)

Holly, Buddy 1936-1959 .... **TCLC 65**

Holmes, Gordon
　　See Shiel, M(atthew) P(hipps)

Holmes, John
　　See Souster, (Holmes) Raymond

Holmes, John Clellon 1926-1988 ...... **CLC 56**
　　See also CA 9-12R; 125; CANR 4; DLB
　　16, 237

Holmes, Oliver Wendell, Jr.
　　1841-1935 .... **TCLC 77**
　　See also CA 114; 186

Holmes, Oliver Wendell
　　1809-1894 .... **NCLC 14, 81**
　　See also AMWS 1; CDALB 1640-1865;
　　DLB 1, 189, 235; EXPP; RGAL 4; SATA
　　34

Holmes, Raymond
　　See Souster, (Holmes) Raymond

Holt, Victoria
　　See Hibbert, Eleanor Alice Burford
　　See also BPFB 2

Holub, Miroslav 1923-1998 .... **CLC 4**
　　See also CA 21-24R; 169; CANR 10; CD-
　　WLB 4; CWW 2; DLB 232

Homer c. 8th cent. B.C.- .... **CMLC 1, 16; PC**
　　23; WLCS
　　See also AW 1; CDWLB 1; DA; DA3;
　　DAB; DAC; DAM MST, POET; DLB
　　176; EFS 1; LAIT 1; RGWL 2; WP

Hongo, Garrett Kaoru 1951- .... **PC 23**
　　See also CA 133; CAAS 22; CP 7; DLB
　　120; EXPP; RGAL 4

Honig, Edwin 1919- .... **CLC 33**
　　See also CA 5-8R; CAAS 8; CANR 4, 45;
　　CP 7; DLB 5

Hood, Hugh (John Blagdon) 1928- . **CLC 15,**
　　28; SSC 42
　　See also CA 49-52; CAAS 17; CANR 1,
　　33, 87; CN 7; DLB 53; RGSF 2

Hood, Thomas 1799-1845 .... **NCLC 16**
　　See also BRW 4; DLB 96; RGEL 2

Hooker, (Peter) Jeremy 1941- .... **CLC 43**
　　See also CA 77-80; CANR 22; CP 7; DLB
　　40

Hope, A(lec) D(erwent) 1907-2000 .... **CLC 3,**
　　51
　　See also BRWS 7; CA 21-24R; 188; CANR
　　33, 74; MTCW 1, 2; PFS 8; RGEL 2

Hope, Anthony 1863-1933 .... **TCLC 83**
　　See also CA 157; DLB 153, 156; RGEL 2;
　　RHW

Hope, Brian
　　See Creasey, John

Hope, Christopher (David Tully)
　　1944- .... **CLC 52**
　　See also AFW; CA 106; CANR 47, 101;
　　CN 7; DLB 225; SATA 62

Hopkins, Gerard Manley
　　1844-1889 .... **NCLC 17; PC 15; WLC**
　　See also BRW 5; BRWR 2; CDBLB 1890-
　　1914; DA; DA3; DAB; DAC; DAM MST,
　　POET; DLB 35, 57; EXPP; PAB; RGEL
　　2; WP

Hopkins, John (Richard) 1931-1998 .. **CLC 4**
　　See also CA 85-88; 169; CBD; CD 5

Hopkins, Pauline Elizabeth
　　1859-1930 .... **TCLC 28; BLC 2**
　　See also AFAW 2; BW 2, 3; CA 141; CANR
　　82; DAM MULT; DLB 50

Hopkinson, Francis 1737-1791 .... **LC 25**
　　See also DLB 31; RGAL 4

Hopley-Woolrich, Cornell George 1903-1968
　　See Woolrich, Cornell
　　See also CA 13-14; CANR 58; CAP 1;
　　CMW 4; DLB 226; MTCW 2

Horace 65B.C.-8B.C. .... **CMLC 39**
　　See also AW 2; CDWLB 1; DLB 211;
　　RGWL 2

Horatio
　　See Proust, (Valentin-Louis-George-Eugene-
　　)Marcel

Horgan, Paul (George Vincent
　　O'Shaughnessy) 1903-1995 .. **CLC 9, 53**
　　See also BPFB 2; CA 13-16R; 147; CANR
　　9, 35; DAM NOV; DLB 102, 212; DLBY
　　1985; INT CANR-9; MTCW 1, 2; SATA
　　13; SATA-Obit 84; TCWW 2

Horn, Peter
　　See Kuttner, Henry

Hornem, Horace Esq.
　　See Byron, George Gordon (Noel)

Horney, Karen (Clementine Theodore
　　Danielsen) 1885-1952 .... **TCLC 71**
　　See also CA 114; 165; DLB 246; FW

Hornung, E(rnest) W(illiam)
　　1866-1921 .... **TCLC 59**
　　See also CA 108; 160; CMW 4; DLB 70

Horovitz, Israel (Arthur) 1939- .... **CLC 56**
　　See also CA 33-36R; CAD; CANR 46, 59;
　　CD 5; DAM DRAM; DLB 7

Horton, George Moses
　　1797(?)-1883(?) .... **NCLC 87**
　　See also DLB 50

Horvath, Odon von 1901-1938 .... **TCLC 45**
　　See also von Horvath, Oedoen
　　See also CA 118; 194; DLB 85, 124; RGWL
　　2

Horvath, Oedoen von -1938
　　See Horvath, Odon von

Horwitz, Julius 1920-1986 .... **CLC 14**
　　See also CA 9-12R; 119; CANR 12

Hospital, Janette Turner 1942- .... **CLC 42,**
　　145
　　See also CA 108; CANR 48; CN 7; RGSF
　　2

Hostos, E. M. de
　　See Hostos (y Bonilla), Eugenio Maria de

Hostos, Eugenio M. de
　　See Hostos (y Bonilla), Eugenio Maria de

Hostos, Eugenio Maria
　　See Hostos (y Bonilla), Eugenio Maria de

Hostos (y Bonilla), Eugenio Maria de
　　1839-1903 .... **TCLC 24**
　　See also CA 123; 131; HW 1

Houdini
　　See Lovecraft, H(oward) P(hillips)

Hougan, Carolyn 1943- .... **CLC 34**
　　See also CA 139

Household, Geoffrey (Edward West)
　　1900-1988 .... **CLC 11**
　　See also CA 77-80; 126; CANR 58; CMW
　　4; DLB 87; SATA 14; SATA-Obit 59

Housman, A(lfred) E(dward)
　　1859-1936 ... **TCLC 1, 10; PC 2; WLCS**
　　See also BRW 6; CA 104; 125; DA; DA3;
　　DAB; DAC; DAM MST, POET; DLB 19;
　　EXPP; MTCW 1, 2; PAB; PFS 4, 7;
　　RGEL 2; WP

Housman, Laurence 1865-1959 .... **TCLC 7**
　　See also CA 106; 155; DLB 10; FANT;
　　RGEL 2; SATA 25

Howard, Elizabeth Jane 1923- ..... **CLC 7, 29**
　　See also CA 5-8R; CANR 8, 62; CN 7

Howard, Maureen 1930- .... **CLC 5, 14, 46,**
　　151
　　See also CA 53-56; CANR 31, 75; CN 7;
　　DLBY 1983; INT CANR-31; MTCW 1, 2

Howard, Richard 1929- .... **CLC 7, 10, 47**
　　See also AITN 1; CA 85-88; CANR 25, 80;
　　CP 7; DLB 5; INT CANR-25

Howard, Robert E(rvin)
　　1906-1936 .... **TCLC 8**
　　See also BPFB 2; BYA 5; CA 105; 157;
　　FANT; SUFW

Howard, Warren F.
　　See Pohl, Frederik

Howe, Fanny (Quincy) 1940- .... **CLC 47**
　　See also CA 117; CAAE 187; CAAS 27;
　　CANR 70; CP 7; CWP; SATA-Brief 52

Howe, Irving 1920-1993 .... **CLC 85**
　　See also AMWS 6; CA 9-12R; 141; CANR
　　21, 50; DLB 67; MTCW 1, 2

Howe, Julia Ward 1819-1910 .... **TCLC 21**
　　See also CA 117; 191; DLB 1, 189, 235;
　　FW

Howe, Susan 1937- .... **CLC 72, 152**
　　See also AMWS 4; CA 160; CP 7; CWP;
　　DLB 120; FW; RGAL 4

Howe, Tina 1937- .... **CLC 48**
　　See also CA 109; CAD; CD 5; CWD

Howell, James 1594(?)-1666 .... **LC 13**
　　See also DLB 151

Howells, W. D.
　　See Howells, William Dean

Howells, William D.
　　See Howells, William Dean

Howells, William Dean 1837-1920 .. **TCLC 7,**
　　17, 41; SSC 36
　　See also AMW; CA 104; 134; CDALB
　　1865-1917; DLB 12, 64, 74, 79, 189;
　　MTCW 2; RGAL 4

Howes, Barbara 1914-1996 .... **CLC 15**
　　See also CA 9-12R; 151; CAAS 3; CANR
　　53; CP 7; SATA 5

Hrabal, Bohumil 1914-1997 .... **CLC 13, 67**
　　See also CA 106; 156; CAAS 12; CANR
　　57; CWW 2; DLB 232; RGSF 2

Hrotsvit of Gandersheim c. 935-c.
　　1000 .... **CMLC 29**
　　See also DLB 148

Hsi, Chu 1130-1200 .... **CMLC 42**

Hsun, Lu
　　See Lu Hsun

Hubbard, L(afayette) Ron(ald)
　　1911-1986 .... **CLC 43**
　　See also CA 77-80; 118; CANR 52; CPW;
　　DA3; DAM POP; FANT; MTCW 2; SFW
　　4

Huch, Ricarda (Octavia)
　　1864-1947 .... **TCLC 13**
　　See also CA 111; 189; DLB 66

Huddle, David 1942- .... **CLC 49**
　　See also CA 57-60; CAAS 20; CANR 89;
　　DLB 130

Hudson, Jeffrey
　　See Crichton, (John) Michael

Hudson, W(illiam) H(enry)
　　1841-1922 .... **TCLC 29**
　　See also CA 115; 190; DLB 98, 153, 174;
　　RGEL 2; SATA 35

DA3; DAM POP; DLB 206; INT CA-134; LAIT 5; MTCW 2; NFS 5, 10, 12; RGAL 4

Kingston, Maxine (Ting Ting) Hong 1940- .... **CLC 12, 19, 58, 121; AAL; WLCS**
See also AAYA 8; AMWS 5; BPFB 2; CA 69-72; CANR 13, 38, 74, 87; CDALBS; CN 7; DA3; DAM MULT, NOV; DLB 173, 212; DLBY 1980; FW; INT CANR-13; LAIT 5; MAWW; MTCW 1, 2; NFS 6; RGAL 4; SATA 53; SSFS 3

Kinnell, Galway 1927- ..... **CLC 1, 2, 3, 5, 13, 29, 129; PC 26**
See also AMWS 3; CA 9-12R; CANR 10, 34, 66; CP 7; DLB 5; DLBY 1987; INT CANR-34; MTCW 1, 2; PAB; PFS 9; RGAL 4; WP

Kinsella, Thomas 1928- .... **CLC 4, 19, 138**
See also BRWS 5; CA 17-20R; CANR 15; CP 7; DLB 27; MTCW 1, 2; RGEL 2

Kinsella, W(illiam) P(atrick) 1935- . **CLC 27, 43**
See also AAYA 7; BPFB 2; CA 97-100; CAAS 7; CANR 21, 35, 66, 75; CN 7; CPW; DAC; DAM NOV, POP; FANT; INT CANR-21; LAIT 5; MTCW 1, 2; RGSF 2

Kinsey, Alfred C(harles) 1894-1956 .... **TCLC 91**
See also CA 115; 170; MTCW 2

Kipling, (Joseph) Rudyard 1865-1936 .. **TCLC 8, 17; PC 3; SSC 5; WLC**
See also AAYA 32; BRW 6; BYA 4; CA 105; 120; CANR 33; CDBLB 1890-1914; CLR 39, 65; CWRI 5; DA; DA3; DAB; DAC; DAM MST, POET; DLB 19, 34, 141, 156; EXPS; FANT; LAIT 3; MAICYA 1; MTCW 1, 2; RGEL 2; RGSF 2; SATA 100; SFW 4; SSFS 8; SUFW; WCH; WLIT 4; YABC 2

Kirk, Russell (Amos) 1918-1994 .. **TCLC 119**
See also AITN 1; CA 1-4R; 145; CAAS 9; CANR 1, 20, 60; HGG; INT CANR-20; MTCW 1, 2

Kirkland, Caroline M. 1801-1864 . **NCLC 85**
See also DLB 3, 73, 74, 250, 254; DLBD 13

Kirkup, James 1918- .... **CLC 1**
See also CA 1-4R; CAAS 4; CANR 2; DLB 27; SATA 12

Kirkwood, James 1930(?)-1989 .... **CLC 9**
See also AITN 2; CA 1-4R; 128; CANR 6, 40; GLL 2

Kirshner, Sidney
See Kingsley, Sidney

Kis, Danilo 1935-1989 .... **CLC 57**
See also CA 109; 118; 129; CANR 61; CDWLB 4; DLB 181; MTCW 1; RGSF 2; RGWL 2

Kissinger, Henry A(lfred) 1923- ..... **CLC 137**
See also CA 1-4R; CANR 2, 33, 66; MTCW 1

Kivi, Aleksis 1834-1872 .... **NCLC 30**

Kizer, Carolyn (Ashley) 1925- ... **CLC 15, 39, 80**
See also CA 65-68; CAAS 5; CANR 24, 70; CP 7; CWP; DAM POET; DLB 5, 169; MTCW 2

Klabund 1890-1928 .... **TCLC 44**
See also CA 162; DLB 66

Klappert, Peter 1942- .... **CLC 57**
See also CA 33-36R; CSW; DLB 5

Klein, A(braham) M(oses) 1909-1972 .... **CLC 19**
See also CA 101; 37-40R; DAB; DAC; DAM MST; DLB 68; RGEL 2

Klein, Joe .... **CLC 154**
See also Klein, Joseph

Klein, Joseph 1946-
See Klein, Joe
See also CA 85-88; CANR 55

Klein, Norma 1938-1989 .... **CLC 30**
See also AAYA 2, 35; BPFB 2; BYA 6, 7, 8; CA 41-44R; 128; CANR 15, 37; CLR 2, 19; INT CANR-15; JRDA; MAICYA 1; SAAS 1; SATA 7, 57; WYA; YAW

Klein, T(heodore) E(ibon) D(onald) 1947- .... **CLC 34**
See also CA 119; CANR 44, 75; HGG

Kleist, Heinrich von 1777-1811 ...... **NCLC 2, 37; SSC 22**
See also CDWLB 2; DAM DRAM; DLB 90; EW 5; RGSF 2; RGWL 2

Klima, Ivan 1931- .... **CLC 56**
See also CA 25-28R; CANR 17, 50, 91; CDWLB 4; CWW 2; DAM NOV; DLB 232

Klimentov, Andrei Platonovich 1899-1951 .... **TCLC 14; SSC 42**
See also CA 108

Klinger, Friedrich Maximilian von 1752-1831 .... **NCLC 1**
See also DLB 94

Klingsor the Magician
See Hartmann, Sadakichi

Klopstock, Friedrich Gottlieb 1724-1803 .... **NCLC 11**
See also DLB 97; EW 4; RGWL 2

Knapp, Caroline 1959- .... **CLC 99**
See also CA 154

Knebel, Fletcher 1911-1993 .... **CLC 14**
See also AITN 1; CA 1-4R; 140; CAAS 3; CANR 1, 36; SATA 36; SATA-Obit 75

Knickerbocker, Diedrich
See Irving, Washington

Knight, Etheridge 1931-1991 . **CLC 40; BLC 2; PC 14**
See also BW 1, 3; CA 21-24R; 133; CANR 23, 82; DAM POET; DLB 41; MTCW 2; RGAL 4

Knight, Sarah Kemble 1666-1727 .... **LC 7**
See also DLB 24, 200

Knister, Raymond 1899-1932 .... **TCLC 56**
See also CA 186; DLB 68; RGEL 2

Knowles, John 1926-2001 .. **CLC 1, 4, 10, 26**
See also AAYA 10; BPFB 2; BYA 3; CA 17-20R; CANR 40, 74, 76; CDALB 1968-1988; CN 7; DA; DAC; DAM MST, NOV; DLB 6; EXPN; MTCW 1, 2; NFS 2; RGAL 4; SATA 8, 89; YAW

Knox, Calvin M.
See Silverberg, Robert

Knox, John c. 1505-1572 .... **LC 37**
See also DLB 132

Knye, Cassandra
See Disch, Thomas M(ichael)

Koch, C(hristopher) J(ohn) 1932- .... **CLC 42**
See also CA 127; CANR 84; CN 7

Koch, Christopher
See Koch, C(hristopher) J(ohn)

Koch, Kenneth 1925- .... **CLC 5, 8, 44**
See also CA 1-4R; CAD; CANR 6, 36, 57, 97; CD 5; CP 7; DAM POET; DLB 5; INT CANR-36; MTCW 2; SATA 65; WP

Kochanowski, Jan 1530-1584 .... **LC 10**
See also RGWL 2

Kock, Charles Paul de 1794-1871 . **NCLC 16**

Koda Rohan
See Koda Shigeyuki

Koda Rohan
See Koda Shigeyuki
See also DLB 180

Koda Shigeyuki 1867-1947 .... **TCLC 22**
See also Koda Rohan
See also CA 121; 183

Koestler, Arthur 1905-1983 ... **CLC 1, 3, 6, 8, 15, 33**
See also BRWS 1; CA 1-4R; 109; CANR 1, 33; CDBLB 1945-1960; DLBY 1983; MTCW 1, 2; RGEL 2

Kogawa, Joy Nozomi 1935- ...... **CLC 78, 129**
See also CA 101; CANR 19, 62; CN 7; CWP; DAC; DAM MST, MULT; FW; MTCW 2; NFS 3; SATA 99

Kohout, Pavel 1928- .... **CLC 13**
See also CA 45-48; CANR 3

Koizumi, Yakumo
See Hearn, (Patricio) Lafcadio (Tessima Carlos)

Kolmar, Gertrud 1894-1943 .... **TCLC 40**
See also CA 167

Komunyakaa, Yusef 1947- .... **CLC 86, 94; BLCS**
See also AFAW 2; CA 147; CANR 83; CP 7; CSW; DLB 120; PFS 5; RGAL 4

Konrad, George
See Konrad, Gyorgy
See also CWW 2

Konrad, Gyorgy 1933- .... **CLC 4, 10, 73**
See also Konrad, George
See also CA 85-88; CANR 97; CDWLB 4; CWW 2; DLB 232

Konwicki, Tadeusz 1926- .... **CLC 8, 28, 54, 117**
See also CA 101; CAAS 9; CANR 39, 59; CWW 2; DLB 232; IDFW 3; MTCW 1

Koontz, Dean R(ay) 1945- .... **CLC 78**
See also AAYA 9, 31; BEST 89:3, 90:2; CA 108; CANR 19, 36, 52, 95; CMW 4; CPW; DA3; DAM NOV, POP; HGG; MTCW 1; SATA 92; SFW 4; YAW

Kopernik, Mikolaj
See Copernicus, Nicolaus

Kopit, Arthur (Lee) 1937- ...... **CLC 1, 18, 33**
See also AITN 1; CA 81-84; CABS 3; CD 5; DAM DRAM; DFS 7; DLB 7; MTCW 1; RGAL 4

Kops, Bernard 1926- .... **CLC 4**
See also CA 5-8R; CANR 84; CBD; CN 7; CP 7; DLB 13

Kornbluth, C(yril) M. 1923-1958 .... **TCLC 8**
See also CA 105; 160; DLB 8; SFW 4

Korolenko, V. G.
See Korolenko, Vladimir Galaktionovich

Korolenko, Vladimir
See Korolenko, Vladimir Galaktionovich

Korolenko, Vladimir G.
See Korolenko, Vladimir Galaktionovich

Korolenko, Vladimir Galaktionovich 1853-1921 .... **TCLC 22**
See also CA 121

Korzybski, Alfred (Habdank Skarbek) 1879-1950 .... **TCLC 61**
See also CA 123; 160

Kosinski, Jerzy (Nikodem) 1933-1991 .... **CLC 1, 2, 3, 6, 10, 15, 53, 70**
See also AMWS 7; BPFB 2; CA 17-20R; 134; CANR 9, 46; DA3; DAM NOV; DLB 2; DLBY 1982; HGG; MTCW 1, 2; NFS 12; RGAL 4

Kostelanetz, Richard (Cory) 1940- .. **CLC 28**
See also CA 13-16R; CAAS 8; CANR 38, 77; CN 7; CP 7

Kotlowitz, Robert 1924- .... **CLC 4**
See also CA 33-36R; CANR 36

Kotzebue, August (Friedrich Ferdinand) von 1761-1819 .... **NCLC 25**
See also DLB 94

Kotzwinkle, William 1938- ..... **CLC 5, 14, 35**
See also BPFB 2; CA 45-48; CANR 3, 44, 84; CLR 6; DLB 173; FANT; MAICYA 1; SATA 24, 70; SFW 4; YAW

Landor, Walter Savage
1775-1864 .... **NCLC 14**
See also BRW 4; DLB 93, 107; RGEL 2

Landwirth, Heinz 1927-
See Lind, Jakov
See also CA 9-12R; CANR 7

Lane, Patrick 1939- .... **CLC 25**
See also CA 97-100; CANR 54; CP 7; DAM
POET; DLB 53; INT 97-100

Lang, Andrew 1844-1912 .... **TCLC 16**
See also CA 114; 137; CANR 85; DLB 98,
141, 184; FANT; MAICYA 1; RGEL 2;
SATA 16; WCH

Lang, Fritz 1890-1976 .... **CLC 20, 103**
See also CA 77-80; 69-72; CANR 30

Lange, John
See Crichton, (John) Michael

Langer, Elinor 1939- .... **CLC 34**
See also CA 121

Langland, William 1332(?)-1400(?) ..... **LC 19**
See also BRW 1; DA; DAB; DAC; DAM
MST, POET; DLB 146; RGEL 2; WLIT 3

Langstaff, Launcelot
See Irving, Washington

Lanier, Sidney 1842-1881 .... **NCLC 6**
See also AMWS 1; DAM POET; DLB 64;
DLBD 13; EXPP; MAICYA 1; PFS 14;
RGAL 4; SATA 18

Lanyer, Aemilia 1569-1645 .... **LC 10, 30**
See also DLB 121

Lao-Tzu
See Lao Tzu

Lao Tzu c. 6th cent. B.C.-3rd cent.
B.C. .... **CMLC 7**

Lapine, James (Elliot) 1949- .... **CLC 39**
See also CA 123; 130; CANR 54; INT 130

Larbaud, Valery (Nicolas)
1881-1957 .... **TCLC 9**
See also CA 106; 152; GFL 1789 to the
Present

Lardner, Ring
See Lardner, Ring(gold) W(ilmer)
See also BPFB 2; CDALB 1917-1929; DLB
11, 25, 86, 171; DLBD 16; RGAL 4;
RGSF 2

Lardner, Ring W., Jr.
See Lardner, Ring(gold) W(ilmer)

Lardner, Ring(gold) W(ilmer)
1885-1933 .... **TCLC 2, 14; SSC 32**
See also Lardner, Ring
See also AMW; CA 104; 131; MTCW 1, 2

Laredo, Betty
See Codrescu, Andrei

Larkin, Maia
See Wojciechowska, Maia (Teresa)

Larkin, Philip (Arthur) 1922-1985 ... **CLC 3,
5, 8, 9, 13, 18, 33, 39, 64; PC 21**
See also BRWS 1; CA 5-8R; 117; CANR
24, 62; CDBLB 1960 to Present; DA3;
DAB; DAM MST, POET; DLB 27;
MTCW 1, 2; PFS 3, 4, 12; RGEL 2

**Larra (y Sanchez de Castro), Mariano Jose
de** 1809-1837 .... **NCLC 17**

Larsen, Eric 1941- .... **CLC 55**
See also CA 132

Larsen, Nella 1893-1963 ...... **CLC 37; BLC 2**
See also AFAW 1, 2; BW 1; CA 125; CANR
83; DAM MULT; DLB 51; FW

Larson, Charles R(aymond) 1938- ... **CLC 31**
See also CA 53-56; CANR 4

Larson, Jonathan 1961-1996 .... **CLC 99**
See also AAYA 28; CA 156

Las Casas, Bartolome de 1474-1566 . **LC 31;
HLCS**
See also Casas, Bartolome de las
See also LAW

Lasch, Christopher 1932-1994 .... **CLC 102**
See also CA 73-76; 144; CANR 25; DLB
246; MTCW 1, 2

Lasker-Schueler, Else 1869-1945 ... **TCLC 57**
See also CA 183; DLB 66, 124

Laski, Harold J(oseph) 1893-1950 . **TCLC 79**
See also CA 188

Latham, Jean Lee 1902-1995 .... **CLC 12**
See also AITN 1; BYA 1; CA 5-8R; CANR
7, 84; CLR 50; MAICYA 1; SATA 2, 68;
YAW

Latham, Mavis
See Clark, Mavis Thorpe

Lathen, Emma .... **CLC 2**
See also Hennissart, Martha; Latsis, Mary
J(ane)
See also BPFB 2; CMW 4

Lathrop, Francis
See Leiber, Fritz (Reuter, Jr.)

Latsis, Mary J(ane) 1927(?)-1997
See Lathen, Emma
See also CA 85-88; 162; CMW 4

Lattimore, Richmond (Alexander)
1906-1984 .... **CLC 3**
See also CA 1-4R; 112; CANR 1

Laughlin, James 1914-1997 .... **CLC 49**
See also CA 21-24R; 162; CAAS 22; CANR
9, 47; CP 7; DLB 48; DLBY 1996, 1997

Laurence, (Jean) Margaret (Wemyss)
1926-1987 . **CLC 3, 6, 13, 50, 62; SSC 7**
See also BYA 13; CA 5-8R; 121; CANR
33; DAC; DAM MST; DLB 53; FW;
MTCW 1, 2; NFS 11; RGEL 2; RGSF 2;
SATA-Obit 50; TCWW 2

Laurent, Antoine 1952- .... **CLC 50**

Lauscher, Hermann
See Hesse, Hermann

Lautreamont 1846-1870 .. **NCLC 12; SSC 14**
See also Lautreamont, Isidore Lucien Du-
casse
See also GFL 1789 to the Present; RGWL 2

Lautreamont, Isidore Lucien Ducasse
See Lautreamont
See also DLB 217

Laverty, Donald
See Blish, James (Benjamin)

Lavin, Mary 1912-1996 . **CLC 4, 18, 99; SSC
4**
See also CA 9-12R; 151; CANR 33; CN 7;
DLB 15; FW; MTCW 1; RGEL 2; RGSF
2

Lavond, Paul Dennis
See Kornbluth, C(yril) M.; Pohl, Frederik

Lawler, Raymond Evenor 1922- .... **CLC 58**
See also CA 103; CD 5; RGEL 2

Lawrence, D(avid) H(erbert Richards)
1885-1930 .... **TCLC 2, 9, 16, 33, 48, 61,
93; SSC 4, 19; WLC**
See also BPFB 2; BRW 7; BRWR 2; CA
104; 121; CDBLB 1914-1945; DA; DA3;
DAB; DAC; DAM MST, NOV, POET;
DLB 10, 19, 36, 98, 162, 195; EXPP;
EXPS; LAIT 2, 3; MTCW 1, 2; PFS 6;
RGEL 2; RGSF 2; SSFS 2, 6; WLIT 4;
WP

Lawrence, T(homas) E(dward)
1888-1935 .... **TCLC 18**
See also Dale, Colin
See also BRWS 2; CA 115; 167; DLB 195

Lawrence of Arabia
See Lawrence, T(homas) E(dward)

Lawson, Henry (Archibald Hertzberg)
1867-1922 .... **TCLC 27; SSC 18**
See also CA 120; 181; DLB 230; RGEL 2;
RGSF 2

Lawton, Dennis
See Faust, Frederick (Schiller)

Laxness, Halldor .... **CLC 25**
See also Gudjonsson, Halldor Kiljan
See also EW 12; RGWL 2

Layamon fl. c. 1200- .... **CMLC 10**
See also Layamon
See also RGEL 2

Laye, Camara 1928-1980 ... **CLC 4, 38; BLC
2**
See also AFW; BW 1; CA 85-88; 97-100;
CANR 25; DAM MULT; MTCW 1, 2;
WLIT 2

Layton, Irving (Peter) 1912- .... **CLC 2, 15**
See also CA 1-4R; CANR 2, 33, 43, 66; CP
7; DAC; DAM MST, POET; DLB 88;
MTCW 1, 2; PFS 12; RGEL 2

Lazarus, Emma 1849-1887 ...... **NCLC 8, 109**

Lazarus, Felix
See Cable, George Washington

Lazarus, Henry
See Slavitt, David R(ytman)

Lea, Joan
See Neufeld, John (Arthur)

Leacock, Stephen (Butler)
1869-1944 .... **TCLC 2; SSC 39**
See also CA 104; 141; CANR 80; DAC;
DAM MST; DLB 92; MTCW 2; RGEL 2;
RGSF 2

Lead, Jane Ward 1623-1704 .... **LC 72**
See also DLB 131

Lear, Edward 1812-1888 .... **NCLC 3**
See also BRW 5; CLR 1, 75; DLB 32, 163,
166; MAICYA 1; RGEL 2; SATA 18, 100;
WCH; WP

Lear, Norman (Milton) 1922- .... **CLC 12**
See also CA 73-76

Leautaud, Paul 1872-1956 .... **TCLC 83**
See also DLB 65; GFL 1789 to the Present

Leavis, F(rank) R(aymond)
1895-1978 .... **CLC 24**
See also BRW 7; CA 21-24R; 77-80; CANR
44; DLB 242; MTCW 1, 2; RGEL 2

Leavitt, David 1961- .... **CLC 34**
See also CA 116; 122; CANR 50, 62, 101;
CPW; DA3; DAM POP; DLB 130; GLL
1; INT 122; MTCW 2

Leblanc, Maurice (Marie Emile)
1864-1941 .... **TCLC 49**
See also CA 110; CMW 4

Lebowitz, Fran(ces Ann) 1951(?)- ... **CLC 11,
36**
See also CA 81-84; CANR 14, 60, 70; INT
CANR-14; MTCW 1

Lebrecht, Peter
See Tieck, (Johann) Ludwig

le Carre, John .... **CLC 3, 5, 9, 15, 28**
See also Cornwell, David (John Moore)
See also AAYA 42; BEST 89:4; BPFB 2;
BRWS 2; CDBLB 1960 to Present; CMW
4; CN 7; CPW; DLB 87; MSW; MTCW
2; RGEL 2

Le Clezio, J(ean) M(arie) G(ustave)
1940- .... **CLC 31, 155**
See also CA 116; 128; DLB 83; GFL 1789
to the Present; RGSF 2

Leconte de Lisle, Charles-Marie-Rene
1818-1894 .... **NCLC 29**
See also DLB 217; EW 6; GFL 1789 to the
Present

Le Coq, Monsieur
See Simenon, Georges (Jacques Christian)

Leduc, Violette 1907-1972 .... **CLC 22**
See also CA 13-14; 33-36R; CANR 69;
CAP 1; GFL 1789 to the Present; GLL 1

Ledwidge, Francis 1887(?)-1917 .... **TCLC 23**
See also CA 123; DLB 20

Lee, Andrea 1953- .... **CLC 36; BLC 2**
See also BW 1, 3; CA 125; CANR 82;
DAM MULT

Lee, Andrew
See Auchincloss, Louis (Stanton)

Lee, Chang-rae 1965- .... **CLC 91**
See also CA 148; CANR 89

DLB 5, 165; EXPP; FW; INT CANR-29; MTCW 1, 2; PAB; PFS 7; RGAL 4; WP

Levi, Jonathan .... **CLC 76**
See also CA 197

Levi, Peter (Chad Tigar)
1931-2000 .... **CLC 41**
See also CA 5-8R; 187; CANR 34, 80; CP 7; DLB 40

Levi, Primo 1919-1987 . **CLC 37, 50; SSC 12**
See also CA 13-16R; 122; CANR 12, 33, 61, 70; DLB 177; MTCW 1, 2; RGWL 2; TCLC 109

Levin, Ira 1929- .... **CLC 3, 6**
See also CA 21-24R; CANR 17, 44, 74; CMW 4; CN 7; CPW; DA3; DAM POP; HGG; MTCW 1, 2; SATA 66; SFW 4

Levin, Meyer 1905-1981 .... **CLC 7**
See also AITN 1; CA 9-12R; 104; CANR 15; DAM POP; DLB 9, 28; DLBY 1981; SATA 21; SATA-Obit 27

Levine, Norman 1924- .... **CLC 54**
See also CA 73-76; CAAS 23; CANR 14, 70; DLB 88

Levine, Philip 1928- .. **CLC 2, 4, 5, 9, 14, 33, 118; PC 22**
See also AMWS 5; CA 9-12R; CANR 9, 37, 52; CP 7; DAM POET; DLB 5; PFS 8

Levinson, Deirdre 1931- .... **CLC 49**
See also CA 73-76; CANR 70

Levi-Strauss, Claude 1908- .... **CLC 38**
See also CA 1-4R; CANR 6, 32, 57; DLB 242; GFL 1789 to the Present; MTCW 1, 2

Levitin, Sonia (Wolff) 1934- .... **CLC 17**
See also AAYA 13; CA 29-32R; CANR 14, 32, 79; CLR 53; JRDA; MAICYA 1; SAAS 2; SATA 4, 68, 119; YAW

Levon, O. U.
See Kesey, Ken (Elton)

Levy, Amy 1861-1889 .... **NCLC 59**
See also DLB 156, 240

Lewes, George Henry 1817-1878 ... **NCLC 25**
See also DLB 55, 144

Lewis, Alun 1915-1944 .... **TCLC 3; SSC 40**
See also BRW 7; CA 104; 188; DLB 20, 162; PAB; RGEL 2

Lewis, C. Day
See Day Lewis, C(ecil)

Lewis, C(live) S(taples) 1898-1963 .... **CLC 1, 3, 6, 14, 27, 124; WLC**
See also AAYA 3, 39; BPFB 2; BRWS 3; CA 81-84; CANR 33, 71; CDBLB 1945-1960; CLR 3, 27; CWRI 5; DA; DA3; DAB; DAC; DAM MST, NOV, POP; DLB 15, 100, 160, 255; FANT; JRDA; MAICYA 1; MTCW 1, 2; RGEL 2; SATA 13, 100; SCFW; SFW 4; SUFW; WCH; WYA; YAW

Lewis, Cecil Day
See Day Lewis, C(ecil)

Lewis, Janet 1899-1998 .... **CLC 41**
See also Winters, Janet Lewis
See also CA 9-12R; 172; CANR 29, 63; CAP 1; CN 7; DLBY 1987; RHW; TCWW 2

Lewis, Matthew Gregory
1775-1818 .... **NCLC 11, 62**
See also DLB 39, 158, 178; HGG; RGEL 2; SUFW

Lewis, (Harry) Sinclair 1885-1951 . **TCLC 4, 13, 23, 39; WLC**
See also AMW; BPFB 2; CA 104; 133; CDALB 1917-1929; DA; DA3; DAB; DAC; DAM MST, NOV; DLB 9, 102; DLBD 1; LAIT 3; MTCW 1, 2; RGAL 4

Lewis, (Percy) Wyndham
1884(?)-1957 .. **TCLC 2, 9, 104; SSC 34**
See also BRW 7; CA 104; 157; DLB 15; FANT; MTCW 2; RGEL 2

Lewisohn, Ludwig 1883-1955 .... **TCLC 19**
See also CA 107; DLB 4, 9, 28, 102

Lewton, Val 1904-1951 .... **TCLC 76**
See also CA 199; IDFW 3, 4

Leyner, Mark 1956- .... **CLC 92**
See also CA 110; CANR 28, 53; DA3; MTCW 2

Lezama Lima, Jose 1910-1976 .... **CLC 4, 10, 101; HLCS 2**
See also CA 77-80; CANR 71; DAM MULT; DLB 113; HW 1, 2; LAW; RGWL 2

L'Heureux, John (Clarke) 1934- ...... **CLC 52**
See also CA 13-16R; CANR 23, 45, 88; DLB 244

Liddell, C. H.
See Kuttner, Henry

Lie, Jonas (Lauritz Idemil)
1833-1908(?) .... **TCLC 5**
See also CA 115

Lieber, Joel 1937-1971 .... **CLC 6**
See also CA 73-76; 29-32R

Lieber, Stanley Martin
See Lee, Stan

Lieberman, Laurence (James)
1935- .... **CLC 4, 36**
See also CA 17-20R; CANR 8, 36, 89; CP 7

Lieh Tzu fl. 7th cent. B.C.-5th cent. B.C. .... **CMLC 27**

Lieksman, Anders
See Haavikko, Paavo Juhani

Li Fei-kan 1904-
See Pa Chin
See also CA 105

Lifton, Robert Jay 1926- .... **CLC 67**
See also CA 17-20R; CANR 27, 78; INT CANR-27; SATA 66

Lightfoot, Gordon 1938- .... **CLC 26**
See also CA 109

Lightman, Alan P(aige) 1948- .... **CLC 81**
See also CA 141; CANR 63, 105

Ligotti, Thomas (Robert) 1953- ...... **CLC 44; SSC 16**
See also CA 123; CANR 49; HGG

Li Ho 791-817 .... **PC 13**

Liliencron, (Friedrich Adolf Axel) Detlev von 1844-1909 .... **TCLC 18**
See also CA 117

Lilly, William 1602-1681 .... **LC 27**

Lima, Jose Lezama
See Lezama Lima, Jose

Lima Barreto, Afonso Henrique de
1881-1922 .... **TCLC 23**
See also CA 117; 181; LAW

Lima Barreto, Afonso Henriques de
See Lima Barreto, Afonso Henrique de

Limonov, Edward 1944- .... **CLC 67**
See also CA 137

Lin, Frank
See Atherton, Gertrude (Franklin Horn)

Lincoln, Abraham 1809-1865 .... **NCLC 18**
See also LAIT 2

Lind, Jakov .... **CLC 1, 2, 4, 27, 82**
See also Landwirth, Heinz
See also CAAS 4

Lindbergh, Anne (Spencer) Morrow
1906-2001 .... **CLC 82**
See also BPFB 2; CA 17-20R; 193; CANR 16, 73; DAM NOV; MTCW 1, 2; SATA 33; SATA-Obit 125

Lindsay, David 1878(?)-1945 .... **TCLC 15**
See also CA 113; 187; DLB 255; FANT; SFW 4; SUFW

Lindsay, (Nicholas) Vachel
1879-1931 .... **TCLC 17; PC 23; WLC**
See also AMWS 1; CA 114; 135; CANR 79; CDALB 1865-1917; DA; DA3; DAC;

DAM MST, POET; DLB 54; EXPP; RGAL 4; SATA 40; WP

Linke-Poot
See Doeblin, Alfred

Linney, Romulus 1930- .... **CLC 51**
See also CA 1-4R; CAD; CANR 40, 44, 79; CD 5; CSW; RGAL 4

Linton, Eliza Lynn 1822-1898 .... **NCLC 41**
See also DLB 18

Li Po 701-763 .... **CMLC 2; PC 29**
See also WP

Lipsius, Justus 1547-1606 .... **LC 16**

Lipsyte, Robert (Michael) 1938- ...... **CLC 21**
See also AAYA 7; CA 17-20R; CANR 8, 57; CLR 23, 76; DA; DAC; DAM MST, NOV; JRDA; LAIT 5; MAICYA 1; SATA 5, 68, 113; WYA; YAW

Lish, Gordon (Jay) 1934- ... **CLC 45; SSC 18**
See also CA 113; 117; CANR 79; DLB 130; INT 117

Lispector, Clarice 1925(?)-1977 .... **CLC 43; HLCS 2; SSC 34**
See also CA 139; 116; CANR 71; CDWLB 3; DLB 113; DNFS 1; FW; HW 2; LAW; RGSF 2; RGWL 2; WLIT 1

Littell, Robert 1935(?)- .... **CLC 42**
See also CA 109; 112; CANR 64; CMW 4

Little, Malcolm 1925-1965
See Malcolm X
See also BW 1, 3; CA 125; 111; CANR 82; DA; DA3; DAB; DAC; DAM MST, MULT; MTCW 1, 2

Littlewit, Humphrey Gent.
See Lovecraft, H(oward) P(hillips)

Litwos
See Sienkiewicz, Henryk (Adam Alexander Pius)

Liu, E. 1857-1909 .... **TCLC 15**
See also CA 115; 190

Lively, Penelope (Margaret) 1933- .. **CLC 32, 50**
See also BPFB 2; CA 41-44R; CANR 29, 67, 79; CLR 7; CN 7; CWRI 5; DAM NOV; DLB 14, 161, 207; FANT; JRDA; MAICYA 1; MTCW 1, 2; SATA 7, 60, 101

Livesay, Dorothy (Kathleen)
1909-1996 .... **CLC 4, 15, 79**
See also AITN 2; CA 25-28R; CAAS 8; CANR 36, 67; DAC; DAM MST, POET; DLB 68; FW; MTCW 1; RGEL 2

Livy c. 59B.C.-c. 12 .... **CMLC 11**
See also AW 2; CDWLB 1; DLB 211; RGWL 2

Lizardi, Jose Joaquin Fernandez de
1776-1827 .... **NCLC 30**
See also LAW

Llewellyn, Richard
See Llewellyn Lloyd, Richard Dafydd Vivian
See also DLB 15

Llewellyn Lloyd, Richard Dafydd Vivian
1906-1983 .... **CLC 7, 80**
See also Llewellyn, Richard
See also CA 53-56; 111; CANR 7, 71; SATA 11; SATA-Obit 37

Llosa, (Jorge) Mario (Pedro) Vargas
See Vargas Llosa, (Jorge) Mario (Pedro)
See also LAIT 5

Lloyd, Manda
See Mander, (Mary) Jane

Lloyd Webber, Andrew 1948-
See Webber, Andrew Lloyd
See also AAYA 1, 38; CA 116; 149; DAM DRAM; SATA 56

Llull, Ramon c. 1235-c. 1316 .... **CMLC 12**

Lobb, Ebenezer
See Upward, Allen

DRAM, MST, NOV; DLB 10, 36, 77, 100, 162, 195; LAIT 3; MTCW 1, 2; RGEL 2; RGSF 2; SATA 54

Maugham, William Somerset
See Maugham, W(illiam) Somerset

Maupassant, (Henri Rene Albert) Guy de 1850-1893 .... NCLC 1, 42, 83; SSC 1; WLC
See also BYA 14; DA; DA3; DAB; DAC; DAM MST; DLB 123; EW 7; EXPS; GFL 1789 to the Present; LAIT 2; RGSF 2; RGWL 2; SSFS 4; SUFW; TWA

Maupin, Armistead (Jones, Jr.) 1944- .... **CLC 95**
See also CA 125; 130; CANR 58, 101; CPW; DA3; DAM POP; GLL 1; INT 130; MTCW 2

Maurhut, Richard
See Traven, B.

Mauriac, Claude 1914-1996 .... **CLC 9**
See also CA 89-92; 152; CWW 2; DLB 83; GFL 1789 to the Present

Mauriac, Francois (Charles) 1885-1970 .... **CLC 4, 9, 56; SSC 24**
See also CA 25-28; CAP 2; DLB 65; EW 10; GFL 1789 to the Present; MTCW 1, 2; RGWL 2

Mavor, Osborne Henry 1888-1951
See Bridie, James
See also CA 104

Maxwell, William (Keepers, Jr.) 1908-2000 .... **CLC 19**
See also AMWS 8; CA 93-96; 189; CANR 54, 95; CN 7; DLB 218; DLBY 1980; INT CA-93-96; SATA-Obit 128

May, Elaine 1932- .... **CLC 16**
See also CA 124; 142; CAD; CWD; DLB 44

Mayakovski, Vladimir (Vladimirovich) 1893-1930 .... **TCLC 4, 18**
See also Maiakovskii, Vladimir; Mayakovsky, Vladimir
See also CA 104; 158; MTCW 2; SFW 4

Mayakovsky, Vladimir
See Mayakovski, Vladimir (Vladimirovich)
See also EW 11; WP

Mayhew, Henry 1812-1887 .... **NCLC 31**
See also DLB 18, 55, 190

Mayle, Peter 1939(?)- .... **CLC 89**
See also CA 139; CANR 64

Maynard, Joyce 1953- .... **CLC 23**
See also CA 111; 129; CANR 64

Mayne, William (James Carter) 1928- .... **CLC 12**
See also AAYA 20; CA 9-12R; CANR 37, 80, 100; CLR 25; FANT; JRDA; MAICYA 1; MAICYAS 1; SAAS 11; SATA 6, 68, 122; YAW

Mayo, Jim
See L'Amour, Louis (Dearborn)
See also TCWW 2

Maysles, Albert 1926- .... **CLC 16**
See also CA 29-32R

Maysles, David 1932-1987 .... **CLC 16**
See also CA 191

Mazer, Norma Fox 1931- .... **CLC 26**
See also AAYA 5, 36; BYA 1, 8; CA 69-72; CANR 12, 32, 66; CLR 23; JRDA; MAICYA 1; SAAS 1; SATA 24, 67, 105; WYA; YAW

Mazzini, Guiseppe 1805-1872 .... **NCLC 34**

McAlmon, Robert (Menzies) 1895-1956 .... **TCLC 97**
See also CA 107; 168; DLB 4, 45; DLBD 15; GLL 1

McAuley, James Phillip 1917-1976 .. **CLC 45**
See also CA 97-100; RGEL 2

McBain, Ed
See Hunter, Evan
See also MSW

McBrien, William (Augustine) 1930- .... **CLC 44**
See also CA 107; CANR 90

McCabe, Patrick 1955- .... **CLC 133**
See also CA 130; CANR 50, 90; CN 7; DLB 194

McCaffrey, Anne (Inez) 1926- .... **CLC 17**
See also AAYA 6, 34; AITN 2; BEST 89:2; BPFB 2; BYA 5; CA 25-28R; CANR 15, 35, 55, 96; CLR 49; CPW; DA3; DAM NOV, POP; DLB 8; JRDA; MAICYA 1; MTCW 1, 2; SAAS 11; SATA 8, 70, 116; SFW 4; WYA; YAW

McCall, Nathan 1955(?)- .... **CLC 86**
See also BW 3; CA 146; CANR 88

McCann, Arthur
See Campbell, John W(ood, Jr.)

McCann, Edson
See Pohl, Frederik

McCarthy, Charles, Jr. 1933-
See McCarthy, Cormac
See also CANR 42, 69, 101; CN 7; CPW; CSW; DA3; DAM POP; MTCW 2

McCarthy, Cormac .... **CLC 4, 57, 59, 101**
See also McCarthy, Charles, Jr.
See also AAYA 41; AMWS 8; BPFB 2; CA 13-16R; CANR 10; DLB 6, 143, 256; TCWW 2

McCarthy, Mary (Therese) 1912-1989 .. **CLC 1, 3, 5, 14, 24, 39, 59; SSC 24**
See also AMW; BPFB 2; CA 5-8R; 129; CANR 16, 50, 64; DA3; DLB 2; DLBY 1981; FW; INT CANR-16; MAWW; MTCW 1, 2; RGAL 4

McCartney, (James) Paul 1942- . **CLC 12, 35**
See also CA 146

McCauley, Stephen (D.) 1955- .... **CLC 50**
See also CA 141

McClaren, Peter .... **CLC 70**

McClure, Michael (Thomas) 1932- ... **CLC 6, 10**
See also CA 21-24R; CAD; CANR 17, 46, 77; CD 5; CP 7; DLB 16; WP

McCorkle, Jill (Collins) 1958- .... **CLC 51**
See also CA 121; CSW; DLB 234; DLBY 1987

McCourt, Frank 1930- .... **CLC 109**
See also CA 157; CANR 97; NCFS 1

McCourt, James 1941- .... **CLC 5**
See also CA 57-60; CANR 98

McCourt, Malachy 1932- .... **CLC 119**
See also SATA 126

McCoy, Horace (Stanley) 1897-1955 .... **TCLC 28**
See also CA 108; 155; CMW 4; DLB 9

McCrae, John 1872-1918 .... **TCLC 12**
See also CA 109; DLB 92; PFS 5

McCreigh, James
See Pohl, Frederik

McCullers, (Lula) Carson (Smith) 1917-1967 .... **CLC 1, 4, 10, 12, 48, 100; SSC 9, 24; WLC**
See also AAYA 21; AMW; BPFB 2; CA 5-8R; 25-28R; CABS 1, 3; CANR 18; CDALB 1941-1968; DA; DA3; DAB; DAC; DAM MST, NOV; DFS 5; DLB 2, 7, 173, 228; EXPS; FW; GLL 1; LAIT 3, 4; MAWW; MTCW 1, 2; NFS 6, 13; RGAL 4; RGSF 2; SATA 27; SSFS 5; YAW

McCulloch, John Tyler
See Burroughs, Edgar Rice

McCullough, Colleen 1938(?)- .. **CLC 27, 107**
See also AAYA 36; BPFB 2; CA 81-84; CANR 17, 46, 67, 98; CPW; DA3; DAM NOV, POP; MTCW 1, 2; RHW

McDermott, Alice 1953- .... **CLC 90**
See also CA 109; CANR 40, 90

McElroy, Joseph 1930- .... **CLC 5, 47**
See also CA 17-20R; CN 7

McEwan, Ian (Russell) 1948- ..... **CLC 13, 66**
See also BEST 90:4; BRWS 4; CA 61-64; CANR 14, 41, 69, 87; CN 7; DAM NOV; DLB 14, 194; HGG; MTCW 1, 2; RGSF 2

McFadden, David 1940- .... **CLC 48**
See also CA 104; CP 7; DLB 60; INT 104

McFarland, Dennis 1950- .... **CLC 65**
See also CA 165

McGahern, John 1934- ... **CLC 5, 9, 48, 156; SSC 17**
See also CA 17-20R; CANR 29, 68; CN 7; DLB 14, 231; MTCW 1

McGinley, Patrick (Anthony) 1937- . **CLC 41**
See also CA 120; 127; CANR 56; INT 127

McGinley, Phyllis 1905-1978 .... **CLC 14**
See also CA 9-12R; 77-80; CANR 19; CWRI 5; DLB 11, 48; PFS 9, 13; SATA 2, 44; SATA-Obit 24

McGinniss, Joe 1942- .... **CLC 32**
See also AITN 2; BEST 89:2; CA 25-28R; CANR 26, 70; CPW; DLB 185; INT CANR-26

McGivern, Maureen Daly
See Daly, Maureen

McGrath, Patrick 1950- .... **CLC 55**
See also CA 136; CANR 65; CN 7; DLB 231; HGG

McGrath, Thomas (Matthew) 1916-1990 .... **CLC 28, 59**
See also AMWS 10; CA 9-12R; 132; CANR 6, 33, 95; DAM POET; MTCW 1; SATA 41; SATA-Obit 66

McGuane, Thomas (Francis III) 1939- .... **CLC 3, 7, 18, 45, 127**
See also AITN 2; BPFB 2; CA 49-52; CANR 5, 24, 49, 94; CN 7; DLB 2, 212; DLBY 1980; INT CANR-24; MTCW 1; TCWW 2

McGuckian, Medbh 1950- ... **CLC 48; PC 27**
See also BRWS 5; CA 143; CP 7; CWP; DAM POET; DLB 40

McHale, Tom 1942(?)-1982 .... **CLC 3, 5**
See also AITN 1; CA 77-80; 106

McIlvanney, William 1936- .... **CLC 42**
See also CA 25-28R; CANR 61; CMW 4; DLB 14, 207

McIlwraith, Maureen Mollie Hunter
See Hunter, Mollie
See also SATA 2

McInerney, Jay 1955- .... **CLC 34, 112**
See also AAYA 18; BPFB 2; CA 116; 123; CANR 45, 68; CN 7; CPW; DA3; DAM POP; INT 123; MTCW 2

McIntyre, Vonda N(eel) 1948- .... **CLC 18**
See also CA 81-84; CANR 17, 34, 69; MTCW 1; SFW 4; YAW

McKay, Claude .... **TCLC 7, 41; BLC 3; PC 2; WLC**
See also McKay, Festus Claudius
See also AFAW 1, 2; AMWS 10; DAB; DLB 4, 45, 51, 117; EXPP; GLL 2; LAIT 3; PAB; PFS 4; RGAL 4; WP

McKay, Festus Claudius 1889-1948
See McKay, Claude
See also BW 1, 3; CA 104; 124; CANR 73; DA; DAC; DAM MST, MULT, NOV, POET; MTCW 1, 2

McKuen, Rod 1933- .... **CLC 1, 3**
See also AITN 1; CA 41-44R; CANR 40

McLoughlin, R. B.
See Mencken, H(enry) L(ouis)
McLuhan, (Herbert) Marshall
1911-1980 .... **CLC 37, 83**
See also CA 9-12R; 102; CANR 12, 34, 61;
DLB 88; INT CANR-12; MTCW 1, 2
McMillan, Terry (L.) 1951- .... **CLC 50, 61,
112; BLCS**
See also AAYA 21; BPFB 2; BW 2, 3; CA
140; CANR 60, 104; CPW; DA3; DAM
MULT, NOV, POP; MTCW 2; RGAL 4;
YAW
McMurtry, Larry (Jeff) 1936- .. **CLC 2, 3, 7,
11, 27, 44, 127**
See also AAYA 15; AITN 2; AMWS 5;
BEST 89:2; BPFB 2; CA 5-8R; CANR
19, 43, 64, 103; CDALB 1968-1988; CN
7; CPW; CSW; DA3; DAM NOV, POP;
DLB 2, 143, 256; DLBY 1980, 1987;
MTCW 1, 2; RGAL 4; TCWW 2
McNally, T. M. 1961- .... **CLC 82**
McNally, Terrence .... **CLC 4, 7, 41, 91**
See also CA 45-48; CAD; CANR 2, 56; CD
5; DA3; DAM DRAM; DLB 7, 249; GLL
1; MTCW 2
McNamer, Deirdre 1950- .... **CLC 70**
McNeal, Tom .... **CLC 119**
McNeile, Herman Cyril 1888-1937
See Sapper
See also CA 184; CMW 4; DLB 77
McNickle, (William) D'Arcy
1904-1977 .... **CLC 89**
See also CA 9-12R; 85-88; CANR 5, 45;
DAM MULT; DLB 175, 212; NNAL;
RGAL 4; SATA-Obit 22
McPhee, John (Angus) 1931- .... **CLC 36**
See also AMWS 3; ANW; BEST 90:1; CA
65-68; CANR 20, 46, 64, 69; CPW; DLB
185; MTCW 1, 2
McPherson, James Alan 1943- .. **CLC 19, 77;
BLCS**
See also BW 1, 3; CA 25-28R; CAAS 17;
CANR 24, 74; CN 7; CSW; DLB 38, 244;
MTCW 1, 2; RGAL 4; RGSF 2
McPherson, William (Alexander)
1933- .... **CLC 34**
See also CA 69-72; CANR 28; INT
CANR-28
McTaggart, J. McT. Ellis
See McTaggart, John McTaggart Ellis
McTaggart, John McTaggart Ellis
1866-1925 .... **TCLC 105**
See also CA 120
Mead, George Herbert 1873-1958 . **TCLC 89**
Mead, Margaret 1901-1978 .... **CLC 37**
See also AITN 1; CA 1-4R; 81-84; CANR
4; DA3; FW; MTCW 1, 2; SATA-Obit 20
Meaker, Marijane (Agnes) 1927-
See Kerr, M. E.
See also CA 107; CANR 37, 63; INT 107;
JRDA; MAICYA 1; MAICYAS 1; MTCW
1; SATA 20, 61, 99; SATA-Essay 111;
YAW
Medoff, Mark (Howard) 1940- .... **CLC 6, 23**
See also AITN 1; CA 53-56; CAD; CANR
5; CD 5; DAM DRAM; DFS 4; DLB 7;
INT CANR-5
Medvedev, P. N.
See Bakhtin, Mikhail Mikhailovich
Meged, Aharon
See Megged, Aharon
Meged, Aron
See Megged, Aharon
Megged, Aharon 1920- .... **CLC 9**
See also CA 49-52; CAAS 13; CANR 1
Mehta, Ved (Parkash) 1934- .... **CLC 37**
See also CA 1-4R; CANR 2, 23, 69; MTCW
1

Melanter
See Blackmore, R(ichard) D(oddridge)
Melies, Georges 1861-1938 .... **TCLC 81**
Melikow, Loris
See Hofmannsthal, Hugo von
Melmoth, Sebastian
See Wilde, Oscar (Fingal O'Flahertie Wills)
Meltzer, Milton 1915- .... **CLC 26**
See also AAYA 8; BYA 2, 6; CA 13-16R;
CANR 38, 92, 107; CLR 13; DLB 61;
JRDA; MAICYA 1; SAAS 1; SATA 1, 50,
80, 128; SATA-Essay 124; WYA; YAW
Melville, Herman 1819-1891 ..... **NCLC 3, 12,
29, 45, 49, 91, 93; SSC 1, 17, 46; WLC**
See also AAYA 25; AMW; AMWR 1;
CDALB 1640-1865; DA; DA3; DAB;
DAC; DAM MST, NOV; DLB 3, 74, 250,
254; EXPN; EXPS; LAIT 1, 2; NFS 7, 9;
RGAL 4; RGSF 2; SATA 59; SSFS 3
Membreno, Alejandro .... **CLC 59**
Menander c. 342B.C.-c. 293B.C. ... **CMLC 9,
51; DC 3**
See also AW 1; CDWLB 1; DAM DRAM;
DLB 176; RGWL 2
Menchu, Rigoberta 1959-
See also CA 175; DNFS 1; HLCS 2; WLIT
1
Mencken, H(enry) L(ouis)
1880-1956 .... **TCLC 13**
See also AMW; CA 105; 125; CDALB
1917-1929; DLB 11, 29, 63, 137, 222;
MTCW 1, 2; RGAL 4
Mendelsohn, Jane 1965- .... **CLC 99**
See also CA 154; CANR 94
Mercer, David 1928-1980 .... **CLC 5**
See also CA 9-12R; 102; CANR 23; CBD;
DAM DRAM; DLB 13; MTCW 1; RGEL
2
Merchant, Paul
See Ellison, Harlan (Jay)
Meredith, George 1828-1909 ... **TCLC 17, 43**
See also CA 117; 153; CANR 80; CDBLB
1832-1890; DAM POET; DLB 18, 35, 57,
159; RGEL 2
Meredith, William (Morris) 1919- .... **CLC 4,
13, 22, 55; PC 28**
See also CA 9-12R; CAAS 14; CANR 6,
40; CP 7; DAM POET; DLB 5
Merezhkovsky, Dmitry Sergeyevich
1865-1941 .... **TCLC 29**
See also CA 169
Merimee, Prosper 1803-1870 ... **NCLC 6, 65;
SSC 7**
See also DLB 119, 192; EW 6; EXPS; GFL
1789 to the Present; RGSF 2; RGWL 2;
SSFS 8; SUFW
Merkin, Daphne 1954- .... **CLC 44**
See also CA 123
Merlin, Arthur
See Blish, James (Benjamin)
Merrill, James (Ingram) 1926-1995 .. **CLC 2,
3, 6, 8, 13, 18, 34, 91; PC 28**
See also AMWS 3; CA 13-16R; 147; CANR
10, 49, 63, 108; DA3; DAM POET; DLB
5, 165; DLBY 1985; INT CANR-10;
MTCW 1, 2; PAB; RGAL 4
Merriman, Alex
See Silverberg, Robert
Merriman, Brian 1747-1805 .... **NCLC 70**
Merritt, E. B.
See Waddington, Miriam
Merton, Thomas 1915-1968 ..... **CLC 1, 3, 11,
34, 83; PC 10**
See also AMWS 8; CA 5-8R; 25-28R;
CANR 22, 53; DA3; DLB 48; DLBY
1981; MTCW 1, 2

Merwin, W(illiam) S(tanley) 1927- ... **CLC 1,
2, 3, 5, 8, 13, 18, 45, 88**
See also AMWS 3; CA 13-16R; CANR 15,
51; CP 7; DA3; DAM POET; DLB 5, 169;
INT CANR-15; MTCW 1, 2; PAB; PFS
5; RGAL 4
Metcalf, John 1938- .... **CLC 37; SSC 43**
See also CA 113; CN 7; DLB 60; RGSF 2
Metcalf, Suzanne
See Baum, L(yman) Frank
Mew, Charlotte (Mary) 1870-1928 .. **TCLC 8**
See also CA 105; 189; DLB 19, 135; RGEL
2
Mewshaw, Michael 1943- .... **CLC 9**
See also CA 53-56; CANR 7, 47; DLBY
1980
Meyer, Conrad Ferdinand
1825-1905 .... **NCLC 81**
See also DLB 129; EW; RGWL 2
Meyer, Gustav 1868-1932
See Meyrink, Gustav
See also CA 117; 190
Meyer, June
See Jordan, June
See also GLL 2
Meyer, Lynn
See Slavitt, David R(ytman)
Meyers, Jeffrey 1939- .... **CLC 39**
See also CA 73-76; CAAE 186; CANR 54,
102; DLB 111
**Meynell, Alice (Christina Gertrude
Thompson)** 1847-1922 .... **TCLC 6**
See also CA 104; 177; DLB 19, 98; RGEL
2
Meyrink, Gustav .... **TCLC 21**
See also Meyer, Gustav
See also DLB 81
Michaels, Leonard 1933- .... **CLC 6, 25; SSC
16**
See also CA 61-64; CANR 21, 62; CN 7;
DLB 130; MTCW 1
Michaux, Henri 1899-1984 .... **CLC 8, 19**
See also CA 85-88; 114; GFL 1789 to the
Present; RGWL 2
Micheaux, Oscar (Devereaux)
1884-1951 .... **TCLC 76**
See also BW 3; CA 174; DLB 50; TCWW
2
Michelangelo 1475-1564 .... **LC 12**
See also AAYA 43
Michelet, Jules 1798-1874 .... **NCLC 31**
See also EW 5; GFL 1789 to the Present
Michels, Robert 1876-1936 .... **TCLC 88**
Michener, James A(lbert)
1907(?)-1997 .. **CLC 1, 5, 11, 29, 60, 109**
See also AAYA 27; AITN 1; BEST 90:1;
BPFB 2; CA 5-8R; 161; CANR 21, 45,
68; CN 7; CPW; DA3; DAM NOV, POP;
DLB 6; MTCW 1, 2; RHW
Mickiewicz, Adam 1798-1855 . **NCLC 3, 101;
PC 38**
See also EW 5; RGWL 2
Middleton, Christopher 1926- .... **CLC 13**
See also CA 13-16R; CANR 29, 54; CP 7;
DLB 40
Middleton, Richard (Barham)
1882-1911 .... **TCLC 56**
See also CA 187; DLB 156; HGG
Middleton, Stanley 1919- .... **CLC 7, 38**
See also CA 25-28R; CAAS 23; CANR 21,
46, 81; CN 7; DLB 14
Middleton, Thomas 1580-1627 .... **LC 33; DC
5**
See also BRW 2; DAM DRAM, MST; DLB
58; RGEL 2
Migueis, Jose Rodrigues 1901- .... **CLC 10**
Mikszath, Kalman 1847-1910 .... **TCLC 31**
See also CA 170

Montaigne, Michel (Eyquem) de
1533-1592 .... **LC 8; WLC**
See also DA; DAB; DAC; DAM MST; EW 2; GFL Beginnings to 1789; RGWL 2

Montale, Eugenio 1896-1981 ... **CLC 7, 9, 18; PC 13**
See also CA 17-20R; 104; CANR 30; DLB 114; EW 11; MTCW 1; RGWL 2

Montesquieu, Charles-Louis de Secondat
1689-1755 .... **LC 7, 69**
See also EW 3; GFL Beginnings to 1789

Montessori, Maria 1870-1952 ...... **TCLC 103**
See also CA 115; 147

Montgomery, (Robert) Bruce 1921(?)-1978
See Crispin, Edmund
See also CA 179; 104; CMW 4

Montgomery, L(ucy) M(aud)
1874-1942 .... **TCLC 51**
See also AAYA 12; BYA 1; CA 108; 137; CLR 8; DA3; DAC; DAM MST; DLB 92; DLBD 14; JRDA; MAICYA 1; MTCW 2; RGEL 2; SATA 100; WCH; WYA; YABC 1

Montgomery, Marion H., Jr. 1925- .... **CLC 7**
See also AITN 1; CA 1-4R; CANR 3, 48; CSW; DLB 6

Montgomery, Max
See Davenport, Guy (Mattison, Jr.)

Montherlant, Henry (Milon) de
1896-1972 .... **CLC 8, 19**
See also CA 85-88; 37-40R; DAM DRAM; DLB 72; EW 11; GFL 1789 to the Present; MTCW 1

Monty Python
See Chapman, Graham; Cleese, John (Marwood); Gilliam, Terry (Vance); Idle, Eric; Jones, Terence Graham Parry; Palin, Michael (Edward)
See also AAYA 7

Moodie, Susanna (Strickland)
1803-1885 .... **NCLC 14**
See also DLB 99

Moody, Hiram F. III 1961-
See Moody, Rick
See also CA 138; CANR 64

Moody, Rick .... **CLC 147**
See also Moody, Hiram F. III

Moody, William Vaughan
1869-1910 .... **TCLC 105**
See also CA 110; 178; DLB 7, 54; RGAL 4

Mooney, Edward 1951-
See Mooney, Ted
See also CA 130

Mooney, Ted .... **CLC 25**
See also Mooney, Edward

Moorcock, Michael (John) 1939- ...... **CLC 5, 27, 58**
See also Bradbury, Edward P.
See also AAYA 26; CA 45-48; CAAS 5; CANR 2, 17, 38, 64; CN 7; DLB 14, 231; FANT; MTCW 1, 2; SATA 93; SFW 4; SUFW

Moore, Brian 1921-1999 ... **CLC 1, 3, 5, 7, 8, 19, 32, 90**
See also Bryan, Michael
See also CA 1-4R; 174; CANR 1, 25, 42, 63; CCA 1; CN 7; DAB; DAC; DAM MST; DLB 251; FANT; MTCW 1, 2; RGEL 2

Moore, Edward
See Muir, Edwin
See also RGEL 2

Moore, G. E. 1873-1958 .... **TCLC 89**

Moore, George Augustus
1852-1933 .... **TCLC 7; SSC 19**
See also BRW 6; CA 104; 177; DLB 10, 18, 57, 135; RGEL 2; RGSF 2

Moore, Lorrie .... **CLC 39, 45, 68**
See also Moore, Marie Lorena
See also AMWS 10; DLB 234

Moore, Marianne (Craig)
1887-1972 .... **CLC 1, 2, 4, 8, 10, 13, 19, 47; PC 4; WLCS**
See also AMW; CA 1-4R; 33-36R; CANR 3, 61; CDALB 1929-1941; DA; DA3; DAB; DAC; DAM MST, POET; DLB 45; DLBD 7; EXPP; MAWW; MTCW 1, 2; PAB; PFS 14; RGAL 4; SATA 20; WP

Moore, Marie Lorena 1957-
See Moore, Lorrie
See also CA 116; CANR 39, 83; CN 7; DLB 234

Moore, Thomas 1779-1852 .... **NCLC 6, 110**
See also DLB 96, 144; RGEL 2

Moorhouse, Frank 1938- .... **SSC 40**
See also CA 118; CANR 92; CN 7; RGSF 2

Mora, Pat(ricia) 1942-
See also CA 129; CANR 57, 81; CLR 58; DAM MULT; DLB 209; HLC 2; HW 1, 2; SATA 92

Moraga, Cherrie 1952- .... **CLC 126**
See also CA 131; CANR 66; DAM MULT; DLB 82, 249; FW; GLL 1; HW 1, 2

Morand, Paul 1888-1976 .... **CLC 41; SSC 22**
See also CA 184; 69-72; DLB 65

Morante, Elsa 1918-1985 .... **CLC 8, 47**
See also CA 85-88; 117; CANR 35; DLB 177; MTCW 1, 2; RGWL 2

Moravia, Alberto .... **CLC 2, 7, 11, 27, 46; SSC 26**
See also Pincherle, Alberto
See also DLB 177; EW 12; MTCW 2; RGSF 2; RGWL 2

More, Hannah 1745-1833 .... **NCLC 27**
See also DLB 107, 109, 116, 158; RGEL 2

More, Henry 1614-1687 .... **LC 9**
See also DLB 126, 252

More, Sir Thomas 1478(?)-1535 .... **LC 10, 32**
See also BRWS 7; DLB 136; RGEL 2

Moreas, Jean .... **TCLC 18**
See also Papadiamantopoulos, Johannes
See also GFL 1789 to the Present

Morgan, Berry 1919- .... **CLC 6**
See also CA 49-52; DLB 6

Morgan, Claire
See Highsmith, (Mary) Patricia
See also GLL 1

Morgan, Edwin (George) 1920- .... **CLC 31**
See also CA 5-8R; CANR 3, 43, 90; CP 7; DLB 27

Morgan, (George) Frederick 1922- .. **CLC 23**
See also CA 17-20R; CANR 21; CP 7

Morgan, Harriet
See Mencken, H(enry) L(ouis)

Morgan, Jane
See Cooper, James Fenimore

Morgan, Janet 1945- .... **CLC 39**
See also CA 65-68

Morgan, Lady 1776(?)-1859 .... **NCLC 29**
See also DLB 116, 158; RGEL 2

Morgan, Robin (Evonne) 1941- .... **CLC 2**
See also CA 69-72; CANR 29, 68; FW; GLL 2; MTCW 1; SATA 80

Morgan, Scott
See Kuttner, Henry

Morgan, Seth 1949(?)-1990 .... **CLC 65**
See also CA 185; 132

Morgenstern, Christian (Otto Josef Wolfgang) 1871-1914 .... **TCLC 8**
See also CA 105; 191

Morgenstern, S.
See Goldman, William (W.)

Mori, Rintaro
See Mori Ogai
See also CA 110

Moricz, Zsigmond 1879-1942 .... **TCLC 33**
See also CA 165; DLB 215

Morike, Eduard (Friedrich)
1804-1875 .... **NCLC 10**
See also DLB 133; RGWL 2

Mori Ogai
See Mori Ogai
See also DLB 180

Mori Ogai 1862-1922 .... **TCLC 14**
See also Mori Ogai; Ogai
See also CA 164; TWA

Moritz, Karl Philipp 1756-1793 .... **LC 2**
See also DLB 94

Morland, Peter Henry
See Faust, Frederick (Schiller)

Morley, Christopher (Darlington)
1890-1957 .... **TCLC 87**
See also CA 112; DLB 9; RGAL 4

Morren, Theophil
See Hofmannsthal, Hugo von

Morris, Bill 1952- .... **CLC 76**

Morris, Julian
See West, Morris L(anglo)

Morris, Steveland Judkins 1950(?)-
See Wonder, Stevie
See also CA 111

Morris, William 1834-1896 .... **NCLC 4**
See also BRW 5; CDBLB 1832-1890; DLB 18, 35, 57, 156, 178, 184; FANT; RGEL 2; SFW 4; SUFW

Morris, Wright 1910-1998 .. **CLC 1, 3, 7, 18, 37**
See also AMW; CA 9-12R; 167; CANR 21, 81; CN 7; DLB 2, 206, 218; DLBY 1981; MTCW 1, 2; RGAL 4; TCLC 107; TCWW 2

Morrison, Arthur 1863-1945 .... **TCLC 72; SSC 40**
See also CA 120; 157; CMW 4; DLB 70, 135, 197; RGEL 2

Morrison, Chloe Anthony Wofford
See Morrison, Toni

Morrison, James Douglas 1943-1971
See Morrison, Jim
See also CA 73-76; CANR 40

Morrison, Jim .... **CLC 17**
See also Morrison, James Douglas

Morrison, Toni 1931- . **CLC 4, 10, 22, 55, 81, 87; BLC 3**
See also AAYA 1, 22; AFAW 1, 2; AMWS 3; BPFB 2; BW 2, 3; CA 29-32R; CANR 27, 42, 67; CDALB 1968-1988; CN 7; CPW; DA; DA3; DAB; DAC; DAM MST, MULT, NOV, POP; DLB 6, 33, 143; DLBY 1981; EXPN; FW; LAIT 2, 4; MAWW; MTCW 1, 2; NFS 1, 6, 8; RGAL 4; RHW; SATA 57; SSFS 5; YAW

Morrison, Van 1945- .... **CLC 21**
See also CA 116; 168

Morrissy, Mary 1958- .... **CLC 99**

Mortimer, John (Clifford) 1923- ..... **CLC 28, 43**
See also CA 13-16R; CANR 21, 69; CD 5; CDBLB 1960 to Present; CMW 4; CN 7; CPW; DA3; DAM DRAM, POP; DLB 13, 245; INT CANR-21; MSW; MTCW 1, 2; RGEL 2

Mortimer, Penelope (Ruth)
1918-1999 .... **CLC 5**
See also CA 57-60; 187; CANR 45, 88; CN 7

Morton, Anthony
See Creasey, John

Morton, Thomas 1579(?)-1647(?) .... **LC 72**
See also DLB 24; RGEL 2

Mosca, Gaetano 1858-1941 .... **TCLC 75**

Mosher, Howard Frank 1943- .... **CLC 62**
See also CA 139; CANR 65

Oliphant, Mrs.
See Oliphant, Margaret (Oliphant Wilson)
See also SUFW
Oliphant, Laurence 1829(?)-1888 .. **NCLC 47**
See also DLB 18, 166
Oliphant, Margaret (Oliphant Wilson)
1828-1897 .... **NCLC 11, 61; SSC 25**
See also Oliphant, Mrs.
See also DLB 18, 159, 190; HGG; RGEL
2; RGSF 2
Oliver, Mary 1935- .... **CLC 19, 34, 98**
See also AMWS 7; CA 21-24R; CANR 9,
43, 84, 92; CP 7; CWP; DLB 5, 193
Olivier, Laurence (Kerr) 1907-1989 . **CLC 20**
See also CA 111; 150; 129
Olsen, Tillie 1912- ... **CLC 4, 13, 114; SSC 11**
See also BYA 11; CA 1-4R; CANR 1, 43,
74; CDALBS; CN 7; DA; DA3; DAB;
DAC; DAM MST; DLB 28, 206; DLBY
1980; EXPS; FW; MTCW 1, 2; RGAL 4;
RGSF 2; SSFS 1
Olson, Charles (John) 1910-1970 .. **CLC 1, 2,
5, 6, 9, 11, 29; PC 19**
See also AMWS 2; CA 13-16; 25-28R;
CABS 2; CANR 35, 61; CAP 1; DAM
POET; DLB 5, 16, 193; MTCW 1, 2;
RGAL 4; WP
Olson, Toby 1937- .... **CLC 28**
See also CA 65-68; CANR 9, 31, 84; CP 7
Olyesha, Yuri
See Olesha, Yuri (Karlovich)
Omar Khayyam
See Khayyam, Omar
See also RGWL 2
Ondaatje, (Philip) Michael 1943- .... **CLC 14,
29, 51, 76; PC 28**
See also CA 77-80; CANR 42, 74; CN 7;
CP 7; DA3; DAB; DAC; DAM MST;
DLB 60; MTCW 2; PFS 8
Oneal, Elizabeth 1934-
See Oneal, Zibby
See also CA 106; CANR 28, 84; MAICYA
1; SATA 30, 82; YAW
Oneal, Zibby .... **CLC 30**
See also Oneal, Elizabeth
See also AAYA 5, 41; BYA 13; CLR 13;
JRDA; WYA
O'Neill, Eugene (Gladstone)
1888-1953 ...... **TCLC 1, 6, 27, 49; WLC**
See also AITN 1; AMW; CA 110; 132;
CAD; CDALB 1929-1941; DA; DA3;
DAB; DAC; DAM DRAM, MST; DFS 9,
11, 12; DLB 7; LAIT 3; MTCW 1, 2;
RGAL 4
Onetti, Juan Carlos 1909-1994 ... **CLC 7, 10;
HLCS 2; SSC 23**
See also CA 85-88; 145; CANR 32, 63; CD-
WLB 3; DAM MULT, NOV; DLB 113;
HW 1, 2; LAW; MTCW 1, 2; RGSF 2
O Nuallain, Brian 1911-1966
See O'Brien, Flann
See also CA 21-22; 25-28R; CAP 2; DLB
231; FANT
Ophuls, Max 1902-1957 .... **TCLC 79**
See also CA 113
Opie, Amelia 1769-1853 .... **NCLC 65**
See also DLB 116, 159; RGEL 2
Oppen, George 1908-1984 ..... **CLC 7, 13, 34;
PC 35**
See also CA 13-16R; 113; CANR 8, 82;
DLB 5, 165; TCLC 107
Oppenheim, E(dward) Phillips
1866-1946 .... **TCLC 45**
See also CA 111; CMW 4; DLB 70
Opuls, Max
See Ophuls, Max
Origen c. 185-c. 254 .... **CMLC 19**
Orlovitz, Gil 1918-1973 .... **CLC 22**
See also CA 77-80; 45-48; DLB 2, 5

Orris
See Ingelow, Jean
Ortega y Gasset, Jose 1883-1955 ... **TCLC 9;
HLC 2**
See also CA 106; 130; DAM MULT; EW 9;
HW 1, 2; MTCW 1, 2
Ortese, Anna Maria 1914- .... **CLC 89**
See also DLB 177
Ortiz, Simon J(oseph) 1941- ..... **CLC 45; PC
17**
See also AMWS 4; CA 134; CANR 69; CP
7; DAM MULT, POET; DLB 120, 175,
256; EXPP; NNAL; PFS 4; RGAL 4
Orton, Joe .... **CLC 4, 13, 43; DC 3**
See also Orton, John Kingsley
See also BRWS 5; CBD; CDBLB 1960 to
Present; DFS 3, 6; DLB 13; GLL 1;
MTCW 2; RGEL 2; WLIT 4
Orton, John Kingsley 1933-1967
See Orton, Joe
See also CA 85-88; CANR 35, 66; DAM
DRAM; MTCW 1, 2
Orwell, George .... **TCLC 2, 6, 15, 31, 51;
WLC**
See also Blair, Eric (Arthur)
See also BPFB 3; BRW 7; BYA 5; CDBLB
1945-1960; CLR 68; DAB; DLB 15, 98,
195, 255; EXPN; LAIT 4, 5; NFS 3, 7;
RGEL 2; SCFW 2; SFW 4; SSFS 4;
WLIT 4; YAW
Osborne, David
See Silverberg, Robert
Osborne, George
See Silverberg, Robert
Osborne, John (James) 1929-1994 .... **CLC 1,
2, 5, 11, 45; WLC**
See also BRWS 1; CA 13-16R; 147; CANR
21, 56; CDBLB 1945-1960; DA; DAB;
DAC; DAM DRAM, MST; DFS 4; DLB
13; MTCW 1, 2; RGEL 2
Osborne, Lawrence 1958- .... **CLC 50**
See also CA 189
Osbourne, Lloyd 1868-1947 .... **TCLC 93**
Oshima, Nagisa 1932- .... **CLC 20**
See also CA 116; 121; CANR 78
Oskison, John Milton 1874-1947 ... **TCLC 35**
See also CA 144; CANR 84; DAM MULT;
DLB 175; NNAL
Ossian c. 3rd cent. - .... **CMLC 28**
See also Macpherson, James
Ossoli, Sarah Margaret (Fuller)
1810-1850 .... **NCLC 5, 50**
See also Fuller, Margaret; Fuller, Sarah
Margaret
See also CDALB 1640-1865; FW; SATA 25
Ostriker, Alicia (Suskin) 1937- ...... **CLC 132**
See also CA 25-28R; CAAS 24; CANR 10,
30, 62, 99; CWP; DLB 120; EXPP
Ostrovsky, Alexander 1823-1886 .. **NCLC 30,
57**
Otero, Blas de 1916-1979 .... **CLC 11**
See also CA 89-92; DLB 134
Otto, Rudolf 1869-1937 .... **TCLC 85**
Otto, Whitney 1955- .... **CLC 70**
See also CA 140
Ouida .... **TCLC 43**
See also De La Ramee, (Marie) Louise
See also DLB 18, 156; RGEL 2
Ouologuem, Yambo 1940- .... **CLC 146**
See also CA 111; 176
Ousmane, Sembene 1923- ... **CLC 66; BLC 3**
See also Sembene, Ousmane
See also BW 1, 3; CA 117; 125; CANR 81;
CWW 2; MTCW 1
Ovid 43B.C.-17 .... **CMLC 7; PC 2**
See also AW 2; CDWLB 1; DA3; DAM
POET; DLB 211; RGWL 2; WP
Owen, Hugh
See Faust, Frederick (Schiller)

Owen, Wilfred (Edward Salter)
1893-1918 ... **TCLC 5, 27; PC 19; WLC**
See also BRW 6; CA 104; 141; CDBLB
1914-1945; DA; DAB; DAC; DAM MST,
POET; DLB 20; EXPP; MTCW 2; PFS
10; RGEL 2; WLIT 4
Owens, Rochelle 1936- .... **CLC 8**
See also CA 17-20R; CAAS 2; CAD;
CANR 39; CD 5; CP 7; CWD; CWP
Oz, Amos 1939- .... **CLC 5, 8, 11, 27, 33, 54**
See also CA 53-56; CANR 27, 47, 65;
CWW 2; DAM NOV; MTCW 1, 2; RGSF
2
Ozick, Cynthia 1928- .... **CLC 3, 7, 28, 62,
155; SSC 15**
See also AMWS 5; BEST 90:1; CA 17-20R;
CANR 23, 58; CN 7; CPW; DA3; DAM
NOV, POP; DLB 28, 152; DLBY 1982;
EXPS; INT CANR-23; MTCW 1, 2;
RGAL 4; RGSF 2; SSFS 3, 12
Ozu, Yasujiro 1903-1963 .... **CLC 16**
See also CA 112
Pacheco, C.
See Pessoa, Fernando (Antonio Nogueira)
Pacheco, Jose Emilio 1939-
See also CA 111; 131; CANR 65; DAM
MULT; HLC 2; HW 1, 2; RGSF 2
Pa Chin .... **CLC 18**
See also Li Fei-kan
Pack, Robert 1929- .... **CLC 13**
See also CA 1-4R; CANR 3, 44, 82; CP 7;
DLB 5; SATA 118
Padgett, Lewis
See Kuttner, Henry
Padilla (Lorenzo), Heberto
1932-2000 .... **CLC 38**
See also AITN 1; CA 123; 131; 189; HW 1
Page, Jimmy 1944- .... **CLC 12**
Page, Louise 1955- .... **CLC 40**
See also CA 140; CANR 76; CBD; CD 5;
CWD; DLB 233
Page, P(atricia) K(athleen) 1916- ...... **CLC 7,
18; PC 12**
See also Cape, Judith
See also CA 53-56; CANR 4, 22, 65; CP 7;
DAC; DAM MST; DLB 68; MTCW 1;
RGEL 2
Page, Stanton
See Fuller, Henry Blake
Page, Stanton
See Fuller, Henry Blake
Page, Thomas Nelson 1853-1922 .... **SSC 23**
See also CA 118; 177; DLB 12, 78; DLBD
13; RGAL 4
Pagels, Elaine Hiesey 1943- .... **CLC 104**
See also CA 45-48; CANR 2, 24, 51; FW
Paget, Violet 1856-1935
See Lee, Vernon
See also CA 104; 166; GLL 1; HGG
Paget-Lowe, Henry
See Lovecraft, H(oward) P(hillips)
Paglia, Camille (Anna) 1947- .... **CLC 68**
See also CA 140; CANR 72; CPW; FW;
GLL 2; MTCW 2
Paige, Richard
See Koontz, Dean R(ay)
Paine, Thomas 1737-1809 .... **NCLC 62**
See also AMWS 1; CDALB 1640-1865;
DLB 31, 43, 73, 158; LAIT 1; RGAL 4;
RGEL 2
Palamas, Kostes 1859-1943 .... **TCLC 5**
See also CA 105; 190; RGWL 2
Palazzeschi, Aldo 1885-1974 .... **CLC 11**
See also CA 89-92; 53-56; DLB 114
Pales Matos, Luis 1898-1959
See Pales Matos, Luis
See also HLCS 2; HW 1; LAW

Simmons, James (Stewart Alexander)
1933- .... **CLC 43**
See also CA 105; CAAS 21; CP 7; DLB 40

Simms, William Gilmore
1806-1870 .... **NCLC 3**
See also DLB 3, 30, 59, 73, 248, 254;
RGAL 4

Simon, Carly 1945- .... **CLC 26**
See also CA 105

Simon, Claude 1913-1984 ... **CLC 4, 9, 15, 39**
See also CA 89-92; CANR 33; DAM NOV;
DLB 83; EW 13; GFL 1789 to the Present;
MTCW 1

Simon, Myles
See Follett, Ken(neth Martin)

Simon, (Marvin) Neil 1927- ... **CLC 6, 11, 31, 39, 70; DC 14**
See also AAYA 32; AITN 1; AMWS 4; CA 21-24R; CANR 26, 54, 87; CD 5; DA3;
DAM DRAM; DFS 2, 6, 12; DLB 7;
LAIT 4; MTCW 1, 2; RGAL 4

Simon, Paul (Frederick) 1941(?)- ..... **CLC 17**
See also CA 116; 153

Simonon, Paul 1956(?)- .... **CLC 30**

Simonson, Rick ed. .... **CLC 70**

Simpson, Harriette
See Arnow, Harriette (Louisa) Simpson

Simpson, Louis (Aston Marantz)
1923- .... **CLC 4, 7, 9, 32, 149**
See also AMWS 9; CA 1-4R; CAAS 4;
CANR 1, 61; CP 7; DAM POET; DLB 5;
MTCW 1, 2; PFS 7, 11, 14; RGAL 4

Simpson, Mona (Elizabeth) 1957- ... **CLC 44, 146**
See also CA 122; 135; CANR 68, 103; CN 7

Simpson, N(orman) F(rederick)
1919- .... **CLC 29**
See also CA 13-16R; CBD; DLB 13; RGEL 2

Sinclair, Andrew (Annandale) 1935- . **CLC 2, 14**
See also CA 9-12R; CAAS 5; CANR 14, 38, 91; CN 7; DLB 14; FANT; MTCW 1

Sinclair, Emil
See Hesse, Hermann

Sinclair, Iain 1943- .... **CLC 76**
See also CA 132; CANR 81; CP 7; HGG

Sinclair, Iain MacGregor
See Sinclair, Iain

Sinclair, Irene
See Griffith, D(avid Lewelyn) W(ark)

Sinclair, Mary Amelia St. Clair 1865(?)-1946
See Sinclair, May
See also CA 104; HGG; RHW

Sinclair, May .... **TCLC 3, 11**
See also Sinclair, Mary Amelia St. Clair
See also CA 166; DLB 36, 135; RGEL 2;
SUFW

Sinclair, Roy
See Griffith, D(avid Lewelyn) W(ark)

Sinclair, Upton (Beall) 1878-1968 ..... **CLC 1, 11, 15, 63; WLC**
See also AMWS 5; BPFB 3; BYA 2; CA 5-8R; 25-28R; CANR 7; CDALB 1929-1941; DA; DA3; DAB; DAC; DAM MST, NOV; DLB 9; INT CANR-7; LAIT 3;
MTCW 1, 2; NFS 6; RGAL 4; SATA 9;
YAW

Singer, Isaac
See Singer, Isaac Bashevis

Singer, Isaac Bashevis 1904-1991 .. **CLC 1, 3, 6, 9, 11, 15, 23, 38, 69, 111; SSC 3; WLC**
See also AAYA 32; AITN 1, 2; AMW;
BPFB 3; BYA 1, 4; CA 1-4R; 134; CANR 1, 39, 106; CDALB 1941-1968; CLR 1;
CWRI 5; DA; DA3; DAB; DAC; DAM MST, NOV; DLB 6, 28, 52; DLBY 1991;

EXPS; HGG; JRDA; LAIT 3; MAICYA 1; MTCW 1, 2; RGAL 4; RGSF 2; SATA 3, 27; SATA-Obit 68; SSFS 2, 12

Singer, Israel Joshua 1893-1944 .... **TCLC 33**
See also CA 169

Singh, Khushwant 1915- .... **CLC 11**
See also CA 9-12R; CAAS 9; CANR 6, 84;
CN 7; RGEL 2

Singleton, Ann
See Benedict, Ruth (Fulton)

Singleton, John 1968(?)- .... **CLC 156**
See also BW 2, 3; CA 138; CANR 67, 82;
DAM MULT

Sinjohn, John
See Galsworthy, John

Sinyavsky, Andrei (Donatevich)
1925-1997 .... **CLC 8**
See also Tertz, Abram
See also CA 85-88; 159

Sirin, V.
See Nabokov, Vladimir (Vladimirovich)

Sissman, L(ouis) E(dward)
1928-1976 .... **CLC 9, 18**
See also CA 21-24R; 65-68; CANR 13;
DLB 5

Sisson, C(harles) H(ubert) 1914- .... **CLC 8**
See also CA 1-4R; CAAS 3; CANR 3, 48, 84; CP 7; DLB 27

Sitwell, Dame Edith 1887-1964 ..... **CLC 2, 9, 67; PC 3**
See also BRW 7; CA 9-12R; CANR 35;
CDBLB 1945-1960; DAM POET; DLB 20; MTCW 1, 2; RGEL 2

Siwaarmill, H. P.
See Sharp, William

Sjoewall, Maj 1935- .... **CLC 7**
See also Sjowall, Maj
See also CA 65-68; CANR 73

Sjowall, Maj
See Sjoewall, Maj
See also BPFB 3; CMW 4; MSW

Skelton, John 1460(?)-1529 ..... **LC 71; PC 25**
See also BRW 1; DLB 136; RGEL 2

Skelton, Robin 1925-1997 .... **CLC 13**
See also Zuk, Georges
See also AITN 2; CA 5-8R; 160; CAAS 5;
CANR 28, 89; CCA 1; CP 7; DLB 27, 53

Skolimowski, Jerzy 1938- .... **CLC 20**
See also CA 128

Skram, Amalie (Bertha)
1847-1905 .... **TCLC 25**
See also CA 165

Skvorecky, Josef (Vaclav) 1924- ...... **CLC 15, 39, 69, 152**
See also CA 61-64; CAAS 1; CANR 10, 34, 63; CDWLB 4; DA3; DAC; DAM NOV; DLB 232; MTCW 1, 2

Slade, Bernard .... **CLC 11, 46**
See also Newbound, Bernard Slade
See also CAAS 9; CCA 1; DLB 53

Slaughter, Carolyn 1946- .... **CLC 56**
See also CA 85-88; CANR 85; CN 7

Slaughter, Frank G(ill) 1908-2001 ... **CLC 29**
See also AITN 2; CA 5-8R; 197; CANR 5, 85; INT CANR-5; RHW

Slavitt, David R(ytman) 1935- ..... **CLC 5, 14**
See also CA 21-24R; CAAS 3; CANR 41, 83; CP 7; DLB 5, 6

Slesinger, Tess 1905-1945 .... **TCLC 10**
See also CA 107; 199; DLB 102

Slessor, Kenneth 1901-1971 .... **CLC 14**
See also CA 102; 89-92; RGEL 2

Slowacki, Juliusz 1809-1849 .... **NCLC 15**

Smart, Christopher 1722-1771 . **LC 3; PC 13**
See also DAM POET; DLB 109; RGEL 2

Smart, Elizabeth 1913-1986 .... **CLC 54**
See also CA 81-84; 118; DLB 88

Smiley, Jane (Graves) 1949- ...... **CLC 53, 76, 144**
See also AMWS 6; BPFB 3; CA 104;
CANR 30, 50, 74, 96; CN 7; CPW 1;
DA3; DAM POP; DLB 227, 234; INT CANR-30

Smith, A(rthur) J(ames) M(arshall)
1902-1980 .... **CLC 15**
See also CA 1-4R; 102; CANR 4; DAC;
DLB 88; RGEL 2

Smith, Adam 1723(?)-1790 .... **LC 36**
See also DLB 104, 252; RGEL 2

Smith, Alexander 1829-1867 .... **NCLC 59**
See also DLB 32, 55

Smith, Anna Deavere 1950- .... **CLC 86**
See also CA 133; CANR 103; CD 5; DFS 2

Smith, Betty (Wehner) 1904-1972 ... **CLC 19**
See also BPFB 3; BYA 3; CA 5-8R; 33-36R; DLBY 1982; LAIT 3; RGAL 4;
SATA 6

Smith, Charlotte (Turner)
1749-1806 .... **NCLC 23**
See also DLB 39, 109; RGEL 2

Smith, Clark Ashton 1893-1961 .... **CLC 43**
See also CA 143; CANR 81; FANT; HGG;
MTCW 2; SCFW 2; SFW 4; SUFW

Smith, Dave .... **CLC 22, 42**
See also Smith, David (Jeddie)
See also CAAS 7; DLB 5

Smith, David (Jeddie) 1942-
See Smith, Dave
See also CA 49-52; CANR 1, 59; CP 7;
CSW; DAM POET

Smith, Florence Margaret 1902-1971
See Smith, Stevie
See also CA 17-18; 29-32R; CANR 35;
CAP 2; DAM POET; MTCW 1, 2

Smith, Iain Crichton 1928-1998 .... **CLC 64**
See also CA 21-24R; 171; CN 7; CP 7; DLB 40, 139; RGSF 2

Smith, John 1580(?)-1631 .... **LC 9**
See also DLB 24, 30; TUS

Smith, Johnston
See Crane, Stephen (Townley)

Smith, Joseph, Jr. 1805-1844 .... **NCLC 53**

Smith, Lee 1944- .... **CLC 25, 73**
See also CA 114; 119; CANR 46; CSW;
DLB 143; DLBY 1983; INT CA-119;
RGAL 4

Smith, Martin
See Smith, Martin Cruz

Smith, Martin Cruz 1942- .... **CLC 25**
See also BEST 89:4; BPFB 3; CA 85-88;
CANR 6, 23, 43, 65; CMW 4; CPW;
DAM MULT, POP; HGG; INT CANR-23; MTCW 2; NNAL; RGAL 4

Smith, Mary-Ann Tirone 1944- .... **CLC 39**
See also CA 118; 136

Smith, Patti 1946- .... **CLC 12**
See also CA 93-96; CANR 63

Smith, Pauline (Urmson)
1882-1959 .... **TCLC 25**
See also DLB 225

Smith, Rosamond
See Oates, Joyce Carol

Smith, Sheila Kaye
See Kaye-Smith, Sheila

Smith, Stevie .... **CLC 3, 8, 25, 44; PC 12**
See also Smith, Florence Margaret
See also BRWS 2; DLB 20; MTCW 2;
PAB; PFS 3; RGEL 2

Smith, Wilbur (Addison) 1933- .... **CLC 33**
See also CA 13-16R; CANR 7, 46, 66;
CPW; MTCW 1, 2

Smith, William Jay 1918- .... **CLC 6**
See also CA 5-8R; CANR 44, 106; CP 7;
CSW; CWRI 5; DLB 5; MAICYA 1;
SAAS 22; SATA 2, 68

Smith, Woodrow Wilson
See Kuttner, Henry
Smolenskin, Peretz 1842-1885 .... **NCLC 30**
Smollett, Tobias (George) 1721-1771 ... **LC 2, 46**
See also BRW 3; CDBLB 1660-1789; DLB 39, 104; RGEL 2
Snodgrass, W(illiam) D(e Witt)
1926- .... **CLC 2, 6, 10, 18, 68**
See also AMWS 6; CA 1-4R; CANR 6, 36, 65, 85; CP 7; DAM POET; DLB 5; MTCW 1, 2; RGAL 4
Snow, C(harles) P(ercy) 1905-1980 ... **CLC 1, 4, 6, 9, 13, 19**
See also BRW 7; CA 5-8R; 101; CANR 28; CDBLB 1945-1960; DAM NOV; DLB 15, 77; DLBD 17; MTCW 1, 2; RGEL 2
Snow, Frances Compton
See Adams, Henry (Brooks)
Snyder, Gary (Sherman) 1930- . **CLC 1, 2, 5, 9, 32, 120; PC 21**
See also AMWS 8; ANW; CA 17-20R; CANR 30, 60; CP 7; DA3; DAM POET; DLB 5, 16, 165, 212, 237; MTCW 2; PFS 9; RGAL 4; WP
Snyder, Zilpha Keatley 1927- .... **CLC 17**
See also AAYA 15; BYA 1; CA 9-12R; CANR 38; CLR 31; JRDA; MAICYA 1; SAAS 2; SATA 1, 28, 75, 110; SATA-Essay 112; YAW
Soares, Bernardo
See Pessoa, Fernando (Antonio Nogueira)
Sobh, A.
See Shamlu, Ahmad
Sobol, Joshua .... **CLC 60**
See also CWW 2
Socrates 470B.C.-399B.C. .... **CMLC 27**
Soderberg, Hjalmar 1869-1941 ...... **TCLC 39**
See also DLB 259; RGSF 2
Soderbergh, Steven 1963- .... **CLC 154**
Sodergran, Edith (Irene)
See Soedergran, Edith (Irene)
See also DLB 259; EW 11; RGWL 2
Soedergran, Edith (Irene)
1892-1923 .... **TCLC 31**
See also Sodergran, Edith (Irene)
Softly, Edgar
See Lovecraft, H(oward) P(hillips)
Softly, Edward
See Lovecraft, H(oward) P(hillips)
Sokolov, Raymond 1941- .... **CLC 7**
See also CA 85-88
Sokolov, Sasha .... **CLC 59**
Solo, Jay
See Ellison, Harlan (Jay)
Sologub, Fyodor .... **TCLC 9**
See also Teternikov, Fyodor Kuzmich
Solomons, Ikey Esquir
See Thackeray, William Makepeace
Solomos, Dionysios 1798-1857 .... **NCLC 15**
Solwoska, Mara
See French, Marilyn
Solzhenitsyn, Aleksandr I(sayevich)
1918- .. **CLC 1, 2, 4, 7, 9, 10, 18, 26, 34, 78, 134; SSC 32; WLC**
See also AITN 1; BPFB 3; CA 69-72; CANR 40, 65; DA; DA3; DAB; DAC; DAM MST, NOV; EW 13; EXPS; LAIT 4; MTCW 1, 2; NFS 6; RGSF 2; RGWL 2; SSFS 9
Somers, Jane
See Lessing, Doris (May)
Somerville, Edith Oenone
1858-1949 .... **TCLC 51**
See also CA 196; DLB 135; RGEL 2; RGSF 2
Somerville & Ross
See Martin, Violet Florence; Somerville, Edith Oenone

Sommer, Scott 1951- .... **CLC 25**
See also CA 106
Sondheim, Stephen (Joshua) 1930- . **CLC 30, 39, 147**
See also AAYA 11; CA 103; CANR 47, 67; DAM DRAM; LAIT 4
Song, Cathy 1955- .... **PC 21**
See also AAL; CA 154; CWP; DLB 169; EXPP; FW; PFS 5
Sontag, Susan 1933- .... **CLC 1, 2, 10, 13, 31, 105**
See also AMWS 3; CA 17-20R; CANR 25, 51, 74, 97; CN 7; CPW; DA3; DAM POP; DLB 2, 67; MAWW; MTCW 1, 2; RGAL 4; RHW; SSFS 10
Sophocles 496(?)B.C.-406(?)B.C. .... **CMLC 2, 47, 51; DC 1; WLCS**
See also AW 1; CDWLB 1; DA; DA3; DAB; DAC; DAM DRAM, MST; DFS 1, 4, 8; DLB 176; LAIT 1; RGWL 2
Sordello 1189-1269 .... **CMLC 15**
Sorel, Georges 1847-1922 .... **TCLC 91**
See also CA 118; 188
Sorel, Julia
See Drexler, Rosalyn
Sorokin, Vladimir .... **CLC 59**
Sorrentino, Gilbert 1929- .. **CLC 3, 7, 14, 22, 40**
See also CA 77-80; CANR 14, 33; CN 7; CP 7; DLB 5, 173; DLBY 1980; INT CANR-14
Soseki
See Natsume, Soseki
See also MJW
Soto, Gary 1952- ... **CLC 32, 80; HLC 2; PC 28**
See also AAYA 10, 37; BYA 11; CA 119; 125; CANR 50, 74, 107; CLR 38; CP 7; DAM MULT; DLB 82; EXPP; HW 1, 2; INT CA-125; JRDA; MAICYAS 1; MTCW 2; PFS 7; RGAL 4; SATA 80, 120; WYA; YAW
Soupault, Philippe 1897-1990 .... **CLC 68**
See also CA 116; 147; 131; GFL 1789 to the Present
Souster, (Holmes) Raymond 1921- .... **CLC 5, 14**
See also CA 13-16R; CAAS 14; CANR 13, 29, 53; CP 7; DA3; DAC; DAM POET; DLB 88; RGEL 2; SATA 63
Southern, Terry 1924(?)-1995 .... **CLC 7**
See also BPFB 3; CA 1-4R; 150; CANR 1, 55, 107; CN 7; DLB 2; IDFW 3, 4
Southey, Robert 1774-1843 .... **NCLC 8, 97**
See also BRW 4; DLB 93, 107, 142; RGEL 2; SATA 54
Southworth, Emma Dorothy Eliza Nevitte
1819-1899 .... **NCLC 26**
See also DLB 239
Souza, Ernest
See Scott, Evelyn
Soyinka, Wole 1934- .... **CLC 3, 5, 14, 36, 44; BLC 3; DC 2; WLC**
See also AFW; BW 2, 3; CA 13-16R; CANR 27, 39, 82; CD 5; CDWLB 3; CN 7; CP 7; DA; DA3; DAB; DAC; DAM DRAM, MST, MULT; DFS 10; DLB 125; MTCW 1, 2; RGEL 2; WLIT 2
Spackman, W(illiam) M(ode)
1905-1990 .... **CLC 46**
See also CA 81-84; 132
Spacks, Barry (Bernard) 1931- .... **CLC 14**
See also CA 154; CANR 33; CP 7; DLB 105
Spanidou, Irini 1946- .... **CLC 44**
See also CA 185

Spark, Muriel (Sarah) 1918- ..... **CLC 2, 3, 5, 8, 13, 18, 40, 94; SSC 10**
See also BRWS 1; CA 5-8R; CANR 12, 36, 76, 89; CDBLB 1945-1960; CN 7; CP 7; DA3; DAB; DAC; DAM MST, NOV; DLB 15, 139; FW; INT CANR-12; LAIT 4; MTCW 1, 2; RGEL 2; WLIT 4; YAW
Spaulding, Douglas
See Bradbury, Ray (Douglas)
Spaulding, Leonard
See Bradbury, Ray (Douglas)
Spelman, Elizabeth .... **CLC 65**
Spence, J. A. D.
See Eliot, T(homas) S(tearns)
Spencer, Elizabeth 1921- .... **CLC 22**
See also CA 13-16R; CANR 32, 65, 87; CN 7; CSW; DLB 6, 218; MTCW 1; RGAL 4; SATA 14
Spencer, Leonard G.
See Silverberg, Robert
Spencer, Scott 1945- .... **CLC 30**
See also CA 113; CANR 51; DLBY 1986
Spender, Stephen (Harold)
1909-1995 .... **CLC 1, 2, 5, 10, 41, 91**
See also BRWS 2; CA 9-12R; 149; CANR 31, 54; CDBLB 1945-1960; CP 7; DA3; DAM POET; DLB 20; MTCW 1, 2; PAB; RGEL 2
Spengler, Oswald (Arnold Gottfried)
1880-1936 .... **TCLC 25**
See also CA 118; 189
Spenser, Edmund 1552(?)-1599 ..... **LC 5, 39; PC 8; WLC**
See also BRW 1; CDBLB Before 1660; DA; DA3; DAB; DAC; DAM MST, POET; DLB 167; EFS 2; EXPP; PAB; RGEL 2; WLIT 3; WP
Spicer, Jack 1925-1965 .... **CLC 8, 18, 72**
See also CA 85-88; DAM POET; DLB 5, 16, 193; GLL 1; WP
Spiegelman, Art 1948- .... **CLC 76**
See also AAYA 10; CA 125; CANR 41, 55, 74; MTCW 2; SATA 109; YAW
Spielberg, Peter 1929- .... **CLC 6**
See also CA 5-8R; CANR 4, 48; DLBY 1981
Spielberg, Steven 1947- .... **CLC 20**
See also AAYA 8, 24; CA 77-80; CANR 32; SATA 32
Spillane, Frank Morrison 1918-
See Spillane, Mickey
See also CA 25-28R; CANR 28, 63; DA3; MTCW 1, 2; SATA 66
Spillane, Mickey .... **CLC 3, 13**
See also Spillane, Frank Morrison
See also BPFB 3; CMW 4; DLB 226; MSW; MTCW 2
Spinoza, Benedictus de 1632-1677 .. **LC 9, 58**
Spinrad, Norman (Richard) 1940- ... **CLC 46**
See also BPFB 3; CA 37-40R; CAAS 19; CANR 20, 91; DLB 8; INT CANR-20; SFW 4
Spitteler, Carl (Friedrich Georg)
1845-1924 .... **TCLC 12**
See also CA 109; DLB 129
Spivack, Kathleen (Romola Drucker)
1938- .... **CLC 6**
See also CA 49-52
Spoto, Donald 1941- .... **CLC 39**
See also CA 65-68; CANR 11, 57, 93
Springsteen, Bruce (F.) 1949- .... **CLC 17**
See also CA 111
Spurling, Hilary 1940- .... **CLC 34**
See also CA 104; CANR 25, 52, 94
Spyker, John Howland
See Elman, Richard (Martin)
Squires, (James) Radcliffe
1917-1993 .... **CLC 51**
See also CA 1-4R; 140; CANR 6, 21

Tuohy, Frank .... **CLC 37**
See also Tuohy, John Francis
See also DLB 14, 139

Tuohy, John Francis 1925-
See Tuohy, Frank
See also CA 5-8R; 178; CANR 3, 47; CN 7

Turco, Lewis (Putnam) 1934- ..... **CLC 11, 63**
See also CA 13-16R; CAAS 22; CANR 24, 51; CP 7; DLBY 1984

Turgenev, Ivan (Sergeevich)
1818-1883 .... **NCLC 21, 37; DC 7; SSC 7; WLC**
See also DA; DAB; DAC; DAM MST, NOV; DFS 6; DLB 238; EW 6; RGSF 2; RGWL 2

Turgot, Anne-Robert-Jacques
1727-1781 .... **LC 26**

Turner, Frederick 1943- .... **CLC 48**
See also CA 73-76; CAAS 10; CANR 12, 30, 56; DLB 40

Turton, James
See Crace, Jim

Tutu, Desmond M(pilo) 1931- .... **CLC 80; BLC 3**
See also BW 1, 3; CA 125; CANR 67, 81; DAM MULT

Tutuola, Amos 1920-1997 ...... **CLC 5, 14, 29; BLC 3**
See also AFW; BW 2, 3; CA 9-12R; 159; CANR 27, 66; CDWLB 3; CN 7; DA3; DAM MULT; DLB 125; DNFS 2; MTCW 1, 2; RGEL 2; WLIT 2

Twain, Mark .... **TCLC 6, 12, 19, 36, 48, 59; SSC 34; WLC**
See also Clemens, Samuel Langhorne
See also AAYA 20; AMW; BPFB 3; BYA 2, 3, 11, 14; CLR 58, 60, 66; DLB 11; EXPN; EXPS; FANT; LAIT 2; NFS 1, 6; RGAL 4; RGSF 2; SFW 4; SSFS 1, 7; SUFW; WCH; WYA; YAW

Tyler, Anne 1941- . **CLC 7, 11, 18, 28, 44, 59, 103**
See also AAYA 18; AMWS 4; BEST 89:1; BPFB 3; BYA 12; CA 9-12R; CANR 11, 33, 53; CDALBS; CN 7; CPW; CSW; DAM NOV, POP; DLB 6, 143; DLBY 1982; EXPN; MAWW; MTCW 1, 2; NFS 2, 7, 10; RGAL 4; SATA 7, 90; YAW

Tyler, Royall 1757-1826 .... **NCLC 3**
See also DLB 37; RGAL 4

Tynan, Katharine 1861-1931 .... **TCLC 3**
See also CA 104; 167; DLB 153, 240; FW

Tyutchev, Fyodor 1803-1873 .... **NCLC 34**

Tzara, Tristan 1896-1963 ..... **CLC 47; PC 27**
See also CA 153; 89-92; DAM POET; MTCW 2

Uhry, Alfred 1936- .... **CLC 55**
See also CA 127; 133; CAD; CD 5; CSW; DA3; DAM DRAM, POP; DFS 11; INT CA-133

Ulf, Haerved
See Strindberg, (Johan) August

Ulf, Harved
See Strindberg, (Johan) August

Ulibarri, Sabine R(eyes) 1919- .... **CLC 83; HLCS 2**
See also CA 131; CANR 81; DAM MULT; DLB 82; HW 1, 2; RGSF 2

Unamuno (y Jugo), Miguel de
1864-1936 . **TCLC 2, 9; HLC 2; SSC 11**
See also CA 104; 131; CANR 81; DAM MULT, NOV; DLB 108; EW 8; HW 1, 2; MTCW 1, 2; RGSF 2; RGWL 2

Undercliffe, Errol
See Campbell, (John) Ramsey

Underwood, Miles
See Glassco, John

Undset, Sigrid 1882-1949 ..... **TCLC 3; WLC**
See also CA 104; 129; DA; DA3; DAB; DAC; DAM MST, NOV; EW 9; FW; MTCW 1, 2; RGWL 2

Ungaretti, Giuseppe 1888-1970 ... **CLC 7, 11, 15**
See also CA 19-20; 25-28R; CAP 2; DLB 114; EW 10; RGWL 2

Unger, Douglas 1952- .... **CLC 34**
See also CA 130; CANR 94

Unsworth, Barry (Forster) 1930- .... **CLC 76, 127**
See also BRWS 7; CA 25-28R; CANR 30, 54; CN 7; DLB 194

Updike, John (Hoyer) 1932- . **CLC 1, 2, 3, 5, 7, 9, 13, 15, 23, 34, 43, 70, 139; SSC 13, 27; WLC**
See also AAYA 36; AMW; AMWR 1; BPFB 3; BYA 12; CA 1-4R; CABS 1; CANR 4, 33, 51, 94; CDALB 1968-1988; CN 7; CP 7; CPW 1; DA; DA3; DAB; DAC; DAM MST, NOV, POET, POP; DLB 2, 5, 143, 218, 227; DLBD 3; DLBY 1980, 1982, 1997; EXPP; HGG; MTCW 1, 2; NFS 12; RGAL 4; RGSF 2; SSFS 3

Upshaw, Margaret Mitchell
See Mitchell, Margaret (Munnerlyn)

Upton, Mark
See Sanders, Lawrence

Upward, Allen 1863-1926 .... **TCLC 85**
See also CA 117; 187; DLB 36

Urdang, Constance (Henriette)
1922-1996 .... **CLC 47**
See also CA 21-24R; CANR 9, 24; CP 7; CWP

Uriel, Henry
See Faust, Frederick (Schiller)

Uris, Leon (Marcus) 1924- .... **CLC 7, 32**
See also AITN 1, 2; BEST 89:2; BPFB 3; CA 1-4R; CANR 1, 40, 65; CN 7; CPW 1; DA3; DAM NOV, POP; MTCW 1, 2; SATA 49

Urista, Alberto H. 1947- .... **PC 34**
See also Alurista
See also CA 45-48, 182; CANR 2, 32; HLCS 1; HW 1

Urmuz
See Codrescu, Andrei

Urquhart, Guy
See McAlmon, Robert (Menzies)

Urquhart, Jane 1949- .... **CLC 90**
See also CA 113; CANR 32, 68; CCA 1; DAC

Usigli, Rodolfo 1905-1979
See also CA 131; HLCS 1; HW 1; LAW

Ustinov, Peter (Alexander) 1921- .... **CLC 1**
See also AITN 1; CA 13-16R; CANR 25, 51; CBD; CD 5; DLB 13; MTCW 2

U Tam'si, Gerald Felix Tchicaya
See Tchicaya, Gerald Felix

U Tam'si, Tchicaya
See Tchicaya, Gerald Felix

Vachss, Andrew (Henry) 1942- .... **CLC 106**
See also CA 118; CANR 44, 95; CMW 4

Vachss, Andrew H.
See Vachss, Andrew (Henry)

Vaculik, Ludvik 1926- .... **CLC 7**
See also CA 53-56; CANR 72; CWW 2; DLB 232

Vaihinger, Hans 1852-1933 .... **TCLC 71**
See also CA 116; 166

Valdez, Luis (Miguel) 1940- ..... **CLC 84; DC 10; HLC 2**
See also CA 101; CAD; CANR 32, 81; CD 5; DAM MULT; DFS 5; DLB 122; HW 1; LAIT 4

Valenzuela, Luisa 1938- .... **CLC 31, 104; HLCS 2; SSC 14**
See also CA 101; CANR 32, 65; CDWLB 3; CWW 2; DAM MULT; DLB 113; FW; HW 1, 2; LAW; RGSF 2

Valera y Alcala-Galiano, Juan
1824-1905 .... **TCLC 10**
See also CA 106

Valery, (Ambroise) Paul (Toussaint Jules)
1871-1945 .... **TCLC 4, 15; PC 9**
See also CA 104; 122; DA3; DAM POET; EW 8; GFL 1789 to the Present; MTCW 1, 2; RGWL 2

Valle-Inclan, Ramon (Maria) del
1866-1936 .... **TCLC 5; HLC 2**
See also CA 106; 153; CANR 80; DAM MULT; DLB 134; EW 8; HW 2; RGSF 2; RGWL 2

Vallejo, Antonio Buero
See Buero Vallejo, Antonio

Vallejo, Cesar (Abraham)
1892-1938 .... **TCLC 3, 56; HLC 2**
See also CA 105; 153; DAM MULT; HW 1; LAW; RGWL 2

Valles, Jules 1832-1885 .... **NCLC 71**
See also DLB 123; GFL 1789 to the Present

Vallette, Marguerite Eymery
1860-1953 .... **TCLC 67**
See also CA 182; DLB 123, 192

Valle Y Pena, Ramon del
See Valle-Inclan, Ramon (Maria) del

Van Ash, Cay 1918- .... **CLC 34**

Vanbrugh, Sir John 1664-1726 .... **LC 21**
See also BRW 2; DAM DRAM; DLB 80; IDTP; RGEL 2

Van Campen, Karl
See Campbell, John W(ood, Jr.)

Vance, Gerald
See Silverberg, Robert

Vance, Jack .... **CLC 35**
See also Vance, John Holbrook
See also DLB 8; FANT; SCFW 2; SFW 4; SUFW

Vance, John Holbrook 1916-
See Queen, Ellery; Vance, Jack
See also CA 29-32R; CANR 17, 65; CMW 4; MTCW 1

Van Den Bogarde, Derek Jules Gaspard Ulric Niven 1921-1999 .... **CLC 14**
See also Bogarde, Dirk
See also CA 77-80; 179

Vandenburgh, Jane .... **CLC 59**
See also CA 168

Vanderhaeghe, Guy 1951- .... **CLC 41**
See also BPFB 3; CA 113; CANR 72

van der Post, Laurens (Jan)
1906-1996 .... **CLC 5**
See also AFW; CA 5-8R; 155; CANR 35; CN 7; DLB 204; RGEL 2

van de Wetering, Janwillem 1931- ... **CLC 47**
See also CA 49-52; CANR 4, 62, 90; CMW 4

Van Dine, S. S. .... **TCLC 23**
See also Wright, Willard Huntington
See also MSW

Van Doren, Carl (Clinton)
1885-1950 .... **TCLC 18**
See also CA 111; 168

Van Doren, Mark 1894-1972 .... **CLC 6, 10**
See also CA 1-4R; 37-40R; CANR 3; DLB 45; MTCW 1, 2; RGAL 4

Van Druten, John (William)
1901-1957 .... **TCLC 2**
See also CA 104; 161; DLB 10; RGAL 4

Van Duyn, Mona (Jane) 1921- ...... **CLC 3, 7, 63, 116**
See also CA 9-12R; CANR 7, 38, 60; CP 7; CWP; DAM POET; DLB 5

DAC; DAM MST, NOV, POP; DLB 2, 8, 152; DLBD 3; DLBY 1980; EXPN; EXPS; LAIT 4; MTCW 1, 2; NFS 3; RGAL 4; SCFW; SFW 4; SSFS 5; TUS; YAW

Von Rachen, Kurt
See Hubbard, L(afayette) Ron(ald)

von Rezzori (d'Arezzo), Gregor
See Rezzori (d'Arezzo), Gregor von

von Sternberg, Josef
See Sternberg, Josef von

Vorster, Gordon 1924- .... **CLC 34**
See also CA 133

Vosce, Trudie
See Ozick, Cynthia

Voznesensky, Andrei (Andreievich)
1933- .... **CLC 1, 15, 57**
See also CA 89-92; CANR 37; CWW 2; DAM POET; MTCW 1

Waddington, Miriam 1917- .... **CLC 28**
See also CA 21-24R; CANR 12, 30; CCA 1; CP 7; DLB 68

Wagman, Fredrica 1937- .... **CLC 7**
See also CA 97-100; INT 97-100

Wagner, Linda W.
See Wagner-Martin, Linda (C.)

Wagner, Linda Welshimer
See Wagner-Martin, Linda (C.)

Wagner, Richard 1813-1883 .... **NCLC 9**
See also DLB 129; EW 6

Wagner-Martin, Linda (C.) 1936- .... **CLC 50**
See also CA 159

Wagoner, David (Russell) 1926- .... **CLC 3, 5, 15; PC 33**
See also AMWS 9; CA 1-4R; CAAS 3; CANR 2, 71; CN 7; CP 7; DLB 5, 256; SATA 14; TCWW 2

Wah, Fred(erick James) 1939- .... **CLC 44**
See also CA 107; 141; CP 7; DLB 60

Wahloo, Per 1926-1975 .... **CLC 7**
See also BPFB 3; CA 61-64; CANR 73; CMW 4; MSW

Wahloo, Peter
See Wahloo, Per

Wain, John (Barrington) 1925-1994 . **CLC 2, 11, 15, 46**
See also CA 5-8R; 145; CAAS 4; CANR 23, 54; CDBLB 1960 to Present; DLB 15, 27, 139, 155; MTCW 1, 2

Wajda, Andrzej 1926- .... **CLC 16**
See also CA 102

Wakefield, Dan 1932- .... **CLC 7**
See also CA 21-24R; CAAS 7; CN 7

Wakefield, Herbert Russell
1888-1965 .... **TCLC 120**
See also CA 5-8R; CANR 77; HGG; SUFW

Wakoski, Diane 1937- ...... **CLC 2, 4, 7, 9, 11, 40; PC 15**
See also CA 13-16R; CAAS 1; CANR 9, 60, 106; CP 7; CWP; DAM POET; DLB 5; INT CANR-9; MTCW 2

Wakoski-Sherbell, Diane
See Wakoski, Diane

Walcott, Derek (Alton) 1930- .... **CLC 2, 4, 9, 14, 25, 42, 67, 76; BLC 3; DC 7**
See also BW 2; CA 89-92; CANR 26, 47, 75, 80; CBD; CD 5; CDWLB 3; CP 7; DA3; DAB; DAC; DAM MST, MULT, POET; DLB 117; DLBY 1981; DNFS 1; EFS 1; MTCW 1, 2; PFS 6; RGEL 2

Waldman, Anne (Lesley) 1945- .... **CLC 7**
See also CA 37-40R; CAAS 17; CANR 34, 69; CP 7; CWP; DLB 16

Waldo, E. Hunter
See Sturgeon, Theodore (Hamilton)

Waldo, Edward Hamilton
See Sturgeon, Theodore (Hamilton)

Walker, Alice (Malsenior) 1944- ... **CLC 5, 6, 9, 19, 27, 46, 58, 103; BLC 3; PC 30; SSC 5; WLCS**
See also AAYA 3, 33; AFAW 1, 2; AMWS 3; BEST 89:4; BPFB 3; BW 2, 3; CA 37-40R; CANR 9, 27, 49, 66, 82; CDALB 1968-1988; CN 7; CPW; CSW; DA; DA3; DAB; DAC; DAM MST, MULT, NOV, POET, POP; DLB 6, 33, 143; EXPN; EXPS; FW; INT CANR-27; LAIT 3; MAWW; MTCW 1, 2; NFS 5; RGAL 4; RGSF 2; SATA 31; SSFS 2, 11; YAW

Walker, David Harry 1911-1992 ...... **CLC 14**
See also CA 1-4R; 137; CANR 1; CWRI 5; SATA 8; SATA-Obit 71

Walker, Edward Joseph 1934-
See Walker, Ted
See also CA 21-24R; CANR 12, 28, 53; CP 7

Walker, George F. 1947- .... **CLC 44, 61**
See also CA 103; CANR 21, 43, 59; CD 5; DAB; DAC; DAM MST; DLB 60

Walker, Joseph A. 1935- .... **CLC 19**
See also BW 1, 3; CA 89-92; CAD; CANR 26; CD 5; DAM DRAM, MST; DFS 12; DLB 38

Walker, Margaret (Abigail)
1915-1998 .... **CLC 1, 6; BLC; PC 20**
See also AFAW 1, 2; BW 2, 3; CA 73-76; 172; CANR 26, 54, 76; CN 7; CP 7; CSW; DAM MULT; DLB 76, 152; EXPP; FW; MTCW 1, 2; RGAL 4; RHW

Walker, Ted .... **CLC 13**
See also Walker, Edward Joseph
See also DLB 40

Wallace, David Foster 1962- ..... **CLC 50, 114**
See also AMWS 10; CA 132; CANR 59; DA3; MTCW 2

Wallace, Dexter
See Masters, Edgar Lee

Wallace, (Richard Horatio) Edgar
1875-1932 .... **TCLC 57**
See also CA 115; CMW 4; DLB 70; MSW; RGEL 2

Wallace, Irving 1916-1990 .... **CLC 7, 13**
See also AITN 1; BPFB 3; CA 1-4R; 132; CAAS 1; CANR 1, 27; CPW; DAM NOV, POP; INT CANR-27; MTCW 1, 2

Wallant, Edward Lewis 1926-1962 ... **CLC 5, 10**
See also CA 1-4R; CANR 22; DLB 2, 28, 143; MTCW 1, 2; RGAL 4

Wallas, Graham 1858-1932 .... **TCLC 91**

Walley, Byron
See Card, Orson Scott

Walpole, Horace 1717-1797 .... **LC 2, 49**
See also BRW 3; DLB 39, 104, 213; HGG; RGEL 2; SUFW

Walpole, Hugh (Seymour)
1884-1941 .... **TCLC 5**
See also CA 104; 165; DLB 34; HGG; MTCW 2; RGEL 2; RHW

Walser, Martin 1927- .... **CLC 27**
See also CA 57-60; CANR 8, 46; CWW 2; DLB 75, 124

Walser, Robert 1878-1956 .... **TCLC 18; SSC 20**
See also CA 118; 165; CANR 100; DLB 66

Walsh, Gillian Paton
See Paton Walsh, Gillian

Walsh, Jill Paton .... **CLC 35**
See also Paton Walsh, Gillian
See also CLR 2, 65; WYA

Walter, Villiam Christian
See Andersen, Hans Christian

Walton, Izaak 1593-1683 .... **LC 72**
See also BRW 2; CDBLB Before 1660; DLB 151, 213; RGEL 2

Wambaugh, Joseph (Aloysius, Jr.)
1937- .... **CLC 3, 18**
See also AITN 1; BEST 89:3; BPFB 3; CA 33-36R; CANR 42, 65; CMW 4; CPW 1; DA3; DAM NOV, POP; DLB 6; DLBY 1983; MSW; MTCW 1, 2

Wang Wei 699(?)-761(?) .... **PC 18**

Ward, Arthur Henry Sarsfield 1883-1959
See Rohmer, Sax
See also CA 108; 173; CMW 4; HGG

Ward, Douglas Turner 1930- .... **CLC 19**
See also BW 1; CA 81-84; CAD; CANR 27; CD 5; DLB 7, 38

Ward, E. D.
See Lucas, E(dward) V(errall)

Ward, Mrs. Humphry 1851-1920
See Ward, Mary Augusta
See also RGEL 2

Ward, Mary Augusta 1851-1920 ... **TCLC 55**
See also Ward, Mrs. Humphry
See also DLB 18

Ward, Peter
See Faust, Frederick (Schiller)

Warhol, Andy 1928(?)-1987 .... **CLC 20**
See also AAYA 12; BEST 89:4; CA 89-92; 121; CANR 34

Warner, Francis (Robert le Plastrier)
1937- .... **CLC 14**
See also CA 53-56; CANR 11

Warner, Marina 1946- .... **CLC 59**
See also CA 65-68; CANR 21, 55; CN 7; DLB 194

Warner, Rex (Ernest) 1905-1986 ...... **CLC 45**
See also CA 89-92; 119; DLB 15; RGEL 2; RHW

Warner, Susan (Bogert)
1819-1885 .... **NCLC 31**
See also DLB 3, 42, 239, 250, 254

Warner, Sylvia (Constance) Ashton
See Ashton-Warner, Sylvia (Constance)

Warner, Sylvia Townsend
1893-1978 .... **CLC 7, 19; SSC 23**
See also BRWS 7; CA 61-64; 77-80; CANR 16, 60, 104; DLB 34, 139; FANT; FW; MTCW 1, 2; RGEL 2; RGSF 2; RHW

Warren, Mercy Otis 1728-1814 ..... **NCLC 13**
See also DLB 31, 200; RGAL 4

Warren, Robert Penn 1905-1989 .. **CLC 1, 4, 6, 8, 10, 13, 18, 39, 53, 59; PC 37; SSC 4; WLC**
See also AITN 1; AMW; BPFB 3; BYA 1; CA 13-16R; 129; CANR 10, 47; CDALB 1968-1988; DA; DA3; DAB; DAC; DAM MST, NOV, POET; DLB 2, 48, 152; DLBY 1980, 1989; INT CANR-10; MTCW 1, 2; NFS 13; RGAL 4; RGSF 2; RHW; SATA 46; SATA-Obit 63; SSFS 8

Warshofsky, Isaac
See Singer, Isaac Bashevis

Warton, Thomas 1728-1790 .... **LC 15**
See also DAM POET; DLB 104, 109; RGEL 2

Waruk, Kona
See Harris, (Theodore) Wilson

Warung, Price .... **TCLC 45**
See also Astley, William
See also DLB 230; RGEL 2

Warwick, Jarvis
See Garner, Hugh
See also CCA 1

Washington, Alex
See Harris, Mark

Washington, Booker T(aliaferro)
1856-1915 .... **TCLC 10; BLC 3**
See also BW 1; CA 114; 125; DA3; DAM MULT; LAIT 2; RGAL 4; SATA 28

Washington, George 1732-1799 .... **LC 25**
See also DLB 31

Yosano Akiko 1878-1942 .... **TCLC 59; PC 11**
  See also CA 161
Yoshimoto, Banana .... **CLC 84**
  See also Yoshimoto, Mahoko
  See also NFS 7
Yoshimoto, Mahoko 1964-
  See Yoshimoto, Banana
  See also CA 144; CANR 98
Young, Al(bert James) 1939- . **CLC 19; BLC 3**
  See also BW 2, 3; CA 29-32R; CANR 26, 65; CN 7; CP 7; DAM MULT; DLB 33
Young, Andrew (John) 1885-1971 ...... **CLC 5**
  See also CA 5-8R; CANR 7, 29; RGEL 2
Young, Collier
  See Bloch, Robert (Albert)
Young, Edward 1683-1765 .... **LC 3, 40**
  See also DLB 95; RGEL 2
Young, Marguerite (Vivian)
  1909-1995 .... **CLC 82**
  See also CA 13-16; 150; CAP 1; CN 7
Young, Neil 1945- .... **CLC 17**
  See also CA 110; CCA 1
Young Bear, Ray A. 1950- .... **CLC 94**
  See also CA 146; DAM MULT; DLB 175; NNAL
Yourcenar, Marguerite 1903-1987 ... **CLC 19, 38, 50, 87**
  See also BPFB 3; CA 69-72; CANR 23, 60, 93; DAM NOV; DLB 72; DLBY 1988; EW 12; GFL 1789 to the Present; GLL 1; MTCW 1, 2; RGWL 2
Yuan, Chu 340(?)B.C.-278(?)B.C. . **CMLC 36**
Yurick, Sol 1925- .... **CLC 6**
  See also CA 13-16R; CANR 25; CN 7
Zabolotsky, Nikolai Alekseevich
  1903-1958 .... **TCLC 52**
  See also CA 116; 164
Zagajewski, Adam 1945- .... **PC 27**
  See also CA 186; DLB 232
Zalygin, Sergei -2000 .... **CLC 59**
Zamiatin, Evgenii
  See Zamyatin, Evgeny Ivanovich
  See also RGSF 2; RGWL 2

Zamiatin, Yevgenii
  See Zamyatin, Evgeny Ivanovich
Zamora, Bernice (B. Ortiz) 1938- .. **CLC 89; HLC 2**
  See also CA 151; CANR 80; DAM MULT; DLB 82; HW 1, 2
Zamyatin, Evgeny Ivanovich
  1884-1937 .... **TCLC 8, 37**
  See also Zamiatin, Evgenii
  See also CA 105; 166; EW 10; SFW 4
Zangwill, Israel 1864-1926 ... **TCLC 16; SSC 44**
  See also CA 109; 167; CMW 4; DLB 10, 135, 197; RGEL 2
Zappa, Francis Vincent, Jr. 1940-1993
  See Zappa, Frank
  See also CA 108; 143; CANR 57
Zappa, Frank .... **CLC 17**
  See also Zappa, Francis Vincent, Jr.
Zaturenska, Marya 1902-1982 ..... **CLC 6, 11**
  See also CA 13-16R; 105; CANR 22
Zeami 1363-1443 .... **DC 7**
  See also DLB 203; RGWL 2
Zelazny, Roger (Joseph) 1937-1995 . **CLC 21**
  See also AAYA 7; BPFB 3; CA 21-24R; 148; CANR 26, 60; CN 7; DLB 8; FANT; MTCW 1, 2; SATA 57; SATA-Brief 39; SCFW; SFW 4; SUFW
Zhdanov, Andrei Alexandrovich
  1896-1948 .... **TCLC 18**
  See also CA 117; 167
Zhukovsky, Vasilii Andreevich
  See Zhukovsky, Vasily (Andreevich)
  See also DLB 205
Zhukovsky, Vasily (Andreevich)
  1783-1852 .... **NCLC 35**
  See also Zhukovsky, Vasilii Andreevich
Ziegenhagen, Eric .... **CLC 55**
Zimmer, Jill Schary
  See Robinson, Jill
Zimmerman, Robert
  See Dylan, Bob

Zindel, Paul 1936- .... **CLC 6, 26; DC 5**
  See also AAYA 2, 37; BYA 2, 3, 8, 11, 14; CA 73-76; CAD; CANR 31, 65, 108; CD 5; CDALBS; CLR 3, 45; DA; DA3; DAB; DAC; DAM DRAM, MST, NOV; DFS 12; DLB 7, 52; JRDA; LAIT 5; MAICYA 1; MTCW 1, 2; SATA 16, 58, 102; WYA; YAW
Zinov'Ev, A. A.
  See Zinoviev, Alexander (Aleksandrovich)
Zinoviev, Alexander (Aleksandrovich)
  1922- .... **CLC 19**
  See also CA 116; 133; CAAS 10
Zoilus
  See Lovecraft, H(oward) P(hillips)
Zola, Emile (Edouard Charles Antoine)
  1840-1902 ...... **TCLC 1, 6, 21, 41; WLC**
  See also CA 104; 138; DA; DA3; DAB; DAC; DAM MST, NOV; DLB 123; EW 7; GFL 1789 to the Present; IDTP; RGWL 2
Zoline, Pamela 1941- .... **CLC 62**
  See also CA 161; SFW 4
Zoroaster 628(?)B.C.-551(?)B.C. ... **CMLC 40**
Zorrilla y Moral, Jose 1817-1893 .... **NCLC 6**
Zoshchenko, Mikhail (Mikhailovich)
  1895-1958 .... **TCLC 15; SSC 15**
  See also CA 115; 160; RGSF 2
Zuckmayer, Carl 1896-1977 .... **CLC 18**
  See also CA 69-72; DLB 56, 124; RGWL 2
Zuk, Georges
  See Skelton, Robin
  See also CCA 1
Zukofsky, Louis 1904-1978 ... **CLC 1, 2, 4, 7, 11, 18; PC 11**
  See also AMWS 3; CA 9-12R; 77-80; CANR 39; DAM POET; DLB 5, 165; MTCW 1; RGAL 4
Zweig, Paul 1935-1984 .... **CLC 34, 42**
  See also CA 85-88; 113
Zweig, Stefan 1881-1942 .... **TCLC 17**
  See also CA 112; 170; DLB 81, 118
Zwingli, Huldreich 1484-1531 .... **LC 37**
  See also DLB 179

PC Cumulative Nationality Index

461

PC- 40 Title Index

Title Index

ISBN 0-7876-5966-5

9 780787 659660

90000